Encyclopedia of Law and Economics
Volume I

Encyclopedia of Law and Economics
Edited by Boudewijn Bouckaert and Gerrit De Geest

Volume I	The History and Methodology of Law and Economics
Volume II	Civil Law and Economics
Volume III	The Regulation of Contracts
Volume IV	The Economics of Public and Tax Law
Volume V	The Economics of Crime and Litigation

Encyclopedia of Law and Economics Volume I

The History and Methodology of Law and Economics

Edited by

Boudewijn Bouckaert

Professor of Law, University of Ghent, Belgium

Gerrit De Geest

Professor of Law and Economics, University of Ghent and University of Antwerp, Belgium and Researcher, Economic Institute/CIAV Utrecht University, The Netherlands

Edward Elgar

Cheltenham, UK • Northampton, MA, USA

Published by
Edward Elgar Publishing Limited
Glensanda House
Montpellier Parade
Cheltenham
Glos GL50 1UA
UK

Edward Elgar Publishing, Inc.
136 West Street
Suite 202
Northampton
Massachusetts 01060
USA

A catalogue record for this book
is available from the British Library

Library of Congress Cataloguing in Publication Data

Encyclopedia of law and economics / edited by Boudewijn Bouckaert,
Gerrit De Geest.
Contents: v. 1. The history and methodology of law and economics — v. 2. Civil law and economics — v. 3. The regulation of contracts — v. 4. The economics of public and tax law — v. 5. The economics of crime and litigation.
Includes bibliographical references.
1. Law and economics Encyclopedias. I. Bouckaert, Boudewijn. II. Geest, Gerrit De.
K487 .E3E53 2000
330—dc 21 99–38062
CIP

ISBN 1 85898 984 1
1 85898 565 X (5 volume set)

Printed and bound in Great Britain by MPG Books Ltd, Bodmin, Cornwall

CONTENTS

EDITORIAL BOARD

Board of Referees

FOREWORD

Richard A. Posner
Chief Judge, US Court of Appeals for the Seventh Circuit
Senior Lecturer, University of Chicago Law School

The law and economics movement was for a long time regarded as an American movement. This was never completely correct. Its origins, certainly, are international. British economists, Adam Smith and Jeremy Bentham to begin with, and later A.C. Pigou and Ronald Coase (among others), played a founding role, as did Max Weber - himself both a lawyer and an economist. Friedrich Hayek and Bruno Leoni are other examples of scholars from outside the Anglo-American sphere whose thought has had an influence on the movement. And there are others. Today, at any rate, it is plain that the movement is international. There are law and economics associations in Europe and Latin America as well as in North America, law and economics scholarship is being produced in every major country and in many minor ones, and several of the leading journals are published outside the United States. Improvements in transportation and communications, and the rapid diffusion of English as the international language of scholarship, has fostered the internationalisation of law and economics. And there is growing recognition that comparative studies are an indispensable tool for gaining a better understanding of the economic nature and consequences of law. It is, for example, most unlikely that we will ever gain an adequate understanding of the efficiency of the Anglo-American 'adversarial' system of legal procedure without comparing it to the 'inquisitorial' system that prevails in Continental Europe; or understand the role of property rights in economic growth without studying the experience of the Central and European nations that have recently emerged from Communism.

Along with the internationalisation of the field has come an extraordinary growth in breadth of coverage and in specialisation of focus. Few areas of legal scholarship remain untouched by economics. Apart from the obvious examples - areas such as taxation and antitrust and securities regulation and (other) regulated industries and commercial law, all areas where the law is explicitly engaged in regulating economic activity - recent decades have seen a broadening of interest to include tort, contract, family, intellectual property, constitutional, criminal, admiralty, labour, arbitration, and antidiscrimination law, among others. But not only have more and more areas of law been brought under the lens of economics; more and more of the increasingly technical tools of economics - itself a field undergoing rapid growth and increased specialisation - have been brought to bear on the law, along with the latest in game theory. An immense and difficult body of monographic and journal scholarship is the result.

When a field becomes large, diverse and technical, it cries out for encyclopedic coverage. Thirty years ago one person, in one book, could map most of the terrain of law and economics. That is no longer possible. It has become infeasible for any single individual to keep fully abreast of the field of law and economics. He or she cannot be fully expert in every area of the field. And yet from time to time the scholar will find it necessary to cross the boundary that demarcates his own area of primary interest. For such a person, the opportunity of getting a quick overview of another part of the field by reading an encyclopedia article is welcome and even essential. It is even more welcome to those scholars, consultants, and practitioners who do not consider themselves 'law and economics' people, but whose work intersects the law and economics field. Law and economics has had interesting things to say about virtually every area of law, and this makes it of potential relevance to anyone working in one of those areas, who might be a practising lawyer, an economic consultant, a sociologist, psychologist, historian, or philosopher. For these 'outsiders', facing a research or practical task to which law and economics may be relevant, the opportunity to consult an encyclopedia article as the initial port of entry into the law and economics field is of immense potential value - as it is to students, and to scholars who are beginning to work in law and economics and want a broader view of the field before they decide where to specialise within it.

The *Encyclopedia of Law and Economics* endeavours, I think very successfully, to provide the kind of encyclopedic coverage - comprehensive and sophisticated but lucid, international without being esoteric, uniform without being monochrome, collective but individual - that the field of law and economics requires. It will help to make the field accessible to outsiders and to promote mutual intelligibility among insiders. It provides a meeting place for and an overview of a vast activity of scholarship, and will thus help to unify and advance the field. It is a milestone in an advancing field.

Introduction

Boudewijn Bouckaert and Gerrit De Geest
General editors

General Aims

The *Encyclopedia of Law and Economics* is an ambitious reference work that attempts to survey the whole law and economics literature in nearly 5,000 pages. Most entries contain two elements: a review of the literature, written by an authority in the field, and a quasi complete bibliography (not just a selection).

Economic analysis of law has expanded dramatically in recent years. In many branches, the literature is now at a 'mature' stage, where scholars agree on basic concepts, theories and even on policy recommendations. Yet, this scholarship does not reach many policymakers, lawyers or judges. Outside the USA, it even does not seem to reach law professors. This is not so much due to the fact that policymakers, judges or law professors are not interested in the economic consequences of legal rules, but rather to the fact that the literature is too inaccessible. There is a clear need for reference works that give a reliable overview of the literature in a way that is understandable also for non-specialists. This is the primary purpose of the *Encyclopedia of Law and Economics*.

Reviews of the Literature

The reviews are relatively lengthy articles (on average nearly 10,000 words) in which the basic questions and items of discussion are explained, the literature is summarized, critical reflections on these publications and on the evolution of the discussion in general are developed, and perhaps suggestions for further research are made.

The authors have been asked not to make their surveys too technical in order to make sure that readers without a mathematical training can still understand them. The result is in-depth and up-to-date syntheses of the literature that are still accessible for non-specialists, like judges, politicians or undergraduate students. All review articles have been anonymously refereed.

Bibliographies

The *Encyclopedia of Law and Economics* is to a great extent also a bibliographical work. In most cases, authors have tried to be quasi-complete.

The bibliographical lists at the end of all entries are not a 'list of cited works'. They list many more references than could be discussed in the text. Beside the bibliography of law and economics studies on the topic itself, many entries contain a second list, entitled 'Other References', which are references cited in the text, but either purely legal, philosophical, sociological, or cited law and economics publications that are not directly related to the very topic (for instance, many authors have cited Coase, 1960).

There is no doubt a need for these such specialized bibliographies. The law and economics literature has exploded in recent years (this Encyclopedia lists over 20,000 law and economics publications). However, to date it has not been so easy for readers to find the relevant publications, because they are spread out over law reviews, economics journals, conference volumes and so on. The fact that economic analysis of law is an interdisciplinary approach means that the specialized bibliographies in economics (like Econlit) or the specialized sources on law (like Lexis or Westlaw) give a very incomplete overview. Moreover, titles of articles or books do not always make clear whether the research was purely legal, purely economic, or truly interdisciplinary.

Quotation Style

As anyone can experience every day, there is no uniformity concerning the quotation style in law and economics, nor in economics or legal science. To make the bibliographies useful for as many scholars and students as possible, it is the policy of the *Encyclopedia of Law and Economics* to provide the maximum of information, but within certain limits. More specifically, the references to articles contain in principle the volume number of the journal and the year of publication, as well as the number of the first and the last pages of an article. Journal titles are written out in full. Titles of works in languages other than English are translated into English.

Structure

The *Encyclopedia of Law and Economics* has a pyramidal structure. The question was what structure had to be chosen. The general division of legal rules into branches differs fundamentally among legal systems. Most continental (European) legal classification systems are based, for instance, on the division between public law and private law. They also unify contract law, tort law and the law on restitution into one branch of law, called 'law of obligations'. American lawyers would have a hard time trying to find their way in such a system. The classification system of Econlit (where K is 'law and economics') was in our opinion no perfect alternative either, since it is not detailed enough and not much common-law oriented to satisfy continental lawyers.

Therefore we decided to elaborate a new, detailed classification system, inspired by both legal theory and law and economics insights. After a methodological and historical part (0000-0900), the law is divided into substantial norms (1000-6000) and meta-norms.

Substantial norms are divided into property (private property 1000 ff., common property 2000 ff.) and the transfer of property (involuntary transfer between private parties - tort law and restitution - 3000 ff.), voluntary transfer of property between private parties (general contract law, 4000 ff., and the regulation of contracts, 5000 ff.) and involuntary transfers between citizens and the state (taxation, social security, takings, 6000 ff.).

Meta-norms include litigation and evidence law (7000 ff.), criminal law (putting some additional incentives on legal rules defined in other branches of law) and rules on the production of legal rules (9000 ff.).

A correct classification system can improve analyses by suggesting what kind of models are to be applied. Medical malpractice, for instance, is considered by Anglo-American rules as a branch of tort law. It is more correct from an economic viewpoint to consider it as a regulation of contracts between physicians and patients (therefore it is treated in the volume on the regulation of contracts and not in the general part on tort law). Marriage law is according to many legal systems a part of 'family law'. Again, it is better to see it as the regulation of a specific contract. Modern economic scholarship on marriage law tries to apply the models on optimal contract remedies to the problem of unstable marriages.

Acknowledgments

A massive undertaking requires the help of an enormous amount of people. We would like to thank, first of all, the members of the editorial board and the board of referees. Second, we owe a lot to the publisher, Edward Elgar, and his staff - especially to Dymphna Evans for supporting the project in many ways. Third, we would like to acknowledge the financial support of the Economic Institute/CIAV of Utrecht University and of the Department of General Jurisprudence and History of Law of the University of Ghent. Finally, we can give no more than a sample of the people that have substantially contributed to this project: Luc Bosman, Olivier Delbecque, Ben Depoorter, Anja De Wilde, Niky D'Hulster, Wim Dubois, Regine Goemaes, Ghislain Hoffman, Steven Mels, Geert Premereur, An Saerens, Gianni Trovisi, Frieda Van Caneghem and Nancy Van Nuffel.

0000
Introductory Books

Bibliography Collected by the Editors

Adams, Michael (1981), *Oekonomische Analyse des Zivilprozesses* (Economic Analysis of Civil Procedure), Koenigstein, Athenaeum-Verlag.

Algra, N.E. (1991), *The Relations Between Law and Economics*, Cahiers Rechtstheorie en Encyclopedie van het recht, Nr. 2.

Arruñada, Benito (1996), 'Analisis contractual de la empresa: Una introduccion aplicada (Contractual Analysis of the Firm: An Applied Introduction)', **5(3)** *Revista Europea de Direccion y Economia de la Empresa*.

Barnes, David W. and Stout, Lynn A. (1992a), *Economic Foundations of Regulation and Antitrust Law*, Minneapolis, West Publishing.

Barnes, David W. and Stout, Lynn A. (1992b), *Economics of Property Rights and Nuisance Law*, Minneapolis, West Publishing.

Barnes, David W. and Stout, Lynn A. (1992c), *Economics of Constitutional Law and Public Choice*, Minneapolis, West Publishing.

Barnes, David W. and Stout, Lynn A. (1992d), *Economic Analysis of Tort Law*, Minneapolis, West Publishing.

Barnes, David W. and Stout, Lynn A. (1992e), *Cases and Materials on Law and Economics*, Minneapolis, West Publishing.

Barnes, David W. and Stout, Lynn A. (1992f), *Economics of Contract Law*, Minneapolis, West Publishing.

Bergel, J.-L. (1989), *Théorie Générale du Droit* (General Theory of Law), Dalloz, Coll. Méthode du droit.

Bowles, Roger A. (1982), *Law and the Economy*, Oxford, Martin Robertson, 239 p.

Cabrillac Remy (1995), *Introduction Générale au Droit* (General Introduction of Law), Dalloz, 23 p.

Cheung, Steven N.S. (1987), *The Words of an Orange Seller* (in Chinese), Taipei: Yuan-Liou Publishing Company, Ltd..

Chiancone, Aldo and Porrini, Donatella (1996), *Lezioni di Analisi Economica del Diritto* (Lessons of Economic Analysis of Law), Torino, Giappichelli.

Cooter, Robert D. and Ulen, Thomas S. (1988), *Law and Economics*, Scott Foresman. Reprinted in Japanese translation by Prof. Shozo Ota, introduction by Prof. Koji Shimdo, published by Shoji-Homu in 1989.

Crafton, Steven M. and Brinig, Margaret F. (1994), *Quantitative Methods for Lawyers*, Durham (NC), Carolina Academic Press.

Dnes, Antony W. (1996), *Economics of Law*, London, Sweet & Maxwell.

Gallo, Paolo (1998), *Analisi Economica del Diritto* (Economic Analysis of Law), Torino, Giappichelli.

Gemtos, Petros A. (1995), *Oikonomika kai Dikaio: Oikonomika gia Nomikous, tomos: Methodologika kai Oikonomika Themelia* (Law and Economics: Economics for Lawyers, vol. I: Methodological and Economic Foundations), Athens-Komotini, Ant. N. Sakkoulas Publications.

Ghestin Jacques (1994), 'Traité de droit civil (Treat of Civil Law)', 84-85.

Hirsch, Werner Z. (1979), *Law and Economics: An Introductory Analysis*, San Diego, Academic Press, 275 p.

Holzhauer, Rudi W., Teijl, Rob et al. (1995), *Inleiding Rechtseconomie* (Introduction to Law and Economics), Arnhem, Gouda Quint.

Holzhauer, Rudi W., Teijl, Rob et al (1989), *Inleiding Rechtseconomie* (Introduction to Law and Economics), Arnhem, Gouda Quint, 345 p.

Hondius, E.H. et al. (1991), *Rechtseconomie en Recht: Kennismaking met een Vakgebied in Opkomst* (Law and Economics and Law: Getting to Know an Emerging Discipline), Zwolle, Tjeenk Willink, 201 p.

Hwang, Chun-Sin and Kan, Steven S. (1994), *Principles of Economics Cooperating for Mutual Prosperity and Progress*, Taipei, Shin Lu Bookstore.

Jovanovic, Aleksandra (1998), *Uvod u Ekonomsku Analizu Prava* (Introduction to Economic Analysis of Law), Belgrade, Pravni fakultet.

Kan, Steven S. (1994), *Principles of Economics Cooperating for Mutual Prosperity and Progress*, Taipei, Shin Lu Bookstore.

Kanniainen, Vesa and Määttä, Kalle (eds) (1996), *Näkökulmia Oikeustaloustieteeseen* (Perspectives on Law and Economics), Helsinki, Gaudeamus.

Kaplow, Louis (1987), *Optimal Transition Policy: Replacing Horizontal Equity with an Ex Ante Incentives Perspective*, Dissertation accepted by Harvard University Department of Economics.

Labus Miroljub (1995), *Osnovi ekonomije: Savremene Teorije i Primena* (Foundation Economics: Contemporary Theories and Application), Jugoslovenska knjiga, Belgrade.

Lande, Robert H., Lafferty, Ronald N. and Kirkwood, John (1984), *Impact Evaluations of Federal Trade Commission Vertical Restraints Cases*, FTC Publication. Nineteen Journal Reprints for *Antitrust Law and Economics* **1** (1986).

Lehmann, Michael (1983), *Buergerliches Recht und Handelsrecht - eine juristische und oekonomische Analyse*, Stuttgart, Poeschel.

Lemennicier, Bertrand (1991), *Economie du Droit* (Economics of Law), Paris, Ed. Cujas, 177 p.

Mackaay, Ejan (1982), *Economics of Information and Law*, Dordrecht, Kluwer, 293 p.

Markovits, Richard S. (1982), *Law and Economic Theory*, Oxford, Centre for Socio-Legal Studies.

Mercado Pacheco, Pedro (1994), *El Análisis Económico del Derecho. Una reconstrucción teórica* (Law and Economics. A Theoretical Reconstruction), Madrid, Centro de Estudios Constitucionales.

Mercuro, Nicholas and Ryan, Tim (1984), *Law, Economics, and Public Policy*, Greenwood, JAI Press.

Miceli, Thomas J. (1996), *Economics of the Law: Torts, Contracts, Property, Litigation*, Oxford, Oxford University Press.

Murphy, Jeffrie G. and Coleman, Jules L. (1984), *The Philosophy of Law: An Introduction to Jurisprudence*, Totowa, Rowman and Allenheld.

Nagel, Bernhard (1993), *Wirtschaftsrecht I, Grundrechte und Einführung in das Bürgerliche Recht, 3 edn* (Basic Rights and an Introduction into the Private Law), München, Lehrbuch.

Nagel, Bernhard (1994), *Wirtschaftsrecht III (Unternehmens-und Konzernrecht)* (Law of Firms and Conglomerates), München, Lehrbuch.

Nentjes, Andries (1993), *Elementaire Rechtseconomie* (Basic Law and Economics), Groningen, Wolters-Noordhoff, 139 p.

Oliver, J.M. (1979), *Law and Economics*, London, Allen and Unwin, 108 p.

Pardolesi, Roberto (1986), *Una introduzione all'Analisi Economica del Diritto con Postfazione* (Translation of A. Mitchell Polinsky's 'Introduction'), Bologna, Zanichelli, 149 p.

Pardolesi, Roberto (1992), 'Postfazione a Polinsky, Mitchell A., Una Introduzione all'Analisi Economica del Diritto (Afterword to Polinsky, Mitchell A., *An Introduction to Economic Analysis of Law*)', *Il Foro Italiano*, 179-199.

Phillips, A. (1962), *Market Structure, Organization and Performance*, Cambridge (MA), Harvard University Press.

Phillips, A. (1971), *Technology and Market Structure: A Study of the Aircraft Industry*, Lexington (MA), Heath.

Phillips, A., Phillips, A.P. and Phillips, T.R. (1994), *Biz Jets: Technology and Market Structure in the Corprate Jet Aircraft Industry*, Boston, Kluwer Academic Publishers.

Polinsky, A. Mitchell (1983), *An Introduction to Law and Economics*, Boston, Little Brown, 183 p.

Polinsky, A. Mitchell (1989), *An Introduction to Law and Economics* (2nd edn), Boston, Little, Brown and Company, 153 p.

Posner, Richard A. (1973), *Economic Analysis of Law*, Boston, Little Brown, 415 p. (1st edn), 1977, 572 p. (2nd edn), 1986, 666 p.

Reumer, Andrés (1996), *Análisis Económico del Derecho* (Economic Analysis of Law), Mexico, Fondo de Cultura Económica, Sociedad Mexicana de geografía y Estadística, e Instituto Technológico Autónome de México.

Roemer, Andrès (1994), *Introdución al Análisis Económico del Derecho* (Introduction to Law and Economics), Mexico, Fondo de Cultura Económica, Sociedad Mexicana de geografía y Estadística, e Instituto Technológico Autónome de México.

Rubin, Paul H. (1983), *Business Firms and The Common Law*.

Rubin, Paul H. (1990), *Managing Business Transactions*, New York, Free Press.

Ryssdal, Stray A.C. (1995), *Legal Realism and Economics as Behavior - A Scandinavian Look at the Economic Analysis of Law*, Oslo, Juridisk Forlag.

Schäfer, Hans-Bernd and Ott, Claus (1995), *Lehrbuch der Ökonomischen Analyse des Zivilrechts, 2. Aufl.* (Textbook on Economic Analysis of Private Law), Berlin.

Stankovic Vladeta (1985), *Privredni Sistem* (Economic System), Belgrade, Pravni fakultet.

Stankovic Vladeta (1995), *Pravo Privrednog Sistema* (Law of the Economic System), Belgrade, Pravni fakultet.

Stephen, Frank H. (1988), *The Economics of the Law*, Ames, Iowa State University Press, 224 p.

Streit, Manfred E. (1991), *Theorie der Wirtschaftspolitik 4. neubearb. u. erweiterte Aufl. (Theory of Economic Policy)*, Düsseldorf.

Tang, Yu-Min (1987), *Translation of Richard A. Posner's Economic Analysis of Law*, Taipei, Commercial Press.

Theeuwes, Jules J.M. et al. (1992), *Recht en Economie*, Amsterdam, Addison-Wesley, 301 p.

Torres Lopez, Juan (1987), *Análisis Económico del Derecho. Panorama doctrinal (Survey on Law and Economics)*, Madrid, Editorial Tecnos.

Tullock, Gordon (1971), *The Logic of the Law*, New York, Basic Books, 278 p.

Van Velthoven, Ben C.J., Van Wijck, Peter W. et al. (1997), *Recht en Efficiëntie* (Law and Efficiency), Deventer, Kluwer, 337 p.

Veljanovski, Cento G. (1990), *The Economics of Law - An Introductory Text*, London, Institute of Economic Affairs, 95 p. (Hobart Paperback).

Vodinelic, V. Vladimir (1991), *Gradjansko Pravo - Uvodne Teme* (Civil Law - Introductory Themes), Belgrade.

Weise, Peter, Eger, Thomas, Brandes, Wolfgang and Kraft, M. (1993), *Neue Mikroökonomie* (New Microeconomics), Heidelberg, Physica.

0010
INTRODUCTORY ARTICLES

Bibliography Collected by the Editors

Adams, Michael (1986), 'Der Irrtum über "künftige Sachverhalte" - Anwendungsbeispiel und Einfürhung in die Ökonomische Analyse des Rechts', *RECHT, Zeitschrift für juristische Ausbildung und Praxis*, 14-23.

Albert, Hans (1986), 'Law as an Instrument of Rational Choice', in Daintith, Terence and Teubner, Gunther (eds), *Contract and Organisation: Legal Analysis in the Law*, Berlin, Walter de Gruyter, 25-51.

Alpa, Guido (1983), 'Interpretazione economica del Diritto (Economic Interpretation of Law)', in X (ed.), *Voce del Novissimo Digesto Italiano*, Torino, UTET, 315-324.

Alpa, Guido (1984), 'Diritto e Analisi Economica (a proposito di un recente libro di R. Bowles) (Law and Economic Analysis, With Regard to a Recent Book by R. Bowles)', *Diritto dell impresa*, 111-120.

Aprile, Ercole (1989), 'Regolamentazione dei Fenomeni Economici e Analisi Economica degli Strumenti Giuridici: Spunti per una Riflessione (Regulation of Economic Phenomena and Economic Analysis of Legal Instruments: Hints for a Reflection)', *Nuovo Diritto*, 505-521.

Arruñada, Benito (1991), 'Nobel al Giro Coasiano (Nobel to the Coasian Turn)', **41** *Revista de Economía*, 122-126.

Assmann, Heinz-Dieter (1989), 'Kommentar on Ott, Allokationseffizienz, Rechtsdogmatik und Rechtsprechung', in Ott, Claus and Schäfer, Hans-Bernd (eds), *Allekationseffizienz in der Rechtsordnung*, Berlin, Springer, 45-49.

Bakker, Luit M. et al. (1996), 'Economie en Recht: van Confrontatie naar Integratie (Economics and Law: From Confrontation to Integration)', in Van de Hoek, M.P. (ed.), *Opstellen aangeboden aan prof. dr. C. Rijnvos*, Groningen, Wolters-Noordhoff, 102-111.

Barbera, Salvador (1989), 'Los derechos individuales en el análisis económico (Individual rights and economic analysis)', **38** *Economistas*.

Behrens, Peter (1981), 'Aspekte einer Ökonomischen Theorie des Rechts (Aspects of an Economic Theory of Law)', **12** *Rechtstheorie*, 472-490.

Behrens, Peter (1988), 'Über das Verhältnis der Rechtswissen schaft zur Nationalökonomie: Die Ökonomischen Grundlagen des Rechts (On the Interrelationship between Law and Economics)', in Boettcher, Erik, Herder-Dorneich, Philipp and Schenk, Karl-Ernst (eds), *Jahrbuch für neue politische Ökonomie 7*, Tübingen, Mohr, 209-228.

Bongaerts, Jan C. (1986), 'Inleiding tot de Economische Analyse van het Recht met Toepassing op het Contractenrecht en het Aansprakelijkheidsrecht, Inzonderheid de Milieuramp te Bhopal (Introduction to Economic Analysis of Law, with Applications to Contract and Tort Law, and in Particular to the Environmental Disaster in Bhopal)', in Van Den Bergh, Roger (ed.), *Verslagboek Eerste Werkvergadering Recht en Economie*, Antwerpen, Leerstoel A. Van Melkebeke, Handelshogeschool, 5-20.

Bouckaert, Boudewijn (1984), 'Efficiëntie of Rechtvaardigheid: het Onvermijdelijk Dilemma? (Efficiency or Justice: the Unavoidable Dilemma?)', **29** *Tijdschrift voor Sociale Wetenschappen*, 101-133.

Bouckaert, Boudewijn (1988), 'L'Analyse Economique du Droit: vers un Renouveau de la Science Juridique? (Economic Analysis of Law: Towards a Renewal of Legal Science?)', **18** *Revue interdisciplinaire d'études juridiques*, 7-47.

Braden, John B. and Bromley, Daniel W. (1981), 'The Economics of Cooperation Over Collective Bads', **8** *Journal of Environmental Economics and Management*, 134-150.

Bromley, Daniel W. (1978), 'Property Rules, Liability Rules, and Environmental Economics', **12** *Journal of Economic Issues*, 43-60.

Bromley, Daniel W. (1989a), 'Entitlements, Missing Markets and Environmental Uncertainty', **17** *Journal of Environmental Economics and Management*, 181-194.

Bromley, Daniel W. (1989b), 'Institutional Change and Economic Efficiency', **23** *Journal of Economic Issues*, 735-759.

Bromley, Daniel W. (1989c), 'Property Relations and Economic Development: The Other Land Reform', **17** *World Development*, 867-877.

Bromley, Daniel W. (1992), 'The Commons, Common Property, and Environmental Policy', **2(1)** *Environmental and Resource Economics*, 1-17.

Bromley, Daniel W. (1993a), 'Regulatory Takings: Coherent Concept or Logical Contradiction', **17** *Vermont Law Review*, 647-682.

Bromley, Daniel W. (1993b), 'The Law, Agency, and Global Climate Change', **3** *International Journal of Environment and Pollution*, 250-268.

Bromley, Daniel W. (1993c), 'Reconstituting Economic Systems: Institutions in National Economic Development', **11** *Development Policy Review*, 131-151.

Bromley, Daniel W. (1994), 'The Enclosure Movement Revisited: The South African Commons', **28** *Journal of Economic Issues*, 357-365.

Bromley, Daniel W. (1995), 'Property Rights and Natural Resource Damage Assessment', **14** *Ecological Economics*, 129-135.

Bromley, Daniel W. (1996), 'The Social Construction of Land', in Hagedorn, Konrad (ed.), *Institutioneller Wandel und Politische Okonomie von Landwirtschaft und Agrapolitik*, Frankfurt am Main, Campus Verlag.

Bromley, Daniel W. and Hodge, Ian (1990), 'Private Property Rights and Presumptive Policy Entitlements: Reconsidering the Premises of Rural Policy', **17** *European Review of Agricultural Economics*, 197-214.

Bruinsma, J.F. and Huls, N.J.H. (1995), 'Recht in de Broze Vernislaag van een Booming Industry (Law as the Fragile Coat of Varnish of a Booming Industry)', **70** *Nederlands Juristen Blad*, 1625-1631.

Brunt, Maureen (1984), 'The Economics of Law: Economic Imperialism in Negligence Law, No Fault Insurance, Occupational Licensing and Criminology: Comment', **67** *Australian Economic Review*, 113-119.

Bulcha, Mekuria, Kibreab, Gaim and Nobel, Peter (1987), 'Sociology, Economy and Law: Views in Common', in Nobel, Peter (ed.), *Refugees and Development in Africa*, Stockholm, Almqvist and Wiksell International, 93-103.

Burow, Patrick (1993), 'Einführung in die Ökonomische Analyse des Rechts (An Introduction into Law and Economics)', **1** *Juristische Schulung*, 8-12.

Cabrillo, Francisco (1987), '?Por Qué un Análisis Económico del Derecho? (Why an Economic Analysis of Law?)', **58** *Revista de Occidente*, 37-46.

Cabrillo, Francisco (1990), 'Una Nueva Frontera: El Análisis Económico del Derecho (A New Frontier: Law and Economics)', **687** *Información Comercial Española*, 9-22.

Calsamiglia, Albert (1988), 'Justicia, Eficiencia y Derecho (Equity, Efficiency and the Law)', **1** *Revista del Centro de Estudios Constitucionales*, 327 ff.

Campbell, C. and Wiles, P. (1976), 'The Study of Law in Society', **10** *Law and Society Review*, 547-578.

Casas Pardo, José, 'Las Estructuras Federal y Fiscal de las Democracias Representativa y Directa como Modelos para una Union Europea Federal (Federal and Fiscal Structures in Representative and Direct Democracies as Models for a Federal European Union)', in X (ed.), *Actas de las Jornadas de Estudio sobre 'La Constitucion española y el ordenamineto comunitario europeo* (II)', Dirección General del Servicio Juridico del Estado, Ministerio de Justicia.

Casas Pardo, José, 'Algunas Consideraciones sobre la Teoría de la Elección Pública (Some Considerations on Public Choice Theory)', in Beltran, Lucas, *Libro Homanaje*, Madrid, Editorial Moneda y Credito.

Casas Pardo, José, 'The Spanish Transition to Democracy: a Public Choice Approach', in Backhaus, Jürgen G. (ed.), *The Political Economy of Structural Change*, Cheltenham, Edward Elgar.

Casas Pardo, José (forthcoming), 'El Contractualismo-Constitucionalismo Liberal de James M. Buchanan (James M. Buchanan's Liberal Contractualism-Constitutionalism)', in Cortina, A. (ed.), *Ética de los Negocios*, Bancaja, Valencia, Fundación Etnor.

Casas Pardo, José (1979), 'El Control de los Efectos Económicos Externos por Medio de la Imposición (Controlling Externalities with Taxation)', *Revista de Derecho Financiero y Hacienda Pública.*

Casas Pardo, José (1984), 'Estudio Introductorio (Introductory Study)', in Buchanan, James M. and Tollison, Robert D. (eds), *Análisis Económico de los Políticos* (Economic Analysis of the Politicians), Madrid, Instituto de Estudios Económicos.

Casas Pardo, José (1987), 'Laudatio Academica', in Casas Pardo, J. and Bru Parra, S. (eds), *Economía y Política* (Economics and Politics), Valencia, Servei de Publicacions, Universitat de Valencia.

Casas Pardo, José (1991), 'Sobre la Relevancia de la Economía Constitucional (About the Relevance of Constitutional Economy)', in X (ed.), *Homenaje al Prof. D. Carlos Otero Díaz*, Universidad de Santiago de Compostela.

Casas Pardo, José (1993), 'Análisis Económico de las Instituciones y de las Reglas (Economic Analysis of the Institutions and Rules)', in Puy Fraga, P. (ed.), *Análisis económico del Derecho y de la Política*, Santiago de Compostela, Fundación Alfredo Brañas.

Casas Pardo, José (1995a), 'Introducción (Introduction)', in Casas Pardo, J. and Schneider, F. (eds), *Current Issues in Public Choice*, Cheltenham, Edward Elgar.

Casas Pardo, José (1995b), 'Does Ethical Proceduralism Underly Buchanan's Constitutional Contractualism?', in Casas Pardo, J. and Schneider, F. (eds), *Current Issues in Public Choice*, Cheltenham, Edward Elgar.

Casas Pardo, José and Brennan, Geoffrey (1978), 'A Reading of the Spanish Constitution', **1** *Constitutional Political Economy.*

Casas Pardo, José and Brennan, Geoffrey (1990), 'La Constitución española a la luz de la Economía política de las constituciones (The Spanish Constitution from the Political Economy of Constitutions Approach)', **116-3** *Hacienda Pública Española.*

Casas Pardo, José and Fernández Cainzos, J., 'Las Contituciones Económica y Fiscal en la Constitución Española de 1978 (The Economic and Fiscal Constitutions into the Spanish Constitution of 1978)', in Alvarez Conde, E. (ed.), *La Constitución española de 1978 diez años despues*, Madrid, Tecnos.

Casas Pardo, José and Fernández Cainzos, J. (1995), 'La Imposición a Traves de la Regulación en España: Un intento de medir la imposición implicita en el sistema financiero español en la década 1977-1987 (Taxation Through Regulation in Spain: An Effort to Measure Implicit Taxation in the Spanish Financial System between 1977-1987)', in X (ed.), *Estudios de Derecho Mercantil en Homenaje al Prof. Manuel Broseta Pont*, Tirant lo Blanch, Valecia.

Casas Pardo, José and Navarro, Puchades M. (forthcoming), 'La Perspectiva de la "Public Choice" en el Análisis de la Actuación de los Entes Públicos (Public Choice Approach and the Behaviour of Public Enterprises)', in X (ed.), *Actas del II Congreso Español de Ciencia Politica y de la Administración.*

Casas Pardo, José and Sainz Sánchez, E. (1995), 'La Coacción de las Instituciones Colectivas (Compelling Collective Institutions)', in Sainz Sánchez, E. (ed.), *Las Organizaciones como sistemas Constitucionales*, Granada, Ensayos sobre el Modelo de Gestión Burocratica de la Universidad Pública, Método Ediciones.

Cherot, Jean-Yves (1987a), 'Trois Thèses de l'Analyses Economique du Droit (Three Theses of Economic Analysis of Law)', *Revue de la Recherche Juridique.*

Cherot, Jean-Yves (1987b), 'Trois Thèses sur l'Analyse Economique du Droit - Quelques Usages de l'Approche Economique des Règles Juridiques (Three Theses on Economic Analysis of Law - Some Uses of the Economic Approach to Legal Rules)', **2** *Revue de la Recherche Juridique.*

Cooter, Robert D. (1982a), 'The Cost of Coase', **11** *Journal of Legal Studies*, 1-33. Reprinted in Donahue, Charles Jr, Kauper, Thomas E. and Martin, Peter W., *Property: An Introduction to the Concept and the Institution*, 1992. Reprinted in Ackerman, Bruce, Ellickson, Robert and Rose, Carol, *Foundations of Property Law*, 1995. Reprinted in Medema, Steven G. (ed.), *The Legacy of Ronald Coase in Economic Analysis*, Aldershot, Edward Elgar Publishing, 96-128.

Cooter, Robert D. (1982b), 'Law and the Imperialism of Economics: An Introduction to the Economic Analysis of Law by Reviewing Some Major Books', **29** *UCLA Law Review*, 1260-1269.

Cooter, Robert D. (1985), 'Prices and Sanctions', **84** *Columbia Law Review*, 1523-1560.

Cooter, Robert D. (1993), 'Diritto ed Economia (Law and Economics)', *Istituto Dell'Enciclopedia Italiana, Fondata Da Giovanni Treccani*, 98-106.

Cooter, Robert D. (1994), 'Laws and Prices: How Economics Contributed to Law By Misunderstanding Morality', **3** *Iuris: Quaderns de Política Jurídica*, 35-36.

Cooter, Robert D. (1995), 'Law and Unified Social Theory', **22** *Law and Society*, 50-67. Reprinted in Galligan, D.J. (ed.), *Socio-Legal Studies in Context: The Oxford Centre Past and Future*, Blackwell Publishers, Oxford, 1995, pp. 50-67.

Cooter, Robert D. and Rubinfeld, Daniel L. (1989), 'Economic Analysis of Legal Disputes and Their Resolution', **27** *Journal of Economic Literature*, 1067-1097.

Reprinted in Posner, Richard A. and Parisi, Francesco (eds), *Law and Economics*, Edward Elgar, 1996 forthcoming.

Cooter, Robert D. and Rubinfeld, Daniel L. (1990), 'Trial Courts: An Economic Perspective', **24** *Law and Society Review*, 533 ff.

Cortenraad, Wouter H.F.M. (1996), 'Rechtseconomie Bestaat Niet (There's no Such Thing as Law and Economics)', **71** *Nederlands Juristen Blad*, 963-967.

Cosentino, Fabrizio (1990), 'Analisi Economica del Eiritto: Ritorno al Futuro? (Economic Analysis of Law: Back to the Future?)', **5** *Foro Italiano*, 153-156.

Crombach, H.F.M. and Van Dun, Frank (1990), 'Recht en Economie in Utopia: een Rechtsfilosofisch Gedachtenexperiment (Law and Economics in Utopia: a Mental Experiment in Legal Philosophy)', **4** *Rechtsgeleerd Magazijn Themis*, 167-176.

De Bock, Ruth (1990), 'Inleiding (Introduction)', **39(10)** *Ars Aequi* in Bock, Ruth de et al. (eds), *Themanummer Rechtseconomie*, 607-613.

De Bock, Ruth et al. (1990), 'Themanummer Rechtseconomie (Special Issue Law and Economics)', **39(10)** *Ars Aequi*, 607-804.

De Geest, Gerrit (1990), 'Public Choice en Rechtseconomie (Public Choice and Law and Economics)', **39(10)** *Ars Aequi* in Bock, Ruth de et al. (eds), *Themanummer Rechtseconomie*, 666-673.

Dnes, Antony W. (1992), 'Franchising', in Eatwell, John, Milgate, Murray and Newman, Peter (eds), *The New Palgrave Dictionary of Money and Finance*, London, Macmillan.

Dnes, Antony W. (1994a), 'Law and Economics', **10** *Policy*, 39-42.

Dnes, Antony W. (1994b), 'Legal Economics', **2** *Hume Papers on Public Policy*, 56-62.

Dooyeweerd, H. (1949), 'De Sociologische Verhouding tussen Recht en Economie en het Probleem van het Zogeheten "Economisch Recht" (The Sociological Relationship Between Law and Economics and the Problem of So-called "Economic Law")', in Dooyeweerd, H. (ed.), *Opstellen op het gebied van Recht, Staat en Maatschappij*, Amsterdam, Bakker, 221-264.

Dorndorf, Eberhard (1995), 'Modelle des Rechtssystems in der Ökonomischen Analyse des Rechts (Models of the Legal System in Law and Economics)', in X. (ed.), *Ökonomie und Gesellschaft. Jahrbuch 11, Markt, Norm und Moral*, Frankfurt/New York, 127-159.

Duggan, A.J. (1989a), 'New Directions in Legal Theory: Law and Economics', **63** *Law Institute Journal*, 852-853.

Duggan, A.J. (1989b), 'Law and Economics in Australia', **1** *Legal Education Review*, 37-41.

Eger, Thomas (1989), 'Einführung in die Ökonomische Analyse des Rechts (Introduction to the Economic Analysis of Law)', in Nagel, B. (ed.), *Wirtschaftsrecht II*, München, Oldenborg, 18-35.

Eide, Erling (1992), 'Rettsøkonomi - en Introduksjon (Law and Economics - an introduction)', **4** *Jussens Venner*, 193-224.

Fezer, Karl-Heinz (1986), 'Aspekte einer Rechtskritik an der Economic Analysis of Law und am Property Rights Approach (Critcal Aspects of the Economic Analysis of Law and the Property Rights Approach from a Lawyer's Viewpoint)', **41** *Juristenzeitung*, 817-824.

Fezer, Karl-Heinz (1988), 'Nochmals, Kritik an der Ökonomischen Analyse des Rechts (More Critics on Law and Economics)', **43** *Juristenzeitung*, 223 ff.

Field, A.J. (1991), 'Do Legal Systems Matter?', **28(1)** *Explorations in Economic History*, 1-35.

Fluet, Claude (1990), 'L'Analyse Economique du Droit (Economic Analysis of Law)', **43(3)** *Économie Appliquée*, 53-66.

Garoupa, Nuno (1997), 'The Theory of Optimal Law Enforcement', **11** *Journal of Economic Surveys*, 267-295.

Gay, David E.R. (1979), 'A Curriculum Note on the New Law and Economics', *Papers and Proceedings of the Southwestern Society of Economists*, 59-66.

Gay, David E.R. (1981a), 'Towards a Theory of Entitlements in Comparative Economics', **25** *Rivista Internazionale di Scienze Economiche e Commerciali*, 1021-1028.

Gay, David E.R. (1981b), 'Entitlements and Public Policy', **18** *Social Science Journal*, 87-100.

Gay, David E.R. (1992), 'Teaching Privatization in the Soviet Union: An Experimental Economics Approach', **1** *Classroom Expernomics*, 5-6.

Gay, David E.R. (1994), 'Incentives and Privatization: An Experimental Economics Approach', **22** *Atlantic Economic Journal*, 79 ff.

Gay, David E.R. and Waters, Alan R. (1982), 'On the Economic Theory of Legal Systems', **29** *Rivista Internazionale di Scienze Economiche e Commerciali*, 433-441.

Gemtos, Petros A. (1998), 'Oi Theoretikes Vaseis tes Oikonomikes Analyses tou Dikaiou (The Theoretical Bases of Economic Analysis of Law)', **46** *Nomiko Vema*.

Georgakopoulos, Nicholas L. (1995), 'Peri Tmematikou Daneismou apo ten Amerikani ke Nomike Skepse (On the Partial Borrowing from the American Legal Thought)', **43** *Nomiko Vema*, 799-807.

Guest, Stephen F.D. (1984), 'The Economics of Law', *Current Legal Problems*, 233-245.

Hatzis, Aristides N. (1996), 'Neofileleutherismos', Dikaio ten Oikonomike Analyse ton Thesmon: Eisagoge ste Melete ton Neon Oikonomikon Theorion gia to Dikaio, ten Koinonia kai ten Politike (The so-called "Neo-Liberalism", the Law and the Economic Analysis of Institutions: Introduction to the Study of the New Economic Theories on Law, Society and Politics)', **6** *Aissymnetes*.

Hatzis, Aristides N. (1997), *Eisagoge sten Oikonomike Analyse tou Dikaiou* (Introduction to the Economic Analysis of Law), Aristotle University of Thessaloniki School of Law and Economics, Department of History, Philosophy and Sociology of Law.

Hayashida, Seimei (1992), 'Ho to Keizai, Keizaibunseki, Hihan to Paradaimu (Law and Economics, Economic Analysis, its Critique and Paradigm)', **42** *Hokudai Hogaku Ronshu* (Hokkaido Law Review), 905-956. Part 2 pp. 1234-1272.

Heyne, Paul (1984), 'The Economics of Law: Economic Imperialism in Negligence Law, No Fault Insurance, Occupational Licensing and Criminology: Comment', **67** *Australian Economic Review*, 109-112.

Hollander, Abraham and Mackaay, Ejan (1980), 'Are Judges Economists at Heart?', in Ciampi, Costanino (ed.), *Artificial Intelligence and Legal Information Systems*, Amsterdam, North Holland, 129-149.

Hondius, E.H., Schippers, Joop J. and Siegers, Jacques J. (eds) (1991), 'Rechtseconomie: Brug tussen twee disciplines (Law and Economics: Bridge between two Disciplines)', in Hondius, E.H., Schippers, J.J. and Siegers, J.J. (eds), *Rechtseconomie en Recht*, Zwolle, Tjeenk Willink, 1-7.

Hotz, Beat (1982), 'Ökonomische Analyse des Rechts - eine Skeptische Betrachtung (Economic Analysis of Law - A Sceptical Reflection)', **34** *Wirtschaft und Recht*, 293-314.

Johnsen, D. Bruce (1994), 'Property Rights to Investment Research: The Agency Costs of Soft Dollar Brokerage', **11** *Yale Journal on Regulation*, 75-113.

Johnsen, D. Bruce (1995), 'The Quasi-Rent Structure of Corporate Entreprise: A Transaction Cost Theory', **44** *Emory Law Journal*, 1277 ff.

Johnsen, D. Bruce, Habib, Michel A. and Naik, Narayan Y. (forthcoming), 'Spin-offs and Information', *Journal of Financial Intermediation*.

Jongbloed, A.W. (1993), 'Recht, Economie en Rechtseconomie (Law, Economics and Law and Economics)', **85(10)** *Rechtsstrijd*, 204-210.

Kanniainen, Vesa, Määttä, Kalle and Heimonen, Matti (1995), 'Oikeustaloustiede - Law and Economics', *Oikeus*, 107-124.

Karakantas, Stylianos (1973), 'Oikonomia kai Dikaion (Law and Economics)', **27** *Harmenopoulos*, 257-265.

Kirby, M.D. (1981), 'Economics and Law: Symbiosis', **23** *Reform*, 86-90.

Kirchner, Christian (1978), 'Ökonomische Analyse des Rechts, Interdisziplinäre Zusammenarbeit von Ökonomie und Rechtswissenschaft (Economic Analysis of Law and Interdisciplinary Cooperation of Jurisprudence and Economics)', in Assmann, Heinz-Dieter, Kirchner, Christian and Schanze, Erich (eds), *Ökonomische Analyse des Rechts*, Kronberg, Athenäum, 75-91.

Kitch, Edmund W. (1983), 'The Intellectual Foundations of "Law and Economics"', **33** *Journal of Legal Education*, 184-196.

Kleinewefers, Henner (1987), 'Ökonomische Theorie des Rechts, Über Unterschiede Zwischen dem Ökonomischen und dem Juristischen Denken (Economic Theory of Law, on the Differences between)', in X (ed.), *Staat und Gesellschaft, Festschrift für Leo Schürm*, Fribourg, Universitätsverlag, 83-116.

Koboldt, Christian, Leder, Mathias and Schmidtchen, Dieter (1992), 'Ökonomische Analyse des Rechts (Law and Economics)', **7** *Wirtschaftswissenschaftliches Studium*.

Koboldt, Christian, Leder, Mathias and Schmidtchen, Dieter (1995), 'Ökonomische Analyse des Rechts (Law and Economics)', in Nobert, Berthold (ed.), *Allgemeine Wirtschaftstheorie*, München, 355-384.

Kornhauser, Lewis A. (1984), 'The Great Image of Authority', **36** *Stanford Law Review*, 349 ff.

Kornhauser, Lewis A. (1985), 'L'analyse Économique Du Droit (The Economic Analysis of Law)', **118-119** *Revue de Synthese*, 313 ff.

Kornhauser, Lewis A. (1986), 'Economic Analysis of Law', **16** *Materiali per una Storia della Cultura Giuridica*, 233 ff.

Kornhauser, Lewis A. (1988), 'Economique (Analyse - du droit)', in Arnaud, André-Jean (ed.), *Dictionnaire Encyclopedique de Theorie et de Sociologie du Droit*, Librairie General de Droit et de Jurisprudence.

Kornhauser, Lewis A. (1992), 'Analise Economica do Direito', **43(2)** *Sub Judica: Justica e Sociedade*.

Kötz, Hein (1993), 'Die Ökonomische Analyse des Rechts (Law and Economics)', *Zeitschrift für die gesamte Versicherungswissenschaft*, 57-70.

Kozyris, Phaedon I. (1991), 'Treis Provlematismoi sten Amerikanike Theoria tou Dikaiou (Three Conjectures in American Jurisprudence)', **39** *Nomiko Vema*, 715-728.

Kozyris, Phaedon I. (1996), 'Protaseis Dianemetikes Dikaiosynes sto 'Telos tes Istorias': Ta Kyria Erotemata me Apla Logia (Proposals of Distributive Justice in the 'End of History': Basic Questions Made Easy)', **3** *Kritike Epitheorese*, 23-81.

Kunz, Harald (1987), 'Recht und Ökonomie (Law and Economics)', **39** *Arbeitgeber*.

Larson, Bruce A. and Bromley, Daniel W. (1990), 'Property Rights, Externalities, and Resource Degradation: Locating the Tragedy', **33** *Journal of Development Economics*, 235-362.

Liakopoulos, Thanases (1982), 'Dikaio kai Oikonomia (Law and Economics)', **2** *Dikaio kai Politike*, 111-133.

Llebot Majo, José Oriol (1996), 'Doctrina y Teoría de la Empresa en el Derecho Mercantil (Una Aproximación al Significado de la Teoría Contractual de la Empresa) (Doctrine and Theory of the Firm in Contract Law Approaching the Meaning of Corporate Contractual Theory)', **210** *Revista de Derecho Mercantil*, 319-388.

Llewellyn, Karl N. (1925), 'The Effect of Legal Institutions upon Economics', **15** *American Economic Review*, 665-683.

Loukopoulos, Andreas D. (1962), 'Emporikon Dikaion kai oi Neoi Prosanatolismoi tes Oikonomias (Commercial Law and the New Directions of Economy)', **29** *Ephemeris ton Hellenon Nomikon*, 353-362.

Mackaay, Ejan (1986), 'La Règle Juridique Observée par le Prisme de l'Economiste - une Histoire Stylisée du Mouvement d'Analyse Economique du Droit (Law Observed through an Economist's Eyeglass - A Stylised History of the Law and Economics Movement)', **1** *Revue internationale de Droit Economique*, 43-88.

Mackaay, Ejan (1988a), 'L'Ordre Spontané Comme Fondement du Droit - un Survol des Modèles de l'Émergence des Règles dans une Société Civile (Spontaneous Order as Foundation of Law - A Survey of Models of the Emergence of Rules in Civil Society)', **22** *Revue Juridique Themis*, 347-383.

Mackaay, Ejan (1988b), 'Het Recht Bezien door de Bril van de Economist - Een Gestyleerd Overzicht van de Rechtseconomie (Law Seen Through Economists' Glasses: An Overview)', *Rechtsgeleerd Magazijn Themis*, 411-452.

Mackaay, Ejan (1991), 'Verschuivingen in De Rechtseconomie (Shifts in Law and Economics)', **66** *Nederlands Juristenblad*, 1505-1521.

Manne, Henry G. (1994), 'Le Origini Intellettuali di una Scuola di Analisi Economica del Diritto', **12** *Rivista Critica del Diritto Privato*, 167-181.

Mantzoufas, Georgios A. (1960), 'Oikonomikon Dikaion (Economic Law)', in X (ed.), *Oikomike kai Logistike Egkyklopedeia* (Encyclopedia of Economics and Accounting), Athens.

Mas-Colell, Andreu (1994), 'L'Anàlisi Econòmica i el Dret (The Economic Analysis and the Law)', **3** *Iuris*, 73-84.

Mengaroni, F. (1988), 'Analisi Economica del Diritto (Economic Analysis of Law)', **1** *Enciclopedia Giuridica*, 1-9.

Mercuro, Nicholas (1986), 'Contributions to Law and Economics: A Survey of Recent Books', **17(4)** *Journal of Economic Education*, 295-309.

Mercuro, Nicholas (1989), 'Towards a Comparative Institutional Approach to the Study of Law and Economics', in Mercuro, Nicholas (ed.), *Law and Economics*, Boston, Kluwer Academic Publishers, 1-26.

Mercuro, Nicholas and Medema, Steven G. (1995), 'Schools of Thought in Law and Economics: A Kuhnian Competition', in Malloy, Robin P. and Braun, Christopher K.

(eds), *Law and Economics: New and Critical Perspectives*, New York, Peter Lang, 65-126.

Mohr, K. and Wehrt, Klaus (1995), 'Einbau der Ökonomischen Analyse des Rechts in ein Juristisches Fallgutachten (Implementing the Economic Analysis of Law into a Legal Opinion)', **10** *JURA*, 536-542.

Mouly, Christian (1987), 'Présentation du Colloque sur l'Analyse Economique du Droit (Introduction to the Symposium of Economic Analysis of Law)', *Revue de la Recherche Juridique*, 413 ff.

Nentjes, Andries (1987), *De Economie van het Recht* (The Economy of the Law), oratie Groningen, s.l., 18 p.

Ogus, Anthony I. (1980), 'Economics, Liberty and the Common Law', **18** *Journal of Society of Public Teachers of Law*, 42-57.

Oker-Blom, Max (1980), 'Jurionomi eller Rätten i Ekonomiskt Perspektiv' (Law and Economics or Law from the Economic Perspective)', *Tidskrift utgiven av Juridiska Föreningen i Finland*, 245-265.

Oppetit, B. (1992), 'Droit et Economie (Law and Economics)', **37** *Archives de Philosophie du Droit. Nouvelle serie*, 17 ff.

Ott, Claus (1989), 'Allokationseffizienz, Rechtsdogmatik und Rechtsprechung - die Immanente Ökonomische Rationalität des Zivilrechts (Allocative Efficiency, Legal Dogmatics and Jurisprudence - The Immanent Rationality of Private Laws)', in Ott, Claus and Schäfer, Hans-Bernd (eds), *Allekationseffizienz in der Rechtsordnung*, Berlin, Springer, 25-44.

Ott, Claus and Schäfer, Hans-Bernd (1988), 'Die Ökonomische Analyse des Rechts. Irrweg oder Chance wissenschaftlicher Rechtserkenntnis? (The Economic Analysis of Law. Wrong Track or Chance)', *Juristenzeitung*, 213-223.

Pardolesi, Roberto (1982), 'Luci ed Ombre Nell Analisi Economica del Diritto (Appunti in Margine ad un Libro Recente) (Lights and Shadows in Law and Economics - Notes about a Recent Book)', **2** *Rivista di Diritto Civile*, 718-728.

Pardolesi, Roberto (1987), 'Analisi Economica del Diritto (Economic Analysis of Law)', **1** *Digesto Civile*, 309-320.

Pardolesi, Roberto (1988), 'Tutela Specifica e Tutela per Equivalente nella Prospettiva dell'Analisi Economica del Diritto (Specific Performance and Damages: An EAL Perspective)', *Quadrimestre*, 76-97.

Pardolesi, Roberto (1989), 'Un Moderno Minotauro: Law and Economics (A Modern Minotaur: Law and Economics)', *Economia, Società e Istituzioni*, 519-534.

Pasquini, Nello (1983), 'Interpretazione Giuridica e Analisi Economica - in Margine ad un "Reading" Recente (Legal Interpretation and Economic Analysis with Recent "Reading")', *Rivista trimestrale di Diritto e Procedura Civile*, 288-300.

Pastor, Santos (1984), 'Una Introducción al Análisis Económico del Derecho (An Introduction to Law and Economics)', **89** *Hacienda Pública Española*.

Pastor, Santos (1989), *Economía y Sistema Jurídico. Una Introducción al Análisis Económico del Derecho* (Economics and the Legal System. An Introduction to Economic Analysis of Law), Madrid, Tecnos.

Pastor, Santos and Pintos, Jesús (1992), 'La Economía y el Derecho: una Colaboración Difícil pero Provechosa (The Interaction Between Law and Economics: Problems and Progress)', **13** *Revista de Economía*, 96-100.

Paz-Ares, Cándido (1985), 'Seguridad Jurídica y Seguridad del Tráfico (Legal Certainty and Exhange Certainty)', *Revista de Derecho Mercantil.*

Phillips, A. (1956), 'Concentration, Scale, and Technological Change in Selected Manufacturing Industries, 1899-1939', **4(3)** *Journal of Industrial Economics*, 179-193.

Phillips, A. (1957), 'Price Discrimination and the Large Firm: Hobson's Choice in the Pectin Industry', **43(5)** *Virginia Law Review*, 685-696.

Phillips, A. (1959), 'A Critique of U.S. Experience with Price-Fixing and the Per Se Rule', **8(3)** *Journal of Industrial Economics*, 13-32. Reprinted in Blumner, S.M. and Hefner, D.L. (eds), *Readings in the Regulation of Business.*

Phillips, A. (1960), 'A Theory of Interfirm Organization', **74(4)** *Quarterly Journal of Economics*, 602-613. Reprinted in Evans, M.D. (ed.), *Interorganizational Relations*, New York, Penguin Books, 1976.

Phillips, A. (1961), 'Policy Implications of the Theory of Interfirm Organization', **51(2)** *American Economic Review*, 245-254.

Phillips, A. (1964a), 'Competition, Confusion and Commercial Banking', **19(1)** *Journal of Finance*, 32-45.

Phillips, A. (1964b), 'Reciprocity Under the Antitrust Laws: Observations on Hales' Comment', **133(1)** *University of Pennsylvania Law Review*, 77-79. Reprinted in **4(4)** *Journal of Reprints for Antitrust Law and Economics*, 1973.

Phillips, A. (1965), 'Market Structure, Innovation and Investment', in Alderson, W., Terpstra, V. and Shapiro, S.V. (eds), *Patents and Progress*, Homewood IL, Richard D. Irwin, 37-58.

Phillips, A. (1967a), 'Structural and Regulatory Reform for Commercial Banking', in Hart, A.G., Pontecorvo, J. and Shay, R. (eds), *Issues in Banking and Monetary Analysis*, New York, Holt, Rinehart and Winston, 7-30.

Phillips, A. (1967b), 'Bank Mergers, Branching and Holding Companies in the Commonwealth of Pennsylvania', **115(4)** *Pennsylvania Law Review*, 560-588.

Phillips, A. (1968), 'An Attempt to Synthesize Some Recent Contributions to the Theory of the Firm', in Phillips, A. and Williamson, O.E. (eds), *Prices: Issues in Theory, Practice and Public Policy*, Philadelphia PA, University of Pennsylvania Press, 32-44. Reprinted in Narver, John C. and Savitt, Ronald (eds), *Conceptual Readings in the Market Economy*, Boston, Holt, Rinehart and Winston, 1971.

Phillips, A. (1970a), 'Structure, Conduct and Performance - and Performance, Conduct and Structure?', in Markham, J.W. and Papanek, G. (eds), *Industrial Organization and Economic Development: Essays in Honor of Edward S. Mason*, Boston, Houghton Mifflin, 26-37.

Phillips, A. (1970b), 'Antitrust Policies: Could they be Tools of the Establishment?', in Sichel, Werner (ed.), *Antitrust Policy and Economy Welfare*, Ann Arbor, University of Michigan Press, 54-80.

Phillips, A. (1971a), 'Technological Change in the Regulated Industries', in Capron, William (ed.), *Technological Change in the Regulated Industries*, Washington, Brookings Institution, 123-165.

Phillips, A. (1971b), 'Patents, Potential Competition and Technological Progress', **56(2)** *American Economic Review*, 301-310. Reprinted in **3** *The Journal of Reprints for Antitrust Law and Economics*, 1971.

Phillips, A. (1972a), 'An Econometric Study of Price-Fixing, Market Structure and Performance in British Industry in the Early 1950s', in Cowlin, Keith (ed.), *Market Structure and Corporate Behavior*, London, Gray-Mills, 176-192.

Phillips, A. (1972b), 'The Objectives of Economic Policy - the Contribution of Antitrust', in X (ed.), *Proceedings of the Conference on Monopolies and Restraints of Trade*, London, Her Majesty's Stationery Office, 84-89.

Phillips, A. (1974a), 'Public Regulation and Corporate Social Behavior: An Application of Managerial Discretion Models', **32(4)** *Review of Social Economy*, 49-61.

Phillips, A. (1974b), 'Commenatry', in Goldschmid, H., Mann, H.M. and Weston, J.F. (eds), *Industrial Concentration: The New Learning*, Boston, Little Brown, 409-413.

Phillips, A. (1974c), 'Regulatory Reform for the Deposit Financial Institutions: Retrospect and Prospects', *Journal of Financial and Quantitative Analysis*, 795-802.

Phillips, A. (1975a), 'Large Scale Investments and Competition', in X (ed.), *Antitrust in a Rapidly Changing Economy*, New York, The Conference Board, 15-21.

Phillips, A. (1975b), 'Some Notes on a Behavioral Theory of Regulation', in Phillips, Charles F., Jr (ed.), *Telecommunications Regulation and Public Choice*, Lexington, VA, Washington and Lee University, 23-33.

Phillips, A. (1975c), 'Competitive Policy for Depoqitory Financial Institutions', in X (ed.), *Promoting Competition in Regulated Markets*, Washington, Brookings Institution, 329-366. Reprinted in **5** *Journal of Reprints for Antitrust Law and Economics*, 1975. Reprinted in Sheperd, William G. (ed.), *Public Policies Toward Business: Readings and Cases,* Homewood, IL, Richard D. Irwin.

Phillips, A. (1976), 'Schwinn Rules and the 'New Economics' of Vertical Relations', **44(3)** *Antitrust Law Journal*, 573-580.

Phillips, A. (1978), 'Regulation and its Alternatives', in X (ed.), *Regulating Business: The Search for an Optimum*, San Francisco, Institute for Contemporary Studies Press, 157-172. Reprinted in *The Economics of Antitrust*, ALI-ABA Course of Study Materials, American Law Institute - American Bar Association Old Sanford and *Antitrust, Government Intervention and Antitrust*, Research Bulletin No. 157, New York, The Conference Board, 1984.

Phillips, A. (1979), 'Organizational Factors in R&D and Technological Change: Market Failure Considerations', in Sahal, D. (ed.), *Perspectives on Research, Development and Technological Innovation*, Lexington, MA, Lexington Books, 105-125.

Phillips, A. (1981), 'Predation and Antitrust Rules: The Complications when Quality is Considered', in Balderston, F.E., Carman, J. and Nicosia, F. (eds), *Regulation of Marketing and the Public Interest: Essay in Honor of Ewald T. Grether*, New York, Pergamon Press, 113-127.

Phillips, A. (1981), 'Airline Mergers in the New Regulatory Environment', **129(4)** *University of Pennsylvania Law Review*, 586-881.

Phillips, A. (1985), 'Unreasonable Rules and Rules of Reason: Economic Aspects of Vertical Price-Fixing', **30(1)** *Antitrust Bulletin*, 99-115.

Phillips, A. (1986), 'Market Concentration and Performance: A Survey of the Evidence', **61(5)** *Notre Dame Law Review*.

Phillips, A. (1990), 'Antitrust Principles and Regulatory Needs', **35** *Antitrust Bulletin*. Reprinted in Kovaleff, T.P. (ed.), *The Antitrust Impulse*, Vol. II, New York, M.E. Sharpe, 1994.

Phillips, A. and Hall, George R. (1960), 'The Salk Vaccine Case: Parallelism, Conspiracy and Other Hypotheses', **45(4)** *Virginia Law Review*, 717-728.

Phillips, A. and Stevenson, Rodney E. (1974), 'The Historical Development of Industrial Organization', **6(3)** *History of Political Economy*, 324-342.

Picot, Arnold and Dietl, Helmut (1993), 'Neue Institutionenökonomie und Recht (New Institutional Economics and Law)', in Ott, Claus and Schäfer, Hans-Bernd (eds), *Ökonomische Analyse des Unternehmensrechts, Beiträge zum 3. Travemünder Symposium zur Ökonomischen Analyse des Rechts*, Heidelberg, Physica Verlag, 306-330.

Polinsky, A. Mitchell (1974), 'Economic Analysis as a Potentially Defective Product: A Buyer's Guide to Posner's Economic Analysis of Law', **87** *Harvard Law Review*, 1655-1681.

Posner, Richard A. (1975), 'The Economic Approach to Law', **53** *Texas Law Review*, 757-782.

Posner, Richard A. (1979), 'Some Uses and Abuses of Economics in Law', **46** *University of Chicago Law Review*, 281-306.

Posner, Richard A. (1987), 'The Law and Economics Movement', **77** *American Economic Review. Papers and Proceedings*, 1-13.

Prasad, Ravi (1993), 'Recent Developments in Regulation and Its Review', *Office of Regulation Review*.

Prasad, Ravi (1995), 'Regulation and its Review 1994-95', *Office of Regulation Review*.

Prisching, Manfred (1979), 'Ökonomische Rechtslehre? Über die Prämissen und Grenzen des "Economic Approach" im Recht (Economic Jurisprudence? On the Premisses and Limits of the Economic Approach to Law)', in Freisitzer, Kurt, Holzer, Hans Ludwig, Mantl, Wolfgang and Höflechner, Walter (eds), *Reformen des Rechts. Festschrift zur 200-Jahr-Feier der Rechtswissenschaftlichen Fakulät der Universität Graz*, Graz, Akademische Druck u. Verlagsanstalt, 995-1020.

Pulitini, Francesco (1967), 'Regole Giuridiche e Teoria Economica (Law and Economic Theory)', *Politica del Diritto*, 297-310.

Raes, Koen (1990), 'Het Recht van de Schaarste (The Law of Scarcety)', **16** *Recht en Kritiek*, 380-394.

Raes, Koen and Willekens, Harry (1994), 'Grondproblemen en Mogelijkheden (Basic Problems and Options)', in Raes, Koen and Willekens, H. (eds), *Economische Verklaringen van het Recht*, Den Haag, VUGA, 9-43.

Rahmsdorf, Detlev W. and Schäfer, Hans-Bernd (1980), 'Ökonomische Analyse des Rechts - Ein Gegentrend? (Economic Analysis of Law - A Controversy?)', in Voigt, R. (ed.), *Verrechtlichung*, Köningstein/Ts., Athenäum, 94-108.

Raiteri, Monica (1988), 'Giustizia Distributiva e Funzione Giudiziaria: Qualche Osservazione nella Prospettiva della Analisi Economica del Diritto (Distributive Justice and the Judicial Function, So)', *Materiali per una storia della cultura giuridica*, 209-228.

Rodano, Giorgio (1989), 'Il Giudice e l'Efficienza del Mercato. Riflessioni di un Economista su un Libro di Diritto Comparato (The Judge and the Efficiency of the Market. An Eco)', *Rivista Critica del Diritto Privato*, 293-312.

Rokas, Ioannis (1980), 'Oikonomike kai Nomike Episteme: Eisagogikes Paratereseis epi ton Scheseon Oikonomias kai Dikaiou (Economics and Legal Science: Introductory Remarks on the Relations between Economy and Law)', in Zepos, P., Rammos G.,

Rokas K. and Loukopoulos A. (eds), *Afieroma eis Alexandron N. Tsirintanin Volume in Honor of Alexandros N. Tsirintanis*, Athens-Komotini, Ant. N. Sakkoulas Publications, 317-347.

Rose-Ackerman, Susan (1988), 'Law and Economics: Paradigm, Politics or Philosophy', in Mercuro, Nicholas (ed.), *Law and Economics*, Boston, Kluwer Academic Publishers, 253-258.

Rose-Ackerman, Susan (1995), 'Economics, Public Policy and Law', *Victoria University of Welington Law Review*.

Sadowski, Dieter (1996), 'Programm und Stand der Betriebswirtschaftlichen Rechtsanalyse (Economic Analysis of Business Law)', in Sadowski et al. (eds), *Regulierung und Unternehmenspolitik*, Wiesbaden, Gabler, 1-20.

Sajó, András (1984), 'Közgazdaságtani Vizsgálódások a Jogról (Analysis of Law from an Economic Point of View)', in Sárközy, Tamás (ed.), *Gazdasági Jogi Tanulmányok II*, Budapest, Közgazdasági és Jogi Könyvkiadó, 5-42.

Sajó, András (1987a), 'Allami Változásipar és a Jog Stabilizáló Ereje (The State Changing Industry and the Stabilizing Ef)', in Hoppal, Mihály and Szecskó, Tamás (eds), *Értékek és változások I*, Budapest, Tömegkommunikációos Kutató Központ, 91-102.

Sajó, András (1987b), 'A Jog a Gazdaság Szabályozástechnikái Közt (Law as One of the Regulating Means of the Economy)', **3** *Jogtudományi Közlöny*, 126-132.

Salje, Peter (1984), *Ökonomische Analyse des Rechts aus deutscher Sicht* (Economic Analysis of Law from a German Point of View).

Samuels, Warren J. (1971), 'Interrelations between Legal and Economic Processes', **14** *Journal of Law and Economics*, 435-450. Reprinted in Samuels, Warren J. and Schmid, A. Allen (eds), *Law and Economics: An Institutional Perspective*, Boston, Nijhoff, 1981.

Samuels, Warren J. (1974), 'The Coase Theorem and the Study of Law and Economics', **14** *Natural Resources Journal*, 1-33.

Santini, Gerardo (1987), *I servizi. Saggio di economia del diritto* (The Services. An Example of an Economic Approach t), Bologna, Il Mulino, 562 p.

Schanze, Erich (1978), 'Ökonomische Analyse des Rechts in den USA. Verbindungslinien zur Realistischen Tradition (Economic Analysis of Law in the US. Connections to the Realistic Tradition)', in Assmann, Heinz-Dieter, Kirchner, Christian and Schanze, Erich (eds), *Ökonomische Analyse des Rechts*, Kronberg, Athenäum, 3-19.

Schanze, Erich (1982), 'Rechtsnorm und Ökonomisches Kalkül (Legal Norm and Economic Calculus)', **138** *Journal of Institutional and Theoretical Economics*, 297-312.

Schippers, Joop J. (1988), 'Rechtseconomie: het Recht van de Economie en de Plicht van het Recht (Law and Economics: Laws of Economics and the Duty of the Law)', **5** *Lust: Onafhankelijk Juridisch Opinieblad*, 104-109.

Schledermann, Helmut (1987), *Rets¢konomi for Jurister* (Law and Economics for Jurists), Aarhus University Press.

Schlicht, Ekkehart (1994), 'Probleme mit dem Ökonomischen Ansatz (Some Problems with the Economic Approach)', **5(2)** *Ethik und Sozialwissenschaften*, 335-337.

Schmidt, Reinhard H. (1996), 'Betriebswirtschaftslehre und Rechtspolitik (Business Administration and Legal Policy)', **41** *Die Aktiengesellschaft*, 250-260.

Sevic, Zeljko (1996), *Law and Economics I: Ekonomska analiza prava svojine u tranziciji* (Law and Economics I: Economic Analysis of the Property Rights in Transition), *Pravni zivot*.

Sevic, Zeljko (1997a), 'Svetska Trgovinska Organizacija: Pravni i institucionalni aspekti (World Trade Organization: Legal and Institutional Aspects)', **52(1-2)** *Finansije*, 139-146.

Sevic, Zeljko (1997b), 'Law and Economics of (Economic) Policy Reform', in Sevic, Zeljko and Wright, Glendal (eds), *Transition in Central and Eastern Europe*, Belgrade, YASF Student Cultural Centre, 152-172.

Sevic, Zeljko and Zorica, Vukasinovic (1997), 'Reforma Drzavne Uprave: Pravno-ekonomska i Finansijska Analiza (Civil Service Reform: Law and Economics and Financial Management Analyses)', **46(9)** *Pravni zivot*, 815-831.

Sinde Monteiro, Jorge (1981), 'Analise Economica do Direito (Economic Analysis of Law)', **57** *Boletim da Faculdade de Direito de Universidade de Coimbra*, 247-251.

Sjaastad, Espen and Bromley, Daniel W. (1997), 'Indigenous Land Rights in Sub-Saharan Africa: Appropriation, Security and Investment Demand', **25** *World Development*, 549-562.

Skogh, Göran (1982), 'Den Osynliga Handen och Lagens Långa Arm (The Invisible Hand and the Law's Long Arm)', **8** *Ekonomisk Debatt*.

Stankovic Vladeta (1991), 'Pravo Privrednog Sistema (Law of the Economic System)', **1-3** *Anali Pravnog fakulteta u Beogradu*, 277-288.

Stolz, Peter (1983), 'Das Wiedererwachte Interesse der Ökonomie an Rechtlichen und Politischen Institutionen (The Renewed Interest of Economics in Legal and Political Institutions)', **119** *Schweizerische Zeitschrift für Volkswirtschaft und Statistik*, 49-67.

Stout, Lynn A. (1981), 'Note: The Case for Mandatory Separate Filing by Married Persons', **91** *Yale Law Journal*, 363-382.

Stout, Lynn A. (1990), 'Are Takeover Premiums Really Premiums? Market Price, Fair Value, and Corporate Law', **99** *Yale Law Journal*, 1235-1296.

Stout, Lynn A. (1992), 'Strict Scrutiny and Social Choice: An Economic Inquiry Into Fundamental Rights and Suspect Classifications', **80** *Georgetown Law Journal*, 1787-1834.

Stout, Lynn A. (1993), 'Poverty and Failure in the Market for Human Capital', *Georgetown Law Journal*, 1947-1959.

Stout, Lynn A. (1996), 'Insurance or Gambling? Derivatives Trading in a World of Risk and Uncertainty', **39** *Brookings Review*.

Strasser, Kurt A., Bard, Robert L. and Arthur, H. Thomas (1982), 'A Reader's Guide to the Uses and Limits of Economic Analysis with Emphasis on Corporation Law', **33** *Mercer Law Review*, 571-593.

Strowel, Alain (1987), 'Utilitarisme et Approche Economique dans la Théorie du Droit. Autour de Bentham et de Posner (Utilitarianism and Economic Approach in Legal Theory. On Bentham and Posner)', **18** *Revue Interdisciplinaire d'Etudes Juridiques*, 1-45.

Supper, Meinhard (1988), 'Das Niederösterreichische Landesrecht und die Ökonomische Analyse des Rechts (The Law of the Province of Lower Austria and the Economic Analysis of Law)', in Funk, Bernd-Christian (Project Management), (ed.), *Deregulierung und Entbürokratisierung am Beispiel*, Vienna, Austrian Economic Publishers Company, 43-48.

Swallow, Brent M. and Bromley, Daniel W. (1994), 'Co-Management or No Management: The Prospects for Internal Governance of Common Property Regimes through Dynamic Contracts', **22** *Oxford Agrarian Studies*, 3-16.

Swallow, Brent M. and Bromley, Daniel W. (1995), 'Institutions, Governance and Incentives in Common Property Regimes for African Rangelands', **6** *Environmental and Resource Economics*, 99-118.

Swan, Peter L. (1984), 'The Economics of Law: Economic Imperialism in Negligence Law, No-Fault Insurance, Occupational Licensing and Criminology?', **0(67)** *Australian Economic Review*, 92-108.

Timonen, Pekka (1998), 'Oikeustiede - Mitä se on?' (Law and economics - what is it about?)', **1** *Lakimies*.

Torres Lopez, Juan (1983a), 'Recensión de la [A Review of] *'International Review of Law and Economics'*, **3** *Revista de la Facultad de Derecho de la Universidad de Granada*.

Torres Lopez, Juan (1983b), 'Recensión del Libro [A Review of] *Law and Economics*, de R. Hirsh', **2** *Revista de la Facultad de Derecho de la Universidad de Granada*.

Torres Lopez, Juan (1985), 'Tradición y Resultados de una Disciplina Novedosa: La Economía del Derecho (Tradition and Outcomes of Law and Economics)', **5** *Revista de la Facultad de Derecho de la Universidad de Granada*.

Torres, Juan (1987), 'Tradición y Resultados de una Disciplina Novedosa: la Economía del Derecho. Una Orientación Bibliográfica (Tradition and Outcome of a New Discipline: The Economics of Law. A Guide to the Literature)', **5** *Revista de la Facultad de Derecho de la Universidad de Granada*.

Trimarchi, Pietro (1987), 'L'Analisi Economica del Diritto: Tendenze e Prospettive (Economic Analysis of Law: Tendencies and Perspecti)', *Quadrimestre*, 563-582.

Tsibris, Michalis R. (1989), 'Oikonomike Analyse tou Dikaiou: To Epomeno Vema (Economic Analysis of Law: The Next Step)', **37** *Nomiko Vema*, 574-586.

Turnbull, Shann (1997), *Evolution of Business and the Corporate Structure*, Corporate Directors' Diploma Course, University of New England, Armidale, Australia, Topic 1.1.

Van den Bergh, Roger (1988), 'Le Droit Civil Face à l'Analyse Economique du Droit (Civil Law Facing Economic Analysis of Law)', *Revue Internationale de Droit Economique*, 229-254.

Van den Bergh, Roger (1991), 'Wat is Rechtseconomie? (What is Law and Economics?)', in Hondius, E.H., Schippers, J.J. and Siegers, J.J. (eds), *Rechtseconomie en Recht*, Zwolle, Tjeenk Willink, 9-49.

Van den Bergh, Roger and Heremans, Dirk (1986), 'Over Krommen en Rechten. Een Reactie op de Kritiek van Kruithof ten Aanzien van de Economische Analyse van het Recht (On Curves and Lines: A Reaction on the Critique of Kruithof on Economic Analysis of Law)', **50** *Rechtskundig Weekblad*, 1649-1668.

Van den Bergh, Roger and Heremans, Dirk (1987), 'Recht en Economie (Law and Economics)', **32** *Tijdschrift voor Economie en Management*, 139-164.

Van den Brink, Rogier, Chavas, Jean-Paul and Bromley, Daniel W. (1995), 'The Economics of Cain and Abel: Agro-Pastoral Property Rights in the Sahel', **31** *Journal of Development Studies*, 373-399.

Veljanovski, Cento G. (1980), 'The Economic Approach to Law - A Critical Introduction', **7** *British Journal of Law and Society*, 158-193.

Veljanovski, Cento G. (1982), 'Cost-Benefit and Law Reform in Australia', **32** *New Law Journal*, 893-897.

Verloren Van Themaat, Pieter (1988), 'Economie Gezien door Juristen (Economics, Seen by Lawyers)', in X (ed.), *Mededelingen van de Afdeling Letterkunde, Nieuwe Reeks*, Amsterdam, Koninklijke Nederlandse Akademie van Wetenschappen, 229-258.

Watrin, Christian (1995), 'Nutzen und Kosten des Rechts (Economics of Law)', in Mantl, Wolfgang (ed.), *Effizienz der Gesetzesproduktion, Abbau der Regelungsdichte im internationalen Vergleich Schriftenreihe des Zentrums für angewandte Politikforschung Bd. 7*, Wien, 239-244.

Weigel, Wolfgang (1990), 'Ökonomie und Recht - Eine Einführung (Economics and Law - An Introduction)', **31(3-4)** *Das öffentliche Haushaltswesen in Österreich*, 169-198.

Weigel, Wolfgang (1991), 'Ökonomie und Recht - Eine Einführung (Law and Economics, a Primer)', in Weigel, Wolfgang (ed.), *Economic Analysis of Law - A Collection of Applications*, Vienna, Österreichischer Wirtschaftsverlag, 13-37.

Weise, Peter (1991), 'Effizienz und Menschenwürde - Ein Gegensatz? Anmerkungen zu einer Kontroverse zwischen Ott/Schäfer und Fezer (Efficiency and Human Dignity - a Contradiction? Remarks on a Controversy between Ott, Schäfer and Fezer)', in Ott, C. and Schäfer, H.-B. (eds), *Ökonomische Probleme des Zivilrechts. Beiträge zur Ökonomischen Analyse des Rechts. Heidelberg/New York, Springer 1991*, Springer, 18-34.

Weth, Stefan (1996), 'Die Justiz - ein Ungeliebtes Kind? (Jurisdiction - an Unloved Kid?)', *Neue Juristische Wochenschrift*, 2427 ff.

Wilberforce, Lord (1978), 'Law and Economics', in Harvey, B.W. (ed.), *The Lawyer and Justice*, London, Sweet and Maxwell.

Williams, A. (1975), 'Collaboration between Economists and Lawyers in Policy Analysis', **13** *Journal of Society of Public Teachers of Law*, 212-218.

Xue-Lascoux, Zhiqun and Bromley, Daniel W. (1996), 'Necessity and Purpose in Chinese Agriculture: 1949-95', **24** *Oxford Development Studies*, 261-280.

0020
MONOGRAPHS

Bibliography Collected by the Editors

Adams, Michael (1980), *Ökonomische Analyse des Sicherungsrechte* (Economic Analysis of Security Law), Königstein/Ts, Athenäum, 322 p.

Adams, Michael (1981), *Ökonomische Analyse des Zivilprozesses* (Economic Analysis of Civil Procedure), Königstein/Ts, Athenäum, 130 p.

Adams, Michael (1985), *Ökonomische Analyse des Gefährdungs- und Verschuldenshaftung* (Economic Analysis of Strict and Fault Liability), Heidelberg, R.v Decker's/C.F. Müller, 310 p.

Alpa, Guido, Pulitini, Francesco, Rodota, Stefano and Romani, Franco (1982), *Interpretazione Giuridica e Analisi Economica* (Legal Interpretation and Economic Analysis), Milano, Giuffrè, 662 p.

Anderson, Martin (1978), *Welfare. The Political Economy of Welfare Reform in the United States*, Stanford, Hoover Institute Press, Stanford University, 251 p.

Anderson, R.W. (1976), *The Economics of Crime*, London, Macmillan, 71 p.

Armentano, Dominick T. (1982), *Antitrust and Monopoly: Anatomy of a Policy Failure*, New York, Wiley, 292 p.

Babic, Blagoje (1994), *Prelaz u Tranziciji* (Deception in Transition), Belgrade, Prometej.

Baird, Charles W. (1980), *Rent Control: The Perennial Folly*, San Francisco, Cato Institute, 101 p.

Baldwin, G.R. and Veljanovski, Cento G. (1982), *Regulation and Cost-Benefit Analysis - The U.S. Experience*, Oxford, Centre for Socio-Legal Studies.

Barzel, Yoram (1989), *Economic Analysis of Property Rights*, Cambridge, Cambridge University Press, 122 p.

Baumol, William J. and Oates, Wallace E. (1988), *The Theory of Environmental Policy*, Cambridge, Cambridge University Press, 299 p.

Baxter, William F. (1974), *People or Penguins: The Case for Optimal Pollution*, New York, Columbia University Press, 110 p.

Becker, Gary S. (1957), *The Economics of Discrimination*, Chicago, University of Chicago Press, 137 p.

Becker, Gary S. (1976), *The Economic Approach to Human Behavior*, Chicago, University of Chicago Press, 314 p.

Becker, Gary S. (1991), *A Treatise on the Family*, Cambridge (MA), Harvard University Press, 288 p.

Beckerman, Wilfred (1990), *Pricing for Pollution: An Analysis of Market Pricing and Government Regulation in Environment Consumption and Policy*, London, Institute of Economic Affairs, 80 p.

Begovic, Boris (1995), *Ekonomika Urbanog Planiranja* (Economics of Urban Planning), Belgrade, CES/MECON.

Berlant, J.L. (1975), *Profession and Monopoly: A Study of Medicine in th*, Berkeley, University of California Press.

Blair, Roger D. and Kaserman, David L. (1983), *Law and Economics of Vertical Integration and Control*, New York, Academic Press, 211 p.

Blumstein, J. et al. (eds) (1978), *Deterrence and Incapacitation: Estimating the Effe*, Washington, National Academy of Sciences.

Bork, Robert H. (1978), *The Antitrust Paradox: A Policy at War with Itself*, New York, Basic Books, 468 p.

Bowman, Ward S., Jr (1973), *Patent and Antitrust Law: A Legal and Economic Approach*, Chicago, University of Chicago Press.

Breyer, Stephen G. (1982), *Regulation and its Reform*, Cambridge, MA, Harvard University Press, 472 p.

Bromley, Daniel W. (1989), *Economic Interests and Institutions: The Conceptual Foundations of Public Policy*, Oxford, Blackwell.

Bromley, Daniel W. (1991), *Environment and Economy: Property Rights and Public Policy*, Cambridge, MA, Blackwell.

Burrows, Paul (1979), *The Economic Theory of Pollution Control*, Oxford, Martin Robertson, 192 p.

Button, Kenneth J. (1990), *Airline Deregulation: International Experiences*, New York, New York University Press, 191 p.

Calabresi, Guido (1970), *The Costs of Accidents: A Legal and Economic Analysis*, New Haven, Yale University Press, 340 p.

Calabresi, Guido and Bobbitt, Philip (1978), *Tragic Choices: The Conflicts Society Confronts in the Allocation of Tragically Scarce Resources*, New York, W.W. Norton, 252 p.

Campbell, David and Clay, Susan, *Long-Term Contracting: A Research Bibliography and Review of the Literature*, Oxford, Centre for Socio-Legal Studies.

Campbell, Rita Ricardo (1976), *Food Safety Regulations: A Study of the Use and Li*, Washington, American Enterprise Institute for Public Policy Research.

Casper, Gerhard and Posner, Richard A. (1976), *The Workload of the Supreme Court*, Chicago, American Bar Foundation.

Cheung, Steven N.S. (1969), *A Theory of Share Tenancy*, Chicago, University of Chicago Press, 188 p.

Cheung, Steven N.S. (1978), *The Myth of Social Costs: A Critique of Welfare Economics and the Implications for Public Policy*, London, Institute of Economic Affairs, 93 p.

Coleman, Jules L. (1988), *Markets, Morals and the Law*, Cambridge, Cambridge University Press, 393 p.

Crain, W. Mark (1980), *Vehicle Safety Inspection Systems - How Effective?*, Washington, American Enterprise Institute for Public Policy Research.

Crandall, Robert W. (1983), *Controlling Industrial Pollution: The Economics and Politics of Clean Air*, Washington, Brookings Institution, 199 p.

Crandall, Robert W. et al. (1986), *Regulating the Automobile*, Washington, Brookings Institution, 202 p.

Crew, Michael A. and Kleindorfer, Paul R. (1986), *The Economics of Public Utility Regulation*, Cambridge (MA), MIT Press, 304 p.

Culyer, A.J. (1973), *The Economics of Social Policy*, London, Martin Robertson, 268 p.

Dahlman, Carl J. (1980), *The Open Field System and Beyond: A Property Right*, Cambridge, Cambridge University Press, 234 p.

Dales, John H. (1968), *Pollution, Property and Prices: An Essay in Policy*, Toronto, University of Toronto Press, 111 p.

Danzon, Patricia M. (1985), *Medical Malpractice: Theory, Evidence, and Public* , Cambridge, MA, Harvard University Press, 264 p.

De Clercq, Marc and Naert, Frank (1985), *De Politieke Markt* (The Political Market), Antwerpen, Kluwer, 163 p.

De Geest, Gerrit (1994), *Economische Analyse van het Contracten- en Quasi-contractenrecht: een Onderzoek naar de Wetenschappelijke Waarde van de Rechtseconomie* (Economic Analysis of Contract Law and Quasi Contract Law: A Study on the Scientic Value of Law and Economics), Antwerpen, Maklu, 568 p.

Demsetz, Harold (1982), *Economic, Legal and Political Dimensions of Competition*, Amsterdam, North-Holland, 125 p.

Derthick, Martha and Quirck, Paul J. (1985), 'Why the Regulators Chose to Deregulate', in Noll, Roger G. (ed.), *Regulatory Policy and the Social Sciences*, Berkeley, University of California Press, 200-231.

Dewees, Donald N., Everson, C.K. and Sims, W.A. (1975), *Economic Analysis of Environmental Policies*, Toronto, University of Toronto Press, 175 p.

Dilnot, Andrew (1989), *The Economics of Social Security*, Oxford, Oxford University Press, 287 p.

Djuricin, Dragan (1994), *Privrede u tranziciji: Privatizacija i Povezane Teme* (Economies in Transition: Privatization and Related Issues), Decije novine, Gornji Milanovac.

Douglas, George W. and Miller, J.C. (1974), *Economic Regulation of Domestic Air Transport: Theory and Policy*, Washington, Brookings Institution.

Dudek, Daniel J. and Wiener, Jonathan Baert (1996), *Joint Implementation, Transaction Costs, and Climate Change*, Paris, OECD.

Eckert, Ross D. (1979), *The Enclosure of Ocean Resources: Economics and the Law of the Sea*, Stanford, Hoover Institute Press, Stanford University, 390 p.

Eggertsson, Thrainn (1990), *Economic Behaviour and Institutions*, Cambridge, Cambridge University Press, 385 p.

Einhorn, Michael A. (ed.) (1991), *Price Caps and Incentive Regulation in Telecommunications*, Dordrecht, Kluwer Academic Publishers, 244 p.

Emons, Winand (1987), *On the Economic Theory of Warranties*, Bonn, 84 p.

Faure, Michael G. and Van den Bergh, Roger (1989), *Objectieve Aansprakelijkheid, Verplichte Verzekering en Veiligheidsregulering* (Strict Liability, Mandatory Insurance and Safety Regulation), Antwerpen, Maklu, 386 p.

Fischel, William A. (1985), *The Economics of Zoning Laws: A Property Rights Approach to American Land Use Controls*, Baltimore , MD, John Hopkins University Press, 372 p.

Fleisher, B. (1966), *The Economics of Delinquency*, New York, Quadrangle.

Frey, Bruno S. (1990), *Ökonomie ist Sozialwissenschaft. Die Anwendung der* (Economics is a Social Science. The Use of Economic), München, Vahlen.

Gaay Fortman, Bastiaan De (1966), *Theory of Competition Policy: A Confrontation of Economic, Political and Legal Principles*, Amsterdam, North-Holland, 341 p.

Gay, David E.R. (1975), 'Property Rights and Adam Smith', **33** *Review of Social Economy*, 177-179.

Gellhorn, Ernest A. (1976), *Antitrust Law and Economics*, St. Paul, West Publishing Company, 472 p.

Ghosh, D., Lees, D. and Seal, W. (1976), *The Economics of Personal Injury*, Westmead, Saxon House, 6 p.

Gibbs, J. (1975), *Crime, Punishment and Deterrence*, New York, Elsevier.

Gimpel-Hinteregger, Monika (1994), *Grundfragen der Umwelthaftung* (Fundamental Issues in Environmental Liabiltiy), Vienna, Manz.

Grabowski, Henry G. (1976), *Drug Regulation and Innovation: Empirical Evidence*, Washington, American Enterprise Institute for Public Policy Research, 82 p.

Grether, David M., Isaac, R. Mark and Plott, Charles R. (1989), *The Allocation of Scarce Resources. Experimental Economics and the Problem of Allocating Airport Slots*, Boulder, CO, Westview Press, 333 p.

Hahn, Robert (1989), *A Primer on Environmental Policy Design*, New York, Harwood Academic, 135 p.

Halpern, Paul J. and Carr, Jack L. (1981), *Liability Rules and Insurance Markets*, Ottawa, Consumer and Corporate Affairs Canada.

Harris, Richard A. and Milkis, Sidney M. (1989), *The Politics of Regulatory Change: A Tale of Two Agencies*, Oxford, Oxford University Press, 331 p.

Hartley, K. and Maynard, Alan (1982), *The Costs and Benefits of Regulating New Product Development in the UK Pharmaceutical Industry*, London, Office of Health Economics.

Hayashida, Seimei (1996), '*Ho to Keizaigaku no Horiron* (Law and Economics as Legal Theory)', Hokudai Tosho Kankokai (Hokkaido University Press).

Hellaman, D.A. (1980), *The Economics of Crime*, New York, St. Martin's Press.

Hellman, Daryl A. and Alper, Neil O. (1990), *Economics of Crime: Theory and Practice*, Needham Heights, Simon and Schuster, Ginn Press, 226 p.

Hess, James D. (1983), *The Economics of Organisation*, Amsterdam, North-Holland, 284 p.

Hiber, Dragor (1998), *Svojina u Tranziciji* (Property in Transition), Belgrade, Pravni fakultet.

Hodgson, Geoffrey M. (1988), *Economics and Institutions*, Cambridge, Polity Press, 365 p.

Huber, Peter W. (1988), *Liability. The Legal Revolution and its Consequences*, New York, Basic Books, 260 p.

Ippolito, Richard A. (1989), *The Economics of Pension Insurance*, Homewood, Irwin for the University of Pennsylvania, Wharton School, Pension Research Council, 270 p.

Ivic, Aleksandar and Maksimovic, Ivan (1984), *Drustvena Svojina i Samoupravljanje I* (Social Property and Self-Management I), Belgrade, Pravni fakultet.

Jackson, Thomas H. (1986), *The Logic and Limits of Bankruptcy Law*, Cambridge (MA), Harvard University Press, 287 p.

Johnson, Bruce M. (1985), *Taking Care of Business: The Economics of Crime by Heroin Abusers*, Lexington, MA, Lexington Books, 278 p.

Joskow, Paul L. and Schmalensee, Richard L. (1983), *Markets for Power: An Analysis of Electric Utility*, Cambridge, MA, MIT Press, 269 p.

Kahn, Alfred E. (1988), *The Economics of Regulation: Principles and Institutions*, Cambridge, MA, MIT Press, 559 p.

Kaufer, Erich (1989), *The Economics of the Patent System*, Chur, Harwood Academic, 66 p.

Kaufmann, Peter J. (1986), *Passing Off and Misappropriation: An Economic and* , Max Planck Institute for Foreign and International Patent, Copyright and Competition Law, VCH-Weinheim, Reerfield Beach.

Kaysen, Carl and Turner, Donald F. (1959), *Antitrust Policy: An Economic and Legal Analysis*, Cambridge, MA, Harvard University Press, 345 p.

Kleiman, Mark A.R. (1989), *Marijuana: Costs of Abuse, Costs of Control*, Westport, Greenwood, 197 p.

Klitgaard, Robert (1988), *Controlling Corruption*, Berkeley, University of California Press, 220 p.

Kneese, Allan V. and Schultze, Charles L. (1975), *Pollution, Prices and Public Policy*, Brookings, Washington, DC, 125 p.

Laband, David N. and Heinbuch, Deborah Hendry (1987), *Blue Laws: The History, Economics, and Politics of Sunday Closing Laws*, Lexington, MA, Lexington Books, 232 p.

Landes, William M. and Posner, Richard A. (1987), *The Economic Structure of Tort Law*, Cambridge, MA, Harvard University Press, 330 p.

Lehmann, Michael (1983), *Bürgerliches Recht und Handelsrecht - eine juristische und Ökonomische Analyse ausgewählter Probleme für Wirtschaftswissenschaftler und interdisziplinär interessierte Juristen unter besonderer Berücksichtigung der "Ökonomischen Analyse des Rechts" und* (Civil Law and Commercial Law - a Legal and Economic Analysis of Selected Problems for Lawyers with an Economic and Interdisciplinary Interest with Special Attention to the 'Economic Analysis of Law' and the "Theory of Property Rights"), Stuttgart, Poeschel, 329 p.

Lepage, Henri (1984), *Pourquoi la propriété?* (Why Property?), Paris, Pluriel.

Leube, Kurt R. and Moore, Thomas Gale (1986), *The Essence of Stigler*, Stanford, Hoover Institute Press, Stanford University, 377 p.

Libecap, Gary D. (1989), *Contracting for Property Rights*, Cambridge, Cambridge University Press, 132 p.

Luken, Ralph A. (1991), *Efficiency in Environmental Regulation*, Dordrecht, Kluwer, 400 p.

Luksetich, William and White, Michael (1982), *Crime and Public Policy: An Economic Approach*, Boston, Little Brown.

Macauley, Molly K. and Portney, Paul R. (1984), *Property Rights in Orbit Regulation*, Washington, American Enterprise Institute for Public Policy Research.

Madzar, Ljubomir (1972), *Osnovi Teorije Proizvodnje* (Basics of the Theory of Production), Belgrade, Institut ekonomskih nauka.

Madzar, Ljubomir (1995), *Svojina i Reforma* (Property and Reform), Belgrade, Institut ekonomskih nauka.

Malloy, Robin Paul (1990), *Law and Economics. A Comparative Approach to Theory and Practice*, St. Paul, West Publishing Company, 166 p.

Mataja, Victor (1888), *Das Recht des Schadenersatzes vom Standpunkte der Nationalökonomie* (The Law of Compensation from the Standpoint of Economics), Leipzig.

Medema, Steven G. (1994), *Ronald H. Coase*, London, MacMillan.

Mendeloff, John M. (1988), *The Dilemma of Toxic Substance Regulation: How Overregulation Causes Underregulation at OSHA*, Cambridge, MA, MIT Press, 321 p.

Mercuro, Nicholas and Medema, Steven G. (1997), *From Posner to Post-Modernism*, Princeton, Princeton University Press.

Mercuro, Nicholas and Ryan, Thimothy P. (1984), *Law, Economics and Public Policy*, Greenwood, JAI Press, 184 p.

Miller, James C., III (1989), *The Economist as Reformer: Revamping the FTC, 1981*, Washington, American Enterprise Institute for Public Policy Research, 110 p.

Moore, Thomas G. (1976), *Trucking Regulation. Lessons from Europe*, Washington, American Enterprise Institute for Public Policy Research, 148 p.

Morrison, Steven A. and Winston, Clifford (1986), *The Economic Effects of Airline Deregulation*, Washington, Brookings Institution, 84 p.

Munch, Patricia (1977), *Costs and Benefits of the Tort System if Viewed as*, Santa Monica, Institute for Civil Justice, Rand Corporation.

Myhrman, Johan, Petrén, Gustav and Strömholm, Stig (1987), *Marknadsekonomins Rättsliga Grundvalar* (The Legal Foundations of the Market Economy), Timbro.

Needham, Douglas (1983), *The Economics and Politics of Regulation: A Behavioral Approach*, Boston, Little Brown, 482 p.

Neely, Richard (1988), *The Product Liability Mess: How Business Can Be Rescued from the Politics of the State Courts*, New York, Free Press, 181 p.

Olson, Walter (ed.) (1988), *New Directions in Liability Law*, New York, The Academy of Political Science, 214 p.

Orlic, V. Miodrag and Rajovic, Veroljub (1984), *Drustvena Svojina i Samoupravljanje II* (Social Property and Self-Management II), Belgrade, Pravni fakultet.

Otto, Hans-Jochen (1982), *Generalprävention und externe Verhaltenskontrolle, Wandel vom Sociologischen zum Ökonomischen Paradigma in der Nordamerikanischen Kriminologie?* (General Prevention and External Control of Behavior, Evolution from Sociological to Economic Paradigm in the North American Criminology?), Freiburg, Max-Planck-Institut für ausländisches internationales Strafrecht, 323 p.

Owen, Bruce M. and Braeutigam, Ronald R. (1978), *The Regulation Game: Strategic Use of the Administrative Process*, Cambridge, MA, Ballinger, 271 p.

Papps, Ivy (1980), *For Love or Money? A Preliminary Economic Analysis*, London, Institute of Economic Affairs, 63 p. (Hobart Paperback No.86).

Pejovich, Svetozar (1990), *The Economics of Property Rights: Towards a Theory*, Dordrecht, Kluwer, 224 p.

Peltzman, Sam (1975), *Regulation of Pharmaceutical Innovation*, Washington, American Enterprise Institute for Public Policy Research, 118 p.

Penrose, E.T. (1951), *The Economics of the International Patent System*, Baltimore, MD, John Hopkins University Press.

Peterson, Wallace C. (1991), *Transfer Spending, Taxes, and the American Welfare*, Dordrecht, Kluwer, 192 p.

Pigou, A.C. (1932), *The Economics of Welfare*, London, Macmillan, 876 p.

Polinsky, A. Mitchell (1989), *An Introduction to Law and Economics* (2nd edn), Boston: Little, Brown and Company, 153 p.

Poole, Robert W., Jr (1982), *Instead of Regulation*, Lexington, KY, Heath, 404 p.

Poole, Robert W., Jr (ed.) (1985), *Unnatural Monopolies: The Case for Deregulating Public Utilities*, Lexington, MA, Lexington Books, 224 p.

Posner, Richard A. (1976), *Antitrust Law: An Economic Perspective*, Chicago, University of Chicago Press, 262 p.

Posner, Richard A. (1981), *The Economics of Justice*, Cambridge, MA, Harvard University Press, 415 p.

Posner, Richard A. (1985), *The Federal Courts: Crisis and Reform*, Cambridge, MA, Harvard University Press, 365 p.

Priddat, Birger (1988), *Das Geld und die Vernunft. Über John Lockes Versuch einer naturrechtlich begründeten Ökonomie* (Money and Reason. On John Locke's Natural Right-Based Economics), Frankfurt am Main, Peter D. Lang.

Priddat, Birger (1993), 'Ökonomie und Macht. John Locke. Neue Aspekte (Economy and Power. John Locke. New Aspects)', in Gephardt, J. and Münclker, H. (eds), *Bürgerschaft und Herrschaft. Zum Verhältnis von Demokratie und Macht im Antiken und Neuzeitlichen Politischen Denken*, Baden-Baden, Nomos.

Pyle, David J. (1983), *The Economics of Crime and Law Enforcement*, London, MacMillan, 216 p.

Pyle, David J. (1989), *Tax Evasion and the Black Economy*, New York, St. Martin's Press, 212 p.

Ramseyer, J. Mark and Rosenbluth, Frances M. (1995), *The Politics of Oligarchy: Institutional Choice in Imperial Japan*, New York, Cambridge University Press.

Raufer, Roger K. and Feldman, Stephen L. (1987), *Acid Rain and Emissions Trading: Implementing a Market Approach to Pollution Control*, Totowa, Rowman and Allenheld, 161 p.

Rea, Samuel A., Jr. (1981), *Disability Insurance and Public Policy*, Toronto, University of Toronto Press.

Rea, Samuel A., Jr. and James E. (1977), *Pesando, Public and Private Pensions in Canada: An Economic Analysis*, Toronto, University of Toronto Press.

Reuter, Peter (1983), *Disorganized Crime: The Economics of the Visible Hand*, London, MIT Press, 233 p.

Ringen, Stein (1987), *The Possibility of Politics: A Study in the Political Economy of the Welfare State*, Oxford, Clarendon, 303 p.

Robert, Philippe and Godefroy, Thierry (1977), *Le Coût du Crime ou l'Economie Poursuivant le Crime* (The Cost of Crime or Economics Prosecuting Crime), Genève, Masson, 225 p.

Rogers, A.J. (1973), *The Economics of Crime*, Illinois, Dryden Press.

Rowley, Charles K. (1966), *The British Monopolies Commission*, London, Allen and Unwin.

Rowley, Charles K. (1973), *Antitrust and Economic Efficiency*, London, Macmillan, 95 p.

Rowley, Charles K. (1992), *The Right to Justice: The Political Economy of Legal Services in the United States*, Aldershot, Edward Elgar.

Rowley, Charles K. and Ogus, Anthony I. (1984), *Prepayments and Insolvency*, London, Office of Fair Trading.

Rowley, Charles K. and Yarrow, G.K. (1978), *Evolution of Concentration in the United Kingdom Cement Industry*, Commission of the European Communities. French edition 1979.

Rubin, Paul H. (1983), *Business Firms and the Common Law. The Evolution of Efficient Rules*, New York, Praeger, 189 p.

Rubin, Paul H. (1993), 'Private Mechanisms for the Creation of Efficient Institutions for Market Economies', in Somogyi, Laszlo (ed.), *The Political Economy of The Transition Process In Eastern Europe*, Cheltenham, Edward Elgar.

Rubin, Paul H. (1994), 'Growing A Legal System in the Post-Communist Economies', **27** *Cornell International Law Journal*, 1-47.

Rubin, Paul H. and Tesche, Jean, 'Enforcement of Agreements in Russia,' in Sachs, Jeffrey (ed.), *The Rule of Law and Economic Reform in Russia*,' Boulder, Westview Press, 912 ff.

Sagoff, Mark (1988), *The Economy of the Earth: Philosophy, Law, and the Environment*, Cambridge, Cambridge University Press, 271 p.

Santini, Gerardo (1979), *Il Commercio* (Trading), Bologna, Il Mulino, 364 p.

Santini, Gerardo (1987), *I Servizi. Saggio di Economia del Diritto* (The Services. An Example of an Economic Approach t), Bologna, Il Mulino, 562 p.

Schenk, Karl-Ernst (1982), *'Institutional Choice' und Ordnungstheorie* ('Institutional Choice' and Theory of Order), Tübingen, Mohr, 39 p.

Scheppele, Kim Lane (1988), *Legal Secrets, Equality and Efficiency in the Common Law*, Chicago, University of Chicago Press, 363 p.

Scherer, Frederic M. (1977), *The Economic Effects of Compulsory Patent Licensing*, New York, New York University Press.

Schmid, A. Allan (1987), *Property, Power, and Public Choice: An Inquiry into Law and Economics*, Westport, Greenwood, 332 p.

Schmidt, Ingo and Rittaler, Jan B. (1989), *A Critical Evaluation of the Chicago School of Antitrust Analysis*, Dordrecht, Kluwer Academic Publishers, 132 p.

Schmidt, Peter and Witte, Ann Dryden (1984), *An Economic Analysis of Crime and Justice: Theory, Methods, and Applications*, New York, Academic Press, 416 p.

Shavell, Steven (1987), *Economic Analysis of Accident Law*, Cambridge, MA, Harvard University Press, 312 p.

Shaviro, Daniel N. (1993), *Federalism in Taxation: The Case for Greater Uniformity*, Washington, AEI Press.

Shaviro, Daniel N. (1995), *Budget Deficits and the Intergenerational Distribution of Lifetime Consumption*, University of Chicago Law and Economics Working Paper, No. 29.

Shepherd, William G. (1985), *Public Policies Toward Business*, Homewood, IL, Richard D. Irwin, 541 p.

Simonich, William L. (1991), *Government Antismoking Policies*, New York, Peter Lang, 300 p.

Smith, Peter and Swann, Dennis (1979), *Protecting the Consumer - An Economic and Legal Analysis*, Oxford, Martin Robertson, 286 p.

Snow, Marcellus S. (1986), *Marketplace for Telecommunications: Regulation and Deregulation in Industrialized Democracies*, New York, Longman, 304 p.

Swann, Dennis (1988), *The Retreat of the State: Deregulation and Privatization in the U.K. and U.S.*, Ann Arbor, University of Michigan Press, 344 p.

Tabasz, Thomas F. (1975), *Toward an Economics of Prisons*, Lexington, KY, Heath.

Taylor, Charles T. and Silbertson, Z.A. (1973), *The Economic Impact of the Patent System*, Cambridge, Cambridge University Press.

Teijl, Rob and Holzhauer, Rudi W. (1997), *Wisselende Perspectieven in de Rechtseconomie* (Changing Perspectives in Law and Economics), Arnhem, Gouda Quint, 431 p.

Thompson, Howard E. (1991), *Regulatory Finance: Financial Foundations of Rate of Return Regulation*, Dordrecht, Kluwer Academic Publishers, 256 p.

Tillman, Georg (1989), *Equity, Incentives, and Taxation*, Berlin, Springer, 132 p.

Trimarchi, Pietro (1961), *Rischio e Responsabilità Oggettiva* (Risk and Strict Liability), Milano, Giuffrè, 383 p.

Tullock, Gordon (1980), *Trials on Trial - The Pure Theory of Legal Procedure*, New York, Columbia University Press, 255 p.

Tullock, Gordon (1983), *Economics of Income Redistribution*, Boston, Kluwer-Nijhoff, 208 p.

Tullock, Gordon (1986), *The Economics of Wealth and Poverty*, New York, Columbia University Press, 210 p.

Tullock, Gordon (1989), *The Economics of Special Privilege and Rent Seeking*, Boston, Kluwer Academic Publishers, 104 p.

Turnbull, Shann (1973), *Time Limited Corporations, Economic Society of Australia and New Zealand (N.S.W. Division)*, Sidney, Monograph, No. 340.

Utton, M.A. (1986), *The Economics of Regulating Industry*, Oxford, Blackwell, 243 p.

Viscusi, W. Kip (1979), *Welfare for the Elderly: An Economic Analysis and Policy Prescription*, New York, Wiley, 251 p.

Vousden, Neil (1990), *The Economics of Trade Protection*, Cambridge, Cambridge University Press, 305 p.

Vracar, K. Stevan (1994), *Preispitivanja Pravne Metodologije: Nagovestaji Drzavno-Pravnog Integralizma* (Reexamination of the Legal Methodology: Indications of State-Legal Integralism), Belgrade, Naucna knjiga.

Vukotic, Veselin (1993), *Privatizacija i Razvoj Trzisne Privrede* (Privatisation and Development of a Market Economy), Belgrade, Institut ekonomskih nauka.

Vukovic, S. (1996), *Cemu privatizacija* (Why Privatization), Belgrade, SDS-IKSI.

Wagstaff, Adam and Maynard, Alan (1988), *Economic Aspects of the Illicit Drug Market and Drug Enforcement Policies in the United Kingdom*, London, Her Majesty's Stationary Office, 156 p.

Waldman, Don E. (1986), *The Economics of Antitrust: Cases and Analysis*, Boston, Little Brown.

Waterson, Michael (1988), *Regulation of the Firm and Natural Monopoly*, Oxford, Blackwell, 164 p.

Weitzman, Lenore J. (1981), *The Marriage Contract: Spouses, Lovers and the Law*, New York, Free Press, 536 p.

Werin, Lars (1982), *Ekonomi Och Rättssystem* (Economy and Legal System), Malmö, Liber.

Whynes, David K. and Bowles, Roger A. (1981), *The Economic Theory of the State*, Martin Robertson, Oxford, 236 p.

Wikström, Kauko (1994), *Oikeus ja Talous* (Law and Economics), Helsi.

Williams, Stephen F. (1973), 'Optimizing Water Use: The Return Flow Issue', **44** *University of Colorado Law Review*, 301-321.

Williamson, Oliver E. (1985), *The Economic Institutions of Capitalism: Firms, Markets, Relational Contracting*, New York, Free Press, 450 p.

Williamson, Oliver E. (1989), *Antitrust Economics: Mergers, Contracting and Strategic Behavior*, Oxford, Basil Blackwell, 363 p.

0030
BOOK REVIEWS

Bibliography Collected by the Editors

Bainbridge, Stephen M. (1990), 'Social Propositions and Common Law Adjudication', **24** *University of Illinois Law Review*, 231 ff.

Bainbridge, Stephen M. (1995), 'The Politics of Corporate Governance', **18** *Harvard Journal of Law and Public Policy*, 671 ff.

Boettke, Peter J. (1997), 'Timur Kuran: Private Truths, Public Lies: The Social Consequences of Preference Falsification', **8(1)** *Constitutional Political Economy*, 89-91.

Brietzke, Paul H. and Whitton, Linda S. (1996), 'An Old(er) Master Stands on the Shoulders of Ageism to Stake another Claim for Law and Economics (Book Review of Richard A. Posner, Aging and Old Age)', **31** *Valparaiso University Law Review*, 89-109.

Brinig, Margaret F. (1993), 'The Law and Economics of No-Fault Divorce', **27** *Family Law Quarterly*, 453-470.

Brinig, Margaret F. (1994), 'Status, Contract and Covenant', **79** *Cornell Law Review*, 1573-1602.

Brinig, Margaret F. (1994), 'Comment on Jana Singer's Alimony and Efficiency', **83** *Georgetown Law Journal*, 2461-2479.

Brinig, Margaret F. (1995), 'Through a Glass Darkly, a Review of Neil Komesar's *Imperfect Alternatives*', **78** *Public Choice*, 190-194.

Campbell, David (1990), 'Review of D. Harris, *Remedies in Contract and Tort*', **17** *Journal of Law and Society*, 254-261.

Campbell, David (1992), 'Review of S. Wheeler, *Reservation of Title Clauses*', 19 *Journal of Law and Society*, 6-12.

Campbell, David (1995), 'Review of R. Tomasic and S. Bottomley, *Directing the Top 500*', **4** *Social and Legal Studies*, 428-432.

Campbell, David (1996), 'Review of B. Fisse and J. Braithwaite, *Corporations, Crime and Accountability*', **5** *Social and Legal Studies*, 549-554.

Chien, Tze-shiou (1997), ''Coase's *The Market, the Firm, and the Law*: A Legal Perspective', **26(2)** *National Taiwan University Law Journal*, 229-246.

Donohue, John J. III and Ayres, Ian (1987), 'Posner's Third Symphony: Thinking about the Unthinkable', **39** *Stanford Law Review*, 791-812.

Dwight, Lee (1997), 'Dennis C. Mueller: *Constitutional Democracy* (Book Review)', **8** *Constitutional Political Economy*, 165-167.

Easterbrook, Frank H. and Fischel, Daniel R. (1993), 'The Economic Structure of Corporate Law', **525** *Annals of American Academy of Political and Social Science*, 200 ff.

Eide, Erling (1981a), 'Heineke, J.M. (ed.), *Economic Models of Criminal Behaviour* (Book Review)', *Economic Journal*, 584-585.

Eide, Erling (1981b), 'Book review of Lars Werin, 1979, *Ekonomi och Rättssystem*', *Tidsskrift for Rettsvitenskap*, 752-754.

Eide, Erling (1984), 'Book review of Göran Skogh, 1982, *Marknadens Villkor*', *Tidsskrift for Rettsvitenskap*, 318-319.

Eide, Erling (1986), 'Book review of Nils Nygaard, 1985, Skatt og Skade', *Tidsskrift for Rettsvitenskap*, 708-712.

Fisch, Jill E. (1995), 'Review Essay: Picking A Winner (reviewing Roberta Romano, *The Genius of American Corporate Law*)', **20** *Journal of Corporate Law*, 451-474.

Gay, David E.R. (1975), 'Book Review of *The Economics of Property Rights*, ed. by Furubotn and Pejovich', **42** *Southern Economic Journal*, 162-164.

Gay, David E.R. (1976), 'Book Review of Henry Manne, *The Economics of Legal Relationships*', **42** *Southern Economic Journal*, 765-766.

Gay, David E.R. (1977a), 'Book Review of *Government Controls and the Free Market*, ed. by Svetozar Pejovich', **44** *Southern Economic Journal*, 407-409.

Gay, David E.R. (1977b), 'Book Review of *Capitalism and Freedom: Problems and Prospects*, ed. by Selden', **37** *Zeitschrift für Nationalokonomie*, 423-424.

Gay, David E.R. (1978), 'Book Review of *Economic Forces at Work*, Armen Alchian', **31** *Kyklos*, 504-505.

Gay, David E.R. (1979), 'Economic Legalism: A Survey of the Naissance of the New Law and Economics', **3** *Midsouth Journal of Economics*, 65-70.

Gay, David E.R. (1979), 'Book Review of *Adam Smith and The Wealth of Nations: Bicentennial Essays 1776-1976*, ed. by Fred Glahe', **32** *Kyklos*, 629-630.

Gay, David E.R. (1981a), 'Book Review of *Regulation, Economics, and the Law*, Bernhard H. Siegan', **39** *Review of Social Economy*, 92-94.

Gay, David E.R. (1981b), 'Book Review of *Moral Revolution and Economic Science: The Demise of Laissez-Faire in Ninteenth Century British Political Economy*, Ellen Frankel Paul', **48** *Southern Economic Journal*, 530-531.

Gay, David E.R. (1982a), 'Book Review of *Mercantilism as a Rent-Seeking Society: Economic Regulation in Historical Perspective*, Robert B. Ekelund and Robert D. Tollison', **35** *Kyklos*, 732-733.

Gay, David E.R. (1982b), 'Book Review of *The Role of Government in a Free Society*, Phil Gramm', **50** *Southern Economic Journal*, 916-917.

Gay, David E.R. (1982c), 'Book Review of *Theories of Property: From Aristotle to the Present*, Anthony Parel and Thomas Flanagan', **15** *History of Political Economy*, 281-283.

Gay, David E.R. and Stanley, Tom D. (1992), 'Introduction Review of the *Fatal Conceit: The Error of Socialism*, Friedrich A. Hayek', **71** *Social Science Quarterly*, 400-401.

Gay, David E.R. and Waligorski, Conrad (1981), 'Book Review of *The State as a Firm: Economic Forces in Political Development*, David Auster and Morris Silver', **34** *Kyklos*, 110-111.

Johnsen, D. Bruce, Easterbrook, Frank H. and Fishel, Daniel R. (1993), 'The Economic Structure of Corporate Law', **525** *Annals of American Academy of Political and Social Science*, 200 ff.

Kitch, Edmund W. (1968), 'Review of Benjamin Kaplan, *An Unhurried View of Copyright*', **20** *Stanford Law Review*, 794 ff.

Kitch, Edmund W. (1981), 'Review of Chapter 11 of Volume XI of the *International Encyclopedia of Comparative Law: Legal Consequences of State Regulation*', **9** *International Journal of Law Libraries*, 230 ff.

Kitch, Edmund W. (1982), 'Review of Kripke, *The SEC and Corporate Disclosure: Regulation in Search of a Purpose*', **47** *University of Chicago Law Review*, 394 ff.

Kitch, Edmund W. (1984), 'Review of Cento G. Veljanovski, *The New Law and Economics: A Research Review*', **4** *International Review of Law and Economics*, 229 ff.

Kitch, Edmund W. (1990), 'Review of Kim Lane Scheppele, *Legal Secrets: Equality and Efficiency in the Common Law*', **28** *Journal of Economic Literature*, 1770 ff.

Kitch, Edmund W. (1993), 'Review of Anne M. Khademian, *The SEC and Capital Market Regulation: The Politics of Expertise*', **10** *Yale Journal on Regulation*, 589-594.

Lande, Robert H. (1988), 'Antitrust Law and Economics: Responding to an Ivory Tower Critique', **57** *University of Cincinnati Law Review*, 235 ff.

Lipford, Jody (1997), 'Lansing Pollock: *The Free Society* (Book Review)', **8** *Constitutional Political Economy*, 169-171.

McGuire, Robert A. (1989), 'Review of *Liberty, Property, and the Foundations of the American Constitution*, by Ellen Frankel Paul and Dickman, Howard', **49** *Journal of Economic History*, 1046-1048.

McGuire, Robert A. (1998), 'Review of *The Constitution in Congress: The Federalist Period, 1789-1801*, by David P. Currie', **58** *Journal of Economic History*.

Mercuro, Nicholas (1977), 'Book Review: *Environmental Controls*, R.A. Leone, Lexington, Lexington Books, 1979', **12(3)** *Review of Business and Economic Research*, 91-92.

Mercuro, Nicholas (1978), 'Book Review: *When Values Conflict*, L.H. Tribe et al. (eds), Cambridge, Ballinger Publishing Co., 1976', **12** *Journal of Economic Issues*, 187-189.

Mercuro, Nicholas (1980), 'Book Review: *The Economics of Natural Resources, Richard Lecomber*, New York, John Wiley and Sons, 1979', **47(1)** *Southern Economic Journal*, 265-267.

Mercuro, Nicholas (1984), 'Book Review: *Ethics, Economics and the Law*, J. Ronald Pennock and John W. Chapman, New York, New York University Press, 1982', **42(2)** *Review of Social Economy*, 192-199.

Mercuro, Nicholas (1986a), 'Book Review: *Research in Law and Economics: Normative Law and Economics*, Vol. 7, ZERBE, Richard O., Jr (ed.), (Greenwich, JAI Press, 1985)', **20** *Journal of Economic Issues*, 146-151.

Mercuro, Nicholas (1986b), 'Contributions to Law and Economics: A Survey of Recent Books', **17(4)** *Journal of Economic Education*, 295-309.

Parisi, Francesco (1994), '*Autonomy and Private Ordering in Contract Law*: Review Essay', **1** *European Journal of Law and Economics*, 213-227.

Parisi, Francesco (1998), 'Book Review: *The New Palgrave Dictionary of Economics and the Law*', **19** *International Review of Law and Economics*.

Parisi, Francesco (1998), '*The Constitutional and Political Economy of Trade Protection*: Review Essay', **5** *European Journal of Law and Economics*, 67-79.

Parisi, Francesco and Ricci, Paolo F. (1991), '*Environmental Policy in the 1990s*: Review Essay', **18** *Ecology Law Quarterly*, 459-484.

Peltzman, Sam (1968), 'Review of Gerald C. Fischer, *American Banking Structure*', **41** *Journal of Business*.

Peltzman, Sam (1970a), 'Review of D. Alhadeff, *Competition and Controls in Commercial Banking*', **43** *Journal of Business*.

Peltzman, Sam (1970b), 'Review of E. Kohn and C. Carlo, '*The Competitive Impact of New Branches*', **43** *Journal of Business*.

Peltzman, Sam (1978), 'Review of D. Schwartzman, *Innovation in the Pharmaceutical Industry*', **16** *Journal of Economic Literature*.

Polinsky, A. Mitchell (1974), 'Economic Analysis as a Potentially Defective Product: A Buyer's Guide to Posner's *Economic Analysis of Law*', **87** *Harvard Law Review*, 1655-1681.

Ramos De Sousa, João (1992a), 'James Buchanan, *Politics without Romance* - Book Review', **2** *Sub Judice*, 50-52.

Ramos De Sousa, João (1992b), 'Frank Easterbrook, *Criminal Procedure as a Market System* - Book Review', **2** *Sub Judice*, 47-49.

Ramos De Sousa, João (1992c), 'Ejan Mackaay, *La Règle Juridique Observée par le Prisme de L'Economiste* - Book Review', **2** *Sub Judice*, 44-46.

Schap, David (1985), 'Review of *Regulatory Decision Making: The Virginia State Corporation Commision*', **52** *Southern Economic Journal*, 591-592.

Schap, David (1987), 'Review of *Electric Power: Deregulation and the Public Interest*', **54** *Southern Economic Journal*, 511-512.

Schap, David (1990a), 'Review of *Economics and Antitrust Policy*', **57** *Southern Economic Journal*, 578-579.

Schap, David (1990b), 'Review of *Competition: The Economics of Industrial Change*', **56** *Southern Economic Journal*, 850-851.

Schap, David (1992), 'Review of *The Economics of Property Rights: Towards a Theory of Comparative Systems*', **58** *Southern Economic Journal*, 845-846.

Schap, David (1993), 'Review of *Recent Developments in the Theory of Industrial Organization*', **60** *Southern Economic Journal*, 531-533.

Schap, David (1994), 'Review of *The Growth of the Public Sector: Theories and International Evidence*', **61** *Southern Economic Journal*, 560-562.

Schap, David (1995), 'Review of *Property Rights and the Limits of Democracy*', **82** *Public Choice*, 193-196.

Schap, David (1996), 'Review of *Economic Thought and Political Theory*', **63** *Southern Economic Journal*, 276-278.

Schap, David (1997), 'Review of *The Limits of Public Choice: A Socological Critique of the Economic Theory of Politics*', **1** *The Independant Review*.

Schmidtchen, Dieter (1997), *Effizienz als Rechtsprinzip. Bemerkungen zu dem gleichnamigen Buch von Horst Eidenmüller* (Center for the Study of Law and Economics), Discussion paper 9708, 1997. Jahrbücher für Nationalökonomie und Statistik

Sousa Franco, António (1992), 'Richard A. Posner, *Economic Analysis of Law* - Book Review', **2** *Sub Judice*, 39-43.

Sunstein, Cass R. (1991), 'After the Rights Evolution: Reconceiving the Regulatory State', **25** *Journal of Economic Issues*, 1191-1195.

Ulen, Thomas S. (1997), 'Book Review: *Regulation: Legal Form and Economic Theory*', **17** *International Review of Law and Economics*, 293-295.

Van den Hauwe, Ludwig (1993), 'Review of Bouckaert and De Geest, *Bibliography of Law and Economics*', **77** *Public Choice*, 917-919.

Van den Hauwe, Ludwig (1995), 'Review of: Flair and de Boussieu, *Fiscal Policy, Taxation and the Financial System in an Increasingly Integrated Europe*', **85** *Public Choice*, 400-405.

Van den Hauwe, Ludwig (1996), '*Economic Methodology and the Economic Analysis of Law* (Book Review)', **3** *European Journal of Law and Economics*, 97-103.

Van den Hauwe, Ludwig (1998), 'German Income Tax Policy Between Equity and Efficiency', **5** *European Journal of Law and Economics*, 267-279.

Verkerke, J. Hoult (1991), 'Free to Search', **105** *Harvard Law Review*, 2080-2097.

Weissel, Erwin (1991), 'Das juristische Denken und das Denken der Juristen. Bemerkungen eines Ökonomen zu K.G. Wurzels 'Rechtswissenschaft als Socialwissenschaftler' (Legal Reasoning and the Reasoning of Lawyers - Some Remarks from an Economists Perspective regarding K.G. Wurzels 'Legal Science as a Social Science'), **6** *Zeitschrift für Rechtsvergleichung*.

Weissel, Erwin (1994), 'Wettbewerb als Pflicht und Recht. Eine Buchbesprechung (Competition as a Duty and a Claim)', **5** *Zeitschrift für Rechtsvergleichung*.

Yandle, Bruce (1997), 'Charles K. Rowley: *The Political Economy of the Minimal State*', **8 (1)** *Constitutional Political Economy*, 93-95.

0040
SYMPOSIA

Bibliography Collected by the Editors

Arnott, Richard J. and Mintz, Jack M. (eds) (1987), *Rent Control: The Internation Experience. Proceedings of a Conference Held at Queen's University, 31 August 4 September 1987*, Kingston, Queen's University, John Deutsch Institute for the Study of Economic Policy, 176 p.

Atias, Christian (1987), 'La Distinction du Patrimonial et de l'Extra-Patrimonial et l'Analyse Economique du Droit: un Utile Face à Face (The Distinction between Patrimonial and Extra-patrimonial Rights and the Economic Analysis of Law)', *Revue de la Recherche Juridique*.

Bebchuck, Lucian Ayre (ed.) (1990), *Corporate Law and Economic Analysis*, Cambridge, Cambridge University Press, 320 p.

Blair, Roger D. and Rubin, Stephen (eds) (1980), *Regulating the Professions: A Public-Policy Symposium*, Lexington, MA, Lexington Books, 328 p.

Buxbaum, Hertig and Hirsch, Hopt (eds), *European Economic and Business Law, Legal and Economic Analyses on Integration and Harmonization*, Berlin, 401 p.

Carmichael, H. Lorne (1988), 'Incentives in Academics: Why is there Tenure?', **96** *Journal of Political Economy*, 453-472.

Centi, Jean-Pierre, 'Quel Critère d'Efficience pour l'Analyse Economique du Droit? (Which Efficiency Criterion for Economic Analysis of Law)', *Revue de la Recherche Juridique*.

Chamberlin, Edward H. (ed.) (1954), *Monopoly, and Competition and Their Regulation*, New York, 549 p.

Cherot, Jean-Yves (1987), 'Trois thèses de l'analyses économique du droit (Three Thesis of Economic Analysis of Law)', *Revue de la Recherche Juridique*.

Conference (1985), 'Critical Issues in Tort Law Reform: A Search for Principles. A Conference Sponsored by the Program in Civil Liability, Yale Law School', **14** *Journal of Legal Studies*, 459-818.

Cranston, Ross and Schick, Anne (eds) (1982), *Law and Economics*, Canberra, Australian National University, 220 p.

Dale, Richard (ed.) (1986), *Financial Deregulation: The Proceedings of a Conference held by the David Hume Institute in May 1986*, Cambridge, Woodhead-Faulkner.

Dorn, James A. and Manne, Henry G. (eds) (1987), *Economic Liberties and the Judiciary*, Fairfax, George Mason University Press, 392 p.

Faure, Michael G. and Van den Bergh, Roger (eds) (1989), *Essays in Law and Economics: Corporations, Accident Prevention and Compensation for Losses*, Antwerpen, Maklu, 232 p.

Gay, David E.R. and Stanley, Tom D. (1992), 'Introduction Review of the Fatal Conceit: The Error of Socialism, Friedrich A. Hayek', **71** *Social Science Quarterly*, 400-401.

Heertje, A. and et al. (1991), *Law and Welfare Economics: op het Raakvlak van Economie en Recht* (Law and Welfare Economics: Where Economics and Law Touch), Bundel n.a.v. het gelijknamige Symposium op 24 oktober 1990.

Ippolito, Pauline M. and Scheffman, David T. (eds) (1986), *Empirical Approaches to Consumer Protection Economics*, Washington, Federal Trade Commission.

Litan, Robert E. and Winston, Clifford (eds) (1988), *Liability: Perspectives and Policy*, Washington, Brookings Institution, 248 p.

Mackaay, Ejan (1987), 'Le Juriste a-t-il le Droit d'Ignorer l'Economiste? (May Lawyers Ignore Economists?)', *Revue de la Recherche Juridique*.

Mathewson, G. Frank, Trebilcock, Michael J. and Walker, Michael A. (eds) (1990), *The Law and Economics of Competition Policy*, Vancouver, Fraser Institute, 443 p.

Mouly, Christian (1987), 'Présentation du Colloque sur l'Analyse Economique du Droit (Introduction to the Symposium of Economic Analysis of Law)', *Revue de la Recherche Juridique*, 413 ff.

Mouly, Christian (1995), 'Analyse Economique du Droit Régissant le Transfert de Propriété (Economic Analysis of Law Governing the Transfer of Property)', in X (ed.), *Faut-il Retarder le Transfert de Propriété ?'*, JCP éd. E, 6 ff.

Nutzinger, Hans G. and Backhaus, Jürgen G. (eds) (1989), *Codetermination: A Discussion of Different Approaches*, Berlin, Springer, 309 p.

Ott, Claus and Schäfer, Hans-Bernd (eds) (1989), *Allekationseffizienz in der Rechtsordnung* (Allocative Efficiency in Legal Order. Contribution), Berlin, Springer, 306 p.

Ott, Claus and Schäfer, Hans-Bernd (eds) (1991), *Ökonomische Probleme des Zivilrechts. Beiträge zum 2. Travemünder Symposium zur Ökonomischen Analyse des Rechts, 21.-26. März 1990* (Economic Problems of Civil Law. Contributions to the Second Travemünder Symposium on Economic Analysis of Law), Berlin, Springer, 347 p.

Ott, Claus and Schäfer, Hans-Bernd (eds) (1994), *Ökonomische Analyse der Rechtlichen Organisation von Innovationen, Beiträge zum 4. Travemünder Symposiun zur Ökonomischen Analyse des Rechts 1994* (Economic Analysis of the Law of Innovations), Heidelberg, Physica.

Pardolesi, Roberto and Van den Bergh, Roger (eds) (1991), *Law and Economics: Some Further Insights*, Milano, Giuffrè, 205 p.

Parisi, Francesco (1998), 'Book Review: The New Palgrave Dictionary of Economics and the Law', **19** *International Review of Law and Economics*.

Pethig, Rudiger and Schlieper, Ulrich (eds) (1987), *Efficiency, Institutions, and Economic Policy: Proceedings of a Workshop Held by the Sonderforschungsbereich 5 at the University of Mannheim*, New York, Springer, 225 p.

Rizzo, Mario J. (ed.) (1987), 'Symposium on Causation in the Law of Torts', **63** *Chicago-Kent Law Review*, 397-680.

Schulenburg, J. Matthias Graf Von Der and Skogh, Göran (eds) (1986), *Law and Economics and the Economics of Legal Regulation*, Dordrecht, Kluwer, 230 p.

Shaviro, Daniel N. (1993), 'Commentary: Uneasiness and Capital Gains', **48** *Tax Law Review*, 393-417.

Skogh, Göran (ed.) (1978), *Law and Economics. Report from a Symposium in Lund*, Lund, Juridiska Föreningen, 231 p.

Slayton, Philip and Trebilcock, Michael J. (eds) (1978), *The Professions and Public Policy*, Toronto, University of Toronto Faculty of Law, 346 p.

Stewart, Marion B. (ed.) (1987), *Energy Deregulation and Economic Growth: Proceedin*, New Brunswick, Rutgers, Bureau of Economic Research.

Stout, Lynn A. (1992), 'Strict Scrutiny and Social Choice: An Economic Inquiry into Fundamental Rights and Suspect Classifications', **80** *Georgetown Law Journal*, 1787-1834.

Stout, Lynn A. (1993), 'Poverty and Failure in the Market for Human Capital', **81** *Georgetown Law Journal*, 1947-1959.

Stout, Lynn A. (1995), 'Betting the Bank: How Derivatives Trading under Conditions of Uncertainty can Increase Risks and Erode Returns in Financial Markets', **21** *Journal of Corporate Law*, 53 ff.

Stout, Lynn A. (1996), 'Type I Error, Type II Error, and the Private Securities Litigation Reform Act', **38** *Arizona Law Review*, 711 ff.

Stout, Lynn A. (1997a), 'How Efficient Markets Undervalue Stocks: CAPM and ECMH in a World of Uncertainty and Disagreement', *Cardozo Law Review*.

Stout, Lynn A. (1997b), 'Technology, Transactions Costs, and Investor Welfare: Is a Motley Fool Born Every Minute?', **75** *Washington University Law Quarterly*, 791 ff.

Stout, Lynn A. (1997c), 'Irrational Expectations', *Journal of Legal Theory*.

Symposium (1970), 'Products Liability: Economic Analysis and the Law', **38** *University of Chicago Law Review*, 1-141.

Symposium (1976), 'Deregulation', **57** *Indiana Law Journal*, 682-755.

Symposium (1977), 'The Economics of Bankruptcy Reform', **41(4)** *Law and Contemporary Problems*.

Symposium (1978), 'Symposium on Posner's Theory of Privacy', *Georgia Law Review*.

Symposium (1979), 'Regulation and Innovation', **43(1)** *Law and Contemporary Problems*.

Symposium (1980a), 'Symposium on Efficiency as a Legal Concern', **8** *Hofstra Law Review*, 485-972.

Symposium (1980b), 'The Law and Economics of Privacy. A Conference Sponsored by the Center for the Study of the Economy and the State', **9** *Journal of Legal Studies*, 621-842.

Symposium (1981a), 'Managing the Transition to Deregulation', **44(1)** *Law and Contemporary Problems*.

Symposium (1981b), 'The Implications of Social Choice Theory for Legal Decision-Making', **9** *Hofstra Law Review*.

Symposium (1983a), 'The Place of Economics in Legal Education', **33** *Journal of Legal Education*, 183-376.

Symposium (1983b), 'Redistribution of Income through Regulation in Housing', **32** *Emory Law Journal*, 767-819.

Symposium (1984a), 'The Ali's Corporate Governance Proposals: Law and Economics', **8** *Delaware Journal of Corporate Law*.

Symposium (1984b), 'Attorney Fees Shifting', **47(1)** *Law and Contemporary Problems*, 1-354.

Symposium (1985a), 'Alternative Compensation Schemes and Tort Theory', **73(3)** *California Law Review*, 548-1042.

Symposium (1985b), 'Symposium on Law and Economics', **85** *Columbia Law Review*, 899-1119.

Symposium (1986), 'Medical Malpractice: Can the Private Sector Find Relief?', **49(2)** *Law and Contemporary Problems*, 1-348.

Symposium (1987), 'Conference on the Law and Economics of Procedure', **3** *Journal of Law, Economics, and Organization*, 143-447.

Symposium (1988a), 'The Crisis in Legal Theory and the Revival of Classical Jurisprudence', **73** *Cornell Law Review*, 281-446.

Symposium (1988b), 'Rent Control and the Theory of Efficient Regulation', **54** *Brooklyn Law Review*, 729-739.

Symposium (1988c), 'Symposium on Takings', **88** *Columbia Law Review*, 1581-1794.

Symposium (1989a), 'Empirical Approaches to Market Power', **32(S)** *Journal of Law and Economics*, 1-275.

Symposium (1989b), 'Symposium on Post-Chicago Law and Economics', **65** *Chicago-Kent Law Review*, 1-191.

Symposium (1989c), 'Non-Posnerian Law and Economics', **12** *Hamline Law Review*, 197-410.

Symposium (1989d), 'Issues in Civil Procedure: Advancing the Dialogue', **69** *Boston University Law Review*, 467-779.

Symposium (1990), 'Different Approaches to the Economics of Institutions', **146** *Journal of Institutional and Theoretical Economics*, 1-235.

Symposium (1991a), 'Symposium on New Views on Antitrust', **147** *Journal of Institutional and Theoretical Economics*, 1-239.

Symposium (1991b), 'The Economics of Liability', **5(3)** *Journal of Economic Perspectives*, 3-136.

Symposium (1996), 'Oikonomike Analyse tou Dikaiou (Economic Analysis of Law)', **6** *Aissymnetes*.

Symposium (Meurer, Michael) (ed.) (1989), 'Economics of Contract Law', *Law and Contemporary Problems*.

Van den Bergh, Roger (ed.) (1986), *Verslagboek Eerste Werkvergadering Recht en Economie* (Conference Volume First Workshop in Law and Economics), Antwerpen, Leerstoel A. Van Melkebeke, Handelshogeschool, 72 p.

Weigel, Wolfgang and Austrian Economic Chamber (eds) (1991), *Economic Analysis of Law - a Collection of Application*, Vienna, Austrian Economic Publishing Company, 295 p.

Williams, Stephen F. (1973), 'Optimizing Water Use: The Return Flow Issue', **44** *University of Colorado Law Review*, 301-321.

X (1979), 'Conference: Private Alternatives to the Judicial Process. Proceedings of A Seminar Sponsored by the Liberty Fund and Administered by the Law and Economics Center of the University of Miami School of Law', **8** *Journal of Legal Studies*, 231-415.

X (1984), 'Conference: Catastrophic Personal Injuries - A Conference Sponsored By the Hoover Institution', **13** *Journal of Legal Studies*, 415-622.

X (1987), 'Conference: Conference on the Law and Economics of Procedure', **3** *Journal of Law, Economics, and Organization*, 143-372.

X (1990), 'Conference: The Organization of Political Institutions', **6(S)** *Journal of Law, Economics, and Organization*, 1-332.

X (1990), 'Conference: The Law and Economics of Risk', **19** *Journal of Legal Studies*, 531-849.

Zerbe, Richard O., Jr (ed.) (1984), 'Symposium: Antitrust and Regulation', **6** *Research in Law and Economics*, 292 ff.

0050
COLLECTIONS OF (NEW) ARTICLES

Bibliography Collected by the Editors

Albon, Robert P. (ed.) (1980), *Rent Control. Costs and Consequences. Essays on the* , St. Leonards, Centre for Independent Studies.

Andreano, Ralph and Siegfried, John J. (eds) (1980), *The Economics of Crime*, Cambridge, Schenkman, 426 p.

Aoki, Masahiko et al. (eds) (1989), *The Firm as a Nexus of Treaties*, London, Sage, 358 p.

Aşsmann, Heinz-Dieter, Kirchner, Christian and Schanze, Erich (eds) (1978), *Ökonomische Analyse des Rechts* (Economic Analysis of Law), Kronberg, Athenäum, 369 p.

Bailey, Elizabeth E. (ed.) (1987), *Public Regulation: New Perspectives on Institution*, Cambridge, MA, MIT Press, 404 p.

Baily, Mary Ann and Cikins, Warren I. (eds) (1985), *The Effects of Litigation on Health Care Costs*, Washington, Brookings Institution.

Becker, Gary S. and Landes, William M. (eds) (1974), *Essays in the Economics of Crime and Punishment*, New York, Columbia University Press, 268 p.

Block, Walter E. (ed.) (1990), *Economics and the Environment: A Reconciliation*, Vancouver, Fraser Institute, 332 p.

Block, Walter E. and Olson, Edgar (eds) (1981), *Rent Control. Myths and Realities. International Evidence of the Effects of Rent Contol in Six Contries*, Vancouver, Fraser Institute, 335 p.

Block, Walter E. and Walker, Michael (eds) (1982), *Discrimination, Affirmative Action, and Equal Opportunity - An Economic and Social Perspective*, Vancouver, Fraser Institute, 271 p.

Boettcher, Erik, Herder-Dorneich, Philipp, Schenk, Karl-Ernst and Schmidtchen, Dieter (eds) (1991), *Jahrbuch für Neue Politische Ökonomie, 10. Band, Systemvergleich und Ordnungspolitik* (Comparative Analysis of Economic Systems and Constitutional Policy), Tübingen.

Bollard, Alan and Buckle, Robert (eds) (1987), *Economic Liberalisation in New Zealand*, Wellington, Allen and Unwin, 364 p.

Bouckaert, Boudewijn and De Geest, Gerrit (eds) (1995), *Essays in Law and Economics II: Contract Law, Regulation, and Reflections on Law and Economics*, Antwerpen, Maklu, 306 p.

Bromley, Daniel W. et al. (eds) (1992), *Making the Commons Work: Theory, Practice, and Policy*, San Francisco, ICS Press.

Bromley, Daniel W. and Segerson, Kathleen (eds) (1992), *The Social Response to Environmental Risk: Policy Formulation in an Age of Uncertainty*, Boston, Kluwer.

Buchanan, James M., Tollison, Robert D. and Tullock, Gordon (eds) (1980), *Toward a Theory of the Rent Seeking Society*, College Station, Texas A&M; University Press.

Burrows, Paul and Veljanovski, Cento G. (eds) (1981), *The Economic Approach to Law*, London, Butterworths, 343 p.

Button, Kenneth J. and Swann, Dennis (eds) (1989), *The Age of Regulatory Reform*, Oxford, Oxford University Press, 339 p.

Calvani, Terry and Siegfried, John J. (eds) (1979), *Economic Analysis and Antitrust*, Boston, Little Brown.

Campbell, David and Vincent-Jones, Peter (eds) (1997), *Contract and Economic Organisation: Socio-legal Initiatives*, Aldershot, Dartmouth.

Clarkson, Kenneth W. and Martin, Donald L. (eds) (1979), *The Economics of Nonproprietary Institutions* (Supplement 1 to Research in Law and Economics), Greenwood, JAI Press, 330 p.

Collard, David (ed.) (1989), *Fiscal Policy: Essays in Honour of Cedric Sandford*, Aldershot, Gower, 173 p.

Comanor, William S. et al. (1991), *Competition Policy in Europe and North America: Economic Issues and Institutions*, New York, Harwood, 260 p.

Crew, Michael A. (ed.) (1985), *Analyzing the Impact of Regulatory Change in Publi*, Lexington, MA, Lexington Books.

Crew, Michael A. (ed.) (1987), *Regulating Utilities in an Era of Deregulation*, New York, St. Martin's Press, 201 p.

Crew, Michael A. (ed.) (1989), *Deregulation and Diversification of Utilities*, Dordrecht, Kluwer, 206 p.

Crew, Michael A. (ed.) (1991), *Competition and the Regulation of Utilities*, Dordrecht, Kluwer, 224 p.

Crew, Michael A. and Kleindorfer, Paul R. (eds) (1991), *Competition and Innovation in Postal Services*, Dordrecht, Kluwer, 304 p.

Daintith, Terence C. (ed.) (1988), *Law as an Instrument of Economic Policy: Comparative and Critical Approaches*, Berlin, Walter de Gruyter, 432 p.

Daintith, Terence C. and Teubner, Gunther (1986), 'Sociological Jurisprudence and Legal Economics: Risks and Rewards', in Daintith, Terence and Teubner, Gunther (eds), *Contract and Organisation: Legal Analysis in the Light of Economic and Social Theory*, Berlin, Walter de Gruyter, 3-22.

Eatwell, John, Milgate, Murray and Newman, Peter (eds) (1987), *The New Palgrave: A Dictionary of Economics*, London, Macmillan, 4093 p.

Eatwell, John, Milgate, Murray and Newman, Peter (eds) (1989), *The New Palgrave: Invisible Hand*, London, Macmillan, 283 p.

Economistas (1989), *Los derechos de propriedad en el análisis económico* (Property Rights in Economic Analysis;(*journal*)).

Einhorn, Michael A. (ed.) (1991), *Price Caps and Incentive Regulation in Telecommunications*, Dordrecht, Kluwer Academic Publishers, 244 p.

Finsinger, Jörg and Pauly, Mark V. (eds) (1986), *The Economics of Insurance Regulation: A Cross-National Study*, New York, St Martin's Press, 300 p.

Gustafsson, B.A. and Klevmarken, N. Anders (eds) (1989), *The Political Economy of Social Security*, Amsterdam, North-Holland, 240 p.

Hardin, Garrett and Baden, John A. (eds) (1977), *Managing the Commons*, San Francisco, Freeman, 294 p.

Heineke, J.M. (ed.) (1978), *Economic Models of Criminal Behaviour*, Amsterdam, North-Holland, 391 p.

Herder-Dorneich, Philipp, Schenk, Karl-Ernst and Schmidtchen, Dieter (eds) (1993), 'Neue Politische Ökonomie von Normen und Institutionen (New Political Economics of Norms and Institutions)', **12** *Jahrbuch für Neue Politische Ökonomie*.

Herder-Dorneich, Philipp, Schenk, Karl-Ernst and Schmidtchen, Dieter (eds) (1994), 'Neue Politische Ökonomie der Regulierung, Deregulierung und Privatisierung (New Political Economics of Regulation, Deregulation, and Privatization)', **13** *Jahrbuch für Neue Politische Ökonomie*.

Johnsen, D. Bruce (1992), 'The Incentive Effects of Soft Dollar Brokerage', in Lehn, Kenneth and Kamphuis, Robert (eds), *Modernizing US Securities Regulations: Economic and Legal Perspectives*, 511-519.

Lange, Peter and Regini, Marino (eds) (1989), *State, Market, and Social Regulation: New Perspectives on Italy*, Cambridge, Cambridge University Press, 295 p.

Litan, Robert E. and Winston, Clifford (eds) (1988), *Liability: Perspectives and Policy*, Washington, Brookings Institution, 248 p.

Magoulas, Georgios and Simon, Jürgen (eds) (1985), *Recht und Ökonomie beim Konsumentenschutz und Konsumentenkredit* (Law and Economics of Consumer Protection and C), Baden-Baden, Nomos, 436 p.

Maksimovic, Ivan (ed.) (1992), *Transformacija Svojinskih Odnosa - Teorijski i Empirijski Aspekti* (Transformation of Property Rights - Theoretical and Empirical Issues), Belgrade, Srpska akademija nauka i umetnosti (SANU).

Martin, Donald L. and Schwartz, Warren F. (eds) (1977), *Deregulating American Industry: Legal and Economic Problems*, Lexington, MA, Lexington Books, 120 p.

McKee, David L. (ed.) (1989), *Hostile Takeovers: Issues in Public and Corporate Policy*, New York, Greenwood Press, 179 p.

McPheters, Lee R. and Strange, W.B. (eds) (1976), *The Economics of Crime and Law Enforcement*, Springfield, Charles Thomas.

Mercuro, Nicholas (ed.) (1989), *Law and Economics*, Boston, Kluwer Academic Publishers, 264 p.

Meyer, John R. and Oster, Clinton V., Jr (eds) (1981), *Airline Deregulation: The Early Experience*, Boston, Auburn House.

Miller, James C., III and Yandle, Bruce (eds) (1979), *Benefit-Cost Analysis of Social Regulation*, Washington, American Enterprise Institute for Public Policy Research.

Mintz, Jack M. and Whalley, John (eds) (1989), *The Economic Impacts of Tax Reform*, Toronto, Canadian Tax Foundation, 463 p.

Moorhouse, John C. (ed.) (1986), *Electric Power: Deregulation and the Public Intere*, San Francisco, Pacific Research Institute for Public Policy.

Moses, Leon N. and Savage, Ian (eds) (1989), *Transportation Safety in an Age of Deregulation*, Oxford, Oxford University Press, 368 p.

Nicklisch, Fritz (ed.) (1987), *Der Komplexe Langzeitvertrag. Strukturen und Internationale Schiedsgerichtsbarkeit* (The Complex Long-Term Contract. Structures and International Arbitration), Heidelberg, Müller Juristischer Verlag, 597 p.

Noll, Roger G. (ed.) (1985), *Regulatory Policy and the Social Sciences*, Berkeley, University of California Press, 400 p.

Parisi, Francesco and Giacobbe, Giovanni (1999), *Analisi Economica e Libertà Contrattuali*, Giuffrè.

Peacock, Alan T. and Forte, Francesco (eds) (1981), *The Political Economy of Taxation*, Oxford, Blackwell, 211 p.

Pennock, J. Roland and Chapman, John W. (eds) (1982), *Ethics, Economics and the Law* (Nomos 24), New York, New York University Press, 323 p.

Peretz, Paul (ed.) (1987), *The Politics of American Economic Policy Making*, New York, Armonk, M.E. Sharpe, 454 p.

Peskin, Henry M., Portney, Paul R. and Kneese, Allan V. (eds) (1981), *Environmental Regulation and the U.S. Economy*, Baltimore, MD, John Hopkins University Press, 163 p.

Phillips, A. (ed.) (1965), *Perpectives on Antitrust Policy*, Princeton, Princeton University Press.

Phillips, A. (1975), *Promoting Competition in Regulated Markets*, Washington, Brookings Institution.

Phillips, A. and Williamson, Oliver E. (eds) (1968), *Prices: Issues in Theory, Practice and Public Policy*, Philadelphia, PA, University of Pennsylvania Press.

Prichard, J. Robert S., Stanbury, W.T. and Wilson, Thomas A. (eds) (1979), *Canadian Competition Policy - Essays in Law and Economics*, Toronto, Butterworths.

Raes, Koen and Willekens, Harry (1994), 'Economische Verklaringen van het Recht (Economic Explanations of Law)', .

Roin, Julie, A. (1988), 'United they Stand, Divided they Fall: Public Choice Theory and the Tax Code', **74** *Cornell Law Review*, 62-134.

Roin, Julie, A. (1989), 'The Grand Illusion: A Neutral System for the Taxation of International Transactions', **75** *Virginia Law Review*, 919 ff.

Roin, Julie, A. (1995), 'Rethinking Tax Treaties in a Strategic World with Disparate Tax Systems', **81** *Virginia Law Review*, 1753 ff.

Roin, Julie, A. (1997), 'The U.S. Response to HIV: Alternative Explanations and the Lessons of Succes', **82** *Virginia Law Review*, 1511 ff.

Rottenberg, Simon (ed.) (1973), *The Economics of Crime and Punishment*, Washington, American Enterprise Institute for Public Policy Research, 232 p.

Rottenberg, Simon (ed.) (1978), *The Economics of Medical Malpractice*, Washington, American Enterprise Institute for Public Policy Research, 293 p.

Rottenberg, Simon (ed.) (1980), *Occupational Licensure Regulation*, Washington, American Enterprise Institute for Public Policy Research, 354 p.

Rottenberg, Simon (ed.) (1981), *The Economics of Legal Mininum Wages*, Washington, American Enterprise Institute for Public Policy Research, 534 p.

Schäfer, Hans-Bernd and Wehrt, Klaus (eds) (1989), *Die Ökonomisierung der Sozialwissenschaften: Sechs Wortmeldungen* (Economics in Social Sciences: Six Contributions), Frankfurt am Main, Campus Verlag, 182 p.

Schelling, Thomas C. (ed.) (1983), *Incentives for Environmental Protection*, Cambridge, MA, MIT Press, 355 p.

Schenk, Karl-Ernst, Schmidtchen, Dieter and Streit, Manfred E. (eds) (1996), *Vom Hoheitsstaat zum Konsensualstaat, Neue Formen der Kooperation zwischen Staat und Privaten Jahrbuch für Neue Politische Ökonomie 15* (From Sovereignity to Consensus, New Forms of Cooperation Between State and Citizens), Tübingen, Mohr.

Schenk, Karl-Ernst, Schmidtchen, Dieter and Streit, Manfred E. (eds) (1997), *Neue Politische Ökonomie der Integration und Öffnung von Infrastrukturnetzen Jahrbuch für Neue Politische Ökonomie 16* (Integration of and Access to Infrastructural Networks), Tübingen, Mohr.

Shogren, Jason F. (ed.) (1989), *The Political Economy of Government Regulation*, Dordrecht, Kluwer, 210 p.

Siegan, Bernard H. (ed.) (1977), *The Interactions of Economics and the Law*, Lexington, MA, Lexington Books, 171 p.

Sirkin, Gerald (ed.) (1981), *Lexeconomics - The Interactions of Law and Economics*, Boston, Nijhoff, 271 p.

Skogh, Göran (ed.) (1978), *Law and Economics. Report from a Symposium in Lund*, Lund, Juridiska Föreningen, 231 p.

Theeuwes, Jules J.M., Van Velthoven, Ben C.J. and Winters, J.K. E.A. (1989), *Recht en Economie* (Law and Economics), Amsterdam, Addison-Wesley, 294 p.

Weidenbaum, Murray L. and Chilton, Kenneth W. (eds) (1988), *Public Policy toward Corporate Takeovers*, New Brunswick, NJ, Transaction, 176 p.

Weisbrod, Burton A., Handler, Joel F. and Komesar, Neil K. (eds) (1978), *Public Interest Law: An Economic and Institutional*, Berkeley, University of California Press, 580 p.

Weiss, Leonard W. and Klass, Michael W. (eds) (1986), *Regulatory Reform: What Actually Happened*, Boston, Little Brown.

Wills, Robert L., Caswell, Julie A. and Culbertson, John D. (eds) (1987), *Issues after a Century of Federal Competition Policy*, Lexington, MA, Lexington Books, 387 p.

X (1990), 'Special Issue on Law and Economics', *Ars Aequi*, 603-804.

Zec, Miodrag, Mijatovic Bosko and Nebojsa Savic (eds) (1994), *Privatizacija Nuznost ili Sloboda Izbora* (Privatization Necessity or Freedom of Choice), Belgrade, Ekonomski institut and Jugoslovenska knjiga.

0060
READERS

Bibliography Collected by the Editors

Alexander, Larry (ed.) (1991), *Contract Law. Volumes I and II*, Aldershot, Dartmouth, 1140 p.

Assmann, Heinz-Dieter, Kirchner, Christian and Schanze, Erich (1978), *Ökonomische Analyse des Rechts* (Economic Analysis of Law), Kronberg, Athenäum.

Coase, Ronald H. (1988), *The Firm, the Market and the Law*, Chicago, University of Chicago Press, 217 p.

Demsetz, Harold (1988), *Ownership, Control, and the Firm. The Organization*, Oxford, Blackwell, 300 p.

Furubotn, Eirik G. and Pejovich, Svetozar (eds) (1974), *The Economics of Property Rights*, Cambridge, MA, Ballinger, 367 p.

Goetz, Charles J. (1984), *Law and Economics: Cases and Materials*, St. Paul, West Publishing Company.

Goldberg, Victor P. (ed.) (1989), *Readings in the Economics of Contract Law*, Cambridge, Cambridge University Press, 252 p.

Kaplan, L.J. and Kessler, P. (eds) (1976), *An Economic Analysis of Crime: Selected Readings*, Springfield, Charles Thomas.

Kronman, Anthony T. and Posner, Richard A. (eds) (1979), *The Economics of Contract Law*, Boston, Little Brown, 274 p.

Kuperberg, Mark and Beitz, Charles R. (eds) (1983), *Law, Economics and Philosophy - A Criticial Introduction; with Applications to the Law of Torts*, Totowa, Rowman and Allenheld, 284 p.

Manne, Henry G. (ed.) (1977), *The Economics of Legal Relationships: Readings in the Theory of Property Rights*, St. Paul, West Publishing Company, 660 p.

Ogus, Anthony I. and Veljanovski, Cento G. (eds) (1984), *Readings in the Economics of Law and Regulation*, Oxford, Clarendon, 361 p.

Parisi, Francesco (1998), *The Economic Structure of the Law* (The Collected Papers of Richard A. Posner: Volume I), Cheltenham and Lyme, Edward Elgar, 354 p.

Parisi, Francesco (1998), *The Economics of Private Law* (The Collected Papers of Richard A. Posner: Volume II), Cheltenham and Lyme, Edward Elgar, 380 p.

Parisi, Francesco (1998), *The Economics of Public Law* (The Collected Papers of Richard A. Posner: Volume III), Cheltenham and Lyme, Edward Elgar, 409 p.

Parisi, Francesco and Giacobbe, Giovanni (1999), *Analisi Economica e Libertà Contrattuali*, Giuffrè.

Parisi, Francesco and Posner Richard A. (1997), *International Library of Critical Writings in Economics, Volume I: Theoretical and Methodological Foundations*, Cheltenham and Lyme, Edward Elgar.

Parisi, Francesco and Posner Richard A. (1997), *International Library of Critical Writings in Europe, Volume II: Contracts, Torts and Criminal Law*, Cheltenham and Lyme, Edward Elgar.

Parisi, Francesco and Posner Richard A. (1997), *International Library of Critical Writings in Europe, Volume III: Other Areas of Private and Public Law*, Cheltenham and Lyme, Edward Elgar.

Posner, Richard A. (ed.) (1977), *Tort Law: Cases and Economic Analysis*, Boston, Little Brown.

Posner, Richard A. and Scott, Kenneth E. (eds) (1980), *Economics of Corporation Law and Securities Regulation*, Boston, Little Brown, 384 p.

Rabin, Robert L. (ed.) (1976), *Perspectives on Tort Law*, Boston, Little Brown.

Rubin, Paul H. (1983), *Business Firms and The Common Law*,.

Schreuders, Wicher and Holzhauer, Rudi W. (1993), *Teksten Rechtseconomie* (Readings in Law and Economics), Arnhem, Gouda Quint, 461 p.

Stigler, George J. (1975), *The Citizen and the State. Essays on Regulation*, Chicago, University of Chicago Press, 209 p.

Stigler, George J. (ed.) (1988), *Chicago Studies in Political Economy*, Chicago, University of Chicago Press, 641 p.

Teijl, Rob and Holzhauer, Rudi W. (eds) (1991), *Teksten Rechtseconomie* (Readings in Law and Economics), Arnhem, Gouda Quint, 549 p.

0070
BIBLIOGRAPHIES

Bibliography Collected by the Editors

Bouckaert, Boudewijn and De Geest, Gerrit (eds.) (1992), *Bibliography of Law and Economics*, Boston, Kluwer Academic Publishers, 684 p.

Buchanan, James M. (1987), 'Bibliography of James M. Buchanan's Publications, 1949-1986', **89** *Scandinavian Journal of Economics*, 17-37.

Campbell, David and Clay, Susan (1976), *Long-Term Contracting: A Research Bibliography and Review of the Literature*, Oxford, Centre for Socio-Legal Studies.

Chiorazzi, Michael and others (1988), 'Empirical Studies in Civil Procedure: A Selected Annotated Bibliography', **51(3)** *Law and Contemporary Problems*, 87-207.

Foley, Patrick, Shaked, Avner and Sutton, John (1981), *The Economics of the Professions. An Introductory Guide to the Literature*, London, London School of Economics, 107 p.

Goehlert, Robert and Gunderson, Nels (1987), *Government Regulation of Business: An Information* , Phoenix, Oryx Press, 425 p.

Hoffman, Elizabeth and Spitzer, Matthew L. (1985), 'Experimental Law and Economics: An Introduction', **85** *Columbia Law Review*, 991-1036.

McGee, Robert W. (1983), 'Data Processing Department Practices', *Bibliography, National Association of Accountants*.

McGee, Robert W. (1983), 'Deferred Taxation', *Bibliography, National Association of Accountants*.

McGee, Robert W. (1984), 'Accounting for Software', *Bibliography, National Association of Accountants*.

McGee, Robert W. and Greaves, Bettina Bien (1993), *Mises: An Annotated Bibliography*, Foundation for Economic Education, 405 p.

Parisi, Francesco (1998a), *The Economic Structure of the Law* (The Collected Papers of Richard A. Posner: Volume I), Ashgate, Edward Elgar, 354 p.

Parisi, Francesco (1998b), *The Economics of Private Law* (The Collected Papers of Richard A. Posner: Volume II), Ashgate, Edward Elgar, 380 p.

Parisi, Francesco (1998c), *The Economics of Public Law* (The Collected Papers of Richard A. Posner: Volume III), Ashgate, Edward Elgar, 409 p.

Parisi, Francesco and Frezza, Giampaolo (1998a), 'Pietro Trimarchi', in Backhaus, Jürgen G. (ed.), *Elgar Companion to Law and Economics*, Ashgate, Edward Elgar.

Parisi, Francesco and Frezza, Giampaolo (1998b), 'Achille Loria (1847-1943)', in Backhaus, Jürgen G. (ed.), *Elgar Companion to Law and Economics*, Ashgate, Edward Elgar.

Parisi, Francesco and Frezza, Giampaolo (1998c), 'Augusto Graziani (1865-1938)', in Backhaus, Jürgen G. (ed.), *Elgar Companion to Law and Economics*, Ashgate, Edward Elgar.

Parisi, Francesco and Frezza, Giampaolo (1998d), 'Cesare Beccaria (1738-1794)', in McCay, Bonnie J. and Acheson, James M. (eds), *The Question of the Commons: The Culture and Ecology of Communal Resources*, Tucson (AZ), University of Arizona.

Parisi, Francesco and Posner, Richard A. (1997a), 'Law and Economics: An Introduction', in Posner, Richard A. and Parisi, Francesco (eds), *Law and Economics*, Ashgate, Edward Elgar, 3-57.

Parisi, Francesco and Posner, Richard A. (1997b), 'Scuole e Tendenze nella Analisi Economica del Diritto', **15** *Rivista Critica del Diritto Privato*.

Parisi, Francesco and Posner Richard A. (1999), 'Analisi Economica del Diritto Pubblico e Commerciale: Una Bibliografia Annotata', in X (ed.), *Biblioteca della Libertá*.

Priddat, Birger (1990), 'Hegel als Ökonom (Hegel as an Economist)', **403** *Volkswirtschaftliche Schriften*.

Pyle, David J. (1979), *The Economics of Crime and Law Enforcement: A Selective Biblipography* (and Supplement 1980), SSRC Public Sector Study Group, Bibliography Series, 216 p.

Samuels, Warren J. (1965), 'Law and Economic Policy: A Bibliographical Survey', **58** *Law Library Journal*, 230-252.

Samuels, Warren J. (1972), 'Law and Economics: A Bibliographical Survey 1965-72', **66** *Law Library Journal*, 96-110.

Sinder, Janet (1987), 'Economists as Judges: A Selective, Annotated Bibliography', **50(4)** *Law and Contemporary Problems*, 279-286.

Snow, Marcellus S. and Jussawalla, Meheroo (1986), *Telecommunication Economics and International Regulatory Policy: An Annotated Bibliography*, New York, Greenwood Press, 216 p.

Stanbury, W.T. and Tretheway, Michael W. (1986), 'Airline Deregulation: A Bibliography', **22** *Logistics and Transportation Review*, 449-489.

Templeton, Virginia Evans and Taubenfeld, Howard J. (1987), *World Environment Law Bibliography: Non Periodical Literature in Law and the Social Sciences Published Since 1970 in Various Languages with Selected Reviews and Annotations from Periodicals*, Littleton, Rothman, 480 p.

Van den Hauwe, Ludwig (1993), 'Review of Bouckaert & De Geest, Bibliography of Law and Economics', **77** *Public Choice*, 917-919.

Veljanovski, Cento G. (1984), *Economics of the Common Law: A Bibliography*, Oxford, Centre for Socio-Legal Studies, 59 p.

0080
DOCTORAL OR MASTER'S THESES

Bibliography Collected by the Editors

Adams, Michael (1981), *Oekonomische Analyse des Zivilprozesses* (Economic Analysis of Civil Procedure), Koenigstein, Athenaeum-Verlag.

Evangelopoulos, Panagiotis (1996), 'E Analyse ton Periousiakon Dikaiomaton kai e Ideologia tes Eleutheres Agoras (Property Rights Analysis and Free-Market Ideology)', 6 *Aissymnetes*.

Fabre-Magnan Muriel (1990), *De l'Obligation d'Information dans les Contrats* (The Obligation of Information in Contracts), L.G.D.J.

Freyer, Susanne (1994), 'Umwelthaftung aus der Sicht der Ökonomischen Analyse des Rechts (Environmental Liability from a Law and Economics Perspective)', *Doctoral Dissertation.*

Garoupa, Nuno (1997), *Essays on the Theory of Optimal Law Enforcement*, University of York, Phil. Thesis.

Hatzis, Aristides N. (1998), *An Economic Theory of Greek Contract Law*, PhD Thesis, University of Chicago Law School.

Manitakis, Antonios (1975), *L'Antinomie entre la Liberté du Commerce et de l'Industrie et la Régulation Administrative de l'Économie: En Droit Belge et en Droit Français*, Bruxelles, Centre Interuniversitaire de Droit Public.

McGee, Robert W. (1993), *Explorations in Law and Economics from a Rights Perspective*, The Union Institute, 221 p.

Moine, I. (1997), *Les choses hors commerce. Une approche de la personne humaine juridique* (Things Apart from Commerce. An Approach of Juridical Humane Persons), L.G.D.J.

Poughon, Jean-Michel (1987), *Histoire doctrinale de l'échange*, (Doctrinal History of Exchange), L.G.D.J.

Raaschou-Nielsen, Agnete (1988), *Institutionel Œndring og ¢konomisk Teori* (Institutional Change and Economic Theory), K¢benhavn, PhD thesis, Det Statsvidenskablige Fagråd.

Riis, Thomas (1996), *Ophavsret og rets¢konomi* (Copyright and Law and Economics), Gadjura, PhD thesis.

Roemer, Andrès (1994), *An Interdisciplinary Approach to Federal Waters and Institutions: The Mexican Case*, UP/Michigan Publishers.

Ryssdal, Stray A.C. (1995), *Legal Realism and Economics as Behavior - A Scandinavian Look at the Economic Analysis of Law*, Oslo, Juridisk Forlag.

Sevic, Zeljko (1994), *Pravni Status Centralne Banke u Savremenoj Trzisnoj Privredi* (Status of the Central Bank in a Contemporary Market Economy), Belgrade, Faculty of Law, University of Belgrade.

Zenati, F. (1981), *Essai sur la Nature Juridique de la Propriété, Contribution à la Théorie Juridique du Droit Subjectif*, (Essay on the Juridical Nature of Property, Contributions to the Juridical Theory of Subjective Rights).

0100
ORGANIZATION OF RESEARCH AND TEACHING

Claus Ott
Professor of Law at the University of Hamburg

Tina Neuling
Research Assistant at the University of Hamburg

Abstract

Law and economics is quite a new field of research but there is a noticeable increase in its influence in both legal and economic scholarship. In the following chapter information is given about different aspects of the organization of research and teaching in this area, in particular about the institutions, the current state of law and economics in academic life all over the world, the basic publications providing more detailed information, Law and Economics Associations, and law and economics on the Internet.
JEL classification: K00
Keywords: law and economics, Academic Programs, Teaching, Research, Research Institutes, law and economics Associations

1. Introduction

Law and economics is a relatively new field of research, and therefore it is only slowly becoming an established part of the curricula at universities and colleges throughout the world. However, there is a clear movement towards employing the tools of law and economics in academic programs and in special research institutes more and more. While most of the literature describing and discussing these influences concentrates on developments at law schools, the field is also being explored in traditional departments of economics. Overall, there is a noticeable increase in the influence of law and economics in both legal and economic scholarship. Nevertheless, the relative importance of the field is still heavily debated. For example, it is often discussed whether or not the economic analysis of law can or cannot provide for a new understanding of the law, and how economic tools have changed the classical study of the law.

One extensive discussion about the role of law and economics in legal education has been published in the *Journal of Legal Education.* In that edition, various opinions are presented in fourteen articles covering about 200 pages. The original debate was held at a symposium in 1983 entitled 'The Place of Economics in Legal Education' (Symposium, 1983). The primary focus of the articles is the relevance of economics on legal thought in general (see Becker, 1983, Breyer, 1983; Calabresi, 1983; Cooter, 1983; Hansmann, 1983; Michelmann, 1983; and Priest, 1983). However, some of the authors also discuss the practical application of law and economics in teaching (see Doyle, 1982; Gelhorn and Robinson, 1983; Klevorick, 1983; Schwartz, M., 1983; Schwartz W., 1983; Summers, 1983; and Trebilcock, 1983). In 1981 a similar symposium was held at Yale University, and in the papers presented at that conference (published in the *Yale Law Journal*) the authors - among them Ackerman (1981), Posner (1981) and Priest (1981), analyzed the current state of legal scholarship. Law and economics was only one of the focuses of discussions there, and the influence of other disciplines which were noticeable in legal scholarship was also discussed. One example of a similar symposium convened outside of the United States is that of the 1991 symposium 'Economic Analysis in Civil Law Countries: Past, Present, Future' (see Cooter and Gordley, 1991). There, scholars from different countries provided information about the influence of law and economics in their respective home countries. See Mattei and Pardolesi (1991) report on Italy, Kirchner (1991) report on Germany, Hertig (1991) report on Switzerland (pointing out the apparent lack of a law and economics movement in Switzerland), Ota (1991) report on Japan, Pastor (1991) report on Spain, Skogh (1991) report on Sweden, and Weigel (1991) report on Austria.

One interesting approach to measuring the actual influence of law and economics has been taken by Landes and Posner (1993). In their article, the authors present a quantitative study in which they analyze citations to show the extent to which economics has in fact influenced legal scholarship.

The following chapters will provide a short overview over different methods of teaching law and economics, and how the research in this area continues to be promoted throughout the world. Since academic programs are constantly changing and many different programs and institutions are still in their developmental stages, only representative examples will be presented here. Much information concerning specific programs or classes can be obtained in detail from the home pages of the respective universities/institutions on the Internet, and can be located through the main search engines. Greater detail about specific countries can furthermore be found in chapters 0305-0395 of this volume, in which the law and economics movements in different countries are presented.

2. Teaching of law and economics - An Overview

Though law and economics is also part of the curricula of many departments of economics, most programs in law and economics are organized by private and public law schools. However, economics scholars often actively participate, and several law schools and departments of economics or business work together in joint programs. Quite often, professors of economics are asked to join law school faculties and to teach there on a permanent basis. Furthermore, there are numerous special institutes formed of both law and economics faculty members.

There are a variety of possibilities to study and teach law and economics at different academic levels and to different audiences. As stated above, it can be taught in law schools, in university-based departments of economics, or at special research institutes. At universities, law and economics can be taught at an undergraduate, graduate or postgraduate level. Finally, law and economics can either be integrated into regular law school courses, or there can be special course offerings either as optional courses or within a separate program.

3. Integration of law and economics into Law or Economics Courses

At law schools, law and economics may be integrated into the traditional law school curriculum. This can be accomplished by first providing an introduction into the basic principles of economics, and later on by encouraging the use of the economic tools learned. This approach is favored by some American law schools where the law and economics approach is an essential tool for understanding the law courses offered in subsequent years. In such programs, basic economics courses and later on economic analysis of different areas of the law are often mandatory requirements.

The most progressive steps so far have been taken by the American George Mason University School of Law in Arlington, Virginia (George Mason University School of Law, 3401 North Fairfax Drive, Arlington, VA 22201-4498, USA). This program emphasizes application of the law and economics approach to the entire study of the law. Almost all of the courses at George Mason use economic theory as their primary method of analysis.

More commonly, however, law schools employ economic tools only within the framework of certain specific courses. Law and economics ideas can and are - at least in the United States - typically treated in the classic law and economic courses (for example antitrust law or corporate law). These courses have served as the traditional forum for the application of the law and economics approach. There exists, however, a growing tendency towards employing law and economics in more and more non-traditional law courses (for example torts, real property, contracts or civil procedure). Today, law and economics is being integrated more and more into the traditional core curricula of legal studies. This expansion is often referred to as the 'New Law and economics'. A brief description of the so-called 'New Law and economics' can be found in Calabresi (1983), and Veljanovski (1982) also gives a good overview over this approach. On the other hand, Kirchner (1991) refers back to the previous tradition in Germany of interdisciplinary research in the field of law and economics which was more or less confined to cartel law, and traces the introduction of 'new law and economics' into legal research and teaching back in the 1970s.

A detailed exposition on what law and economics scholars and economists currently think lawyers should know about economics can be found in Whaples, Morriss and Moorhouse (1998). In preparing this report the authors conducted a survey to find out which concepts the scholars interviewed deemed to be necessary in the teaching of law and economics courses, and what major articles they would recommend for a required reading list.

Law and economics can, of course, be integrated into classical economics courses. However, this approach is more rare and less information about it is available.

4. Special law and economics Courses at Law Schools or in Departments of Economics

As opposed to integrating economic analysis of the law into law or economics courses, there also exist special law and economics courses which are elective in nature and which concentrate more on the field's theoretical aspects. This approach is mostly favored by universities which do not integrate economic analysis of the law into their regular classes. These specialized classes can be found at many American universities as well as elsewhere in the rest of the world.

For example, in Germany such courses can sometimes be found as one of several electives relating to the foundations of the law, the so-called 'Grundlagenveranstaltungen'. It is still, however, rare to find true law and economics lectures. The University of Hamburg is one of the rare exceptions. In Hamburg, fully integrated courses in law and economics are offered to law students as optional classes as part of the regular law school curriculum. Schäfer (1990) explains and discusses the Hamburg model. An early outline of an integrated law and economics course is given by Kötz (1977). At other German Law Schools it is more common to offer classes where pure economics is taught. Kirchner (1991) provides an instructive overview of the general situation in Germany up until the 1990s.

In other countries law and economics classes can be found more often. For example, in Europe such classes are regularly offered in Austria, Belgium, France,

Italy, the Netherlands, Spain, and the United Kingdom. In Austria the University of Innsbruck offers a course in 'Economic Analysis of Law' in addition to fundamental classes in economics for law-students. At the Katholieke Universiteit Leuven in Belgium an English language course entitled 'Economic Analysis of Law' is offered which is based upon a microeconomics and game-theory methodology. Also, the University of Ghent in Belgium offers a course entitled 'Rechtseconomie' to both law and economics students. In France, the University of Montpellier also offers special classes in law and economics. The University of Trento in Italy has an optional class called 'Topics of Economic Analysis of the Law'. All of these are simply examples of current courses being offered in Europe.

The early situation in the Netherlands is described in more detail by Holzhauer and Teijl (1989). Recently, the growing influence of law and economics in the Dutch legal education has become noticeable. Nowadays, law and economics is often offered as a basic introductory course. Examples can be found at the relevant Internet home sites of the Erasmus University of Rotterdam. The earlier status of law and economics at Spanish law schools is described in Pastor (1988) as well as Pastor (1991).

Other countries where the study of law and economics is especially emphasized include the United States, and also Israel, Canada, Australia and New Zealand. Gelhorn and Robinson (1983) review the development of economic science in US law schools and comment on that development's relevance. Lovett (1974) also addresses the role of economics in American law schools and closely examines the curricula at several law schools in the United States. The Buchmann Faculty of Law at Tel-Aviv University has classes where law and economics are combined at the undergraduate level as well as at the graduate level. Trebilcock (1983) provides information about the changes at law schools in Canada. He points out that the influence of law and economics in Canadian legal education is limited as compared to the United States and presents possible explanations for this. The author himself, however, actively participates in promoting law and economics scholarship in Canada. Doyle (1982) extensively examines lecture courses in law and economics offered at an undergraduate level in Australia.

The most recent developments regarding law and economics in various countries are described in the chapter 0300 Survey of Non-English Language Publications. One example of a course in law and economics offered to students of economics is the course 'Analisis Economico del Derecho' at the Universidad Carlos III de Madrid in Madrid, Spain. Professor Santos Pastor, who teaches this class, also wrote the above-cited article 'Teaching Economics to Law Students' (Pastor, 1988).

5. Specific law and economics Programs for Lawyers and Economists

Still another possibility exists, namely the teaching of law and economics in a separate program specializing in law and economics. The ERASMUS Programme in law and economics is a one-year European postgraduate program for lawyers and economists leading to the academic degree of 'European Master in Law and Economics'. It is jointly organized by 19 partner universities within the European Union. The University of Haifa, Israel is also an associate member. Special courses in law and economics are offered at ten of the partner universities. The program's partners (T = partner and teaching unit) are the universities of Aix-en-Provence (T), Berlin, Copenhagen, Ghent (T), Glasgow, Haifa, Hamburg (T), Leiden (T), Linköping (T), Madrid (T), Manchester (T), Milan, Paris, Rome, Rotterdam (T), Stockholm (T), Tampere, Thessaloniki, Valladolid, and Vienna (T). The ERASMUS Programme in law and economics is presently coordinated from the University of Hamburg (C.Ott).

The University of Utrecht is an example of a law school offering a postgraduate program leading to a degree in law and economics (Utrecht LLM Office, Faculty of Law, Utrecht University, Janskerhof 3, 3512 BK Utrecht, The Netherlands). This program is open to both law school and economics program graduates. Students of economics may complete specialized legal courses and are able to obtain a Master of Sciences title.

In the United States, one of the most important programs is the John M. Olin Program in law and economics at the University of Chicago. In that program law and economics ideas have been taught for over 50 years. The significant achievements of that program are described by Coase (1993). At the American College of Law at Syracuse University in New York (Syracuse University College of Law, Office of Admissions and Financial Aid, Suite 212, Syracuse, NY 13244-1030, USA) another form of specialization can be found. Students are able to participate in a program of studies offering a special Law and Economics Concentration. During their normal studies of the law, students are required to take five core courses involving law and economics topics and three elective courses. Once these requirements have been met the students are awarded a special certificate in recognition that they have completed this special concentration.

At the Faculty of Law at the University of Toronto (Faculty of Law, University of Toronto, 78 Queen's Park, Toronto, Ontario, Canada, M5 S 2 C5), where Professor Trebilcock teaches, instructors from the Faculty of Law, the Department of Economics and the Faculty of Management work together. The program offers students special study and research opportunities in a variety of courses, and brings to the Faculty important law and economics scholars through the program's law and economics Workshops and the Visiting Professorship in Law and Economics.

A brief description about an international summer school in law and economics offered in Saarbrücken is presented by Meyer and Müller (1990). In 1988 and in 1989 the Center for the Study of the New Institutional Economics at the University of Saarbrücken organized two international summer schools in cooperation with the University of Texas in Arlington.

The National Law School of India University in Bangalore (Prof. N.L. Mitra, Director, National Law School of India University, Nagarbhavi, Bangalore-560072, India) organizes seminars in law and economics for teaching staff members from Indian law schools and departments of economics.

There are also courses in law and economics available for legal practitioners and professors. A special training program for postgraduates, judges, lawyers, law professors, and academic economists, is offered by the law and economics Center (LEC) founded by Henry Manne in 1974 and located at the George Mason University in Arlington, Virginia. The program is privately funded and offers educational institutes, seminars, and conferences in close cooperation with the University's law school.

6. Teaching Materials

The basic teaching materials for all law and economic classes are the two classic textbooks: Posner, '*Economic Analysis of Law*' (1998), now in its fifth edition, and Cooter and Ulen, '*Law and Economics*' (1996), now in its second edition. In addition, other textbooks intended to provide a basis for academic studies in law and economics have been published. Recent examples include Schäfer and Ott, '*Lehrbuch der Ökonomischen Analyse des Rechts*' (1995), now in its second edition and also available in Spanish, Miceli, '*The Economics of the Law*' (1998), Katz, '*Foundations of the Economic Approach to Law*' (1998), Dau-Schmidt and Ulen, '*Law and Economics Anthology*' (1998), Posner, and Parisi, '*Law and Economics*' (1997) a three volume set, Mercuro and Medema, '*Economics and the Law: From Posner to Post-Modernism*' (1997), and Dnes, '*The Economics of Law*' (1996). Earlier examples of such works include Manne, '*The Economics of Legal Relationships*' (1975), Tullock, '*The Logic of the Law*' (1971), and Bowles, '*Law and the Economy*' (1982). These textbooks all share the common characteristic that they are specifically designed to serve as textbooks for law-students. Other literature - of course - can and is also applied in classrooms. The literature identified above can be found in the bibliography in Chapter 0000 Introductory Books. Examples of how the law and economics approach can be used to analyze specific cases in the classroom are Schäfer and Strück (1983) and Walz and Wienstroh (1983), both published in Walz and Rascher-Friesenhausen (1983), and Wehrt and Mohr (1995).

7. Research in law and economics - An Overview

Research in the area of law and economics is becoming more and more noticeable. There exists an expanding body of literature (books, theses, dissertations, working papers, and journals), and researchers from all over the world regularly meet at academic conferences, workshops and through various law and economics associations. Universities all over the world also host periodic conferences and discussion groups which have a law and economics focus. At several universities special research centers dedicated to law and economics exist.

8. Academic Research in Europe

In Germany there exist two prominent academic research institutes focusing on the topic of law and economics. One is located in the city of Saarbrücken and the other in Hamburg. The 'Forschungsstelle zur ökonomischen Analyse des Rechts' at Saarbrücken (Center for the Study of law and economics, Prof. D. Schmidtchen, Forschungsstelle zur ökonomischen Analyse des Rechts, Universität des Saarlandes, Fachbereich Wirtschaftswissenschaft, Gebäude 31, Postfach 151150, D-66041 Saarbrücken) was founded in 1993 in the Department of Economics of the Universität des Saarlandes. The Center organizes conferences, for example in Wallerfangen, and workshops, invites scholars from all over the world, and provides consultations and advice to numerous private and public authorities. It also publishes a series of theoretical discussion papers. Its particular focus of research is the law and economics of international transactions, constitutional economics, the legal protection of intellectual property, and the evolution of legal rules and conventions in the shadow of the law. The Center also organizes an annual meeting for researchers in the field of New Political Economy. Papers presented at the Center's various conferences are published in the '*Jahrbuch für Neue Politische Ökonomie*'.

In Hamburg, the Institute of law and economics (Universität Hamburg, Fachbereich Rechtswissenschaft, Edmund-Siemers-Allee 1, 20146 Hamburg) founded by Prof. C. Ott and Prof. H.-B. Schäfer as part of the Law Faculty's focus on interdisciplinary research and teaching activities, serves as a forum for guest lecturers, workshops, and seminars. The Institute also publishes a regular series of discussion papers. Since 1988, the Institute has organized a biannual conference of various topics in the field of law and economics at Travemünde (See Conference Volumes (6), edited by C. Ott and H.B. Schäfer). In October 1998, the Institute established a PhD program (*Graduiertenkolleg*) for 15 postgraduate students of law and economics which hosts doctoral candidates from both Europe and the US. (For information regarding other teaching and research centers and academic conferences in Germany please refer to Kirstein 0330 law and economics.)

Another European center for interdisciplinary studies which provides information concerning fundamental topics in law and economics is the Center d'Études Interdisciplinaire Walras Pareto which is part of the Université de Lausanne of Switzerland. An example of a research center located in France is the Department of law and economics within the 'Laboratoire de Droit Privé' of the University of Montpellier (Laboratoire de Droit Privé, 14, rue Cardinal de Cabrières, 34060 Montpellier Cedex 0467615452). That center hosts meetings and conferences in order to promote the exchange of ideas in law and economics. In the Netherlands regular workshops are held in Maastricht, organized by Jürgen Backhaus. In the United Kingdom the David Hume Institute promotes discourse and research on economic and legal aspects of public policy questions. The Hume Institute was founded in Edinburgh in 1985. It publishes a quarterly academic journal and various paper series, and organizes conferences and other events (Contact David Hume Institute, 21 George Square, Edinburgh EH8 9LD, Scotland).

9. Academic Research in Other Countries

In the United States - the birthplace of law and economics - research centers in law and economics are quite common. The universities identified above which offer law and economics courses also maintain extensive research facilities. Thus, at Yale, the University of California-Berkeley or at the University of Chicago research in the field of law and economics is strongly supported and promoted. Workshops and conferences are also currently being offered at the Georgetown University Law Center in Washington, DC. At Georgetown, a law and economics Workshop exists in which students, faculty, and outside speakers regularly present their work. In addition, special academic conferences are organized on a regular basis. Another prominent center of research in the US is the Business, law and economics Center of the John M. Olin School of Business at Washington University in St. Louis, Missouri. The Olin Center, which was founded in 1991, focuses its research on how law, economics, and politics converge to influence private business.

10. Non-University Research

Research in the field of law and economics is not only undertaken at certain universities or law schools. For example, the Institute for Civil Justice in the United States, which is an independent research program within RAND (1700

Main Street, PO Box 2138, Santa Monica, CA 90407-2138, USA), is also known for its interdisciplinary and empirical approach to public policy issues, including economic analysis of the law. RAND is a non-profit institution formed with the goal of improving public policy and public decision making through better research and analysis. The RAND organization employs more than 500 research professionals.

Conferences and other professional meetings which provide researchers from across the world the opportunity to meet and interact are also an important way of ensuring the flow and exchange of ideas and opinions, and provide researchers with the chance to catalog and compare their results with those of other research programs. Annual or biannual conferences are held at several locations throughout the world in order to promote research in the area of law and economics. One such annual international gathering is the mid-term meeting of the Erasmus Program in law and economics. Papers presented at that meeting are published in a series of special publications entitled '*Essays in law and economics*'. In Germany, the biannual Travemünde Symposium provides another opportunity to meet and confer with world class scholars.

Internationally, there exist six distinct professional associations in the area of law and economics. All of these associations organize meetings on a regular basis where working papers are presented and discussed. Thus, they provide a conduit for ongoing exchange and communication amongst professors, research assistants and students. The six existing organizations are: the American Law and Economics Association (ALEA), the Australian Law and Economics Association, the Canadian Law and Economics Association (CLEA), the European Law and Economics Association (EALE), the Latin American Law and Economics Association (LALEA), and the Law and Economics Association of New Zealand Law (LEANZ). Most of these associations can be easily contacted via their home pages on the world wide web.

The American Association of Law and Economics, with its offices located at the Yale Law School in New Haven, Connecticut, organizes numerous conferences. The European Association of Law and Economics was founded in 1984 for the purpose of providing professional assistance to law and economics scholars. It distributes a periodic newsletter, arranges seminars and conferences, and has published several conference volumes in the *International Review of Law and Economics*. In 1994, the New Zealand Association of Law and Economics was established in order to promote law and economics studies in New Zealand. LEANZ also publishes a monthly newsletter and organizes seminars on a regular basis. The Latin-American Law and Economics Association has held its annual meetings since 1995. The Australian Law and Economics Association also organizes regional conferences and meetings.

The growing interest in the field of law and economics can also be measured by the increase in academic publishing. More and more doctoral students are publishing theses emphasizing law and economics. This is a trend which is recognizable throughout the world (see 0080 Doctoral or Masters Theses). The number of professional journals dealing with law and economics topics is also constantly increasing. Some of these journals are now being listed in the world wide web, making it possible for a much larger audience to scan through the publication's table of contents with just a few mouse clicks. The Internet also allows researchers and scholars to exchange information in real time and at a comparably low cost. Since 1994, the George Mason University has established an on-line discussion forum on law and economics topics called 'Econlaw'. Forum participants can easily exchange opinions and download the work of their colleagues from their respective web-sites. All of these developments demonstrate that research as well as teaching in the field of law and economics is becoming more and more a global phenomenon.

Acknowledgements

The authors gratefully acknowledge additional information contributed to this paper by an anonymous referee and the editors. The authors are also grateful to Andre M. Ross, MA (Econ.), Attorney at Law (California), Hamburg, Germany, for improving their English.

Bibliography on Organization of Research and Teaching (0100)

Ackerman, Bruce A. (1981), 'Comment: The Marketplace of Ideas', **90** *Yale Law Journal*, 1131-1148.

Alpa, Guido (1995), *Istituzioni di Diritto privato* (Institutes of private law), Torino, UTET.

Becker, Edward R. (1983), 'The Uses of "Law and Economics" by Judges', **33** *Journal of Legal Education*, 306-310.

Beveridge, W. (1921), 'Economics as a Liberal Education', **1** *Economica*, 2-19.

Breyer, Stephen G. (1983), 'Economics for Lawyers and Judges', **33** *Journal of Legal Education*, 294-305.

Brietzke, Paul H. (1986), 'Another Law and Economics', **9** *Research in Law and Economics*, 57-109.

Calabresi, Guido (1978), 'On the General State of Law and Economics Research Today and Its Current Problems and Prospects', in Skogh, Göran (ed.), *Law and Economics. Report from a Symposium in Lund*, Lund, Juridiska Föreningen, 9-16.

Calabresi, Guido (1983), 'Thoughts on the Future of Economics in Legal Education', **33** *Journal of Legal Education*, 359-364.

Coase, Ronald H. (1993), 'Law and Economics at Chicago', **36** *Journal of Law and Economics*, 239-254.

Cooter, Robert D. (1983), 'Comment', **33** *Journal of Legal Education*, 237-238.

Cooter, Robert D. (1991), 'Economic Theories of Legal Liability (Italian translation:'Le teorie economiche della risponsibilità efficenza produttiva: alcuni contributi su noti argomenti' 379-409)', **5** *Journal of Economic Perspectives*, 11-30. Reprinted in Medema, Steven G. (ed.), *The Legacy of Ronald Coase in Economic Analysis*, Edward Elgar Publishing, Cheltenham and Lyme. Italian translation: 'Le teorie economiche della risponsabilità legale', published in Gianandrea Goisis.

Cooter, Robert D. and Gordley, James (1991), 'Economic Analysis in Civil Law Countries: Past, Present, Future - Introduction to a Symposium', **11** *International Review of Law and Economics*, 261-263.

Doyle, D.A. (1982), 'Alternative Teaching Strategies in Law and Economics Courses: Compression, Thematization and the Corporate Field', in Cranston, Ross and Schick, Anne (eds), *Law and Economics*, Canberra, Australian National University, 208-273.

Gay, David E.R. (1979), 'A Curriculum Note on the New Law and Economics', *XXXPapers and Proceedings of the Southwestern Society of Economists*, 59-66.

Gelhorn, Ernest and Robinson, Glen O. (1983), 'The Role of Economic Analysis in Legal Education', **33** *Journal of Legal Education*, 247-273.

Hansmann, Henry B. (1983), 'The Current State of Law and Economics Scholarship', **33** *Journal of Legal Education*, 217-236.

Hatzis, Aristides N. (1997), *Eisagoge sten oikonomike analyse tou dikaiou* (Introduction to the Economic Analysis of Law), Aristotle University of Thessaloniki School of Law and Economics, Department of History, Philosophy and Sociology of Law.

Hertig, Gerard (1991), 'Law and Economics in Civil Law Countries: Switzerland', **11** *International Review of Law and Economics*, 293-300.

Holzhauer, Rudi W. and Teijl, Rob (1989), 'Rechtseconomie in Nederland (Law and Economics in the Netherlands)', **38(4)** *Ars Aequi*, 248-252.

Kirchner, Christian (1991), 'The Difficult Reception of Law and Economics in Germany', **11** *International Review of Law and Economics*, 277-292.

Kitch, Edmund W. (1980), 'The Law and Economics Programme', **26** *University of Chicago Law School Record*, 42-44.

Klevorick, Alvin K. (1983), 'Reflections on "The Current State of Law-and-Economics Scholarship"', **33** *Journal of Legal Education*, 239-246.

Kötz, Hein (1977), 'Ökonomische analyse van rechtsproblemen - Entwurf einer Lehrveranstaltung für Juristen', in Horn, N. and Tieze, R. (eds), *Sozialwissenschaften im Studium des Rechts*, München, 234-244.

Krier, James E. (1974), 'Economics in the Law School', **22** *University of Pennsylvania Law Review*, 1664-1705.

Lande, Robert H. (1992), 'A Law and Economics Perspective on a "Traditional" Torts Case: Insights for Classroom and Courtroom', **57** *Missouri Law Review*, 399 ff.

Landes, William M. and Posner, Richard A. (1993), 'The Influence of Economics of Law: A Quantitative Study', **36** *Journal of Law and Economics*, 385-424.

Lovett, W.A. (1974), 'Economic Analysis and its Role in Legal Education', **26** *Journal of Legal Education*, 385-421.

Mackaay, Ejan (1987), 'Le juriste a-t-il le droit d'ignorer l'economiste? (May Lawyers Ignore Economists?)', *Revue de la Recherche Juridique*, 419-427.

Manne, Henry G. (1994), 'Le origini intellettuali di una scuola di análisi economica del diritto', **12** *Rivista critica del diritto privato*, 167-181.

Mattei, Ugo and Pardolesi, Roberto (1991), 'Law and Economics in Civil Law Countries: A Comparative Approach', **11** *International Review of Law and Economics*, 265-275.

Meyer, Justus and Müller, Wolfgang (1990), 'Ökonomischen Analyse des Rechts (Report on the Summer Schools in Economic Analysis of Law in Saarbrücken)', **1990** *Juristische Schulung*, 157-157.

Michelman, Frank I. (1983), 'Reflections on Professional Education, Legal Scholarship, and the Law-and-Economics Movement', **33** *Journal of Legal Education*, 197-216.

Ota, Shozo (1991), 'Law and Economics in Japan: Hatching Stage', **11** *International Review of Law and Economics*, 301-308.

Pastor, Santos (1988), 'La enseñanza de la economía en las facultades de Derecho (Teaching Economics to Law Students)', in Ruiz-Huerta, Jesús and Loscos, Javier (eds), Revista de la Facultad de Derecho.

Pastor, Santos (1991), 'Law and Economics in Spain', **11** *International Review of Law and Economics*, 309-317.

Posner, Richard A. and Parisi, Francesco (1997), 'Law and Economics: An Introduction', in Posner, Richard A. and Parisi, Francesco (ed.s), *Law and Economics*, Cheltenham and Lyme, Edward Elgar, 3-57.

Posner, Richard A. (1981), 'The Present Situation in Legal Scholarship', **90** *Yale Law Journal*, 1113-1130.

Posner, Richard A. (1989), 'The Future of Law and Economics: A Comment on Ellickson', **65** *Chicago-Kent Law Review*, 57-62.

Priest, George L. (1981), 'The New Scientism in Legal Scholarship: A Comment on Clark and Posner', **90** *Yale Law Journal*, 1284-1295.

Priest, George L. (1983), 'Social Science Theory and Legal Education: The Law School as University', **33** *Journal of Legal Education*, 437-441.

Priest, George L. (1991), 'Preface: Law and Economics after Europe's Revolution', in Weigel, Wolfgang (ed.), *Economic Analysis of Law - A Collection of Applications*, Vienna, Österreichischer Wirtschaftsverlag, 5-7.

Rose, Jonathan (1995), 'The MacCrate Report: A Restatement of Legal Education - the Need for Reflection and Horse Sense', **44** *Journal of Legal Education*, 548 ff.

Rowley, Charles K. (1981), 'Social Sciences and the Law: The Relevance of Economic Theories', **1** *Oxford Journal of Legal Studies*, 391-405.

Rowley, Charles K. (1985), 'Supreme Court Economic Review', **5** *International Review of Law and Economics*, 107-119.

Salop, Steven C. (1988), 'Evaluating Uncertain Evidence with Sir Thomas Bayes: A Note for Teachers: Response', **2** *Journal of Economic Perspectives*, 178-179.

Schäfer, Hans-Bernd (1990), 'Vom Nutzen und Nachteil der Ökonomie im Rechtsstudium (Advantages and Disadvantages of Economics in Legal Education)', in X (ed.), *Juristenausbildung - erneut überdacht* (New Thoughts on Legal Eduction), 294-321.

Schäfer, Hans-Bernd and Struck, Gerhard (1983), 'Schlammbeseitigung auf der Bundesstrasse. Geschäftsführung ohne Auftrag, Deliktsrecht, negatorische Haftung. Ökonomische Analyse des Rechts (The Case of the Mud Removal at the Federal Highway)', in Walz, W. Rainer and Rascher-Friesenhausen, Hein (eds), *Sozialwissenschaften im Zivilrecht: Fälle und Lösungen in Ausbildung und Prüfung*, Neuwied und Darmstadt, Luchterhand, 119-132.

Schwartz, Murray L. (1983), 'Economics in Legal Education', **33** *Journal of Legal Education*, 365-368.

Schwartz, Warren F. (1983), 'The Future of Economics in Legal Education: The Prospects for a New Model Curriculum', **33** *Journal of Legal Education*, 314-336.

Sheehan, Michael F. (1988), 'Institutionalists Before Regulatory Commissions: The Value of Doing in Thinking, Teaching, and Writing', **22** *Journal of Economic Issues*, 1169-1178.

Sousa Franco, Atónio (1992), 'Análise Económica do Direito: Exercício Intelectual ou Fonte de Ensinamento? (Economic Analysis of Law)', **2** *Sub Judice*, 63-70.

Stevens, Robert (1983), *Law School. Legal Education in America from the 1850s to the 1980s*, Chapel Hill, University of North Carolina Press, 334 p.

Stigler, George J. (1982), 'Economists and Public Policy', **13** *Regulation*, 13-17.

Summers, Robert S. (1983), 'The Future of Economics in Legal Education: Limits and Constraints', **33** *Journal of Legal Education*, 337-358.

Symposium (1983), 'The Place of Economics in Legal Education', **33** *Journal of Legal Education*, 183-376.

Trebilcock, Michael J. (1983), 'The Prospects of "Law and Economics" : A Canadian Perspective', **33** *Journal of Legal Education*, 288-290.

Ulen, Thomas S. (1989), 'Law and Economics: Settled Issues and Open Questions', in Mercuro, Nicholas (ed.), *Law and Economics*, Boston, Kluwer Academic Publishers, 201-231.

Veljanovski, Cento G. (1982), *The New Law and Economics. A Research Review*, Oxford, Centre for Socio-Legal Studies, 169 p.

Vracar, K. Stevan (1994), *Preispitivanja pravne metodologije: Nagovestaji drzavno-pravnog integralizma* (Reexamination of the Legal Methodology: Indications of State-Legal Integralism), Naucna knjiga, Belgrade.

Walz, Rainer W. (1983), 'Die Fehlgeschlagene Investition (The Case of the Investment Failure)', in Walz, Rainer W. And Rascher-Friesenhausen, Hein (eds), *Sozialwissenschaften im Zivilrecht: Fälle und Lösungen in Ausbildung und Prüfung*, Neuwied und Darmstadt, Luchterhand, 52-75.

Walz, W. Rainer and Rascher-Friesenhausen, Hein (eds) (1983), *Sozialwissenschaften im Zivilrecht, Fälle und Lösu* (Social Science in Civil Law, Cases and Answers), Neuwied und Darmstadt, Luchterhand.

Walz, W. Rainer and Wienstroh, Claas (1983), 'Die Fehlgeschlagene Investition (The Case of the Investment Failure)', in Walz, W. Rainer and Rascher-Friesenhausen, Hein (eds), *Sozialwissenschaften im Zivilrecht: Fälle und Lösungen in Ausbildung und Prüfung*, Neuwied und Darmstadt, Luchterhand, 52-75.

Whaples, Robert, Morriss, Andrew P. and Moorhouse, John C. (1998), 'What Should Lawyers Know about Economics?', **48** *Journal of Legal Education*, 120-124.

Wehrt, Klaus and Mohr, Klaus (1995), 'Der Einbau der ökonomischen Analyse des Rechts in ein juristisches Fallgutachten' (Including the Economic Analysis of Law in Legal Reasoning), **1995** *Jura*, 536-542.

Wiegang, Wolfgang (1988), 'Die Rezeption amerikanischen Rechts (The Reception of American Law)', in X (ed.), *Die schweizerische Rechtsordung in ihren internationalen Bezügen*, Bern, Haupt, 229-262.

Wills, Robert L. (1987), 'Economists and Competition Policy: A Case Study', in Wills, Robert L. and Caswell, Julie A. (eds), *Issues after a Century of Federal Competition Policy*, Lexington, MA, Lexington Books, 3-8.

Wilson, G. (1980), *Socio-Legal Research in Germany*, London, Social Science Research Council.

X (1982), 'No Anti-Antitrust "Bias" at the Law and Economics Center: Federal Judges can't be "Brainwashed" ', **14** *Antitrust Law and Economics Review*, 15-70.

X (1983), 'Foreword: Chicago Economics, the FTC, and the Education of the Federal Judiciary', **15** *Antitrust Law and Economics Review*, 1-8.

Other References

Bowles, Roger (1982), *Law and the Economy*, Oxford, Martin Robertson.

Cooter, Robert and Ulen, Thomas S. (1996), *Law and Economics,* Glenview, Scott Foresmann (2nd ed).

Dau-Schmidt, Kenneth and Ulen, Thomas S. (1998), *Law and Economics Anthology*, Ohio, Anderson Publishing

Dnes, Antony W. (1996), *The Economics of Law,* International Thomson Business Press.

Hertig, Gérard (1991), 'Switzerland', **11** *International Review of Law and Economics*, 293-300.

Katz, Avery Wiener (1998), *Foundations of the Economic Approach to Law,* Oxford, Oxford University Press.

Kirchner, Christian (1991), 'The Difficult Reception of Law and Economics in Germany', **11** *International Review of Law and Economics*, 277-292.

Manne, Henry (1975), *The Economics of Legal Relationships. Readings in the Theory of Property Rights*, St. Paul, West Publishing Company.

Mercuro, Nicholas and Medema, Steven G. (1997), *Economics and the Law: from Posner to Post-Modernism*, Princeton, Princeton University Press.

Miceli, Thomas J. (1998), *Economics of the Law: Torts, Contracts, Property, Litigation,* Oxford, Oxford University Press.

Ota, Shozo (1991), 'Law and Economics in Japan: Hatching Stage', **11** *International Review of Law and Economics,* 301-308.

Pastor, Santos (1991), 'Law and Economics in Spain', **11** *International Review of Law and Economics*, 309-317.

Posner, Richard, (1998), *Economic Analysis of Law*, Boston, Aspen Publishers (5th edn).

Posner, Richard A. and Parisi, Francesco (1997), *Law and Economics,* Cheltenham and Lyme, Edward Elgar.

Schäfer, Hans Bernd and Ott, Claus (1995), *Lehrbuch der Ökonomischen Analyse des Rechts* (Handbook of Economic Analysis of Civil Law), Berlin, Springer (2nd edn).

Skogh, Göran (1991), 'Law and Economics in Sweden', **11** *International Review of Law and Economics,* 319-324.

Tullock, Gordon (1971), *The Logic of the Law*, New York, Basic Books.

Weigel, Wolfgang (1991) 'Prospects for Law and Economics in Civil Law Countries: Austria', **11** *International Review of Law and Economics*, 325-329.

0200
HISTORY OF LAW AND ECONOMICS

Ejan Mackaay
Professor of Law
University of Montreal

Abstract

The idea of applying economic concepts to gain a better understanding of law is older than the current movement, which goes back to the late 1950s. Key insights of law and economics can already be found in the writings of the Scottish Enlightenment thinkers. The Historical School and the Institutionalist School, active on both sides of the Atlantic between roughly 1830 and 1930, had aims similar to the current law and economics movement.

During the 1960s and 1970s the Chicago approach to law and economics reigned supreme. After the critical debates in the United States between 1976 and 1983, other approaches came to the fore. Of these, the neo-institutionalist approach and the Austrian approach, both corresponding to schools within economics proper, are worth watching.

Law and economics has progressively found its way to countries outside the United States. From the mid 1970s onwards it reached the English speaking countries, then other countries as well. In no country has law and economics had as much impact as it has in the United States.
JEL classifications: K00, B10, B20
Keywords: law and economics in General, History, Institutions

1. Introduction

The economic analysis of law, or law and economics, may be defined as 'the application of economic theory and econometric methods to examine the formation, structure, processes and impact of law and legal institutions' (Rowley, 1989b, p. 125). It explicitly considers legal institutions not as given outside the economic system but as variables within it, and looks at the effects of changing one or more of them upon other elements of the system. In the economic analysis of law, legal institutions are treated not as fixed outside the economic system, but as belonging to the choices to be explained.

This approach is advocated not merely for legal rules with an obvious link to economic realities such as competition, economic organisation, prices and profits, and income distribution, which translate into competition law, industrial regulation, labour law and tax law. Law and economics has the ambition of applying the economic approach not merely to these areas of economic regulation readily associated with economics, but to *all* areas of law, in particular to the core of the common law.

The current incarnation of law and economics originated in the United States in the late 1950s and found acceptance amongst the legal community from the 1970s onwards, as a result, in particular, of the writings of Richard A. Posner. It has been presented at times as an altogether novel introduction of concepts and methods of a neighbouring science into law, in that it addresses questions across the entire range of legal subject matter, including much non-market behaviour (Posner, 1975a, p. 759).

This view may overstate the originality of the movement. Recent historical research has shown that already in nineteenth century Europe, there existed a broad scholarly movement whose ambition was to show how a better understanding of law could be gained by using economic concepts and methods (Englard, 1990; Pearson, 1997). Holmes's oft-cited exhortation to legal scholars, in 1897, to turn to economics and statistics: 'For the rational study of the law the black-letter man may be the man of the present, but the man of the future is the man of statistics and the master of economics' (Holmes, 1897, p. 469) may have pulled the American branch into the limelight. But if Hovenkamp (1990) is to be believed, Holmes merely gave voice to a development which had already reached the United States in the 1880s and continued well into the twentieth century. This movement is known - rather too little as Pearson contends (1997, pp. 159-161) - as institutional economics (Duxbury; 1995; Pearson, 1997, p. vii; Medema, 1998). But this is not the only connection between law and economics prior to the current movement. At the University of Chicago, where the current movement originated, there was, from 1940s onwards, an earlier infusion of economic ideas into law, associated with the name of Aaron Director.

It is instructive to look at these earlier branches of law and economics to understand the reasons for both their initial attraction and their ultimate decline. In a broader context, the question has recently been raised why the winds turned and intellectual leadership in legal theory moved from Continental Europe to the United States (Mattei, 1994c). For the current movement, a deeper historical perspective should make one wary of the belief that present understanding provides a definitive account of the legal system. Such caution is in order at a time when, in one scholar's words (Ellickson, 1989, p. 26), 'law and economics is no longer growing as a scholarly or curricular force within the leading American law schools. Instead, it is simply holding previously won ground.' Study of the earlier movements may point us to the research agenda to adopt if we wish the current one to continue.

Law and economics borrows concepts and methods from economics proper. It inherits the controversies to which they are subject in the mother discipline.

In economics proper, the question has recently been raised of what has gone wrong in the discipline (Boettke, 1997): even half a generation ago the neoclassical model reigned supreme and virtually unquestioned; now economists appear divided on their theoretical framework.

This debate spills over into the economic analysis of law. Since the 1980s, gone is the beautiful consensus about method and agenda, generated by the first editions of Posner's textbook (1972b, 1977) solidly based on neoclassical economic insights. Besides the Chicago approach, various shades of institutional (Benson, 1994; Mercuro and Medema, 1997, chs 4 and 5; Samuels, 1990, 1998a, 1998b, 1998c; Samuels and Mercuro, 1984; Samuels ans Rutherford, 1998; Samuels and Schmid, 1981; Schmid, 1989a, 1989b, 1994; Teijl and Holzhauer, 1990) or neo-institutional (Alston, Eggertsson and North, 1996; Coase, 1984, 1992; Eggertsson, 1990; Furubotn, 1989, 1993; Furubotn and Richter, 1992, 1997; Knight, 1992; Langlois, 1986; Medema, 1989; Mercuro, 1989; North, 1984, 1986, 1991, 1993, 1994, 1995, 1996; Williamson, 1985, 1986, 1996) approach to law and economics have come to the fore, as has the Austrian approach (Barnett, 1992, 1998; Benson, 1994; Boettke, 1994; Bouckaert, 1984; Boudreaux, 1994; Hayek, 1973, 1976, 1979; Kinsella, 1995; Leoni, 1991; Lepage, 1985; Ogus, 1989; Rizzo, 1979b, 1980a, 1980b, 1980c, 1980d, 1981, 1982a, 1982b, 1985, 1987; Rizzo and Arnold, 1980, 1987; Rowley, 1989a, 1989b; Rowley and Brough, 1987; Schmidtchen, 1993; Teijl and Holzhauer, 1997; Thornton, 1991; Vanberg, 1998a; Voigt, 1992; Wonnell, 1986). These approaches emphasise the interest of historical studies, which received a powerful endorsement when the 1993 Nobel prize for economics was awarded to two economic historians, Douglass North and Robert Fogel (North, 1994).

Since Posner's initial impetus, the sources from which the law and economics movement may draw inspiration have broadened. They now also include the public choice school, bringing an economic approach to political processes, and game theory, which has become a rallying point for the social sciences in that it applies rational choice ideas to the interaction of two or more actors, or indeed a multitude of them with the attendant opportunities for free- rider and hold-out strategies.

For the purpose of exposition, it will be helpful to divide the history of law and economics into phases. Duxbury (1995, p. 340) cautions against the danger of historical reductionism in such periodisation. Simplicity of exposition makes it nonetheless worthwhile in my view.

2. Precursors

Economics as a science may be considered to go back to the late eighteenth century, when Adam Smith wrote his *Inquiry into the Nature and Causes of the*

Wealth of Nations as part of what later came to be called the Scottish Enlightenment (Robertson, 1987). Well before his time one finds writings in which human behaviour is analysed as the result of rational choice, or which undertake rational calculation of the costs and benefits of particular policies or rules, and offer practical economic policy advice to rulers of the day. In this light Macchiavelli (1961; see Pearson 1997, p. 19) should count as an early precursor of law and economics, as should the Cameralists active in Germany from the fifteenth untill the early nineteenth century (Backhaus and Wagner, 1987; Pearson 1997, p. 11). Ridley (1997, p. 54) submits that Hobbes already clearly understood the prisoner's dilemma.

In Adam Smith's own time, David Hume had a clear grasp of the intricacies of human interaction such as game theory formalises them in our day. In his *Treatise* ([1740] 1978) he presents law as a set of conventions which humans have learned to conform to in order to make co-operation possible in a world of scarcity and limited foresight. He understands the paradox of collective action, in his example of the draining of the meadow (Hume, [1740] 1978, Bk 3, Pt 2, Sec. 7) and uses it to justify the provision of some collective goods by the State. Hume's *Idea of a Perfect Commonwealth* provides keen insights in the dynamics of a federal system, as public choice articulates it today ([1777] 1987). Rousseau similarly understood the game of prisoner's dilemma in his description of the stag hunt ([1755] 1971, p. 207).

Adam Smith himself, in his *Inquiry*, saw the crucial role of speculators and the effects of government intervention in the price system and of protectionist policies ([1776] 1937, Bk IV, Ch. 5, p. 493). Speaking of a company of merchants establishing a new trade, who are granted a temporary monopoly, he observes that '[a] temporary monopoly of this kind may be vindicated upon the same principles upon which a like monopoly of a new machine is granted to its inventor, and that of a new book to its author' ([1776] 1937, Bk V, Ch. I, Pt III, Art. 2nd, p. 712). Law is seen here, in utilitarian fashion, as contributing to the public good, indeed as an instrument for promoting it. The incentive effect of law is obvious in the following passage: 'For if the legislature should appoint pecuniary rewards for the inventors of new machines, etc., they would hardly ever be so precisely proportiond to the merit of the invention as this is. For here, if the invention be good and such as is profitable to mankind, he will probably make a fortune by it; but if it be of no value he also will reap no benefit' (Smith, [1776] 1982, p. 83).

Other thinkers of the late eighteenth century also displayed insights now considered part of law and economics. Prominent amongst these are Beccaria and Bellamy ([1764] 1995), for the dissuasive effect of criminal sanctions, and Bentham, in his calculus of pains and pleasures, applied to a variety of legal questions (Bentham, [1789] 1948). But all of these writings did not amount to a systematic understanding of law through a rational choice model.

3. The First Wave

Such an understanding was the ambition of what may be called the first wave of law and economics. This movement, if indeed it may be properly called that, given the relative heterogeneity of viewpoints, was European in origin, but reached the United States through the (older) institutionalist movement. It has been given prominence in a recent historical study entitled *Origins of Law and Economics* by Heath Pearson, with the subtitle *The Economists' New Science of Law Movement 1830-1930* (Pearson, 1997, p. 44, referring to earlier studies). What follows relies mainly on this study to describe the movement(see also Hutter, 1982; Englard, 1990). For the American branch, the (old) institutionalist school, useful sources are Duxbury (1995, pp. 316-330), who questions whether it is proper to speak of a movement (Duxbury, 1995, p. 318), as well as Hovenkamp (1990), Medema (1998) and Mercuro and Medema (1997, Ch. 4).

The key question the proponents of the movement addressed was how property and other rights were determined, historically and functionally, across different societies. The earlier answer of sixteenth and seventeenth century philosophers, that these rights were given as a matter of natural law, logically prior to any positive legal system, seemed to them unsatisfactory. It could not account for the variations of rights in time and space. Changes in property rights, in their view, should be expected to reflect changes in economic conditions. What they were seeking to develop was 'an explanatory science of rights' (Pearson, 1997, p. 33).

The movement originated amongst economists. Prominent amongst them were the Germans belonging to what came to be known as the 'German Historical School' (Pearson, 1997, p. 95). The conjunction of political economy and law in the discipline called *Staatswissenschaft* may have stimulated their contribution. There were contributions in many other countries as well: Austria, Belgium, England, France, Italy, the Netherlands, the United States. Pearson (1997, p. 170-175) lists more than one hundred names of participants in the movement. Only some of these are still remembered today: John R. Commons, Gustave de Molinari, Carl Menger, Gustav Schmoller, Werner Sombart, Adolph Wagner (Hutter, 1982).

The core thesis of the movement, that rights were contingent upon economic and social conditions, came to be widely accepted. When Marx insisted on it in his writings from 1859 onwards, he was expressing accepted wisdom. By the 1870s the movement gained foothold amongst legal scholars: Wilhelm Arnold, Otto von Gierke, Rudolph von Jhering, to mention a few in Germany, and Henry Maine ([1861] 1977), in England. Englard (1990) has drawn attention to the contribution of the Austrian scholar Victor Mataja to the economic analysis of liability for damages a century ago. Scholars in other countries were drawn to the movement as well and one may properly consider it cosmopolitan (Pearson, 1997, p. 33).

The adherents of this approach engaged in a variety of historical studies of rights in land and contractual arrangements for its exploitation. The studies showed how the institutions varied, for instance according to the density of population, the quality of the soil and the type of exploitation. They investigated what was subject to individual rights, what was left as commons and what sharing rules were applicable to the latter. One finds here considerations of relative transactions costs familiar in current law and economics studies, but also acceptance of the wisdom embodied in institutions which have evolved in the course of history, a theme reflected in Hayek's work in our day (Pearson, 1997, pp. 43-70). The explanations proposed may be properly called economic in that they rely on costs and benefits to individuals, who choose rationally in an environment of scarce resources. These are to this day the pillars of economic reasoning.

What caused the decline of the movement? Pearson (1997, p. 131) attributes it mainly to two factors. One is the increasing specialisation amongst social scientists, which led economists to restrict their attention to matters unquestionably related to markets. They studied the workings of the economy within a framework of given legal institutions.

The other factor were the excessive claims made for the movement and the increasing fuzziness of the 'economic' methodology on which it relied. In part, this may be due to the poor state of development of economic science itself: the 'marginalist revolution' took place only in the last part of the nineteenth century. Perhaps as a result, some members of the movement let themselves be tempted to explore explanations that strayed increasingly away from the strictly individualist rational choice model to 'holist concepts' such as 'national spirit', 'socio-psychic motives' and 'collective will' (Commons) or to 'the psychological-moral life of nations' (Schmoller) (Pearson, 1997, pp. 72, 153, 158). As the economics profession specialised, such explanations seemed more and more heretical to economists (Pearson, 1997, p. 153).

The difficulty is well expressed in what Blaug has to say on institutionalism, which is at the root of the American branch of the first wave of law and economics: 'A much better description of the working methodology of institutionalists is *storytelling* ... Storytelling makes use of the method that historians call colligation, the bundling together of facts, low-level generalizations, high level theories, and value judgements in a coherent narrative, held together by a glue of an implicit set of beliefs and attitudes that the author shares with his readers' (Blaug, 1980, p. 126). Coase is even more dismissive: 'The American institutionalists were not theoretical but anti-theoretical, particularly where classical economic theory was concerned.

Without a theory they had nothing to pass on except a mass of descriptive material waiting for a theory, or a fire' (Coase, 1984, p. 230).

The movement fared no better with the legal community than it did with economists. The conclusions which its proponents were able to draw from their model and from their historical investigations did not convince lawyers. The legal community remained of the view that economic factors alone could not account for the fullness of the 'tendencies and aspirations of the human soul' reflected in the law (Pearson, 1997, p. 144, quoting Del Vecchio). This is surely a misreading of the essence of economics (methodological individualism and instrumental rationalism), but one whose persistence must be laid at the doorstep of the proponents of the movement, be it the historical school (Germany) or the (old) institutional school (USA).

By the 1930s, the movement faded away as a distinct contribution of economics to the understanding of law, to make room for the sociology of law and legal realism. Some of its contributions nonetheless live on: Menger's through Hayek in modern neo-Austrian thinking and in the evolutionist theory of Nelson and Winter (1982); Commons' ideas find an echo in Williamson's work (1985, 1996) and live on in that of modern institutionalists such as Samuels (1971, 1972, 1974, 1975, 1976a, 1998a), Samuels and Schmid (1981) and Schmid (1978, 1989). The importance of institutions as constraints on economic activities has been underscored in the 1991 and 1993 Nobel prize lectures in economics: Ronald Coase (1992) and Douglass North (1994).

4. The Second Wave

It will be helpful, in dealing with the current law and economics movement, to distinguish several periods: the beginnings, paradigm proposed (1958-1973), paradigm accepted (1973-1980), paradigm questioned (1976-1983) and the movement shaken (from 1983 onwards).

4.1 Beginnings

As early as the 1930s, there are studies pointing to a revival of the link between law and economics on a different footing. Some of these have remained part of modern day law and economics. In the UK, Arnold Plant looked at the economics of intellectual property (1934a, 1934b and 1953); Ronald Coase, his pupil (Coase, 1994, pp. 176 f.) and one of the founders of the current movement, published as a young researcher his famous study on the nature of the firm (Coase, 1937). But the veritable revival of law and economics occurred at the University of Chicago, in 1940s, under the inspiring leadership of Aaron Director (Duxbury, 1995, p. 341; Levi, 1966; Meltzer, 1966). Economic science itself was by that time undergoing change which led to the 'neo classical synthesis'. The finest overview of this period is unquestionably Duxbury's (1995, Ch. 5).

Aaron Director was in the unusual position of an economist appointed to the Chicago Law School, to succeed Henry Simons, who was also an economist. At the Department of Economics at Chicago, he had a number of remarkable colleagues, amongst whom one counts Frank Knight, George Stigler and Milton Friedman. The Chicago group came to adopt a distinct approach to economic analysis, which insisted on generating testable predictions and on conducting empirical research for the purpose of such tests (Reder, 1987). 'Indeed, the defining traits of Chicago neo-classicals - the suspicion of government and the insistence that markets protect rational individual choice and self-determination - reflect a distinctively American style of individualist ideology' (Duxbury, 1995, p. 418).

Director's problem at the Law School was how to turn his lawyer colleagues round to taking economic analysis seriously. Director, a brilliant economist, applied economic insights to legal cases, in particular in antitrust law (Duxbury, 1995, pp. 343-344; Manne, 1993, p. 5 f.). Accepted wisdom at the time, stemming from the depression and the New Deal, held that in order to achieve effective competition, industry had to be closely supervised and regulated. Director showed this conclusion in most cases to be unwarranted, indeed counterproductive: monopoly was more often alleged than it was effectively present and detrimental to consumer interests. The field has continued to interest Chicagoans (Bork, 1978; Bowman, 1973; Posner, 1976). The battle about the role of antitrust law continues to this day; McChesney and Shughart II (1995) consider the debate in 1997-1998 over the pressure being put on Microsoft for its alleged monopolisation of the computer software market by tying its web browser, called Internet Explorer, with its already domineering Windows operating system. Director's efforts led, during the 1940s and 1950s, to a variety of studies of other legal subjects with clear economic connotations: corporate law, bankruptcy, securities regulation, labour law, income tax, public utility regulation and torts.

Posner and others, writing the history of law and economics at Chicago years later, designate this period as the 'old' law and economics (Posner, 1975a, p. 758; also Ackerman, 1984, p. 63; Kitch, 1983a; Mercuro and Medema, 1997, p. 193; Veljanovski, 1982, p. 7). They contrast it with the 'new' law and economics emerging in the 1960s, whose research agenda was to apply 'economics to core legal doctrines and subjects such as contract, property, tort and criminal law' (Duxbury, 1995, p. 340). About the new movement, Rowley (1989b, p. 125) observes 'its distinctive feature is the application of market economics to legal institutions, rules, and procedures which in certain areas (notably in tort and in crime) are not conventionally seen to influence market behavior, but which indeed are defined in terms of market failure'.

The contrast between the 'old' and the 'new' economics is perhaps overblown (Duxbury, 1995, pp. 340-341), but contains a grain of truth. Several events mark the overstepping of traditional boundaries of economics, characteristic of the 'new' law and economics. One influence is surely Gary Becker's initiatives to analyse non-market behaviour with economic tools: starting with his 1955 doctoral dissertation on *Discrimination in the Market Place* and broadening in his later work on the economics of crime, of the family, on human capital and alleged (ir)rational behaviour (Becker, 1957, 1962, 1975, 1976, 1981). Years later, he summarised his approach as follows: 'Indeed, I have come to the position that the economic approach is a comprehensive one that is applicable to all human behavior, be it behavior involving money prices or imputed shadow prices, repeated or infrequent decisions, large or minor decisions, emotional or mechanical ends' (Becker, 1976, p. 8).

After initial indifference, Becker's thesis came gradually to be seen as a significant contribution to economics and indeed was the justification for the Nobel prize in 1992. Posner is of the view that 'Becker's insistence on the relevance of economics to a surprising range of nonmarket behavior (including charity, love, and addiction), as well as his specific contributions to the economic analysis of crime, racial discrimination, and marriage and divorce, opened to economic analysis large areas of the legal system not reached by Calabresi's and Coase's studies of property rights and liability rules' (Posner, 1998, p. 26; quoted by Duxbury, 1995, p. 396; Posner, 1993).

During the same period - the late 1940s and the 1950s - several other studies opened up fields which later became part of law and economics. For the public choice movement one could point to Duncan Black's writings (1948a, 1948b, 1958) on committees and elections in Britain. In 1954 Scott Gordon (1954, 1958) published a study on the economics of managing a scarce resource in common property, the fisheries, from which the economics of the environment later developed. The next year, Tiebout (1956), studying competition amongst local authorities through expenditures appealing to their taxpayers, unwittingly laid the foundation for what later became the economics of federalism as a system of competition amongst governments. Downs (1957), with his economic theory of democracy, opened the field of the economics of political institutions more broadly and was followed shortly by Buchanan and Tullock's (1962) classic *Calculus of Consent*, which started the public choice school.

Duxbury (1995, pp. 379, 417) emphasises that law and economics should not be considered a direct descendant of American legal realism. While it shares with that movement the view that for a better understanding of law one must rely on the social sciences and on empirical study, practitioners of law and economics are much more precise than were the realists about where to borrow - from economics; from other social sciences to the extent that they adopt the rational choice model - and about the agenda for empirical research flowing from that position. The canons for conducting empirical research have also been considerably refined since the time when the realists were active.

4.2 Paradigm Proposed: Economics into the Main Areas of Law (1958-1973)
A visible step in the emergence of law and economics at Chicago was the creation, in 1958, of the *Journal of Law and Economics*, with Aaron Director as its first editor. Soon afterwards, Coase moved to Chicago and became its editor. In 1960 he published his seminal article on social cost in that journal (Coase, 1960). Demsetz was amongst the earliest scholars realising the significance of the article. He underscored it in a series of perceptive articles (Demsetz, 1964, 1966, 1967, 1972a, 1972b). He first used the term 'the Coase theorem' (1972b, Pt II).

The article is usually taken to stand for the proposition that externalities are no ground for government intervention, but merely indicate that property rights are not adequately specified. When they are, and provided parties to the externality can costlessly negotiate, specification of rights is sufficient for attaining the optimal ('efficient') outcome; the particular way in which the rights are allocated between the parties is indifferent to the economic outcome. The article is also important for drawing attention to the concept of transaction costs. In Coase's examples the concept was simple enough: transaction costs encompass the cost of identifying potential contract partners, of coming to an agreement with them and of 'policing' the solution. Transaction costs prevent apparently profitable deals from being consummated. They concern both information problems and problems of 'strategic behaviour' resulting from the impossibility to fully supervise one's contract partner or from difficulties of 'collective action'. The concept has been extended to regulatory contexts and to the operation of government itself. Its meaning has thereby been singularly expanded. Precisely what is now meant by transaction costs is a matter of debate. One may expect the reduction of transaction costs to be an important concern in law and changes in legal institutions to reflect the discovery of ways to lower transaction costs.

A second seminal article was a paper by Alchian, then at the Rand Corporation in California, on the rationale for property rights, which was circulated in the late 1950s but published only several years later (Alchian, 1965). It looked at the effects of differences between private and public ownership and treated them as economic variables that could be manipulated. Calabresi, at Yale, published a third, equally fundamental, paper on tort law as a system for inducing the proper level of caution in activities liable to cause damage to other persons, considering the cost of the damage as well as the cost of administering the system (Calabresi, 1961).

These papers struck the fancy of a number of economists and became the seeds for a flurry of articles on legal subjects such as property rights, torts, contracts and procedure, for example Alchian and Demsetz (1969, 1972, 1973);

Calabresi (1965a, 1965b, 1970); Calabresi and Melamed (1972); Calabresi and Hirschoff (1972); Cheung (1968, 1969a, 1969b, 1972, 1973); Dales (1968a, 1968b); De Alessi (1969); Demsetz (1964, 1966, 1967, 1968, 1969, 1972a, 1972b); Furubotn and Pejovich (1972, 1974); Landes (1971); McKean (1970a, 1970b); Oi (1973); Pejovich (1971, 1972); Peltzman (1973); Posner (1972a, 1973a, 1973b); Stigler (1970). The *University of Chicago Law Review* published the proceedings of a symposium on product liability in its 1970 issue. Manne (1962, 1965, 1966a, 1966b, 1967) published books and papers on corporation law, controversially taking the defence of insider trading. Samuels (1965, 1973) published two extensive bibliographies of publications dealing with law and economics, broadly casting his net, but showing nonetheless how much literature had been generated in the space of a decade.

The literature in this period was mostly the work of economists. The focus on property rights earned it amongst economists the label 'property rights approach', even where it dealt with contractual practices, products liability or forms of industrial regulation. The term faded away in later years for the more encompassing one of 'economic analysis of law'.

Most contributors in the early days subscribed to the views of the Chicago school of neoclassical economics (Duxbury, 1995, p. 369; Mercuro and Medema, 1997, Ch. 2). The contributions of the 'Chicago group' altogether overshadowed those by economists of other persuasions, such as Leoni, ([1961] 1991); Samuels (1971, 1972); Schmid (1965) or Stewart Macaulay, a lawyer-sociologist, who published a remarkable study on informal contractual relations, which has since become a classic (Macaulay, 1963). The success of the Chicago approach persisted in later periods. Hayek's *Law, Legislation and Liberty* (1973, 1976, 1979) for instance, published contemporaneously with Posner's textbook on law and economics (Posner, 1972b, 1977), went essentially unnoticed at the time amongst the law and economics community, even though Hayek received the Nobel prize for economics in 1974. In retrospect this may seem a regrettable example of tunnel vision; looked at in the perspective of the time, it testifies to the intense enthusiasm generated by the research agenda the Chicago School proposed and to the dynamism and persuasiveness of its proponents.

A few contributors in this early period were lawyers. The names of Calabresi and Manne come to mind. Participation of lawyers is essential since, as we saw above, convincing lawyers turned out to be the critical point in the evolution of the first wave of law and economics, a century earlier. Calabresi played a key role here: 'The distinctive quality of Calabresi's work was to show the power of simple economic principles to rationalise a whole body of law, and to develop a coherent basis for its reform' (Veljanovski, 1990, p. 21). Manne contributed in a different way by organising, from 1971 on, short intensive training seminars in economics for lawyers and judges, and in law for economists (Manne, 1993, p. 10; Duxbury, 1995, p. 359).

4.3 Paradigm Accepted: law and economics into the Law Schools (1973-1980)
Three events signal a change in the movement in the direction of capturing the hearts and imagination of lawyers: the foundation, in 1972, of the *Journal of Legal Studies*; the first publication, of Posner's (1972b; second edition 1977) introduction to the economic analysis of law, both at the Law School of the University of Chicago; the organisation, from 1971 on, of Henry Manne's already mentioned Economics Institutes for Law Professors, short intensive seminars in economics for lawyers, be they judges, practitioners or law teachers (Manne, 1993, p. 10). Together, one might say, they mark the entrance of law and economics into law schools in the United States.

Posner's book was written by a lawyer for lawyers in a clear and straightforward style. It steered clear of economic jargon and adopted the lawyer's well-known distinctions amongst fields of law. It analysed well-known legal doctrines across the entire spectrum of the law. 'Posner's *Economic Analysis of Law*, which first appeared in 1973, sounded most explicitly the modern theme of economic imperialism: You name the legal field, and I will show you how a few fundamental principles of price theory dictate its implicit economic structure' (Epstein, 1997, p. 1168). While these features no doubt contributed to its success, the decisive factor may well have lain in the substance of the book: the efficiency thesis of the common law.

In earlier contributions, law and economics scholars had shown that different institutions - property rights, contractual arrangements, liability rules - could be looked at as in some sense the best option, that is the efficient solution in neo-classical economic terminology. Private property rights generally create better incentives for husbanding scarce resources than do common property or freely available objects. Owners of orchards might be thought to profit freely from the activity of bees pollinating their trees, an externality which some used as a textbook example to show the need for government regulation; closer study showed, however, a practice of contracts between bee keepers and tree owners, making it profitable for both to place beehives near the orchard as needed (Cheung, 1973). Liability rules in tort could be shown not merely to redress the balance disturbed by the tort, but also to create the proper incentives for those whose activity might cause damage to others, to observe care to the extent that its cost is lower than that of the damage thereby prevented (Posner, 1972a).

Posner generalised this idea across the spectrum of the law. Already in the first edition of his book, he put forth the thesis that all rules of the traditional common law reflected such an efficiency logic and that, as a matter of normative judgement, it was desirable that they do so: pursuit of efficiency, here as elsewhere, aims at avoiding waste or maximising the wealth of society. The thesis yields an alluring research agenda: to tease out, using concepts borrowed from neoclassical economics, what would be the 'efficient' rules throughout the domains of the traditional common law and to determine whether the common law in fact conforms to this logic. The research programme was attractive to lawyers because the neoclassical machinery as it was presented in Posner's book looked easy enough to learn and to apply to legal problems.

It is essentially this research programme which has occupied the law and economics community through the 1970s, it is difficult to say whether it is the descriptive or the normative component which provided the greater attraction. Posner himself has been amongst the most ardent defenders of his own thesis. He maintains it, in only slightly weakened form, in the fourth edition of his book, in 1992, presenting the common law as a system of rules 'for inducing people to behave efficiently, not only in explicit markets but across the whole range of social interactions. In settings in which the cost of voluntary transactions is low, common law doctrines create incentives for people to channel their transactions through the market. ... In settings where the cost of allocating resources by voluntary transactions is prohibitively high, making the market an infeasible method of allocating resources, the common law prices behavior in such a way as to mimic the market.' (Posner, 1992a, p. 252; quoted by Duxbury, 1995, pp. 410-411).

4.4 Paradigm Questioned (1976-1983)

Already during the 1970s, the Chicago approach to law and economics was criticised, in particular by the institutionalists (Goldberg, 1976a; Liebhafsky 1976; Samuels, 1976a; Schmid, 1976). Schmid (1976), for instance, made the important point that, since for any distribution of property rights there is a cost-minimising allocation of resources, cost minimisation itself - and by extension the efficiency logic - cannot provide the foundation for the way in which property rights are distributed. Indeed, the allocation of property rights determines what is a cost of what, a conclusion which implicitly follows from the Coase theorem.

These early criticisms went largely unnoticed. The critics made more inroads at the end of the decade, when several symposia were held to examine what law and economics had to contribute to the theory of law (Rizzo, 1980a; Hofstra Symposium 1980; Posner, 1981a; Pennock and Chapman, 1982; Cramton, 1983). The debates brought together the best American minds supporting law and economics and those critical of it. Posner defended law and economics against attacks from legal philosophers such as Dworkin and Fried and critical legal studies thinkers such as Horwitz and Kennedy, and friendlier criticism from lawyers in the Yale tradition such as Calabresi and Kronman and Austrian economists such as Rizzo.

The debates brought out weaknesses of the efficiency thesis as Posner has proposed it (Duxbury, 1995, p. 391; Veljanovski, 1980, pp. 182-187). The first is the point, already mentioned, that efficiency cannot be the foundation of the distribution of property rights, since for any distribution, an efficient allocation of resources can be found. Hence the efficiency thesis is circular. It may be called the circularity thesis and is underscored by several writers besides Schmid (1976) already mentioned: (Baker, 1980; Hart, 1977; Michelman, 1980, p. 448; Samuels and Mercuro 1984, p. 112).

A second difficulty is that the efficiency thesis appears to be non-falsifiable. Where an apparently inefficient arrangement is found, hitherto unnoticed costs can be called in to account for it. This may be useful as a heuristic, but as a way of theory testing, it does not pass muster. To test a theory and expose it to the risk of refutation, one must delimit the set of costs which will be taken into consideration.

A third question pertains to the ahistorical character of the efficiency thesis. (Veljanovski, 1982, p. 97). The thesis suggests that for any given problem there is one efficient solution. Once discovered, there is no reason to move away from it. Yet law tends to evolve over time; a solution considered satisfactory yesterday may no longer seem so today. What explains the change? And what explains that in full knowledge of 'efficient' solutions, we move away from them, as we do in various forms of regulation, such as rent control, minimum wages or environmental regulation? Along similar lines, in the light of the efficiency thesis, persistent differences amongst modern legal systems are puzzling: if there is a tendency towards efficiency and the efficient solution to any legal problem is unique, legal systems should converge. Law and economics needs to address such questions.

A fourth question, raised in particular by Austrian economists, concerns the subjectivity of values. To determine 'efficient' solutions as Posner envisages them requires that the gains resulting from a change of rule are weighed against the losses, in order to choose the rule which promises the optimal result. On what scale are gains and losses occurring to different people to be weighed? Where people transact, their transaction makes such gains and losses comparable, putting them, as it were, for an instant on a single scale which we can observe. In practice, gainers and losers from a particular project do not necessarily transact and compensation of losers by gainers, leading to a Pareto improvement, rarely take place. To arrive nonetheless at policy conclusions, Posner must resort to the Kaldor-Hicks criterion, whereby a rule change is considered an improvement if the gains it procures would be sufficient to offset the losses, both being measured by real or presumed willingness to pay.

Such interpersonal comparisons of value take place all the time in the practice of the law. The judge must put a figure on the losses suffered by a tort victim. If tort rules must serve to induce potential tortfeasors to take proper care, accident costs falling on the side of the victim must be compared to prevention costs falling on the side of the tortfeasor. Common sense accomplishes such comparisons in practice, but, critics argue, they are suspect nonetheless in a scientific sense. This makes problematic, for instance, the policy recommendations Posner derives from the Hand-test in tort law as maximising welfare (Rizzo, 1980b). The criticism has later been amplified by Trebilcock (1987, 1989). Incentive logic and risk-spreading logic do not lead to unambiguous policy conclusions for welfare maximisation: 'Indeed, why not allow the victim to sue *anyone* who ostensibly is a superior risk-bearer to him or to the chairmaker, for example, the latter's banker, law firm, accounting firm, securities underwriter, timber supplier, trucking operator, or indeed a large, well-endowed, well-insured, or well-diversified enterprise totally unconnected to either party? At the limit, it is not clear why, if the courts are committed to spreading accident costs as thinly as possible, there is any logical stopping point short of rendering the state liable for all accident costs ...' (Trebilcock, 1987, pp. 955-956). And he adds a little further down: 'This might be taken to mean, in economic terms, that in cases like the above, accident costs should be internalized to the activity whose level or supply is likely to be most responsive to cost increases (price elastic). While perhaps correct in theory, this criterion seems hopelessly non-operational in all but the most extreme examples' (p. 988).

A fifth question deals with the origin of the perceived efficiency logic. If the common law reflects an efficiency logic, as Posner submits it does, it ought to be possible to formulate a theory accounting for the emergence of that logic. Various attempts have been made to articulate such a theory (Cooter and Kornhauser, 1980; Goodman, 1978; Hirshleifer, 1982; Hollander and Mackaay, 1982; Landes and Posner, 1976, 1979, 1980; Priest, 1977, 1980; Priest and Klein, 1984; Reese, 1989; Rizzo, 1980d; Rubin, 1977, 1982; Terrebonne, 1981). None so far has found general acceptance. It is submitted that the judges operating during the formative years of the common law doctrines a century ago were imbued with laissez faire values congenial to 'efficient' legal rules (Posner, 1992a, p. 255), or that given the constraints in judicial procedure under which judges operate, they are not, unlike Parliament, at liberty to pursue redistributive policies, nor are they subject to intense interest group pressure (Posner, 1992a, p. 524). Yet the judicial policies pursued by modern courts in deciding on the scope to be given to human rights proclaimed in constitutions clearly has distributive effects and their 'efficiency' in Posner's sense would not be easy to demonstrate. Consider also Jules Coleman's observation that what parties demand of the courts is not 'the imposition of an efficient rule, but ... the imposition of any rule that will reduce uncertainty. For such a rule facilitates rational contracting, the long term consequences of which will be efficient' (Coleman (Jules), 1989, p. 190). On this question it is well to remember Sir Arthur Eddington's admonition that '[i]t is also a good rule not to put overmuch confidence in the observational results that are put forward until they are confirmed by theory' (Anonymous, 1978, p. 132).

A final point concerns distributive questions. Even if one grants that the core common law rules reflect an 'efficiency' logic, much modern legislation has an obvious redistributive purpose, and indeed citizens usually seek redistribution through policies they demand from their elected representatives. How this process operates and what its limits are ought to be part of the research agenda of law and economics.

4.5 The Movement Shaken (From 1983 Onwards)

The debates, with their ferocious attacks from all quarters on law and economics, might seem to have left Chicago style law and economics in tatters. But they did not. On the contrary, Posner continues to publish books (Posner, 1981b, 1988a, 1990a, 1990b, 1992a, 1992b, 1992c, 1995a, 1996a, 1996b, 1998; Posner and Silbaugh 1996; Posner and Parisi, 1997). His textbook is currently in its fifth edition (1998). Its closest competitor, by Cooter and Ulen (1996), is in its second edition. The *Journal of Law and Economics* and the *Journal of Legal Studies* continue to flourish. A series of annual research reports, *The Research in Law and Economics* (Carroll, 1979), started in 1979, continues to this day. The main early proponents of law and economics, Bork, Breyer, Calabresi, Easterbrook, Posner and Scalia - some no longer recognising an allegiance to the movement - have been elevated to the bench. About Posner himself, Duxbury muses: 'As he continues to develop and promote his faith in the principle of wealth-maximization, those who stand resolutely opposed to that principle continue, with equal vigour, to demonize him' (Duxbury, 1995, p. 416). For law and economics as a whole, the 1980s have been described as a period of maturation and consolidation in the USA (Veljanovski, 1990, p. 26).

Yet something has changed. The confidence with which the Chicago research agenda for law and economics was taken for granted as the only game in town appears shaken. The debates have allowed viewpoints dissonant from strict neoclassical economics to come out of the shadows. Recent overviews (Mercuro and Medema, 1997; Teijl and Holzhauer, 1990) deal with Chicago Law and Economics, Public Choice Theory, Institutional Law and Economics and Neo-institutional Law and Economics, as well as Austrian Law and Economics.

In 1981, a new journal, the *International Review of Law and Economics*, was created at the initiative of Ogus and Rowley, then at Newcastle-upon-Tyne. Four years later, in 1985, yet another periodical saw the light, at Yale University, the *Journal of Law, Economics, and Organization*. In their opening statement, the editors observe that law and economics 'has expanded ... to take account of the institutional forms within which legal rules and transactions take place' (Leo, 1985, p. 4). In recent issues, this focus is maintained, since the editors 'hold the study of institutions - especially economic, legal and political institutions - to be specifically important and greatly in need of careful analytic study.' (Leo 1997, p. 0)

5. Trends and Themes

Can one discern a pattern amongst the many viewpoints now represented within law and economics broadly written? I venture to list a few common themes, most of them proposed as enrichments of the Chicago law and economics research agenda, rather than as alternatives to it: the role of institutions; historical studies; strategic behaviour in human interaction; limited rationality of human actors; uncertainty and entrepreneurship; the contributions of public choice and game theory; the relationship between the law and economics and the sociology of law.

In considering these possible enrichments, it is well to keep in mind the causes of the decline of the first wave of law and economics. They justify Posner's admonition that 'too many bells and whistles will stop the analytic engine in its tracks. ... A commitment to a relatively simple economic model, one that does not supply a facile explanation for every regularity (or peculiarity) in human behavior, forces the analyst to think hard before discarding the possibility that the behavior under scrutiny may indeed be rational in a straightforward sense. By the same token, a too-great readiness to abandon the simple model in favor of alternative approaches to behavior at the first sign of difficulty carries the risk of overlooking promising avenues for economic analysis' (Posner, 1989, pp. 60, 62). But against it Backhaus and Stephen (1994, pp. 6-7) argue, presenting the new *European Journal of Law and Economics* in 1994, that 'considerable disappointment with the lack of usefulness for practical economic policy of much rigorous theoretical work in economics has resulted in a resurgence of institutionally rich economic work'.

5.1 Institutions

The important role of institutions has been stressed in many corners: the older institutionalists such as Samuels (1971, 1972, 1974, 1975, 1976b), Samuels and Schmid (1981) and Schmid (1965, 1976, 1978); and the newer ones such as Williamson (1985, 1986, 1996), Eggertsson (1990, 1993, 1996), Alston, Eggertsson and North (1996) and Komesar (1997), the economic historians (Bouckaert, 1996, 1997; Libecap, 1986, 1989, 1992, 1993a, 1993b; Milgrom, North and Weingast, 1997; North, 1984, 1986, 1991, 1993, 1994, 1995; North and Wallis, 1994; North and Weingast, 1996; Weingast, 1993, 1995), the management literature (Knight, 1992; Knight and Sened, 1995; Miller, 1992; Gomez, 1996), Austrian economists linking to Carl Menger's contributions (Langlois, 1986, p. 247; Rizzo, 1985), political scientists (Elster, 1989, p. 147).

Coase himself, whose 1937 article on the firm may be considered the first contribution in modern law and economics insisting on the role of institutions, has explicitly sided with these concerns (1937, 1992, 1993): 'It makes little sense for economists to discuss the process of exchange without specifying the institutional setting within which the trading takes place since this affects the incentives to produce and the costs of transacting. I think this is now beginning to be recognised and has been made crystal clear by what is going on in Eastern Europe today.' (Coase, 1994, p. 12). Indeed one may consider that all of law and economics, in as much as it seeks to elucidate the rationale of existing legal rules, engages in institutional analysis.

To understand what an institution is, start with the neoclassical model. The model supposes that agents are informed about potential trades, that profitable agreements are reached without delay or posturing and that deals are faithfully performed. These are, to be sure, simplifying assumptions to make the model manageable. They allow one to construct arguments about how social optimal arrangements (efficiency) come about.

In this model there is no need for the fixity that institutions provide. 'Because most of the formal economic models of competition, exchange, and equilibrium have ignored ignorance and lack of costless full and perfect information, many institutions of our economic system, institutions that are productive in creating knowledge more cheaply than otherwise have been erroneously treated as parasitic appendages. The explanation of use of money, expertise with dealing in a good as a middleman specialist with a trademark or brand name, reputability or goodwill, along with advertising of one's wares (and even unemployment) is often misunderstood. All these can be derived from the same information cost factors that give rise to use of an intermediary medium of exchange' (Alchian, 1977, p. 123). 'If human beings were omniscient, most markets would make no sense. After all, there's no reason to trade stocks if everyone knows the true value of every company. But people are not omniscient. And markets are the best way yet devised to overcome human limitations in deciding what to build, buy, or sell' (Browning and Reiss, 1998, p. 100).

Institutions answer the observation that in reality, situations are often too complicated for ordinary economic actors to find the theoretically optimal arrangement and are simplified to be manageable. 'When it is costly to transact, then institutions matter. And it is costly to transact. ... Institutions are the humanly devised constraints that structure human interaction. They are made up of formal constraints (e.g., rules, laws, constitutions), informal constraints (e.g., norms of behavior, conventions, self-imposed codes of conduct), and their enforcement characteristics' (North, 1996, p. 344). Institutions simplify the decision problem for economic actors, by imposing restraints on each person's conduct which render it substantially predictable to others. 'Institutions are, in an important sense, congealed social knowledge. By following institutionally-sanctioned patterns of behavior, separate individuals are able to coordinate more completely their actions and plans. This is because institutions often limit the options available to an individual thereby reducing the uncertainty about what others are going to do' (O'Driscoll Jr and Rizzo, 1996, p. xxii).

Institutions are rules in a broad sense. Heiner (1983) has attempted to formalise the reasons for using rules, both heuristic rules in individual decision making and social rules in human interactions. Their virtue lies in the relative fixity they provide. But the fixity is also their weakness. At the time of its creation, an institution may be chosen so as to provide generally the best trade-off in the face of the circumstances of the moment. As circumstances change, institutions may come to represent less than optimal trade-offs and yet their fixity prevents them from being instantly adjusted. The benefit of fixity and predictability is bought at the risk of ill fit over time.

Institutions constitute an enrichment of the law and economics agenda. The research programme they imply is not radically incompatible with the 'optimisation' ('efficiency') idea inherent in the neoclassical agenda. But rather than assuming immediate optimisation to be the goal of all decisions within the economic system, an institutional agenda would admit institutions as constraints on optimisation and would consider change of institutions an independent goal. 'The general effort to take account of information asymmetry and other transaction costs, while preserving the assumption that individuals maximize utility, is coming to be called 'neoinstitutional economics' ' (Riker and Weimer, 1993, p. 84)

5.2 History

The institutional agenda sketched above quite logically leads to an increased interest in historical studies: institutions provide fixity in the short run and evolve in the longer run. They leave a trace which we can study. Change of institutions points to a change in the relevant transaction costs visible to interested parties. North (1981, 1986, 1989, 1994, 1995) has explicitly drawn attention to the connection between institutions and history.

Historical studies give an empirical dimension to law and economics work, which may have been lacking in earlier law and economics work, which focused on the function of different legal rules. Law and economics has been too theoretical, says Becker (Roundtable, 1997, p. 1137). To this Epstein (1997, p. 1173) adds that the easy conquests of theory and practice have already been made. ... But precisely because knowledge is so great, the law of diminishing returns explains why new advances are so hard to come by. For Epstein, 'the greatest hope for advancement, barring any major unforeseen conceptual breakthrough, is from more attentive study to the evolution - be it by growth or decline, or both - of particular institutions and social arrangements' (Epstein, 1997, p. 1174)

Quite a few historical studies in law and economics have appeared over the past few years, such as Aftalion (1987, 1990); Alston, Eggertsson and North

(1996); Baechler (1995a, 1995b); Bailey (1992); Beito (1990); Bouckaert (1996, 1997); Ekelund, Hébert and Tollison (1989); Epstein (1994); Green and Shapiro (1994); Greif (1989, 1993, 1997); Greif, Milgrom and Weingast (1994); Hovenkamp (1983); Libecap (1986, 1993b); Mackaay (1997); Milgrom, North and Weingast (1997); North and Weingast (1996); Roe (1994); Rosenberg and Birdzell Jr (1986); Rosenthal (1992); Secretan (1990); Simpson (1975, 1979, 1985, 1988); Umbeck (1977a, 1977b, 1981a, 1981b); Webber and Wildavsky (1986); Weingast (1993, 1995).

5.3 Comparative Law

The reasons for engaging in more comparative work are similar to those for doing historical work. If the economic theory of law is solid, it ought to hold up when applied to the law of different countries, as much as to the law of different epochs. Mattei (1997, pp. ix, 69) complains about 'severe American-centric provincialism' of the law and economics literature and observes poignantly that 'American law and economics has been remarkably parochial, unable to question the presumed need and immutability of a legal process patterned after the American one. ... In the legal context, the mistake is that of accepting the American legal process as an undisputed background and building up models and/or generalizing observations about the efficiency of the law without considering the contingency and relativity of such background. In Europe, the same lack of comparative understanding has prevented committed law and economics scholars from developing original insights capable of shedding new light on the civilian legal process' (ibid., p. 69). Duxbury (1995, p. 409) echoes this concern in observing that 'by and large, however, modern law and economics remains rooted in the common law tradition'. Coase (Roundtable, 1997, p. 1163), in a slightly different context, has also called for more comparative work.

The *International Review of Law and Economics* regularly gives space to comparative studies (Cooter and Gordley, 1991; Mattei and Pardolesi, 1991) and surveys of law and economics in civil law countries. Levmore (1986, 1987) has published detailed comparative studies of particular institutions. Mattei (1994a, 1994b, 1994c, 1995, 1996) and Ajani and Mattei (1995) have focused on the broader aspects of the comparative approach. Scully (1987) purports to develop a general argument that civilian countries, being generally more positivist than those in the common law tradition, offer their citizens less freedom than the latter.

Scully's conclusion points to the question of the reception of law and economics outside of the United States. From the mid 1970s, it reached other English speaking countries and Sweden (Attiyah, 1970; Skogh, 1978; Harris, Ogus and Phillips, 1979; Ogus, 1980; Veljanovski, 1980, 1981, 1982; Burrows 1980; Burrows and Veljanovski, 1981; Ogus and Veljanovski, 1984). By the end of the decade, it had found its way to the German speaking (Horn 1976; Assmann, Kirchner and Schanze, 1978; Opp, 1979; Lehmann, 1983; Schüller, 1983; Behrens, 1984) and the Benelux countries (Mackaay, 1980, 1982; Bouckaert, 1984). Mattei and Pardolesi (1991) mention interest for law and economics comparative law scholars in Italy already in the early 1960s, but without much practical echo until decades later. France has lagged behind, because, most unfortunately, an early contribution to law and economics (Rosa and Aftalion, 1977) became labelled as right-wing ideology without proper claim to scientific status (Andreff et al. 1982; Mackaay 1987). Peculiarities of the French higher education system with its centralised administration and control of appointment and promotion of law professors, providing little incentive for the reception of intellectual ideas originating outside France, may have reinforced this unfortunate development. Remarkable law and economics publications such as Lepage (1985) and Lemennicier (1988) have been by and large ignored by the legal community.

The reception in these countries appears to follow a common pattern. An early sparkling publication triggers broader interest amongst legal scholars. In England (Attiyah, 1970) 'introduced the British reader to Calabresi's economics, igniting interest among lawyers in the reform of the tort system and the efficiency of accident compensation schemes' (Veljanovski, 1990, p. 25). In Germany, this role was played by a small book of readings produced by three young scholars, who spent a year in the US (Assmann, Kirchner and Schanze, 1978). Perhaps reception in Germany was helped by the earlier Ordo-liberal or Freiburg school of law and economics, founded in the 1930s and influential after the Second World War, which included well-known scholars and politicians such as Walter Eucken, Wilhelm Roepke, Ludwig Erhard, Franz Böhm (Backhaus, 1996; Behrens, 1984, p. 8 f., 1993; Grossekettler, 1996; Lenel, 1996; Streit, 1992; Vanberg, 1998b).

Consolidation takes place as law and economics is taught in the law schools (and not only in the economics departments) and young scholars choose a law and economics subject for their thesis. The Erasmus exchange programme in law and economics has probably exerted a positive influence in Europe. So have the European Law and Economics Association and, in its sphere, the Canadian Law and Economics Association.

One must wonder whether law and economics generates outside the United States as much interest as it had earlier on and continues to do in the US. In 1991, Kirchner answered this question in the negative for Germany, in spite of the substantial literature in German on the subject. Looking to the future, Cooter and Gordley (1991, p. 262) conclude that '[b]oth Kirchner and Mattei, however, see the economic approach to law as the opponent of what remains of nineteenth-century formalism. For the economic approach to be successful, then, it must convince its critics that it can avoid the evils of formalism without causing new evils of its own. Its success, then, may require not only openness by traditional legal scholars to a new method, but also creative adaptation of that method by its practitioners'.

5.4 Strategic Behaviour

Williamson (1985, 1986, 1996) in particular has drawn attention to the question of strategic behaviour. The neoclassical model assumes such conduct to be absent. Yet the rules for decision making within corporations or associations of condominium owners or the rules for dealing with conflicts between owners of neighbouring properties are explicable in an economic analysis of law as means to foreclose, or at least reduce, strategic behaviour in these settings of bilateral monopoly. Coleman observes that 'all rules attempt to correct some form of perceived market failing' (Coleman (Jules), 1989, p. 182). Strategic behaviour may be considered a form of market failing and it is a fruitful heuristic for lawyer-economists to consider the threat of such behaviour as the explanation for observed legal institutions. This is a refinement of the institutional agenda (see also Katz, 1998).

5.5 Limited Rationality

Psychologists observe that human reasoning does not in fact conform to the postulates of rational choice in a number of ways (Booth, Booth and Meadwell, 1993; Cook and Levi, 1990; Elster, 1986; Green and Shapiro, 1994; Hahn and Hollis, 1979; Hargreaves Heap, Hollis et al., 1992; Hogarth and Reder, 1986; Hollis, 1987; Hollis and Nell, 1975; Kahneman, Slovic and Tversky, 1982; Mackaay, 1982, Ch. 6; March, 1986; Simon, 1959, 1972, 1979, 1986a, 1986b; Tversky and Kahneman, 1974, 1986a,, 1986b; Tversky, Slovic and Kahneman, 1990). We do not, for instance, intuitively draw the proper statistical inference from a series of occurrences of some event, but attach undue weight to the more recent ones; we ask more for something we sell than we would be willing to pay to acquire it (Kahneman, Knetsch and Thaler, 1991; Knetsch and Sinden, 1984a, 1984b; Knetsch, 1989). Should these observations lead one to reject the rational choice model? That conclusion is generally considered premature. In part this is because market forces induce rationality by penalising random or otherwise irrational choices (Becker, 1962). Until we know how to formalise the bounds on our rationality, Posner's admonition about too many bells and whistles seems apposite.

5.6 Uncertainty, Discovery and Entrepreneurship

Uncertainty, discovery and entrepreneurship are at the heart of the Austrian economics research agenda. They lead to a view of competition law which is distinctly different from that derived from the equilibrium model at the centre of neoclassical economics. The equilibrium model translates a situation in which all knowledge and know-how is presumed given and all potential transactions are presumed to have been considered. For the Austrians, all this knowledge is not given, but must be discovered. The essence of the economic problem is the discovery of new products, services and ways of doing things. The Austrians are concerned to determine the conditions required for that discovery process. This has consequences for the scope of competition law.

The advantage secured by a superior product may initially give a firm something of practical monopoly in its market. In the Austrian view, this is no cause for intervention. So long as the monopoly is contestable, in the sense that no legal impediment stops a newcomer from offering a new product which consumers accept as a substitute for the supposedly monopolistic product, the very success of the apparent monopoly is the carrot which draws competition and drives innovation. Austrians see competition as a discovery process and, one may add, the reverse as well: discovery will most readily take place through competition.

Development of a 'niche' through an innovation and subsequent imitation and dissipation of the 'niche' and search for new ones is the essence of the competitive discovery process. Breaking up such 'monopolies' because of excessive market share would, on an Austrian analysis, have the effect of stifling innovation. The literature on competition law, at least in the United States, is coming round to this dynamic view of competition and innovation, giving credence to the Austrian ideas (Barnett, 1992; Kirzner, 1973, 1979, 1985, 1997; McChesney and Shughart II, 1985; Nelson and Winter, 1982; Schmidtchen, 1993).

The Austrian views differ from the neoclassical synthesis in other important respects as well. Hayek has insisted on the subjective nature of information economic actors use in making their plans and reaching their decisions (Hayek, 1948; Kirzner, 1984; O'Driscoll Jr and Rizzo, 1996; Barnett, 1998). Information about production and consumption plans is revealed and continuously updated through the price mechanism. One cannot correctly gauge this information outside the transactions in which it is revealed through the market. This is no less true for the judges in our system, than it was, fatally, for government officials running the former socialist republics. Austrians generally take a dim view of judicial 're-engineering' of contracts.

How much Austrian and Chicago neoclassical economics actually differ is a matter of debate. Paqué (1985) submits that the distance is smaller than it appears to be. Boettke (1997) sees neoclassical economics as the product of a set of simplifying assumptions about innovation and competition introduced in classical political economy, which made possible the rapid mathematisation of the discipline, but entailed a lack of realism which, in his view, is fatal. Austrian economics has, in his eyes and those of Behrens (1984, p. 22), remained faithful to the older but richer tradition of political economy.

The consequences of the Austrian views for law and economics differ significantly from those reached in a neoclassical perspective (Rizzo, 1980c, 1985; Bouckaert, 1984; Teijl and Holzhauer, 1997). For instance, comparisons of prevention costs for tortfeasors with accident costs for victims, as the Hand test for negligence law would require, are without a foundation on an Austrian view, which for that reason tends to favour strict liability or no liability. The implications of Austrian views for civil law have been explored in some detail and compared to those of Chicago neoclassical views in a recent doctoral thesis in Rotterdam (Teijl and Holzhauer, 1997).

5.7 Public Choice

Public choice is the application of the rational choice model to political phenomena, the field of political science and of public law. It is, to put it another way, a general theory of 'how private interests operate in the public domain' (Ogus, 1994, p. 58). Its core ideas can be traced back at least to Machiavelli. For the current movement the immediate beginnings are works by Duncan Black in the UK and Anthony Downs in the USA (Black, 1948a, 1948b, 1958; Downs, 1957). They were followed by seminal contributions dealing with collective decision making through Parliament, with bureaucracy and with the problems of collective decision making (Buchanan and Tullock, 1962; Olson, 1965; Niskanen, 1971, 1994). There is now a substantial literature on public choice. Readable surveys for lawyers are De Clerq and Naert (1985); Farber and Frickey (1991); Mercuro and Medema (1997, pp. 84-100); Mitchell and Simmons (1994); Stearns (1997); Wagner (1990). Other important surveys can be found in Mueller (1979, 1989, 1997).

Implicit in the neoclassical model underlying mainstream law and economics is the view that government's role is to correct market failure. It is consonant with the broadly held public interest view of government: the government acts as the impartial umpire of social relationships, stepping into the fray to correct whatever has gone astray in the workings of market and other social forces.

Public choice casts doubts on this view. Its proponents question the underlying assumption that actors presumed selfish in private dealings would behave selflessly upon assuming public office. Public choice proposes a private interest view of politics, a world in which actors in political roles act to maximise something of direct interest to them, but defined in ways particular to their roles: politicians are assumed to maximise their chances of re-election; bureaucrats, the size and mandate of their bureaux (Niskanen, 1971; Dunleavy, 1991); voters, the benefits they draw from government programmes and interest groups, the programmes conferring benefits upon their members.

A startling conclusion of public choice is the thesis of the rational ignorance of voters. Since voters cannot expect their individual vote to make a difference between one political programme and another, they have no interest in informing themselves properly on the differences between the two. Political discourse directed at such voters deals in general slogans and in the image of politicians. By contrast, where opposing politicians in an election are divided on a programme which directly affects a particular group of voters, such as farmers, these voters very much have an interest in informing themselves on where the politicians stand on that issue and in promising their vote to those who will benefit them most. Lobby groups channel this interest for their constituents. Olson (1965) has shown that the difficulties of organising lobby groups vary directly with the size and cohesion of the constituent group. Compact groups, as a consequence, are expected to have a disproportionate influence on politicians. Public choice predicts that politicians will generally want to adopt programmes whose benefits are visible and fall upon concentrated groups, while their cost is dispersed as widely and imperceptibly as possible. The actions by interest groups designed to get their members benefits not available in the market have since become known as rent-seeking (Buchanan, Tollison and Tullock, 1980; Krueger, 1974; McChesney, 1997; Posner, 1975b; Rowley, 1988; Rowley et al., 1988a, 1988b; Tollison, 1982, 1987, 1997; Tullock, 1987, 1989, 1993). There is a lively literature on the economics of federations (Breton, 1987, 1989, 1996; Breton and Scott, 1978, 1980; Hamilton, 1987; Kendall and Louw, 1989; Migué, 1993, 1997; Tiebout, 1956; Weingast, 1993, 1995).

5.8 Economic Regulation

Public choice enriches the economic analysis of law in that it provides an understanding of the forces controlling redistribution and of 'economic regulation'. Economic regulation denotes legal restraints upon market actors' behaviour, elaborated by legislators, courts or administrative agencies (Ogus, 1994, p. 1; Hägg, 1997, p. 337). Examples are regulation of state-run utility companies, regulation of transportation, airlines, telecommunications industries, environmental protection, safety and drug regulation, consumer protection, but also 'price-fixing, taxes, subsidies, tariffs, quotas, merger control' (Hägg, 1997, p. 339). All these forms of regulation were seen until the 1960s as attempts to correct market failings, the main justification of government in the neoclassical model.

The question is whether economic regulation in fact improves overall welfare. Within law and economics the answer came increasingly to be seen as negative, in particular with respect to what was until then considered to be the most telling case for government intervention: natural monopoly (Priest, 1993, p. 292). Regulated monopolies were shown often to 'capture' the regulatory agency supervising them, to the detriment of the public, which faced higher than necessary prices. The empirical and theoretical research of these issues centred around the *Journal of Law and Economics*. Coase's article on social cost may be read in this light: the thesis that any form of externality calls for government correction (through liability or taxes) was shown to be mistaken; externalities correct themselves if property rights are properly specified and provided no significant transaction costs stand in the way of negotiations between parties to the externality. Coase (1974) showed, similarly, that lighthouses, thought to be the public good *par excellence*, were in fact for a long time privately run in the UK. Cheung (1973) found that pollination by bees, presumed to be a positive externality and hence source of market failure, was in fact the object of a lively market between beekeepers and farmers.

Burton argues more generally that 'uncontracted or external effects are a pervasive phenomenon of social life' (Burton, 1980, p. 56) and cannot by themselves be sufficient reason for government intervention. What counts as an actionable externality depends on how the boundaries of property rights are defined in a society. There is a lively literature tending to show that the presumed market imperfections are not in fact fatal to the market process or otherwise are circumvented by the ingenuity of market participants (Cowen, 1988). Deregulation of transportation, communication, energy and financial industries in the United States and privatisation of public enterprise from the late 1970s onwards has generally brought benefits to consumers in the form of lower prices and wider diversity of products, lending credence to the 'private interest' view of regulation and casting doubts on the beneficence of government intervention.

If government interventions are not *ipso facto* beneficent, we need a theory to explain how they come about and which are beneficent, which are not. Initially this theory was articulated by Stigler (1971); Posner (1971, 1974) and Peltzman (1976, 1989) at Chicago in terms of interests groups getting their way with politicians. Their approach was consonant with the teachings of the public choice school (Priest, 1993, p. 293). The upshot of this view was that under no circumstances could economic regulation be viewed as beneficent.

From the 1980s onwards, this altogether pessimistic view came to be questioned. Becker showed in two articles that the privileges sought by interest groups would trigger their own counterweight for other interest groups and concluded that the only enduring forms of regulation would benefit all actors at large, rather than specific groups. (Becker, 1983, 1985).

The prevailing view now appears to be that regulation need not always be detrimental to the public interest. Defining and enforcing property rights and contracts and developing tort liability rules sustain the market, rather than hamper it. They are law just as much as the economic regulation of the kind discussed above. Ogus (1994, p. 75) sums up the debate thus: 'public choice theory, and its various offshoots, rightly focus our attention on the way in which regulation affects a variety of private interests. The distributional impact of interventionist measures may be concealed behind the public interest rhetoric which usually accompanies them, but it remains crucial to normative evaluation' (see also Hägg, 1997, pp. 356-357).

5.9 Game Theory

Game theory is a mathematical tool for studying interactions amongst people, in which one person's choice depends on what others choose and vice versa. It has been used in economics and in moral philosophy for quite some time, but has been introduced in legal analysis only recently (Barnett, 1989, p. 9). One use is to detect recurrent patterns in human interaction, leading humans to adopt norms which are models for property rights and contracts. Game theory then provides an understanding of spontaneous order (Axelrod, 1984; Benson, 1994; Birmingham, 1968; Mackaay 1988b, 1991; Parisi, 1995; Picker, 1997; Sugden, 1986, 1989; Ullmann-Margalit, 1977, 1978). Game theory has also been used to shed light on bargaining situations. A helpful overview of the uses of game theory in law is given in (Baird, Gertner and Picker, 1994). There is an ample literature on what game theory can teach with respect to the social contract and the foundation of the state, but this lies outside of law and economics proper (Kerkmeester 1989; Voigt, 1996, 1997).

5.10 Links with the Sociology of Law

In recent years, several authors have called for closer links between law and economics, and the sociology of law. Ellickson for one, in several writings (Ellickson, 1987, 1989, 1990, 1991), with a comment by Posner (1989), pleads for overture to various forms of 'human frailty', a sensibility readily attributed to sociologists, whom he criticises, however, for engaging in much observational work without a proper theory to guide those observations. Others have called for this rapprochement as well: Bouckaert (1994), Cooter (1995), Daintith and Teubner (1986), De Geest (1995), Donohue III (1988) with a comment by Posner (1988b), Johnston (1990). Entire issues of the *European Journal of Law and Economics* (EJLE) and of the *Wisconsin Law Review* (Wisconsin) have been devoted to the matter. The link would seem only natural to sociologists such as Boudon (1977), James Coleman (1987, 1988, 1990a, 1992) and Opp (1979, 1982, 1983, 1988, 1991), who subscribe to the postulate of methodological individualism.

Posner (1988b, 1989, 1995b) is not impressed with what legal sociologists have offered by way of understanding legal phenomena: 'The theories proposed by American sociologists of law, when they propose theories, which is not often, tend to be partial and ad hoc and difficult to test empirically, and modern methods of statistical inference are only rarely in evidence'. He adds that the sociology of law is characterised by 'a dearth of arresting hypotheses to set off against the Coase theorem, the Hand formula, the efficiency theory of the common law, the Modigliani-Miller thesis, the human-capital explanation of employment at will, Ramsey pricing, agency costs, rent-seeking, the selection hypothesis (that plaintiffs tend to win 50 percent of cases litigated to judgment), the concept of complete contingent contracts, the economics of property rights versus liability rules, the activity level theory of strict liability, the efficient-market hypothesis ...' (Posner, 1995b, p. 273). In line with his observation on too many bells and whistles (Posner, 1989, pp. 60, 62), he has little use for the introduction of sociological ideas into the economic analysis of law. Some sociologists (Cranston, 1977; Griffiths, 1995) are critical of the link between the sociology of law and the economic analysis of law as well, but for different reasons. As Coase (1978) reminds us, only experience will tell whether the economic approach as it is has the comparative advantage it claims over other approaches, or whether 'enriched' forms of it do better.

6. Conclusion

This survey leads to two major findings. The first is that the idea of applying economic concepts to gain a better understanding of law is much older than the current movement, which its proponents date back to the late 1950s. The second finding concerns the current movement. After virtually unquestioned dominance and astonishing success of the Chicago approach in the 1960s and 1970s, since about 1980 practitioners of law and economics no longer sing in a single voice.

With respect to the earlier attempts at law and economics, it should be observed that they had declined by the 1930s and find no clear echo in the current movement, outside the work of modern institutionalists such as Samuels and Schmid. Various reasons are given: their methodology became increasingly fuzzy; in the end they failed to convince lawyers, in the absence of a straightforward methodology and telling insights into the nature of legal phenomena. Perhaps, too, the problems they addressed and the solutions they proposed - generally more government intervention - no longer appeared relevant to the legal community.

These observations feed into the second finding, the astounding variety of viewpoints now represented within law and economics broadly written. Will this cacophony drive law and economics into oblivion? It ought not to, since law and economics of whatever stripe still offers insights into a broad range of legal phenomena from contracts, torts and property to commercial law, constitutional law, criminal law and even family law. The task is to convince lawyers that this is a useful, indeed an essential, supplement to traditional lawyering skills. Where law changes rapidly, as it does in our day, lawyers are inevitably involved in policymaking of some sort. The record of lawyers managing such change on the strength of legal skills and legal practice alone is disappointing at best (Posner, 1987b, pp. 769-771).

But can the policy advice proffered by lawyer-economists be relied on? De Alessi (1996, 1997) has formulated a scathing attack on the use of the potential compensation (Kaldor-Hicks) criterion in applied studies and the use of the neoclassical equilibrium model for policy recommendations: 'Actual market solutions in a world of limited private property rights and positive transaction costs always appear to be inefficient relative to some ideal. The result is a bias toward government action to impose rules that, supposedly, move the system toward the ideal. As the application of economics to the analysis of public choices has shown, generations of economists have provided the rhetoric used by rent-seekers in both the private and the public sectors to coopt government regulation and redistribute income to themselves' (De Alessi, 1996, pp. 115-116). To the traditional lawyer, no more is needed to discredit law and economics. For law and economics to prosper, the mainspring of ideas, which is economics proper, must get its house in order (Boettke, 1997).

What then should be the agenda? On the theory of law and economics, Becker's sombre observation is that 'lately, there has been less excitement, less novelty' (Roundtable, 1997, p. 1137). But that, in his view, may be part of the life cycle of scientific theories. In the meantime basic ideas should be absorbed by the practitioners of the discipline. And here lawyers may well ask of law and economics the question Becker put earlier in his remarks: 'What have you done for me lately?' (Roundtable, 1997, p. 1137).

Lawyer-economists must convince lawyers, and even more judges, of the promise of their discipline. They must do this while avoiding being mere rent-seekers on a fad; they must establish the credibility of law and economics as an accurate description of how legal institutions actually work, as well as a generator of hypotheses and insights about law. Cutting through the thicket of established legal doctrine and proposing simpler explanations is one way of doing this. Epstein (1995) is a fine example of that approach. Engaging in empirical work, some of it in the form of historical and comparative studies, is the complementary approach. Only such studies will sort out the debates raging between the various 'schools' of law and economics, as they must be.

Lawyer-economists must distil a straightforward method for applying the economic analysis of law to given legal institutions. Perhaps the method is not always simple and may require a serious learning effort. It should be teachable as a more or less scientific process rather than as a mere art (Katz, 1998, p. v). The benefits of climbing the learning curve should be clear from applications which are telling to lawyers (rather than to economists alone).

One of the remarkable insights coming out of law and economics is that many institutions essential to the functioning of civil society 'have a claim to validity which is independent of specific enactment' (Barry, 1996, p. 617). The institutions produced in the course of evolutionary processes need not be the best conceivable and we may consider reforming them (Buchanan, 1977, p. 131).

But unnecessary and ill-timed interference can do great harm; reform should be undertaken warily and on the basis of the best knowledge available. All theories may turn out to be misguided in the face of later research. Practical policy decisions must be made on the basis of such imperfect knowledge. How essential law and economics is may be gleaned from the experience in Middle and East European countries after the restoration of democracy. Advice about what institutions to create appears to have been given often by economists without appreciation for the dynamics of the law and by lawyers with too little knowledge of the workings of the economy. The pains of transition have been prolonged as a result.

Lawyer-economists should only presume to offer policy advice to minister to the ills of society as the discipline acquires solid empirical bearings. It is not sufficient to criticise accepted wisdom and to propose plausible enrichments of the theory, as the debates around 1980 have done. The crucial point is for the discipline to engage in empirical work capable of disproving false tenets. Only in this way can we hope to discover what is indisputable in law and economics, and make its message last. We shall see whether Coase was right in his assessment that '[i]ndeed, work is going forward at such a pace that I do not consider it overoptimistic to believe that the main outlines of the subject will be drawn within five or ten years.' (Coase, 1994, p. 12).

Acknowledgements

Writing the history of law and economics has turned out to be an arduous task. Sustenance as well as helpful suggestions were provided by Boudewijn Bouckaert, Gerrit De Geest and Frédérick Charette in particular. Eric Schanze, Ronald Kirstein, Stéphane Rousseau, Stefan Voigt and two anonymous referees provided constructive comment. I assume nonetheless full responsibility for the structure of the text and the weight given to different periods and movements.

Bibliography on History of Law and Economics (0200)

Ackerman, Bruce A. (1984), *Reconstructing American Law*, Cambridge, MA, Harvard University Press.

Aftalion, Florin (1987), *L'Économie de la Révolution Française* (The Economics of the French Revolution), Paris, Hachette.

Aftalion, Florin (1990), *The French Revolution - An Economic Explanation*, Cambridge, Cambridge University Press and Paris, Éditions de la Maison de l'Homme.

Ajani, Gianmaria and Mattei, Ugo (1995), 'Codifying Property Law in the Process of Transition: Some Suggestions from Comparative Law and Economics', **19** *Hastings International and Comparative Law Review*, 117-137.

Alchian, Armen A. (1965), 'Some Economics of Property Rights', **30** *Il Politico*, 816-829 reprinted in Alchian, Armen A. (ed.) (1977), Some Economics of Property Rights, *Economic Forces at Work*, Indianapolis, Liberty Press, 127-149.

Alchian, Armen A. (1977), 'Why Money?', in Alchian, Armen A. (ed.), *Economic Forces at Work*, Indianapolis, LibertyPress, 111-123.

Alchian, Armen A. and Demsetz, Harold (1969), 'Corporate Management and Property Rights', in Manne, Henry G. (ed.), *Economic Policy and the Regulation of Corporate Securities,* Washington, DC, American Entreprise Institute, 337-360.

Alchian, Armen A. and Demsetz, Harold (1972), 'Production, Information Costs, and Economic Organization', **62** *American Economic Review*, 777-795.

Alchian, Armen A. and Demsetz, Harold (1973), 'The Property Rights Paradigm', **33** *Journal of Economic History*, 16-27.

Alston, Lee J., Eggertsson, Thráinn and North, Douglass C. (eds) (1996), *Empirical Studies in Institutional Change*, New York, Cambridge University Press.

Andreff, Wladimir et al. (eds) (1982), *L'Économie Fiction - Contre les Nouveaux Économistes*, Paris, François Maspero.

Anonymous (1978), 'Annals of Science - DNA', *The New Yorker*, 4 December 1978.

Assmann, Heinz-Dieter, Kirchner, Christian and Schanze, Erich (eds) (1978), *Ökonomische Analyse des Rechts*, Kronberg/Ts., Athenäum Verlag GmbH.

Atiyah, Patrick S. (1970), *Accidents, Compensation and the Law*, London, Weidenfeld and Nicolson.

Axelrod, Robert (1984), *The Evolution of Cooperation*, New York, Basic Books.

Backhaus, Juergen (1996), 'Franz Böhm Issue', **3** *European Journal of Law and Economics*, 297-376.

Backhaus, Jürgen G. and Stephen, Frank H. (1994), 'The Purpose of the *European Journal of Law and Economics* and the Intentions of Its Editors', **1** *European Journal of Law and Economics*, 5-7.

Backhaus, Jürgen and Wagner, Richard E. (1987), 'The Cameralists: A Public Choice Perspective', **53** *Public Choice*, 3-20.

Baechler, Jean (1995a), *Le Capitalisme - 1. Les Origines* (Capitalism - 1. Origins), Paris, Gallimard.

Baechler, Jean (1995b), *Le Capitalisme - 2. L'Économie Capitaliste* (Capitalism - 2. The Capitalist Economy), Paris, Gallimard.

Bailey, Martin J. (1992), 'Approximate Optimality of Aboriginal Property Rights', **35** *Journal of Law and Economics*, 183-198.

Baird, Douglas G., Gertner, Robert H. and Picker, Randall C. (1994), *Game Theory and the Law*, Cambridge, MA, Harvard University Press.

Baker, C. Edwin (1975), 'The Ideology of Economic Analysis of Law', **5** *Philosophy and Public Affairs*, 3-48.

Baker, C. Edwin (1980), 'Starting Points in the Economic Analysis of Law', **8** *Hofstra Law Review*, 939-972.

Barnett, Randy E. (1989), 'Foreword: Post-Chicago Law and Economics', **65** *Chicago-Kent Law Review*, 1-21.

Barnett, Randy E. (1992), 'The Function of Several Property and Freedom of Contract', in Paul, Ellen Frankel, Jr, Fred D. Miller and Paul, Jeffrey (eds), *Economic Rights,* Cambridge, Cambridge University Press and the Social Philosophy and Policy Foundation, Bowling Green, OH, 62-94.

Barnett, Randy E. (1998), *The Structure of Liberty - Justice and the Rule of Law*, Oxford, Clarendon Press.

Barry, Norman P. (1996), *Classical Liberalism in the Age of Post-Communism*, Cheltenham, UK, Edward Elgar, 6-17.

Beccaria, Cesare and Bellamy, Richard ([1764] 1995), *On Crimes and Punishments and Other Writings*, Cambridge, Cambridge University Press.

Becker, Gary S. (1957), *The Economics of Discrimination*, Chicago, University of Chicago Press.

Becker, Gary S. (1962), 'Irrational Behavior and Economic Theory', **70** *Journal of Political Economy*, 1-18.

Becker, Gary S. (1975), *Human Capital - A Theoretical and Emplrlcal Analysis with Special Reference to Education*, New York, National Bureau of Economic Research, (2nd edn).

Becker, Gary S. (1976), *The Economic Approach to Human Behavior*, Chicago, The University of Chicago Press.

Becker, Gary S. (1981), *A Treatise on the Family*, Cambridge, MA, Harvard University Press.

Becker, Gary S. (1983), 'A Theory of Competition Among Pressure Groups for Political Influence', **98** *Quarterly Journal of Economics*, 371-400.

Becker, Gary S. (1985), 'Public Policies, Pressure Groups, and Dead Weights Costs', **28** *Journal of Public Economics*, 330-347.

Becker, Gary S. (1986), 'The Public Interest Hypothesis Revisited: A New Test of Peltzman's Theory of Regulation', **49** *Public Choice*, 223-234.

Behrens, Peter (1984), *Die ökonomischen Grundlagen des Rechts - Politische Ökonomie als Rationale Jurisprudenz* (The Economic Foundations of Law - Political Economy as Rational Jurisprudence), Tübingen, J.C.B. Mohr (Paul Siebeck).

Behrens, Peter (1993), 'Legalism, Economism, and Professional Attitudes Toward Institutional Design - Comment', **149** *Journal of Institutional and Theoretical Economics*, 141-147.

Beito, David T. (1990), 'Mutual Aid for Social Welfare: The Case of American Fraternal Societies', **4** *Critical Review*, 709-736.

Bentham, Jeremy, ([1789] 1948), *An Introduction to the Principles of Morals and Legislation*, New York, Hafner.

Benson, Bruce L. (1994), 'Legal Philosophy', in Boettke, Peter J. (ed.), *The Elgar Companion to Austrian Economics*, Hants, UK, Edward Elgar, 270-275.

Birmingham, Robert L. (1968), 'Legal and Moral Duty in Game Theory: Common Law Contract and Chinese Analogies', **18** *Buffalo Law Review*, 99-117.

Black, Duncan (1948a), 'The Rationale of Group Decision-Making', **56** *Journal of Political Economy*, 23-34.

Black, Duncan (1948b), 'The Decisions of a Committee Using a Special Majority', **16** *Econometrica*, 245-261.

Black, Duncan (1958), *The Theory of Committees and Elections*, Cambridge, Cambridge University Press.

Blaug, Mark (1980), *The Methodology of Economics - or How Economists Explain*, Cambridge, Cambridge University Press.

Boettke, Peter J. (ed.) (1994), *The Elgar Companion to Austrian Economics*, Hants, UK, Edward Elgar.

Boettke, Peter J. (1997), 'Where did Economics Go Wrong? Equilibrium as a Flight from Reality', **11** *Critical Review*, 11-64.

Booth, William James, Booth, Patrick and Meadwell, Hudson (eds) (1993), *Politics and Rationality*, Cambridge, Cambridge University Press.

Bork, Robert H. (1978), *The Antitrust Paradox: A Policy at War with Itself*, New York, Basic Books.

Bouckaert, Boudewijn (1984), *Recht op Zoek naar Economie? - Prolegomena tot een Economische Analyse van het Recht* (Law Looking for Economics? - Preliminary Considerations for an Economic Analysis of Law), Gent, E.Storia-Scientia.

Bouckaert, Boudewijn (1987), 'L'Analyse Économique du Droit: vers un Renouveau de la Science Juridique? (Economic Analysis of Law: Towards a Renewal in Legal Science?)', **18** *Revue Interdisciplinaire d'Études Juridiques*, 47-61.

Bouckaert, Boudewijn (1990a), 'Jeter un Pont entre Évolution et Droit Naturel' (Building a Bridge Between Evolution and Natural Law), **1** *Journal des Économistes et des Études Humaines*, 193-195.

Bouckaert, Boudewijn (1990b), 'What is Property?', **13** *Harvard Journal of Law and Public Policy*, 775-816.

Bouckaert, Boudewijn (1991), 'La Responsabilité Civile comme Base Institutionnelle d'une Protection Spontanée de l'Environnement, (Tort Law as Institutional Basis for Spontaneous Protection of the Environment)', **2** *Journal des Économistes et des Études Humaines*, 315-335.

Bouckaert, Boudewijn (1994), 'Misschien Geen Vrienden, Waarschijnlijk Wel Bondgenoten. Bedenkingen over de Nauwe Kloof tussen de Rechtssociologie van het Handelen en de Rechtseconomie van de Sociale Cooperatie (Perhaps not Friends, but surely Allies. Reflections on the Narrow Gap beteen the Legal Sociology of Human Action and the Law and Economics of Social Co-operation)', in Raes, K. and Willekens, H. (eds), *Economische Verklaringen van het Recht* (Economic Explanations of Law), Den Haag, Vuga, 44-74.

Bouckaert, Boudewijn (1996), 'City Air Sets One Free: Medieval Cities as Voluntary Political and Economic Communities', in Beito, David (ed.), *The Voluntary City*, San Francisco, The Independent Institute.

Bouckaert, Boudewijn (1997), 'Between the Market and the State: The World of Medieval Cities', in Radnitzky, Gerard (ed.), *Values and Social Order - Vol. 3. Voluntary versus Coercive Orders*, Aldershot, Avebury, 213-241.

Boudon, Raymond (1977), *Effets Pervers et Ordre Social* (Perverse Effects and Social Order), Paris, Presses Universitaires de France.

Boudreaux, Donald J. (1994), 'Law and Economics', in Boettke, Peter J. (ed.), *The Elgar Companion to Austrian Economics*, Hants, UK, Edward Elgar, 264-269

Bowman, Ward S. (1973), *Patent and Antitrust Law: A Legal and Economic Appraisal*, Chicago, University of Chicago Press.

Breton, Albert (1987), 'Towards a Theory of Competitive Federalism', **3** *European Journal of Political Economy*, 263-329.

Breton, Albert (1989), 'The Growth of Competitive Governments', **22** *Canadian Journal of Economics*, 717-749.

Breton, Albert (1996), *Competitive Governments - An Economic Theory of Politics and Public Finance*, Cambridge, Cambridge University Press.

Breton, Albert and Scott, Anthony (1978), *The Economic Constitution of Federal States*, Toronto, University of Toronto Press.

Breton, Albert and Scott, Anthony (1980), *The Design of Federations*, Montreal, The Institute for Research on Public Policy.

Browning, John and Reiss, Spencer (1998), 'Encyclopedia of the New Economy', **6.04** *Wired*, 93-102.

Buchanan, James M. (1977), 'Law and the Invisible Hand', in Siegan, Bernard H. (ed.), *The Interaction of Economics and the Law*, Lexington, MA, Lexington Books, 127-138.

Buchanan, James M. and Tullock, Gordon (1962), *The Calculus of Consent - Logical Foundations of Constitutional Democracy*, Ann Arbor, The University of Michigan Press.

Buchanan, James M., Tollison, Robert D. and Tullock, Gordon (eds) (1980), *Towards a Theory of the Rent-Seeking Society*, College Station, Texas A&M Press.

Burrows, Paul (1980), *The Economic Theory of Pollution Control*, Cambridge, MA, MIT Press.

Burrows, Paul and Veljanovski, Cento G. (eds) (1981), *The Economic Approach to Law*, London, Butterworths.

Burton, John (1980), 'Epilogue: Externalities, Property Rights, and Public Policy: Private Property Rights and the Spoliation of Nature', in Cheung, Steven N.S. (ed.), *The Myth of Social Cost*, San Francisco, CA, Cato Institute, 53-71.

Calabresi, Guido (1961), 'Some Thoughts on Risk-Distribution and the Law of Torts', **70** *Yale Law Journal*, 499-553.

Calabresi, Guido (1965a), 'The Decision for Accidents: An Approach to Nonfault Allocation of Costs', **78** *Harvard Law Review*, 713-774.

Calabresi, Guido (1965b), 'Transaction Costs, Resource Allocation and Liability Rules - A Comment', in Manne, Henry G. (ed.), *The Economics of Legal Relationships - Readings in the Theory of Property Rights*, St. Paul, MN, West Publishing Cy, pp. 204-211.

Calabresi, Guido (1970), *The Cost of Accidents*, New Haven, Yale University Press.

Calabresi, Guido and Hirschoff, Jon T. (1972), 'Toward a Test for Strict Liability in Torts', *Yale Law Journal* **81**, 1055-1085.

Calabresi, Guido and Melamed, Douglas (1972), 'Property Rules, Liability Rules, and Inalienability: One View of the Cathedral', **85** *Harvard Law Review*, 1089-1128.

Carroll, Sidney L. (1979), *Research in Law and Economics - volume 1* (Zerbe general editor), Greenwich, Conn., JAI Press.

Cheung, Steven N.S. (1968), 'Private Property Rights and Sharecropping', *Journal of Political Economy* **76**, 1107-1122.

Cheung, Steven N.S. (1969a), *The Theory of Share Tenancy*, Chicago, The University of Chicago Press.

Cheung, Steven N.S. (1969b), 'Transaction Costs, Risk Aversion, and the Choice of Contractual Arrangements', **12** *Journal of Law and Economics*, 23-42.

Cheung, Steven N.S. (1970), 'The Structure of a Contract and the Theory of a Non-Exclusive Resource', **13** *Journal of Law and Economics*, 49-70.

Cheung, Steven N.S. (1972), 'The Enforcement of Property Rights in Children, and the Marriage Contract', **82** *Economic Journal*, 641-657.

Cheung, Steven N.S. (1973), 'The Fable of the Bees: An Economic Investigation', **16** *Journal of Law and Economics*, 11-33.

Cheung, Steven N.S. (1980), *The Myth of Social Cost*, San Francisco, CA, Cato Institute.

Coase, Ronald H. (1937), 'The Nature of the Firm', **4** *Economica* (n.s.), 386-405 reproduced in Coase 1988, p 33-55.

Coase, Ronald H. (1960), 'The Problem of Social Cost', **3** *Journal of Law and Economics*, 1-44 (reprinted in Coase, Ronald H. (1988), *The Firm, the Market and the Law*, Chicago, The University of Chicago Press 95-156).

Coase, Ronald H. (1974), 'The Lighthouse in Economics', **17** *Journal of Law and Economics*, 357-376 (reprinted in Coase, Ronald H. (1988), *The Firm, the Market and the Law*, Chicago, The University of Chicago Press 187-213).

Coase, Ronald H. (1978), 'Economics and Contiguous Disciplines', **7** *Journal of Legal Studies*, 201-210.

Coase, Ronald H. (1984), 'The New Institutional Economics', **140** *Journal of Institutional and Theoretical Economics*, 229-231.

Coase, Ronald H. (1988), *The Firm, the Market and the Law*, Chicago, The University of Chicago Press.

Coase, Ronald H. (1992), 'The Institutional Structure of Production', **82** *American Economic Review*, 713-719.

Coase, R.H. (1993), 'Law and Economics at Chicago', **36(1)** *Journal of Law and Economics*, 239-254.

Coase, Ronald H. (1994), *Essays on Economics and Economists*, Chicago, The University of Chicago Press.

Coleman, James S. (1987), 'Norms as Social Capital', in Radnitzky, Gerard and Bernholz, Peter (eds), *Economic Imperialism - The Economic Method Applied Outside the Field of Economics*, New York, Paragon House, 133-155.

Coleman, James S. (1988), 'The Problem of Order: Where are Rights to Act Located?', **144** *Journal of Institutional and Theoretical Economics*, 367-373.

Coleman, James (1990a), 'Norm-Generating Structures', in Cook, Karen S. and Levi, Margaret (eds), *The Limits of Rationality*, Chicago, The University of Chicago Press, 250-273.

Coleman, James S. (1990b), 'Natural Persons, Corporate Actors, and Constitutions', **2** *Constitutional Political Economy*, 81-106.

Coleman, James S. (1990c), *Foundations of Social Theory*, Cambridge, MA, Belknap Press of Harvard University Press.

Coleman, James S. (1991), 'Constructed Organization: First Principles', **7** *Journal of Law, Economics, and Organization*, 7-23.

Coleman, James S. (1992), 'The Economic Approach to Sociology (An ICUS Book)', in Radnitzky, Gerard (ed.), *Universal Economics - Assessing the Achievements of the Economic Approach*, New York, Paragon House, 133-148.

Coleman, Jules L. (1982), 'The Economic Analysis of Law', in Pennock, J. Roland and Chapman, John W. (eds), *Ethics, Economics and Law*, New York, New York University Press, 83-103.

Coleman, Jules L. (1989), 'Afterword: The Rational Choice Approach to Legal Rules', **65** *Chicago-Kent Law Review*, 177-191.

Cook, Karen S. and Levi, Margaret (1990), *The Limits of Rationality*, Chicago, The University of Chicago Press.

Cooter, Robert D. (1995), 'Law and Unified Social Theory', **22** *Journal of Law and Society*, 50-67.

Cooter, Robert D. and Gordley, James (1991), 'Economic Analysis in Civil Law Countries: Past, Present, Future', **11** *International Review of Law and Economics*, 261-263.

Cooter, Robert and Kornhauser, Lewis (1980), 'Can Litigation Improve the Law Without the Help of Judges?', **9** *Journal of Legal Studies*, 139-163.

Cooter, Robert and Ulen, Thomas (1996), *Law and Economics*, New York, HarperCollins, (2nd edn).

Cowen, Tyler (1988), *The Theory of Market Failure*, Fairfax, VA, George Mason University Press.

Cramton, Roger C. (1983), 'The Place of Economics in Legal Education (Symposium)', **33** *Journal of Legal Education*, 183-368.

Cranston, R. (1977), 'Creeping Economism: Some Thoughts on Law and Economics', **4** *British Journal of Law and Society*, 103-115.

Daintith, Terence C. and Teubner, Gunther (1986), 'Sociological Jurisprudence and Legal Economics: Risks and Rewards', in Daintith, Terence and Teubner, Gunther (eds), *Contract and Organisation: Legal Analysis in the Light of Economic and Social Theory*, Berlin, Walter de Gruyter, 3-22.

Dales, J.H. (1968a), 'Land, Water, and Ownership', **1** *Canadian Journal of Economics*, 791.

Dales, J.H. (1968b), *Pollution, Property and Prices - An Essay in Policy-Making and Economics*, Toronto, University of Toronto Press.

De Alessi, Louis (1969), 'Implications of Property Rights for Government Investment Choices', **59** *American Economic Review*, 13-24.

De Alessi, Louis (1996), 'Value, Economic Efficiency, and Rules: Some Implicit Biases Against Individual Liberty', in Bouillon, Hardy (ed.), *Libertarians and Liberalism - Essays in Honour of Gerard Radnitzky,* Aldershot, Ashgate, 112-122.

De Alessi, Louis (1997), 'Value, Efficiency, and Rules: The Limits of Economics', in Radnitzky, Gerard (ed.), *Values and Social Order - Vol. III. Voluntary versus Coercive Orders,* Aldershot, Avebury, 283-304.

De Clerq, Marc and Naert, Frank (1985), *De Politieke Markt* (The Political Market), Antwerpen, Kluwer.

De Geest, Gerrit (1995), 'Toward an Integration of Economic and Sociological Approaches', **2** *European Journal of Law and Economics*, 301-308.

Demsetz, Harold (1964), 'The Exchange and Enforcement of Property Rights', **7** *Journal of Law and Economics*, 11-26.

Demsetz, Harold (1966), 'Some Aspects of Property Rights', **9** *Journal of Law and Economics*, 61-70.

Demsetz, Harold (1967), 'Towards a Theory of Property Rights', **57** *American Economic Review*, 347-373.

Demsetz, Harold (1968), 'The Cost of Transacting', **82** *Quarterly Journal of Economics*, 33-53.

Demsetz, Harold (1969), 'Information and Efficiency: Another Viewpoint', **12** *Journal of Law and Economics*, 1-22.

Demsetz, Harold (1972a), 'Wealth Distribution and the Ownership of Rights', **1** *Journal of Legal Studies*, 223-232.

Demsetz, Harold (1972b), 'When Does the Rule of Liability Matter?', **1** *Journal of Legal Studies*, 13-28.

Donohue III, John J. (1988), 'Law and Economics: The Road not Taken', **22** *Law and Society Review*, 903-926.

Downs, Anthony (1957), *An Economic Theory of Democracy*, New York, Harper and Row.

Dunleavy, Patrick (1991), *Democracy, Bureaucracy and Public Choice - Economic Eplanations in Political Science*, Hertfordshire, Harvester Wheatsheaf.

Duxbury, Neil (1995), *Patterns of American Jurisprudence*, Oxford, Clarendon Press, ch. 5.

Eggertsson, Thráinn (1990), *Economic Behavior and Institutions*, Cambridge, Cambridge University Press.

Eggertsson, Thráinn (1993), 'The Economics of Institutions - Avoiding the Open-Field Syndrome and the Perils of Path Dependence', **36** *Acta Sociologica*, 3-37.

Eggertsson, Thráinn (1996), 'A Note on the Economics of Institutions', in Alston, Lee J., Eggertsson, Thráinn and North, Douglass C. (eds), *Empirical Studies in Institutional Change*, New York, Cambridge University Press, 6-24.

EJLE (1995), **2(4)** *European Journal of Law and Economics*, 263-394.

Ekelund, Robert B., Hébert, Robert F. and Tollison, Robert D. (1989), 'An Economic Model of the Medieval Church: Usury as a Form of Rent Seeking', **5** *Journal of Law, Economics, and Organization*, 307-331.

Ellickson, Robert C. (1987), 'A Critique of Economic and Sociological Theories of Social Control', **16** *Journal of Legal Studies*, 67-99, reprinted in Levmore, Saul (ed.) (1994), *Foundations of Tort Law*, New York, Oxford University Press, 265-276.

Ellickson, Robert C. (1989), 'Bringing Culture and Human Frailty to Rational Actors: A Critique of Classical Law and Economics', **65** *Chicago-Kent Law Review*, 23-55.

Ellickson, Robert C. (1990), 'Three Systems of Land-Use Control', **13** *Harvard Journal of Law and Public Policy*, 67-71.

Ellickson, Robert C. (1991), *Order without Law - How Neighbors Settle Disputes*, Boston, Harvard University Press.

Elster, Jon (1986), *Rational Choice*, New York, New York University Press.

Elster, Jon (1989), *Nuts and Bolts for the Social Sciences*, Cambridge, Cambridge University Press.

Englard, Izhak (1990), 'Victor Mataja's *Liability for Damages from an Economic Viewpoint*: A Centennial to an Ignored Economic Analysis of Tort', **10** *International Review of Law and Economics*, 173-191.

Epstein, Richard A. (1994), 'On the Optimal Mix of Private and Common Property', in Paul, Ellen Frankel, Miller Jr, Fred D. and Paul, Jeffrey (eds), *Property Rights*, Cambridge, Cambridge University Press, 17-41.

Epstein, Richard A. (1995), *Simple Rules for a Complex World*, Cambridge, MA, Harvard University Press.

Epstein, Richard A. (1997), 'Law and Economics: Its Glorious Past and Cloudy Future', **64** *University of Chicago Law Review*, 1167-1174.

Farber, Daniel A. and Frickey, Philip P. (1991), *Law and Public Choice - A Critical Introduction*, Chicago, The University of Chicago Press.

Fuller, Lon L. (1968), *The Anatomy of the Law* (Mentor Books), New York, The New American Library.

Fuller, Lon L. (1969), *The Morality of Law*, New Haven, Yale University Press.

Fuller, Lon L. (1971), 'Human Interaction and the Law', in Wolff, Robert Paul (ed.) *The Rule of Law*, New York, Simon and Schuster, 171-217.

Furubotn, Eirik (1989), 'The New Institutional Approach to Economic History', **145** *Journal of Institutional and Theoretical Economics/ Zeitschrift für die Gesammte Staatswissenschaft*, 1-5.

Furubotn, Eirik G. (1993), 'The New Institutional Economics. Recent Progress: Expanding Frontiers', **149** *Journal of Institutional and Theoretical Economics/ Zeitschrift für die Gesammte Staatswissenschaft*, 1-10.

Furubotn, Eirik G. and Pejovich, Svetozar (1972), 'Property Rights and Economic Theory: A Survey of Recent Literature', **10** *Journal of Economic Literature*, 1137-1172.

Furubotn, Eirik G. and Pejovich, Svetozar (1974), *The Economics of Property Rights*, Cambridge, MA, Ballinger Publishing Cy.

Furubotn, Eirik G. and Richter, Rudolf (1992), *The New Institutional Economics : A Collection of Articles from the Journal of Institutional and Theoretical Economics*, Ann Arbor, Texas A&M University Press.

Furubotn, Eirik G. and Richter, Rudolf (eds) (1997), *Institutions and Economic Theory: The Contribution of the New Institutional Economics*, Ann Arbor, University of Michigan Press.

Goetz, Charles J. (1987), 'Public Choice and the Law: The Paradox of Tullock', in Rowley, Charles K. (ed.), *Democracy and Public Choice: Essays in Honor of Gordon Tullock*, Oxford, Blackwell, 171-180.

Goldberg, Victor P. (1976a), 'Toward an Expanded Economic Theory of Contract', in Samuels, Warren J. (ed.), *The Chicago School of Political Economy*, East Lansing, Mich., Association of Evolutionary Economics and Michigan State University, 259-275. Also in **10** *Journal of Economic Issues*, 45-61.

Goldberg, Victor P. (1976b), 'Commons, Clark, and the Emerging Post-Coasian Law and Economics', **10** *Journal of Economic Issues*, 877-893.

Gomez, Pierre-Yves (1996), *Le Gouvernement de l'Entreprise - Modèles Économiques de l'Entreprise et Pratiques de Gestion* (The Governance of Business - Economic Models of the Enterprise and Management Practices), Paris, InterÉditions,Masson.

Goodman, John C. (1978), 'An Economic Theory of Evolution of the Common Law', **7** *Journal of Legal Studies*, 393-406.

Gordon, H. Scott (1954), 'The Economic Theory of a Common Property Resource: The Fishery', **62** *Journal of Political Economy*, 124-142.

Gordon, H. Scott (1958), 'Economics and the Conservation Question', **1** *Journal of Law and Economics*, 110-121.

Green, David G. (1995), 'Welfare Before the Welfare State: The British Experience', in Ebeling, Richard M. (ed.), *American Perestroika: The Demise of the Welfare State*, Hillsdale, Michigan, Hillsdale College Press, 73-87.

Green, Donald P. and Shapiro, Ian (1994), *Pathologies of Rational Choice Theory - A Critique of Applications in Political Science*, New Haven, Yale University Press.

Greif, Avner (1989), 'Reputation and Coalitions in Medieval Trade: Evidence on Maghribi Traders', **49** *Journal of Economic History*, 857-882.

Greif, Avner (1993), 'Contract Enforceability and Economic Institutions in Early Trade: The Maghribi Traders' Coalition', **83** *American Economic Review*, 525-548.

Greif, Avner (1997), 'Reputation and Coalitions in Medieval Trade: Evidence on Maghribi Traders, in Klein, Daniel B. (ed.), *Reputation: Studies in the Voluntary Elicitation of Good Conduct*, Ann Arbor, The University of Michigan Press, 137-163.

Greif, Avner, Milgrom, Paul R. and Weingast, Barry R. (1994), 'Coordination, Commitment, and Enforcement: The Case of the Merchant Guild', **102** *Journal of Political Economy*, 745-776.

Griffiths, John (1995), 'Normative and Rational Choice Accounts of Human Social Behavior', **2** *European Journal of Law and Economics*, 285-299.

Grossekettler, Heinz (1996), 'Franz Böhm as a Pioneering Champion of an Economic Theory of Legislative Science', **3** *European Journal of Law and Economics*, 309-329.

Hägg, P. Göran T. (1997), 'Theories on the Economics of Regulation: A Survey of the Literature from a European Perspective', **4** *European Journal of Law and Economics*, 337-370.

Hahn, Frank and Hollis, Martin (eds) (1979), *Philosophy and Economic Theory*, Oxford, Oxford University Press.

Hamilton, Bruce W. (1987), 'Tiebout: Hypothesis', in Eatwell, John, Milgate, Murray and Newman, Peter (eds), *The New Palgrave - The World of Economics*, New York, W.W. Norton, 672-677.

Hargreaves Heap, Shaun, Hollis, Martin et al. (1992), *The Theory of Choice - A Critical Guide*, Oxford, Blackwell.

Harris, Donald R., Ogus, A.I. and Phillips, J. (1979), 'Contract Remedies and the Consumer Surplus', **95** *Law Quarterly Review*, 581-610.

Hart, H.L.A. (1977), 'American Jurisprudence Through English Eyes: The Nightmare and the Noble Dream', **11** *Georgia Law Review* , 969-990.

Hayek, F.A. (1948), 'The Use of Knowledge in Society', in Hayek, F.A. (ed.), *Individualism and Economic Order,* Chicago, Henry Regnery Cy, 77-91.

Hayek, F.A. (1968), 'Competition as a Discovery Procedure', in Hayek, F.A. (ed.), *New Studies in Philosophy, Politics, Economics and the History of Ideas,* Chicago, The University of Chicago Press, 179-190.

Hayek, Friedrich A. (1973), *Law, Legislation and Liberty - Volume 1: Rules and Order*, Chicago, The University of Chicago Press.

Hayek, Friedrich A. (1976), *Law, Legislation and Liberty - Volume 2: The Mirage of Social Justice*, Chicago, The University of Chicago Press.

Hayek, Friedrich A. (1979), *Law, Legislation and Liberty - Volume 3: The Political Order of a Free People*, Chicago, The University of Chicago Press.

Heiner, Ronald A. (1983), 'The Origin of Predictable Behavior', **73** *American Economic Review*, 560-595.

Hirshleifer, Jack (1982), 'Evolutionary Models in Economics and Law: Cooperation versus Conflict Strategies', in Rubin, Paul H. (ed.), *Research in Law and Economics, vol. 4 - Evolutionary Models in Economics and Law,* Greenwich, Conn., JAI Press, 1-60.

Hofstra Symposium (1980), 'Symposium on Efficiency as a Legal Concern', **8** *Hofstra Law Review*, 485-972.

Hogarth, Robin M. and Reder, Melvin W. (1986), *Rational Choice - The Contrast between Economics and Psychology*, Chicago, The University of Chicago Press.

Hollander, Abraham and Mackaay, Ejan (1982), 'Are Judges Economists at Heart?', in Ciampi, C. (ed.), *Artificial Intelligence and Legal Information Systems, Volume I,* Amsterdam, North-Holland Publishing, 129-149.

Hollis, Martin (1987), *The Cunning of Reason*, Cambridge, Cambridge University Press.

Hollis, Martin and Nell, Edward (1975), *Rational Economic Man - A Philosophical Critique of NeoClassical Economics*, Cambridge, Cambridge University Press.

Holmes, Oliver Wendell (1897), 'The Path of the Law', **10** *Harvard Law Review*, 457-478.

Horn, Norbert (1976), 'Zur ökonomischen Rationalität des Privatrechts. Die Privatrechts Theoretische Verwertbarkeit der Economics Analysis of Law' (On the Economic

Rationality of Private Law. On Private-Law Assessment of the Economics Analysis of Law), **176** *Archiv für die Civilistische Praxis*, 307-333.

Hovenkamp, Herbert (1983), 'The Economics of Legal History', **67** *Minnesota Law Review*, 645-697.

Hovenkamp, Herbert (1990), 'The First Great Law and Economics Movement', **42** *Stanford Law Review*, 993-1058.

Hume, David ([1740] 1978), *A Treatise of Human Nature*, Oxford, Clarendon Press, (2nd edn).

Hume, David ([1777] 1987), 'Idea of a Perfect Commonwealth', in Hume, David (ed.), *Essays Moral, Political and Literary*, Indianapolis, Liberty Fund, 512-519.

Hutter, Michael (1982), 'Early Contributions to Law and Economics - Adolf Wagner's Grundlegung', **16** *Journal of Economic Issues*, 131-147.

Johnston, Jason Scott (1990), 'Law, Economics, and Post-Realist Explanation', **24** *Law and Society Review*, 1217-1254.

Kahneman, Daniel, Slovic, Paul and Tversky, Amos (1982), *Judgment under Uncertainty: Heuristics and Biases*, Cambridge, Cambridge University Press.

Kahneman, Daniel, Knetsch, Jack L. and Thaler, Richard H. (1991), 'The Endowment Effect, Loss Aversion, and Status Quo Bias', **5** *Journal of Economic Perspectives*, 193-206.

Katz, Avery Wiener (1998), *Foundations of the Economic Approach to Law*, New York, Oxford University Press.

Kendall, Frances and Louw, Leon (1989), *Let the People Govern*, Norwood (South Africa), Amagi Publications.

Kerkmeester, Heico (1989), *Recht en Speltheorie - Een Economisch Model voor het Ontstaan van Staten en Recht* (Law and Game Theory - an Economic Model of the Emergence of States and Law), Lelystad (Pays-Bas), Koninklijke Vermande.

Kinsella, N. Stephan (1995), 'Legislation and the Discovery of Law in a Free Society', **11** *Journal of Libertarian Studies*, 132-181.

Kirchner, Christian (1991), 'The Difficult Reception of Law and Economics in Germany', **11(3)** *International Review of Law and Economics*, 277-292.

Kirzner, Israel M. (1973), *Competition and Entrepreneurship*, Chicago, The University of Chicago Press.

Kirzner, Israel M. (1979), *Perception, Opportunity, and Profit - Studies in the Theory of Entrepreneurship*, Chicago, The University of Chicago Press.

Kirzner, Israel M. (1984), 'Prices, the Communication of Knowledge, and the Discovery Process', in Leube, Kurt R. and Zlabinger, Albert H. (eds), *The Political Economy of Freedom - Essays in Honor of F.A. Hayek*, München, Philosophia Verlag, 193-206.

Kirzner, Israel M. (1985), *Discovery and the Capitalist Process*, Chicago, The University of Chicago Press.

Kirzner, Israel M. (1997), *How Markets Work - Disequilibrium, Entrepreneurship and Discovery*, London, Institute of Economic Affairs.

Kitch, Edmund W. (1983a), 'The Fire of Truth: A Remembrance of Law and Economics at Chicago, 1932-1970', **26** *Journal of Law and Economics*, 163-234.

Kitch, Edmund W. (1983b), 'The Intellectual Foundations of Law and Economics', **33** *Journal of Legal Education*, 184-196.

Knetsch, Jack L. (1989), 'The Endowment Effect and Evidence of Nonreversible Indifference Curves', **79** *American Economic Review*, 1277-1284.

Knetsch, Jack L. and Sinden, J.A. (1984a), 'Willingness to Pay and Compensation Demanded: Experimental Evidence of an Unexpected Disparity in Measures of Value', **99** *Quarterly Journal of Economics*, 507-521.

Knetsch, Jack L. and Sinden, J.A. (1984b), 'The Persistence of Evaluation Disparaties', **99** *Quarterly Journal of Economics*, 691-695.

Knight, Jack (1992), *Institutions and Social Conflict*, Cambridge, Cambridge University Press.

Knight, Jack and Sened, Itai (eds) (1995), *Explaining Social Institutions*, Ann Arbor, University of Michigan Press.

Komesar, Neil K. (1997), 'Exploring the Darkness: Law, Economics, and Institutional Choice', **1997** *Wisconsin Law Review*, 465-474.

Krueger, Anne O. (1974), 'The Political Economy of the Rent-Seeking Society', **64** *American Economic Review*, 291-303.

Landes, William M. (1971), 'An Economic Analysis of the Courts', **14** *Journal of Law and Economics*, 61-107.

Landes, William M. and Posner, Richard A. (1976), 'Legal Precedent: A Theoretical and Empirical Analysis', **19** *Journal of Law and Economics*, 249-307.

Landes, William M. and Posner, Richard A. (1979), 'Adjudication as a Private Good', **8** *Journal of Legal Studies*, 235-284.

Landes, William M. and Posner, Richard A. (1980), 'Legal Change, Judicial Behavior and the Diversity Jurisdiction', **9** *Journal of Legal Studies*, 367-386.

Langlois, Richard N. (1986), 'Rationality, Institutions, and Explanation', in Langlois, Richard N. (ed.), *Economics as a Process - Essays in the New Institutional Economics*, Cambridge, Cambridge University Press, 225-255.

Lehmann, Michael (1983), *Bürgerliches Recht und Handelsrecht - eine Juristische und Ökonomische Analyse* (Civil and Commercial Law - A Legal and Economic Analysis), Stuttgart, C.E. Poeschel Verlag.

Lemennicier, Bertrand (1988), *Le Marché du Mariage et de la Famille* (The Market of Marriage and the Family), Paris, Presses Universitaires de France.

Lenel, Hans Otto (1996), 'The Life and Work of Franz Böhm', **3** *European Journal of Law and Economics*, 301-307.

Leo (1985), 'Editor's Foreword', **1** *Journal of Law, Economics, and Organization*, 3-4.

Leo (1997), 'Mission statement', **13** *Journal of Law, Economics, and Organization*, 0 (inside cover).

Leoni, Bruno ([1961] 1991), *Freedom and the Law*, Indianapolis, LibertyPress, (3rd edn).

Lepage, Henri (1985), *Pourquoi la Propriété* (Why Property?), Paris, Hachette.

Levi, Edward H. (1966), 'Aaron Director and the Study of Law and Economics', **9** *Journal of Law and Economics*, 3-4.

Levmore, Saul (1986), 'Rethinking Comparative Law: Variety and Uniformity in Ancient and Modern Tort Law', **61** *Tulane Law Review*, 235-287.

Levmore, Saul (1987), 'Variety and Uniformity in the Treatment of the Good-Faith Purchaser', **16** *Journal of Legal Studies*, 43-65.

Libecap, Gary D. (1986), 'Property Rights in Economic History: Implications for Research', **23** *Explorations in Economic History*, 227-252.

Libecap, Gary D. (1989), *Contracting for Property Rights*, Cambridge, Cambridge University Press.

Libecap, Gary (1992), 'Douglass C. North: Institutions and Economic Performance', in Samuels, Warren J. (ed.), *New Horizons in Economic Thought: Appraisals of Leading Economists*, Aldershot, Edward Elgar, 227-298.

Libecap, Gary (1993a), 'Politics, Institutions, and Institutional Change', **149** *Journal of Institutional and Theoretical Economics*, 29-35.

Libecap, Gary (1993b), 'What Really Happened at Teapot Dome?', in McCloskey, Donald N. (ed.), *Second Thoughts - Myths and Morals of US Economic History*, New York, Oxford University Press,157-162.

Liebhafsky, Harold H. (1976), 'Price Theory as Jurisprudence: Law and Economics Chicago Style', **10** *Journal of Economic Issues*, 23-43.

Macaulay, Stewart (1963), 'Non-Contractual Relations in Business. A Preliminary Study', **28** *American Sociological Review*, 55-67.

Machiavelli, Niccolò (1961), *The Prince*, Harmondsworth, UK, Penguin Books.

Mackaay, Ejan (1980), 'Veranderingen in het Stelsel van Vergoeding en Verhaal van Schade - Economische Kanttekeningen (Changes in the System of Compensation and Recourse for Damages - Economic Considerations)', in: *Schade lijden en Schade dragen*, Zwolle, W.E.J. Tjeenk Willink, 147-174.

Mackaay, Ejan (1982), *Economics of Information and Law*, Boston, Kluwer.

Mackaay, Ejan (1986), 'La Règle Juridique Observée par le Prisme de l'Économiste. Une Histoire Stylisée du Mouvement de l'Analyse Économique du Droit (The Legal Rule Observed Through the Glasses of the Economist. A Stylised History of the Law and Economics Movement)', **1986** *Revue Internationale de Droit Économique*, 43-83.

Mackaay, Ejan (1987), 'Le Juriste a-t-il le Droit d'Ignorer l'Économiste? (May Lawyers Ignore Economists?)', **2** *Revue de la Recherche Juridique - Droit Prospectif*, 419-427.

Mackaay, Ejan (1988a), 'Het Recht Bezien door de Bril van de Economist (The Law Observed Through the Economist's Eyeglass)', **1988** *Rechtsgeleerd Magazijn Themis*, 411-452.

Mackaay, Ejan (1988b), 'L'Ordre Spontané Comme Fondement du Droit - Un Survol des Modèles de l'Émergence des Règles dans la Société Civile (Spontaneous Order as the Foundation of Law - An Overview of Models of the Emergence of Norms in Society)', **22** *Revue Juridique Thémis*, 347-383 and (1989) **3** *Revue Internationale de Droit Économique*, 247-287.

Mackaay, Ejan (1991), 'Le Droit Saisi par le Jeu' (Law as a Game), **17-18** *Droit et Société*, 57-81.

Mackaay, Ejan (1997), 'The Emergence of Constitutional Rights', **8** *Constitutional Political Economy*, 15-36.

Maine, Henry Sumner ([1861] 1977), *Ancient Law*, London, Everyman's Library.

Manne, Henry G. (1962), 'The Higher Criticism of the Modern Corporation', **62** *Columbia Law Review*, 399-432.

Manne, Henry G. (1965), 'Mergers and the Market for Corporate Control', **73** *Journal of Political Economy*, 110-120.

Manne, Henry G. (1966a), 'In Defense of Insider Trading', **44** *Harvard Business Review*, 113-122.

Manne, Henry G. (1966b), *Insider Trading and the Stock Market*, New York, Free Press.

Manne, Henry G. (1967), 'Our Two Corporate Systems: Law and Economics', **53** *Virginia Law Review*, 259-284.

Manne, Henry G. (1993), *An Intellectual History of the School of Law George Mason University*, Rapport, Law and Economics Center, School of Law, George Mason University.

March, James G. (1986), 'Bounded Rationality, Ambiguity, and the Engineering of Choice (Readings in Social and Political Theory)', in Elster, Jon (ed.), *Rational Choice,* New York, New York University Press, 143-170.

Mashaw, Jerry L. (1997), *Greed, Chaos, and Governance - Using Public Choice to Improve Public Law*, New Haven, Yale University Press.

Mattei, Ugo (1994a), 'Efficiency as Equity: Insights from Comparative Law and Economics', **18** *Hastings International and Comparative Law Review*, 157-173.

Mattei, Ugo (1994b), 'Efficiency in Legal Transplants: An Essay in Comparative Law and Economics', **14** *International Review of Law and Economics*, 3-19.

Mattei, Ugo (1994c), 'Why the Wind Changed: Intellectual Leadership in Western Law', **42** *American Journal of Comparative Law*, 195-218.

Mattei, Ugo (1995), 'The Comparative Law and Economics of Penalty Clause in Contracts', **43** *American Journal of Comparative Law*, 427-444.

Mattei, Ugo (1996), 'Aspects of Reception of Law', **44** *American Journal of Comparative Law*, 335-351.

Mattei, Ugo (1997), *Comparative Law and Economics*, Ann Arbor, University of Michigan Press.

Mattei, Ugo and Pardolesi, Robert (1991), 'Law and Economics in Civil Law Countries: A Comparative Approach', **11** *International Review of Law and Economics*, 265-275.

McAdams, Richard H. (1997), 'Comment: Accounting for Norms', **1997** *Wisconsin Law Review*, 625-637.

McChesney, Fred S. (1987), 'Rent Extraction and Rent Creation in the Economic Theory of Regulation', **16** *Journal of Legal Studies*, 101-118.

McChesney, Fred S. (1997), *Money for Nothing - Politicians, Rent Extraction and Political Extortion*, Cambridge, Harvard University Press.

McChesney, Fred S. and Shughart II, William F. (1995), *The Causes and Consequences of Antitrust - The Public-Choice Perspective*, Chicago, The University of Chicago Press.

McKean, Roland N. (1970a), 'Products Liability: Implications of Some Changing Property Rights', **84** *Quarterly Journal of Economics*, 611-626.

McKean, Roland N. (1970b), 'Products Liability: Trends and Implications', **38** *University of Chicago Law Review*, 3-63.

Medema, Steven G. (1989), 'Discourse and the Institutional Approach to Law and Economics: Factors that Separate the Institutional Approach to Law and Economics From Alternative Approaches', **23** *Journal of Economic Issues*, 417-425.

Medema, Steven G. (1997), 'The Trial of *Homo Economicus*: What Law and Economics Tells Us about the Development of Economic Imperialism', in John B. Davis (ed.), *New Economics and Its History, History of Political Economy*, **29** (supplement), 122-142.

Medema, Steven G. (1998), 'Wandering the Road from Pluralism to Posner: The Transformation of Law and Economics in the Twentieth Century', in Mary Morgan and Malcolm Rutherford (eds), *The Transformation of American Economics: From Interwar Pluralism to Postwar Neoclassicism, History of Political Economy*, **30** (supplement), 202-224.

Meltzer, Bernard D. (1966), 'Aaron Director: A Personal Appreciation', **9** *Journal of Law and Economics*, 5-6.

Mercuro, Nicholas (1989), *Law and Economics*, Boston, Kluwer Academic Publishers.

Mercuro, Nicholas and Medema, Steven G. (1997), *Economics and the Law: From Posner to Post-Modernism*, Princeton, Princeton University Press.

Michelman, Frank I. (1980), 'Constitutions, Statutes, and the Theory of Efficient Adjudication', **9** *Journal of Legal Studies*, 431-461.

Migué, Jean-Luc (1993), *Federalism and Free Trade*, London, Institute of Economic Affairs.

Migué, Jean-Luc (1997), 'Public Choice in a Federal System', **90** *Public Choice*, 235-254.

Milgrom, Paul R., North, Douglass C. and Weingast, Barry R. (1997), 'The Role of Institutions in the Revival of Trade: Law Merchant, Private Judges, and the Champagne Fairs', in Klein, Daniel B. (ed.), *Reputation: Studies in the Voluntary Elicitation of Good Conduct,* Ann Arbor, The University of Michigan Press, 243-266.

Miller, Gary J. (1992), *Managerial Dilemmas: The Political Economy of Hierarchy* (Political Economy of Decisions and Institutions), Cambridge, Cambridge University Press.

Mitchell, William C. (1988), 'Virginia, Rochester and Bloomington: Twenty-five Years of Public Choice and Political Science', **56** *Public Choice*, 101-119.

Mitchell, William C. and Simmons, Randy T. (1994), *Beyond Politics - Markets, Welfare, and the Failure of Bureaucracy*, Boulder, Westview Press.

Mueller, Dennis C. (1979), *Public Choice*, Cambridge, Cambridge University Press.

Mueller, Dennis C. (1989), *Public Choice II - A revised edition of Public Choice*, Cambridge, Cambridge University Press.

Mueller, Dennis C. (ed.) (1997), *Perspectives on Public Choice - A Handbook*, Cambridge, Cambridge University Press.

Nelson, Richard R. and Winter, Sidney G. (1982), *An Evolutionary Theory of Economic Change*, Cambridge, MA, The Belknap Press.

Niskanen, William A. (1971), *Bureaucracy and Representative Government*, Chicago, Aldine Press.

Niskanen Jr, William A. (1994), *Bureaucracy and Public Economics*, Aldershot, Edward Elgar.

North, Douglass C. (1981), *Structure and Change in Economic History*, New York, W.W. Norton and Co.

North, Douglass C. (1984), 'Transaction Costs, Institutions, and Economic History', **140** *Journal of Institutional and Theoretical Economics/Zeitschrift für die Gesammte Staatswissenschaft*, 7 ff.

North, Douglass C. (1986), 'The New Institutional Economics', **142** *Journal of Institutional and Theoretical Economics/Zeitschrift für die Gesammte Staatswissenschaft*, 230-237.

North, Douglass C. (1989), 'A Transaction Cost Approach to the Historical Development of Polities and Economics', **145** *Journal of Institutional and Theoretical Economics/ Zeitschrift für die Gesammte Staatswissenschaft*, 661-668.

North, Douglass C. (1991), 'Institutions', **5** *Journal of Economic Perspectives*, 97-112.

North, Douglass C. (1993), 'Institutions and Credible Commitment', **149** *Journal of Institutional and Theoretical Economics/Zeitschrift für die Gesammte Staatswissenschaft*, 11-23.

North, Douglass C. (1994), 'Economic Performance Through Time', **84** *American Economic Review*, 359-368.

North, Douglas C. (1995), 'Five Propositions about Institutional Change', in Knight, Jack and Sened, Itai (eds), *Explaining Social Institutions*, Ann Arbor, University of Michigan Press, 15-26.

North, Douglass C. (1996), 'Economic Performance Through Time', in Alston, Lee J., Eggertsson, Thráinn and North, Douglass C. (eds) *Empirical Studies in Institutional Change*, New York, Cambridge University Press, 342-355.

North, Douglass C. and Wallis, J.J. (1994), 'Integrating Institutional Change and Technical Change in Economic History. A Transaction Cost Approach', **150** *Journal of Institutional and Theoretical Economics*, 609-624.

North, Douglass C. and Weingast, Barry R. (1996), 'Constitutions and Commitment: The Evolution of Institutions Governing Public Choice in Seventeenth-Century England', in Alston, Lee J., Eggertsson, Thráinn and North, Douglass C. (eds), *Empirical Studies in Institutional Change*, New York, Cambridge University Press, 134-165.

O'Driscoll Jr, Gerald P. and Rizzo, Mario J. (1996), *The Economics of Time and Ignorance*, London, Routledge (2nd edn).

Ogus, Anthony I. (1980), 'Economics, Liberty and the Common Law', **15** *Journal of the Society of Public Teachers of Law*, 42-57.

Ogus, Anthony I. (1989), 'Law and Spontaneous Order: Hayek's Contribution to Legal Theory', **16** *Journal of Law and Society*, 393-409.

Ogus, Anthony I. (1994), *Regulation - Legal Form and Economic Theory*, Oxford, Clarendon Press.

Ogus, A.I. and Veljanovski, C.G. (1984), *Readings in the Economics of Law and Regulation*, Oxford, Clarendon Press.

Oi, Walter J. (1973), 'The Economics of Product Safety', **4** *Bell Journal of Economics and Management*, 3-28.

Olson, Mancur (1965), *The Logic of Collective Action - Public Goods and the Theory of Groups*, Cambridge, MA, Harvard University Press.

Opp, Karl-Dieter (1979), 'Emergence and Effects of Social Norms - A Confrontation of Some Hypotheses of Sociology and Economics', **32** *Kyklos*, 775-801.

Opp, Karl-Dieter (1982), 'Evolutionary Emergence of Norms', **21** *British Journal of Social Psychology*, 139-149.

Opp, Karl-Dieter (1983), *Die Entstehung sozialer Normen*, Tübingen, J.C.B. Mohr.

Opp, Karl-Dieter (1988), 'Spontaneous Order and Tit for Tat. Some Hypotheses and an Empirical Test', **144** *Journal of Institutional and Theoretical Economics*, 374-385.

Opp, Karl-Dieter (1991), 'Economie et Sociologie: Les Fondements Communs', **2** *Journal des Économistes et des Études Humaines*, 63-82.

Paqué, Karl-Heinz (1985), 'How Far is Vienna from Chicago - An Essay on the Methodology of Two Schools of Dogmatic Liberalism', **38** *Kyklos*, 412-434.

Parisi, Francesco (1995), 'Toward a Theory of Spontaneous Law', **6** *Constitutional Political Economy*, 211-231.

Pearson, Heath (1997), *Origins of Law and Economics - The Economists' New Science of Law, 1830-1930*, Cambridge, Cambridge University Press.

Pejovich, Svetozar (1971), 'Towards a General Theory of Property Rights', **31** *Zeitschrift für Nationalökonomie*, 141-155.

Pejovich, Svetozar (1972), 'Towards an Economic Theory of the Creation and Specification of Property Rights', **30** *Review of Social Economics*, 309 ff.

Peltzman, Sam (1973), 'An Evaluation of Consumer Protection Legislation: The 1962 Drug Amendments', **81** *Journal of Political Economy*, 1049-1091.

Peltzman, Sam (1976), 'Toward a More General Theory of Regulation', **19** *Journal of Law and Economics*, 211-240.

Peltzman, Sam (1989), 'The Economic Theory of Regulation after a Decade of Deregulation', in Bailey, Martin and Winston, Clifford (eds), *Brookings Papers on Economic Activity: Microeconomics,* Washington DC, Brookings Institution, 1-41.

Pennock, J. Roland and Chapman, John W. (1982), *Ethics, Economics and Law*, New York, New York University Press.

Picker, Randal C. (1997), 'Simple Games in a Complex World: A Generative Approach to the Adoption of Norms', **64** *University of Chicago Law Review*, 1225-1288.

Plant, Arnold (1934a), 'The Economic Aspects of Copyright in Books', **1** *Economica*, 167-195.

Plant, Arnold (1934b), 'The Economic Theory Concerning Patents in Inventions', **1** *Economica*, 30-51.

Plant, Arnold (1953), *The New Commerce in Ideas and Intellectual Property*, London, University of London.

Posner, Richard A. (1971), 'Taxation by Regulation', **2** *Bell Journal of Economics and Management Science*, 22-50.

Posner, Richard A. (1972a), 'A Theory of Negligence', **1** *Journal of Legal Studies*, 29-96.

Posner, Richard A. (1972b), *Economic Analysis of Law*, Boston, Little, Brown and Co.

Posner, Richard A. (1973a), 'An Economic Approach to Legal Procedure and Judicial Administration', **2** *Journal of Legal Studies*, 399 ff.

Posner, Richard A. (1973b), 'Strict Liability: A Comment', **2** *Journal of Legal Studies*, 205-221.

Posner, Richard A. (1974), 'Theories of Economic Regulation', **5** *Bell Journal Economics and Management Science*, 335-358.

Posner, Richard A. (1975a), 'The Economic Approach to Law', **53** *Texas Law Review*, 757-782.

Posner, Richard A. (1975b), 'The Social Cost of Monopoly and Regulation', **83** *Journal of Political Economy*, 807-827.

Posner, Richard A. (1976), *Antitrust Law*, Chicago, University of Chicago Press.

Posner, Richard A. (1977), *Economic Analysis of Law*, Boston, Little, Brown and Co (2nd edn).

Posner, Richard A. (1981a), 'A Reply to Some Recent Criticisms of the Efficiency Theory of the Common Law', **9** *Hofstra Law Review*, 775-794.

Posner, Richard A. (1981b), *The Economics of Justice*, Cambridge, MA, Harvard University Press.

Posner, Richard A. (1986), *Economic Analysis of Law*, Boston, Little, Brown and Co (3rd edn).

Posner, Richard A. (1987a), 'The Law and Economics Movement', **77** *American Economic Review* (Papers and Proceedings), 1-13.

Posner, Richard A. (1987b), 'The Decline of Law as an Autonomous Discipline: 1962-1987', **100** *Harvard Law Review*, 761-780.

Posner, Richard A. (1988a), *Law and Literature - A Misunderstood Relation*, Cambridge, MA, Harvard UP.

Posner, Richard A. (1988b), 'Comment on Donohue', **22** *Law and Society Review*, 927-929.

Posner, Richard A. (1988c), 'Conventionalism: The Key to Law as an Autonomous Discipline', **38** *University of Toronto Law Journal*, 333-354.

Posner, Richard A. (1989), 'The Future of Law and Economics: A Comment on Ellickson', **65** *Chicago-Kent Law Review*, 57-62.

Posner, Richard A. (1990a), *The Problems of Jurisprudence*, Cambridge, MA, Harvard University Press.

Posner, Richard A. (1990b), *Cardozo - A Study in Reputation*, Chicago, The University of Chicago Press.

Posner, Richard A. (1992a), *Economic Analysis of Law*, Boston, Little, Brown and Co (4th edn).

Posner, Richard A. (1992b), *Sex and Reason*, Cambridge, Harvard University Press.

Posner, Richard A. (ed.) (1992c), *The Essential Holmes: Selections from the Letters, Speeches, Judicial Opinions, and Other Writings of Oliver Wendell Holmes, Jr.*, Chicago, The University of Chicago Press.

Posner, Richard A. (1993), 'Gary Becker's Contributions to Law and Economies', **22** *Journal of Legal Studies*, 211-215.

Posner, Richard A. (1995a), *Aging and Old Age*, Chicago, The University of Chicago Press.

Posner, Richard A. (1995b), 'The Sociology of the Sociology of Law: A View from Economics', **2** *European Journal of Law and Economics*, 263-284.

Posner, Richard A. (1996a), *The Federal Courts: Challenge and Reform*, Cambridge, MA, Harvard University Press, (2nd edn).

Posner, Richard A. (1996b), *Law and Legal Theory in England and America*, Oxford, Clarendon Press.

Posner, Richard A. (1998), *Economic Analysis of Law*, Aspen Law and Business (5th edn).

Posner, Richard A. and Parisi, Francesco (1997), *Law and Economics - Vol. 1 Theoretical and Methodological Issues; Vol. 2 Contracts, Torts and Criminal Law; Vol. 3 Other Areas in Private and Public Law*, Cheltenham, Edward Elgar.

Posner, Richard A. and Silbaugh, Katharine B. (1996), *A Guide to America's Sex Laws*, Chicago, The University of Chicago Press.

Priest, George L. (1977), 'The Common Law Process and the Selection of Efficient Rules', **6** *Journal of Legal Studies*, 65-82.

Priest, George L. (1980), 'Selective Characteristics of Litigation', **9** *Journal of Legal Studies*, 399-421.

Priest, George L. (1993), 'The Origins of Utility Regulation and the 'Theories of Regulation' Debate', **36** *Journal of Law and Economics*, 289-323.

Priest, George L. and Klein, Benjamin (1984), 'The Selection of Disputes for Litigation', **13** *Journal of Legal Studies*, 1-55.

Reder, Manfred (1987), 'Chicago School', in Eatwell, John, Milgate, Murray and Newman, Peter (eds), *The New Palgrave - The World of Economics*, New York, W.W. Norton, 40-50.

Reese, David A. (1989), 'Does the Common Law Evolve?', **12** *Hamline Law Review*, 321-353.

Ridley, Matt (1997), *The Origins of Virtue - Human Instincts and the Evolution of Cooperation*, New York, Viking Press.

Riker, William H. and Weimer, David L. (1993), 'The Economic and Political Liberalization of Socialism: The Fundamental Problem of Property Rights', in Frankel

Paul, Ellen, Miller Jr, Fred D. and Paul, Jeffrey (eds), *Liberalism and the Economic Order,* Cambridge, Cambridge University Press, 79-102.

Rizzo, Mario J. (ed.) (1979a), *Time, Uncertainty, and Disequilibrium - Exploration of Autrian Themes*, Lexington, MA, D.C. Heath and Co (Lexington Books).

Rizzo, Mario J. (1979b), 'Uncertainty, Subjectivity, and the Economic Analysis of Law', in Rizzo, Mario J. (ed.), *Time, Uncertainty, and Disequilibrium - Exploration of Austrian Themes,* Lexington, MA, D.C. Heath and Co (Lexington Books), 71-95.

Rizzo, Mario J. (1980a), 'Change in the Common Law: Legal and Economic Considerations (Symposium)', **9** *Journal of Legal Studies*, 189-429.

Rizzo, Mario J. (1980b), 'Law Amid Flux: The Economics of Negligence and Strict Liability in Tort', **9** *Journal of Legal Studies*, 291-318.

Rizzo, Mario J. (1980c), 'The Mirage of Efficiency', **8** *Hofstra Law Review*, 648-658.

Rizzo, Mario J. (1980d), 'Can There be a Principle of Explanation in Common Law Decisions: A Comment on Priest', **9** *Journal of Legal Studies*, 423-427.

Rizzo, Mario J. (1981), 'The Imputation Theory of Proximate Cause: An Economic Framework', **15** *Georgia Law Review*, 1007-1038.

Rizzo, Mario J. (1982a), 'The Economic Loss Problem: A Comment on Bishop', **2** *Oxford Journal of Legal Studies*, 197-206.

Rizzo, Mario J. (1982b), 'A Theory of Economic Loss in the Law of Torts', **11** *Journal of Legal Studies*, 281-310.

Rizzo, Mario J. (1985), 'Rules versus Cost-Benefit Analysis in the Common Law', **4** *Cato Journal*, 865-884.

Rizzo, Mario J. (1987), 'Foreword - Fundamentals of Causation', **63** *Chicago-Kent Law Review*, 397-680.

Rizzo, Mario J. and Arnold, F.S. (1980), 'Causal Apportionment in the Law of Torts: An Economic Theory', **80** *Columbia Law Review*, 1399-1429.

Rizzo, Mario J. and Arnold, Frank S. (1987), 'An Economic Framework for Statutory Interpretation', **50** *Law and Contemporary Problems*, 165-180.

Robertson, John (1987), 'Scottish Enlightenment', in Eatwell, John, Milgate, Murray and Newman, Peter (eds), *The New Palgrave - The World of Economics,* New York, W.W. Norton, 634-639.

Roe, Mark J. (1994), *Strong Managers, Weak Owners - The Political Roots of American Corporate Finance*, Princeton, Princeton University Press.

Rosa, Jean-Jacques and Aftalion, Florin (1977), *L'Economie Retrouvée - Vieilles Critiques et Nouvelles Méthodes*, Paris, Economica.

Rosenberg, Nathan and Birdzell Jr, L.E. (1986), *How the West Grew Rich - The Economic Transformation of the Industrial World,* New York, Basic Books.

Rosenthal, Jean-Laurent (1992), *The Fruits of Revolution - Property Rights, Litigation and French Agriculture, 1700-1860 (Political Economy of Institutions and Decisions)*, Cambridge, Cambridge University Press.

Roundtable (1997), 'The Future of Law and Economics: Looking Forward - Roundtable Discussion', **64** *University of Chicago Law Review*, 1132-1165.

Rousseau, Jean Jacques ([1755] 1971), *Discours sur Les Sciences et Les Arts - Discours sur l'Origine des Inégalités*, Paris, Flammarion.

Rowley, Charles K. (1988b), 'Rent-Seeking versus Directly Unproductive Profit-Seeking Activities', in Rowley, Charles K., Tollison, Robert D. and Tullock, Gordon (eds), *The Political Economy of Rent-Seeking,* Boston, Kluwer, 15-25.

Rowley, Charles K. (1989a), 'The Common Law in Public Choice Perspective: A Theoretical and Institutional Critique', **12** *Hamline Law Review*, 355-383.

Rowley, Charles K. (1989b), 'Public Choice and the Economic Analysis of Law', in Nicholas Mercuro (ed.), *Law and Economics,* Boston, Kluwer Academic Publishers, 123-173.

Rowley, Charles K. and Brough, Wayne (1987), 'The Efficiency of the Common Law: A New Institutional Economics Perspective', in Pethig, Rudiger and Schlieper, Ulrich (eds), *Efficiency, Institutions and Economic Policy: Proceedings of a Workshop held by the Sonderforschungsbereich 5 at the University of Mannheim, June 1986,* Berlin, Springer-Verlag, 103-121.

Rowley, Charles K., Tollison, Robert D. and Tullock, Gordon (1988), *The Political Economy of Rent-Seeking*, Boston, Kluwer.

Rubin, Paul (1977), 'Why is the Common Law Efficient?', **6** *Journal of Legal Studies*, 51-63.

Rubin, Paul H. (1982), 'Common Law and Statute Law', **11** *Journal of Legal Studies*, 205-223.

Samuels, Warren J. (1965), 'Legal-Economic Policy: A Bibliographical Survey', **58** *Law Library Journal*, 230-252.

Samuels, Warren J. (1971), 'The Interrelationship between Legal and Economic Processes', **14** *Journal of Law and Economics*, 435-450.

Samuels, Warren J. (1972), 'In Defense of a Positive Approach to Government as an Economic Variable', **15** *Journal of Law and Economics*, 453-459.

Samuels, Warren J. (1973), 'Legal-Economic Policy: A Bibliographical Survey, 1965-1972', **66** *Law Library Journal*, 96-110.

Samuels, Warren J. (1974), 'The Coase Theorem and the Study of Law and Economics', **14** *Natural Resources Journal*, 1-33.

Samuels, Warren J. (1975), 'John Henry Beale's Lectures on Jurisprudence, 1909', **29** *University of Miami Law Review*, 260-280.

Samuels, Warren J. (ed.) (1976a), *The Chicago School of Political Economy*, East Lansing, Mich., Association of Evolutionary Economics and Michigan State University.

Samuels, Warren J. (1976b), 'Introduction: Commons and Clark on Law and Economics', **10** *Journal of Economic Issues*, 743-749.

Samuels, Warren J. (1976c), 'Further Limits to Chicago School Doctrine', in Samuels, Warren J. (ed.), *The Chicago School of Political Economy,* East Lansing, Mich., Association of Evolutionary Economics and Michigan State University, 397-457.

Samuels, Warren J. (1990), 'Old versus the New Institutionalism', **2** *Review of Political Economy*, 83-86.

Samuels, Warren J. (1998a), *Founding of Institutional Economics*, London, Routledge.

Samuels, Warren J. (1998b), *Law and Economics: The Early Journal Literature*, London, Pickering and Chatto Ltd.

Samuels, Warren J. (1998c), *European Economists of the Early 20th Century vol. 1: Studies of Neglected Thinkers of Belgium, France, the Netherlands*, Cheltenham, Edward Elgar Publishers.

Samuels, Warren J. and Mercuro, Nicholas (1984), 'Posnerian Law and Economics on the Bench', **4** *International Review of Law and Economics*, 107-130.

Samuels, Warren J. and Rutherford, Malcolm (1998), *Classics in Institutional Economics: The Founders - 1890-1945 (5 vols)*, London, Pickering and Chatto Ltd.

Samuels, Warren J. and Schmid, A. Allan (1981), *Law and Economics: An Institutional Perspective*, Boston, Martinus Nijhoff Publishing.

Schmid, A. Allen (1965), 'Property, Power and Progress', **41** *Land Economics*, 275 ff.

Schmid, A. Allen (1976), 'The Economics of Property Rights: A Review Article', in Samuels, Warren J. (ed.), *The Chicago School of Political Economy*, East Lansing, Mich., Association of Evolutionary Economics and Michigan State University, 469-479.

Schmid, A. Allan (1978), *Property, Power, and Public Choice - An Inquiry into Law and Economics*, New York, NY, Praeger Publishers.

Schmid, A. Allan (1989a), 'Economy and State: An Institutional Theory of Process and Learning', in Samuels, Warren (ed.), *Fundamentals of the Economic Role of Government*, Westport, CT, Greenwood.

Schmid, A. Allan (1989b), 'Law and Economics: An Institutional Perspective', in Mercuro, Nicholas (ed.), *Law and Economics*, Boston, Kluwer Academic Publishers, 57-86.

Schmid, A. Allan (1994), 'Institutional Law and Economics', **1** *European Journal of Law and Economics*, 33-51.

Schmidtchen, Dieter (1993), 'Time, Uncertainty, and Subjectivism: Giving More Body to Law and Economics', **13** *International Review of Law and Economics*, 61-84.

Schüller, Alfred (ed.) (1983), *Property Rights und ökonomische Theorie* (Property Rights and Economic Theory), München, Verlag Franz Vahlen.

Scully, Gerald W. (1987), 'The Choice of Law and the Extent of Liberty', **143** *Journal of Institutional and Theoretical Economics*, 595-615.

Secretan, Catherine (1990), *Les Privilèges Berceau de la Liberté - La Révolte des Pays-Bas: aux Sources de la Pensée Politique Moderne (1566-1619)* (Privileges as the Mainspring of Liberty - The Dutch Revolt: Return to the Sources of Modern Political Thought (1566-1619)), Paris, Vrin.

Simon, Herbert A. (1959), 'Theories of Decision-Making in Economics and Behavioral Science', **49** *American Economic Review*, 253-283.

Simon, Herbert A. (1972), 'Theories of Bounded Rationality', in McGuire, C.B. and Radner, Roy (eds), *Decision and Organization: A Volume in Honor of Jacob Marschak*, Minneapolis, University of Minnesota Press (2nd edn), 161-176.

Simon, Herbert A. (1979), 'From Substantive to Procedural Rationality', in Hahn, Frank and Hollis, Martin (eds), *Philosophy and Economic Theory*, Oxford, Oxford University Press, 65-85.

Simon, Herbert A. (1986a), 'Rationality in Psychology and Economics', in Hogarth, Robin M. and Reder, Melvin W. (eds), *Rational Choice - The Contrast between Economics and Psychology*, Chicago, The University of Chicago Press, 25-40.

Simon, Herbert A. (1986b), 'Theories of Bounded Rationality', in McGuire, C.B. and Radner, Roy (eds), *Decision and Organization*, Minneapolis, University of Minnesota Press (2nd edn), 161-176.

Simpson, A.W.B. (1975), 'Innovations in Nineteenth Century Contract Law', **91** *Law Quarterly Review*, 247 ff.

Simpson, A.W.B. (1979), 'The Horwitz Thesis and the History of Contracts', **46** *University of Chicago Law Review*, 533-601.

Simpson, A.W.B. (1985), 'Quackery and Contract Law: The Case of the Carbolic Smoke Ball', **14** *Journal of Legal Studies*, 345-389.

Simpson, A.W.B. (1988), 'Legal Reasoning Anatomized: On Steiner's Moral Argument and Social Vision in the Courts', **13** *Law and Social Inquiry*, 637 ff.

Skogh, Göran (ed.) (1978), *Law and Economics - Report from a Symposium in Lund, Sweden 24 - 26 August 1977*, Lund, Juridiska Föreningen i Lund.

Smith, Adam ([1776] 1937), *An Inquiry into the Nature and Causes of the Wealth of Nations*, New York, The Modern Library.

Smith, Adam ([1776] 1982), *Lectures on Jurisprudence*, Indianapolis, LibertyClassics.

Stearns, Maxwell L. (ed.) (1997), *Public Choice and Public Law - Readings and Commentary*, Cincinnati, Anderson Publishing Co.

Stigler, George J. (1970), 'The Optimum Enforcement of Laws', **68** *Journal of Political Economy*, 526-536.

Stigler, George J. (1971), 'The Theory of Economic Regulation', **2** *Bell Journal of Economics and Management Science*, 3-21.

Streit, Manfred E. (1992), 'The Freiburg School of Law and Economics', **148** *Journal of Institutional and Theoretical Economics*, 675-704.

Sugden, Robert (1986), *The Economics of Rights, Co-operation and Welfare*, Oxford, Basil Blackwell.

Sugden, Robert (1989), 'Spontaneous Order', **3** *Journal of Economic Perspectives*, 85-97.

Teijl, Rob and Holzhauer, Rudi W. (1990), 'Pluriformiteit in de Rechtseconomie: een Verkenning van Scholen (Pluriformity in Law and Economics: An Exploration of the Schools)', **39** *Ars Aequi*, 617-631.

Teijl, Rob and Holzhauer, Rudi W. (1997), *Wisselende Perspectieven in de Rechtseconomie* (Varying Perspectives in Law and Economics), Arnhem, Gouda Quint.

Terrebonne, R.P. (1981), 'A Strictly Evolutionary Model of Common Law', **10** *Journal of Legal Studies*, 397-407.

Thornton, Mark (1991), *The Economics of Prohibition*, Salt Lake City, University of Utah Press.

Tiebout, Charles M. (1956), 'A Pure Theory of Local Expenditures', **64** *Journal of Political Economy*, 416-424.

Tollison, Robert D. (1982), 'Rent-Seeking: A Survey', **35** *Kyklos*, 575-602.

Tollison, Robert D. (1987), 'Is the Theory of Rent-Seeking Here to Stay?', in Rowley, Charles K. (ed.), *Democracy and Public Choice - Essays in Honor of Gordon Tullock*, Oxford, Basil Blackwell, 143-157.

Tollison, Robert D. (1997), 'Rent Seeking', in Mueller, Dennis C. (ed.), *Perspectives on Public Choice - A Handbook*, Cambridge, Cambridge University Press, 506-525.

Trebilcock, Michael J. (1987), 'The Social Insurance-Deterrence Dilemma of Modern American Tort Law: A Canadian Perspective on the Liability Insurance Crisis', **24** *San Diego Law Review*, 929-1002.

Trebilcock, Michael J. (1989), 'The Future of Tort Law: Mapping the Contours of the Debate', **15** *Canadian Business Law Journal*, 471-488.

Tullock, Gordon (1987), 'Rent Seeking', in Eatwell, John, Milgate, Murray and Newman, Peter (eds), *The New Palgrave - The World of Economics*, New York, W.W. Norton, 604-609.

Tullock, Gordon (1989), *Economics of Special Privilege and Rent Seeking*, Hingham, MA, Kluwer Academic Publishers.

Tullock, Gordon (1993), *Rent Seeking* (The Shaftesbury Papers, 2), Aldershot, Hants, UK, Edward Elgar.

Tversky, Amos and Kahneman, Daniel (1974), 'Judgment under Uncertainty: Heuristics and Biases', **185** *Science*, 1124-1131.

Tversky, Amos and Kahneman, Daniel (1986a), 'The Framing of Decisions and the Psychology of Choice (Readings in Social and Political Theory)', in Elster, Jon (ed.), *Rational Choice,* Elster, New York University Press, 123-141.

Tversky, Amos and Kahneman, Daniel (1986b), 'Rational Choice and the Framing of Decisions', in Hogarth, Robin M. and Reder, Melvin W. (eds), *Rational Choice - The Contrast between Economics and Psychology,* Chicago, The University of Chicago Press, 67-94.

Tversky, Amos, Slovic, Paul and Kahneman, Daniel (1990), 'Rational Choice and the Framing of Decisions', **80** *American Economic Review*, 215 ff.

Ullmann-Margalit, Edna (1977), *The Emergence of Norms*, Oxford, Clarendon Press.

Ullmann-Margalit, Edna (1978), 'Invisible Hand Explanations', **39** *Synthese*, 263-291.

Umbeck, John R. (1977a), 'A Theory of Contract Choice and the California Gold Rush', **20** *Journal of Law and Economics*, 421–437.

Umbeck, John R. (1977b), 'The California Gold Rush: A Study of Emerging of Property Rights', **14** *Explorations in Economic History*, 197-226.

Umbeck, John R. (1981a), 'Might Makes Right: A Theory of the Foundation and Initial Distribution of Property Rights', **19** *Economic Inquiry*, 38-59.

Umbeck, John R. (1981b), *A Theory of Property Rights with Application to the California Gold Rush*, Ames, Iowa State University Press.

Vanberg, Viktor J. (1994), 'Carl Menger's Evolutionary and John R. Common's Collective Approach to Institutions: A Comparison', in Vanberg, Viktor J. (ed.), *Rules and Choice in Economics,* London, Routledge, 144-163.

Vanberg, Viktor (1998a), 'Austrian School of Economics and the Evolution of Institutions', in Newman, Peter (ed.), *The New Palgrave Dictionary of Economics and the Law, Vol. 1,* London, MacMillan, 134-140.

Vanberg, Viktor (1998b), 'Freiburg School of Law and Economics', in Newman, Peter (ed.), *The New Palgrave Dictionary of Economics and the Law, Vol. 2,* London, Mac Millan, 172-179.

Veljanovski, Cento G. (1980), 'The Economic Approach to Law - A Critical Introduction', **7** *British Journal of Law and Society*, 158-193.

Veljanovski, Cento G. (1981), 'Wealth Maximization, Law and Ethics - On the Limits of Economic Efficiency', **1** *International Review of Law and Economics*, 5-28.

Veljanovski, Cento G. (1982), *The New Law-and-Economics - A Research Review*, Oxford, Centre for Socio-Legal Studies.

Veljanovski, Cento G. (1990), *The Economics of Law - An Introductory Text*, London, Institute of Economic Affairs.

Voigt, Stefan (1992), 'On the Internal Consistency of Hayek's Evolutionary Oriented Constitutional Economics - Some General Remarks', **3** *Journal des Économistes et des Études Humaines*, 461-476.

Voigt, Stefan (1996), 'Pure Eclecticism - The Tool Kit of the Constitutional Economist', **7** *Constitutional Political Economy*, 177-196.

Voigt, Stefan (1997), 'Positive Constitutional Economics: A Survey', **90** *Public Choice*, 11-53.

Wagner, Richard E. (1990), *To Promote The General Welfare - Market Processes vs. Political Transfers*, San Francisco, CA, Pacific Research Institute for Public Policy.

Webber, Carolyn and Wildavsky, Aaron (1986), *A History of Taxation and Expenditure in the Western World*, New York, Simon and Schuster.

Weingast, Barry R. (1993), 'Constitutions as Governance Structures: The Political Foundations of Secure Markets', **149** *Journal of Institutional and Theoretical Economics*, 286-311.

Weingast, Barry R. (1995), 'The Economic Role of Political Institutions: Market-Preserving Federalism and Economic Development', **11** *Journal of Law, Economics, and Organization*, 1-31.

Williamson, Oliver E. (1985), *The Economic Institutions of Capitalism - Firms, Markets, Relational Contracting*, New York, The Free Press.

Williamson, Oliver E. (1986), *Economic Organization - Firms, Markets and Policy Control*, New York, New York University Press.

Williamson, Oliver E. (1996), *The Mechanisms of Governance*, Oxford, Oxford University Press.

Windisch, Rupert (1984), 'Politische Verfügungsrechte, Umverteilung und konstitutionelle Budgetreform (Political Disposition rights, Redistribution and Constitutional Budget Reform)', in Neumann, Manfred (ed.), *Ansprüche, Eigentums- und Verfügungsrechte*, Berlin, Duncker and Humblot, 569-607.

Wisconsin (1997), 'Special Issue on Law and Society and Law and Economics: Common Ground, Irreconciliable Differences, New Directions', **1997** *Wisconsin Law Review*, 375-627.

Wonnell, Christopher T. (1986), 'Contract Law and the Austrian School of Economics', **54** *Fordham Law Review*, 507-543.

0305
LAW AND ECONOMICS IN AUSTRIA

Wolfgang Weigel
University of Vienna

Abstract

This note concentrates on the state of 'law and economics' in Austria after the emergence of the economic analysis of law. The long tradition of research in bringing together legal and economic aspects particularly in the field of regulation and dating back to the eighteenth century is also adressed. Moreover, some reasons why modern law and economics have encountered a fairly weak reception for almost two decades are suggested. Finally, the quite encouraging development both in teaching and research during the 1990s is emphasized.
JEL classification: A12, K00
Keywords: Austria, law and economics, Paradigms, Teaching, Research

1. General Observations

In Austria, the mutual dependence of economics and law has been recognized literally for more than two hundred years. However, from the beginning, public law and, more specifically, regulation - or 'Wirtschaftsverwaltungsrecht', to use the appropriate German term - received much more attention than civil law. Evidence for this assertion is provided by a textbook, entitled *The Principles of Police, Action and Finance*, written by one of the most influential counsellors to the sovereign of the Austrian empire, Joseph von Sonnenfels, which was published in three volumes beginning in the year 1765, where the term police refers to public administration, action to private trade and finance to fiscal issues of government. Here, and in most of the later work treating these issues, however, there was no common denominator in terms of a distinct methodology. On the contrary, one of the particular features of modern law and economics is that legal issues are approached by means of the tools of microeconomic theory. Taking the latter characteristic as the essential feature of law and economics, as it is understood nowadays, contrary to the general concern about economic issues in legal reasoning, the interest in that field of research in Austria is not very great.

Its reception in the academic sphere is, however, considerably ahead of that in the secular world. Among scientists, lawyers appear to be more concerned than economists. This is not surprising, since it is mainly for lawyers that the methodology involved gives rise to a radical change in the way of approaching legal problems, whereas economists are traditionally more accustomed to deriving policy conclusions from their analysis, which may very well comprise changes in prevailing regulations. A typical example is the work on opening hours of shops by the economists Clemenz and Inderst (1989). Following the said tradition, among lawyers those working in the field of public law (constitutional law, administrative law as well as regulation) are generally more interested than those in private law. In the latter, the main attitude is scepticism if not prejudice, as can be seen from quotations by, for example Mayer-Maly (1991, p. 220, note to p. 129) and Bydlinski (1988, pp. 282 passim). This conclusion rests upon three sources: first, the examination and classification of existing literature; second, quotations by leading scientists; and third, the response to a mail survey in the course of the preparation for this paper.

The information which follows will illustrate and explain the views expressed above.

2. Predominant Paradigms

One reason for the weak impact of law and economics both in the academic sphere and civil practice of law seems to be the predominant role of distinct paradigms in educational training. Legal scholars are basically brought up in the spirit of legal positivism. Even more recent ideas such as that of a value-related understanding of law (Bydlinski, 1982) leave hardly any space for the economic approach to law. Dissenting approaches are rarely considered. Even in applied research conventional juridical craftsmanship is used; one typical example is that by the lawyers Aicher and Lessiak (1989) on discount and competition, which does not contain even one single reference to the economic analysis of law.

Economists in turn are mainly trained in neoclassical economic theory, as far as microeconomics is concerned, whereas late Keynesian views predominate in macroeconomics until recently at least (see Frey and Kirchgässner, 1994, p. 477). Nevertheless, the research programs suggested by scholars of modern law and economics are occasionally adopted. This can be inferred from the lists of publications submitted to the present author following a call for submission: in many of the accompanying letters it is stated that the publications enlisted are understood as being related to law and economics, without taking into account the methodology underlying the economic approach to law.

3. Professional Structure

Lawyers play a predominant role in the Austrian economy. They still hold most of the leading positions in public administration and in private business. More recently economists have caught up to some extent, but most of them received their degrees in business administration, not in economics proper.

However, lawyers receive educational training in basic economics (both macro and micro) whereas economists are taught basic private and public law in turn. Moreover, civil servants, who seek achievement to higher posts, must take supplementary courses in economics as well as distinct fields of law at the federal academy of administration, irrespective of their university degree.

4. Prejudices and Ignorance

One reason for the weak reception of the economic approach to law seems to be a general lack of knowledge about the state of the art. More specifically, the entire approach is generally associated with the 'Chicago school', which is held to be primarily efficiency-orientated, taking the Pareto-efficient allocations of competitive markets as a reference standard. It is generally agreed that therefore issues of (social) justice do not receive the attention they deserve in legal reasoning. These conjectures are supported by the fact that the predominant references which can be found in the literature are to criticise Richard Posner, as, for example, in the writings of the most influential authors, Bydlinsky (1988) and Mayer-Maly (1991).

Consequently it is generally ignored that many outstanding scholars of law and economics have taken a much broader view than that of the Chicago school for a long time. It is disturbing to see that their basic ideas have hardly yet entered university classrooms. Fortunately, there is one exception: the closely related 'property rights - public choice approach', as it has been termed by Goldberg (1980, p. 402) is actually being promoted now in the economic departments of the universities of Linz, Innsbruck, and Vienna and also in the department of sociology of the University of Graz. From here, it would only be a short step to adopt law and economics more generally.With the exception of the University of Vienna, where regular lectures and seminars are held, this step has not be taken.

Unfortunately, responses to the questionaire mentioned earlier show that the situation with respect to teaching is even worse in law schools. There, the ideas underlying the economic analysis of law are taught only occasionally in the course of classes held on topics which are traditionally in the domain of law and economics, such as corporate law, environmental law and criminal law.

5. Challenges by Legal and Economic Practice

Contrary to the weak overall interest in modern law and economics, the Austrian economy would offer itself as an ideal playground for scholary work in that field. It is still highly regulated, with regulations applying to competition, barriers to entry and administered prices, to name but a few issues. There is also growing concern about environmental standards accompanied by an ever-increasing number of legal measures.

More recently predominant policy issues such as privatization of public utilities and deregulation, as well as the harmonization of the Austrian legal framework with that of the European Union, create new challenges for both economists and lawyers. The problems associated with these newly emerging issues would call for appropriate tools of analysis and advice. Therefore, time may prepare the ground for a larger perception of the fruitfulness of the economic approach to law.

6. A Necessarily Brief History

In adressing the history of economic thought in the field of modern law and economics, one must be aware that it is both rooted in and therefore closely related to a variety of other fields of research. These are nowadays frequently summarized under the label of New Institutional Economics, and they comprise many very important contributions, for example on the evolution of social order and the economic theory of democracy. The most prominent authors associated with these contributions are Hayek and Schumpeter respectively. Unfortunately it is beyond the scope of this article to take full account of their work. Moreover, although they are Austrians by birth and from origin, these authors - like several others - received adequate acknowledgement for their pathbreaking contributions abroad only after their emigration from Austria. Therefore, their pioneering work should be attributed to Austria only with reservations.

But even with respect to law and economics in a narrow sense, despite its generally weak reception, Austria may be looked at as an important post of forerunners: as far back as 1897, Herrmann published a book on *Theorie der Versicherung* (Theory of Insurance), in which he introduced ideas which are quite close to those which a century later became known as the Coase theorem. Another pioneering work was *Rechte und Verhältnisse vom Standpunkt der Volkswirthschaftslehre* (Rights and Relations from the Point of View of Economics) by Eugen Böhm-Bawerk in 1881. In this small book, Böhm-Bawerk acknowledges rights and entitlements to be valuable assets. The title of Victor Mataja's book *Das Recht des Schadenersatzes vom Standpunkt der Nationalökonomie* (The Law of Damages from an Economic Perspective), published in 1888, ought to sound familiar to present day scholars. Finally, the work of K.G. Wurzel deserves attention here. Writing at the time of World War One, Wurzel strongly advocated interdisciplinary reasoning for lawyers (see also Weissel, 1991).

After World War Two, questions of property and wealth were discussed in the course of both the adoption of ORDO-liberalism and a newly emerging general interest in the catholic doctrine on social justice and the distribution of private property (see for example Streissler, 1973). These writings can be seen as loosely linked to the subject at hand.

During the 1980s, the first writings were published which explicitly contained reference to the economic analysis of law. A landmark for Austria, unfortunately with weak impact on the interest in general, however, was the 7th annual conference of the European Association for law and economics, held in Vienna in 1989, arranged by the author. It was not until the early 1990s, though, that the economic analysis of law was explicitly taught for the first time in classes in the economics department of Vienna university. Occasionally interdisciplinary seminars were held, and in the Technical University of Vienna, a group of scientists who had assumed Neoinstitutionalism started a critical dispute about the relevance of the modern property-rights doctrine.

In Vienna as well as Graz, books by Hafner (1987), Huber (1995) and Gimpel-Hinteregger (1994) were published, which were basically revised versions of 'Habiltation' theses and contained reflections on law and economics.

A research program on 'Dynamic Models of Optimal Law Enforcement' was established at the Institute for Econometrics, Operation Research and Systems Theory, University of Technology, which is devoted to the application of game theory and operations research to the economics of crime, more specifically corruption and illicit drugs.

Also, more recently, the first doctoral theses have been written explicitly adressing the approach: Grabenwarter (1994) and Freyer (1994).

Law and economics was finally accepted as complementary course for the study of both law and economics in 1994. Approximately 20 to 25 scientists are now working in this field.

Bibliography on law and economics in Austria (0305)

Böhm, Stephan (1987), 'Handlungsrechte, Wettbewerb und Privatisierung (Property Rights, Competition and Privatization)', **34** *Wirtschaftspolitische Blätter*, 576-583.

Clemenz, Gerhard and Inderst, Alfred (1989), *Ökonomische Analyse der Ladenöffnungszeiten* (Economic Analysis of Shop Opening Hours), Vienna, Manz Publishers, 128 p.

Dawid, H. and Feichtinger, G. (1995), 'On the Persistence of Corruption', **186** *Forschungsbericht/Research Memorandum*, Institute for Econometrics, Operation Research and System Theory, University of Technology, Vienna.

Feichtinger, Gustav (1995), 'Crime and Punishment: A Dynamic Approach', **195** *Forschungsbericht/Research Memorandum*, Institute for Econometrics, Operation Research and System Theory, University of Technology, Vienna.

Feichtinger, G., Forst, Ch.V. and Piccardi, C. (1993), 'A Nonlinear Dynamic Model for the Dynastic Cycle', **165** *Forschungsbericht/Research Memorandum*, Institute for Econometrics, Operation Research and System Theory, University of Technology, Vienna.

Freyer, Susanne (1994), 'Umwelthaftung aus der Sicht der Ökonomischen Analyse des Rechts (Environmental Liability from a Law and Economics Perspective)', Doctoral Dissertation, University of Vienna.

Gantner, Manfried, (1984), 'Schwierigkeiten der Verrechtlichung ökonomischer Tatbestände (The Difficulty of Transforming Economic Issues into Law)', **31** *Wirtschaftspolitische Blätter*, 423-430.

Gantner, Manfred (1988), 'Die neue Luftverkehrsordnung der Europäischen Gemeinschaft und ihre Auswirkungen auf die Austrian Airlines und die EG-Integrationspolitik (New European Community Air Transport Regulation and its Impact on Austrian Airlines and Integration Policies)', **14** *Wirtschaft und Gesellschaft*, 337-357.

Gantner, Manfred (1988), 'Öffentliche (De-)Regulierung im Zusammenhang mit der österreichischen Post- und Telegraphenverwaltung (Public Deregulation of Postal Serevices)', **8** *Finanzwissenschaftliche Diskussionsreihe*.

Gantner, Manfried (ed.) (1991), *Handbuch des öffentlichen Haushaltswesens* (The Handbook of Public Budgeting), Vienna, Manz Publishers, 416 p.

Gantner, Manfried (1993), 'Anmerkungen zur Universitätsreform aus finanzwissenschafltichen Sicht (Notes on Reforming Universities from a Public Finance Perspective)', in Strasser, R. (ed.), *Beiträge zum Universitätsrecht*, Vienna, 119-139.

Gantner, Manfried (ed.) (1994), *Budgetausgliederung - Fluch(t) oder Segen?* (Budgetary Disembodiment - Vice or Virtue?), Vienna, Manz Publishers, 232 p.

Gantner, Manfried (1995), 'Energieabgaben als Ländersteuern? Wirkungsanalyse und finanzverfassungsrechtliche Überlegungen am Beispiel des Feldversuch Vorarlbergs (Duties on Energy as Provincial Taxes?)', **21** *Wirtschaft und Gesellschaft*, 47-76.

Genser, Bernd (ed.) (1987), *Abfertigungsregeln im Spannungsfeld der Wirtschaftspolitik* (Rules of Indemnification as a Current Problem in Economic Policy), Vienna, Manz Publishers, 272 p.

Gimpel-Hinteregger, Monika (1994), *Grundfragen der Umwelthaftung* (Fundamental Issues in Environmental Liabiltiy), Vienna, Manz Publishers.

Grabenwarter, Christoph (1992), *Ladenschlußrecht* (Regulation of Shopping Hours), Vienna-New York , 1992.

Grabenwarter, Christoph (1994), *Rechtliche und ökonomische Überlegungen zur Erwerbsfreiheit* (Legal and Economic Considerations on the Freedom of Enterprise), Vienna.

Gragnani, A., Feichtinger, G. and Rinaldi, S. (1994), *Dynamics of Drug Consumption: A Theoretical Model*, 94-77, Working Paper, International Institute for Applied Systems Analysis, Laxenburg.

Gragnani, A., Rinaldi, S. and Feichtinger, G. (1995), 'Slow-Fast Limit Cycles in Controlled Drug Markets', **185** *Forschungsbericht/Research Memorandum*, Institute for Econometrics, Operation Research and System Theory, University of Technology, Vienna.

Hafner, Gerhard (1987), *Seerechtliche Verteilung von Nutzungsrechten* (The Assignment of Property Rights on the Sea), Vienna-New York, Springer Publishers, 533 p.

Hanreich, Hanspeter (1983), 'Verbraucherpolitik durch Wettbewerbsrecht (Consumer Policy by Competition Law)', in Korinek, Karl (ed.), *Beiträge zum Wirtschaftsrecht*, Vienna, Orac Publishers, 539-560.

Huber, Christian (1990), 'Schadensbemessung und ökonomische Analyse des Rechts (The Measurement of Damage and the Economic Analysis of Law)', in Harald Baum, Christoph Engel, Oliver Remien and Manfred Wenchstern (eds), *Jahrbuch Junger Zivilrechtswissenschaftler 1990, Kapitalmarktrecht, Schadensrecht, Privatrecht und deutsche Einheit*, Richard Boorberg Verlag, 133-150.

Huber, Christian (1995), *Fragen der Schadensberechnung* (Issues in Calculating Damages), Vienna, Manz, 2nd edn.

Lewisch, Peter (1989), *Erwerbsfreiheit und Bedarfsprüfung* (The Freedom to Earn one's Living as Subjected to Regulations Concerning Needs), Vienna, Marktwirtschaftliche Schriften des Carl Menger Institutes, 47 p.

Lewisch, Peter (1995), *Punishment, Public Law Enforcement and the Protective State*, Vienna-New York, Springer.

Musger, Gottfried (1991), 'Ökonomische Analyse der Umwelthaftung (Economic Analysis of Environmental Liability)', in Haureich, Hanspeter and Schwarzer, Stephan (eds), *Umwelthaftung*, Vienna, Austrian Economic Publishers Company, 22-41.

Prisching, Manfred (1979), 'Ökonomische Rechtslehre? Über die Prämissen und Grenzen des Economic Approach im Recht (Economic Jurisprudenz? On the Premisses and Limits of the Economic Approach to Law)', in Freisitzer, Kurt, Holzer, Hans Ludwig, Mantl, Wolfgang and Höflechner, Walter (eds), *Reformen des Rechts. Festschrift zur 200-Jahr-Feier der Rechtswissenschaftlichen Fakulät der Universität Graz*, Graz, Akademische Druck u. Verlagsanstalt, 995-1020.

Prisching, Manfred (1982), 'Sozioökonomische Bedingungen der Kriminalität. Über empirische Divergenzen und theoretische Kontroversen (Socio-economic Conditions of Criminality. On Empirical Divergencies and Theoretical Controversies)', **65** *Monatsschrift für Kriminologie und Strafrechtsreform*, 163-176.

Prisching, Manfred (1983), 'Über die Karriere einer Handlungstheorie. Der ökonomische Weg auf dem Weg durch die Sozialwissenschaften (On the Career of a Behavioral Theory. The Economic Way on the way through the Social Sciences)', **37** *Zeitschrift für philosophische Forschung*, 256-274.

Prisching, Manfred (1987), 'Regeln für das Handeln. Soziale Entscheidungsmechanismen im Modernisierungsprozess (Rules for Behavior. Social Decision Mechanisms in Modernization Process)', **18** *Rechtstheorie. Zeitschrift für Logik, Methodenlehre, Kybernetik und Soziologie des Rechts*, 151-181.

Rinaldi, S., Feichtinger, G. and Wirl, F. (1994), 'Corruption Dynamics in Democratic Systems', **168** *Forschungsbericht/Research Memorandum*.

Roth, Gabriel (1977), 'Der Schutzzweck richterlicher Kontrolle von AGB' (The Protection Goal of the Judicial Control of Standard Term Clauses), **4** *Österreichische Zeitschrift für Wirtschaftsrecht*, 32-37.

Roth, Günter H. (1994), 'Kommentar zu Bernd Oppermann: Marktransparenz und Marktaufschließung durch Werbung im Recht des unlauteren Wettbewerbs (Transparency of the Market, Market Entry by Advertising and the Law of Unfair Competition - A Comment on Bernd Oppermann's Paper)', in Claus Ott and Hans-Bernd Schäfer, *Ökonomischer Analyse der rechtliche Organisation von Innovationen*, Tübingen, J.C.B. Mohr.

Schneider, Friedrich and Bartel, Rainer (1989), *Gemein Wirtschaft versus Privatwirtschaft* (Collective Economics versus Private Economics), Vienna, Manz Publishers, 315 p.

Schwarzer, Stephan (1984), 'Die Änderung der Gewerbeordnung durch das Umweltfondsgesetz - eine versäumte Gelegenheit (The Amendment of the Industrial Code via the Environmental Funds Act - a Foregone Chance)', *Österreichische Zeitschrift für Wirtschaftsrecht*, 11-16.

Schwarzer, Stephan (1985), 'Wirtschaftsrecht und ökonomische Effizienz (Commercial Law and Economic Efficiency)', *Wirtschaftspolitische Blätter*, 26-31.

Schwarzer, Stephan (1985), 'Zur Lastenverteilung im österreichischen Luftreinhaltungsrecht (Sharing the Burden in Austrian Clean Air Regulation)', *UPR*, 305-314.

Schwarzer, Stephan (1987a), 'Wirtschaftslenkung durch das Umweltrecht? (Commercial Regulation via Environmental Law?)', *Österreichische Zeitschrift für Wirtschaftsrecht*, 101-110.

Schwarzer, Stephan (1987b), 'Die Finanzierung des Umweltschutzes im österreichischen Wirtschaftsrecht (On Financing Environment Protection in Austrian Commercial Regulations)', in Joseph Marko and Armin Scholz (eds), *Demokratie und Wirtschaft*, Studien zu Politik und Verwaltung, Vienna - Cologne - Graz, 209-237.

Schwarzer, Stephan (1989), 'Gedanken zur Effizienz und Effektivität des österreichischen Umweltrecht (Thoughts on the Efficiency and Effectiveness of Austrian Environmental Regulations)', *Wirtschaftspolitische Blätter*, 454-462.

Schwarzer, Stephan (1992a), *Die Genehmigung von Betriebsanlagen* (The Approval of Plants), Vienna.

Schwarzer, Stephan (1992b), 'Der Umgang mit Altlasten in Österreich (The Treatment of Containments in Austria)', in Edmung Brandt (ed.), *Altlasten. Bewertung - Sanierung - Finanzierung*, 3. Auflage, Taunusstein, 282-298.

Schwarzer, Stephan (1993a), 'Rechtsprobleme der Verringerung der CO_2-Emissionen von Kleinfeuerungsanlagen - luftreinhaltungsrechtliche und energierechtliche Aspekte (Legal Problems of Reduction of Carbon dioxide in Small Furnaces)', *Jahresbericht 1992 der Österreichischen CO_2-Kommission*, Akademie für Umwelt und Energie, 243-257.

Schwarzer, Stephan (1993b), 'Nationale und internationale Verpackungsreglementierung als Unternehmensdatum (National and International Regulations on Packages as a Constraint for Entrepreneurship)', *Österreichische Zeitschrift für Wirtschaftsrecht*, 16-23.

Schwarzer, Stephan (1995a), 'Marktwirtschaftliche Instrumente als Alternative zum Ordnungsrecht in der Umweltpolitik? (Market-Prone Instruments as Substitute for Directives in Environmental Policy?)', *Wirtschaftspolitische Blätter*, 317-325.

Schwarzer, Stephan (1995b), 'Die Bedeutung der Richtlinie der EU über Verpackungen und Verpackungsabfälle für die österreichische Abfallpolitik (The Consequences of the EU-Directive about Packages and Package-Wast for the Austrian Waste-Disposal Policy)', *Österreichische Zeitschrift für Wirtschaftsrecht*, 97-104.

Schwarzer, Stephan (1996), 'Die Beschleunigung von Genehmigungsverfahren als Wirtschafts- und umweltpolitisches Anliegen - zugleich ein Vorwort (The Acceleration of Approval Processes as a Policy Issue - a Preface)', in Schwarzer, Stephan (ed.), *Die Beschleunigung von Genehmigungsverfahren für Betriebsanlagen - Möglichkeiten nach geltendem Recht und Reformansätze*, in Druck.

Supper, Meinhard (1988), 'Das niederösterreichlische Landesrecht und die ökonomische Analyse des Rechts (The Law of the Province of Lower Austria and the Economic Analysis of Law)', in Funk, Bernd-Christiaen (ed.) (project management), *Deregulierung und Entbürokratisierung am Beispiel von Niederösterreich*,Vienna, Austrian Economic Publishers Company, 43-48.

Weigel, Wolfgang (1990a), 'Ökonomie und Recht - Eine Einführung (Economics and Law - An Introduction)', **31** *Das öffentliche Haushaltswesen in Österreich*, 169-198.

Weigel, Wolfgang (1990b), 'Grenzen der Wettbewerbspolitik (The Limits of Competition Policy)', **37** *Wirtschaftspolitische Blätter*, 560-566.

Weigel, Wolfgang (1991a), 'Ökonomie und Recht - Eine Einführung (Law and Economics, a Primer)', in Weigel, Wolfgang (project managment) and Austrian Economic Chanmber (ed.), *Economic Analysis of Law - A Collection of Applications*, Vienna, Austrian Economic Publishing Company, 13-37.

Weigel, Wolfgang (1991b), 'Prospects for Law and Economics in Civil Law Countries: Austria', **11** *International Review of Law and Economics*, 325-329.

Weigel, Wolfgang and Austrian Economic Chamber (eds) (1991), *Economic Analysis of Law - a Collection of Application*, Vienna, Austrian Economic Publishing Company, 295 p.

Weissel, Erwin (forthcoming), 'Zurück zu den Quellen (der Ökonomischen Analyse des Rechts) (Back to the Roots (of Economic Analysis of Law))', *Zeitschrift für Rechtsvergleichung*.

Weissel, Erwin (1990), 'Zur Problematik der Kartellrechtlichen Behandlung von Vertriebsbindungen bei Markenartikeln (The Problem of Vertical Restraints of Brands in Cartel Law)', **6** *Österreichische Blätter für Gewerblichen Rechtsschutz und Urheberrecht*.

Weissel, Erwin (1991a), 'Das juristische Denken und das Denken der Juristen. Bemerkungen eines Ökonomen zu K.G. Wurzels 'Rechtswissenschaft als Socialwissenschaftler' (Legal Reasoning and the Reasoning of Lawyers - Some Remarks from an Economists Perspective regarding K.G. Wurzels 'Legal Science as a Social Science')', **6** *Zeitschrift für Rechtsvergleichung*.

Weissel, Erwin (1991b), 'Kommentar zum Sicherheitspolizeigesetz 1991: Praeceps legibus solutus? Zur Politischen Ökonomie des Polizeiwesens (Comment on the Security Forces Act)', *Zeitschrift für Rechtsvergleichung*, in print.

Weissel, Erwin (1994a), 'Wettbewerb als Pflicht und Recht. Eine Buchbesprechung (Competition as a Duty and a Claim)', **5** *Zeitschrift für Rechtsvergleichung*.

Weissel, Erwin (1994b), 'Der Rechtsbruch als Regel- oder Sonderfall (Unlawfulness as a Normal or a Special Case)', **6** *Zeitschrift für Rechtsvergleichung*.

Other References

Aicher, Josef and Lessiak, Rudolf (1989), *Rabattgesetz contra Wettbewerb* (The Law of Dscounts versus Competition), Vienna, Carl Menger Institut.

Böhm-Bawerk, Eugen v. (1881), *Rechte und Verhältnisse vom Standpunkte der volkswirtschaftlichen Güterlehre* (Rights and Relationships from the Viewpoint of the Economic Theory of Commodities), Innsbruck.

Bydlinski, Franz (1982), *Juristische Methodenlehre und Rechtsbegriff* (Legal Methodology and the Meaning of the Term Law), Vienna and New York, Springer Publishers.

Bydlinski, Franz (1988), *Fundamentale Rechtsgrundsätze* (Fundamental Principles of Law), Vienna and New York, Springer Publishers, 133-290 (ch.III).

Frey, Bruno and Kirchgässner, Gebhard (1994), *Demokratische Wirtschaftspolitik* (Economic Policy in a Democracy), 2nd edn, Munich, Vahlen.

Goldberg, Victor (1980), 'Public Choice - Property Rights', in Samuels, Warren J., *The Methology of Economic Thought*, New Brunswick and London, Transaction Books, 402-426.

Herrmann, Emanuel (1897), *Theorie der Versicherung* (Theory of Insurance), 2nd edn, Vienna.

Mataja, Victor (1888), *Das Recht des Schadenersatzes vom Standpunkte der Nationalökonomie* (The Law of Compensation from the Standpoint of Economics), Leipzig.

Mayer-Maly, Theodor (1991), *Rechtswissenschaft* (The Science of Law), 5th edn, Munich and Vienna, Oldenbourg.

Sonnenfels, Joseph von (1765), *Principien von Polizey, Handlung und Finanz* (The Principles of Police, Action and Finance), 3 Volumes, 1st printing, Vienna.

Streissler, Erich (1973), *Macht und Freiheit in der Sicht des Liberalismus* (Power and Liberty from a Liberal Perspective), Vienna.

Wurzel, K.G. (1991), *Rechtswissenschaft als Sozialwissenschaft* (Law as a Social Science), reprint, Vienna, Springer.

0310
LAW AND ECONOMICS IN BELGIUM

Gerrit De Geest
Professor at the University of Ghent
Researcher at the Economic Institute/CIAV Utrecht University

Abstract

This chapter concentrates on the state of law and economics (narrowly defined) in Belgium. As in most European countries, traditional law professors - who believe in the idea of law as an autonomous science - were initially rather critical towards this new approach. This early scepticism seems to have disappeared in more recent years.

Optional courses are now taught at most Belgian universities, and law and economics articles have been published in traditional law reviews. There is one specialized book series on law and economics. Several national workshops and international conferences have been organized at the Universities of Antwerp, Gent and Leuven.
JEL classification: K00
Keywords: Law and Economics, Belgium, Research, Education, Conferences

1. Introduction. Reception of Law and Economics in Belgium

Law and economics (narrowly defined) was introduced in Belgium by Cousy (1976), when he applied the brand new economic theory on product liability to Belgian law. Cousy had been confronted with this new approach during a stay in the USA. The true start was given by Bouckaert (1984a) who devoted his inaugural lecture to law and economics, and by Faure and Van den Bergh who organized the first of a series of Flemish workshops in 1986.

As in most European countries, traditional law professors were initially rather critical towards this new approach. A lively debate between the legal doctrinist Kruithof (1986, 1987) and the legal economists Van den Bergh and Heremans (1987a, 1987b) took place. Kruithof criticized law and economics mainly for its unrealistic assumptions and for the inferiority of economic values to moral values.

This early scepticism seems to have disappeared in more recent years. Optional courses are now taught at most Belgian universities, and law and economics papers have been accepted by traditional law reviews. In 1995, the University of Ghent awarded an honorary doctorate to Richard Posner.

Yet the average law professor is still not very familiar with the approach. In the first introductory lectures of their courses, Belgian law professors traditionally refer to historical and sometimes philosophical literature. In rare cases only, a Belgian law professor will briefly introduce the students to the economics of the legal rules. Belgium is of course not unique in this respect. As in most continental countries, legal science is generally seen as an autonomous science. In Belgium and France, the Exegetic School, although officially dead, still has some influence. According to this view, judges and legal scientists had to follow the legislation as faithfully as possible and had to leave improvements of the law (*de lege ferenda*) entirely to the legislator.

The following sections will survey the current state of law and economics with respect to education, research and organized conferences and workshops. Law and economics will be narrowly defined. There is, of course, much more law and economics in Belgium, if the term includes, for instance, regulation of industries and industrial organization. In other words, this survey will pay more attention to 'new law and economics' than to 'old law and economics'.

2. Education

At no Belgian university is law and economics a mandatory course, although, it is offered as an optional course at most universities. At the University of Ghent such an optional course for law students has existed since the early 1980s (first under a different name, 'Algemene en Kritische Rechtstheorie' - General and Critical Legal Theory). At the university of Antwerp, there is an optional course for law students. In Leuven, there is a similar introductory course, taught in English (also offered in the LL M programme). Robert Cooter has taught a law and economics course at Louvain-la-neuve on various occasions. At the economics faculty of Namur there is a course as well.

The University of Ghent is a partner in the Erasmus Programme on Law and Economics and offers five specialized courses. The Catholic University of Brusssels and the Facultés Saint-Louis offer a joint Master's programme on legal theory, which introduces the students to nearly all branches of legal theory, including law and economics.

There has been a (part-time) professor on law and economics and legal theory at the University of Ghent since 1997 (De Geest). In addition, some other professors (Van den Bergh, Bouckaert, Van Cayseele, Heremans, Vereecke and others) are devoting at least part of their research time to law and economics.

3. Research

The first introductory (little) monograph on law and economics was Bouckaert's inaugural lecture (1984a). Faure and Van den Bergh (1989, on tort law and insurance) was the first longer monograph in Belgium. The first PhD based on law and economics research broadly defined was De Clercq (1983). De Geest (1994a) was the first PhD on new law and economics. In the PhDs of Byttebier (1993), Peeters (1989) and Strowel (1987) some chapters were devoted to law and economics literature.

There is one book series on law and economics at Maklu publishers, first edited by Heremans and Van den Bergh, and since 1997 by Heremans and Bouckaert. In this series, books were published on federalism (Vanderveeren et al., 1987), tort law and compulsory insurance (Faure and Van den Bergh 1989), contract law (De Geest, 1994a), and competition law (Van Cayseele, 1994).

There is no specialized Belgian journal on law and economics. Law and economics papers have been published in traditional law reviews (for example Faure and Van den Bergh, 1987; Van den Bergh, 1992; Bouckaert, 1993), traditional economics reviews (for example Van den Bergh, 1980), in journals devoted to legal theory and legal philosophy (Bouckaert, 1986; Van den Bergh, 1988; De Geest, 1990a), and a sociology of law journal (Bouckaert, 1994; De Geest, 1994b; Raes, 1994; Strowel, 1994). A special issue of the Vlaamse Jurist Vandaag (the journal of the Flemish lawyers' association) was devoted to law and economics (1987).

Research has focused on tort law and insurance (for example Faure and Van den Bergh, 1989), property law (for example Bouckaert, 1990b; De Geest, 1994b), contract law (De Geest, 1994a), consumer protection (for example Van den Bergh, 1980), and competition law (for example Van Cayseele, 1994; Van den Bergh, 1993). Quite some energy has gone into methodological discussions (for example Bouckaert, 1984b; Kruithof 1986, 1987; Van den Bergh and Heremans, 1987a, 1987b; Strowel, 1987; De Geest, 1994a; Raes, 1994).

4. Conferences and Workshops

Workshops on law and economics have been held in Antwerp (1986, 1987, organized by Faure and Van den Bergh), in Ghent (1989, 1994, 1996, 1998 organized by Bouckaert and De Geest), Leuven (1991, organized by Heremans and Van Cayseele). While the first three were meant to introduce law and economics to Belgian lawyers, the later workshops were set up for a more specialized and international audience.

The annual conference of the European Association of Law and Economics took place in Antwerp in 1988 (organized by Faure and Van den Bergh) and in Leuven in 1994 (organized by Cousy and Heremans). In 1995 a conference on law and economics versus sociology of law was held in Ghent (Bouckaert and De Geest). The annual conference of Belgian economists in 1986 at Brussels was devoted to the economics of regulation.

Acknowledgements

The author would like to thank Roger Van den Bergh for having organized the anonymous refereeing procedure.

Bibliography on Law and economics in Belgium (0310)

Andersen, Cecilia (1986), 'Het Octrooirecht ten dienste van Kleine en Middelgrote Ondernemingen (Patent Law at the Service of Small and Middle Sized Entreprises)', **40** *Economisch en Sociaal Tijdschrift*, 613-629.

Baeck, L., Ongena, H. and Cools, J.P. (1987), 'Begripsbepaling en Situering van het Dereguleringsverschijnsel in de Geschiedenis van het Economisch Denken (Definition and Situation of the Deregulation Phenomenon)', in X (ed.), *18de Vlaams Wetenschappelijk Economisch Congres, Brussel 8 en 9 mei 1987, Sociaal-economische Deregulering*, Brussel, V.E.H.U.B., 29-47.

Blauwens, Gust and Van De Voorde, Eddy (1986), 'Onderzoek naar de Economische Kost van de Regulering van het Goederenvervoer in België (An Investigation into the Economic Cost of the Regulation of the Transport of Goods in Belgium)', **40** *Economisch en Sociaal Tijdschrift*, 575-592.

Blauwens, Gust and Van De Voorde, Eddy (1988), 'Deregulering en de Vraag naar Luchtvervoer (Deregulation and the Demand for Air Transport)', **32** *Tijdschrift voor Economie en Management*, 127-142.

Blonk, W.A.G. (1987), 'Vervoer (Transport)', in X (ed.), *18de Vlaams Wetenschappelijk Economisch Congres, Brussel 8 en 9 mei 1987, Sociaal-economische Deregulering*, Brussel, V.E.H.U.B., 543-560.

Bongaerts, Jan C. (1986), 'Inleiding tot de Economische Analyse van het Recht met Toepassing op het Contractenrecht en het Aansprakelijkheidsrecht, Inzonderheid de Milieuramp te Bhopal (Introduction to Economic Analysis of Law, with Applications to Contract and Tort Law, and in Particular to the Environmental Disaster in Bhopal)', in Van den Bergh, Roger (ed.), *Verslagboek Eerste Werkvergadering Recht en Economie*, Antwerpen, Leerstoel A. Van Melkebeke, Handelshogeschool, 5-20.

Bongaerts, Jan C. (1987), 'Milieubeleid: Regulering of Aansprakelijkheidsregel? (Environmental Policy: Regulation or Liability?)', *Vlaams Jurist Vandaag*, 17-22.

Bouckaert, Boudewijn (1984a), *Recht op Zoek naar Economie? Prolegomena tot een Economische Analyse van het Recht* (Law in Search of Economics? Introduction to an Economic Analysis of Law), Gent, Story-Scientia.

Bouckaert, Boudewijn (1984b), 'Efficiëntie of Rechtvaardigheid: het Onvermijdelijk Dilemma? (Efficiency or Justice: the Unavoidable Dilemma?)', **29** *Tijdschrift voor Sociale Wetenschappen*, 101-133.

Bouckaert, Boudewijn (1986), 'Is de Prins een Goede Herder van de Mededinging? Grondslagen van het Internationaal Europees Economisch Recht (Is the Prince a Good Shepherd of Competition? Foundations of International European Economic Law)', **15** *Rechtsfilosofie en Rechtstheorie*, 8-27.

Bouckaert, Boudewijn (1987), 'Het Aansprakelijkheidsrecht tussen Rechtvaardigheid en Efficiëntie (Liability Law between Justice and Efficiency)', **1** *Vlaams Jurist Vandaag*, 23-26.

Bouckaert, Boudewijn (1988a), 'L'Analyse Économique du Droit: vers un Renouveau de la Science Juridique? (An Economic Analysis of Law: Towards a Renewal of Legal Science?)', **18** *Revue Interdisciplinaire d'Études Juridiques*, 7-47.

Bouckaert, Boudewijn (1988b), 'Economische Analyse van het Stadsverval in België: naar een Geïntegreerd Stadsrenovatiebeleid? (An Economic Analysis of City Decline in Belgium: Towa)', *Planologische Discussiebijdragen*, 53-61.

Bouckaert, Boudewijn (1990a), 'Zin of Onzin van Planning', (Sense or Nonsense of Planning)', **2** *Ruimtelijke Planning*.

Bouckaert, Boudewijn (1990b), 'Eigendomsrechten vanuit Rechtseconomisch Perspectief (Property Rights from an Economic Perspective)', **39** *Ars Aequi*, 777-786.

Bouckaert, Boudewijn (1993), 'Verdwaald in de Jungle van de Wet. Biedt Rechtsdwaling een Uitkomst? (Lost in the Jungle of the Law. Does the Concept Legal Mistake Provide a Solution?)', *Tijdschrift voor Privaatrecht*, 1347-1407.

Bouckaert, Boudewijn (1994), 'Misschien Geen Vrienden, Waarschijnlijk Wel Bondgenoten. Bedenkingen over de Nauwe Kloof tussen de Rechtssociologie van het Handelen en de Rechtseconomie van de Sociale Coöperatie (Possibly No Friends, but Probably Partners: Reflections on the Narrow Gap Between the Legal Sociology of Action and the Legal Economics of Social Cooperation)', **2** *Recht der Werkelijkheid*, 44-74.

Bourgoignie, Thierry (1973), 'Overheid en Bedrijfsleven/3 La Reglementation des Prix en Belgique (Price Regulation in Belgium)', **27** *Economisch en Sociaal Tijdschrift*, 387-400.

Bracke, F. (1987), 'Deregulering en Algemeen Belang: 1. Bronnen en Doelstellingen (Deregulation and General Interest: Sources and Purposes)', in X (ed.), *18de Vlaams Wetenschappelijk Economisch Congres, Brussel 8 en 9 mei 1987, Sociaal-economische Deregulering*, Brussel, V.E.H.U.B., 101-122.

Bulcke, J. (1987), 'Industrie en Energie: 3. Electriciteit' (Industry and Energy: Electricity)', in X (ed.), *18de Vlaams Wetenschappelijk Economisch Congres, Brussel 8 en 9 mei 1987, Sociaal-economische Deregulering*, Brussel, V.E.H.U.B., 421-440.

Byttebier, Koen (1993), *Het Vijandige Overnamebod* (Hostile Takeovers), Antwerpen, Maklu.

Cousy, Herman (1976), 'Produktenaansprakelijkheid. Proeven van een Juridisch-Economische Analyse (Product Liability. Attempt of a Legal-Economic Analysis)', *Tijdschrift voor Privaatrecht*, 995-1035.

D'alcantara, G. (1987), 'Telecommunicatie. Economische aspecten (Telecommunication: Economic Aspects)', in X (ed.), *18de Vlaams*

Wetenschappelijk Economisch Congres, Brussel 8 en 9 mei 1987, Sociaal-economische Deregulering, Brussel, V.E.H.U.B., 565-579.

D'Ursel, Laurent (1985), 'L'Analyse Économique du Droit des Contracts (An Economic Analysis of Contract Law)', **14** *Revue Interdisciplinaire d'Études Juridiques*, 45-88.

Daems, H. and De Grauwe, Paul (1981), 'Determinanten van de Overheidsreglementering (Determinants of Government Regulation)', in X (ed.), *Overheidsinterventies, Effectiviteit en Efficiëntie. Vijftiende Vlaams Wetenschappelijk Economisch Congres*, Leuven, Departement Toegepaste Economische Wetenschappen, 25-41.

Dauw, C. (1987), 'Financiële Deregulering en Financiering der Investeringen (Financial Deregulation and Financing of Investment)', in X (ed.), *18de Vlaams Wetenschappelijk Economisch Congres, Brussel 8 en 9 mei 1987, Sociaal-economische Deregulering*, Brussel, V.E.H.U.B., 695-730.

De Bondt, Raymond and Van Herck, G. (1981), 'Prijsbeleid en Economische Efficiëntie (Price Policy and Economic Efficiency)', in X (ed.), *18de Vlaams Wetenschappelijk Economisch Congres, Brussel 8 en 9 mei 1987, Sociaal-economische Deregulering*, Brussel, V.E.H.U.B., 253-278.

De Bruyne, G. (1987), 'Inkomensvorming en Deregulering van de Arbeidsmarkt: 2. Indexering (Income Formation and Deregulation in the Labour Market: Indexation)', in X (ed.), *18de Vlaams Wetenschappelijk Economisch Congres, Brussel 8 en 9 mei 1987, Sociaal-economische Deregulering*, Brussel, V.E.H.U.B., 249-263.

De Clercq, Marc (1983), *Economische Aspecten van het Vervuilingsbeleid (Deel I. Theorie, Deel II. Praktijk)* (Economic Aspects of Pollution Policy), Leiden, Spruyt, van Mantgen en Does, p. 493.

De Clercq, Marc (1984), 'Liberaal Milieubeleid', (Liberal Environmental Policy)', **69** *Economisch-Statistische Berichten*, 488-493.

De Clercq, Marc and Naert, Frank (1985), *De Politieke Markt* (The Political Market), Antwerpen, Kluwer, 163 p.

De Geest, Gerrit (1987), 'James Buchanan, Nobelprijswinnaar Economie 1986 (James Buchanan, Nobel Laureate for Economics 1986)', *De Vlaamse Gids*, 44-49.

De Geest, Gerrit (1990a), 'Public Choice, Mensbeeld en Ideologie (Public Choice, Model of Man and Ideology)', **19** *Rechtsfilosofie en Rechtstheorie*, 109-122.

De Geest, Gerrit (1990b), 'Public Choice en Rechtseconomie (Public Choice and Law-and- Economics)', **39(10)** *Ars Aequi* in Bock, Ruth de, et al. (eds), *Themanummer Rechtseconomie*, 666-673.

De Geest, Gerrit (1994a), *Economische Analyse van het Contracten- en Quasi-Contractenrecht: een Onderzoek naar de Wetenschappelijke Waarde van de Rechtseconomie* (An Economic Analysis of Contract Law and Quasi Contract Law: A Study on the Scientific Value of Law and Economics), Antwerpen, Maklu, 568 p.

De Geest, Gerrit (1994b), 'Private versus Gemene Eigendom: de 'Tragedy of the Commons' Herbekeken (Private versus Common Property: The 'Tragedy of the Commons' Reconsidered)', **1994(2)** *Recht der Werkelijkheid*, 132-146. Reprinted in Raes, Koen and Willekens, Harry (eds), *Economische Verklaringen van het Recht*, 's-Gravenhage, Vuga, 1994.

De Kock, S. (1978), 'De Vervuiler Betaalt: Slogan of Noodzaak? (The Polluter Pays: Slogan or Necessity?)', **23** *Tijdschrift voor Economie en Management*, 99-124.

Degadt, J. (1985), 'Het Leefmilieu: Relevantie van Economische Analyses voor een Doelmatig Overheidsbeleid in het Geregionaliseerde België (The Environment:

Relevance of Economic Analyses for an Effective Governmental Policy in Federalized Belgium)', **30** *Tijdschrift voor Economie en Management*, 367-386.

Demin, P. (1987), 'Industrie en Energie: 1. Industrie (Industry and Energy: 1. Industry)', in X (ed.), *18de Vlaams Wetenschappelijk Economisch Congres, Brussel 8 en 9 mei 1987, Sociaal-economische Deregulering*, Brussel, V.E.H.U.B., 387-398.

Engelen, Peter-Jan (1996), 'De Regelgeving omtrent Handel met Voorkennis: een Juridisch-Economische Benadering (The Legal Rules on Insider Trading: a Legal and Economic Approach)', **51(24)** *Weekberichten, Kredietbank*, 1-7. Translated and reprinted as 'La Reglementation en Matière de Delit d'Initie: une Approche Économico-Juridique', **51(24)** *Bulleting Hebdomadaire, Kredietbank*, 1-7.

Faure, Michael G. (1986), 'Commentaar bij de Paper van Dr. Jan C. Bongaerts: Coase en Produktenaansprakelijkheid (Commentary to the paper by Dr. Jan C. Bongaerts: Coase and Product Liability)', in Van Den Bergh, Roger (ed.), *Verslagboek Eerste Werkvergadering Recht en Economie*, Antwerpen, Leerstoel A. Van Melkebeke, Handelshogeschool, 31-37.

Faure, Michael G. (1993), *(G)een Schijn van Kans. Beschouwingen over het Statistisch Causaliteitsbewijs bij Milieugezondheidsschade* (Not a chance. Reflections on Statistical Causation and Environmental Health Damage), Antwerpen, Maklu, 68 p.

Faure, Michael G. and Van Buggenhout, Willy (1987), 'Produktenaansprakelijkheid. De Europese Richtlijn: Harmonisatie en Consumentenbescherming? (The European Directive Concerning Product Liability, Harmonization and Consumer Protection?)', **51** *Rechtskundig Weekblad*, 33-88.

Faure, Michael G. and Van den Bergh, Roger (1987), 'Efficiënties van het Foutcriterium in het Belgisch Aansprakelijkheidsrecht (Efficiencies of the Fault Criterion in Belgian Liability Law)', **51** *Rechtskundig Weekblad*, 11-19.

Faure, Michael G. and Van den Bergh, Roger (1989), *Objectieve Aansprakelijkheid, Verplichte Verzekering en Veiligheidsregulering* (Strict Liability, Mandatory Insurance and Safety Regulation), Antwerpen, Maklu, 386 p.

Faure, Michael G., Van den Bergh, Roger, Hartlief, T. and Tjittes, R. (1990), *De Invloed van Verzekering op de Civiele Aansprakelijkheid, Preadviezen Uitgebracht voor de Vereniging voor Burgerlijk Recht* (The Influence of Insurance on Civil Liabilty, Recommendations for the Association of Civil Law), Lelystad, Vermande, 118 p.

Gathon, Henry Jean (1988), 'La Distribution de l'Eau en Belgique: Prix, Coût et Efficacité (The Distribution of Water in Belgium: Price, Cost and Efficiency)', **0(119)** *Cahiers Economiques de Bruxelles*, 371-384.

Germain, Marc (1989), 'Externalités, Taxation et Traitement de la Pollution dans le Cadre d'un Duopole de Cournot (Externalities, Taxation and Dealing with Pollution in the Case of a Cournot Duopoly)', **55** *Recherches Economiques de Louvain*, 273-292.

Holderbeke, F., Pernot, A. and Denys, J. (1987), 'Inkomensvorming en Deregulering van de Arbeidsmarkt: 3. Arbeidsvoorwaarden (Income Formation and Deregulation of the Labour Market: Labour Conditions)', in X (ed.), *18de Vlaams Wetenschappelijk Economisch Congres, Brussel 8 en 9 mei 1987, Sociaal-economische Deregulering*, Brussel, V.E.H.U.B., 265-303.

Huyse, Luc (1987), 'Deregulering en Algemeen Belang: 2. Deregulering als Maatschappelijke Reconstructie (Deregulation and General Interest: Deregulation as Social Reconstruction)', in X (ed.), *18de Vlaams Wetenschappelijk Economisch*

Congres, Brussel 8 en 9 mei 1987, Sociaal-economische Deregulering, Brussel, V.E.H.U.B., 123-140.

Kruithof, Robert (1986), 'Leven en Dood van het Contract (Life and Death of Contract)', **49** *Rechtskundig Weekblad*, 2761-2768.

Kruithof, Robert (1987), 'Naschrift (Epilogue)', **50** *Rechtskundig Weekblad*, 1669-1680.

Langerwerf, Etienne (1986), 'De Sociaal-Economische Ontwikkeling en de Procesvoeringsratio's van de Burgerlijke Rechtbanken tussen 1950 en 1980 (The Social and Economic Development and the Litigation Ratios of the Civil Courts Between 1950 and 1980)', **40** *Economisch en Sociaal Tijdschrift*, 87-102.

Lemieux, Pierre (1983), *Du Libéralisme à l'Anarcho-Capitalisme* (From Liberalism to Anarcho-Capitalism), Paris, Presses Universitaires de France (PUF).

Leunis, J. and De Vos, G. (1986), 'De Wet betreffende de Handelsvestigingen: De Eerste 10 Jaar (The Licensing Law: The First 10 Years)', **31** *Tijdschrift voor Economie en Management*, 309-333.

Mackaay, Ejan (1986), 'La Règle Juridique Observée par le Prisme de l'Économiste - une Histoire Stylisée du Mouvement d'Analyse Économique du Droit (Law Observed through an Economist's Eyeglass - A Stylised History of the Law and Economics Movement)', **1** *Revue internationale de Droit Economique*, 43-88.

Meyers, Jan and Steenbergen, Jacques (1987), 'Deregulering, Europese Eenmaking en Bescherming van het Nationaal Belang (Deregulation, European Unification and Protection of National Interest)', in X (ed.), *18de Vlaams Wetenschappelijk Economisch Congres, Brussel 8 en 9 mei 1987, Sociaal-economische Deregulering*, Brussel, V.E.H.U.B., 51-75.

Michielssen, F. and Van Hecke, M. (1973), 'Prijsbeleid (Price Policy)', in X (ed.), *18de Vlaams Wetenschappelijk Economisch Congres, Brussel 8 en 9 mei 1987, Sociaal-economische Deregulering*, Brussel, V.E.H.U.B., 189-223.

Naert, Frank (1984), 'De Politieke Economie van Pressiegroepen (The Political Economy of Pressure Groups)', **69** *Economisch-Statistische Berichten*, 56-61.

Naert, Frank (1987), 'Overheidsuitgaven en Pressiegroepen in België (Government Expenditure and Lobby Groups in Belgium)', **32** *Tijdschrift voor Economie en Management*, 165-187.

Pacolet, J. (1987), 'Financiële Instellingen en Markten: 1. Deposito-instellingen (Financial Institutions and Markets: Deposit Offices)', in X (ed.), *18de Vlaams Wetenschappelijk Economisch Congres, Brussel 8 en 9 mei 1987, Sociaal-economische Deregulering*, Brussel, V.E.H.U.B., 623-647.

Peeters, Bruno (1989), *De Continuïteit van het Overheidsondernemen: een Begrippenanalyse en een Kritiek op de Uitvoeringsimmuniteit* (The Continuity Principle of Governmental Activities: A Concept Analysis and a Critique on Execution Immunity), Antwerpen, Maklu, 559 p.

Peeters, Ch., Verbeke, A. and Winkelmans, W. (1987), 'Een Geïntegreerd Overheidsbeleid voor de Belgische Binnenvaartsector (An Integrated Governmental Policy for the Belgian Inland Shipping Sector)', **32** *Tijdschrift voor Economie en Management*, 19-37.

Pollefliet, E. (1987), 'Prijsvorming en Mededingingsbeleid: 1. Economische Aspecten (Price Formation and Competition Policy: Economic Aspects)', in X (ed.), *18de Vlaams Wetenschappelijk Economisch Congres, Brussel 8 en 9 mei 1987, Sociaal-economische Deregulering*, Brussel, V.E.H.U.B., 145-170.

Pollefliet, E. (1988), '1992: Regulering of Deregulering van de Financiële Sector? (1992: Regulation or Deregulation of the Financial Sector?)', **42** *Economisch en Sociaal Tijdschrift*, 631-654.

Poulmans, G. (1987), 'Inkomensvorming en Deregulering van de Arbeidsmarkt: 1. Arbeidsflexibiliteit (Income Formation and Deregulation in the Labour Market: Flexibility)', in X (ed.), *18de Vlaams Wetenschappelijk Economisch Congres, Brussel 8 en 9 mei 1987, Sociaal-economische Deregulering*, Brussel, V.E.H.U.B., 229-248.

Raes, Koen (1988a), 'Recht en Neo-Klassieke Economie (Law and Neo-classical Economics)', **17** *Rechtsfilosofie en Rechtstheorie*, 29-30.

Raes, Koen (1988b), 'Onrechtmatige Daad en de Markt van Pijn en Smart (Torts and the Market of Pain and Suffering)', **14** *Recht en Kritiek*, 102-125.

Raes, Koen (1990), 'Het Recht van de Schaarste (The Law of Scarcity)', **16** *Recht en Kritiek*, 380-394.

Raes, Koen (1994), 'Economische Verklaringen van het Recht: Grondproblemen en - Mogelijkheden (Economic Explanations of Law: Fundamental Problems and Potential Opportunities)', **2** *Recht der Werkelijkheid*, 9-44.

Raes, Koen and Willekens, Harry (eds) (1994), *Economische Verklaringen van het Recht* (Economic Explanations of Law)', 's-Gravenhage, Vuga.

Rosiers, Marc (1986), 'De Effecten van Leegstand op de Huisvesting (The Effects of Unoccupied Houses on Housing)', **40** *Economisch en Sociaal Tijdschrift*, 67-85.

Sjegers, R., Faes, P. and Segebarth, K. (1987), 'Deregulering van de Handels-en Dienstenstromen en van de Rechtstreekse Investeringen: 3. Dienstverlening (Deregulation of Trade and Service Flows and of Direct Investments: Services)', in X (ed.), *18de Vlaams Wetenschappelijk Economisch Congres, Brussel 8 en 9 mei 1987, Sociaal-economische Deregulering*, Brussel, V.E.H.U.B., 797-839.

Spinnewyn, F. (1987), 'Inkomensvorming en Deregulering van de Arbeidsmarkt: 4. Sociale Zekerheid (Income Formation and Deregulation of the Labour Market: Social Security)', in X (ed.), *18de Vlaams Wetenschappelijk Economisch Congres, Brussel 8 en 9 mei 1987, Sociaal-economische Deregulering*, Brussel, V.E.H.U.B., 305-320.

Strowel, Alain (1987), 'Utilitarisme et Approche Économique dans la Théorie du Droit. Autour de Bentham et de Posner (Utilitarianism and Economic Approach in Legal Theory. On Bentham and Posner)', **18** *Revue interdisciplinaire d'études juridiques*, 1-45.

Strowel, Alain (1990), 'A la Recherche de l'Intérêt en Économie. De l'Utilitarisme à la Science Économique Néo Classique (Searching for Interest in Economics. From Utilitarism to Neo-classical Economics)', in Gerard, Philippe, Ost, François and Et Van De Ker (eds), *Droit et intérêt*, Bruxelles, Fac. Univ. St-Louis, 37-87.

Strowel, Alain (1994), 'De Economische Analyse van de Intellectuele Rechten: een Les voor de Jurist? (An Economic Analysis of Intellectual Rights: A Lesson for the Lawyer?)', **2** *Recht der Werkelijkheid*, 178-202. Reprinted in Raes, Koen and Willekens, Harry (eds), *Economische Verklaringen van het Recht*, 's Gravenhage, Vuga.

Trojan, C. (1987), 'Landbouw (Agriculture)', in X (ed.), *18de Vlaams Wetenschappelijk Economisch Congres, Brussel 8 en 9 mei 1987, Sociaal-economische Deregulering*, Brussel, V.E.H.U.B., 475-504.

Van Cayseele, Patrick (1994), *De Belgische Wet op de Mededinging. Concentraties in een Industrieel Economisch en Internationaal Juridisch Perspectief* (The Belgian

Competition Act: Concentrations in an Industrial-Economic and International Legal Perspective), Antwerpen, Maklu, p. 152.

Van Den Bergh, P. (1987), 'Deregulering van de Internationale Financiële Stromen en Valutastelsel (Deregulation of the International Financial Flows and Exchange System)', in X (ed.), *18de Vlaams Wetenschappelijk Economisch Congres, Brussel 8 en 9 mei 1987, Sociaal-economische Deregulering*, Brussel, V.E.H.U.B., 845-878.

Van den Bergh, Roger (1980), 'Over de Mededingingsbeperkende Werking van de Wet Handelspraktijken of het Verhaal van Concurrenten die Tegen de Concurrentie Beschermd Willen Worden (On the Competition Limiting Effect of the Law on Trade Practices or the Story of Competitors who Want to be Protected Against Competition)', **34** *Economisch en Sociaal Tijdschrift*, 421-446.

Van den Bergh, Roger (1986), 'De Economische Reguleringstheorie en de Belgische Vestigingswetgeving voor Kleine en Middelgrote Handels- en Ambachtsondernemingen (The Economic Theory of Regulation and the Belgian Licensing Law for Small and Middle-Sized Entreprises)', in Van Den Bergh, Roger (ed.), *Verslagboek Eerste Werkvergadering Recht en Economie*, Antwerpen, Leerstoel A. Van Melkebeke, Handelshogeschool, 38-49.

Van den Bergh, Roger (ed.) (1986), *Verslagboek Eerste Werkvergadering Recht en Economie* (Conference Proceedings of the First Workshop on Law and Economics), Antwerpen, Leerstoel A. Van Melkebeke, Handelshogeschool, 72 p.

Van den Bergh, Roger (1988), 'Le Droit Civil Face à l'Analyse Économique du Droit (Civil Law Facing Economic Analysis of Law)', *Revue internationale de Droit Economique*, 229-254.

Van den Bergh, Roger (1990), 'Economische Analyse van het Consumentenrecht (An Economic Analysis of Consumer Protection Law)', **39** *Ars Aequi*, 787-793.

Van den Bergh, Roger (1991), 'Wat is Rechtseconomie? (What is Law and Economics?)', in Hondius, E.H., Schippers, J.J. and Siegers, J.J. (eds), *Rechtseconomie en Recht*, Zwolle, Tjeenk Willink, 9-49.

Van den Bergh, Roger (1992), 'Ongelijkheid en Discriminatie in de Verhouding tussen Leveranciers en Afnemers (Inequality and Discrimination in the Relationship between Supplier and Buyer' (Preadvies van het XXXVe Rechtscongres Georganiseerd door de Vlaamse Juristenvereniging te Leuven op 9 mei 1992), **56** *Rechtskundig Weekblad*, 1229-1239.

Van den Bergh, Roger (1993), *Economische Analyse van het Mededingingsrecht. Een Terreinverkenning* (An Economic Analysis of Competion Law: An Exploration), Arnhem, Gouda Quint, p. 120.

Van den Bergh, Roger (1994), *Subsidiariteit Rechtseconomisch Bekeken. Adieu Bruxelles?* (Subsidiarity from an Economic Viewpoint: Goodbye Brussels?), Arnhem, Gouda Quint, 105 p.

Van den Bergh, Roger (1995), 'Is Verkeersveiligheid te Duur? (Is Traffic Safety too Expensive?)', **59** *Rechtskundig Weekblad*, 1313-1323.

Van den Bergh, Roger and Faure, Michael G. (1990), 'De Invloed van Verzekering op de Civiele Aansprakelijkheid, een Rechtseconomische Analyse (The Influence of Insurance on Tort Liability, an Economic Analysis)', *XXX Preadviezen uitgebracht voor de Vereniging voor Burgerlijk Recht*, 9-53.

Van den Bergh, Roger and Heremans, Dirk (1987a), 'Over Krommen en Rechten. Een Reactie op de Kritiek van Kruithof ten Aanzien van de Economische Analyse van het Recht (On Curves and Lines: A Reaction to the Criticism of Kruithof towards an Economic Analysis of Law)', **50** *Rechtskundig Weekblad*, 1649-1668.

Van den Bergh, Roger and Heremans, Dirk (1987b), 'Recht en Economie (Law and Economics)', **32** *Tijdschrift voor Economie en Management*, 139-164.

Van Den Berghe, Lutgart (1987), 'Financiële Instellingen en Markten: 3. Verzekeringen (Financial Institutions and Markets: Insurance)', in X (ed.), *18de Vlaams Wetenschappelijk Economisch Congres, Brussel 8 en 9 mei 1987, Sociaal-economische Deregulering*, Brussel, V.E.H.U.B., 665-692.

Van Gerven, Walter (1986), 'Herijken van Economische Wetgeving (over reguleren en dereguleren) (Re-Stamping of Economic Regulation - on Regulating and Deregulating)', **49** *Rechtskundig Weekblad*, 286-308.

Van Gerven, Yves (1991), 'Regulering van Vijandige Overnames. De Amerikaanse Ervaring (Regulation of Hostile Takeovers: The American Experience)', *Rechtskundig Weekblad*, 791-833.

Van Hulle, K. (1987), 'Informatie en Markttransparantie (Information and Market Transparency)', in X (ed.), *18de Vlaams Wetenschappelijk Economisch Congres, Brussel 8 en 9 mei 1987, Sociaal-economische Deregulering*, Brussel, V.E.H.U.B., 79-97.

Van Oevelen, Aloïs (1986), 'Enige Bedenkingen van een Jurist bij de Economische Analyse van het Aansprakelijkheidsrecht (Some Considerations of a Jurist on Economic Analys)', in . Van den Bergh, Roger (ed.), *Verslagboek Eerste Werkvergadering Recht en Economie*, Antwerpen, Leerstoel A. Van Melkebeke, Handelshogeschool, 21-30.

Vanbuggenhout, Willy (1987), 'De Economische Benadering van het Recht. Haar Nut en Grenzen voor de Praktijk(bedrijfs)jurist (The Economic Approach of Law: Its Use and Limits for the Practising Company Lawyer)', *Vlaams Jurist Vandaag*, 27-30.

Vanderveeren, Christine, Van Rompuy, Paul, Heremans, Dirk and Heylen, E. (1987), *De Economische en Monetaire Unie in de Belgische Staatshervorming: Juridische en Economische Aspecten* (The Economic and Monetary Union in the Belgian State Reform: Legal and Economic Aspects), Antwerpen, Maklu, 250 p.

Vanwildemeersch, J. (1987), 'Industrie en Milieu (Industry and Environment)', in X (ed.), *18de Vlaams Wetenschappelijk Economisch Congres, Brussel 8 en 9 mei 1987, Sociaal-economische Deregulering*, Brussel, V.E.H.U.B., 399-405.

Vermoes, J. (1987), 'De Programmaovereenkomst: Regulering of Deregulering? (The Program Contract: Regulation or Deregulation?)', in X (ed.), *18de Vlaams Wetenschappelijk Economisch Congres, Brussel 8 en 9 mei 1987, Sociaal-economische Deregulering*, Brussel, V.E.H.U.B., 441-454.

Vuchelen, J. En Praet, P. (1987), 'Diensten en Vrije Beroepen (Services and Free Professions)', in X (ed.), *18de Vlaams Wetenschappelijk Economisch Congres, Brussel 8 en 9 mei 1987, Sociaal-economische Deregulering*, Brussel, V.E.H.U.B., 507-541.

0315
LAW AND ECONOMICS IN DENMARK

Henrik Lando
Associate Professor of Law and Economics at Copenhagen Business School

Abstract

Law and economics is a small but growing area of research and teaching in Denmark.

Economic reasoning applied especially to tort law has a long precedent in Denmark, but often meets with opposition. At the universities, only little research in law and economics is done within the law faculties and there is no chair in law and economics. At the business schools the interest among legal scholars seems greater, as is manifested by the establishment of a law and economics programme at some of the major business schools. Economists show an increasing interest in law, and this is largely due to developments within the theory of industrial organization, mechanism design/contract theory, and institutional economics.
JEL classification: K00
Keywords: Law and Economics, Research, Teaching

1. Ussing's Early Contribution

Around 1900, there was a wave of interest in law and economics reasoning among Scandinavian tort scholars. The inspiration was a book by lawyer-economist Victor Mataja (a student of Menger) who advocated strict liability on the basis of the principle of internalization. The wave may be said to have culminated in the doctoral dissertation of the Danish jurist Henry Ussing in 1914. He analyzed the question of strict liability vs. negligence in tort law against the background of neoclassical economic principles. Ussing advocated strict liability for 'extraordinary acts which involve unusual danger'.

Much of his reasoning was couched in today's modern terms of prevention, risk-allocation and administration costs. His arguments are modern. For example, with respect to prevention he mentioned as an argument for strict liability the problem of 'non-observability' (though he does not use this term), that is the difficulty for the judge of knowing the particulars of a case, which means that not all 'truly sensible precautions' will be made under the negligence rule. He also mentioned that strict liability may induce more innovation in safety. Ussing's main argument for restricting the scope of limited liability to extraordinary acts concerned the administrative costs of insurance, including 'not only the expense of enforcing claims but also of administration expenses in the widest sense'. In conclusion, Ussing's analysis is an early example of the application of economic principles to tort law.

However, Ussing's (and Mataja's) analysis was met with scepticism by most Danish jurists. Even today, most leading Danish tort scholars seem sceptical of the law and economics approach. For example, in the leading textbook on tort law (Von Eyben et al., 1995, p. 35) one reads: this theory - like all other prevention theories - in the end rest on a speculative foundation'.

2. More Recent Contributions

Since Ussing's doctoral dissertation in 1914, three doctoral law theses (to be distinguished from PhD dissertations, the doctorate thesis is usually larger than a PhD) and one PhD thesis have combined law and economics.

Bo Von Eyben, in 'Kompensation for personskade' (Compensation for Personal Injury) (1983) discussed the economic approach to tort law at some length, including references to the works of Ussing, Calabresi and Posner. As in the textbook mentioned above, the author was sceptical of the value of the economic approach.

Jens Fejø's dissertation (1985) in English translation (1990) was entitled 'Monopoly Law and the Market - studies of EC competition law with US American Antitrust Law as a frame of reference and supported by basic market economics'. He compared American competition policy with that of the European Common Market (in particular with respect to the use of 'per se' prohibitions versus 'the rule of reason') and made extensive reference to economic theory in his attempt to derive prescriptions.

Jan Schans Christensen's doctoral dissertation from 1991, 'Contested Take-overs in Danish Law - A Comparative Analysis based on a Law and Economic Approach' discussed the need for legal reform in Denmark to facilitate contested take-overs.

Thomas Riis's PhD thesis 'Ophavsret og Retsøkonomi' (Intellectual Property and Law and Economics) (1996) deals, within an economic model, with the optimal law of copyrights. His thesis is the first to be written by a cand.merc.jur which combines law and economics.

The history of Danish economists' contributions to law and economics is difficult to write. Naturally, many economists have been active in designing laws and regulations, as members for example of expert committees. However, we will refrain from delving into how economic thought on law has developed 'in practice', so to speak. Basic economic research in law seems a recent phenomenon in Denmark.

3. Present Research

As in other countries, both law scholars and economists show an increased interest in law and economics. Law scholars are doing work on the law and economics of intellectual property, contract law, company law and competition law. Among economists, work is done in competition law, property rights, tort law, tax law, environmental law and company law. However, the total number of researchers in these fields amounts to a handful of law scholars and perhaps a few more economists. There is at present no research in such areas as the economics of litigation, criminal law, or family law. Law faculties of universities have no chair in law and economics and it is not part of their research agenda.

Two positive developments are worth mentioning. First, an increasing number of economists work on subjects which have a clear connection to law. Industrial organization, the theory of contracts and the theory of mechanism design (institutional design) have, as in other countries, become new major fields of study. This has already spilled over into law and economics research. A few economists with a background in industrial organization and contract theory are at present applying formal economic modelling to competition law, tort law and environmental law. This is a new development. Second, it is widely recognized that more research needs to be done in this area. At present, there are good incentives for going into this area of research both, it seems, in terms of future faculty positions and in terms of the funding available from different sources.

On the negative side, development of the field seems hampered by misconceptions and misunderstandings between jurists and economists. Communication difficulties certainly exist between the two paradigms, as in other countries.

4. Courses in Law and Economics

The teaching of law and economics has mainly expanded at the Business School of Copenhagen, the Business School of Aarhus and at Ålborg University. In the middle of the 1980s, the three institutions began a law and economics programme, consisting of a 3-year undergraduate study and 2½ years of graduate studies. This is perhaps the main positive development within law and economics and it is hence worth giving some details about the study.

At the Copenhagen Business School, 588 students are at present enrolled as law and economics students (373 undergraduate and 215 graduate students), in Århus the number is 251 (177 undergraduate and 74 graduate students), and in Ålborg University the number is approximately 250. At the Copenhagen Business School the total number of students who have finished their graduate studies from the beginning to the present is 163, in Århus it is 124 and in Ålborg it is approximately 160.

Some of the graduate courses are taught jointly by a law scholar and an economist, for example Tort and Insurance Law and Competition Law, at the Copenhagen Business School. The programme enjoys a good reputation and candidates have in general had no problems finding jobs in the private or public sector. However, it is fair to say that the students are given more training in law and legal method than in economics. In particular, economic modelling is given very little attention.

Outside the business schools little is happening in terms of incorporating law and economics into education, though there are signs of an increasing interest. At the law faculty of Copenhagen University, a course in law and economics was established last year, but so far with only a low attendance. In Aarhus (the second largest city), a similar course was begun some years ago but it has been abandoned since.

Students of economics are rarely taught law, with the exception of a course in business law at the undergraduate level at the business schools. Economic students may, however, obtain credit during their graduate studies for following courses at the law faculty. In general, however, economists' knowledge of law is very limited at the time they finish their education. Formerly, law was a first-year mandatory course, but this is no longer so.

Law students are generally taught a first-year course of elementary economics (although it looks like this course may be cancelled soon at Aarhus University).

5. The PhDs

It is worth paying attention to the number of PhD students which the subject attracts, since this number (and the quality of the students in combination with the quality of the PhD education) is likely to be important for the future of law and economics in Denmark, even though it must be remembered that some of the best students study abroad. One can hope, and it seems likely, that the latter will be of importance in importing law and economics into Denmark.

The number of PhDs working in the field of law and economics is expanding. As a result of the establishment of the law and economics line of education mentioned above, this is particularly the case in the business schools. A handful of graduates with a law and economics degree are presently writing PhDs, most of them at business schools. Only a couple of these PhDs, however, combine law and economics in their research, while the rest have mainly specialized in law. At the law faculties of universities, there is at present only one PhD student in the field of law and economics (at Copenhagen University, in contract law).

6. Conclusion

Law and economics, that is, the application of economic theory to the field of law, is a growing area of research and teaching in Denmark. However, the area is at present small, even in relation to the size of the country.

The following features stand out: economic reasoning applied to law has a long history in Denmark, but has often met with opposition. At the universities, only little research in law and economics is done within the law faculties. At the business schools, the interest among legal scholars seems greater, as is manifested by the establishment of a law and economics programme at some of the major business schools.

Bibliography on Law and Economics in Denmark (0315)

Albæk, Svend, Molgaard, H. Peter and Baltzer Overgaard, Per (1995), 'Dansk Konkurrenceret og Vertikal Kontrol (Danish Competition Law and Vertical Control)', **133** *Nationaltokonomisk Tidsskrift*, 268-283.

Andersen, Peder, Jensen, Vibeke and Birk Mortensen, Jørgen (eds) (1993), *Governance by Legal and Economic Measures*, Copenhagen, Gad.

Blegvad, Britt-Mari and Collin, Finn (eds) (1987), 'Virksomheden mellem Økonomi og jura (The Firm between Law and Economics)', in *Samfundslitteratur 1987*.

Christensen, J.S. (1991), 'Contested Take-overs in Danish Law - A Comparative Analysis based on a Law and Economic Approach' doctoral dissertation discussing the need for legal reform in Denmark to facilitate contested take-overs, Gad, K¢benham.

Collin, Finn (1987), 'Integration af Juridiske og Økonomiske Beslutningsmodeller (Integration of Legal and Economic Decision models)', in Blegvad, Britt-Mari and Collin, Finn (eds), *Virksomheden mellem ¢konomi og jura*.

Daintith, Terence C. (1987), 'Oprettelse og anvendelse af langfristede kontrakter (The Creation and Use of Longterm Contracts)', in Blegvad, Britt-Mari and Collin, Finn (eds), *Virksomheden mellem ¢konomi og jura*.

Davis, Jerome, Breinholt Larsen, Finn and Pagh Nielsen, Karen Marie (1984), *Offentlig Styring af Olie-gas Aktiviteter i Grønland* (Public Regulation of Oil and Gas Activities in Greenland), Aarhus University Press.

Davis, Lee N. (1989), 'Skydd for Innovationer (Protecting Innovations)', in Bjurggren, Per-Olof and Skogh, Göran, *Foretaget - et Kontraksekonomisk Analys*, Stockholm, SNS forlag, 151-158.

Davis, Lee N. (1991), *Patenter og innovationer: Mod et Strategisk Perspektiv*. (Patents and Innovations: Aiming for a Strategic Perspective).

Fejø, Jens (1985), *Monopol-ret og Marked* (Monopoly Law and Market), København, HHK.

Jeppesen, Tim (1995), 'Miljøpolitiske Muligheder i EF (Framing Environmental Policy in the EC)', *Nordisk Administrativt Tidsskrift*.

Krenchel, Jens Valdemar (1996), 'Okonomisk ret - om den Retsøkonomiske Analyse (Analysis of Law and Economics)', **4** *Justitia*.

Lando, Henrik (1996), 'Hvornår bør Objektivt ansvar Gælde? Det Retsøkonomiske bud på et sæt af Kriterier for Objketivt Ansvar (When Should Strict Liability Apply? The Law and Economics Answer)', Under Review with *Tidsskrift for Retsvidenskab*.

Lando, Henrik (1996), 'Tre Essays om Principper i Rrstatningsretten: Objektivt Ansvar, Culpa-ansvar og det Offentliges Erstatningsansvar (Three Essays on Tort Law: Strict Liability, Negligence and Liability of the Public Sector)', Working Paper, Institute of Finance.

Larsen, Anders and Olsen, Ole Jess (1995), 'Konkurrence i Energisektoren og Statslig Regulering (Competition in the Energy Sector and State Regulation)', *AKF rapport*.

Molgaard, H. Peter, Baltzer Overgaard, Per and Ohlenschlæger Madsen, Ole (1996), *Den Danske Konkurrencelov i Moderne Industriøkonomisk Belysning* (The Danish Law of Competition analysed in the Perspective of Modern Industrial Economics), Aarhus University Press.

Moller, Michael (1996), 'Inskydergarantifonden og Redning af Konkurstruede Pengeinstitutter (Devising a System to Rescue Failing Banks)', **5** *Finans/Invest*.

Moller, Michael and Nielsen, Niels Chr. (1993), 'En Økonomisk Analyse af Københavns Kommunes Hjemfaldspolitik (An Economic Analysis of Repurchase Declarations of the Copenhagen Community)', **2** *Nationalokonomisk Tidsskrift*.

Moller, Michael and Nielsen, Niels Chr. (1994), 'Okonomers og Juristers Syn på arv (Economist's and Lawyer's View of Inheritance)', in Lynge Andersen, Lennart and Mogelvang-Hansen, Peter (eds), G.E.C. Gad.

Mortensen, Jorgen Birk and Olsen, Ole Jess (1991), 'Privatisering og Deregulering (Privatisation and Deregulation)', *Jurist- og Økonomforbundets Forlag, 1993*.

Nielsen, Niels Chr. (1987), 'Okonomi, jura og Markedsmekanismer (Law, Economics and the Market Mechanism)', in Blegvad, Britt-Mari and Collin, Finn (eds), *Virksomheden mellem Økonomi og jura*.

Nielsen, Niels Chr. (1993), 'Minoritetsaktionærbeskyttelse - eller et Velfungerende Marked for Virksomhedskontrol (Minority Protection or a Well-functioning Market for Corporate Control)', *Revision og Regnskabsvæsen*.

Nielsen, Niels Chr. and Ebbesen, Jan (1993), 'Stemmelofter - En Økonomisk Analyse af den Retlige Analyse (Restrictions on Voting Rights, an Economic Analysis of the Legal Analysis)', **6** *Juristen*, 251-264.

Olsen, Ole Jess (1993), 'Regulering af Offentlige Forsyningsvirksomheder i Danmark (The Regulation of Public Utilities in Denmark)', *Jurist- og Økonomforbundets Forlag*.

Raaschou-Nielsen, Agnete (1988), (Institutional Change and Economic Theory), K¢benhavn, PhD thesis, Det Statsvidenskablige Fagråd.

Riis, Thomas (1994), 'Ophavsret og Kulturøkonomi i EF (Copyright and the Economics of Culture in EC)', *NIR*.

Riis, Thomas (1996), *Ophavsret og Retsøkonomi* (Intellectual Property and Law and Economics), PhD thesis.

Riis, Thomas (1996), *Copyright and Law and Economics*, Gadjura, PhD thesis.

Schledermann, Helmut (1987), *Retsøkonomi for Jurister* (Law and Economics for Jurists), Aarhus University Press.

Svendsen, Gert Tinggaard (1993), 'Fordele ved et Marked for CO_2 -kvoter (Advantages in CO_2 Emissions Trading)', **7** *SamfundsØkonomen*, 5-9.

Svendsen, Gert Tinggaard (1994), 'Globalt CO_2 -marked', **1** *Fremtidsorientering*, 35-36.

Svendsen, Gert Tinggaard (1994), 'Kvoter og Syreregn (Quotas and Acid Rain)', **3** *Okonomi & Politik*, 33-39.

Svendsen, Gert Tinggaard (1995), 'Den Stationære Bandit - og Lobbyisme (The Stationary Bandit and Lobbyism)', **3** *Okonomi & Politik*, 24-31.

Von Eyben et al. (1995), *Laerebog i Erstatningsret* (Textbook in Tort Law), Jurist s Økonom¢abindets Forlag, p. 35.

Wegener, Morten (1996), *Franchising i EU-Konkurrenceretten* (Franchising in Perspective of the EU-Law of Competiton), Forthcoming report winter.

0320
LAW AND ECONOMICS IN FINLAND

Risto Nuolimaa and Pekka Timonen
University of Tampere

Abstract

This chapter gives an overview of law and economics in Finland and seeks an explanation for why law and economics arrived late in Finland and then spread only slowly. In Finland as in the other Nordic countries, legal formalism was superseded by Scandinavian realism and by the 'analytical' legal research influenced by this realist school as long ago as the 1940s and 1950s.

In addition, scholars who in a country as small as Finland are few in number, have had to devote all their efforts to Finnish issues and changes in the Finnish legal system. European economic integration, however, has been the main reason for the awakening of interest in law and economics in Finland.
JEL classification: K00
Keywords: Law and Economics, Finland, Legal Realism

1. Background

Until the middle of the 1990s legal research in the field of law and economics was sporadic in Finland. In economics the situation has been better, though it has been a field in which only a few scholars have been interested. Since 1994, however, the gradually increasing volume of research has been produced mainly by legal scholars and it is this body of work on which this essay will concentrate. It is based largely on the study by Timonen (1998).

There are several interlinked reasons why law and economics arrived late in Finland and then spread only slowly.

(1) Jurisprudence in Finland has traditionally been influenced by developments in the other Nordic countries and in Germany. Thus awareness of law and economics, yet alone active interest in it, did not spread very quickly.

(2) Law and economics is intimately connected with the Anglo-American common law system and so this way of thinking as well as its application seem somewhat alien in a statute-based legal system. In the Finnish tradition the written law and travaux préparatoires carry much greater weight than case law and so research has focussed on the interpretation of current statutory law. This being the case, it has been possible only to a very limited extent to evaluate the

central question in the common law system: what would be the best (most efficient) way on a general level to form legal rules.

(3) In the USA law and economics is seen as part of a continuum covering various trends critical of legal doctrinalism. This is a point emphasized in particular by Mercuro and Medema (1997). In Finland, as in the other Nordic countries, legal formalism was superseded by Scandinavian realism and by the 'analytical' legal research influenced by this realist school as long ago as the 1940s and 1950s (see Stray Ryssdal, 1995, pp. 29-57). A very considerable part of the pressures for change that Posner (1987) has shown lay behind law and economics, were dealt with then.

(4) Throughout the 1990s Finnish researchers have been wrestling with the new legislation and the new questions arising from the EEA agreement and full EU membership. At the same time the exceptionally severe depression in the domestic Finnish market and the problems that it caused have given rise to a debate about reforming or dismantling the Nordic welfare state and this debate has inevitably raised important legal issues. In other words, scholars, who in any case in a country as small as Finland are few in number, have had to devote all their efforts to Finnish issues and changes in the Finnish legal system. They simply have not had the time and energy to take up new ideas such as law and economics until they had got a grip on the changes taking place in the Finnish legal environment and understood their significance. European economic integration, however, has forced Finnish scholars to seek out a new analytical apparatus. As Timonen (1997) stresses, this has been the main reason for the awakening of interest in law and economics in Finland.

2. Law and Economics research in Finland

The law and economics approach was first presented in Finland in an article published in 1980 (see Oker-Blom, 1980). It did not, however, arouse much interest and the whole theme was forgotten in Finland for nearly a decade and a half, although Timo Rapakko did publish the doctoral thesis he had done in the USA (Stanford) in Finland (Rapakko, 1987). It might be helpful to point out here that in Finland doctoral theses have been relatively rare and highly appreciated. In many subjects they have been written not by young academics embarking on a career, but by mature scholars in mid-career. Almost without exception doctoral theses are published. Considerable efforts are now being made to increase the number of PhDs and to reduce the number of years spent on doctoral research.

Law and economics research can be said to have got under way in Finland in 1994. The first economics-based doctoral theses in the field were published in 1994 and 1995 (see Högholm, 1994 and Sundgren, 1995). The first law- based doctoral theses were published in 1997 (see Timonen, 1997 and Määttä, 1997). So far interdisciplinary discussion and research cooperation has been meagre.

Otherwise, presentations of the subject for Finnish readers and reports on research in progress can be found in scholarly articles. In 1995 and 1996 several works were published that presented the approach, see especially Kanniainen, Määttä and Heimonen (1995). Mostly they describe the mainstream of law and economics research and explain the basic economic terminology. The first Finnish textbook on law and economics, Kanniainen and Määttä (1996) is also a collection of articles, in which each writer treats the subject from his or her own perspective, the team of writers including experts in economics as well as law.

From a comparative perspective it is interesting that work on the law and economics approach in legal studies has begun by using two modes of analysis that lie outside the mainstream. In Timonen (1997) the questions posed belong to the branches of law dealing with market behaviour (company, securities and competition law). The writer questions the suitability of Chicago law and economics thinking, rooted as it is in neoclassical economics, as a point of departure for the study of statute-based law and proposes in its place an approach based on neo-institutional economics. Making use of this, the work gives a general evaluation of the relationship between markets and regulation and of the significance of the efficiency argument in legal analysis. Määttä (1997) applies regulation theory to evaluate environmental taxes and their efficiency and to examine the development of environmental politics. Of the trends current within law and economics he has relied most on public choice thinking.

The first studies that clearly emphasize efficiency arguments and thus best represent the law and economics approach have yet to see the light of day in Finland and it is not yet possible to present any overall evaluation. The approach is, however, spreading rapidly and it can be expected that it will establish its place as a rightful recognised part of law studies in Finland before the end of the century.

Bibliography on Law and Economics in Finland (0320)

Högholm, Kenneth (1994), *Essays in the Market for Corporate Control*, Helsinki, Swedish School of Economics and Business Administration.

Kanniainen, Vesa and Määttä, Kalle (eds) (1996), *Näkökulmia oikeustaloustieteeseen* (Perspectives on Law and Economics), Helsinki, Gaudeamus.

Kanniainen, Vesa, Määttä, Kalle and Heimonen, Matti (1995), 'Oikeustaloustiede - law and economics (Law and Economics)', *Oikeus*, 107-124.

Määttä, Kalle (1997), *Environmental Taxes. From an Economic Idea to a Legal Institution*, Helsinki, Finnish Lawyers' Publishing.

Oker-Blom, Max (1980), 'Jurionomi eller rätten i ekonomiskt perspektiv (Law and Economics or Law from the Economic Percpective)', *Tidskrift utgiven av Juridiska Föreningen i Finland*, 245-265.

Rapakko, Timo (1987), *Corporate Control and Parent Firms' Liability for their Controlled Subsidiaries: A Study on the Regulation of Corporate Conduct*, Helsinki, Helsinki School of Economics.

Sundgren, Stefan (1995), *Bankruptcy Costs and Bankruptcy Code*, Helsinki, Swedish School of Economics and Business Administration.

Timonen, Pekka (1997), *Määräysvalta, hinta ja markkinavoima - Julkisesti noteeratun yrityksen määräysvallan siirtymisen oikeudellinen sääntely* (Control, Price and Market Power - The judicial regulation of transfers of control in quoted companies), Helsinki, Finnish Lawyers' Publishing.

Timonen, Pekka (1998), 'Oikeustaloustiede - mitä se on? (Law and Economics - What is it About?)', *Lakimies*, 100-114.

Other References

Mercuro, Nicholas and Medema, Steven G. (1997), *Economics and the Law. From Posner to Post-Modernism*, Princeton, Princeton University Press.

Posner, Richard (1987), 'The Decline of Law as an Autonomous Discipline: 1962-1987', **100** *Harvard Law Review*, 761-780.

Stray Ryssdal, A.C. (1995), *Legal Realism and Economics as Behaviour. A Scandinavian Look at Economic Analysis of Law*, Oslo, Juridisk Forlag.

0325
LAW AND ECONOMICS IN FRANCE

Lionel Montagné
Assistant in Civil Law
Université de Montpellier - Faculty of Law

Abstract

Even if economic reasoning applied to law is sometimes used by economists, the majority of jurists in France have some difficulties in accepting this tool as a complement to legal thought. So, there is no chair in law and economics in our French University of law, even though an effort seems to be made by the University of law in Montpellier, which includes some lectures in law and economics in its training for postgraduates students in law. But, in spite of that, prejudices and a lack of knowledge of law and economics, among jurists have slowed down the process of development of this matter.
JEL classification: A12, K00
Keywords: France, Research, Education.

1. Introduction

Even if the economic analysis of law has been developed well in most common law countries, as well in countries such as Germany or Sweden on the European continent, it must be noted that in France this tool is still underestimated by lawyers. Initially put forward by economists (A) the economic approach to law did not have the hoped-for success. As the matter of fact, we just have to look at the number of works published in this field, to see that the challenge has been ignored by the legal community (B).

A. Economic Analysis of Law: A Challenge for the French Jurist

The economic analysis of law aims at a better understanding of the logic of legal rules and judicial decisions. It is supposed to enlighten the jurist, whatever his or her discipline, as to the construction and the finality of the law. However, in France this tool was developed by economists and not by jurists (section 2), and the legal community did not examine the assets of such an instrument until some time later. In studying questions traditionally dealt with by lawyers, economists raised a real challenge that has been taken up only in the last few years by certain authors from Montpellier and Aix-en-Provence (section 3). Despite those efforts, the majority of the legal profession today seems to remain insensible to this tool.

2. The Economist and the Law

Economics is defined by Lionel Robbins as 'the science which studies human behavior in terms of the relationships between ends and means'. Therefore, it is evident that the rules of law, in so far as they organize the means in a world of scarcity and uncertainty, will sooner or later also become the object of study by economists in France. As elsewhere, this is precisely what happened, and in that process important notions, such as the notion of transaction costs, were established that shed light on legal doctrines. Different fields, until now the private domain of jurists, have come under the scrutiny of the economic community. Hence the development of an economic approach to property rights (Lepage, 1984), contract law or matrimonial law (Lemennicier, 1991). Nonetheless, this was not enough to stimulate the curiosity of the French legal community, at least not until 1986 when a symposium was organized on the economic analysis of law at Aix-en-Provence. For the first time, a degree of enthusiasm for applying economic reasoning to law became apparent.

Indeed, Professor Savatier in his lesson on the theory of liabilities in economic private law (Savatier, 1974) had already underlined the utility and the efficiency of economic tools in the development of legal reasoning. Professor Mouly, too, was convinced, especially after the 1986 conference, that a reflection on the mutual contributions of economy and law was both necessary and beneficial (Mouly, 1987, p. 413). But, in spite of this, and contrary to what was happening in other European countries, law and economics was still not taken up in France. If economists show a continued interest in this subject, very few legal authors refer directly to this instrument, even if incontestably they sometimes use a Posnerian approach to law in their writings (see Mousseron, 1987). Among the few exceptions, mention should be made of authors such as Mouly (1995, p. 377), Atias (1987, p. 477) or Chérot (1987a, p. 443), who occasionally use this tool. But, to this day, no work has been written by a jurist in this domain. The only existing work remains that of Lemennicier (1991), Professor of Economics.

3. The Jurist and the Economy

In the early 1990s one began to see an implicit recognition by various legal authors of the utility of the economic analysis of the law as a complement to legal thought, on the same level as sociology or morality. Hence, in the last edition of his civil law treaty, Ghestin (1994, pp. 84-85) dedicated some pages to law and economics in order to better situate the position of civil law among the legal disciplines. Fabre-magnan, in her thesis (1990, pp. 50-117) on the obligation of information in contracts, suggests an economic analysis of this obligation after having explained the basics of the economic analysis of law. Also , Cabrillac (1995, p. 23) in his general introduction of law, summarizes in a few lines the three functions (normative, predictive, critical) of an economic analysis of law. Finally, on the initiative of economists in Aix-en-Provence, '*Le Journal des Economistes et des Etudes humaines*' was founded, including, and this is noteworthy, some professors of law in its scientific committee.

In 1994 an important event occurred that led us to believe that the challenge set to the legal community more than thirty years ago had finally been accepted. Indeed, while the economic analysis of law was not taught in any of the French universities of law (except, perhaps, the 'DEA Analyse économique des institutions' which, however, depends on the University of Economics and is intended for students in economics), Professor C. Mouly started to introduce his postgraduate students to the utilization of economic tools in legal reasoning, and at the same time took part in the third-term university Erasmus (now called Socrates) Program in law and economics. The department of economic theory of law at the university of law in Montpellier, of which he was the creator and the director, became the privileged meeting place for economists and jurists whose common research on the economic approach to contract law and property rights, augured a much awaited success. Unfortunately, two years later, Professor Mouly's tragic and premature demise was to slow down the process of development of law and economics in the French legal culture.

B. The Economic Analysis of Law: a Challenge Ignored by the French Jurist

The study of legal questions often requires the use of different elements taken from sociology, history or logical analysis. The jurist uses these for the same reason that he/she refers to legal linguistics or philosophy of law. But curiously enough, the utilization of the economic approach to law is neglected. Some authors assign this marginalization to the absence of publications in French (see Mackaay 1987a), but this imbalance, we believe, is also, and firstly, due to a bias jurists have against economics (section 4) and the specific choice of economic instruments made by the advocate of an economic analysis of law (section 5).

4. The Subjective Obstacles to the Development of an Economic Analysis of Law

The intuitive perception of what is economics, acquired through the multitude of economic acts that they accomplish every day, leads most jurists to believe that they have enough knowledge of economics to fulfill their task. For others, the economic analysis of law is too narrow in its approach, and so must be excluded from legal discussions.

Such attitudes are easily explained. A first reason is the separation of the legal and economic disciplines in our academic system; jurists have little knowledge of economic analytical tools. Today, a law student does not receive the basic economic training that he had in the past. Also, the internal division within the legal discipline increases the effect of a separation between law and economics. Thus, the only jurists who use economics are those who follow a training in patrimonial law or in antitrust law.

Secondly, the jurist dislikes in modern economics what he perceives as a utilitarian approach. Convinced that economists are motivated only by the study of efficiency, he quickly turns away from their works. This belief is also reinforced by the use of mathematical or rationalistic language in economics, and tools that from the point of view of most jurists are incompatible with social studies. Not having completely mastered the tools of law and economics, legal authors therefore prefer to ignore this challenge.

Finally, due to insufficient knowledge of the field and his a priori judgment, the jurist was not in a position to appreciate the latest evolutions in economics. Hence, he was unable to notice the new conceptions, such as the Austrian School, according to which, for example, the criteria of efficiency used in law and economics must not be static but should be dynamic (Centi, 1987). So, according to this new view, one cannot appreciate the quality of legal rules only through its capacity to organize the efficient management of the scarcity. One must also verify whether our legal system adjusts itself appropriately to change in our environment. Through its recent development the economic analysis of law could thus oblige the jurist to question the foundations of institutions, instead of dogmatically affirming solutions directly translated from Latin adages which are sometimes obsolete.

5. The Objective Obstacles to the Development of an Economic Analysis of Law

The idea of a commercial activity whose object would be the persons themselves provokes a strong hostility from classical jurists. There are border lines which should not be crossed, and a law regarding persons cannot be analysed in the same way as law to be applied to ordinary assets. However, even if, for example, the prohibition to sell civil clienteles and ministerial offices is constantly affirmed, the jurisprudence did not hesitate to allow their indirect commercialization. Does not the patronymic name, which in France is imprescriptible and not transferable (inalienable), become itself the object of transactions which sanction this commercialization ? In view of this fact some economists proposed to submit the law of persons and the law of assets to the economic approach, without discrimination, with the risk of violating this *summa divisio* to which every French jurist is so attached. The American origin of the movement, as well as its slight respect for legal assumptions was, therefore, the object of diatribes from the legal community. The economic approach was blamed for being an imperialistic tool like sociology under the influence of Durkheim. But if we look at today's economic analysis of law, this argument is no longer true; Posner himself has moderated his positions (see Posner 1992, p. 25) and other movements have been born admitting that the economic analysis of the law is just a means among others to appreciate the quality of certain legal rules.

However, the neoclassic foundations on which the movement is founded further add to the reasons to ignore the economic analysis of the law. The rationality of the economic agent who is perfectly aware of prices, and operates calculated choices in order to maximize his pleasure at the least cost, is a disconcerting model for one who searches solutions in equity and not in utility. *Homo economicus* would not be the model of jurists who think the law and economics to be incompatible, and presume the collaboration between jurists and economists to be impossible through lack of a common language.

As Mackaay 1987a has written, the language represents a further obstacle to this collaboration. Indeed, depending on the disciplines, words have different meanings. The 'exchange', for example, represents for economists the general act by which a person gives up a good against another good, whereas for the jurist it defines a very particular contract. Inversely, some equivalent notions are expressed using different words: depending on whether the contract allows one to get rid of uncertainties or not, the economist will use the terms 'complete' or 'incomplete' contract where the jurist will use the terms 'perfect' or 'imperfect' contract. Finally, the legal vocabulary finds its origins in Roman law whereas the economist uses a more recent terminology adapted to a present and evolutionary world.

C. Conclusion

The lack of communication and the existence of prejudices are regrettable stumbling blocks to the development of law and economics in France. In spite of the efforts of economists to propose a fruitful collaboration in the development of the field, only some jurists have responded. Others still prefer to ignore this tool and the situation will remain thus so long as the French Law Universities do not make an effort to demonstrate an interest in the use of this tool of analysis, a natural complement to the conventional training of a lawyer.

Acknowledgements

Special thanks to Prof. Pierre Garello for his help and patience.

Bibliography on Law and Economics in France (0325)

Ackerman, Bruce A. (1986), *Deux Sortes de Recherche en Droit et Économie* (Two Sorts of Research in Law and Economics), Revue de la Recherche Juridique, Droit prospectif: l'Analyse Économique du Droit, 2 colloques, Aix-en-Provence, mai 1986 et Corte, janvier 1986, Presses Universitaires d'Aix-Mareille.

Atias, Christian (1987), *La Distinction du Patrimonial et de l'Extra-Patrimonial et l'Analyse Économique du Droit: un Utile Face à Face* (The Distinction between Patrimonial and Extra-patrimonial Rights and the Economic Analysis of Law), Revue de la Recherche Juridique, Droit prospectif: l'Analyse économique du Droit, 2 colloques, Aix-en-Provence, mai 1986 et Corte, janvier 1986, Presses Universitaires d'Aix-Mareille, p. 477.

Bastiat, F. (1983), *Propriété et Loi* (Property and Law), Paris.

Bauch, Matthias (1996), *Unternehmensinsolvenzen, Prophylaxe und Bewältigung in Frankreich - Darstellung und Ökonomische Analyse von Procédure d'Alerte, Règlement Amiable und Redressement et Liquidation Judiciaires* (Bankruptcy of Corporations in France - Discussion and Economic Analysis), Dissertation, Regensburg.

Bergel, J.-L. (1989), *Théorie Générale du Droit* (General Theory of Law), Dalloz, Coll. Méthode du Droit.

Bergel, J.-L. (1994), *La Propriété* (Property), Dalloz.

Bienayme, A., 'Défense et Illustration d'une Réflexion Juridique Intégrant l'Économie (Defense and Illustration of a Legal Reflexion Integrating Economics)', **64(6)** *La Semaine Juridique*.

Cabrillac Remy (1995), *Introduction Générale au Droit* (General Introduction of Law), Dalloz, 23 p.

Carbonnier, J. (1983), *Flexible Droit, Textes pour une Sociologie du Droit sans Rigueur.* (Flexible Law, Texts for Sociology of Law without Rigour), L.G.D.J.

Carbonnier, J. (1995), *Droit Civil. Les Biens* (Civil Law. Goods), T. III, P.U.F.

Centi, Jean-Pierre (1987), 'Quel Critère d'Éfficience pour l'Analyse Économique du Droit (Which Efficiency Criterion for Economic Analysis of the Law)', in *Revue de la Recherche Juridique, Droit Prospectif: l'Analyse Économique du Droit*, 2 colloques, Aix-en-Provence, mai 1986 et Corte, janvier 1986, Presses Universitaires d'Aix-Mareille, p. 456.

Cherot, Jean-Yves (1987a), 'Trois Thèses sur l'Analyse Économique du Droit - Quelques Usages de l'Approche Économique des Règles Juridiques (Three Theses on Economic Analysis of Law - Some Uses of the Economic Approach to Legal Rules)', in *Revue de la Recherche Juridique, Droit Prospectif: l'Analyse Économique du Droit*, 2 colloques, Aix-en-Provence, mai 1986 et Corte, janvier 1986, Presses Universitaires d'Aix-Mareille, p. 443.

Cherot, Jean-Yves (1987b), 'Elements pour une Théorie de la Réglementation (Elements for a Theory of Regulation)', *Revue de la Recherche Juridique, Droit Prospectif: l'Analyse Économique du Droit*, 2 colloques, Aix-en-Provence, mai 1986 et Corte, janvier 1986, Presses Universitaires d'Aix-Mareille.

Cherot, Jean-Yves (1990), *Les Évolutions du Droit Économique* (The Evolutions of Law and Economics).

Coulange, Pierre (1990), 'La Production de Droit (The Production of Legal Rules)', **3** *Journal des Economistes et des Etudes Humaines*, 277-302.

Dubouchet, P. (1994), 'Herméneutique et Théorie Normative du Droit (Hermeneutic and Normative Theory of Law)', Presses Universitaires d'Aix-Marseille, R.R.J., p. 735.

Dubouchet, P. (1994), *La théorie Normative et le Langage du Juge* (The Normative Theory and the Language of Judge), Presses Universitaires d'Aix-Marseille, p. 658 .

Duharcourt, Pierre (1988), ''Théories' et 'Concept' de la Régulation (Regulation as a Theory and as a Concept)', **22(5)** *Economies et Sociétés*, 135-161.

Encaoua, David and Koebel, Philippe (1987), 'Réglementation et Déréglementation des Télécommunications: Leçons Anglo-saxonnes et Perspectives d'Évolution en France (Regulation and Deregulation of Telecommunications, Anglo-Saxon Lessons and Evolutionary Perspectives in France)' , **38** *Revue Economique*, 475-520.

Encaoua, David and Moreaux, Michel (1987), 'L'Analyse Théorique des Problèmes de Tarification et d'Allocation des Costs dans les Télécommunications (The Theoretical Approach to Pricing and Cost Allocation for Telecommunication Services)', **38** *Revue Economique*, 375-413.

Fabre-magnan Muriel (1990), *De l'Obligation d'Information dans les Contrats* (The Obligation of Information in Contracts), L.G.D.J.

Farjat, G. (1963), *L'Ordre Public Économique* (Economic Public Order), Bibliothèque de Droit Privé.

Farjat, G. (1982), *Droit Economique* (Economic Law), P.U.F.

Fluet, Claude (1987), 'Fraude Fiscale et Offre de Travail au Noir (Tax Evasion and the Supply of Unofficial Labour)', **63** *L'Actualité Economique*, 225-242.

Fluet, Claude (1990), 'L'Analyse Économique du Droit (Economic Analysis of Law)', **43(3)** *Économie Appliquée*, 53-66.

Fortier, V. (1991), *La Fonction Normative des Notions Floues* (The Normative Functions of the Vagueness Notions), Presses Universitaires d'Aix-Marseille, p. 755.

Garello, Jacques, Lemennicier, Bertrand and Lepage, Henri (1990), *Cinq Questions sur les Syndicats* (Five Questions on Labor Unions), Paris, Presses Universitaires de France (PUF).

Garello, P. (1995), *Présentation d'un Débat Fondamental en Science Économique et ses Implications pour les Rapports entre Droit et Économie* (Presentation of Fundamental Debate in Economics and its Implication in the Relationship between Law and Economics), R.R.J. , Presses Universitaires d'Aix-Marseille., 419 p.

Ghestin Jacques (1994), 'Traité de Droit Civil (Treate of Civil Law)', LGDJ , 84-85.

Gridel, J.-P. (1994), *Introduction au Droit et au Droit Français., Notions Fondamentales. Méthodologie. Synthèses* (Introduction to the Law and the French Law, Fundamentals notions. Methodology. Synthesis), Dalloz.

Hannequart, Achille and Greffe, Xavier (1985), *Economie des Interventions Sociales* (Economics of Social Interventions), Paris, Economica, 264 p.

Husson, B. (1987), *Le Prise de Contrôle d'Entreprises* (Takeovers), Paris, Presses Universitaires de France (PUF).

Josserand, L. (1937), *Un Ordre Juridique Nouveau* (A New Juridical Order), Dalloz, 41 p.

Kornhauser, Lewis A. (1985), 'L'analyse Economique Du Droit (The Economic Analysis of Law)', **118-119** *Revue de Synthese*, 313 ff.

Laveleye, Emile De (1891), 'De la Propriété et de ses Formes Primitives (Property and its Primitive Forms)', in Rottenberg, Simon (ed.), *Occupational Licensure and Regulation*, Washington (DC), American Enterprise Institute.

Lemennicier, Bertrand (1980), *La Spécialisation des Rôles Conjugaux, les Gains du Mariage et la Perspective du Divorce* (Specialization of Conjugal Role, Marital Gains, and Perspective of Divorce), consommation.

Lemennicier, Bertrand (1982), *Les Déterminants de la Mobilité Matrimoniale* (The Determinants of Matrimonial Mobility), consommation.

Lemennicier, Bertrand (1987), 'Indemnités de Licenciement: Assurances tous Risques, Réparation d'un Préjudice ou Impact sur la Liberté de Contracter (Damages of Licensing: All Risk Insurance, Retrieving a Loss or Taxation on the Freedom of Contract)', *Revue de la Recherche Juridique Droit Perspectif.*

Lemennicier, Bertrand (1988), *Le Marché du Mariage et de la Famille* (The Marriage Market and the Family), Paris, Presses Universitaires de France (PUF), Collection Libre Echange.

Lemennicier, Bertrand (1990), 'Bioéthique et Liberté (Bio-Ethics and Liberty)', **13** *Droits: Revue Française de Théorie Juridique*, 111-122.

Lemennicier, Bertrand (1991), *Economie du Droit* (Economics of Law), Paris, Ed. Cujas, 177 p.

Lemennicier, Bertrand and Levy-Garboua (1981), *L'Arbitrage Autarcie-marché: une Explication du Travail Féminin* (Arbitration Autarchy-Market: An Explanation of Female Work), consommation.

Lepage, Henri (1984), *Pourquoi la Propriété?* (Why Property?), Paris.

Liggio, L. P. (1990), 'Evolution of French Liberal Thought', **1** *Journal des Economistes et des Etudes Humaines*, 101 ff.

MacKaay, Ejan (1986), 'La Règle Juridique Observée par le Prisme de l'Économiste - une Histoire Stylisée du Mouvement d'Analyse Économique du Droit (The Legal Rule Viewed from the Perspective of the Economist - A Stylized History of the Law and Economics Movement)', **1** *Revue Internationale de Droit Economique*, 43-88.

MacKaay, Ejan (1987a), 'Le Juriste a-t-il le Droit d'Ignorer l'Economiste? (May Lawyers Ignore Economists?)', *Revue de la Recherche Juridique*, 419-427.

MacKaay, Ejan (1987b), 'Le Paradoxe des Droits Acquis (The Paradox of Acquired Rights)', in X (ed.), *De 'l'Ancienne' à la 'Nouvelle' Économie. Essais à l'Occasion de la Dixième Université d'été de la Nouvelle Économie*, Aix-en-Provence, Librairie de l'Université, 205-219.

MacKaay, Ejan (1989), 'Les Droits Intellectuels - entre Propriété et Monopole (Intellectual Property Rights - Between Property and Monopoly)', **1** *Journal des Economistes et des Etudes Humaines.*

Moine, I. (1997), *Les Choses hors Commerce. Une Approche de la Personne Humaine Juridique.* (Things Apart from Commerce. An Approach of Juridical Human Person), LGDJ.

Mouly, Christian (1987), 'Présentation du Colloque sur l'Analyse Économique du Droit (Introduction to the Symposium of Economic Analysis of Law)', *Revue de la Recherche Juridique*, 413 ff.

Mouly, Christian (1995), 'La Propriété (Property)', in X (ed.), *Droits et Libertés Fondamentaux, 2nd edn*, Dalloz.

Mouly, Christian (1995), 'Analyse Économique du Droit Régissant le Transfert de Propriété (Economic Analysis of Law Governing the Transfer of Property)', in X (ed.), *Faut-il Retarder le Transfert de Propriété?'*, JCP éd. E, 6 ff.

Mousseron, Jean-Marc (1987), 'La Gestion des Risques par le Contrat (Risk Management by Contract)', *Revue Trimestrielle de Droit Civil*, 481 ff.

Naudet, Jean-Yves and Serment, Laurent (1990), 'Le Droit de Propriété Garanti par la Convention Européenne des Droits de l'Homme face à l'Analyse Économique (Property Law Guaranteed by the European Convention of Human Rights, in the Light of Economic Analysis)', **15** *Revue de la Recherche Juridique Droit Perspectif*, 15-50.

Oppetit, B. (1992), 'Droit et Economie (Law and Economics)', **37** *Archives de Philosophie du Droit. Nouvelle serie*, 17 ff.

Patault, A.-M (1989), *Introduction Historique au Droit des Biens.* (Historical Introduction to the Property), Paris, Presses Universitaires de France.

Picard, Pierre (1988), 'La Tarification Optimale des Télécommunications: une Présentation Synthetique (Optimal Pricing for Telecommunications: An Overview)', **0(12)** *Annales d'Economie et de Statistique*, 27-62.

Playoust, O. (1993), *Normativité et Légitimité du Droit* (Normativism and Legitimacy of Law), Presses Universitaires d'Aix-Marseille, 193 p.

Point, Patrick (1990), 'Entreprises, Normes d'Environnement et Incitations à Reduire les Delais de Mise en Conformité (Firms, Environmental Standards and Incentives to Promote Compliance)', **100** *Revue d'Économique Politique*, 260-282.

Posner, Richard A. (1992), *Economic Analysis of Law, 4th edn*, Little, Brown and Company.

Poughon, Jean-Michel (1987), *Histoire Doctrinale de l'Échange,* (Doctrinal History of Exchange), LGDJ.

Poughon, Jean-Michel (1990), 'Une Constante Doctrinale: l'Approche Économique du Contract', **12** *Droits: Revue Française de Théorie Juridique*, 47-59.

Prychitko, David L. (1990), 'Methodological Individualism and the Austrian School', **1** *Journal des Economistes et des Etudes Humaines*, 171 ff.

Riboud, M. (1988), 'Altruisme au Sein de la Famille, Croissance Économique et Démographie (Altruism in the Family, Economic Growth and Demography)', *Revue Economique*.

Rosa, J.J. (1984), 'Deréglementation et Théorie du Droit (Deregulation and Legal Theory)', **33** *Politique Economique*.

Rothbard, Murray N. (1991), *L'Éthique de la Liberté.* (The Ethics of Liberty), Les Belles Lettres.

Rouland, Norbert (1985), 'Lecture Anthropologique et Inter-Culturelle des Systèmes Fonciers (Anthropology and Inter-cultural Reading of Systems of Property)', **1** *Destins du Droit de Propriété*, 73 ff.

Salaun, Fabienne (1990), 'Privatisation et Reglementation: le Cas du British Gas (Privatization and Regulation: The Case of British Gas)', **24** *Economies et Sociétés*, 453-469.

Savatier René (1959), *Les Méthamorphoses Économiques et Sociales du Droit Civil Aujourd'hui* (The Economic and Sociologic Metamorphoses of Civil Law Today), Paris, Dalloz.

Savatier René (1974), *La Théorie des Obligations en Droit Privé Économique* (The Theory of Obligations in Private Economic Law), Paris, Dalloz.

Sayag, Alain and Serbat, Henri (1982), *L'Application du Droit de la Faillite. Eléments pour un Bilan* (The Application of Bankruptcy Law. Data for an Evaluation), Paris, Librairies Techniques.

Schweitzer, Serge (1987), 'De 'l'Ancienne' à la 'Nouvelle' Economie: Comment Passe-t-on d'un Paradigme à l'Autre (From 'Old' to 'New' Economics: How One Goes From One Paradigm to Another)', in X (ed.), *De 'l'Ancienne' à la 'Nouvelle' Économie. Essais à l'Occasion de la Dixième Université d'été de la Nouvelle Économie. Aix-en-Provence 1978-1987*, Aix-en-Provence, Librairie de l'Université, 257-274.

Seurot, François (1987), 'Analyse Économique de la Liberté des Contrats (Economic Analysis of Freedom of Contracts)', in X (ed.), *De 'l'Ancienne' à la 'Nouvelle' Économie. Essais à l'Occasion de la Dixième Université d'été de la Nouvelle Économie. Aix-en-Provence 1978-1987*, Aix-en-Provence, Librairie de l'Université, 275-281.

Sofer, C. (1985), *La Division du Travail entre Hommes et Femmes* (The Division of Labour Between Men and Women), Paris, Economica.

Théret, Bruno (1990), 'La Place de l'État dans les Théories Économiques Françaises de la Régulation: Éléments Critiques et Repositionnement à la Lumière de l'Histoire (The

Place of the State in French Economic Theories of Regulation; Critical Arguments and New Posture Brought to Light by History)', **43(2)** *Économie Appliquée*, 43-81.

Waline, M. (1965), 'Quelques Facteurs Sociologiques de l'Évolution Actuelle du Droit (Some Sociologic Factors of Actual Evolution of Law)', in X (ed.), *Mélanges Offerts à René Savatier*.

Zenati, F. (1981), *Essai sur la Nature Juridique de la Propriété, Contribution à la Théorie Juridique du Droit Subjectif.* (Essay on the Juridical Nature of Property, Contribution to the Juridical Theory of Subjective Rights), Thèse, Lyon.

Zenati, F. (1993), Pour une Rénovation de la Théorie de Propriété (For a Renovation of the Theory of Property), RTD civ., 305 p.

Other References

Atias, C. (1993), *Droit Civil. Les Biens.* (Civil law. Goods), Litec.

Berra, D. (1969), *Le Principe de Libre Disposition des Biens en Droit Civil* (The Principe of Free Disposal of Goods), Nancy.

Brocard, L. (1934), *Propriété Privée et Économie Nationale* (Property and National Economy), Mélanges Geny, p. 145.

Fromont, M. (1984), 'Le Droit de Propriété et la Constitution en Allemagne et en France (Property Rights and Dutch and French Constitution)' in Pequignot, G.D. (ed.), *L'Interventionnisme Économique de la Puissance Publique, Études en l'Honneur*, p. 267.

Gilli, J.-P. (1975), *Redéfinir le Droit de Propriété.* (To Redefine Property Rights), Centre de Recherche en Urbanisme.

Goyard-fabre, S. (1981), *Kant et le Problème du Droit* (Kant and the Problem of Law), Coll. Bibliothèque d'Histoire de la Philosophie.

Mazeaud, H., L. Mazeaud, et al. (1994), *Leçons de Droit Civil, Biens, Droits de Propriété et ses Démembrements.* (Lessons of Civil Law, Goods, Property Rights and their Decomposition), Montchrestien Tome II..

Ripert, G. (1951), *Aspects Juridiques du Capitalisme Moderne* (Juridical Aspects of Modern Capitalism), L.G.D.J.

0330
LAW AND ECONOMICS IN GERMANY

Roland Kirstein
Center for the Study of Law and Economics
University of Saarland

Abstract

Law and economics in Germany was dominated by regulation, competition and 'German Ordnungspolitik' until the early 1970s. Since then, German scholars have published a broad body of work in German and in the English language, covering fields like contract law, environmental law, labor law, public law, bankruptcy law, constitutional economics and legal procedure. Also in the 1970s, teaching activities were started at German universities. In addition to this, several (bi)annual conferences on law and economics were launched. The foundation of some research centers gave a further impetus to the German law and economics movement.
JEL classification: K00, A20
Keywords: German Literature, Teaching Activities, Conferences, Research Institutes on Law and economics

1. Introduction

Until 25 years ago, research in the field of law and economics in Germany mainly focussed on competition and regulation. Discussions on the relation between jurisprudence and economics took place only occasionally, see for example Stützel (1966) and Jahr (1966). Since the late 1970s however, the first German books on other law and economics topics were published, such as Kunz (1976a) on the economics of individual and collective crime, Behrens (1986) on Political Economics, and Adams (1981) on procedural law. A collection of seminal law and economics papers, translated into German, was published by Assman, Kirchner and Schanze (1978).

Since then, publications by German scholars have covered all fields of law and economics. Teaching programs were installed and new research institutions were founded. A lot of these publications were published in English, although the bibliography attached to this chapter is limited to contributions in German. Of course, the discussion as well as the bibliography can only give a brief overview, which does not claim to be complete.

2. German 'Ordnungspolitik'

German research on competition policy traditionally focussed on 'Ordnungspolitik', a term that can roughly be translated as 'Institutional Policy' or as 'Constitutional Political Economics'. The term refers to the legal and organizational means governments can use to influence the institutional framework of the economy. Within this framework, the economic actors are free to pursue their own goals. W. Eucken, E. Hoppmann, C. Watrin and H. Willgerodt are among the early contributors to this traditional approach. Since 1949, the 'ORDO. Jahrbuch fuer die Ordnung von Wirtschaft und Gesellschaft' annually publishes papers on ordnungspolitik.

Not only economists but also lawyers contributed to this field of research, see for example Boehm (1980), Mestmaecker (1978) and Möschel (1988), who wrote many papers on German and European competition law with a clear economic focus. Law scholars as well as economists serve in several federal commissions, which turned out to be an important interface for the interdisciplinary transmission of research results. Ingo Schmidt developed an early expertise in the comparison of US and German competition law, see for example Schmidt (1973a).

The 10th volume of the *Jahrbuch fuer Neue Politische Oekonomie* provides an overview of newer ideas on 'ordnungspolitik', see Boettcher et al. (1991). In 1979, the first Symposion on 'New Political Economics als Ordnungstheorie' took place. These papers were published in 1980.

3. New Law and Economics in Germany

3.. Basic Concepts

German law scholars sometimes criticize the law and economics movement for focussing on efficiency, and argue against its usage as a legal principle for the judicature, such as Fezer (1986). Ott and Schäfer (1988) and Weise (1991) discussed Fezer's article. Eidenmueller (1995a) has written a comprehensive book on this important debate, with a detailed review by Schmidtchen (1997). Kunz (1985a) was one of the first books in German on the evolution of norms and orders, followed by Hutter (1989). Witt (1988) und Kerber (1992) examine the impact that institutions have on competition and innovation. The evolution of judge-made law was analyzed by Wangenheim (1995).

3.2 Contract Law and Externalities

An important field for German law and economic scholars is environmental economics, see for example Lehmann (1992b) on Environmental Liability Law. Endres (1993) has analyzed instruments of Environmental Policy in a project on

International Environmental Contracts. He also does research into Tort and Liability Law (see Endres, 1991b). A game theoretic approach to this subject was chosen by Jost (1997a).

Lawyers as well as economists broadly covered the field of workers' participation and labor law (see Nagel, 1988b or Eger (1995b) analyzed long-term contracts. Workers participation as a mean to protect quasi-rents from sunk investments was analyzed by Schmidtchen (1987a). Adomeit (1996) covers labor regulation.

Weck-Hannemann (1996) wrote about female employment and family taxation. Walwei (1993) provides an analysis of the regulation of private employment agencies.

Druckarzcyk started to do research into insolvency law and reorganization in 1980 (see for example Druckarczyk, 1987c). An early contribution to the economic analysis of insolvency law was made by R. Schmidt, see also Schmidt (1981b). On the regulation of finance and loans, see Herrmann (1994) or Terberger (1987). Intellectual Property Rights are discussed by Koboldt and Schmidtchen (1991) and Tietzel (1994). The economics of international trade and the territoriality of law is the subject of Schmidt-Trenz (1990a), who tried to explain the role of international trade firms from an institutional economics viewpoint. Kötz (1986) analyzes international private law harmonization.

3.3 Public Law and Procedural Law

Besides the work on 'ordnungspolitik', German scholars also contributed to the economic analysis of constitutions, see for example Vanberg (1982b). The relevance of constitutional economics for economic policy is discussed by Voigt (1996). Leschke (1993) relates economic theory of constitutions to the concept of democracy. Schmidt-Trenz (1996) points out the two basic dilemmas institutions have to solve simultaneously: the contribution and the delegation problem. *The Jahrbuch fuer Neue Politische Oekonomie* vol. 15 collects articles that were presented during a symposium on 'New Forms of Cooperation Between State and Citizens' (see Schenk, Schmidtchen and Streit, 1996).

An application of constitutional economics to drug policy was provided by Erlei (1992) and Koboldt (1995c). Adams (1994) wrote on the costs and benefits of drug liberalization, whereas Frank (1995) analyzed smoking bans. Contributions to the economic analysis of the welfare and health care system were provided by Schulenburg (1993) and Seidl (1988a). Schöffski (1995) writes about the regulation of German pharmacies.

Civil and criminal procedure seem to be less attractive as subjects of economic research than substantive law. After some contributions by Adams that were published in the early 1980s, only a few papers on this topic followed, such as Schäfer and Kötz (1992). Schäfer (1995) points out the productive function of jurisdiction for the creation of cooperation rents. Only recently, had this field gained more attention, see for example Ott and Schäfer (1996) on plea bargaining, or Schmidtchen and Kirstein (1997), who analyze the motivational impact of procedural rules on potential litigants.

4. Teaching Activities, Research Centers and Conferences

One of the oldest institutions in Germany working in the field of law and economics is the Institut fuer Genossenschaftswesen in Münster, which was founded in 1947. Nowadays, it is concerned with analyzing different forms of cooperation, such as franchise contracts, or 'Genossenschaften' (buyer or seller cooperatives), making use of the framework of New Institutional Economics, see Bonus (1981b). Also in Münster, Grossekettler edits the *Schriften zur wirtschaftswissenschaftlichen Analyse des Rechts*.

Teaching activities in law and economics started in the early 1970s. Some interdisciplinary courses have been organized, such as seminars on competition and cartel law in Stuttgart or in Tübingen. The annual workshop in law and economics in Maastricht (the Netherlands) was launched by the German scholar Jürgen Backhaus in 1987. Since 1984, Backhaus has co-edited the *European Journal of Law and Economics*.

In Hamburg, Ott and Schäfer installed an Erasmus program for postgraduate students from 18 European countries, and integrated law and economics into the Law Faculty. Their textbook (Ott and Schäfer, 1996) was recently published in the 4th edition. Since 1988, Ott and Schäfer have organized a biannual conference on law and economics in Travemuende. Together with R. van den Bergh, they founded an Institute of law and economics at the University of Hamburg. The same university also hosts a Center for Research in Law and Innovation, founded by W. Hoffmann-Riem. Also in Hamburg, P. Behrens, M. Holler, C. Ott, H.-B. Schäfer, and W. Walz edit a law and economics publication series, called 'Schriftenreihe zur oekonomischen Analyse des Rechts'.

The first annual meeting on New Political Economics took place in 1981. Nowadays it is organized by K.-E. Schenk, D. Schmidtchen and M. Streit. The papers of this conference are published in the *Jahrbuecher fuer Neue Politische Oekonomie*. D. Schmidtchen has founded the Forschungsstelle fuer die oekonomische Analyse des Rechts (Center for the Study of Law and Economics) at the University of Saarbruecken. The recently founded Max-Planck Institute for Research into Economic Systems in Jena is mainly concerned with transition economics. Its starting point in the attempt to explain the change of economic systems is the idea that economic development mainly depends on the institutional framework (see for example Streit, 1996). The Walter-Eucken Institut in Freiburg publishes lectures and papers on economic policy.

In 1994, B. Nagel, P. Weise and T. Eger founded an Institut fuer Recht und Oekonomis (Institut for Law and Economics) at the University in Kassel. I. Schmidt has founded a center for research into competition policy and cartel law at the university of Stuttgart. In Trier, the Institut fuer Arbeitsrecht und Arbeitsbeziehungen in der Europäischen Gemeinschaft (Institute for Labor Law and Labor Relations in the EU) uses institutional economics to perform empirical comparisions of the labor law of different European countries (see Sadowski and Kurth, 1991).

R. Richter is the founder of the Wallerfangen summer school (nowadays organized by U. Schweizer), and started the annual Wallerfangen conference, which in part covers law and economics subjects. The papers presented in this conference are published in the *Journal of Theoretical and Institutional Economics* (JITE), which is now edited by E. Schlicht.

Bibliography on Law and Economics in Germany (0330)

Adams, Michael (1980), *Ökonomische Analyse des Sicherungsrechte* (Economic Analysis of Security Law), Königstein/Ts, Athenaeum, 322 p.

Adams, Michael (1981), *Ökonomische Analyse des Zivilprozesses* (Economic Analysis of Civil Procedure), Königstein/Ts, Athenaeum, 130 p.

Adams, Michael (1983a), 'Eine Wohlfahrtstheoretische Analyse des Zivilprozesses und der Rechtsschutzversicherungen (A Welfare Analysis of Civil Procedure and Legal Costs Insurance)', *Zeitschrift für Schweizerisches Recht*, 187-208.

Adams, Michael (1983b), 'Streitgespräch Adams/Blankenburg über den Einfluß der Rechtsschutzversicherungen auf den Geschäftsanfall der Gerichte, veranstaltet vom Bundesministerium der Justiz (Discussion on the Influence of Legal Costs Insurances on the Caseload of the Courts)', *Deutsche Richterzeitung*, 353-362.

Adams, Michael (1985), *Ökonomische Analyse des Gefährdungs- und Verschuldenshaftung* (Economic Analysis of Strict and Fault Liability), Heidelberg, R.v Decker's/C.F. Müller, 310 p.

Adams, Michael (1986a), 'Zur Aufgabe des Haftungsrechts im Umweltschutz (On the Task of Liability Law for the Protection of the Environment)', **99** *Zeitschrift für Zivilprozess*, 129-165.

Adams, Michael (1986b), 'Der Zivilprozess als Folge strategischen Verhaltens (On Civil Procedure as a Consequence of Strategic Behavior)', **7** *Zeitschrift für Rechtssoziologie*, 212-225.

Adams, Michael (1986c), 'Zur Behandlung von Irrtümern und Offenbarungspflichten im Vertragsrecht (On Mistake and Information Revelation Duties in Contract Law)', **186** *Archiv für die civilistische Praxis*, 453-489.

Adams, Michael (1986d), 'Der Irrtum über Künftige Sachverhalte. Anwendungsbeispiel und Einführung indie Ökonomische Analyse des Rechts (Error about Future Facts)', *RECHT, Zeitschrift für juristische Ausbildung und Praxis*, 14-23.

Adams, Michael (1987a), 'Ökonomische Analyse der Produkthaftung (Economic Analysis of Product Liability)', **87** *Der Betriebs-Berater*.

Adams, Michael (1987b), 'Produkthaftung - Wohltat oder Plage - Eine Ökomische Analyse (Product Liability - Benefit or Plague - An Economic Analysis)', **3124** *Der Betriebs-Berater*.

Adams, Michael (1989a), 'Das Verursacherprinzip als Leerformel (The Polluter Pays Principe as Empty Formula)', *Juristenzeitung*, 789-790.

Adams, Michael (1989b), 'Ökonomische Begründung des AGB-Gesetzes - Verträge bei Asymetrischer Information (The Economic Basis of the German Unfair Contract T)', *Der Betriebs-Berater*, 781-788.

Adams, Michael (1989c), 'Warum kein Ersatz von Nichtvermögensschäden? (Why No Damages for Nonpecuniary Losses?)', in Ott, Claus and Schäfer, Hans-Bernd (eds), *Allekationseffizienz in der Rechtsordnung*, Berlin, Springer, 210-217.

Adams, Michael (1989d), 'Der Markt für Unternehmenskontrolle und sein Missbrauch (The Market of Corporate Control and Its Abuse)', *Die Aktiengesellschaft*, 333-338.

Adams, Michael (1990a), 'Warum das 'Verursacherprinzip' eine leere Worthülse darstellt und von feinsinnigen Juristen bei Haftungslastentscheidungen im Umweltrecht als ungeeignetes Kriterium verworfen werden sollte (Why the 'Polluter Pays Principle' Is an Empty Formula and Should be Disregarded by Sensitive Lawyers when Making Decisions on Liability in Environment Law)', in Haller, M., Hauser, H. and Zäch, R. (eds), *Ergängzungen, Festschrift Erweiterungsbau der Hochschule St. Gallen*, Haupt, 605-612.

Adams, Michael (1990b), 'Was spricht gegen eine unbehinderte Übertragbarkeit der in Unternehmengebundenen Ressourcen durch ihre Eigentümer (Arguments against an Unlimited Transferability of a Firm's Resources)', *Die Aktiengesellschaft*, 243-252.

Adams, Michael (1990c), 'Zur Nichtigkeit von Preisaufschlagverboten in Kreditkartenverträgen gemäß § 15 GWB (On the Voidness of Supplementary Charges Prohibition Clauses in Contracts on Credit Cards)', *Zeitschrift für Wirtschaftsrecht*, 632-635.

Adams, Michael (1990d), 'Höchststimmrechte, Mehrfachstimmrechte und sonstige wundersame Hindernisse auf dem Markt für Unternehmenskontrolle (Maximum Voting Right, Multiple Voting Right, and some Wonderfull Obstacles from the Market of Corporate Control)', **35** *Die Aktiengesellschaft*, 63-78.

Adams, Michael (1991a), 'Normen, Standards, Rechte (Norms, Standards, Rights)', *Juristenzeitung*, 941-955.

Adams, Michael (1991b), 'Wie zerstört man den Markt für Rauschgifte? (How to Destroy the Drug Markets?)', **Juni** *Zeitschrift für Rechtspolitik*, 202-204, unveränderter Nachdruck in, *Magazin für die Polizei*, 9/1992 P. 4-6

Adams, Michael (1991c), 'Das bürgerlich-rechtliche Benachteiligungsverbot gemäß § 612 III BGB (The Prohibition of Discrimination in the German Private Law)', *Juristenzeitung*, 534-539.

Adams, Michael (1991d), 'Eigentum, Kontrolle und Beschränkte Haftung (Property, Control and Limited Liability)', in Ott, Claus and Schäfer, Hans-Bernd (eds), *Ökonomische Probleme des Zivilrechts*, Berlin, Springer, 193-225.

Adams, Michael (1992), 'Den Teufel mit Belzebub austreiben - Wie man den Markt für Rauschgiftezerstört (Excorcise one Evil with Another - How to Destroy the Drug Markets)', **12** *Kriminalistik, Zeitschrift für die gesamte kriminalistische Wissenschaft und Praxis*, 757-761.

Adams, Michael (1993), 'Neues vom Drogenmarkt? (News from the Drug Market)', **12** *Kriminalistik, Zeitschrift für die gesamte kriminalistische Wissenschaft und Praxis*, 755-757.

Adams, Michael (1994a), 'Das Bundesarbeitsgericht und das Recht zur Täuschung (The Federal Labor Court and the Right to Deceive)', **April** *Zeitschrift für Wirtschaftsrecht*, 499 ff.

Adams, Michael (1994b), 'Beseitigung der steuerlich bedingten Machtzentralisierung bei Versicherungsunternehmen durch Einführung eines 'qualifizierten Kontos' (Elimination of the Centralization of Power due to Tax Law by Introducing a 'Qualified Account')', *Zeitschrift für Wirtschaftsrecht*, 1434-1437.

Adams, Michael (1994c), 'Die Usurpation von Aktionärsbefugnissen mittels Ringverflechtung in der 'Deutschland-AG' - Vorschläge für Reformen im Wettbewerbs-, Steuer- und Unternehmensrecht (The Ursupation of Shareholder's Rights by Circle Interlinks in the 'Germany Stock Corporation'. Proposals for a Reform in Competition Law, Tax Law, and Cooperations Law)', *Die Aktiengesellschaft*, 148-156.

Adams, Michael (1994d), 'Heroin an Süchtige? - Ein abschließender Schlagabtausch (Heroin for Addicts?)', *Zeitschrift für Rechtspolitik*, 421-426.

Adams, Michael (1994e), 'Rechte und Normen als Standards', in Tietzel, M. (ed.), *Homo Oeconomicus, XI (3), Ökonomik der Standardisierung*, 501-553.

Adams, Michael (1994f), 'Heroin vom Staat - Kollektiver Wahnsinn oder das gesuchte Konzept zur Zerstörung des Drogenmarktes? (Provision of Heroin by the State - Social Madness or a Concept to Destroy the Drug Market)', **März** *Zeitschrift für Rechtspolitik*, 106-111.

Adams, Michael (1994g), 'Macht von Banken und Versicherungen - Wettbewerb im Finanzdienstleistungssektor-, Stellungnahme zur öffentlichen Anhörung des Deutschen Bundestages - Ausschuß für Wirtschaft, 8 Dezember 1993 (Power of Banks and Insurances)', *Zeitschrift für Bank- und Börsenrecht*, 77-86.

Adams, Michael (1996), 'Bankenmacht und Deutscher Juristentag - Es empfehlen sich gesetzliche Maßnahmen zur Einschränkung des Einflusses der Kreditinstitute auf Aktiengesellschaften (Recommendations to Limit the Influence of Banks on Stock Corporations)', *Zeitschrift für Wirtschaftsrecht*, 1590-1602.

Adams, Michael (1997), 'Heroin an Süchtige? - Die Ergebnisse des schweizerischen Versuchs einer kontrollierten Opiatabgabe an Süchtige und ihr Vergleich mit den Einwänden der Versuchsgegner in Deutschland (Heroin for Addicts? Results of a Swiss Experiment of Controlled Distribution of Opiates and a Comparision to the Objections of the Opponents in Germany)', *Zeitschrift für Rechtspolitik*.

Adams, Michael and Shavell, Steven (1990), 'Zur Strafbarkeit des Versuchs (On the Criminal Liability for Attempts)', *Goltdammer's Archiv für Strafrecht*, 337-386.

Adomeit, Klaus (1996), *Regelungen von Arbeitsbedingungen und Ökonomische Notwendigkeiten - Eine Untersuchung zu aktuellen Fragen des Deutschen Tarifrechts* (Regulations on the Conditions of Labour and Economic Constraints), München, Verlag Aktuell, Landsberg am Lech.

Alsmöller, Horst (1982), *Wettbewerbspolitische Ziele und Kooperationstheoretische Hvpothesen im Wandel der Zeit: Eine Dogmengeschichtliche Untersuchung von Einstellungen zu Verbundsystemen und von Grunden für diese Einstellun gen* (Competition Policy Purpose and Cooperation-Theoretical Hypotheses Through the Times: A Historical Investigation of the Institutions for Alliance Systems and for the Causes of these Institutions), Tübingen, Mohr, 337 p.

Assmann, Heinz-Dieter (1978), 'Die Transformationsprobleme des Privatrechts und die Ökonomische Analyse des Rechts. Chancen und Grenzen der privatrechlichen Verwertbarkeit der Ökonomischen Analyse des Rechts (Chances and Limitations of the Usability Economic Analysis of Law with Respect to Private Law))', in Assmann, Heinz-Dieter, Kirchner, Christian and Schanze, Erich (eds), *Ökonomische Analyse des Rechts*, Kronberg, Athenäum, 21-74.

Assmann, Heinz-Dieter (1983), 'Entwicklungstendenzen der Prospekthaftung (Tendencies of Liability for Misleading Information)', *WM*, 138-144.

Assmann, Heinz-Dieter (1985), *Prospekthaftung* (Liability for Misleading Information Included in Prospectuses), Köln, Heymann, 456 p.

Assmann, Heinz-Dieter (1988), 'Multikausale Schäden im deutschen Haftungsrecht (Multicausal Injuries in German Tort Law)', in Fenyves, Attila and Weyers, Hans-Leo (eds), *Multikausale Schäden im modernen Haftungsrechten*, Frankfurt A.M., Metzner, 99-151.

Assmann, Heinz-Dieter (1989), 'Kommentar on Ott, Allokationseffizienz, Rechtsdogmatik und Rechtsprechung', in Ott, Claus and Schäfer, Hans-Bernd (eds), *Allekationseffizienz in der Rechtsordnung*, Berlin, Springer, 45-49.

Assmann, Heinz-Dieter (1990), 'Privatrechtliche Tatbestände der Umwelthaftung in ökonomischer Analyse (Economic Analysis of Civil Liability for Pollution)', in Wagner, Gerd Rainer (ed.), *Unternehmung und ökologische Umwelt*, München, Vahlen, 201-219.

Assmann, Heinz-Dieter, Kirchner, Christian and Schanze, Erich (eds) (1978), *Ökonomische Analyse des Rechts* (Economic Analysis of Law), Kronberg, Athenäum, 369 p.

Backhaus, Jürgen G. (1979), *Ökonomik der partizipativen Unternehmung I* (Economics of Enterprises under Worker Participation), Tübingen, Mohr/Siebeck.

Backhaus, Jürgen G. (1980), *Arbeitsverhältnis und Beschäftigung, Politisch-ökonomische Analyse zur Bekämpfung der Arbeitslosigkeit* (Labor Relation and Employment, A Political Economic Anaylsis of Actions against Unemployment), Frankfurt, Campus.

Backhaus, Jürgen G. (1980a), 'Wirtschaftsreformen und Unternehmensverfassung, Fortentwicklung der Institutionen der Mitbestimmung (Economic Reforms and Constitution of Enterprises. Development of Worker Participation)', in Wagener, Hans-Juergen (ed.), *Demokratisierung der Wirtschaft, Möglichkeiten und Grenzen im Kapitalismus*, Frankfurt, Campus.

Backhaus, Jürgen G. (1980b), 'Wirtschaftliche Analyse der Entwicklungsmöglichkeiten mitbestimmter Wirtschaftssysteme (Economic Analysis of Co-Determination)', in Kappler, Ekkehard (ed.), *Unternehmensstruktur und Unternehmensentwicklung*, Freiburg, Rombach, 266-289.

Backhaus, Jürgen G. (1980c), 'Kein Aufruf zur Verteidigung des organisierten Verbrechens (No Call for a Defence of Organised Crime)', **136(4)** *Zeitschrift für die Gesamte Staatswissenschaft*, 658-672.

Backhaus, Jürgen G. (1980d), *Öffentliche Unternehmen, Zum Wirtschaftsrecht, den Funktionen und Rechtsformen öffentlicher Unternehmen* (On the Business Law, the Functions, and the Legal Types of Public Enterprises), Frankfurt, Haag und Herchen.

Backhaus, Jürgen G. (1981), 'Die Funktionsfähigkeit der mitbestimmten Großunternehmung (The Functionability of Large Corporations under Worker Participation)', in Issing, Ottmar (ed.), *Zukunftsprobleme der Sozialen Marktwirtschaft. Verhandlungen auf der Jahrestagung der Gesellschaft fuer Wirtschafts- und Sozialwissenschaften/Verein fuer Socialpolitik, in Nürnberg 1980*, Berlin, Duncker and Humblot, 213-228.

Backhaus, Jürgen G. (1987), *Mitbestimmung im Unternehmen*, Göttingen, Vandenhoeck and Ruprecht, 306 p. Reprinted in *Co-Determination: A Legal and Economic Analysis*.

Backhaus, Jürgen G. (1990), 'Die politische Ökonomie der Schutzzolltheorie (Political Economics of the Protection Tariff Theory)', in Schefold, Bertram (ed.), *Studien zur Entwicklung der oekonomischen Theorie X*, Berlin, Duncker and Humblot, 103-113.

Backhaus, Jürgen G. and Nutzinger, Hans G. (1982), *Eigentumsrechte und Partizipation - Property Rights and Participation* (Property Rights and Participation), Frankfurt, Haag und Herchen.

Backhaus, Jürgen G. and Schneider, Friedrich (1990), 'Das Coase Theorem (The Coase Theorem)', **9(4)** *Wirtschaftswissenschaftliches Studium*, 162-184.

Backhaus, Jürgen G., Eger, Thomas and Nutzinger, Hans G. (1978), *Partizipation in Betrieb und Gesellschaft, 15 theoretische und empirische Studien* (Participation in Enterprise and Society), Frankfurt, Campus.

Bartling, Hartwig (1974), 'Zur Ökonomie der Kriminalitätsbekämpfung. Eine Integration der Resozialisierung in die Kriminalökonomie (On the Economics of Criminal Policy: An Integration of Resocialisation in Economics of Criminal Law)', *Zeitschrift für Wirtschafts- und Sozialwissenschaften*, 313-333.

Bauch, Matthias (1996), *Unternehmensinsolvenzen, Prophylaxe und Bewältigung in Frankreich - Darstellung und ökonomische Analyse von Procédure d'Alerte, Règlement Amiable und Redressement et Liquidation Judiciaires* (Bankruptcy of Corporations in France - Discussion and Economic Analysis), Dissertation, Regensburg, 1996.

Baum, Herbert (1976), 'Das Stabilisierungspotential Staatlich Administrierter Preise (On the Stabilization Effects of Public Regulated Prices)', **190** *Jahrbuch für Nationalökonomie und Statistik*, 349-376.

Baum, Herbert (1978), 'Verteilungswirkungen der staatlichen Preispolitik (Effects of Public Regulated Prices on Distribution of Income)', **193** *Jahrbuch für Nationalökonomie und Statistik*, 220-243.

Behrens, Peter (1981), 'Aspekte einer ökonomischen Theorie des Rechts (Aspects of an Economic Theory of Law)', **12** *Rechtstheorie*, 472-490.

Behrens, Peter (1986), *Die ökonomischen Grundlagen des Rechts. Politische Ökonomie als rationale Jurisprudenz* (The Economic Foundations of the Law), Tübingen, Mohr, 386 p.

Behrens, Peter (1988), 'Über das Verhältnis der Rechtswissen schaft zur Nationalökonomie: Die ökonomischen Grundlagen des Rechts (On the Interrelationship between Law and Economics)', in Boettcher, Erik, Herder-Dorneich, Philipp and Schenk, Karl-Ernst (eds), *Jahrbuch für Neue Politische Ökonomie 7*, Tübingen, Mohr, 209-228.

Behrens, Peter (1989), 'Die Bedeutung der ökonomischen Analyse des Rechts für das Arbeitsrecht (The Importance of Economic Analysis of Law for Labour Law)', **20** *Zeitschrift für Arbeitsrecht*, 209-238.

Beier, Friedrich-Karl (1979), 'Die Bedeutung des Patentsystems für den Technischen, Wirtschaftlichen und Sozialen Fortschritt (The Significance of Patent Law for the Technical,)', *Gewerblicher Rechtsschutz und Urheberrecht - Internationaler Teil*, 227-235.

Beimowski, Joachim (1989), *Zur ökonomischen Analyse Allgemeiner Geschäftsbedingungen* (Economic Analysis of General Business Clauses), München.

Bialek, Axel (1994), *Perspektiven der Genossenschaft als Organisationsform Schriften zur ökonomischen Analyse des Rechts* (Perspectives of Cooperatives as Type of Organization), Berlin, Duncker and Humblot.

Bittlingmayer, George (1987), 'Die wettbewerbspolitische Vorstellungen der Chicago School (Competition Policy According to the Chicago School)', **37** *Wirtschaft und Wettbewerb*, 709-718.

Blaschczok, Andreas (1993), *Gefährdungshaftung und Risikozuweisung* (Strict Liability and Allocation of Risks), Köln, Berlin, Bonn, München, Carl Heymanns Verlag.

Böbel, Ingo (1988), *Eigentum, Eigentumsrechte und Institutioneller Wandel* (Property, Property Rights and Institutional Change), Berlin, Springer, 360 p.

Boehm, F. (1980), *Freiheit und Ordnung in der Marktwirtschaft* (Freedom and Constitution in a Market Economy), Baden-Baden, Nomes.

Boettcher, Erik, Herder-Dorneich, Philipp, Schenk, Karl-Ernst and Schmidtchen, Dieter (eds) (1991), *Jahrbuch für Neue Politische Ökonomie, 10. Band, Systemvergleich und Ordnungspolitik* (Comparative Analysis of Economic Systems and Constitutional Policy), Tübingen.

Bongaerts, Jan C. and Heinrichs, Dirk (1986), 'Deutsche Umweltschutzgesetze und Umweltschutzinvestitionen des produzierenden Gewerbes (German Environmental Protection Legislation and Environmental Investment by West German Manufacturing Industries)', **32(3)** *Konjunkturpolitik*, 151-163.

Bongaerts, Jan C., Meyerhoff, Jürgen, Thomasberger, Claus and Wittke, Anja (1989), *Lösungsansätze für ein ganzheitliches System von Umweltsteuern und Sonderabgaben in der Bundesrepu blik Deutschland* (A Solution for a Total Environmental System and Special Taxes in the Federal Republic of Germany), Berlin, Schriftenreihe des Instituts für Oekologische Wirtschaftsforschung Nr. 31.

Bonus, Holger (1975), 'Steuern als Instrumente des Umweltschutzes - Weitere Bemerkungen zu Richard Zwintz (Taxes as an Instrument of Environmental Protection)', **131(3)** *Zeitschrift für die Gesamte Staatswissenschaft*, 540-549.

Bonus, Holger (1976), 'Der Schutz des Schwächeren in der Umweltökonomie (The Protection of the Weaker in Environmental Economics)', **40(3-4)** *Rabels Zeitschrift für Ausländisches und Internationales Privatrecht*, 409-429.

Bonus, Holger (1978), 'Ordnungspolitische Aspekte öffentlicher Güter (Constitutional Aspects of Public Goods)', **98** *Schriften des Vereins für Socialpolitik, Neue Folge*, 51-73.

Bonus, Holger (1979), 'Öffentliche Güter, Verführung und Gefangenendilemma (Public Goods, Temptation and the Prisoners' Dilemma)', **10(2)** *List Forum*, 69-102. Reprinted in Grundtexte zur Sozialen Marktwirtschaft, Stuttgart/New York, Gustav Fischer Verlag. 1979/80, pp. 283-305

Bonus, Holger (1980a), 'Neue Politische Ökonomie und Öffentliche Güter (New Political Economics and Public Goods)', in X. (ed.), *Neue Politische Ökonomie als Ordnungstheorie*, Tübingen, Mohr/Siebeck, 153-172.

Bonus, Holger (1980b), 'Öffentliche Güter und Gefangenendilemma (Public Gooods and the Prisoners' Dilemma)', in Dettling, W. (ed.), *Die Zähmung des Leviathan. Neue Wege der Ordnungspolitik*, Baden-Baden, Nomos Verlagsgesellschaft, 129-160.

Bonus, Holger (1981a), 'Emissionsrechte als Mittel der Privatisierung öffentlicher Ressourcen aus der Umwelt (Emission Rights as a Means of Privatization of Public Resources)', in Wegehenkel, L. (ed.), *Marktwirtschaft und Umwelt*, Tübingen, J.C.B. Mohr (Paul Siebeck), 54-77.

Bonus, Holger (1981b), 'Zur Transformation der Marktwirtschaft durch Sozialkomponente und Demokratisierung (On the Transformation of Market Economy by Social Components and Democratization)', **116** *Schriften des Vereins für Socialpolitik*, 233-253.

Bonus, Holger (1981c), 'Wettbewerbswirkungen umweltpolitischer Instrumente (The Effects of Environmental Policy Instruments on Competition)', **1-2** *Ifo-Schnelldienst*, 20-28.

Bonus, Holger (1982a), 'Emissionsrechte als Mittel der Privatisierung öffentlicher Ressourcen aus der Umwelt (Emission Rights as a Means of Privatization of Public Resources)', in Möller, Osterkamp and Schneider (eds), *Umweltökonomik*, Verlag Anton Hain, 295-314.

Bonus, Holger (1982b), 'Wettbewerbspolitische Implikationen umweltpolitischer Instrumente (The Implications of Environmental Policy Instruments on Competition Policy)', in Gutzler, H. (ed.), *Umweltpolitik und Wettbewerb*, Baden-Baden, Nomos Verlagsgesellschaft, 103-121.

Bonus, Holger (1983), 'Darstellung und Bewertung der neuen flexiblen Auflagen-Konzepte der US-Luftreinhaltepolitik (Evaluation of the New Flexible Condition Policy against Air Pollution)', in Pohl, H. G. (ed.), *Saubere Luft als Marktprodukt*, Bonn, Bonn aktuell, 53-83.

Bonus, Holger (1984), 'Zwei Philosophien der Umweltpolitik, Lehren aus der amerikanischen Luftreinhaltepolitik (Two Philosophies of Environmental Policy, Lessons from the American Policy against Air Pollution)', **12(5)** *List Forum*, 323-340.

Bonus, Holger (1986a), 'Eine Lanze für den Wasserpfennig (Taking up the Cudgel for the 'Waterpenny')', **9** *Wirtschaftsdienst*, 451-455.

Bonus, Holger (1986b), 'Don Quichotte, Sancho Pansa und der Wasserpfennig (Don Quixote, Sancho Pansa, and the 'Waterpenny')', **12** *Wirtschaftsdienst*, 625-629.

Bonus, Holger (1987), 'Illegitime Transaktionen, Abhängigkeit und Institutioneller Schutz (Illegitimate Transactions, Dependency, and Protective Institutions)', **32** *Hamburger Jahrbuch für Wirtschaft und Gesellschaftspolitik*, 87-107.

Bonus, Holger (1991), 'Schöne Müllerin. Heiratsmarkt, Vor- und Nachteile der Ehe aus ökonomischer Sicht (Advantages and Disadvantages of Marriage from the Economist's Viewpoint)', **12** *Wirtschaftswoche*, 44-49.

Bonus, Holger (1992), 'Standard und Wert in ökonomischer Sicht (Standard and Value from the Economist's Viewpoint)', in Bonus, H., Hoppe, W. and Schreiber, K.-F. (eds), *Umweltverträglichkeitsprüfung - Gibt es Standards?*, Münster, Zentrum für Umweltforschung der Westfälischen Wilhelms-Universität, Vorträge und Studien, 139-153.

Bonus, Holger (1994a), 'Nationalökonomie auf neuen Wegen (National Economics on New Pathes)', in Jäger, W. (ed.), *Neue Wege der Nationalökonomie*, Münster, Aschendorf, 14-48.

Bonus, Holger (1994b), 'Marktwirtschaftliche Instrumente als Alternative zu hoheitlichem Vollzug (Market Oriented Instruments as an Alternative to Sovereign Execution)', in Barz, W., Brinkmann, B., Ewers, H.-J. and Hoppe, W. (eds), *Vollzugsfragen im Umweltschutz*, Münster, 13-22.

Bonus, Holger (1996), 'Die Langsamkeit von Spielregeln (The Slowness of Rules)', in Backhaus, K. and Bonus, H. (eds), *Die Beschleunigungsfalle oder der Triumph der Schildkröte, 2, Auflage*, Stuttgart, Schäffer-Poeschl Verlag, 3-18.

Borchert, Manfred and Grossekettler, Heinz (1985), *Preis- und Wettbewerbstheorie: Marktprozesse als analystische Problem un Ordnungspolitische Gestalungsaufgabe* (Price Theory and Competition Theory: Market Processes as Analytical Problem and Policy Recomandations), Verlag W. Kohlhammer, 371 p.

Brandes, Wolfgang, Buttler, Friedrich, Dorndorf, Eberhard and Walwei, U. (1991), 'Grenzen der Kündigungsfreiheit - Kündigungsschutz zwischen Stabilität und Flexibilität (Limits of the Freedom to Terminate Employment Contracts)', in Semlinger, K. (ed.), *Flexibilität des Arbeitsmarktes, Interessen, Wirkungen, Perspektiven*, Frankfurt/Main und New York, Campus-Verlag, 111-131.

Brinkmann, Thomas and Kübler, Friedrich (1981), 'Überlegungen zur Ökonomischen Analyse im Unternehmensrecht (Thoughts on an Economic Analysis of Company Law)', **137** *Journal of Institutional and Theoretical Economics*, 681-688.

Brüggemeier, Gert (1989), 'Die Gefährdungshaftung der Produzenten nach der EG-Richtlinie - ein Fortschritt der Rechtsentwicklung? (Strict Liability of Producers according to the EC-)', in Ott, Claus and Schäfer, Hans-Bernd (eds), *Allekationseffizienz in der Rechtsordnung*, Berlin, Springer, 228-247.

Buhbe, Matthes (1980), *Ökonomische Analyse von Eigentumsrechten - Der Beitrag der Economics of Property Rights zur Theorie der Institutionen* (Economic Analysis of Property Rights - The Contribution of the Property Rights Approach to the Theory of Institutions), Frankfurt am Main, Peter D. Lang, 185 p.

Bund, Dorothee (1984), *Die Ökonomische Theorie der Verfassung* (The Economic Theory of the Constitution), Baden-Baden, Nomos, 96 p.

Burow, Patrick (1993), 'Einführung in die ökonomische Analyse des Rechts (An Introduction into Law and Economics)', **1** *Juristische Schulung*, 8-12.

Buttler, Friedrich and Walwei, U. (1990), 'Effizienzwirkungen des Kündigungsschutzes (Impacts of Protection against Dismissal on Efficiency)', **23(3)** *MittAB*, 386-393.

Dorndorf, Eberhard (1979), *Freie Arbeitsplatzwahl und Recht am Arbeitsergebnis. Zur rechtlichen Bedeutung des Konflikts zwischen Arbeitsmobilität und Aneignungsfähigkeit des Arbeitsprodukts* (Free Choice of Employment and the Property Rights on the Output), Frankfurt, Metzner-Verlag.

Dorndorf, Eberhard (1986), *Kreditsicherungsrecht und Wirtschaftsordnung. Zur materiell- und konkursrechtlichen Dogmatik der Mobiliarsicherungsrechte* (Security Law and Economic Constitution), Heidelberg, Müller Juristischer Verlag.

Dorndorf, Eberhard (1989), 'Arbeitsmarkttheorie und Arbeitsrechtswissenschaft, Analoge Probleme und Diskussionsschwerpunkte im Hinblick auf die Funktionsfähigkeit der Arbeitsmärkte (Theory of Labor Markets and Jurisprudence)', in X. (ed.), *Währungsreform und Soziale Marktwirtschaft, Arbeitstagung des Vereins für Socialpolitik in Freiburg 1988*, Berlin, Duncker and Humblot.

Dorndorf, Eberhard (1992a), 'Mehr Individualvertragsfreiheit im Arbeitsrecht? (More Freedom for Individual Employment Contracts?)', in Däubler, Wolfgang, Bobke, Manfred and Kehrmann, Karl (eds), *Festschrift für Albert Gnade*, Köln, Bund-Verlag.

Dorndorf, Eberhard (1992b), 'Ökonomische Analyse des Rechts und Betriebsverfassungsrecht (Law and Economics and the German 'Betriebsverfassungsgesetz')', **75** *Kritische Vierteljahresschrift für Gesetzgebung und Rechtswissenschaft*, 416-432.

Dorndorf, Eberhard (1995), 'Modelle des Rechtssystems in der ökonomischen Analyse des Rechts (Models of the Legal System in Law and Economics)', in X. (ed.), *Ökonomie und Gesellschaft. Jahrbuch 11, Markt, Norm und Moral*, Frankfurt/New York, 127-159.

Dorndorf, Eberhard and Frank, Jürgen (1985), 'Reform des Rechts der Mobiliarsicherheiten. Unter besonderer Berücksichtigung der öknomischen Analyse der Sicherungsrechte (Economic Analysis of Security Law)', *Zeitschrift für Wirtschaftsrecht*, 65-84.

Dorndorf, Eberhard, Brandes, Wolfgang and Buttler, Friedrich (1991), 'Grenzen der Kündigungsfreiheit - Kündigungsschutz zwischen Stabilität und Flexibilität (Limits of the Right to Terminate Employment Contracts)', in Semlinger, K. (ed.), *Flexibilität des Arbeitsmarktes, Interessen, Wirkungen, Perspektiven*, Frankfurt/Main und New York, Campus-Verlag.

Drukarczyk, Jochen (1973), 'Zum Problem der Angemessenen Barabfindung bei Zwangsweise Ausscheidenden Anteilseignern (The problem of an adequate lump-sum compensation for shareholders who are frozen out)', **18** *Arbeitgeber*, 357-365.

Drukarczyk, Jochen (1979a), 'Begrenzte Haftung, Gläubigerrisiko und Gesellschafterdarlehen - Zur Vorschrift des § 32a eines neuen GmbHG (Limited liability, creditors' risk, and proprietors' loans - Comments to § 32a of a new GmbHG)', in Heigl, A. and Uecker, P. (eds), *Betriebswirtschaftslehre und Recht*, Wiesbaden, Gabler.

Drukarczyk, Jochen (1979b), 'Bilanzielle Überschuldungsmessung - Zur Interpretation der Vorschriften von § 92(2) AktG und § 64(1) GmbHG (Measurement of overindebtedness - Interpretation of § 92(2) AktG and § 64(1) GmbHG)', *Zeitschrift für Unternehmens- und Gesellschaftsrecht*, 553-582.

Drukarczyk, Jochen (1981a), 'Zum Problem der Auslösung insolvenzrechtlicher Verfahren (The Problem of Triggering Bankruptcy Proceedings)', **51** *ZfB*, 235-257.

Drukarczyk, Jochen (1981b), 'Verschuldung, Konkursrisiko, Kreditverträge und Marktwert von Aktiengesellschaften (Debt Financing, Bankruptcy Risk, Credit Agreements and the Market Value of Stock Corporations)', in Ehrlicher, W. and Krümmel, H.-J. (eds), *Kredit und Kapital*, Berlin, 287-319.

Drukarczyk, Jochen (1983), 'Kreditverträge, Mobiliarsicherheiten und Vorschläge zu ihrer Reform im Konkursrecht (Credit Agreements, Personal Securities and Suggestions for a Reform of Bankruptcy Law)', **53** *ZfB*, 328-349.

Drukarczyk, Jochen (1984a), 'Reorganisation und Gläubigeransprüche (Reorganization and creditors' claims)', **44(3)** *DBW*, 371-391.

Drukarczyk, Jochen (1984b), 'Mobiliarsicherheiten, Kreditverträge und Insolvenzrecht (Collateralization of Debt, Credit Agreements and Bankruptcy Law)', in Neumann, M. (ed.), *Ansprache, Eigentums- und Verfügungsrechte*, Berlin, Duncker and Humblot, 681-704.

Drukarczyk, Jochen (1986a), 'Was kann der Tatbestand der Überschuldung leisten? (Overindebtedness as a Trigger of Insolvency Proceedings)', **38** *ZfbF*, 207-234.

Drukarczyk, Jochen (1986b), 'Zum Problem der 'wirtschaftlichen Vertretbarkeit' von Sozialplänen (The Problem of 'Economic Feasibility' of Social Compensation Plans)', **39** *Recht der Arbeit*, 115-120.

Drukarczyk, Jochen (1987a), 'Ökonomische Analyse der Rechtsprechung des BGH zur Sittenwidrigkeit von Sanierungskrediten (Economic Analysis of the Jurisprudence of the Bund)', in X (ed.), *Kapitalmarkt und Finanzierung*, Jahrestagung des Vereins für Socialpolitik in München, 379-397.

Drukarczyk, Jochen (1987b), 'Kreditsicherheiten und Insolvenzverfahren (Collateralized Debt and Insolvency Proceedings)', **8** *Zeitschrift für Wirtschaftsrecht*, 205-217.

Drukarczyk, Jochen (1987c), *Unternehmen und Insolvenz - Zur effizienten Gestaltung des Kreditisicherungs- und Insolvenzrechts* (Entrepreneurship and Insolvency - On the Efficient Shape of Safeguarding of Credits Law and Insolvency Law), Wiesbaden, Gabler, 424 p.

Drukarczyk, Jochen (1988), 'Zum Verhältnis von Markt und Regulierung in einem neuen Insolvenzrecht - Besprechung des Ersten Berichts der Kommission für Insolvenzrecht (The Relation of Market and Regulation in the new Bankruptcy Law - Discussion of the first report by the 'Kommission für Insolvenzrecht')', **1** *DBW*, 3-25.

Drukarczyk, Jochen (1989), 'Insolvenzrecht als Versuch marktkonformer Gestaltung von Verwertungsentscheidungen und Verteilungsregeln (Bankruptcy Law as an Attempt to Organize Insolvency Proceedings in Line with Market Rules)', **10** *Zeitschrift für Wirtschaftsrecht*, 341-351.

Drukarczyk, Jochen (1992a), 'Insolvenzrechtsreform, Reformkonzeptionen und Aktueller Stand (Reform of the Bankruptcy Law, Concepts of Reform and State of the Art)', **52** *DBW*, 161-183.

Drukarczyk, Jochen (1992b), 'Mobiliargesicherte Gläubiger, Verfahrensbeitrag im Insolvenzverfahren und Kreditkonditionen (Secured Creditors, Contributions to Bankruptcy Proceedings and Credit Terms)', **46** *WM*, 1136-1144.

Drukarczyk, Jochen (1993), 'Soll das Insolvenzrecht eine Reorganisation zulassen? (Should Bankruptcy Law allow Reorganization?)', in Gerke, W. (ed.), *Planwirtschaft am Ende - Marktwirtschaft in der Krise? Festschrift für Wolfram Engels*, Stuttgart, 109-137.

Drukarczyk, Jochen (1994a), 'Kapitalerhaltungsrecht, Überschuldung und Konsistenz - Besprechung der Überschuldungs-Definition in BGH WM 1992, 1650 (Capital Maintenance, Overindebtedness and Consistency - Discussion of the Statutory Definition of Overindebtedness by the German Supreme Court)', **48** *WM*, 1737-1746.

Drukarczyk, Jochen (1994b), 'Überschuldung, Zur Konstruktion eines Insolvenztatbestandes im Spannungsfeld von Kapitalerhaltungsrecht und Kreditmarkt (Overindebtedness, Construction of an Insolvency Trigger Given the Constraints of Capital Maintenance and Credit Markets)', in Ballwieser, W., Bücking, H.-J., Drukarczyk, J. And Schmidt, R.H. (eds), *Bilanzrecht und Kapitalmarkt. Festschrift für Adolf Moxter*, Düsseldorf, 1231-1258.

Drukarczyk, Jochen (1995a), 'Verwertungsformen und Kosten der Insolvenz (Asset Use and Bankruptcy Costs)', **1** *BFuP*, 40-58.

Drukarczyk, Jochen (1995b), 'Gesellschafterdarlehen, Rechtsprechungsgrundsätze des BGH und § 32a GmbHG - Einige kritische Anmerkungen (Proprietors' Loans, Principles of Jurisdiction of the German Supreme Court and § 32a GmbHG - Critical comments)', in Elschen, R., Siegel, Th. and Wagner, F.W. (eds), *Unternehmenstheorie und Besteuerung. Festschrift für Dieter Schneider*, Wiesbaden, Gabler, 173-202.

Drukarczyk, Jochen and Rieger, Reinhard (1986), 'Zu den Entscheidungswirkungen von § 613a BGB vor und nach Insolvenz (Consequences of § 613a BGB Before and After Insolvency)', **2** *KTS*, 209-242.

Drukarczyk, Jochen, Duttle, Josef and Rieger, Reinhard (1985), 'Mobiliarsicherheiten - Arten, Verbreitung,Wirksamkeit (Firms and Collateralization of Debt - Types and Effectiveness)', in X. (ed.), *Rechtstatsachenforschung*, Köln, Bundesministerium der Justiz.

Duttle, Josef (1986), *Ökonomische Analyse dinglicher Sicherheiten - Die Reform der Mobiliarsicherheiten und Probleme ihrer Behandlung in insolvenzrechtlichen Verfahren* (Economic Analysis of Collateral Securities - The Reform of Personal Securities and Problems of their Treatment in Bankruptcy Proceedings), Dissertation, Marchal und Matzenbacher, Wissenschaftsverlag, Krefeld, 1986.

Eger, Thomas (1989), 'Einführung in die Ökonomische Analyse des Rechts (Introduction to the Economic Analysis of Law)', in Nagel, B. (ed.), *Wirtschaftsrecht II*, München, Oldenborg, 18-35.

Eger, Thomas (1991a), 'Veränderungen von Rechtsnormen im Systemvergleich. Eine Ökonomische Analyse (Changes of Legal Norms in Different Economic Systems. An Economic Analysis)', in Wagener, H.-J. (ed.), *Anpassung durch Wandel. Evolution und Transformation von Wirtschaftssystemen. Schriften des Vereins für Socialpolitik*, Berlin, Duncker and Humblot, 81-99.

Eger, Thomas (1991b), 'Kommentar (Comment on Finsinger and von Randow, *Neue Akivität*)', in Ott, Claus and Schäfer, Hans-Bernd (eds), *Ökonomische Probleme des Zivilrechts*, Berlin, Springer, 109-114.

Eger, Thomas (1992), 'Eine Ökonomische Analyse der Zulieferbeziehungen in der Automobilindustrie (An Economic Analysis of the Relations between Suppliers and Manufacturers in Automotive Industry)', in Nagel, Bernhard, *EG-Wettbewerbsrecht und Zulieferbeziehungen in der Automobilindustrie, Gutachten im Auftrag der EG-Kommission, Generaldirektion Wettbewerb (IV)*, Brussel, 1-35.

Eger, Thomas (1994), 'Kommentar zu Helmut Köhler, Erweiterung des gewerblichen Rechtsschutzes durch UWG-Normen (Comment on Helmut Köhler, Extension of Legal Protection of Industrial Property by UWG-norms)', in Ott, Claus and Schäfer, Hans-Bernd (eds), *Okonomische Analyse der rechtlichen Organisation von Innovationen*, Tübingen, Mohr, 270-280.

Eger, Thomas (1995a), 'Wieviel Normierung braucht der Markt? Ökonomische Aspekte der Vertragsfreiheit (How Many Norms are Necessary for the Market to Operate? Economic Aspects of Freedom of Contract)', in X. (ed.), *Ökonomie und Gesellschaft. Jahrbuch 11, Markt, Norm und Moral*, Frankfurt/New York, 45-88.

Eger, Thomas (1995b), *Eine ökonomische Analyse von Langzeitverträgen* (An Economic Analysis of Long-Term-Contracts), Marburg, Metropolis, 263 p.

Eger, Thomas (1996a), 'Die Evolution von Recht als Prozeß der Selbstorganisation (The Evolution of Law as a Process of Self-organization)', in Priddat, B.P. and Wegner, G. (eds), *Zwischen Institution und Evolution. Neue Ansätze in der ökonomischen Theorie*, Marburg, Metropolis, 211-244.

Eger, Thomas (1996b), 'Möglichkeiten und Grenzen des Reputationsmechanismus (Possibilities and Constraints of Reputation Mechanism)', *Wirtschaftspraxis, Verwaltungspraxis, Wirtschaftswissenschaften*, 1-10.

Eger, Thomas and Weise, Peter (1990a), 'Innovation, Imitation und Patentrecht im Systemvergleich (Innovation, Imitation, and Patent Law in Different Economic Systems)', in Gramatzki, H.-E., Klinger, F. and Nutzinger, H.G. (eds), *Wissenschaft, Technik und Arbeit, Innovationen in Ost und West*, Kassel, VWL-inform, 107-133.

Eger, Thomas and Weise, Peter (1990b), 'Normen als gesellschaftliche Ordner (Norms as Social Co-ordination Parameters)', in X. (ed.), *Ökonomie und Gesellschaft, Jahrbuch 8, Individuelles Verhalten und kollektive Phänomene*, Frankfurt/New York, 65-111.

Eger, Thomas and Weise, Peter (1995), 'Die Evolution von Normen aus Unordnung, Ein synergetisches Modell (The Evolution of Norms out of Disorder, Synergetic Model)', in X. (ed.), *Ökonomie und Gesellschaft. Jahrbuch 11, Markt, Norm und Moral*, Frankfurt/New York, 192-209.

Eger, Thomas, Nagel, Bernhard and Weise, Peter (1991), 'Effizienz und Menschenwürde - Ein Gegensatz? (Efficiency and Human Dignity - An Opposition?)', in Ott, Claus and Schäfer, Hans-Bernd (eds), *Ökonomische Probleme des Zivilrechts*, Berlin, Springer, 18-34.

Eger, Thomas, Nutzinger, Hans G. and Weise, Peter (1993), 'Eine ökonomische Analyse der mitbestimmten Unternehmung (An Economic Analysis of Codetermined Enterprise)', in Ott, C. and Schäfer, H.-B. (eds), *Ökonomische Analyse des Unternehmensrechts*, Heidelberg, Physica, 78-116.

Eggerstedt, Harald (1987), 'Wettbewerb and Regulierung auf Versicherungsmarkten (Competition and Regulation in Insurance Markets)', **107** *Zeitschrift für Wirtschafts- und Sozialwissenschaften*, 397-416.

Eggerstedt, Harald (1988), 'Uber Regulierung und Deregulierung von Versicherungsmarkten. Eine Replik (On Regulation and Deregulation of Insurance Markets. A Reply)', **58** *Zeitschrift für Betriebswirtschaft*, 704-707.

Eickhof, Norbert (1986), 'Versorgungswirtschaft und Wettbewerbsordnung (Public Utilities and the Competitive System)', in Eucken, Walter and Bohm, Franz (eds), *Ordo: Jahrbuch fur die Ordnung von Wirtschaft und Gesellschaft*, Stuttgart, Gustav Fischer, 201-218.

Eidenmüller, Horst (1993), 'Ökonomische Effizienzkonzepte in der Rechtsanwendung (The Use of Efficiency Concepts in Adjudication)', in Breidenbach, S., Grundmann, S., Mülbert, P. and Singer, R. (eds), *Jahrbuch Junger Zivilrechtswissenschaftler 1992, Rechtsfortbildung jenseits klassischer Methodik - Privatautonomie zwischen Status und Kontrakt - Privatrecht und Europa 1992*, Stuttgart et al., Boorberg, 11-28.

Eidenmüller, Horst (1995a), *Effizienz als Rechtsprinzip, Möglichkeiten und Grenzen der ökonomischen Analyse des Rechts* (Efficiency as a Legal Principle - Possibilities and Limitations of the Economic Analysis of Law), Tübingen, Mohr/Siebeck.

Eidenmüller, Horst (1995b), 'Neuverhandlungspflichten bei Wegfall der Geschäftsgrundlage (Renegotiation Duties Following a Fundamental Change of Circumstances)', **16** *Zeitschrift für Wirtschaftsrecht*, 1063-1071.

Eidenmüller, Horst (1995c), 'Marktwirtschaft, Privatrecht und Verteilungsgerechtigkeit (Market Economy, Private Law and Distributive Justice)', in Pies, I. and Leschke, M. (ed.), *John Rawls' politischer Liberalismus*, Tübingen, Mohr/Siebeck, 123-127.

Eidenmüller, Horst (1996a), 'Die Banken im Gefangenendilemma, Kooperationspflichten und Akkordstörungsverbot im Sanierungsrecht (The Banks in a Prisoners' Dilemma, Duties to Cooperate in Bankrupty Workouts)', **160** *Zeitschrift für das gesamte Handels- und Wirtschaftsrecht*, 343-373.

Eidenmüller, Horst (1996b), 'Der Insolvenzplan als Vertrag (The Insolvency Plan as a Contract)', in Schenk, Karl-Ernst, Schmidtchen, Dieter and Streit, Manfred E. (eds), *Vom Hoheitsstaat zum Konsensualstaat, Neue Formen der Kooperation zwischen Staat und Privaten Jahrbuch für Neue Politische Ökonomie 15*, Tübingen, Mohr, 164-192.

Eidenmüller, Horst (1997a), 'Ökonomische und spieltheoretische Grundlagen von Verhandlung/Mediation (Economic and Game Theoretic Foundations of Negotiation and Mediation)', in Breidenbach, S. and. Henssler, M. (ed.), *Mediation für Juristen, Konfliktbehandlung ohne gerichtliche Entscheidung*, Köln, Otto Schmidt.

Eidenmüller, Horst (1997b), 'Insolvenzbewältigung durch Reorganisation (Reorganization as a Mode of Coping with Insolvency)', in Ott, Claus and Schäfer, Hans-Bernd (ed.), *5. Travemünder Symposium zur ökonomischen Analyse des Rechts*, Tübingen, Mohr/Siebeck.

Eidenmüller, Horst (1997c), 'Rechtsanwendung, Gesetzgebung, und Ökonomische Analyse (Adjudication, Lawmaking, and Economic Analysis)', **197** *Archiv für die Civilistische Praxis*, 80-135.

Emrich, Heinrich Maria (1978), *Die Problematik der Fusionskontrolle bei Konglomeraten, Eine Untersuchung der rechtlichen Schwierigkeiten und ihrer wirtschaftlichen Grundlage unter besonderer Berücksichtigung der Einzelmarktbetrachtung und des Marktanteilskriteriums in den § 24, 22 GWB* (The Problem of Merger Control in Conglomerates), Berlin.

Endres, Alfred (1976), 'Das Coase-Theorem bei langfristiger Betrachtung (The Coase Theorem in a Long Term Perspective)', **27** *Jahrbuch für Sozialwissenschaft*, 430-433.

Endres, Alfred (1977), 'Die Coase-Kontroverse (The Coase Controversy)', **133** *Journal of Institutional and Theoretical Economics*, 637-651.

Endres, Alfred (1985), *Umwelt- und Ressourcenökonomie* (Environmental and Resources Economics), Darmstadt, 193 p.

Endres, Alfred (1988), 'Staatliche Regulierung und Ökonomische Theorie (Regulation and Economic Theory)', **17(4)** *Wirtschaftswissenschaftliches Studium*, 197-198.

Endres, Alfred (1989), 'Allokationswirkungen des Haftungsrechts (Allocative Effects of Liability Law)', **40(1)** *Jahrbuch für Sozialwissenschaft*, 115-129.

Endres, Alfred (1991a), 'Haftungsregeln für gentechnologische Unfälle - Das Problem der Haftungsobergrenze (Liability Rules in Biotechnology - Problems of Liability Limitation)', **42(1)** *Jahrbuch für Sozialwissenschaft*, 131-143.

Endres, Alfred (1991b), *Ökonomische Grundlagen des Haftungsrechts* (Economic Foundations of Liability Law), Heidelberg, Physica.

Endres, Alfred (1992), *Die Bedeutung von Gesetzgebung und Rechtsprechung für die Internalisierung externer Effekte* (The Role of Legislation and Jurisdiction in the Internalisation of Externalities), Gutachten für die Prognos AG, Basel, 1992.

Endres, Alfred (1993), 'Internationale Vereinbarungen zum Schutz der globalen Umweltressourcen - Der Fall Proportionaler Emissionsreduktion (International Agreements for the Protection of the Global Environment)', **48(1)** *Aussenwirtschaft*, 51-76.

Endres, Alfred (1995), 'Zur Ökonomie internationaler Umweltschutzvereinbarungen (The Economics of International Environmental Agreements)', **18(2)** *Zeitschrift für Umweltpolitik und Umweltrecht*, 143-178.

Endres, Alfred and Gäfgen, Gerard (1988), 'Wettbewerb und Regulierung auf dem Bundesdeutschen Lebensversicherungsmarkt (Competition and Regulation in the West German Life Insurance Market)', **205** *Jahrbuch für Nationalökonomie und Statistik*, 11-29.

Endres, Alfred and Gäfgen, Gerard (1989), 'Regulierung und Versicherungswirtschaft - Die Ökonomische Perspektive in Forschungsgesellschaft für Wettbewerb und Unternehmensorganisation (Regulation and the Insurance Industry - The Economic Perspective)', in Fwu (eds), *Versicherungsmärkte im Wettbewerb*, Baden-Baden, Nomos, 11-42.

Endres, Alfred and Marburger, P. (1993), *Umweltschutz durch gesellschaftliche Selbststeuerung* (Environmental Protection by Social Self-Regulation), Economica, Schriftenreihe des Kollegs 'Umweltstaat' der Gottlieb Daimler-und Karl Benz-Stiftung, Bonn, 1993.

Endres, Alfred and Schwarze, Reimund (1991), 'Allokationswirkungen einer Umwelt-Haftpflichtversicherung (Allocative Effects of an Environmental Liability Insurance)', **14** *Zeitschrift für Umweltpolitik und Umweltrecht*, 1-25.

Endres, Alfred, Rehbinder, E. and Schwarze, Reimund (1992), *Haftung und Versicherung für Umweltschäden aus ökonomischer und juristischer Sicht* (Liability and Insurance for Environmental Damages - A Law and Economics Perspective), Berlin (Springer), Schriftenreihe des Kollegs 'Umweltstaat' der Gottlieb Daimler-und Karl Benz-Stiftung, 1992.

Endres, Alfred, Rehbinder, E. and Schwarze, Reimund (1994), *Umweltzertifikate und Kompensationslösungen aus Ökonomischer und Juristischer Sicht* (Transferable Discharge Permits and Emissions Trading - A Law and Economics Perspective), Economica, Schriftenreihe des Kollegs 'Umweltstaat' der Gottlieb Daimler-und Karl Benz-Stiftung, Bonn, 1994.

Engelhardt, Günther (1991), 'Strafzuschlag zum Schadensersatz, Kommentar (Punitive Damages, Comment on Köndgen, Immaterial)', in Ott, Claus and Schäfer, Hans-Bernd (eds), *Ökonomische Probleme des Zivilrechts*, Berlin, Springer, 183-190.

Erlei, Mathias (1992), *Meritorische Güter. Die theoretische Konzeption und ihre Anwendung auf Rauschgifte als demeritorische Güter* (Meritoric Goods. Theory and Application on Drugs as Demeritoric Goods), Lit-Verlag Münster, Hamburg.

Erlei, Mathias (1994), 'Recht auf Selbstschädigung oder Recht auf Selbstschutz? Eine Betrachtung der Rauschgiftproblematik aus ökonomischer Sicht (Right on Self-Damaging or Right on Self-Protection? The Drug Problem from the Economists' Viewpoint)', **20** *List-Forum für Wirtschafts- und Finanzpolitik*, 144-153.

Erlei, Mathias (ed.) (1995), *Mit dem Markt gegen Drogen!? Lösungsansätze für das Drogenproblem aus ökonomischer Sicht* (Market against Drugs?), Schäfer-Poeschel.

Eschenburg, Rolf (1978a), 'Mikroökonomische Aspekte von Property Rights (Micro-economic Aspects of Property Rights)', in Schenk, K.E. (ed.), *Ökonomische Verfügungsrechte und Allokationsmechanismen in Wirtschafsystemen*, Berlin, Duncker and Humblot, 9-27.

Eschenburg, Rolf (1978b), 'Vertragstheoretisches Denken in der Ökonomie (Contractual Theory in Economics)', **23** *Hamburger Jahrbuch für Wirtschaft und Gesellschaftspolitik*, 221-236.

Farny, Dieter (1987), 'Uber Regulierung und Deregulierung von Versicherungsmarkten (On Regulating and Deregulating Insurance Markets)', **57** *Zeitschrift für Betriebswirtschaft*, 1001-1023.

Fezer, Karl-Heinz (1986), 'Aspekte einer Rechtskritik an der Economic Analysis of Law und am Property Rights Approach (Critcal Aspects of the Economic Analysis of Law and the Property Rights Approach from a Lawyer's Viewpoint)', **41** *Juristenzeitung*, 817-824.

Fezer, Karl-Heinz (1988), 'Nochmals, Kritik an der Ökonomischen Analyse des Rechts (Once More, Critique on Law and Economics)', **43** *Juristenzeitung*, 223-228.

Finsinger, Jörg (1988a), 'Zur Deregulierung von Versicherungsmarkten (On the Deregulation of Insurance Markets)', **58** *Zeitschrift für Betriebswirtschaft*, 698-703.

Finsinger, Jörg (1988b), *Verbraucherschutz auf Versicherungs märkten* (Consumer Protection in Insurance Markets), München, Florentz, 219 p.

Finsinger, Jörg (1989), 'Kommentar' Die Zivilrechtliche Haftung für Werbeangaben bei der Vertragsanbahnung als Problem der Allokationseffizienz (Comment on Lehmann, Die Zivilrechtliche Haftung für Werbeangaben bei der Vertragsanbahnung als Problem der

Allokationseffizienz)', in Ott, Claus and Schäfer, Hans-Bernd (eds), *Allekationseffizienz in der Rechtsordnung*, Berlin, Springer, 185-187.

Finsinger, Jörg and Schulenburg, J. Matthias Graf Von Der (1989), 'Der Sonntagsverkauf (The Effects of Sunday Trading)', **109** *Zeitschrift für Wirtschafts- und Sozialwissenschaften*, 119-128.

Finsinger, Jörg and Simon, Jürgen (1987), 'Vertragsbruch und Schadensersatz (Breach of Contract and Damages)', **2** *Kritische Vierteljahresschrift für Gesetzgebung und Rechtswissenschaft*, 262-274.

Finsinger, Jörg and Simon, Jürgen (1988), *Eine ökonomische Bewertung der EG-Produkthaftu* (An Economic Appreciation of the EC- Product Li), Lüneburg, Arbeitsbericht Hochschule Lüneburg, Fachbereich Wirtschafts- und Sozialwissenschaften, 44 p.

Finsinger, Jörg and Von Randow, Philip (1991), 'Neue Aktivitäten und Haftungsregeln - Zugleich ein Beitrag zur ökonomischen Analyse des privaten Nachbarrechts (New Activities and Liability Rules - Also a Contri)', in Ott, Claus and Schäfer, Hans-Bernd (eds), *Ökonomische Probleme des Zivilrechts*, Berlin, Springer, 87-108.

Frank, Björn (1995), 'Ökonomische Analyse von Rauchverboten (Economic Analysis of Smoking Bans)', **46(1)** *Jahrbuch für Wirtschaftswissenschaften*, 109-119.

Frank, Jürgen (1986), 'Die 'Rationalität' einer ökonomischen Analyse des Rechts (The 'Rationality' of an Economic Analysis of Law)', **2** *Zeitschrift für Rechtssoziologie*, 191-211.

Frank, Jürgen (1987), 'Ökonomische Modelle der Abschreckung (Economic Models of Deterrence)', **1** *Kriminologisches Journal*, 55-65.

Frank, Jürgen (1989), 'Kollektive Oder Individuelle Steuerung Der Umwelt? (Collective or Individual Control of the Environment?)', **1** *Kritische Justiz*, 36-55.

Fröhlich, P. (1975), *Marktabgrenzung in der Wettbewerbspolitik: Die* (Market Definition in Competition Policy: The P), Göttingen.

Fuchs, Maximilian (1979), 'Die Behandlung von Ehe und Scheidung in der 'Ökonomischen Analyse des Rechts' (The Treatment of Marriage and Divorce in the 'Economic Analysis of Law')', **7** *Zeitschrift für das gesamte Familienrecht*, 553-557.

Funke, Stefan (1995), *Die Verschuldungsordnung. Ein Beitrag zur finanzwirtschaftlichen Ordnungspolitik Schriften zur ökonomischen Analyse des Rechts* (Regulation of Public Debt. A Contribution to the Fiscal Economics Constitutional Policy), Berlin, Duncker and Humblot.

Gäfgen, G'rad (1983), 'Entwicklung und Stand der Theorie der Property Rights. Eine kritische Bestandsaufnahme (Development and Actual Situation of the Property R)', in Neumann, M. (ed.), *Ansprache, Eigentums- und Verfügungsrechte*, Berlin, Duncker and Humblot, 43-62.

Ganal, Michael (1986), *Die handels- und kartellrechtliche Beurteilung von Agentursystemen. Eine Juristische und Ökonomische Analyse, Schriftenreihe Law and Economics, Vol. 1* (Evaluation of Agency Systems from the Viewpoint of Mercantile Law and Anti-Trust Law), München, Florentz, 379 p.

Gebhard, Joachim (1985), *Finanzierungsleasing über Mobilien - Versuch einer Analyse eines expandierenden Finanzmarktes* (Financial Leasing - An Analysis of an Expanding Capital Market), Wiesbaden, Gabler.

Gotthold, Jürgen (1980), 'Zur ökonomischen 'Theorie des Eigen tums'. Eine kritische Einfuhrung (The Economic Theory of Property - A Critical Introduction)', **144** *Zeitschrift für das gesamte Handels- und Wirtschaftsrecht*, 545-562.

Gotthold, Jürgen (1981), 'Neuere Entwicklungen der Wettbewerbstheorie: Kritische Bemerkungen zur neo-liberalen Theorie der Wettbewerbspolitik (New Developments in Competition Theory: Critical Remarks on the Neo-Liberal Theory of Competition Policy)', **145** *Zeitschrift für das gesamte Handels- und Wirtschaftsrecht*, 286-340.

Greipel, E. and Taeger, U. (1981), 'Auswirkungen des Patentschutzes und der Lizenz (Effects of Patent Protection and License Practice Activity on Competition in Specific Areas of Economic Activity with Special Reference to the Market Position of Small and Middle Size Companies), Gutachten erstellt für das Bundeswirtschaftsministeriu)', *Gutachten erstellt für das Bundeswirtschaftsministerium*.

Grossekettler, Heinz (1978), 'Der Fall 'Deutsche SB-Kauf kontra adidas'. Volkswirtschaftliche Analyse einer Liefervereinigung (Economic Analysis of a Supply Relation)', **9** *Wettbewerb in Recht und Praxis*, 619-634.

Grossekettler, Heinz (1981), 'Die Gesamtwirtschaftliche Problematik Vertraglicher Vertriebssysteme (The Economic Impact of Contractual Supply Systems)', in Ahlert, D. (ed.), *Vertragliche Vertriebssysteme Zwischen Industrie und Handel, Grundzüge einer Betriebswirtschaftlichen, Rechtlichen und Volkswirtschaftlichen Beurteilung*, Wiesbaden, Gabler, 225-314.

Grossekettler, Heinz (1984), 'Verwaltungsstrukturpolitik (Public Administration Structure Policy)', in Ewers, H.-J. and Schuster (ed.), *Probleme der Ordnungs- und Strukturpolitik*, Göttingen, 16-51.

Grossekettler, Heinz (1986), 'Options- und Grenzkostenpreise für Kollektivgüter unterschiedlicher Art und Ordnung. Ein Beitrag zu den Bereitstellungs- und Finanzierungsregeln für öffentliche Leistungen (Option Pricing and Marginal Prices for Collective Goods)', **43(2)** *Finanzarchiv*, 211-253.

Grossekettler, Heinz (1989), 'Deregulierung und Privatisierung. Erscheinungsformen, Legitimationskriterien und politische Verhaltenstendenzen (Deregulation and Privatization)', **18(10)** *Wirtschaftswissenschaftliches Studium*, 437-445.

Grossekettler, Heinz (1991a), 'Zur theoretischen Integration der Wettbewerbs- und Finanzpolitik in die Konzeption des ökonomischen Liberalismus (On the Integration of Competition Policy and Public Finance into the Economic Liberalism)', **10** *Jahrbuch für Neue Politische Ökonomie*, 103-144.

Grossekettler, Heinz (1991b), 'Die Versorgung mit Kollektivgütern als ordnungspolitisches Problem (Public Goods as a Problem of Constitutional Economics)', **42** *Ordo*, 69-89.

Grossekettler, Heinz (1991c), 'Deregulierung, Entbürokratisierung und Privatisierung (Deregulation, Debureaucratization, and Privatization)', **2** *Wirtschafts- und Umweltrecht*, 303-310.

Grossekettler, Heinz (1992), 'Wettbewerb Soweit wie Möglich, Planung Soweit wie Nötig. Über Voraussetzungen und Entwicklungsmöglichkeiten der Schillerschen Beweislastregel (Competition as far as Possible, Planning as far as Necessary)', **73** *Schriften der Gesellschaft zur Förderung der Westfälischen Wilhelms-Universität Münster*, 18-36.

Grossekettler, Heinz (1995), *Ökonomische Analyse der interkommunalen Kooperation* (Economic Analysis of Intermunicipal Cooperation), Arbeitspapiere des Instituts für Genossenschaftswesen der Universität Münster, No. 5, 1995.

Grossekettler, Heinz (1996), 'Kommentar zu, Klaus-Werner Schatz, Reform von Planungs- und Genehmigungsverfahren (Comment on, Klaus-Werner Schatz, Reform of Public Planning and Approval Processes)', **15** *Jahrbuch für Neue Politische Ökonomie*, 31-37.

Hauschka, Christoph E. (1990), 'Zielkonflikte zwischen Unternehmenkontrolle und Wirtschaftsförderung in den Wettbewerbspolitischen Programmaussagen der EG-Kommission (Conflict of Goals between Enterprise Control and Economic Imperatives in the Competition Programme of the EC-Commission)', **40** *Wirtschaft und Wettbewerb*, 205-216.

Henning-Bodewig, Frauke (1985), 'Die Qualitätsfunktion der Marke im Amerikanischen Recht (The Quality Function of Trademarks in American Law)', **7** *GRUR Int.*, 445-453.

Herder-Dorneich, Philipp, Schenk, Karl-Ernst and Schmidtchen, Dieter (eds) (1993), 'Neue Politische Ökonomie von Normen und Institutionen (New Political Economics of Norms and Institutions)', **12** *Jahrbuch für Neue Politische Ökonomie*.

Herder-Dorneich, Philipp, Schenk, Karl-Ernst and Schmidtchen, Dieter (eds) (1994), 'Neue Politische Ökonomie der Regulierung, Deregulierung und Privatisierung (New Political Economics of Regulation, Deregulation, and Privatization)', **13** *Jahrbuch für Neue Politische Ökonomie*.

Herdzina, Klaus (1985), 'Marktentwicklung und Wettbewerbsverhalten (Market Development and Competition Attitude)', in Bombach, G., Gahlen, B. and Ott, A.E. (eds), *Industrieökonomik: Theorie und Empirie*, Tübingen, Mohr, 105-123.

Herdzina, Klaus (1987), *Wettbewerbspolitik* (Competition Policy), Stuttgart, Gustav Fischer, 237 p.

Herrmann, Harald (1976), 'Die Grundsätze ordnungsgemäßer Buchführung im Licht einer entscheidungswissenschaftlichen Rechtstheorie (The Generally Accepted Principles of Book-Keeping in the Light of a Decision Theory of Law)', *Zeitschrift für Unternehmens- und Gesellschaftsrecht*, 203-238.

Herrmann, Harald (1977), 'Organisations- und Entscheidungslehre im Unternehmensverfassungsrecht (Organization- and Decision-Theory in the Law of Corporations)', in Horn, N. and Tieze, R. (ed.), *Sozialwissenschaften im Studium des Rechts*, München, 151-172.

Herrmann, Harald (1979), 'Verbandskonzentration und Großunternehmen. Zur Bedeutung des Vereinsrechts für die Organisation von Großunternehmen in den Interessenverbänden der deutschen und englischen Industrie (1871-1914) (Concentration of Trade Associations and Big Enterprises. The Impact of the Law of Associations for the Organisation of Big Enterprises in the Trade Associations of the German and British Industry (1981-1914))', in Horn, N. and Kocka, J. (eds), *Recht und Entwicklung der Großunternehmen im 19. und 20. Jahrhundert. Wirtschafts-, sozial- und rechtshistorische Untersuchungen zur Industrialisierung in Deutschland, Frankreich, England und den USA*, Göttingen, 676 ff.

Herrmann, Harald (1981), 'Der Trigger-Preismechanismus der USA. Erfahrungen des amerikanischen Wirtschaftsministeriums und antitrustrechtliche Grenzen interessenverbandlicher Einflußnahme (The Trigger-Price Mechanism of the USA. The Experience of the U.S.-American Commerce Department and Antitrust Limits of Lobbying)', *Recht der Internationalen Wirtschaft*, 525-533.

Herrmann, Harald (1982), 'Anzapfverbote im Einzelhandel und Privatrechtlicher Verbraucherschutz (Predatory Pricing by Retail Companies and the Private Law of Consumer Protection)', *Gewerblicher Rechtsschutz und Urheberrecht*, 917 ff.

Herrmann, Harald (1983a), 'Kaufrechtliche Grenzen der Händlerwerbung. Ein Marktbezogener Vorschlag zur Haftung für 'stillschweigende' Zusicherung und positive Vertragsverletzung (Sale's Law Limits of Advertising of Retailers. An Antitrust Proposal on the Liability for Implied Warranties and Breach of Contract)', *Archiv für die Civilistische Praxis*, 248-278.

Herrmann, Harald (1983b), 'Die Sachverwalterhaftung vermögenssorgender Berufe. Zu den berufssoziologischen und wirtschaftsrechtlichen Grundlagen der culpa in contrahendo (The Liability of Professional Contract Mediators. To the culpa in contrahendo and its Basis in the Profession's Sociology and the Law of Commerce)', *Juristenzeitung*, 422-430.

Herrmann, Harald (1984a), *Interessenverbände und Wettbewerbsrecht. Ein deutsch-amerikanischer Vergleich zum Recht der unberechtigten Verfahrenseinleitung, Selbstbeschränkungsabkommen und Wettbewerbsregeln* (Trade Associations and Antitrust Law. A German-American Comparison for the Law of Harrassing, Self-Regulation and Trade Practice Rules), Baden-Baden, Nomos.

Herrmann, Harald (1984b), 'Sanierungsfusion und Behinderungsmißbrauch. Zum Rechtsmodell funktionsfähigen Wettbewerbs im GWB und im Montanvertrag (Pre-Insolvenca-Merger and Monopoly Practices. To the Concept of Workable Competition in the German Antitrust Law and in the EG-Treaty of Coal and Steel)', *Die Aktiengesellschaft*, 1-12.

Herrmann, Harald (1985a), 'Wettbewerbliche und Kartellrechtliche Aspekte der Herstellerhaftung für Mangelschäden (Aspects of Competition and Antitrust in Cases of Product Liability for 'Mangelschäden')', *Gewerblicher Rechtsschutz und Urheberrecht*, 896-909.

Herrmann, Harald (1985b), 'Die Rückrufhaftung des Produzenten. Zum vorbeugenden Rechtsschutz bei Vertrags- und Verkehrspflichtverletzungen sowie bei sittenwidrigem Wettbewerb (The Call-back-Liability of Producers. To the Anticipating Effects of the Law of Contracts and of Torts and in Cases of Unfair Competition)', *Der Betriebs-Berater*, 1801-1818.

Herrmann, Harald (1986a), 'Die gefährdungstatbestandliche Auslegung des § 23a Abs. 1 Nr. 1 a/b GWB bei Marktverkettungsfusionen. Ein deutsch-amerikanischer Rechtsvergleich (The Prospective Interpretation of § 23a Sec.1 No.1a/b GWB in Cases of Tying Markets by Vertical Mergers. A German-American Law)', *Recht der Internationalen Wirtschaft*, 253-269.

Herrmann, Harald (1986b), 'Gesellschafterklagen auf Unterlassen in der OHG und KG (Suits on Cease and Desist Orders by Partners of Commerce Partnerships and Limited Partnerships)', *JURA*, 511-520.

Herrmann, Harald (1987), 'Vertrags- und wettbewerbsrechtliche Grenzen der Zinsanhebung beim Hypothekenkredit (Limits of Interest Adaptation Clauses in Contract Law and the Law of Competition)', *Wertpapiermitteilungen* in Frech, H.E. (ed.), *Regulating Doctors' Fees: Competition, Benefits, and Controls under Medicare*, Washington, DC, American Enterprise Institute, 1029-1062.

Herrmann, Harald (1988a), 'Vertragsanpassung - Ein Problem des Freiheitsschutzes nach Vertragsschluß (Contract Adaptation - A Problem of the Protection of Liberty after Contract Conclusion)', *JURA*, 505-511.

Herrmann, Harald (1988b), 'Vertragliche Preisvorbehalte bei Beschränktem und unlauterem Wettbewerb (Contract Clauses on Price Adaptation in Cases of Restricted and Unfair Competition)', *Recht und Risiko*, 325-364.

Herrmann, Harald (1989a), 'Der ungedeckte Fehlbetrag nach § 268 Abs. 3 HGB und die Folgepflichten des Abschlußprüfers und der Gesellschaftsorgane in der AG und GmbH (The Statement of Losses under § 268 Sec. 3 HGB and the Concurring Duties of the

Public Accountant and the Board Members of Public and Closed Corporations)', *ZGR*, 273-304.

Herrmann, Harald (1989b), 'Wettbewerbsgefahren von Konglomeratfusionen (Dangers to Competition in Cases of Conglomerate Mergers)', *BB*, 1213-1217.

Herrmann, Harald (1989c), 'Handelsbilanzrechtliche Probleme des Quasi-Eigenkapitals in der GmbH und KG (Problems of the Accounting Law of Mezzanine Financing in the Closed Corporation and the Limited Partnership)', in Albers, S., Herrmann, H., Kahle, E., Kruschwitz, C. and Perlitz, M. (eds), *Elemente Erfolgreicher Unternehmenspolitik in Mittelständischen Unternehmen*, Stuttgart, 301-322.

Herrmann, Harald (1993), 'Kreditvertragsrecht und funktionsfähiger Wettbewerb im neuen Bundesgebiet (Law of Borrowing and Workable Competition in the Ex-GDR)', *Zeitschrift für Wirtschaftsrecht*, 54-63.

Herrmann, Harald (1994), 'Wettbewerbliche Transparenzgebote im AGB-Gesetz und UWG (Provisions of Market Transparence in the Law of Adheasion Contracts and of Fair Trade)', *Zeitschrift für Wirtschaftsrecht*, 45-102.

Herrmann, Harald (1996a), *Recht der Kammern und Verbände Freier Berufe in der Europäischen Union und den USA* (Law of Chambers and Associations of the Professions in the European Community and the United States), Baden-Baden, Nomos.

Herrmann, Harald (1996b), 'Quasi-Eigenkapital im Kapitalmarkt- und Unternehmensrecht.-Ein deutsch-amerikanischer Rechtsvergleich und Beitrag zum internationalen Wirtschaftsrecht (Mezzanine Financing in the Law of Securities Regulations and in the Law of Corporations. An Analysis of German-American Comparative Law and of International Commerce Law)', **17** *Recht des internationalen Wirtschaftverkehrs*.

Hesse, Günter (1980), 'Der Property-Rights-Ansatz. Eine ökonomische Theorie der Veränderung des Rechts? (The Property Rights Approach. An Economic Theory of Legal Change?)', **195** *Jahrbuch für Nationalökonomie und Statistik*, 481 ff.

Hesse, Günter (1982), 'Die Änderung von Rechten im Property-Rights-Ansatz (The Change of Institutions in the Property Rights Paradigm)', **11(6)** *Wirtschaftswissenschaftliches Studium*, 249-257.

Hesse, Günter (1983), 'Zur Erklärung der Änderung von Handlungsrechten mit Hilfe der ökonomischen Theorie (The Explanation of the Change of Property Rights w)', in Schüller, Alfred (ed.), *Property Rights und Ökonomische Theorie*, München, Vahlen, 79-109.

Hesse, Günter (1992), 'Innovative Anpassung in sozio-ökonomischen Systemen - Ein Beispiel, Landnutzungssysteme und Handlungsrechte bezüglich Boden (Innovative Adaptation in Socio-Economic Systems - An Example, Land Use Systems and Property Rights)', in Bievert, B. and Held, M. (ed.), *Evolutorische Ökonomik, Neuerungen, Normen, Institutionen*, Frankfurt a.M./New York, 110-142.

Hesse, Günter (1997), 'Effiziente Institutionen und wirtschaftlicher Rückschritt (Efficient Institutions and Economic Descent)', in Fehl, U. and Delhaes-Günther, K. von (ed.), *Dimensionen des Wettberwerbs*, Stuttgart.

Hofmann, E. and Wehrt, Klaus (1992), 'Die Reform der Kfz-Steuer - wirtschaftspolitisch betrachtet (Economic Analysis of the Reform of the Motor Vehicle Tax)', **4** *Zeitschrift für Verkehrswissenschaft*, 263-271.

Holler, Manfred J. (1984a), 'Moral, Markt und Norm. Thesen zur ökonomischen Theoriebildung (Morals, Market, and Norms. Theses on the Creation of Economic Theories)', in Holler, Manfred J. (ed.), *Homo Oeconomicus 2*, München, Leudemann, 512-558.

Holler, Manfred J. (1984b), 'Norm, Normsetzung und Wissenschaft (Norms, Norm Setting, and Science)', **39** *Universitas*, 1145-1152.

Holler, Manfred J. (1989a), 'Ethik, Ökonomie, Arbeit und der Triumph der Medizin (Ethics, Economics, Labor, and the Victory of Medicine)', in Wieland, K. (ed.), *Homo Oeconomicus 5*, München, Accedo, 41-63.

Holler, Manfred J. (1989b), 'Komplexe Entscheidungen in Sozialen Institutionen (Complex Decisions in Social Institutions)', in Boettcher, Erik, Herder-Dorneich, Philipp and Schenk, Karl-Ernst (eds), *Jahrbuch für Neue Politische Ökonomie*, Tübingen, Mohr, 219-228.

Holler, Manfred J. (1996), 'Die Rationalität Strategischer Normierung in Europa (The Rationality of Strategic Standardization in Europe)', in Schenk, Karl-Ernst, Schmidtchen, Dieter and Streit, Manfred E. (eds), *Vom Hoheitsstaat zum Konsensualstaat, Neue Formen der Kooperation zwischen Staat und Privaten Jahrbuch für Neue Politische Ökonomie 15*, Tübingen, Mohr, 137-153.

Holler, P. (1979), 'Probleme der Utilitaristischen Strafrechtfertigung (Problems of Utilitarian Criminal Law Making)', *Zeitschrift für die Gesamte Strafrechtswissenschaften*, 45-95.

Hoppmann, Erich (1966), 'Das Konzept der optimalen Wettbewerbsintensität (The Concept of Optimal Competition Intensity)', **180** *Jahrbuch für Nationalökonomie und Statistik*, 286-323.

Hoppmann, Erich (1967a), 'Wettbewerb als Norm der Wettbewerbspolitik (Competition as Norm for Competition Policy)', **18** *Ordo: Jahrbuch für die Ordnung von Wirtschaft und Gesellschaft*, 77-94.

Hoppmann, Erich (1967b), 'Die Funktionsfähigkeit des Wettbewerbs: Bemerkungen zu Kantzenbachs Erwiderung (The Functionality of Competition: Remarks on Kantzenbach's Reaction)', **181** *Jahrbuch für Nationalökonomie und Statistik*, 251-264.

Hoppmann, Erich (1968), 'Zum Problem einer Wirtschaftpolitischen praktikablen Definition des Wettbewerbs (On the Problem of an Economic and Practical Defin)', in Schneider, H.K. (ed.), *Grundlagen der Wettbewerbspolitik*, Berlin, 9-49.

Hoppmann, Erich (1970), 'Neue Wettbewerbspolitik: Vom Wettbewerb zur staatlichen Mikro-Steuerung: Bemerkungen zu einem 'neuen Leitbild' der Wettbewerbspolitik (New Competition Policy: From Competition to Govern)', **184** *Jahrbuch für Nationalökonomie und Statistik*, 397-416.

Hoppmann, Erich (1988), *Wirtschaftsordnung und Wettbewerb* (Economic Order and Competition), Baden-Baden, Nomos, 566 p.

Horn, Norbert (1976), 'Zur ökonomischen Rationalität des Privatrechts. Die privatrechts theoretische Verwertbarkeit der 'Economics Analysis of Law' (The Economic Rationality of Private Law. On the)', **176** *Archiv für die Civilistische Praxis*, 307-333.

Horst, Peter M. (1987), *Kapitalanlegerschutz. Haftung bei Emissionen und Vertrieb von Kapitalanlagen. Eine Juristische und Ökonomische Analyse, Schriftenreihe Law and Economics, Bd. 2* (Protection of Capital Investors), München.

Hüderpohl, Astrid (1996), *Organisation der Wohlfahrtspflege. Eine ökonomische Analyse ausgewählter Nationaler und internationaler Organisationen, Schriften zur ökonomischen Analyse des Rechts* (Organization of Welfare. An Economic Analysis of Selected National and International Organizations), Berlin, Duncker and Humblot.

Hummel, Berger (1988), *Die volkswirtschaftliche Bedeutung von Kunst und Kultur* (The Economic Significance of Art and Culture), München.

Hutter, Michael (1979), *Die Gestaltung von Property Rights als Mittel gesellschaftlichwirtschaftlicher Allokation* (The Structure of Property Rights as a Means of Social-Economic Allocation), Göttingen, Vandenhoeck and Ruprecht, 245 p.

Hutter, Michael (1980), 'Über eine Alternative zur Neoklassischen Ökonomischen Analyse des Rechts (On an Alternative for Neo-classical Economic Analysis)', **144** *Zeitschrift für das gesamte Handels- und Wirtschaftsrecht*, 642-651.

Hutter, Michael (1989), *Die Produktion von Recht. Eine selbstreferentielle Theorie der Wirtschaft, angewandt auf den Fall des Arzneimittelpatentrechts* (The Production of Law. A Selfreferential Theory of the Economy, applied to the Case of Pharmaceutical Patent Law), Tübingen, Mohr, 213 p.

Isay, H. (1927), *Die Funktion der Patente im Wirtschaftskampf* (Patent Functions in Economic Battle), Berlin, Franz Vahlen.

Jahr, Günther (1966), 'Funktionsanalyse von Rechtsfiguren als Grundlage einer Begegnung von Rechtswissenschaft und Wirtschaftswissenschaft (Functional Analysis of Legal Ideas as a Base for Encounters of Lawyers and Economists)', **36(12)** *Zeitschrift für Betriebswirtschaft*, 757-768.

Jost, Peter J. (1992), *Schadensausgleich und Präventivwirkung im neuen deutschen Umwelthaftungsrecht. Eine ökonomische Analyse* (Damage Compensation and Preventive Effects of the New German Environment Liability Laws. An Economic Analysis), Basel, Wirtschaftswissenschaftliches Zentrum Sonderdruck 10.

Jost, Peter J. (1997a), 'Koordinationsverhalten bei Umweltdelikten. Eine spieltheoretische Argumentation (Coordination and Environment Damages)', in Weber, Jürgen (ed.), *Umweltmanagement. Aspekte einer umweltbezogenen Unternehmensführung*, Stuttgart, Schäffer-Poeschel.

Jost, Peter J. (1997b), *Effektivität von Recht aus ökonomischer Sicht* (Effectivity of Law from the Economist's Viewpoint), Berlin, Duncker and Humblot.

Kallfass, Hermann H. (1980), 'Die Chicago School: Eine Skizze des 'neuen' amerikanisches Ansatzes für die Wettbewerbspolitik (The Chicago School: A Sketch of the 'New' American Approach for Competition Policy)', **30** *Wirtschaft und Wettbewerb*, 596-601.

Kallfass, Hermann H. (1997), 'Konzepte und Indikatoren zur Abgrenzung räumlicher Märkte in der europäischen Zusammenschlußkontrolle (Indicators for the Definition of Local Markets)', in Kruse, Jörn, Stockmann, Kurt and Vollmer, Lothar (eds), *Wettbewerbspolitik im Spannungsfeld nationaler und internationaler Kartellrechtsordnungen. Festschrift für Ingo Schmidt zum 65. Geburtstag*, Baden-Baden, Nomos, 111 ff.

Kantzenbach, Erhard (1967), 'Das Konzept der optimalen Wettbewerbsintensität: Eine Erwiderung auf den gleichnamigen Besprechungsaufsatz von Erich Hoppmann (The Concept of Optimal Competition Intensity: A Reaction on Erich Hoppman's Comment of the Same Title)', **181** *Jahrbuch für Nationalökonomie und Statistik*, 193-241.

Kantzenbach, Erhard (1977), 'Ein wirtschaftspolitisches Leitbild für die Gestaltung der Energiewirtschaft (An Economic Policy Model for Structuring the Power Supply Industry)', **1** *Zeitschrift für Energiewirtschaft*, 38-46.

Kantzenbach, Erhard (1984), 'Zehn Jahre Monopolkommission (Ten Years Monopoly Commission)', **34** *Wirtschaft und Wettbewerb*, 297-301.

Kantzenbach, Erhard (1985), 'Mehr Wettbewerb im Rundfunk? (More Competition in Broadcasting?)', in Lüder, K. (ed.), *Rundfunk im Umbruch*, Berlin, 161-167.

Kantzenbach, Erhard (1987), 'Die Vorschläge der Monopolkommission (The Proposals of the Monopoly Commission)', in Röper, B. (ed.), *Wettbewerb im Medienbereich Schriften des Vereins für Socialpolitik N.F. 162*, Berlin, 143-153.

Kantzenbach, Erhard (1988), 'Zur Anwendbarkeit des Wettbewerbsrechts auf den Rundfunk und zum Verhältnis von publizistischem und ökonomischem Wettbewerb (On the Applicability of Competition Law on Broadcasting and on the Relation of Journalistic and Economic Competition)', in Hoffmann-Riem, Wolfgang (ed.), *Materialien zur interdisziplinären Medienforschung 20*, Baden-Baden, 78-83.

Kantzenbach, Erhard (1995), 'Wettbewerbsrecht und Wettbewerbspolitik in der Europäischen Union. Diskussionsbeitrag zum gleichnamigen Referat von Ernst Joachim Mestmäcker (Competition Law and Competition Policy in the European Union. Comment)', in Gerken, Lüder (ed.), *Europa zwischen Ordnungswettbewerb und Harmonisierung*, Berlin, 213-217.

Kantzenbach, Erhard (1996), 'Wettbewerbspolitik versus Industriepolitik (Competition Policy vs. Industrial Policy)', in X. (ed.), *Maastricht II - Entwicklungschancen und Risiken der EU. Tagungsband zur Jahresversammlung der Arbeitsgemeinschaft deutscher wirtschaftswissenschaftlicher Forschungsinstitute Beihefte der Konjunkturpolitik 44*, Berlin, 43-47.

Kantzenbach, Erhard and Greiffenberg, G. (1980), 'Die Übertragung des Modells des 'funktionsfähigen Wettbewerbs' auf die Presse (Transferring the Concept of 'Functional Competition' on the Press)', in Klaue, S. u.a. (eds), *Probleme der Pressekonzentration*, Baden-Baden, 189-202.

Kantzenbach, Erhard and Kinne, Konstanze (1997), 'Nationale Zusammenschlußkontrolle und internationale Wettbewerbsfähigkeit von Unternehmen (National Merger Control and International Competitive Power of Firms)', in Kruse, Jörn, Stockmann, Kurt and Vollmer, Lothar (eds), *Wettbewerbspolitik im Spannungsfeld nationaler und internationaler Kartellrechtsordnungen. Festschrift für Ingo Schmidt zum 65. Geburtstag*, Baden-Baden, Nomos, 67 ff.

Kantzenbach, Erhard and Krüger, Reinald (1990), 'Zur Frage der richtigen Abgrenzung des sachlich relevanten Markten bei der wettbewerbspolitischen Beurteilung von Unternehmenszusammenschlüssen (On the Question of the Correct Definition of the Relevant Market at the Judgment of Mergers)', **40** *Wirtschaft und Wettbewerb*, 472-481.

Kantzenbach, Erhard and Kruse, J. (1989), 'Kollektive Marktbeherrschung (Collective Market Power)', in Jürgensen, H. And Kantzenbach, E. (eds), *Wirtschaftspolitische Studien aus den Instituten für Europäische Wirtschaftspolitik und für Industrie- und Gewerbepolitik der Universität Hamburg 75*, Göttingen.

Kantzenbach, Erhard and Otremba, W. (1983), 'Vertikale Integration und Wettbewerb in der Mineralölindustrie und Petrochemie (Vertical Integration and Competition in the Oil and Petrochemical Industries)', **7** *Zeitschrift für Energiewirtschaft*, 74-77.

Kantzenbach, Erhard, Kottmann, Elke and Krüger, Reinald (1996), *Kollektive Marktbeherrschung. Neue Industrieökonomik und Erfahrungen aus der Europäischen Fusionskontrolle, Veröffentlichungen des HWWA-Instituts für Wirtschaftsforschung Hamburg 28* (Collective Market Power. New Industrial Economics and Experiences from the European Anti-Merger Policy), Baden-Baden.

Kaufer, Erich (1966), 'Kantzenbachs Konzept des funktionsfähigen Wettbewerbs: Ein Kommentar (Kantenbach's Concept of Functional Competition: A Comment)', **179** *Jahrbuch für Nationalökonomie und Statistik*, 481-492.

Kaufer, Erich (1968), 'Das Konzept der optimalen Wettbewerbsintensität: Eine Replik (The Concept of Optimal Competition Intensity: A Reply)', **181** *Jahrbuch für Nationalökonomie und Statistik*, 242-250.

Kaulmann, Peter (1987), 'Property rights und Unternehmungstheorie. Stand und Weiterentwicklung der empirischen Forschung (Property Rights and the Theory of the Firm)', **3** *Schriftenreihe Law and Economics*.

Kerber, Wolfgang (1992), 'Innovation, Handlungsrechte und Evolutionärer Marktprozeß (Innovation, Property Rights and Evolutionary Market Process)', in Witt, Ulrich (ed.), *Studien zur Evolutorischen Ökonomik II*, Berlin, 171-195.

Kerber, Wolfgang (1996), 'Recht als Selektionsumgebung für evolutorische Wettbewerbsprozesse (Law as Selection Environment for Evolutionary Competition Processes)', in Priddat, B.P. and Wegner, G. (eds), *Zwischen Institution und Evolution. Neue Ansätze in der ökonomischen Theorie*, Marburg, Metropolis, 297-326.

Kilian, W, Picot, Arnold, Neuburger, R., Niggl, J., Scholtes, K.-L. and Seiler, W. (1994), *Electronic Data Interchange (EDI), Aus ökonomischer und juristischer Sicht, Forschungsbericht zu dem von der Volkswagen-Stiftung geförderten Forschungsprojekt ELTRADA (Elektronische Transaktionen von Dokumenten zwischen Organisationen* (Electronic Data Interchange EDI from the Viewpoint of Economic and Law), Baden-Baden, Nomos.

Kirchner, Christian (1978), 'Ökonomische Analyse des Rechts, Interdisziplinäre Zusammenarbeit von Ökonomie und Rechtswissenschaft (Economic Analysis of Law and Interdisciplinary Cooperation of Jurisprudence and Economics)', in Assmann, Heinz-Dieter, Kirchner, Christian and Schanze, Erich (eds), *Ökonomische Analyse des Rechts*, Kronberg, Athenäum, 75-91.

Kirchner, Christian (1980), '"Ökonomische Analyse des Rechts' und Recht der Wettbewerbsbeschränkungen (Economic Analysis of Law' and Antitrust Law)', **144** *Zeitschrift für das gesamte Handels- und Wirtschaftsrecht*, 563-588.

Kirchner, Christian (1984), 'Ansatze zu einer Ökonomischen Analyse des Konzernrechts (Starting Point for an Economic Analysis of Large Companies Law)', in Boettcher, Erik, Herder- Dorneich, Philipp and Schenk, Karl-Ernst (eds), *Jahrbuch für Neue Politische Ökonomie*, Tübingen, Mohr, 223-251.

Kirchner, Christian (1989), 'Kommentar (Comment on Brüggemeier, Die Gefährdungshaftung der)', in Ott, Claus and Schäfer, Hans-Bernd (eds), *Allekationseffizienz in der Rechtsordnung*, Berlin, Springer, 248-253.

Kirchner, Christian (1991a), 'The Difficult Reception of Law and Economics in Germany', **11** *International Review of Law and Economics*, 277-292.

Kirchner, Christian (1991b), 'Comment (on Eger, Nagel and Weise, *Effizienz und Menschenwürde*)', in Ott, Claus and Schäfer, Hans-Bernd (eds), *Ökonomische Probleme des Zivilrechts*, Berlin, Springer, 35-38.

Kirchner, Christian (1997), 'Kartellrecht und neue Institutionenökonomik. Interdisziplinäre Überlegungen (Antitrust Law and New Institutional Economics. Some Interdisciplinary Ideas)', in Kruse, Jörn, Stockmann, Kurt and Vollmer, Lothar (eds), *Wettbewerbspolitik im Spannungsfeld Nationaler und Internationaler Kartellrechtsordnungen. Festschrift für Ingo Schmidt zum 65. Geburtstag*, Baden-Baden, Nomos, 33 ff.

Kirstein, Roland (1997), *Rechtsschutzversicherungen, Glaubwürdigkeit und die Entscheidung zu klagen* (Legal Costs Insurances, Credibility and the Decision to Bring Suit), Center for the Study of Law and Economics, Discussion Paper, Saarbrücken, No. 9703.

Klaus, J. (1987), 'Umweltökonomie und Umweltpolitik (Environmental Economics and Environmental Politics)', in Wenz, E., Issing, O. and Hofmann, H. (eds), *Oekologie, Oekonomie und Jurisprudenz*, München, Florentz.

Kleinmann, Werner (1997), 'Die Umsatzschwellen für Zusammenschlüsse von gemeinschaftsweiter Bedeutung in der Europäichen Fusionskontrolle und ihre Revision (Return Thresholds for Mergers of Unionwide Relevance in the European Merger Control)', in Kruse, Jörn, Stockmann, Kurt and Vollmer, Lothar (eds), *Wettbewerbspolitik im Spannungsfeld nationaler und internationaler Kartellrechtsordnungen. Festschrift für Ingo Schmidt zum 65. Geburtstag*, Baden-Baden, Nomos, 131 ff.

Klemm, Günter (1983), *Ökonomische Analyse von Streik und Ausperrung im Rahmen einer marktwirtschaftlichen Ordnung* (Economic Analysis of Strike and Lock-out in the Context of a Market Economy), 214 p.

Koboldt, Christian (1991a), 'Kommentar on Schanze, Stellvertretung und Ökonomische Agentur-Theorie', in Ott, Claus and Schäfer, Hans-Bernd (eds), *Ökonomische Probleme des Zivilrechts*, Berlin, Springer, 76-86.

Koboldt, Christian (1991b), 'Stellvertretung und ökonomische Agentur-Theorie, Probleme und Wechselbezüge, Kommentar (Representation and the Economic Agency Theory, Problems and Relations)', in Ott, Claus and Schäfer, Hans-Bernd (eds), *Ökonomische Probleme des Zivilrechts*, Berlin, Springer.

Koboldt, Christian (1992), 'Legitimitätsaspekte der Prohibitionspolitik: Individuelle Handlungsbeschränkungen und ökonomische Sozialvertragstheorie (Aspects of Legitimacy of Prohibition Policy, Individual Constraints and Economic Social Contract Theory)', in Homann, K. (ed.), *Wirtschaftsethische Perspektiven des Drogenproblems*, Berlin.

Koboldt, Christian (1993), 'Zeitinkonsistenz, Separabilität und Teilspielperfektheit, vom möglichen Segen der 'beschränkten' Rationalität (Time Inconsitstency, Separability, ans Subgame Perfectness, On the Possible Blessing of the 'Bounded' Rationality)', **10** *Homo Oeconomicus*.

Koboldt, Christian (1995a), 'Property Rights und Urheberschutz (Property Rights and Copyright)', in Ott, Claus and Schäfer, Hans-Bernd (eds), *Okonomische Analyse der rechtlichen Organisation von Innovationen*, Tübingen, Mohr.

Koboldt, Christian (1995b), 'Konstitutionenökonomische Aspekte der Prohibitionspolitik (Constitutional Economics of Prohibition Policy)', in Erlei, Matthias (ed.), *Mit dem Markt gegen Drogen*, Stuttgart.

Koboldt, Christian (1995c), *Ökonomik der Versuchung, Sozialvertragstheorie und Drogenverbot* (Economics of Temptation), Tübingen.

Koboldt, Christian (1996), 'Die Rationalität strategischer Normierung in Europa - Kommentar (The Rationality of Strategic Standardization in Europe. Comment)', in Schenk, Karl-Ernst, Schmidtchen, Dieter and Streit, Manfred E. (eds), *Vom Hoheitsstaat zum Konsensualstaat, Neue Formen der Kooperation zwischen Staat und Privaten Jahrbuch für Neue Politische Ökonomie 15*, Tübingen, Mohr.

Koboldt, Christian and Schmidtchen, Dieter (1991), 'Copyrights, A und O in Literatur und Musik? (Copyrights, The Essentials in Literature and Music?)', **42** *Ordo: Jahrbuch für die Ordnung von Wirtschaft und Gesellschaft*.

Koboldt, Christian, Leder, Mathias and Schmidtchen, Dieter (1992), 'Ökonomische Analyse des Rechts (Law and Economics)', **7** *Wirtschaftswissenschaftliches Studium*, 334-342.

Koboldt, Christian, Leder, Mathias and Schmidtchen, Dieter (1995), 'Ökonomische Analyse des Rechts (Law and Economics)', in Nobert, Berthold (ed.), *Allgemeine Wirtschaftstheorie*, München, 355-384.

Koch, Hans-Joachim (1983), 'Die wirtschaftliche Vertretbarkeit nachträglicher Anordnungen (The Economic Justification of Additional Orders)', *Wirtschaft und Verwaltung*, 158-173.

Koch, Harald (1981), 'Die Ökonomie der Gestaltungsrechte. Möglichkeiten und Grenzen der Ökonomische Analyse des Rechts am Beispiel von Kündiging und Anfechtung (The Economics of Dispositive Right. Possibilities)', in Bernstein, H., Drobnig, U. and Kötz, H. (eds), *Festschrift für Konrad Zweigert zum 70. Geburtstag*, Tübingen, Mohr, 851-877.

Koch, Lambert T. (1996), *Evolutorische Wirtschaftspolitik, Eine elementare Analyse mit entwicklungspolitischen Beispielen* (Evolutionary Economic Policy, An Elementary Analysis with Examples of Development Policies), Tübingen, Mohr/Siebeck.

Koch, Manfred (1992), *Die wirtschaftliche Betätigung der Gemeinden. Ein Beitrag zur finanzwirtschaftlichen Ordnungspolitik Schriften zur ökonomischen Analyse des Rechts* (Economic Activities of Local Authorities. A Contribution to the Constitutional Politics of Public Economics), Berlin, Duncker and Humblot.

Koch, Walter A.S. (1984), 'Negative Einkommensteuern und Konjunkturpolitik (Negative Income Taxes and Stabilization Policy)', **30** *Konjunkturpolitik*, 348-373.

Kohl, Helmut (1991), 'Das Allgemeine Persönlichkeitsrecht als Ausdruck oder Grenze des Effizienzdenkens im Zivilrecht? (The General Right of Privacy as Expression or Limit To Efficiency in Private Law?)', in Ott, Claus and Schäfer, Hans-Bernd (eds), *Ökonomische Probleme des Zivilrechts*, Berlin, Springer, 41-51.

Kohl, Helmut, Kübler, Friedrich, Walz, W. Rainer and Wüstrich, Wolfgang (1974), 'Abschreibungsgesellschaften, Kapitalmarkteffizienz und Publizitätszwang - Plädoyer für ein Vermögensanlagegesetz (Tax Shelter Companies, Efficiency of Capital Markets)', **138** *Zeitschrift für das gesamte Handels- und Wirtschaftsrecht*, 1-49.

Köhler, Helmut (1980), 'Vertragsrecht und 'Property Rights' - Theorie, Zur Integration ökonomischer Theorien in das Privatrecht (Contract Law and Property Rights Theory - On the Integration of Economic Theories into Private Law)', **144** *Zeitschrift für das gesamte Handels- und Wirtschaftsrecht*, 589-607.

Köhler, Helmut (1989), 'Zur Ökonomischen Analyse der Regeln über die Geschäftsgrundlage (On the Economic Analysis of the Rules of the Implicit Basis of a Contract)', in Ott, Claus and Schäfer, Hans-Bernd (eds), *Allokationseffizienz in der Rechtsordnung*, Berlin, Springer, 148-162.

Koller, Ingo (1979), *Die Risikozurechnung bei Vertragsstörungen in Austauschverträgen* (The Risk Allocation of Contract Disturbances in Bilateral Contracts), München, C.H. Beck, 474 p.

Koller, Ingo (1981), 'Die Verteilung des Scheckfälschungsrisikos zwischen Kunde und Bank (The Division of the False Cheque Risk Between Client and Bank)', *Neue Juristische Wochenschrift*, 2433 ff.

Köndgen, Johannes (1977), 'Ökonomische Aspekte des Schadensproblems. Bemerkungen zur Kommerzialisierungsmethode des Bundesgerichtshofes (Economic Aspects of the Damage Problem. Remarks on the 'Commercializing Method' of the Bundesgerichtshofes)', **177** *Archiv für die civilistische Praxis*, 1-34.

Köndgen, Johannes (1991), 'Immaterialschadenersatz, Gewin nabschöpfung oder Genugtuung in Geld bei vorsätzlichen Vertragsbruch? (Damages for Nonpecuniary Losses, Skimming-off of E)', in Ott, Claus and Schäfer, Hans-Bernd (eds), *Ökonomische Probleme des Zivilrechts*, Berlin, Springer, 169-182.

Köndgen, Johannes and Von Randow, Philipp (1989), 'Sanktionen bei Vertragsverletzung (Sanctions for Breach of Contract)', in Ott, Claus and Schäfer, Hans-Bernd (eds), *Allekationseffizienz in der Rechtsordnung*, Berlin, Springer, 122-140.

Koslowski, Peter (1989), 'Grenzen der Verkehrsfähigkeit und der Privatrechtsautonomie in der Verfügung über den menschlichen Leib - Kommentar (Limits of the Marketability and Private Autonomy in the Disposition over the Human Body - Comment)', in Ott, Claus and Schäfer, Hans-Bernd (eds), *Allekationseffizienz in der Rechtsordnung*, Berlin, Springer, 115-119.

Kötz, Hein (1983a), 'Haftungsausschluss der Chemischreiniger (Exemption Clauses in Cleaning Contracts, Legal Validity and Economic Efficiency)', in Walz, W. Rainer and Rascher-Friesenhausen, Hein (eds), *Sozialwissenschaften im Zivilrecht: Fälle und Lösungen in Ausbild und Prüfung*, Neuwied und Darmstadt, Luchterhand, 76-88.

Kötz, Hein (1983b), 'Haftungsausschlussklauseln, Eine Juristisch-Ökonomische Analyse (Exemption Clauses, a Legal-Economic Analysis)', *25 Jahre Karlsruher Forum. Beiheft zu Versicherungsrecht*, 145-152.

Kötz, Hein (1986), 'Rechtsvereinheitlichung - Nutzen, Kosten, Methoden, Ziele (Law Harmonization - Benefits, Costs, Methods, Goals)', **50** *Rabels Zeitschrift für Ausländisches und Internationales Privatrecht*, 483-507.

Kötz, Hein (1989a), 'Zur Effizienz von Haftungsausschlussklauseln (On the Efficiency of Exemption Clauses)', in Ott, Claus and Schäfer, Hans-Bernd (eds), *Allekationseffizienz in der Rechtsordnung*, Berlin, Springer, 189-200.

Kötz, Hein (1989b), 'Zivilrechtliche Haftung aus Ökonomischer Sicht (Civil Liability from an Economic Perspective)', in Schäfer, Hans-Bernd and Wehrt, Klaus (eds), *Die Ökonomisierung der Sozialwissenschaften: Sechs Wortmel dungen*, 149-167.

Kötz, Hein (1990a), 'Schadenszurechnung und Schadensverteilung aus Juristischer und Ökonomischer Sicht (Allocation and Distribution of Loss from a Legal and Economic Perspective)', *Karlsruher Forum, Beiheft zur Zeitschrift Versicherungsrecht*, 14-43.

Kötz, Hein (1990b), 'Ziele des Haftungsrechts (Purposes of Civil Liability)', in Baur, Jürgen F., Hopt, Klaus J. and Mailänder (eds), *Festschrift für Ernst Steindorff*, Berlin, De Gruyter, 643-666.

Kötz, Hein (1993), 'Die Ökonomische Analyse des Rechts (Law and Economics)', *Zeitschrift für die gesamte Versicherungswissenschaft*, 57-70.

Kötz, Hein and Schäfer, Hans-Bernd (1989), 'Schadensverhütung durch Ökonomische Anreize. Eine Empirische Untersuchung (Damage Prevention by Economic Incentives. An Empirical Investigation)', **189** *Archiv für die Civilistische Praxis*, 501-525.

Kruse, J. (1997), 'Vertikale Integration als Wettbewerbsproblem (Vertical Integration as a Problem of Competition)', in Kruse, Jörn, Stockmann, Kurt und Vollmer, Lothar (eds), *Wettbewerbspolitik im Spannungsfeld Nationaler und Internationaler Kartellrechtsordnungen. Festschrift für Ingo Schmidt zum 65. Geburtstag*, Baden-Baden, Nomos, 247 ff.

Kruse, J., Stockmann, Kurt and Vollmer, Lothar (eds) (1997), *Wettbewerbspolitik im Spannungsfeld nationaler und internationaler Kartellrechtsordnungen. Festschrift für Ingo Schmidt zum 65. Geburtstag*, Baden-Baden, Nomos.

Krüsselberg, Hans-Günter (1983), 'Property Rights-Theorie und Wohlfartsökonomik (Property Rights Theory and Welfare Economics)', in Schüller, Alfred (ed.), *Property Rights und Ökonomische Theorie*, München, Vahlen, 45-75.

Kübler, Friedrich (1983), 'Was leistet die Konzeption der Property Rights für Aktuelle Rechtspolitische Probleme? (What is the Use of the Conception of Property Rights for Current Political Problems?)', in Neumann, M. (ed.), *Ansprache, Eigentums- und Verfügungsrechte*, Berlin, Duncker and Humblot, 105-122.

Kübler, Friedrich (1989), 'Schlußwort: Vergleichende Überlegungen zur rechtspraktischen Bedeutung der Ökonomischen Analyse (Closing Word: Comparitive Considerations on the Meaning of Law and Economics for Legal Practice)', in Ott, Claus and Schäfer, Hans-Bernd (eds), *Allekationseffizienz in der Rechtsordnung*, Berlin, Springer, 293-306.

Kübler, Friedrich (1990), 'Effizienz als Rechtsprinzip - Überlegungen zum Rechtspraktischen Gebrauch Ökonomischer Argumente (Efficiency as Legal Principle - Considerations for the Legal Practice Use of Economic Arguments)', in Baur, Jürgen F., Hopt, Klaus J. and Mailänder (eds), *Festschrift für Ernst Steindorff*, Berlin, De Gruyter, 687-704.

Kübler, Friedrich, Mendelson, Morris and Mundheim, Robert H. (1990), 'Die Kosten des Bezugsrechts - Eine rechtsökonomische Analyse des Amerikanischen Erfahrungsmaterials (The Costs of the Subscription Right - A Legal Economic Analysis of the American Experience)', *Die Aktiengesellschaft*, 461-475.

Kunz, Harald (1976a), *Die Ökonomik Individueller und Organisierter Kriminalität* (The Economics of Individual and Organized Crime), Köln, Berlin, Bonn, München, Carl Heymanns Verlag.

Kunz, Harald (1976b), 'Von einer neuen Ökonomik der Kriminalität (On a New Economics of Crime)', **132** *Zeitschrift für die Gesamte Staatswissenschaft*, 282-299.

Kunz, Harald (1976c), 'Die Ökonomik von Strafverfolgung und Strafvollzug (Economics of Enforcement and Punishment)', **132** *Zeitschrift für die Gesamte Staatswissenschaft*, 535-548.

Kunz, Harald (1985a), *Marktsystem und Information, 'Konstitutionelle Unwissenheit' als Quelle von 'Ordnung'* (Market System and Information), Tübingen, Mohr/Siebeck.

Kunz, Harald (1985b), 'Zur Entstehung und Verhaltenswirkung sozialer Normen, mit einigen Argumenten für eine Ökonomisch rationale Kriminalpolitik (On the Evolution and the Incentive Effect of Social Norms, with Some Arguments for an Economic Rational Crime Policy)', **68** *Monatsschrift für Kriminologie und Strafsrechtsreform*, 202-215.

Kunz, Harald (1987), 'Recht und Ökonomie (Law and Economics)', **39** *Arbeitgeber*.

Kunz, Harald (1993), 'Kriminalität (Crime)', in Ramb, B.-T. and Tietzel, M. (ed.), *Ökonomische Verhaltenstheorie*, München, Vahlen.

Kurz, Rudi and Rall, Lothar (1983), *Behinderungsmißbrauch, Probleme einer ordnungskonformen Konkretisierung* (Abuse of Market Power), Tübingen.

Lampe, Hanes-Eckhard (1979), *Wettbewerb. Wettbewerbsbeziehungen. Wettbewerbsintensität* (Competition. Competition Relations, Competition Intensity), Baden-Baden, Nomos, 317 p.

Leder, Mathias (1992), 'Der Transaktionskostenansatz - Möglichkeiten und Grenzen (The Transaction Cost Approach - Possibilities and Boundaries)', in Schlieper, Ulrich and Schmidtchen, Dieter (eds), *Makro, Geld und Institutionen*, Tübingen, 106-108.

Leder, Mathias (1993), 'Kommentar zu 'Rational Choice vs. Adaptive Rule-Following, on the Behavioral Foundations of the Social Sciences' von Victor Vanberg (Comment on Viktor Vanberg, Rational Choice vs. Adaptive Rule-Following, on the Behavioral Foundations of the Social Sciences)', **12** *Jahrbuch für Neue Politische Ökonomie*, 116-121.

Leder, Mathias (1994), *Eingeschränkt rationales Verhalten, Optimizing versus Satisficing und regelgebundenes Verhalten* (Bounded Rationality, Optimizing versus Satisficing and Rule Governed Behavior), Discussion Paper der Universität Witten/Herdecke, 1994.

Leder, Mathias (1996), 'Kommentar zu 'Plea-bargaining - der Deal im Strafprozeß' von Claus Ott/Hans-Bernd Schäfer (Comment on Claus Ott and Hans-Bernd Schäfer, Plea-bargaining - the 'deal' in criminal proceedings)', **15** *Jahrbuch für Neue Politische Ökonomie*, 132-134.

Leder, Mathias and Schmidtchen, Dieter (1990), 'Die Produktion von Recht. Ein Literaturaufsatz (The Production of Law. A Survey)', **146** *Journal of Institutional and Theoretical Economics*, 749-757.

Lehmann, Michael (1980), 'Die Untersuchungs- und Rügepflicht des Käufers in BGB und HGB. Rechtsvergleichender Überblick - Ökonomische Analyse (The Duty to Examine and Notify a Defect in the German Civil and Commercial Code. A Comparative Survey - Economic Analysis)', *Wertpapiermitteilungen*, 1162-1169.

Lehmann, Michael (1981a), *Vertragsanbahnung durch Werbung* (Contract Preparing through Promotion), München, C.H. Beck.

Lehmann, Michael (1981b), 'Die bürgerlich-rechtliche Haftung für Werbeangaben. Culpa in contrahendo als Haftungsgrundlage für Vertragsanbahnende Erklärungen', **36** *Der Betriebs-Berater*, 1233-1242.

Lehmann, Michael (1982), 'Ökonomie, Sozialbiologie - Humanwissenschaften. Über die Notwendigkeit und Möglichkeit einer Interdisziplinären Grundlagenforschung (Economics, Social Biology - Human Sciences. About the Necessity and Possibility of an Interdisciplinary Fundamental Re)', *Der Betriebs-Berater*, 1997-2004.

Lehmann, Michael (1983a), *Bürgerliches Recht und Handelsrecht - eine juristische und Ökonomische Analyse ausgewählter Probleme für Wirtschaftswissenschaftler und interdisziplinär interessierte Juristen unter besonderer Berücksichtigung der 'Ökonomischen Analyse des Rechts' und* (Civil Law and Commercial Law - a Legal and Economic Analysis of Selected Problems for Lawyers with an Economic and Interdisciplinary Interest with a Special Attention for the 'Economic Analysis of Law' and the 'Theory of Property Rights'), Stuttgart, Poeschel, 329 p.

Lehmann, Michael (1983b), 'Eigentum, geistiges Eigentum, gewerbliche Schutzrechte, Property Rights als Wettbewerbsbeschränkungen zur Förderung des Wettbewerbs (Property, Intellectual Property, Commercial Rights of Protection, Property Rights as Restraints of Competition to promote the Competition)', in X (ed.), *Gewerblicher Rechtsschutz und Urheberrecht, InternationalerTeil (Festschrift für E. Ulmer)*, 356-362.

Lehmann, Michael (1983c), 'Patentrecht und Theory der Property Rights, eine Ökonomische und Juristische Analyse (Patent Law and Property Rights Theory, an Economic and Legal Analysis)', in X (ed.), *Festschrift für R. Franceschelli*, Mailand, 35-51.

Lehmann, Michael (1983d), 'Die missglückte Probefahrt. Vertragsrecht, Quasivertragsrecht, Deliktrecht. Ökonomische Analyse des Rechts (The Failed Excursion. Contract Law, Quasi-Contract Law Economic Analysis of Law)', in Walz, W. Rainer and

Rascher-Friesenhausen, Hein (eds), *Sozialwissenschaften im Zivilrecht: Fälle und Lösungen in Ausbild und Prüfung*, Neuwied und Darmstadt, Luchterhand, 35-51.

Lehmann, Michael (1983e), *Buergerliches Recht und Handelsrecht - eine Juristische und Ökonomische Analyse*, Stuttgart, Poeschel.

Lehmann, Michael (1984), 'Theorie der Property Rights und Schutz des geistigen und gewerblichen Eigentums - Wettbewerbsbeschränkungen zur Förderung des Wettbewerbs (Property Rights Theory and the Protection of Intellectual Property)', in X (ed.), *Ansprüche, Eigentums- und Verfügungsrechte*, Berlin, Duncker and Humblot, 519-535.

Lehmann, Michael (1986a), 'Evolution in Biologie, Ökonomie und Jurisprudenz (Evolution in Biology, Economics and Jurisprudence)', **17** *Rechtstheorie*, 463-477.

Lehmann, Michael (1986b), 'Das Privileg der beschränkten Haftung und der Durchgriff im Gesellschafts- und Konzernrecht. Eine Juristische und Ökonomische Analyse (The Privilege of Limited Liability and the Peircing of the Corporate Veil in Association and Trust Law)', **3** *Zeitschrift für Unternehmens- und Gesellschaftsrecht*, 345-370.

Lehmann, Michael (1987), 'Die UWG-Neuregelungen 1987 - Erläuterungen und Kritik (The New UWG Unfair Competition Rules - Explanations and Critique)', **89** *Gewerblicher Rechtsschutz und Urheberrecht*, 199-214.

Lehmann, Michael (1988a), 'Verbraucherschutz und Schutz des Schwächeren im Zivilrecht. Eine juristische und Ökonomische Analyse (Consumer Protection and Protection of the Weaker Party by the Private Law)', in Finsinger and Simon (eds), *Recht und Risiko. Juristische und Ökonomische Analysen*, München, Florentz, 365-389.

Lehmann, Michael (1988b), 'Juristisch-ökonomische Kriterien zur Berechnung des Verletzergewinns bzw. des entgangenen Gewinns (Legal-Economic Criteria for the Calculation of the Profit of the Injurer Respectively the Lost Profit)', **25** *Der Betriebs-Berater*, 1680-1687.

Lehmann, Michael (1989), 'Die Zivilrechtliche Haftung für Werbeangaben bei der Vertragsanbahnung als Problem der Allokationseffizienz (Civil Liability for Advertising as a Problem of Allocative Efficiency)', in Ott, Claus and Schäfer, Hans-Bernd (eds), *Allekationseffizienz in der Rechtsordnung*, Berlin, Springer, 169-184.

Lehmann, Michael (1990a), 'Just in time: Handels- und ABG- rechtliche Probleme (Just in Time: Problems in the Law of Commerce and of Unfair Contract Terms)', **27** *Der Betriebs-Berater*, 1849-1855.

Lehmann, Michael (1990b), 'Das Prinzip Wettbewerb (The Principle of Competition)', **2** *Juristenzeitung*, 61-67.

Lehmann, Michael (1991), 'Umwelthaftungsrecht dient der Internalisierung negativer Extemalitäten, Kommentar (Environmental Liability Law is to Internalize Negative Externalities. A Comment)', in Ott, Claus and Schäfer, Hans-Bernd (eds), *Ökonomische Probleme des Zivilrechts*, Berlin, Springer, 290-294.

Lehmann, Michael (1992a), 'Schranken der beschränkten Haftung. Zur Ökonomischen Legitimation des Durchgriffs bei der GmbH (Limits of Limited Liability)', **4** *GmbH-Recht*, 200-206.

Lehmann, Michael (1992b), 'Umwelthaftungsrecht. Ein Beitrag zur Internalisierung von negativen Externen Effekten (Environmental Liability Law)', in Schulz (ed.), *Ökologie und Recht*, Köln, Berlin, Bonn, München, Carl Heymanns Verlag, 81-89.

Lehmann, Michael (1993), 'Das Prinzip Wettbewerb. Ein gemeinsames Gesetz der Evolution für Biologie, Ökonomie und Wirtschaftsrecht (The Competition Principle. A Common Law of Evolution for Biology. Economics and Commercial Law)', in McGuire, Michäl T. (ed.), *Der Faktor Mensch im neuen Europa*, Luchterhand, Neuwied et al., 241-258.

Leidig, Guido (1979), *Dominante Werbung. Ziele, Wirkungen, rechtliche Gestaltung* (Advertising. Objectives, Effects, Legal Aspects), Frankfurt/M., Bern, Cirencester.

Leidig, Guido (1984a), 'Aspekte einer Ökologisch-ökonomischen Rechtswissenschaft (Aspects of an Ecologic-Economic Jurisprudence)', **39(7)** *Universitas*, 759-765.

Leidig, Guido (1984b), *Ökologisch-ökonomische Rechtswissenschaft* (Ecologic-Economic Jurisprudence), Frankfurt/M., Bern, New York.

Leidig, Guido (1991), 'Perspektiven einer Ökologisch-ökonomischen Rechtswissenschaft (Perspectives of an Ecologic-Economic Oriented Jurisprudence)', in Voigt, R. (ed.), *Das Recht und seine Wissenschaft 3. ed.*, Siegen, 105-122.

Leschke, Martin (1993), *Ökonomische Verfassungstheorie und Demokratie* (Constitutional Economics and Democracy), Berlin, Duncker and Humblot.

Leschke, Martin (1995a), 'Konstitutionelle Demokratie und die Europäische Union (Constitutional Democracy and the European Union)', **4** *List Forum*, 394-412.

Leschke, Martin (1995b), 'Neue Richtlinien für Europa. Das Urteil des Bundesverfassungsgerichts zum Vertrag von Maastricht aus Sicht der Konstitutionellen Ökonomik (New Restrictions in Europe, An Analysis of the Maastricht Judgement of the German Bundesverfassungsgericht from the View of Constitutional Economics)', **44(1)** *Zeitschrift für Wirtschaftspolitik*, 3-28.

Leschke, Martin (1996), 'Zur institutionellen Ausgestaltung der Europäischen Union (How Should the Institutional Structure of the European Union be Designed?)', in Streit, M.E. and Voigt, St. (ed.), *Europa reformieren - Ökonomen und Juristen zur zukünftigen Verfaßtheit Europas*, Baden-Baden, Nomos, 100-112.

Levmore, Saul and Stuntz, William J. (1991), 'Rechtsfolgen im Privatrecht und im öffentlichen Recht: Rechtsvergleichung unter einem Law-and-Economics Blickwinkel (Legal Consequences in Private and Public Law: Comparative Law from a Law and Economics Viewpoint)', in Ott, Claus and Schäfer, Hans-Bernd (eds), *Ökonomische Probleme des Zivilrechts*, Berlin, Springer, 297-314.

Linder, Ludwig (1980), *Privatklage und Schadensersatz im Kartellrecht, Eine vergleichende Untersuchung zum deutschen und amerikanischen Recht* (Civil Suit and Damage Compensation in Antitrust Law, A Comparision of German and American Law), Baden-Baden, Nomos.

Lutter, Marcus and Wahlers, Henning W. (1989), 'Der Buyout: Amerikanische Fälle und die Regeln des deutschen Rechts (The Buyout: American Cases and the German Rules)', **34** *Die Aktiengesellschaft*, 1-17.

Magoulas, Georgios (1985), 'Zur Ökonomischen Analyse des Konsumentenschutzes - unter besonderer Berücksichtigung Informations- und Risikobezogener Probleme von Konsumen tenmärkten (On the Economic Analysis of Consumer Protection - With Special Attention for Information and Risk)', in Magoulas, Georgios and Simon, Jürgen (eds), *Recht und Ökonomie beim Konsumentenschutz und Konsumentenkredit*, Baden-Baden, Nomos, 23-57.

Magoulas, Georgios (1986), 'Privatrechtlicher Immissionsschutz, Wucher und Ökonomische Analyses des Rechts (Civil Law Protection against Harmful Effects on the Environment, Usury and Economic Analysis)', in Simon, Jürgen (ed.), *Regulierungsprobleme im Wirtschaftsrecht*, Neuwied und Darmstadt, Luchterhand, 1-24.

Magoulas, Georgios (1989), 'Verbraucherschutz als Problem Asymmetrischer Informationskosten (Consumer Protection as a Problem of Asymmetric Information)', in Ott, Claus and Schäfer, Hans-Bernd (eds), *Allekationseffizienz in der Rechtsordnung*, Berlin, Springer, 70-80.

Magoulas, Georgios and Schwartze, Andreas (1986), 'Das Gesetz über den Widerruf von Haustürgeschäften und ähnlichen Geschäften: Eine Rechtliche und Ökonomische Analyse (The Law Regarding Revocation of Door-to-Door Dealings and Similar Transactions: A Legal and Economic Analysis)', **18(5)** *Jüristische Arbeitsblätter*, 225-235.

Magoulas, Georgios and Simon, Jürgen (eds) (1985), *Recht und Ökonomie beim Konsumentenschutz und Konsumentenkredit* (Law and Economics of Consumer Protection and C), Baden-Baden, Nomos, 436 p.

Markert, Kurt (1997), 'Deutsche Fusionskontrolle im Energeiversorgungsbereich (Merger Control in the German Public Utilities Sector)', in Kruse, Jörn, Stockmann, Kurt and Vollmer, Lothar (eds), *Wettbewerbspolitik im Spannungsfeld nationaler und internationaler Kartellrechtsordnungen. Festschrift für Ingo Schmidt zum 65. Geburtstag*, Baden-Baden, Nomos, 231 ff.

Meinberg, Volker (1988), 'Empirische Erkentnissen zum Vollzug des Umweltstrafrechts (Empirical Insights Concerning the Enforcement of Environmental Criminal Law)', **100** *Zeitschrift für die Gesamte Strafrechtswissenschaften*, 112-157.

Meran, Georg (1988), 'Zur Kontroverse uber die Wettbewerbswirkungen eines Umweltlizenzmarktes (The Controversy on the Competition on a Market for Environmental Licenses)', **108** *Zeitschrift für Wirtschafts- und Sozialwissenschaften*, 439-450.

Mestmäcker, Ernst-Joachim (1978), *Recht und Ökonomisches Gesetz. Über die Grenzen von Staat, Gesellschaft und Privatautonomie* (The Law and Economic Laws), Baden-Baden, Nomos.

Mestmäcker, Ernst-Joachim (1988), 'Fusions Kontrolle im Gemeinsamen Markt zwischen Wettbewerbspolitik und Industriepolitik (Merger Control in the Common Market Between Compet)', *Europarecht*, 349-377.

Mestmäcker, Ernst-Joachim (ed.) (1993), *Recht in der offenen Gesellschaft. Hamburger Beiträge zum Deutschen, Europäischen und Internationalen Wirtschafts- und Medienrecht Wirtschaftsrecht und Wirtschaftspolitik 125* (Law in an Open Society), Baden-Baden, Nomos.

Meyer, Dirk (1989), 'Rent Seeking durch Rationalisierungsschutz oder die Wohlfahrtsverluste einer Kostensenkungssteuer (Rent Seeking through Regulations Protecting Human Capital from Devaluation Due to Technological Innovation)', **35** *Konjunkturpolitik*, 188-1200.

Mohr, K. and Wehrt, Klaus (1995), 'Einbau der Ökonomischen Analyse des Rechts in ein Juristisches Fallgutachten (Implementing the Economic Analysis of Law into a Legal Opinion)', **10** *JURA*, 536-542.

Möschel, Wernhard (1972), 'Das Wirtschaftsrecht der Banken. Die währungs-, bankaufsichts-, kartell- und EWG-rechtliche Sonderstellung der Kreditinstitute (Banking Law)', in X. (ed.), *Schriftenreihe 'Wirtschaftsrecht und Wirtschaftspolitik', Band 29*, Frankfurt. Reprinted by now Nomos Verlagsgesellschaft Baden-Baden

Möschel, Wernhard (1975a), 'Kreditwirtschaft und Bereichsausnahme nach õ 102 GWB (Credit Markets and Areas Exempt from Competition under õ 102 GWB [German Antitrust Law])', **139** *Zeitschrift für das gesamte Handels- und Wirtschaftsrecht*, 347-361.

Möschel, Wernhard (1975b), 'Bankenrecht und Wirtschaftsordnung (Law of Banking and Economic Order)', *BB*, 1025-1030.

Möschel, Wernhard (1975c), *Rechtsordnung zwischen Plan und Markt. Am Beispiel von Preiskontrollen nach õ 22 GWB. Heft 54 der Schriftenreihe 'Vorträge und Aufsätze' des Walter Eucken Instituts* (Law between Plan and Market), Tübingen.

Möschel, Wernhard (1978), 'Wettbewerb im Schnittfeld von Rechtswissenschaft und Nationalökonomie (Competition at the Crossing of Legal Science and National Economy)', *Wirtschaftwissenschaftliche Studien*, 351-357.

Möschel, Wernhard (1981a), 'Neuere Entwicklungen der Wettbewerbstheorie. Kritische Bemerkungen zu kritischen Bemerkungen (Recent Developments in Competition Theory)', **145** *Zeitschrift für das Gesamte Handels- und Wirtschaftsrecht*, 590-598.

Möschel, Wernhard (1981b), 'Zur wettbewerbstheoretischen Begründbarkeit von Ausnahmebereichen (Areas Exempt from Competition and Competition Theory)', **32** *Ordo*, 85-102.

Möschel, Wernhard (1983), 'Divergierende Entwicklungen im Amerikanischen und Europäischen Kartellrecht (Conflicting Developments in American and European Antitrust Law)', *Wirtschaftwissenschaftliche Studien*, 603-609.

Möschel, Wernhard (1986a), 'Effizienz und Wettbewerbspolitik (Efficiency and Policy of Competition)', *Wirtschaftswissenschaftliches Studium*, 341-346.

Möschel, Wernhard (1986b), 'Ökonomische Kriterien in der Anwendung des Kartellgesetzes (Views of Economic Evidence in Antitrust Litigation)', *JA*, 525-533.

Möschel, Wernhard (1988), *Wettbewerbspolitik aus ordoliberaler Sicht, in Strafrecht, Unternehmensrecht, Anwaltsrecht. Festschrift für Gerd Pfeiffer zum Abschied aus dem Amt als Präsident des Bundesgerichtshofes* (Competition Policy from an Ordo-liberal Point of View), Köln, Berlin, Bonn, München, Carl Heymanns Verlag.

Möschel, Wernhard (1990), *Internationaler Freihandel in Bankdienstleistungen, in Festschrift für Ernst Steindorff* (International Free Trade in Banking Services), Berlin.

Möschel, Wernhard (1992a), *Wettbewerbspolitik vor neuen Herausforderungen, in Ordnung in Freiheit* (Competition Policy Faced by New Challenges), Symposium aus Anlaß des 100. Jahrestages des Geburtstages von Walter Eucken am 17. Januar 1991, Tübingen.

Möschel, Wernhard (1992b), *EG-Industriepolitik nach Maastricht, in Festschrift für Rudolf Nirk* (EC Industrial Policy after 'Maastricht'), München.

Möschel, Wernhard (1993a), *Privatisierung als ordnungspolitische Aufgabe, in Festschrift für Joachim Gernhuber* (Privatization as a Task of Policy), Tübingen.

Möschel, Wernhard (1993b), 'Privatisierung der Sparkassen. Zu den jüngsten Vorschlägen der Monopolkommission (The Privatization of Savings Banks)', *WM*, 93-99.

Möschel, Wernhard (1993c), 'Zum Subsidiaritätsprinzip im Vertrag von Maastricht (The Principle of Subsidiarity in the Maastricht-Treaty)', in Gerken, L. (ed.), *Europa 2000 - Perspektive wohin? Die europäische Integration nach Maastricht*, Freiburg, Max-Planck-Institut für ausländisches internationales Strafrecht, 93-105.

Möschel, Wernhard (1995), *Den Staat an die Kette legen - Gegen die Aushöhlung des Wettbewerbs durch den Staat, Frankfurter Institut - Kleine Handbibliothek - Band 13* (Chaining up the State - Against the Undermining of Competition by the State), Bad Homburg vdH, 94 p.

Möschel, Wernhard (1996a), *Kartellrecht in der Reform, in Festschrift für Ernst-Joachim Mestmäcker* (The Reform of Antitrust Law), Baden-Baden.

Möschel, Wernhard (1996b), 'Ist die Tarifautonomie noch zeitgemäß? (Is the German System of Autonomous Wage Bargaining Still up to Date?)', **45** *Zeitschrift für Wirtschaftspolitik*, 39-48.

Möschel, Wernhard (1996c), *Rabattgesetz und Deregulierung, Frankfurter Institut - Kleine Handbibliothek - Band 19* (Discounts Act and Deregulation), Bad Homburg vdH.

Möschel, Wernhard (1997), 'Notwendigkeit und Potentiale der Aufgabenprivatisierung (Privatization)', in Kruse, Jörn, Stockmann, Kurt and Vollmer, Lothar (eds), *Wettbewerbspolitik im Spannungsfeld nationaler und internationaler Kartellrechtsordnungen. Festschrift für Ingo Schmidt zum 65. Geburtstag*, Baden-Baden, Nomos, 351 ff.

Mueller, Dennis C. (1986), 'Das Antitrustrecht der Vereinigten Staaten am Scheideweg (The Antitrust Law of the United States at the Parting of the Ways)', **36** *Wirtschaft und Wettbewerb*, 533-555.

Nagel, Bernhard (1979a), 'Kann die Fusionskontrolle ihren Anspruch einlösen? (Is the Merger Control Able to Achieve its Goals)', *DB*, 1021-1025.

Nagel, Bernhard (1979b), 'Die Verlagerung der Probleme um die Unternehmensmitbestimmung auf das Informationsproblem (Transferring the Problems of Worker Participation to the Information Problem)', *BB*, 1799-1804.

Nagel, Bernhard (1980), 'Beschaffung und Weitergabe von Informationen durch Mitbestimmungsträger im Aufsichtsrat (Collection and Transmission of Information by Workers' Representatives in the Board of Directors)', in Diefenbacher and Nutzinger (eds), Frankfurt/M., Bern, Cirencester, 249-269.

Nagel, Bernhard (1981a), 'Rechtsauslegung und Rechtssetzung zur Mitbestimmung (Interpretation of Law and Law Making Concerning Worker Participation)', *Blätter für Steuer-, Sozialversicherungs- und Arbeitsrecht*, 344-350.

Nagel, Bernhard (1981b), 'Fusion und Fusionskontrolle (Merger and Merger Control)', in Cox, Jens and Markert (eds), *Handbuch des Wettbewerbs*, München.

Nagel, Bernhard (1982a), 'Zusammensetzung mitbestimmter Aufsichtsratsausschüsse und Unternehmensinteresse (Composition of the Board of Directors under Worker Participation and the Goals of the Firm)', *DB*, 2677-2681.

Nagel, Bernhard (1982b), 'Fusionskontrolle und Schutz von Arbeitsplätzen (Merger Control and Job Protection)', *Arbeit und Recht*, 207-215.

Nagel, Bernhard (1982c), 'Der Schutz von Arbeitsplätzen im Kartell- und Wettbewerbsrecht (Protection of Jobs in Anti-Trust- and Competition Law)', in Kittner (ed.), *Arbeitsmarkt - Ökonomische, soziale und rechtliche Grundlagen*, Heidelberg, Müller Juristischer Verlag.

Nagel, Bernhard (1984a), *Konzentration und kartellrechtliche Kontrolle von Marktmacht in der Brauwirtschaft, 2. Aufl.* (Concentration and Control of Market Power in the Brewery Sector), Kassel.

Nagel, Bernhard (1984b), 'Informationsrechte und Mitbestimmungsträger nach dem Mitbestimmungsgesetz 1976 und dem Betriebsverfassungsgesetz (Rights on Information and Worker Participation according to the German Law of 1976)', in Koubek and Schredelseker (eds), *Information, Mitbestimmung und Unternehmenspolitik*, Frankfurt/M..

Nagel, Bernhard (1984c), 'Informationsrechte und Informationspolitik in mitbestimmten Unternehmen (Rights on Information and Information Policy in Firms under Worker Participation)', in Diefenbacher and Nutzinger (eds), *Mitbestimmung, Theorie, Geschichte, Praxis*, Heidelberg, Müller Juristischer Verlag.

Nagel, Bernhard (1988a), 'Der Lieferant on line - unternehmensrechtliche Probleme der Just-in-Time-Produktion am Beispiel der Automobilindustrie (Delivery online. Legal Problems of Just-in-Time Production in the Automobile Sector)', *DB*, 2291-2294.

Nagel, Bernhard (1988b), *Mitbestimmung und Grundgesetz* (Worker Participation and the German Basic Law), Baden-Baden.

Nagel, Bernhard (1989), *Wirtschaftsrecht II Eigentum, Delikt, Vertrag* (Property, Tort, Contract), München.

Nagel, Bernhard (1990), 'Erosion der Mitbestimmung und EG- Kommissionsentwürfe zur Europa-AG (Erosion of Worker Participation)', *Arbeit und Recht*, 205-213.

Nagel, Bernhard (1991a), 'Kommentar (Comment on Wehrt, Die Qualitätshaftung des Verkäuf)', in Ott, Claus and Schäfer, Hans-Bernd (eds), *Ökonomische Probleme des Zivilrechts*, Berlin, Springer, 260-264.

Nagel, Bernhard (1991b), 'Schuldrechtliche Probleme bei Just-in-Time-Lieferbeziehungen - dargestellt am Beispiel der Automobilindustrie (Problems with Law of Contract in Just-in-Time Delivery Relations)', *DB*, 319-326.

Nagel, Bernhard (1991c), 'Der EG-Richtlinienentwurf zum Europäischen Betriebsrat (The EG-Guideline on the European Workers Committee)', *Arbeit und Recht*, 161-172.

Nagel, Bernhard (1992a), *EG-Wettbewerbsrecht und Zulieferbeziehungen der Automobilindustrie, Gutachten im Auftrag der EG-Kommission* (EU Competition Law and the Delivery Relations in the Automobile Industry), Veröffentlichungen der Kommission, Luxemburg und Brüssel, 1992.

Nagel, Bernhard (1992b), 'Von der Lex Mercatoria zur Lex Laboris, zur Rechtlichen Bewältigung der Internationalen Arbeitsbeziehungen (Lex Mercatoria and Lex Laboris. On the Legal Analysis of International Work Relations)', in Däubler, Wolfgang, Bobke, Manfred and Kehrmann, Karl (ed.), *Festschrift für Albert Gnade*, Köln, Bund-Verlag.

Nagel, Bernhard (1992c), 'Zulieferbeziehungen der Automobilindustrie und Wettbewerbsrecht der EG (Delivery Relations in the Automobile Industry and the Competition Law of the EG)', *Wirtschaft und Wettbewerb*, 818-829.

Nagel, Bernhard (1993a), 'Die Produkt und Umwelthaftung im Verhältnis von Herstellern und Zulieferern (Product and Environment Liability in the Relation to Suppliers)', *DB*, 2469-2474.

Nagel, Bernhard (1993b), 'Die Marken der Hersteller von Autoteilen und das Wettbewerbsrecht der EG (Brands of Automobile Parts and the Competition Law of the EG)', *Zeitschrift für Wirtschaftsrecht*, 987-993.

Nagel, Bernhard (1993c), *Wirtschaftsrecht I, Grundrechte und Einführung in das Bürgerliche Recht, 3. Ed.* (Basic Rights and an Introduction into the Private Law), München.

Nagel, Bernhard (1994), *Wirtschaftsrecht III (Unternehmens-und Konzernrecht)* (Law of Firms and Conglomerates), München, Lehrbuch.

Nagel, Bernhard (1995a), 'Gewährleistung und Produkthaftung im internationalen Produktionsverbund (Guarantee and Product Liability in International Cooperations)', *DB*, 2581-2590.

Nagel, Bernhard (1995b), 'Autonomie, Abhängigkeit und Wettbewerb, rechtliche und Ökonomische Analyse (Law and Economics of Autonomy, Dependence and Competition)', in X. (ed.), *Ökonomie und Gesellschaft. Jahrbuch 11, Markt, Norm und Moral*, Frankfurt/New York, 89-126.

Nagel, Bernhard (1996), 'Wie effizient sind Tarifvertrag und Mitbestimmung? (How Efficient are Wage Agreements and Worker Participation?)', **2** *Gewerkschaftliche Monatshefte*, 97-111.

Neumeyer, F. (1969), 'Patent und Beschränkung des Wettbewerbs (Patent and Limitation of Competition)', **12** *Wirtschaft und Recht*, 240-251.

Nieder-Eichholz, Markus (1993), *Die Subventionsordnung. Ein Beitrag zur finanzwirtschaftlichen Ordnungspolitik Schriften zur Ökonomischen Analyse des Rechts* (Regulation of Subsidies. A Contribution to the Constitutional Politics of Public Economics), Berlin, Duncker and Humblot.

Oberender, Peter and Ruter, Georg (1987), 'Innovationsforderung: Einige grundsätzliche ordnung spolitische Bemerkungen (The Promotion of Innovation: Some Basic Remarks from the Viewpoint of Constitutional Economics)', in Lenel, Hans Otto (ed.), 143-154.

Oppenländer, K.H. (ed.) (1974), *Patentwesen, technischer Fortschritt und Wettb* (Patents, Technical Progress and Competition), Göttingen, Otto Schwartz.

Ott, Claus (1989), 'Allokationseffizienz, Rechtsdogmatik und Rechtsprechung - die immanente Ökonomische Rationalität des Zivilrechts (Allocative Efficiency, Legal Dogmatics and Jurisprudence - The immanent Rationalism of Private Laws)', in Ott, Claus and Schäfer, Hans-Bernd (eds), *Allekationseffizienz in der Rechtsordnung*, Berlin, Springer, 25-44.

Ott, Claus (1991), 'Vorvertragliche Aufklärungspflichten im Recht des Güter- und Leistungsaustausches (Precontractual Obligation to Provide Information in the Law)', in Ott, Claus and Schäfer, Hans-Bernd (eds), *Ökonomische Probleme des Zivilrechts*, Berlin, Springer, 142-162.

Ott, Claus (1994), 'Entwicklung und Konstruktion effizienter Normen im Rechtssystem des deutschen Zivilrechts (Development and Construction of Efficient Norms in the German Private Law System)', **11(2)** *Homo Oeconomicus*, 293-329.

Ott, Claus and Schäfer, Hans-Bernd (1986), 'Begründung und Bemessung des Schadensersatzes wegen entganger Sachnutzung (Foundation and Rating of the Compensation for Damage Because of Lost Utility of Property)', **7** *Zeitschrift für Wirtschaftsrecht*, 613-624.

Ott, Claus and Schäfer, Hans-Bernd (1988), 'Die ökonomische Analyse des Rechts. Irrweg oder Chance wissenschaftlicher Rechtserkenntnis? (The Economic Analysis of Law. Wandering or Chance for Scientific Insights?)', *Juristenzeitung*, 213-223.

Ott, Claus and Schäfer, Hans-Bernd (eds) (1989), *Allekationseffizienz in der Rechtsordnung* (Allocative Efficiency in Legal Order. Contribution), Berlin, Springer, 306 p.

Ott, Claus and Schäfer, Hans-Bernd (1990), 'Schmerzensgeld bei Körperverletzungen. Eine Ökonomische Analyse (Compensation for Physical Injury)', *Juristenzeitung*, 563-573.

Ott, Claus and Schäfer, Hans-Bernd (eds) (1991a), *Ökonomische Probleme des Zivilrechts. Beiträge zum 2. Travemünder Symposium zur Ökonomischen Analyse des Rechts, 21.-26. März 1990* (Economic Problems of Civil Law. Contributions to the Second Travemünder Symposium on Economic Analysis of Law), Berlin, Springer, 347 p.

Ott, Claus and Schäfer, Hans-Bernd (1991b), 'Ökonomische Auswirkungen der EU Insider Regulierung in Deutschland (Economic Consequences of the EG-Insider-Regulation in Germany)', *Zeitschrift für Bankrecht und Bankwirtschaft*, 226-241.

Ott, Claus and Schäfer, Hans-Bernd (1993a), 'Unternehmenspublizität, Umweltschadensbilanz und Haftung für Unternehmen', in Ott, C. and Schäfer, H.-B. (eds), *Ökonomische Analyse des Unternehmensrechts*, Heidelberg, Physica, 217 ff.

Ott, Claus and Schäfer, Hans-Bernd (eds) (1993b), *Ökonomische Analyse des Unternehmensrechts, Beiträge zum 3. Travemünder Symposium zur Ökonomischen Analyse des Rechts 1992* (Economic Analysis of the Law of Firms), Heidelberg, Physica.

Ott, Claus and Schäfer, Hans-Bernd (eds) (1994), *Ökonomische Analyse der Rechtlichen Organisation von Innovationen, Beiträge zum 4. Travemünder Symposiun zur Ökonomischen Analyse des Rechts 1994* (Economic Analysis of the Law of Innovations), Heidelberg, Physica

Ott, Claus and Schäfer, Hans-Bernd (1996), 'Plea-Bargaining', der 'Deal' im Strafprozeß (Plea-Bargaining)', in Schenk, Karl-Ernst, Schmidtchen, Dieter, Streit, Manfred E. (eds), *Vom Hoheitsstaat zum Konsensualstaat, Neue Formen der Kooperation zwischen Staat und Privaten Jahrbuch für Neue Politische Ökonomie 15*, Tübingen, Mohr, 107-126.

Otto, Hans-Jochen (1982), *Generalprävention und externe Verhaltenskontrolle, Wandel vom Sociologischen zum Ökonomischen Paradigma in der Nordamerikanischen Kriminologie?* (General Prevention and External Control of Behavior, Evolution from Sociological to Economic Paradigm in the North American Criminology?), Freiburg, Max-Planck-Institut für ausländisches internationales Strafrecht, 323 p.

Panther, Stephan (1991), 'Zivilrecht und Umweltschutz (Civil Law and Environmental Protection)', in Ott, Claus and Schäfer, Hans-Bernd (eds), *Ökonomische Probleme des Zivilrechts*, Berlin, Springer, 267-289.

Picot, Arnold and Dietl, Helmut (1993), 'Neue Institutionenökonomie und Recht (New Institutional Economics and Law)', in Ott, Claus and Schäfer, Hans-Bernd (eds), *Ökonomische Analyse des Unternehmensrechts, Beiträge zum 3. Travemünder Symposium zur Ökonomischen Analyse des Rechts*, Heidelberg, Physica Verlag, 306-330.

Pies, Ingo and Leschke, Martin (eds) (1995), *Ökonomische Gesellschaftstheorie in der Diskussion, John Rawls Politischer Liberalismus. Theoretische Grundlagen demokratischer Wirtschafts- und Gesellschaftspolitik* (Economic Theory of Society and John Rawls Political Liberalism), Tübingen.

Pies, Ingo and Leschke, Martin (ed.) (1996), *James Buchanans konstitutionelle Ökonomik (Konzepte der Gesellschaftstheorie, Bd. 2)* (James Buchanan's Constitutional Economics), Tübingen, Mohr, 281 p.

Priddat, Birger (1988), *Das Geld und die Vernunft. Über John Lockes Versuch einer naturrechtlich Economics)*, Frankfurt am Main, Peter D. Lang.

Priddat, Birger (1990), 'Hegel als Ökonom (Hegel as an Economist)', **403** *Volkswirtschaftliche Schriften*.

Priddat, Birger (1993a), 'Ökonomie und Macht. John Locke. Neue Aspekte (Economy and Power. John Locke. New Aspects)', in Gephardt, J. and Münclker, H. (eds), *Bürgerschaft und Herrschaft. Zum verhältnis von Demokratie und Macht im antiken und neuzeitlichen politischen Denken*, Baden-Baden, Nomos.

Priddat, Birger (1993b), 'Staat (The State)', in Homann, K. and Enderle, G. (eds), *Lexikon der Wirtschaftsethik*, Freiburg, 1020-1025.

Priddat, Birger (1997), 'Konstituanten deutscher Politischer Ökonomie. Zur Geschichte der Parafiski im 19. Jahrhundert (On the Sources of German Political Economics. The Genesis of 'Parafisci' in the 19th Century)', in Tiepelmann, K. and van der Beek, G. (eds), *Parafiski Vol. 2*, Hamburg.

Prosi, G. (1971), *Ökonomische Theorie des Buches. Volkswirtschaftiche Aspekte des Urheber- und Verlegerschutzes* (The Economic Theory of Books, Copyright and Publisher's Rights), Düsseldorf.

Rahmsdorf, Detlev W. (1986), 'Zur Renaissance der Sozialver tragstheorien in den Wirtschaftswissenschaften und ihrer interdisziplinären Relevanz (The Renaissance of the Social Contract in Political Economies and their Interdisciplinary Significance)', *Der Staat*, 269-284.

Rahmsdorf, Detlev W. (1987), 'Ökonomische Analyse des Rechts, Utilitarismus und die klassische deutsche Philosophie (Economic Analysis of Law, Utilitarianism and the Classical German Philosophy)', **18** *Rechtstheorie*, 487-501.

Rahmsdorf, Detlev W. and Schäfer, Hans-Bernd (eds) (1988), *Ethische Fragen der Wirtschaftspolitik und des Rechts* (Ethical Questions of Political Economics and Law), Berlin, Dietrich-Reimer-Verlag, 219 p.

Ramb, B.T. and Tietzel, Manfred (eds) (1993), *Ökonomische Verhaltenstheorie* (Economic Theory of Behavior), München.

Ribhegge, Hermann (1994), 'Ökonomische Theorie des effizienten Vertragsbruchs und die normativen Grundlagen der Ökonomischen Theorie des Rechts (The Economic Theory of Efficient Breach of Contracts and the Normative Foundations of the Economic Analysis of Law)', **11** *Homo Oeconomicus*, 113-141.

Richter, Rudolf (1991a), 'Institutionenökonomische Aspekte der Theorie der Unternehmung (Institutional Economics of the Theory of the Firm)', in Ordelheide, D., Rudolph, B., Büsselmann, E. (ed.), *Betriebswirtschaftslehre und Ökonomische Theorie*, Stuttgart, Poeschel.

Richter, Rudolf (1991b), 'Bankenregulierung aus der Sicht der Neuen Institutionenökonomik (Regulation of Banks from the Viewpoint of the New Institutional Economics)', in Siebke, J. (ed.), *Finanzintermediation, Bankenregulierung und Finanzmarktintegration*, Berlin, Duncker and Humblot, 43-64.

Richter, Rudolf (1992), 'Institutionen Ökonomisch analysiert. Zur jüngsten Entwicklung auf dem Gebiete der Wirtschaftstheorie (Economic Analysis of Institutions)', in Landeszentralbank im Saarland (ed.), *Wissenschaftliche Hefte*, Saarbrücken.

Richter, Rudolf (1993), 'Ökonomische Theorie des Privateigentums, Thema und Variationen (Economics of Property Rights)', *Jahrbuch für Sozialwissenschaft.*

Richter, Rudolf and Furubotn, Eirik G. (1996), *Neue Institutionenoekonomik. Eine Einfuehrung und kritische Wuerdigung* (Institutions and Economic Theory - Contributions of the New Institutional Economics), Tübingen, Mohr/Siebeck.

Röper, Bernd (1982), *Die Mi brauchaufsicht vor dem Hintergrund der* (The Abuse Aspect as Background for the Development of a New Competition Theory), Berlin, Humboldt.

Roth, Günter H. (1986), 'Zur 'economic analysis' der beschränk ten Haftung (On the 'Economic Analysis' of Limited Liability)', **3** *Zeitschrift für Unternehmens- und Gesellschaftsrecht*, 371-382.

Roth, Günter H. (1991), 'Kommentar (Comment on Adams, Eigentum, Kontrolle und beschrän)', in Ott, Claus and Schäfer, Hans-Bernd (eds), *Ökonomische Probleme des Zivilrechts*, Berlin, Springer, 226-233.

Rowe, Gerard C. (1992), 'Sachenrechtliche Ersitzungsregeln aus Ökonomischer Sicht (An Economic Perspective on Limitations of Actions in Property Law)', **75** *Kritische Vierteljahresschrift der Gesetzgebung und Rechtswissenschaft*, 390-415.

Ruppelt, Hans-Joachim (1989), 'Der Verordnungsentwurf für eine europäische Fusionskontrolle im EG-Ministerrat (The Regulation Bill for a European Fusion Control in the EC-Cabinet Council)', **39** *Wirtschaft und Wettbewerb*, 187-202.

Sadowski, Dieter (1988), 'Währt ehrlich am längsten? Personalpolitik zwischen Arbeitsrecht und Unternehmenskultur (Is Honesty the Best Policy? Personal Management Between Labor Law and Corporate Culture)', in Budäus, Dietrich, u.a. (ed.), *Betriebswirtschaftslehre und Theorie der Verfügungsrechte*, Wiesbaden, Gabler, 219-238.

Sadowski, Dieter (1996), 'Programm und Stand der betriebswirtschaftlichen Rechtsanalyse (Economic Analysis of Business Law)', in Sadowski et al. (ed.), *Regulierung und Unternehmenspolitik*, Wiesbaden, Gabler, 1-20.

Sadowski, Dieter et al. (1993), *Vollzugsdefizite des Schwerbehindertengesetzes* (Deficits in the Execution of the Handicapped Law), Bonn, Schriftenreihe des Bundesministers für Arbeit und Soziales, 1993.

Sadowski, Dieter and Frick, Bernd (1990), 'Betriebsräte und Gesetzesvollzug (Labor Representatives and Execution of Laws)', **4** *Zeitschrift für Personalforschung*, 165-178.

Sadowski, Dieter and Frick, Bernd (1992), *Die Beschäftigung Schwerbehinderter - Betriebswirtschaftliche Analysen und politische Empfehlungen* (Employment of Severely Handicapped), Idstein, Schulz-Kirchner.

Sadowski, Dieter and Kurth, Elke (1991), 'Wettbewerbsverzerrung trotz europäischen Arbeitsrechts? Ein Ökonomischer Vergleich des Arbeitnehmerschutzes beim Unternehmensverkauf in Deutschland und Großbritannien (Distortions of Competition despite the European Labor Law?)', in Marr, R. (ed.), *Eurostrategisches Personalmanagement*, München und Mering, 423-446.

Sadowski, Dieter, Backes-Gellner, Uschi and Frick, Bernd (1995), 'Betriebsräte in Deutschland, Gespaltene Rationalitäten? (Labor Representatives in Germany)', **14** *Jahrbuch für Neue Politische Ökonomie*, 157-182.

Sadowski, Dieter, Czap, Hans and Wächter, Hartmut (eds) (1996), *Regulierung und Unternehmenspolitik - Methoden und Ergebnisse der betriebswirtschaftlichen Rechtsanalyse* (Regulation and Business Policy), Wiesbaden, Gabler.

Salje, Peter (1984), *Ökonomische Analyse des Rechts aus deutscher Sicht* (Economic Analysis of Law from a German Point of View),.

Sauerland, Dirk (1997), *Föderalismus zwischen Freiheit und Effizienz*, Berlin, Duncker and Humblot, 288 p.

Sauter, Herbert (1989), 'Gruppenfreistellungs-Verordnung für Know-how-Vereinbarungen (The Group Exemption Regulation for Know-How Agreements)', **39** *Wirtschaft und Wettbewerb*, 383-391.

Schäfer, Hans-Bernd (1989), 'Allokationseffizienz als Grundprinzip des Zivilrechts (Allocative Efficiency as Basic Principle of Civil Law)', in Ott, Claus and Schäfer, Hans-Bernd (eds), *Allekationseffizienz in der Rechtsordnung*, Berlin, Springer, 1-24.

Schäfer, Hans-Bernd (1991), 'Ökonomische Analyse von Auf klärungspflichten (Economic Analysis of the Duty to Provide Informati)', in Ott, Claus and Schäfer, Hans-Bernd (eds), *Ökonomische Probleme des Zivilrechts*, Berlin, Springer, 117-141.

Schäfer, Hans-Bernd (1995), 'Kein Geld für die Justiz - Was ist uns der Rechtsfrieden wert? (No Money for the Jurisdiction - What is the Value of Peace under the Law?)', *Deutsche Richterzeitung*, 461 ff.

Schäfer, Hans-Bernd and Kötz, Hein (1992), 'Iudex, calcula! (Judge, calculate!)', *Juristenzeitung*, 355 ff.

Schäfer, Hans-Bernd and Ott, Claus (1986a), 'Begründung und Bemessung des Schadensersatzes wegen entgangener Sachnutzung (Cause and Calculation of Damages for Loss of Use)', *Zeitschrift für Wirtschaftsrecht*, 613 ff.

Schäfer, Hans-Bernd and Ott, Claus (1986b), *Lehrbuch der Ökonomischen Analyse des Zivilrechts* (Handbook of Economic Analysis of Civil Law), Berlin, Springer, 367 p.

Schäfer, Hans-Bernd and Ott, Claus (1988), 'Die Ökonomische Analyse des Rechts. Irrweg oder Chance wissenschaftlicher Rechtserkenntnis? (Economic Analysis of Law - Wandering or Chance for Scientific Insights?)', *Juristenzeitung*, 213 ff.

Schäfer, Hans-Bernd and Ott, Claus (1990), 'Schmerzengeld bei Körperverletzungen. Eine Ökonomische Analyse (Damages for Pain and Suffering)', *Juristenzeitung*, 563-573.

Schäfer, Hans-Bernd and Ott, Claus (1991), 'Ökonomische Auswirkungen der EG-Insider-Regulierung in Deutschland (Economic Effects of the EU Insider Regulation)', **3** *Zeitschrift für Bankrecht und Bankwirtschaft*, 226 ff.

Schäfer, Hans-Bernd and Ott, Claus (1994), 'Entwicklung und Konstruktion effizienter Normen im Rechtssystem des deutschen Zivilrechts (Development and Construction of Efficient Norms in the Legal System of German Private Law)', *Homo Oeconomicus*, 293 ff.

Schäfer, Hans-Bernd and Ott, Claus (1995), *Lehrbuch der Ökonomischen Analyse des Zivilrechts, 2. Aufl.* (Textbook on Economic Analysis of Private Law), Berlin.

Schäfer, Hans-Bernd and Rölike, A. (1997), *Kosten-Nutzen-Analyse der Rechtssprechung unter besonderer Berücksichtigung der Vorschläge zur Kostenreduzierung in der Justiz, Handbuch der außergerichtlichen Konfliktbeilegung* (Cost-Benefit Analysis of Jurisdiction and Cost Reduction),.

Schäfer, Hans-Bernd and Struck, Gerhard (1983), 'Schlammbeseitigung auf der Bundesstrasse. Geschäftsführung ohne Auftrag, Deliktsrecht, negatorische Haftung. Ökonomische Analyse des Rechts (The Case of the Mud Removal at the Federal Highway)', in Walz, W. Rainer and Rascher-Friesenhausen, Hein (eds), *Sozialwissenschaften im Zivilrecht: Fälle und Lösungen in Ausbildung und Prüfung*, Neuwied und Darmstadt, Luchterhand, 119-132.

Schäfer, Hans-Bernd and Wehrt, Klaus (1989a), 'Ökonomische Analyse des Schadensrechts. Ein Überblick (Economic Analysis of Tort Law. A Survey)', **34** *Hamburger Jahrbuch für Wirtschaft und Gesellschaftspolitik*, 81-106.

Schäfer, Hans-Bernd and Wehrt, Klaus (eds) (1989b), *Die Ökonomisierung der Sozialwissenschaften: Sechs Wortmeldungen* (Economics in Social Sciences: Six Contributions), Frankfurt am Main, Campus Verlag, 182 p.

Schanze, Erich (1977), 'Anlegerschutz bei Aktienfonds, Das Indexfonds-Konzept (Shareholder Protection)', **22** *Die Aktiengesellschaft*, 102-107.

Schanze, Erich (1978a), 'Ökonomische Analyse des Rechts in den U.S.A./Verbindungslinien zur realistischen Tradition (Economic Analysis of Law in the U.S.A. - Origins a)', in Assmann, Heinz-Dieter, Kirchner, Christian and Schanze, Erich (eds), *Ökonomische Analyse des Rechts*, Kronberg, Athenäum, 3-19.

Schanze, Erich (1978b), 'Ökonomische Analyse des Rechts in den USA. Verbindungslinien zur realistischen Tradition (Economic Analysis of Law in the US. Connections to the Realistic Tradition)', in Assmann, Heinz-Dieter, Kirchner, Christian and Schanze, Erich (eds), *Ökonomische Analyse des Rechts*, Kronberg, Athenäum, 3-19.

Schanze, Erich (1981), 'Der Beitrag von Coase zu Rechte und Ökonomie des Unternehmens (Coase's Contribution to Law and Economics of Business Organizations)', **137** *Journal of Institutional and Theoretical Economics*, 694-701.

Schanze, Erich (1982), 'Rechtsnorm und Ökonomisches Kalkül (Legal Norm and Economic Calculus)', **138** *Journal of Institutional and Theoretical Economics*, 297-312.

Schanze, Erich (1983), 'Theorie des Unternehmens und Ökonomische Analyse des Rechts (Theory of the Firm and Economic Analysis of Law)', in Boettcher, Erik, Herder-Dorneich, Philipp and Schenk, Karl-Ernst (eds), *Jahrbuch für neue politische Ökonomie*, Tübingen, Mohr, 161-180.

Schanze, Erich (1986a), *Investitionsverträge im internationalen Wirtschaftsrecht* (Investment Contracts in International Economics), Frankfurt a.M., Metzner, 305 p.

Schanze, Erich (1986b), 'Untemehmensrechtliche Koordination von Staat und Wirtschaft bei internationalen Gro Projekten in Entwicklungsländern (Corporate Coordination of State and Economy Concerning Project Investment in Developing Countries)', **6** *Jahrbuch für Neue Politische Ökonomie*, 269-287.

Schanze, Erich (1989), *Langzeitverträge im Spannungsfeld von Vertrags-, Gesellschafts-, Wettbewerbs- und Arbeitsrecht, Symbiotische Bezugs- und Absatzsysteme, Vorlage für die Tagung für Rechtsvergleichung Würzburg 1989* (Long-Term Contracts between Contract, Corporation, Competition, and Labor Law), Fachgruppe für Grundlagenforschung, Arbeitssitzung, 14 Sept 1989.

Schanze, Erich (1991), 'Stellvertretung und Ökonomische Agentur-Theorie - Probleme und Wechselbezüge (The Law of Agency and Agency Theory - Problems and Relations)', in Ott, Claus and Schäfer, Hans-Bernd (eds), *Ökonomische Probleme des Zivilrechts*, Berlin, Springer, 60-75.

Schanze, Erich (1993), 'Rechtswissenschaft und Betriebswirtschaftslehre (Jurisprudence and Business Administration)', in Wittmann, W., Kern, W., Köhler, R., Küpper, H.-U., Wysocki, K.v. (ed.), *Handwörterbuch der Betriebswirtschaft, 5. Aufl.*, Stuttgart, 3760-3774.

Schanze, Erich (1995a), 'Rechtsvorschriften für die Produktion (Regulation of Production)', in Kern, W., Schröder, H.-H. And Weber, J. (eds), *Handwörterbuch der Produktionswirtschaft, 2. Aufl.*, 1779-1788.

Schanze, Erich (1995b), 'Franchising im öffentlichen Sektor (Franchising in the Public Sector)', in Naschold, F. u.a. (ed.), *Leistungstiefe im Öffentlichen Sektor, Kap. 7*, Berlin.

Schatz, Klaus-Werner (1996), 'Reform von Planungs- und Genehmigungsverfahren (Reform of Planning and Permission Procedures)', in Schenk, Karl-Ernst, Schmidtchen, Dieter and Streit, Manfred E. (eds), *Vom Hoheitsstaat zum Konsensualstaat, Neue Formen der Kooperation zwischen Staat und Privaten Jahrbuch für Neue Politische Ökonomie 15*, Tübingen, Mohr.

Schenk, Karl-Ernst (1970), 'Ein organisationstheoretisches Konzept der Regelungsvorgänge in Wirtschaftssystemen und seine Anwendung (An Organization-Theoretical Concept of Control Processes in Economic Systems and its Application)', in Boettcher, E. (ed.), *Beiträge zum Vergleich von Wirtschaftssystemen, Schriften des Vereins für Socialpolitik, N.F. Bd. 57*, Berlin, 174-216.

Schenk, Karl-Ernst (1971a), 'Gedanken zur Untersuchung von Koordinationsmechenismen mit sytemanalytischen Methoden (Thoughts on the Analysis of Coordination Mechanisms from the Systems Approach)', in Schenk, K.-E. (ed.), *Systemanalyse in den Wirtschafts und Sozialwissenschaften, Reihe 'Wirtschaftskybernetik und Systemanalyse', Bd. 1*, Berlin.

Schenk, Karl-Ernst (1971b), 'Wirtschaftsordnungen zwischen Konvergenz und Unvereinbarkeit (Economic Constitutions between Convergence and Incompatibility)', **17** *Monatsblätter für freiheitliche Wirtschaftspolitik*, 530-536.

Schenk, Karl-Ernst (1976a), 'Eine neue Variante des Marktsozialismus. Zu den Reformvorschlägen von J. K. Galbraith (A New Variant of Market Socialism. About the Reform Ideas of J. K. Galbraith)', in Watrin Chr. (ed.), *Studien zum Marktsozialismus, Schriften des Vereins für Socialpolitik, N.F., Bd. 86*, Berlin, 109-118.

Schenk, Karl-Ernst (1976b), 'Demokratie oder Bürokratie? Dezentralisierung - Selbstverwaltung - Entbürokratisierung (Democracy or Bureaucracy? Decentralization, Self-administration, De-bureaucratisation))', in Geißler, H. (ed.), *Verwaltete*

Bürgergesellschaft in Fesseln. Bürokratisierung und ihre Folgen für den Staat, Wirtschaft und Gesellschaft, Frankfurt (M), Berlin Wien.

Schenk, Karl-Ernst (1978a), 'Ökonomische Theorie der Bürokratisch Organisierten Produktion (Economic Theory of Bureaucratic Organized Production)', in Helmstädter, E. (ed.), *Neuere Entwicklungen in den Wirtschaftswissenschaften, Schriften des Vereins für Socialpolitik, N.F., Bd. 98*, Berlin, 591-608.

Schenk, Karl-Ernst (1978b), 'Bürokratie und Wirtschaftsordnung - Endogene Faktoren für die Veränderung (Bureaucracy and Economic Order. Endogenous Factors of Change)', **23** *Hamburger Jahrbuch für Wirtschaft und Gesellschaftspolitik*, 141-154.

Schenk, Karl-Ernst (1978c), 'Grenzüberschreitende Unternehmensformen in den Ost-West-Wirtschaftsbeziehungen (Transnational Forms of Enterprises in East-West Economic Relations), mit A. Wass von Czege', in Schiller, Karl (ed.), *Technolgietransfer durch Ost-West-Kooperation, Ökonomische Studien aus den Institut für Außenhandel und Überseewirtschaft, Bd. 27*, Stuttgart/New York, 1-12.

Schenk, Karl-Ernst (1980a), 'Marktversagen und Bürokratieversagen (Market Failure and Bureaucracy Failure)', in Boettcher, E., Herder-Dorneich, Ph. and Schenk, K.-E. (ed.), *Neue Politische Ökonomie als Ordnungstheorie*, Tübingen, 192-199.

Schenk, Karl-Ernst (1980b), 'Rationale Ordnungspolitik (Rational Constitutional Policy)', in Dettling, W. (ed.), *Die Zähmung des Leviathan. Neue Wege der Ordnungspolitik*, Baden-Baden, Nomos Verlagsgesellschaft, 207-225.

Schenk, Karl-Ernst (1981a), 'Das Spektrum der existierenden Wirtschaftsordnungen (The Spectrum of Existing Economic Constitutions)', in Issing, D. (ed.), *Zukunftsprobleme der sozialen Marktwirtschaft, Schriften des Vereins für Socialpolitik, N.F. Bd. 116*, Berlin, 412-419.

Schenk, Karl-Ernst (1981b), 'Märkte und Hierarchien. Anreiz-und Kontrollmechanismen in der Theorie der Wirtschaftssysteme (Markets and Hierarchies. Incentive and Control Mechanisms in the Theory of Economic Systems)', in Hedtkamp, G. (ed.), *Anreiz-und Kontrollmechanismen in Wirtschaftssystemen, Schriften des Vereins für Socialpolitik, N.F., Bd. 117*, Berlin, 11-27.

Schenk, Karl-Ernst (1981c), *Märkte, Hierarchien und Wettbewerb. Elemente einer Theorie der Wirtschaftsordnung* (Markets, Hierarchies and Competition. Elements of a theory of economic constitution), München.

Schenk, Karl-Ernst (1982a), 'Institutional Choice' und Transaktionsökonomik. Perspektiven der systemanalytischen und industrieökonomischen Anwendung (Institutional Choice and Transaction Economics, Perspectives of System-Analytic and Industrial-Economic Application)', in Schiller, K. (ed.), *Studien zur Politischen Ökonomie, Ökonomische Studien aus dem Institut für Außenhandel und Überseewirtschaft, Bd. 32*, Stuttgart/New York.

Schenk, Karl-Ernst (1982b), *'Institutional Choice' und Ordnungstheorie* ('Institutional Choice' and Theory of Order), Tübingen, Mohr, 39 p.

Schenk, Karl-Ernst (1983a), 'Second Economy und Wirtschaftsordnung - Ein systemübergreifender, transaktionsökonomischer Erklärungsansatz (Second Economy and Economic Constitution. An explanation approach encompassing different systems on the basis of transaction economics ' mit A. Wass von Czege), in Hedtkamp, G. (ed.), *Beiträge zum Problem der Schattenwirtschaft, Schriften des Vereins für Socialpolitik N.F., Bd. 132*, Berlin, 33-51.

Schenk, Karl-Ernst (1983b), 'Vergleichende System und Industriestudien - Ein 'Institutional Choice'- Ansatz (Comparative Systems and Industrial Studies - An Institutional Choice approach)', in Schiller, K. (ed.), *Ökonomische Studien aus dem Institut für Außenhandel und Überseewirtschaft, Bd. 34*, Stuttgart-New York, 1-20.

Schenk, Karl-Ernst (1983c), ''Institutional Choice' - Entwicklungen und Hauptanwendungen (Institutional Choice - Developments and Main Applications)', in Boettcher, E., Herder-Dorneich, Ph. Schenk, K.-E. (eds), *Jahrbuch für Neue Politische Ökonomie, Bd. 2*, Tübingen, 70-85.

Schenk, Karl-Ernst (1985), ''Institutional Choice', Wirtschaftsordnung und Industrieorganisation, Ein Beitrag zur Analyse komplexer arbeitsteiliger Systeme (Institutional Choice, Economic Constitution and Industrial Organisation. A contribution to the analysis of complex economic systems)', in Schiller, K. (ed.), *Industrieorganisation und Koordination - Theorien und Ländervergleiche, Ökonomische Studien aus den Institut für Außenhandel und Überseewirtschaft, Bd. 36*, Stuttgart-New York, 1-25.

Schenk, Karl-Ernst (1988a), 'Technologietransfer, Joint Ventures und Transaktionskosten. Möglichkeiten und Grenzen strategischer Allianzen von Unternehmen in und zwischen Ost und West (Transfer of Technologies, Joint Ventures and Transaction Costs. Opportunities and boundaries of strategic alliances by enterprises of East and West)', in Dürr, E. Sieber, H. (eds), *Weltwirtschaft im Wandel, Festgabe für E. Tuchtfeldt*, Bern-Stuttgart, 595-606.

Schenk, Karl-Ernst (1988b), 'Die ordnungspolitische Funktion des Rechts in der modernen Wirtschaftstheorie (Law and its Constitution-Political Functions in Modern Economic Theory)', in X. (ed.), *Das Recht in einer freiheitlichen Industriegesellschaft, Veröffentlichungen der Walter-Raymond-Stiftung, Bd. 26*, Köln, 179-202.

Schenk, Karl-Ernst (1988c), 'Property Rights und Theorie der Institutionen (Property Rights and Theory of Institutions)', *Das Wirtschaftsstudium*.

Schenk, Karl-Ernst (1991a), 'Bemerkungen zum Stand der Neuen Politischen Ökonomie (Remarks about the Achievements of the New Political Economics)', **10** *Jahrbuch für Neue Politische Ökonomie*, 7-10.

Schenk, Karl-Ernst (1991b), 'Internationale Kooperationen und Joint Ventures. Theoretische und strategische Grundlagen ((International cooperations and joint ventures. Theoretical and strategical foundations)', in Schoppe, S. G. (ed.), *Kompendium der Internationalen Betriebswirtschaftslehre*, München-Wien, 153-184.

Schenk, Karl-Ernst (1992a), 'Ordnungstheorie auf Entscheidungstheoretischer Grundlage. Zum Buch von Bruno Jeitziner unter diesem Titel (Theory of Economic Constitutions on Decision-Theoretical Basis. About the book of Bruno Jeitziner)', in X. (ed.), *ORDO, Jahrbuch für Ordnung von Wirtschaft und Gesellschaft, Bd, 43*, Stuttgart, Franz Steiner, 515-517.

Schenk, Karl-Ernst (1992b), 'Die neue Institutionenökonomie - Ein Überblick über wichtige Elemente und Probleme der Weiterentwicklung (New Institutional Economics - A Review of Important Elements and Problems of further Developments)', *Zeitschrift für Wirtschafts- und Sozialwissenschaften*, 339-378.

Schenk, Karl-Ernst (1996a), 'Genossenschaftsverbund und Netzwerk-Externalitäten (Confederations of Cooperatives and Network Externalities)', in Bonus, H., Grossekettler, H., Großfeld, B. and Wagner, H. (ed.), *Humanität und Genossenschaften. Festschrift für Wilhelm Jäger*, Münster, 157-167.

Schenk, Karl-Ernst (1996b), 'Neue Politische Ökonomie (NPÖ) (New Political Economics)', in X. (ed.), *Wirtschaftslexikon, 8. Aufl.*, München, 509-511.

Schenk, Karl-Ernst and Porschen, D. (1979), 'Ansätze zu einer Ökonomischen Theorie der Einparteiensysteme Osteuropas (Approaches to an Economic Theory of Eastern Europe's Political Party Systems)', in von Weizsäcker, C.C. (ed.), *Staat und Wirtschaft, Schriften des Vereins für Socialpolitik, N.F., Bd. 102*, Berlin.

Schenk, Karl-Ernst, Schmidtchen, Dieter and Streit, Manfred E. (eds) (1996), *Vom Hoheitsstaat zum Konsensualstaat, Neue Formen der Kooperation zwischen Staat und Privaten Jahrbuch für Neue Politische Ökonomie 15* (From Sovereignity to Consensus, New Forms of Cooperation Between State and Citizens), Tübingen, Mohr.

Schenk, Karl-Ernst, Schmidtchen, Dieter and Streit, Manfred E. (eds) (1997), *Neue Politische Ökonomie der Integration und Öffnung von Infrastrukturnetzen Jahrbuch für Neue Politische Ökonomie 16* (Integration of and Access to Infrastructural Networks), Tübingen, Mohr.

Scherer, Frederic M. (1985), 'Stand und Perspektiven der Industrieökonomik (S and Perspectives of Industrial Economics)', in Bombach, G., Gahlen, B. and Ott, A.E. (eds), *Industrieökonomik: Theorie und Empirie*, Tübingen, Mohr, 3-19.

Schlicht, Ekkehart (1974), 'Die Theorie der kollektiven Entscheidung und der individualistische Ansatz (Theory of Collective Choice and Individualism)', **2** *Leviathan*, 265-280.

Schlicht, Ekkehart (1984), 'Bemerkungen zum Zusammenwirken 'Ökonomischer' und 'sozialer' Einflüsse auf das Verhalten (On the Interaction of 'Social' and 'Economic' Influences)', in Birg, H., Wingen, M. and Zimmermann, K. (eds), *Zusammenhänge zwischen Bevölkerungs- und Wirtschaftsentwicklung in der Bundesrepublik Deutschland, Deutsche Gesellschaft für Bevölkerungswissenschaft e.V.*, Wiesbaden, Gabler, 119-124.

Schlicht, Ekkehart (1990), 'Individuelles Bestreben und kulturelles Gefüge (Individual Striving in the Cultural Context)', in Weise, Peter (ed.), *Ökonomie und Gesellschaft Jahrbuch 8, Individuelles Verhalten und kollektive Phänomene*, Frankfurt am Main, Campus, 112-127.

Schlicht, Ekkehart (1993), 'Koordinationskosten und 'Social Capital' (Co-ordination Costs and Social Capital)', in Schlieper, Ulrich and Schmidtchen, Dieter (eds), *Makro, Geld and Institutionen*, Tübingen, 95-100.

Schlicht, Ekkehart (1994a), 'Die emotive und die kognitive Gerechtigkeitsauffassung (The Emotive and the Cognitive View of Justice)', **2** *Ökonomie und Gesellschaft*, 141-154.

Schlicht, Ekkehart (1994b), 'Probleme mit dem Ökonomischen Ansatz (Some Problems With the Economic Approach)', **5(2)** *Ethik und Sozialwissenschaften*, 335-337.

Schlicht, Ekkehart and Kubon-Gilke, Gisela (1993), 'Gefordertheit und Institutionelle Analyse am Beispiel des Eigentums ('Requiredness' and Institutional Analysis)', **15** *Gestalt Theory*, 256-273.

Schmidt, Ingo (1963a), 'Die öffentliche Hand als Unternehmen im Sinne des GWB (The Government as an Enterprise with Respect to Competition Law)', **18** *Der Betriebs-Berater*, 1404 ff.

Schmidt, Ingo (1963b), 'Markttransparenz als Voraussetzung für Wettbewerbsbeschränkungen (Market Transparency as a Prerogative for Competition Distortions)', **13** *Wirtschaft und Wettbewerb*, 97 ff.

Schmidt, Ingo (1964a), 'Preismeldestellen - Kartelle im Tarnanzug (Price Announcement Authorities - Cartels in Disguise)', **18** *Der Volkswirt*, 652 ff.

Schmidt, Ingo (1964b), 'Zum Begriff des Preiswettbewerbs nach õ 16 GWB (Price Competition)', **14** *Wirtschaft und Wettbewerb*, 120 ff.

Schmidt, Ingo (1965a), 'Preisbindung und Preiswettbewerb (Price Fixings and Price Competition)', **27** *Der Markenartikel*, 435 ff.

Schmidt, Ingo (1965b), 'Das Verhältnis von Patent- und Kartellrecht - Folgerungen aus der Konzentrationsenquete für die Patentreform (The Relation of Patent Law and Competition Law)', *Die Aussprache*, 155 ff.

Schmidt, Ingo (1965c), 'Relevanter Markt, Marktbeherrschung und Mißbrauch in õ 22 GWB und Art. 86 EWGV (Relevant Market, Domination, and Abuse according to German and European Competition Law)', **15** *Wirtschaft und Wettbewerb*, 453 ff.

Schmidt, Ingo (1966), 'Neuere Entwicklungen in der Wettbewerbstheorie unter Berücksichtigung wachstumspolitischer Zielsetzungen (New Developments in the Competition Theory)', **16** *Wirtschaft und Wettbewerb*, 699 ff.

Schmidt, Ingo (1967), 'Zum Nachweis des Mißbrauchs einer Rechtlichen oder Faktischen Wettbewerbsbeschränkung, Eine Analyse der im amerikanischen Recht entwickelten Theorien und Kriterien zur Schadenshöhe in den 'civil damage suits' und zur 'performance'-Kontrolle in den 'public (On Proving the Abuse of a Legal or Factual Restraints of Competition: An Analysis of the American Theories)', **17** *Wirtschaft und Wettbewerb*, 635 ff.

Schmidt, Ingo (1968), 'Zum Schutzzweck der Mißbrauchsaufsicht über marktbeherrschende Unternehmen (The Goal of Abuse Control)', **21** *Der Betriebs-Berater*, 1795 ff.

Schmidt, Ingo (1969), 'Reform des GWB - Aufgabe des nächsten Bundestages (Reform of the German Anti-Trust Law)', **49** *Zeitschrift für Wirtschaftspolitik*, 450 ff.

Schmidt, Ingo (1970), 'Erweiterter Schutz kleiner und mittlerer Unternehmen (Extended Protection for Small and Medium Firms)', *Marktwirtschaft*, 21 ff.

Schmidt, Ingo (1972), 'Entwicklung der Antitrustrechtsprechung gegenüber Konglomeraten (The Development of the Anti-Trust Judicature on Conglomerates)', **18** *Außenwirtschaftsdienst des Betriebs-Beraters*, 275 ff.

Schmidt, Ingo (1973a), 'US-amerikanische und Deutsche Wettbewerbspolitik Gegenüber Marktmacht, Eine vergleichende Untersuchung und kritische Analyse der Rechtsprechung gegenüber Tatbeständen des externen und internen Unternehmenswachstums sowie des Behinderungswettbewerbs (Competition Policy and Market Power in the US and in Germany)', in Besters, Hans (ed.), *Quaestiones Oeconomicae Band 6*, Berlin.

Schmidt, Ingo (1973b), 'Wie kann Marktmacht kontrolliert werden? (How Can Market Power be Controlled?)', **23** *Der Bürger im Staat*, 252 ff.

Schmidt, Ingo (1976a), 'Die Zusammenhänge von relevantem Markt, Marktbeherrschung und Marktergebnis am Beispiel der Mißbrauchsaufsicht des Bundeskartellamtes bei Arzneimitteln (The Federal Anti-Trust Authority's Abuse Control of the Pharmaceutical Market as an Example for the Relation of Relevant Market, Market Dominance und Market Results)', **190** *Jahrbuch für Nationalökonomie und Statistik*, 67 ff.

Schmidt, Ingo (1976b), 'Geplanter Verschleiß (Intended Wear)', in Arbeitsgemeinschaft der Verbraucher and Deutscher Gewerkschaftsbund (ed.), *Handbuch des Verbraucherrechts*, Neuwied/Rhine.

Schmidt, Ingo (1981a), 'Per se Rule oder Rule of Reason (Per-se rules or Rules of Reason)', **10** *WiSt*, 282 ff.

Schmidt, Ingo (1981b), 'Wettbewerbspolitik in den USA (Competition Policy in the US)', in Cox, Jens and Markert (eds), *Handbuch des Wettbewerbs*, München, 533-556.

Schmidt, Ingo (1981c), 'Preiskontrolle in Deutschland (Price Control in Germany)', **50** *Annalen der Gemeinwirtschaft*, 491 ff.

Schmidt, Ingo (1981d), 'Obsoleszenz als Mißbrauch wirtschaftlicher Macht (Obsolescence as an Abuse of Economic Power)', **21** *Wirtschaft und Wettbewerb*, 868 ff.

Schmidt, Ingo (1986), 'Ist Größe an sich gefährlich (Is Bigness Dangerous Per Se?)', **36** *Wirtschaft und Wettbewerb*, 193 ff.

Schmidt, Ingo (1990a), *Wettbewerbspolitik und Kartellrecht: Eine Einführung*, (3rd edn) (Competition Policy and Antitrust Law: An Introduction), Stuttgart, Gustav Fischer, 330 p.

Schmidt, Ingo (1990b), 'Die Europäische Fusionskontroll-Verordnung (The European Merger Control Law)', **70** *Zeitschrift für Wirtschaftspolitik*, 90 ff.

Schmidt, Ingo (1992a), 'EG-Integration, Industrie- versus Wettbewerbspolitik (European Integration, Industrial Policy vs. Competition Policy)', **72** *Zeitschrift für Wirtschaftspolitik*, 628 ff.

Schmidt, Ingo (1992b), 'Die Wettbewerbsordnung (The Competition Restraint)', in Adams, W.P. et al. (eds), *Länderbericht USA I, Geographie, Geschichte, Politische Kultur, Politisches System, Wirtschaft, Schriftenreihe vol. 293/I der Bundeszentrale für politische Bildung, 2nd ed.*, Bonn, 606 ff.

Schmidt, Ingo (1995), 'Europäische Industriepolitik - ein Widerspruch zur Wettbewerbsordnung? (European Industrial Policy - Contradiction to the Competition Law System?)', **45** *Wirtschaft und Wettbewerb*, 971 ff.

Schmidt, Ingo (1996a), 'Pro und Contra Konzentrationsprivileg, Die unterschiedlichen Wirkungen von Kartellen und Fusionen auf Wettbewerb und Effizienz (Pro and Contra Privileged Concentration, The Different Impacts of Cartels and Mergers on Competition and Efficiency)', in Kruse, Jörn and Mayer, Otto G. (eds), *Aktuelle Probleme der Wettbewerbs- und Wirtschaftspolitik, Erhard Kantzenbach zum 65. Geburtstag*, Baden-Baden, 119 ff.

Schmidt, Ingo (1996b), 'Wettbewerbspolitik versus Industriepolitik in der EG, Korreferat zu Erhard Kantzenbach (Industrial Policy vs. Competition Policy, Comment)', **44** *Applied Economics Quarterly*, 59 ff.

Schmidt, Ingo and Binder, Steffen (1996), *Wettbewerbspolitik im internationalen Vergleich, Die Erfassung wettbewerbsbeschränkender Strategien in Deutschland, England, Frankreich, den USA und der EG* (An International Comparision of Competition Policy), Heidelberg.

Schmidt, Ingo and Elßer, Stefan (1990), 'Innovationsoptimale Unternehmensgrößen und Marktstrukturen (Innovation Optimal Firm Sizes and Market Structures)', **19** *WiSt*, 556 ff.

Schmidt, Ingo and Elßer, Stefan (1992), 'Die Rolle des Markenartikels im marktwirtschaftlichen System (The Role of Brands in the Market Economy)', in Dichtl, Erwin and Eggers, Walter (eds), *Marke und Markenartikel als Instrumente des Wettbewerbs*, München, 47 ff.

Schmidt, Ingo and Engelke, Heinz (1989), 'Marktzutrittsschranken und Potentieller Wettbewerb (Market Entry Barriers and Potential Competition)', **18** *WiSt*, 399 ff.

Schmidt, Ingo and Kirschner, Ulrich (1985), 'Darstellung und wettbewerbspolitische Würdigung der U.S. Vertical Restraints Guidelines (Critical Evaluation of the US Vertical Restraint Guidelines)', **35** *Wirtschaft und Wettbewerb*, 781 ff.

Schmidt, Ingo and Kirschner, Ulrich (1987), 'Capture Theory, Ein Erklärungsansatz für die mangelnde Effizienz der Regulierung (Capture Theory as an Approach to Explain the Lack of Efficiency of Regulation)', **16** *WiSt*, 293 ff.

Schmidt, Ingo and Richard, Sabine (1989), 'Unternehmensgröße, Ausdruck von Macht oder Effizienz? (Size of Firms as an Indicator for Efficiency or Power?)', *gdi impuls*, 26 ff.

Schmidt, Ingo and Richard, Sabine (1991), 'Zum Verhältnis von Dumpingrecht und Kartellrecht in der EG (On the Relation of Anti-Dumping Law and Antitrust Law)', **41** *Wirtschaft und Wettbewerb*, 665 ff.

Schmidt, Ingo and Ries, W. (1983), 'Der Hirschman-Herfindahl-Index (HHI) als wettbewerbspolitisches Instrument in den US-Fusionsrichtlinien 1982 (The Hirschmann-Herfindah Index as an Instrument of Competition Policy in the US Merger Guidelines)', **33** *Wirtschaft und Wettbewerb*, 525 ff.

Schmidt, Ingo and Rittaler, Jan B., *Das wettbewerbstheoretische und -politische Credo der sog. Chicago School* (The Guidelines of the So-alled Chicago School on Competition Theory and Competition Policy), Diskussionsbeiträge aus dem Institut für VWL No. 23/85.

Schmidt, Ingo and Rittaler, Jan B. (1986a), *Die Chicago School of Antitrust Analysis: Wett* (The Chicago School of Antitrust Analysis: Competition Theoretical and Political Analysis of a Credo), Baden-Baden, Nomos, 119 p.

Schmidt, Ingo and Rittaler, Jan B. (1986b), 'Chicago School of Antitrust Law, Ökonomische Analyse des Wettbewerbsrechts (Chicago School of Antitrust Law, Economic Analysis of Competition Law)', **15** *WiSt*, 283 ff.

Schmidt, Ingo and Rittaler, Jan B. (1987), 'Marktphasen und Wettbewerb (Market phases and Competition)', **16** *WiSt*, 597 ff.

Schmidt, Ingo and Röhrich, Martina (1992), 'Kompetitive Marktstrukturen und externes Unternehmenwachstum (Competitive Market structures and External Firm Growth)', **29** *WiSt*, 179 ff.

Schmidt, Ingo and Schmidt, Andr (1996), 'X-Ineffizienz, Lean Production und Wettbewerbsfähigkeit (X-Inefficiency, Lean Production, and Ability to Compete)', **25** *WiSt*, 65 ff.

Schmidt, Reinhard H. (1981a), 'Kreditsicherung und Konkursrecht (Credit Security and Insolvency Law)', in Göppl, Hermann and Henn, Rudolf (eds), Geld, Banken und Versicherungen, Königstein/Ts. 1981, *Geld, Banken und Versicherungen*, Königstein/Ts., 569-573.

Schmidt, Reinhard H. (1981b), *Ökonomische Analyse des Insolvenzrechts (Economic Analysis of Insolvency Law)*, Wiesbaden, Gabler, 155 p.

Schmidt, Reinhard H. (1981c), 'Die Ökonomische Grundstruktur des Insolvenzrechts (The Economic Struckture of the Insolvency Law)', **26** *Die Aktiengesellschaft*, 35-44.

Schmidt, Reinhardt H. (1981d), 'Die Ökonomische Grundstruktur der Insolvenz Recht (The Economic Basic Structure of Bankruptcy Law)', *Die Aktiengesellschaft*, 35-44.

Schmidt, Reinhard H. (1984), 'Asymmetrische Information und Gläubigerverfügungsrechte in der Insolvenz (Asymmetric Information and Creditor's Rights during Insolvency)', **54** *Zeitschrift für Betriebswirtschaft*, 717-742.

Schmidt, Reinhard H. (1996), 'Betriebswirtschaftslehre und Rechtspolitik (Business Administration and Legal Policy)', **41** *Die Aktiengesellschaft*, 250-260.

Schmidt, Reinhard H. and Koch, Hans-Dieter (1981), 'Ziele und Instrumente des Anlegerschutzes (Goals and Means of Investor Protection)', **33(3)** *Betriebswirtschaftliche Forschung und Praxis*, 29-48.

Schmidt, Reinhard H. and Kübler, Friedrich (1988), *Gesellschaftsrecht und Konzentration* (Company Law and Concentration), Berlin, Duncker and Humblot, 225 p.

Schmidt, Reinhard H., Ballwieser, W., Böcking, H.-J. and Drukarczyk, Jochen (1994), *'Bilanzrecht und Kapitalmarkt', Festschrift zum 65. Geburtstag von Adolf Moxter* (Accounting Law and Capital Markets), Düsseldorf.

Schmidtchen, Dieter (1973a), 'Politische Ökonomie staatlicher Preisinterventionen. Dargestellt am Beispiel der 'politischen Preise' im Nachrichtenverkehr (Political Prices in the News Business as an Example for the Politcal Economics of Public Price Interventions)', .

Schmidtchen, Dieter (1973b), 'Für eine konsequente Wettbewerbspolitik und über die Wege dorthin, Bemerkungen zum Wettbewerbsverständnis des Sachverständigenrates (For a Consistent Competition Policy and How to Achieve It)', **129** *Zeitschrift für die Gesamte Staatswissenschaft*, 102 ff.

Schmidtchen, Dieter (1974a), 'Der 'politische Preis' (The 'Political Price')', **1** *Wirtschaftswissenschaftliches Studium*, 17 ff.

Schmidtchen, Dieter (1974b), 'Politische Ökonomie (Political Economics)', **24** *Jahrbuch für die Ordnung von Wirtschaft und Gesellschaft*, 233 ff.

Schmidtchen, Dieter (1978), *Wettbewerbspolitik als Aufgabe: Methodologisch* (Competition Policy as Task: Methodological and System Theoretical Foundations for a Reorientatation), Baden-Baden, Nomos.

Schmidtchen, Dieter (1979), 'Ausbeutung aufgrund einer Wettbewerbsbeschränkung durch Zustand? Kritische Analyse der theoretischen Grundlagen einer freiheitsgefährdenden Wettbewerbspolitik (Expropriation through a Competition Restraint by State? A Critical Analysis of the Theoretical Foundations of a Competition Policy that Threatens Freedom)', **30** *Ordo: Jahrbuch für die Ordnung von Wirtschaft und Gesellschaft*, 273 ff.

Schmidtchen, Dieter (1981), 'Leitungspartizipation, Wettbewerb und Funktionsfähigkeit des Marktsystems (Management Participation)', in Issing, D. (ed.), *Zukunftsprobleme der sozialen Marktwirtschaft, Schriften des Vereins für Socialpolitik, N.F. Bd. 116*, Berlin, 191 ff.

Schmidtchen, Dieter (1982a), 'Property Rights, Freiheitsschutz und die Logik staatlicher Preisinterventionen: Kritische Analyse der theoretischen Grundlagen einer freiheits gefährdenden Wettbewerbspolitik (Property Rights, Protection of Liberty and the Logic of Governmental Price)', in Die Mi Brauchsaufsicht Vor Dem Hintergrund Der En (ed.), *Schriften des Vereins für Socialpolitik, Vol. 124.*

Schmidtchen, Dieter (1982b), 'Theorie des 'politischen Preises' (Theory of Political Prices)', in Böcker, F. (ed.), *Preistheorie und Preisverhalten*, München, 279 ff.

Schmidtchen, Dieter (1985), 'Monopol und Institutional Choice (Monopoly and Institutional Choice)', in Schenk, K.-E. (ed.), *Wirtschaftsordnung, Industrieorganisation und Koordination - Theorie und Ländervergleiche*, Stuttgart, 180-211.

Schmidtchen, Dieter (1987a), ''Sunk Costs', Quasirenten und Mitbestimmung (Sunk Costs, Quasirents, and Worker Participation)', **6** *Jahrbuch für Neue Politische Ökonomie*, 139 ff.

Schmidtchen, Dieter (1987b), ''Unsichtbare-Hand-Erklärung' und die Theorie der komparativen Kosten (Invisible-Hand Explanations and the Theory of Comparative Costs)', in Borchert, M., Fehl, U. und Oberender, P. (ed.), *Markt und Wettbewerb, Festschrift für Ernst Heuß Bern*, Stuttgart, 287 ff.

Schmidtchen, Dieter (1987c), 'Gebührenpolitik der DBP und Ordnungspolitik (Pricing Policy of the Deutsche Bundespost and Constitutional Policy)', in Diederich, H., Hamm, W. and Zohlnhöfer, W. (eds), *Die deutsche Bundespost im Spannungsfeld der Wirtschaftspolitik*, Heidelberg, 221-281.

Schmidtchen, Dieter (1988), 'Fehlurteile über das Konzept der Wettbewerbsfreiheit (Wrong Conclusions on the Concept of Competitive Freedom)', **39** *Ordo: Jahrbuch für die Ordnung von Wirtschaft und Gesellschaft*, 111-135.

Schmidtchen, Dieter (1989), 'Evolutorische Ordnungstheorie oder: die Transaktionskosten und das Unternehmertum (The Theory of Evolutionary Order, or: Transaction Costs and Entrepreneurship)', *Ordo: Jahrbuch für die Ordnung von Wirtschaft und Gesellschaft*, 161-182.

Schmidtchen, Dieter (1990), 'Die Produktion von Recht. Ein Literaturaufsatz (The Production of Law. An Overview)', **146(4)** *Journal for Institutional and Theoretical Economics*, 749-757.

Schmidtchen, Dieter (1991), 'Jenseits von Maximierung, Gleichgewicht und Effizienz: Neuland für die Ökonomische Analyse des Rechts? (Beyond Maximization, Balance and Efficiency: New L)', in Ott, Claus and Schäfer, Hans-Bernd (eds), *Ökonomische Probleme des Zivilrechts*, Berlin, Springer, 316-343.

Schmidtchen, Dieter (1993), 'Neue Institutionenökonomik internationaler Transaktionen (New Institutional Economics of International Transactions)', in Schlieper, Ulrich and Schmidtchen, Dieter (eds), *Makro, Geld and Institutionen*, Tübingen, 57-84.

Schmidtchen, Dieter (1994a), 'Vom nichtmarginalen Charakter der Steuermoral (On the Non-marginal Character of Tax Morals)', in Chr. Smekal and Theurl, E. (eds), *Stand und Entwicklung der Finanzpsychologie*, Baden-Baden, 185-211.

Schmidtchen, Dieter (1994b), 'Ökonomik des Vertrauens (Economics of Trust)', in Hof, H. (ed.), *Recht und Verhalten, Verhaltensgrundlagen des Rechts - zum Beispiel Vertrauen. Interdisziplinäre Studien zu Recht und Staat, Bd. 1*, Baden-Baden, 129-163.

Schmidtchen, Dieter (1994c), 'Antitrust zwischen Marktmachtphobie und Effizienzeuphorie, Alte Themen - neue Ansätze (Antitrust between Fear of Market Power and Euphoria about Efficiency)', in Möschel, W., Streit M. and Witt, U. (eds), *Marktwirtschaft und Rechtsordnung, Festschrift für Erich Hoppmann*, Baden-Baden, 143-166.

Schmidtchen, Dieter (1995a), 'Territorialität des Rechts, Internationales Privatrecht und die privatautonome Regelung internationaler Sachverhalte. Grundlagen eines interdisziplinären Forschungsprogramms (Territoriality of Law, International Private Law, and Private Autonomous Order of International Relations)', **59(1)** *Rabels Zeitschrift für ausländisches und internationales Privatrecht*, 56-112.

Schmidtchen, Dieter (1995b), 'Die Zwillingsideen der Evolution und der spontanen Bildung einer Ordnung (The Twin Ideas of Evolution and Spontaneous Order)', in Francke, H.-H. (ed.), *Ökonomischer Individualismus und freiheitliche Verfassung*, Freiburg, 239-271.

Schmidtchen, Dieter (1997), *Effizienz als Rechtsprinzip. Bemerkungen zu dem gleichnamigen Buch von Horst Eidenmüller* (Center for the Study of Law and Economics), Discussion paper 9708, 1997. Jahrbücher für Nationalökonomie und Statistik

Schmidtchen, Dieter and Fehl, E.U. (1986), 'Wettbewerbstheoretische Aspekte der Mißbrauchsaufsicht über Autobahntankstellen (Competition Theoretical Approach of the Abuse Control Concerning Highway Gas Stations)', *Wirtschaft und Wettbewerb*, 572 ff.

Schmidtchen, Dieter and Kirstein, Roland (1997), 'Abkoppelung der Prozeßkosten vom Streitwert? Eine Ökonomische Analyse von Reformvorschlägen (Separation of Litigation Costs and the Value of the Case? An Economic Analysis of Reform Proposals)', in Prütting, H. and Rüssmann, H. (eds), *Verfahrensrecht am Ausgang des 20. Jahrhunderts. Festschrift für Gerhard Lüke zum 70. Geburtstag, München 1997*, München, 741-766.

Schmidtchen, Dieter and Koboldt, Christian (1991), 'Copyrights - A und O in Literatur und Musik? (Copyrights in Literature and Music)', **42** *Ordo: Jahrbuch für die Ordnung von Wirtschaft und Gesellschaft.*

Schmidtchen, Dieter, Koboldt, Christian and Kirstein, Roland (1997), 'Rechtsvereinheitlichung beim 'droit de suite'? Ökonomische Analyse des Richtlinienentwurfs der Europäischen Kommission Center for the Study of Law and Economics (Harmonization of a Droit de Suite? An Economic Analysis of a Proposal of the European Commission)'

Schmidtchen, Dieter, Schmidt Trenz, Hans Jorg and Utzig, S. (1988), 'Zwang oder nicht Zwang - das ist hier die Frage. Der Verein für Socialpolitik und seine Mitgliederzeitschrift (Coercion or not - that's the Question. On the Member Journal of the Verein für Socialpolitik)', **204** *Jahrbuch für Nationalökonomie und Statistik*, 423-436.

Schmidt-Trenz, Hans-Joerg (1987), 'Der 'state of nature' im Schatten von Erwartungen über die Bildung und Verteilung von Eigentumsrechten. Ergebnisse einer spieltheoretischen Analyse der Vertragstheorie von J. M. Buchanan (The State of Nature in the Shadow of Expectations on Creation and Distribution of Property Rights)', *Diskussionsbeiträge Fachbereich Wirtschaftswissenschaft der Universität des Saarlandes.*

Schmidt-Trenz, Hans-Joerg (1990a), *Außenhandel und Territorialität des Rechts. Grundlegung einer Neuen Institutionenökonomik des Außenhandels* (Trade and Territoriality of Law), Baden-Baden, Nomos.

Schmidt-Trenz, Hans-Joerg (1990b), 'Kammern und Verbände als spontane 'Hilfssheriffs', (Ansätze zu einer Neuen Institutionenökonomik von Kammern und Verbänden, Teil I) (Chambers and Non-profit Organizations as spontaneous 'Deputy Sheriffs')', **15** *Verbandsmanagement*, 21-28.

Schmidt-Trenz, Hans-Joerg (1990c), 'Kammern und Verbände als 'Organisatoren von Wählerinteressen', (Ansätze zu einer Neuen Institutionenökonomik von Kammern und Verbänden, Teil II) (Chambers and Non-profit Organizations to Organize Voters' Interests)', **15/3** *Verbandsmanagement*, 52-59.

Schmidt-Trenz, Hans-Joerg (1991), 'Kammern und Verbände als 'Nicht-Marktliche Institutionen' (Hierarchien), (Ansätze zu einer Neuen Institutionenökonomik von Kammern und Verbänden, Teil III) (Chambers and Non-profit Organizations as Non-market Institutions)', **16** *Verbandsmanagement*, 19-24.

Schmidt-Trenz, Hans-Joerg (1992a), 'Systemwandel und vertrauensbildende Maßnahmen. Der Transformationsprozeß der 'DDR'-Wirtschaft im Lichte einer Neuen Institutionenökonomik von Kammern und Verbänden (System Transition and Trustbuilding Means)', **11** *Jahrbuch für Neue Politische Ökonomie*, 145-163.

Schmidt-Trenz, Hans-Joerg (1992b), *Systemwandel und vertrauensbildende Maßnahmen. Der Transformationsprozeß der 'DDR'-Wirtschaft im Lichte einer Neuen Institutionenökonomik von Kammern und Verbänden* (System Transition and Trustbuilding Means), Diskussionsbeiträge Fachbereich Wirtschaftswissenschaft der Universität des Saarlandes A 9203, Saarbrücken, No. A 9203.

Schmidt-Trenz, Hans-Joerg (1995), *Ökonomische Analyse der Reform des Rechts der privaten Schiedsgerichtsbarkeit. Was nutzt die Straffung des Vollstreckbarerklärungsverfahrens?* (Economic Analysis of the Reform of Private Arbitration Law), Diskussionsbeiträge der Forschungsstelle zur Ökonomischen Analyse des Rechts der Universität des Saarlandes 9505, Saarbrücken, 1995.

Schmidt-Trenz, Hans-Joerg (1996), *Die Logik kollektiven Handelns bei Delegation. Das Organisationsdilemma der Verbände am Beispiel des Beitragszwangs bei den Industrie- und Handelskammern* (The Logic of Collective Action with Delegation), Tübingen, Mohr/Siebeck.

Schmidt-Trenz, Hans-Joerg and Schmidtchen, Dieter (1994), 'Theorie optimaler Rechtsräume. Die Regulierung sozialer Beziehungen durch die Kontrolle von Territorium (Theory of Optimum Legal Areas)', **13** *Jahrbuch für Neue Politische Ökonomie*, 7-29.

Schmitz-Herscheidt, Friedhelm, 'Ansätze zu einer Ökonomischen Theorie des Gesellschaftsrecht (Initial Stages to an Economic Theory of Company Law)', in Boettcher, Erik, Herder-Dorneich, Philipp and Schenk, Karl-Ernst (eds), *Jahrbuch für Neue Politische Ökonomie*, Tübingen, Mohr.

Schneider, Jens-Peter (1996), 'Kooperative und Konsensuale Formen Administrativer Entscheidungsprozesse (Cooperative and Consensual Forms of Administrative Decision Making)', **15** *Jahrbuch für Neue Politische Ökonomie*, 82-102.

Schneider, Jens-Peter (1997), 'Das Neue Steuerungsmodell als Innovationsimpuls für Verwaltungsorganisation und Verwaltungsrecht (New Public Management as an Innovative Impulse for Administrative Organisation and Adminstrative Law)', in Eberhard Schmidt-Aßmann and Wolfgang Hoffmann-Riem (eds), *Organisationsrecht als Steuerungsressource (Band 5 der Schriften zur Reform des Verwaltungsrechts)*, Baden-Baden, Nomos.

Schneider, Jens-Peter and Hoffmann-Riem, Wolfganf (1995), 'Wettbewerbs- und umweltorientierte Re-Regulierung im Großhandels-Strommarkt (Re-Regulation of wholesale electricity markets towards competition and environmental protection)', in Hoffmann-Riem/Schneider (eds), *Umweltpolitische Steuerung in einem liberalisierten Strommarkt*, Baden-Baden, Nomos, 13-94.

Schöch, Heinz (1985), 'Empirische Grundlagen der Generalprävention (Empirical Foundations of General Prevention)', in Vogler, T. (ed.), *Festschrift für Hans- Heinrich Jescheck zum 70. Ge*, Berlin, Duncker and Humblot, vol. II, 1081-1105.

Schöffski, Oliver, 'Gedanken zur Deregulierung des deutschen Apothekenwesens (Ideas for the Deregulation of the German Pharmacy System)', **45(2)** *Zeitschrift für Wirtschaftspolitik*, 216-248.

Schöffski, Oliver (1995), *Die Regulierung des deutschen Apothekenwesens. Eine Ökonomische Analyse* (Regulation of German Pharmacies. An Economic Analysis), Baden-Baden, Nomos.

Schöffski, Oliver and Zhang, J. (1992), 'Überlegungen zur Einführung einer Krankenversicherung in der Volksrepublik China (Reflections about the Introduction of Health Insurance in the People's Republic of China)', **81** *Versicherungswissenschaft*, 249-260.

Schröder, Michael (1997), *Betriebliche Vollzugskosten der Arbeits- und Sozialgesetzgebung. Ein internationaler und intertemporaler Vergleich* (Execution Costs of Labor and Social Laws), Frankfurt, Campus.

Schröder, Roland (1996), *Sind kleine Bundesländer zu teuer?* (Federal States in Germany, Are the Small ones too Expensive?), Diskussionspapiere für liberale Politik Nr. 1, 1996.

Schulenburg, J. Matthias Graf Von Der, 'Demographischer Wandel und Umverteilung via Gesetzliche Krankenversicherung (Demographic Change and Redistribution via Statutory Health Insurance)', in Gäfgen, G. and Oberender, P. (eds), *Verteilungsziele und Verteilungswirkungen im Gesundheitswesen, Gesundheitsökonomische Beiträge Band 6*, Baden-Baden, Nomos.

Schulenburg, J. Matthias Graf Von Der (1982), 'Health Maintenance Organizations - Eine interessante Alternative zur traditionellen Krankenversicherung? (Health Maintenance Organizations - An Alternative for Traditional Health Insurance)', **71** *Zeitschrift für die gesamte Versicherungswissenschaft*, 27-648.

Schulenburg, J. Matthias Graf Von Der (1984), 'Wettbewerb und Regulierung im Gesundheitswesen - Property Rights als Ziel und Restriktion ärztlicher Honorarpolitik (Competition and Regulation in the Health Care Sector)', in Neumann, M. (ed.), *Ansprache, Eigentums- und Verfügungsrechte*, Berlin, Duncker and Humblot, 435-456.

Schulenburg, J. Matthias Graf Von Der (1985), ''Pro-Competitive-Strategy' im Gesundheitswesen, Eine kritische Stellungnahme aus deutscher Sicht ('Pro-Competitive-Strategy' in the Health Care Sector, A Critical Statement from the German Point of View)', in Hamm, W. and0 Neubauer, G. (eds), *Wettbewerb im Gesundheitswesen, Bd. 7 der Beiträge zur Gesundheitsökonomie*, Gerlingen, Bleicher, 325-353.

Schulenburg, J. Matthias Graf Von Der (1987), 'Marktstruktur und Wettbewerb in der ambulanten Versorgung, Die 'Ärzteschwemme' und ihre Auswirkungen auf die ambulante Versorgung (Market Structure and Competition in Out-Patient Care, The Glut of Physicians and and Effects on Ambulatory Care)', in Brennecke, R. and Schach, E. (eds), *Ambulante Versorgung, Nachfrage und Steuerung*, Berlin, Springer, 125-172.

Schulenburg, J. Matthias Graf Von Der (1988), 'Mehr Markt im Gesundheitswesen (More Market in the Health Care Sector)', **144** *Zeitschrift für die Gesamte Staatswissenschaft*, 396-402.

Schulenburg, J. Matthias Graf Von Der (1989), *Probleme der Gesundheitspolitik in Frankreich und Deutschland* (Problems of Health Politics in France and Germany), Frankfurt, Campus.

Schulenburg, J. Matthias Graf Von Der (1990), 'Demographischer Wandel, intergenerationale Gerechtigkeit und Stabilität des Generationenvertrages (Demographic Change, Intergenerational Justice and Stability of the Contact Between Generations)', in Gahlen, B., Hesse, H. and Ramser H.J. (eds), *Theorie und Politik der Sozialversicherung, Schriftenreihe des Wirtschaftswissenschaftlichen Seminars Ottobeuren Bd. 19*, Tübingen, Mohr/Siebeck, 269-300.

Schulenburg, J. Matthias Graf Von Der (1992), 'Wie souverän darf der Konsument auf Versicherungmärkten sein? Nachfragerverhalten und Regulierung auf Versicherungsmärkten (How Sovereign is a Consumer on Insurance Markets Allowed to be? Behaviour of Consumers and Regulation on Insurance Markets)', in Jacob, H., Adam, D., Hansmann, K.-H., Hilke, W., Müller, W., Preßmar, D.B. and Scheer, A.-W. (eds), *Schriften zur Unternehmensführung, Band 45*, Wiesbaden, Gabler, 3-18.

Schulenburg, J. Matthias Graf Von Der (1993), 'Kann der moderne Wohlfahrtsstaat die Konflikte zwischen medizinischen Möglichkeiten, sozialer Verantwortung und wirtschaftlicher Machbarkeit lösen? (Is the Modern Welfare State Able to Solve the Conflicts Between Medical Possibilities, Social Responsibility and Economic Possibilities?)', **2** *Staatwissenschaften und Staatspraxis*, 256-269.

Schulenburg, J. Matthias Graf Von Der and Breyer, F. (1989), 'Umlagefinanzierte Rentenversicherung bei abnehmender Bevölkerung unter den Bedingungen eines demokratischen Wahlmechanismus (Pension Insurance Financed by Contributions in Times of Decreasing Population Under the Conditions of a Democratic Election Mechanism)', in Boettcher, Erik, Herder-Dorneich, Philipp and Schenk, Karl-Ernst (eds), *Jahrbuch für Neue Politische Ökonomie*, Tübingen, Mohr, 126-139.

Schulenburg, J. Matthias Graf Von Der and Finsinger, Jorg (1989), 'Der Sonntagsverkauf (Selling on Sunday)', **109** *Zeitschrift für Wirtschafts- und Sozialwissenschaften*, 119-228.

Schulenburg, J. Matthias Graf Von Der and Hauser, Heinz (1988), 'Health Maintenance Organizations - Eine Reformkonzeption für die Gesetzliche Krankenversicherung in der Bundesrepublik Deutschland (Health Maintenance Organizations - A New Concept for the Statutory Health Insurance in Germany)', **19** *der von der Robert Bosch Stiftung herausgegebenen Beiträge zur Gesundheitsökonomie*.

Schulenburg, J. Matthias Graf Von Der and Kleindorfer, P. (1986), 'Wie stabil ist der Generationenvertrag in der Krankenversicherung? Zum Problem der Gerechtigkeit und der Akzeptanz intergenerativer Umverteilung (How Stable is the Contract Between Generations in the German Statutory Health Insurance?)', in Gäfgen, G. (ed.), *Ökonomie des Gesundheitswesens, Schriften des Vereins für Socialpolitik*, Berlin, Duncker and Humblot, 413-434.

Schulenburg, J. Matthias Graf Von Der and Schöffski, Oliver (1994a), 'Überweisungs- und Einweisungsverhalten von Primärärzten nach dem GSG (Referrals and Hospital Admissions of Primary Care Physicians After the Health Care Reform Act of 1992)', **136(14)** *Münchener Medizinische Wochenschrift*, 202-205.

Schulenburg, J. Matthias Graf Von Der and Schöffski, Oliver (1994b), 'Transformation des Gesundheitswesens im Spannungsfeld zwischen Kostendämpfung und Freiheit, Eine Ökonomische Analyse des veränderten Überweisungs- und Einweisungsverhaltens nach den Arzneimittelregulierungen des GSG (Transformation of the Health Care System, An Economic Analysis of the Changes in Referrals and Hospital Admissions after the Drug Budget of the Health Care Reform Act of 1992)', in Oberender, P. (ed.), *Probleme der Transformation im Gesundheitswesen*, Baden-Baden, Nomos, 45-81.

Schulenburg, J. Matthias Graf Von Der and Wagner, Michael J. (1990), 'Protektionismus, Marktstruktur und Importkonkurrenz, Eine vergleichende Ökonometrische Studie für die Bundesrepublik Deutschland und die USA (Protectionism, Market Structure and Import Competition)', **36(4)** *Ifo-Studien zur Industriewirtschaft*, 267-291.

Schüller, Alfred (1978), 'Property Rights, Unternehmerische Legitimation und Wirtschaftsordnung. Zum vermögenstheoretischen Ansatz einer allgemeinen Theorie der Unternehmung (Property Rights, Entrepreneurial Legitimation and Economic System. On the Property Rights Approach of a General Theory of the Enterprise)', in Schenk, K.E. (ed.), *Ökonomische Verfügungsrechte und Allokationsmechanismen in Wirtschafsystemen*, Berlin, Duncker and Humblot, 29-87.

Schüller, Alfred (1979), 'Eigentumsrechte, Unternehmenskontrollen und Wettbewerbsordnung (Property Rights, Corporate Control and Competition)', **30** *Ordo: Jahrbuch für die Ordnung von Wirtschaft und Gesellschaft*, 325-364.

Schüller, Alfred (1983), 'Theorie der Firma und wettbewerbliches Marktsystem (Theory of the Firm and Competitive Market System)', in Schüller, Alfred (ed.), *Property Rights und Ökonomische Theorie*, München, Vahlen, 145-183.

Schüller, Alfred (1985), 'Zur Ökonomik der Property Rights (On the Economics of Property Rights)', **14(5)** *Das Wirtschaftsstudium*, 259-265.

Schulz, Andreas (1984), 'Überlegungen zur Ökonomischen Analyse des Haftungsrechts (Considerations on the Economic Analysis of Liability Law)', **35** *Versicherungsrecht*, 608-618.

Schumann, Joachim (1978), ''Neue Mikroökonomik' und Theorie des Eigentumsrechte. Ansätze zur Ergänzung der mikroökonomischen Theorie (New Microeconomics' and Property Rights Theory. An Introduction to the Completion of Microeconomic Theory)', **7** *Wirtschaftswissenschaftliches Studium*, 307-311.

Schwark, Eberhard (1997), 'Wirtschaftssubventionen im Spannungsfeld von nationalem Recht und Gemeinschaftsrecht (Subsidies between National and European Law)', in Kruse, Jörn, Stockmann, Kurt, Vollmer, Lothar (eds), *Wettbewerbspolitik im Spannungsfeld nationaler und internationaler Kartellrechtsordnungen. Festschrift für Ingo Schmidt zum 65. Geburtstag*, Baden-Baden, Nomos, 325 ff.

Schwartze, Andreas (1988), 'Die Beseitigung des Wegfalls der Geschäftsgrundlage: Zur wirtschaftlichen Effizienz und zur juristischen Konsistenz eines Ökonomischen Modells (The Abolition of the Frustration of Contract: On Economic Efficiency and Legal Consistency of an Economic Model)', *Recht und Risiko*, 155-170.

Seidl, Christian (1979a), 'Reform der Steuern auf Einkommen und Ertrag, Novellierung des herrschenden Steuersystems oder Systemänderung durch eine modifizierte analytische Einkommensteuer? (Reforming the Income Tax, Improving the Traditional Tax or Tax Reform by a Schedule Income Tax?)', **6(4)** *Freie Argumente, Freiheitliche Zeitschrift für Politik*, 1-56.

Seidl, Christian (1979b), 'Das Konzept einer modifizierten analytischen Einkommensteuer als Alternative zum herrschenden System direkter Steuern (A Schedule Income Tax as an Alternative to the Traditional System of Direct Taxation)', **26(5)** *Wirtschaftspolitische Blätter*, 49-62.

Seidl, Christian (1980a), 'Die Individual- versus die Kollektiventscheidung, Freiheit in marktwirtschaftlichen Ordnungen (Individual Decisions versus Collective Decisions, Freedom in Market Economies)', in Streißler, E. and Watrin, Ch. (eds), *Zur Theorie marktwirtschaftlicher Ordnungen*, Tübingen, Mohr, 386-435.

Seidl, Christian (1980b), 'Ein analytisches Einkommensteuerkonzept mit flankierenden Steuern (A Schedule Income Tax with Matching Other Taxes)', in Helige, O. (ed.), *Dokumentation zur Steuerreformkommission, Wirtschaftsverlag Dr. Anton Orac*, Wien, 128-155.

Seidl, Christian (1980c), 'Historischer Abriß österreichischer Steuerstrukturen und Steuerreformen (A History of Austrian Tax Structures and Tax Reforms)', in Helige, O. (ed.), *Dokumentation zur Steuerreformkommission, Wirtschaftsverlag Dr. Anton Orac*, Wien, 219-231.

Seidl, Christian (1986), 'Kollektiventscheidung und Liberalismus (Collective Choice and Liberalism)', **33** *Wirtschaftspolitische Blätter*, 217-229.

Seidl, Christian (1988a), 'Ausgestaltungsformen der Sozialversicherung und ihre Ökonomischen Wirkungen (Varieties of Social Security and Its Economic Impacts)', in Holzmann, R. (ed.), *Ökonomische Analysen der Sozialversicherung, Bd. 3 der Schriftenreihe des Ludwig Boltzmann-Instituts für Ökonomische Analysen wirtschaftspolitischer Aktivitäten, Manzsche Verlags- und Universitätsbuchhandlung*, Wien, 53-99.

Seidl, Christian (1988b), 'Welfarismus versus Liberalismus. Sind Demokratie und individuelle Rechte unvereinbar? (Welfarism versus Liberalism. Are Democracy and Individual Rights Contradictory?)', in Rahmsdorf, Detlef and Schäfer, Hans-Bernd (eds), *Ethische Grundfragen der Wirtschafts- und Rechtsordnung, Bd. 4 der 'Hamburger Beiträge zur öffentlichen Wissenschaft'*, Dietrich Reiner Verlag, Berlin-Hambug, 143-204.

Seidl, Christian (1989a), 'Kommentar (Comment on Kötz, Zur Effizienz von Haftungsausschl)', in Ott, Claus and Schäfer, Hans-Bernd (eds), *Allekationseffizienz in der Rechtsordnung*, Berlin, Springer, 201-207.

Seidl, Christian (1989b), 'Betriebssteuer und Neutralität (On the Neutrality of a Business Tax)', **66/4** *Steuer und Wirtschaft*, 350-357.

Seidl, Christian (1991a), 'Kommentar zur Arbeit von Helmut Kohl, Das Allgemeine Persönlichkeitsrecht als Ausdruck oder Grenze des Effizienzdenkens im Zivilrecht? (A Comment on the Paper by Helmut Kohl, Individual Rights as a Phenomenon or a Limit on Efficiency Considerations in Private Law?)', in Ott, Claus and Schäfer, Hans-Bernd (eds), *Ökonomische Probleme des Zivilrechts*, Berlin, Springer, 52-57.

Seidl, Christian (1991b), 'Kommentar (Comment on Kohl, Das Allgemeine Persönlichkeitsrec)', in Ott, Claus and Schäfer, Hans-Bernd (eds), *Ökonomische Probleme des Zivilrechts*, Berlin, Springer, 52-57.

Seidl, Christian (1994), 'Marktgerechte versus kollektivistische Sozialpolitik (Libertarian versus Collectivist Social Policy)', in Hermann-Pillath, Carsten, Schlecht, Otto and Wünsche, Horst F. (eds), *Marktwirtschaft als Aufgabe, Wirtschaft und Gesellschaft im Übergang vom Plan zum Markt, Bd. III der Grundtexte zur Sozialen Marktwirtschaft der Ludwig-Erhard-Stiftung*, Stuttgart, Gustav Fischer, 363-376.

Seidl, Christian (1997), 'Das Wesen liberaler Rechte (On the Essence of Liberal Rights)', in Ott, Claus and Schäfer, Hans-Bernd (eds), *Ökonomische Analyse des Rechts, Fünftes Travemünder Symposium zur Analyse des Rechts*.

Seidl, Christian, Binder, Martin, Ruppe, Hans-Georg, Steinhöfler, Karl and Tichy, Gunther (1981), *Sozialpolitik und Umverteilung. Eine kritische Analyse der Ökonomischen und juristischen Probleme aus österreichischer Sicht* (Social Policy and Redistribution. A Critical Analysis of the Legal and Economic Conditions in Austria), Wien.

Siekmann, Hans (1996), 'Corporate Governance und öffentlich-rechtliche Unternehmen (Corporate Governance and Public Enterprises)', in Schenk, Karl-Ernst, Schmidtchen, Dieter and Streit, Manfred E. (eds), *Vom Hoheitsstaat zum Konsensualstaat, Neue Formen der Kooperation zwischen Staat und Privaten Jahrbuch für Neue Politische Ökonomie 15*, Tübingen, Mohr.

Sinn, Hans-Werner (1989), 'Kommentar on Magoulas, Verbraucherschutz als Problem asymmetrischer Informationskosten', in Ott, Claus and Schäfer, Hans-Bernd (eds), *Allekationseffizienz in der Rechtsordnung*, Berlin, Springer, 81-90.

Spindler, Gerald (1988), 'Geschäftsgrundlage und Steuerrechtsänderungen (Changes of Tax Law and their Impact on Long Term Contracts - an Economic Analysis)', in Finsinger and Simon (eds), *Recht und Risiko. Juristische und Ökonomische Analysen*, München, Florentz, 288-325.

Spindler, Gerald (1993), *Recht und Konzern - Interdependenzen der Rechts- und Unternehmensentwicklung in Deutschland und den USA zwischen 1870 und 1933* (The Evolution of Corporate Law, Tax Law and Antitrust Law and their Impact on the Structures of Corporations Comparing the History of the US to Germany), Tübingen, Mohr.

Spindler, Gerald (1996), 'Umweltschutz durch private Prüfungen von Unternehmensorganisationen, Die EG-Öko-Audit-VO (Environmental Protection by Auditing the Organization Structure of Corporations)', in Schenk, Karl-Ernst, Schmidtchen, Dieter and Streit, Manfred E. (eds), *Vom Hoheitsstaat zum Konsensualstaat, Neue Formen der Kooperation zwischen Staat und Privaten Jahrbuch für Neue Politische Ökonomie 15*, Tübingen, Mohr, 205-230.

Spindler, Gerald (1997a), *Unternehmensorganisationspflichten - zivilrechtliche und öffentlich-rechtliche Regulierungskonzepte* (Organization of the Enterprise - Regulatory Approaches in Private and Public Administrative Law), Tübingen, Mohr.

Spindler, Gerald (1997b), 'Deregulierung des Aktienrechts? (Deregulation of Mandatory Corporate Law in Germany)', **2** *Die Aktiengesellschaft.*

Starnecker, Hermann (1995), *Englische Insolvenzverfahren - Administrative Receivership und Administration Order vor dem Hintergrund der deutschen Insolvenzordnung* (Bankruptcy proceedings in Great Britain - Administrative Receivership and Administration Order on the back of the German bankruptcy code), Frankfurt am Main, Lang Verlag.

Stockmann, Kurt (1997), 'Das Wettbewerbselement in der Spruchparixis des vergabeüberwachungsausschusses des Bundes (Competition as a Decision Factor of a Federal Licensing Commission)', in Kruse, Jörn, Stockmann, Kurt and Vollmer, Lothar (eds), *Wettbewerbspolitik im Spannungsfeld nationaler und internationaler Kartellrechtsordnungen. Festschrift für Ingo Schmidt zum 65. Geburtstag*, Baden-Baden, Nomos, 379 ff.

Streit, Manfred E. (1991), *Theorie der Wirtschaftspolitik 4. neubearb. u. erweiterte Aufl.* (Theory of Economic Policy), Düsseldorf.

Streit, Manfred E. (1994), 'Europäische Industriepolitik nach Maastricht - Eine ordnungspolitische Analyse (European Industrial Policy after Maastricht)', in Möschel, W., Streit, M. and Witt, U. (eds), *Marktwirtschaft und Rechtsordnung, Festschrift für Erich Hoppmann*, Baden-Baden, 189-211.

Streit, Manfred E. (1996), 'Zur Interdependenz der Ordnungen - marktwirtschaftliche Ordnungspolitik im Sozialstaat (The Interdependency of Orders)', **22(3)** *List-Forum für Wirtschafts- und Finanzpolitik*, 1-18.

Streit, Manfred E., Wegner, G., Kasper, W. and Voigt, Stefan (1995), *Freiburger Beiträge zur Ordnungsökonomik* (Freiburger Contributions to Economics of Legal Frameworks), Tübingen, Mohr/Siebeck.

Stützel, Wolfgang (1966), 'Entscheidungstheoretische Elementarkategorien als Grundlage einer Begegnung von Wirtschaftswissenschaft und Rechtswissenschaft (Elementary Categories of Decision Theory as a Base for Encounters of Economics and Legal Theory)', **12** *Zeitschrift für Betriebswirtschaft*, 769-789.

Sullivan, Lawrence A. (1983), 'Warenzeichen und Behinderungspratiken in den USA: Eine vorläufige Analyse (Product Marks and Hindrance Practices in the USA: A Preliminary Analysis)', **9** *GRUR Int.*, 714-721.

Taeger, U.C. (1979), 'Untersuchung der Aussagefähigkeit von Patentstatistiken hinsichtlich technologischer Entwicklungen (Research into the Informal Value of Patent Statistics with Respect to Technological Developments)', **17** *Ifo-Studien zur Industriewirtschaft.*

Terberger, Eva (1987), *Der Kreditvertrag als Instrument zur Lösung von Anreizproblemen -Fremdfinanzierung als Principal/Agent-Beziehung* (Debt Contracts and Incentive Problems), Heidelberg.

Terberger, Eva (1994a), 'Kommentar zu Picot, Arnold/Dietl, Helmut, Informations (de-) regulierung am Kapitalmarkt aus InstitutionenÖkonomischer Sicht (New Institutional Economics and the (De-)Regulation of Insider Trading)', **13** *Jahrbuch für Neue Politische Ökonomie*, 143-148.

Terberger, Eva (1994b), *Neo-institutionalistische Ansätze, Entstehung und Wandel - Anspruch und Wirklichkeit* (New Institutional Economics - Origin and Change, Scientific Claims and Achievements), Wiesbaden, Gabler.

Terberger, Eva (1995), 'Bankenaufsicht (Regulation of Banks)', in Gerke, Wolfgang and Steiner, Manfred (eds), *Handwörterbuch des Finanz- und Bankwesens, Band 6, 2. Aufl.*, Stuttgart, 151-163.

Terberger, Eva (1996), 'Kommentar zu Siekmann, Helmut, Corporate Governance und Öffentlich-rechtlich organisierte Unternehmen (Corporate Governance and Public Enterprises)', **15** *Jahrbuch für Neue Politische Ökonomie*.

Terhart, Peter (1995), *Chapter 11 Bankruptcy Code, Eine Alternative für Deutschland*? (Chapter 11 Bankruptcy Code, An alternative for Germany?), Frankfurt an Main, Lang Verlag.

Teutemann, Manfred (1992), *Rationale Kompetenzverteilung im Rahmen der europäischen Integration. Ein Beitrag zur finanzwirtschaftlichen Ordnungspolitik* (Rational Allocation of Competency and the European Integration. A Contribution to the Constitutional Politics of Public Economics), Berlin, Duncker and Humblot.

Tietzel, Manfred (1981a), 'Die Rationalitätsannahme in den Wirtschaftswissenschaften oder Der homo oeconomicus und seine Verwandten (The Rationality Assumption in Economics or the Homo Oeconomicus and his Relatives)', **32** *Jahrbuch für Sozialwissenschaft*, 115-136.

Tietzel, Manfred (1981b), 'Die Ökonomie der Property Rights, Ein Überblick (Economics of Property Rights)', **30** *Zeitschrift für Wirtschaftspolitik*, 207-243.

Tietzel, Manfred (1981c), 'Die Ökonomie Der Property Rights: Ein Überblick (The Economics of Property Rights: A Survey)', **30** *Zeitschrift für Wirtschaftspolitik*, 207-243.

Tietzel, Manfred (1982), 'Was kann man von der Theorie rationaler Erwartungen rationalerweise erwarten? (Rational Expectations about the Theory of Rational Expectations)', **15(4)** *Kredit und Kapital*, 492-516.

Tietzel, Manfred (1983), 'Wirtschaftstheorie als allgemeine Theorie des menschlichen Verhaltens. Eine Analyse der New Home Economics (Economic Theory as a General Theory of Human Behavior)', **32(3)** *Zeitschrift für Wirtschaftspolitik*, 225-242.

Tietzel, Manfred (1986), 'Zur Entstehung des Privateigentums (On the Evolution of Private Property)', **37** *Ordo*, 105-127.

Tietzel, Manfred (1988), 'Zur Ökonomischen Theorie des Betrügens und Fälschens (On the Economic Theory of Fraud and Counterfeiting)', **204** *Jahrbuch für Nationalökonomie und Statistik*, 17-34.

Tietzel, Manfred (1989), 'Probleme der asymmetrischen Informationsverteilung beim Güter- und Leistungstausch (Problems of Asymmetric Information in the Trade of Goods and Services)', in Ott, Claus and Schäfer, Hans-Bernd (eds), *Allekationseffizienz in der Rechtsordnung*, Berlin, Springer, 52-63.

Tietzel, Manfred (1991a), 'Kommentar' (on Schäfer, Ökonomische Analyse von Aufklärungspflichten and Ott, Vorvertragliche Aufklärungspflichten) (Comment)', in Ott, Claus and Schäfer, Hans-Bernd (eds), *Ökonomische Probleme des Zivilrechts*, Berlin, Springer, 163-166.

Tietzel, Manfred (1991b), 'Der Neue Institutionalismus auf dem Hintergrund der alten Ordnungsdebatte (The New Institutionalism and the Old Debate on Economic Order)', **10** *Jahrbuch für Neue Politische Ökonomie*, 3-37.

Tietzel, Manfred (1994), 'Urheberrechte im Zeitalter der Fotokopie. Die Ökonomik von Verwertungsgesellschaften am Beispiel der VG Wort (Copyright Law in the Age of the Photocopy, The Economics of Resale Royalty Organizations)', in Ott, Claus and Schäfer, Hans-Bernd (eds), *Okonomische Analyse der rechtlichen Organisation von Innovationen*, Tübingen, Mohr, 128-147.

Tietzel, Manfred and Weber, M. (1991), 'Von Betrügern, Blendern und Opportunisten. Eine Ökonomische Analyse (Betrayers, Cheaters, and Opportunists)', **40** *Zeitschrift für Wirtschaftspolitik*, 109-137.

Todt, Horst (1991), 'Freiheit und Utilitarismus (Freedom and Utilitarianism)', in Ott, Claus and Schäfer, Hans-Bernd (eds), *Ökonomische Probleme des Zivilrechts*, Berlin, Springer, 1-17.

Trimarchi, Pietro (1972), 'Die Regelung der Vertragshaftung aus Ökonomischer Sicht (The Regulation of Contractual Liability from an Economic Point of View)', **136** *Zeitschrift für das gesamte Handels- und Wirtschaftsrecht*, 118-138.

Trimarchi, Pietro (1989), 'Der Wegfall der Geschäftsgrundlage aus allokativer Sicht - Kommentar (The Frustration of Contract from an Allocative Sig)', in Ott, Claus and Schäfer, Hans-Bernd (eds), *Allekationseffizienz in der Rechtsordnung*, Berlin, Springer, 163-167.

Vanberg, Viktor J. (1982a), *Verbrechen, Strafe und Abschreckung, die Theor* (Crime, Sanction and Deterrence: The Theory of), Tübingen, Mohr, 50 p.

Vanberg, Viktor J. (1982b), *Markt und Organisation. Individualistische Sozialtheorie und das Problem korporativen Handelns* (Market and Organization. Individualist Social Theory and the Problem of Corporate Action), Tübingen.

Vanberg, Viktor J. (1982c), 'Das Unternehmen als Sozialverband. Zur Sozialtheorie der Unternehmung und zur juristsichen Diskussion um ein neues Unternehmensrecht (The Firm as a Social Organization. The Social Theory of the Firm and the Legal Discussion on a New Law of Business Corporations)', **1** *Jahrbuch für Neue Politische Ökonomie*, 276-307.

Vanberg, Viktor J. (1983a), 'Organisationsziele und individuelle Interessen (Organizational Goals and Individual Interests)', **34** *Soziale Welt*, 171-187.

Vanberg, Viktor J. (1983b), 'Der individualistische Ansatz zu einer Theorie der Entstehung und Entwicklung von Institutionen (The Individualistic Approach to a Theory of the Emergence and the Development of Institutions)', **2** *Jahrbuch für Neue Politische Ökonomie*, 50-69.

Vanberg, Viktor J. (1984), ''Unsichtbare Hand Erklärung' und soziale Normen ('Invisible Hand Explanation' and Social Norms)', in Todt, H. (ed.), *Normgeleitetes verhalten in den Sozialwissenschaften Schriften des VEreins für Socialpolitik*, Berlin, 115-144.

Vanberg, Viktor J. (1995), 'Ordnungspolitik und die Unvermeidbarkeit des Wettbewerbs (Constitutional Politics and the Unavoidability of Competition)', in Francke, H.-H. (ed.), *Ökonomischer Individualismus und freiheitliche Verfassung*, Freiburg, 187-211.

Väth, Andreas (1987), *Die Wettbewerbskonzeption des Europäischen Ger* (The Competition Concept of the European Court), Bayreuth, P.C.O.-Verlag, 298 p.

Voigt, Stefan (1991), 'Die evolutionsorientierte Theorie der Verfassung - Bemerkungen zum Ansatz von Hayeks (The Evolutionary Theory of Constitution. Remarks on Hayek's Approach)', **40** *Zeitschrift für Wirtschaftspolitik*, 93-107.

Voigt, Stefan (1992a), *Die Welthandelsordnung zwischen Konflikt und Stabilität - Konfliktpotentiale und Konfliktlösungsmechanismen* (The World Trade System between Conflict and Stability), Freiburg.

Voigt, Stefan (1992b), 'Das Lizenzauktionsverfahren, Ein zielkonformes Instrument zur Regulierung lokaler Kabelfernsehstationen? Eine Analyse der anglo-amerikanischen Diskussion und Praxis (The Licence Auctioning System as an Instrument to Regulate Local Cable Stations)', **17** *The European Journal of Communications*, 67-90.

Voigt, Stefan (1994a), 'Die kontraktorientierte Theorie der Verfassung - Anmerkungen zum Ansatz Buchanans (A Contractarian Theory of Constitution. Remarks on Buchanan's Approach)', **11** *Homo Oeconomicus*, 173-209.

Voigt, Stefan (1994b), 'Der Weg zur Freiheit - Mögliche Implikationen Hayekscher Hypothesen für die Transformation der Wirtschaftssysteme Mittel- und Osteuropas (The Road to Freedom. Possible Implications of Hayekian Hypothesises for the Transformation of the Economies in Middle- and Eastern Europe)', in Hölscher, J. et al (ed), *Bedingungen Ökonomischer Entwicklung in Zentralosteuropa, Bd. 2*, Marburg, Metropolis, 63-105.

Voigt, Stefan (1996), 'Die konstitutionelle Ökonomik als Herausforderung für die Theorie der Wirtschaftspolitik - zugleich eine Skizze zur Weiterentwicklung einer Ökonomischen Theorie der Verfassung erscheint (Constitutional Economics as a Challenge for the Theory of Economic Policy)', in Pies, Ingo and Leschke, Martin (eds), *James Buchanans konstitutionelle Ökonomik*, Tübingen, Mohr/Siebeck.

Voigt, Stefan and Kiwit, Daniel (1995), 'Überlegungen zum institutionellen Wandel unter Berücksichtigung des Verhältnisses interner und externer Institutionen (Reflections on Institutional Change with Respect to the Relation between Internal and External Institutions)', **46** *Ordo*, 117-147.

Vollmer, Lothar (1997), 'Die Sondermärkte im Spannungsfeld von nationalen und europäischen Regulierungs- und Deregulierungsaktivitäten (Tensions between national and European Regulation and Deregulation)', in Kruse, Jörn, Stockmann, Kurt and Vollmer, Lothar (eds), *Wettbewerbspolitik im Spannungsfeld nationaler und internationaler Kartellrechtsordnungen. Festschrift für Ingo Schmidt zum 65. Geburtstag*, Baden-Baden, Nomos, 289 ff.

Von Randow, Philipp (1989), 'Kommentar (On Adams, Warum kein Ersatz von Nichtvermögensschäden)', in Ott, Claus and Schäfer, Hans-Bernd (eds), *Allekationseffizienz in der Rechtsordnung*, Berlin, Springer, 218-225.

Von Weizsäcker, Carl-Christian (1984), 'Was leistet die Property Rights Theorie für aktuelle wirtschaftspolitische Fragen? (What Brings the Property Rights Theory for Economi)', in Neumann, M. (ed.), *Ansprache, Eigentums- und Verfügungsrechte*, Berlin, Duncker and Humblot, 123-152.

Von Weizsäcker, Carl-Christian (1987), 'Der Markt für unternehmensgebundene Ressourcen (The Market for Enterprise Restricted Resources)', **126** *XXXStrukturwandel und Wirtschaftsord nung, Referate des XX.FIW-Symposiums - FIW Schriftenreihe*, 31-42.

Walwei, U., 'Ökonomische Analyse arbeitsrechtlicher Regelungen am Beispiel des Kündigungsschutzes (Economic Analysis of Protection Against Dismissal as an Example for Worker Protection Laws)', **63(6)** *WSI-Mitteilungen*, 392-400.

Walwei, U. (1989), *Ansätze einer Ökonomischen Analyse des Arbeitsrechts - Debatte um Deregulierung und Flexibilisierung des Arbeitsrechts aus Ökonomischer Sicht* (Economic Analysis of Labor Markets. The Debate on Deregulation and Flexibilization of the Labor Law), Arbeitspapiere aus dem Arbeitskreis Sozialwissenschaftliche Arbeitsmarktforschung (SAMF), 1989.

Walwei, U. (1990), 'Ökonomisch-rechtliche Analyse befristeter Arbeitsverhältnisse (Law and Economics of Temporary Employment)', .

Walwei, U. (1993), 'Zum Regulierungsbedarf bei Zulassung privater Arbeitsvermittlung (On the Need for Regulation of Admission of Private Employment Agencies)', **26(3)** *Mitteilungen aus der Arbeitsmarkt- und Berufsforschung*, 285-293.

Walwei, U. (1995), 'Atypische Beschäftigungsformen, Kongruenz und Divergenz der Interessen (Non-typical Forms of Employment)', in Keller, B.and Seifert, H. (eds), *Atypische Beschäftigung. Verbieten oder gestalten?*, Köln, 9-24.

Walwei, U. (1996), 'Befristung von Arbeitsverhältnissen, Mehr Beschäftigung durch weniger Kündigungsschutz? (Temporary Employment, More Employment by Less Protection Against Dismissal?)', in Montada, L. and Dieter, A. (eds) *Gerechtigkeitsprobleme der Arbeitslosigkeit. Berichte aus dem Zentrum für Gerechtigkeitsforschung an der Universität Potsdam, Nr. 3*, 127-154.

Walz, W. Rainer (1974), 'Marktbezogener Umweltschutz und Privatrechtlicher Immissionsschutz - Kann Umweltökonomie einen Beitrag zur Funktionsbestimmung Privatrechtlicher Immissionsschutzregeln leisten? (Market Related Environmental Protection and Private Law Protection agai), *Funktionswandel der Privatrechtsinstitutionen, Festschrift für Ludwig Raiser*, 185-222.

Walz, W. Rainer (1986), 'Sachenrecht für Nichtsachen? Kritik einer Systemanalogie (Property Law for Immaterial Goods? Critique on a System Analogy)', **1** *Kritische Vierteljahresschrift für Gesetzgebung und Rechtswissenschaft*, 131-164.

Walz, W. Rainer (1988), 'Rechtssicherheit und Risikozuweisung bei Steuerrechtsänderungen - Verbotene Rückwirkung, gebotene Übergangsregelung, richterliche Vertragsanpassung (Legal Certainty and Risk Allocation for Changes in Tax Law - Illegal Retroaction, Transitional Rules)', *Recht und Risiko*, 252-286.

Walz, W. Rainer (1989), 'Ökonomische und rechtssystematische Überlegungen zur Verkehrsfähigkeit von Gegenständen (Economic and Legal Dogmatic Considerations in Mark)', in Ott, Claus and Schäfer, Hans-Bernd (eds), *Allekationseffizienz in der Rechtsordnung*, Berlin, Springer, 93-114.

Walz, W. Rainer (1990), 'Sachenrechtliches Systemdenken im Wandel - Die Ökonomischen Determinanten des Verfügungstatbestandes (Property Law System Thinking in Change - The Economic Determinants of the Disposition General Findings)', **5** *Kritische Vierteljahresschrift für Gesetzgebung und Rechtswissenschaft*, 374-405.

Walz, W. Rainer (1993), 'Ökonomische Regulierungstheorie vor den Toren des Bilanzrechts (Economic Theory of Regulation and Accounting Law)', **82** *Zeitschrift für Betriebswirtschaftliche Forschung*.

Walz, W. Rainer (1994), 'Privatautonomie oder rechtliche Intervention bei der Ausstattung und □nderung von Gesellschafterrechten? (Private Autonomy or Legal Intervention when Creating or Modifying the Corporation Law?)', in Ott, C. and Schäfer, H.-B. (eds), *Ökonomische Analyse des Unternehmensrechts*, Heidelberg, Physica, 50-75.

Walz, W. Rainer (1996a), 'Rechtspolitik und Betriebswirtschaftslehre angesichts der Internationalisierung des Bilanzrechts (Legal Policy, Business Administration, and the Internationalization of Accounting Law)', in Sadowski, D., Czap, H. and Wächter, H.

(eds), *Regulierung der Unternehmenspolitik. Methoden und Kritik der betriebswirtschaftlichen Rechtsanalyse*, Wiesbaden, Gabler, 23-49.

Walz, W. Rainer (1996b), 'Ökonomische und soziologische Unternehmensleitbilder vor den Toren des Gesellschaftsrechts (Economic and Sociologic Images of the Firm and the Coorpration Law)', *Die Aktiengesellschaft*, 161-169.

Walz, W. Rainer and Rascher-Friesenhausen, Hein (ed.) (1983), *Sozialwissenschaften im Zivilrecht, Fälle und Lösu* (Social Science in Civil Law, Cases and Answers), Neuwied und Darmstadt, Luchterhand.

Walz, W. Rainer and Wienstroh, Claas (1983), 'Die Fehlgeschlagene Investition (The Case of the Investment Failure)', in Walz, W. Rainer and Rascher-Friesenhausen, Hein (eds), *Sozialwissenschaften im Zivilrecht: Fälle und Lösungen in Ausbild und Prüfung*, Neuwied und Darmstadt, Luchterhand, 52-75.

Wangenheim, Georg v. (1995), *Die Evolution von Recht. Ursachen und Wirkungen haeufigkeitsabhaengigen Verhaltens in der Rechtsfortbildung* (The Evolution of Law. Causes and Effects of Frequency Dependent Behaviour in Legal Evolution), Tübingen, Mohr/Siebeck.

Wangenheim, Georg v. (1996), 'Verwaltungsinterne Durchsetzbarkeit neuer Formen des Verwaltungshandelns (New Forms of Administrative Behaviour and its Enforcement Within the Administration)', **15** *Jahrbuch für Neue Politische Ökonomie*.

Watrin, Christian (1975a), 'Politische Ökonomie der demokratisierten Gesellschaft (The Political Economy of a Democraticized Society)', in Lutz, Friedrich A. (ed.), *Der Streit um die Gesellschaftsordnung. Sozialwissenschaftliche Studien für das Schweizerische Institut für Auslandsforschung. Bd. 3 (N.F.)*, Zürich, 113-142.

Watrin, Christian (1975b), 'Gesellschaftliches Eigentum und Arbeiterselbstverwaltung - ein Weg zur Humanisierung der Gesellschaft? (Collective Property and Workers Self-Government - The Road to a More Human Society?)', **26** *Ordo*, 79-96.

Watrin, Christian (1976), 'Selbstverwaltete Unternehmen und Produktionsmitteleigentum. (Labor Managed Enterprises and Private Property of Capital)', in Watrin, Christian, Willgerodt, Hans (eds), *Widersprüche der Kapitalismuskritik. Festgabe für Alfred Müller-Armack. Wirtschaftspolitische Chronik, Heft 2/3*, 157-178.

Watrin, Christian (1977), 'Ordnungspolitische Aspekte des Sozialstaates (The Institutional Framework of the Social State)', in Külp, Bernhard and Haas, Hans-Dieter (eds), *Soziale Probleme der modernen Industriegesellschaft, Schriften des Vereins für Socialpolitik N.F. Bd. 92/II*, Berlin, 963-985.

Watrin, Christian (1978), 'Der Sozialstaat als Ordnungsproblem in der freien Gesellschaft', in Lammert, Norbert (ed.), *Wirtschaft in der Gesellschaft. Entwicklungslinie und Problemfelder, München*, Wien, 31-45.

Watrin, Christian (1980), 'Vom Wirtschaftsdenken der Klassiker zu den neoliberalen Ordnungsvorstellungen (From Classical Economic Liberalism to Modern Neoliberalism)', in Linder, Willy, Helbing, Hanno and Bütler, Hugo (eds), *Liberalismus - nach wie vor. Grundgedanken und Zukunftsfragen. Aus Anlaß des zweihundertjährigen Bestehens der Neuen Zürcher Zeitung. Buchverlag der Neuen Zürcher Zeitung. Zürich 1980*, Zürich, 81-102.

Watrin, Christian (1986), 'Eigentum. IV, Wirtschaftliche Probleme (The Economics of Property Rights)', **2(7)** *Staatslexikon, hrsg. von der Görres-Gesellschaft*, 162-178.

Watrin, Christian (1989), 'Epilog, James M. Buchanans Entwurf einer konstitutionellen Ökonomik (Epilog, James M. Buchanan's *Theory of Constitutional Economics*)', in

Peacock. Alan and Willgerodt, Hans (eds), *Germany's Social Market Economy, Origins and Evolution*, London, Macmillan, 106-123.

Watrin, Christian (1990a), 'Ordnungspolitische Defizite der DDR-Wirtschaft und Möglichkeiten zu deren Überwindung durch marktwirtschaftliche Reformen (Central Planning and the Transformation to a Market Order)', **37** *Beihefte der Konjunkturpolitik*, 9-22.

Watrin, Christian (1990b), 'Vom sozialistischen zum privaten Eigentum (From Socialist to Private Property)', **35** *Hamburger Jahrbuch für Wirtschaft und Gesellschaftspolitik*, 119-128.

Watrin, Christian (1994), 'Die Gesellschaft freier Menschen - Bemerkungen zu Erich Hoppmanns Arbeiten über Freiheit und marktwirtschaftliche Ordnung (The Free Society - Erich Hoppmann on Freedom and Economic Order)', in Möschel, W., Streit, M. and Witt, U. (ed.), *Marktwirtschaft und Rechtsordnung, Festschrift für Erich Hoppmann*, Baden-Baden, 211-223.

Watrin, Christian (1995), 'Nutzen und Kosten des Rechts (Economics of Law)', in Mantl, Wolfgang (ed.), *Effizienz der Gesetzesproduktion, Abbau der Regelungsdichte im internationalen Vergleich Schriftenreihe des Zentrums für angewandte Politikforschung Bd. 7*, Wien, 239-244.

Watrin, Christian (1996), 'Der Wettbewerb der Ordnungen als Entdeckungsverfahren für eine nachhaltige Entwicklung (Korreferat) (Sustainable Development and Competition Among Economic Systems as a Discovery Process)', in Gerken, Lüder (ed.), *Ordnungspolitische Grundfragen einer Politik der Nachhaltigkeit/Walter Eucken Institut*, Baden-Baden, 103-113.

Weck-Hannemann, Hannelore (1991), 'Politische Ökonomie des Protektionismus. Eine Institutionelle Analyse (Political Economics of Protectionism. An Institutional Analysis)', in Siebke, Jürgen (ed.), *Monetäre Konfliktfelder der Weltwirtschaft. Schriftenreihe des Vereins für Socialpolitik, NF 210*, Berlin, Duncker and Humblot, 125-142.

Weck-Hannemann, Hannelore (1992), 'Politische Ökonomie des Protektionismus. Eine Institutionelle und Empirische Analyse (Political Economics of Protectionism. An Institutional and Empirical Analysis)', **17** *Wirtschaftswissenschaft*.

Weck-Hannemann, Hannelore (1996), 'Frauenerwerbstätigkeit und Familienbesteuerung (Female Employment and Family Taxation)', in Thöni, Erich and Winner, Hannes (eds), *Die Familie im Sozialstaat. Familienbesteuerung aus Ökonomischer und juristischer Sicht Veröffentlichungen der Universität Innsbruck 216*, Innsbruck, 191-207.

Weck-Hannemann, Hannelore and Pommerehne, Werner W. (1989), 'Einkommenssteuerhinterziehung in der Schweiz. Eine empirische Analyse (An Empirical Analysis of Income Tax Evasion in Switzerland)', **125(4)** *Schweizerische Zeitschrift für Volkswirtschaft und Statistik*, 515-556.

Wegehenkel, Lothar (1980a), *Transaktionskosten, Wirtschaftssystem und Unternehmertum* (Transaction Costs, Economic System and Entrepreneurship), Tübingen, Mohr, 77 p.

Wegehenkel, Lothar (1980b), *Coase Theorem und Marktsystem* (Coase Theorem and the Market System), Tübingen, Mohr, 138 p.

Wegehenkel, Lothar (1989), 'Kommentar (on Köndgen and van Randow, Sanktionen bei Vertragsverletzung)', in Ott, Claus and Schäfer, Hans-Bernd (eds), *Allekationseffizienz in der Rechtsordnung*, Berlin, Springer, 141-145.

Wehrt, Klaus (1991a), 'Die Qualitätshaftung des Verkäufers aus Ökonomischer Sicht (Economic Analysis of the Seller's Liability for the Quality of his Good)', in Ott, Claus and Schäfer, Hans-Bernd (eds), *Ökonomische Probleme des Zivilrechts*, Berlin, Springer, 235-259.

Wehrt, Klaus (1991b), 'Die BGH-Urteile zur Tilgungsverrechnung - Nur die Spitze des Eisbergs, Der korrekt abgerechnete Hypothekenbankkredit (The Judgements of the German Supreme Court Concerning the Reimbursement of Wrongly Calculated interest Payments, a Critical Economic Review)', **24** *Betriebs-Berater*, 1645-1655.

Wehrt, Klaus (1991c), 'Die Qualitätshaftung des Verkäufers aus Ökonomischer Sicht (The Quality Liability of Sellers from an Economic Point of View)', in Ott, Claus and Schäfer, Hans-Bernd (eds), *Ökonomische Probleme des Zivilrechts*, Berlin, Springer, 235-259.

Wehrt, Klaus (1992), 'Das Ökonomische Vertragsmodell, Theorie und Anwendung (The Economic Model of Contract, Theory and Application)', **4** *Kritische Vierteljahresschrift für Gesetzgebung und Rechtswissenschaft*, 359-373.

Wehrt, Klaus (1993), 'Gewährleistungsregeln als Instrument der Informationsübertragung (Rules of Warranty as an Instrument of Information Transfer)', **1** *Zeitschrift für Wirtschafts- und Sozialwissenschaften*, 77-113.

Wehrt, Klaus (1994a), 'Zur Zinsfälligkeitsabrede, die eine unterjährige Zahlungsverpflichtung enthält, Anmerkung zum BGH-Urteil vom 5.10.93 - XI ZR 35/93 (An Interest Clause which Fixes the Periods for the Interest Payments, a Remark to a Judgement of the German Supreme Court)', **3** *Juristenzeitung*, 155-157.

Wehrt, Klaus (1994b), 'Die wettbewerbliche Funktion transparenter Zinsfälligkeitsabreden (The Competitive Function of Transparent Interest Clauses)', **2** *Zeitschrift für Bankrecht und Bankwirtschaft*, 161-171.

Wehrt, Klaus (1997), 'Vorfälligkeitsentschädigung und Wettbewerb, Mögliche Wettbewerbliche Auswirkungen der Rechtsprechung zur vorzeitigen Ablösung von Festzinsdarlehen (Possible Competitive Effects of the Jurisdiction According the Prepayment of Mortgages)', **1** *Zeitschrift für Bankrecht und Bankwirtschaft*.

Weise, Peter (1991), 'Effizienz und Menschenwürde - Ein Gegensatz? Anmerkungen zu einer Kontroverse zwischen Ott/Schäfer und Fezer (Efficiency and Human Dignity - a Contradiction? Remarks on a Controversy between Ott, Schäfer and Fezer)', in Ott, C. and Schäfer, H.-B. (eds), *Ökonomische Probleme des Zivilrechts. Beiträge zur Ökonomischen Analyse des Rechts. Heidelberg/New York, Springer 1991*, Springer, 18-34.

Weise, Peter (1994), 'Property Rights und Urheberschutz, Kommentar (Property Rights and Copyright, Comment)', in Ott, Claus and Schäfer, Hans-Bernd (eds), *Okonomische Analyse der rechtlichen Organisation von Innovationen*, Tübingen, Mohr, 115-125.

Weise, Peter (1996a), 'Verhaltenskoordination durch soziale Normen und Kräfte (Co-ordination of Behaviour by Social Norms and Forces)', in Priddat, B. P. and Wegner, G. (eds), *Zwischen Institution und Evolution. Neue Ansätze in der Ökonomischen Theorie*, Marburg, Metropolis, 187-209.

Weise, Peter (1996b), 'Insolvenzbewältigung durch Reorganisation, Kommentar zu dem gleichnamigenBeitrag von H. Eidenmüller (Handling of Insolvency by Reorganization, Comment)', in Ott, C. and Schäfer, H.-B. (ed), *Effiziente Verhaltenssteuerung und Kooperation im Zivilrecht*, Tübingen, Mohr, 214-221.

Weise, Peter (1996c), 'Peter, Reform von Planungs- und Genehmigungsverfahren, Kommentar zu dem gleichnamigen Beitrag von K.-W. Schatz (Reform of Planning and Permission Procedures, Comment)', in Schenk, Karl-Ernst, Schmidtchen, Dieter and Streit, Manfred E. (eds), *Vom Hoheitsstaat zum Konsensualstaat, Neue Formen der*

Kooperation zwischen Staat und Privaten Jahrbuch für Neue Politische Ökonomie 15, Tübingen, Mohr, 38-42.

Weise, Peter and Eger, Thomas (1990a), 'Innovation, Imitation und Patentrecht im Systemvergleich (Innovation, Imitation, and Patent Law in Different Economic Systems)', in Gramatzki, H.-E., Klinger, F. and Nutzinger, H.G. (eds), *Wissenschaft, Technik und Arbeit, Innovationen in Ost und West*, Kassel, VWL-inform, 107-133.

Weise, Peter and Eger, Thomas (1990b), 'Normen als gesellschaftliche Ordner (Norms as Social Co-ordination Parameters)', **8** *Ökonomie und Gesellschaft*, 65-111.

Weise, Peter and Eger, Thomas (1995), 'Die Evolution von Normen aus Unordnung, Ein Synergetisches Modell (The Evolution of Norms out of Disorder, A Synergetic Model)', **11** *Ökonomie und Gesellschaft*, 192-209.

Weise, Peter, Eger, Thomas, Brandes, Wolfgang and Kraft, M. (1993), *Neue Mikroökonomie* (New Microeconomics), Heidelberg, Physica.

Weise, Peter, Nutzinger, Hans G. and Eger, Thomas (1993), 'Eine Ökonomische Analyse der Mitbestimmten Unternehmung (An Economic Analysis of Codetermined Enterprise)', in Ott, C. and Schäfer, H.-B. (eds), *Ökonomische Analyse des Unternehmensrechts*, Heidelberg, Physica, 78-116.

Weth, Stefan (1996), 'Die Justiz - ein ungeliebtes Kind? (Jurisdiction - an Unloved Kid?)', *Neue Juristische Wochenschrift*, 2427 ff.

Weth, Stefan (1997), 'Prämien für gute Richter (Bonuses for Good Judges)', in Prütting, H. and Rüssmann, H. (eds), *Verfahrensrecht am Ausgang des 20. Jahrhunderts. Festschrift für Gerhard Lüke zum 70. Geburtstag, München 1997*, München, 961 ff.

Wieckhorst, Thomas (1994), *Recht und Oekonomie des Produkthaftungsgesetzes. Eine an den recthlichen Zielvorgaben und am Effizienzkriterium orientierte Analyse* (Law and Economics of the Product Liability Law. Legal Goals and Efficiency), Baden-Baden, Nomos.

Willeke, Frans-Ullrich (1980), *Wettbewerbspolitik* (Competition Policy), Tübingen, Mohr.

Witt, Ulrich (1988), 'Eine individualistische Theorie der Entwicklung Ökonomischer Institutionen (An Individualistic Theory of the Evolution of Economic Institutions)', **9** *Jahrbuch für Neue Politische Ökonomie*, 72-95.

Witt, Ulrich (1993), 'Multiple Gleichgewichte und kritische Massen - das Problem der Verfassungstreue (Multiple Equilibria, Critical Masses, and the Problem of Constitutional Loyality)', **14** *Jahrbuch für Neue Politische Ökonomie*, 229-246.

Wohlgemuth, M. (1991), 'Ordnungspolitische Anmerkungen zum 'Einigungsvertrag' (Constitutional Political Remarks on the 'Einigungsvertrag')', **70** *Wirtschaftsdienst*, 507-511.

Wohlgemuth, M. and Mussler, Werner (1995), 'Institutionen im Wettbewerb - Ordnungstheoretische Anmerkungen zum Systemwettbewerb in Europa (Institutional Competition)', in Peter Oberender and Manfred E. Streit (eds), *Europas Arbeitsmärkte im Integrationsprozeß*, Baden-Baden, Nomos, 9-45.

Wolff, Birgitta (1996a), 'Public-Private Partnerships', in Schenk, Karl-Ernst, Schmidtchen, Dieter and Streit, Manfred E. (eds), *Vom Hoheitsstaat zum Konsensualstaat, Neue Formen der Kooperation zwischen Staat und Privaten Jahrbuch für Neue Politische Ökonomie 15*, Tübingen, Mohr.

Wolff, Birgitta (1996b), *Trittbrettfahren im System sozialer Sicherung, Contribution to the Symposium Öffentliches Recht als ein Gegenstand Ökonomischer Forschung, 10.-12.10.1996 in Wünneberg* (Free-Riding in the Social Security System), Tübingen, Mohr.

Wortmann, Gerhard (1983), *Geplanter Produkt-Verschleiß als Rechtsproblem* (Intended Wear as a Legal Problem), Frankfurt.

0335
LAW AND ECONOMICS IN GREECE

Aristides N. Hatzis
University of Chicago Law School

Abstract

In Greece there is no established discipline of law and economics yet, if by this we mean a coherent body of work and a group of scholars dedicated to its promotion. There are only some recent and hesitant attempts by some scholars to introduce law and economics to Greek legal bibliography and a number of dispersed studies. However, the substantial body of work of an eminent social scientist and the first samples of writing by young scholars, combined with the first informal courses at a graduate level and the first references to law and economics in textbooks, bear promise of a brighter future.
JEL classification: A11, A23, K00, K10
Keywords: Greek Legal Scholarship, Economic Law, Law and Economics: Teaching and Scholarship, Graduate Studies.

1. Introduction

Economic analysis of law (EAL) is at a nascent level in Greece. It is virtually unknown to the great majority of lawyers and economists (including academics), who think of it as something as exotic and elusive as sociology of law (which is established as a course in the three public law schools of Athens, Thessaloniki and Komotini). For some lawyers, economic analysis of law (the term 'law and economics' is not employed) is similar to economic law, an all-encompassing term for the sum of commercial, banking, company, and so on, laws. For economists, EAL is equally vague, perhaps something they hear about in a conference, although most of them are familiar with the Coase theorem and theories of regulation. There is definitely no Greek EAL, if by this we mean a coherent body of work and a relevant group of scholars dedicated to its promotion.

However, there is a small number of scholars who have, over the last few years, begun to publish articles (mainly introductory ones) presenting the new theory to Greek lawyers and economists. Most of them have studied law in the United States and have become familiar with the movement-turned-discipline there. A great number of Greek legal scholars have conducted their doctoral research in Germany and even those who have written their theses in Greece have used mostly German bibliography. This is largely the result of the heavy influence of German law on Greek law (especially civil law). As a result, the Greek scholars with a doctorate from a common law country (especially from the United States) are very few in number. This is the basic reason for the embryonic status of law and economics in Greece.

2. Research in Law and Economics

Many papers have been published from 1960 to the early 1980s studying the relationship between law and economics and emphasizing the need for a broader collaboration. These papers were often overly theoretical, without potential application to actual legal problems and with no discussion of the developments in the Anglo-Saxon legal world. The discussion revolved around the work of Weber, Stammler and Marx, with some references to the 'socialization' of the economy after World War II (particularly the excellent papers by Mantzoufas, 1960; Karakantas, 1973; Rokas, 1980, all three professors of civil law in economic departments, Loukopoulos, 1962, as well as Liakopoulos, 1982, for a typical Marxist, critical-legal approach). Another extensively discussed problem was state intervention in the economy and the ensuing constitutional issues from the antinomies created in a mixed economic system (see Manitakis, 1975; Stathopoulos, 1981; Gemtos, 1990b). Finally, a number of legal scholars have treated purely economic problems with the intention of informing their colleagues of parallel developments in another social science (see in particular the brief discussion of the Laffer curve by Rodios, 1986, and the excellent survey by Gavrielidou, 1990, of the economic literature on taxation and the work of four scholars: Milton Friedman, Nicholas Kaldor, Firmin Oules and Maurice Allais). The scholar who first introduced EAL to the Greek legal world is the former Rector of the University of Athens, Prof. Petros Gemtos. Gemtos (a specialist in the philosophy and methodology of science and a holder of two doctorates, one in law and another in economics from the University of Tübingen) is also the central figure of Greek EAL. Prof. Gemtos was not only the first Greek EAL scholar, but made original contributions, presented almost simultaneously with the expansion of EAL in the USA in the early 1970s.

In his first and seminal EAL paper (Gemtos, 1976) on the legal problems created by hyperinflation (in constitutional, tax and contract law), he not only studied a legal problem using the tools of economics, but he extensively discussed the usefulness of positive economics to the analysis and solution of legal problems (see p. 833 for some insightful remarks and also pp. 836-846). This paper was an exemplary application of his research program (formulated and expounded as early as 1974, see Gemtos, 1974) for the association of legal science with positive social science. In a second endeavor to treat legal problems under an economic prism, Gemtos (1990b) dealt with consumer protection legislation as a necessary restraint of economic freedom. He also briefly criticized the proliferation of products liability legislation as leading to inefficient results that can harm consumers.

In a series of publications (see Gemtos, 1988, 1990a, 1991, 1998 and Gemtos, 1995 for a definitive treatment of the issues discussed in the previous articles), he elaborated extensively on the relations between law and economics, and especially between legal reasoning and economic methodology, not only critically presenting the literature see especially Gemtos (1998), but also offering considerable original insights.

Gemtos's theoretical and methodological views on the interdisciplinary cooperation between law and economics are applied to his major contribution to EAL. In an article on the 'property rights' theory he critically introduces the older institutional theories of economics and the new institutional theory of property rights (in his view, the most successful attempt to incorporate institutional analysis in economics). By supplying neoclassical economics with the necessary concept of transaction costs that replaces the unrealistic assumption of perfect information, new institutional economics lend a more realistic nature to economic analysis and facilitate its use by lawyers and other social scientists who have to work with complex actual situations.

Gemtos identifies himself clearly with the neo-institutional school, but with some reservations rooted in the relevant discourse taking place in Germany. He places the theory of property rights at the central stage of his EAL, giving 'property rights' a broader meaning than the one they have in both economics and law. He uses the word 'praxeological rights' to include the 'right to damage someone or something' (which of course might produce the obligation for restitution), the opposite 'right to defend oneself from the damage', and so on. Every good is accompanied by a bundle of praxeological rights, not restricted to the well-known rights recognized by property law (Gemtos, 1988, pp. 1201-1202).

Prof. Gemtos remains the leader in the field, not only because of his writings, but also because of his active support for the institutionalization of EAL at the University of Athens. In 1995 he published the first textbook on law and economics in Greek. It consists of two volumes (the second one is forthcoming) and its purpose is twofold: to introduce basic economic concepts (including macroeconomics) to lawyers and law-students and to present EAL (and the contemporary economic analysis of institutions in the broad sense) to the Greek legal world see also Gemtos (1998).

Besides Gemtos, and at the same time with him, a number of scholars specializing in economic or commercial law and with graduate studies mainly in the USA, published introductory EAL articles. The first of these articles was a general treatment of the relation between law and economics by a commercial law scholar, Ioannis Rokas (1980), who completed his graduate studies in Germany (Berlin) and now teaches at the Athens University of Economics and Business. Rokas, like Gemtos, draws heavily upon German bibliography for the relations between economy and law and briefly discusses the new 'field' of EAL. Although his intention was not to present EAL as a separate discipline or school, his target was the lack of communication between law and economics. These two disciplines are related internally to such an unusual degree that it creates problems to both lawyers and economists who deal mainly with the same object. Rokas calls for a 'standing interdisciplinary contact', citing a number of examples where the convergence of law and economics is inevitable. Rokas defends the 'old' law and economics with clarity and zeal.

This lack of communication between lawyers and economists is bridged temporarily by the first and only attempt in Greek legal scholarship (after Gemtos, 1976, but also see Delivanes, 1954, for an early treatment of a legal issue by an economist) of Phanes Christophorou (1986), a lawyer with the European Commission (LL.M. from Harvard), to use economic analysis in treating a legal issue, that is antitrust law (what else!). His interpretation of Greek antitrust law is informed by an extensive critical discussion of the economic literature (*ibid.*, pp. 898-909) with the purpose of influencing the implementation of the law (pp. 900, 906-907) (Similarly, see the brief discussion of the economics of crime by Calliope Spinellis, 1992, a criminal law professor with a doctorate from the University of Chicago).

Michalis Tsibris (1989) was the first to present an up-to-date introduction to EAL. His paper consists of a fair presentation and discussion of the leading theories and basic concepts and discusses various examples from torts and property law (with an extensive reference to the Coase theorem). Tsibris has many reservations concerning the use of efficiency as a criterion and the compatibility of the two discourses, and although he is outright negative to the normative EAL, he is decisively positive toward the use of economic analysis by lawyers. Tsibris (a commercial law scholar) holds an LL.M. degree from Harvard, where the influence of Frank Michelman on his thinking has proven greater than that of Steven Shavell, as this article reveals.

A similar introductory paper has been written by another American-educated scholar, Thanos Papaioannou (LL.M. and doctorate on labor law from the University of Pennsylvania). This article is the most typical of the attitude of Greek legal scholars (especially the ones specializing in 'economic' law), who are receptive to the use of economics by lawyers, but at the same time quite suspicious of both the unintended and the intended effects of the application of economic theories to what they perceive as the coherent logical construct of Greek law. The title of the article is telling and, starting from the first introductory paragraph, Papaioannou (1991) informs the reader that EAL is a movement parallel and congenial to the wave of the reappraisal of free-market ideas by economists and the dominance of New Right ideas in the USA, personified by President Reagan and the judges he appointed to the federal courts. However, Papaioannou is generally favorable to EAL, especially when applied to contract law, commercial law or torts. Notwithstanding, he is critical of the economics of crime and especially of any attempt to attack individual rights on economic grounds.

In the same vein with the three aforementioned articles, we should consider the work of Prof. Phaedon Kozyris (1991). Kozyris, then professor at Ohio State University School of Law (with graduate studies at Chicago and Cornell and a doctorate from Pennsylvania) is now Professor of International Law at the University of Thessaloniki. This article is a critical evaluation of the prevalent schools of legal philosophy in the United States, including a presentation of EAL of the 'free-market Chicago School', as he mentions several times in the text. He emphasizes the political elements in the law and economics discourse, discussing very briefly (and with a faultfinding mind) some EAL proposals. In spite of his hesitation, he acknowledges the usefulness of economic analysis as a 'tool and method for the revision of the law'. In a more recent paper, Kozyris (1996) takes a more positive stand towards EAL (pp. 58-68, and especially pp. 73-74), characterizing it as 'innovative and fruitful'.

The last and most recently published article is also the most friendly towards EAL, not surprisingly, since the author, Nicholas Georgakopoulos (a Professor at the University of Connecticut Law School with graduate studies and a doctorate from Harvard) is a well-known legal scholar in the USA with significant work on EAL. Georgakopoulos wrote his article because of the 'minimal' impact of EAL in Greece. He deplores the reception of critical legal theory by Greek constitutional scholars and holds that, if it is generalized, it can destroy Greek legal scholarship as long as it is not offset by a parallel dissemination of EAL that will reinforce the scientific character of legal science. Georgakopoulos emphasizes the success of EAL in the USA and its pragmatic character, urging for the incorporation of EAL in law school curricula.

Georgakopoulos is also the translator of Richard Posner's *Cardozo: A Study in Reputation*, in Greek (Posner, 1997). Given the scarcity of translations of foreign legal works in Greek (particularly from the Anglo-Saxon world), this translation is important not only for the introduction of the Greek legal world to the mechanisms of common law by two famous American judges, but also for the introduction to EAL and Richard Posner's recent work. Georgakopoulos (1997a, 1997b) in two extensive notes accompanying the lively translation, extensively discusses relevant philosophical and doctrinal issues but also the development of Posner's legal theory in the direction of a singular 'liberal' pragmatism.

The original contributions to EAL are analogous to its influence on Greek legal scholarship. With the exception of the work by Gemtos (see above), the original work is meager. There are only two young scholars specializing in EAL:

Panagiotis Evangelopoulos, an economist (holding a doctorate degree from the University of Athens, under the supervision of Prof. Gemtos) who is working in the field of property rights theory; and Aristides Hatzis, a lawyer, who is studying the economics of contract law at the University of Chicago, under the supervision of Judge Richard Posner. However, their approaches are disparate. Evangelopoulos is an economist with an interest in political philosophy. His principal work (1997) is in no way an application of property rights theory towards the study of Greek property law (or any particular property law for that matter), but rather a philosophical examination of the institution of property. Evangelopoulos constructs a theory of property rights that is more in tune with neoclassical theory and influenced by the libertarian theories of justice (Nozick and Buchanan) and free-market economics (Austrian but Chicago school as well) to a greater degree than the majority of works in this tradition.

This becomes clear in a piece that is a statement of his philosophical position and his methodological stance (Evangelopoulos, 1996) as well as in an insightful recent article, where he develops the argument that all kinds of rights (even basic human rights) are subsumed under the hyper-set of property rights. Property rights are mainly allocated by majority rule via state intervention and by independent individuals via market mechanism. If the former is dominant, then the political process has the upper hand; if the latter is dominant, then a spontaneous order emerges. Property rights must be determined mainly by the market and away from state intervention, since the former combines rationality and liberty, while the latter inefficiency and coercion (Evangelopoulos, 1998). On the other hand, Hatzis (the author of this survey) is, perhaps, the only adherent of EAL in the narrow sense. The basic goal of his thesis (1998b) is the construction of an economic theory of Greek contract law, which will help in evaluating the existing legal rules in terms of efficiency, in creating legal rules that are more consistent with the objectives of contract law and consequently in solving a number of allegedly 'unresolved' problems of Greek contract law theory. The comparative study (in Greek and American contract law) of contract formation, unconscionability, commercial impracticability and liquidated damages under the prism of EAL leads to some useful conclusions, not only towards the efficient solution of the aforementioned much-discussed problems, but also towards the problem of the existence of an inherent economic logic in civil law, similar to that of common law (see Hatzis, 1997, for a summary of his thesis and also Hatzis ,1997c, on the comparative efficiency of civil and common law).

Hatzis' contribution to Greek bibliography is of a more introductory nature. In an article published in 1991, he presents the life and work of Ronald Coase, with a detailed critical presentation of the Coase theorem. He did the same in Hatzis (1998a) for the work of Mancur Olson. In a lengthy paper, Hatzis (1996) introduces the 'rational choice' revolution and the new schools that use neoclassical microeconomic methodological tools for the study of political science, sociology and legal theory. He examines the various consequentialist libertarian philosophical approaches to society and institutions, and explores the relation that each of them maintains to the particular elements of rational choice theory (see also Hatzis 1993, 1999a and 1999b for similar introductory papers and surveys in English).

Another young scholar whose work is relevant is Aspasia Tsaoussis-Hatzis (1999a), a sociologist of law whose work on the economic consequences of divorce draws heavily on the theories of Nobel laureate Prof. Gary Becker (who is also the supervisor of her thesis (1999b) at the University of Chicago Law School) on the economics of the family.

3. Education

The discussion thus far has shown that Greek EAL is a newly-emergent field, still taking hesitant infantile steps. There is a small number of scholars who work in the field (or who at least have an interest in the field), largely due to the nature of 'technical doctrinalism' that characterizes Greek legal theory and the absence of institutionalization. It is extremely difficult to expect a change of attitude on the part of the great majority of Greek lawyers (even scholars) who are both formalists and positivists. Nevertheless, some recent developments, such as the founding of the School of Judges in Thessaloniki (that emphasizes the study of social science), as well as the increasing specialization and the tendency for the continuation of legal studies at the graduate level displayed by Greek lawyers, are promising signs for the future.

Starting from the academic year 1995-1996, Nikolaos Intzessiloglou (Professor of Sociology of Law at the University of Thessaloniki and the Greek coordinator of the Erasmus Programme in Law and Economics) has dedicated the second year of the graduate course of Sociology of Law to EAL. In collaboration with Aristides Hatzis, he introduced the basic concepts of EAL with a parallel discussion of philosophical, epistemological and methodological issues. The readings consisted mainly of Cento Veljanovski's *The Economics of Law: An Introductory Text* (London, IEA, 1990) and also included a number of introductory articles in English, French and Greek, and notes prepared by Hatzis (1997a). The first courses of EAL in Greece were very successful, mainly because they were addressed to graduate students (all of them being lawyers or judges) with a manifested interest in jurisprudence (most of them had sociology of law as their major). After the completion of the course, many graduate students showed a particular interest in continuing their studies in EAL.

Prof. Intzessiloglou, as the founder and editor of *Aissymnetes* (an interdisciplinary law journal) has promoted the discussion on EAL, dedicating the sixth volume of the journal to this discussion (see Evangelopoulos, 1996; Hatzis, 1996; Reynolds, 1996). This symposium includes an article by the Professor of the University of Macedonia Vaios Lazos (1996) on the economics of crime. Lazos, an economist who is not at all influenced by EAL or the work of Gary Becker, comes to essentially similar conclusions.

4. Prospects

The prospects for EAL in Greece are more than favorable. In the following years, the first special chairs for EAL are expected to be established by the Universities of Athens and Thessaloniki. There is already a number of graduate students with a great interest in the field and the number of publications is steadily growing.

But the most significant development is the use of economic analysis by mainstream legal scholars. In 1991, Prof. Panagiotis Papanikolaou, a contract law scholar at the University of Athens, published a remarkable monograph on freedom of contracts, using the findings of EAL in his discussion (Magoulas and Jost, 1985, preceded him but they are professors in Germany). His book (together with all the aforementioned work) managed to familiarize the Greek legal world with EAL. As a result, in recent textbooks by some of the most prominent civil and commercial law professors at the University of Athens, there were many references to EAL (see for example Michales Stathopoulos, *General Law of Obligations*, 2nd edn, Athens-Komotini, Ant. N. Sakkoulas, 1993, pp. 11-13, Leonidas Georgakopoulos, *Handbook of Commercial Law*, vol. 1.1, 2nd edn, Athens, P. Sakkoulas, 1995 and Apostolos Georgiades, *General Principles of Civil Law*, Athens-Komotini, Ant. N. Sakkoulas, 2nd edn, 1997, pp. 67-68, all in Greek). This is more important than it appears. Greek legal scholars are hostile to almost any interdisciplinary or philosophical treatment of private law. These scholars present (particularly in textbooks, not treatises) EAL, and EAL alone, as a very interesting (but also dangerous if misused) theory of adjudication and interpretation.

The much-needed next step for economic analysis of law in Greece is its full institutionalization and its extensive use for the analysis of legal problems. However, such a prospect seems quite remote today.

Acknowledgments

I would like to express my appreciation to Gerrit De Geest, Panos Evangelopoulos, Petros Gemtos, Nicholas Georgakopoulos, Nikolaos

Intzessiloglou, Aspasia Tsaoussis-Hatzis and an anonymous referee, whose comments on the first draft of this paper were very helpful.

Bibliography on Law and Economics in Greece (0335)

Christoforou, Phanes (1986), 'Prostasia tou Antagonismou kai Oikonomike Analyse sta Plaisia tou Nomou 703/77 (Protection of Market Competition and Economic Analysis under Law 703/77)', **6** *Ellenike Epitheorese Europaikou Dikaiou*, 879-927.

Delivanes, D.I. (1954), 'Ai Oikonomikai Synepeiai tou Enoikiostasiou (The Economic Consequences of Rent Control)', **21** *Ephemeris ton Hellenon Nomikon*, 1106-1111.

Evangelopoulos, Panagiotis (1996), 'E Analyse ton Periousiakon Dikaiomaton kai e Ideologia tes Eleutheres Agoras (Property Rights Analysis and Free-Market Ideology)', **6** *Aissymnetes*.

Evangelopoulos, Panagiotis (1997), *Oikonomike Analyse ton Periousiakon Dikaiomaton kai o Mechanismos tes Agoras (Economic Analysis of Property Rights and the Market Mechanism)*, PhD Thesis, University of Athens, Dept. of Economics. Reprinted as monograph: Athens, Libro, 1999.

Evangelopoulos, Panagiotis (1998), 'O Kanon tes Pleiopsefias kai o Prosdiorismos ton Dikaiomaton (The Majority Rule and the Stipulation of Rights)', **1** *Episteme kai Koinonia*, 69-81.

Gavrielidou, Alexandra A. (1990), 'Enallaktikes Protaseis sto Phoro Eisodematos (Alternative Proposals to the Income Tax)', **38** *Nomiko Vema*, 382-400.

Gemtos, Petros A. (1974), 'E Provlematike ton Axiologikon Kriseon stis Koinonikes Epistemes (The Problem of Normative Judgments in the Social Sciences)', **4** *Philosophia*, 120-136.

Gemtos, Petros A. (1976), 'Antimetopises tou Plethorismou os Oikonomikon kai Nomikon Provlema. Sygchronos Symvole eis ten Diereunesin ton Themeliakon Scheseon ton Pragmatologikon kai ton Kanonistikon Epistemon (The Treatment of Inflation as an Economic and Legal Problem. Contemporary Contribution to the Examination of the Fundamental Relations between the Positive and Normative Sciences)', **30** *Harmenopoulos*, 830-846.

Gemtos, Petros A. (1988), 'Methodologika Programmata sten Oikonomike kai te Nomike Episteme kai to Provlema tes Diepistemonikes tous Synergasias (Methodological Programs in Economics and Legal Science and the Problem of their Interdisciplinary Collaboration)', **36** *Nomiko Vema*, 1192-1202, reprinted in (1990), **39** *Cyprus Law Review*, 4627-4643.

Gemtos, Petros A. (1990a), 'Law and Economics: Methodological Problems in their Interdisciplinary Cooperation', in Nicolacopoulos, Pantelis D. (ed.), *Greek Studies in the Philosophy and History of Science (Boston Studies in the Philosophy of Science, vol. 121)*, Dordrecht, Kluwer, 239-250.

Gemtos, Petros A. (1990b), 'Oikonomike Eleutheria kai Prostasia tou Katanalote se mia Sygxrone Demokratike Koinonia (Economic Freedom and Consumer Protection in a Contemporary Democratic Society)', **16** *Syntagma*, 19-29.

Gemtos, Petros A. (1991), 'Thesmikes Analyseis sten Oikonomike: E Theoria ton Praxiakon Dikaiomaton (Institutional Analyses in Economics: The Property Rights Theory)', **4** *Aissymnetes*, 27-48.

Gemtos, Petros A. (1995), *Oikonomika kai Dikaio: Oikonomika gia Nomikous, tomos A: Methodologika kai Oikonomika Themelia* (Law and Economics: Economics for Lawyers, vol. I: Methodological and Economic Foundations), Athens-Komotini, Ant. N. Sakkoulas Publications.

Gemtos, Petros A. (1998), 'Oi Theoretikes Vaseis tes Oikonomikes Analyses tou Dikaiou (The Theoretical Bases of Economic Analysis of Law)', **46** *Nomiko Vema*.

Georgakopoulos, Nikos L. (1995), 'Peri Tmematikou Daneismou apo ten Amerikanike Nomike Skepse (On the Partial Borrowing from the American Legal Thought)', **43** *Nomiko Vema*, 799-807.

Georgakopoulos, Nikos L. (1997a), 'O *Cardozo* tou Posner san Eisagoge sten Amerikanike Nomike Skepse (Posner's *Cardozo* as an Introduction to American Legal Theory)', in Posner (1997), i-xi.

Georgakopoulos, Nikos L. (1997b), 'Kritiko Semeioma: O Pragmatismos tou Posner (Critical Note: Posner's Pragmatism)', in Posner (1997), 175-198.

Hatzis, Aristides N. (1991), 'Ronald H. Coase: Nobel Oikonomikon 1991 (Ronald H. Coase: Nobel Laureate in Economics, 1991)', **68** *Epikentra*, 77-84.

Hatzis, Aristides N. (1993), 'Comments on Bertrand Lemmenicier's paper 'Social Justice and its Controversies', **4** *Journal des Economistes et des Etudes Humaines*, 263-268.

Hatzis, Aristides N. (1996), ''Neofileleutherismos', Dikaio kai Oikonomike Analyse ton Thesmon: Eisagoge ste Melete ton Neon Oikonomikon Theorion gia to Dikaio, ten Koinonia kai ten Politike (The so-called 'Neo-Liberalism', the Law and the Economic Analysis of Institutions: Introduction to the Study of the New Economic Theories on Law, Society and Politics)', **6** *Aissymnetes*.

Hatzis, Aristides N. (1997a), *Eisagoge sten Oikonomike Analyse tou Dikaiou* (Introduction to the Economic Analysis of Law), Aristotle University of Thessaloniki School of Law and Economics, Department of History, Philosophy and Sociology of Law.

Hatzis, Aristides N. (1997b), *Krise tou Dikaiou e Krise tes Theorias tou? Prolegomena se mia Oikonomike Theoria tou Dikaiou ton Symvaseon* (A Crisis of Law or a Crisis of its Theory? Prolegomena of an Economic Theory of Contract Law), working paper presented in a workshop under the auspices of Panteios University.

Hatzis, Aristides N. (1997c), *The Absence of Theory: Common vs. Civil Contract Law*, paper presented at the XIVth Annual Conference of the European Association of Law and Economics, held at Barcelona, September 4-6, 1997.

Hatzis, Aristides N. (1998a), 'Mancur Olson, Jr. (1932-1998)', **1** *Episteme kai Koinonia*, 195-202.

Hatzis, Aristides N. (1998b), *An Economic Theory of Greek Contract Law*, PhD Thesis, University of Chicago Law School.

Hatzis, Aristides N. (1999a), 'Crime', in O'Hara, Phillip (ed.), *Encyclopedia of Political Economy*, London, Routledge, Vol. I, 163-166.

Hatzis, Aristides N. (1999b), 'Rent-Seeking and Vested Interests', in O'Hara, Phillip (ed.), *Encyclopedia of Political Economy*, London, Routledge, Vol. II, 974-977.

Karakantas, Stylianos (1973), 'Oikonomia kai Dikaion (Law and Economics)', **27** *Harmenopoulos*, 257-265.

Kozyris, Phaedon I. (1991), 'Treis Provlematismoi sten Amerikanike Theoria tou Dikaiou (Three Deliberations in American Jurisprudence)', **39** *Nomiko Vema*, 715-728.

Kozyris, Phaedon I. (1996), 'Protaseis Dianemetikes Dikaiosynes sto 'Telos tes Istorias': Ta Kyria Erotemata me Apla Logia (Proposals of Distributive Justice in the 'End of History': Basic Questions Made Easy)', **3** *Kritike Epitheorese*, 23-81.

Lazos, Vaios (1996), 'E Kampyle Adiaforias enos Eglematos (The Indifference Curve of a Crime)', **6** *Aissymnetes*.

Liakopoulos, Thanases (1982), 'Dikaio kai Oikonomia (Law and Economics)', **2** *Dikaio & Politike*, 111-133.

Loukopoulos, Andreas D. (1962), 'Emporikon Dikaion kai oi Neoi Prosanatolismoi tes Oikonomias (Commercial Law and the New Directions of Economy)', **29** *Ephemeris ton Hellenon Nomikon*, 353-362.

Magoulas, Georgios and Fritz, Jost (1985), 'Oikonomike Analyse tou Dikaiou. - Provlemata ton Katanalotikon Pistoseon se Allodapous Ergazomenous kai Symvole sten Ermeneia tes § 138 GermAK (Problems of Consumer Credit to Foreign Employees and a Contribution to the Interpretation of § 138 of the German Civil Code)', **6** *Scientific Review of the Thessaloniki Bar Association*, 203-217.

Manitakis, Antonios (1975), *L'antinomie entre la liberté du commerce et de l'industrie et la régulation administrative de l'économie (en droit belge et en droit français)*, Bruxelles, Centre Interuniversitaire de Droit Public.

Mantzoufas, Georgios A. (1960), 'Oikonomikon Dikaion (Economic Law)', in *Oikomike kai Logistike Egkyklopedeia* (Encyclopedia of Economics and Accounting), Athens.

Papaioannou, Thanos (1991), 'E Oikonomike Analyse tou Dikaiou: Mia Endiaferousa alla kai Epikindyne Theoria (Economic Analysis of Law: An Interesting but Dangerous Theory)', **4** *Aissymnetes*, 51-65.

Papanikolaou, Panagiotis A. (1991), *Peri ton Orion tes Prostateutikes Paremvaseos tou Dikaste ste Symvase: Pros mia Genike Theoria Peri Katachreseos tes Symvatikes Eleutherias* (On the Boundaries of the Paternalistic Intervention of the Judge to a Contract: Towards a General Theory on the Abuse of Freedom of Contracts), Athens-Komotini, Ant. N. Sakkoulas Publications.

Posner, Richard A. (1997), *O Dikastes Cardozo: Mia Melete tes Physes tes Phemes* (translation in Greek of Richard Posner's *Cardozo, A Study in Reputation,* Chicago: University of Chicago Press, 1991, by Nikos L. Georgakopoulos), Athens-Komotini, Ant. N. Sakkoulas.

Provopoulos, George and Zambaras, Athanassios (1991), 'Testing for Causality Between Government Spending and Taxation', **68** *Public Choice*, 277-282.

Reynolds, Noel B. (1996), 'Rule of Law in Legal and Economic Theory' (Translated in Greek and published in Aissymnetes, 6), in Kotsiris, L.E. (ed.), *Law at the Turn of the 20th Century*, Thessaloniki, Sakkoulas Publications, 355-374.

Rodios, Nikos D. (1986), 'E Kampyle tou Laffer e Peri tes Phthinousas Apodoseos tes Phorologias (The Laffer Curve or On the Diminishing Return of Taxation)', **53** *Ephemeris ton Hellenon Nomikon*, 216-218.

Rokas, Ioannis (1980), 'Oikonomike kai Nomike Episteme: Eisagogikes Paratereseis epi ton Scheseon Oikonomias kai Dikaiou (Economics and Legal Science: Introductory Remarks on the Relations between Economy and Law)', in Zepos, P., Rammos, G., Rokas, K. and Loukopoulos, A. (eds), *Afieroma eis Alexandron N. Tsirintanin* (Volume in Honor of Alexandros N. Tsirintanis), Athens-Komotini, Ant. N. Sakkoulas Publications, 317-347.

Spinellis, Calliope D. (1992), 'Victim-Oriented Crime Prevention through the Prism of the (New) School of Social Defense and the School of Economic Analysis of Law', in X (ed.), *Panegyrikos Tomos gia ta Eikosachrona tou Hellenikou Tmematos tes Diethnous Etairias Koinonikes Amynes* (Commemorative Volume for the Twenty Years of the Greek Section of the International Society of Social Defense), Thessaloniki.

Stathopoulos, Michales (1981), 'Oikonomike Eleutheria, Oikonomiko Systema kai Syntagma (Economic Freedom, Economic System and the Constitution)', **7** *Syntagma*, 517-532.

Symposium (1996), 'Oikonomike Analyse tou Dikaiou (Economic Analysis of Law)', **6** *Aissymnetes*.

Tsaoussis-Hatzis, Aspasia (1999a), 'Changes in Greek Marriage and Divorce Law: The Impact of the Family Law Reform of 1983', in Miller, Robin R. and Browning, Sandra Lee, *Till Death Do Us Part: A Multicultural Anthology on Marriage*, Greenwich: JAI Press.

Tsaoussis-Hatzis, Aspasia (1999b), *The Social and Economic Consequences of the Greek Divorce Law Reform of 1983*, PhD Thesis, University of Chicago Law School.

Tsibris, Michalis R. (1989), 'Oikonomike Analyse tou Dikaiou: To Epomeno Vema (Economic Analysis of Law: The Next Step)', **37** *Nomiko Vema*, 574-586.

0340
Law and Economics in Hungary

András Sajó and Kinga Pétervári
Central European University (Budapest) - Legal Studies

Abstract

This chapter describes the state of law and economics in Hungary in 1996. Its main conclusion is that little work has been done in this field. Earlier it was the socialist economic system which hindered the introduction of this sort of analysis. But - contrary to our expectations expressed in the 1992 precursor of this article - the creation of a market economy did not lead to the establishment of law and economics in Hungary as a side-effect. The main factors which prevented this were the nature of the Hungarian legal system and legal thinking and the rigid divisions within the academic system.
JEL classification: K00
Keywords: Hungarian Legal System, Research, Teaching, Hungarian Academic System

1. Introduction

As you will see below the numbers of items in the bibliography of this chapter is smaller than that of the 1992 list. The main reason for this is that we have decided to change the principle upon which the selection is based. When compiling the 1992 bibliography we construed law and economics in a very broad sense, which now seems to be far too broad. The reason why this broad construction seemed justified to us back then had to do with some promising starts at the ELTE Law School, for example the extra-curriculum seminars on law and economics in 1987 held by András Sajó, which are no longer available.

2. Past and Present Situation

In the 1970s and very early 1980s the non-conceptual, 'case-by-case oriented command market system' was often referred to. This term implies a softened planned economy, in which state enterprises have some degree of legally guaranteed autonomy in executing the central plans, as opposed to the strict command economy characteristic of the 1950s and early 1960s, in which the state exercises discretionary and direct control. However mild the system had gradually become, it was still in control of the economic regulations, thus leaving no room for considerations of efficiency analysis. Even though students of law had to study economics, the kind of economics they were exposed to was Marxist economic theory, the spirit of which is quite alien to that of law and economics.

After the fall of the communist regime, economic legislation got from the ground and an enormous number of new laws were introduced (for example the Company Act of 1988, the Income Tax Act, the VAT Act, and so on in 1989, and so on). This frenzy of economic legislation has of course given rise to serious theoretical reflections and the 1992 bibliography is the record of that. Certainly, some of that literature does not belong to law and economics proper, but it dealt with related topics and had the promise of developing into law and economics in a narrow sense. To put it briefly, it seemed to us then that the economic analysis-related legal literature of the late 1980s and early 1990s constituted the rudiments of a session study of law and economics. This expectation proved to be wrong.

The more recent literature, voluminous as it still is, shows little signs of the assimilation of the theoretical principles, explanatory models, argumentative strategies, methodological approaches, and so on characteristic of law and economics in its narrow sense. The most significant common feature of the Hungarian articles, comments and textbooks is that they focus on the mere interpretation of the new laws, the explanation of new legal institutions and the description of enforcing specific provisions. Because of that, new legal periodicals have been established in the past few years (for example Gazdaság és Jog, *Economy and Law*), which despite their inspiring titles show no inclination to apply the method of analysis of law and economics. We might have continued to construe law and economics broadly and put together a bibliography as long as (or even longer than) that of 1992, but this would have been thoroughly misleading.

3. Explanations for Lack of Success

Clearly, the application of the same principles of selection, which may have been charitable in 1992, would now be straightforwardly deceptive. At this juncture one may naturally inquire into the reasons of why the economics-related legal literature has failed to develop into an economic analysis of law. It seems that the main factors include the following:

(a) The predominance of traditional German legal thought in Hungarian legal thinking. It must be emphasised that this involves traditional German legal thought. Recent developments in German legal thinking incorporating law and economics approach are little known.

(b) Not only Hungarian legal thinking as such but the whole *Hungarian legal system* follows traditional German legal thought (even though it is just as heavily influenced by Roman law). Whereas the exact nature of the connection between law and economics and the Anglo-American legal system is still a question of dispute, it seems clear that it is difficult to adopt a mode of analysis when the circumstances are quite different from those under which it has usually been applied. So the differences between the Anglo-American and the Hungarian legal systems constitute a barrier, even if it is not an insurmountable one

(c) For historical reasons, Hungarian higher education has not provided people with a sufficient background in both law and economics to be able to conduct this sort of analysis. The university system, modelled after the Russian one, preferred relatively small, specialised units of higher education. As it happens, economics and law have ended up in different institutions. Since all other scholarly institutions have been organised along the same disciplinary boundaries as higher education, the institutional separation of law and economics has spread over the whole of Hungarian intellectual life. Therefore the interdisciplinary approach of law and economics not only has little scholarly support, it was virtually defined out of existence by the rigidity of the academic system.

Furthermore, lawyers have increasing difficulties with the increasingly mathematicised economic analysis of law. As a corollary, the lack of significant legal research in the field contributes to a great extent to the poor publication list in law.

4. Prospects

Even so it does not seem justified to conclude from all this that the chances of law and economics are meagre. Integration into the international community of legal scholars has increased and the Hungarian students of law are aware of the issues which have the focus of attention of the international community. A good example to that may be that there are more articles in English on law and economics now than in Hungarian. So, whereas five years ago the great majority of Hungarian scholars had not yet heard of law and economics, this is not the case any longer. The community of Hungarian legal scholars has a fairly good basic understanding of the basic issues and approaches associated with law and economics, which seems to provide a strong enough basis for the future development of law and economics research.

Bibliography on Law and Economics in Hungary (0340)

Ábel, István and Szakadát, László (1995), 'Csd a Piacgazdasági Átmenetben (Insolvency in the Transitional Economy)', **10** *Közgazdasági Szemle*, 942-954.

Berde Éva (1994), 'Közjavak és Potyautasok (Public Goods and Free Riders)', **5** *Közgazdasági Szemle*, 431-443.

Lendvai, Balázs and Nyíri, Viktor (1994), 'Az Üzlethelyiségek Bérleti Jogának Egyes Kérdései (Some Questions on Lease Rights of Retail Premises)', **12** *Jogtudományi Közlöny*, 498 ff.

Major, Éva (1994), 'Iparjogvédelem Gazdaságtana (Economics of Intellectual Property)', in X (ed.), *Iparjogvédelmi Kézikönyv* (Handbook of Intellectual Property), Budapest, Közgazdasági és Jogi Könyvkiadó, 188-197.

Mátyás, Antal (1996), *A Modern Közgazdaságtan Története* (History of Modern Economics), Budapest, Aula.

Mátyás, Antal (1996), 'A Hagyományos Közgazdaságtan Bírálata és Kutatási Körének Kiszélesítése az új Intézményi Iskola Képviseli Részérl (Criticism and Extension of the Scope of Research of Traditional Economics as Carried out by the Neoinstitutionalists)', **7-8** *Közgazdasági Szemle*, 614-628.

Szakadát, László (1991), 'A Tulajdonjogok Problémája a Bankrendszerben (Problems of Property Rights in the Banking System)', in X (ed.), *Ki Fizet a Végén?*, Budapest, MTA Közgazdaságtudományi Intézet.

Szakadát, László (1995), 'Ronald Coase és a Közgazdaságtan Módszertana (Ronald Coase and the Methodology of Economics)', **11** *Közgazdasági Szemle*, 1044-1051.

Urbán, László (1995), 'Közcélú Szabályozás Hatáselemzése Public Policy Elemzés (Efficiency Analysis of Public Policy (Public Policy Analysis))', **3** *Közgazdasági Szemle*, 270-278.

0345
Law and Economics in Italy

Roberto Pardolesi
University of Roma (Luiss)

Giuseppe Bellantuono
University of Trento

Abstract

Law and economics in Italy is still an underdeveloped subject. Despite the early contributions of the 1960s and 1970s, most Italian lawyers and economists have displayed a marked indifference towards the economic approach to law. After reviewing some initiatives which promise to foster the spread of law & economics, we show that the hindrances encountered by the economic analysis of law stem from a misconception of both the economic and the comparative method.
JEL classification: K0
Keywords: Law and economics, Italy, Comparative Law, Interdisciplinary Education.

1. Introduction

The origins and subsequent development of law and economics in Italy can be described as a history with some lights and many shadows. In the following sections we shall see that since the 1960s the economic approach to law has attracted increasing attention, but it has not succeeded becoming a prominent part of Italian legal doctrine. The second section briefly reviews the earliest Italian contributions to EAL and summarizes the debate on its transplantation to a civil law country. Sections 3 and 4 discuss the reasons why large sectors of the legal and economic profession have chosen not to follow the path that has proved so fruitful in the United States.

2. Italian Law and Economics Between the Past and the Future

At the same time as Ronald Coase and Guido Calabresi were working on their seminal articles, an Italian scholar, Pietro Trimarchi, published a pathbreaking book on strict liability (Trimarchi, 1961) entirely based on concepts such as the allocation of risks to the least cost insurer or recourse to strict liability to induce potential wrongdoers to adopt optimal precautions. A later article, also translated into German, applied the tools already employed in the field of tort law to breach of contract cases (Trimarchi, 1970).

These contributions marked the first appearance of EAL in Italy. However, they did not prompt an immediate reaction. It was not until the late 1970s that systematic EAL research and teaching began in Italy. Even at this late stage, moreover, the economic approach to law was largely confined to the margins of the legal profession.

Some years ago the spread of the economic approach to law in Italy was the subject of a detailed analysis by Ugo Mattei and Roberto Pardolesi (1991). The authors remarked that the hindrances encountered by the economic analysis of law stemmed, above all, from a misconception of both the economic and the comparative method.

With regard to the former, Mattei and Pardolesi stressed that Italian economists had devoted their energies mostly to the study of post-Keynesian economics. Yet, it is well known that the law and economics movement sprang from the development and revision of the neoclassical paradigm during the decades following the end of the Second World War. The choice of a different line of research was probably one of the factors that most seriously hampered the dialogue between lawyers and economists.

As far as the comparative method is concerned, Mattei and Pardolesi dismissed the claim that EAL is useless in civil law systems because of its American origin. To be sure, the great dichotomy between civil law and common law is still a distinctive feature of the Western legal tradition. Today, however, few scholars (if any) would be willing to reject the doctrines developed on the other side of the Atlantic because of fundamental differences in the American legal system. The phenomenon of legal transplants, which modern comparative studies have emphasised and explored (see for example, Watson, 1974; Sacco, 1991; Ewald, 1995) is the best evidence that each tradition borrows from the other when confronted with the same problems.

If common and civil lawyers are able to communicate in many fields, explanation is still required as to why, in the late 1990s, the economic analysis of law has still not gained widespread acceptance in Italian legal culture. In the following two sections we shall see that the answer probably differs between lawyers and economists. Both groups of social scientists may have been heavily influenced by EAL, but each chose not to cultivate the interaction between algebra and pandects. The reasons why lawyers and economists have been deaf to the lessons of Coase et al. shed light on the evolution of these two branches in Italy.

3. Why Italian Lawyers do not Listen

Lest we give a distorted portrayal of the Italian situation, we must immediately specify that recent years have witnessed a growing interest in the economic approach to law. As the Italian Bibliography makes clear, the number of authors applying the microeconomics categories to the study of legal problems is now much greater than it was in the recent past. Even more importantly, the subjects dealt with by these writings are highly diversified, ranging from classical antitrust themes to environmental issues to the market for works of art.

Other initiatives have been planned to foster the spread of EAL. Il Mulino, a prominent Italian publisher, is about to issue a journal entirely devoted to law and economics. This undertaking will be backed by a textbook on law and economics, presently being compiled, which should link with the Italian translation/adaptation of the second edition of the famous textbook by Cooter and Ulen. The purpose of the Italian version is to enable Italian students to grasp the main features of the economic approach to law through their application to the Italian legal system. However, the courses in comparative law and private law offered by the Law Faculties of Rome and Trento are already being taught with an eye to the concepts arising from law and economics. As further evidence of interest in this subject we may cite the law and economics meetings held in Siena in 1992 (see the papers collected by Mattei and Pulitini 1994) and 1996, attended by more than one hundred Italian lawyers and economists, and the conference organized in Milan in October 1995 with the joint participation of American and Italian lawyer-economists (see the papers by Monateri, 1995; Gambaro, 1996; Pardolesi, 1996).

Although these projects confirm the impression of lively debate, explanation is still required for the indifference displayed by most of the Italian legal doctrine (not to mention the courts). A host of reasons apparently hamper complete acceptance of the economic approach to law. None of them, however, is compelling.

To begin with, lawyer-economists must still contend with the perennial claim that the notion of efficiency is politically biased. The choice of efficiency as the reference point or crucial paradigm of a value judgment is regarded with suspicion by those who believe that the law cannot neglect distributive concerns (see, for example, Zaccaria, 1995). Suffice it to say that the traditional distinction between positive and normative economics is now in crisis and the notion of efficiency is no longer regarded as neutral (see Blaug, 1992; Hovenkamp, 1990). It is worth noting, moreover, that even an influential scholar clearly extraneous to the law and economics movement acknowledges the possibility of a reconciliation between cost-benefit analysis and the principles of egalitarianism (Dworkin, 1986, p. 276ff.). Hence, in economics as well as in law, the usefulness of the concept of efficiency should be judged according to the problem at hand.

However, rejection of the ideologically oriented approach believed to be prevalent in Chicago-style law and economics hampers thorough understanding of other currents of thought which shape the economic analysis of law. In other words, it is a mistake to identify EAL with Posner and his followers. The success of law and economics is largely due to the variety of research programs on which it is able to draw. The neoclassical paradigm of the Chicago school, for example, is now - at least, from a certain point of view - far less interesting than the comparative institutional analysis conducted by Oliver Williamson and other scholars in the area of new institutional economics (for discussion of the relationship between new institutional economics and law and economics see Williamson, 1993). It is worth mentioning that many Italian economists are now deeply involved in this research program (see, for references, the survey by Rizzello, 1996).

There are those who already suggest the existence of post-Chicago law and economics (see Symposium, 1989; Rubin, 1996). We prefer to speak of numerous competing lines of inquiry which sometimes yield conflicting results. A prominent role is now played by game theory, whose first applications to legal problems date back to the early 1970s. The analysis of strategic interactions among individuals, the main concern of game theory, has progressively undermined traditional beliefs about the role of the market and governmental regulation (see, for example, Ayres, 1990; Hovenkamp, 1995; for an updated list of game theory applications to legal problems see Huang, 1995). In the light of these developments, nothing could today be further from the truth than the monolithic vision of EAL often displayed by Italian scholars.

These remarks take us to another debated aspect of the reception of EAL in Italy. In many quarters the economic approach to law is regarded as simply irrelevant to better understanding of legal problems. Why study economics, the argument goes, if the solutions it provides are more or less coincident with the ones reached by means of the familiar legal methods? Statements of this kind reveal a patent misconception of the purposes that EAL seeks to accomplish. The prestige which surrounds economics - often regarded as the leading social science - may have prompted the belief that the economic approach to law is able to provide a definitive answer to any doubtful matter. By contrast, it is more realistic to recognize that law and economics provides useful tools with which to check the arguments that lawyers employ by shedding light on the economic contest in which a legal dispute arises. Therefore, the main contribution of law and economics is the enhanced understanding of the interests at stake it supplies.

A brief survey of the Italian literature lends support to this view. In nuisance cases, for example, the notion of externality explains why Italian courts grant a sum of money to the injured party even when the wrongdoer is allowed to pollute (Pardolesi, 1977 and, more recently, Mattei 1995; Gambaro, 1995). In tort law the age-old debate on the content of fault gains a new and stimulating meaning when analysed through the lens of economics (Cafaggi, 1996). Needless to say, the new Italian antitrust law of October 1990 would be impossible to understand without the support of an economic apparatus (see Pardolesi, 1993).

Although its results are hardly original law and economics exerts a powerful influence on the style of legal reasoning. The new rhetoric of EAL is best seen as a device which shows the lawyers which elements of a legal controversy are relevant and which are not (see Ackerman, 1984; McCloskey, 1988). This feature, however, can be regarded as a primary reason for its appeal as well as for its uneasy reception in Italy. Indeed, the economic argument compels lawyers to look at legal disputes from an unprecedented point of view, one almost at odds with the supposedly orthodox attitude. Instead of talking about rights and entitlements, lawyers are forced to assess the consequences of each rule on the allocation of resources. Apart from the complexity of the analysis, it is clear how far it diverges from the traditional reasoning of the Western legal tradition. The clash between the Western legal tradition and the Posnerian version of law and economics has recently been highlighted by Monateri (1995). By contrast, the usefulness of instrumental reasoning in the Italian legal system has been reaffirmed by the constitutional judge Mengoni (1994).

In short, Italian legal culture finds itself caught in a paradox. Law and economics promises valuable insights into legal problems, but at the same time it requires in-depth understanding of its techniques. Lawyers can take advantage of the economic approach to law only if they choose to invest in this field. Unfortunately, though, they lack the data with which to gauge the benefits available until that investment is made. This paradox is largely due to the scant attention paid to economics in lawyers' training. The Italian law faculties normally include only one course of economics on their programs, which is clearly inadequate to tackle the complexity of modern mathematical economics.

Of course, Italian lawyers have occasionally displayed deep understanding of the economic issues underlying legal matters. For their part, many Italian economists have been keenly aware of the interaction between law and economics (for references to the works of nineteenth-century Italian lawyers and economists see Cosentino, 1990). It is clear, however, that this tradition has been unable to lay the basis for more systematic study. It may be that one of the reasons for this lack of communication has been the role played by social scientists in Italian society and culture, but we believe that the present situation can be explained mainly by the shortcomings of academic training.

In short, the lack of a formal training is a problem that cannot be postponed any longer. It is at this point that Italian economists should enter the scene. Unfortunately, they have listened no more than Italian lawyers have done.

4. Why Italian Economists do not Listen

About two decades ago Ronald Coase suggested that the expansion of economics into contiguous fields would come to an end when social scientists in those fields were able to master its techniques. The number of American lawyers who now have a PhD in economics seems to confirm his forecast (Coase, 1978, 1996). Nevertheless, it is clear that law and economics in the United States would have had less impact if economists had not involved themselves in the enterprise. It is hardly an exaggeration to state that the cooperation between lawyers and economists has been a fundamental factor in the development of the economic approach to law (for information on the involvement of economists in law and economics see Ellickson, 1989; Landes and Posner, 1993; Stigler, 1992).

What about Italy? The indifference of economists towards legal institutions is so manifest that it is not worth dwelling upon. Suffice it to say that a recent introduction to a collection of papers by Ronald Coase does not include the slightest reference to his influence on the economic analysis of law or to Italian contributions in that field (Grillo, 1995, pp. 7ff.). Judging from these writings, it seems that economics and law in Italy do not communicate at all.

This situation is even more surprising if we look at the training provided by Italian schools of economics. Their programs include a wide range of law courses, and economics students have ample opportunity to become fully conversant in both disciplines. Why this does not happen is not clear. One might suggest that the jobs market is highly specialized and young graduates with hybrid skills do not find employment easily. Whatever the case may be, on the eve of the twenty-first century the Italian Bibliography of Law and Economics lists only a few contributions by Italian economists.

It is difficult to say whether the present situation will to change in the near future. Since the last century, political debate on the reform of administrative agencies and governmental regulation has been the main concern of economic thinkers in Italy (see, for example, the essays on market and democracy collected in Bocciarelli and Ciocca, 1994). In accordance with this tradition, current analysis appears to be dominated by macroeconomics issues (for a recent survey of the Italian situation by a French economist see Bartoli, 1996).

This is not to say, however, that hopeful signs of a renewed interest in legal institutions are entirely lacking. The presence of economists in the law faculties has recently begun to yield fruitful interdisciplinary studies. Some courses in economics, for example, have applied insights from law and economics to Italian laws and institutions (see Chiancone and Porrini, 1996; Galeotti 1995), and there are encouraging signals from the already mentioned Italian economists working in the field of the New Institutional Economics. Even more importantly, modern economics textbooks are now devoting more space to such subjects as transaction costs, asymmetric information, strategic interactions and institutional constraints (see, for example, Del Bono and Zamagni, 1996).

Since the 1980s, moreover, there has been a growing interest in game theory. The activities of the Interuniversitary Centre for Game Theory and Applications, established in 1990 in Florence, range from the development of research programs to the spread of game theory in the scientific community. Unfortunately, Italian economists at work in this field are unaware of the applications of game theory to legal problems. For example, a recent introductory textbook notes that game theory has been applied outside economics in such areas as political science, philosophy, computer science, engineering and evolutionary biology (Costa and Mori, 1994, pp. 10f.). Law, of course, is not even mentioned.

Italian scholars are equipping themselves with the theoretical instruments employed in the economic analysis of the American legal system. In the short period the institutional dimension - be it the theory of the firm or the structure of administrative agencies and public utilities - will probably attract more attention than private law topics like contract, tort and property. Needless to say, even this development would be a giant step towards the interdisciplinary study of law and economics.

Bibliography on Law and Economics in Italy (0345)

Alpa, Guido (1976), 'Colpa e Responsabilit... Oggettiva nella Prospettiva dell Analisi Economica del Diritto (Negligence and Strict Liability In An EAL Perspective)', *Politica del Diritto*, 431-448.

Alpa, Guido (1983), 'Interpretazione Economica del Diritto (Economic Interpretation of Law)', in X (ed.), *Voce del Novissimo Digesto Italiano*, Torino, UTET, 315-324.

Alpa, Guido (1984), 'Diritto e Analisi Economica (a proposito di un recente libro di R. Bowles) (Law and Economic Analysis, With Regard to a Recent Book by R. Bowles)', *Diritto dell Impresa*, 111-120.

Alpa, Guido (1995), *Istituzioni di Diritto Privato* (Institutes of Private Law), Torino, UTET.

Alpa, Guido (1996), 'Lo Snobismo degli Economisti e il Rifiuto del Dialogo con i Giuristi (a Proposito dell'introduzione alla Versione Italiana di 'Impresa, Mercato e Diritto' di R.H. Coase) (The Economists' Snobbery and the Refusal of Dialogue with Lawyers)', *Economia e Diritto del Terziario*, 745-749.

Alpa, Guido and Giampieri, Alberto (1996), 'Analisi Economica del Diritto e Analisi del Metodo: la Questione del Danno Contrattuale (Economic Analysis of Law and Methodological Analysis: the Problem of Contractual Damages)', *Rivista Trimestrale di Diritto e Procedura Civile*, 717-723.

Alpa, Guido, Pulitini, Francesco, Rodota, Stefano and Romani, Franco (1982), *Interpretazione Giuridica e Analisi Economica* (Legal Interpretation and Economic Analysis), Milano, Giuffrè, 662 p.

Antoniolli Deflorian, Luisa (1996), *La Struttura Istituzionale del Nuovo Diritto Comune*

Europeo: Competizione e Circolazione dei Modelli Giuridici (The Institutional Structure of the new European Common Law: Competion and Transplants of Legal Models), Trento, Dipartimento di Scienze guiridiche.

Aprile, Ercole (1989), 'Regolamentazione dei Fenomeni Economici e Analisi Economica degli Strumenti Giuridici: Spunti per una Riflessione (Regulation of Economic Phenomena and Economic Analysis of Legal Instruments: Hints for a Reflection)', *Nuovo Diritto*, 505-521.

Bellantuono, Giuseppe (1995), 'Polizza Fideiussoria, Reticenza e Obblighi di Informazione (Performance Bond, Non-Disclosure and Duties of Information)', *Il Foro Italiano*, 1905-1909.

Bessone, Mario (1984), ''Gli standards' dei contratti di impresa e l'analisi economica del diritto (The 'Standards' in Contracts and Economic Analysis)', *Giurisprudenza di merito*, 982-987.

Cafaggi, Fabrizio (1995), 'La nozione di difetto ed il ruolo dell'informazione. Per l'adozione di un modello dinamico-relazionale di difetto in una prospettiva di riforma (The notion of defect and the role of information. For the adoption of a dynamic-relational model of defect in a perspective of reform)', *Rivista Critica del Diritto Privato*, 447-480.

Cafaggi, Fabrizio (1995b), 'Pubblicit... commerciale (Commercial Advertising)', **XI** *Digesto commerciale*, 433-500.

Cafaggi, Fabrizio (1996), *Profili della Colpa Relazionale* (Outlines of Relational Fault), Padova, CEDAM.

Cafaggi, Fabrizio, Cuffaro, Vincenzo and Di Via Luciano (1993), 'Attuazione della Direttiva n. 450/84/Cee in Materia di Pubblicit... ingannevole (decreto legislativo 25 gennaio 1992 n. 74) (Implementation of EC Directive no. 450/84 on Misleading Advertising)', *Le Nuove Leggi Civili Commentate*, 671-761.

Carbone, Paolo (1991), 'Nuovi Illeciti Attinenti alla Negoziazione di 'Valori Mobiliari'. Profili della disciplina. Spunti critici (New Torts concerning Securities Exchange. Outlines of the rules. Critical hints)', **V** *Il Foro Italiano*, 466-490.

Carbone, Paolo (1993), *Tutela Civile del Mercato e Insider Trading* (Private Law Protection of the Market and Insider Trading), Padova, CEDAM.

Carriero, Giuseppe (1992), *Informazione, Mercato, Buona Fede: il Cosiddetto Insider Trading* (Information, Market, Good Faith: the socalled Insider Trading), Milano, Giuffré.

Carriero, Giuseppe (1997), Norme di Protezione dell'Utente dei Servizi Bancari e Finanziari: Taluni Effetti Economici (Legal Protection of the Consumer of Bank and Financial Services: Some Economic Effects), *Rivista di diritto dell'impresa*, 79 ff.

Caruso, Daniela (1991), 'Relazioni Precontrattuali e Teoria dei Giochi (Precontractual Relations and Game Theory)', *Quadrimestre*, 810-832.

Caruso, Daniela (1991b), 'Note in Tema di Danni Precontrattuali (Nota a Cass., 11 maggio 1990, n. 4051, Bellucci c. Min. difesa) (Notes about Precontractual Damages)', **1** *Il Foro Italiano*, 188-200.

Caruso, Daniela (1993), *La Culpa in Contrahendo - L'Esperienza Statunitense e Quella Italiana* (Culpa in Contrahendo - The American and Italian Experience), Milano, Giuffrè.

Castronovo, Carlo (1981), 'Inattuazione Della Prestazione di Lavoro e Responsabilit... Del Danneggiante (Employee's Non-Performance and Tortfeasor's Liability)', *Massimario di Giurisprudenza del Lavoro*, 370-377.

Chianale, Angelo (1992), *L'Atto Pubblico: Contributo allo Studio dei Costi Transattivi* (The Document under the Seal of a Public Officer: Contribution to the Study of Transaction Costs), Torino, Giappichelli.

Chianale, Angelo (1993), *Diritto Soggettivo e Tutela in Forma Specifica. Indagine in Tema di Responsabilità Extracontrattuale* (Subjective Right and Specific Performance. An Inquiry in Tort Law), Milano, Giuffrè.

Chiancone, Aldo and Porrini, Donatella (1996), *Lezioni di Analisi Economica del Diritto* (Lessons of Economic Analysis of Law), Torino, Giappichelli.

Chiassoni Pierluigi (1991), 'L'Analisi Economica del Diritto negli Stati Uniti: Formalismo o Realismo? (Economic Analysis of Law in the United States: Formalism or Realism?)', *Quadrimestre*, 473-525.

Chiassoni, Pierluigi (1992), *Economic Analysis of Law. L'analisi economica del diritto negli Stati Uniti* (The Economic Analysis of Law in the United States), Torino, Giappichelli.

Clerico, Giuseppe (1992), 'Inadempienza Contrattuale e Determinazione del Risarcimento Monetario (Breach of Contract and Quantification of Monetary Damages)', *Economia Pubblica*, 267-276.

Clerico, Giuseppe (1994), 'Raccolta e Allocazione diSsangue: Donazione, Mercato e Intervento Pubblico (Gathering and Allocation of Blood: Gift, Market and Public Intervention)', **4** *Rassegna Giuridica della Sanità*, 140-152.

Clerico, Giuseppe (1995), 'Prodotto Difettoso e Responsabilità delDanno: i Dilemmi della Scelta Pubblica (Defective Product and Liability for Damages: the Dilemma of the Public Choice)', *Economia Pubblica*, 25-70.

Clerico, Giuseppe (1996), 'Produzione e Rischio di Danni: regolamentazione Pubblica versus Regole di Responsabilità (Production and Risk of Damages: Public Regulation vs. Liability Rules)', *Economia e Diritto del Terziario*, 491-518.

Cosentino, Fabrizio (1988), 'Autonomia Privata e Paternalismo del Legislatore Nella Prospettiva dell'Analisi Economica del Diritto (Individual Autonomy and the Paternalism of the Legislator: An EAL Perspective)', *Rivista Critica del Diritto Privato*, 473-511.

Cosentino, Fabrizio (1989), 'Responsabilità da Prodotto Difettoso: Appunti di Analisi Economica del Diritto (nota a U.S. Supreme Court California, 31 marzo 1988, Brown c. Abbott Laboratories) (Liability for Defective Products: An Economic Analysis of Law)', **4** *Foro Italiano*, 137-143.

Cosentino, Fabrizio (1990a), 'Analisi Economica del Diritto: Ritorno al Futuro? (Economic Analysis of Law: Back to the Future?)', **5** *Foro Italiano*, 153-156.

Cosentino, Fabrizio (1990b), 'Il Contratto di Servizio delle Cassette di Sicurezza: Clausole di Limitazione della Responsabilità della Banca e Dichiarazione di Valore (The Contract for Services Related to Safety Deposit Boxes: Exemption Clauses for the Bank and Statement of Value)', **1** *Foro Italiano*, 1292-1298.

Cosentino, Fabrizio (1990c), 'L'Inadempimento Efficiente Nuovamente al Vaglio della Cassazione (Nota a Cass., 21 marzo 1989, n. 1403, Allione c. Greco) (The Efficient Breach again Under Scrutiny Before the Court of Cassation)', **I** *Il Foro Italiano*, 223-227.

Cosentino, Fabrizio (1992), 'Trasporto di Merci su Strada e Limitazione della Responsabilità: Osservazioni in Chiave di Analisi Economica del Diritto, (Nota a Corte costit., 22 novembre 1991, n. 420, Soc. Dafne et Cloe c. Autotrasp. bestiame Melano) (Carriage of Goods by Road and Limitation of Liability: Remarks from the Point of View of the

Economic Analysis of Law)', **1** *Il Foro Italiano*, 647-655.

Cosentino, Fabrizio (1992b), 'Alla Ricerca della Raccomandata Perduta: Modificate le Regole Sulla 'Posta In Gioco' (Nota a Corte costituzionale 28 febbraio 1992, n. 74, Soc. Sapri Broker assicuraz. c. Min. Poste) (Searching for the Lost Registered Letter: Rules on Mail Amended)', **I** *Il Foro Italiano*, 1354-1356.

Cosentino, Fabrizio (1993), 'Il Paternalismo del Legislatore nelle Norme di Limitazione dell'Autonomia dei Privati (The Paternalism of the Legislator in the Rules Limiting Private Autonomy)', *Quadrimestre*, 119-139.

Cosentino, Fabrizio (1995), 'Il Dilemma dell'Economia Informale: Proibizione o Deregolamentazione? (The Dilemma of Informal Economy: Prohibition or Deregulation?)', *Politica del Diritto*, 635-653.

Cosentino, Fabrizio (1996a), 'La Responsabilita Civile e Le Ragioni dell'Analisi Economic (Tort Law and the Arguments of Economic Analysis)', in X (ed.), *Danno e Responsabilità Civile*, 403-415.

Cosentino, Fabrizio (1996b), 'Neil Komesar, il Danno da Immissioni e la Responsabilità Civile: una Storia di Alternative Imperfette? (Neil Komesar, Damage from Nuisance and Tort Law: A Story of Imperfect Alternatives?)', *Politica del Diritto*, 321-329.

De Lorenzi, Valeria (1993), 'Il Mandato alla Luce dell'Analisi Economica del Diritto (Agency Law in the Light of Economic Analysis of Law)', *Contratto e Impresa*, 965-1013.

De Lorenzi, Valeria (1997), 'La Rappresentanza Diretta Volontaria. Problemi e Soluzioni alla Luce dell'Analisi Economica del Diritto (Agency Law. Problems and Solutions in the Light of Economic Analysis of Law)', *Contratto e Impresa*, 595-669.

Denozza, Francesco (1987), 'Il mercato dei 'Limoni', la Teoria degli Ostaggi e la Risoluzione del Contratto di Leasing (The Market for Lemons, Theory of Hostages and Breach of the Leasing)', *Rivista Italiana del Leasing*, 682-691.

Denozza, Francesco (1990), *Antitrust: Leggi Antimonopolistiche e Tutela dei Consumatori nella CEE e negli USA* (Antitrust: Antitrust Laws and Consumer Protection in the EC and USA), Bologna, il Mulino.

Denozza, Francesco (1991), 'La Cassazione e la Risoluzione del Leasing (The Court of Cassation and the Breach of Leasing)', *Giurisprudenza Commerciale*, 845-857.

Enriques, Luca (1996), 'L'Economia delle Società per Azioni di Frank Easterbrook e Daniel Fischel: Diritto societario, efficienza dei mercati e analisi economica', *Rivista Critica del Diritto Privato*, 563-578.

Fazio, Antonio and Capriglione, Francesco (1983), 'Governo del Credito e Analisi Economica del Diritto (Governing Credit and Economic Analysis of Law)', **1** *Banca, Borsa, e Titoli di Credito*, 310-346.

Ferrarese, Maria Rosaria (1992), *Diritto e Mercato: il Caso degli Stati Uniti* (Law and Market: the Case of the United States), Torino, Giappichelli.

Ferrarini, G. (1977), *La Locazione Finanziaria* (Leasing), Milano, Giuffrè, 261 p.

Franzosi, Mario (1989), *Monopolio - Oligopolio - Concentrazioni* (Monopoly - Oligopoly - Concentrations), Milano, Giuffrè.

Frignani, Aldo, Pardolesi, Roberto, Patroni Griffi, Antonio and Ubertazzi, Luigi Carlo (eds) (1993), *Diritto Antitrust Italiano, Commento alla l. 10 ottobre 1990 n. 287, 2 vol.* (Italian Antitrust Law), Bologna, Zanichelli.

Galeotti, Ginaluigi (1995), *Appunti Introduttivi ad una Analisi Economica delle Istituzioni*, Unpublished Lessons, Rome.

Gallo, Paolo (1992), 'Errore sul Valore, Giustizia Contrattuale e Trasferimenti Ingiustificati di Ricchezza alla Luce dell'Analisi Economica del Diritto (Mistake on Value, Contractual Justice and Unjust Enrichment)', *Quadrimestre*, 656-703.

Gallo, Paolo (1993), 'Appunti in Tema di Colpevolezza, Colpa Soggettiva ed Efficienza Economica (in occasione di alcune recenti pubblicazioni) (Notes about Liability, Subjective Fault and Economic Efficiency on the Occasion of Some Recent Publications)', *Quadrimestre*, 712-732.

Gallo, Paolo (1995), 'Immissioni, usi Incompatibili e Problemi di Allocazione di Risorse Scarse (Nuisance, Incompatible Uses and Problems of Allocation of Scarce Resources)', **1** *Rivista di Diritto Civile*, 657-693.

Gallo, Paolo (1998), *Analisi Economica del Diritto (Economic Analysis of Law)*, Torino, Giappichelli.

Gambaro, Antonio (1979), *La Legittimazione Passiva alle Azioni Possessorie* (Standing to Be Sued in Ownership Litigation), Milano, Giuffrè, 163 p.

Gambaro, Antonio (1995), *Il Diritto di Propriet (Property Law)*, Milano, Giuffrè.

Gambaro, Antonio (1996), 'L'Analisi Economica e la Ricerca della Logica Proprietaria (Economic Analysis and the Search for the Rationale of Ownership)', *Rivista Critica del Diritto Privato*, 235-244.

Grillo, Michele (1995), 'Introduzione to Coase, Impresa Mercato e Diritto (Introduction to Coase, Law and Economics)', *il Mulino, Bologna*, 7-38.

Grillo, Michele (1996), 'Lo Snobismo degli Economisti e il Rifiuto del Dialogo con i Giuristi. Una Risposta a Guido Alpa (The Economists' Snobbery and the Refusal of Dialogue with Lawyers. A reply to Guido Alpa)', *Economia e Diritto del Terziario*, 751-754.

Guatri, Luigi (1986), *Crisi e Risanamento delle Imprese* (Crisis and Reorganization of the Firms), Milano, Giuffrè, 339 p.

Ichino, Pietro (1998), 'Il Diritto del Lavoro e i Modelli Economici (Labour law and economic models)', *Lavoro e Diritto*, 309-322.

Macario, Francesco (1996), *Adempimento e Rinegoziazione nei Contratti a Lungo Termine* (Performance and Renegotiation in Long-Term Contracts), Napoli, Jovene.

Maccabruni, Franco (1995), 'Insider Ttrading e Analisi Economica del Diritto (Insider Trading and Economic Analysis of Law)', **1** *Giurisprudenza Commerciale*, 598-622.

Marella, Maria Rosaria (1994), 'Onerosità del Risarcimento in Forma Specifica (Onerousness of Specific Performance)', **I,2** *Giurisprudenza Italiana*, 1067-1074.

Marini, Giovanni (1986), 'Ingiustizia dello Scambio e Lesione Contrattuale (Unfairness of the Exchange and Contractual Lesion)', *Rivista Critica del Diritto Privato*, 257-315.

Marini, Giovanni (1990), *Promessa ed Affidamento nel Diritto dei Contratti* (Promise and Reliance in Contract Law), Napoli, Jovene, 317 p.

Marini, Giovanni (1995), *Promessa e Affidamento nel Diritto dei Contratti* (Promise and Reliance in Contract Law), Napoli, Jovene.

Mastrorilli, Annachiara (1994), 'Originalit... nelle opere compilative e informazione (Nota a Cass. 10 marzo 1994, n. 2345 e 2 dicembre 1993, n. 11953) (Originality in Compiled Works and Information)', **I** *Il Foro Italiano*, 2417-2422.

Mattei, Ugo (1985),'I Modelli nella Tutela dell'Ambiente (The Models for the Protection of the Environment)', **2** *Rivista di Diritto Civile*, 389-427.

Mattei, Ugo (1987),'Diritto e Rimedio nell'Esperienza Italiana ed in quella Statunitense: un Primo Approccio (Law and Remedies Related to Italian and American Experiences: A First Approach)', *Quadrimestre*, 341-359.

Mattei, Ugo (1987b), *Tutela Inibitoria e Tutela Risarcitoria* (Injunctive Relief and Damages), Milano, Giuffrè, 419 p.

Mattei, Ugo (1995), *La Proprietà Immobiliare* (Real Property), Torino, Giappichelli.

Mattei, Ugo (1996), 'Analisi Economica e Comparata delle Clausole Penali nel Diritto dei Contratti (Comparative Law and Rconomics of Penalty Clauses in Contracts)', *Rivista Critica del Diritto Privato*, 603-627.

Mattei, Ugo and Pulitini, Francesco (1990), 'Modelli Competitivi, Regole Giuridiche ed Analisi Economica (Competitive Models, Legal Norms and Economic Analysis)', *Quadrimestre*, 77-102.

Mattei, Ugo and Pulitini, Francesco (eds) (1994), *Consumatore, Ambiente, Concorrenza - AnalisiEeconomica del Diritto* (Consumer, Environment, Competition - Economic Analysis of Law), Milano, Giuffrè.

Mengaroni, F. (1988), 'Analisi Economica del Diritto (Economic Analysis of Law)', **1** *Enciclopedia giuridica*, 1-9.

Mengoni, Luigi (1994), 'L'argomentazione Orientata alle Conseguenze (The argumentation Oriented to the Consequences)', *Rivista Trimestrale di Diritto e Procedura Civile*, 1-18.

Monateri, Pier Giuseppe (1989), *Cumulo di Responsabilità Contrattuale ed extra Contrattuale* (Overlap of Contractual and Extracontractual Liability), Padova, CEDAM, 315 p.

Monateri, Pier Giuseppe (1995), 'Risultati e Regole. (Un'Analisi Giuridica dell'Analisi Economica del Diritto) (Rules and Outcomes. A Legal Analysis of the Economic Analysis of Law)', *Rivista Critica del Diritto Privato*, 605-619.

Monateri, Pier Giuseppe (1998), *La responsabilitá Civile (Tort Law)*, Torino, Utet.

Monateri, Pier Giuseppe (1998), 'Responsabilitá Civile (Tort Law)', **17** *Digesto Civile*, 1-12.

Monti, Andrea (1998), 'Learned Hand Formula e Buona Fede nell'Esecuzione del Contratto. Analisi economica e comparata (Learned Hand Formula and Good Faith in Contract. Comparative and Economic Analysis, *Rivista Critica del Diritto Privato*, 125-147 (4400).

Nogler, Luca (1992), 'Una Ventata di Analisi Economica del Diritto in Tema di Contratto di Lavoro a Termine (Nota a Cass., sez. lav., 21 febbraio 1992, n. 2153, Matteucci c. Cassa risp. Citt... di Castello) (A Wave of Economic Analysis of Law on Forward Employment Contract)', **I** *Giustizia Civile*, 2104-2105.

Osti, Cristoforo (1995), *Antitrust e Oligopolio: Concorrenza, Cooperazione e Concentrazione (Antitrust and Oligopoly: Competition, Cooperation and Merger)*, Bologna, Il Mulino.

Pacces, Alessio and Pardolesi, Roberto (1997), 'Clausole Vessatorie in Crisi d 'Identità. Appunti di Analisi Economica del Diritto (The Identity Crisis of Unfair Terms. Remarks of Economic Analysis of Law), in Furgiuele (ed.), *Diritto Privato*, II1996, Padova.

Paganelli, Maurizio (1989), 'Alla Volta di Frankenstein: Biotecnologie e propriet... (di parti) del corpo (Toward Frankenstein: Biotechnology and Property Rights in Body Parts)', **4** *Foro Italiano*, 417-441.

Panella, Giorgio (1994), 'Responsabilità Civile ed 'Effetti Esterni': un'Applicazione ai Problemi dell'Inquinamento (Tortious Liability and 'External Effects': an Application to the Problems of Pollution)', *Economia e Diritto del Terziario*, 631-653.

Pardolesi, Roberto (1977), 'Azione Reale e Azione di Danni nell Art. 844 C.C. Logica Economica e Logica Giuridica Nella Composizione Del Conflitto Tra Usi Incompatibili Delle Propriet ... Vicine (Property Rule and Liability Rule in Article 844 Codice Civile:

Economic Arguments, Legal Arguments and Litigation for Inconsistent Uses of Neighbours Lands)', **1** *Foro Italiano*, 1144-1154.

Pardolesi, Roberto (1982), 'Luci ed Ombre nell analisi economica del diritto (Appunti in Margine Ad Un Libro Recente) (Lights and Shadows in Law and Economics - Notes about a Recent Book)', **2** *Rivista di Diritto Civile*, 718-728.

Pardolesi, Roberto (1985), 'Invalidità Temporanea del Dipendente, Illecito del Terzo Rivalsa' del Datore di Lavoro (ovvero: l'analisi economica del diritto in cassazione) (Temporary Disability of Employees, Tortuous Conduct by Third Party Employer's Remedies)', **1** *Foro Italiano*, 2286-2291.

Pardolesi, Roberto (1986), *Una Introduzione all'Analisi Economica del Diritto con Postfazione* (Translation of A. Mitchell Polinsky's 'Introduction'), Bologna, Zanichelli, 149 p.

Pardolesi, Roberto (1987), 'Analisi Economica del Diritto (Economic Analysis of Law)', **1** *Digesto Civile*, 309-320.

Pardolesi, Roberto (1988), 'Tutela Specifica e Tutela per Equivalente nella Prospettiva dell'Analisi Economica del Diritto (Specific Performance and Damages: An EAL Perspective)', *Quadrimestre*, 76-97.

Pardolesi, Roberto (1989), 'Un Moderno Minotauro: Law and Economics (A Modern Minotaur: Law and Economics)', *Economia, Società e Istituzioni*, 519-534.

Pardolesi, Roberto (1991), 'Energia (Energy)', **VII** *Digesto Civile*, 444-448.

Pardolesi, Roberto (1992), 'Postfazione a Polinsky, Mitchell A., Una Introduzione all'Analisi Economica del Diritto, (Afterword to Polinsky, Mitchell A., An Introduction to Economic Analysis of Law)', *Il Foro Italiano*, 179-199.

Pardolesi, Roberto (1993), 'Analisi Economica della Legislazione Antitrust Italiana (Economic Analysis of Italian Antitrust Law)', **V** *Il Foro Italiano*, 1-18.

Pardolesi, Roberto (1994), 'Parallelismo e Collusione Oligopolistica: il Lato Oscuro dell' Antitrust (Parallelism and Oligopolistic Collusion: the Dark Side of Antitrust)', **IV** *Il Foro Italiano*, 65-76.

Pardolesi, Roberto (1996), 'Regole di Default eRazionalit. Limitata: per un (diverso) Approccio diAnalisiEconomicaa l Diritto dei Contratti (Default Rules and Bounded Rationality: for a Different Economic Approach to Contract Law)', *Rivista Critica del Diritto Privato,*451-466.

Pardolesi, Roberto and Motti, Cinzia (1990), 'L'Idea è Mia!': Lusinghe e Misfatti dell'Economics of Information ('The Idea is Mine!': Enticements and Misdeeds of the Economics of Information)', *Diritto dell'Informazione e dell'Informatica*, 345-359.

Pardolesi, Roberto and Osti, Cristoforo (1996), 'Avvisi di Burrasca: Antitrust e Diritti Tv suManifestazioni Sportive (Storm Warnings: Antitrust and Television Rights on Sport Events)', *Rivista di Diritto Sportivo*, 1-31.

Parisi, Francesco, and (1990), 'Sviluppi nell'Elemento Soggettivo del Tort of Negligence', **36** *Rivista di diritto civile*, 545-599.

Parisi, Francesco (1991), 'Interpretazione Giuridica ed Analisi Economica - IlTeorema di Coase Trenta Anni Dopo (Legal Interpretation and Economic Analysis - The Coase Theorem Thirty Years Later)', *Rivista Critica del Diritto Privato*, 643-676.

Parisi, Francesco (1993), 'Learned Hand Formula of Negligence', **X** *Digesto Civile*, 4th ed., 436-443; reprinted in *Materiali di Economia e Diritto*, 1997, Università di Roma La Sapienza, 285-292.

Parisi, Francesco (1998), 'The Market for Votes: Coasian Bargaining in an Arrovian

Setting', **6** *George Mason Law Review*, 745-766.

Parisi, Francesco (1998),'La Genesi della Responsabilità nel Diritto Antico', in Parisi, Francesco and Giacobbe, Giovanni (ed.), *Analisi Economica e Libertà Contrattuali*, Guiffrè.

Parisi, Francesco (1998),'Teorema di Coase', **16** *Digesto Italiano* (Diritto Civile).

Parisi, Francesco (1998), 'Teorema di Arrow', **16** *Digesto Italiano* (Diritto Civile).

Parisi, Francesco and Frezza, Giampaolo (1998), 'Rischio e Causalita nel Concorso di Colpa', **44** *Rivista di diritto civile*.

Parisi, Francesco and Frezza, Giampaolo (1998), 'La Responsabilita Stocastica', **63** *Responsabilita Civile e Previdenza*, 824-847.

Parisi, Francesco and Frezza, Giampaolo (1998), 'Crisi e Proposte di Riforma nel Sistema dei Torts', **63** *Responsabilita Civile e Previdenza*, 555-563.

Parisi, Francesco and Frezza, Giampaolo (1998), 'Il Concorso di Colpa: Analisi Economico-Comparata', *Rivista di diritto civile*.

Parisi, Francesco and Posner Richard A. (1998), 'Scuole e Tendenze nella Analisi Economica del Diritto', *Biblioteca dellla Livertà*.

Parisi, Francesco (1999), 'Autonomia e Ordinamento Privato nella Legislazione Contrattuale', in Parisi, Francesco and Giacobbe, Giovanni (ed.), *Analisi Economica e Libertà Contrattuali*, Guiffrè.

Parisi, Francesco (1999), 'Family Law and Successions', in U. Mattei (ed.), *Introduction to Italian Law*, Boston, Kluwer Law International, forthcoming.

Parisi, Francesco and Giacobbe, Giovanni (1999), *Analisi Economica e Libertà Contrattuali*, Giuffrè.

Parisi, Francesco and Posner Richard A. (1999), 'Analisi Economica del Diritto Pubblico e Penale: Una Bibliografia Annotata', in X (ed.), *Biblioteca della Libertá*.

Parisi, Francesco and Posner Richard A. (1999), 'Analisi Economica del Diritto Privato e Commerciale: Una Bibliografia Annotata', in X (ed.), *Biblioteca della Libertá*.

Parisi, Francesco and Frezza, Giampaolo (1999), 'Cesare Beccaria (1738-1794)', in Backhaus J.G. (ed.), *Elgar Companion to Law and Economics*, Ashgate, Edward Elgar.

Parisi, Francesco and Frezza, Giampaolo (1999), 'Achille Loria (1847-1943)', in Backhaus, J.G. (ed.), *Elgar Companion to Law and Economics*, Ashgate, Edward Elgar.

Parisi, Francesco and Frezza, Giampaolo (1999), 'Augusto Graziani (1865-1938)', in Backhaus, J.G. (ed.), *Elgar Companion to Law and Economics*, Ashgate, Edward Elgar.

Pasquini, Nello (1983), 'Interpretazione Giuridica e Analisi Economica - inMargine ad un 'Reading' Recente (Legal Interpretation and Economic Analysis with Recent 'Reading')', *Rivista Trimestrale di Diritto e Procedura Civile*, 288-300.

Podda, Oscar (1990), 'Bad Deals: Acquisto di Partecipazioni Societarie e Garanzie del Venditore (Bad Deals: Sale of Shares and Seller's Warranties)', *Quadrimestre*, 548-564.

Pontiroli, Luca (1995), 'Il Declino dell'Autonomia Privata nei Contratti Bancari: Spunti per Riflessione Critica (The Fall of Private Autonomy in Bank Contracts: Hints for a Critical Reflection)', *Contratto e Impresa*, 804 ff.

Pontiroli, Luciano (1997), 'La posizione del 'contraente debole' nei *Principles of International Commercial Contracts* di Unidroit: much ado about nothing? (The Position of the 'Weak Party')' in the Unidroit *Principles of International Commercial Contracts*: Much Ado About Nothing?, **I** *Giurisprudenza Commerciale*, 566-606.

Ponzanelli, Giulio (1991), 'Limitazione di Responsabilità, Analisi Economica e Giudizio di Costituzionali... (Nota a Corte cost. 22 novembre 1991, n. 420, Soc. Dafne et Cloe c.

Autotrasp. bestiame Melano) (Limitation of Liability, Economic Analysis and Constitutional Judgement)', I *Il Foro Italiano*, 643-647.

Ponzanelli, Giulio (1992), *La Responsabilità Civile. Profili di Diritto Comparato* (Tort Law. Outlines of Comparative Law), Bologna, Il Mulino.

Pozzo, Barbara (1996), *Danno Ambientale ed Imputazione della responsabilità. Esperienze giuridiche a confronto* (Environmental Damage and Charge of Liability. Legal Experiences Compared), Milano, Giuffrè.

Pradi, Andrea (1997), 'Proprietà Privata e PubblicaUtilità: il Modello dei Costi Transattivi (Private Property and Public Utility: the Model of Transaction Costs)', *Rivista Critica del Diritto Privato*, 421-441.

Preite, Disiano (1986), 'In Tema di Sollecitazione del Pubblico Risparmio (Enhancing Public Savings)', *Giurisprudenza Commerciale*, 217-245.

Preite, Disiano (1987), 'Sovrapprezzo, aste Competitive e Mercato mobiliar' (Overpricing, Competitive Auctions and Security Market)', *Giurisprudenza Commerciale*, 882-924.

Preite, Disiano (1988), *La Destinazione dei Risultati nei Contratti Associativi* (The Destination of the Results in Partnership Contracts), Milano, Giuffrè, 456 p.

Preite, Disiano (1992), *L'Abuso della Regola di Maggioranza nelle Deliberazioni Assembleari delleSocietà per azioni* (The Abuse of the Rule of Majority in the Decisions of Shareholders' Meetings), Milano, Giuffrè.

Preite, Disiano (1993), *Abuso di Maggioranza e Conflitto di Interessi del Socio nella Società per Azioni* (Abuse of the Majority and Conflict of Interests of the Shareholder in the Corporation), in Colombo e Portale (eds), Trattato delle Società perAzioni, 3, 2, Torino, Utet, 3-182.

Pulitini, Francesco (1967), 'Regole Giuridiche E Teoria Economica (Law and Economic Theory)', *Politica del Diritto*, 297-310.

Raiteri, Monica (1988), 'Giustizia Distributiva e Funzione Giudiziaria: Qualche Osservazione nella Prospettiva della Analisi Economica del Diritto (Distributive Justice and the Judicial Function, Some Observations in an Economic and Law Perpective)', *Materiali per una Storia della Cultura Giuridica*, 209-228.

Raiteri, Monica (1992), 'La Funzione Giurisdizionale tra Redistribuzione Economica e Tutela dei Diritti (The Jurisdictional Office Between Economic Redistribution and Protection of Rights)', *Materiali per una Storia della Cultura Giuridica*, 475-518.

Renda, Andrea (1997), 'Prime Contratuals: una Occasione Maneata? (Preliminary Annotatious on the Directive about Contractual Warranties: A Lost Chance?)', *Diritto del Impresa*, 55-614.

Resta, Giorgio (1996), 'Scarsità delle Risorse e Funzione Allocativa del Diritto: il Caso dei Trapianti d'Organo (Scarsity of Resources and Allocative Function of the Law: the Case of Organ Transplants)', *Rivista Critica del Diritto Privato*, 111-159.

Rodano, Giorgio (1989), 'Il giudice e l'efficienza del Mercato. Riflessioni di un Economista su un Libro di Diritto Comparato (The Judge and the Efficiency of the Market. An Economist's Reflections on a Comparative Law Book)', *Rivista Critica del Diritto Privato*, 293-312.

Romani, Franco (1985), 'Appunti sull'Analisi Economica dei Contratti (Notes about the Economic Analysis of Contract Law)', *Quadrimestre*, 15-29.

Romani, Franco (1990), 'Diritto ed economia: la Prospettiva di un Economista (Law and Economics: the Perspective of an Economist)', *Sociologia del Diritto*, 245 ff.

Rossello, Carlo (1990), *Il Danno Evitabile. La Misura della Responsabilità ... tra Diligenza ed Efficienza* (Avoidable Damage: The Measure of Liability Between Due Care and Efficiency), Padova, CEDAM, 320 p.

Russo, Enzo (1992), 'L'Impatto Amministrativo della Riforma del Contenzioso: Spunti di Analisi Economica del Diritto (The Administrative Impact of the Reform of the Contentious Procedure: Hints of Economic Analysis of Law)', *Il Fisco*, 10471-10479.

Santagata, Walter (1995), 'Istituzioni per il Mercato dell'Arte: Artisti e Mercanti tra Regole, Convenzioni e Allocazioni dei Diritti (Institutions for the Market of Works of Art: Artists and Merchants among Rules, Conventions and Allocation of Rights)', *Economia Pubblica*, 87-115.

Santini, Gerardo (1979), *Il Commercio* (Trading), Bologna, Il Mulino, 364 p.

Santini, Gerardo (1987), *I Servizi. Saggio di Economia del Diritto* (The Services. An Example of an Economic Approach to Law), Bologna, Il Mulino, 562 p.

Savona, Ernesto (1990), 'Un Settore Trascurato: l'Analisi Economica della Criminalit .., del Diritto Penale e del Sistema di Giustizia Penale (A Neglected Sector: Economic Analysis of Crime, Criminal Law and the System of Criminal Justice)', *Sociologia del Diritto*, 255-277.

Tarzia, Giuseppe (1983), 'Credito Bancario e Risanamento dell'Impresa nella Procedura di Amministrazione Straordinaria (Credit and the Reorganization of the Firm)', *Giurisprudenza Commerciale*, 340-352.

Toffoletto, Alberto (1996), *Il Risarcimento del Danno nel Sistema delleSanzioni per La violazione della Normativa Antitrust* (The Compensation for Damages in the Liability System for the Infringment of Antitrust Law), Milano, Giuffrè.

Tricoli, Clara (1981), 'Per una Teoria Economica dell Espropriazione e dell Indennizzo (An Economic Theory of Takings and Compensation)', *Rivista di Diritto Commerciale*, 335-357.

Trimarchi, Pietro (1961), *Rischio e responsabilità oggettiva* (Risk and Strict Liability), Milano, Giuffrè, 383 p.

Trimarchi, Pietro (1970), 'Sul Significato Economico dei Criteri di Responsabilit ... Contrattuale (Economic Meaning of Contract-Liability Criteria)', *Rivista Trimestrale di Diritto e Procedura Civile*, 512-531.

Trimarchi, Pietro (1987), 'L'Analisi Economica del Diritto: Tendenze e Prospettive (Economic Analysis of Law: Tendencies and Perspectives)', *Quadrimestre*, 563-582.

Trimarchi, Pietro (ed.) (1994), *Per una Riforma della Responsabilit.. Civile per Danno all'Ambiente* (The Reform of Tort Law for Environmental Damage), Milano, Giuffrè.

Troiano, Onofrio (1996), *I Servizi Elettronici di Pagamento. Addebiti in Conto non Autorizzati: un'Analisi Comparata* (Electronic Payment Systems: A Comparative Analysis), Milano, Giuffrè (5850).

Ventura, Andrea (1990), 'Il Ruolo del Teorema di Coase nell'Analisi Economica del Diritto di G. Calabresi (The Role of the Coase Theorem in G. Calabresi's Economic Analysis of Law)', *Economia Pubblica*, 27-34.

Villa, Gianroberto (1988), 'Errore Riconosciuto, Annullamento del Contratto ed Incentivi alla Ricerca di Informazioni (Known Mistake, Contract Avoidance and Incentives towards Information Acquisition)', *Quadrimestre*, 286-300.

Villa, Gianroberto (1992), 'Contratto Illecito ed Irripetibilità della Prestazione - Una Analisi Economica (Unlawful Contract and Non Repayable Performance - An Economic Analysis)', *Quadrimestre*, 19-64.

Zaccaria, Giuseppe (1995), 'Una Teoria del Pragmatismo Prescrittivo. Sulla Jurisprudence di Richard A. Posner (A Theory of Prescriptive Pragmatism. On the Jurisprudence of Richard A. Posner)', in Furgiuele (ed.), *Diritto Privato 1995, I, Il Trasferimento di Propriet*, Padova, 451-475.

Other References

Ackerman, Bruce (1984), *Reconstructing American Law*, Harvard University Press. Cambridge, Mass.

Ayres, Ian (1990), 'Playing Games with the Law', **42** *Stanford Law Review*, 1291-1317.

Bartoli (1996), 'Chronique de la Pensée Économique en Italie (Chonicle of Economic Thinking in Italy', **47** *Revue Économique*, 1013 ff.

Blaug, Mark (1992), *The Methodology of Economics, or, How Economics Explain*, Second Edition, Cambridge, Cambridge University Press.

Bocciarelli, Rossella and Ciocca, Pierluigi (1994), *Scrittori Italiani di Economia* (Italian Writing in Economics), Laterza, Roma-Bari.

Coase, Ronald H. (1978), 'Economics and Contiguous Disciplines', **7** *Journal of Legal Studies*, 201 ff.

Coase, Ronald H. (1996), 'Law and Economics and A.W. Brian Simpson', **25** *Journal of Legal Studies*, 103-119.

Costa, Giacomo and Mori, Pier Angelo (1994), *Introduzione alla Teoria dei Giochi* (Introduction to the Theory of Giochi), Bologna, Il Mulino.

Delbono, Flavio and Zamagni, Stefano (1996), *Lezione di Microeconomia* (Lessons in Microeconomics), Bologna, Il Mulino.

Dworkin, Ronald (1986), *Law's Empire*, Cambridge (MA), Harvard University Press.

Ellickson, Robert (1989), 'Bringing Culture and Human Frailty to Rational Actors: A Critique of Classical Law and Economics', **65** *Chicago-Kent Law Review*, 23-55.

Ewald (1995), 'Comparative Jurisprudence: The Logic of Legal Tranplants', **43** *American Journal of Comparative Law*, 489 ff.

Hovenkamp, Herbert (1990), 'Positivism in Law and Economics', **78** *California Law Review*, 815.

Hovenkamp, Herbert (1995), 'Law and Economics in the United States: A Brief Historical Survey', **19** *Cambridge Journal of Economics*, 331-352.

Huang, Peter H. (1995), 'Strategic Behavior and the Law: A Guide for Legal Scholars to Game Theory and the Law and Other Game Theory Texts', **36** *Jurimetrics Journal*, 99-114.

Landes, William and Posner, Richard (1993), 'The Influence of Economics on Law: A Quantitative Study', **36** *Journal of Law and Economics*, 385 ff.

Mattei, Ugo and Pardolesi, Roberto (1991), 'Law and Economics in Civil Law Countries: A Comparative Approach', **11** *International Review of Law and Economics*, 265-275.

McCloskey, Donald (1988), 'The Rhetoric of Law and Economics', **86** *Michigan Law Review*, 752 ff.

Rizzello, Salvatore (1996), 'Mente Organizzazioni Istituzioni. I Fondamenti Microeconomici del Neoistituzionalismo', *Economia Politica*, 225-263.

Rubin, Edward L. (1996), 'The New Legal Process, the Synthesis of Discourse, and the Microanalysis of Institutions', **109** *Harvard Law Review*, 1393-1438.

Sacco, Rodolfo (1991), 'Legal Formants, A Dynamic Approach to Comparative Law', **39**

American Journal of Comparative Law, 1-349.

Stigler, George (1992), 'Law or Economics?', **35** *Journal of Law and Economics*, 455-468.

Symposium (1989), 'Post-Chicago Law and Economics', **65** *Chicago-Kent Law Review*, 3 ff.

Watson, Alan (1974), *Legal Transplants: An Approach to Comparative Law*, Cambridge (MA), Harvard University Press.

Williamson, Oliver (1993), 'Transactions Cost Economics Meets Posnerian Law and Economics', **149** *Journal of Institutional and Theoretical Economics*, 99-118.

0350
LAW AND ECONOMICS IN MEXICO

Andrès Roemer and José Diego Valadés

Abstract

Despite its almost exponential growth, particularly since 1983, economic analysis of law is still an area of minor importance in Mexico. Economic analysis of law is still not an integral part of legal education. Legal scholarship is formalistic in general, and is concerned more with definitions that with the purposes of legal provisions.

This discipline's main achievement in the academic community has been its contribution to forming a different juridical mentality, whether of research, policy or analysis.

Since its establishment on April 6, 1995, the Mexican Academy of Law and Economics has carried out several academic, teaching and research activities.
JEL classification: K00.
Keywords: Research, Teaching, Mexican Academy of Law and Economics.

1. Introduction

Despite its almost exponential growth, particularly since 1983, economic analysis of law is still an area of minor importance in Mexico. However, its growth rate and the weakness of its adversaries are indications that economic analysis of law will soon become an important trend in legal research and in public policy matters.

There are approximately 40 people working in this field. Some are full-time academicians and most of them work for the federal government. Their writings are concerned mainly with the problems of the Mexican regulation system and are almost always written in Spanish. Because of their small number and their relatively high demand, research tends to cover a considerable diversity of topics instead of concentrating on particular areas. Among others, we can mention the following topics that have been the object of analysis in this field: regulation, law and economics, education, the economics of water, contracts, ownership, institutions, public services, labor legislation and domestic trade.

It should be mentioned that legal knowledge in Mexico is formalistic in general, and Mexican legal scholars have a greater relationship with scholars of continental Europe, particularly with Spanish, Italian and French academicians, than with Americans, the ones who substantially inspired this discipline. On the other hand, the participation by legal scholars in the political process is remarkable. This influence is characterized by different routes, significantly through members of courts, the executive branch, the Congress, and the high-level bureaucracy.

Based on the foregoing, in Mexico a large part of the evolution of economic analysis of law has grown significantly from public sector parameters. Lawyers and economists, particularly specialists in microeconomics theory, keep in mind the usefulness of economic analyses of law in the field of public policy. An important example in this respect is the new agrarian legislation that, without ignoring the principles of justice, was clearly revised using standards of economic efficiency.

2. Law and Economics at Mexican Universities

In the academic community there are few Mexican universities that show any interest in economic analysis of law. Among them we can mention the Autonomous Technological Institute of Mexico (ITAM), Center for Economic Research and Teaching (CIDE). Likewise, a certain interest has been detected in the Law School of the National Autonomous University of Mexico (UNAM) (since the new curriculum of 1993, there exists a course related to economic matters in each of the 10 semesters), the National Institute of Public Administration (INAP), and the University of the Americas in Puebla (UDLA).

This discipline's main achievement in the academic community has been its contribution to forming a different juridical mentality, whether of research, policy or analysis. Students often see the emphasis on the real or potential effects of law and economics through the incentives it produces and the importance of the costs of the legal system as the main contribution of the economic approach to law.

In law schools, most teaching related to economics is given in courses that concern economic theory, history of economic thought and economic law (part of Mexican social law). These courses are part of the law schools' curriculum (first, second and seventh semesters respectively). This teaching lasts approximately four months per term.

3. The Mexican Academy of Law and Economics

As regards economic analysis as a movement, the Mexican Association of Law and Economics (called Mexican Academy of Law and Economics since

May of 1997) (AMDE) was founded on April 6, 1995 with the important support of professors Robert Cooter and Albert Fishlow, as well as of the former President of Mexico, Miguel de la Madrid Hurtado, the former Federal Attorney of Mexico, Pedro Ojeda Paullada, the President of the ITAM, Dr Arturo Fernández, and Andrès Roemer. Being part of the Latin American and Caribbean Association of Law and Economics, the AMDE has more than 30 founding members, 27 numerary members (who have presented academic papers and are current with their fees), as well as 25 supernumerary members (who are current with payments but have not presented any related academic paper) and another 400 people interested in the Academy (who attend congresses and seminars).

Since its establishment on April 6, 1995, the Mexican Academy of Law and Economics has carried out academic, teaching and research activities among which the following should be mentioned:

To date more than 137 research papers have been compiled that address 'Economic Analysis of Sexual Commingling and Regulation', 'Microeconomics of Civil Liability and the Marriage Contract', to 'Analysis of the Free Trade Agreement'.

- A data base in the subject has been formed with 9000 academic essays from more than fourteen countries, indexed by place, topic and author.
- Two National Congresses have been held with more than 200 participants in each one.
- Economic Analysis of Law courses have been implemented in the Autonomous Technological Institute of Mexico (ITAM), in the Center for Economic Research and Teaching (CIDE) and in the Autonomous Metropolitan University (UAM), as well as seminars in the National Institute of Public Administration (INAP), the University of the Americas, Puebla Campus and in the Law School of the National Autonomous University of Mexico (UNAM).
- The Annual National Law and Economy award was established for the best research paper in the area, as well as the Robert Cooter Award for the best academic paper in Law and Economics from the ITAM.
- The respective Academies were likewise formed in the States of Puebla, Coahuila, Chiapas, Jalisco, Oaxaca and Veracruz.

4. Perspectives

As regards publishing services, no single journal has been created dedicated specifically to the economic analysis of laws. Lawyers are critical of economic analysis of law. One of the reasons could be that Mexican academic lawyers lack an understanding of quantitative methods; another reason is that there has been scant contribution by Mexican economists to law, although some economists have taught in the law schools and, more significantly, a number of legal scholars question the essential deontological bases and the fundamental validity of economic analysis in general.

As can be seen, economic analysis of law is still not an integral part of legal education. Mexican juridical training and some other institutional circumstance can explain the reason why. Juridical formalism in Mexico is concerned more with definitions that with the purposes of legal provisions. On the other hand, the economic approach to law would seem instrumental and deals mainly with how certain aims can be achieved by giving the member or members of a society incentives. However, we should not be pessimistic as to the future of economic analysis of law in Mexico. The positive factors must not be overlooked. In the first place, as mentioned previously, academic lawyers and economists have an interest in applying economics to law. In the second place, in some law schools there seems to be a dissatisfaction with the traditional teaching of law as an autonomous discipline. Thirdly, a considerable number of young academicians are interested in the international perspectives, and consequently in the new juridical perspectives. Lastly, as was shown, the application of economic analysis of the legislation in force in Mexico has produced fruits and is being practiced profusely. This will probably be reflected in legal education in the medium and long terms.

Thus, the presence and influence of economic analysis of law will continue to grow, both from the legal and from the social point of view. The future of law and economics in Mexico depends crucially on the ability of this discipline to show in a simple way, not just the potential but the real value of this approach. It must also show its own limitations and reciprocities with the science of law: the what and the how of legal knowledge can contribute to the development of law and of economics. This kind of cooperation is necessary for an interdisciplinary approach such as law and economics. Meanwhile, public policies will continue to be the main source of demand (and inspiration) for economic analysis of law in this country.

Bibliography on Law and Economics in Mexico (0350)

Alcudia Goya, Hector, 'The Social Convenience of a Disincorporation from Federal Government of the "Almacenes Generales De Deposito"', Mexican Association of Law and Economics Working Series Papers of Law and Economics, no. 14.

Acosta Rivera, Jose De Jesus, Culebro Moreno, Jorge and Rosillo Iglesias, Jose Gabriel, 'Economic Analysis on Voting', Mexican Association of Law and Economics Working Series Papers of Law and Economics, no. 64.

Acosta, Francisco Antonio, 'Market Power and Institutional Assignation of a Transferable Permissions System For Polluting Emissions', Mexican Association of Law and Economics Working Series Papers of Law and Economics, no. 06.

Agiss Bitar, Fernando, 'The Law of Economic Competence: A Judicial and Economic Approximation on the Competence Law in Mexico', Mexican Association of Law and Economics Working Series Papers of Law and Economics, no. 84.

Aguirre Pablo, Karla, 'Economic Analysis on Tributary Law on Trade Taxes and its Relation with Nafta', Mexican Association of Law and Economics Working Series Papers of Law and Economics, no. 40.

Alba, Pilar, Ocaña, Alan and Suarez, Diana, 'Analysis on the New Fishing Law', Mexican Association of Law and Economics Working Series Papers of Law and Economics, no. 88.

Arias De La Mora, Roberto, 'The Participation of the Citizenship in Mexico City', Mexican Association of Law and Economics Working Series Papers of Law and Economics, no. 49.

Barraza Llorenz, Mariana, 'The New Law on Agriculture In Mexico', Mexican Association of Law and Economics Working Series Papers of Law and Economics, no. 86.

Barrera Flores, Raymundo, 'Economic Analysis of the Regulation of Lethal Weapons', Mexican Association of Law and Economics Working Series Papers of Law and Economics, no. 25.

Barria Macera, Rodrigo, 'Economic Analysis on Article 27 of the Constitution of Mexico', Mexican Association of Law and Economics Working Series Papers of Law and Economics, no. 87.

Bravo Ruiz, Maria Lilia and Presser Valdes, Soren, 'Economic Analysis on Institutional Aspects of Mexico City's Water Supply', Mexican Association of Law and Economics Working Series Papers of Law and Economics, no. 55.

Caceres Nieto, Enrique, 'Economic Analysis on Law: An Integral Theory', Mexican Association of Law and Economics Working Series Papers of Law and Economics, no. 88.

Cambero Garcia, Gerardo and Covil Princivil, Donald, 'Economic Analysis on Intellectual Property Rights', Mexican Association of Law and Economics Working Series Papers of Law and Economics, no. 56.

Carrera Paniso, Sofia and Peralta Sanchez, J. Ignacio, 'Analysis of the Education System in Mexico and its Legal Perspective', Mexican Association of Law and Economics Working Series Papers of Law and Economics, no. 89.

Castro, Mariana and Rodriguez, Manuel, 'Economic Analysis on Voting', Mexican Association of Law and Economics Working Series Papers of Law and Economics, no. 67.

Chavez Mondragon, Rafael, 'The Problem of Milk Production', Mexican Association of Law and Economics Working Series Papers of Law and Economics, no. 03.

Cuellar Trewartha, Ana Leticia, 'The Mexican Federalism Case: Public Choice vs Republicanism', Mexican Association of Law and Economics Working Series Papers of Law and Economics, no. 90.

Diarte Martinez, Heriberto, 'The Mexican Federalism From an Economic and Legal Perspective', Mexican Association of Law and Economics Working Series Papers of Law and Economics, no. 91.

Dominguez Diaz, Deisy Gabriela, 'Intellectual Property Rights in Mexico', Mexican Association of Law and Economics Working Series Papers of Law and Economics, no. 92.

Dudet Bellanger, Federico and Rios Piter, Armando, 'Economic Analysis of Law: Possibilities of An Alternative Banking System In Mexico', Mexican Association of Law and Economics Working Series Papers of Law and Economics, no. 58.

Elenes, Vanessa, 'Economic Analysis on Prostitution', Mexican Association of Law and Economics Working Series Papers of Law and Economics, no. 66.

Fragoso, Edna, 'Consequenses of Nafta', Mexican Association of Law and Economics Working Series Papers of Law and Economics, no. 93.

Galindo Suarez, Rosa Maria, 'Economic Analysis on Law', Mexican Association of Law and Economics Working Series Papers of Law and Economics, no. 84.

Garcia Salgo, Claudio, 'Law and Development', Mexican Association of Law and Economics Working Series Papers of Law and Economics, no. 25.

Garcia Verdu, Rodrigo, 'The Irreversible Investment Under Uncertainty Theory: An Economic Analysis on Law Application', Mexican Association of Law and Economics Working Series Papers of Law and Economics, no. 95.

Garcia Villegas Sanchez Cordero, Olga 'Economic Analysis on Judges on Creation of Efficient Juridical Rules, Mexican Association of Law and Economics Working Series Papers of Law and Economics, no. 13.

Garcia Villegas Sanchez Cordero, Paula Maria, 'Economic Analysis on Article 28 of the Constitution of Mexico', Mexican Association of Law and Economics Working Series Papers of Law and Economics, no. 96.

Gomez Martinez, Juan Carlos, 'The Public Policies Elaboration on the Federal Public Administration', Mexican Association of Law and Economics Working Series Papers of Law and Economics, no. 97.

Gonzalez Burelo, Juan Alejandro, 'The Problem of a Getting Degree', Mexican Association of Law and Economics Working Series Papers of Law and Economics, no. 27.

Gonzalez De Alba, Ivan Guillermo, 'Economic Analysis of Environmental Policy', Mexican Association of Law and Economics Working Series Papers of Law and Economics, no. 60.

Gutierrez Fernandez, Geronimo and Islas Torres, Alberto, 'The Federal Taxes', Mexican Association of Law and Economics Working Series Papers of Law and Economics, no. 98.

Hernadez Pintado, Fausto Jose, 'An Independent Central Bank: An Economic Analysis of the Law of the Bank of Mexico', Mexican Association of Law and Economics Working Series Papers of Law and Economics, no. 83.

Hernandez Murillo, Ruben, 'Civil Contracts' Regime: the Unfulfilment', Mexican

Association of Law and Economics Working Series Papers of Law and Economics, no. 99.

Karam, Daniel, 'Economic Analysis on the Relation between Federal Government And the Press', Mexican Association of Law and Economics Working Series Papers of Law and Economics, no. 44.

Leipen Linares, Elizabeth and Garcia Franco, Jose Carlos, 'Analysis on Mining Regulation in Mexico', Mexican Association of Law and Economics Working Series Papers of Law and Economics, no. 100.

Leon Oviedo, Fernando, 'Economic Analysis on the Bankruptcy Law', Mexican Association of Law and Economics Working Series Papers of Law and Economics, no. 28.

Levy, Gabriel, 'Selected Topics on Soller', Mexican Association of Law and Economics Working Series Papers of Law and Economics, no. 30.

Lobeira, Santiago, 'Economic Analysis of Environmental Legislation in the Matter of Pollution', Mexican Association of Law and Economics Working Series Papers of Law and Economics, no. 31.

Lopez G., Cesar Miguel, 'Economic Analysis of Aids', Mexican Association of Law and Economics Working Series Papers of Law and Economics, no. 46.

Lopez Hoyo, Jose Gerardo, 'The Collective Contract System in Mexico', Mexican Association of Law and Economics Working Series Papers of Law and Economics, no. 101.

Madero, Samantha, 'Law and Economics of the Regulation of Illegal Drugs', Mexican Association of Law and Economics Working Series Papers of Law and Economics, no. 36.

Marin Suarez, Anouk, 'Analysis of the Regime of Rental Apartments in Mexico City', Mexican Association of Law and Economics Working Series Papers of Law and Economics, no. 102.

Marquez Heine, Luis Antonio, 'Economic Analysis of Antitrust Laws', Mexican Association of Law and Economics Working Series Papers of Law and Economics, no. 103.

Martin Del Campo Flores and David, Erik, 'The Lords of War', Mexican Association of Law and Economics Working Series Papers of Law and Economics, no. 104.

Martinez Lopez, Andres and Quintero Ramirez Horacio, 'Economic Analysis on the Jewish-Christian Divine Pact', Mexican Association of Law and Economics Working Series Papers of Law and Economics, no. 61.

Martinez, Luis Danton, 'The Creation of a Mortgage Backed Securities Market on Mexico', Mexican Association of Law and Economics Working Series Papers of Law and Economics, no. 82.

Mejica Rosales, Ricardo, ''El Chopo' Economic Analysis on a Non-regulated Market', Mexican Association of Law and Economics Working Series Papers of Law and Economics, no. 20.

Mendoza Justo, Gustavo Hernandez O., Ma. Eugenia, 'Economic Analysis on Guerrillas', Mexican Association of Law and Economics Working Series Papers of Law and Economics, no. 62.

Meneses Cazares, Julio, 'Who Should I Vote For?', Mexican Association of Law and Economics Working Series Papers of Law and Economics, no. 38.

Meritano Corrales, Sergio, 'Economic Analysis on a New Federalism', Mexican

Association of Law and Economics Working Series Papers of Law and Economics, no. 17.

Messmacher Linatas, Miguel and Yañez Sandoval, Armando, 'Economic Analysis on the Federal Hunting Law', Mexican Association of Law and Economics Working Series Papers of Law and Economics, no. 105.

Meza Parra, Isaac Omar, 'The Limit of the Autonomy of the Central Bank in Mexico', Mexican Association of Law and Economics Working Series Papers of Law and Economics, no. 63.

Milo Caraza, Alexis and Valencia Alvarez Donaji, 'Economic Analysis of Art', Mexican Association of Law and Economics Working Series Papers of Law and Economics, no. 64.

Mir, Claudia, Zarate, Graciela and Ripol, Alex, 'Economic Analysis of the Federalization of the Health Services in Mexico City', Mexican Association of Law and Economics Working Series Papers of Law and Economics, no. 65.

Montaño Fernandez, Carlos, 'Analysis on the Regulation of the Federal Law of Environmental Balance And Environment Protection in the Matter of Prevention and Control of Air Pollution', Mexican Association of Law and Economics Working Series Papers of Law and Economics, no. 106.

Montesinos Cordoba, Jorge Luis and Araujo Papilla, Agustin, 'Economic Analysis on Divorce', Mexican Association of Law and Economics Working Series Papers of Law and Economics, no. 66.

Obregon Roa, Hector Manuel, 'Economic Analysis of Internet', Mexican Association of Law and Economics Working Series Papers of Law and Economics, no. 01.

Ordoñes Bustos, Dora Irene, 'Economic Analysis of Theft', Mexican Association of Law and Economics Working Series Papers of Law and Economics, no. 67.

Orejas R., Miguel A. 'Economic Analysis of the Mexican Legislation', Mexican Association of Law and Economics Working Series Papers of Law and Economics, no. 43.

Ortega Gilly, Federico, 'Management of Prisons in Mexico From Governmental To Private Sector', Mexican Association of Law and Economics Working Series Papers of Law and Economics, no. 52.

Ortega Ortiz, Hiquingari, 'Economic Analysis on Artificial Insemination in Humans', Mexican Association of Law and Economics Working Series Papers of Law and Economics, no. 23.

Ortiz Alonso, Maria Guadalupe, 'Efficiency on Family Law', Mexican Association of Law and Economics Working Series Papers of Law and Economics, no. 35.

Perez Gavila, Fernando, 'An Economic Analysis of the Mexican System of Public Education', Mexican Association of Law and Economics Working Series Papers of Law and Economics, no. 11.

Perez Lara, Delfino, 'The Reform on House-living Funds: the Infonavit Case', Mexican Association of Law and Economics Working Series Papers of Law and Economics, no. 41.

Pinto, Jesus, 'Economic Analysis of the Cocaine Market', Mexican Association of Law and Economics Working Series Papers of Law and Economics, no. 68.

Pizaña Treviño, Karla, 'Economic Analysis on the Law of Investment Societies', Mexican Association of Law and Economics Working Series Papers of Law and Economics, no. 107.

Pliega Zapata, Alejandra, 'Economic Analysis on Basic Education: Economic and Social Development', Mexican Association of Law and Economics Working Series Papers of Law and Economics, no. 69.

Pulido Rincon, Rodrigo, 'Economic Analysis on the Living-houses Renting Problem of Mexico City: A Comparison Between the Former and the Actual Renting Law', Mexican Association of Law and Economics Working Series Papers of Law and Economics, no. 10.

Quiyond Jimenez, Alejandro, 'Be Ware!', Mexican Association of Law and Economics Working Series Papers of Law and Economics, no. 26.

Ramirez Rodales, Alejandro, 'Economic Analysis on the Federal Fishing Law', Mexican Association of Law and Economics Working Series Papers of Law and Economics, no. 34.

Ramirez Salazar, Eduardo, 'Comparison Between Two Proposals To Solve the Intermediatism', Mexican Association of Law and Economics Working Series Papers of Law and Economics, no. 70.

Remes Tello De Meneses, Roberto, 'Economics, Law an Urban Transportation From Individual To Collective Transportation', Mexican Association of Law and Economics Working Series Papers of Law and Economics, no. 09.

Rendon Ojeda, Victor Armando, 'Analysis on the Efficiency of Corruption Against Inefficient Laws', Mexican Association of Law and Economics Working Series Papers of Law and Economics, no. 16.

Rios Gonzalez, Rogelio, 'Personal Economic Analysis on Public Policy: Make a Decision', Mexican Association of Law and Economics Working Series Papers of Law and Economics, no. 71.

Rivera, Miguel Angel, 'The Gossip Market', Mexican Association of Law and Economics Working Series Papers of Law and Economics, no. 37.

Rocha, Carolina, 'Economic Analysis on Abortion', Mexican Association of Law and Economics Working Series Papers of Law and Economics, no. 19.

Roemer, Andrès (1989), *Análisis Económico-Jurídico de le Acuacultura de Camerón, el Caso Mexicano* (Economic Analysis of the Shrimp Market in Mexico), Mexico, UNAM.

Roemer, Andrès (1989), *Evaluacion Juridica, Finmanciera, y Economicade la Camaronicultura en Mexico*, Instituto Tecnologico Autonomo de Mexico.

Roemer, Andrès (1992), *Importancia del Análisis Económico del Derecho*, Mexico, SUMMA de la Sociedad Mexicana de Geografía en México y Estadística.

Roemer, Andrès (1993), *Introduccion al Analisis Economico del Derecho*, Mexico City, Fondo de Cultura Economica.

Roemer, Andrès (1994), *Introdución al Análisis Económico del Derecho* (Introduction to Law and Economics), Mexico, Fondo de Cultura Económica, Sociedad Mexicana de geografía y Estadística, e Instituto Technológico Autónome de México.

Roemer, Andrès (1996), *Economía y Derecho: Políticas Públicas del Agua* (Economics and Law: Public Policy of Water), Centro de Investigación y Docencia Económica, la Sociedad Mexicana de Geografía y Estadística and Porrùa.

Roemer, Andrès, 'An Eclectic Approach To Property Rights', Mexican Association of Law and Economics Working Series Papers of Law and Economics.

Roemer, Andrès, *Economic Analysis of Law: Markets For Water In Mexico*, Porrua, Cide.

Roemer, Andrès, *Introduction To Law and Economics*, Fce, Smge, Itam (1994).

Roemer, Andrès, *Privatization: the Mexican Versus the French Case*.

Roemer, Andrès, *The Game of Law And Economics*, Smge, Itam.

Rosas Chavez, Patricia, 'Economic Analysis on the Federal Law of Public Security in Mexico', Mexican Association of Law and Economics Working Series Papers of Law and Economics, no. 72.

Ruiz Aguila, Silvia, 'Economic Analysis on Juvenile Criminal's Behavior', Mexican Association of Law and Economics Working Series Papers of Law and Economics, no. 73.

Ruiz Chagoya, Aleida, 'Economic Analysis of Civil Law', Mexican Association of Law and Economics Working Series Papers of Law and Economics, no. 07.

Salazar Jasso, Ruben, 'Issues To Consider on the Solution of the Negative Effects Caused by Illegal Drugs Abuse', Mexican Association of Law and Economics Working Series Papers of Law and Economics, no. 74.

San Sebastian, Sergio and Pastrana, Jorge, 'Economic Analysis of Post-Modernism', Mexican Association of Law and Economics Working Series Papers of Law and Economics, no. 75.

Sanchez Garcia, Antonio, 'An Economic Analysis: Public Demonstrations in Mexico City', Mexican Association of Law and Economics Working Series Papers of Law and Economics, no. 12.

Sanders, Mauricio, 'Economic Analysis on the Rules of Soccer', Mexican Association of Law and Economics Working Series Papers of Law and Economics, no. 48.

Sanjurjo Rivera, Enrique, 'An Economic Analysis of the Old Testament', Mexican Association of Law and Economics Working Series Papers of Law and Economics, no. 25.

Santana Cartas, Sandra Alicia, 'Law and Economics of Euthanasia', Mexican Association of Law and Economics Working Series Papers of Law and Economics, no. 45.

Santos Garcia, Isabel Guadalupe and Perez Meres, Mario Alejandro, 'Economic Analysis on the Mexican Chamberof Deputies: Institutions, Incentives and Management', Mexican Association of Law and Economics Working Series Papers of Law and Economics, no. 76.

Schwandi, Michel, 'Inefficiencies and Alternatives on Garbage: A Market Economic Analysis', Mexican Association of Law and Economics Working Series Papers of Law and Economics, no. 22.

Sepulveda Mestres, Nuria, 'Property Rights on Retirement Funds' Collective Fund System vs Personal Account System', Mexican Association of Law and Economics Working Series Papers of Law and Economics, no. 39.

Solis Angulo, Liliana, 'Economic Analysis on the Regulation of Surrogated Motherhood', Mexican Association of Law and Economics Working Series Papers of Law and Economics, no. 84.

Soria Sierra, Gabriela, 'Economic Analysis on Criminal Law', Mexican Association of Law and Economics Working Series Papers of Law and Economics, no. 51.

Suarez Cardera, Victor, 'Public Policies on Mexican Agriculture: A Five-year Term Agricultural Law', Mexican Association of Law and Economics Working Series Papers of Law and Economics, no. 04.

Taracena Ble, Heberto, 'Analysis of Public Lands', Mexican Association of Law and Economics Working Series Papers of Law and Economics, no. 108.

Torres Fragoso, Jaime, 'The Application In Mexico of the Death Penalty', Mexican

Association of Law and Economics Working Series Papers of Law and Economics, no. 77.

Torres Rivera, Alma Delia and Ponce Lazaro, Reyna, 'Economic Analysis of the Criminal Code An the Criminal Procedure Code: the State of Morelos Proposal', Mexican Association of Law and Economics Working Series Papers of Law and Economics, no. 78.

Treviño Goirgulli, Alfonso, 'Economic Analysis on Civil Law Regulation', Mexican Association of Law and Economics Working Series Papers of Law and Economics, no. 42.

Urritia, Luis, 'Economic Reasons for a Financial Regulation in Mexico', Mexican Association of Law and Economics Working Series Papers of Law and Economics, no. 02.

Valades, Jose Diego, 'Economic Analysis on Flirting', Mexican Association of Law and Economics Working Series Papers of Law and Economics, no. 79.

Valderrama Lopez, Juan Carlos and Diaz Tapia, Juan, 'A Negotiation Project To Accomplish An Agreement of Economic Partnership And Political Arrangement Between Mexico And the European Community', Mexican Association of Law and Economics Working Series Papers of Law and Economics, no. 41.

Valdes Palacio, Yailen and Romo Morales, Gerardo, 'Abortion in Mexico: An Economic Analysis', Mexican Association of Law and Economics Working Series Papers of Law and Economics, no. 109.

Varela Pineda, Flavio, 'Institutional Change And Internal Reform In the P.r.i.', Mexican Association of Law and Economics Working Series Papers of Law and Economics, no. 63.

Vargas Diaz, Jaime Fernando, 'The Deregulation in the Electrical Industry in Mexico: Causes and Consequenses', Mexican Association of Law and Economics Working Series Papers of Law and Economics, no. 04.

Vazquez Ochoa, David, 'Economic Effects on the Rural Production System Under the Law of January 15th of 1915, and Under the Reform of Article 27 of the Constitution of Mexico', Mexican Association of Law and Economics Working Series Papers of Law and Economics, no. 33.

Vega Godines, Alejandro, 'Law and Neo-instututional Economics of the Budgetary System of Education', Mexican Association of Law and Economics Working Series Papers of Law and Economics, no. 80.

Vernon, Andres, 'The Last Chance: Reforms on Article 27 of the Mexican Constitution and a New Law on Forests', Mexican Association of Law and Economics Working Series Papers of Law and Economics, no. 110.

Villa Rodriguez, Jose Manuel, 'Games', Mexican Association of Law and Economics Working Series Papers of Law and Economics, no. 18.

Willie, Thomas, 'An Economic Analysis of the Market For Diamonds', Mexican Association of Law and Economics Working Series Papers of Law and Economics, no. 81.

Yunes Zorrilla, Jeso, 'The Human Capital: Municipalities', Mexican Association of Law and Economics Working Series Papers of Law and Economics, no. 08.

Zavala Pavila, Adolfo, 'Economic Analysis on Crime', Mexican Association of Law and Economics Working Series Papers of Law and Economics, no. 32.

Zepeda Lecuona, Guillermo Raul, 'Law on Environmental and Protection Policies',

Mexican Association of Law and Economics Working Series Papers of Law and Economics, no. 111.

Zepeda Leucona, Guillermo Raul, 'Analysis on the Reform of the Legal Regime of the 'Ministerio Publico' (Public Ministry) on Justice Prosecution, 'Mexican Association of Law and Economics Working Series Papers of Law and Economics, no. 50.

Zepeda Leucona, Guillermo Raul, 'Economic Analysis of the Judiciary System in the State of Jalisco', Mexican Association of Law and Economics Working Series Papers of Law and Economics, no. 01.

0355
Law and Economics in the Netherlands

Rudi W. Holzhauer
Erasmus University of Rotterdam

Rob Teijl
Dutch Ministry of Justice

Abstract

The rise of law and economics in the Netherlands has been a mixed lawyers and economists effort. Budget cuts during recent years put pressure on economics departments in law faculties to focus more on 'the law' and hence law and economics became an interesting issue for these departments. Adoption by the regular law professors is fairly slow and fairly reluctant. The cautious positioning of law and economics by its early (and later) proponents avoided any major confrontative philosophical or political debates.
JEL classification: K00.
Keywords: Research, Education, Teaching.

1. Introduction - Overview

The proper activities in new law and economics started in the Netherlands in 1987. Leiden University (Franken, Hol) then organised a nationwide meeting, with the aims to make an inventory of all law and economics activities in the Netherlands, and to see what options were open to cooperate with and coordinate research and teaching. Approximately 40 academics attended that meeting.

One of the results was the plan to cooperate in writing a student text book. Representatives of three faculties (Franken and Hol from Leiden, Backhaus from Maastricht and Holzhauer and Teijl from Rotterdam) agreed to write a text that was embedded in Dutch law and that used examples from the Dutch legal system. A first student textbook by Holzhauer and Teijl was published in June 1989; a second edition appeared in 1995. Other textbooks followed: Theeuwes et al. (1989), Hondius (1991), Nentjes (1993b) and Van Velthoven and Van Wijck (1997).

The Dutch judiciary has a centre for permanent education. In 1992 a first two day seminar was organised, which basically is repeated bi-annually. There is some - be it limited - interest (15 to 20 participants).

The major general Dutch law review (*Nederlands Juristen Blad*) has had a special editor for law and economics since the 1980s (Ejan Mackaay). The main student law journal (*Ars Aequi*) has had a one page column twice a year since 1992 (Holzhauer, Teijl). The major general Dutch economists' journal (*Economisch Statistische Berichten*) intends to accommodate a regular column from 1998 onwards.

So far the Society for Civil Law (Van den Bergh and Faure, 1990) and the Society for Procedural Law (Holzhauer, 1993) have explicitly put the law and economics approach at the centre of an annual meeting.

2. Research - General

The first PhD thesis in the field of law and economics in the Netherlands is Mackaay (1982). Mackaay has also published several overview articles of (1985, 1988, 1989, 1991). Kaufmann wrote his PhD thesis in 1985 on 'Passing off and misappropriation in the law of unfair competition' (thesis Utrecht); Kneppers-Heynert in 1988 on 'An economic and legal analysis of franchising' (thesis Groningen); Kerkmeester in 1989 on 'Law and game theory: an economic model for the emergence of state organization and law' (thesis Rotterdam); Hol on 'Law in balance' (1993; thesis Leiden) and Teijl and Holzhauer in 1997 on 'Changing Perspectives in Law and Economics' (thesis Rotterdam). By now several law and economics oriented research projects have been started.

In 1988 it was decided to found the Centre for Law and Economics. Its goal is to promote research and teaching in law and economics. Its information adress is Erasmus University Rotterdam - law faculty, PO box 1738, 3000 DR Rotterdam, Netherlands.

In 1988 the first workshop on law and economics was held in Maastricht (Backhaus). The workshop had five lectures. And Gordon Tullock was as a guest-speaker invited. His keynote lecture was on 'Economic analysis of legal procedure'. By now there is a firm tradition: in April 1998 the eleventh Workshop was held in Maastricht.

All law faculties now regularly focus on the economic implications of (changes in) legal rules.

In 1991 a Dutch language law and economics series was started by Franken, Holzhauer and Teijl (Series Rechtseconomische Verkenningen, published by Gouda Quint, Arnhem). The purpose is to offer a forum for publishing contributions of 75-150 pages. On average one volume a year has been published: Teijl and Holzhauer (1991b), Richters (1991), Kerkmeester (1993a), Van den Bergh (1993, 1994, 1997c), Gaakeer and Kerkmeester (1997).

3. Research - Topics

Property Law

Limited attention is paid to institutional property arrangements. Bouckaert (1990) gives a summary outline. Meijs and Jansen (1989) relate ownership to politics and economics. De Geest (1994) discusses private versus common ownership. Economic ownership and legal ownership are confronted by Slagter (1968), Colijn et al. (1981) and Huijgen (1995). For a more sociological setting see von Benda-Beckman (1992).

Hol (1993) touches nuisance issues. Environmental topics are discussed by Faure (1990b, 1993, 1994). Wiersma (1989) and Peeters (1992) focus on tradeable (pollution) permits. Ownership of the company is analysed by Moerland (1995c) and Timmerman (1996). See *Company Law* below.

Teijl and Holzhauer (1991b) provide an overview of the economic analysis of intellectual property. An economic perspective on intellectual property can also be found in Koopmans (1983, 1994) and Strowel (1994). Van Dijk (1994) concentrates on the economics of patent protection, and Kaufmann (1986) on the economics of trademarks. For an economic approach on copyright on the Internet see Richard (1996).

Contracts

There is no literature on the economics of contracts in general. Du Perron (1990) and Theeuwes (1996) are summary attempts. Franchising is dealt with in depth by Kneppers-Heynert (1988). Aelen (1990) examines the EC block exemption for franchise agreements. Castermans and Notermans (1985) look at disclosure rules in contract formation.

Tort

Basic outlines are Mackaay (1990) and Van Schilfgaarde (1990). Hol (1993) offers a fairly thorough economic analysis of general tort principles, including a philosophical perspective. Van Dam (1989) touches on law and economics. Causation issues are discussed in Faure (1993), Ietswaart (1995) and Kerkmeester (1993b, 1994b). Law professor and Supreme Court Judge Nieuwenhuis (1991) has always been rather sceptical. More opposition can be found in Hol (1991) and Bloembergen (1996). Raes (1988b) criticizes the economic approach to personal harm on humanistic/philosophical grounds.

Traffic liability is the topic in two early reports by the Justice Department Ministerie van Justitie (1978, 1980). Nentjes and Dijkstra (1993) and Van den

Bergh (1997a) relate the neoclassical economic model of liability to a proposed change in traffic liability law, as do Visscher (1998), Visscher and Van den Bergh (1998). Liability and insurance is the theme in Van den Bergh and Faure (1990).

Company Law

By way of introduction read De Kluiver (1994, 1996). The 'ownership' of the firm and the relationship between shareholders, management and supervisors are discussed in Boot (1995), Brink (1994), Rietkerk (1992), Slagter (1988, 1989, 1993), Van der Grinten (1994), Wildenberg and Zwetsloot (1994).

Different systems of remuneration are analysed by Eigenhuizen et al. (1987) and Bruining et al. (1989).

In 1995 and 1996 there was a fairly extensive discussion of Corporate Governance issues: see Boot (1994), Crist (1995), Frentrop (1995), Frijns et al. (1995), Mendel (1995), Moerland (1995b and 1995e), Slagter (1994), Tabaksblatt (1995), Wallage (1995), Wiggers (1995), Commissie Corporate Governance (1996) and Raaijmakers et al. (1996). This discussion is likely to continue. Moerland (1995a) analyses alternative disciplinary mechanisms in different corporate systems.

Insider dealing is discussed in Doorenbos and Roording (1990). More law than economics (on insider dealing) are Beckman and Herst (1988), Corstens (1989), Doorenbos (1989), Dreese (1984), Groenhuijsen (1995), Slagter (1996) and Voûte (1989).

Economic analyses of takeovers can be found in Rietkerk (1988) and Moerland (1988), facts on the Netherlands in Vogelzang and Dotsch (1988). See Braakman (1988) for the role of European competition law. Bruining (1992) shows the effects of takeovers on share prices. De Jong (1988) relates protective measures to takeovers.

Theoretical and empirical concentration issues in De Jong (1992), Dorsman (1992) and Langendijk (1992).

Tax Law

Contributions on the economics of tax law are Caanen and Essers (1990), Hessing and Elffers (1994) and Zwemmer (1995).

Competition Law/Anti Trust

The divide in writings on competition law is the New Dutch Competition Act, that came into force on 1 January 1998. It marked a period where the Netherlands were said to be a cartel-paradise. Since that date there is an anti-trust authority, and hence more explicit attention for breaking down all sorts of anti-competitive situations.

A general law and economics overview on competition law is Van den Bergh (1997c). More specific on the new act are Van den Bergh (1997b) and De Vreugd (1993). See also Biesheuvel et al. (1996), Bos (1996), De Jong (1997), Van der Ploeg (1996) and Schenk (1997).

Criminal Law

Basic analyses in line with Gary Becker's approach: Meester and Wesemann (1976), Franken (1983, 1991) and Nentjes (1988).

The economic and non-economic factors of crime are analysed in Theeuwes and Van Velthoven (1994a). Their conclusion is that economic determinants like unemployment, probability of apprehension and punishment significantly explain the decrease in criminality, but that social norm variables at the same time have a relatively more substantial effect. An economic model of the criminal law system is developed by Van Tulder (1994). In a non-model way see Steenhuis (1984). Of special interest is Van Tulder's finding that extra expenditures later on in the system (for example on prisons) are more effective. Kleemans (1996) focusses on the possibilities to describe urban crime patterns using choice behaviour of those who commit the specific crime. Economic offences are discussed in Van Altena et al. (1990).

Critique on the rational choice model with respect to criminal law can be found in Franken (1983), Wladimiroff (1991), Baerveldt (1993), Bruinsma and Van de Bunt (1993), Van Dijk (1993), Hesseling (1993), Kleemans (1993) and Moerland (1993). The latter six references are in a special issue of the *Tijdschrift voor Criminologie* (*Journal of Criminology 1993/2*) rational choice and criminal behaviour.

Administrative/Constitutional Law

An economic model for the emergence of state organization and law in a game theoretical approach is offered by Kerkmeester (1989). The same author presents an introduction into constitutional economics in Kerkmeester (1993a). For an economic analysis of constitutional law see also Backhaus (1991) and Ten Berge (1991). Van Ommeren (1990) looks at administrative compensation and financial capacity from a law and economics angle. Jansen (1996) discusses administrative fines in the new Dutch Competition Act.

Regulation

Early notes on deregulation are De Kraan (1982a, 1982b) (general), Mok (1983), Slot (1983) and Bolkestein (1985) (competition law). Deregulation in working conditions legislation is discussed in Faure (1995a). In 1994 the Minister of Economic Affairs initiated a research project on the functioning of the market in the Netherlands. It has boosted the writings on regulation in general and furthermore resulted in some reports on the possible impact of deregulation and privatization in some economic sectors. See on this (de-) regulation debate: Bernardt and Canoy (1997), Bos (1995), Van Damme (1996, 1997), Geelhoed (1993), Gestel et al. (1996), Jacobs (1996), Koedijk (1994), Mol and Verbon (1997), Peeters (1994), Van der Ploeg (1994), Van Waarden and Unger (1992), Verhaegen and Volkers (1996).

Public Choice
The economic theory of political decisionmaking is presented by Groenewegen et al. (1988), De Geest (1990), Van Winden (1990) and Schreuders (1990).

Environmental Law
In a very general way Nentjes (1993a) discusses who owns the environment. The efficiency of an environmental policy in accordance with market principles is discussed in Wiersma (1989).

Faure (1990b) takes up the Shavell model for the choice of protecting the environment through liability law or through regulation. The first use rule is analysed in Faure (1994), and reflections on probabilistic causal evidence for environmental health damage are made in Faure (1993). Nieuwenhuis (1991) offers three ways of balancing interests in environmental law, including a critique on the economic approach (see also Nieuwenhuis, 1997).

A comparative study regarding the transferability of pollution rights is to be found in Peeters (1992). Nentjes (1996) compares tradeable permits to covenants.

Legal Procedure
Van Velthoven and Van Wijck (1996, 1997) apply the Shavell model on suits and settlements. Authors that should be mentioned here in a more general way are Van Tulder, Van Koppen, Ten Kate and Malsch. All their work is more or less on efficiency and effectiveness in the area of adjudication. Their empirical approach partly stems from a sociological background. More purely sociological in nature are the contributions of Blankenburg (1984, 1990). Klijn (1988, 1996) are somewhere in between. Contributions from lawyers are Van Dijk (1987) and Snijders (1987).

4. Teaching

In a number of law faculties attention is paid to law and economics. Sometimes this is done in a (compulsory) course on economics, sometimes in another form. Mention can be made of the faculties in Groningen, Leiden,

Maastricht, Rotterdam and Utrecht. There is a tendency for economics in law faculties to increasingly focus on law/legal topics. In this way at Leiden university law faculty law and economics material was developed for the second year (compulsory) course in economics. Those materials are now in the book by Van Velthoven, Van Wijck et al. (1997). In Groningen and Rotterdam we see a similar move. In Maastricht law and economics is offered in a much more limited way later on in the curriculum.

In the early 1990s several joint study weekends were held at an undergraduate level, with law and economics students from Ghent, Antwerp and Rotterdam.

Together with the Ghent Law Faculty (Bouckaert, De Geest) the Rotterdam Law Faculty (Holzhauer, Teijl) founded the one-year English taught Erasmus Programme in Law and Economics in 1990. The network of participating faculties expanded throughout Europe and is at present (1998) some 20. The coordination of the Programme shifted to Hamburg (Ott, Schäfer) in 1995. In this Programme Rotterdam teaches two terms; Leiden one term. Utrecht created a separate one-year English taught postgraduate LL.M. Programme in (European) Law and Economics in 1997 and founded the first part-time chair in law and economics (held by Roger Van den Bergh). The Rotterdam law faculty will have the first chair in law and economics in 1998.

5. Prospects for Law and Economics in the Netherlands

The rise of law and economics in the Netherlands has been a mixed effort by lawyers and economists. Most law faculties (there are eight in the Netherlands) have their own chair in economics (as well as in sociology and - often - psychology). Budget cuts during recent years put pressure on economics departments in law faculties to focus more on 'the law' and hence law and economics became an interesting issue for these departments. Adoption by the regular law professors is - as one could expect - fairly slow and fairly reluctant. The cautious positioning of law and economics by its early (and later) proponents avoided any major confrontative philosophical or political debates.

So far, faculties of economics hardly seem to take an interest in law and economics. Most contributions came and come from (economists and lawyers in) law faculties.

For a moment, in the mid 1990s, the already mentioned budget cuts threatened the existence of economics (and all other non-law disciplines) in those faculties. However, there are now (1997/98) signs for a renewed interest in interdisciplinary research and teaching. Thus, we may see regular economics chairs being transformed into law and economics. On the whole we nevertheless seriously doubt whether law and economics will ever establish itself acedemically in the 'American' way, for example appear in many/most/all students and practitioners law books.

The Department of Justice takes some interest in law and economics issues. There are several private consultants that practice law and economics, usually under the heading of 'policy analysis'. The firms/foundations 'Research en Beleid' in Leiden; 'Stichting voor Economisch Onderzoek (SEO)' in Amsterdam and the 'Nederlands Economisch Instituut (NEI)' in Rotterdam all regularly produce economic analyses of legal issues on demand.

Bibliography on Law and Economics in the Netherlands (0355)

This list consists of contributions to law and economics in Dutch publications. Occasionally an article or book is in the English Language (for example originally published in English). If in Dutch, the author may occasionally be non-Dutch (for instance, Belgian).

ABN (1989), *Octrooien en Licenties* (Patents and Licences), Algemene Bank Nederland, 35 p.

ABN (1989), *Kwekersrecht* (Plant Breeders Right), Algemene Bank Nederland, 12 p.

ABN (1990), *Octrooien in het Midden- en Kleinbedrijf* (Patents in Middle-sized and Small Companies), Algemene Bank Nederland, 11 p.

Aelen, L.O.M. (1990), 'De EEG-Groepsvrijstelling voor Franchise-Overeenkomsten (The EX Block Exemption for Franchise Agreements)', **38** *Sociaal-Economische Wetgeving: Tijdschrift voor Europees en Economisch Recht*, 3-16.

Akkermans, A. (1995), 'Statistisch Causaliteitsbewijs bij Toxische Schadeveroorzaking (Statistical Causation and Toxic Damage)', *Verzekeringsarchief*, 44-53.

Algra, N.E. (1991), *The Relations Between Law and Economics*, Cahiers Rechtstheorie en Encyclopedie van het Recht, Nr. 2.

Aretz, Edward M. (1993), *Efficient Law*, Limburg, Rijksuniversiteit, 181 p.

Baarslag, A.D. (1990), 'Octrooibeleid van de Onderneming (Patent Policy of the Firm)', in X (ed.), *Octrooien in Nederland en Europa*, Kamer van Koophandel en Fabrieken voor Rotterdam en de Beneden-Maas, 22 mei.

Backhaus, Jürgen G. (1990), 'De Eis tot Correctie van Ondoelmatig Recht (The Need to Correct Inefficient Law)', **39(10)** *Ars Aequi*, 660-665.

Backhaus, Jürgen G. (1991), 'Een Economische Analyse van het Constitutionele Recht (An Economic Analysis of Constitutional Law)', in Hondius, E.H., Schippers, J.J. and Siegers, J.J. (eds), *Rechtseconomie en Recht*, Zwolle, Tjeenk Willink, 107-148.

Baerveldt, Chris (1993), 'Het Gebruik van Rationele Keuzereconstructies bij de Effect-evaluatie van Interventies (The Use of Rational Choice Constructs in Evaluating the Consequences of Interventions)', **35(2)** *Tijdschrift voor Criminologie*, 158-176.

Bakker, Luit M. et al. (1996), 'Economie en Recht: van Confrontatie naar Integratie (Economics and Law: From Confrontation to Integration)', in Van de Hoek, M.P.

(ed.), *Opstellen Aangeboden aan prof. dr. C. Rijnvos*, Groningen, Wolters-Noordhoff, 102-111.

Bakker, Luit M. and Holzhauer, Rudi W. (1998), *Parallel Import*, Rechtseconomische Verkenningen, Arnhem, Gouda Quint.

Bakker, Luit M. and Ridder, Ronald K. De (1990), 'Het EG- Mededingingsbeleid en de Samenwerking en Concentratie Binnen het Europese Bankwezen (EC Competition Policy and European Banking Cooperation and Concentration)', **39(11)** *Bank- en Effectenbedrijf*, 42-46.

Barents, R. (1986), 'Enige Recente Ontwikkelingen in het Europese Mededingingsbeleid (1980-1985) (Some Recent Developments in European Competition Policy)', **29** *TVVS Maandblad voor Ondernemingsrecht en Rechtspersonen*, 192-198.

Beckman, H. and Herst, H.C.C. (1988), 'Handel met Voorwetenschap (Insider Dealing)', **66(2)** *De Naamloze Vennootschap*, 71-75.

Bekkers, V.J.J.M. (1996), 'De Schutkleuren van het Dereguleringsbeleid (The Camouflage of Deregulation Policy)', in Van Gestel, R.A.J. et al. (eds), *Markt en Wet*, Deventer, W.E.J. Tjeenk Willink, 59-77.

Bernardt, Y. and Canoy, M. (1997), 'Hordenlopen van Monopolie naar Markt (The Hurdle-Race from Monopoly to Market)', **82** *Economisch-Statistische Berichten*.

Biesheuvel, M.B.W. et al. (1996), *Van Ordening naar Marktwerking: Kanttekeningen bij het Ontwerp-Mededingingswet* (From a Regulatory to a Market Approach: Notes on the Competion Bill), 's-Gravenhage, SDU, 172 p.

Blankenburg, E. (1984), 'Bevorderen Rechtshelpers de Groeiende Neiging tot Procederen of Remmen zij deze Juist af? (Does Legal Aid Promote or Curb the Increasing Tendency to go to Trial)', in X (ed.), *De Jonge Balie Congres 1984, Congresbundel: Deformalisering in de rechtspraktijk*, Zwolle, Tjeenk Willink, 110-123.

Blankenburg, E. (1990), 'Naar een Planeconomie voor de Rechtshulp (Towards a Planned Economy for Legal Aid)', *Nederlands Juristen Blad*, 879-882.

Blankenburg, E. and Verwoerd, J.R.A. (1987), 'Vermijden en Benutten van Civielrechtelijke Procedures in Nederland en Omringende Landen (The Use and Avoidance of Private Law Proceedings in Surrounding Countries)', **7-2** *Justitiële Verkenningen*, 20-35.

Bleeker, K.A.M. (1989), 'De Geheimhoudingsplicht volgens art. 42 WEM in het Licht van het EEG-Verdrag (The Secrecy Duty According to s. 42 WEM in the Light of the EC Treaty)', **37** *Sociaal-Economische Wetgeving: Tijdschrift voor Europees en Economisch Recht*, 714-722.

Bloembergen (1972), *Duizend Botsingen: Een Kwantitatieve Analyse van Civiele Rechtbankvonnissen in Verkeerszaken* (Thousand Accidents: A Quantitative Analysis of Civil Court Decisions on Traffic Matters), Deventer, Kluwer, 74 p.

Bloembergen, A.R. (1996), 'Wolfsbergen en de Rechtseconomie (Wolfsbergen and Law and Economics)', in Franke, M.E. et al. (eds), *Onrechtmatige Daad*, Deventer, Gouda Quint, 25-38.

Bloembergen, A.R. and Van Wersch, P.J.M. (1973), *Verkeersslachtoffers en hun Schade* (Victims of Traffic Accidents and Their Damage), Deventer, Kluwer, 241 p.

Bolkestein, Frits (1985), *Freedom and Regulation: A Liberal View on Competition Policy* (Vrijheid en Regeling: Een Liberale Visie op de Mededingingspolitiek), s-Gravenhage, 35 p.

Booij, J.T. (1993), *De Economische Betekenis van het Auteursrecht in 1989: Rapportage 1993* (The Economic Role of Copyright Law in 1989: Report 1993), Amsterdam, Stichting voor Economisch Onderzoek, 61 p.

Boot, Arnoud, W.A. (1994), 'Corporate Governance, Structuurregime en de Financiering van het Bedrijfsleven (Corporate Governance, Supervisory Boards and Corporate Finance)', **68** *Maandblad voor Accountancy en Bedrijfseconomie*, 724-736.

Boot, Arnoud, W.A. (1995), 'Naar een Dynamischer Structuurregime (Towards More Dynamic Supervisory Boards)', **73** *De Naamloze Vennootschap*, 280-284.

Bos, P.V.F. (1994), 'Van Ontvoogding naar Ontgoocheling of van Interstatelijkheid naar Communautaire Dimensie? (From Guardianship to Illusion or From a State to a Community Perspective)', **69** *Nederlands Juristen Blad*, 906-911.

Bos, D.I. (1995), *Marktwerking en Regulering: Theoretische Aspecten en Ervaringen in Nederland en het Buitenland* (Market Forces and Regulation: Theoretical Aspects and Experiences in the Netherlands and Abroad), Den Haag, Ministerie van Economische Zaken, 130 p.

Bos, P.V.F. (1996), 'Het Voorstel voor een Nieuwe Mededingingswet: De Sprong van Us Men naar het Paard van Troje (The New Competion Bill: From Like Knows Like to the Trojan Horse)', **71** *Nederlands Juristen Blad*, 1237-1243.

Bos, P.V.F. and Fierstra, Marc A. (1989), *Europees Mededingingsrecht* (European Competition Law), Deventer, Kluwer, 274 p.

Bos, P.V.F. and Stuyck, J.H.V. (1989), 'Concentratiecontrole naar EEG-recht (Concentration Control in EC-Law)', **37** *Sociaal-Economische Wetgeving: Tijdschrift voor Europees en Economisch Recht*, 300-404.

Bouckaert, Boudewijn (1990), 'Eigendomsrechten vanuit Rechtseconomisch Perspectief (Property Rights from an Economic Perspective)', **39** *Ars Aequi* in Bock, Ruth de, et al. (ed), *Themanummer Rechtseconomie*, 777-789.

Boukema, C.A. (1991), 'Economische en Juridische Aspecten van Hoofdstuk I Fusiecode (Economic and Legal Aspects of Chapter I Dutch Merger Rules)', in Coljee, P.D., Franken, H., Heertje, A. and Kanning, W. (eds), *Law and Welfare Economics*, Amsterdam, VU Amsterdam.

Bouckaert, Boudewijn (1994), 'Misschien Geen Vrienden, Waarschijnlijk Wel Bondgenoten: Bedenkingen over de Nauwe Kloof tussen de Rechtssociologie van het Handelen en de Rechtseconomie van de Sociale Coöperatie (Perhaps not Friends but Probably Allies: Considerations Regarding the Narrow Gap Between Legal Sociology of Action and Legal Analysis of Social Cooperation)', in Raes, Koen and Willekens, H. (eds), *Economische Verklaringen van het Recht*, Den Haag, VUGA, 44-74.

Bovens, M.A.P. and Witteveen, W.J. (1987), 'Bruce Ackerman over Sociale Rechtvaardigheid, de Rol van de Rechter en 'Law and Economics' (Bruce Ackerman on Social Justice, the Role of the Judiciary and 'Law and Economics')', *Staatkundig Jaarboek, Ars Aequi Libri*, 255-278.

Braakman, A.J. (1988), 'Europees Kartelrecht als Strijdmiddel bij Overnames (European Anti-trust Law as Takeover Combat Mechanism)', **73** *Economisch-Statistische Berichten*, 854-858.

Brink, M. (1994), 'De Discussie over de Structuurwet Anders Bezien (A Different View on the Supervisory Boards Act)', **72** *De Naamloze Vennootschap*, 240-246.

Brinkhof, Jan J. (1990), 'Over Octrooirecht en Economie (On Patent Law and the Economy)', **39(10)** *Ars Aequi*, 794-802.

Bruin, A.C.N. (1995), 'Fusietoezicht: Derde Pijler van het Mededingingsbeleid (Merger Control: Third Leg of Competition Policy)', **80** *Economisch-Statistische Berichten*, 489-492.

Bruining, J. (1992), 'De Effecten van Overnames op Aandelenrendementen in Fusies en Overnames (The Effects of Take-Overs on Share Prices in Mergers and Take-Overs)', in X (ed.), *Fusies en Overnames: Liber Amicorum aangeboden aan Prof. dr. L.A. Ankum*, Schoonhoven, Academic Service, 35-50.

Bruining, J. et al. (1989), 'Prestatieverbetering na Management Buy-out in het Licht van de Agency Theorie (Improvement of Performance After Management Buy-Out in View of the Agency Theory)', **67** *De Naamloze Vennootschap*, 229-234.

Bruinsma, G.J.N. and Van de Bunt, H.G. (1993), 'Misdrijven uit Berekening (Calculated Crimes)', **35(2)** *Tijdschrift voor Criminologie*, 99-109.

Bruinsma, J.F. and Huls, N.J.H. (1995), 'Recht in de Broze Vernislaag van een Booming Industry (Law as the Fragile Coat of Varnish of a Booming Industry)', **70** *Nederlands Juristen Blad*, 1625-1631.

Caanen, Ch. and Essers, P.H.J. (1990), 'Rechtseconomie en Belastingrecht (Law and Economics and Taxation Law)', **39(10)** *Ars Aequi*, 677-681.

Cantrijn, A., Jeunink, A. and Kabir, R. (1993), 'Beschermingsconstructies en de Rol van de Aandeelhouder (Protection Schemes and the Role of the Shareholder)', *Nederlands Instituut voor het Bank-en Effectenbedrijf.*

Castermans, A.G. (1989), 'Schadevergoeding bij Dwaling (Damages for Misrepresentation)', *Rechtsgeleerd Magazijn Themis*, 136-146.

Castermans, A.G. and Notermans, R. (1985), 'Naar een economische analyse van de mededelingsplicht bij dwaling (Towards an Economic Analysis of the Duty to Inform in Misrepresentation Law)', 141-155.

Chao-Duyvis, M.A.B. (1990), 'Vergelding als Schadevergoeding (Retribution as Damages)', *Nederlands Juristen Blad*, 513-520.

Cohen Jehoram, Herman (1979), 'Industriële Eigendom en Innovatie (Industrial Property and Innovation)', *Nederlands Juristen Blad*, 609-612.

Cohen Jehoram, Herman (1989), 'Het Economisch Belang van het Auteursrecht en de Gevaren Daarvan (The Economic Importance of Copyright and its Dangers)', **13** *Informatierecht AMI*, 91-95.

Colijn, P.J. et al. (eds) (1981), *Economische Eigendom* (Economic Ownership), Deventer, Kluwer, 92 p.

Coljee, P.D. (1991), 'Het Economisch Adviesrecht van de Ondernemingsraad, Quo Vadis? Artikel 25 WOR nader beschouwd (The Workers Council Economic Right of Advice, Quo Vadis)', in Coljee, P.D., Franken, H., Heertje, A. and Kanning, W. (eds), *Law and Welfare Economics*, Amsterdam, VU Amsterdam, 77-99.

Commissie Corporate Governance (1996), *Corporate Governance in Nederland* (Corporate Governance in the Netherlands), Amsterdam, Secretariaat Corporate Governance, 40 p.

Corstens, G.J.M. (1989), 'De Strafbaarstelling van Misbruik van Voorwetenschap (Penalization of Insider Dealing)', in X (ed.), *Misbruik van Voorwetenschap, serie Monografieën Van der Heijden Instituut*, Deventer, Kluwer, 19-38.

Cortenraad, Wouter H.F.M. (1996), 'Rechtseconomie Bestaat Niet (There's no Such Thing as Law and Economics)', **71** *Nederlands Juristen Blad*, 963-967.

Cramer, Meijering, Nijssen (1986), *De Economische Betekenis van het Auteursrecht 1* (The Economic Importance of Copyright 1), Amsterdam, Stichting voor Economisch Onderzoek Universiteit van Amsterdam.

Crist, William D. (1995), 'The Corporate Governance Impact of US Pension Funds as Large Global Investors', **73** *De Naamloze Vennootschap*, 257-264.

Crol, Conrad-Jan E. (1988), 'Beschermingsconstructies: Overbodig (Protective Measures: Superfluous)', **73** *Economisch-Statistische Berichten*, 862-864.

Crombag, H.F.M. and Van Dun, Frank (1990), 'Recht en Economie in Utopia: een Rechtsfilosofisch Gedachtenexperiment (Law and Economics in Utopia: a Mental Experiment in Legal Philosophy)', **4** *Rechtsgeleerd Magazijn Themis*, 167-176.

Cuelenaere, L.M. and Leen, A.R. (1989), 'Een Rechtseconomisch Aspect van de Positie van de Crediteur in een Faillissement. Is Afschaffing van de Maximum Rente een Oplossing? (A Law and Economics Aspect of the Creditor's Position)', **38(10)** *Ars Aequi*, 834-836.

De Beus, J.W. (1989), *Markt, Democratie en Vrijheid* (Market, Democracy and Liberty), Zwolle, Tjeenk Willink, 682 p.

De Bock, Ruth (1990), 'Inleiding (Introduction)', **39(10)** *Ars Aequi* in Bock, Ruth de, et al. (eds), *Themanummer Rechtseconomie*, 607-613.

De Bock, Ruth et al. (1990), 'Themanummer Rechtseconomie (Special Issue Law and Economics)', **39(10)** *Ars Aequi*, 607-804.

De Geest, Gerrit (1990), 'Public Choice en Rechtseconomie (Public Choice and Law and Economics)', **39(10)** *Ars Aequi* in Bock, Ruth de et al. (eds), *Themanummer Rechtseconomie*, 666-673.

De Geest, Gerrit (1994), 'Private Versus Gemene Eigendom: de "Strategy of the Commons" Herbekeken (Private versus Common Ownership: the "Strategy of the Commons" revisited)', in Raes, Koen and Willekens, H. (eds), *Economische Verklaringen van het Recht*, Den Haag, VUGA, 132-146.

De Jong, Hendrik W. (1981), 'Marktorganisatie, Mededinging en Prijsvorming (Market Organisation, Competition and Price-Making)', **66** *Economisch-Statistische Berichten*, 1268-1280.

De Jong, Hendrik W. (1982), 'De Europese Mededingingspolitiek: Overzicht en Beoordeling (European Competition Policy: Overview and Assessme)', *Beleid en Maatschappij*, 230-240.

De Jong, Hendrik W. (1988), 'Fusies, Overnames en Beschermingsconstructies (Mergers, Take-overs and Protective Devices)', **73** *Economisch-Statistische Berichten*, 842-847.

De Jong, Hendrik W. (1989a), 'Concurrentie, Concentratie en het Europese Mededingingsbeleid (Competition, Concentration and European Competition Policy)', **74** *Economisch-Statistische Berichten*, 1182-1187.

De Jong, Hendrik W. (1989b), 'Concurrentie en Concentratie in de Markteconomie (Competition and Concentration in the Market Economy)', **37** *Sociaal-Economische Wetgeving: Tijdschrift voor Europees en Economisch Recht*, 664-688.

De Jong, Hendrik W. (1989c), *Dynamische Markttheorie* (Dynamic Market Theory), Leiden, Stenfert Kroese, 334 p.

De Jong, Hendrik W. (1990), 'Nederland: Het Kartelparadijs van Europa (The Netherlands: European Anti-trust Paradise)', **75** *Economisch-Statistische Berichten*, 244-248.

De Jong, Hendrik W. (1992), 'Theorie en Empirie van het Concentratieproces (Theorie and Empiricism of the Process of Concentration)', in X (ed.), *Fusies en Overnames: Liber Amicorum aangeboden aan Prof. dr. L.A. Ankum*, Schoonhoven, Academic Service, 119-135.

De Jong, Hendrik W. (1997), *Monopoliseren of Rivaliseren: Opstellen over Concurrentie, Kartelvorming en Economische Machtsposities* (Monopolizing or Competing: Essays on Competition, Cartelization and Dominant Positions), Weteringbrug, Edclusa, 115 p.

De Kluiver, H.J. (1996), 'Mag het nog Ietsje Meer Zijn? Over Tekort, Overvloed en Onbehagen in het Ondernemingsrecht (Could We Have Some More? On Shortage, Abundance and Dissatisfaction in Company Law)', **71** *Nederlands Juristen Blad*, 1439-1451.

De Kluiver, H.J. (1994), 'Het Vennootschapsrecht Dient te Worden Versoepeld ... en Verscherpt (Company Law Should Be Relaxed ... and Tightened)', **37** *TVVS Maandblad voor Ondernemingsrecht en Rechtspersonen*, 174-180.

De Kraan, D.J. (1982a), 'Deregulering: een Begripsbepaling (Deregulation: A Definition)', **9** *Beleid en Maatschappij*, 177-181.

De Kraan, D.J. (1982b), 'Deregulation', **62** *Economisch-Statistische Berichten*, 692-696.

De Laat, Eric (1997), *Essays on Patent Policy. The Multi-dimensionality of Patents and Asymmetric Information*, Tinbergen Institute Research Series Nr. 137.

De Vreugd, Kees (1993), *Overheidsingrijpen ter Bevordering van Marktwerking? De Kartelwetgeving in Nederland met Behulp van de Rechtseconomie nader Bekeken* (Government Intervention in Furtherance of the Market? Dutch Anti Trust Legislation Analysed from a Law and Economics Perspective), Rotterdam, Erasmus University, 127 p.

Degenkamp, J.Th. and Heynen, H.M. (1980a), 'Juridische en Economische Eigendom. Een Formele Analyse (Legal and Economic Ownership. A Formal Analysis)', in X (ed.), *Tolvrije gedachten*, Deventer, Kluwer, 117-129.

Degenkamp, J.Th. and Heynen, H.M. (1980b), *Tolvrije Gedachten* (Free Thoughts), Deventer, Kluwer, 304 p.

Doel, J. v.d. and Van Velthoven, Ben C.J. (1990), *Democratie en Welvaartstheorie* (3rd edn) (Democracy and Welfare Economics), Alphen a.d. Rijn, Samsom H.D. Tjeenk Willink, 232 p.

Doel, J. v.d. and Van Velthoven, Ben C.J. (1993), *Democracy and Welfare Economics: an Introduction into New Political Economy*, 2nd edn, Cambridge, Cambridge University Press, 212 p.

Doorenbos, D.R. (1989), 'Misbruik van Voorwetenschap: Schade en Schande (Insider Dealing: Once Bitten, Twice Shy)', **67** *De Naamloze Vennootschap*, 164-166.

Doorenbos, D.R. and Roording, J.F.L. (1990), 'Rechtseconomie en Strafrecht: een Rechtseconomische Analyse van de Bestrijding van Misbruik van Voorwetenschap bij de Handel in Rffecten (Law and Economics and Criminal Law: A Law and Economics Analysis of Insider Trading in Securities)', **39** *Ars Aequi*, 733-742.

Dooyeweerd, H. (1949a), 'De Sociologische Verhouding tussen Recht en Economie en het Probleem van het Zogeheten "Economisch Recht" (The Sociological

Relationship Between Law and Economics and the Problem of So-called "Economic Law")', in Dooyeweerd, H. (ed.), *Opstellen op het gebied van Recht, Staat en Maatschappij*, Amsterdam, Bakker, 221-264.

Dooyeweerd, H. (ed.) (1949b), *Opstellen op het Gebied van Recht, Staat en Maatschappij* (Essays on Law, State and Society), Amsterdam, Bakker, 471 p.

Dorsman, A.B. (1992), 'Concentratietendensen in de Financiële Sector (Concentration Tendencies in the Financial Sector)', in X (ed.), *Fusies en Overnames: Liber Amicorum aangeboden aan Prof. dr. L.A. Ankum*, Schoonhoven, Academic Service, 161-177.

Dreese, A. (1984), *Misbruik van Voorwetenschap bij Effectenbeurstransacties. An Outsider's View on Insider Trading* (Insider Dealing on the Stock Exchange. An Outsiders View), 's-Gravenhage, Vereniging voor Effectenbescherming, 127 p.

Drijber, B.J. (1989), 'Groepsvrijstelling Know-How Licenties: Rechtszekerheid of Onduidelijkheid (Block Exemption Know-How Licences: Legal Certainty or Vagueness)', **37** *Sociaal-Economische Wetgeving: Tijdschrift voor Europees en Economisch Recht*, 200-216.

Eigenhuizen, H.G. et al. (1987), 'Aandelenopties voor Management en Personeel Sterk in Opkomst (The Increasing Use of Stock Options for Management and Staff)', **65(1)** *De Naamloze Vennootschap*, 1-16.

Eijlander, Ph. (1996), 'Regulering van de Kwaliteit van Zorginstellingen (Regulating the Quality of Care Organizations)', in Van Gestel, R.A.J. et al. (eds), *Markt en Wet*, Deventer, W.E.J. Tjeenk Willink, 209-219.

Faure, Michael G. (1990a), 'De Verzekering van Geldboeten bij Zeewaterverontreiniging door Olie (The Insurance of Fines with Respect to the Oil-Pollution in Sea Waters)', in X (ed.), *Grensoverschrijdend Strafrecht. Opstellen*, Arnhem, Gouda Quint, 203-221.

Faure, Michael G. (1990b), 'Milieubescherming door Aansprakelijkheidsrecht of Regulering (Protecting the Environment through Liability Law or Regulation)', **39(10)** *Ars Aequi*, 759-769.

Faure, Michael G. (1991), 'Rechtseconomie en Privaatrecht: Kunnen Rechtsregels Bijdragen tot de Reductie van Ongevalskosten (Law and Economics and Private Law: Can Legal Rules)', in Hondius, E.H., Schippers, J.J. and Siegers, J.J. (eds), *Rechtseconomie en Recht*, Zwolle, Tjeenk Willink, 51-93.

Faure, Michael G. (1993), *(G)een Schijn van Kans* ((Not) A Shadow of a Chance), Antwerpen, Maklu, 68 p.

Faure, Michael G. (1994), 'Eerstingebruikneming in het Milieurecht: een Rechtseconomische Analyse (First Use in Environmental Law: a Law and Economics Analysis)', in Raes, Koen and Willekens, H. (eds), *Economische Verklaringen van het Recht*, Den Haag, VUGA, 147-178.

Faure, Michael G. (1995a), 'Rechtseconomische Kanttekeningen bij de Deregulering van de Arbeidsomstandighedenwetgeving (A Law and Economics Note on Deregulation in Working Conditions Legislation)', **10(5)** *Sociaal Recht*, 140-149.

Faure, Michael G. (1995b), 'Over Beschermde Slachtoffers, Vrijgevige Rechters en Zuchtende Verzekeraars (On Protected Victims, Generous Judges and Yearning Insurers)', **70(33)** *Nederlands Juristen Blad*, 1227-11235.

Faure, Michael H. (1998), 'Is aansprakelijkheid 'met terugwerkende kracht' efficiënt en verzekerbaar? (Is Rectrocative Liability Efficient and Insurable?', *Aansprakelijkheid en Verzekering*, 1-11.

Faure, Michael G. and Hartlief, T. (eds) (1995), *Verzekering en de groeiende aansprakelijkheidslast. Een juridisch, gezondheidskundig en economisch onderzoek naar ontwikkelingen met betrekking tot de aansprakelijkheidslast en de consequenties voor verzekeraars naar aanleiding van de werkgeversaansprakelijkheid voor bedrijfsongevallen en beroepsziekten* (Insurance and Increasing Liability), Deventer, Kluwer.

Faure, Michael G. and Van den Bergh, Roger (1993), 'Het toelaten van kartels op de Europese verzekeringsmarkt: hogere premies, lagere kwaliteit en meer ongevallen? (Allowing Cartels on the European Insurance Market: Higher Premiums, Lower Quality and More Accidents?)', *Nederlands Juristen Blad*, 261-267.

Feenstra, J.J. (1988), 'Fusiecontrole door de EEG na het Philip Morris arrest (EC Merger Control after the Philip Morris Case)', **66** *De Naamloze Vennootschap*, 60-67.

Fierstra, Marc A. (1990), 'Communautaire Concentratiecontrole: Een Nieuwe Fase in een Ontwikkeling (Community Concentration Control: A New Development Stage)', **38** *Sociaal-Economische Wetgeving: Tijdschrift voor Europees en Economisch Recht*, 330-350.

Franken, Hans (1983), 'Economische Analyse van het Strafrecht (Economic Analysis of Criminal Law)', in X (ed.), *Bij deze stand van zaken. Opstellen aangeboden aan A.L. Melai*, Arnhem, Gouda Quint, 117-131.

Franken, Hans (1987), 'Voorkomen is Beter dan Genezen (Prevention is Better Than Cure)', *RMThemis*, 469-471.

Franken, Hans (1991), 'Rechtseconomie en Strafrecht (Law and Economics and Criminal Law)', in Hondius, E.H., Schippers, J.J. and Siegers, J.J. (eds), *Rechtseconomie en Recht*, Zwolle, Tjeenk Willink, 163-179.

Frentrop, P.M.L. (1995), 'Corporate Governance: Snijvlak van Paradigma's (Corporate Governance: Intertwining Paradigms)', **73(12)** *De Naamloze Vennootschap*, 252-256.

Frijns, J.M.G., Mensonides, J. and Schreurs, R.J. (1995), 'Institutionele Beleggers en Corporate Governance (Institutional Investors and Corporate Governance)', **73(12)** *De Naamloze Vennootschap*, 265-270.

Gaakeer, Jeanne (1994), 'De Taal van het Recht en de Taal van de Economie, ofwel Integratie en het Gevaar van Steno (Law's Language and Economic's Language, or Integration and the Danger of Shorthand)', in Foqué, R. et al. (eds), *Geïntegreerde Rechtswetenschap*, Arnhem, Gouda Quint, 423-441.

Gaakeer, Jeanne and Kerkmeester, Heico (1997), *De Toenadering tussen Law and Economics en Law and Literature* (The Rapproachement of Law and Economics and Law and Literature), Gouda Quint, Arnhem.

Geelhoed, L.A. (1983), *De Interveniërende Staat* (The Intervening State), s-Gravenhage, Staatsuitgeverij.

Geelhoed, L.A. (1993), 'Deregulering, Herregulering en Zelfregulering (Deregulation, Re-regulation and Selfregulation)', in Eijlander, Ph. (ed.), *Government and Selfregulation*, Deventer, W.E.J. Tjeenk Willink, 33-51.

Gestel, R.A.J. et al. (1996), *Markt en Wet* (The Market and The Law), Deventer, W.E.J. Tjeenk Willink, 224 p.

Gestel, R.A.J. and Verschuuren (1996), 'Marktwerking, Deregulering en Wetgevingskwaliteit ... en de Kwaliteit van het Milieu? (The Market, Deregulation and The Quality of Legislation ... and The Quality of The Environment?)', in Gestel, R.A.J. van et al. (eds), *Markt en Wet*, Deventer, W.E.J. Tjeenk Willink, 151-172.

Ghering, M., Puffelen, F. Van and Schilthuis, F. (1989), *De Economische Betekenis van het Auteursrecht* (The Economic Importance of Copyright 2), Amsterdam, Stichting voor Economisch Onderzoek Universiteit van Amsterdam, 58 p.

Glasz, J.R. (1994), 'De Commissaris en het Structuurregime (The Outside Director and the Supervisory Regime)', **37(5)** *TVVS Maandblad voor Ondernemingsrecht en Rechtspersonen*, 117-120.

Goedbloed, Aad (1993), 'Beschermingsconstructies en Aandeelkoersen (Protective Measures and Share Prices)', **3** *Pecunia Magazine*, 23-28.

Grapendaal, M. (1990), 'De Paradox en het Dilemma. Effecten van Politieoptreden op de Zeedijk (Paradox and Dilemma. Effects of Police Action at the Zeedijk)', **39(10)** *Ars Aequi*, 714-720.

Griffiths, J. (1991), 'De Rechtbank als Fietsenfabriek (The Court as Bicycle Manufacturer)', **66** *Nederlands Juristenblad*, 129-130.

Groenewegen, John (1990), 'Transactiekosten (Transactions Costs)', *Tijdschrift voor politieke economie*, 50-76.

Groenewegen, John, Van Paridon, Kees and Schreuders, Wicher (1988), 'The Economic Theory of Political Decision Making', **22(3)** *Journal of Economic Issues*, 831-835.

Groenhuijsen, M.S. (1995), 'De Hoge Raad over Misbruik van Voorwetenschap in de HCS-zaak (The Supreme Court on Insider Dealing in the HCS Case)', **70(27)** *Nederlands Juristen Blad*, 987-990.

Grosheide, F.W. and Frequin, M.J. (1990), 'Uitgeversrecht (Publishers Right)', **14** *Informatierecht AMI*, 43-47.

Hartlief, Ton (1998), *Ieder draagt zijn eigen schade* (Everybody Bears His Own Damage), Deventer, Kluwer.

Heertje, A. (1966), 'Conflictstof voor Juristen en Economen (Conflict Material for Lawyers and Economists)', **15** *Ars Aequi*, 14-16.

Heertje, A. (1990), 'Speltheorie als Economische Analyse van het Recht (Game Theory as Economic Analysis of Law)', in Maris, C.W. et al. (eds), *Recht, Rechtvaardigheid en Doelmatigheid*, Arnhem, Gouda Quint, 90-100.

Heertje, A. et al. (1991), *Law and Welfare Economics: op het Raakvlak van Economie en Recht* (Law and Welfare Economics: Where Economics and Law Touch), Bundel n.a.v. het gelijknamige Symposium op 24 oktober 1990.

Heertje, A. and Wabeke, J.W. (1989), 'Het Dreigende Faillissement van Justitie en Politie (The Near Bankrupcty of Prosecution and Police)', **74** *Economisch-Statistische Berichten*, 1152-1155.

Hellingman, K. and Mortelmans, K.J.M. (1989), *Economisch Publiekrecht: Rechtswaarborgen en Rechtsinstrumenten* (Economic Public Law: Guarantees in Law and Instrumentality), Deventer, Kluwer, 363 p.

Hendrikse, G.W.J. and Schreuder, H. (1987), 'Economische Organisatietheorieën (Organisational Theories in Economics)', **72** *Economisch-Statistische Berichten*, 810-815.

Hendrikse, G.W.J. and Schreuder, H. (1990), 'Economische Organisatietheorie (Organisational Theories in Economics)', in Van der Geest, L. (ed.), *Economische Theorie: de Stand van Zaken*, Schoonhoven, Academic Service, 277-290.

Hertog, Johan A. and Kraamwinkel, Margriet M. (1991), 'Pensioennadelen in Het Licht van de Contracttheorie (Pension Disadvantages in the Light of Contract Theory)', *Economisch-Statistische Berichten*, 908-912.

Hessel, B. (1990), 'De Mogelijke Rol van de Rechtseconomie in een Moderne Rechtsstaat (The Possible Role of Law and Economics in a State with a Rule of Law)', **39(10)** *Ars Aequi*, 645-653.

Hesseling, René (1993), 'Verplaatsing: een Pleidooi voor het Rationele Keuzeperspectief (Moving: a Plea for the Rational Choice Perspective)', **35(2)** *Tijdschrift voor Criminologie*, 143-157.

Hessing, D.J. and Elffers, H. (1994), 'Een Belasting voor de Rechtseconomie? Een Blik op Twintig Jaar Onderzoek naar Belastingontduiking (A Burden for Law and Economics? A Look Into Twenty Years of Tax Evasion Research)', in Raes, Koen and Willekens, H. (eds), *Economische Verklaringen van het Recht*, Den Haag, VUGA, 93-108.

Hol, A.M. (1990), 'Efficiëntie als Instrument en als Norm. Enkele Rechtstheoretische Kanttekeningen bij de Economische Analyse van het Recht (Efficiency as Instrument and Norm: Some Remarks on the Economic Analysis of Law)', **39(10)** *Ars Aequi*, 632-644.

Hol, A.M. (1991), 'Rechten en Doeleinden. Enkele Morele Aspecten van Juridische Aansprakelijkheid (Rights and Goals. Some Moral Aspects of Legal Liability)', in X (ed.), *Dilemma's van Aansprakelijkheid*, Zwolle, Tjeenk Willink, 127-142.

Hol, A.M. (1993), *Gewogen Recht: Billijkheid en Efficiëntie bij Onrechtmatige Daad* (Law in Balance: Justice and Efficiency in Tort Law), Deventer, Kluwer, 231 p.

Holzhauer, Rudi W. (1993), 'Een Economische Analyse van de Allocatie van Proceskosten (An Economic Analysis of Cost Allocation Rules)', in X (ed.), *De Kosten van een Procedure*, Deventer, Kluwer, 25-47.

Holzhauer, Rudi W. (1998a), 'The Costs of Languages and IP-Rights Protection in the European Union. The Case of Patents', in Ott, Claus and von Wangenheim, Georg (eds), *Essays in Law and Economics IV*, Antwerpen, Maklu.

Holzhauer, Rudi W. (1998b), 'Jenever and Jumping Wild Cats, The Scope of Trademark Protection in Law and in Economics', working paper (forthcoming).

Holzhauer, Rudi W. and Bakker, Luit M. (1998), 'Parallel Imports between Law and Economics', in Ott, Claus and von Wangenheim, Georg (eds), *Essays in Law and Economics IV*, Antwerpen, Maklu.

Holzhauer, Rudi W. and Biemans, Denise Y.M. (1993), 'Een Economisch-Juridische Benadering van Reclame (A Law and Economics Approach to Advertising)', **42(11)** *Ars Aequi*, 786-795.

Holzhauer, Rudi W. and Teijl, Rob (1988), 'Geschillenbeslechting als Economisch Alternatief (Dispute Settlement as Economic Alternative)', in Snijders, H.J. et al. (eds), *Overheidsrechter Gepasseerd*, Arnhem, Gouda Quint, 489-499.

Holzhauer, Rudi W. and Teijl, Rob (1989a), 'Rechtseconomie in Nederland (Law and Economics in the Netherlands)', **38(4)** *Ars Aequi*, 248-252.

Holzhauer, Rudi W., Teijl, Rob et al. (1989b), *Inleiding Rechtseconomie* (Introduction to Law and Economics), Arnhem, Gouda Quint, 345 p.

Holzhauer, Rudi W., Teijl, Rob et al. (1995), *Inleiding Rechtseconomie* (Introduction to Law and Economics), Arnhem, Gouda Quint.

Hondius, E.H. (1991), 'Rechtseconomie en Privaatrecht: Enige Kanttekeningen (Law and Economics and Private Law: Some Remarks)', in Hondius, E.H., Schippers, J.J. and Siegers, J.J. (eds), *Rechtseconomie en Recht*, Zwolle, Tjeenk Willink, 95-105.

Hondius, E.H., Schippers, J.J. and Siegers, Jacques J. (eds) (1991), 'Rechtseconomie: Brug tussen twee disciplines (Law and Economics: Bridge between two Disciplines)', in Hondius, E.H., Schippers, J.J. and Siegers, J.J. (eds), *Rechtseconomie en Recht*, Zwolle, Tjeenk Willink, 1-7.

Hondius, E.H. et al. (1991), *Rechtseconomie en Recht: Kennismaking met een Vakgebied in Opkomst* (Law and Economics and Law: Getting to Know an Emerging Discipline), Zwolle, Tjeenk Willink, 201 p.

Hoogenboom, B. (1990), 'Rechtseconomie en Particuliere Beveiliging: "Policing for profits" als Voorloper van Strafrechtelijke Hervormingen (Law and Economics and Private Security: "Policing for Profit" as Precursor of Criminal Reform)', **39(10)** *Ars Aequi*, 721-732.

Hoogendoorn, Ms.N. (1995), 'De Accountant in het Spanningsveld tussen Rechtsregels en Economische Werkelijkheid (The Accountant in the Area of Tension between Legal Rules and Economic Reality)', in X (ed.), *Ondernemen tussen Macht en Ordening: Opstellen op het Grensvlak van Economie en Recht*, Amsterdam, Thesis Publishers, 57-72.

Huijgen, W.G. (1995), *Economische Eigendom* (Economic Ownership), Deventer, W.E.J. Tjeenk Willink, 120 p.

Huls, N.J.H. (1988), *Van Liquidatie tot Rehabilitatie* (From Liquidation to Rehabilitation), s-Gravenhage, Ministerie van Economische Zaken, 106 p.

Hulst, W.G.J. Van and Willems, J.G.L.M. (1989), *Externe Organisatie: Een Kennismaking met het Ondernemingsgedrag in Markteconomische Stelsels (External Organisation: An Introduction to Firm Behaviour in Market Systems)*, Leiden, Stenfert Kroese, 284 p.

Huyghen, Annelies and Theeuwes, Jules (1997), 'Electriciteit wordt duur betaald (Electricity doesn't come Cheap)', *Economisch-Statistische Berichten*, 84-86.

Ietswaart, Heleen F.P. (1995), 'Boekbespreking: Michael Faure, (G)een Schijn van Kans, Beschouwingen over het Statistisch Causaliteitsbewijs bij Milieugezondheidsschade (Book Review: Michael Faure, (Not) A Shadow of a Chance), Reflections on Probabilistic Causal Evidence for Environmental Health Damage)', **156** *Rechtsgeleerd Magazijn Themis*, 35-38.

Jacobs, A.T.J.M. (1996), 'Deregulering, Economische Flexibiliteit en het Arbeidsrecht (Deregulation, Economic Flexibility and Labour Law)', in Gestel, R.A.J. van et al. (eds), *Markt en Wet*, Deventer, W.E.J. Tjeenk Willink, 195-207.

Jansen, O.J.D.M.L. (1996), 'De Bestuurlijke Boete in het Wetsvoorstel Mededingingswet (Administrative Fines in the Competition Bill)', **71(31)** *Nederlands Juristen Blad*, 1250-1254.

Jeunink, A. and Kabir, R. (1993), 'De Relatie tussen Aandeelhoudersstructuur en Beschermingsconstructies (The Relation between the Shareholder's Structure and Protection Schemes)', **71** *De Naamloze Vennootschap*, 90-95.

Jongbloed, A.W. (1993), 'Recht, Economie en Rechtseconomie (Law, Economics and Law and Economics)', **85(10)** *Rechtsstrijd*, 204-210.

Kabir, R. (1988), 'De Invloed van Regulering op de Effectenmarkt', in Kemna, A. (ed.), *Financiering en Belegging : Stand van zaken anno 1988*, Rotterdam, Erasmus University, 111-131.

Kabir, R. (1991), 'Het Opschorten van de Handel op de Amsterdamse Effectenbeurs', **63** *Bedrijfskunde*, 65-71.

Kanning, W. (1991), 'Een non-cooperatieve benadering van het Coase-theorema (A Non Co-operative Approach to the Coase Theorem)', in Coljee, P.D., Franken, H., Heertje, A. and Kanning, W. (eds), *Law and Welfare Economics*, Amsterdam, VU Amsterdam, 39-48.

Kaufmann, Peter J. (1986), *Passing Off and Misappropriation*, Weinheim (Germany), IIC Studies, 178 p.

Kaufmann, Peter J. and Gemser, G. (1994), 'De Lof der Nabootsing Revisited (The Glory of Imitation Revisited)', **62(4)** *Bijblad bij de Industriële Eigendom*, 106-111.

Kaufmann, Peter J. and Wijnberg, N.M. (1990), 'Het Decca Arrest: Bescherming van Prestatie en Imitatie (The Decca Case: Protecting Activities and Imitation)', *Intellectuele Eigendom en Reclamerecht*, 77-81.

Kerkmeester, Heico (1989a), *Recht en Speltheorie: een Economisch Model voor het Ontstaan van Staten en Recht* (Law and Game Theory: an Economic Model for the Emergence of State Organization and Law), Rotterdam, Erasmus University, 212 p.

Kerkmeester, Heico O. (1989b), *Recht en Speltheorie* (Law and Game Theory), diss. Rotterdam, 212 p.

Kerkmeester, Heico (1991), 'De Inefficiëntie van de Vrederechter: een Economische Theorie van Rechtspraak Getoetst (The Inefficiency of the Peace Court: Testing an Economic Theory of the Common Law)', in Doré, J.P. (ed.), *Au Jour d'Amour: Opstellen Aangeboden aan Prof. Dr. C.M.G. ten Raa*, Rotterdam, Erasmus University.

Kerkmeester, Heico (1992), 'De Veronderstellingen in de Rechtseconomie: Wanneer Zij Bruikbaar Zijn en Wanneer Niet (The Assumptions in Law and Economics: When Can They be Used and When Not)', **21(2)** *Tijdschrift voor Rechtsfilosofie en Rechtstheorie*, 126-143.

Kerkmeester, Heico (1993a), *De Grondwet als Sociaal Contract: een Inleiding in de Constitutionele Economie* (The Constitution as a Social Contract: an Introduction Into Constitutional Economics), Rechtseconomische Verkenningen, Part 3, Gouda Quint, 130 p.

Kerkmeester, Heico (1993b), 'De Betekenis van het Waarschijnlijkheidsbegrip voor de Aansprakelijkheid uit Onrechtmatige Daad: Meijers Geactualiseerd (The Meaning of the Concept of Probability for Tort Liability: Meijers Updated)', **6111** *Weekblad voor Privaatrecht, Notarisambt en Registratie*, 767-773.

Kerkmeester, Heico (1993c), 'De Strafrechtstheory van Gary Becker (Gary Becker's Economic Theory of Crime)', **1993** *Delikt en Delinkwent*, 225-239.

Kerkmeester, Heico (1994a), 'Boekbespreking: Faure, M.G., *(G)een Schijn van Kans* (Book Review Faure, M.G., *(Not) A Shadow of a Chance*)', **2** *Tijdschrift voor Milieuaansprakelijkheid*, 45-48.

Kerkmeester, Heico (1994b), 'Public Choice avant la Lettre? Economische Kanttekeningen bij de Geschiedenis van de artt. 50 en 67 lid 3 Grondwet (Public Choice avant la Lettre? Economic Comments on the History of Sections 50 and 60 ss. 3 Dutch Constitution)', in Pieterman, R. et al. (eds), *Bijdragen tot de Rechtsgeschiedenis van de Negentiende Eeuw*, Arnhem, Gouda Quint, 235-254.

Kerkmeester, Heico (1994c), 'Economie als Integratieve Wetenschap (Economics as a Science of Integration)', in Foqué, R. et al. (eds), *Geïntegreerde Rechtswetenschap*, Arnhem, Gouda Quint, 379-402.

Kerkmeester, Heico (1996a), 'Boekbespreking: Baird, D.C., Gertner, R.H. and Picker, R.C., *(Book review) Game Theory and the Law*', **25** *Tijdschrift voor Rechtsfilosofie en Rechtstheorie*, 72-75.

Kerkmeester, Heico (1996b), 'Evolutionaire Rechtseconomie: naar een Herwaardering van Gewoonterecht? (Evolutionary Law and Economics: Towards a Reassessment of Customary Law)', **22** *Recht en Kritiek*, 335-355.

Kerkmeester, Heico (1996c), 'Bespreking van R.P. Malloy en J. Evensky (red.), Adam Smith and the Philosophy of Law and Economics and van R.H. Coase, Essays on Economics and Economists (Book Reviews)', **22** *Recht en Kritiek*, 290-296.

Kerkmeester, Heico (1996d), 'Bespreking van G. De Geest, Economische Analyse van het Contracten- en Quasi-contractenrecht: Een Onderzoek naar de Wetenschappelijke Waarde van de Rechtseconomie (Book Review)', **25** *Tijdschrift voor Rechtsfilosofie en Rechtstheorie*, 216-219.

Kerkmeester, Heico (1996e), 'Bespreking van F.P. van Tulder, Van Misdaad tot Straf: een Economische Benadering van de Strafrechtelijke Keten (Book Review)', **26** *Delikt en Delinkwent*, 892-903.

Kerkmeester, Heico (1997), 'De Retoriek van de Rechtseconomie (The Rhetorics of Law and Economics)', in Feteris, E.T. et al. (eds), *Op Goede Gronden*, Nijmegen, Ars Aequi Libri, 207-213.

Kerkmeester, Heico and De Mulder, R.V. (1987), 'Statistiek en Bewijsrecht (Statistics and the Law of Evidence)', **62** *Nederlands Juristen Blad*, 73-81.

Kerkmeester, Heico and Holzhauer, Rudi W. (1998), *Rechtseconomische Annotaties* (Law and Economics Case Comments), Rechtseconomische Verkenningen, Arnhem, Gouda Quint.

Kerkmeester, Heico O. and Mulder, R.V. De (1988), 'Beslissingstheoretische Criteria voor de Beslechting van een Juridisch Geschil door een Onafhankelijke Derde (Theoretical Decisionmaking Criteria in Settling a Legal Dispute by a Third Party)', in Snijders, H.J. (ed.), *Overheidsrechter Gepasseerd*, Arnhem, Gouda Quint, 501-511.

Kernkamp, F.H. (1985), 'Risk Appraisal', in Van Dunné, Jan M. et al. (eds), *Iustitia et Amicitia*, Arnhem, Gouda Quint, 61-74.

Kleemans, Edward R. (1993), 'Misdaadanalyse en de Rationele Keuzebenadering (Crime Analysis and the Rational Choice Perspective)', **35(2)** *Tijdschrift voor Criminologie*, 127-142.

Kleemans, Edward R. (1996), *Strategische Misdaadanalyse en Stedelijke Criminaliteit* (Strategical Crime Analysis and City Crime), Enschede, Internationaal Politie Instituut Twente, 291 p.

Klijn, A. (1988), *Duurder Recht, Minder Vraag: De Prijsverhoging van Rechtsverzorging en de Gevolgen daarvan voor Lagere Inkomens* (More Costly Law, Lesser Demand: The Increased Price of Legal Assistance and its Consequences for Lower Incomes), 's-Gravenhage, SDU, 96 p.

Klijn, A. et al. (1996), *Rechtsbijstand: Krimpende Markten* (Legal Assistence: Shrinking Markets), 's-Gravenhage, SDU.

Kneppers-Heynert, E.M. (1988), *Een Economische en Juridische Analyse van Franchising tegen de Achtergrond van een Property Rrights- en Transactiekosten Benadering* (An Economic and Legal Analysis of Franchising in the Light of a Property and Transaction Costs Approach), Groningen, Van Denderen, 268 p.

Kneppers-Heynert, E.M. (1995), 'Juridische en Economische Aspecten van Partnerships (Legal and Economic Aspects of Partnerships)', in X (ed.), *Ondernemen tussen Macht en Ordening: Opstellen op het Grensvlak van Economie en Recht*, Amsterdam, Thesis Publishers, 15-35.

Koedijk, C.G. (1994), *Nooit meer Slapen: Over Deregulering en Verantwoordelijkheid* (No More Sleeping: About Deregulation and Responsibility), Maastricht, Universitaire Pers, 34 p.

Koopmans, T. (1983), 'Mini-monopolies (Mini-monopolies)', *Rechtsgeleerd Magazijn Themis*, 342-344.

Koopmans, T. (1994), 'Intellectuele Eigendom, Economie en Politiek (Intellectual Property, Economics and Politics)', **18** *Informatierecht*, 107-111.

Lambers, H.W. (1962), 'Mededingingspolitiek (Competition Policy)', in Andriessen, J.E. and Van Meerhaeghe, M.A.G. (eds), *Theorie van de Economische Politiek*, Leiden, Stenfert Kroese, 307-338.

Langendijk, H.P.A.J. (1992), 'Concentratie op de Markt voor Zakelijke Dienstverlening (Concentration on the Market for Commercial Services)', in X (ed.), *Fusies en Overnames: Liber Amicorum aangeboden aan Prof. dr. L.A. Ankum*, Schoonhoven, Academic Service, 137-159.

Le Blanc, L.J.C.M. (1990), 'Bismarck als Benchmark. Enkele Rechtseconomische Beschouwingen over Publieke Sector en Sociale Zekerheid in Nederland (Bismarck as Benchmark. Some Law and Economics Considerations on the Public Sector and Social Welfare in the Netherlands)', **39(10)** *Ars Aequi*, 654-659.

Le Blanc, L.J.C.M. (1990), 'Bismarck als Benchmark: enkele Rechtseconomische Beschouwingen over Publieke Sector en Sociale Zekerheid in Nederland (Bismarck as Benchmark: Some Law and Economics Considerations on the Public Sector and Social Welfare in the Netherlands)', **39(10)** *Ars Aequi*, 654-6100.

Lindner, G.L. (1985), 'Arreststraf of Geldboete (Detention or Fine)', *Dissertatie Rijks Universiteit Leiden*.

Linneman, M.J.T. (1990), 'Sportrechten, artikel 15 en Marktopdeling (Sports Rights, Section 15 and Splitting up the Market)', **14** *Informatierecht AMI*, 63-66.

Linssen, G.J. (1973), 'De Rol van de Commissie bij de toepassing van het Europese mededingingsrecht (The Role of the Commission in Applying European Competition Law)', in Verloren Van Themaat, Pieter (ed.), *Europees Kartelrecht anno 1973*, Deventer, Kluwer, 23-45.

Linssen, G.J. (1981), 'De Verhouding Tussen het Formele en het Informele Kartelbeleid in Nederland en de Plaats van de Commissie Economische Mededinging (The Interrelationship between the Formal and Informal Dutch Anti-trust Policy and the Position of the Economic Competition Commission)', **24** *TVVS Maandblad voor Ondernemingsrecht en Rechtspersonen*, 255-259.

Mackaay, Ejan (1980), 'Veranderingen in het Stelsel van Vergoeding en Verhaal van Schade (Changes in the System of Compensation and Recoupment of Damages)', **55** *Nederlands Juristen Blad*, 813-825. Reprinted in *Schade lijden en schade dragen*, Zwolle, Tjeenk Willink, Nederlands Juristenblad Boekenreeks No. 6, 1981.

Mackaay, Ejan (1982), *Economics of Information and Law*, Boston, Kluwer-Nijhoff, 293 p.

Mackaay, Ejan (1985), 'Rechtseconomie - Hora Est (Law and Economics - The Time Has Come)', *Nederlands Juristenblad*, 1347 ff.

Mackaay, Ejan (1988), 'Het Recht Bezien door de Bril van de Economist - Een gestyleerd overzicht van de rechtseconomie (Law Seen Through Economist's Glasses: An Overview)', *Rechtsgeleerd Magazijn Themis*, 411-452.

Mackaay, Ejan (1989), 'Rechtseconomie Behind the Dikes (Law and Economics Behind the Dikes)', *Nederlands Juristenblad*, 921-922.

Mackaay, Ejan (1990), 'Het Aansprakelijkheidsrecht (Liability Law)', **39(10)** *Ars Aequi*, 743-749.

Mackaay, Ejan (1991), 'Verschuivingen in De Rechtseconomie (Shifts in Law and Economics)', **66** *Nederlands Juristenblad*, 1505-1521.

Maijoor, Steven J. (1991), *The Economics of Accounting Regulation*, Maastricht, Datawyse, 213 p.

Maijoor, Steven J. (1994), 'Economische Analyses van de Regelgeving van de Externe Verslaggeving: een Beschrijving van Onderzoeksresultaten (Economic Analyses of External Accounting Rules: a Description of Research Results)', **68** *Maandblad voor Accountancy en Bedrijfseconomie*, 112-118.

Maijoor, Steven J. (1995), *Dominees op de Markt: een Economische Analyse van de Markt, het Kantoor en het Controleproces van Accountants* (Preachers on the Market: an Economic Analysis of the Market, the Office and the Monitoring by Accountants), Maastricht, Universitaire Pers, 39 p.

Malsch, Marijke (1990), *Advocaten Voorspellen de Uitkomst van hun Zaken* (Lawyers' Predictions of Judicial Decisions: A Study on Calibration of Experts), Lisse, Swets & Zeitlinger, 109 p.

Malsch, Marijke (1997), 'De Uitkomst van de Zaak Voorspellen (Predicting the Outcome of Judicial Decisions)', in Van Koppen, Peter J. et al. (eds), *Het Hart van de Zaak*, Deventer, Gouda Quint, 532 ff.

Meester, G. and Wesemann, P. (1976), 'Kosten-baten Analyse en Strafrecht (Cost Benefit Analysis and Criminal Law)', in X (ed.), *Portret van de Juridische Faculteit Rotterdam 12 1/2*, Deventer, Kluwer, 217-228.

Meijs, Paul and Jansen, Wim (1989), *Eigendom tussen Politiek en Economie* (Ownership between Politics and Economy), Groningen, Wolters-Noordhoff, 195 p.

Melai, A.L. (1973), 'De Straf en het Gezichtspunt van de Econometristen (Punishment and the Econometrist Perspective)', in X (ed.), *Speculum Langemeyer*, Zwolle, Tjeenk Willink, 315-331.

Mendel, M.M. (1995), 'Wetsontwerp Beschermingsmaatregelen VEUO-beurs uit Oogpunt van Rechtsbedeling en Corporate Governance (Protective Measures Bill from a Justice and from a Corporate Governance Perspective)', **73** *De Naamloze Vennootschap*, 271-273.

Ministerie Van Justitie (1978), *Rapport van de Studiegroep Verkeersaansprakelijkheid, Deel I, Vergoeding van Schade door Dood en Letsel* (Report of the Commission Traffic Liability, Part I, Compensation of Damages through Death and Injury), s-Gravenhage, Staatsuitgeverij, 1978 p.

Ministerie Van Justitie (1980), *Rapport van de Studiegroep Verkeersaansprakelijkheid, Deel II, Vergoeding van Zaakschade* (Report of the Commission Traffic Liability,

Part I, Compensation of Damages Caused to Things), s-Gravenhage, Staatsuitgeverij, 1980 p.

Moerland, H. (1991), *Winkeldiefstal, een te Riskante Zaak?* (Theft in Shops, a too Risky Business?), Arnhem, Gouda Quint, 342 p.

Moerland, H. (1993), 'Afschrikking, de Bakermat van de Rationele Keuzebenadering in de Criminologie (Deterrence, the Cradle of the Rational Choice Approach)', **35(2)** *Tijdschrift voor Criminologie*, 110-126.

Moerland, H. and Rodermond, J.G. (1987a), 'Ontwikkelingen in het Afschrikkingsonderzoek (Developments in Deterrence Research)', *Panopticon*, 59-75.

Moerland, H. and Rodermond, J.G. (1987b), 'Winkeldiefstal, een (te) Riskante Zaak? Onderzoek naar een mogelijke samenhang tussen het plegen van winkeldiefstal en de verwachte gevolgen (Theft in Shops, a (too) Risky Business? Investigation of a Possible Relationship between Theft in Shops and the Expected Consequences)', *Panopticon*, 335-349.

Moerland, P.W. (1988), 'De Overnamemarkt in Theorie en Praktijk (The Take-Over Market in Theory and Practice)', **73** *Economisch-Statistische Berichten*, 848-853.

Moerland, P.W. (1992), 'Economische Theorievorming omtrent de Onderneming (Economic Theory of the Firm)', **66** *Maandblad voor Accountancy en Bedrijfseconomie*, 57-65.

Moerland, P.W. (1995a), 'Alternative Disciplinary Mechanisms in Different Corporate Systems', **26** *Journal of Economic Behavior and Organization*.

Moerland, P.W. (1995b), 'Vennootschappelijke Systemen en Disciplineringsmechanismen in Internationaal Perspectief (Corporate Systems and Disciplinary Mechanisms in International Perspective)', **69** *Maandblad voor Accountancy en Bedrijfseconomie*, 242-252.

Moerland, P.W. (1995c), 'Corporate Ownership and Control Structures: an International Comparison', **10** *Review of Industrial Organization*.

Moerland, P.W. (1995d), 'Eigendoms- en Beheersstructuren van de Beursvennootschap (Structures for Ownership and Control of Quoted Companies)', **69** *Maandblad voor Accountancy en Bedrijfseconomie*, 545-554.

Moerland, P.W. (1995e), 'Corporate Governance en Marktwerking (Corporate Governance and the Market)', **73** *De Naamloze Vennootschap*, 247-251.

Mok, M.R. (1976), 'Kartelbeleid nu en in de toekomst (Present and Future Anti-trust Policy)', in Mok, M.R., (ed.), *Nieuwe Ontwikkelingen in het Europese Kartel Recht*, Kluwer, Deventer, 1-15.

Mok, M.R. (1978), '20 jaar WEM (20 Years WEM)', **26** *Sociaal-Economische Wetgeving: Tijdschrift voor Europees en Economisch Recht*, 737-760.

Mok, M.R. (1983), 'Het Paard achter de Wagen: Deregulering en Kartelrecht (The Cart Before the Horse: Deregulation and Anti-trust Law)', **31** *Sociaal-Economische Wetgeving: Tijdschrift voor Europees en Economisch Recht*, 666-678.

Mok, M.R. (1996), 'Het Voorstel-Mededingingswet (The Competition Bill)', **39** *TVVS Maandblad voor Ondernemingsrecht en Rechtspersonen*, 157-161.

Mol, N.P. and Verbon, Harrie A.A. (1997), *Neo-Institutionele Economie en Openbaar Bestuur: Perspectieven op de Verzelfstandiging van Overheidsdiensten* (Neo-Institutional Economics and Public Control: Perspectives on Privatization of Public Services), 's-Gravenhage, Vuga, 144 p.

Nagelkerke, J.J. (1979), 'Beschouwingen over Economische Wetenschap en haar Betekenis voor de Rechtsvorming (Considerations about Economic Science and its Use)', *RMThemis*, 356-385.

Nederlands Economisch Instituut (1989), *Naar een Economische Benadering van Criminaliteit en Veiligheidszorg* (Towards an Economic Approach of Delinquency and Security Provision), Rotterdam, Nederlands Economisch Instituut.

Nederlands Economisch Instituut (1991), *Verhuur- en leenrecht EG. Commentaar op het SEO-rapport 'Naar een Verhuur- en Leenrecht in de Europese Gemeenschap'* (EC Rental and Lending Rights. Commentary on the SEO-report 'Towards a Rental and Lending Right in the European Community'), Rotterdam, Nederlands Economisch Instituut, 24 p.

Nederlof, H.P. (1994), 'Gevolgen van de Toepassingsdrempel van Vijf Miljard Ecu voor de Beleidsconsistentie bij Concentratiecontrole (Consequences of the Five Billion Ecu Threshold for Policy-consistency in Concentration Controle)', **42** *Sociaal-Economische Wetgeving: Tijdschrift voor Europees en Economisch Recht*, 83-96.

Nentjes, Andries (1987), *De Economie van het Recht* (The Economy of the Law), oratie Groningen, s.l., 18 p.

Nentjes, Andries (1988), 'De Welvaartseffecten van het Strafrecht (Welfare Effects of Criminal Law)', **2** *Justitiële Verkenningen*, 34-52.

Nentjes, Andries (1993a), 'Van Wie is het Milieu? (Who Owns the Environment?)', **39(10)** *Ars Aequi* in Bock, Ruth de et al. (eds), *Themanummer Rechtseconomie*, 706-713.

Nentjes, Andries (1993b), *Elementaire Rechtseconomie (Basic Law and Economics)*, Groningen, Wolters-Noordhoff, 139 p.

Nentjes, Andries (1996), 'Meer Markt in het Milieubeleid: Convenanten Versus Verhandelbare Vergunningen (More Market in Environmental Policy: Covenants Versus Tradeable Permits)', in Van de Hoek, M.P. (ed.), *Opstellen aangeboden aan prof. dr. C. Rijnvos*, Groningen, Wolters-Noordhoff, 112-126.

Nentjes, Andries and Dijkstra, J. (1993), 'Verkeersaansprakelijkheid: Slachtoffercompensatie of Ongevallenpreventie (Traffic Liability: Compensating Victims or Preventing Accidents)', **68** *Nederlands Juristen Blad*, 951-954.

Nieuwenhuis, J.H. (1984), 'Recht en Belang (Law and Interests)', *Flores Debitorem*, 65-74.

Nieuwenhuis, J.H. (1988), 'Ieder het Zijne (Each His Own)', **2** *RMThemis*, 73-84.

Nieuwenhuis, J.H. (1991), 'Blinddoek En Balans in Het Milieurecht. Drie Manieren Om Belangen af te Wegen (Blindfold and Balance in Environmental Law. Three Ways of Balacing Interests)', in X (ed.), *Dilemma's van Aansprakelijkheid*, Zwolle, Tjeenk Willink, 37-51.

Nieuwenhuis, J.H. (1997), *De Ramp op het Pikmeer* (The Pikmeer Disaster), Deventer, Kluwer, 22 p.

Ommeren, F.J. Van (1990), 'Bestuurscompensatie, Draagkracht en Rechtseconomie (Administrative Compensation, Financial Capacity and Economic Analysis of Law)', **39(10)** *Ars Aequi*, 682-691.

Ottervanger, T.R. (1996), 'Concentratietoezicht (Monitoring Concentrations)', **71** *Nederlands Juristen Blad*, 1245-1249.

Pagie, Katja (1993), *Wel of Niet Fuseren? Een Onderzoek vanuit Rechtseconomisch Perspectief* (To Merge or Not To Merge? A Law and Economics Perspective), thesis.

Peeperkorn, Luc (1987), 'Mededingingsbeleid op klompen (Competition Policy on Wooden Shoes)', **10** *Tijdschrift voor politieke economie*, 57-75.

Peeperkorn, Luc (1988), 'Openbaarheid van Kartels (The Public Nature of Cartels)', **73** *Economisch-Statistische Berichten*, 212-214.

Peeperkorn, Luc (1989a), 'Het EG-mededingingsbeleid (EC Competition Policy)', **74** *Economisch-Statistische Berichten*, 1139-1142.

Peeperkorn, Luc (1989b), 'Fusiecontrole in de EG (EC Merger Control)', **74** *Economisch-Statistische Berichten*, 1163-1165.

Peeters, Marjan G.W.M. (1992), *Marktconform Milieurecht. Een Rechtsvergelijkende Studie naar de Verhandelbaarheid van Vervuilingsrechten* (Market Conform Environmental Law. A Comparative Study Regarding the Transferability of Pollution Rights), Zwolle, Tjeenk Willink, 438 p.

Peeters, Marjan G.W.M. (1994), 'Marktconforme Regulering (Market Conform Regulation)', in Eijlander, Ph. et al. (eds), *Wetgeven en de Maat van de Tijd*, Deventer, W.E.J. Tjeenk Willink, 125-135.

Perron, Edgar Du (1990), 'De rechtseconomische Analyse van het Verbintenissenrecht (A Law and Economics Analysis of the Law of Obligations)', **39(10)** *Ars Aequi*, 770-776.

Pijnacker Hordijk, E.P.H. and Snoep, T.M. (1996), 'De Overheid als Ondernemer: Kanttekeningen vanuit Mededingingsrechtelijk Perspectief (The Government as Entrepreneur: Notes From a Competion Law Perspective)', **71** *Nederlands Juristen Blad*, 923-929.

Praet, Patrick (1992), 'De List van de Economische Rede: de Ethische Constructie in Law and Economics (The Lure of Economic Reasoning: the Ethical Construction in Law-and-Economics)', **18** *Recht en Kritiek*, 343-359.

Quaedvlieg, Antoon A. (1992), 'The Economic Analysis of Intelletual Property Law', in Korthals Altes, Willem F., Dommering, Egbert J., Hugenholtz, P. Bernt and Kabel, Jan J.C. (eds), *Information Law Towards the 21st Century*, Deventer, Kluwer, 379-393.

Raaijmakers, M.J.G.C. et al. (1996), *'Corporate Governance' in Nederland: Besluitvorming en Verantwoording in Beursondernemingen* ('Corporate Governance' in the Netherlands: Decisionmaking and Answerability in Quoted Companies), Den Haag, Stichting Maatschappij en Onderneming, 117 p.

Raes, Koen (1988a), 'Rechtstheorie als Ideologiekritiek (Law and Economics as Ideological Criticism)', in Kamstra, O.W.M. et al. (eds), *Nederlandsche Rechtswetenschap*, Zwolle, Tjeenk Willink, 283-298.

Raes, Koen (1988b), 'Onrechtmatige Daad en de Markt van Pijn en Smart (Torts and the Market for Pain and Suffering)', **14** *Recht en Kritiek*, 102-125.

Raes, Koen (1990), 'Het Recht van de Schaarste (The Law of Scarcety)', **16** *Recht en Kritiek*, 380-394.

Raes, Koen and Willekens, Harry (1994a), 'Grondproblemen en -Mogelijkheden (Basic Problems and Options)', in Raes, Koen and Willekens, H. (eds), *Economische Verklaringen van het Recht*, Den Haag, VUGA, 9-43.

Raes, Koen (1994), 'Economische verklaringen van het recht: grondproblemen en -mogelijkheden' (Economic Explanations of Law: Fundamental Problems and

Potential)', **2** *Recht der Werkelijkheid*, 9-44. Reprinted in Raes, Koen and Willekens, Harry (eds.), *Economische verklaringen van het recht*, 's-Gravenhage, Vuga, 1994

Resius, F.J. (1990), 'Uitgeversbescherming' (The Protection of Publishers)', **14** *Informatierecht*, 67-69.

Richard, Th.A.M. (1996), 'Naar een Economische Benadering van het Auteursrecht op Internet (Towards an Economic Approach of Copyright on Internet)', **71** *Nederlands Juristen Blad*, 957-962.

Richters, H.W. (1991), *Schikkingen en Proceskansen* (Settlements and Expected Proceedings Outcome), diss. Rotterdam, 171 p.

Rietkerk, G. (1988), 'Bestuursonvriendelijke Onderneming: een Countervailing Power. Een Economische Analyse (Management Unfriendly Take-over: A Countervailing Power. An Economic Analysis)', **66** *De Naamloze Vennootschap*, 45-54.

Rietkerk, G. (1992), 'Structuurregeling aan Heroverweging Toe (Supervisory Rules to be Reconsidered)', **77** *Economisch-Statistische Berichten*.

Rovens, R. and Prinsen, P.J. (1984), 'Extra Politie-inzet en Rijden onder Invloed (More Police and Drunken Driving)', **52** *WODC*.

Ru, H.J. De (1987), *Staat, Markt en Recht* (The State, the Market and the Law), Zwolle, Tjeenk Willink, 93 p.

Ru, H.J. De (1988), *Prijst de Wet zich uit de Markt?* (Does the Law Price Itself Out of the Market?), Zwolle, Tjeenk Willink.

Ryan, Bernard (1994), 'Law and Economics and Employment Law', in Raes, Koen and Willekens, H. (eds), *Economische Verklaringen van het Recht*, Den Haag, VUGA, 109-131.

Scheiwe, Kirsten (1991), 'Costs and Benefits of Housework: Winners and Losers', **17(2)** *Recht en Kritiek*, 283-297.

Schenk, Hans (1997), 'Fusies, Efficiëntie en Mededingingsbeleid: Mogelijkheden en Beperkingen van het Nieuwe Concentratietoezicht (Mergers, Efficiency and Competition Policy: Options and Limitations of the New Concentration Monitoring)', in Dankbaar, Ben and Becker, F. (eds), *Economisch Beleid in een Ondernemende Samenleving*, Houtem/Diegem, Bohn Stafleu/Van Loghum, 111-148.

Schippers, J.J. (1988), 'Rechtseconomie: het Recht van de Economie en de Plicht van het Recht (Law and Economics: Laws of Economics and the Duty of the Law)', **5** *Lust: Onafhankelijk Juridisch Opinieblad*, 104-109.

Schreuders, Wicher (1990), 'Het Formatie Dillemma: Nieuwe Variant op het Prisoner's Dilemma (The Formation Dilemma, A New Variant on the Prisoner's Dilemma)', **5** *Namens*, 13-17.

Schreuders, Wicher (1994), 'Globale Grenzen (Global Frontiers)', in Department of Economic Affairs (ed.), *Internationaal Platform Globalisering*, Den Haag, Ministerie van Economische Zaken, 105-110.

Schreuders, Wicher and Holzhauer, Rudi W. (eds) (1993), *Teksten Rechtseconomie* (Readings in Law-and-Economics), Arnhem, Gouda Quint, 461 p.

SEO (1982), *De Economische Betekenis van het Auteursrecht in Nederland* (The Economic Importance of Copyright in the Netherlands), Amsterdam, Stichting voor Economisch Onderzoek, 241 p.

SEO (1989), *Naar een Verhuur- en Leenrecht in de Europese Gemeenschap* (Towards a Rental and Lending Rights in the European Community), Amsterdam, Stichting voor Economisch Onderzoek, 203 p.

Simon, Henk (1993), *Publiekrecht of Privaatrecht? Een Geschiktheidsonderzoek aan de Hand van het Nutsmaximalisatiebeginsel Toegespitst op het Gebruik van het Privaatrecht door het Bestuur* (Public Law or Private Law. Looking at Suitability From a Utility Maximizing Principle, with Special Reference to the Use of Private Law by the Public Administration), Zwolle, Tjeenk Willink, 466 p.

Slagter, Wiek J. (1968), *Juridische en Economische Eigendom* (Legal and Economic Ownership), Deventer, Kluwer, 66 p.

Slagter, Wiek J. (1988), *Macht en Onmacht van de Aandeelhouder* (Shareholder's Lack of Power), Deventer, Kluwer, 47 p.

Slagter, Wiek J. (1989), *Schaarse Rechten. Afscheidscollege Rotterdam (Scarce Rights)*, Deventer, Kluwer, 42 p.

Slagter, Wiek J. (1993), 'Verslag van de Presentatie "Renovatie van het Structuurregime" op het congres "Naar nieuwe machtsverhoudingen in de Nederlandse Vennootschap"', op 15 juni 1993 te Rotterdam (Account of the Presentation "Renewing the Supervisory Rules" in the Symposium "Towards a New Balance of Power in the Dutch Company", held in Rotterdam on June 15 1993)', **36(8)** *TVVS Maandblad voor Ondernemingsrecht en Rechtspersonen*, 194-197.

Slagter, Wiek J. (1994), 'Institutional Investors and Corporate Governance in The Netherlands', in Baums, Th., Buxbaum, R.M. and Hopt, K.J. (eds), *Institutional Investors and Corporate Governance*, Berlin, De Gruyter, 329-346.

Slagter, Wiek J. (1995), 'Grensoverschrijdingen en Grensgeschillen tussen de Economische en Rechtswetenschap (Border-crossings and Border-differences Between Economic and Legal Science)', in Slagter, Wiek J. et al. (eds), *Ondernemen Tussen Macht en Ordening: Opstellen op het Grensvlak van Economie en Recht*, Amsterdam, Thesis Publishers, 1-14.

Slagter, Wiek J. (1996), 'Misbruik van Voorwetenschap (Insider Dealing)', **39** *TVVS Maandblad voor Ondernemingsrecht en Rechtspersonen*, 69-71.

Slagter, Wiek J. et al. (eds) (1995), *Ondernemen tussen Macht en Ordening: Opstellen op het Grensvlak van Economie en Recht* (Entrepreneurship Between Power and Regulation: Essays on the Borderline of Economics and Law), Amsterdam, Thesis Publishers, 80 p.

Slot, P.J. (1983a), *Regelen en Ontregelen. Oratie Leiden (Regulating and De-regulating)*, Kluwer, Deventer.

Slot, P.J. (1983b), *Regelen en Ontregelen: over Deregulering en Economisch Recht* (Regulating and De-regulating: on Deregulation and Economic Law), Inaugural Lecture, Rijksuniversiteit Leiden.

Snijders, H.J. (1987), 'Prijzig Recht, Kwetsbaar Recht. Preadvies voor de 35e jaarvergadering van de Nederlandse Orde van Advocaten (Expensive Law, Vulnerable Law)', *Advocatenblad*, 325-342.

Snijders, W.L. (1975), 'Misbruikstoezicht en Verbodsbeginsel in het Kartelrecht (I) (Supervising Abuse and the Principle of Banning Orders in Anti-trust Law I)', **40** *Maandschrift Economie*, 133-154.

Snijders, W.L. (1982), 'Het Optreden tegen Economische Machtsposities op Grond van de Wet Economische Mededinging (The Action against Economic Position of Powers on the Basis of the Economic Competition Act)', in X (ed.), *In Orde: Liber Amicorum Pieter Verloren van Themaat*, Deventer, Kluwer, 267-293.

Sociaal Cultureel Planbureau (1990), *Doelmatig Rechtspreken* (Efficient Administration of Justice, *S.C.P., Cahier no. 88*, s-Gravenhage, Staatsdrukkerij, 1990 p.

Sociaal-Economische Raad (1994), *Advies Nieuwe Mededingingswet* (Recommendations for the New Competion Bill), SER-publicatie, 94/13.

Soetenhorst, W.J. (1989), 'Wettelijke Bescherming van de Uitgeefprestatie in Nederland, Duitsland, Zwitserland en Groot- Brittannië (Legal Protection of Publishers Activities in the Netherlands, Germany, Switzerland and Great Britain)', **13** *Informatierecht*, 55-57.

Soetenhorst, W.J. (1993), *De Bescherming van de Uitgeefprestatie* (Legal Protection of Publishers), Zwolle, Tjeenk Willink, 283 p.

Spittje, Petra J. (1991), 'De hinderwetgeving (Nuisance Legislation)', in Coljee, P.D., Franken, H., Heertje, A. and Kanning, W. (eds), *Law and Welfare Economics*, Amsterdam, VU Amsterdam, 115-132.

Steenhuis, D.W. (1984), 'Strafrechtelijk Optreden: Stapje Terug en een Sprong Voorwaarts (Criminal Policy: A Step Backwards and a Jump Ahead)', in X (ed.), *Delikt en Delinkwent*, Arnhem, Gouda Quint, 4-5.

Stichting voor Economisch Onderzoek (1982), *De Economische Betekenis van het Auteursrecht in Nederland* (The Economic Importance of Copyright in the Netherlands), Amsterdam, Stichting voor Economisch Onderzoek, 241 p.

Stichting voor Economisch Onderzoek (1989), *Naar een Verhuur- en Leenrecht in de Europese Gemeenschap* (Towards Rental and Lending Rights in the European Community), Amsterdam, Stichting voor Economisch Onderzoek, 203 p.

Strowel, Alain (1994), 'De Economische Analyse van de Intellectuele Rechten: een Les voor de Jurist? (Economic Analysis of Intellectual Property Rights: a Lesson for Lawyers?)', in Raes, Koen and Willekens, H. (eds), *Economische Verklaringen van het Recht*, Den Haag, VUGA, 179-202.

Tabaksblatt, M. (1995), 'Corporate Governance in Internationaal Perspectief (Corporate Governance in International Perspective)', **73** *De Naamloze Vennootschap*, 242-246.

Teijl, Rob and Holzhauer, Rudi W. (1990), 'Pluriformiteit in de Rechtseconomie: een Verkenning van Scholen (Multiformity in Law and Economics: an Exploration)', **39(10)** *Ars Aequi*, 617-631.

Teijl, Rob and Holzhauer, Rudi W. (eds) (1991a), *Teksten Rechtseconomie* (Readings in Law and Economics), Arnhem, Gouda Quint, 549 p.

Teijl, Rob and Holzhauer, Rudi W. (1991b), 'De Toenemende Complexiteit van het Intellectuele Eigendomsrecht. Een Economische Analyse' (The Growing Complexity of Intellectual Property Law. An Economic Analysis), in *Rechtseconomische Verkenningen Deel 1*.

Teijl, Rob and Holzhauer, Rudi W. (1992), 'Sturen in de Mist (Steering in the Fog)', *Landelijk Overleg Juridische Faculteitsbladen*, 27-28.

Teijl, Rob and Holzhauer, Rudi W. (1993), 'There's No Such Thing as a Free Rule', in Soeteman, A. et al. (eds), *Om de Norm: een Kwestie van Regels en Handhaving*, Lelystad, Vermande, 145-150.

Teijl, Rob and Holzhauer, Rudi W. (1994), *De Betekenis van de Oostenrijkse School voor de Rechtseconomie* (The Impact of the Austrian School on Law-and-Economics), Arnhem, Gouda Quint.

Teijl, Rob and Holzhauer, Rudi W. (1995), 'The Impact of the Austrian School on Law and Economics', in Bouckaert, Boudewijn and De Geest, Gerrit (eds), *Essays in Law and Economics II: Contract Law, Regulation, and Reflections on Law and Economics*, Antwerpen, Maklu, 247-266.

Teijl, Rob and Holzhauer, Rudi W. (1997), *Wisselende Perspectieven in de Rechtseconomie* (Changing Perspectives in Law and Economics), Arnhem, Gouda Quint, 431 p.

Ten Berge, J.B.J.M. (1991), 'Rechtseconomie en Staatsrecht/bestuursrecht (Law and Economics and Constitutional/Administrative Law)', in Hondius, E.H., Schippers, J.J. and Siegers, J.J. (eds), *Rechtseconomie en Recht*, Zwolle, Tjeenk Willink, 149-162.

Ten Kate, J. (1989), 'Schikkingen tijdens Civielrechtelijke Geschillen (Settlements in Private Law Disputes)', **10(1)** *Recht der Werkelijkheid*, 63-79.

Ten Kate, J. and Koppen, P.J. Van (1984), *Determinanten van Privaatrechtelijke Beslissingen* (Determinants of Civil Decisions), Arnhem, Gouda Quint, 123 p.

Ten Kate, J. and Koppen, P.J. Van (1997), 'Schikken of Niet (To Settle or Not To Settle)', in Van Koppen, Peter J. et al. (eds), *Het Hart van de Zaak*, Deventer, Gouda Quint, 44-62.

'T Gilde, A.P.J. and Haank, D.J. (1985), *De Praktijk van de Wet Economische Mededinging* (The Competition Act in Practice), 's-Gravenhage, SWOKA, Onderzoeksrapport, 38 p.

Theeuwes, Jules J.M. (1996), 'Economische Analyse van het Overeenkomstenrecht (Economic Analysis of Contract Law)', in Van de Hoek, M.P. (ed.), *Opstellen aangeboden aan prof. dr. C. Rijnvos*, Groningen, Wolters-Noordhoff, 127-152.

Theeuwes, Jules J.M. and Van Velthoven, Ben C.J. (1994a), 'Een Economische Visie op de Ontwikkeling van de Criminaliteit (An Economic Look at the Development of Criminality)', **20** *Justitiële Verkenningen*, 42-65.

Theeuwes, Jules J.M. and Van Velthoven, Ben C.J. (1994b), *De Ontwikkeling van de Criminaliteit in Nederland, 1950-1990: een Economische Analyse* (The Development of Criminality in the Netherlands, 1950-1990: an Economic Analysis), Research Memorandum 94-07, Faculty of Law, Department of Economics.

Theeuwes, Jules J.M., Van Velthoven, Ben C.J. and Winters, J.K. E.A. (1989), *Recht en Economie* (Law and Economics), Amsterdam, Addison-Wesley, 294 p.

Theeuwes, Jules J.M. et al. (1992), *Recht en Economie* (Law and Economics), Amsterdam, Addison-Wesley, 301 p.

Timmerman, L. (1990), 'Onderneming en Vennootschap (Enterprise and Firm)', in X (ed.), *Piercing Van Schilfgaarde*, Deventer, Kluwer, 3-11.

Timmerman, L. (1993), 'Enkele Opmerkingen over Vennootschapsrecht in EG-Perspectief (Some Remarks on Company Law in an EC-Perspective)', **6094** *Weekblad voor Privaatrecht, Notarisambt en Registratie*, 436-438.

Timmerman, L. (1996), 'Doorbraak van Aansprakelijkheid, de Kern van Enige Recente Ontwikkelingen (Lifting the Veil: the Core of Some Recent Developments)', **39** *TVVS Maandblad voor Ondernemingsrecht en Rechtspersonen*, 134-137.

Tinbergen, J. (1982), 'Kan de Economische Wetenschap Bijdragen tot de Ontwikkeling van het Recht? (Can the Economic Science Contribute to Legal Development?)', in X (ed.), *In Orde: Liber Amicorum Pieter Verloren van Themaat*, Deventer, Kluwer, 295-300.

Uitermark, P.J. (1972), 'Maximumprijzen: een Vergeten Hoofdstuk? (Maximum Prices: A Forgotten Chapter?)', **36** *Maandschrift Economie*, 465-484.

Uitermark, P.J. (1986), 'Het Nederlandse Mededingingspolitieke Regime: Over de Verhouding tussen Verbod, Misbruik, Misstand en Casuïstisch Beleid (Dutch Competition Policy: On the Interrelationship between Banning, Abuse, Wrongs and Case-to-Case Policy)', **29** *TVVS Maandblad voor Ondernemingsrecht en Rechtspersonen*, 108-115.

Uitermark, P.J. (1987a), 'Over Economische Mededinging (On Economic Competition)', **35** *Sociaal-Economische Wetgeving: Tijdschrift voor Europees en Economisch Recht*, 339-372.

Uitermark, P.J. (1987b), 'Over Informeel Mededingingsbeleid (On Informal Competition Policy)', **2** *Recht der Werkelijkheid*, 30-53.

Uitermark, P.J. (1990), *Economische Mededinging en Algemeen Belang: Een onderzoek naar de economisch-theoretische fundering van de mededingingspolitiek* (Economic Competition and Public Interest: An Investigation into the Economic-theoretical Foundations of Competition Policy), Groningen, Wolters-Noordhoff, 475 p.

Van Altena, A.R., Schippers, J.J. and Siegers, Jacques J. (1990), 'Rechtseconomie en Economisch Strafrecht (Law and Economics and Economic Criminal Law)', in X (ed.), *Facetten van Economisch Strafrecht: Opstellen over Economisch Strafrecht*, Arnhem, Gouda Quint, 163-182.

Van Asselt, Henk Th. (1989a), *Octrooiduur en Innovatie in de Geneesmiddelenindustrie* (Patent Term and Innovation in the Pharmaceutical Industry), Management Report Series.

Van Asselt, Henk Th. (1989b), 'Balanceren tussen Innovatie en Monopolie: Octrooiduur en Innovatie in de Geneesmiddelenindustrie (Balancing Innovation and Monopoly: The Patent Term and Innovation in the Pharmaceutical Industry)', **57(6)** *Intellectuele eigendom en reclamerecht*, 143-147.

Van Dam, C.C. Van (1989), *Zorgvuldigheidsnorm en Aansprakelijkheid* (The Duty of Care and Liability), Deventer, Kluwer, 333 p.

Van Damme, E.E.C. (1996), 'Marktwerking en Herregulering (Markets and Re-regulation)', in Gestel, R.A.J. van et al. (eds), *Markt en Wet*, Deventer, W.E.J. Tjeenk Willink, 19-43.

Van Damme, E.E.C. (1997), 'Tien Misverstanden over Veilingen (Ten Misunderstandings about Auctions)', **82** *Economisch-Statistische Berichten*, 24-28.

Van de Kerkhof, Marie-José A. (1993), *Economische Efficiëntie van Octrooibescherming* (Economic Efficiency of Patent Protection), thesis.

Van den Berg, P.J. (1996), 'Rechtseconomie als Cultuurwetenschap (Law and Economics as Cultural Science)', **25(2)** *Tijdschrift voor Rechtsfilosofie en Rechtstheorie*, 95-112.

Van den Bergh, P. and Faure, Michael (1990), *De Invloed van Verzekering op de Civiele Aansprakelijkheid: Een rechtseconomische Analyse* (The Influence of Insurance on Civil Liability: An Economic Analysis), Lelystad, Vermande.

Van den Bergh, Roger (1990), 'Economische Analyse van het Consumentenrecht (Economic Analysis of Consumer Law)', **39(10)** *Ars Aequi*, 787-793.

Van den Bergh, Roger (1991), 'Wat is Rechtseconomie? (What is Law and Economics?)', in Hondius, E.H., Schippers, J.J. and Siegers, J.J. (eds), *Rechtseconomie en Recht*, Zwolle, Tjeenk Willink, 9-49.

Van den Bergh, Roger (1993), *Economische Analyse van het Mededingingsrecht: een Terreinverkenning* (Economic Analysis of Competition Law: an Exploration), Rechtseconomische Verkenningen, Arnhem, Gouda Quint, 120 p.

Van den Bergh, Roger (1994), *Subsidiariteit Rechtseconomisch Bekeken: Adieu Bruxelles?* (Subsidiarity from an Economic Perspective: Adieu Bruxelles), Rechtseconomische Verkenningen, Arnhem, Gouda Quint, 105 p.

Van den Bergh, Roger (1997a), *Automatische Vergoeding van Schade Geleden door Zwakke Verkeersdeelnemers: een Rechtseconomische Kritiek (Automatic Compensation of Damages Suffered by Weak Parties in Traffic Accidents)*, Paper gepresenteerd op de studiedag Verkeersaansprakelijkheid in België en Nederland.

Van den Bergh, Roger (1997b), 'Van Nederlands Kartelparadijs naar Europees Kartelparadijs: een Kritische Rechtseconomische Kijk op het Wetsvoorstel voor een Nieuwe Mededingingswet (From a Dutch Cartel Paradise to an European Cartel Paradise)', **72(4)** *Nederlands Juristen Blad*, 149-153.

Van den Bergh, Roger (1997c), *Economische Analyse van het Mededingingsrecht: een Terreinverkenning* (Economic Analysis of Competition Law: an Exploration), Rechtseconomische Verkenningen, Arnhem, Gouda Quint, 164 p.

Van den Bergh, Roger (1998), 'Automatische vergoeding van schade geleden door zwakke verkeersdeelnemers: een rechtseconomische kritiek (Automatical Compensation to Weak Parties in Traffic Accidents: An Economic Critique', in Faure, Michael and Hartlief, T. (eds), *Verkeersaansprakelijkheid in België en Nederland*, Antwerp, Intersentia, 27-74.

Van den Broek, Jan H.G. (1991), 'Nieuwe Instrumenten voor Energiebesparing (New Instruments for Energy Savings)', in Coljee, P.D., Franken, H., Heertje, A. and Kanning, W. (eds), *Law and Welfare Economics*, Amsterdam, VU Amsterdam, 59-76.

Van den Hof, Daniëlle (1994), *Instrumenten van Milieubeheer. Een onderzoek vanuit Rechtseconomisch Perspectief* (Instruments of Environmental Policy. A Law and Economics Perspective), thesis.

Van der Grinten, W.C.J. (1994), 'De Structuurvennootschap in Discussie (The Supervised Company under Discussion)', **69(3)** *Nederlands Juristen Blad*, 85-89.

Van der Ploeg, Frederick (1994), 'Regulering: Zegen of Vloek? Van Deelbelang naar Algemeen Belang (Regulation: Blessing or Curse? From Private to General Interest)', in Bos, D.I. (ed.), *Deregulering in Nederland: Economische Uitdagingen voor de Nieuwe Regering*, Rotterdam, Erasmus University, 9-38.

Van der Ploeg, Frederick (1996), 'Vijf Kanttekeningen bij de Nieuwe Mededingingswet (Five Comments on the New Competition Act)', **81** *Economisch-Statistische Berichten*, 652-653.

Van der Weijden, Carel J. (1987), 'Over toetreding, uittreding en effectieve mededinging (Entry, Exit and Effective Competition)', in *Van alle markten thuis*, Rotterdam, Universitaire Pers, 97-106.

Van der Weijden, Carel J. (1995), *Te Laag Geprijsd* (At What Price), Rotterdam, Erasmus University, 22 p.

Van der Woude, M.H. (1995), 'Nederlands en Europees Kartelrecht (Dutch and European Anti-trust Law)', **5** *Rechtsgeleerd Magazijn Themis*, 198-204.

Van der Woude, M.H. (1996), 'Decentralisatie en Mededinging (Decentralization and Competition)', **2** *Nederlands Tijdschrift voor Europees Recht*, 255-259.

Van der Zijpp, I. (1995), 'Wetgeving en Rechtsvervaging in de Zakenwereld (Legislation and Fading Law in the Business Community)', in X (ed.), *Ondernemen tussen Macht en Ordening: Opstellen op het Grensvlak van Economie en Recht*, Amsterdam, Thesis Publishers, 47-55.

Van Dijk, J.J.M. (1984), 'Financieel Economische Aspecten van Misdaad en Misdaadbestrijding (Financial Economic Aspects of Crime and Prevention)', **69** *Economisch-Statistische Berichten*, 1248-1252.

Van Dijk, J.J.M. (1987), 'Over de Wenselijkheid van Overheidsinterventies op de Markt van Recht en Orde (On the Desirability of Governmental Intervention on the Market for Law and Order)', **67** *Advocatenblad*, 343-352.

Van Dijk, J.J.M. (1993), 'Het Calculerende Slachtoffer (The Calculating Victim)', **35(2)** *Tijdschrift voor Criminologie*, 177-188.

Van Dijk, J.J.M. and Röell, A. (1988), 'Criminaliteit in Tal en Last (Crime in Scores and Costs)', **14(2)** *Justitiële Verkenningen*, 7-33.

Van Dijk, T.W.P. (1994), *The Limits to Patent Protection, Essays on the Economics of Intellectual Property Rights*, Maastricht, Universitaire Pers, 201 p.

Van Eldijk, Ab (1992), 'Collectieve Goederen en Private Rechten (Collective Goods and Private Rights)', **13(1)** *Recht der Werkelijkheid*, 4-7.

Van Koppen, Peter J. and Malsch, Marijke (1991), 'Defendants and One-shotters Win After All: Compliance with Court Decisions in Civil Cases', **25** *Law and Society Review*, 803-820.

Van Koppen, P.J. (1990), 'Cassatieadvocaten en de Selectiekamer (Cassation Lawyers and the Chamber of Selection)', *Nederlands Juristen Blad*, 14-26.

Van Koppen, P.J., Richters, H.W. and Ten Kate, J. (1989), 'Schikken of Procederen: Psychologische kanttekeningen bij de Economie van Civielrechtelijke Geschillen (Settlement vs. Trial: Psychological Notes on the Economy of Private Law Disputes)', *Rapport aangeboden aan de Minister van Justitie*.

Van Koppen, Peter J. and Malsch, Marijke (1992), 'Hoe de Verliezer Wint (How the Loser Wins)', **67** *Nederlands Juristen Blad*, 1101-1104.

Van Koppen, Peter J. and Malsch, Marijke (1997), 'De Waarde van Civiele Vonnissen (The Value of Civil Judgments)', in Van Koppen, Peter J. et al. (eds), *Het Hart van de Zaak*, Deventer, Gouda Quint, 611-621.

Van Manen, Niels F. (1994), 'Eigenbelang, Chaos en Sociale Orde (Self-interest, Chaos and Social Order)', in Raes, Koen and Willekens, H. (eds), *Economische Verklaringen van het Recht*, Den Haag, VUGA, 75-92.

Van Plompen, P.M.A.L. (1996), 'Het Ontwerp-Mededingingswet (The Competition Bill)', **74** *De Naamloze Vennootschap*, 158-167.

Van Schilfgaarde, E. Van (1990), 'Economische Analyse van het Nederlands Aansprakelijkheidsrecht uit Onrechtmatige Daad (Economic Analysis of Dutch Tort Liability Law)', **39(10)** *Ars Aequi*, 750-758.

Van Tulder, Frank (1985), *Criminaliteit, pakkans en politie* (Criminality, Chance of Being Caught and Police), *Sociaal Cultureel Planbureau, Cahier no. 45*, 's-Gravenhage, Staatsdrukkerij, 1985 p.

Van Tulder, Frank (1986), 'Kosten en baten van twee vormen van criminaliteitsbestrijding (Costs and Benefits of Two Types of Crime Combat)', **71** *Economisch-Statistische Berichten*, 172-179.

Van Tulder, Frank (1990), 'Rechtshulp in Economisch Perspectief (Legal Aid from an Economic Perspective)', **39(10)** *Ars Aequi*, 692-705.

Van Tulder, Frank (1991), 'Over Fietsen en Recht (On Bicycles and Law)', **66** *Nederlands Juristenblad*, 444-445.

Van Tulder, Frank (1994), *Van Misdaad tot Straf* (From Crime to Penalty), Serie Sociale en Culturele Studies, 's-Gravenhage, Vuga, 319 p.

Van Tulder, Frank and Janssen, S. (1988b), 'De Prijselasticiteit van het Recht (The Price Elasticity of Law)', **73** *Economisch-Statistische Berichten*, 19-22.

Van Tulder, Frank and Janssen, S. (1988a), *De Prijs van de Weg naar het Recht* (The Price of the Road to the Law), Sociaal Cultureel Planbureau Stukwerk, No. 45.

Van Tulder, Frank P. and Spapens, A.C. (1990), *Doelmatig Rechtspreken (Efficient Administration of Justice)*, 's-Gravenhage, Vuga, 74 p.

Van Veen, P. (1995), *Naar een Nieuwe Mededingingswet (Towards a New Competition Act)*, Rotterdam, Erasmus University, 31 p.

Van Velthoven, Ben C.J. (1994), *De Economie van Misdaad en Straf: een Overzicht van de Literatuur* (The Economics of Crime and Punishment: a Literature Review), Research Memorandum 94-08, Faculty of Law, Department of Economics.

Van Velthoven, Ben C.J. and Van Wijck, Peter W. (1996), *De Economie van Civiele Geschillen: Rechtsbijstand Versus No Cure No Pay* (The Economics of Civil Suits: Legal Aid versus No Cure No Pay), Research Memorandum 96-02, Faculty of Law, Department of Economics.

Van Velthoven, Ben C.J. and Van Wijck, Peter W. (1997), 'De Economie van Civiele Geschillen (The Economics of Civil Suits)', **18** *Recht der Werkelijkheid*, 18-52.

Van Velthoven, Ben C.J., Van Wijck, Peter W. et al. (1997), *Recht en Efficiëntie* (Law and Efficiency), Deventer, Kluwer, 337 p.

Van Waarden, F. and Unger, B. (1992), 'Marktfalen, Kartellering en Economische Efficiëntie (Market Failure, Cartelization and Economic Efficiency)', **77** *Economisch-Statistische Berichten*, 916-920.

Van Welderen Rengers, W.J. (1861), *Beschouwingen over het Verband tusschen het Burgerlijk Recht en de Staatshuishoudkunde* (Reflections on the Relationship Between Civil Law and Economics), Utrecht, P.W. v.d. Weijer, 120 p.

Van Wijck, Peter W. and Van Velthoven, Ben C.J. (1996), *Een Economische Analyse van het Amerikaanse en het Continentale Systeem van Proceskostentoerekening* (An Economic Analysis of American and Continental Systems of Cost Allocation Rules), Research Memorandum, Faculty of Law, Department of Economics, 96-04.

Van Winden, Frans A.A.M. (1990), 'De Economische Theorie van de Politieke Besluitvorming (The Economic Theory of Political Decisionmaking)', in Van der Geest, L. (ed.), *Economische Theorie: de Stand van Zaken*, Schoonhoven, Academic Service, 125-148.

Van Winden, Frans A.A.M. (1997), *On The Economic Theory of Interest Groups*, Discussion paper, 97-117/1.

Verhaegen, P.H.A.M. and Volkers, A.B. (1996), 'Kosten en Baten van Regelgeving (Costs and Benefits of Rulemaking)', in Gestel, R.A.J. van et al. (eds), *Markt en Wet*, Deventer, W.E.J. Tjeenk Willink, 45-57.

Verhoef, B.M., Verster, A.C.P. and Klaassen, L.H. (1989), *Naar een Economische Benadering van Criminaliteit en Veiligheidszorg* (Towards an Economic Approach of

Delinquency and Security Provision), Dordrecht, Stichting Maatschappij en Politie, 138 p.

Verloren Van Themaat, Pieter (1978), 'Het Wetsontwerp-Lubbers tot Wijziging van de Wet Economische Mededinging (The Lubbers Bill on a Change of the Economic Competition Act)', **26** *Sociaal-Economische Wetgeving: Tijdschrift voor Europees en Economisch Recht*, 178-192.

Verloren Van Themaat, Pieter (1988a), 'Economie Gezien door Juristen (Economics, Seen by Lawyers)', in X (ed.), *Mededelingen van de Afdeling Letterkunde, Nieuwe Reeks*, Amsterdam, Koninklijke Nederlandse Akademie van Wetenschappen, 229-258.

Verloren Van Themaat, Pieter (1988b), 'Nieuw Leven in de Wet Economische mededinging of terug naar Abtsweg? (New Life in the Economic Competition Act or Back to Abtsweg?)', **36** *Sociaal-Economische Wetgeving: Tijdschrift voor Europees en Economisch Recht*, 4-15.

Visscher, L.T. (1998), 'The Problem of Uncompensated Losses. The Case of Dutch Traffic Liability', in Ott, Claus and von Wangenheim, Georg (eds), *Essays in Law and Economics IV*, Antwerpen, Maklu.

Visscher, L.T. and Kerkmeester, Heico (1996), 'Kenbaarheidsvereiste en Gewoonte als Verweren Tegen een Actie uit Onrechtmatige Daad, een Rechtseconomische Benadering (The Knowledge Requirement and Custom as Defences Against a Tort Action, a Law and Economics Approach)', **3** *Tijdschrift voor Milieuaansprakelijkheid*, 48-57.

Visscher, L.T. and Van den Bergh, Roger (1998), 'Over Fietsende Juristen en Autorijdende Rechtseconomen (On Cycling Lawyers and Driving Legal Economists)', **73** *Nederlands Juristen Blad*, 122-127.

Vogelzang, P.J. and Dotsch, S.J. (1988), 'Fusies en Overnames in Nederland, 1971-1988 (Mergers and Take-Overs in the Netherlands, 1971-1988)', **73** *Economisch-Statistische Berichten*, 859-861.

von Benda-Beckmann, Franz (1992), 'Uncommon Questions about Property Rights', **13** *Recht der Werkelijkheid*, 8-14.

Voogd, R.P. (1989), *Statutaire Beschermingsmiddelen bij Beursvennootschappen* (Protective Measures in the Memorandum of Quoted Companies), Deventer, Kluwer, 499 p.

Voûte, J. (1989), 'Enige Civielrechtelijke Aspecten van Misbruik van Voorwetenschap (Some Civil Aspects of Insider Dealing)', in X (ed.), *De Maris-Bundel*, Deventer, Kluwer, 219-230.

Wallage, Ph. (1995), 'Corporate Governance en de Rol en Functie van de Accountant (Corporate Governance and the Role and Function of the Accountant)', **73** *De Naamloze Vennootschap*, 274-276.

Walther, Sylvia R.B. (1991), 'Eigen schuld slachtoffer en schadevergoedingsmaatregel. Een civielrechtelijke verdeelsleutel in het strafrecht (Victims Fault and Damage Orders. A Civil Law Distributive Code in Criminal Law)', **66** *Nederlands Juristenblad*, 90-94.

Wassenaer Van Catwijck, A.J.O. Baron Van (1977), *Verkeersverzekering* (Traffic Insurance), Zwolle, Tjeenk Willink, 78 p.

Wassenaer Van Catwijck, A.J.O. Baron Van (1988), 'Verkeersverzekering in Noord-Amerika (Traffic Insurance in North America: No-fault in Action)', *Het Verzekerings-Archief*, 321-377.

Wassenaer Van Catwijck, A.J.O. Baron Van (1991), 'Op zeker spelen. Invloeden van zekerheden in het NBW op het financieringsbedrijf (Play it Safe. Influence of Dutch New Civil Code Se)', in Coljee, P.D., Franken, H., Heertje, A. and Kanning, W. (eds), *Law and Welfare Economics*, Amsterdam, VU Amsterdam, 133-150.

Weijden, Carel J. Van Der (1962), *Toegang en Toetreding: Facetten van de Mededinging* (Entry and Entrance: Aspects of Competition), Den Haag.

Weijden, Carel J. Van Der (1981), 'Toestaan of verbieden? Een beschouwing rond de Wet economische mededinging (Allowing or Banning? Considerations about the Economic Competition Act)', **66** *Economisch-Statistische Berichten*, 1281-1284.

Weijden, Carel J. Van Der (1987), 'Werkzame mededinging (Workable Competition)', **72** *Economisch-Statistische Berichten*, 1194-1199.

Wertheimer, H.W. (1983), 'De Europese Concentratiecontrole in De Revisie (European Concentration Control in Revision)', **31** *Sociaal-Economische Wetgeving: Tijdschrift voor Europees en Economisch Recht*, 66-84.

Wichers Hoeth, L. (1984), 'Mini-monopolies: Een Reactie (Mini-monopolies: A Response)', *Rechtsgeleerd Magazijn Themis*, 356-357.

Wiersma, D. (1989), 'De Efficiëntie van een Marktconform Milieubeleid (The Efficiency of an Environmental Policy in Accordance with Market Principles)', *Dissertatie Groningen*.

Wiggers, Willem J.H. (1995), *Corporate Governance, Rechtsvergelijkende Beschouwingen over Kwaliteit van Bestuur en Toezicht in de Onderneming* (Corporate Governance, Comparitive Considerations on Quality of Management and Supervision in the Firm), Working Paper Juridische Faculteit.

Wildenberg, I.W. and Zwetsloot, F.J.M. (1994), *Naar een Nieuwe Machtsindeling in de Nederlandse Vennootschap (Towards a New Division of Power in the Dutch Company)*, Deventer, Kluwer, 69 p.

Wladimiroff, M. (1991), 'Rechtseconomie en Strafrecht: Enige Kritische Kanttekeningen (Law and Economics and Criminal Law: Some Critical Remarks)', in Hondius, E.H., Schippers, J.J. and Siegers, J.J. (eds), *Rechtseconomie en Recht*, Zwolle, Tjeenk Willink, 181-186.

Woude, M.H. Van Der (1989), 'Kartelrechtelijke beschikkingen EG-Commissie 1985-1987 (Commission Anti-trust Orders 1985-1987)', **37** *Sociaal-Economische Wetgeving: Tijdschrift voor Europees en Economisch Recht*, 2-27.

X (1990), 'Special Issue on Law and Economics', *Ars Aequi*, 603-804.

Zijlstra, Jelle and Goudzwaard, Bob (1966), *Economische politiek en concurrentieproblematiek in de EEG en de lidstaten* (Economic Policy and Competition Problems in the EC and the Member States), Serie Concurrentie, Brussel.

Zwemmer, J.W. (1995), 'Belastingrecht op het Grensvlak van Economie en Recht (Tax Law on the Borderline of Economics and Law)', in X (ed.), *Ondernemen tussen Macht en Ordening: Opstellen op het Grensvlak van Economie en Recht*, Amsterdam, Thesis Publishers, 37-45.

0360
LAW AND ECONOMICS IN NORWAY

Erling Eide
Professor of Economics, Faculty of Law, University of Oslo

Abstract

The growing interest in law and economics among academic lawyers is demonstrated by the fact that the subject now has become compulsory for law students at the Faculty of Law in Oslo. A number of PhD theses at the same faculty are wholly or partially of a law and economics character. Economists have contributed on various issues within economics of crime, product liability, constitutional law, environmental law, and industrial organization.
JEL classification: K00
Keywords: Product Liability, Economics of Crime, Litigation, Constitutional Law, Environmental Law

1. Research

Although economic analysis occasionally has appeared in the traditional Norwegian law literature, it was not until Trine-Lise Wilhelmsen's study on 'Egenrisiko i skadeforsikring' (Retained Risk in Casualty Insurance) in 1989 that such analysis became part of a major work by an academic lawyer. Since then, Anders C. Stray Ryssdal (1995a, 1996b) has written a two volume dissertation, one on *Legal Realism and Economics as Behaviour: A Scandinavian Look at Economic Analysis of Law*, and the other on *Economic Analysis of Civil Suits and Appeals.* Another major contribution is *Avtalelovens § 36 og økonomisk effektivitet* (Section 36 of the Nordic Contract Acts and Economic Efficiency) by Trine-Lise Wilhelmsen (1995). Economic theory also plays an important role in three PhD dissertations that are about to be completed at the University of Oslo, one on antitrust law and two on environmental law.

Apart from the questions of monopolies, competition and so on analysed in the old law and economics literature, economists have only recently entered the more modern field of law and economics. Prevalent topics studied are regulation, product liability, crime, environmental law and industrial organization. Alf E. Risa has in several papers analyzed health and safety, in particular product liability, Risa (1994). Constitutional issues are analysed by Hylland (1984). A number of contributions to the economics of crime literature started with Allingham and Sandmo (1972) and Sandmo (1981) on tax evasion, followed by Isachsen and

Strøm (1980) on the underground economy, Andvig and Moene (1990) on corruption, Andvig (1995) on organized crime and Eide (1994a) on criminal behavior in general. An eleven-year program (1991-2001) on economic crime by the Research Council of Norway had by the end of 1997 produced 42 reports, mostly on tax evasion, bankruptcy and economic crime in financial markets. Some of these reports, in particular Knivsflå (1993) and Langli (1994), are more of a law and economics type than most of the others.

A manifestation of the growing interest in law and economics was the invitation to a group of academic lawyers and economists to spend a year at the Centre for Advanced Study at The Norwegian Academy of Science and Letters in 1994-95. Five scholars spent most of the year in Oslo, whereas several others were invited for shorter periods, some attending a conference on the Law and Economics of the Environment. A conference volume edited by Van den Bergh and Eide was published.

2. Education

In connection with a major reorganization of the study of law at the University of Oslo law and economics has been substituted for the traditional introductory course in micro and macro economics. A compulsory course in law and economics for public law must be taken in the second year, and the students may also choose to take a more extensive course (one quarter of a year's work) at the end of the study. At other institutions no courses in law and economics are offered, except courses for economists where industrial organization and regulation are main topics.

Two textbooks have been published by Erling Eide. One on *Kriminaløkonomi* (Economics of Crime) has been written for a course in economics, whereas one on *Rettsøkonomi for offentlig rett* (Law and Economics for Public Law) has been written for a compulsory course at the Faculty of Law in Oslo.

Bibliography on Law and Economics in Norway (0360)

Allingham, M. and A. Sandmo (1972), 'Income Tax Evasion: A Theoretical Analysis', **1** *Journal of Public Economics*, 323-338.

Andvig, Jens C. (1989), 'Korrupsjon i Utviklingsland (Corruption in Developing Countries)', **23** *Nordisk Tidsskrift for Politisk Ekonomi*, 51-70.

Andvig, Jens C. (1995), 'Corruption in the North Sea Oil Industry: Issues and Assessment', **23** *Crime, Law and Social Change*, 289-313.

Andvig, Jens C. and Karl Ove Moene (1990), 'How Corruption may Corrupt', **13** *Journal of Economic Behavior and Organization*, 63-76.

Eide, Erling (1981a), 'Kritikk av noen forutsetninger i Kriminalmeldingen (Critique of Some Assumptions in the Report on Crime)', *Lov og Rett*, 312-323.

Eide, Erling (1981b), 'Book Review of Lars Werin,1979, Ekonomi och Rettssystem', **94** *Tidsskrift for Rettsvitenskap*, 752-754.

Eide, Erling (1981c), 'Heineke, J.M. (Ed.), Economic Models of Criminal Behaviour (Book Review)', *Economic Journal*, 584-585.

Eide, Erling (1983), 'Realbeskatning og Nominalismen i Norsk Rett (Real Tax Rates and Nominalism in Norwegian Law)', **37** *Sosialøkonomen*, 5-10.

Eide, Erling (1984a), 'Book Review of Göran Skogh, 1982, Marknadens Villkor', **95** *Tidsskrift for Rettsvitenskap*, 318-319.

Eide, Erling (1984b), 'Renter og Verdisikring av Pengekrav (Interest Rates and Security against Inflation in Monetary Claims)', **97** *Tidsskrift for Rettsvitenskap*, 477-533.

Eide, Erling (1986), 'Book Review of Nils Nygaard, 1985, Skatt og Skade', **96** *Tidsskrift for Rettsvitenskap*, 708-712.

Eide, Erling (1987), 'Ekspropriasjonserstatning i en Inflasjonstid: Valg av Kapitaliseringsrente (Compensation for Expropriation in Times of Inflation)', *Lov og Rett*, 165-177.

Eide, Erling (1992), 'Rettsøkonomi - en Introduksjon (Law and Economics - an Introduction)', *Jussens Venner*, 193-224.

Eide, Erling (1994a), *Kriminaløkonomi (Economics of Crime)*, Stavanger, Rogaland Mediesenter.

Eide, Erling (1994b), *Economics of Crime: Deterrence and the Rational Offender*, Amsterdam, North-Holland.

Eide, Erling (1995a), 'Valg av Investeringsobjekt for Erstatningsbeløp (Choice of Type of Investment for Compensatory Damages)', *Lov og Rett*, 58-64.

Eide, Erling (1995b), 'Kapitaliseringsrenten - ny Episode (The Discount Rate - New Episode)', *Lov og Rett*, 351-358.

Eide, Erling (1997, 2. utg.), *Rettsøkonomi for offentlig rett*, Bergen, Grafisk Hus.

Heyerdahl, H. Cristopher (1991), *En Økonomisk Analyse av de Ulovfestede Ansvarsreglene i Erstatningsretten, for Risikonøytrale Aktører* (An Economic Analysis of Common Law Liability Rules in Tort Law for Risk-Neutral Agents).

Hylland, Aanund (1984), 'Bør politikerne binde sin egen handlefrihet? - Om grunnlovfestet budsjettbalanse, oljefond og politisk hestehandel (Should Politicians Restrict Their Freedom of Action?)', *Bergen Bank Kvartalsskrift*, 87-101.

Isachsen, Jon Arne and Steinar Strøm (1980), 'The Hidden Economy: The Labour Market and Tax Evasion', **82** *Scandinavian Journal of Economics*, 305-311.

Isachsen, Arne Jon and Strøm, Steinar (1981), *Skattefritt. Svart Sektor i Vekst* (Taxfree. The Growth of the Black Sector), Oslo, Universitetsforlaget.

Knivsflå, Kjell Henry (1993), 'Illegal Insider Trading and the Stock Market Reaction', **10** *The Research Council of Norway*, Research on Economic Crime.

Langli, Christian (1994), 'Konkurskriminalitet: En Empirisk Analyse av Aksjeselskaper som har Gått Konkurs (Bankruptcy Crime: An Empirical Analysis of Corporations that Have Gone Bankrupt), **17** *The Research Council of Norway*, Research on Economic Crime.

Risa, Alf Erling (1994), 'Preference Revelation in Strict Liability Product Safety Markets', **14** *International Review of Law and Economics*, 41-52.

Ryssdal, Stray A.C. (1993), 'Antitrust Enforcement - An Inquiry into Policy Analysis of Competition Law', Working Paper, **89** *Centre for Research in Economics & Business Administration*, Bergen.

Ryssdal, Anders C. Stray (1995a), *Legal Realism and Economics as Behaviour: A Scandinavian Look at Economic Analysis of Law*, Oslo, Juridisk Forlag.

Ryssdal, Anders C. Stray (1995b), *An Economic Analysis of Civil Suits and Appeals*, Oslo, Juridisk Forlag.

Ryssdal, Stray A.C. (1996), 'Towards a Nordic Competition Law?', **109** *Tidsskrift for Rettsvitenskap*, 332-357.

Sandmo, Agnar (1981), 'Income Tax Evasion. Labour Supply, and the Equity-efficiency Tradeoff', **16** *Journal of Public Economics*.

Stavang, Endre (1992), *Verdiskapningshensyn og juridisk argumentasjon: Særlig om kompensasjon for lokale miljøskader* (The Relation between Efficiency Analysis and Legal Reasoning, with Special Reference to Local Pollution Damage), Stensilserie Nr. 139, Institutt for privatrett, Universitetet i Oslo.

Stavang, Endre (1996), 'Legal Economics: How Cautious Should Lawyers Be?', Working Paper, **3** *Law and Economics*, Institutt for privatrett, Universitetet i Oslo.

Stavang, Endre (1997), 'Tolerance Limits and Temporal Priority in Environmental Civil Liability', Working Paper, **4** *Law and Economics*, Institutt for privatrett, Universitetet i Oslo.

Van den Bergh, Roger and Erling, Eide (1994), *Law and Economics of the Environment*, Oslo, Juridisk Forlag.

Wilhelmsen, Trine-Lise (1989), *Egenrisiko i Skadeforsikring* (Retained Risk in Casualty Insurance), Sjørettsfondet, Grafisk Hus, Bergen.

Wilhelmsen, Trine-Lise (1995), 'Avtalelovens 36 og økonomisk effektivitet (Section 36 of the Nordic Contract Acts and Economic Efficieny)', **108** *Tidsskrift for Rettsvitenskap*, 1-246.

0365
LAW AND ECONOMICS IN PORTUGAL

Miguel Moura e Silva
Assistente, Faculdade de Direito da Universidade de Lisboa

Abstract

This short chapter presents an overview of the current state of law and economics in Portugal. Whereas no specific courses are taught on this subject, researchers in the field have been relatively active. An account is given of some of the research done so far in Portugal.
JEL classification: K00
Keywords: Portugal, Law and Economics, Teaching, Research

1. Introduction

At present, law and economics seems to remain the province of a few scholars, mainly teaching at the University of Coimbra and University of Lisbon Law Schools and the Economics departments of the University of Coimbra, Universidade Nova and Universidade Católica, as well as the ISEG - Economics and Business School. With a few exceptions, such as a special issue by a law review, Sub Iudice, dedicated to Law and Economics, published in 1992, there seems to be a lack of institutionalized communication channels between scholars, particularly between lawyers and economists.

2. Law and Economics Courses

No specialized courses on law and economics exist in the current curricula at undergraduate level in either Economics or Law degrees. In Portugal, Law is taught as a five year degree following high school. The Economics degree has the same structure (although it may be completed in four years in some universities). The legal curriculum is mandatory during the first three years and there is no possibilitity of undergraduate interdisciplinary studies in other university departments. The economic training of law students consists, in most law schools, in a first-year, two semesters, course on Political Economy and a second-year, one semester, course on International Economic Relations. These courses tend to focus more on institutional and historical aspects rather than on applied economic theory even at an elementary level. No formal economic theory is normally taught and only a few law schools adopt elementary textbooks such as Nordhaus/Samuelson. This is hardly surprising as lecturers and assistants of economic subjects are usually lawyers with no specific economic background.

On the other hand, economics students are typically taught two law courses of one semester each. The first course consists of an introduction to law, a simplified version of a similar subject taught to first-year law students. The second is an upper-class course, normally dealing with basic corporate and trade regulation law.

At graduate level, to my knowledge the only experiment so far has been in the Masters degree at the University of Lisbon Law School where a research seminar was held two years ago on basic game theory concepts by Emeritus Prof. Soares Martinez.

Despite this bleak outlook, law and economics basic concepts are fairly well known among legal scholars and they are reflected in their academic work.

The introduction of a specialized Law and Economics course in undergraduate curricula at law schools seems to be a remote prospect. A traditional approach to legal education tends to keep curricula unchanged for many years and there is at present no proposal for change in existing law schools. This may yet change as the Universidade Nova in Lisbon is in the process of setting up a new law school opening in 1997. Since this university has a well reputed economics department one may expect a greater inclination to innovate legal education by incorporating law and economics. At the time of writing the curricula was not yet available for comment.

As to the use of law and economics as a tool in specific subjects taught at law schools, this is greatly undermined by law students' general lack of any serious undergraduate economics background.

3. Research

3.1 Methodology and Fundamental Concepts

Professor Jorge Sinde Monteiro of the University of Coimbra Law School is one of the pioneers of law and economics in Portugal. In an article published in 1981 (Sinde Monteiro, 1981) he considers several methodological questions regarding the place of economic analysis of law in the context of the 'science of law' (jurisprudence). The author considers the role of values, and concludes that 'justice' as defined by law and economics scholars such as Guido Calabresi is not the same as lawyers' 'justice'. For the latter 'justice' is what the author terms a constitutive and regulative principle and not a merely empirical fact. His conclusion is that the economic analysis of law may usefully constitute an auxiliary science of law, but not science of law itself.

Professor Sousa Franco, of the University of Lisbon Law School and the Portuguese Catholic University Law School, emphasizes the role of economic analysis of law in overcoming legal positivism by providing a framework for the analysis of the content and purpose of legal rules (Sousa Franco, 1992). Nevertheless, he cautions against an excessive enthusiasm for economic analysis of law due to what he terms its materialistic and individualistic bias. The preservation of the particular values established by the legal system is necessary to prevent an instrumentalization of law and the replacement of non-economic or 'supra-economic' values. Despite these methodological issues, the author argues cogently for the role of economic analysis in overcoming a certain narrow-mindedness of legal studies and in bringing together law and its practice.

3.2 Civil Procedure

In the field of civil procedure, Justice Ribeiro Mendes of the Portuguese Constitutional Court has written one of the most interesting pieces of economic analysis of Portuguese law (Ribeiro Mendes, 1992). Setting out from Richard Posner's analysis of civil procedure, Justice Ribeiro Mendes examines some of the economic effects of the Portuguese rules regarding debt collection (executive procedure). The division between declarative procedure (mandatory for creditors that do not have an executive title) and the increased costs of this two-tier procedure create incentives to look for alternative ways of securing debt, such as guaranty cheques, hidden property guarantees, negative guarantees and withholding of title. Another significant problem examined by Justice Ribeiro Mendes is that of the sale of debtors' assets. In Portugal this sale is made by order of the courts and the tender takes place before a judge. According to the author, this system has developed into a collusive market, where bid-rigging is rampant, thus defrauding creditors and the State.The author envisages central sales agencies, managed by the State or by specially-regulated firms.

3.3 Antitrust

Moura e Silva (1993) attempts to show the tension and the interplay between intellectual property law with its concern for the protection of incentives to innovate and antitrust with its goal of maintaining competitive markets. The 1991 EC software directive incorporated this concern in the form of a decompilation exception which allows access to the elements of a computer program which are necessary to achieve interoperability. However, this delicate balance may be upset by the use of EC competition law in order to prevent the exercise of such intellectual property rights as a mean to foreclose competitors, as evidenced by the Magill case. Using the tools of economic analysis of intellectual property, he argues for moderation in the use of antitrust when competitive concerns have already been reflected in the mechanism design of intellectual property laws, as is the case of EC software protection.

Moura e Silva (1994) analyses the application of the EC merger regulation until 1993, under the light of current industrial economics and compares the Commission's approach to that used by US antitrust enforcement agencies under the 1992 Merger Guidelines. An argument is made for greater use of economic analysis, especially regarding market definition, and for an explicit efficiencies defence.

3.4 Consumer Protection

Teixeira (1994) sets out from MacNeil's relational contract theory to study the structure of contracts involving different legal orders from the perspective of the choice of law and consumer protection. The impact of consumer protection goals in the context of rules on conflict of laws on the contractual balance between the parties is then analysed. The author argues, from a conflict of laws point of view, that the concept of market plays a pivotal role in defining the applicable law in the case of international consumer contracts within the European Union, particularly in light of the regime of the Rome and Brussels conventions, as this market construct is not merely economic but also has a social content protecting the legitimate expectations of consumers regardless of their nationality or country of origin.

4. Conclusion

In conclusion, law and economics is well disseminated among academia, particularly in those fields with greater contact with economic science, such as tax law or public finance. A growing number of private law scholars use economic analysis of law in their research work as evidenced in some of the research reviewed above. However, at academic level, law and economics in Portugal seems to suffer from two communication problems. One is the lack of a 'workshop' tradition in legal academia which could contribute to bring together the different scholars working in the field. The other is the divide between lawyers and economists in academia. Furthermore, the growing interest of academia in law and economics has yet to translate into a more common use of law and economics as a teaching method at both undergraduate and graduate levels.

Bibliography on Law and Economics in Portugal (0365)

Confraria, João (1989), 'Aspectos de Abordagem Económica do Comportamento Criminal (Aspects of the Economic Analysis of Criminal Behaviour)', *Scientia Juridica*, 171-182.

Martins, Manuel Victor (1992), 'Ronald Coase: Na Fronteira de Economia e do Direito', **2** *Sub Judice*, 29-30.

Moura e Silva, Miguel (1993), 'Protecção de Programas de Computador na Comunidade Europeia', **7** *Revista Direito e Justiça*, 253-310.

Moura e Silva, Miguel (1994), 'Controlo de Concentraçõas na Comunidade Europeia', **8** *Revista Direito e Justiça*, 133-139.

Ramos De Sousa, João (1992a), 'Ejan Mackaay, La Règle Juridique Observée par le Prisme de L'Economiste - Book Review', **2** *Sub Judice*, 44-46.

Ramos De Sousa, João (1992b), 'Frank Easterbrook, Criminal Procedure as a Market System - Book Review', **2** *Sub Judice*, 47-49.

Ramos De Sousa, João (1992c), 'James Buchanan, Politics without Romance - Book Review', **2** *Sub Judice*, 50-52.

Ribeiro Mendes, Armindo (1992), 'Processo Executivo e a Economia', **2** *Sub Judice*, 51-62.

Sinde Monteiro, Jorge (1981), 'Analise económica do direito (Economic Analysis of Law)', **57** *Boletim da Faculdade de Direito de Universidade de Coimbra*, 247-251.

Sousa Franco, António (1992), 'Richard A. Posner, Economic Analysis of Law - Book Review', **2** *Sub Judice*, 39-43.

Sousa Franco, António (1992), 'Análise Económica do Direito: Exercício Intelectual ou Fonte de Ensinamento?', **2** *Sub Judice*, 63-70.

Teixeira, Pedro Gustavo (1994), 'A Questão da Protecção dos Consumidores nos Contratos Plurilocalizados (Consumer Protection in International Contracts)', **54** *Revista da Ordem dos Advogados*, 181-343.

0370
LAW AND ECONOMICS IN QUEBEC

Frédérick Charette
Research Fellow
University of California, Berkeley

Abstra. t

Although law and economics has had a definitive impact on legal studies in the United States and English-speaking Canada, and continues to make inroads in Europe, the Province of Quebec remains insulated. Not only is institutional recognition of the discipline absent, its practitioners are also few and isolated. In this short chapter, I try to offer an up-to-date picture of the field within Quebec's law schools as well as some hypotheses that could explain the current state of affairs.
JEL classification: K00
Keywords: Canada, Quebec, Research, Education, Teaching, French

1. Introduction

Writing on the status of law and economics in Quebec has proven to be a worthy challenge. Although the movement has had a definitive impact on legal studies in the United States and English-speaking Canada, and continues to make inroads in Europe, the Province of Quebec remains insulated. Not only is institutional recognition of the discipline absent, its practitioners are also few and isolated. In this short review, I will try to offer an up-to-date picture of the field within Quebec's law schools as well as some hypotheses that could explain the current state of affairs. We will see that language alone cannot fully account for the lack of interest in the field. Finally, I will try and provide some hope for the future by pointing to the possibility of a wider recognition of the field and to the uniqueness of Quebec's legal system as a potentially rich source for comparative studies.

2. Law and Economics Education and Research in Law Schools and Economics Departments

In the introduction to the second edition of their Law and Economics, Cooter and Ulen (1996, p. 2) list ten criteria by which one can measure the impact of economics on law. None of the six Quebec law schools (Laval, McGill, Montreal, Sherbrooke, UQAM, to which I add the civil law section of the University of Ottawa) pass all these tests. There are no Economics PhD programmes in the faculty of any law school. There is no joint degree program (PhD econ./LL.B.). There are evidently no journals devoted to the field and Quebec law journals only exceptionally publish law and economics articles. The few articles that were published, are cited only rarely by other Quebec legal scholars, despite their quality. Not only is the field often ignored, but only four law schools out of six have an Economic Analysis of Law course on their curriculum (McGill and UQAM being the exceptions), and only two of them (Montreal and Laval) have been offering the course on a yearly basis since it was added to the curriculum. Finally, there is no professional organization in Quebec equivalent to the Canadian Law and Economics Association (CLEA), in spite of the fact that in most fields there are French-speaking organizations in Quebec duplicating the corresponding Canadian organizations.

Contrary to lawyers, Quebec economists fully consider themselves to be part of an international profession. Economics has developed into a truly international field, with a common language and a shared hierarchy of schools and departments. Quebec economists are not, contrary to civil lawyers, insulated from foreign influences: they study abroad, candidates for teaching positions come from all over the world and faculty members engage actively in economic research whose quality they expect to be measured by world standards. Hence, economics departments should provide more opportunities for studies in law and economics. However, the fact remains that, as is the case with legal scholars, most economists do not seem to have expressed any special interest in studying Quebec law, except perhaps with regard to some special legislation such as the introduction of the provincial no-fault automobile insurance bill.

Two notable exceptions must be mentioned here. Reuven Brenner, who holds the Repap Chair at McGill's Faculty of Management, and Jean-Luc Migué of the Ecole Nationale d'Administration Publique (ENAP) are two scholars of international stature whose involvement in law and economics must be pointed out. Although not strictly associated with the law and economics movement, Prof. Brenner has made a distinctive use of law and economics tools throughout his oeuvre to explain why people innovate or gamble on new ideas. Prof. Migué's involvement with law and economics has been more explicit and more accessible, as he has written in both French and English. His most important contribution must be his studies on the economics of language and the economics of federalism.

Reasons as to why so few scholars have made distinctive contributions to the field are not readily forthcoming. As is the case with Prof. Brenner, it might be that the economic papers discussing legal issues are not written in French but in English, and that they could be found in the appropriate section of the encyclopedia. Even with that caveat in mind, one would be hard pressed to find more than twenty articles published by Quebec scholars in economics reviews. So there is a real puzzle with regard to the lack of involvement in law and economics by Quebec scholars, be they legal scholars or economists.

Common prejudiced views advanced as explanations for this puzzle simply do not resist a comparative perspective. For example, the language differential or the presence of a civil code cannot be part of the explanation: most Quebec economists publish in English, and the language barrier has not prevented German and Dutch jurists from applying the economic model to their own civil code.

A more plausible hypothesis would focus on the lack of competition between Quebec universities. Not only is the system completely public with no private university in operation, but studies are heavily subsidized, with the lowest tuition fees in all of North America, and teachers fully unionized. Because civil law schools are so few in number, and because full employment security is provided after a five year probation period, there is very little movement between the faculties and hence an utter lack of competition. Professors' appointment fees are exclusively based on experience rather than on performance and there is consequently a relative uniformity of treatment among faculty members. Chairs are exceedingly rare. Incentives to innovate by researching new fields of study are mostly indirect.

As in any other field, publications remain paramount for prestige and promotions. However, in law schools, the criteria of international publications is not retained, perhaps because of the civil character of the profession. The pressure to perform at the international level remains low. As long as this will be the case, incentives to innovate and excel will be likely to be lower in Quebec than elsewhere. Because competition leads to a discovery process, its absence often explains a lack of entrepreneurship. For the moment, the few steps on the academic ladder can be easily climbed by producing commentaries on case law or legislative notes affecting one's field; there is nothing to gain from ventures in new studies far from the comforts of one's home turf.

3. Future Prospects

Nevertheless, there may be some hope. The expansion of law and economics into public law and international law, and especially the economics of federalism, is bound to influence Quebec jurists working in those fields. Contrary to private law, and despite the language barrier, public law in Quebec is traversed by Canadian and American influences. Moreover, funding cuts, declining admission prospects and a relatively high unemployment rate have forced law schools to require a doctoral degree as a condition of employment. Aspiring professors are now more likely to have received training in the US and hence to have been exposed to law and economics. Finally, since there will be growing uncertainty regarding employment security, it is likely that those new and highly mobile professors will have to distinguish themselves in order to keep a high profile; the law and economics field continues to offer enormous possibilities in this regard.

Much as law and economics might catch on and attract new practitioners in Quebec, this is still a far cry from becoming a standard part of the curriculum in law schools. One essential step in that direction is the first general introduction to law and economics in French (in addition to the brief survey of core private law subjects by Bertrand Lemennicier in his Économie du Droit, Paris, Cujas, 1991), currently being written by Prof. Ejan Mackaay and the undersigned. Prof. Mackaay, who teaches at the Faculté de Droit de l'Université de Montréal, must be considered as one of the pioneers of the field and the leading figure of law and economics in Quebec. His writings in French, English and Dutch can all be praised for their clarity and soundness.

The book is aimed at the civilian legal community, both in Quebec and elsewhere in the French-speaking world. The publication of this book should help to establish law and economics as an integral part of the legal curriculum in those countries. Beyond this upcoming introductory work, however, the prospects for the development of French language literature on the subject are dim. Economists already publish in English, and new professors at law schools are more likely than their seniors to write in English, not only because they have often been trained in that language, but especially because they want to keep their job options open beyond provincial and national boundaries.

This does not mean that there is no hope for the study of Quebec private law institutions. The recent growth of a distinct comparative law and economics field could spur interest in the unique civil law system of Quebec, and with good reason. First of all, there is an official English version of all legislative texts, as well as of some court decisions and textbooks. Moreover, and contrary to the French system, Quebec's private law has borrowed its civil procedure styles of judicial reasoning from British common law and has developed a large body of case law. Finally, Quebec having been more influenced by the European model of the welfare state than by the American one, it provides a stark contrast to the latter, a useful beginning for any comparative study.

4. Conclusion

All is not gloomy about the state of the field in Quebec. As the following bibliography will show, there are scholars of great quality in Quebec, and the new generation of professors will be better trained and more outward looking than their predecessors. The development of a body of convincing comparative and constitutional law and economics studies may be just what is needed to help Quebec jurists overcome their initial reservations about the field. We may yet be heading for a new quiet revolution.

Bibliography on Law and Economics in Quebec (0370)

Belley, Jean-Guy (1996), 'Le Contrat Comme Phénomène d'Internormativité (The Contract as a Phenomenon of Inter-Normativity)', in Belley, Jean-Guy (ed.), *Le Droit Soluble - Contributions Québècoises à l'Étude de la Normativité,* Paris, Librairie Générale de Droit et de Jurisprudence, 195-232.

Bourbeau, Robert (1983), *Les Accidents de la Route au Québec 1926-1978: Étude Démographique et Épidémiologique* (Road Accidents in Quebec, 1926-1978: A Demographic and Epidemiologic Study), Montréal, Presses de l'Université de Montréal.

Boyer, Marcel (1995), *La Réglementation Incitative* (Inciting Regulations), Montréal, Centre Interuniversitaire de Recherche en Analyse des Organisations.

Boyer, Marcel and Dionne, Georges (1985), 'Sécurité Routière: Responsabilité pour Négligence et Tarification (Road Safety: Responsibility for Negligence and Pricing)', **18** *Canadian Journal of Economics*, 814-830.

Boyer, Marcel, Dionne, Georges and Vanasse, Charles (1991), 'Infractions au Code de la Sécurité Routière, Infractions au Code Criminel et Gestion Optimale de la Sécurité Routière (Infractions to the Road Safety Code, Infractions to the Criminal Code and Optimal Management of Road Safety)', **67** *L'actualité Economique*, 279-305.

Brenner, Gabrielle A. and Brenner, Reuven (1989), *Les Innovations et la Loi sur la Concurrence* (Innovations and the Competition Law), Montréal, Ecole des hautes Études Commerciales, Institut D'économie Appliquée. Actualité Economique 65, 146-63 (1990)

Brenner, Reuven (1990a), *Les Choix du Québec* (The Choices of Québec), Commission sur l'Avenir Politique et Constitutionnel du Québec (Commission Bélanger-Campeau), Les avis des spécialistes invités à répondre aux huit questions par la Commission (Commission Bélanger-Campeau).

Brenner, Reuven (1990b), 'Inventions et Innovations dans le Monde des Affaires et des Sciences (Inventions and Innovations in Business and Science)', **26** *Etudes Françaises*, 51-78.

Brenner, Reuven (1990c), 'Pays de l'Est: d'abord les Réformes Légales, Ensuite les Politiques Monétaires et Macroéconomiques (Eastern European Countries: First the Legal Reforms, Then the Monetary and Macroeconomic Policies)', **1** *Journal des Économistes et des Études Humaines: Bilingual Journal of Interdisciplinary Studies*, 253-277.

Brenner, Reuven (1991), 'Les Choix du Québec', in X (ed.), *Les Avis des Spécialistes Invités à Répondre aux Huit Questions Posées par la Commission*, Assemblées Nationale, Documents parlementaires, 119-156.

Brenner, Reuven (1995), 'Quebec and Canada: In the Locks of a Financial Embrace', **1(8)** *Choix, Institute for Research on Public Policy*, 5-30.

Brenner, Reuven and Brenner, Gabrielle A. (1988), 'Entrepreneurship - Le Nouveau Nom d'un Vieux Phénomène (Entrepreneurship - A New Name for an Old Phenomenon)', *Revue Internationale de Gestion.*

Breton, Albert (1978), *Le Bilinguisme: une Approche Économique* (Bilingualism: An Economic Approach), Montréal, Institut de recherche C.D. Howe.

Charette, Frédérick (1992a), 'L'illusion du Droit Moral, telle que Révélée par le Droit de l'Informatique (The Illusion of a Moral Right, as Revealed by a Study of Computer Law)', **4** *Cahiers de Propriété Intellectuelle*, 161-185.

Charette, Frédérick (1992b), 'Libéraliser la Publicité des Avocats: Fondements et Conséquences (Liberalizing Lawyers' Advertising: Foundations and Consequences)', **71** *Canadian Bar Review*, 508-551.

Courchene, Thomas J. (1986), *La Gestion Économique et le Partage des Pouvoirs* (Management and the Separation of Powers), Ottawa, Commission royale sur l'union économique et les perspectives de développement du Canada.

Courchene, Thomas J. (1987), *Les Offrandes des Rois Mages : Etat-providence ou Etat Providentiel?* (The Magi's Offerings: Welfare State or Providential State?), Toronto, C.D. Howe Institute.

Courchene, Thomas J. (1991), *Eloge du Fédéralisme Renouvelé* (Praise for a Renewed Federalism), Toronto, C.D. Howe Institute.

Cousineau, Jean-Michel (1991), 'L'Effet du Salaire Minimum sur le Chômage des Jeunes et des Femmes au Québec: une Réestimation et un Réexamen de la Question (The Impact of a Minimum Wage on Unemployment of Young People and Women in Quebec: A New Look at the Question)', **67** *Actualite Economique*, 144-165.

Dion, Michel (1992a), 'Le Raisonnement Éthique en Affaires (Ethics Reasoning in Business)', in Dion, Michel (ed.), *L'éthique ou le Profit*, Montréal, Fides, 13-98.

Dion, Michel (ed.) (1992b), *L'Ethique ou le Profit* (Ethics or Profit), Montréal, Fides.

Fluet, Claude (1990), 'L'Analyse Economique du Droit (Economic Analysis of Law)', **43(3)** *Economie Appliquée*, 53-66.

Fortin, Bernard, Garneau, Gaétan, Lacroix, Guy, Lemieux, Thomas and Montmarquette, Claude (1996), *L'Économie Souterraine au Québec - Mythes et Réalités* (The Underground Economy in Quebec - Myths and Realities), Sainte-Foy, Presses de l'Université Laval.

Fortin, Pierre (1980), *Les Conditions Minimales de Travail: Leurs Conséquences Économiques* (The Fixation of Minimum Working Conditions: Their Economic Consequences), 35e congrès des relations industrielles, La détermination des conditions minimales de travail par l'Etat: une loi: son économie et sa portée.

Gaudry, Marc (1977), 'Quelques Problèmes de Tarification du Transport des Voyageurs à Montréal (Some Tarification Problems Regarding Public Transit in Montreal)', **III** *Canadian Public Policy*, 307-314.

Gaudry, Marc (1986), *Un Abrégé de DRAG, un Modèle de la Demande Routière, des Accidents et de leur Gravité, appliqué au Québec de 1956 à 1982* (A Summary of DRAG, a model of Road Demand and of Accidents and their Seriousness, Applied to Quebec from 1956 to 1982), Montréal, Centre de recherche sur les transports.

Gaudry, Marc (1995), *Sur une Application à la Région Métropolitaine de Montréal des Recommandations de la Commission Royale sur le Transport des Voyageurs au Canada* (Of an Application to the Montreal Metropolitan Area of the Recommendations of the

Royal Commission on Public Transit in Canada), Montréal, Centre de recherche sur les transports.

Gaudry, Marc, Fournier, François and Simard, Robert (1995), *DRAG-2, un Modèle Économétrique Appliqué au Kilométrage, aux Accidents et à leur Gravité au Québec - Synthèse des résultats* (DRAG-2, An Econometric Model Applied to Mileage and to Accidents and their Seriousness in Quebec - Summary of Results), Québec, Société de l'assurance automobile du Québec.

Hébert, Gérard (1986), 'Les Normes du Travail à Caractère Économique au Canada et au Québec (Labor Rules of an Economic Nature in Canada and Quebec)', **17** *Revue Générale de Droit*, 45-84.

Krauss, Michael I. (1986), 'L'affaire Lapierre: vers une Théorie Économique de l'Obligation Quasi-contractuelle (The Lapierre Case: Toward an Economic Theory of the Quasi-Contractual Obligation)', **31** *McGill Law Journal*, 683-721.

Krauss, Michael I. (ed.) (1989), *Action Positive - Théorie et Conséquences* (Affirmative Action - Theory and Consequences), Cowansville (QC), Yvon Blais.

Krauss, Michael I. (1994), 'La Réglementation contre le Marché dans le Développement de Normes (Regulation against the Market in Norms Formation)', **5** *Journal des Économistes et des Études Humaines*, 573-599.

Landry, Raymond A. (1991), 'La Priorité Fiscale sur les Meubles et le Projet de Code Civil du Québec (Fiscal Priority on Movables and the Quebec Civil Code Bill)', **22** *Revue générale de droit*, 649-658.

Lemieux, Pierre (1983), *Du Libéralisme à l'Anarcho-capitalisme* (From Liberalism to Anarcho-Capitalism), Paris, Presses Universitaires de France (PUF).

Lemieux, Pierre (1987), *La Souveraineté de l'Individu* (The Sovereignty of the Individual), Paris, Presses Universitaires de France (PUF).

Lemieux, Pierre (1988), *L'Anarcho-capitalisme* (What is Anarcho-Capitalism?), Paris, Presses Universitaires de France (PUF).

Lemieux, Pierre (1991), *Apologie des Sorcières Modernes* (An Apology of Modern Witches), Paris, Belles Lettres.

Lemieux, Pierre (1993), *Le Droit de Porter des Armes* (The Right to Bear Arms), Paris, Belles Lettres.

Lemieux, Vincent (1991), *Les Relations de Pouvoir dans les Lois - Comparaison entre les Gouvernements du Québec de 1944 à 1985 (Power Relations in Laws - Comparison Between Quebec Governments from 1944 to 1985)*, Sainte-Foy, Presses de l'Université Laval.

Mackaay, Ejan (1979), 'Les Notions Floues ou l'Économie de l'mprécision (Fuzzy Concepts or the Economics of Imprecision)', **12** *Langages*, 33-50.

Mackaay, Ejan (1980), 'Le Droit Relatif aux Accidents - une Interprétation Économique (The Law of Accidents - An Economic Approach)', **15** *Revue Juridique Themis*, 383-415.

Mackaay, Ejan (1986a), 'Les Biens Informationnels ou le Droit de Suite dans les Idées (Information Goods or the Sequel Right in Ideas)', **12** *Informatica e Diritto*, 45-65.

Mackaay, Ejan (1986b), 'La Règle Juridique Observée par le Prisme de l'Économiste - une Histoire Stylisée du Mouvement d'Analyse Économique du Droit (The Legal Rule Viewed from the Perspective of the Economist - A Stylized History of the Law and Economics Movement)', **1** *Revue Internationale de Droit Économique*, 43-88.

Mackaay, Ejan (1987a), 'Tableau Synoptique de l'Analyse Économique du Droit (Synoptic Table of the Economic Analysis of Law)', **1987** *Revue de la Recherche Juridique Droit Perspectif*, 637 ff.

Mackaay, Ejan (1987b), 'Courants de Pensée Juridique à l'Origine de l'Analyse Économique du Droit (tableaux) (Legal Currents at the Origin of the Economic Analysis of Law (Tables)', **1987** *Revue de la Recherche Juridique Droit Perspectif*, 635-636.

Mackaay, Ejan (1987c), *Le Paradoxe des Droits Acquis. De l'Ancienne à la Nouvelle Économie - Essais à l'Occasion de la Dixième Université d'été de la Nouvelle Économie, Aix-en-Provence 1978-1987 (The Paradox of Vested Rights)*, Aix-en-Provence, Librairie de l'Université.

Mackaay, Ejan (1987d), 'Le Juriste a-t-il le Droit d'Ignorer l'Economiste? (May Lawyers Ignore Economists?)', *Revue de la Recherche Juridique*, 419-427.

Mackaay, Ejan (1988), 'L'ordre Spontané comme Fondement du Droit - un Survol des Modèles de l'Émergence des Règles dans une Société Civile (Spontaneous Order as Foundation of Law - A Survey of Models of the Emergence of Rules in Civil Society)', **22** *Revue Juridique Themis*, 347-383.

Mackaay, Ejan (1989), 'L'ordre Spontané comme Fondement du Droit - un Survol des Modèles de l'Émergence des Règles dans la Société Civile (Spontaneous Order as the Foundation of Law - A Survey of Models of the Emergence of Rules in Civil Society)', **3** *Revue Internationale de Droit Economique*, 247-287.

Mackaay, Ejan (1990), 'Les Droits Intellectuels - entre Propriété et Monopole (Intellectual Property Rights - Between Property and Monopoly)', **1** *Revue des Économistes et des Études Humaines*, 61-358.

Mackaay, Ejan (1991a), 'La Propriété Est-elle en Voie d'Extinction? (Is Property about to Become Extinct?)', in Mackaay, Ejan (ed.), *Nouvelles Technologies et Propriété*, Montréal, Ed. Thémis, Paris, LITEC, 217-247.

Mackaay, Ejan (1991b), 'Le Droit Saisi par le Jeu (Game-Theory Applied to Law)', *Droit et Société*, 57-81.

Mackaay, Ejan (ed.) (1991c), *Nouvelles Technologies et Propriétés* (New Technologies and Property), Montréal, Ed. Thémis, Paris, LITEC.

Mackaay, Ejan (1992a), 'Penser l'Informatique Génétique en Droit Québécois (Thinking about Genetic Computing in Quebec Law)', in Knoppers, Bartha Maria; Cadiet, Lo‹c and Laberge, Claude M. (eds), *La Génétique Humaine: de l'Information à l'Informatisation* (Human Genetics: From Information to Computerization), Montréal et Paris, Thémis et LITEC, 25-38.

Mackaay, Ejan (1992b), 'Le Droit Saisi par le Jeu (Game-Theory Applied to Law)', in Ost, François and Van De Kerkhove, Michel (eds), *Le Jeu: un Paradigme pour le Droit*, Paris, Librairie Générale de Droit et de Jurisprudence, 81-110.

Mackaay, Ejan (1992c), 'Règle et Décision en Droit (Rule and Decision in Law)', in Bourcier, Danièle and Mackay, Pierre (eds), *Lire le Droit - Langue, Texte, Cognition*, Paris, Librairie Générale de Droit et de Jurisprudence, 41-69.

Mackaay, Ejan (1993), 'Assurances Sociales et Responsabilité (Social Welfare and Responsibility)', **4** *Journal des Économistes et des Études Humaines*, 135-157.

Mackaay, Ejan and Trudeau, Hélène (eds) (1995), *L'environnement - à Quel Prix?* (Protecting the Environment - At What Price?), Montréal, Editions Thémis.

Migué, Jean-Luc (1956), *Histoire des Finances Canadiennes, 1866-1939* (History of Canadian Public Finances), Université de Montréal.

Migué, Jean-Luc (1970), 'Le Nationalisme, l'Unité Nationale et la Théorie Économique de l'Information (Nationalism, National Unity and the Economic Theory of Information)', **3** *Canadian Journal of Economics*, 183-198.

Migué, Jean-Luc (1971), *Le Québec d'aujourd'hui: Regards d'universitaires* (Quebec Today: Perspectives from Academics), Montréal, Hurtubise HMH.

Migué, Jean-Luc (1977), 'Méthodologie Économique et Économie Non Marchande (Economic Methodology and Non-Trading Economics)', *Revue d'Économique Politique*, 506 ff.

Migué, Jean-Luc (1979a), *Les Nationalismes au Canada: Perspective Économique* (Nationalisms in Canada: An Economic Perspective), Montréal, Institut de recherche C.D. Howe.

Migué, Jean-Luc (1979b), *L'économiste et la Chose Publique* (The Economist and Public Policy), Sillery (QC), Presses de l'Université du Québec.

Migué, Jean-Luc (1989), 'Action Positive et Égalité des Femmes au Travail (Affirmative Action and Women's Equality in the Workplace)', in Krauss, Michael (ed.), *Action Positive: Théorie et Conséquences* (Affirmative Action: Theory and Consequences), Cowansville (QC), Yvon Blais, 85-109.

Migué, Jean-Luc (1990), *Retour au Vrai Fédéralisme: Institutionnalisation de la Concurrence entre Gouvernements* (Return to a True Federalism: The Institutionalization of Competition Between Governments), Commission sur l'avenir politique et constitutionnel du Québec (Commission Bélanger-Campeau), Les avis des spécialistes invités à répondre aux huit questions par la Commission (Commission Bélanger-Campeau).

Migué, Jean-Luc (1994), *Une Société Sclérosée - Quand le Mal Européen gagne le Canada* (An Ossified Society - When the European Illness Wins Over Canada), Montréal and Paris, L'Etincelle.

Migué, Jean-Luc and Bélanger, Gérard (1972), *Le Prix de la Santé* (The Cost of Health), Montréal, Hurtubise HMH.

Migué, Jean-Luc and Marceau, Richard (1989), *Le Monopole Public de l'Éducation: l'Économie Politique de la Médiocrité (*The Public Monopoly on Education: The Political Economy of Mediocrity), Sillery (QC), Presses de l'Université du Québec.

Migué, Jean-Luc, Bélanger, Gérard and Boucher, Michel (1978), *Le Prix du Transport au Québec* (The Cost of Transport in Quebec), Québec, Editeur officiel du Quebec.

Montmarquette, Claude (1988), *Le Marché Politique: qu'est-ce qui est Produit? Qui y Participe? Qui en Profite?* (The Political Market: What is Produced? Who Plays? Who Profits?), Montréal, Centre de recherche et développement en économique.

Nadeau, Richard (1989), 'La Réforme du Droit des Obligations - Le Point de Vue du Barreau du Québec (The Opinion of the Quebec Bar on the Reform of Contract Law)', **30** *Cahiers de Droit*, 647-656.

Noreau, Pierre (1993), *Droit Préventif - Le Droit au-delà de la Loi* (Preventive Law - Law Beyond Legislation), Montréal, Editions Thémis.

Pestieau, Joseph (1984), *Guerre et Paix sans Etat - Anarchie et Ordre Coutumier* (War and Peace Outside the State - Anarchy and Customary Order), Montréal, Hexagone.

Pestieau, Joseph (1989), 'Droit, Éthique, Économie (Law, Ethics, Economy)', in Lafrance, Guy (ed.), *Ethique et Droits Fondamentaux/Ethics and Basic Rights*, Ottawa, Presses de l'Université d'Ottawa, 195-200.

Sosoe, Lukas (1992), 'Le Contractualisme et la Question des Nationalités (Contractualism and the Question of Nationalities)', **19** *Philosophiques*, 29-40.

Vaillancourt, François (ed.) (1985), *Economie et Langue* (Economy and Language), Québec, Editeur officiel du Quebec.

Vaillancourt, François (1988), *Langue et Disparités de Statut Économique au Québec, 1970 et 1980* (Language and Disparities of Economic Status in Quebec, 1970 and 1980), Montréal, Office de la langue française.

Vaillancourt, François (1991), *Réponses aux Questions Posées par la Commission sur l'Avenir Politique et Constitutionnel du Québec* (Answers to the Questions Asked by the Commission on the Political and Constitutional Future of Quebec), in *Commission sur l'avenir politique et constitutionnel du Québec (Commission Bélanger-Campeau), Les avis des spécialistes invités à répondre aux huit questions par la Commission (Commission Bélanger-Campeau),* Québec, Editeur officiel du Quebec, 1117-1133.

Vaillancourt, François and Carpentier, Josée (1989), *Le Contrôle de l'Économie du Québec: la Place des Francophones en 1987 et son Évolution depuis 1961* (The Control of the Economy of Quebec: The Status of Francophones in 1987 and its Evolution since 1961), Montréal, Office de la langue française.

Other References

Cooter, Robert and Ulen, Thomas S. (1996), *Law and Economics*, 2nd edition, Addison-Wesley.

0375
LAW AND ECONOMICS IN TAIWAN

Steven S. Kan
Professor at the Department of Economics
National Tsing Hua University, Hsin Chu, Taiwan

Abstract

The purpose of this chapter is to show how law and economics has taken roots in Taiwan, which authors have played primary roles in teaching and research, and what have been the recent research topics. The chapter first presents a brief description of Taiwan's economic-social-political background. This is then followed by an introduction to Taiwan's education and research in law and economics.
JEL classification: K00
Keywords: Economics, Law, Taiwan

1. Economic-Social-Political Background

Taiwan has changed from a traditional Chinese agricultural economy to an industrialized economy in the last 50 years. Though geographically remote from Western industrialized economies, the small island succeeded in the late 1970s being their trading partner in textiles, electronics, machine tools, and so on. Today, it is catching on in the information age and has fast-growing industries in computer peripherals and semi-conductors. Because of its economic success many of the citizens have been able to go abroad for business, education and vocation. They return home with aspirations for greater individual freedom and a pluralistic society. Social relationships have thus been transformed in many ways and a life under an authoritarian regime is no longer acceptable. As a result, Taiwan has undertaken a series of constitutional reforms since 1992 and is now moving towards a more democratic society. It is in this dynamic economic-social-political setting that Taiwan's study of law and economics has taken roots.

2. Education

Economics professors in Taiwan are primarily returnees with an American doctoral degree. In contrast, law professors hold law degrees in almost even proportions from the US, Germany and Japan. In the past, economics students were required to take an introductory law course, but law students were not required to take any economics courses. Laws and regulations enacted since the early 1980s have helped to bring about a change. They were promulgated to meet new economic and social problems in employment, fair trade, finance, environmental protection, and so on. Responding to the development, law departments soon initiated specialized programs in financial and economic law. To prepare students to deal with such legal matters, these programs require first-year students to take four credit hours in economics principles, which are taught by the economics faculty. For the same reason, more economics students would like to start taking elective law courses to help their career development. Both the economics and the law students know that there are substantial differences not only between economics and law but also between the English-American and Continental systems of law. However, not until recently were they able to find a connection between economics and law, because few scholars were familiar with Ronald H. Coase's insights in the firm, the market, and the law.

It was only ten years ago that the modern law and economics field became known in Taiwan. Yu-Min Tang (1987) deserves special credit for translating the first edition of Posner's *Economic Analysis of Law*. The translated work was well-received and reprinted after two years. Another special credit should go to Steven Cheung (1987). His popular writings on private property rights and contracts were published when privatization and economic liberalization were hot issues in Taiwan. They soon became best-sellers and they helped popularize the names of Coase, Alchian and Demsetz with Taiwan's college students.

Taiwan's first undergraduate law and economics course was offered in September 1987 to juniors by the economics department of National Tsing Hua University. A graduate sequel, the economic analysis of law, debuted in 1990. Coase's winning of the Nobel Prize in 1991 further boosted students' interests. A course on economic organization along Oliver E. Williamson's line was started up as a response to graduate students' requests in 1992. However, the demands of freshmen and sophomores could not be met because of a lack of adequate teaching materials and teachers. Hwang and Kan (1994) published a principles textbook emphasizing new institutional economics in the summer of 1994. With the arrival of a new faculty member, the department started to offer courses on new economic history and new institutional economics. In addition to fulfilling these teaching responsibilities, Liu (1994, 1995) translated Douglass C. North's two major books. Finally, with Chen and Li (1995) translation of Coase's book, there are now basic Chinese materials for students of all departments that can open the door to law and economics.

In the meantime several scholars have also contributed to promoting the central message of law and economics. Bing-Yuang Hsiung of National Taiwan

University and George S. Wang of National Chengchi University have included Coase's ideas in their public economics course. Huei-Lin Wu of Chung-Hua Institute of Economic Research has written introductory essays in magazines and newspapers for lay readers. Tze-Chien Wang, who is now a grand justice, arranged a seminar and invited me to introduce law and economics to his colleagues at the law department of National Taiwan University. These educational and promotional efforts are now taking effect. For example, Soochow University's law department, which specializes in common law, has started an undergraduate law and economics course in its night program. The law department of National Taiwan University is now offering a graduate course in tort law along Posner, Landes and Shavell's line. The department is also planning to have undergraduate law and economics courses in the near future.

3. Research: Activities and Scope

A few institutions and foundations have in recent years sponsored the visits of distinguished foreign scholars to promote academic research in economics. For example, the visitors included Gary Becker, James Buchanan, Issac Ehrlich, Douglass North and Gordon Tullock. Their visits have helped stimulate research in law and economics. A special day was marked on January 19, 1991 when Cyrus C. Chu successfully organized Taiwan's first academic conference on the economic analysis of law. The conference not only brought together various researchers in law and economics but also opened up a dialogue between legal scholars and economists. The effect of these activities is clear in that legal scholars and professional lawyers are now invited to help with an economics student's thesis. Likewise, economists are invited to be members of a law student's thesis committee. As a result, there is more vigorous research in law and economics and more research results are appearing in professional journals.

The law and economics research community in Taiwan is small. There are two types of research related to law and economics. The first type deals with financial and economic laws and is mainly conducted by legal scholars. It is related to law and economics because more of the substance is involved but less of the methodology is used. The second type of research involves rigorous economic analysis and belongs to the narrowly defined field of law and economics. It is conducted by economists and several areas of law have been taken up. To illustrate Taiwan's recent interest in law and economics a select bibliography is appended at the end of this overview. The bibliography shows that recent research topics can be classified into four groups: financial and economic law, criminal law, environmental law and others. While the volume cannot warrant a full survey, I will try in the following to give a brief guide and show that Taiwanese scholars can actively contribute to law and economics research.

4. Research: Some Recent Research Topics

In the area of financial and economic law, research topics are concerned with current economic conflicts. Li and Chen (1995), Hwang (1995, 1996) and Chen (1997) focus on antitrust issues of intra-industry alliance in product designs, intra-industry mutual holdings of stocks, vertical mergers, and collusive pricing. The issues of foreign competition and financial disclosure have been investigated by Juang (1997) and Tseng (1996). Fong (1997) and Tan (1991) discuss issues related to intellectual property rights such as the corporate name, the trademark, and counterfeits. Aoki and Hu (1997) have also investigated the effect of a legal system on incentives to innovate. They are mostly written in Chinese and some of their research results have wider implications that are not limited to Taiwanese cases. However, no law and economics research related to employment laws is being published, perhaps reflecting the fact that Taiwan has been able to maintain full employment.

The most active law and economics research is on criminal law and purely conducted by economists. The results of this line of research are especially interesting and some of them have been published in international journals. They are interesting because the researchers have utilized Chinese cases to shed light on some less attended topics in Western literature. For examples, two articles by Chu (1990a, 1990b) explicitly consider venal tax officials and plea bargaining with respect to the problem of tax evasion. As law enforcement efforts in Taiwan have been oscillatory, Chu (1991) makes a case that oscillatory enforcement is optimal under some conditions. On the proposition that fines are more efficient than imprisonment, Chu and Jiang (1993) present an opposite case by considering wealth. Imprisonment serves the dual functions of deterrence and incapacitation; yet little work has been done to address the latter function. For criminal offenses involving bodily parts that cannot be deterred, Kan (1996) finds that imprisonment is less efficient than corporal punishment because it incapacitates other productive parts as well. As a life sentence involves a permanent incapacitation of the whole body, he also finds that its abolition would hinge on whether a society accepts temporary incapacitation as a substitute punishment. Chu (1991), Chu et. al. (1997), Chen et al. (1997), Koo (1991) and Shea and Wu (1994) have embarked on other important topics such as criminal proceedings, litigation procedure, repeat offenses, the allocation of legal costs and anti-monitoring activities. There are also empirical studies written in Chinese. Adopting a Bayesian approach, Yang and Chen (1996) find that a life sentence had no deterrence effect.

An unfortunate aspect of Taiwan's economic development is that it was achieved at the expense of its environment. Despite the environmental regulations that are now in place, much remains to be done. There are significant law and economics papers on the problems related to environmental law. Taking hints from Taiwan's poor enforcement of environmental regulations, Huang (1996a, 1996b) has explicitly considered incomplete enforcement, a firm's avoidance behavior and hierarchical governments in his studies. He sheds new light on the effectiveness of environmental regulations and the complex relationships among legislators, regulators and firms. Yeh (1992) used a special Taiwanese case, in which the central government set up a compensation fund for the victims nearby a petroleum cracking plant, to discuss the problems associated with the de facto sales of pollution rights. Shaw (1992) compared Pigovian taxation and strict liability as methods to control externalities in Taiwan. Fu et. al. (1993), on the other hand, adopted the property rights and contractual approach to discuss sustainable development. Shaw (1995) has also translated Anderson and Leal's *Free Market Environmentalism.*

While other research topics in law and economics are important as well, they have so far only received limited attention from Taiwanese researchers. For example, Chu and Qian (1995) and Hsieh (1991) seem to be the only two discussing vicarious liability and medical malpractice in the area of tort law. Research in other areas is the same. Koo and Sung (1993) is the only study on the public funding aspect of Taiwan's election and recall law. Wu and Huang (1994) presents the only theoretical work on norms and cultures. Kan and Hwang (1991a, 1991b, 1995) are also alone in considering ancient Chinese economic and legal thoughts in a modern light.

Most of the research works we have introduced so far, however, do not touch on property rights and transaction costs. The fact indicates that Coase, Cheung and Williamson's insights are yet to make a strong impact on Taiwan's research, as Chien (1997) has indicated in his recent book review. Despite being few in numbers, the research results are quite significant. There were two papers on transaction costs and Coase theorem. Kan (1993) elucidates the subjective nature of transaction cost and emphasizes the much neglected entrepreneurship in exchanges. With an effort to reconcile Buchanan's criticism on the celebrated the Coase theorem, Hsiung (1993) was able to clarify several issues of the debate. On property rights, Su (1991) used law and economics argument to discuss the conditions for or against the principle of *numerus clausus*. Other works are involved with the application of transaction cost analysis to Taiwanese cases. The empirical test of Kan and Hsiao (1996) shows that peasants' choices of irrigation contracts in the Tsing Dynasty were consistent with transaction cost economics. The paper also echoes Coase's view that public works need not require government intervention. Chien (1995) relates the common use and abuse of a condominium's top space to transaction costs and property rights.

Finally, Taiwan's ongoing democratization process has spurred Hwang and Kan's (1995) and Kan and Hwang's (1996, 1997) significant contributions to constitutional law. They adopt a *super-firm* approach to focus on the organization of a democratic government. As there are transaction costs between representatives and officials and between them and the people, they think that checks and balances are mechanisms to prevent the collusion of officials and representatives. However, the costs associated with checks and balances have been neglected. Applying Fama and Jensen's distinction of decision control and decision management powers in the firm, they elucidate that different concerns over the two types of transaction costs can lead to various forms of presidential, parliamentary and hybrid governments. A testable implication of their transaction cost analysis is that the number of check-and-balance mechanisms decreases with the development of competitive mass media and the technological advances in transportation as well as telecommunication. The research not only breaks away from current models in political science, but also shows that transaction cost economics can shed significant insights into the organization of a democratic government.

Acknowledgments

The author would like to thank Sheng C. Hu, Ruey-Hua Liu and Daigee Shaw for their comments and suggestions.

Bibliography on Law and Economics in Taiwan (0375)

Aoki, Reiko and Hu, Jin-Li (1997), 'Licensing vs. Litigation: Effect of the Legal System on Incentives to Innovate', unpublished manuscript.

Chen, C.M. (1997), 'Basing-Point Pricing, Parallel Behavior, and Colluding Behavior: From American Anti-Trust Law' (in Chinese), **5(1)** *Fair Trade Quarterly*, 65-96.

Chen, K.M. and Li, H.H. (1995), Chinese Translation of Ronald H. Coase's *The Firm, the Market, and the Law,* Taipei, Yuan-Liou Publishing Company, Ltd.

Chen, Kong-pin, Chien Hung-ken and Chu, Cyrus C.Y. (1997), 'Sequential versus Unitary Trials with Asymmetric Information', **26(1)** *Journal of Legal Studies*, 239-258.

Cheung, Steven N.S. (1987), *The Words of An Orange Seller* (in Chinese) Taipei, Yuan-Liou Publishing Company, Ltd.

Chien, Tze-shiou (1995), 'A Study on the Property Right of a Condominium's Top Space' (in Chinese), **41(10)** *Military Law Journal*, 8-15.

Chien, Tze-shiou (1997), 'Coase's The Market, the Firm, and the Law: A Legal Perspective' (in Chinese), **26(2)** *National Taiwan University Law Journal*, 229-246.

Chu, Cyrus C.Y. (1990a), 'A Model of Income Tax Evasion with Venal Tax Officials: The Case of Taiwan', **45(3)** *Public Finance*, 392-408.

Chu, Cyrus C.Y. (1990b), 'Plea Bargaining with the IRS', **41(3)** *Journal of Public Economics*, 1319-1333.

Chu, Cyrus C.Y. (1991), 'An Economic Analysis of the Criminal Proceedings in Civil Law Countries', **11(1)** *International Review of Law and Economics*, 111-116.

Chu, Cyrus C.Y. (1993), 'Oscillatory vs. Stationary Enforcement of Law', **13(3)** *International Review of Law and Economics*, 303-315.

Chu, Cyrus C.Y. and Jiang, Neville (1993), 'Are Fines More efficient Than Imprisonment?', **51** *Journal of Public Economics*, 391-413.

Chu, Cyrus C.Y. and Qian, Yingyi (1995), 'Vicarious Liability under a Negligence Rule', **15(3)** *International Review of Law and Economics*, 305-322.

Chu, Cyrus C.Y., Sheng-Cheng Hu and Ting-Yuan Huang (1997), 'Punishing Repeat Offenders More Severely!', IEAS Working paper No. 9703, Academia Sinica.

Fong, Jerry G. (1997), 'Corporate Name, Trade Name, Trade Mark, and Domain Name' (in Chinese), **5(2)** *Fair Trade Quarterly*, 65-96.

Fu, Tsu-tan, Shaw, Daigee and Yu, B.T. (1993), 'A Property Rights and Contractual Approach to Sustainable Development', Discussion Paper No. 9334, The Institute of Economics, Academia Sinica.

Hsieh, Chee-Ruey (1991), 'Medical Liability, Dispute, and Litigation: Theory and Evidence of Taiwan' (in Chinese), **19(1)** *Taiwan Economic Review*, 87-114.

Hsiung, Bing Yuang (1993), 'The Scale of the Market and the Scale of the Heart: Reconciling Coase and Buchanan on the Coase Theorem' (in Chinese), **21(2)** *Academia Economic Papers*, 331-356.

Huang, Chung-Huang (1996a), 'Hierarchical Government, Environmental Regulations, Transfer Payments, and Incomplete Enforcement', in Mendelsohn, Robert and Shaw, Daigee (eds), *The Economics of Pollution Control in the Asia Pacific*, 253-272. Vermont, Edward Elgar Publishing Company.

Huang, Chung-Huang (1996b), 'Effectiveness of Environmental Regulations under Incomplete Enforcement and the Firm's Avoidance Behavior', **8** *Environmental and Resource Economics*, 182-204.

Hwang, Chun-Sin and Kan, Steven S. (1994), *Principles of Economics-Cooperating for Mutual Prosperity and Progress*, Vol. 1 (in Chinese), published by the authors and distributed by Shin Lu Bookstore, Taipei.

Hwang, Chun-Sin and Kan, Steven S. (1995), 'Democracy and the Principle for the Division of Labor in Government Organization' (in Chinese), in Chien, Sechin Y.S. and Tai, Terence H. (eds), *Philosophy and Public Norms*, Book Series 34, Sun Yat-sen Institute for Social Sciences and Philosophy,163-200. Taipei, Academia Sinica.

Hwang, L.T. (1996), 'The Anti-Competitive Effect of Intra-Industry Mutual Holdings of Stocks: A Discussion on Fair Trade Law' (in Chinese), **4(2)** *Fair Trade Quarterly*, 1-14.

Hwang, L.T. (1995), 'The Paradoxical Regulation of Fair Trade Law on Vertical Merger: An Economic Analysis' (in Chinese), **3(3)** *Fair Trade Quarterly*, 19-31.

Juang, C.F. (1997), 'Foreign Competition and the Demarcation of Geographical Market' (in Chinese), **5(1)** *Fair Trade Quarterly*, 1-47.

Kan, Steven S. (1993), 'Entrepreneurship, Transaction Costs, and Subjectivist Economics', **1(2)** *Journal of Enterprising Culture*, 159-182

Kan, Steven S. (1996), 'Corporal Punishments and Optimal Incapacitation', **25(1)** *Journal of Legal Studies*, 121-130.

Kan, Steven S. and Hsiao, Ding-Way (1996), 'Contracts in Tsing Dynasty to Build Irrigation System at Lan-Yang Plain: A Transaction Cost Analysis' (in Chinese), **59** *Journal of Agricultural Economics*, 111-157, National Chung Hsing University.

Kan, Steven S. and Hwang, Chun-Sin (1991a), 'Hsun-Tzu's Theory of Justice' (in Chinese), in Tai, Hua T. and Cheng, Hsiao-Shih (eds), *Justice and Related Concepts*, Monograph Series 28, Sun Yat-sen Institute for Social Sciences and Philosophy, 93-130. Taipei, Academia Sinica.

Kan, Steven S. and Hwang, Chun-Sin (1991b), 'Economic Thoughts of Law in Ancient China', unpublished manuscript.

Kan, Steven S. and Hwang, Chun-Sin (1994), *Principles of Economics-Cooperating for Mutual Prosperity and Progress*, Vol. 2 (in Chinese), published by the authors and distributed by Shin Lu Bookstore, Taipei.

Kan, Steven S. and Hwang, Chun-Sin (1995), 'The Break and the Link between Cofucius' and Mo-Tzu's Public Norms' (in Chinese), in Chien, Sechin Y.S. and Tai, Terence H. (eds), *Philosophy and Public Norms*, Monograph Series 34, Sun Yat-sen Institute for Social Sciences and Philosophy, 135-162. Taipei, Academia Sinica.

Kan, Steven S. and Hwang, Chun-Sin (1996), 'A Form of Government from the Perspective of Transaction Cost Economics', **7(3)** *Constitutional Political Economy*, 197-220.

Kan, Steven S. and Hwang, Chun-Sin (1997), 'Check-and-Balance or the Separation of Decision Control and Decision Management Powers' (in Chinese), **25(3)** *Economic Essays*, 375-406. Taipei, Academia Sinica.

Koo, Hui-Wen (1991), 'Allocation of Legal Costs: American Rule vs. British Rule', **19(2)** *Taiwan Economic Review*, 197-218.

Koo, Hui-Wen and Png, I.P.L. (1994), 'Private Security: Deterrent or Diversion?', **14** *International Review of Law and Economics*, 87-101.

Koo, Hui-Wen and Sung, Yusen D. (1993), 'The Public Financing of Private Election Expenditures: An Economic Analysis of the Taiwanese Election and Recall Law' (in Chinese), **21(1)** *Taiwan Economic Review*, 25-44.

Li, Y.M. and Chen, H.M. (1995), 'An Economic Analysis of Intra-Industry Alliance in Product Designs' (in Chinese), **3(4)** *Fair Trade Quarterly*, 109-125.

Liu, Ruey-Hua (1994), Translation of Douglass C. North's *Institution, Institutional Change, and Economic Performance*, Taipei, China Times Publishing Company.

Liu, Ruey-Hua (1995), Translation of Douglass C. North's *Structure and Change in Economic History*, Taipei, China Times Publishing Company.

Shaw, Daigee (1992), 'Controlling Environmental Externalities: Pigouvian Tax vs. Strict Liability' (in Chinese), **2(1)** *Humanities and Social Sciences*, 35-44.

Shaw, Daigee (1995), Translation of T.L. Anderson and R. Leal's *Free Market Environmentalism*, Taipei, Chu Liu Book Company.

Shea, Jia-Dong and Wu, Jy-Wen (1994), 'Tax Evasion, Anti-Monitoring Activities, and the Imapcts of Government Policies' (in Chinese), **22(1)** *Academia Economic Papers*, 81-100.

Su, Yeong-Chin (1991), 'Rethinking of the Principle of Numerus Clausus-in the light of Development of Civil Law and Economic Theory of Property Right' (in Chinese), **19(2)** *Taiwan Economic Review*, 219-257.

Tan, Leslie L.T. (1991), 'Informative Advertising with Counterfeits' (in Chinese), **19(2)** *Academia Economic Papers*, 217-231.

Tang, Yu-Min (1987), Translation of Richard A. Posner's *Economic Analysis of Law*, Taipei, Commercial Press.

Tseng, Wang-Run (1996), 'Capital Structure and the Regulation of Disclosure', **25(4)** *National Taiwan University Law Journal*, 279-317.

Yang, Hao-Yen and Chen, Jong-Rong (1996), 'A Bayesian Approach of the Deterrent Effect of Life Sentence' (in Chinese), **24(1)** *Academia Economic Papers*, 115-133.

Yeh Jiunn-rong (1992), 'Selling Environmental Rights: From the Fifth Cracking Project to the Compensation Fund' (in Chinese), **2(1)** *Humanities and Social Sciences*, 17-34.

Wu, Ho-Mou and Huang, Peter (1994), 'More Order without More Law: A Theory of Social Norms and Organizational Cultures', **10** *Journal of Law, Economics and Organization*, 390-406.

0380
LAW AND ECONOMICS IN SERBIA

Zeljko Sevic
Senior Lecturer
Business School - University of Greenwich

Abstract

This chapter aims to present an overview of the development of law and economics as a scientific and academic discipline in Serbia from its very beginnings. It starts with an historical introduction describing the beginning of legal education in Serbia in the mid-nineteenth century, and the early development of legal and economic sciences and teaching in Serbia, until the fall of the socialist self-management system. The most prominent works in law and economics are discussed briefly by giving the prospective reader a broad idea of the state-of-the-art literature in the field published in Serbian (Serbo-Croatian) in the last few decades. All of this supports the final conclusion that law and economics in Serbia may be a very fast growing field of economic and legal literature in the years to come.
JEL classification: K00, B2, B3, K1
Keywords: Serbia, Law and Economics, Belgrade Law School, Legal Transition

1. Introduction

From the early 1990s onwards Yugoslav scholars have increasingly begun to recognise the importance of the economic analysis of legal institutions and practice.

In the former Republic of Yugoslavia, the development of legal and social science disciplines was strictly influenced and monitored by political bodies, but probably less so than in other socialist countries; hence the need to analyze this legal and economic development within the political and cultural frameworks of these countries. Given the traditional influence of universities on social life in Serbia, the teaching of these disciplines will be analyzed as well.

First, a brief chronicle of the developments in law and economics against the background of the changes in social and political structures in Serbia will be given. Second, the major works in law and economics in Serbia will be presented, and finally a conclusion will be provided (Section 4).

2. Historical Developments

Legal sciences have been taught in Serbia since the establishment of the Faculty of Law in 1841 (more correctly it concerned the legal division of the Great School). A number of economic subjects also were taught in courses from the mid-1850s onwards, to provide students with the broad educational background necessary for future employment, mainly in the civil service. With the reorganisation of higher education and the establishment of the University of Belgrade in 1905, a separate Department of National Economy and Finance was established within the Faculty of Law. The Faculty of Law educated aspiring lawyers, some of whom were specialising in economics and finance.

Until 1937, the Faculty of Law was the only institution offering training in economics, but only as a supplementary subject. The main degree (which was) granted to successful students was a classical LLB degree. A number of the best performing students continued their studies abroad, at the faculties of economics, and gained doctoral degrees in economics (political economy). In 1937, the Higher Economics and Commerce School (analogous to a polytechnic) was established. Although after World War II this school became the University of Belgrade's Faculty of Economics, the Faculty of Law retained its economics department.

After the socialist revolution during World War II, both institutions suffered great changes in their educational programmes and lost a number of 'unsuitable' staff (that is, despite their academic merit, a number of academics were arrested or expelled from the university). The syllabi were changed to be in line with mainstream socialist doctrine. Immediately after World War II the Soviet textbooks were simply translated and used for teaching. Even after the break with the Soviet Union in 1948, a few authors were still largely influenced by Stuchka-Pashukanis' legal, and Kondratyev's economic doctrine.

With the introduction of market reforms in 1965, changes in the universities' educational programmes were introduced. Some Western theories were slowly integrated into both legal and economic theory, and scholars gradually reestablished links with research institutions in Western countries. This resulted in a huge increase in the number of publications. Although these reforms lasted a year or so, it did not improve the openness of the research institutions. However, some academics, particularly lawyers, passed the 'Rubicon' of socially allowed political dissidence determined by the political censors, with their strong criticism of a final draft of the Federal constitution drawn up in 1973. Some of the scholars, for the first time, began to analyze the welfare effects of proposed legal acts from the point of view of comparative constitutional law, the legal system, social logic, social justice, and so on. But, it turned out that Tito's regime did not support academic freedom fully, and some academics were either imprisoned or isolated from the academic community. Others simply fled the country. Fifteen years later the predictions of these academics proved to be correct, when the constitutional crisis caused the former Republic of Yugoslavia to disintegrate. The introduction of a concept of self-management, in connection with the institutions of 'associated labour' and 'social ownership without owners' ('non-ownership concept of social property') severely affected the universities' educational programmes.

3. Current Situation

The fall of the communist regimes in Eastern Europe has shown that the Yugoslav concept of 'socialism with a human face' was not socially sustainable either. The transition requires change, new proposals and social solutions. This implies both the return to the positive pre-socialist traditions and a critical adoption of advanced Western theory. In this respect, the 1990s marked the birth of law and economics literature in Serbia. A number of authors adopted a more or less economically-based approach to legal and economic phenomena. Generally, these works were devoted to the problems of property rights and their (social) efficiency. Some of the authors apply simultaneously both law and economics and the public choice approaches (Sevic).

Professor Vodinelic of Belgrade University's Faculty of Law first mentioned law and economics in his textbook 'Civil Law - Introductory Themes', in 1991. With simple and generalistic explanations of law and economics concepts, he introduced them to the first-year law students. The second and more significant move was made by Professor Labus, also from Belgrade's Faculty of Law, in his recent textbook: 'Foundation Economics: Contemporary Theory and Application', published in 1995. This book was aimed at second-year law students, and presented in an exhaustive fashion the Coase theorem and its possible application in legal practice with reference to the Yugoslav legal order. It also stressed, as had been done many times before, that the judge is more constrained by law in a continental legal system than in the Anglo-Saxon (Common Law) system. The author provided his students with many splendid examples referring to Yugoslav positive law and practice, especially in the field of torts. Until this work the economic aspects of damage had not been considered from the point of view of the classic restitution rules. Currently, law students are informed about the basics of 'the economic analysis of law' (in Professor Labus' words: 'Legal School in Economics'). In contrast, at the Faculty of Economics there is no mention of law and economics. Even the course in 'Contemporary Economic Thought' does not consider this discipline, and only one page is devoted to public choice. Economics students are taught positive commercial (or international commercial) law but they do not have an opportunity to learn about law and economics.

Professor Vracar's book: 'Reexamination of the Legal Methodology: Indications of State-Legal Integralism' published in 1994 as a textbook for masters and doctoral students in law is a very interesting publication worth mentioning as well. This book is, in fact, a collection of Professor Vracar's previously published and unpublished papers, written between the early 1960s and mid-1990s. The renowned Yugoslav legal philosopher, legal theoretician and methodologist did not try to solve all the existing controversies in law and its related disciplines, but simply to share his thoughts with colleagues. One of the most famous critics of the draft for the Federal Constitution in the 1970s, and a victim of state terror, he returned to his theoretical roots and to his favourite legal thinker Professor Hans Kelsen. In addition to the promotion of a socio-politically (and economically) efficient concept of legal system and legal order, the book revealed that Professor Vracar had been a proponent of the use of game theory in law and political science as early as 1962. It is a real discovery to find out that he tried to introduce 'game theory' (which he called 'theory of competition') as a method of legal research at that time. The paper on advanced mathematics might, at first sight, seem descriptive today, but in fact it is very analytical and rather overwhelming in its complex legal logic applications.

A recent work which should, certainly be mentioned is the textbook 'Tax Science and Tax Law' by Professor Dejan Popovic (1997), former Dean of Belgrade Faculty of Law. In a delightful manner he introduces basic and more advanced topics on taxation, utilising both legal and economic methodologies. However, the majority of recently published books using law and economics methodology are concerned property right problems in the light of the transition in Yugoslavia. The voluminous work by Professor Madzar, entitled 'Property and Reform', published in 1995, is certainly one of them. He examines the role of property in socialism and its shortcomings, arguing for the overall reform of property and privatisation, stressing the importance of property rights for the final outcome of the transition process in Yugoslavia. Recently, in 1998, a number of books were published under the auspices of the project 'Constituting Serbia as a Legal State', generously funded by the Serbian Ministry of Science and Technology. The book by Dr Hiber on 'Property in Transition' (1998) is one of those which may enrich the literature on property rights issues in Serbia. The author analyses the different aspects of property and modes of privatisation. However, he could not omit an analysis of the socialist and self-management property concepts as a point of departure in property reform in Serbia. The work is predominantly practice-oriented, focusing on the criticism of some positive legal provisions. Another important work is the book entitled 'Introduction to the Economic Analysis of Law' by Dr Jovanovic (1998). Written in a textbook manner, the monograph slowly introduces the reader to *some* basic concepts of law and economics within the Yugoslav context. It may be that the book lacks proper academic rigour, but it certainly fills a gap in Serbian/Yugoslav legal and economic literature. As the first book of its kind, it really reaches its aims, and provides a basis to build upon. The main objection beside its over-simplicity may be the lack of use of up-to-date literature, and support of only some 'streams' in modern law and economics, equalising Law and Economics with New Institutional Economics, which the author refers to as 'Economics of Property Rights'.

The application of principles of law and economics is still not accepted in court procedures, even though an improvement in the field may be expected. At present a number of economists are sworn court experts (appointed by the Minister of Justice). They are supposed to formulate opinions on different economic, financial and accountancy issues, but in most cases they just estimate the losses. The sworn expert's opinion is not obligatory but (optional demonstrative) as the final decision is always in the hands of the court council, usually consisting of the presiding professional judge and two so-called 'jury judges'. Although experts only apply a classical utilitarian cost-benefit analysis, the judges usually base their sentence on the experts' opinion. Practice is not a formal source of law in Serbia, but lower courts take into account previous acknowledged decisions in order to avoid cancellation of the sentence in the appeal procedure later on. Although it is widely believed that judges in continental legal systems firmly stick to the legal norms stipulated in the law (Statute, Act), practice has recently shown a wide variety in sentencing, at least in Serbia.

What are the possible reasons for the present state of law and economics in Serbia? Besides the previously noted influence of a dominant socialist model in the past, a divergence of academic lawyers and economists can be observed. Both professions seem to try to keep their respective disciplines clearly separated from one another. For a while, there was open reluctance towards authors who tried to connect the two disciplines in their research. Historically, there has also been rivalry between the Faculty of Law and Faculty of Economics. The Faculty of Law kept its own department of economics, which is usually staffed very well. Even a well-known American property rights economist, Professor Svetozar (Steve) Pejovich, graduated from Belgrade's Faculty of Law in 1955.

4. Conclusion

It seems that Serbian law and economics is on its way to developing its own distinctive identity, rather than merely following the dominant American path. It is more European, and as a result more conservative with respect to certain typically Anglo-Saxon applications. The introduction of efficiency in the analysis of law, which comprises all three analyses (predictive, explanatory and normative) can undoubtedly influence the further development not only of legislative activities, but also of legal and economic thought as a whole in the country. However, it is not clear whether legislators in Serbia understand that law enforcement is not free and whether they know how to deal with the existence of 'externalities'. At present, it seems that the Serbian/Yugoslav legislators strongly believe that the implementation of law and law enforcement does not bring about any costs. This can, consequently, influence the path of administrative and legal reforms. More particularly, the size of the state apparatus may be more important for the legislator than its actual efficiency level. However, some authors have recently pointed out this problem, and the legislation policy stance will hopefully change in the future.

The mid-1990s appeared to be a turning point in the development of law and economics in Serbia. Up to this moment the main subjects of interest in terms of research have been property rights and privatisation, given that these issues are crucial for the transition process. Papers dealing with the efficiency of (commercial) law and its influence on the dynamics of economic change can be found as well. Authors who started to show an interest in law and economics at the beginning of the 1990s are currently very research-productive. They have also obtained senior positions in academia, and it can be expected that law and economics as an academic discipline will have a prominent future in Serbia in the years to come.

Bibliography on Law and Economics in Serbia (0380)

Andjelkovic, Mileva (1995a), 'Savremene Tendencije u Finansiranju Socijalno-politicke FunkcijeDrzave (Contemporary Tendencies in Financing State's Socio-Political Functions)', **50(1-2)** *Finansije*, 1-11.

Andjelkovic, Mileva (1995b), 'Koncept Zloupotrebe Prava u Poreskoj Materiji (Concept of Abuse of Law in Fiscal Matters)', **50** *Finansije*, 269-277.

Antic, Slavoljub (1994), 'Alternativni Pristup Regulaciji Elektroprivrede (An Alternative Approach to the Electricity Sector Regulation)', **47(3-4)** *Ekonomist*, 197-204.

Babic, Blagoje (1994), *Prelaz u Tranziciji* (Deception in Transition), Belgrade, Prometej.

Bandin, Tomislav (1988), 'Politicko Jedinstvo kao Faktor Ostvarivanja Dogovorene Ekonomske i Razvojne Politike (Political Unity as a Factor of Implementation of Agreed Economic and Development Policy)', **41(1)** *Ekonomist*, 29-31.

Begovic, Boris (1993), 'Urbanisticko Planiranje kao Oblik Drzavne Intervencije (Urban Planning as a Type of State's Intervention)', **26** *Ekonomska misao*, 71-86.

Begovic, Boris (1995), *Ekonomika Urbanog Planiranja* (Economics of Urban Planning), Belgrade, CES/MECON.

Begovic, Boris (1996), 'Prihvatljiv nivo Drzavne Intervencije Tokom Tranzicije - Slucaj Urbanog Planiranja (Acceptable Level of State Intervention During the Transition: The Case of Urban Planning)', in Nada Lazarevic (ed.), *Urbano Planiranje i Politika*, Belgrade, Arhitektonski fakultet, 73-78.

Begovic, Boris (1996), 'Smece u Ekonomskoj Teoriji: Slucaj Prirodnog Monopola (Garbage in the Economic Theory: The Case of Natural Monopoly)', **29** *Ekonomska Misao*, 35-47.

Begovic, Boris and Mijatovic Bosko (1991), 'Predlog Reforme Sistema Korišcenja Gradskog Zemljišta (A Proposal for a Reform of the Use of Urban Building Sites)', **24(2)** *Ekonomska Misao*, 175-186.

Begovic, Boris and Mijatovic Bosko (1991), 'Predlog Strategije Privatizacije Gradskog Zemljišta (A Proposal for the Privatisation Strategy of Urban Building Sites)', **24(3)** *Ekonomska Misao*, 289-300.

Bozovic Radoman (1988), 'Svojinski Odnosi i Ustavne Promene (Ownership Relations and the Constitutional Changes)', **21(2)** *Ekonomska Misao*, 11-20.

Cok, Vida (1989), 'Svojina kao Pravo Coveka (Property as a Human Right)', **35** *Jugoslovenska Revija za Medjunarodno Pravo*, 38-49.

Djuricin, Dragan (1994), *Privrede u Tranziciji: Privatizacija i Povezane Teme* (Economies in Transition: Privatization and Related Issues), Decije novine, Gornji Milanovac.

Gligorov, Vladimir (1990), 'Zavisnost i Reforme (Dependency and Reforms)', in Vladimir Gligorov and Jovan Teokarevic (eds), *Napustanje Socijalizma*, Belgrade, Institut za medjunarodni radnicki pokret i Strucna knjiga, 257-274.

Gligorov, Vladimir (1990), 'Nejednakost i Efikasnost: Modernizacija sa Socioloskog i Ekonomskog Stanovista (Inequality and Efficiency: Modernisation from Sociological and Economic Perspectives)', in Teokarevic Jovan (ed.), *Modernizacija i drustveni razvoj*, Belgrade, Institut za medjunarodni radnicki pokret, 29-38.

Hiber, Dragor (1993), 'Privatizacija - moc Drzave i Vladavina Prava (Privatization - Power of the State and Rule of Law)', **35(1)** *Sociologija*, 39-52.

Hiber, Dragor (1998), *Svojina u Tranziciji* (Property in Transition), Belgrade, Pravni fakultet.

Ilic Bogdan (1992), 'Primat Preduzetnistva ili Svojine u Savremenoj Trzisnoj Privredi (Superiority of Entrepreneurship or Property in a Contemporary Market Economy)', **45** *Ekonomist*, 47-58.

Ivic, Aleksandar and Maksimovic, Ivan (1984), *Drustvena Svojina i Samoupravljanje I* (Social Property and Self-Management I), Belgrade, Pravni fakultet.

Jelic, Ranko (1995), *Drustvena i Drzavna Svojina* (Social and State Property), Belgrade, Nomos.

Jovanovic, Aleksandra (1993), *Participativna Ekonomija: Uticaj Tipa Svojine na Ponasanje (Efikasnost) Preduzeca* (Participatory Economics: Influence of a Property Form on Behaviour (Efficacy) of a Firm), Belgrade, Pravni fakultet.

Jovanovic, Aleksandra (1994), 'Transakcioni Troskovi Privatizacije (Transaction Costs of Privatisation)', **43** *Pravni Zivot*, 895-905.

Jovanovic, Aleksandra (1996), 'Ekonomski Efekti Nekih Ekonomskih Prava', in Svetislav, Taborosi (ed.), *Srbija u Tranziciji*, Belgrade, Pravni fakultet, 113-125.

Jovanovic, Aleksandra (1998), *Uvod u Ekonomsku Analizu Prava* (Introduction to Economic Analysis of Law), Belgrade, Pravni fakultet.

Jovanovic, Aleksandra and Hiber, Dragor (1996), 'Postupak Izvrsenja na Imovini Drustvenog Preduzec a i Moralni Hazard (Execution Procedure on the Property of a Social Enterprise and Moral Hazard)', in *Svojina i Slobode - Aspekti Tranzicije*, Belgrade, Institut ekonomskih nauka, 202-208.

Jovanovic, Aleksandra and Mijatovic, Bosko (1996), 'Preduzece i Moralni Hazard (Firm and Moral Hazard)', **45** *Pravni Zivot*, 404-415.

Labus, Miroljub (1988), *Drustvena ili Grupna Svojina* (Social or Group Property), Belgrade, Naucna knjiga.

Labus, Miroljub (1990), 'Devalvacija i Administrativna Kontrola Cena (Devaluation and Administrative Control of Prices)', **23(1)** *Ekonomska Misao*, 1-24.

Labus, Miroljub (1995), *Osnovi Ekonomije: Savremene Teorije i Primena* (Foundation Economics: Contemporary Theories and Application), Jugoslovenska knjiga, Belgrade.

Madzar, Ljubomir (1972), *Osnovi Teorije Proizvodnje* (Basics of the Theory of Production), Belgrade, Institut ekonomskih nauka.

Madzar, Ljubomir (1995), *Svojina i Reforma* (Property and Reform), Belgrade, Institut ekonomskih nauka.

Maksimovic, Ivan (ed.) (1992), *Transformacija Svojinskih Odnosa - Teorijski i Empirijski Aspekti* (Transformation of Property Rights - Theoretical and Empirical Issues), Belgrade, Srpska akademija nauka i umetnosti (SANU).

Mihajlovic, Kosta (1991), 'Svojina i Efikasnost (Property and Efficiency)', **39** *Pravni Zivot*, 561-575.

Mijatovic, Bosko (1993a), 'Mogucnosti Privatizacije (Possibilities for Privatization)', **35(1)** *Sociologija*, 23-38.

Mijatovic, Bosko (1993b), *Privatizacija* (Privatization), Belgrade, Ekonomski institut.

Mijatovic, Bosko (1994), 'Privatizacija Gradskog Gradjevinskog Zemljista (Privatisation of Urban Building Sites)', **43(9-10)** *Pravni zivot*, 875-893.

Milovanovic, Milic (1993), 'Teorijski Izvori i Metodi Privatizacije (Theoretical Sources and Methods of Privatisation)', **35(1)** *Sociologija*, 5-22.

Milovanovic, Milic (1994), 'Privatizacija i Ekonomska Efikasnost (Privatization and Economic Efficiency)', **27(1-2)** *Ekonomska Misao*, 1-20.

Orlic, V. Miodrag (1993), *Zakljucivanje Ugovora* (Conclusion of Contracts), Institut za uporedno pravo, Beograd.

Orlic, V. Miodrag and Rajovic, Veroljub (1984), *Drustvena Svojina i Samoupravljanje II* (Social Property and Self-Management II), Belgrade, Pravni fakultet.

Petrovic, Milenko (1995), 'Funkcije Drzave u Savremenoj Trzisnoj Privredi (State Functions in a Contemporary Market Economy)', **28(3-4)** *Ekonomska Misao*, 207-224.

Popovic, Dejan (1997), *Nauka o Porezima i Poresko Pravo* (Tax Science and Tax Law), Savramena administracija and Open Society Institute/COLPI, Belgrade and Budapest.

Sevic, Zeljko (1994a), 'Socijalisti i Svojina: Prilog Pravnoj i Ekonomskoj Teoriji (Prava) Svojine (Socialists and Property: Contribution to the Legal and Economic Theory of Property Rights)', in Suvakovic, Uros (ed.), *Evropska Levica Danas* (European Left Today), Belgrade, SPS.

Sevic, Zeljko (1994b), *Komisioni Posao u Bankarskom Pravu* (Undisclosed Agency Operations Commission Transactions in the Banking Law), Belgrade, CiP-stampa.

Sevic, Zeljko (1994c), *Pravni Status Centralne Banke u Savremenoj Trzisnoj Privredi* (Status of the Central Bank in a Contemporary Market Economy), Belgrade, Faculty of Law, University of Belgrade.

Sevic, Zeljko (1995), 'Svojinski Oblici i Efikasnost Funkcionisanja Bankarskog Sistema (Property Forms and the Banking System Efficiency)', **44(9)** *Pravni Zivot*, 647-660.

Sevic, Zeljko (1996a), 'Ekonomska Analiza Prava Svojine u Tranziciji (Economic Analysis of the Property Rights in Transition)', **45(10)** *Pravni Zivot*, 964-977.

Sevic, Zeljko (1996b), *Centralna Banka: Polozaj - Organizacija - Funkcije* (Central Bank: Position - Organization - Functions), Belgrade, Cigoja-stampa.

Sevic, Zeljko (1996c), 'Odnos Centralne Banke i Izvrsne Vlasti (Relationship between the Central Bank and Executive Power)', **26(1-2)** *Jugoslovensko Bankarstvo*, 29-36.

Sevic, Zeljko (1996d), 'Bankarstvo i Bankarsko Pravo: Neka Otvorena Pitanja Samostalnosti Bankarskog Prava (Banking and Banking Law: Some Open Questions on Banking Law Independence)', **51(11-12)** *Finansije*, 964-977.

Sevic, Zeljko (1997), 'Svetska Trgovinska Organizacija: Pravni i Institucionalni Aspekti (World Trade Organization: Legal and Institutional Aspects)', **52** *Finansije*, 139-146.

Sevic, Zeljko and Sevic, Aleksandar (1997), 'Centralna Banka i Finansijska Trzista (Central Bank and Financial Markets)', **27** *Jugoslovensko Bankarstvo*, 28-34.

Sevic, Zeljko and Zorica, Vukasinovic (1997), 'Reforma Drzavne Uprave: Pravno-Ekonomska i Finansijska Analiza (Civil Service Reform: Law and Economics and Financial Management Analyses)', **46(9)** *Pravni Zivot*, 815-831.

Soskic, Dragutin (1983), 'Kriticki Osvrt na Sustinu Samoupravno Dogovorene cene Obrazovanja (Critical Notices on the Core on Self-Management Agreed Price of Education)', **31** *Anali Pravnog fakulteta u Beogradu*, 756-771.

Stankovic, Vladeta (1985), *Privredni Sistem* (Economic System), Belgrade, Pravni fakultet.

Stankovic, Vladeta (1991), 'Pravo Privrednog Sistema (Law of the Economic System)', **39** *Anali Pravnog Fakulteta u Beogradu*, 277-288.

Stankovic, Vladeta (1995), *Pravo Privrednog Sistema* (Law of the Economic System), Belgrade, Pravni fakultet.

Vasic, B. Vukasin (1986), 'Makroekonomska Politika kao Javno Dobro (Macroeconomic Policy as a Public Good)', **39(3)** *Ekonomist*, 429-430.

Vodinelic, V. Vladimir (1991), *Gradjansko Pravo - uvodne Teme* (Civil Law - Introductory Themes), Belgrade, Nomos.

Vracar, K. Stevan (1994), *Preispitivanja Pravne Metodologije: Nagovestaji Drzavno-Pravnog Integralizma* (Reexamination of the Legal Methodology: Indications of State-Legal Integralism), Naucna knjiga, Belgrade.

Vukadin, Emilija (1988), 'Instrument Kompenzacije u Jugoslovenskom Privrednom Sistemu: Karakter Uslova i Mogucnost Primene (Compensation as an Instrument in Yugoslav Economic System: Character of Conditions and its Feasibility)', **36(4)** *Anali Pravnog Fakulteta u Beogradu*, 386-398.

Vukotic, Veselin (1993a), *Privatizacija i Razvoj Trzisne Privrede* (Privatisation and Development of a Market Economy), Belgrade, Institut ekonomskih nauka.

Vukotic, Veselin (1993b), 'Privatizacija, Pravicnost i Efikasnost (Privatization, Justice, and Efficiency)', **46(1-2)** *Ekonomist*, 81-88.

Vukovic, S. (1996), *Cemu privatizacija* (Why Privatization), Belgrade, SDS-IKSI.

Zec, Miodrag, Mijatovic Bosko and Nebojsa Savic (eds) (1994), *Privatizacija Nuznost ili Sloboda Izbora* (Privatization Necessity or Freedom of Choice), Belgrade, Ekonomski institut and Jugoslovenska knjiga.

0385
LAW AND ECONOMICS IN SPAIN

Santos Pastor
Universidad Complutense de Madrid y Centro de Investigaciones en Derecho, Economiá y Administración de Empresas

Jesús Pintos
Instituto de la Rioja et Instituto de Derecho y Economiá

Abstract

This chapter addresses the evolution and current situation of law and economics in Spain along four major dimensions: teaching, academic research, legal policy and judicial practice. A glance at trends and likely extensions is also included. Furthermore, an accompanying Spanish bibliography in law and economics provides detailed information on a wide variety of research fields and authors, following the guidelines provided by the editors.
JEL classification: K00, H0, L5
Keywords: Law and Economics in Spain, Public Choice, Economics of Regulation, Public Economics.

1. Introduction

Although, as usual, one can trace the roots further back, in Spain what can be narrowly defined as new Law and Economics started in the 1980s. At that time, some academics started to introduce basic ideas of the movement as they were evolving (mainly in the United States), and tried to apply them to Spanish legal institutions. As time went by, the emphasis tended to be placed more on the applications and less on the review or importing of existing developments from abroad. At the present time, one may well conclude that at least one third of legal scholars 'have heard' about this business, and at least one tenth are well acquainted with the approach. On the other hand, about half of the academic economists know the approach well and more than 10 percent are familiar with it and use it on a more regular basis.

This short report concerns law and economics in a broader sense, that is, it reflects not only (although mainly) works pertaining to what has been named *new Law and Economics*, but also publications related to Public Choice and Constitutional Economics, Economic Regulation and (only a few) General Public

Economics. Such a broad scope is a consequence of the wide table of contents suggested by the editors.

As a framework for this report, we will take into account as a starting point the article that one of us wrote in 1991 on the situation and future of law and economics. According to the prediction made then on the likely evolution of this movement, there would be a fast growing progress from the economics side of law and economics, in sharp contrast with a slower evolution on the law side (see Pastor, 1991). As expected, one of the apparent features of the current situation turned out to be the confirmation of that prediction. Of course, the legal literature, both explicitly and implicitly, has also grown at a relatively fast pace.

The number of scholars now doing research in law and economics has become big enough and the fields covered so wide that, unlike in that 1991 article, we do not personally know quite a number of the individuals listed below. An increasing number of fields of law have been addressed by the economic approach. In order to figure out where law and economics is practiced and the extent to which this is being done, the affiliation institutions of the scholars listed below may serve as a good clue. By the way, it is remarkable that the 1997 Annual Conference of the European Association of Law and Economics was held at Barcelona (Univ. Pompeu Fabra).

Despite the abovementioned progress, the economic approach to law is still practiced by a minority within the academic world. The encouraging increase comes, on the one hand, from the fact that more scholars (specially younger ones) master foreign languages (English in particular) which enables them to follow progress made abroad, and on the other hand, from the strength of the approach.

The consistency of the approach should be shown in practice. Unfortunately this is often not the case as fireworks and paraphernalia have taken the place of actual substantial contributions.

2. Teaching Law and Economics

Undergraduate Studies in Law

Recent changes in the law curriculum have caused a reduction in the length of a compulsory course on principles of economics (it lasts now one semester instead of two) at the expense of the introduction of several non-compulsory courses, law and economics being one of them (the governmental regulation of the curriculum explicitly mentioned law and economics as one of the fields to cover in the one semester course in principles of economics. Although the actual coverage greatly depends on the lecturer's knowledge and on time constraints it has been of some help in establishing the presence and expansion of this discipline in the law schools). To our knowledge, such a course is already being taught in the law schools at the University Carlos III and Universidad Autónoma, both in Madrid. It is also contemplated at the University of Santiago de Compostela (including public choice), at the University of Extremadura, and may soon be adopted as part of the curriculum at the Universidad Complutense in Madrid.

In addition, law and economics topics are being taught as part of the course on principles of economics in several universities: for instance, at the University of La Coruña, and Complutense (Madrid). Topics in Public Choice and Constitutional Economics are also taugth at the Universities of Valladolid, Valencia and Santiago de Compostela Law Schools.

Undergraduate Studies in Economics and Business Administration
Although topics in law and economics are definitely part of a number of courses in Public Economics, Industrial Organization, and Microeconomics, the only formal courses in Law and Economics in a curriculum in Economics are taught at the University Carlos III de Madrid, as an elective course for the last year students, and at the University Pompeu Fabra in Barcelona, as an elective for second-year students of the Graduate Program in Economics and Management.

Similarly, some topics of law and economics are covered in the Business Administration curriculum as part of the courses in Business Organization (University Pública de Navarra, Zaragoza, and Pompeu Fabra).

Graduate Studies in Law
Public Universities Complutense, Autónoma and Carlos III, all of them in Madrid, offer graduate courses in Law and Economics, some of them as part of European programmes.

Graduate Studies in Economics
The theory of contracts, property rights, and economic regulation are part of most PhD programmes. Optional courses on topics in Law and Economics are offered at the University Carlos III (which includes a course in Insurance Law and Economics) and at the University Pompeu Fabra.

3. Scholarly Work

In addition to the attached list, other substantial legal scholarship applies elements of law and economics. Actually, we suspect that this part of the literature (which only slightly appears in our list) shall be of great relevance in the future. To mention just one area, most conventional works in bankruptcy law involve substantial economic reasoning and, to a lesser extent, that could also be applied to a great deal of commercial law, torts and contract law. We can expect this direction to be further developed most rapidly in the next years.

The setting up of the specialized Center of Law and Economics, Instituto de Derecho y Economía at the University Carlos III and the newest Centro de Investigaciones en Derecho, Economiá y Administración de Empresas (Cinde) at University Complutense, may be an important achievement for the scholarly work as well as for the policy implementation of this approach.

4. Law and Economics and Legal Policy

To some extent, economic reasoning is present in important parts of legal reform. Procedural Law, Bankruptcy Law, Tort Law and Court Administration are some of the areas covered, although one can seldom see explicit mention of Law and Economics.

5. Law and Economics, Law Practice and Judge Decisions

Although some efforts have been made, there is no substantial achievement in the appropriation of this approach by legal practitioners. Two hypotheses can explain such a failure. One is the academic nature of the predominant output produced so far. The other may have to do with the 'continental' European, that is civil law, tradition and the way the role of judges is perceived in this tradition. We believe that difficult cases deserve economic attention because in those cases the law is open to different interpretations, and the economic one could then be most competitive.

6. Final Remarks

Language barriers are dropping, and this will open up the market for ideas. It is also an advantage that the law and economics practitioners, at least in Europe, are nowadays more realistic and practice-oriented than before.

We still believe that the expansion of the approach greatly depends on its involvement and application to specific areas (sometimes called disciplines) of law. Economics will be more fruitful as Economics of Corporate Law, Criminal Law, Contract Law and the like. When some sound economics is placed in the hands of a good legal scholar, the productivity is more that duplicated in any respect, that is, for the law itself, for the law and economics approach and sometimes even for economics as well. We need to know more about the legal industry to be able to produce something sound. And for that, co-authorship could be a good strategy.

Although the achievements so far are worth the effort, the emphasis in training and joint legal and economics efforts sound to us as something worthwhile to be seriously taken into account. In that respect, joint support and supervision of PhD theses by a legal scholar and an economics scholar may be a good policy both for purposes of training candidates and for the research itself. Some of our preliminary results confirm the mutual gains of such a proposal.

7. Note on the Bibliography

To elaborate the Spanish Bibliography we asked the scholars we knew were working in this field to inform us of any other scholar using the law and economics approach. We may have been unable to reach every contributor, and for that we apologize. Subsequent updates may restore our unconscious omissions.

On the other hand, we refrain from including in the list translations of books and articles, mainly from English, but also some from German. The books by Calabresi on accidents, the introduction to law and economics by Polinsky, the textbook on private law by Ott and Shaffer, are some of those which come to our minds. A number of articles written in non-Spanish languages have also been published. (A number of them are collected in Santos Pastor (ed.), *Lecturas de Análisis Económico del Derecho*, (Reading Materials in Law and Economics), Instituto de Derecho y Economía, Universidad Carlos III de Madrid, Documento de Trabajo, 2/97, 1997).

Bibliography on Law and Economics in Spain (0385)

Alejo, M. Enrique (1987), 'La Efectividad de la Política de Competencia (The Effectiveness of Competition Policy)', **687** *Información Comercial Española*, 51-66.

Alfaro Aguila-Real, Jesús (1991), *Las Condiciones Generales de la Contratación, Estudio de las Disposiciones Generales* (Standard Form Contracts: Why Are They Binding?), chapter 1, Madrid, ED; Civitas, Prólogo Cándidio, 507 p.

Alfaro Aguila-Real, Jesús (1993), 'Autonomía Privada y Derechos Fundamentales (Freedom of Contract and Fundamental Rights)', **46(2)** *Anuario de Derecho Civil*, 57-122.

Alfaro Aguila-Real, Jesús (1994), 'Protección de los Consumidores y Derecho de los Contratos (Consumer Protection and Contract Law)', **47(2)** *Anuario de Dericho Civil*, 305-323.

Alfaro Aguila-Real, Jesús (1995a), 'Voces de la Enciclopedia jurídica Básica (Voices in the Basic Encyclopedia of Law)', *Cívitas, Madrid 1995, Franchising, tomo II*, 3153-3158.

Alfaro Aguila-Real, Jesús (1995b), *Interés Social y Derecho de Suscripción Preferente. Una Aproximación Económica* (Economic Efficiency of a Strict Construction of the 'Interest of the Corporation' Clause in Corporate Law), Madrid, Ed. Cívitas, 160 p.

Alfaro Aguila-Real, Jesús (1996a), 'Los Costes de Transacción (Transaction Costs)', in Iglesias, Prada (ed.), *Estudios Jurídicos en Homenaje al Profesor Aurelio Menéndez*, Madrid, Ed. Civitas, Tomo-I, 131-162.

Alfaro Aguila-Real, Jesús (1996b), 'Los Justos Motivos Como Causa Legal no Escrita de Exclusión y Separación de Socios en la Sociedad de Responsabilidad Limitada. Cómo Deshacerse de un Socio Molesto (How to exclude an annoying shareholder)', **222** *Revista de Derecho Mercantil*, 1079-1142.

Alonso Gonzalez, Luis Alberto (1995), 'Ideas para una Teoría de la Corrupción (Some Ideas for a Theory of Corruption)', **741** *Información Comercial Española*, 71-83.

Arruñada, Benito (1991), 'Market vs. Regulation in the Market for Corporate Control: Interactions Between Takeovers and Industrial Policiy in Spain', in Pardolesi, Roberto and Van Den Bergh, Roger (eds), *Law and Economics: Some Further Insights*, Milano, Giuffrè, 71-106.

Arruñada, Benito (1988a), 'Tiburones y Sanguijuelas en la Plaza de la Lealtad (Sharks and Spongers in the Stockmarket)', **2123** *Boletín del ICE*, 771-772.

Arruñada, Benito (1988b), 'Un Análisis Económico de la Regulación de la Sociedad Anónima en España (An Economic Analysis of the Regulation of the Joint-Stock Society in Spain)', **3** *Anales de Estudios Económicos y Empresariales*, 191-224.

Arruñada, Benito (1990a), *Control y Regulación de la Sociedad Anónima* (Control and Regulation of Joint-Stock Companies), Madrid, Alianza Editorial, 390 p.

Arruñada, Benito (1990b), *Economía de la empresa: un Enfoque Contractual* (The Economics of the Firm: A Contractual Approach) ,Barcelona, Ed. Ariel, 398 p.

Arruñada, Benito (1990c), 'La Regulación de la Información Empresarial (Regulation of Corporate Information)', **51** *Boletín del Círculo de Empresarios*, 11-42.

Arruñada, Benito (1990d), 'Control y Propiedad: Límites al Desarrollo de la Empresa Española (Corporate Control and Ownership: Limits to its Growth in Spain)', **687** *Información Comercial Española*, 67-88.

Arruñada, Benito (1991), 'Nobel al Giro Coasiano (Nobel to the Coasian Turn)', **41** *Revista de Economía*, 122-126.

Arruñada, Benito (1992a), 'La Conversión Coactiva de Acciones Comunes en Acciones sin Voto para Lograr el Control de las Sociedades Anónimas: De cómo la ingenuidad legal prefigura el fraude (Mandatory Conversion of Common Shares into Non-Voting Shares to Reach Corporate Control over Joint-Stock Companies: How legal Simplicity Leads to Fraud)', **71** *Revista Española de Financiación y Contabilidad*, 283-314.

Arruñada, Benito (1992b), '¿Hacia un 'Mercado Unico' de Control Societario? (Towards a Common Market of Corporate Control)', **703** *Información Comercial Española*, 144-170.

Arruñada, Benito (1992c), 'Tiburones Sólo en el Diccionario (Sharks only in the Dictionary)', **56** *Boletín del Círculo de Empresarios*, 15-30.

Arruñada, Benito (1992d), 'Crítica a la Regulación de las Opas (A Critique on the Regulation of Takeovers)', **203-4** *Revista de Derecho Mercantil*, 29-67.

Arruñada, Benito (1992e), 'Profesionales del Monopolio (Professionals of Monopoly)', **14** *Revista de Economía*, 95-101.

Arruñada, Benito (1993), 'Pintando la Caja Negra: Notas a 'La Empresa en el Análisis Económico' de V. Salas (Painting the Black Box: A Note on 'The Firm in V. Salas' Economic Analysis)', **57** *Papeles de Economía Española*, 156-169.

Arruñada, Benito (1994a), 'Competencia y Privatización en el Mercado Educativo (Competition and Privatization in the Education Market)', **59(2)** *Boletín del Círculo de Empresarios*, 265-275.

Arruñada, Benito (1994b), 'El Reparto del Monopolio: Obreros y Empresarios en la Historia de Asturias (Sharing the Monopoly: Workers and Managers in the History of Asturias)', in García Delgado, J.L. and Fernández de la Buelga, L. (eds), *Economía y Empresa en Asturias: Homenaje al Marqués de Aledo*, Madrid, Editioral Cívitas, 690-720.

Arruñada, Benito (1995a), 'Diseño Organizativo y Gestión de Personal en la Sanidad Pública (Organization and Management of Human Resources in the Public Healthcare System)', in A.E.S. (ed.), *Cambios en la Regulación Sanitaria*, Barcelona, SG Editores, 64-119.

Arruñada, Benito (1995b), 'Colegios Profesionales y Diseño Institucional (Professional Corporation and Institutional Design)', **63** *Economistas*, 86-90. Reproduced in Velarde J. et al. (dirs.) *Regulación y competencia en la economía española*, Cívitas, Madrid, 1995, 65-75.

Arruñada, Benito (1995c), 'The Search for Efficiency in the Spanish Healthcare System', in X (ed.), *A Mixed Market in Healthcare, A New European Convergence*, Londres, European Policy Forum, 52-64.

Arruñada, Benito (1995d), *Análisis Económico del Notariado* (Economic Analisis of the Notary), Madrid, Consejo General del Notariado, 166 p.

Arruñada, Benito (1996a), 'Liberalización de Servicios y Colegios Profesionales (Liberalization of Professional Services and Associations)', in Arruñada, B. et al. (eds), *Reforma de estructura*, Barcelona, Sociedad de Estudios Económicos, 49-71.

Arruñada, Benito (1996b), 'The Economics of Notaries', **3(1)** *European Journal of Law and Economics*, 5-37.

Arruñada, Benito and Paz Ares, Cándido (1995), 'Conversion of Ordinary Shares into Non-Voting Shares', **15(4)** *International Review of Law and Economics*.

Arruñada, B. and Paz-Ares, Cándido (1996), 'Mandatory Rotation of Company Auditors - A Critical Examination', **16** *International Review of Law and Economics*, 31-61.

Barbera, Salvador (1989), 'Los Derechos Individuales en el Análisis Económico (Individual Rights and Economic Analysis)', **38** *Economistas*, 6-9.

Bisbal Méndez, Joaquim (1970), *Prólogo Técnico de: Guido Calabresi, The Costs of Accidents* (Technical Foreword to Guido Calabresi's 'The Cost of Accidents'), New Haven, Yale University Press. Reprinted in *El Coste de los accidentes*, Ed., Ariel, Barcelona, 1984.

Bisbal Méndez, Joaquim (1983), 'La Responsabilidad Extracontractual y la Distribución de los Costes del Progreso (Tort Law and the Allocation of the Costs of Progress)', **167-168** *Revista de Derecho Mercantil*, 76-125.

Bisbal Méndez, Joaquím (1986), *La Empresa en Crisis y el Derecho de Quiebras* (The Crisis of the Firm and Bankruptcy Law), Bolonia, Real Colegio de España, 383 p.

Bisbal Méndez, Joaquim (1994), 'La Insoportable Levedad del Derecho Concursal (The Unbearable Lightness of Bankruptcy Law)', **214** *Revista de Derecho Mercantil*, 843-872.

Bustos Gisbert, Antonio (1995), *El Debate Sobre la Legalización de las Drogas Blandas: un Análisis Formalizado* (Making Drugs Legal: A Formal Analysis), 155 p.

Cabrillo, Francisco (1986), 'Adam Smith on Bankruptcy Law? New Law and Economics in the Glasgow Lectures?', **8** *History of Economics Society Bulletin*, 40-41.

Cabrillo, Francisco (1987a), *Análisis económico de Derecho Concursal Español*, (An Economic Analysis of Spanish Bankruptcy Law), Madrid, Fundación Juan March, 53 p.

Cabrillo, Francisco (1987b), '?Por Qué un Análisis Económico del Derecho? (Why an Economic Analysis of Law?)', **58** *Revista de Occidente*, 37-46.

Cabrillo, Francisco (1989), *Quiebra y Liquidación de Empresas* (Bankruptcy and Closing Down of Firms), Madrid, Unión Editorial, 151 p.

Cabrillo, Francisco (1990), 'Una Nueva Frontera: El Análisis Económico del Derecho (A New Frontier: Law and Economics)', **687** *Información Comercial Española*, 9-22.

Cabrillo, Francisco (1993), 'La Teoría Económica de la Reorganización de las Empresas en Quiebra (Economic Theory of the Reorganization of Bankrupty Firms)', **58** *Economistas*, 62-67.

Cabrillo, Francisco (1994), 'Industrialización y Derecho de Daños en la España del Siglo XIX (Industrialization and Tort Law in XIXth Century Spain)', **12** *Revista de Historia Económica*, 591-609.

Cabrillo, Francisco (1996), *Matrimonio, Familia y Economía* (Marriage, Family and Economics), Madrid, Minerva Ediciones, 335 p.

Cabrillo, Francisco and Vazquez Vega, Pablo (1995), 'Reforma de las Estructuras y Eficiencia Económica: la Nueva Regulación (Reforming Structures and Economic Efficiency: The New Regulation)', **60** *Boletín del Círculo de Empresarios*.

Calsamiglia, Albert (1988), 'Justicia, Eficiencia y Derecho (Equity, Efficiency and the Law)', **1** *Revista del Centro de Estudios Constitucionales*, 327 ff.

Carbajo, Domingo and Ruesca, Santos M. (1994), 'La Incidencia de la Fiscalidad Sobre Bienes Inmuebles en la Movilidad de los Factores Productivos en el Mercado nico Europeo (Especial referencia a la movilidad del capital) (The Effect of Real State Taxes on the Mobility of the Factors in the E.U. Market, Special Regard to Capital Mobility)', **18** *Actualidad Tributaria*, 475-490.

Casas Pardo, José (1979), 'El Control de los Efectos Económicos Externos por Medio de la Imposición (Controlling Externalities with Taxation)', **29** *Revista de Derecho Financiero y Hacienda Pública*.

Casas Pardo, José (1982), 'Algunas Consideraciones sobre la Teoría de la Elección Pública (Some Considerations on Public Choice Theory)', in Beltrán, Lucas, *Libro Homenaje*, Madrid, Editorial Moneda y Crédito.

Casas Pardo, José (1984), 'Estudio Introductorio (Introductory Study)', in Buchanan, James M. and Tollison, Robert D. (eds), *Análisis Económico de los Políticos* (Economic Analysis of the Politicians), Madrid, Instituto de Estudios Económicos.

Casas Pardo, José (1987), 'Laudatio Academica', in Casas Pardo, J. and Bru Parra, S. (eds), *Economía y Política (Economics and Politics)*, Valencia, Servei de Publicacions, Universitat de Valencia.

Casas Pardo, José (1991), 'Sobre la Relevancia de la Economía Constitucional (About the Relevance of Constitutional Economy)', in Puy Fraga, P. (ed.), *Homenaje al Prof. D. Carlos Otero Díaz*, Universidad de Santiago de Compostela.

Casas Pardo, José (1993), 'Análisis Económico de las Instituciones y de las Reglas (Economic Analysis of the Institutions and Rules)', in Puy Fraga, P. (ed.), *Análisis Económico del Derecho y de la Política*, Santiago de Compostela, Fundación Alfredo Brañas.

Casas Pardo, José (1995a), 'Does Ethical Proceduralism Underly Buchanan's Constitutional

Contractualism?', in Casas Pardo, J. and Schneider, F. (eds), *Current Issues in Public Choice*, Cheltenham, Edward Elgar.

Casas Pardo, José (1995b), 'Introducción (Introduction)', in Casas Pardo, J. and Schneider, F. (eds), *Current Issues in Public Choice*, Cheltenham, Edward Elgar.

Casas Pardo, José (1995c), 'Las Estructuras Federal y Fiscal de las Democracias Representativa y Directa como Modelos para una Unión Europea Federal (Federal and Fiscal Structures in Representative and Direct Democracies as Models for a Federal European Union)', in X (ed.), *Actas de las Jornadas de Estudio sobre 'La Constitución española y el ordenamiento comunitario europeo (II)'*, Dirección General del Servicio Jurídico del Estado, Ministerio de Justicia.

Casas Pardo, José (1998), 'The Spanish Transition to Democracy: a Public Choice Approach', in Backhaus, Jürgen G. (ed.), *The Political Economy of Structural Change*, Cheltenham, Edward Elgar.

Casas Pardo, José (1998), 'El Contractualismo-Constitucionalismo Liberal de James M. Buchanan (James M. Buchanan's Liberal Contractualism-Constitutionalism)', in Cortina, A. (ed.), *Ética de los Negocios*, Bancaja, Valencia, Fundación Etnor, forthcoming.

Casas Pardo, José and Brennan, Geoffrey (1990a), 'A Reading of the Spanish Constitution (1978)', **1** *Constitutional Political Economy*.

Casas Pardo, José and Brennan, Geoffrey (1990b), 'La Constitución Española a la luz de la Economía Política de las Constituciones (The Spanish Constitution from the Political Economy of Constitutions Approach)', **116** *Hacienda Pública Española*, 53-67.

Casas Pardo, José and Fernández Cainzos, J. (1989), 'Las Contituciones Económica y Fiscal en la Constitución Española de 1978 (The Economic and Fiscal Constitutions into the Spanish Constitution of 1978)', in Alvarez Conde, E. (ed.), *La Constitución Española de 1978 diez Años Después*, Madrid, Tecnos.

Casas Pardo, José and Fernández Cainzos, J. (1995), 'La Imposición a Traves de la Regulación en España: Un Intento de Medir la Imposición Implicita en el Sistema Financiero Español en la Década 1977-1987 (Taxation Through Regulation in Spain: An Effort to Measure Implicit Taxation in the Spanish Financial System between 1977-1987)', in X (ed.), *Estudios de Derecho Mercantil en Homenaje al Prof. Manuel Broseta Pont*, Tirant lo Blanch, Valencia.

Casas Pardo, José and Navarro, Puchades M. (1996), 'La perspectiva de la 'Public Choice' en el Análisis de la Actuación de los Entes Públicos (Public Choice Approach and the Behaviour of Public Enterprises)', in X (ed.), *Actas del II Congreso Español de Ciencia Politica y de la Administración (forthcoming)*.

Casas Pardo, José and Sainz Sánchez, E. (1995), 'La coacción de las instituciones colectivas (Compelling Collective Institutions)', in Sainz Sánchez, E. (ed.), *Las Organizaciones como Sistemas Constitucionales*, Ensayos Sobre el Modelo de Gestión Burocrática de la Universidad Pública, Granada, Ed. Método.

Chiappori, P.A. and Macho-Stadler, I. (1990), 'Contrats de Travail Repetes: la Memoire (Repeated Labour Contracts:The Memory)', **17** *Annales d'Economie et de Statistique*, 47-70.

Chiappori, P.A., Macho-Stadler, I., Rey, P. and Salanie, B. (1994), 'Repeated Moral Hazard: the Role of Memory, Commitment, and the Access to Credit Markets', **38** *European Economic Review*, 1527-1553.

Chiappori, P.A., Pérez-Castillo, J. David and Verdier, T. (1995), 'Spatial Competition in the Banking System: Localization, Cross Subsidies and the Regulation of Interest Rates', **39**

European Economic Review, 889-918.

Coll Martin, Sebastián (1982), 'La Minería del Carbón en España a Finales del Antiguo Régimen (Coal Mining in Spain at the End of the Old Regime)', in Tedde, Pedro (ed.), *La Economía Española al final del Antiguo Régimen. II, Manofacturas*, Madrid, Alianza Editorial, 239-335.

Coll Martin, Sebastián (1984), *Jovellanos y la Minería Asturiana (Textos inéditos de Don Gaspar Melchor de Jovellanos)* (Jovellanos and the Asturian Mining), **13** Colección Textos y Estudios del Siglo XVIII, Oviedo, Universidad de Oviedo.

Coll Martin, Sebastián and Sudrii I Triay, Carles (1987), *El Carbón en España, 1770-1961. Una Historía Económica* (Coal in Spain, 1770-1961, An Economic History), Madrid, Turner, 624 p.

Desdentado, Aurelio and Durán, Almudena (1996), *Las Causas Económicas para la Extinción Objetiva del Contrato de Trabajo. Un Análisis Jurídico y Económico* (Objective Causes for Breach of Labour Contracts. An Economic and Legal Analysis), Cuadernos de Derecho Judicial, 55-116.

Economistas (1989), *Los Derechos de Propriedad en el Análisis Económico* (Property Rights in Economic Analysis).

Espinosa, M.P. and Macho-Stadler, I. (1989), 'Coordinación de Política Industrial en el Marco de la CEE (Industrial Policy Coordination in the EEC)', **2** *De Economía Pública*, 61-77.

Estrada, Javier (1993), 'A Note on the Optimality of Strict Liability', **41** *Economics Letters*, 187-191.

Estrada, Javier (1994), 'Insider Trading: Regulation, Deregulation, and Taxation', **5** *Swiss Review of Business Law*, 209 ff.

Estrada, Javier (1995), 'Insider Trading: Regulation, Securities Markets, and Welfare Under Risk Aversion', **35** *Quarterly Review of Economics and Finance*, 421-449.

Gallastegui, M.C., Ibarra, E. and Macho-Stadler, I. (1993), 'Contratos De pesca Desde la Perspectiva de la Teoría de la Agencia (Fishing Contracts from a Principal-Agency Viewpoint)', **20** *Estudios de Economía, número especial sobre La Economía de la Incertidumbre y la Información*, 329-354.

Ganuza Fernandez, Juan José (1995), 'Procurement Contract with Observable Quality', *Revista Española de Economía* (Monografico sobre regulación), 153-164.

Garciá De Enterría, Javier (1989), 'Sobre la Eficiencia delMercado de Capitales. Una aproximación al 'securities law' de los Estados Unidos (The Efficiency of the Capital Market. Approaching U.S. Securities Law)', **193-194** *Revista de Derecho Mercantil*, 653-678.

Garciá De Enterría, Javier (1993), 'El Control del Poder Societario en la Gran Empresa y la Función Disciplinar de las OPAS (Corporate Control of Large Companies and the Disciplinary Role of Takeovers)', **47** *Revista de Derecho Bancario y bursatil*, 665-689.

Garciá De Enterría, Javier (1996), *La Opa Obligatoria* (Mandatory Takeovers), Madrid, Editorial Cívitas, 324 p.

Garciá Gallego, Aurora and Georgantzis, Nikolaos (1992), *On the Antitrust Implications of Information Sharing: An Overview of the Theoretical Findings and Possible Applications to the Tractors Industry Case*, Report for the A-3 Unit (Economic Questions and Studies) of DG IV (Competition) of the European Comission.

Garciá Gallego, Aurora and Georgantzis, Nikolaos (1995), *Competitive and Predatory Multi-Plant Location Decisions*, Instituto Valenciano de Investigaciones Económicas,

Valencia, Spain, No. WP-EC95-03, 22 p.

Garciá Gallego, Aurora and Georgantzis, Nikolaos (1996a), 'Competition Intensity vs. Service Quality: On the Distribution of Para-Pharmaceutical Products in Spain', in Martin, Stephen (ed.), *Interaction of Member State and EU Competition Policy*, Amsterdam, forthcoming.

Garciá Gallego, Aurora and Georgantzis, Nikolaos (1996b), 'Multiproduct Activity and Competition Policy: The Tetra Pak Case', **31** *European Journal of Law and Economics*, 83-95.

Garciá Sanz, Angel (1994), 'El siglo XVIII: entre la Prosperidad de la Trashumancia y la Crítica Antimestaña de la Ilustración (The Mesta in Spain, XVIIIth Century)', in Gonzalo Anes y Angel García Sanz (eds), *Mesta, Trashumancia y vida Pastoril*, Madrid, Sociedad V Centenario del Tratado de Tordesillas, 137-158.

Garcia Viñuela, Enrique (1992), 'La Distribución de la Renta y el Criterio de Justicia de Rawls (Income Distribution and Rawls' Justice)', **123** *Hacienda Pública Española*, 77-83.

Garciá Viñuela, Enrique (1995), 'Búsqueda de Rentas a Través del Sector Público (Rent Seeking Through the Public Sector)', **133** *Hacienda Pública Española*, 107-114.

Garcia Viñuela, Enrique (1996a), 'La Financiación de los Partidos Políticos: un Enfoque de Elección Pública (Financing Political Parties: A Public Choice Approach)', **92** *Revista de Estudios Políticos*, 281-297

Garcia Viñuela, Enrique (1996b), 'Una Nota Sobre la Teoría del Estado de Anthony de Jasay (A Note on Anthony de Jasay's Theory of the State)', **136** *Hacienda Pública Española.*

Garciá Viñuela, Enrique (1996c), 'Una Estimación de la Búsqueda de Rentas en los Presupuestos de Gastos de Algunos Paises de la Unión Europea durante los años 80 (An Estimation of Rent Seeking in Some E.E.C. Countries' Budgets during the 80s)', *Hacienda Pública Española*, 49-54.

Garciá Viñuela, Enrique and Vázquez Vega, Pablo (1996), 'Financing the Political Parties: A Public Choice Approach', **2-3** *Ecomonia delle Scette Pubbliche*, 139-153

Garciá Villarejo, Avelino and Salinas Sánchez, Janvier (1993), *Manual de Hacienda Pública general y de España* (Public Treasury Manual), Madrid, Tecnos, 671 p.

Garcimartin Alférez, Francisco Javier (1995), 'El Régimen Normativo de las Transacciones Privadas Internacionales: una Aproximación Económica (The Regulation of International Private Transactions: an Economic Approach)', **47** *Revista Española de Derecho Internacional*, 11-39.

Garcimartin Alférez, Francisco Javier (1996), 'El Coste de la ley Helms-Burton para las Empresas Españolas (The Costs of Helms-Burton Rule for Spanish Companies)', **306** *Derecho de los Negocios*, 13-27 .

Georgantzis, Nikolaos (1992a), *The Social Aspects of Telecommunications: Targeted Subsidies as a Means to Achieve Universal Basic Services*, Report for the A-3 Unit (Economic Questions and Studies) of DG IV (Competition) of the European Comission.

Georgantzis, Nikolaos (1992b), *The Effect of Mergers on Potential Competition under Economies or Diseconomies of Joint Production*, Istituto Universitario Europeo, EUI Working Paper ECO, Florence, Italy, No. 92/67.

Georgantzis, Nikolaos and Garciá Gallego, Aurora (1995), *La Actividad Multiproducto y sus Implicaciones para la Politica de la Competencia* (Multiproduct Activity and Competiton Policy Implications), Instituto Valenciano de Investigaciones Economicas, WP EC 95-04, 40 p.

Gimeno Ullastres, Juan A. (1975), 'Las Causas del Déficit Público (Trying to Explain Public

Deficit)', **88** *Hacienda Pública Española*, 85-105.

Gimeno Ullastres, Juan A. (1975), 'La Reforma del Impuesto sobre la Renta de las Personas Físicas (Reforming the Personal Income Tax)', *Revista de Economía Aplicada e Historia Económica*, 23-44.

Gimeno Ullastres, Juan A. (1975), *La situación de las Facultades de Derecho y Económicas: análisis y propuestas* (Analysis and Proposals for Law and Economics Schools), Secretaría de Estado de Universidades e Investigación, Ministerio de Educación y Ciencia, 67 p.

Gimeno Ullastres, Juan A. (1975), *¿A Quién Beneficia el Gasto Público?* (Who Does Public Expenditure Favour?), **4** Número Monográfico de la Revista de Economía Pública e Historia Económica.

Gimeno Ullastres, Juan A. (1975), 'Política de Empleo en España (Labour Policy in Spain)', **12** *Contrapunto*, 10-15.

Gimeno Ullastres, Juan A. (1976), 'Reforma Fiscal y Sistema Tributario (Reforming the Tax System)', in Figuero, J. (ed.), *Las Reformas Urgentes*, Madrid, Taller Ediciones JB, 481-490.

Gimeno Ullastres, Juan A. (1980), *Imposición Sobre el Consumo y Distribución Personal de Rentas* (Consumption Taxes and Personal Distribution of Income), Madrid, Instituto de Estudios Fiscales, 341 p.

Gimeno Ullastres, Juan A. (1984a), 'Los Recargos Locales sobre Impuestos Estatales (Local Overcharges on Central Taxes)', **1114** *La Ley*, 1-4.

Gimeno Ullastres, Juan A. (1984b), 'Los Presupuestos Familiares (Family Budgets)', **1** *Estudios Sobre el Consumo*, 39-54.

Gimeno Ullastres, Juan A. (1985), 'La Incidencia del I.V.A. Sobre los Consumidores (How V.A.T. Affects Consumers)', **4** *Estudio sobre le Consumo*, 37-55.

Gimeno Ullastres, Juan A. (1986), 'Rentas Familiares y Equidad (Equity and Family Income)', **99** *Hacienda Pública Española*, 289-300.

Gimeno Ullastres, Juan A. (1993), 'La Incidencia del Gasto Público por Niveles de Renta: España 1990 vs. 1980 (The Effect of Public Expenditure by Levels of Income: Spain 1990 vs. 1980)', in X (ed.), *I Simposio Sobre la Igualdad y Distribución de la Renta y la Riqueza*, Madrid, Fundación Argentaria, 63-121.

Gimeno Ullastres, Juan A. (1994), *La Fiscalidad delTtabaco en la CEE* (Taxing Tobacco in the E.C.), Madrid, Editorial Cívitas, 127 p.

Gimeno Ullastres, Juan A. (1995a), 'Sector Público y Patrocinio (Public Sector and Sponsorship)', in Linde, Paniagua (ed.), *Cultura y Desarrollo*, Madrid, Ministerio de Cultura, 116-132.

Gimeno Ullastres, Juan A. (1995b), 'Los Beneficios de los Gastos Indivisibles (Benefits of Indivisible Expenses)', **133** *Hacienda Pública Española*, 115-130.

Gimeno Ullastres, Juan A. and Ruiz Huerta, Jesús (1981), *El nuevo Estado Fiscal Español* (The New Spanish Fiscal State), Madrid, H. Blume, 315 p.

Gimeno Ullastres, Juan A. and Ruiz Huerta, Jesús (1986), 'Reforma Fiscal y Financiación del las CCAA: El Régimen Especial (Financing the Communities and Tax Reform: The Special Regime)', in Ruiz-Huerta, J. and Muñoz de Bustillo, R. (eds), *Estado Federal/Estado Regional: La Financianción de las Comunidades Autónomas*, Salamanca, Ediciones de la Diputación de Salamanca, 245-263.

Gimeno Ullastres, Juan A. and Ruiz Huerta, Jesús (1989), 'Los Costes de los Servicios Universitarios (The Cost of Universities)', in Alewell (ed.), *La Financiación de la*

Enseñanza Superior, Madrid, Consejo de Universidades, 181-209.

Gimeno Ullastres, Juan A. and Ruiz Huerta, Jesús (1991), 'Financiación Autonómica: Un Modelo Alternativo de Corresponsabilidad Fiscal (Financing the Communities: An Alternative Model for Tax Corresponsability)', **15** *Revista Valenciana de Hacienda Pública*, 149-179.

Gimeno Ullastres, Juan A. and Ruiz Huerta, Jesús (1993), 'Descentralización Fiscal y Corresponsablidad a Través de las Grandes Figuras Tributarias (Tax Descentralization and Corresponsability)', **3** *Cuadernos Aragoneses de Economía*, 29-40.

Gimeno Ullastres, Juan A., Ruiz Huerta, Jesús and Olleros, Jaime (1977), *Una Reforma Fiscal para España* (Tax Reform in Spain), Madrid, Moneda y Credito S.A.

Gómez-Pomar, Fernando (1989), 'Reglas de Transacción y Derechos de Propiedad Intellectual (Transaction Rules and Intellectual Property Rights)', **38** *Economistas*, 40-46.

Gómez-Pomar, Fernando (1990a), 'Tutela de la Apariencia y Reglas de Responsabilidad: los arts. 1164 y 1527 del código civil (Protection of Appearance and Liability Rules: Articles 1164 and 1527 of the Code Civil)', **4** *Revista de Derecho Privado*, 255-274.

Gómez-Pomar, Fernando (1990b), 'La Producción de Copias y los Derechos de Autor: el Caso de la Fotocopiadora (Copy Production and Copyright: The Photocopy Machine)', **687** *Información Comercial Española*, 43-50.

Gómez-Pomar, Fernando (1990c), 'Copias, Fotocopias y Derechos de Autor (Copies, Photocopies and Copyrights)', *Revista de la Facultad de Derecho de la Universidad Complutense*.

Gómez-Pomar, Fernando (1990d), 'La Producción de Copias y los Derechos de Autor: el Caso de la Fotocopia (Photocopy and Author's Copyright)', **687** *Información Comercial Española*, 43-50.

Gómez-Pomar, Fernando (1991), 'Un Modelo de los Efectos de la Copia Sobre los Derechos de Autor (A Model on the Effects of Copies on the Author's Copyright)', **77** *Revista de la Facultad de Derecho de la Universidad Complutense*, 247-259.

Gómez-Pomar, Fernando (1992), 'Las Entidades de Gestión de la Propiedad Intellectual: una Aproximación Económica (Managment Units of Intellectual Property: An Economic Approach)', **14** *Revista de Economía*, 85-88.

Gómez-Pomar, Fernando (1993a), 'La Función de la Propiedad Intelectual y el Régimen de la Fotocopia (The Role of Intellectual Property and Regulation of the Photocopies)', **614** *Revista Crítica de Derecho Inmobiliario*, 165-216.

Gómez-Pomar, Fernando (1993b), 'El Derecho de Accidentes y el Análisis Económico: Presupuestos e Implicaciones Básicas (Tort Law and Economic Analysis: Basic Implications)', in Puy Fraga, P. (ed.), *Análisis Económico del Derecho y de la Política*, Santiago de Compostela, Fundación Alfredo Brañas.

Gómez-Pomar, Fernando (1996a), *La Responsabilidad por daño Ecológico: Ventajas, Costes y Alternativas* (Environmental Torts: Advantages, Costs and Alternatives), Madrid, 80 p.

Gómez-Pomar, Fernando (1996b), 'Insurance Benefits, Insurance Subrogation, and Imperfects Liability Rules', *International Review of Law and Economics*.

Gómez-Pomar, Fernando and Pastor, Santos (1990), 'El Derecho de Accidentes y la Responsabilidad Civil: Un Análisis Jurídico y Económico (Accident Law and Liability Rules: A Legal and Economic Analysis)', **43** *Anuario de Derecho Civil*, 495-538.

Herguera, Iñigo and Martinelli, César (1995), 'Regulacion de Precios de Interconexion (Price

Regulation in Commun)', **747** *Información Comercial Española*, 73-86.

Herguera, Iñigo and Rodríguez Romero, Luis (1995), 'Regulación de las Telecomunicaciones en la Unión Europea: Competencia en Servicios y en Redes (The European Regulation of the Telecommunication Industry)', **747** *Información Comercial Española*, 9-22.

Huerta Arribas, Emilio (1986), 'Restricciones Verticales y Política de Defensa de la Competencia (Vertical Restrictions and Competition Law Policy)', *Investigaciones Económicas*, 315-330.

Huerta Arribas, Emilio (1987a), 'Eficiencia en los Sistemas de Distribución: Un Modelo de Duopolio Sucesivo (Efficiency in Distribution Systems: A Consecutive Duopoly Model)', **15** *Cuadernos de Economía*, 205-218.

Huerta Arribas, Emilio (1987b), 'Política de Competencia en España y Organización Industrial (Competition Policy in Spain and Industrial Organization)', **650** *Información Comercial Española*, 42-55.

Huerta Arribas, Emilio (1988), '¿Necesitaremos una Política de Defensa de la Competencia? (Shall we Need a Competition Policy?)', *Investigaciones Económicas*, 89-95.

Huerta Arribas, Emilio (1989), 'Análisis de la Integración Vertical de Empresas en España (Analysis of Firm's Vertical Integration in Spain)', **39-40** *Papeles de Economía Española*, 149-164.

Huerta Arribas, Emilio (1991), 'La Competitividad de las Empresas y la Politica de Defensa de la Competencia (Firms' Competitiveness and Competition Policy)', **21** *Revista Vasca de Ecomomía Ekonomiaz*, 51-69.

Huerta Arribas, Emilio (1994), 'La Política de Defensa de la Competencía en España: Algunos ejemplos (Competition Policy in Spain: Some Examples)', **57** *Cuadernos Económicos de ICE*, 213-229.

Huerta De Soto, Jesús (1982), 'Método y Crisis en la Ciencia Económica (Method and Crisis in Economics)', **74** *Hacienda Pública Española*, 33-48.

Huerta De Soto, Jesús (1989), 'Los Planes de Pensiones Privados y sus Fondos Financieros (Private Pensions and their Financial Funding)', in Martinez Lafuente, Antonio (ed.), *Estudios Sobre Planes y Fondos de Pensiones*, Ariel, Barcelona, 169-187.

Huerta De Soto, Jesús (1992), *Socialismo, Cálculo Económico y Función Empresarial* (Socialism, Economic Calculation and Enterpreneurship), Madrid, Unión Editorial, 442 p.

Huerta De Soto, Jesús (1994a), 'A Propósito del Proceso de Unificación en Europa (About the European Process of Monetary Union)', in Ramón Febrero (ed.), *España y la Unificación Monetaria Europea: una Reflexión Crítica*, Madrid, Abacus Editorial, 289-302.

Huerta De Soto, Jesús (1994b), *Planes de Pensiones Privados* (Private Pension Plans), Madrid, San Martín, 294 p.

Huerta De Soto, Jesús (1994c), 'Banque Central ou Banque Libre: Le Debat Theorique sur les Reserves Fractionaires', **5(2-3)** *Journal des Economistes et des Etudes Humaines*, 379-391.

Huerta De Soto, Jesús (1994d), 'Ahorro y Previsión en el Seguro de Vida', in Huerta De Soto (ed.), *Estudios de Economía Política*, Madrid, Unión Editorial, 334-338.

Huerta De Soto, Jesús (1994e), 'Ecología de Mercado (Free Market Environmentalism)', in Huerta De Soto (ed.), *Estudios de Economía Política*, Madrid, Unión Editorial, 229-249.

Huerta De Soto, Jesús (1994f), 'Génesis, Esencía y Evolución de la Escuela Austríaca de Economía (Genesis, Essence and Evolution of the Austrian School of Economics)', in

Huerta De Soto (ed.), *Estudios de Economía Política*, Madrid, Unión Editorial, 17-55.

Huerta De Soto, Jesús (1994g), 'The Crisis of Social Security: An Economic Analysis from the Austrian Perspective', **5** *Journal des Economistes et des Etudes Humaines*, 127-155.

Huerta De Soto, Jesús (1995a), 'A Critical Analysis of Central Banks and Fractional-Reserve Free Banking from the Austrian Perspective', **8(2)** *Review of Austrian Economics*, 25-38.

Huerta De Soto, Jesús (1995b), 'Entrepreneurship and the Economic Analysis of Socialism', in Gerrit Meijer (ed.), *New Perspectives on Austrian Economics*, Routledge, London, 228-253.

Huerta De Soto, Jesús (1995c), 'A Theory of Liberal Nationalism', **9** *Il Politico, Università Pavia, Italy*, 583-598.

Huerta De Soto, Jesús (1996a), 'Socialismo, Corrupción Etica y Economía de Mercado (Socialism, Ethical Corruption and the Market Economy)', in Noñez Ladeveze, Luis (ed.), *Etica Pública y Moral Social*, Madrid, Noesis, 101-132.

Huerta De Soto, Jesús (1996b), 'Derechos de Propiedad y Gestión Privada de los Recursos de la Naturaleza (Property Rights and Private Management of Environmental Resources)', **2** *Cuadernos del Pensamineto Liberal*, 13-30.

Huerta De Soto, Jesús (1996c), 'New Light on the Prehistory of the Theory of Banking and the School of Salamanca', **9** *Review of Austrian Economics*, 59-61.

Lafuente, Alberto (1987), 'Aspectos Económicos de la Definición de Mercado (Some Economic Aspects of the Market Definition)', **687** *Información Comercial Española*, 70-82.

Lehmann, Michael (1990), 'La Teoría de los 'Property Rights' y la Protección de la Propriedad Intellectual e Industrial (The Property Rights Theory and the Protection of Intellectual and Industrial Property)', *Revista General de Derecho*, 544-545.

Llebot Majo, José Oriol (1996a), 'El Sistema de la Responsabilidad de los Administradores, Doctrina y Jurisprudencia (Manager's Liability System, Doctrine and Jurisprudence)', **7(4)** *Revista de Derecho de Sociedades*, 49-70.

Llebot Majo, José Oriol (1996b), 'Doctrina y Teoría de la Empresa en el Derecho Mercantil (Una Aproximación al Significado de la Teoría Contractual de la Empresa) (Doctrine and Theory of the Firm in Contract Law Approaching the Meaning of Corporate Contractual Theory)', **210** *Revista de Derecho Mercantil*, 319-388.

Macho-Stadler, I. (1987), 'Contratos Basados en Mecanismos de Control y Sanciones Severas: Modelización y Limitaciones (Contracts based on Monitoring and Severe Punishment)', **4(2)** *Revista Española de Economía*, 291-310.

Macho-Stadler, I. (1991), 'Riesgo Moral con Varios Agentes: Contratos Optimos y Diseño Organizativo de la Relación (Moral Hazard with Multiple Agents: Optimal Contract Design)', **8** *Revista Española de Economía*, 255-283.

Macho-Stadler, I. (1993), 'Penalties within the Moral Hazard Problem', **44** *Metroeconomica*, 239-257.

Macho-Stadler, I. and Pérez-Castrillo, J. David (1988), 'Sobre los Compromisos Multiperíodo en los Modelos de Riesgo Moral Repetido (Multiple Period Commitments in Repeated Moral Hazard Models)', **5** *Revista Española de Economía*, 143-158.

Macho-Stadler, I. and Pérez-Castrillo, J. David (1991a), 'Moral Hazard and Cooperation', **35** *Economics Letters*, 17-20.

Macho-Stadler, I. and Pérez-Castrillo, J. David (1991b), 'Contrats de Licence et Asymetrie d'Information (Licensing Contracts and Asymmetric Information)', **24** *Annales* *d'Economie et de Statistique*, 189-208.

Macho-Stadler, I. and Pérez-Castrillo, J. David (1991c), 'Double Risque Moral et Delegation (Double Moral Hazard and Delegation)', **57** *Recherches Économiques de Louvain*, 277-296.

Macho-Stadler, I. and Pérez-Castrillo, J. David (1992), 'Le Regle de la Derogation dans une Relation d'Agence (Derogation Rule in an Agent-Principal Relationship)', **102-103** *Economie et Prévision*, 67-77.

Macho-Stadler, I. and Pérez-Castrillo, J. David (1993a), '¿Delegar o Centralizar? Qué dice la Economía de la Información? (What Economics of Information Say about Delegation and Decentralization?)', **52** *Cuadernos Económicos de ICE*, 25-46.

Macho-Stadler, I. and Pérez-Castrillo, J. David (1993b), 'Moral Hazard with Several Agents: the Gains from Cooperation', **11(1)** *International Journal of Industrial Organization*, 73-100.

Macho-Stadler, I. and Pérez-Castrillo, J. David (1994), *Random Audits in Tax Evasion Models*, W.P. UAB-IAE, No. 287.94.

Macho-Stadler, I. and Pérez-Castrillo, J. David (1996), 'Optimal Tax Auditing when Some Individuals Need Not File', *Economic Design*.

Macho-Stadler, I. and Pérez-Castrillo, J. David (1997a), *An Introduction to the Economics of Information: Incentives and Contracts*, Oxford, Oxford University Press, 277 p.

Macho-Stadler, I. and Pérez-Castrillo, J. David (1997b), 'Optimal Auditing Policy with Heterogeneous Income Sources', **38** *International Economic Review*, 951-968.

Macho-Stadler, I. and Verdier, T. (1989), 'Aspectos Estrategicos de la Separación Accionista-Gestor (Strategic Aspects between Corporate Ownership and Control)', **2(3)** *De Economía Pública*, 25-44.

Macho-Stadler, I., Martinez-Giralt, X. and Pérez-Castillo, J. David (1996), 'The Role of Information in Licensing Contract Design', **25** *Research Policy*, 25-40.

Macho-Stadler, I., Olivella-Cunill, P. and Pérez-Castillo, J. David (1993), *Tax Amnesties in a Dynamic Model of Tax Evasion*, W.P. UAB-IAE, No. 247.94.

Macho-Stadler, I., Pérez-Castillo, J. David and Ponsati, C. (1994), *Stable Multilateral Trade Agreements*, W.P. UAB-IAE, No. 281.94.

Mas-Colell, Andreu (1994), 'L'Anàlisi Econòmica i el Dret (The Economic Analysis and the Law)', **3** *Iuris*, 73-84.

Massaguer, Josep María (1994), 'La Regulación de Servisios Profesionales, (un Análisis de Racionalidad Económica y Legitimidad Antitrust) (The Regulation of the Professions' Economic Rationality and Antitrust Legitimacy)', **3** *Iuris*, 85-120.

Mercado Pacheco, Pedro (1994), *El Análisis Económico del Derecho. Una Reconstrucción Teórica* (Law and Economics. A Theoretical Reconstruction), Madrid, Centro de Estudios Constitucionales, 292 p.

Naharro Quirós, Elena (1987), 'La Regulación Jurídica de las Comarcas de alta Montaña y la Definición de los Derechos de Propiedad (The Law of the Highlands and the Definition of Property Rights)', **647** *Información Comercial Española*, 93-109.

Nugent, Jeffrey B. and Sanchez, Nicolás (1989), 'The Efficiency of the Mesta: A Parable', **26(3)** *Explorations in Economic History*, 261-284.

Ocaña, Carlos (1995), 'Mergers and Takeovers in Spain: Empirical Evidence on Abnormal Returns and Insider Trading', (forthcoming) *Journal of Business Accounting and Finance*.

Olivella, P. (1990), 'Una Introducción a la Delegación como Mecanismo de Compromiso

(An Introduction to Delegation to force Commitment)', **7-2** *Economía Pública*, 37-52.

Olivella, P. (1992a), 'Un Estudio de la Evasión Fiscal desde la Perspectiva de las Relaciones Principal-Agente (A Principal-Agent Approach to Tax Evasion)', **9-2** *Revista Española de Economía*.

Olivella, P. (1992b), *Las Amnistias Fiscales: Descripcion y Analisis Economico* (Economic Analysis of Tax Amnesties), Universitat autonoma de Barcelona.

Olivella, P. (1995), 'Information Structures and the Delegation of Monitoring', **39** *Annales d'Economie et de Statistique*, 1-32.

Olivella, P. (1996), *Tax Amnesties and Tax Evasion Inertia*, mimeo UAB.

Olivella, P. and Aron, D. (1994), 'Bonus and Penalty Schemes as Equilibrium Incentives Devices with Application to Manufacturing Systems', **10** *Journal of Law, Economics, and Organization*, 1-34.

Paredes, José Manuel (1995), *El Límite entre Imprudencia y Riesgo Permitido en Derecho Penal: ¿es Posible Determinarlo con Criterios Utilitarios?* (The Limit Between Negligence and Allowed Risk in Criminal Law: Is Utilitarianism of Any Help?).

Pastor, Santos (1982a), 'La Construcción Naval Española Veinte Años Después (The Shipbuilding Industry Twenty Years After: Dinamics and Regulation)', in Raga, José T. (ed.), *Homenaje al Profesor Lucas Beltrán*, Madrid, IEF.

Pastor, Santos (1982b), 'El Mercado de Transporte Marítimo en los Primeros Ochenta (The Maritime Transport in the Eighties: Problems and Policies)', **2** *Anuario de Derecho Marítimo*.

Pastor, Santos (1984a), 'Política Marítima Española: Valoración e Implicaciones de Futuro (The Regulation of the Shipping Industry)', in X (ed.), *Jornadas Sobre Transporte Marítimo y Política Económica*, Madrid, IETC-Ministerio de Transportes.

Pastor, Santos (1984b), 'Una Introducción al Análisis Económico del Derecho (An Introduction to Law and Economics)', **89** *Hacienda Pública Española*, 153-177.

Pastor, Santos (1986), 'Heroína y Política Criminal: Un Enfoque Alternativo (Heroin and Criminal Policy: An Alternative Approach)', in X (ed.), *La Problemática de la Droga en España; Análisis y Propuestas Político-Criminales*, Madrid, IUC y Edersa.

Pastor, Santos (1988a), 'Las Políticas de no Intervención Estatal en Economía: una Revisión (The State in a Market Economy: A Review)', **113** *Hacienda Pública Española*, 147-159.

Pastor, Santos (1988b), 'Estado, Mercado, Eficiencia y Equidad (The Market, the State, Efficiency and Equity)', in Corcuera, J. and Garcia Herrera, M.A. (eds), *Derecho y Economía en el Estado Social*, Tecnos & Gobierno Vasco.

Pastor, Santos (1989a), 'Derecho Penal, Política Criminal y Economía: un Intento de Generalización (Criminal Law, Criminal Policy and Economics)', **11** *Revista de la Facultad de Derecho de la UCM*.

Pastor, Santos (1989b), 'Fundamentos de Política Judicial (Foundations of Judicial Policy)', **1541** *Boletín de Información del Ministerio de Justicia*.

Pastor, Santos (1989c), *Economía y Sistema Jurídico. Una Introducción al Análisis Económico del Derecho* (Economics and the Legal System. An Introduction to Economic Analysis of Law), Madrid, Tecnos, 263 p.

Pastor, Santos (1989d), 'Derechos de Propiedad y Análisis Económico: ¿Nuevas Luces a Viejas Sombras? (Economics of Property Rights: Shading Lights?)', **38** *Economistas*, 28-35.

Pastor, Santos (1989e), 'Economía de la Justicia (I) (Economics of Litigation I)', **5** *Revista* *de Economía Pública*, 131-169.

Pastor, Santos (1990a), 'Elementos para un Análisis Económico de la Justicia: el Gasto Público en Justicia en España (Public Expenditure in the Courts: Reflections on Method and Scope)', *Hacienda Pública Española*, 155-174.

Pastor, Santos (1990b), 'A Propósito de la Eficacia del Gasto Público. Notas Sobre una Asignatura Pendiente del Sector Público Español (The Efficiency of Public Expenditure)', **680** *Información Comercial Española*, 151-157.

Pastor, Santos (1990c), 'Economía de la Justicia (II) (Economics of Litigation II)', **6** *Revista de Economía Pública*, 69-86.

Pastor, Santos (1990d), 'Economía de la Justicia en España (Problems in the Spanish Courts)', **4** *Revista de Economía*, 65-69.

Pastor, Santos (1990e), 'El Análisis Económico del Acceso a la Justicia (The Economics of Access to Justice)', **687** *Información Comercial Española*, 23-42.

Pastor, Santos (1991a), 'Informe Sobre la Litigación, Recursos y Acceso de los Cuidadanos a la Justicie (Report on Litigation, Courts Inputs and Access to Justice)', in Ministerio De Justicia (ed.), *Materiales Para una Reforma Procesal*, Madrid.

Pastor, Santos (1991b), 'Elementos para la Reforma Procesal: Análisis de la Litigación, oferta de Tutela Judicial, Dilación, Recursos Económicos y Acceso de los Ciudadanos a la Justicia (The Supply and Demand of the Courts Services: Empirical Evidence)', in Comisión General de Codificación (ed.), *Materiales Para Una Reforma Procesal*, Ministerio de Justicia, 87-353.

Pastor, Santos (1991c), 'Gasto Público en Justicia: una Nota Comparativa (Government Expenditure in the Court System: Comparative Evidence)', **3** *Presupuesto y Gasto Público*, 115-120.

Pastor, Santos (1991d), 'Law and Economics in Spain', **11** *International Review of Law and Economics*, 309-317.

Pastor, Santos (1993), 'Composición, Estructura y Características de la Litigiosidad Contencioso-Administrativa: Un Análisis Muestral (Litigation in Contentious -Administrative Courts. An Empirical Analysis)', **111** *Boletín de Información del Consejo General del Poder Judicial*, 205-288.

Pastor, Santos (1994), 'La Exigibilidad de las Normas y la Resolución de Conflictos (Law Enforcement and Dispute Resolution)', **3** *Iuris: Quaderns de Política Jurídica*, 155-174.

Pastor, Santos (1995), '¿Qué Hacer en los Conflictos Fiscales? Un Análisis Económico de las Propuestas de Actas de Conformidad (The Resolution of Tax Disputes)', **132** *Hacienda Pública Española*, 225-244.

Pastor, Santos (1997), 'El Impacto Económico de la Reforma (The Economic Impact of Judicial Reform)', in Jarquin, E. and Carrillo, F. (eds), *La Economía Política de la Reforma Judicial*, New York, Banco Interamericano de Desarrollo, 85-97.

Pastor, Santos and Gomez-Pomar, Fernando (1990), 'El Derecho de Accidentes y la Responsabilidad Civil: un Análisis Económico y Jurídico (Tort Law and Economics,)', **43-2** *Anuario de Derecho Civil*, 495-538.

Pastor, Santos and Pintos, Jesús (1992), 'La Economía y el Derecho: una Colaboración Difícil Pero Provechosa (The Interaction Between Law and Economics: Problems and Progress)', **13** *Revista de Economía*, 96-100.

Pastor, Santos, Ruiz-Huerta, Jesús and Loscos, Javier (1988), 'La Enseñanza de la Economía en las Facultades de Derecho (Teaching Economics to Law Students)', **73** *Revista de la Facultad de Derecho*, 595-607.

Pastore, Mario H. (1990), 'La Hipotesis de Domar sobre las Causas de la Sevidumbre o la Esclavitud en una Colonia Hispanoamericana: Contraste y Reformulación (Domar's Hypothesis on the Origins of Slavery in a Spanish Colony in America)', **8** *Revista de Historia Económica*, 575-589.

Paz-Ares, Cándido (1981), 'La Economía Política Como Jurisprudencia Racional (Political Economy as Rational Jurisprudence)', **34** *Anuario de Derecho Civil*, 601-707.

Paz-Ares, Cándido (1983a), 'Sobre la Infracapitalización de las Sociedades (On Infra-Capitalization of Corporations)', **36** *Anuario de Derecho Civil*, 1587-1369.

Paz-Ares, Cándido (1983b), 'Una Teoría Económica Sobre la Mercantilidad de la Compraventa (An Economic Theory for Sale Being Contract Law)', **36** *Anuario de Derecho Civil*, 943-996.

Paz-Ares, Cándido (1985a), 'Seguridad Jurídica y Seguridad del Tráfico (Legal Certainty and Exhange Certainty)', **175-176** *Revista de Derecho Mercantil*, 7-41.

Paz-Ares, Cándido (1985b), 'Seguridad Jurídica y Seguridad del Tráfico (Certainty in the Law and Secure Trade)', *RDM*, 7-41.

Paz-Ares, Cándido (1993), 'Principio de Eficiencia y Derecho Privado (Efficiency and Private Law)', in AA.VV., *Derecho, Moral y Eficiencia, III*, Jornadas de Filosofía del Derecho, Palma de Mallorca. Revisado en Estudios en homenaje a M. Brocheta Pont, Valencia 1995, III pp.

Paz-Ares, Cándido (1994a), 'Seguridad Jurídica y Sistema Notarial (Certainty in the Law and the Notarial System)', in X (ed.), *El Libro Colectivo de la Fé Pública*, Madrid, 73-134. Igualmente publicado el Iuris 1, 1994, pp. 351-372.

Paz-Ares, Cándido (1994b), 'La Infracapitalización. Una Aproximación Contractual (A Contractual Approach to Infracapitalization)', *Revista de Derecho de Sociedades, Número Extraordinario*, 253-269.

Paz-Ares, Cándido (1995a), *El Sistema Notarial. Una Aproximación Económica (An Economic Approach to The Notarial System)*, Madrid, Consejo General del Notariado, 153 p.

Paz-Ares, Cándido (1995b), 'The Conversión of Ordinary Shares into Non Voting Shares', **15** *International Review of Law and Economics*, 351-372.

Paz-Ares, Cándido (1996a), *La Ley, el Mercado y la Indepencia del Auditor* (The Law, the Market and Auditor's Independence), Madrid, Ed. Cívitas, 120 p.

Paz-Ares, Cándido (1996b), *¿Dividendos a Cambio de Votos? (Assessments for Votes)*, Madrid, McGraw-Hill, 180 p.

Pedraja, Francisco and Salinas, Javier (1995), 'La Eficiencia de la Justicia (The Efficiency of the Contentious-Administrative Courts)', **8** *Revista de Economía Aplicada*, 163-196.

Pérez-Castrillo, J. David (1990), 'Procesos de I+D y Estructura Industrial: un Panorama de Modelos Teóricos (Theoretical Models for R&D Procedures and Industrial Structure)', **6** *Economía Pública*, 171-214.

Pérez-Castrillo, J. David (1993), 'Una Panorámica de la Literatura de Contratos de Licencia (Survey on Licensing Contracts)', *Revista Española de Economía (Número Monográfico sobre Investigación y Desarrollo)*, 109-126.

Pérez-Castrillo, J. David and Verdier, T. (1992), 'A General Analysis of Rent Seeking Games', **73(3)** *Public Choice*, 335-350.

Pérez-Castrillo, J. David and Verdier, T. (1993), 'On Subsidizing R&D', *Revista Española de Economía (Número Monográfico sobre Investigación y Desarrollo)*, 9-20.

Pérez-Castrillo, J. David. and Sandons, J. (1996), 'Disclosure of Know-How in Research Joint Ventures', **4** *International Journal of Industrial Organization*.

Pintos Ager, Jesús (1998a), *Responsabilidad Civil y Reparación sin Culpa. Un Análisis Jurídico y Económico de las Alternativas Globales y las Reformas Parciales Mediante Baremos*, Tesis Doctora inédita en el departamento de derecho privado y de la empresa de la universidad Carlos III de Madrid.

Pintos Ager, Jesús (1998b), 'Sobre la Convenienca y la Constitucionalidad del Sistema de Valoración del Daño Personal de la Ley 30/1995', **4458** *La Ley*.

Portellano, Pedro (1995a), *La imitación en el Derecho de la Competencia Desleal* (Mimic in Competition Law), Madrid, Editorial Cívitas, 645 p.

Portellano, Pedro (1995b), 'La Valoración del Sistema de Patentes: una Enseñanza para el Derecho de la Competencia Desleal (Valuing the Patent System: a Lesson for Competition Law)', **604-605** *Revista General de Derecho*, 625-637.

Portellano, Pedro (1996), *Deber de Fidelidad de los Administradores de Sociedades Mercantiles y Oportunidades de Negocio* (Fidelity Commitment of Corporation Managers and Bussiness Oportunities), Madrid, Editorial Cívitas, 143 p.

Puy Fraga, Pedro (1987), 'El Programa de la Economía Constitucional: Una Síntesis (The Constitutional Economics Program: an Abstract)', **192** *Revista de Derecho Financiero y Hacienda Pública*, 1181-1194.

Puy Fraga, Pedro (1988), 'A Framework for a Public Choice Analysis of the European Community', in Faiña Medén, J. Andrés, *Economia delle Scelte Pubbliche*, 141-158.

Puy Fraga, Pedro (1991a), 'Contractualismo y Justicia (Contractualism and Justice)', in Otero, M., Rovira, C. and Segura, M. (eds), *Problemas de la Ciencia Jurídica. Homenaje a Francisco Puy Muñoz*, Santiago, Servicio de Publicacións da Universidade de Santiago de Compostela, 269-289.

Puy Fraga, Pedro (1991b), 'La Influencia de la Economía en el Derecho, Veinticinco Años Después (The Influence of Economics on the Law)', in Puy Fraga, P. (ed.), *Estudios en Homenaje al Profesor Carlos Otero Díaz*, Santiago, Servicio de Publicaciones de la Universidad de Santiago, 541-575.

Puy Fraga, Pedro (1992a), 'La Economía Política del Servicio Militar (Political Economy of Recruiting)', **219** *Revista de Derecho Financiero y Hacienda Pública*, 471-500. edición, Boletín de Información del Ministerio de Defensa, n§ 227, 1992, p. 9-29. 2nd edn, Monografías del Ceseden: Cuatro aspectos de la defensa nacional, Ministerio de Defensa, Madrid, 1993, páxs. 137-165.

Puy Fraga, Pedro (1992b), 'Comment on the Political Economy of Current European Integration', in Vosgerau, H.J., *European Integration in the World Economy*, Heildelberg, Springer, 707-716.

Puy Fraga, Pedro (1992c), 'Presentación a El Modelo Económico del Comportamiento Humano (Presentation to the Economic Model of Human Behaviour)', in Frey, B.S. and A. Serna, Dereito, *Revista Xurídica da Universidade de Santiago de Compostela, vol. I*, 197-200.

Puy Fraga, Pedro (1993a), *Análisis Económico del Derecho y la Política* (Economic Analysis of Law and Politics), Santiago de Compostela, Fundación Alfredo Brañas, 224 p.

Puy Fraga, Pedro (1993b), 'Busqueda de Rentas en el Sector Público, o una Teoría Económica de la Corrupción Política (Rent Seekers in the Public Sector: An Economic Theory for Corruption)', in Puy Fraga, P. (ed.), *Análisis Económico del Derecho y de la Política*, Santiago de Compostela, Fundación Alfredo Brañas, 149-172.

Puy Fraga, Pedro (1993c), 'O Procedemento Administrativo como Factor na toma de Decisións Públicas, (Comentarios desde a economía política á Lei 30/1992 do 26 de

Novembro, de réxime xurídico das administracións públicas e do procedemento administrativo común) (The Role of Administrative Procedure in Public Decision Making)', **5** *Revista Galega de Administracion Publica*, 163-181.

Puy Fraga, Pedro (1994a), 'Elección Pública y Estado del Bienestar (Public Choice and Welfare State)', in Caramés, Luis (ed.), *La Crisis del Estado del Bienestar*, Santiago de Compostela, Asociación Galega de Estudios de Economía do Sector Público, 481-506.

Puy Fraga, Pedro (1994b), 'Corrupción Pública e Economía Política (Public Corruption and Political Economy)', **19** *Análise Empresarial*, 13-21.

Puy Fraga, Pedro (1994c), 'Indices de Voluntariedad para el Servicio Militar: Una visión desde la economía política (Voluntary Indexes from a Political Economy Approach to the Mandatory Military Service)', in F. Fernández Segado (ed.), *El Servicio Militar: Aspectos Jurídicos y Socioeconómicos*, Madrid, Editorial Dikynson, 275-295. Reedición e traducción do artig.: 'Indices de voluntariedade e custos do servicio militar: Unha visión desde a economía política', Revista Galega da Economía, vol. 2, n§ 1, 1993, páxs. 231-243.

Puy Fraga, Pedro (1995a), 'Democracia Representativa e Reforma Constitucional (Representative Democracy and Constitutional Reform)', in Fernández Leiceaga, Jordán Rodríguez, M., Iglesias, E. López, Deza, X. Vence (eds), *Estudos en Homenaxe ó profesor Xose Manuel Beiras Torrado*, Universidade de Santiago de Compostela, 141-161.

Puy Fraga, Pedro (1995b), *Economía y Política en Yugoslavia (1945-1990): el Fracaso de un Experimento de Organización Económica y Social* (Economics and Politics in Jugoslavia (1945-1990): A failed Experiment of Social and Economic Organization;La crisis de los Balcanes, monografías del CESEDEN), Madrid, Ministerio de Defensa.

Puy Fraga, Pedro (1995c), *Economía Constitucional y Constitución Española de 1978* (Constitutional Political Economy and The Spanish Constitution of 1978*)*, Santiago de Compostela, edición en microficha, Servicio de Publicaciones da Universidade de Santiago de Compostela.

Puy Fraga, Pedro (1995d), *Economía en Broma y en Serio* (Economics for Fun and Serious), Madrid, Minerva, Fundación Alfredo Brañas, 163 p.

Puy Fraga, Pedro (1995e), 'Economía en Broma y en Serio Consideraciones sobre la Aplicabilidad del Homo Economicus (Economics for Fun and Serious)', in Corona, Ramón and Puy, Fraga (eds), *Economía en Broma y en Serio*, Madrid, Minerva - Fundación Alfredo Brañas, 29-57.

Puy Fraga, Pedro, Suárez, A. Iglésias and Ron Romero, Ron J. (1985), 'Una Nota Sobre los Problemas que Plantea la Imposición Autonómica y la Municipal (A note on Autonomic and Local Taxes)', in X (ed.), *Actas de la X Reunión de Estudios Regionales, T. II, Asociación Española de Ciencia Regional - Junta de Castilla León*, 901-909.

Reumer, Andrés (1996), *Análisis Económico del Derecho* (Economic Analysis of Law), Mexico, Fondo de Cultura Económica, Sociedad Mexicana de geografía y Estadística, e Instituto Technológico Autónome de México.

Ruesca, Santos M. (1982), 'La Economía Irregular en el Mercado de Trabajo (Irregular Economy in the Labour Market)', **587** *Información Comercial Española*, 91-102.

Ruesca, Santos M. (1986), 'Economía Oculta: de la Definición y los Métodos de Estimación (Underground Economy: Definition and Estimation Methods)', in X (ed.), *Problemas Estadísiticos de la Economía Sumergida*, Madrid, Instituto Nacional de Estadística, 25-48.

Ruesca, Santos M. (1987), *La Economía Sumergida en España* (Underground Economy in

Spain), Revista del Instituto de Estudios Económicos.

Ruiz-Huerta Carbonell, Jesús (1992), 'Vigencia y Operatividad del Principio de la no Confiscatoriedad de los Tributos en el Ordenamiento Español (The Principle of Non Confiscation of Taxes: Enforcement in Spain)', **64** *Crónica Tributaria*.

Ruiz-Huerta Carbonell, Jesús (1994), 'The Dimension, Effectiveness and Efficiency of Public Expenditure', in X (ed.), *National Budgeting for Economic and Monetary Union*, European Institute of Public Administration, 195-199.

Ruiz-Huerta Carbonell, Jesús (1995), 'Las Rentas de las Personas Mayores (Eldest Citizens' Income)', in X (ed.), *Las Actividades Económicas de las Personas Mayores*, Madrid, Secot, 201-234.

Ruiz-Huerta Carbonell, Jesús and Giménez, Antonio (eds) (1993), *Estructura Institucional y Gestión del Gasto Público en Algunos Páises de la OCDE* (Institutional Structure and Managment of Public Expenditure in Some Countries), Madrid, Instituto de Estudios Fiscales, 591 p.

Ruiz-Huerta Carbonell, Jesús, Alvarez, Jesús, Ayala, Luis, Iriondo, Iñaki, Martinez, Rosa and Palacios, Juan Ignacio (1996), *La Distribución Funcional y Personal de la Renta en España* (Functional and Personal Distribution of Income in Spain), Premio de investagión 1995 del Consejo Económico y Social.

Saiz Gonzalez, J. Patricio (1996), *Invención, Patentes e Innovación en España (1759-1878)* (Invention, Patents and Innovation in Spain 1759-1878), Tesis doctoral en el Departamento de Historia Contemporanea, Universidad Autónoma de Madrid.

Salas, Vicente (1987), *Economía de la Empresa. Decisiones y Organizaciones* (Economics of Business Decisions and Organizations), Barcelona, Ed. Ariel, 411 p.

Salinas, Javier (1994), *Presupuestos y Financiación de la Unión Europea* (Coordination of Budget Policy Through Legislation), Valladolid, Editorial Lex Nova.

Salinas, Javier (1980), 'Traducción e Introducción a la Versión Española (The Calculation of Consensus)', in Buchanan, James M. and Tullock, Gordon (eds), *El Cálculo delConsenso*, Madrid, Ed. Espasa Calpe.

Salinas, Javier (1991), *Economía Política del Federalismo Fiscal Español* (Political Economy of the Spanish Fiscal Federalism), Madrid, Instituto de Estudios Fiscales, 179 p.

Salinas, Javier (1993), *Economía Política Constitucional de los Presupuestos Públicos* (Constitutional Political Economy of the Budget), Madrid, Tecnos.

Salinas, Javier (1994), *Pensiones y Seguridad Social. ¿Un futuro incierto?* (Pensions and Social Security: An Uncertain Future?), Madrid, Barklays Pensiones.

Salinas, Javier (1995a), 'Racionalidad Económica y Derecho Presupuestario (Economic Rationality and Budget Law)', **132** *Hacienda Pública Española*, 245-252.

Salinas, Javier (1995b), 'Economía Constitucional de la Descentralización del Sector Público en España (Constitutional Economy of Descentralization of the Spanish Public Sector)', in Capítulo del libro, *La Financiación de las Comunidades Autonomas, Análisis y Orientación desde la Teoría del Federalismo Fiscal*, Valladolid, Consejeria de Economía, Junta de Castilla y León, 29-54.

Salinas, Javier (1995c), 'La Financiación del Sector Público en España: el Bienestar de los Ciudadanos y el Estado de Bienestar (Financing the Public Sector in Spain: Citizens Welfare and Welfare System)', in X (ed.), *La Financiación de la Economía Española*, 54-70.

Salinas, Javier (1995d), 'Gasto Público y Bienestar Social: el Caso Español (Public Expenditure and Welfare State: The Spanish Case)', **45** *Revista de Derecho Financiero* *y Hacienda Pública*, 743-761.

Salinas, Javier (1996a), 'Economía Constitucional de la Política Fiscal Española y la Convergencia Europea (Constitutional Economy of Spanish Tax Policy and European Covergence)', in X (ed.), *Proceedings, XVIII Jornadas de la Dirección General del Servicio Juridico del Estado sobre la Constitución Española y el Ordenamiento Comunitario Europeo*, Madrid, Ministerio de Justicia.

Salinas, Javier (1996b), *Elementos Institucionales de la Organización Territorial del Sector Público en Castilla y León* (Institutional Elements of the Public Sector's Territorial Organization in Castilla and Leon), Valladolid, Consejería de Economía, Junta de Castilla y León.

Salvador Coderch, Pablo (1987), *¿Qué es Difamar?. Libelo Contra la ley del Llibelo* (Defamation. The Law on Libel), Madrid, Editioral Cívitas, 114 p.

Salvador Coderch, Pablo (1990), *El Mercado de las Ideas* (The Market for Ideas), Madrid, Centro de Estudios Constitucionales, 549 p.

Salvador Coderch, Pablo (1993), *El Derecho de la Libertad* (Liberty Rights), Madrid, Centro de Estudios Constitucionales, 64 p.

Salvador Coderch, Pablo, Lloveras, Ferrer et al. (1995), 'Del Servicio Público al Servicio a la Comunidad (From Public Service to Service for the Community)', **136** *Revista de Administración Pública*, 69-117.

Sánchez, Isabel (1990), 'Evasión Fiscal, Regulación y Mecanismos Optimos de Inspección (Tax Evasion, Regulation, and Optimal Auditing Mechanisms)', **45** *Cuadernos Económicos de ICE*, 121-143.

Sánchez, Isabel (1991), 'Provisión Voluntaria de Bienes Públicos: Resultados Experimentales (Volutantary Contributions to Public Goods: Experimental Results)', **11** *Economía Pública*, 191-218.

Sánchez, Isabel (1993), 'Hierarchical Design and Enforcement of Income Tax Policies', **50** *Journal of Public Economics*, 345-369.

Sánchez, Isabel (1994), *Determinantes Individuales de la Evasión Fiscal: un Enfoque Experimental* (Individual determinants of Tax Evasion: an Experimental Approach), monografía, Instituto de Estudios Fiscales.

Sánchez, Isabel (1995a), 'Experimental Analysis of Individuals' Tax Compliance Rate', in de Juan, A. (ed.), *Frontiers in Economic Psychology, proceedings of the IAREP Conference*, Agosto.

Sanchez, Isabel (1995b), 'Unravelling the Puzzle of Tax Compliance Using Experimental Methods', **48** *Kyklos*, 3-18.

Sánchez, Isabel and Zapater, I. (1986), 'Diseño Dinámico de Contratos (Dynamic Contract Design)', *Investigaciones Económicas,* 117-142.

Sanjiao Otero, Francisco Javier (1991), 'Una Aproximación al Estudio de los Ciclos Político Económicos (Political-Economic Cycles)', in Puy Fraga, P. (ed.), *Estudios en Homenaje al Prof. Carlos G. Otero Diaz*, Universidade de Santiago de Compostela, 657-673.

Sanjiao Otero, Francisco Javier (1993), 'Decisións Políticas e Ciclos Económicos (Political Decisions and Economic Cycles)', in X (ed.), *Análisis Económico del Derecho y de la Política*, Fundación Alfredo Brañas, 173-190.

Sanjiao Otero, Francisco Javier (1994), 'Economía de las Instituciones: Análisis de la Política Museística en 'Galicia (Economics of Institutions: Policy on Museums in Galicia)', **3** *Dereito, Revista Xurídica da Universidade de Santiago de Compostela*, 127-158.

Sanjiao Otero, Francisco Javier (1995a), 'El Dinero de Talía y Melpómene: un Análisis

Económico del Mundo 'Teatral (Talia and Melpomene's Money: Economic Analysis of the Theatre)', in Corona, Ramón and Puy, Fraga (eds), *Economía en Broma y en Serio*, Madrid, Minerva - Fundación Alfredo Brañas, 107-132.

Sanjiao, Otero and Francisco, Javier (1995b), 'Análise Económico das Medidas Públicas para o Fomento do Teatro Privado Galego (Economic Analysis of Public Policy to Promote Private Galician Theatre)', in Leiceaga, Fernández, Jordán, Rodríguez, López, Iglesias and Vence, Deza (eds), *Estudos en homenaxe ó profesor Xose Manuel Beiras Torrado*, Universidade de Santiago de Compostela, 439-460.

Torres López, Juan (1983a), 'Recensión del Libro (A Review of) Law and Economics, de R. Hirsh', **2** *Revista de la Facultad de Derecho de la Universidad de Granada.*

Torres López, Juan (1983b), 'Recensión de la (A Review of) 'International Review of Law and Economics', **3** *Revista de la Facultad de Derecho de la Universidad de Granada.*

Torres López, Juan (1984a), 'Recensión del Libro, El Coste de los Accidentes (A Review of, The Cost of Accidents)', **4** *Revista de la Facultad de Derecho de la Universidad de Granada*, 175-179.

Torres López, Juan (1984b), 'Tradición y Resultados de una Disciplina Novedosa: La Economía del Derecho (Tradition and Outcomes of Law and Economics)', **5** *Revista de la Facultad de Derecho de la Universidad de Granada*, 27-40.

Torres López, Juan (1985), 'Las Críticas a la Corriente Mayoritaria en el Análisis Económico del Derecho (Critizisms Against the Mainstream in Law and Economics)', *Valladolid.*

Torres López, Juan (1987a), *Análisis Económico del Derecho. Panorama doctrinal* (Survey on Law and Economics), Madrid, Editorial Tecnos, 108 p.

Torres López, Juan (1987b), 'Tradición y Resultados de una Disciplina Novedosa: la Economía del Derecho. Una Orientación Bibliográfica (Tradition and Outcome of a New Discipline: The Economics of Law. A Guide to the Literature)', **5** *Revista de la Facultad de Derecho de la Universidad de Granada.*

Torres López, Juan (1989), 'Derechos de Propiedad, Poder y Mercado (Property Rights, Power and Market)', **38** *Economistas*, 22-26.

Torres López, Juan (1992), 'Regular la Información, Problemas Económicos, Perspectivas Jurídicas (Economic and Legal Issues in the Regulation of Information)', **14** *Revista de Economía*, 89-94.

Valdeón Buruque, Julio (1994), 'La Mesta y el Pastoreo en Castilla en la Baja Edad Media, 1273-1473 (The Mesta in the Low Medieval Age 1273-1473)', in Gonzalo Anes y Angel García Sanz (eds), *Mesta, Trashumancia y vida Pastoril*, Madrid, Sociedad V Centenario del Tratado de Tordesillas, 49-64.

Vázquez Vega, Pablo (1990), 'Grupos de Interés en la Comunidad Económica Europea. Apuntes Sobre un Regulación Actual (The Regulation of Interest Groups in the European Community)', **687** *Información Comercial Española*, 89-102.

Vázquez Vega, Pablo (1992), *Análisis Económico de las Organizaciones Internacionales* (Economic Analysis of International Organizations), Universidad Complutense.

Vázquez Vega, Pablo (1995), *Institutions and Postwar Economic Growth in Europe*, Working Paper, Departamento de Economía Universidad de Cantabria, n.95.06.

Vázquez Vega, Pablo (1996), '¿Discriminación Positiva? La Reforma del Impuesto de Sociedades en el Pais Vasco (Positive Discrimination? Corporate Tax Reform in Euskadi)', *Revista de la Camara de Comercio, Industria y Navegación.*

0390
LAW AND ECONOMICS IN SWEDEN

Göran Skogh
Professor of Economics, Department of Managment and Economics, Linköping University

Abstract

The European law and economics movement started early in Sweden. However, the dialogue between economists and lawyers has developed slowly, if at all. The reluctance toward economics in the law schools can be explained by the strong influence emanating from 'legal realism and positivism'. Moreover, scholars with a law degree have most limited training in social sciences. Although law and economics has only exerted a marginal impact on legal education, it has nonetheless influenced the Swedish political debate.
JEL classification: K00
Keywords: Law and Economics, Scandinavian Realism, Education, Research.

1. Introduction

During 1974-77, a Law and Economics seminar took place at the Department of Economics and at the Faculty of Law at the University of Lund. The first international conference in Law and Economics in northern Europe was held in 1977, and a conference volume ensued, *Acta Societatis Juridicae Lundensis* (1977). Thus, the European law and economics movement started early in Sweden.

The first doctoral dissertation in law and economics in Sweden was defended at the University of Lund (see Skogh, 1973). Thereafter, several dissertations have been presented by economists, for example Soeria-Atmadja (1983), Bjuggren (1985), Schuller (1986), Fahlbeck (1996), Bolin (1996), Berggren (1997), Hägg (1998) and by lawyers, for example Samuelsson (1991), Runesson (1996) and Domeij (1998).

Nevertheless, the dialogue between academic economists and lawyers has developed slowly, if at all. Nowadays, there are no regular law and economics seminars at any Swedish university. Nonetheless, there are three fully accredited law schools in Sweden: at the universities of Lund, Stockholm and Uppsala. Other universities and colleges offer partial programs in law. There is one chair in Economics (shared with the economics department) at the Faculty of Law at the University of Stockholm. There used to be a similar chair in Economics at the law faculties of the Universities of Lund and Uppsala, but the chairs have been withdrawn.

Law students traditionally take an obligatory introductory course in economics. This course was reduced in the 1970s from around ten weeks to four weeks of full-time study. Swedish textbooks in economics for law students are Skogh (1977), Werin (1982, 1997), Höglund (1984), Bjuggren and Skogh (1990), Skogh and Lane (1993), and Bergström and Samuelsson (1997). Also international textbooks are used. Law students are, thus, to some extent acquainted with the economics of property rights, risk-sharing, and so on. The normal period of study for a law degree is four-and-a-half years. Swedish law students have no previous university training (such as the bachelor's degree in the USA). Hence, the Swedish lawyer gains very little training in the social sciences.

2. Scandinavian Realism

The reluctance to include more than rudimentary courses in economics in the law schools can be explained by the strong influence emanating from the 'legal realist' school in Sweden. Scandinavian legal realism is sometimes called the 'Uppsala School'. Its founding father was Axel Hägerström, a philosopher at the University of Uppsala during the first decades of the century. Hägerström's attention was directed to law and ethics as sources of metaphysics, which he found meaningless and unscientific. Important members of the Uppsala School were Alf Ross (1968, 1971) and Karl Olivecrona (1939). For an overview of Scandinavian realism, including selected translations into English, see Lloyd (1972, pp. 497-560), and Ryssdal (1995).

According to Olivecrona, the scientific study of the law should be a study of empirical facts. He dismissed notions such as the existence of (natural) individual rights or property rights as fantasies of the mind. Scandinavian realists were extreme positivists in that they tried to eliminate all metaphysical, ideological and normative elements in the study of the legal order.

Scandinavian legal realism has influenced legal thinking and legal education for most of the twentieth century. Lawyers and legal philosophers who wanted to protect natural, traditional, or moral rights were regarded as conservative, backward, or sometimes even misled by legal or moral metaphysics. Teaching at the law faculties was largely the positive study of actual law *de lege lata*, while the study of the philosophy of law and the social function of law *de lege ferenda* was limited. Courses in jurisprudence were short and were dominated by legal realism, at least until the mid 1970s. The possibility of using scientific principles to study general (natural) principles of law was ruled out in elementary textbooks (see Malmström, 1986). Thus, the academic lawyer was trained as a technician, a specialist in knowledge of the actual legal documents and in interpretation of the aims of legislators. The study of law in society was left to sciences and arts outside the law faculties, such as Philosophy, History, Sociology, Political Science and Economics. This does not say that the Scandinavian realists did not take part in the legal policy debate. Indeed, from the 1920s to the 1960s, several of the most influential realists were members of Parliament and/or ministers in several Social Democratic governments.

3. The Legal and Economic Profession

As noted above, the study of social sciences at law schools is minimal. Consequently, most scholars with a law degree have limited knowledge of social sciences, mathematics, or statistics. This may appear somewhat paradoxical, given realism's advocacy of a purely positive and empirical legal science.

The recruitment of lawyers to the courts is made within the judicial system. Besides legal training, other qualifications have low value, which tends to isolate judges from other professional groups (see Ryberg, 1989). Lawyers in high-level positions in public administration are to a large extent recruited from the courts. Hence, there may be a similar bias in public administration. There may also be a political bias among lawyers - all higher positions are filled through appointment by the government. Loyalty to the general ideology on which the welfare state is based may thus be maintained. The same tendencies exist in law schools. Law professors are commissioned to appoint professors to faculties of law, which may favour the preponderance of traditional, welfare-oriented lawyers. There are no private law schools.

The separation of the study of economics from law is mainly a post-war phenomenon. Earlier, research in economics, and especially in public finance, took place at law faculties. For instance, Knut Wicksell (1958), who made seminal contributions to the economics of constitutional and tax law, was professor of Economics at the Faculty of Law in Lund in the beginning of the twentieth century. The presence of economics at law faculties might have helped to spread the law and economics movement in Sweden. However, just the opposite has occurred. The common pool of knowledge between lawyers and economists diminished as economics became more and more influenced by mathematics and statistics. For a long time now, the two disciplines have isolated themselves from each other, even though they once coexisted within the same faculty. Economics research has adapted Anglo-American scientific values, with results normally published in international journals. Most law professors, on the other hand, do not publish in English. Their writing is generally limited to legal investigations and to textbooks written in Swedish (see Ståhl, 1989). Because of this difference, some economists occasionally question the competence of lawyers. Lawyers, on the other hand, are critical of economic analysis of law. Exceptions, however, are Hellner (1988) and Roos (1981, 1990) that notes the relevance of economic analysis of law. One reason for the reluctance may be that Swedish academic lawyers lack understanding of economic methods, and another may be that the contributions Swedish economists have made to law have been limited.

The mutual distrust has to some extent been transmitted to law and economics research. Economic analysis of law is not regarded as mainstream economics. Nevertheless, there is an interest in institutional economics, and as long as the analysis of institutions is based on generally accepted methods, economic analysis of law is accepted within the profession.

Applied economics, in cooperation with lawyers or adapted for them, has little professional status among academic economists. Similarly, cooperation with economists is of low professional value in the legal profession. Nevertheless, a number of scholars are working on law and economics problems at various institutions. In addition to what has been mentioned above, work by Holmén (1993), Eklund (1995) and Bjuggren (1992, 1995) should be noted. Moreover, the Stockholm School of Economics has an Economics Department and a Law Department interested in the field. Some smaller business schools and universities have also shown an interest in law and economics, especially Linköping University and Jönköping International Business School. Finally, the private Center for Business and Policy Studies (SNS) has conducted a number of law and economics projects: see, for instance, Bergström and Rydqvist (1992) and Macey (1994).

4. The Impact of Law and Economic Thinking

The Political Debate

Although law and economics has only exerted a marginal impact on legal education, it has nonetheless influenced Swedish society in a number of ways.

Legal rule-making is based mainly on legislation, prepared by public administrators and adopted by Parliament. Politics, lobbying and public opinion are important determinants of the outcome of this process. Here, economics plays an important role. The impact of lawyers on legal rules is mainly indirect, occurring through administration and through the wording and interpretation of statutes. To the extent that lawyers participate in the general political debate, they do so either as specialists in a defined field of law or as contributors to the general political debate.

For a long time the main issue in Swedish politics has been the public sector. The Social Democrats in power have expanded the public sector, while the conservative (non-Socialist) parties generally argue in favour of a smaller public sector, decentralisation and increased reliance on markets. The opposition also favours protecting private property and constraining the government through constitutional reforms. Economists have been influential in this debate. Arguments resting on public choice, the economics of regulation, the theory of property rights and law and economics have frequently been used to attack the Social Democrats. A few years ago, when the bourgeoisie parties came into power, they included the protection of property rights in the constitution. This has contributed to giving law and economics an image of being right-wing.

Criminal Law

Economic reasoning has also influenced specific legal fields. Until the early 1970s, the criminological debate was dominated by 'sociological' and 'medical' schools, which held that the purpose of sanctions was to treat the individual and to make the criminal less inclined to commit crimes. Punishment did not appear to deter, and general deterrence was not analysed in detail. In the mid 1970s, the 'classical' school experienced a renaissance: punishment was to be proportional to the harm of the crime and not only related to the criminal's need for treatment. General deterrence was again regarded as important (see Brottsförebyggande Rådet, 1975), and the criminal code was adjusted, accordingly.

Although it is not possible to identify clearly the connection between changes in criminal policy and the economics of crimes, it can be argued that the connection existed. The first publications in law and economics in Swedish were on the economics of crime (see Skogh, 1973; Skogh and Stuart, 1982a, 1982b). Swedish criminologists and criminal lawyers in the Ministry of Justice were familiar with Gary Becker's (1968) work and the subsequent empirical literature on deterrence. The Swedish debate was also influenced indirectly through international changes in favour of the 'classical' school's belief that punishment should parallel harm.

National factors also had an impact on the rapid change in Swedish attitudes toward general prevention. One such factor was that criminals formed an association, KRUM, which claimed to represent prisoners. KRUM rejected the idea that criminals were mentally ill or incapable of rational decisions. It wanted prisoners to be regarded as rational and argued in favour of time-limited sentences instead of time-unlimited treatment. In the 1970s, there was also an increased interest in white-collar crimes, drug-related crimes, tax evasion, and other 'calculated' crimes. For such crimes, deterrence may be the most obvious reason for punishment.

Tort law

One of the major goals of the Social Democratic party has been to build up an extensive public insurance system. Health insurance, disability insurance, unemployment insurance, and pension schemes today cover most personal economic losses. Such insurance is mainly financed through taxes and is independent of negligence.

Opponents have argued that damages are an important tool for preventing accidents. The counter-argument from Social Democratic politicians and some influential lawyers has been that the tort system is slow, unsophisticated, and expensive. It has also been argued that the preventive effect of damages is unproved, (see Hellner, 1985).

Economic analysis of accident law was introduced in Sweden two decades ago, (see Skogh, 1977, 1998a, 1998b). In general, there has been a political reluctance to change the public system of undifferentiated, no-fault insurance schemes. However, attitudes have changed among lawyers, (see Roos, 1990). One reason for the change in political attitudes is that costs of compensating people for losses of earnings due to sickness have increased sharply. A reform instituting deductibles for employees and employers has been introduced and extended. An immediate effect was a significant reduction in the absence at the workplace. The traffic and disability insurance systems are now under debate (see Bladini, 1994).

5. Concluding Remarks

Although law and economics came to Sweden more than two decades ago, it has not yet become an integral part of legal research. The Scandinavian doctrine of legal realism, together with various institutional obstacles, may explain why. There is no reason, however, to be overly pessimistic about the future of law and economics in Sweden. Several positive factors ought not be overlooked. First, especially young academic lawyers are interested in applying economics to law. In the law schools, there appears to be dissatisfaction with traditional legal realism and formalistic positivism. Second, membership in the EU and the presence of international common law trends influence the legal scholars. Third, the application of economic analysis to ongoing legislation is fruitful, which is likely to have an impact on legal education and research in the long run.

Bibliography on Law and Economics in Sweden (0390)

Acta Sociatatis Juridicae Lundensis (1977), 'Law and Economics. Report from a Symposium in Sweden', **28** *Juridiska Föreningen i Lund.*

Berggren, Niclas (1997), *Essays in Constitutional Economics. Dissertation*, Stockholm School of Economics.

Bergström, Clas and Rydquist, Kristian (1992), *Marknaden för Företagskontroll* (The Market for Corporate Control), Stockholm, SNS förlag.

Bergström, Clas and Samuelsson, Per (1997), *Aktiebolagets Grundproblem* (Basic Problems of the Limited Liability Firm), Nerenius & Santérus Stockholm.

Bjuggren, Per-Olof (1985), *A Transaction Cost Approach to Vertical Integration: The Case of the Swedish Pulp and Paper Industry*, Lund Economic Studies.

Bjuggren, Per-Olof (1992), 'The Effects of Contractual Restriction on Industrial Organization: The Case of Swedish Pulpwood Transactions', *International Review of Law and Economics*, 517-532.

Bjuggren, Per-Olof (1995), 'A Transaction Costs Perspective on Financial Distress and Capital Structure', *International Review of Law and Economics*, 395-404.

Bjuggren, Per-Olof and Skogh, Göran (eds) (1990), *Företaget. En Kontraktsekonomisk Analys* (The Firm. A Contractual Approach), SNS Publishing company.

Bladini, Filip (1994), 'Trafik och Arbetsskador - ett Reformförslag Utifrån Läran om Ekonomisk Prevention (Damages in Traffic and at the Workplace - a Reform Based on the Theory of Economic Prevention)', *Svensk Juristtidning*, 632-672.

Bolin, Kristian (1996), *An Economic Analysis of Marriage and Divorce*, Lund Economic Studies.

Brottsförebyggande Rådet (1975) , 'General Deterrence', **2** Report, 2 ff.

Domeij, B. (1998), *Läkemedelspatent* (Pharmaceutical Patents in Europe), Dissertation, Department of Law, Stockholm University.

Eklund, Ronnie (1995), 'Contract Labour in the Nordic Countries', **3** *Juridisk Tidskrift*.

Fahlbeck, Erik (1996), *Essays in Transaction Costs Economics' Dissertation*, Swedish University of Agricultural Sciences.

Hägg, Göran, P.T. (1998), *An Institutional Analysis of Insurance Regulation. The Case of Sweden. Dissertation*, Department of Economics, University of Lund.

Hannesson, Rögnvaldur (1974), 'Varför Fiskegränserna bör Utvidgas (Why the Fishing Borders Have to be Expanded)', **5** *Ekonomisk Debatt*.

Hellner, Jan (1978), 'Rättsekonomi, Avbeställning och Coase-Teorem (Law and Economics, Cancellation and Coase Theorem)', **24** *Juridiska föreningen i Lund*.

Hellner, Jan (1985), *Skadeståndsrätt*, 4th edn (Law of Torts), Stockholm, Almqvist and Wiksell International.

Hellner, Jan (1988), 'Lagstiftning och Forskning inom den Centrala Förmögenhetsrätten (Legislation and Research in Civil Law)', *Svensk Juristtidning*, 169-180.

Höglund, Bengt (1984), *Spelet om Resurserna i den Svenska Blandekonomin* (The Swedish Mixed Economy), Lund, Dialogos.

Holmén, Camilla (1993), *Rätten till Offentliga Personuppgifter. En Kontraktsekonomisk Analys* (The Right to Personal Information in Public Registers. A Contractual Analysis), Department of Economics, University of Lund.

Lundgren, Nils and Lönn, H. (1980), 'Gör Hyresrätt till Bostadsrätt (Transform Rent Contract to Ownership)', *Ekonomisk Debatt*.

Macey, Jonathan R. (1994), *Svenskt Bankväsendes Framtida Utveckling* (Future Development of the Swedish Banking System), Stockholm, SNS forlag.

Myhrman, Johan (1981), 'Kontraktsrätt och löntagarfonder (Contractual Rights and Labour Funds)', **6** *Ekonomisk Debatt*.

Myhrman, Johan, Hörngren, Lars, Viotti, Staffan and Eliasson, Gunnar (1987), *Kreditmarknadens spelregler (The Rules of the Game on the Credit Market)*, SNS Publishing Company.

Myhrman, Johan, Petrén, Gustav and Strömholm, Stig (1987), *Marknadsekonomins Rättsliga Grundvalar* (The Legal Foundations of the Market Economy), Timbro.

Roos, Carl Martin (1981), *On Insurer Generosity*, Scandinavian Studies in Law.

Roos, Carl Martin (1990), *Ersättningsrätt och Ersättningssystem* (Compensation Right and Compensation System), Stockholm, Nordstedts.

Runesson, Eric M. (1996), *Rekonstruktion av oFullständiga Avtal. Särskilt om Köplagens Reglering av Risken för Okade Prestationskostnader* (Reconstruction of Incomplete Contracts in Trade Law), Juristförlaget, Stockholm.

Ryberg, Lena (1989), *Domarkarriären* (The Career of Judges), Juristförlaget, Stockholm.

Samuelsson, Per (1991), *Information och Ansvar. Om Börsbolagens Ansvar* (Information and Remedies. Listed Companies and Their Responsibility for False and Misleading Information in the Stock Market), Stockholm, Norstedt.

Samuelsson, Per and Skogh, Göran (1989), 'Juridisk Forskning i Gränsområdet mot Ekonomi - Exemplet Insiderhandel (Legal Research and Economics - The Example of Insider Trading)', in Basse, Ellen Margrethe (ed.), *Regulering og Styring - en Juridisk Teori og Metode-bog*, 91-110.

Schuller, Bernd Joachim (1986), *Ekonomi och Kriminalitet. En Empirisk Undersökning av Brottsligheten i Sverige* (Economics and Crime. Emperical Research in Sweden), **17** Economic Studies.

Skogh, Göran (1971), *En Samhällsekonomisk Mål-Medel-Analys Av Butikssnatterie, Appendix 1* (An Economic Analysis of Shoplifting), SOU.

Skogh, Göran (1973), *Staffrätt och Samhällsekonomi* (Criminal Law and the Economy), Lund Economic Studies.

Skogh, Göran (1975), 'Vilken är den Rättvisa Räntan? Kritisk kommentar till förslag om räntelag (What is the Fair Interest Rate? Critical Commentary on a Law Proposal Concerning Interest Rates)', *Svensk Juristtidning*, 116-121.

Skogh, Göran (1976), 'Ett Alternativ till den Föreslagna Konsumentkreditlagen (An Alternative to the Proposed Consumer Credit Law)', *Svensk Juristtidning*, 542-547.

Skogh, Göran (1977), *Priser, Skadestånd och Straff* (Prices, Damages and Penalties), Malmö, Liber.

Skogh, Göran (1978), 'Konsumentlagstiftningen i Rättsekonomisk Belysning (The Consumer Legislation from a Law and Economics Perspective)', in X (ed.), *Festskrift till Per Stiernquist*, Juridiska Föreningen i Lund.

Skogh, Göran (1979), 'Kontraktsteoretisk Oversikt (Contract Theory - a Survey)', **1** *Statsökonomisk tidskrift*.

Skogh, Göran (1980), 'Straffvärdering enligt Välfärdsekonomiska Principer (Penalty Assessment According to Welfare-economic Principles)', **2** *Påföljdsval, Straffmätning och Straff värde*.

Skogh, Göran (1982a), 'Public Insurance and Accident Prevention', **2** *International Review of Law and Economics*.

Skogh, Göran (1982b), 'Den Osynliga Handen och Lagens Långa Arm (The Invisible Hand and the Law's Long Arm)', **8** *Ekonomisk Debatt*.

Skogh, Göran (1982c), *Marknadens Villkor* (The Terms of the Market), Stockholm, Timbro.

Skogh, Göran (ed.) (1984), *Vem Skall Bestämma Over skog och Mark? (Who is Going to Decide Over Forest and Land?)*, Lund, Dialogos.

Skogh, Göran (1985a), 'Äganderätten och Lagstiftningen om Markresurserna (Property Rights and Legislation on Land Resources)', *Svensk Juristtidning*.

Skogh, Göran (1985b), 'Rättssäkerhet i Marknadsekonomin (Legal Certainty in the Market Economy)', in Segerstedt, Tetal (ed.), *Rättssäkerhet och Demokrati*, Ratios Förlag.

Skogh, Göran (1988), 'Äganderättens Ekonomi och Politik (The Economics and Politics of Property Rights)', *Politiskt-Filosofiska Sällskapets årsskrift.*

Skogh, Göran (1991), 'Law and Economics in Sweden', **11** *International Review of Law and Economics*, 319-324.

Skogh, Göran (1995), *Ekonomiskt Ansvar vid Kärnkraftsolyckor* (Liability at Nuclear Accidents), Rapport till Energikommissionen, SOU 1995:140, bil. 25.

Skogh, Göran (1998a), 'Development Risks and the Insurability of Industrial Hazards', **a** *Geneva Papers on Risk and Insurance*, 247-265.

Skogh, Göran (1998b), 'Insurance and Liability', in X., *Encyclopedia of Law and Economics*, Edward Elgar and University of Gent.

Skogh, Göran and Lane, Jan Erik (1993), *Äganderätten i Sverige. En Lärobok i Rättsekonomi* (Property Rights in Sweden), SNS Förlag.

Skogh, Göran and Samuelsson, Per (1985a), *Konsumentpolitik* (Consumer Policy), Stiftelsen Marknadsekonomiskt Alternativ för Sverige.

Skogh, Göran and Samuelsson, Per (1985b), *Splittring eller Sammanhållning i Svensk Försäkring* (Disruption or Unity in Swedish Insurance? An Economic and Legal Analysis of the Marketing Agreements etc.), Lund, Dialogos.

Skogh, Göran and Stuart, Charles (1982a), 'A Contractarian Theory of Property Rights and Crime', **1** *Scandinavian Journal of Economics.*

Skogh, Göran and Stuart, Charles (1982b), 'An Economic Analysis of Crime Rates, Punishments and the Consequences of Crime', **39** *Public Choice.*

Skogh, Göran, P.O. Bjuggren et al. (1989), *Företaget. En Kontraktsekonomisk Analys* (The Firm. A Contractual Analysis), SNS Förlag.

Soeria-Atmadja, S. (1982), 'Handlar Konsumentombudsmannen Alltid i Konsumenternas Intresse?' (Do the Consumers' Representatives Always Protect the Consumers' Interests?)', **4** *Ekonomisk Debatt.*

Soeria-Atmadja, S. (1983), *Product Guarantees and Liability Rules: an Economic Analysis. Disseration*, Department of Economics. University of Stockholm.

Ståhl, Ingemar (1976), 'Ägande och Makt i Företagen - en Debattinledning, Nationalekonomiska Föreningens Förhandlingar (Ownership and Power in the Firms - An Introduction to Debate, the Economics Association's Negotiations)', **1** *Ekonomisk Debatt.*

Ståhl, Ingemar (1989), *Några Data om Forskning och Utbildning vid Juridiska Fakulteter* (Some Data on Research and Education at Law Faculties), Unpublished, Department of Economics, Lund University.

Werin, Lars (1978), 'Expropriation - en Studie i Lagstiftningsmotiv och Ersättningsrättsliga Grundprinciper (Expropriation - A Study in Legislative Motives and Compensatory Basic Principles)', *Svensk Juristtidning*, 81-120.

Werin, Lars (1982), *Ekonomi och Rättssystem* (Economy and Legal System), Malmö, Liber.

Werin, Lars (1997), *Economic Incentives and the Legal Order*, Unpublished manuscript.

Wicksell, Knut (1958), 'A New Principle of Just Taxation', *Finanztheoretische Untersuchungen.* Musgrave and Peacock, 1958, 72-118

Wijkman, P.M. (1974), 'Kampen om Jordens Allmänningar (The Struggle for the Common Land on Earth)', *Ekonomisk Debatt.*

Other References

Becker, Gary (1968), 'Crime and Punishment: An Economic Approach', *Journal of Political Economy*, 169-217.

Lloyd, Lord of Hampstead (1972), *Introduction to Jurisprudence*, 3th Edition, London, Steams and Son.

Macey, Jonathan (1993), *Corporate Law and Corporate Governance in Sweden*, SNS förlag, Stockholm.

Malmström, Åke (1986), *Civilrätt* (Civil Law), Malmö, Liber.

Olivecrona, Karl (1939), *Law as Facts, 2nd edn*, 1971, Copenhagen and London.

Ross, Alf (1968), 'Directive and Norms', in Honderick, T. (ed.), *International Library of Philosophy and Scientific Method.*

Ross, Alf (1971), *Om Ret og Retfaerdighet. En införelse i den analytiske retsfilosofi* (On rights and Justice. An introduction to the Analytical Legal Philosophy), *3rd edn*, Nyt Nordisk Forlag, Copenhagen.

Ryssdal, Stray A.C. (1995), *Legal Realism and Economic Behaviour. A Scandinavian Look at Economic Analysis of Law*, Oslo, Juridisk Forlag.

0395
LAW AND ECONOMICS IN SWITZERLAND

Bibliography Collected by the Editors

Adams, Michael (1985), *Ökonomische Analyse des Gefährdungs- und Verschuldenshaftung* (Economic Analysis of Strict and Fault Liability), Heidelberg, R.v Decker's/C.F. Müller, 310 p.

Adams, Michael (1986), 'Der Irrtum über "künftige Sachverhalte" - Anwendungsbeispiel und Einfürhung in die ökonomische Analyse des Rechts', *RECHT, Zeitschrift für Juristische Ausbildung und Praxis*, 14-23.

Baudenbacher, Carl (1983), 'Echtliche Grundprobleme der Allgemeinen Geschäftsbedingungen (Standard Term Clauses: Basic Problems of Economic, Liability and Procedural Law)', in Zurich, Schulthess (ed.), *Wirtschafts- Schuld- und Verfahrens*.

Baudenbacher, Carl (1985), *Rechtsverwirklichung als ökonomisches Problem? Zur Überlastung der Zivilgerichte* (Enforcement of Law as an Economic Problem? On the Overload of the Civil Courts, Zurich) Schulthess.

Borner, Silvio (1979), 'Wirtschafts- Sozial- und Eigentumsord nung um Verfassungsentwurf: Ein Diskussionsbeitrag aus ökonomi scher Sicht (Economic, Social and Property Structure in the Constitutionial Bill: A Contribution to the Discussion from an Economic Viewpoint)', **98** *Zeitschrift für Schweizerisches Recht*, 463-479.

Eisen, Roland (1986), 'Wettbewerb und Regulierung in der Versicherung Die Rolle asymmetrischer Information (Competition and Regulation in Insurance: The Role of Asymmetrical Information)', **122** *Schweizerische Zeitschrift für Volkswirtschaft und Statistik*, 339-358.

Felder, St. (1989), 'Sind Externalitäten in Jeden Fall zu Internalisieren? (Are Externalities Always to Internalize?)', **125** *Schweizerische Zeitschrift für Volkswirtschaft und Statistik*, 189-193.

Frey, Bruno S. (1990), *Ökonomie ist Sozialwissenschaft. Die Anwendung der* (Economics is a Social Science. The Use of Economic), München, Vahlen.

Frey, Rene L. (1987), 'Wirtschaftswachstum und Umweltqualitat: Auf der Suche nach einer neuen Wachstumspolitik (Economic Growth and Environmental Quality: In Search of a New Growth Policy)', **123** *Schweizerische Zeitschrift für Volkswirtschaft und Statistik*, 289-315.

Frey, René L. and Leu, Robert E. (1987), 'Waldsterben: von der Naturwissenschaftlichen Analyse zur Umweltpolitik (The Death of the Forest: From a Natural Sciences Analysis to Environmental Policy)', **39** *Wirtschaft und Recht*, 58-72.

Hertig, Gerard (1991), 'Law and Economics in Civil Law Countries: Switzerland', **11** *International Review of Law and Economics*, 293-300.

Iten, R., Maggi, R., Schelbert-Syfrig, Heidi and Zimmerman, Andreas J. (1989), 'There is no Such Thing as a Free Lunch', **125** *Schweizerische Zeitschrift für Volkswirtschaft und Statistik*.

Janssen, Martin and Hummler, Konrad (1979), *Bundesverfassung und Verfassungsentwurf, Eine ökonomisch-rechtliche Analyse* (Constitution and Revision of the Constitition, An Economic and Legal Analysis), Schriften des Schweizerischen Aufklärungs-Dienstes.

Junod, Charles-André (1988), 'L'Indexation des Crédits Hypothécaires Pourrait-elle à la Fois Améliorer le Fonctionnement du Marché du Logement et Servir de Correctif à l'Inflation? (Could the Indexation of Mortgage debt Improve the Functioning of the Housing Market and Serve to Correct the Inflation)', **40** *Wirtschaft und Recht*, 88-123.

Kleinewefers, Henner (1987), 'Ökonomische Theorie des Rechts, Über Unterschiede Zwischen dem Okonomischen und dem Juristischen Denken (Economic Theory of Law, On the Differences between)', in X (ed.), *Staat und Gesellschaft, Festschrift für Leo Schürm*, Fribourg, Universitätsverlag, 83-116.

Kramer, Ernst A. (1979), 'Konsumentenschutz als neue Dimension des Privat- und Wirtschaftsrecht (Consumer Protection as a New Dimension of Private and Economic Law)', **98** *Zeitschrift für Schweizerisches Recht*, 49-92.

Meier-Schatz, Christian (1987), 'Unternehmenszusammenschlüsse mittels Übernahmeangebot (Mergers by Takeover Bid)', **39** *Wirtschaft und Recht*, 16-39.

Meier-Schatz, Christian (1988), 'Über die Notwendigkeit Gesellschaftsrechtlicher Aufsichtsregeln, Ein Beitrag zur Ökonomischen Analyse des Gesellschaftsrechts (On the Necessity of Rules for the Supervision of Corporations, A Contribution to the Economic Analysis of Company Law)', **1** *Zeitschrift für Schweizerisches Recht*, 1-241.

Meier-Schatz, Christian (1989a), *Wirtschaftsrecht und Unternehmenspublizität* (Economic Legislation and Enterprise Publicity), Zurich, Schulthess.

Meier-Schatz, Christian (1989b), 'Europäische Harmonisierung des Gesellschafts- und Kapitalmarktrechts (European Harmonization of Company and Capital Market Law)', **41** *Wirtschaft und Recht*, 84-110.

Pommerehne, Werner W. (1983), 'Steuerhinterziehung und Schwarzarbeit als Grenzen der Staatstatigkeit (Tax Evasion and Underground Activities as Limits of Government's Growth)', **119** *Schweizerische Zeitschrift für Volkswirtschaft und Statistik*, 261-284.

Richli, Paul (1985), 'Handels- und Gewerbefreiheit contra Energiepolitik (Freedom of Trade and Industry versus Energy Policy)', **86** *Schweizerisches Zentralblatt für Staats- und Verwaltungsrecht*, 1-14.

Robert, Philippe and Godefroy, Thierry (1977), *Le Coût du Crime ou l'Economie Poursuivant le Crime* (The Cost of Crime or Economics Prosecuting Crime), Genève, Masson, 225 p.

Ruffner, Markus (1990), *Neue Wettbewerbstheorie und schweizerisches Ka* (New Competition Theory and Swiss Antitrust Law, Possibilities and Limitations of a Market and Institutionalist Foundation of Competition Policy), Zurich, Schulthess.

Schelbert-Syfrig, Heidi and Zimmermann, Andreas J. (1988), 'Konkurrenz und Umweltschutz. Wald und Holzwirtschaft zwischen Okonomie und Okologie (Competition and Environment Protection. Forest and Forestry Between Economics and Ecology)', **124** *Schweizerische Zeitschrift für Volkswirtschaft und Statistik*, 289-302.

Schelbert-Syfrig, Heidi, Lang, Th., Buse, I., Henzman, J., Maggi, R. and Iten, R. (1988), *Wertvolle Umwelt* (Valuable Environment), Zurich, Schriftenreihe Wirtschaft und Gesellschaft der Zürcher Kantonalbank, September.

Schürmann, Leo (1976), 'Konjunkturpolitik und freie Wechselkur se (Conjuncture Policy and Free Exchange Rate)', in X (ed.), *Schweizerische Wirtschaftspolitik zwischen gestern*, Bern, Haupt, 265-277.

Schürmann, Leo (1990), 'Der Wettbewerb im Urteil der Staatswissenschaft (The Competition in the Judgment of Economics)', **42** *Wirtschaft und Recht*, 35-41.

Sieber, Hugo (1981), 'Wirtschaftsfreiheit und Wirtschaftspolitik (Festschrift für Hans Huber zum 80. Geburtstag) (Economic Freedom and Economic Policy)', in X (ed.), *Recht als Prozess und Gefüge*, Bern, Haupt, 447-465.

Stolz, Peter (1983), 'Das Wiedererwachte Interesse der Ökonomie an Rechtlichen und Politischen Institutionen (The Renewed Interest of Economics in Legal and Political Institutions)', **119** *Schweizerische Zeitschrift für Volkswirtschaft und Statistik*, 49-67.

Vuaridel, Roger (1986), 'L'Objet et le Niveau de la Concurrence dans la Théorie Economique et dans la Jurisprudence (The Object and Level of Competition in Economic Theory and in Jurisprudence)', **20** *Wirtschaft und Recht*, 111-128.

Weck-Hannemann, Hannelore and Pommerehne, Werner W. (1989), 'Einkommenssteuerhinterziehung in der Schweiz. Eine empirische Analyse (An Empirical Analysis of Income Tax Evasion in Switzerland)', **125(4)** *Schweizerische Zeitschrift für Volkswirtschaft und Statistik*, 515-556.

Wiegang, Wolfgang (1988), 'Die Rezeption Amerikanischen Rechts (The Reception of American Law)', in X (ed.), *Die Schweizerische Rechtsordung in ihren Internationalen Bezügen*, Bern, Haupt, 229-262.

0400
METHODOLOGY: GENERAL

Heico Kerkmeester
Associate Professor
Erasmus University of Rotterdam

Abstract

Most disputes on the methodology of law and economics have been initiated by critical scholars from disciplines outside the field itself, such as practitioners of law and literature and critical legal studies. This chapter reviews the literature on the methododology of law and economics.

It discusses, among others, the following issues: the object of law and economics, the measuring rod (money versus utility), positive and normative law and economics, and the scientific value of law and economics
JEL classification: K00.
Keywords: Positive and Normative Law and Economics, Scientific Value, Method and Object.

1. Law and Economics: Method and Object

Law and economics does not differ from other fields of study in the respect that over time different schools of thought have come into existence. Such schools include Chicago Law and Economics, Public Choice Theory, Institutional Law and Economics and Neoinstitutional Law and Economics (Mercuro and Medema, 1997). It has been argued, however, that most legal economists follow a pragmatic, eclectic, approach and that with a few exceptions, it is hard to fit them in a particular school of which they faithfully follow the rules. The economic approach to law is based on a limited number of assumptions that themselves may be amended if an alternative set of assumptions would fit the particular object of study better (De Geest, 1994). Therefore, a review of the methodology of law and economics must concentrate on the ideas that are shared by the vast majority of the people working in this field, although attention will be paid to the cases in which alternative viewpoints have been defended by major scholars. Remarkably, most disputes on the methodology of law and economics have been initiated by critical scholars from disciplines outside the field itself, such as practitioners of law and literature and critical legal studies.

Disputes on the proper definition of object and method of law and economics are not completely absent, but there seems to be a consensus among most of its practitioners. The fundament of this consensus is Gary Becker's (1976) argument that economics should be defined according to its method, rather than to its object of study. According to Becker, this method is the rational choice approach. Students of law and economics sometimes summarize this approach in just four words - 'people maximize, markets clear' (Baird, 1997) - but besides maximizing behavior and market equilibrium, the economic rational choice approach also comprises the assumption of stable preferences.

The rational choice approach can be and is applied to almost any object of study where choices are made, including for example criminal activities, sexual behavior and animal behavior. The notion of market clearance or market equilibrium refers to the fact that because demand rises if prices go down, supply rises if prices go up, and vice versa, the market will tend towards a situation where supply equals demand at a particular equilibrium price.

Equilibria will not only result on explicit markets such like the stock exchange, but also on implicit markets such as the market for criminal activities or the marriage market, which in law and economics are more than just metaphors. If the price of criminal activities goes up, due to for example a stricter criminal law, demand will go down, and similarly the demand for marriages will go down if the price rises (Becker, 1991).

Law and economics can be defined as the economic analysis of law, and therefore as the application of the rational choice approach to law. In accordance with the textbook definitions, the term law here refers to statutes, judge-made law, treaties and customary law. However, not only the law itself is studied, but also the way it came into existence and, in particular, its effects.

Law and economics is closely related to neo-institutional economics, but as Ronald Coase (1994) has shown, it is possible to distinguish both. Coase argues that while law and economics demonstrates how economics is important for the study of the law, neo-institutional economics focuses on the importance of institutions - mainly the firm, the market, and of course the law - that are important for the understanding of the economic system. Coase predicts that over time the fields will diverge from each other and increasingly will become the domain of specialists. Initially, a lot of insight in the law is gained by the understanding that people make choices and, therefore, economists are able to contribute to the understanding of the law. Once lawyers get familiar with the basic concepts of economics, however, their superior understanding of the object of study will enable them to surpass economists working in the same field. Lawyers will be able to refine the method and thereby improve on the study of the particular object. Over time this will be required in order to advance law and economics.

The people who are assumed to maximize are individual people. This is to say that the individual action is the basic unit of analysis, so that the action of collective actors like firms or states should be analyzed in individual terms. This principle, known as methodological individualism, is just an analytical tool and in itself does not have ethical implications in the sense that the interests of individuals *ought* to be maximized.

Moreover, methodological individualism does not require that individuals are nontuistic in the sense that they only take their own wellbeing into account when they make decisions. It is true that in most economic analysis of law the assumption of rationality implies nontuism, but this is clearly an example of an assumption that may be amended without violating the essence of an economic analysis. In the context of family law, for example, it is usually assumed that parents are altruistic towards their children (Becker, 1991). Neither does methodological individualism imply that individuals are assumed to make their decisions in isolation from others. The idea that individuals choose in the context of social interactions is made explicit when game theory is used as a method of economic analysis, as nowadays is often the case (Kerkmeester, 1995).

It has been argued that human rationality is bounded in the sense that it is limited by a lack of information or of abilities to process information. An alleged consequence is that people do not maximize but are satisfied with reaching a certain aspiration level of utility. However, in mainstream law and economics issues of information may be taken into account by acknowledging that acquiring and processing information is costly and that, therefore, a rational individual deliberately will limit the collection of information (Posner, 1993a).

Recent developments in law and economics extend its realm beyond the context of markets by analyzing the consequences of social norms. The existence of social norms can be the basis for an explanation of human behavior, alternative to the rational choice approach. In some cases the best predictions may be yielded by the assumption that individuals choose certain acts because it is the norm to do so, rather than that they would base their actions on an outcome-oriented evaluation of costs and benefits (Elster, 1989). Within law and economics, social norms have particularly attracted attention since Ellickson (1991) showed that, different from what the Coase theorem predicts, individuals do not bargain towards an efficient solution on the basis of clearly defined rights that function as starting point for negotiations. Rather they simply follow social norms that often, although not always, help to obtain efficient outcomes.

Many attempts have been made to show that social norms themselves may be the results of rational choices (Becker, 1996; Cooter, 1998).

2. The Measuring Rod: Money Versus Utility

If people maximize, *what* do they maximize? Two 'measuring rods' are widely used in law and economics.

The first is utility, a term referring to the preferences of individuals: the more a particular item is preferred, the higher is by definition the utility that it yields to the individual. Everything can be measured in terms of utility, including for example leisure, love, altruistic feelings, the adherence to norms, and so on. It is even conceivable that someone derives utility from losing his money. What individuals prefer and to which extent they do so, is a matter of personal taste in which economics does not interfere: *de gestibus non est disputandum* (Becker, 1996).

The most important arguments for the use of utility rather than money are derived from the axiom of diminishing marginal utility, that says that the utility gained from successive units of a commodity diminishes. The same can be argued with regard to money, in the sense that an additional euro will yield less utility than the last one. If the axiom holds, this has consequences for the attitude of individuals toward risk. If twice the amount of money does not yield twice the amount of utility, an individual will prefer the certainty of a particular amount of money above a gamble with a 50 percent chance of getting the double amount and a 50 percent chance of receiving nothing. However, the axiom does not always hold and, moreover, in some contexts individuals may not be risk-avoiders but be neutral towards risk, or even risk-seekers in the sense that they prefer a gamble with a certain expected value over the certainty of this value.

An important drawback of utility is that it is hard to make interpersonal comparisons if such a subjective measuring rod for utility is used. This is why the use of the Pareto criterion is defended. The definition that a change will result in a Pareto improvement if at least one person will be better off and no person will be worse off than before avoids the need for making interpersonal comparisons. A solution is Pareto optimal if no further Pareto improvements can be made. The Pareto criterion is to be distinguished from the Kaldor-Hicks criterion that states that a change results in a wealth improvement if the winners gain more than enough to compensate the losers, whereby however such a compensation need not take place in fact.

While as a logical statement the assumption that an individual is engaged in the maximization of utility is true by definition and therefore a truism, the same assumption clearly is unrealistic as an empirical statement. Ronald

Coase (1994) compares the use of the term utility in economic models with the use of the term aether in classical physics. It is not observable, but only called in because it is required to make the traditional model work.

The fact that all behaviors can be explained in terms of utility is an advantage, but at the same time another drawback of its use. The only way to determine someone's utility function is to observe his behavior. If, however, the utility function thus derived will be used to predict the behavior of the same individual, circularities are bound to occur. No matter how unusual one's behavior, it always can be 'explained' by assuming that it maximizes utility. This helps to understand the importance of rational choice theory's assumption that preferences are stable during the period under consideration.

The most obvious alternative for the use of utility is money, as is preferred by both Coase and Posner, and this use has clearly some advantages. In the first place the assumption that, other things being constant, people prefer more money over less and always like to have more, is among the most realistic assumptions that can be made. Because, however, some individuals may form an exception to this rule, the circularity inherent in the statement that individuals maximize utility is avoided. Interpersonal comparisons are easier to make with money than with utility. Although a dollar may not mean the same to person A as to person B, at least it is the same dollar. This possibility is particularly important in normative law and economics. In order to avoid the restrictions of the Pareto criterion that as was noted above, only allows for a change if nobody is worse off as a result, Richard Posner (1992) defends the use of the principle of wealth maximization. The measure is the willingness to pay: if goods and other resources are in the hands of the persons who were willing and able to pay the highest amount for this, wealth is maximized. Willingness to pay is not a pure expression of the preferences that an individual has towards a particular item. It may be the case that although A has more intense preferences with regard to an item than B has, still B may be willing to pay more for it, for the simple reason that he has more money available. There is a speculative element in it since the offering prices one needs to know to determine willingness to pay are not always observable.

Alternatives

There has not been much attention for the use of alternatives to money or utility in law and economics. This neglect contrasts with the extensive discussions in economics and in ethical discourses. A source of alternatives for money is fed by some authors' argument against welfarism, that is the idea that the social ordering of different situations should depend on the utility that individuals derive in those different states of the world (Roemer, 1996). An important problem is that individuals may have 'perverse' preferences, for example deriving utility from torturing someone else, or expensive tastes. For positive purposes this is not a point, but it causes difficulties as soon as utility maximization is regarded as something that should be promoted (Posner, 1979).

The alternatives presented not only counter welfarism, but also provide better opportunities for interpersonal comparisons. Examples are John Rawls' well-known concept of primary goods and Amartya Sen's functionings. Functionings refer to what goods can do for people, which is not only yielding individual utility, but also escaping death, being nurtured, getting self-respect, participating in community life, and so on. The point is not that those functionings could be measured in terms of utility, because of course they can, but that they themselves can be measured more objectively than is possible with utility. However, for most economic analyses of law, it is doubtful whether the advantages just mentioned outweigh the costs of a more complicated approach.

Criticisms

The economic assumptions regarding utility or wealth maximization have been the main objects of attacks by critics of law and economics. The criticisms have focused on the positive as well as the normative use of the assumptions.

The mainstream ideas about maximizing behavior are based on the assumption that desires and opportunities are independently given (Kerkmeester, 1992). It may, however, be the case that desires are influenced by opportunities. Dworkin (1980) points at the possibility that because of the familiar 'grass is greener' phenomenon, social wealth may be increased by a transfer from A to B, but because of the resulting change in preferences then again may be increased by transferring the item back from B to A. Even more common is the situation in which on the contrary someone will ask more for something he owns than he would pay to acquire it. This has become known as the endowment effect and as such it has received its place in the economic analysis of law (Sunstein 1997a).

Particularly vexing for economists is the sour grapes effect, named after the fable of the fox who, when he discovered that he could not reach certain grapes, did not want them because they were sour anyway (Elster, 1979). The effect is important for a judgement of the assumption of wealth maximization but it conflicts with the equally important assumption that preferences are stable.

Some authors have argued that the unidimensionality of measuring in terms of utility or money fails to take the complexity of human motivation into account. Martha Nussbaum (1997) argues that in law and economics too much attention is paid to variables that are measurable, at the expense of other factors that may play no lesser role in determining human action. According to Robin West (1988) legal economists fail to reckon with the warmth and empathy that characterizes human relations. The use of Kaldor-Hicks efficiency in law and economics, however, implies the assumption that it is possible to obtain sufficient insight in the preferences of others to determine what one needs to get in order to be compensated for a loss (De Geest 1994). Therefore, it is doubtful whether West's criticism holds against mainstream law and economics.

All the previous remarks are based on the idea that the assumptions regarding utility or wealth maximization do not provide for a realistic description of the complexities of human behavior in the real world. One response from law and economics could be that its assumptions can be - and often are - made to be more in accordance with reality. In particular, Gary Becker's (1996) recent work on tastes shows willingness to incorporate the possibility of changes in preferences into the economic model. A different response, however, could be that unrealism of assumptions is not necessarily a bad thing. The latter point will be returned to in Section 4.

Most reactions have been provoked by Richard Posner's principle of wealth maximization. The most influential of these reactions is Ronald Dworkin's (1980) comment.

In the first place Dworkin notes that willingness to pay for an item is not only determined by preferences for the item, but also by ability to pay. Therefore, a scarce item may end up in the hands of a rich man who barely needs it, rather than with a poor soul who desperately needs it, but simply cannot afford to pay the same amount. This situation is in accordance with the principle of wealth maximization, while total utility is not maximized.

In the second place, wealth maximization may lead to outcomes that can be regarded as unfair. This is the case in the example mentioned above, but outcomes can also be unfair in cases in which total utility is maximized but unequally divided.

In the third place, Dworkin argues that the principle of wealth maximization interferes with individual autonomy as would be guaranteed by individual rights. He mentions a case in which A attaches a higher value to an item than owner B does. A benevolent dictator then would maximize wealth by taking the item from B and giving it to A.

The allegation that law and economics does not recognize rights that is implicit in the last remark is clearly unjustified, and Dworkin himself mitigated his criticism in this respect. As the importance of the notion of property rights within law and economics shows, rights do play an important role. Dworkin's remarks certainly have their merits, but it should be noted that a normative law and economics does not stand or fall with Posner's wealth maximization. Posner (1980) himself insisted that the principle of wealth maximization is in accordance with individual autonomy.

3. Positive and Normative Law and Economics

Due to the discussion above it has become obvious that it is important to try to distinguish between positive and normative law and economics. This issue is particularly important for an evaluation of the position of law and economics as a scientific discipline. In other words: it should be clear whether law and economics regards statements about how the law and its effects are, or about how they ought to be.

A possible point of view is that both are possible (Friedman, 1987). A positive analysis explains the law, predicts its effects and thereby indicates which legal rule as a matter of fact will be efficient. These results of a positive analysis can then be used for normative purposes, such as the prescription of the efficient rule.

The approach leading to normative statements has been aptly characterized by James Buchanan's (1990) words 'the ought is derived from the presumed is'. A legal economists starts with assumptions about human behavior. Correct predictions of human behavior and the way it is influenced by the law are required for decisions on how the law should be. Therefore, the discussion about the realism of assumptions that will follow in the next paragraph will be relevant for both positive and normative law and economics.

However, not everyone is satisfied with the idea of a co-existence of positive and normative law and economics. Some argue that only a positive economic analysis of law is possible (De Geest 1994). The efficiency of a legal rule is regarded to be a factual issue, and that it thus can be determined objectively. To argue that therefore this rule is desirable is to add a value judgement that is not a part of an economic analysis.

A point of view that is even more radical is that economics is a strictly positive science, while law is a strictly normative undertaking, and that therefore law and economics cannot go together (Couwenberg et al. 1980).

The opinions just cited lose ground, however, as soon as it is acknowledged that a science is not necessarily positive and that this is particularly true for the economic science. Coase gives the example of an economist predicting that a certain measure, namely collectivization of agriculture, will lead to mass starvation. In Coase's opinion it is absurd to state that the economist is not able to make a statement about whether this particular measure is desirable or not. The idea that the making of value judgements is better left to others is rejected by Coase (1994), since he believes that economists and others share many values and economists thus are able to make acceptable value judgements on their own.

Coase's opinion is supported by the fact that nowadays many economists are no longer reluctant to acknowledge that they are engaged in a normative undertaking. In particular, the relation between economics and ethical issues as the just distribution of welfare has been the subject of study (Roemer, 1996). It could well be argued that if economics could be normative anywhere it is in the context of the economic analysis of law.

Several authors (for example Raes 1990) even argue that an economic analysis always is normative, at least implicitly. Their argument is that if legal economists focus so much on efficiency, this shows that they believe laws *should be* efficient or that at least efficiency is an important and desirable characteristic. An even more critical approach to the allegedly normative contents of law and economics is put forward from critical legal studies and law and literature. Both are currents in American legal theory that have been particularly aimed at unmasking law and economics as a biased - inherently conservative, right-wing - movement (Kelman, 1987; Duxbury, 1995; Mercuro and Medema, 1997).

4. The Scientific Value of Law and Economics

Inductive versus Deductive Approaches

In the previous paragraph it was argued that the relation between theory and the empirical world is not only important in positive law and economics, but also if a normative point of view is taken. According to the famous words of Oliver Wendell Holmes, which are often quoted in law and economics: 'experience not logic is the life of the law'.

Two extreme viewpoints are possible as to the relation mentioned above. The most common is the application of the deductive method, of which the rational choice approach is an example. Deduction implies that the focus is from theory to reality, that is starting with making assumptions, deriving hypotheses from them, and testing these hypotheses by confronting them with the results of empirical observations.

The alternative is an inductive approach, that is to say focusing from reality to theory. One starts with making empirical observations, making generalizations in order to develop a theory. In his criticisms on the use of assumptions in law and economics, which use is inherent to the deductive approach, Ronald Coase defends the inductive alternative that he has been practicing himself. Coase accuses the followers of the deductive approach of practicing 'blackboard economics', that is having the conviction that a model that is drawn on the blackboard obviously has meaning for the real world. An example is given by the provision of lighthouses, which according to economic models are classical examples of public goods for which the government should provide. Coase (1988) showed that empirical, inductive, research led to the conclusion that in fact in England for centuries there been a profitable private provision of lighthouses.

The predominance of deductive approaches in law and economics has also resulted in criticisms from law and literature (Gaakeer and Kerkmeester, 1997). By focusing on generalizations rather than on individual cases, law and economics allegedly overlooks aspects that make every case unique (White, 1987).

Given the dominance of the deductive approach in law and economics, the debate on the position of assumptions in law and economics deserves closer scrutiny. The usual point of view is that for several reasons the realism of assumptions is irrelevant. In the first place an economic theory of law that captures its full complexity would not be a theory, but a description (Posner, 1992).

The most principled as well as influential counterargument is based on Milton Friedman's (1953) ideas about the role of assumptions in positive economics that have become part of the dominant methodology in law and economics. Friedman argues that the realism of a model should not be tested on the level of the assumptions underlying it, but on the level of the hypotheses derived from the model. Therefore, what counts is whether a model predicts well, in other words whether the predictions derived from the model (the hypotheses) are in accordance with empirical observations.

A frequent comment on the rationality assumption, namely that real people are not rational in the sense that they make deliberate calculations, calculating with lightning speed can be countered by pointing at Friedman's argument. It is not relevant whether people really calculate, but whether their behavior can be predicted correctly on the basis of a model that is made *as if* those calculations are made and decisions are based upon them.

An extreme viewpoint of Friedman that has become known as the 'F-twist', is that assumptions even *should be* unrealistic, because that is what makes them general enough to yield fruitful predictions.

Friedman's methodological paper has evoked a large amount of comments. An argument against the use of Friedman's methodology is the assertion that - at least in a number of contexts - unrealistic assumptions fail to yield correct predictions about the empirical world, and thus the F-twist certainly does not hold. The most important defender of this view is Cass Sunstein, who pleas for a 'behavioral law and economics'.

Based on empirical research that found anomalies in rational choice theory, Sunstein (1997b) develops a catalogue of complications that law and economics should take into account, in particular if it comes to estimation of probabilities, changes of preferences, and addiction. This is not to say that behavior is unpredictable. On the contrary, deviations from the predictions of rational choice theory often happen in a systematic way and inductive research of these deviations can help to build economic models that yield better predictions.

Another point to be mentioned is that in Friedman's view correct predictions are useful because they help confirm to a theory. However, the logical-positivist idea that the confirmation of theories is relevant has come under attack from the philosophy of science known as critical realism, with Karl Popper as its founder. Popper argued that confirmations never are able to prove that a theory is correct. One should therefore strive for the falsification of his theory, looking for empirical observations that are *not* in accordance with the predictions of the model. If a model is falsified in a confrontation with reality, the assumptions of the model can be adjusted and attempts at falsification can start anew. Ideally, deduction and induction will follow each other in an 'empirical cycle'.

The methodological prescriptions of critical rationalism have found wide support (Teijl and Holzhauer, 1997). Critics of this viewpoint, however, have argued that although the falsification principle is adhered to in theory, it is not followed in practice. Usually, scholars look for confirmations of their theory and in case a discrepancy between reality and the predictions of the theory is found, this is blamed on anomalies that require further study (Coase, 1994).

Alternatives to Critical Rationalism

Observing the failure of critical rationalism to describe the practice of law and economics as a scientific discipline, alternative models have been sought. Thomas Kuhn presented an alternative in his *The Structure of Scientific Revolutions* (Coase, 1994). Kuhn noted that indeed isolated discrepancies do not lead to the abandonment of a generally accepted paradigm. Whether a new paradigm will replace the old will not only be determined on the basis of empirical results. Of no less importance is the ability of the adherents of the new paradigm to gain key posts at universities and at the boards of important journals. Legal economists choose between competing theories and empirical research plays a role in showing the attractiveness or unattractiveness of a theory.

The fact that Kuhn stresses an institutional perspective implies that the success of law and economics to a large extent depends on the ability of lawyer-economists to obtain positions at law schools and to get their articles accepted in prestigious legal journals. A complicating point hereby is, however, that the amount of success will depend on the attractiveness of law and economics as a *normative* theory. Of old, the legal academia has been less interested in positive studies than in normative arguments that state how a case should be decided or how a law should be written.

Another alternative that attracted attention in law and economics is Lakatos's *Methodology of Scientific Research Programmes* (De Geest 1994; Teijl and Holzhauer 1997). According to Lakatos, theories have a hard core that is maintained, even if some elements have been falsified. A layer of additional hypotheses, ceteris paribus clauses and empirical observations protects this hard core. In practice, several research programs compete with each other. A research program is regarded as progressive if it yields new and correct predictions. A theory is only regarded to be falsified when it is replaced by a new and better theory.

De Geest (1994) has developed a theory that does not stress the importance of the truth of a theory but its plausibility, defined as the probability that its statements about the reality are true. For the plausibility of a theory not only empirical confirmations are relevant, but also the accordance of its statements with self-observation and life experience of the specialists that give a judgement of the theory. The latter is important for law and economics because empirical confirmations in the form of observable data are still limited in number. The same line of reasoning is followed by Coase (1994) in his effort to reconcile the main works of Adam Smith, namely *The Theory of Moral Sentiments* and *The Wealth of Nations*. If the complicated theory of motivation as developed in *The Theory of Moral Sentiments* is used as the starting point of an economic analysis the conclusions from *The Wealth of Nations* still hold, but are made more plausible. In this respect the problem with the use of unrealistic assumptions as defended by Friedman is that they do not contribute to the plausibility of a theory.

Ronald Coase (1994) further argues that even if predictions on the basis of unrealistic assumptions are correct, a theory based upon them may fail in providing insight in the working of the economic (or legal) system. An important factor in judging the importance of realism of assumptions is the goal one is aiming for. If it is only prediction and control, the use of unrealistic assumptions is fine, as long as they indeed predict well. If, however, the goal is explanation, an approach based on unrealistic assumptions is not really helpful in providing insight in what really moves a person and in how legal rules really have effects. There is an additional need for a 'mechanism' that shows how something could have happened. Not only the predictions, but also the beauty, elegance and internal consistency of an economic model determine its value for the analysis of law. Therefore, the life of law and economics is not just experience; it is logic as well.

Bibliography on Methodology: General (0400)

Adams, Michael (1984), 'Ist die Ökonomie eine imperialistische Wissenschaft? - Über Nutz und Frommen der Ökonomischen Analyse des Rechts (Is Economics an Imperialist Science? On the Usefulness and Forms of Economic Analysis of Law)', **7** *JURA*, 337-349.

Adelstein, Richard P. (1981a), 'The Plea Bargain in England and America: A Comparative Institutional View', in Burrows, Paul and Veljanovski, Cento G. (eds), *The Economic Approach to Law*, London, Butterworths, 226-252.

Adelstein, Richard P. (1981b), 'Institutional Function and Evolution in the Criminal Process', **76** *Northwestern University Law Review*, 1-99.

Adelstein, Richard P. and Peretz, Steven I. (1985), 'The Competition of Technologies in Markets for Ideas: Copyright and Fair Use in Evolutionary Perspective', **5** *International Review of Law and Economics*, 209-238.

Alpa, Guido (1996), 'Lo Snobismo degli Economisti e il Rifiuto del Dialogo con i Giuristi (a Proposito dell'Introduzione alla Versione Italiana di 'Impresa, Mercato e Diritto' di R.H. Coase) (The Economists' Snobbery and the Refusal of Dialogue with Lawyers)', *Economia e Diritto del Terziario*, 745-749.

Backhaus, Jürgen G. (1996), *Good Economics, Bad Economics, and European Economics*, Meteor Research Memorandum, Maastricht, No. RM/96/007.

Baird, Douglas G. (1997), 'The Future of Law and Economics: Looking Forward', **64** *University of Chicago Law Review*, 1129-1165.

Becker, Gary S. (1976), *The Economic Approach to Human Behavior*, Chicago: University of Chicago Press.

Becker, Gary S. (1991), *A Treatise on the Family,* Enlarged edition, Cambridge, MA, Harvard University Press.

Becker, Gary S. (1996), *Accounting for Tastes*, Cambridge, MA, Harvard University Press.

Brenner, Reuven (1980), 'Economics: An Imperialistic Science?', **9** *Journal of Legal Studies*, 184 ff.

Brietzke, Paul H. and Whitton, Linda S. (1996), 'An Old(er) Master Stands on the Shoulders of Ageism to Stake Another Claim for Law and Economics (Book Review of Richard A. Posner, Aging and Old Age)', **31** *Valparaiso University Law Review*, 89-109.

Bruce, Christopher J. (1989), 'A Positive Analysis of Methodology in the Law and Economics Literature', *Hamline Law Review*, 197-228.

Buchanan, James M. (1990), 'The Domain of Constitutional Economics', **1** *Constitutional Political Economy*, 1-18.

Campbell, David (1994), 'Ayres versus Coase: An Attempt to Recover the Issue of Equality in Law and Economics', **21** *British Journal of Law and Society*, 434-463.

Campbell, David (1996), 'On What is Valuable in Law and Economics', **8** *Otago Law Review*, 489-514.

Campbell, David (1997), 'The Relational Constitution of Contract and the Limits of Economics: Kenneth Arrow on the Social Background of Markets', in Deakin, Simon and Michie, Jonathan (eds), *Contracts, Co-operation and Competition: Studies in Economics, Management and Law*, Oxford, Oxford University Press, 529-596.

Coase, Ronald H. (1988), *The Firm, the Market, and the Law*, Chicago, University of Chicago Press.

Coase, Ronald H. (1994), *Essays on Economics and Economists*, Chicago, University of Chicago Press.

Cooter, Robert (1998), 'Expressive Law and Economics', **27** *Journal of Legal Studies*, 585-608.

Cosentino, Fabrizio (1988), 'Autonomia Privata e Paternalismo del Legislatore nella Prospettiva dell'Analisi Economica del Diritto (Individual Autonomy and the Paternalism of the Legislator: An EAL Perspective)', *Rivista Critica del Diritto Privato*, 473-511.

Cotter, Thomas F. (1996), 'Legal Pragmatism and the Law and Economics Movement', **84** *Georgetown Law Journal*, 2071-2141.

Couwenberg, S.W., Nagelkerke, J.J. and Slagter, Wiek J. (1980), *Recht en Economie* (Law and Economics), Rotterdam.

De Geest, Gerrit (1994), *Economische Analyse van het Contracten- en Quasi-Contractenrecht: een Onderzoek naar de Wetenschappelijke Waarde van de Rechtseconomie* (Economic Analysis of Contract Law and Quasi Contract Law: A Study on the Scientic Value of Law and Economics), Antwerpen, Maklu, 568 p.

De Geest, Gerrit (1996), 'The Debate on the Scientific Status on Law and Economics', **40** *European Economic Review*, 999-1006.

Duxbury, Neil (1995), *Patterns of American Jurisprudence*, Oxford, Clarendon.

Dworkin, Ronald M. (1980), 'Is Wealth a Value?', **9** *Journal of Legal Studies*, 191-226.

Ellickson, R.C. (1991), *Order Without Law: How Neighbors Settle Disputes*, Cambridge, MA, Harvard University Press.

Elster, Jon (1979), *Sour Grapes*, Cambridge, Cambridge University Press.

Elster, Jon (1989), *The Cement of Society. A Study of Social Order*, Cambridge, Cambridge University Press.

Elster, Jon (1997), 'More Than Enough. Review of G.S. Becker, Accounting for Tastes', **64** *University of Chicago Law Review*, 749-764.

Epstein, Richard A. (1997), 'Law and Economics: Its Glorious Past and Cloudy Future', **64** *University of Chicago Law Review*, 1167-1174.

Feichtinger, Gustav (1995), 'Crime and Punishment: A Dynamic Approach', **195** *Forschungsbericht/Research Memorandum*.

Feichtinger, G., Forst, Ch.V. and Piccardi, C. (1993), 'A Nonlinear Dynamic Model for the Dynastic Cycle', **165** *Forschungsbericht/Research Memorandum*.

Ferrarese, Maria Rosaria (1992), *Diritto e Mercato: il Caso degli Stati Uniti* (Law and Market: the Case of the United States), Torino, Giappichelli.

Fezer, Karl-Heinz (1986), 'Aspekte einer Rechtskritik an der Economic Analysis of Law und am Property Rights Approach (Critical Aspects of the Economic Analysis of Law and the Property Rights Approach from a Lawyer's Viewpoint)', **41** *Juristenzeitung*, 817-824.

Fezer, Karl-Heinz (1988), 'Nochmals, Kritik an der Ökonomischen Analyse des Rechts (More Critics on Law and Economics)', **43** *Juristenzeitung*, 223 ff.

Frech, H. Edward III (1995), 'European versus American Economics, Artificial Intellegence and Scientific Content', **48** *Kyklos*, 219-226.

Friedman, David D. (1987), 'Law and Economics', in X (ed.), *The New Palgrave: Invisible Hand*, London, Macmillan, 173-182.

Friedman, Milton (1953), 'The Methodology of Positive Economics', in X (ed.), *Essays in Positive Economics*, Chicago, University of Chicago Press.

Gaakeer, Jeanne and Kerkmeester, Heico (1997), *De Toenadering tussen Law and Economics en Law and Literature. Liaisons Dangereuses of De Werking van Adam Smiths Onzichtbare Hand?* (The Rapproachement between Law and Economics and Law and Literature. Laisons Dangereuses or Adam Smith's Invisible Hand), Deventer, Gouda Quint.

Gay, David E.R. (1981), 'Book Review of Moral Revolution and Economic Science: The Demise of Laissez-Faire in Ninteenth Century British Political Economy, Ellen Frankel Paul', **48** *Southern Economic Journal*, 530-531.

Gay, David E.R. (1982), 'Book Review of The Role of Government in a Free Society, Phil Gramm', **50** *Southern Economic Journal*, 916-917.

Gemtos, Petros A. (1974), 'E Provlematike ton Axiologikon Kriseon stis Koinonikes Epistemes (The Problem of Normative Judgments in the Social Sciences)', **4** *Philosophica*, 120-136.

Gemtos, Petros A. (1988), 'Methodologika Programmata sten Oikonomike kai te Nomike Episteme kai to Provlema tes Diepistemonikes tous Synergasias (Methodological Programs in Economics and Legal Science and the Problem of their Interdisciplinary Collaboration)', **36** *Nomiko Vema*, 1192-1202, reprinted in *Cyprus Law Review*, 39, 4627-4643 (1990)

Gemtos, Petros A. (1990), 'Law and Economics: Methodological Problems in their Interdisciplinary Cooperation', in Nicolacopoulos, Pantelis D. (ed.), *Greek Studies in the Philosophy and History of Science* (Boston Studies in the Philosophy of Science, vol. 121), Dordrecht, Kluwer, 239-250.

Gemtos, Petros A. (1995), *Oikonomika kai Dikaio: Oikonomika gia Nomikous, tomos: Methodologika kai Oikonomika Themelia* (Law and Economics: Economics for Lawyers, vol. I: Methodological and Economic Foundations), Athens-Komotini, Ant. N. Sakkoulas Publications.

Gragnani, A., Feichtinger, G. and Rinaldi, S. (1994), 'Dynamics of Drug Consumption: A Theoretical Model', **94-77** Working Paper.

Gragnani, A., Rinaldi, S. and Feichtinger, G. (1995), 'Slow-Fast Limit Cycles in Controlled Drug Markets', **185** *Forschungsbericht/Research Memorandum*.

Gridel, J.-P. (1994), *Introduction au droit et au droit français. Notions fondamentales. Méthodologie. Synthèses.* (Introduction to the Law and the French Law. Fundamentals notions. Methodology. Synthesis), Dalloz.

Grillo, Michele (1996), 'Lo Snobismo degli Economisti e il Rifiuto del Dialogo con i Giuristi. Una Risposta a Guido Alpa (The Economists' Snobbery and the Refusal of Dialogue with Lawyers. A Reply to Guido Alpa)', *Economia e Diritto del Terziario*, 751-754.

Hatzis, Aristides N. (1997), *Eisagoge sten Oikonomike Analyse tou Dikaiou* (Introduction to the Economic Analysis of Law), Aristotle University of Thessaloniki School of Law and Economics, Department of History, Philosophy and Sociology of Law.

Hol, A.M. (1991), 'Rechten En Doeleinden. Enkele Morele Aspecten Van Juridische Aansprakelijkheid (Rights and Goals. Some Moral Aspects of Legal Liability)', in X (ed.), *Dilemma's van Aansprakelijkheid*, Zwolle, Tjeenk Willink, 127-142.

Huerta De Soto, Jesús (1982), 'Método y Crisis en la Ciencia Económica (Method and Crisis in Economics)', **74** *Hacienda Pública Española*, 33-48.

Johnsen, D. Bruce (1986), 'Wealth is Value', **15** *Journal of Legal Studies*, 263-288.

Katz, Avery (1996a), 'Taking Private Ordering Seriously', **144** *University of Pennsylvania Law Review*.

Katz, Avery (1996b), 'Positivism and the Separation of Law and Economics', **94** *Michigan Law Review*.

Kelman, Mark G. (1987), *A Guide to Critical Legal Studies*, Cambridge, MA, Harvard University Press.

Kerkmeester, Heico (1992), 'De Veronderstellingen in de Rechtseconomie: Wanneer Zij Bruikbaar Zijn en Wanneer Niet', **21** *Nederlands Tijdschrift voor Rechtsfilosofie en Rechtsrtheorie*, 126-143.

Kerkmeester, Heico (1995), 'Game Theory as a Method in Law and Economics', in Bouckaert, Boudewijn and De Geest, Gerrit (eds), *Essays in Law and Economics II: Contract Law, Regulation, and Reflections on Law and Economics*, Antwerpen, Maklu, 267-285.

Kerkmeester, Heico (1996), 'Bespreking van R.P. Malloy en J. Evensky (red.), Adam Smith and the Philosophy of Law and Economics en van R.H. Coase, Essays on Economics and Economists (Book Reviews)', **22** *Recht en Kritiek*, 290-296.

Kerkmeester, Heico (1997), 'De Retoriek van de Rechtseconomie (The Rhetorics of Law and Economics)', in Feteris, E.T. et al. (eds), *Op Goede Gronden*, Nijmegen, Ars Aequi Libri, 207-213.

Kitch, Edmund W. (1983), 'Intellectual Foundations of Law and Economics', **33(2)** *Journal of Legal Education*, 183-209.

Kitch, Edmund W. (1992), 'The Framing Hypothesis', in Newman, Peter, Milgate, Murray and Eatwell, John (eds), *The New Palgrave Dictionary of Money and Finance*, London, MacMillan.

Kornhauser, Lewis A. (1984), 'The Great Image of Authority', **36** *Stanford Law Review*, 349 ff.

Kornhauser, Lewis A. (1986), 'Economic Analysis of Law', **16** *Materiali per una Storia della Cultura Giuridica*, 233 ff.

Kornhauser, Lewis A. (1988), 'Economique (Analyse - du droit)', in Arnaud, André-Jean (ed.), *Dictionnaire Encyclopedique de Theorie et de Sociologie du Droit*, Librairie General de Droit et de Jurisprudence.

Kornhauser, Lewis A. (1989), 'The New Economic Analysis of Law: Legal Rules as Incentives', in Mercuro, Nicholas (ed.), *Law and Economics*, Boston, Kluwer Academic Publishers.

Kornhauser, Lewis A. (1992), 'Analise Economica do Direito', **43(2)** *Sub Judica: Justica e Sociedade*.

Kronman, Anthony T. (1980), 'Wealth Maximization as a Normative Principle', **9** *Journal of Legal Studies*, 227-242.

Lande, Robert H. (1989), 'Commentary: Implications of Professor Scherer's Research for the Future of Antitrust', **29** *Washburn Law Journal*, 256 ff.

Leff, Arthur A. (1974), 'Economic Analysis of Law: Some Realism About Nominalism', **60** *Virginia Law Review*, 78 ff.

Malloy, Robin Paul and Evensky, Jerry (eds) (1995), *Adam Smith and the Philosophy of Law and Economics*, Dordrecht, Kluwer Academic Publishers.

Mercuro, Nicholas and Medema, Steven G. (1997), *Economics and the Law. From Posner to Post-Modernism*, Princeton, Princeton University Press.

Mercuro, Nicholas and Ryan, Timothy P. (1984), *Law, Economics, and Public Policy*, Greenwood, JAI Press.

Migué, Jean-Luc (1977), 'Méthodologie Économique et Économie Non Marchande (Economic Methodology and Non-Trading Economics)', *Revue d'Économique Politique*, 506 ff.

Monateri, Pier Giuseppe (1995), 'Risultati e Regole. (Un'Analisi Giuridica dell'Analisi Economica del Diritto) (Rules and Outcomes. A Legal Analysis of the Economic Analysis of Law)', *Rivista Critica del Diritto Privato*, 605-619.

Nussbaum, Martha C. (1997), 'Flawed Foundations. The Philosophical Critique of (a Particular Type of) Economics', **64** *University of Chicago Law Review*, 1197-1214.

Parisi, Francesco (1998), *The Economic Structure of the Law (The Collected Papers of Richard A. Posner: Volume I)*, Cheltenham and Lyme, Edward Elgar, 354 p.

Parisi, Francesco and Posner Richard A. (1997a), 'Law and Economics: An Introduction', in Posner, Richard A. and Parisi, Francesco (ed.), *Law and Economics*, Cheltenham and Lyme, Edward Elgar, Ashgate, 3-57.

Parisi, Francesco and Posner Richard A. (1997b), 'Scuole e Tendenze nella Analisi Economica del Diritto', **15** *Rivista Critica del Diritto Privato*.

Parisi, Francesco and Posner Richard A. (1997c), *International Library of Critical Writings in Economics, Volume I: Theoretical and Methodological Foundations*, Cheltenham and Lyme, Edward Elgar.

Pastor, Santos (1984), 'Una Introducción al Análisis Económico del Derecho (An Introduction to Law and Economics)', **89** *Hacienda Pública Española*.

Pastor, Santos (1989), 'Derechos de Propiedad y Análisis Económico: ¿Nuevas Luces a Viejas Sombras? (Economics of Property Rights: Shading Lights?)', **38** *Economistas*, 28-35.

Polinsky, A. Mitchell (1974), 'Economic Analysis as a Potentially Defective Product: A Buyer's Guide to Posner's Economic Analysis of Law', **87** *Harvard Law Review*, 1655-1681.

Posner, Richard A. (1979), 'Utilitarianism, Economics, and Legal Theory', **8** *Journal of Legal Studies*, 103-140.

Posner, Richard A. (1980), 'The Value of Wealth: A Comment on Dworkin and Kronman', **9** *Journal of Legal Studies*, 243-252.

Posner, Richard A. (1992), *Economic Analysis of Law*, 4th edn, Boston, Little Brown.

Posner, Richard A. (1993a), 'The New Institutional Economics Meets Law and Economics', **149** *Journal of Institutional and Theoretical Economics*, 73-87.

Posner, Richard A. (1993b), 'Ronald Coase and Methodology', *Journal of Economic Perspectives*, 195-210.

Raes, Koen (1990), 'Het Recht van de Schaarste (The Law of Scarcity)', **16** *Recht en Kritiek*, 380-394.

Reumer, Andrés (1996), *Análisis Económico del Derecho* (Economic Analysis of Law), Mexico, Fondo de Cultura Económica, Sociedad Mexicana de geografía y Estadística, e Instituto Technológico Autónome de México.

Rinaldi, S., Feichtinger, G. and Wirl, F. (1994), 'Corruption Dynamics in Democratic Systems', **168** *Forschungsbericht/Research Memorandum*.

Roemer, Andrès (1992), *Importancia del Análisis Económico del Derecho*, Mexico, SUMMA de la Sociedad Mexicana de Geografía en México y Estadística.

Roemer, John E. (1996), *Theories of Distributive Justice*, Cambridge, MA, Harvard University Press.

Romani, Franco (1990), 'Diritto ed Economia: la Prospettiva di un Economista (Law and Economics: the Perspective of an Economist)', *Sociologia del Diritto*, 245-254.

Rowley, Charles K. (1981), 'Social Sciences and the Law: The Relevance of Economic Theories', **1** *Oxford Journal of Legal Studies*, 391-405.

Slagter, Wiek J. (1995), 'Grensoverschrijdingen en Grensgeschillen tussen de Economische en Rechtswetenschap (Border-crossings and Border-differences Between Economic and Legal Science)', in Slagter, Wiek J. et al. (eds), *Ondernemen Tussen Macht en Ordening: Opstellen op het Grensvlak van Economie en Recht*, Amsterdam, Thesis Publishers, 1-14.

Sousa Franco, Atónio (1992), 'Análise Económica do Direito: Exercício Intelectual ou Fonte de Ensinamento?', **2** *Sub Judice*, 63-70.

Stake, Jeffrey E. (1991), 'Status and Incentive Aspects of Judicial Decisions', **79** *Georgetown Law Journal*, 1447-1497.

Stout, Lynn A. (1997), 'Irrational Expectations', (forthcoming) *Journal of Legal Theory*.

Sunstein, Cass R. (1997a), *Free Markets and Social Justice*, Oxford, Oxford University Press.

Sunstein, Cass R. (1997b), 'Behavioral Analysis of Law', **64** *University of Chicago Law Review*, 1175-1195.

Teijl, Rob and Holzhauer, Rudi W. (1997), *Wisselende Perspectieven in de Rechtseconomie* (Changing Perspectives in Law and Economics), Deventer, Gouda Quint.

Trebilcock, Michael J. (1983), 'The Prospects of 'Law and Economics': A Canadian Perspective', **33** *Journal of Legal Education*, 288-290.

Turnbull, Shann (1977), *Impact of Mining Royalties on Aboriginal Communities in the Northern Territory*, First Report, Parliamentary Paper, Canberra, Australian Government Publishing Service, No. 135/1978.

Turnbull, Shann (1978), *Economic Development of Aboriginal Communities in the Northern Territory Second Report, Self-sufficiency (with Land Rights)*, Parliamentary Paper, Canberra, Australian Government Publishing Service, No. 438/1978.

Turnbull, Shann (1980), *Economic Development of Aboriginal Communities in the Northern Territory: A Study in two parts, Department of Aboriginal Affairs*, Canberra, Australian Government Publishing Service.

Turnbull, Shann (1992), 'Economics and the Laws of Nature', in Marston, Alan (ed.), *The Other Economy: Economics Nature Can Live With*, LBD Publishers, Auckland, 81-138.

Turnbull, Shann (1994), 'Stakeholder Democracy: Redesigning the Governance of Firms and Bureaucracies', **23(3)** *Journal of Socio-Economics*, 321-360.

Turnbull, Shann (1997), 'Stakeholder Governance: A Cybernetic and Property Rights Analysis', **5(1)** *Corporate Governance: An International Review*, 11-23.

Weise, Peter (1991), 'Effizienz und Menschenwürde - Ein Gegensatz? Anmerkungen zu einer Kontroverse zwischen Ott/Schäfer und Fezer (Efficiency and Human Dignity - a Contradiction? Remarks on a Controversy between Ott/Schäfer and Fezer)', in Ott,

C. and Schäfer, H.-B. (eds), *Ökonomische Probleme des Zivilrechts, Beiträge zur ökonomischen Analyse des Rechts,* Heidelberg/New York, Springer, 18-34.

West, Robin (1988), 'Economic Man and Literary Woman: One Contrast', **39** *Mercer Law Review*, 867-878.

White, James Boyd (1987), 'The Language and Culture of Economics', **54** *Tennessee Law Review*, 161-202.

Williamson, Oliver E. (1991), 'Intellectual Foundations: The Need for a Broader View', **33** *Journal of Legal Education*, 210-216.

0500
SCHOOLS: GENERAL

Ejan Mackaay
Professor of Law
University of Montreal

Abstract

The concept of schools is used to summarise the ideas of thinkers who share common premises on how and what to research, and to contrast them with those of other schools. It is an expositional convenience and should be used only when the differences touch fundamental matters of the field of research. The differences between schools focus attention on questions to be resolved by further research.

Within the current law and economics movement, besides the mainstream, the institutionalists, the neoinstitutionalists and the Austrians constitute distinct schools. Whether the New Haven School constitutes a distinct school is debatable.
JEL classification: K00
Keywords: Law and Economics in General, Schools

1. Introduction: Schools in General

1.1 Schools

A school of thought in scientific endeavour is a group of thinkers who adopt a common approach, including shared theoretical premises, on how and what to research in a particular field. The term is also used as shorthand for the ideas those thinkers defend.

Originally the term school may have designated a major thinker, founder of the school, and his or her disciples. In current usage the link to a common intellectual leader is no longer essential. The members of a school of thought may, but need not, themselves claim allegiance to the school. Members of a school may consider that the adherence to a set of common precepts allows them to build on each other's work and so to attain economies of scale in research not available if they worked in isolation.

When should we distinguish schools? To speak of schools, one must see groups of scholars defending contrasting, even incompatible, views about fundamental aspects of a field of research and these views must have a certain complexity and logical coherence (De Geest, 1995, p. 458). Classifying such views into schools facilitates exposition (Teijl and Holzhauer, 1990, p. 622; Teijl and Holzhauer, 1997, p. 8). We understand through contrasts. Presentation of schools focuses attention on their differences, which further research, theoretical as well as empirical, should aim at resolving.

The convenience of summarising the thinking within a school through the common ideas should not lead one to disregard the differences amongst the thinkers belonging to that school. Menger, Mises and Hayek, all belonging to the Austrian school of economics, share ideas of spontaneous order and a reluctance towards government intervention designed to correct its imperfections. But they differ in that, for instance, Mises is clearly more aprioristic and deductive in his reasoning than is Hayek and sees no room for empirical testing of his ideas, something Hayek admitted (Teijl and Holzhauer, 1997, pp. 121-128). Whether the Austrian school itself should be distinguished from the neoclassical mainstream is sometimes questioned within economics proper: 'With all the respect due to 'Austrian' economics, its latter-day insistence to differentiate itself from the neoclassical mainstream seems more important to a small band of its practitioners than to the bystander. What matters is that Menger and Wieser argued within the same rational choice 'paradigm' as Marshall and Edgeworth' (de Jasay, 1992, p. 337).

Legal theory shows many instances of schools. The legal realists in the United States, associated with the names of Holmes, Frank, Llewellyn and others, were united in their reaction against what they presented as the excesses of positivism in American law schools of the late nineteenth and early twentieth century. During the same period in France, the '*école de la libre recherche scientifique*' (Free scientific research school) of Gény and Saleilles was a comparable reaction against the earlier '*école de l'exégèse*' (exegetic school), to whom they attributed the view that law was strictly to be found in the Code and statutes. The historical school of Savigny and others in Germany, followed by Maine, Maitland and others in the UK, reacted against what was considered excessive reliance on logic and aprioristic reasoning in German legal thinking at the time. In their view law was to be seen 'as something which evolved from the instinctive sense of right of the community and developed in and by reason of particular social, economic, and other contexts' (Walker, 1980, p. 1106).

1.2 Movements

It is useful to consider a few related terms. Movement is a broader term than school of thought. It designates a large grouping of people loosely sharing scientific or practical and, in particular, political aims. One could speak of the law and economics movement, but scarcely of the law and economics school.

1.3 Paradigms

Since the 1960s, two new terms, paradigm and research programme, are used to describe aspects of the evolution of scientific thinking (De Geest, 1995, p. 389 f.). Paradigm in normal usage is a very clear or typical example of something. With respect to the evolution of the sciences, it acquired a different meaning as a result of Thomas Kuhn's book (Kuhn, 1970). The term 'research programme' is due to Lakatos, writing in reaction to Kuhn (Lakatos, 1970).

The puzzle Kuhn sought to explain is how science grows. The collapse of the best-corroborated scientific theory of all times, Newton's mechanics and gravitation theory, in favour of Einstein's ideas, had scattered the view of scientific growth 'by accumulation of eternal truths' (Lakatos, 1970, p. 92). Popper had used this and like episodes to argue that the best way forward in science is not so much by seeking confirmation of one's ideas through observation, but by seeking ruthlessly to disprove them. The force of scientific theories lies in the attempted refutations they have so far withstood.

Do scientists effectively proceed in this manner? Kuhn's reading of the history of science leads him to argue that they do not. During periods of what Kuhn terms 'normal science', the practitioners of a scientific discipline let themselves be guided by a shared fundamental theory and view of 'methods, problem-field, and standard of solution' (Kuhn, 1970, p. 103). These shared ideas Kuhn termed the paradigm (Kuhn, 1970, p. 10). To attract a following amongst scientists, the paradigm must account for observations and regularities considered certain within the discipline, and for some new ones; it must also be open-ended enough to set a range of new puzzles to be solved. During this period of 'normal science', scientists are engaged in puzzle-solving and the discipline advances without the paradigm being questioned (Kuhn, 1970, p. 10).

As research proceeds and empirical results accumulate, one finds observations tending to support the theory, but also some which tend to disconfirm it. If the latter concern puzzles at the periphery of the theory, one attempts to refine it to yield predictions that better accord with observation. But the contrary evidence may also concern more fundamental aspects of the theory. Such observations do not immediately lead one to consider the current theory refuted. Rather such instances are provisionally set aside as anomalies.

As the number of known anomalies grows, there comes a point when some practitioners of the discipline no longer consider the current paradigm tenable and start looking for a modified or improved one. As this sentiment spreads, the discipline enters into a crisis: practitioners are no longer convinced that their theory and associated research procedures are well-founded. An outsider may have the impression that research stagnates and that there are interminable discussions about foundations and methodology.

As the crisis deepens the stage is set for a new paradigm to be proposed. The acceptance of the new paradigm bring about what Kuhn calls a scientific revolution. The fundamental advances in science are in his view the result of such revolutions.

1.4 Research Programmes

In Lakatos's eyes scientific advances do not all come by way of revolutions and Kuhn's view suffers furthermore from the difficulty that the transition from one paradigm to another appears to be based on the psychology of researchers rather than on reason. Lakatos sees within any discipline or sub-discipline several competing 'research programmes' which specify at their 'hard core' a set of unquestioned premises about the discipline (Lakatos, 1970, p. 133) and at their periphery a 'protective belt' of matters for which the theory may be further elaborated and which may be subjected to empirical testing. At the periphery, one accepts negative test results without considering the theory refuted. They invite further refinement of the theory.

On this view, scientists adhere to a research programme because of its plausibility and the research agenda it implies. Progressive research programmes, offering a wide open research agenda, attract many practitioners, 'degenerating' or declining research programmes are progressively abandoned. Growth of scientific knowledge in this view is more like the competitive process with which economists are familiar rather than like a 'religious conversion' (Lakatos, 1970, p. 93) or 'a bandwagon effect' (Lakatos, 1970, p. 178).

1.5 Paradigms and Research Programmes in Law and Economics?

Do the concepts of paradigms and research programmes apply to law and economics? Kuhn himself is doubtful about the application of his ideas to the social sciences generally, which he consider pre-scientific. He concedes that any group of scientists may adopt common beliefs and practices to guide their endeavours (even a phlogiston theory), but stresses the difference between such a paradigm and the one guiding the activity of the practitioners of a 'mature' science.

About the 'the transition from the pre- to the post-paradigm period in the development of a scientific field' he writes: 'Before it occurs, a number of schools compete for the domination of a given field. Afterward, in the wake of some notable scientific achievement, the number of schools is greatly reduced, ordinarily to one, and a more efficient mode of science practice begins. The latter is generally esoteric and oriented to puzzle-solving, as the work of a group can be only when its members take the foundations of their field for granted' (Kuhn, 1970, p. 178) and he continues '[w]hat changes with the transition to maturity is not the presence of a paradigm but rather its nature. Only after the change is normal puzzle-solving research possible. Many of the attributes of a developed science which I have above associated with the acquisition of a paradigm I would therefore now discuss as consequences of the acquisition of the sort of paradigm that identifies challenging puzzles, supplies clues to their solution, and guarantees that the truly clever practitioner will succeed.' (Kuhn, 1970, p. 179).

Blaug (1980) considers paradigms and research programmes for economics at large. He concludes that a presentation in terms of competing and partly overlapping research programmes is apposite and to be preferred to one in terms of revolutions. He speaks nonetheless of the marginalist revolution in the latter part of the nineteenth century and of the Keynesian Revolution in the 1930s. Wolin (1980) applies Kuhn's ideas to political science, but adopts as the criterion for the merit of a theory the extent to which it is acceptable to various political actors. The approach allows him to demonstrate what he considers to be a paradigm shift in his discipline. But it leaves the reader with the uncomfortable question of what distinguishes a scientific paradigm from a shared social or religious outlook, or even a mere fashion. Surely the distinction must ultimately rest on the possibility to account for observations and to make testable predictions.

Can these concepts of paradigms and research programmes be usefully applied to law and economics? Several writers have recently considered this question (Rubin, 1985; Veljanovski, 1985; De Geest, 1995, p. 389 f.; van den Hauwe, 1996; Teijl and Holzhauer, 1997, p. 7 f.; Ellickson, 1998; Posner, 1998). If the answer is affirmative, further questions concern the scope of the paradigm or research programme and the grounds for preferring one paradigm or research programme to another.

In the piece on the History of Law and Economics (0200) the term 'paradigm' was loosely used in describing different periods of the latest wave of law and economics. The 1950s, 1960s and 1970s might be described, loosely again, as periods of 'normal science': the research agenda seemed clear and researchers spent their time solving puzzles indicated by the 'paradigm'. The 1980s brought debates about various foundational questions. Since then several competing 'schools' present themselves in the law and economics literature. In Kuhn's terms, that could indicate attempts to establish a first scientific paradigm or a crisis in the existing paradigm.

To accept the latter hypothesis, one would have to be able to point to a set of unquestionable scientific accomplishments and to anomalies giving rise to the crisis. Ellickson (1998, p. 551) professes to see the latter in the blindness of the 'classical law and economics' to 'social norms' (which, in his view, would give an entirely different twist to the problem situations envisaged in the Coase theorem). Posner (1998, p. 565) sees no crisis but merely new puzzles to be solved within the existing research programme, the core of which, in his view, is the rational choice theory. 'A paradigm shift occurs when a theory no longer furnishes acceptable answers to the questions that trouble current researchers, not when it is modified or enriched to cope with new questions or questions previously beyond the grasp of the theory' (Posner, 1998, p. 564).

The question of the criteria to be used for choosing amongst competing theories or research programmes is debated in Rubin (1985); Veljanovski (1985); De Geest (1995, pp. 389 f.); van den Hauwe (1996); Teijl and Holzhauer (1997, pp. 7 f.); Posner (1998). Posner (1998, p. 555) recalls Friedman's prediction test in writing that 'a theory that does not generate predictions is difficult to feel comfortable with'. De Geest, after a lengthy discussion of the issue, proposes what he terms a 'plausibility theory' (1995, pp. 407 f.), which is criticised by van den Hauwe (1996). In De Geest's view, the 'mainstream approach' to law and economics is sufficiently open-ended to absorb, by way of puzzles to be solved, the ideas which are now put forward by competing 'schools'. This view appears close to Posner's (1998).

Teijl and Holzhauer (1997) undertake a comparison of what the 'Chicago school' and the 'Austrian School' have to contribute to law and economics. The Austrian School considers that the optima on which much Chicago law and economics relies are indeterminable. The approaches appear to be radically incompatible and this obliges the authors squarely to face the question of the criteria for choosing between rival approaches. The difficulty is to avoid judging the performance of one approach in terms set by the other. Teijl and Holzhauer opt for the framework of research programmes put forth by Lakatos and propose to examine what each approach has to say on a range of practical legal puzzles within the fields of contracts, tort liability and litigation. In each case, they seek answers to three questions: what are the effects of legal rules can be explained? To what extent do they contribute to society's welfare? How can the emergence and contents of legal rules be explained? (Teijl and Holzhauer, 1997, p. 35). At the end of their study, Austrian economics is presented as perhaps more like the 'armchair economics' than its practitioners would like to admit. Nonetheless the authors profess, in conclusion, to be unable to state a preference between these theories on objective grounds. Ultimately the choice is a matter of acceptance within the scientific community (Teijl and Holzhauer, 1997, p. 365).

Before examining the different schools within law and economics, it may be helpful to summarise the common principles which set law and economics approaches off against other intellectual currents such as Critical Legal Studies, and feminism. As for the sociology of law, popular in Europe in particular as a link between the social sciences and the law, there is debate about the extent to which its practitioners share the premises set out below, in particular the postulate of methodological individualism.

2. Common Ground in Law and Economics

All law and economics research is aimed at gaining new insights in the law by applying economic concepts and theories. The underlying premises are those of economics proper.

2.1 Methodological Individualism

The first premise is the postulate of *methodological individualism.* According to this postulate all analyses must ultimately be couched in terms of the behaviour of individuals; all collective phenomena must be explained as compositions or perverse effects of individual decisions.

By way of an example, consider the 'urban war' in Amsterdam in the late 1970s and early 1980s opposing about 3000 squatters and their sympathisers amongst the public at large to the police. One might be tempted to attribute this to the climate of the times, in Amsterdam in particular, to large unemployment amongst the young and to the housing crisis. All of these factors have some plausibility but do not touch the heart of the matter. They do not explain how individual participants in this development could rationally act as they did and yet arrive at a collective disaster.

The source of the problem was the rent control policy then in force in the Netherlands. It granted tenants fixed rents and almost unassailable occupancy of rented premises, and placed severe restrictions on what landlords could do with their property. This led landlords recovering possession of their premises to leave them empty while waiting for permission to renovate. As a result there were a lot of vacant buildings in the city. This in turn led squatters forcibly to occupy such buildings, a practice which the courts were reluctant to stop. Once legal ways had been found to secure eviction of squatters, there remained the practical problem of enforcing the judgements. The police called in to enforce were facing a determined group defending a vested interest.

This explanation accounts for the 'climate' which developed in Amsterdam in that period. Each step of the development is the result of transparent rational choices made by actors in this game. The overall disaster is a perverse 'composition' effect which the law should seek to avoid.

2.2 Rational Choice

Individual decision makers are presumed, secondly, to be rationally maximising their satisfactions, or their benefits over costs, as they see them (the *rational choice hypothesis*). This hypothesis is essential for scientific work in that '[i]f people do not behave in predictable ways, then the idea that we can regulate society by laws and incentives becomes untenable' (Veljanovski, 1990, p. 35). It allows one to flesh out predictions of how individuals are expected to react to changes in their environment.

The realism of the rational choice hypothesis is questioned principally on two grounds. Psychological research tends to show that people's decisions tend to deviate from the rational choice model in situations involving in particular small probabilities or great complexity. We do not appear to have the intellectual hardware to perform the calculations that the full rationality assumption attributes to us. Furthermore in real life individuals face decisions fraught with risk or uncertainty. They are often imperfectly informed about the stakes. There is debate about what rationality means in a context where decision makers cannot assess the extent of their own ignorance. As we shall see, these difficulties are the focus of criticism by both the institutional and Austrian schools. The critics propose to attenuate the rationality postulate, but not to reject it. It is one of the matters on which the survey of the history of law and economics (0200) sees room for further research.

2.3 Stable Preferences

A third premise is that of *stable preferences* (Becker, 1976, p. 5). Admittedly, preferences are not given at birth, by biological necessity, to remain fixed during one's lifetime; they are shaped or reshaped during one's youth and may shift more slowly during later life. Cultural influences may thus be accounted for (Becker, 1996, p. 3; Sowell, 1998). Yet to make predictions of how individuals will react to change, one must presume their preferences to remain constant in the short run. Whoever submits that preferences have changed must adduce evidence to that effect.

2.4 Equilibrium

A fourth premise concerns what happens in human interaction. Barring disturbance, interactions are presumed to tend towards an *equilibrium*, described in bare form by game theory and more elaborately by economic theory dealing with markets, in which (implicit) price adjustments in the process of competition tend to equalise supply and demand for a good or service. Becker (1976, p. 5f.) considers the premise of market equilibrium to be applicable to implicit markets in politics, marriage and other areas as much as to markets in which transactions involving money take place.

3. Schools in Law and Economics

Within a community as large as the law and economics movement, one must expect differences of opinion about research matters. They may concern such questions as whether particular anomalies should count as tolerable within the existing theoretical framework, rather than as refutations calling for rejection or revision of the theory, or what is admissible simplification of reality within a model as opposed to unacceptable reductionism. In law and economics, different views are expressed, for instance, on whether inconsistencies in choice or the practice of rule following should call into question the postulate of rational choice.

Not all differences of opinion indicate distinct schools. The term schools ought to be reserved for situations in which several fundamental differences of opinion coalesce to form incompatible approaches at a relatively fundamental level.

The Encyclopedia itself distinguishes in its classification several schools and approaches: Austrian School, Institutionalism, New Institutional Economics, Property Rights Approach, Game Theory Applied to Law, Comparative Law and Economics, Experimental Law and Economics, Law and Economics and Development. Some authors profess to discern even further schools: 'Law and economics and critical legal studies are richly diverse intellectual movements involving a multitude of individual views, methodologies, 'schools', and diverse theoretical traditions. There are, however, other 'schools' [than the Chicago school] within law and economics that exhibit different perspectives. The New Haven school, of Yale University, for instance, has attracted liberal practitioners who adopt the common methodology of the Chicago school but believe that there is a larger need for state intervention in order to cure problems involving market failure' (Minda, 1989, pp. 111-112).

Let us briefly look at each of these 'schools', to determine whether the term school is justified. For convenience we begin with the last item of the classification in the Encyclopedia.

'Law and Economics and Development' is a field to be investigated with the tools of law and economics, but should not be seen as a distinct school. 'Comparative Law and Economics' too is a field for the application of law and economics. It is all the more promising as it exposes law and economics methodology to the test of being applied to legal systems different from its home base of American law and possibly being found wanting. This is not a distinct school, but rather a focus which gives larger scope to existing approaches. 'Game Theory Applied to Law' and 'Experimental Law and Economics' are promising tools or approaches with which to broach law and economics questions. They are not in opposition to older approaches, but complement them.

3.1 The Property Rights Approach

The 'Property Rights Approach' is presented in the chapter on History (0200) as the name economists gave to their attempts at solving a puzzle in economics proper. In neoclassical economic theory - till according to Demsetz (1997, p. 1) 'the central theory of economics' - organizations and the behaviour of individuals within them are puzzling. In studying decentralised socialist enterprises in the former Yugoslavia, for example, one does not get far by examining policies adopted by the owner of the capital goods, which is to say the State or the bureaucrats nominally in charge of the enterprise (Furubotn and Pejovich, 1974b, p. 250; Barzel, 1989, pp. 98-113). It is more instructive to look at the preferences and decisions of the workers, who were in charge, through the Workers Council, of the policy decisions for their firm. Focusing on the workers, one can readily explain why such firms were loath to let workers go in circumstances which would make such a decision seem logical for a comparable Western firm: the workers making such decisions would cut the branch on which they were sitting.

More puzzling is the question why the firms did not maximise worker salaries, but instead retained some profit as savings for future investments. Why would workers invest in capital goods they did not own? As Furubotn and Pejovich explain, workers would find this to be in their interest in so far as it maximised the present value of the future income stream paid to the average employee. Their conclusion is that the behaviour of the Yugoslav firm is explicable in terms of rational decisions by persons who actually control the use of the resources in the firm. The heuristic Furubotn and Pejovich draw from this insight is that to explain the behaviour of the firm, one must look at the 'property-rights structure' at all levels (Furubotn and Pejovich, 1974b, p. 251).

It is clear that the term 'property-rights structure' is not used here in its legal sense. Property rights, in this usage, mean 'decision authority' (Libecap, 1989, p. 1), the actual power to control the use of a good and to appropriate the fruits. Property rights in this economic sense are a descriptive term, more general than 'right of ownership' (Furubotn and Pejovich, 1974a, p. 4). When one speaks of 'my office', 'my secretary' or when a gang speaks of 'its territory' the possessive term is used in this sense.

The term 'property rights' used in the 'property rights approach' has created confusion with the legal meaning of the term. Be that as it may, the approach no longer seems to constitute a separate school. Its insights have been absorbed into law and economics proper as Posner first unified it.

3.2 The Austrian and Institutionalist Schools

The clearest case for distinct schools within the classification adopted in the Encyclopedia could be made for the Austrians and for the old and the new Institutionalist approaches, in contrast to the mainstream or Chicago approach to law and economics. The distinctions correspond to 'schools' in economics proper.

Readers are referred to the chapters on these three schools (0510, 0520 and 0530) for detailed accounts of what these schools stand for and the differences with the mainstream approach. The differences between schools and the mainstream point to matters that are part of the agenda for future research presented in the conclusion of the piece on the History of Law and Economics (0200): the role of institutions, historical research, the place of uncertainty, discovery and entrepreneurship, strategic behaviour and bounded rationality.

3.3 The New Haven School

Minda sees room for the New Haven school: 'There are, however, other 'schools' within law and economics that exhibit different perspectives. The New Haven school, of Yale University, for instance, has attracted liberal practitioners who adopt the common methodology of the Chicago school but believe that there is a larger need for state intervention in order to cure problems involving market failure' (Minda, 1989, pp. 111-112). The school warrants an 'Aside' in Mercuro and Medema's chapter on Chicago Law and Economics (Mercuro and Medema, 1997, pp. 79-83).

The New Haven school goes back to the writings of Calabresi (see review of History of Law and Economics - 0200), whose views are quite distinct from the Chicago law and economics (Duxbury, 1995, p. 393). Without taking issue with any of the postulates of the neoclassical model, Calabresi believes that efficiency which the model stresses could never be the whole story in so far as legal rules are concerned. Justice and distributional concerns would always have to have their due (Duxbury, 1995, p. 393).

Susan Rose-Ackerman articulates what she sees as the central tenets of the 'school' following in Calabresi's footsteps (Mercuro and Medema, 1997, p. 79-83; Rose-Ackerman, 1989, 1992). Distributional concerns remain central. Market failure is held to be more prevalent than Chicago law and economics would make it out to be and government intervention is expected to be capable of correcting it, although it may not succeed in all circumstances. The overall philosophy of this group is presented as less 'politically conservative' than the Chicago law and economics group and the public choice group.

On the whole, the differences seem to be a matter of political colour. The theoretical premises and methods the New Haven group adopt are insufficiently distinct from the mainstream view to constitute a separate school.

3.4 The Freiburg School

The Ordo-Liberal or Freiburg school of law and economics is now mainly of historical interest. It was founded in the 1930s and influential in the years immediately following the Second World War. It included well-known scholars and politicians such as Walter Eucken, Wilhelm Roepke, Ludwig Erhard, Franz Böhm. The school has only recently been recognised internationally as an interesting intellectual current of law and economics, as a result of the translation of the major works of Böhm and Eucken in particular. (Vanberg, 1998, p. 172). Several articles on the movement as a whole and on individual members have appeared recently (Backhaus, 1996; Behrens, 1984, p. 8, 1993; Grossekettler, 1996; Lenel, 1996; Streit, 1992).

The Freiburg school focused on the proper role of government in an open society which had evolved out of the earlier feudal structures, on preventing factions from controlling the state and on competition policy as fostered by the state. The paradox of the state as grantor of special privileges and at the same time as guarantor of competition was, in their view, to be solved by constitutional design. This focus brings them close to the agenda of the public choice and the constitutional political economy groups.

4. Conclusion

Schools are an expositional convenience to summarise the ideas of thinkers who share common premises on how and what to research, and to contrast these with those of other schools. They focus attention on questions for further research. One should not lay too much stress on the alleged differences amongst schools (De Geest, 1995, p. 468). It may be worthwhile to see them as puzzles to be solved within a broadly defined 'mainstream approach' (Posner, 1998).

Within the current law and economics movement, the mainstream, the institutionalists, the neoinstitutionalists and the Austrians may be regarded as distinct schools, as they are in economics proper. Whether the New Haven School constitutes a distinct school is a moot point.

The differences between the schools point to questions which should be part of the agenda for future research: the role of institutions, historical research, the place of uncertainty, discovery and entrepreneurship, strategic behaviour and bounded rationality. These matters have been presented in the piece on the History of Law and Economics (0200).

Bibliography on Schools: General (0500)

Backhaus, Juergen (1996), Franz Böhm issue, **3** *European Journal of Law and Economics*, 297-376.

Barzel, Yoram (1989), *Economic Analysis of Property Rights*, Cambridge, Cambridge University Press.

Becker, Gary S. (1976), *The Economic Approach to Human Behavior*, Chicago, The University of Chicago Press.

Becker, Gary S. (1996), *Accounting for Tastes*, Cambridge, MA, Harvard University Press.

Behrens, Peter (1984), *Die Ökonomischen Grundlagen des Rechts - Politische Ökonomie als Rationale Jurisprudenz* (The Economic Foundations of Law - Political Economy as Rational Jurisprudence), Tübingen, J.C.B. Mohr (Paul Siebeck).

Behrens, Peter (1993), 'Legalism, Economism, and Professional Attitudes Toward Institutional Design - Comment', **149** *Journal of Institutional and Theoretical Economics*, 141-147.

Blaug, Mark (1980), 'Kuhn versus Lakatos, or Paradigms versus Research Programmes in the History of Economics', in Gutting, Gary (ed.), *Paradigms and Revolutions - Appraisals and Applications of Thomas Kuhn's Philosophy of Science,* Notre Dame, University of Notre Dame Press, 137-159.

De Geest, Gerrit (1995), *Economische Analyse van het Contracten- en Quasi-Contractenrecht - Een Onderzoek naar de Wetenschappelijke Waarde van de Rechtseconomie* (Economic Analysis of Contract and Quasi-Contract Law - An Inquiry into the Scientific Merit of the Economic Analysis of Law), Antwerpen, Maklu Uitgevers.

de Jasay, Anthony (1992), 'Rational Choice in Conflict', in Radnitzky, Gerard (ed.), *Universal Economics - Assessing the Achievements of the Economic Approach,* New York, Paragon House, 327-338.

Demsetz, Harold (1997), *The Economics of the Business Firm - Seven Critical Commentaries*, Cambridge, Cambridge University Press.

Duxbury, Neil (1995), *Patterns of American Jurisprudence*, Oxford, Clarendon Press.

Ellickson, Robert C. (1998), 'Law and Economics Discovers Norms', **27** *Journal of Legal Studies*, 537-552.

Friedman, Milton (1953), 'The Methodology of Positive Economics', in Friedman, Milton (ed.), *Essays in Positive Economics,* Chicago, The University of Chicago Press, 1-43.

Furubotn, Eirik G. and Pejovich, Svetozar (1974a), *The Economics of Property Rights*, Cambridge, MA, Ballinger Publishing Cy.

Furubotn, Eirik G. and Pejovich, Svetozar (1974b), 'Property Rights and the Behavior of the Firm in a Socialist State: The Example of Yugoslavia', in Furubotn, Eirik G. and Pejovich, Svetozar (eds), *The Economics of Property Rights,* Cambridge, MA, Ballinger Publishing Cy, 227-251.

Grossekettler, Heinz (1996), 'Franz Böhm as a Pioneering Champion of an Economic Theory of Legislative Science', **3** *European Journal of Law and Economics*, 309-329.

Kuhn, Thomas S. (1970), *The Structure of Stientific Revolutions*, Chicago, The University of Chicago Press (1962), 2nd edn.

Lakatos, Imre (1970), 'Falsification and the Methodology of Scientific Research Programmes', in Lakatos, Imre and Musgrave, Alan (eds), *Criticism and the Growth of Knowledge,* Cambridge, Cambridge University Press, 91-196.

Lenel, Hans Otto (1996), 'The Life and Work of Franz Böhm', **3** *European Journal of Law and Economics*, 301-307.

Libecap, Gary D. (1989), *Contracting for Property Rights* (Political Economy of Institutions and Decisions), Cambridge, Cambridge University Press.

Mercuro, Nicholas and Medema, Steven G. (1997), *Economics and the Law: From Posner to Post-Modernism*, Princeton, Princeton University Press.

Minda, Gary (1989), 'The Law and Economics and Critical Legal Studies Movements in American Law', in Mercuro, Nicholas (ed.), *Law and Economics,* Boston, Kluwer Academic Publishers, 87-122.

Posner, Richard A. (1998), 'Social Norms, Social Meaning, and Economic Analysis of Law: A Comment', **27** *Journal of Legal Studies*, 553-565.

Rose-Ackerman, Susan (1989), 'Law and Economics: Paradigm, Politics, or Philosophy', in Mercuro, Nicholas (ed.), *Law and Economics,* Boston, Kluwer Academic Publishers, 233-258.

Rose-Ackerman, Susan (1992), *Rethinking the Progressive Agenda: The Reform of the American Regu!atory State*, New York, Free Press.

Rubin, Paul H. (1985), 'Some Notes on Methodology in Law and Economics', **7** *Research in Law and Economics*, 29-39.

Sowell, Thomas (1998), *Conquests and Cultures - An International History*, New York, Basic Books.

Streit, Manfred E. (1992), 'The Freiburg School of Law and Economics', **148** *Journal of Institutional and Theoretical Economics*, 675-704.

Streit, Manfred E. (1994), 'The Freiburg School of Law and Economics', in Boettke, Peter J. (ed.), *The Elgar Companion to Austrian Economics,* Hants, Cheltenham, Edward Edgar Publishing Co., 508-515.

Teijl, Rob and Holzhauer, Rudi W. (1990), 'Pluriformiteit in de Rechtseconomie: een Verkening van Scholen' (Pluriformity in Law and Economics: An Exploration of the Schools), **39(10)** *Ars Aequi*, 617-631.

Teijl, Rob and Holzhauer, Rudi W. (1997), *Wisselende Perspectieven in de Rechtseconomie* (Varying Perspectives in Law and Economics), Arnhem, Gouda Quint.

van den Hauwe, Ludwig (1996), 'Book Review : Economic Methodology and theEconomic Analysis of Law, Gerrit De Geest, MAKLU: Antwerpen-Apeldoorn, 1994', **3** *European Journal of Law and Economics*, 97-103.

Vanberg, Viktor (1998), 'Freiburg School of Law and Economics', in Newman, Peter (ed.), *The New Palgrave Dictionary of Economics and the Law, Vol. 2,* London, Macmillan, 172-179.

Veljanovski, Cento G. (1985), 'The Role of Economics in the Common Law', **7** *Research in Law and Economics*, 41-64.

Veljanovski, Cento G. (1990), *The Economics of Law - An Introductory Text*, London, Institute of Economic Affairs.

Walker, David M.(1980), *The Oxford Companion to Law*, Oxford, Clarendon Press.

Wolin, Sheldon S. (1980), 'Paradigms and Political Theories', in Gutting, Gary (ed.), *Paradigms and Revolutions - Appraisals and Applications of Thomas Kuhn's Philosophy of Science,* Notre Dame, University of Notre Dame Press, 160-191.

0510
AUSTRIAN SCHOOL

Bibliography Collected by the Editors

Adelstein, Richard P. (1992), 'Charles E. Lindblom', in Samuels, Warren J. (ed.), *New Horizons in Economic Thought: Appraisals of Leading Economists*, Cheltenham, Edward Elgar, 202-226.

Barry, Norman P. (1984), 'The 'Austrian' Perspective', in Whynes, David K. (ed.), *What Is Political Economy? Eight Perspectives*, New York, Blackwell, 33-58.

Benson, Bruce L. (1991), 'An Evolutionary Contractarian View of Primitive Law: The Institutions and Incentives Arising Under Customary American Indian Law', **5** *Review of Austrian Economics*, 65-89.

Benson, Bruce L. (1993), 'The Impetus for Recognizing Private Property and Adopting Ethical Behavior in a Market Economy: Natural Law, Government Law, or Evolving Self-Interest', **6** *Review of Austrian Economics*, 43-80.

Benson, Bruce L. (1994), 'Legal Philosophy', in Boettke, Peter J. (ed.), *The Elgar Companion to Austrian Economics*, London, Edward Elgar, 270-275.

Crafton, Steven M. and Brinig, Margaret F. (1994), *Quantitative Methods for Lawyers*, Durham, NC, Carolina Academic Press.

Dnes, Anthony W. (1988), 'The Efficiency of Central Planning', **35(4)** *Scottish Journal of Political Economy*, 404-410.

Dnes, Anthony W. (1989), 'Rent Seeking, Entrepreneurship, Subjectivism and Property Rights: A Comment', **144** *Journal of Institutional and Theoretical Economics*, 891-893.

Garello, P. (1995), *Présentation d'un Débat Fondamental en Science Economique et ses Implications pour les Rapports entre Droit et Economie* (Presentation of Fundamental Debate in Economics and its Implication in the Relationship between Law and Econnomics), R.R.J. , Presses Universitaires d'Aix-Marseille., 419 p.

Hayek, Friedrich A. von (1973), *Law, Legislation, and Liberty*, Chicago, University of Chicago Press.

Huerta De Soto, Jesús (1994), 'Génesis, Esencía y Evolución de la Escuela Austríaca de Economía (Genesis, Essence and Evolution of the Austrian School of Economics)', in X (ed.), *Estudios de Economía Política*, Madrid, Unión Editorial, 17-55.

Kan, Steven S. (1993), 'Entrepreneurship, Transaction Costs, and Subjectivist Economics', **1(2)** *Journal of Enterprising Culture*, 159-182.

Kan, Steven S. and Hwang, Chun-Sin (1996), 'A Form of Government Organization from the Perspective of Transaction Cost Economics', **7** *Constitutional Political Economy*, 197-220.

Kirzner, Israel M. (ed.) (1986), *Subjectivism, Intelligibility and Economic Understanding: Essays in Honor of Ludwig M. Lachmann on His Eighteenth Birthday*, London, Macmillan.

Krecke, E.l. (1996), 'Law and the Market Order - An Austrian Critique of Economic Analysis of Law', **8** *Journal des Economistes et des Etudes Humaines*, 19 ff.

Leoni, Bruno (1991), *Freedom and the Law*, Indianapolis, Liberty Fund.

McGee, Robert W. and Greaves, Bettina Bien (1993), *Mises: An Annotated Bibliography*, Foundation for Economic Education, 405 p.

Paqué, Karl-Heinz (1985), 'How Far is Vienna from Chicago? An Essay on the Methodology of Two Schools of Dogmatic Liberalism', **38** *Kyklos*, 412-434.

Prychitko, David L. (1990), 'Methodological Individualism and the Austrian Shool', **1** *Journal des Economistes et des Etudes Humaines*, 171 ff.

Schmidtchen, Dieter (1993), 'Time, Uncertainty, and Subjectivism: Giving More Body to Law and Economics', **13** *International Review of Law and Economics*, 61-84.

Schwartzstein, Linda A. (1992), 'Austrian Economics and the Current Debate between Critical Legal Studies and Law and Economics', **20** *Hofstra Law Review*, 1105 ff.

Schwartzstein, Linda A. (1994), 'An Austrian Economic View of Legal Process', **55** *Ohio State Law Journal*.

Teijl, Rob and Holzhauer, Rudi W. (1994), *De Betekenis van de Oostenrijkse School voor de Rechtseconomie* (The Impact of the Austrian School on Law and Economics), Arnhem, Gouda Quint.

Teijl, Rob and Holzhauer, Rudi W. (1995a), 'The Impact of the Austrian School on Law and Economics', in Bouckaert, Boudewijn and De Geest, Gerrit (eds), *Essays in Law and Economics II: Contract Law, Regulation, and Reflections on Law and Economics*, Antwerpen, Maklu, 247-266.

Teijl, Rob and Holzhauer, Rudi W. (1995b), 'The Impact of the Austrian School of Law and Economics', in Bouckaert, Boudewijn and De Geest, Gerrit (eds), *Essays in Law and Economics II: Contract Law, Regulation, and Reflections on Law and Economics*, Antwerpen, Maklu, 247-265.

Van den Hauwe, Ludwig (1998a), 'German Income Tax Policy Between Equity and Efficiency', **5** *European Journal of Law and Economics*, 267-279.

Van den Hauwe, Ludwig (1998b), 'Evolution and the Production of Rules - Some Preliminary Remarks', **5** *European Journal of Law and Economics*, 81-117.

Wonnell, Christopher T. (1986), 'Contract Law and the Austrian School of Economics', **54** *Fordham Law Review*, 507-543.

0520
INSTITUTIONAL LAW AND ECONOMICS

Steven G. Medema
Associate Professor of Economics, University of Colorado at Denver

Nicholas Mercuro
College of Natural Sciences, Michigan State University

Warren J. Samuels
Professor of Economics, Michigan State University

Abstract

From its beginnings in the late nineteenth century, institutional economics has been concerned with the analysis of the interrelations between legal and economic processes. The institutional approach to law and economics examines both the influence of economy upon law and legal reasoning and the influence of law and legal change upon economic activity and performance. This essay examines the central tenants of institutional law and economics, dating from the early work of individuals such as Robert Lee Hale and John R. Commons and through its modern manifestations. As such, it emphasizes the evolutionary nature of law and economy, the tension between continuity and change, the problem of order, the reciprocal nature of legal-economic problems and the attendant dual nature of rights, the problematic nature of efficiency, and the need for a comparative institutional approach to the practice of law and economics. By recognizing the multiplicity of potential solutions to legal-economic problems and the underlying value premises attending each, the comparative institutional approach to law and economics attempts to flesh out both what is actually going on within the legal-economic nexus and the alternative possibilities open to society within the legal-economic decision-making process.
JEL classification: K00
Keywords: Law and Economics, Institutional Economics, Efficiency, Rights, Government

1. Introduction

From its beginnings in the late nineteenth century, institutional economics has been concerned with the analysis of the interrelations between nominally legal and economic processes. The earliest roots of law and economics are in part within the institutionalist tradition of economics but, as recognized by Warren J. Samuels (1993), go well beyond that school of economic analysis. Early contributions to the institutional approach to law and economics include the work of Henry Carter Adams (1897) on economics and jurisprudence, Richard T. Ely (1914) on the relation of property and contract to the distribution of wealth, and, especially, John R. Commons (1924, 1925) on the legal foundations of the economic system. Important elements of the institutional approach to law and economics can also be found in the work of Thorstein Veblen (1899, 1904), lawyer-economists Robert Lee Hale (1952) and Walton H. Hamilton (1932), and legal scholars such as Karl Llewellyn (1925), Jerome Frank (1930), and Roscoe Pound (1911a, 1911b, 1912). Institutional economics is essentially an American contribution to economic thought, one that, like Legal Realism in jurisprudence, is said to have 'had its heyday in the 1920s and early 1930s' (Bell, 1967). Nonetheless, it continues to have a relatively strong presence today in both the US and Europe.

A. Institutional Economics

2. Overview

Institutional economics developed as a rather heterodox approach to the study of economic society and has been amply reviewed by Bell (1967, pp. 539-571), Gordon (1964, pp. 123-147), Kapp (1976), Mitchell (1937), Rutherford (1994), Spiegel (1971, pp. 628-641), Srivastava (1965, pp. 470-487), and more recently by Pribram (1983, pp. 355-62; 424-29) and Whalen (1996). There also are extensive overviews/anthologies of institutional economics including those by Hodgson, Samuels and Tool (1994), Samuels (1988), and Tool (1988, 1993). As its name implies, institutional economics places at the center of analysis the study of the institutions of the economic system. Institutions are variously and broadly defined within institutional economics. Commons (1934) defined an institution as 'collective action in control of individual action' and as 'collective action in restraint, liberation, and expansion of individual action' thereby emphasizing the social bases of the individual which orthodox economists took as given and self-subsistent. Veblen (1899) defined institutions as 'widely followed habits of thought and the practices which prevail in any given period', thereby emphasizing their problematic and belief-oriented nature. Herbert J. Davenport essentially combined the two definitions in his description of an institution as 'a working consensus of human thought or habits - a generally-established attitude of mind and a generally-adopted custom of action as for example, private property, inheritance, government, taxation, competition, and credit' (cited in Srivastava, 1965, p. 470).

Institutional economics has often been described as part of 'a revolt against formalism' (Spiegel, 1971, p. 629), a revolt that took place in law, in history, and in economics at about the same time. Institutional economics, as part of that revolt, was led by a group of young American scholars who, after World War I, engaged in a critique of the predominate, formalistic economic doctrines of the day. In economics, formalism was taken to be the abstract *deductive* reasoning of orthodox economic analysis that enthroned universally valid reason, assumed passive, rational utility-maximizing behavior, and demonstrated an inordinate concern over the equilibria of comparative statics (in particular utility analysis of consumer behavior and the marginal productivity theory of distribution).

Reflecting their belief that this methodology was inadequate for understanding many important facets of the economic system, institutionalists focused their attention on *inductive* analyses of specific institutional aspects of the American economy. While their principal emphasis was on using the inductive method to describe the constituent elements of the economy, the institutionalists never employed the inductive method to extremes and thereby were still able to make substantive theoretical generalizations. As noted by Buckingham (1958, pp. 107-108), 'the development of generalizations gave institutional economics more of a theoretical content than the largely descriptive [German] historical school was ever able to attain. Institutional theory is by no means as refined and exact as orthodox theory, but is not so abstract and lacking in empirical content either'.

3. Factors Contributing to the Institutionalist School of Thought

Whalen (1996) has traced the emergence of institutional economics to three distinct sources of influence. One was the German historical school, which influenced such early institutionalist thinkers as Richard T. Ely. The German historical school, founded by Wilhelm Roscher (1817-94) and later dominated by Gustav von Schmoller (1838-1917), emerged at least in part as a reaction against classical economic thinking in the mid-nineteenth century. The historical school emphasized the dynamics of economic development, the need to use empirical data (rather than abstract ideas) to ground economic theories, and the necessity of paying particular attention to human institutions. This emphasis on gathering facts and studying them in relation to their historical significance rather than as isolated, objective data in static, timeless models had a direct bearing on the methodology of emerging institutionalist economics.

The second influence was from American pragmatic philosophy as set forth by, among others, Charles Peirce, William James and John Dewey. Proponents of American pragmatic philosophy recognized an uncertainty inherent in understanding and looked for philosophical methods for establishing the meaning of concepts and beliefs. The analysis of social phenomena had to be conducted within systems of relationships among individuals in their empirical settings. They largely replaced *a priori* abstract reasoning with empirical studies. Contrary to the narrow, uniform 'rational behavior' assumption in orthodox microeconomics, choices were pragmatically perceived - to be made in a world of ever-changing empirical objects and emerging economic, political, and social institutions. 'True' ideas are those to which responsible investigators would assent after thorough examination - that is, after considering what conceivable effects of a practical kind a theory or object holds. Thus, only those hypotheses that contributed to organizing data garnered through sense perceptions related to the real world (that is, held practical significance), and did so in a progressive and unifying manner, were taken to be legitimate. In short, an idea was right if it had 'fruitful' consequences. The pragmatist emphasis on the uncertainty inherent in understanding served to provide an epistemological foundation and a social philosophy upon which to erect the basic tenets of institutional economic thought.

The third influence came through Thorstein Veblen's turn-of-the century writings focusing on the Darwinian, non-teleological evolutionary nature of economic change to which one can trace many of the origins of and early insights into institutional economic thought. After short sojourns at a variety of universities, including Johns Hopkins, a doctorate degree in philosophy from Yale University in 1884, and several years (1891-96) as an economics fellow at Cornell University and the University of Chicago, Veblen was given a teaching post at the University of Chicago in 1896, becoming an assistant professor of economics in 1900 at the age of 43. The previous year he published his first and most renowned book, *The Theory of the Leisure Class* (Veblen 1899).

Here, as in his other writings, Veblen emerged a strong critic of orthodox economic thinking, rejecting the mechanistic view of economic society as reflected in static equilibrium analysis. As observed by Spiegel (1971, pp. 631-632), Veblen rejected the orthodox 'hedonistic conception of man as a lightning calculator of pleasures and pain' as overly narrow and outmoded.

Consequently, he characterized the conventional approach to economics as taxonomic, overly concerned with classification and systematization that depicted human behavior in passive, inert, hedonic terms and, at the same time, brushed aside the 'disturbing factors' that did not fit into the received doctrine's pursuit of truth. With respect to conventional economics' pursuit of truth, in a revealing statement in an address in 1908, Veblen asserted that 'the outcome of any serious research can only be to make two questions grow where one question grew before' (Spiegel, 1971, pp. 631).

Veblen focused on what he called an evolutionary method of economic analysis. He believed that the material environment, technology, and propensities of human nature condition the emergence and growth of institutions. Because he believed that social change implied changes in habits of thought and customs as crystallized in institutions, he insisted on a critical examination of capitalistic institutions - especially what he termed *industry* and *business*, along with the economic power they were able to exercise - to better comprehend economic society. Toward that end, he emphasized that it was necessary to understand both the 'widespread social habits' and the institutions, and not merely how prevailing institutions worked, but with finding out how the institutions of capitalism evolved.

In another of his books, *The Theory of Business Enterprise* (1904), Veblen identifies the price system as the leading economic institution in the so-called pecuniary economy. Many contributing factors, most of which are inherent in the economic system including 'businesslike technicians', 'labor organizations', 'technological advances', and so on, lead to economic tensions among the interrelated forces of production and profit. These tensions manifested themselves in a class system - (1) the productive class, comprised of those who were socially productive, and (2) the leisure class, comprised of those who came to depend upon acquisition. And, as described by Bell (1967, pp. 548-549), these manifested themselves in 'custodians of absentee-credit' who were certain to engage in 'capitalistic sabotage' and further, that 'the struggle for economic advantage for their own vested interests' would result in both labor and business technicians engaging in a 'conscious withdrawal of efficiency'. 'Cultural lags' brought on by technological change altered the institutions and human behavior resulting in an ever-present class conflict (Srivastava, 1965, pp. 474-475). Thus, as Veblen described it, it is the very factors within the institution of the price system that led business to experience fewer intervals of short-term depressions that ultimately gave way to more chronic stagnation. For Veblen, the pecuniary aspects of life are all-pervading and become an integral part of the analysis of the evolution of society.

4. Modern Elements of Institutional Economics

From the writings of Thorstein Veblen and other contributors (to be reviewed below) such as Wesley C. Mitchell, Clarence E. Ayres, Walton H. Hamilton, Robert Lee Hale and John R. Commons, institutional economics emerged as a rather heterodox approach to analyzing economic society. As will become evident, many of the founders of and present contributors to institutional economics stress the evolutionary facet of institutions and, thus, the economy. This continuing concern with the evolutionary nature of the economy underlies the name of the association - The Association For Evolutionary Economics - that has maintained some intellectual continuity and focus among this group of economists. The Association publishes its own journal, the *Journal of Economic Issues*. The *Review of Political Economy* regularly publishes work embodying the institutionalist perspective (often with a somewhat more European flavor), as do the *Cambridge Journal of Economics*, *Economy and Society*, *Industrial and Corporate Change* and the *Review of International Political Economy*.

In its modern form institutional economics, as set forth by Gordon (1964, pp. 124-125), is embodied in a series of propositions defining an approach both alternative to and complementary to mainstream economic analysis. These propositions, together with the particular and specific focus contributed by Commons, provide the foundation upon which institutional law and economics rests.

1. Economic behavior is strongly conditioned by the institutional environment within which economic activity takes place and, simultaneously, economic behavior affects the structure of the institutional environment.
2. The mutual interaction between the institutions and the behavior of economic actors is an evolutionary process, hence the need for an 'evolutionary approach' to economics.
3. In analyzing the evolutionary processes contained therein, emphasis is directed to the role played by the conditions imposed by modern technology and the monetary institutions of modern, mixed-market capitalism.
4. Emphasis is centered upon conflicts within the economic sphere of society as opposed to harmonious order inherent within the cooperative, spontaneous, and unconscious free play of economic actors within the market.
5. There is a clear and present need to channel the conflicts inherent in economic relationships by structuring institutions to establish a mechanism of social control over economic activity.

6. Institutionalism requires an interdisciplinary approach calling on psychology, sociology, anthropology, and law to help understand the behavior of economic actors and thereby generate more accurate assumptions in describing their behavior.

These propositions offer a partial rejection of the mechanistic price-theoretic approach proffered by the more orthodox neoclassical microeconomics. The propositions are a manifestation of the institutionalist position that the framework of orthodox economic analysis does not allow it to get at certain fundamentally important features of economic activity.

Further, evolutionary institutional economics is proffered as being based on more 'realistic' behavioral assumptions derived from a broad array of social science knowledge and a fuller appreciation for and understanding of the institutions driving a mixed-market economy. This drive for realistic assumptions led the early institutionalists to extensive data-collection efforts. A pioneer in this regard, and a leading institutionalist, was Wesley C. Mitchell, a student of Veblen's at the University of Chicago. Mitchell spent most of his academic career at Columbia University (from 1913-1944). His book, *Business Cycles* (Mitchell, 1928) was his greatest research work. In it, he maintained that all institutions were subject to forces that brought about change in response to changing conditions and behavior. His concern was with the behavior of institutional factors which would provide a basis for generalizations; thus the need to produce the empirical evidence (statistical records and quantitative verification of change) that would thereby permit the development of more realistic theories of economic change (Bell, 1967, p. 565). The book was a historical description of the economic organizations of four countries (US, Germany, Great Britain and France) and of the pecuniary aspects of their economies. In his research he compiled all of the data necessary to recount the business cycle theories within each country. Mitchell demonstrated that trade cycles were not accidental disruptions in the economy but were instead systematic fluctuations brought on by the changing economic organization of the economy together with its changing culture. It should be noted in passing that in furtherance of this tradition Mitchell founded the National Bureau of Economic Research, which has become a major center for empirical work in economics. Mitchell succeeded in helping to expand the scope of economics beyond static equilibrium analysis thereby fulfilling his mission 'to explain at once the current working and the cumulative changing of economic processes' (Mitchell, 1914, p. 37).

B. Institutional Law and Economics: Origins and Development

5. Ayres and Hale

Because institutional economics has always been concerned with legal facets of the economy (that is the relationship between the law and the development and performance of the economy), there is no clear dividing line or simplistic transition between institutional economics and institutional law and economics. Thus, an understanding of the nature of the analyses and the concerns of the major contributors to institutional economics concomitantly provides an understanding and appreciation of the scope and content of present-day institutional law and economics. This and the next section are intended to help make this transition.

Certain of Thorstein Veblen's ideas described above were given further development by Clarence E. Ayres. Ayres received his PhD in philosophy from the University of Chicago in 1917 writing on the relationship between ethics and economics. He started his teaching career at Amherst College assisting the legal-economist, Walton H. Hamilton in his course, 'Social and Economic Institutions'. After brief sojourns at the University of Wisconsin and New York University, in 1930, his former colleague, Hamilton, was influential in urging Ayres to move to the University of Texas at Austin where he influenced a generation of institutionalist scholars.

Ayres's perspective on the economy is found in his treatise *The Theory of Economic Progress* (Ayres, 1944). As described by Breit (1973), it is a theoretical work that attempts to explain the forces that have shaped the economy, focusing on those factors that accelerated the economy's development as well as those that have impeded it. For Ayres, the challenge confronting economics is to 'devise new organizational forms, to pragmatically develop organizational arts to match, rather than contradict, our science and technology' (Breit, 1973, pp. 255-256).

Ayres saw human activity as reflective of two basic and ever-present forces: 'technological' behavior, a productive and progressive force, and 'ceremonial' behavior (as manifested in, for example, hierarchies, mores, culture and ideology), which is counterproductive and inhibits change, acting as a curb on technological progress. The central theme of this work is that an exponentially expanding and advancing 'technology' (defined broadly as all human activities involving the use of tools, and thus including both human and physical capital) is responsible for the enormous changes in the welfare of society. The focus is not so much on the individuals, but on technological progress as related to the advancement of the tools (that is, the objective instruments capable of being variously combined) and the role of technology in enhancing economic progress. Since the ceremonial institutions resist change, he argued, progress is a function of the relative strength of these progressive and inhibiting forces, with the variance of their relative strengths helping to explain the differential rates of development across societies and cultures.

Robert Lee Hale received his LLB from Harvard University in 1909 and his PhD in economics from Columbia University in 1918. As recounted by Dorfman (1959), Samuels (1973) and Duxbury (1990, 1995), Hale initially held a joint appointment in the economics department and the law school at Columbia University and then moved to the law school on a full-time basis in 1928. His emphasis on the integration of economics and law was reflected both in his teaching - particularly his course on 'Legal Factors in Economic Society' - and in his writing, much of which dealt with the regulation of railroads and public utilities, fields in which an understanding of the interface between economics and law has always been fundamental. Hale wrote extensively on the legal and economic theory of rate-base valuation, as well as on the regulation of rate structure and level. His writings were instrumental in the adoption by the courts of the 'prudent investment' doctrine of valuation for public utilities (Dorfman, 1959, p. 161).

Hale is perhaps best described as a legal realist who drew upon the emerging tradition of institutionalism (Duxbury 1995, pp. 107-108). Consistent with the realists of the day, Hale's work was very much a challenge to and critique of the dominant tradition of *laissez-faire* capitalism. And, while Richard Posner (1995, p. 3) contends that the legal realists had little influence on the contemporary law and economics movement, he does allow that Hale 'anticipated some of the discoveries ... of law and economics' as we know it today.

Like John R. Commons (whose contributions will be reviewed below), Hale was influenced by Wesley H. Hohfeld's articulation of 'fundamental legal conceptions', which, in Hohfeld's mind, were the 'lowest common denominators of law' (Cotterrell, 1989, p. 88). Hale's paradigm was comprised of the concepts of voluntary freedom, volitional freedom, coercion, power and government. Legal and economic processes were viewed as inseparable and the economy described as a structure of coercive power arrangements and relationships which necessitated an understanding of the formation and structure of the underlying distribution of economic power. As such, the economy was seen as a system of power operating through a system of coercion, and thus the economic freedom expressed by the courts of the day was merely freedom to engage in economic coercion (Samuels, 1973).

Hale did not view coercion as something to be condemned, but rather as a basic fact of economic life. For example, he argued that if income is in fact acquired through coercion, abetted actively or passively by government, then it cannot be said that overt coercive redistributions of income by government are themselves wrong (Dorfman, 1959, pp. 162-163). Hale's Hohfeldian perspective on rights led him to view nearly every statute with economic implications as impacting negatively upon someone's liberty or property. Given this, he believed that it was essential for the courts to undertake an intelligent balancing of the gains and losses brought about by the particular statutes brought before them - a process which, he said, requires 'a realistic understanding of the economic effect of the legislation' (quoted in Dorfman, 1959, p. 163). While Hale believed that ethical judgments must ultimately be the basis upon which the court's decisions are made, he felt that the judicial application of economic principles was necessary in order to ascertain the economic consequences - allocative and distributive - of the legislation whose constitutionality the court was asked to evaluate (Hale, 1924, 1927). Hale's brand of legal economics - as reflected in both his writing and his teaching - gradually evolved into a 'theory of the economy as a system of mutual coercion and the legal basis thereof' (Samuels, 1973, p. 25), with his perspective being most fully spelled out in his classic book *Freedom Through Law* (Hale, 1952).

6. John R. Commons and his Impact on the Development of Institutional Law and Economics

John R. Commons stands as the central figure in the development of the institutional approach to law and economics. Unlike his contemporaries, Commons never earned a PhD degree and after a slowly developing academic career, in 1904, at the age of 42, he was given an appointment at the University of Wisconsin where he and his associates quickly brought the economics department to the forefront of the discipline (Spiegel, 1971, p. 630).

Commons became associated with the progressive government of the State of Wisconsin, engaging in what he termed 'investigational economics' (preparatory fact-finding reports produced by Commons and his students) necessary for the drafting of legislation and the formulation of innovative policies in a wide variety of areas including industrial relations, labor law reform (including workmen's compensation and unemployment insurance), public utility regulation and price stabilization. Besides teaching and writing at the University of Wisconsin, he was also very involved in public life serving on an array of state and federal commissions. In his distinguished academic career, Commons wrote several books, two of which now serve as a benchmark for institutional law and economics: *Legal Foundations of Capitalism* (Commons, 1924) and *Institutional Economics: Its Place in Political Economy* (Commons, 1934).

As Spiegel (1971, pp. 628-629) has pointed out, there was a pronounced linkage between Commons' institutional economics and the German historical school (due in part to his teacher Ely's attachment to the German school). The influence of the American pragmatic philosophers on his thinking was much less significant, although its presence is evidenced in his emphasis on the pragmatic importance of using inductive analysis. And unlike Thorstein Veblen, who sought a near total rejection of orthodox economic theory, Commons (as well as Wesley C. Mitchell) held a much more conciliatory position seeing institutional economics as a complement to, rather than a substitute for, neoclassical analysis.

Commons' institutional economics was conceived as a broad synthesis of law, economics and ethics; it recognized both conflicts of interest and their mutual dependencies as well as the need for security of expectations and order (Spiegel, 1971, p. 638). In contrast to the strict methodological individualism and the harmony of interests paradigm that imbued orthodox economics, Commons placed a greater emphasis on the role of collective and corporate activities in the economy and centered his analysis on the conflicts of interest inherent in a modern economy. Human action was seen to be socially or culturally determined; that is, human action and cultural determinants were seen to interact with each other. Consequently, the free will of individuals contributes to the cultural environment and is, in turn, molded by that environment (Buckingham, 1958, p. 104).

As characterized by Parsons (1957, p. 23), for Commons, the main task of economics consisted of determining the 'reasonableness of the working rules underlying the general economic order in an age in which citizens, corporations, and labor unions have economic power' (see also Parsons, 1985). Institutional economics for Commons was an economics of rights, duties, liberties and exposures and he looked at the economy as a series of intended and purposeful changes - so-called 'managed equilibria'. He believed that the primary economic institutions were formed on the basis of definite patterns of socially sanctioned habits and could be reshaped. This belief led him to probe extensively the impact of institutions, particularly the operation of the legal system (including the judiciary, the legislature and the regulatory commissions) in working out solutions to conflicts and the impact of those solutions on economic structure and performance.

In *Legal Foundations of Capitalism* (Commons, 1924) Commons's chief concern was with uncovering the development, evolution and workings of the institutions that ultimately impact the performance of the economic system. It was a theoretical work that examined the legal foundations of the capitalist economic system. The treatise was unlike anything that had come before and benefited from Commons's close contact with law through his extensive aforementioned involvement with the courts, his service on government commissions and his drafting of legislation. The emphasis of the book is on the role of law and the courts and how they determine the structural elements of an economic system. Like his predecessors, Commons believed all economic institutions are subject to evolution. Whether describing the institution of capitalism, private property, or the state itself, each was shown to receive its sanction from the authorities - the church, the state, the courts - through an evolutionary process.

Commons analysis showed, on the one hand, how economy influences law as the economic system brings to bear pressures on political and legal systems for legal change that facilitates a particular evolutionary path and, on the other hand, how law influences the economy - that is, how legal change facilitates the development of economic activity in a particular direction. In order to bring out the nature and extent of this mutual interdependence, he undertook an analysis of a wide variety of cases, working rules and statutes to probe their impacts on the development of modern capitalism and thereby to illuminate the interrelations between legal and economic processes. Of particular import here is his analysis of the role played by rights and working rules within the economic system, where he lays out, in a systematic way, why rights (and thus law) matter within the economic system and why the development of economic theory should proceed with attention to the role of law and legal change in structuring economic activity and performance.

Commons was particularly concerned in *Legal Foundations* to uncover the values both underlying and ensconced in the working rules that govern social-economic relations. He found them in the courts' use of the term 'reasonable value' - whether reasonable value in public utility regulation, the reasonable wage in labor law, the reasonable safety as related to workmen's compensation, or the reasonable conduct of private and public citizens. He observed that legal history demonstrated certain well-defined tendencies on the part of the courts to eliminate those practices of capitalistic institutions deemed destructive, while at the same time to reaffirm the 'reasonable' policies that should be encouraged and followed in a competitive system. Determinations have to be made as to whose interests are to count or, said another way, to determine whose preferred practices would be given protected status. 'Reasonable value' could be used by the courts to ground policies that would bring about compromises in arenas of economic conflict, including labor disputes, public utility rate-making, tax policy, pricing, and so on (Bell, 1967, pp. 556-557). As the definition of what types of activities were considered reasonable evolved over time, so too did the legal rules governing social-economic relations, the structure of markets and the structure of capitalism itself, as seen in the effects of the transformation of the legal definition of property and its impact on business and the effects of law on the employment relation within the firm, on the market mechanism and on the wage bargain. Thus, in the West, a movement was engendered from a feudal and agrarian society to a capitalist system, with economic change driving legal change, which in turn facilitated the economic transformations. (See Samuels (1996) for a 'Reader's Guide' to the *Legal Foundations of Capitalism.*)

7. Contemporary Institutional Law and Economics: The Commons Tradition

Virtually all of contemporary institutional law and economics follows in the tradition of Commons and much of this emanates from Michigan State University through the work of Warren J. Samuels and A. Allan Schmid, both trained at the University of Wisconsin by students of Commons. Others at Michigan State University who continue to contribute to this tradition are Harry Trebing, whose works exhibit many of the same concerns as Hale with regard to the analysis of regulation and public utilities (Trebing, 1976, 1989; Trebing and Estabrooks, 1993); and Robert A. Solo, much of whose work focuses on monopoly regulation and institutional change (Solo, 1967, 1974, 1982). Former students of Samuels and Schmid who have gone on to focus their research on the relations between legal (or governmental) and economic processes rather than the application of microeconomic theory to the law, include Steven G. Medema and Nicholas Mercuro writing individually and together on topics including the Coase theorem (Medema, 1994, 1996a; Medema and Zerbe, 1997), the policy implications of Coasean economics (Medema and Samuels, 1997), the commonalities between the work of the Institutionalists and the work of Coase (Medema, 1996b), law, economics and public policy (Mercuro and Ryan, 1984), the comparative institutional approach to law and economics (Mercuro, 1989b) and on the various schools of thought comprising law and economics, including the institutionalist school (Mercuro, 1989a; Mercuro and Medema, 1995, 1997); Philip Wandschneider (1984,1986) on water rights; and Josef Broder (1981, 1983) on the judicial process.

Other examples of the institutional approach to law and economics can be found in Bromley (1989), Carter (1985), Kanal (1985), Liebhafsky (1987), Ostrom (1986), Parsons (1974), and Seidman (1973).

Much, though not all, of the work of A. Allan Schmid and Warren J. Samuels (see the extensive references to their respective work at the end of this essay) can be best understood in the context of the structure-conduct-performance paradigm:

> △ law or legal structure → △ behaviour or conduct in the mixed market economy → △ economic peformance

For institutional law and economics, the emphasis is on the interrelations and *mutual* interaction between government and the economy, with the effect that its perspective is described by the relation

> △ law or legal structure ⇔ △ behaviour or conduct in the mixed market economy ⇔ △ economic performance

Both Samuels's and Schmid's practices of institutional law and economics are avowedly positive. As they describe it in the 'introduction' to their book on institutional law and economics (Samuels and Schmid 1981, p. 1), 'Our principal goal is quite simply to understand what is going on - to identify the instrumental variables and fundamental issues and processes - in the operation of legal institutions of economic significance' and to promote 'the development of skills with which to analyze and predict the performance consequences of alternative institutional designs'. The focus of their institutional approach is on delving into the workings of the legal-economic nexus in order to understand its processes and thereby analyze the processes and consequences of choice. Resource allocation and the distribution of income and wealth are explained 'in terms of a complex causal chain involving both allocation and distribution as functions of market forces that depend in turn on power, rights and the use of government' (Samuels and Schmid, 1981, p. 4).

Samuels and Schmid's respective approaches are best understood as two complementary branches that differ only with respect to the relative emphasis given to 'structure' and 'conduct'. The work of Schmid has tended to concentrate on the interdependence of structure and performance, with an emphasis on empirical work that explores the economic impact of alternative legal structures. A concise statement of Schmid's approach to institutional law and economics is contained in his book *Property, Power and Public Choice: An Inquiry Into Law and Economics* (Schmid, 1987), which includes examples of empirical studies undertaken by Schmid (see Schmid, 1987, pp. 257-291). In his approach, he brings to the forefront the many varieties of human interdependence, focusing both on (1) the various types of transactions - bargained, administrative and status and grant transactions and (2) the varied interdependencies that emerge - technological, pecuniary and political externalities. Schmid's analysis takes place under a situation-specific structure-conduct-performance paradigm, in which alternative institutional structures (for example, different definitions and assignments of property rights) are identified, together with the (dis)incentives created, their consequences for individuals, firms and government behavior are identified and their effects on economic performance and quality of life are assessed. As such, it reflects a 'total' approach to policy analysis (Schmid, 1987, pp. 257-258), one that emphasizes the link between structure and performance. As posed by Schmid (1987, p. 188), the institutional approach to law and economics must ask: How do the rules of property structure human relationships and affect participation in decisions when interests conflict or when shared objectives are to be implemented? How do the results affect performance of the economy?

The work of Samuels, in contrast, has tended to concentrate on describing the interdependence between conduct/behavior of individuals and groups and legal-economic performance. For Samuels, the organizing concept is that of the legal-economic nexus, wherein 'the law is a function of the economy and the economy (especially its structure) is a function of law ... [Law and economy] are jointly produced, not independently given and not merely interacting' Samuels (1989a, p. 1567). Through the legal-economic nexus are worked out the structures of the law and the economic system, where each serves as both dependent and independent variable in the construction of legal-economic reality. Legal rules govern 'the terms of access to and participation in the economy by potential economic actors' and 'property and other rights ... govern whose preferences will be given effect through the market' (Samuels, 1975, p. 66).

C. Central Themes of Institutional Law and Economics

8. The Evolutionary Nature of Law and Economy

As noted above, one of the factors emphasized by the institutionalists and especially John R. Commons in his discussion of the legal foundations of the capitalist economic system is the evolutionary nature of the economic system. The import of the evolutionary perspective is that it broadens the frame of analysis beyond the 'idea of mechanistic maximization under static constraints' (Hodgson, 1994, p. 223) to the longer-run processes (gradual or in leaps) of economic development - structural transformations owing to technical, legal, or other forces, knowledge acquisition, and so on. While not eschewing static analysis or denying its value, the role of legal change in affecting the course of this evolution makes the institutional approach to law and economics inherently evolutionary, as exemplified in Commons' analysis and in particular in his discussion of the evolution of the law of property.

Prior to the late nineteenth century, the US courts held to a physical conception of property, a view that defined property as value in use rather than value in exchange (Commons, 1924, p. 12). One of the implications of this definition of property was that governmental deprivations of exchange value did not require compensation under the Fifth and Fourteenth amendments. As Commons (1924, pp. 12-14) points out, it was only in the 1870s that the idea of property as value in exchange first began to creep into dissenting opinions of the US Supreme Court and it was not until the 1890s that the Court finally made the transition from a definition of property as a thing having only use value to a definition that conceived of property as the exchange value of something. In making this transition, the Court was saying not only that physical things are property, but that 'the *expected earning power* of those things is property' and thus '[t]o deprive the owners of the *exchange value* of their property is equivalent to depriving them of their property' (Commons, 1924, p. 16, emphasis in original). No longer were physical seizures of property the only 'takings' requiring compensation; it now became the case that activities (including government regulations) that reduced the exchange value of things could give rise to claims for compensation. The concept of property was further expanded in the *Allgeyer* case of 1897 to include liberty of access to markets, an important component in the determination of exchange values (Commons, 1924, p. 17). The received definition of property as corporeal property had been expanded to include both incorporeal property - for example, debt instruments or promises to pay - and intangible property - 'anything that enables one to obtain from others an income in the process of buying and selling, borrowing and lending, hiring and hiring out, renting and leasing, in any of the transactions of the modern business' (Commons, 1924, p. 19).

The import of this expanded definition of property for the development of the capitalist system is set forth by Commons in the context of farming:

> The isolated, colonial or frontier farmer might produce and consume things, attentive only to their use value, but the modern farmer lives by producing 'social-use-values' and buying other social-use-values produced and sold by other business men. In this way he also 'produces' exchange-value, that is, assets. He farms for sale, not for use and while he has the doubtful alternative of falling back on his own natural resources if he cannot sell his products, yet his farm and crops are valuable because they are business assets, that is, exchange-values, while his liabilities are his debts and his taxes, all of them measured by his expectations and realizations on the commodity markets and money markets, in terms of exchange-value or price. (Commons, 1924, p. 21)

That is, what in part distinguishes capitalism from the colonial and feudal systems it replaced is the transition from production for one's own use to 'production for the use of others and acquisition for the use of self' (Commons, 1924, p. 21) and it was the adoption of this more expansive definition of property that helped to facilitate this economic transition.

Following Commons, the contemporary institutional approach to law and economics is evolutionary, emphasizing the importance of historical process and evolutionary change of law through time. As described by Samuels (1989a, p. 1578), the legal-economic nexus 'is a continuing, explorative and emergent process through which are worked out ongoing solutions to legal problems'. The legal-economic nexus is that sphere of decision making that reflects the working out of whose interests are to count as rights, whose values are to dominate and who is to make these decisions. The resolution of these issues determines not just rights, but the allocation and distribution of resources in society and hence power, income and wealth. The structure of legal-economic institutions - the state (whether in the context of the legislature, the bureaucracy, or the judiciary), the firm and the market - channels legal-economic decision making and this structure is seen as the outcome of an evolutionary process of legal-economic change rather than as movement to a steady-state equilibrium (Schmid, 1989, p. 66). Legal change, while gradual, has been continuous and 'has led to major transformations of the legal system and of the pattern of rights and, thereby, of the system of economic organization and control' (Samuels and Mercuro, 1979, p. 167). The pervasiveness of legal change and the ongoing process of legal-economic reconstruction through the nexus process thus makes necessary an evolutionary-historical approach that accounts for the array of factors and forces promoting both continuity and change over time. Illustrative examples of this type of analysis are provided by Field (1979, 1981, 1984, 1991) and Bromley (1989).

Field (1979, 1984) argues that a meaningful analysis and explanation of rules structures that organize and regulate economic activity cannot be accomplished by incorporating the rules into an endogenous neoclassical model. Rather, he asserts, a thorough understanding of the determinants and consequences of institutions and rules requires a case-by-case approach that maintains particular sensitivities to the historical, cultural and legal facets of the particular legal-economic institution being studied, including the norms that influence legal-economic behavior. In an analysis critical both of Chicago law and economics and of neoinstitutionalist law and economics (particularly the works of Posner and North and Thomas), Field (1981) asserted that some subset of institutional structures needs to be treated as parametric in the general equilibrium models and granted an explanatory status analogous to that traditionally accorded tastes, technology and endowments in the neoclassical model. More recently, Field (1991) has urged that legal-economic scholars devote more extensive attention to the effects of legal rules (particularly through income-expenditure effects) on aggregate or macroeconomic variables.

Bromley (1989), too, criticizes the narrowness of the Chicago and neoinstitutional (or new institutional) models of institutional change - particularly their contention that institutional change is driven solely by considerations of efficiency. Against this, he presents an analysis of institutional change that makes such change hinge on four factors: (1) the alteration of the economy's productive efficiency, (2) the redistribution of income, (3) the reallocation of economic opportunity and (4) the reallocation of economic advantage - all worked out over time in the context of individuals and collectivities pursuing their interest within a larger social-political context.

9. Continuity versus Change

The recognition of the evolutionary nature of legal-economic relations brings to the fore a second fundamental theme of institutional law and economics: the ever-present tension between continuity and change in legal-economic relations. The evolutionary path of the legal-economic system is derivative of the legal-economic policy *choices* that are made over time. Continuity and change are the outcome of the policymaking process, more specifically, of the interaction between the groups supporting the respective forces of continuity and change and the power that each can bring to bear on this process (Samuels, 1966, pp. 267-273). Within this policymaking process (be it legislative, bureaucratic, or judicial) arise and operate forces that, through acts of commission or omission, serve to maintain the *status quo* structure of legal-economic institutions and relations - that is, continuity - while other forces promote an alteration in these institutions and relations - that is, change. The ongoing choice process within the legal-economic arena determines both the institutional structures that obtain at any given point in time and whether the *status quo* institutional structures, or some other, will prevail in the future, that is, whether there will be change and if so how much.

10. Mutual Interdependence, Conflict and the Problem of Order

Institutional law and economics views the legal-economic system as a system of mutual interdependence rather than one of atomistic independence. The economy, says Schmid (1989, p. 59), is 'a universe of human relations', not merely 'a universe of commodities' and within this world each individual has scarcity relationships with others. While it may be that part of life deals with movements from positions off of contract curves to positions on contract curves in the process of exhausting gains from trade, the institutionalist approach places strong emphasis on (1) who gets to play, (2) where one starts in the game and (3) the rules governing the game.

Given the importance of human interdependence and the emphasis on who plays and what are the starting points, the focus of institutional law and economics is on conflict rather than harmony, where '[t]he role of the legal system, including both common and constitutional law, is to provide a framework or a process for conflict resolution and the development of legal rights' (Samuels and Mercuro, 1979, p. 166). The fundamental problem here is that of order, which Samuels (1972a, p. 584) defines as 'the reconciling of freedom and control, or autonomy and coordination including hierarchy and equality, with continuity and change'. 'The ultimate meaning of the legal and economic processes' says Samuels (1971, p. 449), 'is in terms of their functioning toward resolving the problem(s) of order'. The existence of conflicting interests necessitates both a process (or processes) for deciding between these competing interests and a method (or methods) for determining how these conflicts are to be resolved.

At the micro level, the firm is seen as something more than a nexus of contracts among isolated individual agents. It is a community designed in part to suspend narrow, individualistic calculations of advantage and facilitate the learning of standard objectives. This is more fully explored by Hodgson (1988), Eisenberg (1990), Lazonick (1991) and Leibenstein (1987), who focus not only on the social origins of individual preferences and goals but on the complex processes by which individual utility functions are constructed and revised and by which the meaning of 'profit maximization' is worked out by agents within the firm. Present within this and other literature is a rich array of analyses of individual psychology, going beyond the simplistic rationality assumption; of organizations, going beyond their treatment as homogeneous, predetermined entities; of behavior in general, going beyond the singular focus on isolated individuals to the institutional and organizational environment in which they operate; and so on. Among the sources of these analyses are modern Darwinian evolutionary theory, cognitive psychology, organization theory and comparative economic systems. Some of the analyses can appear to be either extensions of or departures from neoclassical economic theory, while other analyses are intended to be alternatives to mainstream economics. One result is the showing that the unique determinate optimal equilibrium solutions of the neoclassical research protocol are both presumptive and forced, heuristically useful for analytical exercises but not representative of actual economic processes in all their evolutionary complexity.

In all this, society is recognized, at least in part, as a cooperative venture for mutual advantage where there are both identities and conflicts of interests in ongoing human relations. Within this system of mutual interdependence, societal institutions, including the legal system, both enhance the scope of cooperative endeavors and channel political-legal-economic conflict toward resolution (Mercuro, 1989b, p. 2). The resolution of these conflicts, of whose interests government will give effect through law and otherwise, is the resolution of the problem of order in society - a working out of a societal structure that promotes coherence, security and orderliness in human relations. Indeed, the manner by which a society comes to channel conflict says much about its ultimate character.

11. Rights, Power and Government

Law is fundamentally a matter of rights creation and recreation. Consistent with the positive, descriptive nature of their approach, institutionalists are concerned with the rights (re)creation process and the impact of this process on legal-economic decision making and activity. To understand the importance of rights from the institutional perspective, it is first necessary to understand the sphere of activities open to individuals and the institutionalist conception of the determination of the individual choice process.

Individual decision making is a function of one's opportunity set, which 'consists of the available alternatives for action or choice, each with a relative opportunity cost, which are open to the individual' (Samuels, 1974, p. 120). However, these opportunity sets are limited in their scope: owing to human interdependence and scarcity, each individual's opportunity set is constrained and shaped by the opportunity sets of others in society. Since each individual desires to make choices from a set that is as unconstrained as possible, individuals will wish to control the choices and hence opportunity sets, of others who may constrain their choice. The extent of each individual's ability to determine his or her own choices and to influence the opportunity sets and hence choices, of others is the outcome of a process of mutual coercion, where the ability to coerce is simply the ability of A to impact B's opportunity set without B's consent. An individual's capacity to exercise coercion is, in turn, a function of that individual's power, defined as 'the means or capacity with which to exercise choice' and this power is relative to the power of others. Thus, '[t]he opportunity set of the individual, within which he attempts a constrained maximizing equilibrium, is a function of the total structure of mutual coercion, grounded upon relative power'. Moreover, power is also a dependent variable in this process, being a function of the choices made from opportunity sets that exist and evolve through time (Samuels, 1972b, pp. 65-66). Opportunity sets, then, are endogenously worked out rather than being exogenously given.

The ongoing attempts to delineate and redefine opportunity sets, through the machinations of power and mutual coercion in the face of conflicts, give rise to disputes which necessitate resolution. For example, the upstream polluting factory's choice of production technology impacts and conflicts with the choice of activities of the downstream water user and conversely. The upstream user cannot exercise choice without impacting the choice of downstream users and conversely. The resolution of such conflicts comes through the creation and assignment (or reassignment) of legal rights, which define the scope of choices open to each individual and the degree to which each is exposed to the choices of others. Thus, power and hence coercion and the resulting opportunity sets and choices, are a function of rights.

The origin of rights, as well as the (re)defining and the (re)assigning of rights through the resolution of conflicts of interest bring to the fore the point that rights have a dual nature - 'the opportunity set enhancement of those who have rights and the opportunity set restriction of those who are exposed to them' (Samuels, 1974, p. 122). Virtually every legal change imposes both benefits and costs, the enhancement of some opportunity sets and the simultaneous restriction of others. Externalities are thus ubiquitous and reciprocal - any (re)definition, (re)assignment, or change in the degree of enforcement of rights benefits some interests and harms others; the externality remains in different form; it is merely shifted, as was made clear by Ronald Coase in 'The Problem of Social Cost', (1960). From the institutionalist perspective, systems of property, tort and contract law, then, do not provide solutions to situations of externality but rather only resolutions, as externalities and hence benefit and harm are channeled in a particular direction through the legal delimitation of rights.

Government is seen to play a central and inevitable role within this process, for rights are not rights because they are preexisting, but rather are rights because they are protected by government. As Warren J. Samuels has written, 'Rights are whatever interests government protects vis-à-vis other interests when there is a conflict' (Samuels, 1974, pp. 118-119, 127). Rights are thus relative to and contingent upon 'the legal limitations inherent in their identification and interpretation, the exercise by others of their rights and legal and nonlegal change' (Samuels, 1974, p. 118). Each of these factors is a function of the rights-creation (and re-creation) process and hence of the ability of individuals to secure rights (or a change therein) through the use and control of government. Government thus becomes an object of control for those seeking private legal-economic gain or advantage, 'a mode through which relative rights and therefore relative market (income securing) status is given effect' (Samuels, 1971, pp. 441-442). The question is not, then, one of more versus less government, but rather of whose interests government gives effect to through law - that is, through the process of rights creation and recreation. Contributors to institutional law and economics thus see terms such as regulation, deregulation and government intervention as misleading, in that government is omnipresent. For example, it is often said that the adoption of workplace safety regulations constitutes an intervention of government into the market, yet such activity represents merely a change of the interests to which government gives effect, as rights - a movement which expands the rights/opportunity sets of workers and reduces the rights/opportunity sets of employers. The issue as to who will have rights thus turns on whose interests government allows to be realized and who is able to use government for what ends. The critical matter is who is able to control and use the legal-economic nexus in order to control legal-economic continuity or change (Samuels, 1971, p. 440; Samuels, 1989a, p. 1578).

The central implication of the reciprocal nature of externalities is that the decision over whose interests are protected as rights is necessarily a function of a choice process - choice as to who will have rights and who will be exposed to the exercise of those rights, of who will be able to inflict gains and losses on others and to what extent (Samuels and Mercuro, 1979, pp. 172-174). This inevitable necessity of choice reveals that law is not something that is given or to be discovered, but is instead a human artifact marked by deliberative and nondeliberative human choice (Samuels, 1981, p. 168). The fact that law is a human choice process means that value judgments will necessarily be introduced in choosing between competing interests and legal-economic outcomes are thus 'an expression of the values of those who have participated and prevailed at each stage of choice in the political-legal-economic arena' - that is, those who are able to most effectively use government to further their own ends (Mercuro, 1989b, p. 10). Justice, then, reflects not some given set of high foundational principles, but rather a normative valuational process that determines the laws, norms and values that are to govern living (Samuels, 1971, p. 444; Samuels and Mercuro, 1979, pp. 160-163).

12. The Problematic Nature of Efficiency

Institutional law and economics has, on occasion, been characterized as rejecting outright Chicago law and economics. This is not so. Indeed while the institutional law and economics literature has been quite critical of certain facets of the Chicago approach, Samuels (1981, pp. 148-149), for one, has praised Posner for the usefulness of his analysis in once again bringing to the attention of economists and legal scholars alike how economic conditions affect the law and conversely. Nonetheless, one of the hallmarks of the institutional approach to law and economics is the rejection of the Chicago and general neoclassical emphasis on the determination of *the* efficient resolution of legal disputes. The institutionalists do not reject efficiency as an important variable in legal-economic analysis, but rather maintain that efficiency alone cannot and should not, determine the assignment of rights (Samuels, 1989a, p. 1563).

The starting point for the institutionalist critique of the efficiency criterion is the recognition that economic activity - prices, costs, outputs, risk, income, wealth, and so on - is not some sort of natural phenomenon, but rather is determined by the structure of rights that exists in society, with the levels of and changes in each of these variables being in part a function of the legal structure and legal change over time (Samuels, 1971, p. 440, 1989a, p. 1565; and Schmid 1989, p. 67). Each particular rights structure will give rise to a particular set of prices, costs, outputs, and so on and thus to a particular efficient allocation of resources. Hence, there is no unique efficient result. For the institutionalists, the purportedly positivist Chicago-school rhetoric of 'atomistic industries' or 'contestable markets' and the associated concept of 'price-taking behavior' is exposed as nothing more than deeply normative 'rights-taking behavior' (Samuels and Mercuro, 1984). The institutionalists maintain that inasmuch as rights underlie product prices and thus costs, to talk of 'price-takers' bypasses virtually all that is (or should be) important in Chicago law and economics and much of public choice theory.

Because efficiency is a function of rights and not the other way around, it is circular to maintain that efficiency alone can determine rights. Since costs, prices, outputs, wealth and so on are derivative of a particular rights structure, so too are cost minimization, value-of-output maximization and wealth maximization. (For a detailed examination of the determination of costs in this regard, see Samuels and Schmid, 1997.) Different specifications of rights will lead to different (and economically noncomparable) minimizing or maximizing valuations. The result is that an outcome that is claimed to be efficient is efficient only with regard to the assumed initial structure of rights (Schmid, 1989, pp. 68-69) the latter of which is often the very matter at issue. Thus, as Samuels (1981, p. 154) asserts, '[t]o argue that wealth maximization [or any other efficiency criterion] can determine rights serves only to mask a choice of which interests to protect as rights. Legal decisions or changes can be said to be efficient only from the point of view of the party whose interests are given effect through the identification and assignment of rights.'

Moreover, the definition of 'output' - of what it is that one is to be efficient about - requires an antecedent normative specification as to the appropriate performance goal for society. Social output (the aggregate well-being of society), consumptive output (the value of goods from the consumer point of view) and productive output (the value of goods from the producer point of view, that is, profits) are three examples of the alternatives that are available. The value-laden choice of a particular definition of output as the maximand, which in effect is the choice of a particular social welfare function where many are possible, will drive the decision as to what constitutes the efficient allocation (Samuels, 1978, pp. 102-104).

Further, due to the non-uniqueness of efficiency, efficiency is inevitably bound up with distribution; as Samuels and Schmid (1981, p. 2) describe it, 'the concept of efficiency as separate from distribution is false'. Rights determination is a normative activity with both efficiency and distributional consequences, determining which efficient allocation and which distribution of benefits and costs will carry the day. Rights determine the distribution of income and wealth, which in turn determines the efficient solution that is reached. But at the same time, the specification of rights and the resulting efficient outcome, structure the future distribution of income and wealth in society. The choice of rights, then, is ultimately a distributional issue: 'With no unique optimal use of resources and opportunities independent of rights identification and assignment, the legal system must select the [distributional] result to be pursued: *the definition of the efficient solution is both the object and the subject of the legal system*' (Samuels, 1978, p. 106, emphasis in original). In institutional law and economics '[t]he distribution problem, viz., of power, income, wealth, opportunity, exposure and sacrifice, is critical to legal-economic research and policy' (Samuels, 1975, p. 70). Thus, as described by Schmid (1989, p. 69), 'the whole point is that global welfare maximization is meaningless' and '[t]o recommend one right over another, analysts must take their stand as naked normativists without the comfort of the Pareto-better cloak or any other formalism'.

The recognition of the multiplicity of efficient solutions and the contingency of any given efficient solution on the presumed structure of rights (the definition and assignment) and the definition of output reveals the inherent normative element that is present in efficiency-based decision making. Each possible legal solution points to a different efficient outcome and '[t]here is no independent test by which the law's solutions can be said to be the efficient solution' (Samuels, 1981, p. 155). The determination of a particular efficient solution involves a normative and selective choice as to whose interests will be accommodated, who will realize gains and who will realize losses.

This line of reasoning leads institutionalists to reject the efficiency theory of the common law. Any given rights structure will produce an efficient or wealth-maximizing outcome and thus '[t]he so-called efficiency of the common law is an 'empirical regularity' only in the sense that every common law specification of rights can produce a unique, wealth-maximizing outcome' (Samuels, 1981, p. 162). If different interests had been protected as rights, different efficient outcomes would have occurred. The choice of certain rights structures reflects a normative choice for a particular efficient pattern of law and economic development over time, where different decisions would have led to different patterns of efficient development. Thus, the literature purporting to explain the efficient development of the common law 'explains everything and nothing' Samuels (1981, p. 162). 'Wealth maximization cannot ... explain the evolution of the common law: any developmental logic concerning rights in a market economy would have led the common law to some wealth-maximizing result' (Samuels, 1981, p. 154).

In a similar vein, proponents of institutional law and economics also reject the standard theory of rent seeking, which defines rent-seeking activities as 'resource-wasting activities of individuals in seeking transfers of wealth through the aegis of the state' (Buchanan, Tollison and Tullock, 1980, p. ix). Rent-seeking theory thereby argues that expenditures of scarce resources by agents in an attempt to garner a privileged position (for example, an exclusive monopoly franchise) from the state, or, the use of the state (for example, through legislative activities or lobbying) to alter product price and/or factor prices to enhance profits without a concomitant increase in output, is wasteful in that resources are expended solely for the purpose of effecting a transfer of rents from one party to another. The normative thrust of this theory thus becomes one of promoting policies designed to avoid wasteful, rent-seeking activities, which often involves a greater, more exclusive reliance on markets and a scaling back of government.

The intellectual construct employed by proponents of the rent-seeking literature is that of the competitive market economy and the legitimized product and factor prices and thus profits that obtain therefrom. Prices and profits that occur consequent standard marketplace phenomena - such as the entering and exiting of firms into and from industries, adopting new technologies, altering the scale of plant, and so on - are all legitimate. However, when prices and profits are altered by and/or through the aegis of the state, this is said to result in waste.

From the standpoint of institutional law and economics, this characterization of rent seeking is an exercise in selective perception and market legitimation (Samuels and Mercuro, 1984, pp. 55-70). As the institutionalists have pointed out, to use today's market prices and profits as a basis to determine rents and wastes is to give propriety to extant laws governing the production of goods while at the same time selectively culling out one subset of rights to make claims of wasteful, rent-seeking activity. It is the proponents' reliance on the model of competition that gives effect to this selective perception. As is made clear in institutional law and economics, models of the economy predicated on price-taking behavior are in reality models of rights-taking behavior. Market prices are not absolute, predetermined and independent of law, but, rather, are a partial function of rights - the latter related directly to the government's ubiquitous role in creating, defining, assigning, enforcing and altering rights. Moreover, today's prevailing market prices of products and factors of production are all predicated upon the past use of the state and past rent-seeking activities. Market-generated product and factor prices that make up a firm's revenue-cost calculation are property-rights specific; as a consequence, so too is its net revenue calculation a function of rights. The government's role in the economy remains ubiquitous and, accordingly, a theory that purports to identify rent-seeking behavior and the economic wastes therefrom is question begging. There are no *correct* rights, prices, profits, or correct structure of rents. Thus, rent-seeking theory is characterized as an artificial, misguided normative theory that will 'mislead positive analysis and generate artificial distinctions and thereby provide no real basis for distinguishing between permissible and impermissible activities' (Samuels and Mercuro, 1984, p. 67; see also Medema, 1991).

13. Toward a Comparative Institutional Analysis

The driving force behind institutional law and economics is the need to come to grips with the interrelations between legal and economic processes. Samuels (1975, p. 72) identifies three efforts that are central to this process: (1) 'models of legal-political and economic interaction' must be developed; (2) 'objective, positive, empirical studies of government as both a dependent and independent variable and of economic activity as both an input and an output of political-legal processes' must be undertaken; and (3) efforts must be made 'to wed both theoretical and empirical analyses toward a self-consciously objective, positive comprehension of law and economics'. Such analysis will serve the twin purposes of deepening the understanding of legal and economic processes and their interrelations and providing a more sound basis upon which to predict the potential consequences of legal-economic change.

The import of this becomes clear in the institutionalist assertion that the essential normative element in political-legal-economic decision making means that a choice must be made between alternative efficiency-distributional results and hence between alternative political-legal-economic institutional structures. This, in turn, necessitates a comparative institutional approach to legal-economic analysis. The institutional structure cannot, in this view, merely be assumed away or taken as given. Rather, it must be the subject of study and, more specifically, the legal-economic decision-making process must involve a comparison of the effects of institutional alternatives on social well-being. The need for a comparative institutional approach to legal-economic policy and not only by the institutionalists, has long been recognized. Other proponents of a comparative institutional approach, coming from somewhat different perspectives include Coase (1960, esp. pp. 42-44), Demsetz (1969), Komesar (1981, 1994), Stewart (1987) and Shepsle and Weingast (1984) generally, though not exclusively, working under the banner of the New Institutional Law and Economics.

The comparative institutional approach is general rather than partial (Samuels 1972a, pp. 582, 585) and consists of describing and analyzing the systematic relationship between (1) the structure of political-legal-economic institutions, focusing on the rights and rules by which they operate; (2) the conduct or observed behavior in light of the incentives (penalties and rewards) created by the structure of institutions; (3) the consequent economic performance, i.e., the allocation *and* distribution of resources that determine the character of economic life under these institutions (Mercuro, 1989b, p. 11, emphasis in original).

Within this structure-conduct-performance paradigm the object, then, is to explain and compare the outcomes that will occur under real, discrete, alternative institutional structures. A comparative institutional approach to law and economics emphasizes the need to explain and analyze the available alternatives and the consequences of choice at three distinct stages: (1) the constitutional stage of choice - the social contract that binds people together, which is subject to reinterpretation and revision; (2) the institutional stage of choice - the structuring and restructuring of political-legal-economic institutions; and (3) the economic impact stage of choice - describing the economic impacts of existing or potentially revised legal-economic relations, be they in the form of private property rights, status rights, communal property (Mercuro, 1989b, pp. 3-6) and open-acces resources (Mercuro, 1997).

The analysis must be done at each of these levels and not solely in terms of efficiency, but also in terms of the distribution of income and wealth, employment rates and any other factors that may affect the quality of life or the productive capacity of firms. As Samuels (1981, p. 165) has argued, '[f]or law to be preoccupied solely with economic maximization would rob law of life and of much of what makes for human meaning and significance'. The goal here is not normative judgment, but description: 'A viable approach to the study of the interrelations between law and economics should be content with describing the full array of economic impacts (including both the allocation and distribution of resources) of alternative institutions and legal arrangements together with an articulation of whose interests will be served and at whose expense' (Mercuro, 1989b, p. 12). Such analysis will not privilege one set of interests over others, but it will enable those who study and participate in the processes of the legal-economic nexus to better understand these processes and their resulting effects on law and economy (Samuels, 1989a, p. 1578). Institutionalist-oriented case studies include the works of Carter (1985), Schmid (1985), Seidman (1973) and Wandschneider (1986). Carter (1985) criticizes the neoclassical microeconomic explanation of institutional arrangements as at best partial and at worst mystifying. Employing a Wisconsin institutionalist perspective that recognizes both the relevance of economic power and the historical context within which exchange occurs, Carter revisits Commons's analysis of 'yellow dog' labor contracts and analyzes the interlinked tenure-credit contracts. Seidman (1973) contrasts the classical and anticlassical perspectives on facilitative law and finds the latter, which recognizes the asymmetric status and power of parties to a contract to be controlling, to better describe what transpired in the colonial African economies of Kenya and Ghana. Schmid (1985), writing on biotechnology-related property rights issues in the agricultural sector, demonstrates that attempts to provide exclusivity may inadvertently create added costs and affect the choice of breeding method and agricultural technologies, was well as the division of rents between inventors and the public. Wandschneider (1986) analyzes the property rights institutions that allocate water in the northwest US. He finds that, as compared to the EPR (efficient property rights) model, an institutionalist model that recognizes (1) that social norms may supersede economic rationality and (2) that conflict over distributional issues may block Pareto-better outcomes, is better able to explain the development of rights to water in the US.

Of course normative judgments must be made in the process of reaching legal decisions. Recognizing this, the institutional approach emphasizes the need for openness and value clarification in the political-legal-economic decision-making process, clearly a legacy of the legal realist movement within the field of law (Samuels, 1989a, p. 1573). Economists, legal scholars, policymakers and judges should strive to make the value premises underlying their conclusions as explicit as possible, so that the choice process can be effectuated 'carefully and overtly' rather than 'carelessly and covertly'

(Samuels, 1978, p. 113; 1989b). This call for openness is clearly tied to the comparative institutional method:

> Not only should normative premises be made explicit, but an array of studies should be conducted on the basis of *alternative* normative (and factual) assumptions. To do only one study is to give effect to only one perception and specification of outputs, costs, benefits and rights. Alternative studies call attention to the subtle intrusion of ideology and partisanship, emphasize the necessary and inevitable critical choice of underlying values, highlight the fundamental distributional consequences that depend on the political determination of output definitions and so forth. (Samuels 1978, p. 112, emphasis in original)

The obfuscation of values and underlying normative premises within so much of the Chicago school of law and economics and public choice theory is the bane of the comparative institutional approach. Relying solely on the Pareto efficiency criterion serves to obfuscate and impede the normative choice process that is necessarily at work in the legal-economic nexus. Examples of scholarship that avoid much of the obfuscation brought on by solely relying on Pareto-efficiency analysis include Bromley (1989), Calabresi (1985, 1991), Lang (1980), Griffin (1991, 1995) and Mishan (1972).

Calabresi (1991) demonstrates that the frequently-made distinction between removing inefficiencies (making moves *to* the Pareto frontier) and innovating (pushing the Pareto frontier *outward*) is a false dichotomy. He argues that moves from the status quo are not possible without either (1) disadvantaging at least one party (hence making distributional considerations unavoidable), or (2) trying to shift the frontier outward (a process that also typically entails distributional consequences). As a consequence, Calabresi, in a combined concern for efficiency and distribution, calls for a method of analysis that attempts to answer the following question: Which actions are most likely, at least cost, to shift the frontier outward and who will gain and who will lose from such moves?

Calabresi (1985) also argues that ideals, beliefs and attitudes matter in shaping the law. Recognizing that legal entitlements alter our perception of benefits and costs, he examines the legal response to beliefs and attitudes. The focus on ideals, beliefs and attitudes highlights the limitations inherent in the economic analysis of legal rules. Calabresi poses the hypothetical question: How does or should a society contemplate 'improvements' - be it the automobile or any such improvement that spreads benefits and costs across society? He asks: 'Is it worth the price we pay as a society?' 'Who should pay the price?' And, given law's commitment to the concept of reasonableness, he asks: 'Who's value system determines what is reasonable?' The thrust of the book is to compel society to understand and articulate the tradeoffs being made between the values of different segments of society as we embrace new technologies or ways of life. Consequently, the call is for an honest and open approach to resolving issues involving conflicting values and beliefs.

Lang (1980) critically examines several concepts of efficiency as related to policy analysis, exposing their normative content and thereby demonstrating the limits to efficiency-based policy analysis. He observes that property rights issues arise from different sets of values which, if reflected in policy, lead to different Pareto-efficient allocations of resources. He calls for policy analysis to (1) undertake a greater use of economic analysis to determine the *incidence* of benefits and costs associated with alternative remedies, or (2) pursue an 'instrumental economics' which places a greater degree of emphasis on the design of policies and institutions which will achieve a specified social and economic end. In a similar vein, Mishan (1972) critically examines Hochman and Rodgers' (1969) position that one can resolve the distribution problem for society by promoting Pareto-efficient redistributions. After exploring the undesirability of efficiency-derived distributions, Mishan concludes that economists ought to concede that welfare economics is founded on ethics and make policy recommendations or proposals consistent with the ethics of the society for which the policy is intended.

Griffin (1991) critiques the traditional market- and price-guided policies for internalizing externalities offered within the context of neoclassical theory - policies which, he argues, are insufficient for this purpose. He contends that the major omission in neoclassical theory is a mechanism to incorporate institutional options (and their associated transaction costs) to resolve the problems brought on by negative externalities and he advances a method of explicitly incorporating institutional transaction costs into welfare diagrammatics. In a later paper, Griffin (1995) examined the differences between the economic criteria of potential Pareto improvements and Pareto improvements as normative foundations from which to assess public policy. He demonstrates that potential Pareto criteria have greater disciplinary acceptance than their normative foundations merit and that the Pareto criterion has suffered undue criticism consequent the former.

14. Summary

In contrast to some other approaches to law and economics, the institutional approach draws no distinction between jurisprudential, legislative, bureaucratic, or regulatory treatments. All are seen as particular parts or manifestations of the interrelation of government and the economy, or of legal and economic processes. Underlying the major thrust of the institutional approach to law and economics are two complementary modes of analysis. Instead of concentrating on a unidirectional sequence in which the law or legal structure governs behavior or conduct in the mixed market economy which in turn drives economic performance, for institutional law and economics the emphasis is on the interpenetration and interrelations between government and the economy, so that law or legal structure and behavior or conduct in the mixed market economy and economic performance are dependent on each other in a process of circular and cumulative causation.

Correlatively, whereas some of the more orthodox approaches to law and economics seek unique, determinate optimal equilibrium solutions, institutional law and economics finds such solutions to be question-begging and concentrates on identifying and analyzing the processes by which the various legal structures, the conduct and the economic performance are worked out. Similarly, those contributing to institutionalist law and economics do not feel obliged to identify particular legal arrangements as 'optimal'. They argue that putatively optimal solutions to problems of policy only give effect to selective preconceptions and assumptions as to whose interests are to count, for which economists have no particular basis on which to choose, especially given that so-called optimal solutions are driven by and specific to the choice of rights and so on which produce them - ironically with those very rights structures which are at center stage in virtually all schools of thought of law and economics.

Although institutionalists are interested in identifying the alternatives open to policy and trying to say something of their consequences, they are reluctant to substitute their preferences for those of actual legal and economic actors engaged in the processes of working solutions out by and for themselves. Along comparable lines, institutional law and economics distinguishes between (1a) a *market economy* (typically a mixed-market economy, often somewhat vague on 'the mix'), (1b) a *conceptual market* (a market typically characterized with a vaguely described 'minimalist government' in the context of 'pure competition') and (1c) *markets in general* (typically a euphemism invoked to avoid the important factors and details inherent in the previous two conceptions of the market) on the one hand and (2) *actual institutionalized markets* on the other. Accordingly, they question the blind reliance on 'the market' - whether type a, b, or c to solve problems inasmuch as institutionalized markets, in their view, are a function of the institutions and power structures which form and operate through them. To affirm a solution by a 'market' together with the outcome which obtains and is purported to be optimal, is to give effect to a particular structure of law, rights and therefore power, and thus beg the operative issue(s). For those who narrowly seek markets and putatively optimal solutions to problems of policy, institutional law and economics will be disappointing.

It may well be that since the overtly positive and even agnostic approach of institutional law and economics is not comforting to those who would seek refuge in determinate solutions to the questions of legal-economic policy, then some may be inclined to dismiss it on this ground. Against this, Schmid responds: 'If [institutional law and economics] has no dispositive answer to resolve policy arguments, what is it good for? It can identify many less than obvious sources of power in an economy so that people can know where their welfare comes from. It can raise the level of normative debate so that issues can be joined and people can live with tragic choices rather than ignoring and dismissing them' (Schmid, 1994, pp. 36-37). While singular solutions to legal-economic issues reflect only one particular set of value premises and one particular conception of the facts, benefits and costs at issue, the comparative institutional approach, by recognizing the multiplicity of potential solutions and underlying value premises, attempts to flesh out both what is actually going on in the legal-economic nexus and the alternative possibilities that are open to society in the ongoing social construction and reconstruction of legal-economic reality.

Acknowledgments

We wish to thank the Fritz Thyssen Foundation for its generous support and the faculty and staff of the Erasmus Program in Law and Economics at the University for Hamburg in providing Professor Mercuro a productive environment in the time during which this project was completed. We are indebted to A. Allan Schmid, the editors and two anonymous referees for their insightful comments on earlier drafts of this material. The excellent research assistance of Mary Therese Cogeos is also gratefully acknowledged.

Bibliography on Institutional Law and Economics (0520)

Adams, Henry C. (1897), 'Economics and Jurisprudence', Reprinted in Dorfman, Joseph (ed.), *Two Essays By Henry Carter Adams: Relation of the State to Industrial Action and Economics and Jurisprudence*, New York, Augustus M. Kelley, 1969, 135-75.

Broder, Josef (1981), 'Citizen Participation in Michigan District Courts', in Samuels, Warren J. and Schmid, A. Allan (eds) *Law and Economics: An Institutional Perspective*, Boston, Martinus Nijhoff, 166-78.

Broder, Josef and Schmid, A. Allan (1983) 'Public Choice in Local Judicial Systems', **40** *Public Choice*, 7-19.

Bromley, Daniel W. (1989), *Economic Interests and Institutions*, New York, Basil Blackwell.

Carter, Michael R. (1985), 'A Wisconsin Institutionalist Perspective on Microeconomic Theory of Institutions: The Insufficiency of Pareto Efficiency, **19** *Journal of Economic Issues*, 797-813.

Commons, John R. (1924), *Legal Foundations of Capitalism*, New York, Macmillan. Reprinted, Clifton, NJ, Augustus M. Kelley, 1974.

Commons, John R. (1925), 'Law and Economics', **34** *Yale Law Journal*, 371-82.

Commons, John R. (1934), *Institutional Economics*, New York, Macmillan.

Duxbury, Neil (1990), 'Robert Hale and the Economy of Legal Force', **53** *The Modern Law Review*, 421-44.

Ely, Richard T. (1914), *Property and Contract in Their Relation to the Distribution of Wealth*, 2 vols, New York, Macmillan.

Field, Alexander J. (1979), 'On the Explanation of Rules Using Rational Choice Models', **13** *Journal of Economic Issues*, 49-72.

Field, Alexander J. (1981), 'The Problem with Neoclassical Institutional Economics', **18** *Explorations in Economic History*, 174-98.

Field, Alexander J. (1984), 'Microeconomics, Norms and Rationality', **32** *Economic Development and Cultural Change*, 683-711.

Field, Alexander J. (1991), 'Do Legal Systems Matter?', **28** *Explorations in Economic History*, 1-35.

Griffin, Ronald (1991), 'The Welfare Analysis of Transaction Costs, Externalities and Institutional Choice', **73** *American Journal of Agricultural Economics*, 601-14.

Griffin, Ronald (1995), 'On the Meaning of Economic Efficiency in Policy Analysis', **71** *Land Economics*, 1-15.

Hale, Robert Lee (1924), 'Economic Theory and the Statesman', in Tugwell, Rexford G. (ed.), *The Trend of Economics*, New York, Knopf.

Hale, Robert Lee (1927), 'Economics and the Law', in Ogburn, William F. and Goldenweiser, Alexander A. (eds), *The Social Sciences and Their Interrelations*, Boston, Houghton Mifflin.

Hale, Robert Lee (1952), *Freedom Through Law*, New York, Columbia University Press.

Hamilton, Walton H. (1932), 'Property According to Locke', **41** *Yale Law Journal*, 864-80.

Kanal, Don (1985), 'Institutional Economics: Perspectives on Economy and Society', **19** *Journal of Economic Issues*, 815-28.

Komesar, Neil K. (1981), 'In Search of a General Approach to Legal Analysis: A Comparative Institutional Alternative', **79** *Michigan Law Review*, 1350-92.

Komesar, Neil K. (1994), *Imperfect Alternatives: Choosing Institutions in Law, Economics and Public Policy*, Chicago, University of Chicago Press.

Lang, Mahlon G. (1980), 'Economic Efficiency and Policy Comparisons', **62** *American Journal of Agricultural Economics*, 772-77.

Liebhafsky, H.H. (1987), 'Law and Economics from Different Perspectives', **21** *Journal of Economic Issues*, 1809-36.

Llewellyn, Karl N. (1925), 'The Effect of Legal Institutions upon Economics', **15** *American Economic Review*, 655-83.

Medema, Steven G. (1991), 'Another Look at the Problem of Rent Seeking', **25** *Journal of Economic Issues*, 1049-65.

Medema, Steven G. (1994), *Ronald H. Coase*, London and New York, Macmillan and St Martin's Press.

Medema, Steven G. (1996a), 'Of Pangloss, Pigouvians and Pragmatism: Ronald Coase and Social Cost Analysis', **18** *Journal of the History of Economic Thought*, 96-114.

Medema, Steven G. (1996b), 'Ronald Coase and American Institutionalism', **14** *Research in the History of Economic Thought and Methodology*, 51-92.

Medema, Steven G. and Samuels, Warren J. (1997), 'Ronald Coase and Coasean Economics: Some Questions, Conjectures and Implications', in Samuels, Warren J., Medema, Steven G. and Schmid, A. Allan (eds), *The Economy as a Process of Valuation*, Aldershot, Edward Elgar.

Medema, Steven G. and Zerbe, Richard O., Jr. (1997), 'The Coase Theorem', in Bouckaert, Boudewijn and De Geest, Gerrit (eds), *Encyclopedia of Law and Economics*, Aldershot, Edward Elgar.

Mercuro, Nicholas (ed.) (1989a), *Law and Economics*, Boston, Kluwer Academic Publishers.

Mercuro, Nicholas (1989b), 'Toward a Comparative Institutional Approach to the Study of Law and Economics', in Mercuro, Nicholas (ed.), *Law and Economics*, Boston, Kluwer Academic Publishers, 1-26.

Mercuro, Nicholas (1997), *Ecology, Law and Economics*, Lanham, University Press of America.

Mercuro, Nicholas and Medema, Steven G. (1995), 'Schools of Thought in Law and Economics: A Kuhnian Competition', in Malloy, Robin Paul and Braun, Christopher K. (eds), *Law and Economics: New and Critical Perspectives*, New York, Peter Lang, 65-126.

Mercuro, Nicholas and Medema, Steven G. (1997), *Economics and the Law: From Posner to Post-Modernism*, Princeton, Princeton University Press.

Mercuro, Nicholas and Ryan, Timothy P. (1980), 'Property Rights and Welfare Economics: *Miller et al. v. Schoene* Revisited', **56** *Land Economics*, 202-12.

Mercuro, Nicholas and Ryan, Timothy P. (1984), *Law, Economics and Public Policy*, Greenwich, CT, JAI Press.

Ostrom, Elinor (1986), 'A Method of Institutional Analysis', in Kaufman, Franz-Xarer (ed.), *Guidance, Control and Evaluation in the Public Sector*, Berlin, Walter de Gruyter.

Rutherford, Malcolm (1994), *Institutions in Economics: The Old and the New Institutionalism*, Cambridge, Cambridge University Press.

Samuels, Warren J. (1966), *The Classical Theory of Economic Policy*, Cleveland, World.

Samuels, Warren J. (1971), 'Interrelations Between Legal and Economic Processes', **14** *Journal of Law and Economics*, 435-50.

Samuels, Warren J. (1972a), 'Ecosystem Policy and the Problem of Power', **2** *Environmental Affairs*, 580-96.

Samuels, Warren J. (1972b), 'Welfare Economics, Power and Property', in Wunderlich, Gene and Gibson, W.L., Jr. (eds), *Perspectives of Property*, University Park, PA, Institute for Research on Land and Water Resources, Pennsylvania State University, 61-127.

Samuels, Warren J. (1973), 'The Economy as a System of Power and its Legal Bases: The Legal Economics of Robert Lee Hale', **27** *University of Miami Law Review*, 261-371.

Samuels, Warren J. (1974), 'Commentary: An Economic Perspective on the Compensation Problem', **21** *Wayne Law Review*, 113-34.

Samuels, Warren J. (1975), 'Approaches to Legal-Economic Policy and Related Problems of Research', in Nagel, Stuart (ed.), *Policy Studies and the Social Sciences*, Lexington, MA, Lexington Books, 65-73.

Samuels, Warren J. (ed.) (1976), *The Chicago School of Political Economy*, East Lansing, Graduate School of Business, Michigan State University.

Samuels, Warren J. (1978), 'Normative Premises in Regulatory Theory', **1** *Journal of Post Keynesian Economics*, 100-14.

Samuels, Warren J. (1981), 'Maximization of Wealth as Justice: An Essay on Posnerian Law and Economics as Policy Analysis', **60** *Texas Law Review*, 147-72.

Samuels, Warren J. (ed.) (1988), *Institutional Economics*, 3 Vols, Aldershot, Edward Elgar Publishing.

Samuels, Warren J. (1989a), 'The Legal-Economic Nexus', **57** *George Washington Law Review*, 1556-78.

Samuels, Warren J. (1989b), 'The Methodology of Economics and the Case for Policy Diffidence and Restraint', **42** *Review of Social Economy*, 113-33.

Samuels, Warren J. (1992), *Essays on the Economic Role of Government*, 2 Vols, New York, New York University Press.

Samuels, Warren J. (1993), 'Law and Economics: Some Early Journal Contributions', in Samuels, Warren J., Biddle, Jeff and Patchak-Schuster, Thomas W. (eds), *Economic Thought and Discourse in the Twentieth Century*, Aldershot, Edward Elgar Publishing, 217-85.

Samuels, Warren J. (1995), 'Reflections on the Intellectual Context and Significance of Thorstein Veblen', **29** *Journal of Economic Issues*, 915-22.

Samuels, Warren J. (1996), 'Reader's Guide to John R. Commons, *Legal Foundations of Capitalism*', *Research in the History of Economic Thought and Methodology, Archival Supplement* 5, 1-61.

Samuels, Warren J. and Mercuro, Nicholas (1979), 'The Role and Resolution of the Compensation Principle in Society: Part One - The Role', **1** *Research in Law and Economics*, 157-94.

Samuels, Warren J. and Mercuro, Nicholas (1980), 'The Role and Resolution of the Compensation Principle in Society: Part Two - The Resolution', **2** *Research in Law and Economics*, 103-28.

Samuels, Warren J. and Mercuro, Nicholas (1984), 'A Critique of Rent-Seeking Theory', in Colander, David C. (ed.), *Neoclassical Political Economy: The Analysis of Rent-Seeking and DUP Activities*, Cambridge, MA, Ballinger Publishing, 55-70.

Samuels, Warren J. and Schmid, A. Allan (eds) (1981), *Law and Economics: An Institutional Perspective*, Boston, Martinus-Nijhoff Publishing, 268 p.

Samuels, Warren J. and Schmid, A. Allan (1997), 'The Concept of Cost in Economics', in Samuels, Warren J., Medema, Steven G. and Schmid, A. Allan, *The Economy as a Process of Valuation*, Aldershot, Edward Elgar Publishing.

Schmid, A. Allan (1985), 'Biotechnology, Plant Variety Protection and Changing Property Institutions in Agriculture', **7** *North Central Journal of Agricultural Economics*, 129-38.

Schmid, A. Allan (1987), *Property, Power and Public Choice: An Inquiry into Law and Economics*, 2nd edn, New York, Praeger.

Schmid, A. Allan (1989), 'Law and Economics: An Institutional Perspective', in Mercuro, Nicholas (ed.), *Law and Economics*, Boston, Kluwer Academic Publishers, 57-85.

Schmid, A. Allan (1994), 'Institutional Law and Economics', **1** *European Journal of Law and Economics*, 33-51.

Seidman, Robert (1973), 'Contract Law, the Free Market and State Intervention: A Jurisprudential Perspective', **7** *Journal of Economic Issues*, 553-76.

Shepsle, Kenneth A. and Weingast, Barry (1984), 'Political Solutions to Market Problems', **78** *American Political Science Review*, 417-34.

Solo, Robert A. (1974), *The Political Authority and the Market System*, Cincinnati, South-Western.

Trebing, Harry M. (ed.) (1976), *New Dimensions in Public Utility Pricing*, East Lansing, Institute of Public Utilities, Michigan State University.

Trebing, Harry M. (1989), 'Telecommunications Regulation - The Continuing Dilemma', in Nowotym, K., Smith, D.B. and Trebing, H.M. (eds), *Public Utility Regulation*, Boston, Kluwer Academic Publishers, 120-22.

Trebing, Harry M. and Estabrooks, Maurice (1993), 'Telecommunications Policy in the Global Information Economy of the Nineties', in Stevinson, Rodney, Oum, T.H. and Oniki, H. (eds), *International Perspectives on Telecommunications Policy*, Greenwich, CT, JAI Press, 17-37.

Wandschneider, Philip (1984), 'Managing River Systems: Centralization versus Decentralization', **24** *Natural Resources Journal*, 1043-66.

Wandschneider, Philip (1986), 'Neoclassical and Institutionalist Explanations of Changes in Northwest Water Institutions', **20** *Journal of Economic Issues*, 87-107.

Other References

Ackerman, Bruce A. and Stewart, Richard B. (1988), 'Reforming Environmental Law: The Democratic Case for Market Incentives', **13** *Columbia Journal of Environmental Law*, 171-99.

Ayres, Clarence E. (1944), *The Theory of Economic Progress*, Chapel Hill, University of North Carolina Press.

Baumol, William J. and Oates, Wallace E. (1988), *The Theory of Environmental Policy* (2nd edn), Cambridge, Cambridge University Press.

Bell, John F. (1967), 'Institutional Economics', in *A History of Economic Thought*, New York, Ronald Press, 539-71.

Breit, William (1973), 'The Development of Clarence Ayres's Theoretical Institutionalism', **54** *Social Science Quarterly*, 244-57.

Buchanan, James M., Tollison, Robert and Tullock, Gordon (1980), *Toward a Theory of the Rent-Seeking Society*, College Station, Texas A&M University Press.

Buckingham, Walter S. (1958), *Theoretical Economic Systems: A Comparative Analysis*, New York, Ronald Press Company, 89-124.

Calabresi, Guido (1985), *Ideals, Beliefs, Attitudes and the Law: Private Law Perspectives on a Public Law Problem*, Syracuse, NY, Syracuse University Press.

Calabresi, Guido (1991), 'The Pointlessness of Pareto: Carrying Coase Further', **100** *Yale Law Journal*, 1211-37.

Coase, Ronald H. (1960), 'The Problem of Social Cost', **3** *Journal of Law and Economics*, 1-44.

Cotterrell, Roger (1989), *The Politics of Jurisprudence*, London, Butterworths.

Demsetz, Harold (1969), 'Information and Efficiency: Another Viewpoint', **12** *Journal of Law and Economics*, 1-22.

Dorfman, Joseph (1959), *The Economic Mind in American Civilization, Volumes IV and V: 1918-1933*, New York, The Viking Press. Reprinted by Augustus M. Kelley Publishers, 1969.

Duxbury, Neil (1995), *Patterns of American Jurisprudence*, Oxford: Oxford University Press.

Eisenberg, Melvin A. (1990), 'An Overview of Law and Economics', *Working Paper* No. 90-9, School of Law, University of California, Berkeley.

Frank, Jerome (1930), *Law and the Modern Mind*, New York, Brentano's.

Gordon, Robert A. (1964), *Institutional Economics*, Berkeley, University of California Press.

Hochman, Harold and Rodgers, J.D. (1969), 'Pareto-Optimal Redistributions', **59** *American Economic Review*, 542-57.

Hodgson, Geoffrey M. (1988), *Economics and Institutions*, Philadelphia, University of Pennsylvania Press.

Hodgson, Geoffrey M. (1994), 'Evolution, Theories of Economic', in Hodgson, Geoffrey M., Samuels, Warren J. and Tool, Mark R. (eds), *The Elgar Companion to Institutional and Evolutionary Economics*, Aldershot, Edward Elgar Publishing, 218-24.

Hodgson, Geoffrey M., Samuels, Warren J. and Tool, Mark R. (eds) (1994), *The Elgar Companion to Institutional and Evolutionary Economics*, Aldershot, Edward Elgar Publishing.

Kapp, K. William (1976), 'The Nature and Significance of Institutional Economics', **29** *Kyklos*, 209-32. Reprinted in Samuels, Warren J. (ed.) (1988), *Institutional Economics*, Vol. 1, Aldershot, Edward Elgar Publishing.

Lazonick, William (1991), *Business Organization and the Myth of the Market Economy*, Cambridge, Cambridge University Press.

Leibenstein, Harvey (1987), *Inside the Firm*, Cambridge, MA, Harvard University Press.

Mishan, Ezra (1972), 'The Futility of Pareto-Efficiency in Policy Analysis', **62** *American Economic Review*, 971-76.

Mitchell, Wesley C. (1914), 'Human Behaviour and Economics: A Survey of Recent Literature', **29** *Quarterly Journal of Economics* 29, 1-47.

Mitchell, Wesley C. (1928), *Business Cycles: The Problem and its Setting*, New York, National Bureau of Economic Research.

Mitchell, Wesley C. (1937), *The Backward Art of Spending Money and Other Essays*, New York, McGraw-Hill.

Parsons, Kenneth H. (1957), 'A New Look at Institutionalism', **47** *American Economic Review*, 21-26.

Parsons, Kenneth H. (1974), 'The Institutional Basis for an Agricultural Market Economy', **8** *Journal of Economic Issues*, 737-57.

Parsons, Kenneth H. (1985), 'Commons' Relevance to Contemporary Economics', **19** *Journal of Economic Issues*, 755-78.

Posner, Richard A. (1995), *Overcoming Law*, Cambridge, MA, Harvard University Press.

Pound, Roscoe (1911a), 'The Scope and Purpose of Sociological Jurisprudence, Part I', **24** *Harvard Law Review*, 591-619.

Pound, Roscoe (1911b), 'The Scope and Purpose of Sociological Jurisprudence, Part II', **25** *Harvard Law Review*, 140-68.

Pound, Roscoe (1912), 'The Scope and Purpose of Sociological Jurisprudence, Part III', **25** *Harvard Law Review*, 489-516.

Pribram, Karl (1983), *A History of Economic Reasoning*, Baltimore, Johns Hopkins University Press.

Solo, Robert A. (1967), *Economic Organization and Social Systems*, New York, Bobbs-Merrill.

Solo, Robert A. (1982), *The Positive State*, Cincinnati, South-Western.

Spiegel, Henry William (1971), *The Growth of Economic Thought*, Durham (NC), Duke University Press.

Srivastava, Sik (1965), *History of Economic Thought*, Delhi, Atma Ram & Sons.

Stewart, Richard B. (1987), 'Crisis in Tort Law? The Institutional Perspective', **54** *University of Chicago Law Review*, 184-99.

Stewart, Richard B. (1988), 'Controlling Environmental Risks Through Economic Incentives', **13** *Columbia Journal of Environmental Law*, 153-69.

Tool, Marc R. (1988), *Evolutionary Economics*, 2 Vols, Armonk, NY, M.E. Sharpe.

Tool, Marc R. (ed.) (1993), *Institutional Economics: Theory, Method, Policy*, Boston, Kluwer.

Veblen, Thorstein B. (1899), *The Theory of the Leisure Class*, New York, Macmillan.

Veblen, Thorstein B. (1904), *The Theory of Business Enterprise*, New York, Charles Scribner's Sons.

Veblen, Thorstein B. (1923), *Absentee Ownership and Business Enterprise in Recent Times*, New York, B.W. Huebsch.

Whalen, Charles J. (1996), 'The Institutionalist Approach to Economics', in Foldvary, Fred (ed.), *Beyond Neoclassical Economics: Heterodox Approaches to Economic Theory*, Aldershot: Edward Elgar.

Cases

Allgeyer v. Louisiana

0530
NEW INSTITUTIONAL ECONOMICS

Peter G. Klein
Department of Economics, University of Georgia

Abstract

This chapter surveys the new institutional economics, a rapidly growing literature combining economics, law, organization theory, political science, sociology and anthropology to understand social, political and commercial institutions tries to explain what institutions are, how they arise, what purposes they serve, how they change and how they may be reformed. Following convention, I distinguish between the institutional environment (the background constraints, or 'rules of the game', that guide individuals' behavior) and institutional arrangements (specific guidelines designed by trading partners to facilitate particular exchanges). In both cases, the discussion here focuses on applications, evidence and policy implications.
JEL classification: D23, D72, L22, L42, O17
Keywords: Institutions, Firms, Transaction Costs, Specific Assets, Governance Structures

1. Introduction

The new institutional economics (NIE) is an interdisciplinary enterprise combining economics, law, organization theory, political science, sociology and anthropology to understand the institutions of social, political and commercial life. It borrows liberally from various social-science disciplines, but its primary language is economics. Its goal is to explain what institutions are, how they arise, what purposes they serve, how they change and how - if at all - they should be reformed. This essay surveys the wide-ranging and rapidly growing literature on the economics of institutions, with an emphasis on applications and evidence. The survey is divided into eight sections: the institutional environment; institutional arrangements and the theory of the firm; moral hazard and agency; transaction cost economics; capabilities and the core competence of the firm; evidence on contracts, organizations and institutions; public policy implications and influence; and a brief summary.

Until recently, 'institutional economics' usually referred to the writings of Thorstein Veblen, John R. Commons, Wesley C. Mitchell, Clarence Ayres and their followers. This is a diverse group, but their work reflects several common themes, mostly criticisms of orthodox economics: (1) a focus on collective rather than individual action; (2) a preference for an 'evolutionary' rather than mechanistic approach to the economy; and (3) an emphasis on empirical observation over deductive reasoning. (For a sampling of the secondary literature see Seckler, 1975; Gruchy, 1972; Gruchy, 1987; Rutherford, 1983; Langlois, 1989; and Hodgson, 1998. On the German roots of American institutionalism, see Richter, 1996.) Whatever their contributions, the older institutionalists are little known to most contemporary economists. Coase's (1984, p. 230) dismissal is typical: 'Without a theory they had nothing to pass on except a mass of descriptive material waiting for a theory, or a fire'. Still, this tradition (broadly defined) continues in such outlets as the *Journal of Economic Issues*, the *Cambridge Journal of Economics* and the *Review of Political Economy*.

The term 'new institutional economics' was originated by Williamson (1975). NIE, which began to develop as a self-conscious movement in the 1970s, traces its origins to Coase's analysis of the firm (Coase, 1937), Hayek's writings on knowledge (Hayek, 1937, 1945) and Chandler's history of industrial enterprise (Chandler, 1962), along with contributions by Simon (1947), Arrow (1963), Davis and North (1971), Williamson (1971, 1975, 1985), Alchian and Demsetz (1972), Macneil (1978), Holmström (1979) and others. Its best-known representatives are Coase, Williamson and North. For overviews and commentaries see Eggertsson (1990), Furubotn and Richter (1991), Coase (1992), Werin and Wijkander (1992), Pejovich (1995), Drobak and Nye (1997); and annual symposium issues of the *Journal of Institutional and Theoretical Economics*.

Like its older counterpart, the new institutional economics is interested in the social, economic and political institutions that govern everyday life. However, the new institutional economics eschews the holism of the older school. NIE follows strict methodological individualism, always couching its explanations in terms of the goals, plans and actions of individuals. Of course, NIE appreciates social phenomena like corporate culture, organizational memory, and so on. Still, NIE takes these as *explananda*, not the *explanans*.

NIE differs from mainstream neoclassical economics, however, in insisting that policy analysis be guided by what Coase (1964) calls 'comparative institutional analysis'. Orthodox welfare analysis typically compares real-world outcomes with the hypothetical benchmark of perfectly competitive general equilibrium. It is unsurprising, then, that actual market outcomes will come up short. The relevant question, Coase explains, is whether a feasible alternative can be devised:

> Contemplation of an optimal system may provide techniques of analysis that would otherwise have been missed and, in certain special cases, it may go far to providing a solution. But in general its influence has been pernicious. It has directed economists' attention away from the main question, which is how alternative arrangements will actually work in practice. It has led economists to derive

> conclusions for economic policy from a study of an abstract of a market situation. It is no accident that in the literature ... we find a category 'market failure' but no category 'government failure'. Until we realize that we are choosing between social arrangements which are all more or less failures, we are not likely to make much headway. (Coase, 1964, p. 195)

Coase's own investigation of British lighthouses (Coase, 1974) is a well-known comparative-institutional study. Coase discovered that before the 1830s, the typical British lighthouse - the classic, textbook example of a 'public good', which presumably the market cannot supply and therefore the state must provide - was privately owned and operated. Coase pointed out that here, public ownership does not overcome the 'free-rider problem' any better than does private ownership. Thus we should not be surprised to see private entrepreneurs providing this public good - at least until it was nationalized and provided thereafter by the state. (For other examples of public goods that were privately provided, but later nationalized - typically to raise revenue for the sovereign - see Benson, 1994 on police services and public highways, Benson, 1992 on criminal law and Selgin and White, forthcoming on money.)

To organize the various strands of the NIE, it is useful to begin with Davis and North's (1971) distinction between the 'institutional environment' and 'institutional arrangements'. The former refers to the background constraints, or 'rules of the game', that guide individuals' behavior. These can be both formal, explicit rules (constitutions, laws, property rights) and informal, often implicit rules (social conventions, norms). While these background rules are the product of - and can be explained in terms of - the goals, beliefs and choices of individual actors, the social result (the rule itself) is typically not known or 'designed' by anyone. Institutional arrangements, by contrast, are specific guidelines - what Williamson (1985, 1996b) calls 'governance structures' - designed by trading partners to mediate particular economic relationships. Business firms, long-term contracts, public bureaucracies, nonprofit organizations and other contractual agreements are examples of institutional arrangements.

2. The Institutional Environment

The institutional environment forms the framework in which human action takes place. 'Institutions reduce uncertainty by providing a structure to everyday life', writes North (1990, p. 3). 'In the jargon of the economist, institutions define and limit the set of choices of individuals. Institutional constraints include both what individuals are prohibited from doing and, sometimes, under what conditions some individuals are permitted to undertake certain activities. ... They are perfectly analogous to the rules of the game in a competitive team sport' (North, 1990, pp. 3-4). Unlike the rules in team sports, however, these guidelines often arise 'spontaneously', as by-products of individual choices, rather than deliberately through collective action (Hayek, 1967, 1973).

The Legal Environment and Property Rights

Of these sets of rules, the legal environment has received the most attention. Economists have long been interested in the economic effects of laws (for instance, the effects of a price ceiling on equilibrium price and quantity), but only in the last few decades has economics been applied to the design of legal rules and the legal system itself. Beginning with the early literature on the efficiency of the common law (Rubin, 1977; Priest, 1977), economics has been used to study not only the character and effects of law but the mechanisms by which legal rules change. In this sense, law and economics may therefore be considered a part of NIE, although it is customary to speak of law and economics and NIE as separate movements. (See the exchange between Posner, 1993, and Williamson, 1993, for contrasting views on the relationship between these two literatures. See also Williamson, 1996c, on the relationship between NIE and legal realism.)

NIE has been particularly interested in contract law (Llewellyn, 1931; Macneil, 1974, 1978; Langbein, 1987) and property law (Alchian, 1961; Demsetz, 1967; Furubotn and Pejovich, 1972, 1974; De Alessi, 1980; Barzel, 1989). However, unlike the 'legal centralism' tradition, which holds that disputes are primarily settled by the courts as official agents of the state, NIE often focuses on private solutions, holding that 'in many instances the participants can devise more satisfactory solutions to their disputes than can professionals constrained to apply general rules on the basis of limited knowledge of the dispute' (Galanter, 1981, p. 4). The recent studies on decentralized law and its evolution by Benson (1990), Ellickson (1991) and Cooter (1994), for example, are examples of this 'private ordering' tradition.

Norms and Social Conventions

Equally important are the informal and often tacit, rules that structure social conduct. '[F]ormal rules ... make up a small ... part of the sum of constraints that shape choices; ... the governing structure is overwhelmingly defined by codes of conduct, norms of behavior and conventions' (North, 1990, p. 36).

Such rules, once established, form constraints for individual actors. Yet how can the rules themselves be explained in terms of purposeful individual choices? In Menger's (1883, p. 146) words: 'How can it be that institutions which serve the common welfare and are extremely significant for its development come into being without a common will directed toward establishing them?'

One approach is to interpret social conventions as noncooperative Nash-equilibrium solutions to a variety of repeated games ('supergames') faced by individuals in social settings. An example is the coordination game made famous by Schelling (1960). Two friends arrange to meet one day at 5:00 p.m. in New York City. As the time of the meeting approaches, however, neither can remember where the meeting was to take place. Furthermore, the friends cannot contact each other to verify the location of the meeting; each must guess, independently, a likely meeting place. What can they do? Obviously, this game has multiple Nash equilibria: any outcome in which both friends choose the same location - say, the corner of 34th Street and 5th Avenue - is a Nash equilibrium to the game. According to Schelling, when faced with this kind of problem, agents rely on cultural information outside the structure of the game. Everyone simply *knows*, for example, that the logical place to meet in New York City is beneath the clock in the main terminal of Grand Central Station. This equilibrium is what Schelling called a 'focal point.' Over time, he argued, behavioral regularities develop so agents can solve these kinds of coordination problems.

Ullman-Margalit (1977) calls these equilibria 'norms'; Sugden (1986) calls them 'conventions'; Schotter (1981) calls them 'social institutions'. In Schotter's (1981, p. 11) words, a social institution is 'a regularity in social behavior that is agreed to by all members of society, specifies behavior in specific recurrent situations and is either self-policed or policed by some external authority'. These regularities are presumed to arise over time as agents interact repeatedly. Game theory itself, however, usually says little about how a particular convention is chosen; it only identifies combinations of strategies that are mutual best responses. More recently, some explicitly evolutionary models (Witt, 1989; Wärnereyd, 1990; Boyer and Orlean, 1992) have tried to explain the dynamic process by which particular equilibria are chosen. Axelrod (1984) has shown experimentally that strategies of repeated cooperation tend to be established relatively quickly.

Ellickson (1991) explains that social norms, as 'customary law', can be superior to administrative or judicial dispute resolution among people with close social ties. Ellickson studied disputes between cattle ranchers and farmers in Shasta County, California and found that these disputes were usually resolved by appeal to generally accepted social rules, not by bargaining over legal rights (as the Coase Theorem would predict). '[M]embers of a close-knit group develop and maintain norms whose content serves to maximize the aggregate welfare that members obtain in their workaday affairs with one another' (Ellickson, 1991, p. 167). That is, through repeated play, agents tend to converge on strategies of cooperation that improve joint well being. These strategies replace traditional legal remedies. 'Law solves the problem of cooperation by altering the payoff structure in each game; relationships solve the problem by repeating the game. In Shasta County, where both solutions are available, relationships prevail over law' (Cooter, 1993, p. 423). Informal norms, in these cases, replace law.

Norms and law are not necessarily substitutes, however. Law can shape the outcome of private bargaining by serving as a backup mechanism for resolving disputes that cannot be resolved privately. If the alternative to private dispute resolution is resolution in court, then the expected outcome at trial determines the parties' 'threat values' in bargaining. Bargaining typically takes place 'in the shadow of the law' (Cooter, Marks and Mnookin, 1982). Moreover, norms can help shape the law, if judges look to social norms as guidelines for legal decisions. The traditional account of the medieval law merchant illustrates this phenomenon. During the commercial revolution merchants developed a system of private courts to resolve disputes among themselves. The rules of these courts became general merchant practice, enforced by the threat of ostracism. As the English legal system developed, judges began to hear commercial disputes once handled privately. In resolving these disputes, English common-law judges tended to enforce the merchant customs already in place. In this way the common law came to embody the principles that already existed, principles developed through private interaction among merchants. (On the law merchant see Trakman, 1983 and Benson, 1989). Today, many commercial disputes are resolved privately, through organizations such as the VISA Arbitration Committee (Solove, 1986; Cooter, 1994).

Economic History and Economic Growth

Attention to the institutional environment has become increasingly common in economic history and it has deeply enriched our understanding of how economies develop through time (North and Thomas, 1973; North, 1990; Drobak and Nye, 1997). Economic development is no longer regarded as a gradual, inevitable transformation from local autarky to specialization and the division of labor. Instead, development is seen as a response to the evolution of institutions that support social and commercial relationships. Economic growth thus depends on the degree to which the potential hazards of trade (shirking, opportunism and the like) can be controlled by institutions, which reduce information costs, encourage capital formation and capital mobility, allow risks to be priced and shared and otherwise facilitate cooperation.

In early societies, agency problems were typically solved through kinship or other close social ties. Greif (1989), for example, has shown how eleventh-century Jewish traders in the Mediterranean trade enforced codes of conduct by maintaining close social relationships, using the threat of ostracism as a disciplinary device. Later, standardized weights and measures, units of account, media of exchange and procedures to resolve disputes (such as merchant law courts) supported the expansion of trade by lowering information costs. Capital markets could flourish only in societies where rulers could credibly commit not to expropriate private wealth; North and Weingast (1989) show how capital markets emerged in Britain after the Glorious Revolution of 1688 placed parliamentary limits on the authority of the Crown. The growth of product and factor markets depends similarly on establishing secure property rights. Furthermore, as an economy industrializes, more and more commercial activity involves 'transacting': trade, finance, banking, insurance and management (Wallis and North, 1986). Industrialization requires institutions to mitigate the costs associated with these transactions.

Economic development, then, is institutional development. 'The central issue of economic history and of economic development is to account for the evolution of political and economic institutions that create an economic environment that induces increasing productivity' (North, 1991, p. 98).

Positive Political Theory
Political institutions have also received much attention in NIE. The rational-choice approach to politics, as outlined in public choice (Buchanan and Tullock, 1962; Mueller, 1979, 1989) and positive political theory (McKelvey, 1976; Riker, 1981; Enelow and Hinich, 1984), holds that political institutions can be explained in terms of purposeful human choice. This framework has been applied to constitutions, legislatures, executives, bureaucracies, courts and elections. Spatial models of voting, for example, show how different voting rules (such as which party can set the agenda) affect the outcome. Among the better-known applications of the spatial model are studies of the committee structure in Congress, under which committees have agenda-setting power (Denzau and Mackay, 1983; Shepsle and Weingast, 1987). The rational-choice perspective is also used to explain the effects of political institutions on public policy, including macroeconomic policy, welfare policy, budgets, regulation and technology policy (see Weingast, 1996, for an overview).

Why, however, do political institutions take one form or another? One approach is to identify particular political institutions that are self-perpetuating, meaning that those individuals or groups which can modify the institution have no incentive to do so (Ordeshook, 1993; Weingast, 1995). Antebellum American federalism is one example; it survived, arguably, because it was supported by institutions such as the territorial 'balance rule' established by the Missouri Compromise of 1820 (Weingast, 1994). Another approach identifies institutions that allow bureaucrats to make their policy choices last beyond their own tenures (Moe, 1989).

Complexity and Cognitive Science
A few recent papers have focused on the relationship between the institutional environment and cognitive processes in forming a framework for decision making under uncertainty (Denzau and North, 1994; Clark, 1997). Denzau and North (1994) argue that ideology, along with institutions, helps agents cope with complex decisions. They define ideology as a shared set of mental models possessed by groups of individuals. These mental models are 'the internal representations that individual cognitive systems create to interpret the environment'; institutions are 'the external (to the mind) mechanisms individuals create to structure and order the environment' (Denzau and North, 1994, p. 4). Together, ideology and institutions form a framework for economic activity under conditions of uncertainty. If social learning is path-dependent, as they maintain, then economic development will be gradual and uneven. This may explain why some economies continue to perform poorly for long periods.

3. Institutional Arrangements and the Theory of the Firm

These rules and customs that make up the institutional environment are primarily economy-side phenomena. Another aspect of the new institutional economics focuses on agreements made by specific individuals to govern their own relationships. Such institutional arrangements - what Williamson (1996b, p. 5) calls the institutions of governance - include contracts and organizations and in particular, the business firm. The study of governance is more prosaic than the study of the institutional environment. 'Mundane questions of whether to make or buy a component to be used in the manufacture of an automobile or whether to expand the hospital into outpatient and home health services are ones that arise at the level of governance. By contrast, composite economic growth and income distribution are more apt to be the objects of interest in an inquiry into the institutional environment' (Williamson, 1996b, p. 5). However, the study of governance - in particular, the theory of the firm - is arguably more developed than the study of the institutional environment.

Coase once described his 1937 paper on the firm as 'much cited and little used' (Coase, 1972, p. 56). Today, the theory of the firm is one of the fastest-growing areas in applied microeconomics. For overviews of the modern theory of the firm, see Holmström and Tirole (1989), Milgrom and Roberts (1992), Radner (1992), Holmström and Milgrom (1994), Hart (1995) and Buckley and Michie (1996). For critiques and alternative perspectives see Langlois and Robertson (1995) and Foss (1997).

The Conventional Theory of The Firm

What economists usually mean by 'the theory of the firm' is the theory of production, not the theory of the firm as a legal entity. In economics textbooks, the 'firm' is a production function or production possibilities set, a 'black box' that transforms inputs into outputs. Given technology, input prices and a demand schedule, the firm maximizes money profits subject to the constraint that its production plans must be technologically feasible. The firm is modeled as a single actor, facing a series of straightforward decisions: what level of output to produce, how much of each factor to hire, and so on. Similarly, the firm's size and product range are usually explained in terms of production costs: economies of scale imply larger firms, while economies of scope justify the multiproduct firm (Spulber, 1989, pp. 113-20).

The conventional theory has proved highly useful for understanding pricing and output decisions and how these vary with competitive conditions. It also has the appeal of analytical tractability along with its elegant parallel to neoclassical consumer theory (profit maximization is like utility maximization, isoquants are indifference curves, and so on). However, the production-function approach provides little insight into the boundaries of the firm. For example, cost subadditivity (as reflected in economies of scale and scope) implies that certain quantities of output can be produced more efficiently when they are produced together. Yet this does not explain why the joint production must take place in a single firm; absent transactional difficulties, two independent firms could simply contract to share the same plant or facility and jointly produce the efficient level of output (Teece, 1980, 1982). Whether the firms will integrate thus depends on the cost of writing and enforcing contracts, not only on the underlying productive technology.

The black-box model is really a theory about a *plant* or production process, not a *firm*. Textbook treatments frequently blur the distinction between firm and plant (for a welcome exception, see Sharkey, 1982, pp. 73-83), but the two are quite distinct. A single firm can own and operate multiple production processes, just as two or more firms can contract to operate jointly a single production process (as in a research joint venture). For this reason, the production-function approach cannot fully explain such real-world business practices as vertical and lateral integration, acquisitions, geographic and product-line diversification, franchising, long-term commercial contracting, transfer pricing and joint ventures, nor is it an adequate guide for antitrust and regulatory policy. Instead, the new institutional economics sees the firm as a set of arrangements - as an *organization* - itself worthy of economic analysis.

Coase and Transaction Costs

The new institutional approach to the firm is usually traced to Coase's celebrated 1937 paper on 'The Nature of the Firm'. Coase was the first to explain that the boundaries of the organization depend not only on the productive technology, but on the costs of transacting business. In the Coasian framework, as developed and expanded by Williamson (1975, 1985, 1996b), Klein, Crawford and Alchian (1978), Grossman and Hart (1986) and Hart and Moore (1990), the decision to organize transactions within the firm as opposed to on the open market - the 'make or buy decision' - depends on the relative costs of internal and external exchange. The market mechanism entails certain costs: discovering the relevant prices, negotiating and enforcing contracts, and so on. Within the firm, the entrepreneur can reduce these 'transaction costs' by coordinating these activities himself. However, internal organization brings another kind of transaction costs, namely problems of information flows, incentives, monitoring and performance evaluation. More generally, all feasible modes of economic organization incur costs. The nature of the firm, then, is determined by the relative costs of organizing transactions under alternative institutional arrangements.

This transformation of economists' thinking about the firm is nicely summarized by Roe (1994, p. vii):

> Economic theory once treated the firm as a collection of machinery, technology, inventory, workers and capital. Dump these inputs into a black box, stir them up and one got outputs of products and profits. Today, theory sees the firm as more, as a management structure. The firm succeeds if managers can successfully coordinate the

firm's activities; it fails if managers cannot effectively coordinate and match people and inputs to current technologies and markets. At the very top of the firm are the relationships among the firm's shareholders, its directors and its senior managers. If those relationships are dysfunctional, the firm is more likely to stumble.

With this new orientation, economic theory is playing an increasingly visible role in finance, accounting, management and other areas once thought to be beyond the purview of economics.

4. Moral Hazard and Agency

The modern theory of the firm comprises several approaches. The moral-hazard or agency-theoretic approach begins with Berle and Means's (1932) identification of the 'separation of ownership and control' in the large firm. The modern corporation, they claimed, is run not by owners (shareholders), but by salaried managers, whose goals often differ from those of the owners. Managers may use their discretion to 'shirk' or otherwise pursue personal objectives (firm growth, personal power, entrenchment, perquisites) at the expense of shareholder value.

The Berle-Means account omits the possibility that competition might impose discipline on shirking managers. Product-market competition, competition in the internal market for managers (Fama, 1980) and competition in the market for corporate control (Manne, 1965) all place limits on managerial discretion. Still, their basic model of conflict between shareholders and managers - what we would now call a principal-agent problem - remains a powerful lens for viewing the internal organization of the firm. Agency theory, as developed by Jensen and Meckling (1976), Fama (1980), Fama and Jensen (1983) and Jensen (1986), has become the standard language of corporate finance.

Agency theory studies the design of ex-ante incentive-compatible mechanisms to reduce agency costs in the face of potential moral hazard (malfeasance) by agents. Agency costs are defined by Jensen and Meckling (1976, p. 308) as the sum of '(1) the monitoring expenditures of the principal, (2) the bonding expenditures by the agent and (3) the residual loss'. The residual loss represents the potential gains from trade not realized because principals cannot provide perfect incentives for agents when the agents' actions are unobservable. In a typical agency model, a principal assigns an agent to do some task (producing output, for instance), but has only an imperfect signal of the agent's performance (for example, effort). The agency problem resembles the signal-extraction problem popularized in macroeconomics by Lucas (1972): how much of the observable outcome (output) is due to the agent's effort and how much is due to factors beyond the agent's control? The optimal incentive contract balances the principal's desire to give the agent incentives to increase effort (for example, by basing compensation on the outcome) with the agent's desire to be insured from the fluctuations in compensation that come from these factors beyond his control.

In the agency literature, the firm itself is not the subject of attention. According to Alchian and Demsetz (1972) and Jensen and Meckling (1976), the 'firm' is simply a convenient label for the collection of contracts between owners and managers, managers and employees and the firm and its customers and suppliers. The firm is a nexus of a set of contracting relationships. ... The firm is a legal fiction which serves as a focus for a complete process in which the conflicting objectives of individuals ... are brought into equilibrium within a framework of contractual relations' (Jensen and Meckling, 1976, pp. 311-12).

The question of interest is thus the degree to which various contracts can mitigate these conflicts; the boundary of the firm is a secondary issue.

5. Transaction Cost Economics

Transaction cost economics (TCE) represents another approach to studying institutional arrangements. Here, the emphasis is on governing transactions. TCE holds that all but the simplest transactions require some kind of mechanism - what Williamson (1985) calls a governance structure - to protect the transacting parties from various hazards associated with exchange. The appropriate governance structure depends on the characteristics of the transaction, so TCE implies an applied research program of comparative contractual analysis: how do different forms of governance work in various circumstances? For this reason, TCE (associated mainly with Williamson) is sometimes described as the 'governance' branch of the NIE, as opposed to the 'measurement' branch (associated with Alchian and Demsetz, 1972).

The governance approach is distinguished by its emphasis on incomplete contracts. In the transaction cost framework, economic organization imposes costs because complex contracts are usually incomplete. A complete contract specifies a course of action, a decision, or terms of trade contingent on every possible future state of affairs. In the textbook model of competitive general equilibrium, all contracts are assumed to be complete. The future is not known with certainty, but the probability distributions of all possible future events are known (what Knight, 1921, would call 'risk' rather than 'uncertainty'). In an important sense, the model is 'timeless': all relevant future contingencies are considered in the ex ante contracting stage, so there are no decisions to be made - no actions to be taken at all, really - as the future plays itself out.

TCE relaxes this assumption and holds that all complex contracts are unavoidably incomplete. In a world of 'true' uncertainty, the future holds genuine surprises and this limits the available contracting options. In simple transactions - for instance, procuring an off-the-shelf component - uncertainty may be relatively unimportant and spot-market contracting works well. For more complex transactions, such as the purchase and installation of specialized equipment, a more sophisticated contract is needed. However, such a contract will typically be incomplete - it will provide remedies for only some possible future contingencies. One example is a *relational contract*, an agreement that describes shared goals and a set of general principles that govern the relationship (Goldberg, 1980). Another is an *implicit contract* - an agreement that while unstated, is assumed to be understood by all sides.

Williamson attributes contractual incompleteness to cognitive limits or 'bounded rationality', following Simon's (1961, p. xxiv) interpretation of human action as 'intendedly rational, but only limitedly so'. Other NIE economists are more agnostic, assuming only that some quantities or outcomes are unobservable (or not verifiable to third parties, such as the courts), in which case contracts cannot be made contingent on these variables or outcomes.

Specific Investments and the Holdup Problem

Contractual incompleteness exposes the contracting parties to certain risks. Primarily, if circumstances change unexpectedly, the original governing agreement may no longer be effective. The need to adapt to unforeseen contingencies constitutes an additional cost of contracting; failure to adapt imposes what Williamson (1991a) calls 'maladaptation costs'. The most-often-discussed example of maladaptation is the 'holdup' problem associated with relationship-specific investments. Investment in such assets exposes agents to a potential hazard: If circumstances change, their trading partners may try to expropriate the rents accruing to the specific assets. Suppose an upstream supplier tailors its equipment for a particular customer. After the equipment is in place, the customer may demand a lower price, knowing that the salvage value of the specialized equipment is lower than the net payment it offers. This creates an underinvestment problem: Anticipating the customer's behavior, the supplier will be unwilling to install the custom machinery without protection for such a contingency, even if the specialized technology would make the relationship more profitable for both sides.

One way to safeguard rents accruing to specific assets is vertical (or lateral) integration, where a merger eliminates any adversarial interests. Less extreme options include long-term contracts (Joskow, 1985, 1987, 1988, 1990), partial ownership agreements (Pisano, Russo and Teece, 1988; Pisano, 1990), or agreements for both parties to invest in offsetting relationship-specific investments (Heide and John, 1988). Overall, several governance structures may be employed. TCE holds that parties tend to choose the governance structure that best controls the underinvestment problem, given the particulars of the relationship.

The holdup problem is the best-known example of a contractual hazard. More generally, contractual difficulties can arise from several sources: '(1) bilateral dependence; (2) weak property rights; (3) measurement difficulties and/or oversearching; (4) intertemporal issues that can take the form of disequilibrium contracting, real-time responsiveness, long latency and strategic abuse; and (5) weaknesses in the institutional environment' (Williamson, 1996b, p. 14). Each of these has the potential to impose maladaptation costs. Foreseeing this possibility, agents seek to reduce the potential costs of maladaptation by matching the appropriate governance structure with the particular characteristics of the transaction.

In this way, TCE may be considered the study of *alternative institutions of governance*. Its working hypothesis, as expressed by Williamson (1991c, p. 79), is that economic organization is mainly an effort to 'align transactions, which differ in their attributes, with governance structures, which differ in their costs and competencies, in a discriminating (mainly, transaction cost economizing) way'. Simply put, TCE tries to explain how trading partners choose, from the set of feasible institutional alternatives, the arrangement that protects their relationship-specific investments at the least cost.

Institutions as Governance Structures

Transactions differ in several ways: the degree to which relationship-specific assets are involved, the amount of uncertainty about the future and about other parties' actions, the complexity of the trading arrangement and the frequency with which the transaction occurs. Each matters for the preferred institution of governance, although the first - asset specificity - is particularly important. Williamson (1985, p. 55) defines asset specificity as 'durable investments that are undertaken in support of particular transactions, the opportunity cost of which investments is much lower in best alternative uses or by alternative users should the original transaction be prematurely terminated'. This could describe a variety of relationship-specific investments, including both specialized physical and human capital, along with intangibles such as R&D and firm-specific knowledge or capabilities.

Governance structures can be described along a spectrum, with 'market' and 'hierarchy' at the poles. At one end lies the pure anonymous spot market, which suffices for simple transactions such as basic commodity sales. Market prices provide powerful incentives for exploiting profit opportunities and market participants are quick to adapt to changing circumstances as information is revealed through prices. When relationship-specific assets are at stake, however and when product or input markets are thin, bilateral coordination of investment decisions may be desirable and combined ownership of these assets may be efficient. At the other end of the spectrum from the simple, anonymous spot market thus lies the fully integrated firm, where trading parties are under unified ownership and control. TCE posits that such hierarchies offer greater protection for specific investments and provide relatively efficient mechanisms for responding to change where coordinated adaptation is necessary. Compared with decentralized structures, however, hierarchies provide managers with weaker incentives to maximize profits and normally incur additional bureaucratic costs. Between the two poles of market and hierarchy are a variety of 'hybrid' modes, such as complex contracts and partial ownership arrangements. The movement from market to hierarchy thus entails a tradeoff between the high-powered incentives and adaptive properties of the market and the safeguards and central coordinating properties of the firm.

The general theoretical framework of TCE is now sufficiently accepted to have been incorporated in several textbook treatments (Kreps, 1990, pp. 744-90; Rubin, 1990; Milgrom and Roberts, 1992; Acs and Gerlowski, 1996; and Besanko, Dranove and Shanley, 1990).

6. Capabilities and the Core Competence of the Firm

An alternative approach to explaining institutional arrangements focuses on the 'core competence' or 'capabilities' of the firm. The capabilities view, which traces its roots to Alfred Marshall and Joseph Schumpeter, was first stated explicitly by Edith Penrose in her *Theory of the Growth of the Firm* (1959). It has been developed further by Teece (1980, 1982) and by Nelson and Winter in their *Evolutionary Theory of Economic Change* (1982). The capabilities view regards the firm not as a nexus of contracts (as in Alchian and Demsetz, 1972), or as a set of residual control rights (as in Grossman and Hart, 1986), but as a stock of knowledge. The firm's capabilities depend on the tacit knowledge it contains, as manifested in organizational memory or routines. This knowledge is considered technologically inseparable; it is firm-specific, not transaction-specific and thus helps determine the boundary of the firm (Chandler, 1992). In this sense, 'firms exist because they are superior institutional arrangements for accumulating specialized productive knowledge, quite independently of considerations of opportunism, incentive alignment and the like' (Foss, 1996, p. 2).

In the field of strategic management, organizational capabilities have been examined from within the 'resource-based' view of the firm. In the resource-based view, competitive advantage comes from having unique factors of production, resources that are not easily imitable or transferable (and thus cannot be purchased in factor markets). Excess profits or supranormal returns are seen as rents accruing to these unique resources (Rumelt, 1984; Wernerfelt, 1984). Firm-specific resources may include organizational capabilities, managerial skill, technological innovation and reputational capital. When firms have excess capacity in these unique factors, they expand and diversify into product lines whose manufacture employs similar capabilities or routines. The resource-based view is thus concerned as much about economic change, or 'evolution', as it is about the design and use of optimal contracts. For this reason, the capabilities approach is often associated with the 'evolutionary' theory of the firm. (See Langlois and Robertson, 1995, for an overview.)

The capabilities perspective is intriguing and offers many useful insights into firm organization and behavior. However, research in this area often proceeds at a very high level of abstraction. While there have been several applied studies (Kogut and Chang, 1991; Langlois and Robertson, 1989; Langlois, 1992a, 1992b;

Teece et al., 1994; Argyres, 1996) further empirical work is needed to develop the economics of firm capabilities.

7. Evidence on Contracts, Organizations and Institutions

The same criticism has been leveled at the theory of the firm more generally. Simon (1991, p. 27), for example, has charged the new institutional economics and transaction cost economics in particular, with lacking sufficient empirical support. Until the relevant empirical studies have been done, he says, 'the new institutional economics and related approaches are acts of faith, or perhaps of piety'. However, much empirical work has already been carried out. (Shelanski and Klein, 1995, provide a comprehensive survey; Masten, 1996, collects many of the important articles.) On balance, a remarkable amount of this empirical work is consistent with TCE - much more so, perhaps, than is the case with most of industrial organization (Joskow, 1991, p. 81). As Williamson (1996a, p. 55) puts it: 'TCE is an empirical success story'.

Much of the empirical research in TCE follows the same basic model. The efficient form of organization for a given economic relationship - and, therefore, the likelihood of observing a particular organizational form or governance structure - is a function of certain properties of the underlying transaction or transactions: asset specificity, uncertainty, complexity and frequency. Organizational form is the dependent variable, while asset specificity, uncertainty, complexity and frequency are independent variables. Specifically, the probability of observing a more integrated governance structure depends positively on the amount or value of the relationship-specific assets involved and, for significant levels of asset specificity, on the degree of uncertainty about the future of the relationship, on the complexity of the transaction and on the frequency of trade.

Empirical work in TCE implicitly assumes that market forces work to cause an 'efficient sort' between transactions and governance structures, so that exchange relationships observed in practice can be explained in terms of transaction cost economizing. Williamson (1988, p. 174) acknowledges this, while recognizing that the process of transaction cost economizing is not automatic:

> The [transaction cost] argument relies in a general, background way on the efficacy of competition to perform a sort between more and less efficient modes and to shift resources in favor of the former. This seems plausible, especially if the relevant outcomes are those that appear over intervals of five and ten years rather than in the very near term. This intuition would nevertheless benefit from a more fully developed theory of the selection process. Transaction cost arguments are thus open to some of the same objections that evolutionary economists [for example, Nelson and Winter] have made of orthodoxy.

Still, he maintains that the efficiency presumption is reasonable, offering the argument - analogous to Friedman's famous (1953) statement on the selection process - that inefficient governance arrangements will tend to be discovered and undone. Concerning vertical integration, for example, Williamson (1985, pp. 119-20) writes that 'backward integration that lacks a transaction cost rationale or serves no strategic purposes will presumably be recognized and will be undone', adding that mistakes will be corrected more quickly 'if the firm is confronted with an active rivalry'. Silverman, Nickerson and Freeman (1997) have shown that transaction cost efficiency is positively correlated with firm survival in the for-hire trucking industry, though evidence from other industries is scant.

Despite such concerns, most empirical literature inspired by TCE takes as given an economizing framework, assuming that we can draw inferences about the efficiency of organizational forms by observing what organizations actually do. Unlike earlier traditions in industrial organization, which presumed that complex contracts and similar deviations from perfect competition are usually attempts to gain monopoly power, TCE follows the common-law presumption that such contracts 'serve affirmative economic purposes' (Williamson, 1985, p. 200). Furthermore, such contracts are objectionable only if some feasible alternative exists (Coase, 1964).

Organizational form is often modeled as a binary variable - 'make' or 'buy', for example - though it can sometimes be represented by a continuous variable. Of the independent variables, asset specificity is the most difficult to measure. Williamson (1991a) distinguishes among six types of asset specificity. The first is site specificity, in which parties are in a 'cheek-by-jowl' relationship to reduce transportation and inventory costs and assets are highly immobile. The second, physical asset specificity, refers to relationship-specific equipment and machinery. The third is human asset specificity, describing transaction-specific knowledge or human capital, achieved through specialized training or learning-by-doing. The fourth is brand-name capital, reflected in intangible assets reflected in consumer perceptions. The fifth is 'dedicated assets', referring to substantial, general-purpose investments that would not have been made outside a particular transaction, the commitment of which is necessary to serve a large customer. The sixth is temporal specificity, describing assets which must be used in a particular sequence.

Among the common empirical proxies for asset specificity are component 'complexity', qualitatively coded from survey data, as a proxy for physical asset specificity (Masten, 1984); worker-specific knowledge, again coded from survey data, as a proxy for human asset specificity (Monteverde and Teece, 1982); physical proximity of contracting firms, as a proxy for site specificity (Joskow, 1985, 1987, 1988, 1990; Spiller, 1985); and R&D expenditure, as a proxy for physical asset specificity. Other proxies, such as fixed costs or 'capital intensity', have more obvious limitations and are rarely used.

Vertical Integration

Vertical integration, or the 'make-or-buy' decision, was the first topic studied extensively within the TCE framework. Traditionally, economists viewed vertical integration as an attempt to earn monopoly rents by gaining control of input markets or distribution channels. But in the early 1980s a few authors began to investigate transaction-cost (that is, efficiency) rationales for vertical integration. Monteverde and Teece (1982) made one of the first systematic efforts to test a contractual interpretation of vertical integration. They examined the effects of asset specificity, defined as worker-specific knowledge or 'applications engineering effort', on the decision to produce components in-house or to obtain them from outside suppliers. They found applications engineering effort to be a statistically significant determinant of backwards integration. The results are consistent with case-study evidence from Globerman (1980) on firm-specific technical knowledge and integration in the Canadian telecommunications industry. Globerman studied evidence from public hearings and found a tendency toward common ownership of telephone lines and equipment as the research and development demands of a carrier on its equipment suppliers become more complex and uncertain and require more relationship-specific investments.

Other studies of component procurement have found similar support for transactional explanations of vertical relationships. Two studies by Walker and Weber (1984, 1987) focus on uncertainty as a determinant of vertical integration in the auto industry. Like Monteverde and Teece, they worked with a list of automobile components, coded as made or bought, as the dependent variable. They found that greater uncertainty about production volume raises the probability that a component is made in-house, but that 'technological uncertainty', measured as the frequency of changes in product specification and the probability of technological improvements, has little effect. Their second (1987) study included measures of market competition, testing the interactive effects of both uncertainty in production and competition among suppliers and added the qualification that volume uncertainty matters only when supply markets are thin.

In a further refinement, Masten, Meehan and Snyder (1989) distinguished among types of specific assets, comparing the relative importance of relationship-specific human and physical capital. They also studied automobile component production, finding that engineering effort, as a proxy for human asset specificity, appears to affect the integration decision more than physical or site specificity. Klein (1988), in a discussion of the G.M.-Fisher Body case, also suggests that specific human capital in the form of technical knowledge was a major determinant of G.M.'s decision to buy out Fisher.

The relationship between G.M. and Fisher Body in the 1920s is a frequently discussed application of TCE. Both Klein, Crawford and Alchian (1978) and Williamson (1985, pp. 114-15) explain G.M.'s buyout of Fisher in terms of the specific physical assets that accompanied the switch from wooden- to metal-bodied cars. The account in Klein (1988) is somewhat different, emphasizing specific human capital. Langlois and Robertson (1989) also criticize the earlier TCE account of the G.M.-Fisher relationship, arguing that systemic uncertainty, rather than asset specificity, accounts for the failure of long-term contracting there. Helper, MacDuffie and Sabel (1997) propose another alternative: G.M. acquired Fisher to promote collaborative learning, not to avoid hold-up. Obviously, this case continues to stimulate interest.

Other studies have documented a similar link between integration and R&D, which usually involves specific human capital (Armour and Teece, 1980; Joskow, 1985; Pisano, 1990). Site specificity, dedicated assets and the need for specifically tailored products or production facilities have been shown to increase vertical integration in a variety of industries, including electricity generation (Joskow, 1985), aerospace (Masten, 1984), aluminum (Stuckey, 1983; Hennart, 1988), forestry (Globerman and Schwindt, 1986), chemicals (Lieberman, 1991) and offshore oil gathering (Hallwood, 1991).

These papers are case studies of particular industries or production processes. As such, they avoid the problem of inconsistent measurement across industries, but have measurement difficulties of their own. The classification of dichotomous variables like 'make-or-buy', for example, is typically based on survey data, requiring more discretion by the researcher than economists are comfortable with. Nonetheless, most of the empirical work in TCE on vertical integration has been of this type. While generalizing the results is of course difficult, the cumulative evidence from different studies and industries is quite consistent with the basic theory. Also, there do exist some cross-sectional studies on transactional determinants of vertical integration using multi-industry data and most have been supportive (Levy, 1985; MacMillan, Hambrick and Pennings, 1986).

Long-term Contracts and 'Hybrid' Forms

Long-term contracts can be interpreted as intermediate or 'hybrid' forms of organization, neither market nor hierarchy. A series of papers by Joskow (1985, 1987, 1988, 1990) investigates the effects of asset specificity on contract duration and price adjustment in agreements between coal suppliers and coal-burning electrical plants. He examined a large sample of coal contracts and found that contracts tended to be longer, all else equal, when relationship-specific investments (here, site specificity and dedicated assets) are at stake. Crocker and Masten (1988) found the same result for the natural gas industry. More generally, they argue that efficient contract duration depends on the costs of contracting; contract terms become shorter, for example, as uncertainty increases. Goldberg and Erickson (1987) analysed contracts for petroleum coke and concluded that many provisions of the contracts can best be interpreted as efforts by the parties to protect themselves against expropriation of specialized investments. Other relevant studies on natural gas contracts have been done by Crocker and Masten (1991) and Hubbard and Weiner (1991).

DeCanio and Frech (1993) tried to measure more precisely the efficiency gains from long-term contracts in natural gas. Relationship-specific investments are critical for transactions between wellhead owners and pipelines. For that reason, 'take-or-pay' contracts, in which the buyer must pay for some minimum quantity even if delivery is not taken, are often used to safeguard against buyer (pipeline) opportunism. In 1987, the Federal Energy Regulatory Commission (FERC) outlawed take-or-pay contracts. The authors used data from before and after the FERC order to test its effect on spot gas prices and prices at the wellhead. They found that FERC's interference with parties' ability to craft long-term governance mechanisms raised natural gas prices between 21 percent and 31 percent in the year following FERC's order. The results support TCE explanations for the relative efficiency of long-term contracts where asset specificity is required, while representing an effort to quantify that efficiency gain. (Mulherin, 1986, and Masten and Crocker, 1985, also examine 'take-or-pay' contracts.)

Another hybrid form of organization is a partial ownership agreement or 'equity linkage'. Pisano (1990) asks why firms may rely on equity linkages instead of contracts to support certain transactions. He argues that partial ownership will dominate contractual governance when a relationship involves uncertainty, transaction-specific capital and other variables. He hypothesizes that equity linkages are more likely when R&D is to be done during collaboration and when collaboration encompasses multiple projects and less likely when there are more potential collaborators. His study of collaborative arrangements in the biotechnology industry supported all these claims. Pisano, Russo and Teece (1988) applied a similar analysis to the telecommunications equipment business and found that the same basic framework can explain the choice between equity linkages and other forms of cooperative ventures (joint ventures, consortiums, or other non-equity linkages).

Allen and Lueck (1993) studied 'cropshare' contracts between farmers and landowners. Such contracts specify sharing rules for both inputs and outputs; in doing so, they pool enforcement costs by making both the farmer and the landowner residual claimants. This reduces the farmer's incentive to deplete the capital value of the soil. Allen and Lueck show that optimal sharing rules will involve either full payment of inputs by farmers or sharing input costs in proportion to the output-sharing rule. Nee (1992) studied hybrid governance structures in China's transitional economy such as small, family-owned firms run by peasant entrepreneurs ('cadre-entrepreneurs') and collectively owned enterprises leased to private operators ('marketized firms'). On hybrids see also Gallick (1984), Masten and Snyder (1993), Lafontaine and Masten (1995) and Menard (1996).

Informal Agreements

Like other parts of the new institutional economics, TCE pays special attention to the importance of private solutions to resolve disputes, in contrast to the older tradition of legal centralism. Several studies have investigated whether informal trade arrangements, which are not legally enforceable, may also be motivated by the desire to make exchange more efficient. Important work in this area has been done by Palay (1984, 1985). In two closely related papers, Palay studied the role of informal, legally unenforceable agreements between rail-freight carriers and shippers. He argues that ICC regulation of the industry, which prohibits vertical integration of carriers and shippers, was geared to 'classical contracting' (Macneil, 1978) but is inappropriate for transactions requiring more complex agreements. Shipment of items like automobile parts and chemicals, for example, requires specially designed rail cars and equipment that cannot be easily redeployed for other uses. Palay claims that informal agreements, substituting for combined ownership, would emerge both to encourage and to protect these relationship-specific investments. Furthermore, he argues that the underlying characteristics of a transaction predict whether it will be supported by an informal agreement. Evidence from case studies of shipper-carrier transactions reveals a pattern of informal agreements highly consistent with TCE. Equipment tailored for particular users - custom carrier racks for automobile parts, tank and covered hopper cars for specific volatile chemicals, and so on - was owned by individual shippers. For more standardized shipments, these would be owned by rail carriers. The informal agreements also provided handling procedures for unusual circumstances related to shipment. The transactions that did not use informal contracting all involved non-specialized capital such as standard box cars. All of this suggests the importance of asset specificity for complex contracting.

Two studies of New England fishing industries also examined the role of transaction costs in determining trade agreements and market structure. Wilson (1980) conducted an intensive study of the New England fresh-fish market. He found that underlying the smooth functioning of the market was a system of mutual dependence created by the particular trade arrangements there; reputation effects provided an enforcement mechanism. Acheson's (1985) study of the Maine lobster market reached similar conclusions, finding the lobster market to be characterized by long-term, informal relationships between fishermen and lobster-pound operators. Fisherman and pound operators typically crafted agreements to reduce the costs of information and the possibility of opportunistic use of informational asymmetries. The agreements were reinforced by reputation considerations and interdependencies arising from sharing scarce resources, such as market information, boat fuel and bait. Informal agreements and norms in eighteenth- and nineteenth-century whaling have been studied similarly by Ellickson (1989) and Gifford (1993).

Finally, in an interesting application of TCE to the context of personal relationships, Brinig (1990) employed transaction cost reasoning to explain the sudden increase in the demand for diamond engagement rings in the mid-1930s. The increase, she argues, can be traced to the abolition in several states of the 'breach of promise to marry action' around the same time. Before this action was abolished, a broken engagement could trigger a lawsuit, because a woman in this situation faced considerable loss of reputation. Once the cause of action was eliminated, however, another arrangement was needed to ensure the credibility of the marriage commitment. Diamond engagement rings filled that role. In this way, rings may be seen as a governance structure: They safeguard the future bride's relationship-specific investment - her good reputation.

Franchise Contracting

Williamson's (1976) case study of the Oakland, California Cable TV (CATV) franchise was an early empirical study using transactional reasoning. Responding to the Posner-Demsetz argument that competitive bidding for monopoly franchises would result in competitive prices, Williamson claimed that once idiosyncratic investments are in place, what was a large-numbers bargaining situation during the bidding process is transformed into a bilateral monopoly. Because of this change, the terms of the original contract may no longer be suitable. Williamson outlined the difficulties faced by Oakland in the early 1970s over its CATV franchise. The franchise was awarded to the lowest bidder in 1970. After the franchise was awarded, however, the construction process went more slowly than expected, fewer households signed up than predicted and costs escalated. Consequently, the franchisee requested a renegotiation of the contract. A complex dual-source agreement was eventually reached, but this outcome was far different from that specified in the initial agreement.

Two later studies of CATV have looked for similar problems, with mixed results. Zupan (1989) examined a series of public cable franchise agreements, comparing the terms of trade struck during the original franchise agreement with those prevailing at the time of renewal, after relationship-specific investments had been made; he found no significant differences in those terms. Prager (1990), however, found that opportunistic behavior by the franchisee, as perceived by cable customers, was higher for franchises awarded through competitive bidding.

Of course, it is not always the franchisee who is opportunistic; the franchiser may be as well. Grandy's (1989) examination of nineteenth-century railroad regulation in New Jersey found that the railroads in that state were willing to make large specialized investments only when they were protected by 'special corporation charters' limiting state action against them. Levy and Spiller's (1994) comparative study of telecommunications regulation in Argentina, Chile, Jamaica, the Philippines and the UK shows that private investment is forthcoming only when regulators can commit not to pursue arbitrary administrative actions. Furthermore, many private franchise contracts can also be explained through TCE (Norton, 1989; Dnes, 1992).

Besides these contractual phenomena, TCE has been brought to bear on such diverse topics as labor market contracts and regulation (Barker and Chapman, 1989), tie-ins and 'block booking' (Kenney and Klein, 1983), international trade and the multinational corporation (Yarbrough and Yarbrough, 1987; Gatignon and Anderson, 1988; Hennart, 1989; Klein, Frazier and Roth, 1990), company towns and company stores (Fishback, 1986, 1992), land tenure agreements (Roumasset and Uy, 1980; Alston and Higgs, 1982; Alston, Datta and Nugent, 1984; Datta, O'Hara and Nugent, 1986) and even indentured prostitution (Ramseyer, 1991). These and other 'non-standard' contracting practices, when viewed through a transaction cost lens, often turn out to have efficiency properties, particularly in offering safeguards for specific investments.

Is the Empirical Evidence Reliable?

The discussion here presents only a sampling of the empirical literature on contracts, organizations and institutions (see the Appendix to Shelanski and Klein, 1995, for a more complete list). While the vast majority of these studies are consistent with transaction cost reasoning, some difficulties remain. Besides the measurement difficulties discussed above, empirical research on the institutions of governance is often hampered by confusion about the definitions of and therefore the empirical proxies for, key variables, especially uncertainty. Asset specificity has been more successfully treated in the empirical literature; relationship-specific physical, site and human capital investments have all been studied, both independently and comparatively. However, further refinement and analysis need to be done here, particularly concerning measurement. Proxies such as capital intensity or fixed costs are very imperfect and may not capture whether the investment has value outside the transaction for which it was initially made. Another concern is that asset-specificity effects may be confused with market power. While specific investment may lead to bilateral monopoly, a small-numbers bargaining situation is not by itself evidence of relationship-specific investment.

Besides these difficulties of measurement and definition, empirical research on the institutions of governance is also subject to the problem found in empirical work generally: alternate hypotheses that could also fit the data are rarely stated and compared. Usually, the data are found only consistent or inconsistent with the hypothesis at hand. Undoubtedly, studies that explicitly compare competing, observationally distinct hypotheses about contractual relationships are needed, because rival theories commonly posit mutually exclusive outcomes. One example is Spiller's (1985) comparison of asset-specificity and market-power explanations for vertical mergers, explanations that have rival predictions about the size of the gains from mergers under various competitive conditions. Another prototype for such a project might be MacDonald's (1985) cross-sectional study of vertical integration, which incorporated elements of both TCE and Stigler's theory of the vertical 'life-cycle' of the firm (though it did not attempt to distinguish between them). Poppo and Zenger (1997) compare transaction-cost and resource-based explanations for the make-or-buy decision, finding greater empirical support for the former.

A more general concern is that most of the empirical studies discussed here establish correlations, not causal relations, between asset specificity and internal governance. These studies typically test a reduced-form model where the probability of observing a more hierarchical form of governance increases with the degree of relationship-specific investments. Plausibly, if the presence of such investments reduces the costs of internal organization, then asset specificity could lead to integration, independent of the holdup problem or other maladaptation costs (Masten, 1994, p. 10). Masten, Meehan and Snyder (1991) attempt to distinguish these two effects in the context of human capital. They find that specific human capital investments appear to reduce internal governance costs more than they increase market governance costs. Further studies of this type would be valuable in assessing the implications of the evidence for the reduced-form version of the basic theory. However, we do not yet have a general theory of how relationship-specific assets might reduce the costs of internal organization. By contrast, the underinvestment problem associated with specific assets and market governance is fairly well understood.

8. Public Policy Implications and Influence

Theoretical and empirical research in the NIE has strong implications for antitrust, regulation and other aspects of public policy. This is particularly true for the studies of institutional arrangements discussed in the previous section. A basic conclusion of transaction cost economics is that vertical mergers, even when there are no obvious technological synergies, may enhance efficiency by reducing governance costs. Hence Williamson (1985, p. 19) takes issue with what he calls the 'inhospitality tradition' in antitrust - namely, that firms engaged in non-standard business practices like vertical integration, customer and territorial restrictions, tie-ins, franchising, and so on, must be seeking monopoly gains. In the ten years between the celebrated *Schwinn* (1967) and *GTE-Sylvania* (1977) cases, Williamson argues, economists began to incorporate transaction cost considerations into their understanding of vertical restrictions. This change in the intellectual climate was reflected in the Supreme Court's reversal in *GTE-Sylvania* of its earlier position that vertical restraints are necessarily anticompetitive.

Joskow (1991, pp. 79-80) points out that this change may reflect sensitivity to claims that vertical integration and restraints need not reduce competition, rather than to claims that such arrangements provide contractual safeguards. While the NIE argued that nonstandard business practices may reduce transaction costs, Chicago-school writers like Posner, Peltzman and Bork were maintaining that such practices do not necessarily result in reduced competition. Of course, these arguments are largely complementary. Moreover, the Chicago position on vertical restraints relies largely (though not explicitly) on transaction-cost reasoning (Meese, 1997). In this sense, NIE has played an important role in recent changes in antitrust enforcement, even if its contribution has not always been recognized.

NIE and transaction cost economics in particular, also has direct implications for many other contracting practices and regulations, though it does not yet appear to have influenced those areas. Barker and Chapman (1989) argue, for example, that closed-shop agreements in labor markets may serve to protect workers' job-specific training rather than to exploit a monopoly position. They attack New Zealand's 'blanket coverage clause', which effectively prohibits the closed shop, supporting their claims with arguments based on TCE. Studies of optimal contract design such as Crocker and Reynolds's (1993) examination of Air Force procurement contracts are also relevant as a guide to public policy toward government purchases of goods and services. Other contracts between government agencies and private firms, such as franchise contracts for the provision of public utilities (like cable TV), can be evaluated using TCE reasoning. TCE also points out how the potential for opportunism by the state affects private incentives to make specific investments (Levy and Spiller, 1994). This is particularly important for economic and political reform in the former communist countries, where the need to provide incentives for private investment is paramount.

9. Summary

Speaking of Lionel Robbins's influential *Nature and Significance of Economic Science* (1932), Coase (1992, p. 714) remarked that 'in Robbins's view, an economist does not interest himself in the internal arrangements within organizations but only in what happens on the market'. Even Coase himself believed, as late as 1988, that '[w]hy firms exist, what determines the number of firms, what determines what firms do ... are not questions of interest to most economists' (Coase, 1988, p. 5).

Today, this is clearly no longer the case. The preceding survey provides a brief (and admittedly unbalanced) sketch of the new institutional economics. The literature in NIE is expanding rapidly and gaining increasing adherents and influence in economics, political science, law, strategy, sociology, growth and development, history and other disciplines. It is a highly diverse field and its many branches are rich in theoretical insight, relevant for policy and empirically useful.

Acknowledgements

I am grateful to Nicholas Argyres, John Drobak, Richard Langlois, Jackson Nickerson, David Robinson and Oliver Williamson for helpful suggestions and clarifications. This paper draws on material in Shelanski and Klein (1995) and Klein and Shelanski (1996).

Bibliography on New Institutional Economics (0530)

Acheson, James A. (1985), 'The Maine Lobster Market: Between Market and Hierarchy', **1** *Journal of Law, Economics, and Organization*, 385-398.

Acs, Zoltan J. and Gerlowski, Daniel A. (1996), *Managerial Economics and Organization*, Englewood Cliffs, NJ, Prentice-Hall.

Alchian, Armen A. (1961), *Some Economics of Property*, Santa Monica, Rand Corporation.

Alchian, Armen A. and Demsetz, Harold (1972), 'Production, Information Costs, and Economic Organization', **62** *American Economic Review*, 777-795.

Allen, Douglas W. and Lueck, Dean (1993), 'Transaction Costs and the Design of Cropshare Contracts', **24** *Rand Journal of Economics*, 78-100.

Alston, Lee J. and Higgs, Robert (1982), 'Contractual Mix in Southern Agriculture since the Civil War: Facts, Hypotheses, and Tests', **42** *Journal of Economic History*, 327-353.

Alston, Lee J., Datta, S. and Nugent, Jeffrey B. (1984), 'Tenancy Choice in a Competitive Framework with Transaction Costs', **92** *Journal of Political Economy*, 1121-1133.

Argyres, Nicholas (1996), 'Evidence on the Role of Firm Capabilities in Vertical Integration Decisions', **17** *Strategic Management Journal*, 129-150.

Armour, Henry O. and Teece, David J. (1980), 'Vertical Integration and Technological Innovation', **62** *Review of Economics and Statistics*, 470-474.

Axelrod, R. (1984), *The Evolution of Cooperation*, New York, Basic Books.

Bardhan, Pranab K. (1989), 'The New Institutional Economics and Development Theory: A Brief Critical Assessment', **17(9)** *World Development*, 1389-1395.

Barker, George R. and Chapman, Ralph B. (1989), 'Evaluating Labor Market Contracting and Regulation: A Transaction Costs Perspective with Particular Reference to New Zealand', **145** *Journal of Institutional and Theoretical Economics*, 317-342.

Barzel, Y. (1989), *Economic Analysis of Property Rights*, Cambridge, Cambridge University Press.

Benson, Bruce L. (1989), 'The Spontaneous Evolution of Commercial Law', **55** *Southern Economic Journal*, 644-661.

Benson, Bruce L. (1990), *The Enterprise of Law: Justice Without the State*, San Francisco, Pacific Research Institute for Public Policy.

Benson, Bruce L. (1992), 'The Development of Criminal Law and its Enforcement: Public Interest or Political Transfers?', **3** *Journal des Economistes et des Etudes Humaines*, 79-108.

Benson, Bruce L. (1994), 'Are Public Goods Really Common Pools? Considerations of the Evolution of Policing and Highways in England', **32** *Economic Inquiry*, 249-271.

Besanko, D., Dranove, D. and Shanley, Mark (1990), *Economics of Strategy*, New York, Wiley.

Boyer, Robert and Orlean, Andre (1992), 'How Do Conventions Evolve?', **2** *Journal of Evolutionary Economics*, 165-177.

Brinig, Margaret F. (1990), 'Rings and Promises', **6** *Journal of Law, Economics, and Organization*, 203-215.

Buchanan, James M. and Tullock, Gordon (1962), *The Calculus of Consent: Logical Foundations of Constitutional Democracy*, Ann Arbor, University of Michigan Press.

Buckley, Peter J. and Michie, Jonathan (1996), *Firms, Organizations, and Contracts: A Reader in Industrial Organization*, Oxford, Oxford University Press.

Chandler, Alfred D., Jr (1992), 'Organizational Capabilities and the Economic History of the Industrial Enterprise', **6** *Journal of Economic Perspectives*, 79-100.

Clark, Andy (1997), 'Economic Reason: The Interplay of Individual Learning and External Structure', in Drobak, John N. and Nye, John V.C. (eds), *The Frontiers of the New Institutional Economics*, San Diego, Academic Press, 269-290.

Coase, Ronald H. (1937), 'The Nature of the Firm', in Coase, Ronald H. (ed.), *The Firm, the Market, and the Law*, Chicago, University of Chicago Press, 33-55.

Coase, Ronald H. (1964), 'The Regulated Industries: Discussion', **54** *American Economic Review*, 194-197.

Coase, Ronald H. (1972), 'Industrial Organization: A Proposal for Research', in Coase, Ronald H. (ed.), *The Firm, the Market, and the Law*, Chicago, University of Chicago Press, 57-74.

Coase, Ronald H. (1974), 'The Lighthouse in Economics', in Coase, Ronald H. (ed.), *The Firm, the Market, and the Law*, Chicago, University of Chicago Press, 187-213.

Coase, Ronald H. (1984), 'The New Institutional Economics', **140** *Journal of Institutional and Theoretical Economics*, 229-232.

Coase, Ronald H. (1988), 'The Firm, the Market, and the Law', in Coase, Ronald H. (ed.), *The Firm, the Market, and the Law*, Chicago, University of Chicago Press, 1-31.

Coase, Ronald H. (1992), 'The Institutional Structure of Production', **82** *American Economic Review*, 713-719.

Cooter, Robert D. (1993), 'Against Legal Centralism', **81** *California Law Review*, 417-429.

Cooter, Robert D. (1994), 'Structural Adjudication and the New Law Merchant: A Model of Decentralized Law', **14** *International Review of Law and Economics*, 215-231.

Cooter, Robert D., Marks, Stuart and Mnookin, Robert H. (1982), 'Bargaining in the Shadow of the Law: A Testable Model of Strategic Behavior', **11** *Journal of Legal Studies*, 225-251.

Crocker, Keith J. and Masten, Scott E. (1988), 'Mitigating Contractual Hazards: Unilateral Options and Contract Length', **19** *Rand Journal of Economics*, 327-343.

Crocker, Keith J. and Masten, Scott E. (1991), 'Pretia Ex Machina? Prices and Process in Long-Term Contracts', **24** *Journal of Law and Economics*, 69-99.

Crocker, Keith J. and Reynolds, Kenneth J. (1993), 'The Efficiency of Incomplete Contracts: An Empirical Analysis of Air Force Engine Procurement', **24** *Rand Journal of Economics*, 126-146.

Datta, Samar K., O'Hara, Donald J. and Nugent, Jeffrey B. (1986), 'Choice of Agricultural Tenancy in the Presence of Transaction Costs', **62** *Land Economics*, 145-158.

Davis, Lance E. and North, Douglass C. (1971), *Institutional Change and American Economic Growth*, Cambridge, Cambridge University Press.

De Alessi, Louis (1980), 'The Economics of Property Rights: A Review of the Evidence', *Research in Law and Economics*, 1-47.

DeCanio, Stephen J. and Frech, H.E. III (1993), 'Vertical Contracts: A Natural Experiment in Natural Gas Pipeline Regulation', **149** *Journal of Institutional and Theoretical Economics*, 370-392.

Demsetz, H. (1967), 'Toward a Theory of Property Rights', **57** *American Economic Review*, 347-359.

Denzau, Arthur and North, Douglass C. (1994), 'Shared Mental Models: Ideologies and Institutions', **47** *Kyklos*, 3-31.

Dnes, Antony W. (1992), ''Unfair' Contractual Practices and Hostages in Franchise Contracts', **148** *Journal of Institutional and Theoretical Economics*, 484-504.

Drobak, John N. and Nye, John V.C. (1997), *The Frontiers of the New Institutional Economics*, San Diego, Harcourt Brace Jovanovich.

Eggertsson, Thrainn (1990), *Economic Behavior and Institutions*, Cambridge, Cambridge University Press.

Ellickson, R.C. (1989), 'A Hypothesis of Wealth-Maximizing Norms: Evidence from the Whaling Industry', **5** *Journal of Law, Economics, and Organization*, 83-97.

Ellickson, R.C. (1991), *Order Without Law: How Neighbors Settle Disputes*, Cambridge, MA, Harvard University Press.

Enelow, James M. and Hinich, Melvin J. (1984), *The Spatial Theory of Voting*, New York, Cambridge University Press.

Fama, Eugene F. (1980), 'Agency Problems and the Theory of the Firm', **88** *Journal of Political Economy*, 288-307.

Fama, Eugene F. and Jensen, Michael C. (1983), 'Separation of Ownership and Control', **26** *Journal of Law and Economics*, 301-326.

Fishback, P.V. (1986), 'Did Coal Miners 'Owe Their Souls to the Company Store'? Theory and Evidence from the Early 1900s', **46** *Journal of Economic History*, 1011-1029.

Fishback, P.V. (1992), 'The Economics of Company Housing: Historical Perspectives from the Coal Fields', **8** *Journal of Law, Economics, and Organization*, 346-365.

Foss, Nicolai J. (1996), *On the Relations Between Evolutionary and Contractual Theories of the Firm*, Department of Industrial Economics and Strategy, Copenhagen Business School.

Foss, Nicolai J. (1997), *Resources, Firms, and Strategy: A Reader in the Resource-Based Approach*, Oxford, Oxford University Press.

Furubotn, Eirik and Pejovich, Svetozar (1972), 'Property Rights and Economic Theory: A Survey of Recent Literature', **10** *Journal of Economic Literature*, 1137-1162.

Furubotn, Eirik and Pejovich, Svetozar (1974), *The Economics of Property Rights*, Cambridge, MA, Ballinger.

Furubotn, Eirik and Richter, Rudolf (1991), *The New Institutional Economics: An Assessment*, College Station, TX, Texas A&M University Press.

Furubotn, Eirik and Richter, Rudolf (1997), *Institutions and Economic Theory: The Contribution of the New Institutional Economics*, Ann Arbor, University of Michigan Press.

Galanter, Marc (1981), 'Justice in Many Rooms: Courts, Private Ordering, and Indigenous Law', **19** *Journal of Legal Pluralism*, 1-47.

Gallick, Edward C. (1984), *Exclusive Dealing and Vertical Integration: The Efficiency of Contracts in the Tuna Industry*, Washington, DC, Bureau of Economics, Federal Trade Commission.

Gatignon, Hubert and Anderson, Erin (1988), 'The Multinational Corporation's Degree of Control over Foreign Subsidiaries: An Empirical Test of a Transaction Cost Explanation', **4** *Journal of Law, Economics, and Organization*, 305-336.

Gifford, Adam, Jr. (1993), 'The Economic Organization of 17th- through mid-19th-Century Whaling and Shipping', **20** *Journal of Economic Behavior and Organization*, 137-150.

Globerman, S. (1980), 'Markets, Hierarchies, and Innovation', **14** *Journal of Economic Issues*, 977-998.

Globerman, S. and Schwindt, R. (1986), 'The Organization of Vertically Related Transactions in the Canadian Forest Products Industries', **7** *Journal of Economic Behavior and Organization*, 199-212.

Goldberg, Victor P. (1980), 'Relational Exchange: Economics and Complex Contracts', **23** *American Behavioral Scientist*, 337-352. Reprinted in Putterman, Louis (ed.), *The Economic Nature of the Firm: A Reader*, New York, Cambridge University Press, 1986.

Goldberg, Victor P. and Erickson, John R. (1987), 'Quantity and Price Adjustment in Long-Term Contracts: A Case Study of Petroleum Coke', **30** *Journal of Law and Economics*, 369-398.

Grandy, Christopher (1989), 'Can Government be Trusted to Keep its Part of a Social Contract? New Jersey and the Railroads, 1825-1888' **5** *Journal of Law, Economics, and Organization*, 249-269.

Greif, Avner (1989), 'Reputation and Coalitions in Medieval Trade: Evidence on the Maghribi Traders', **49** *Journal of Economic History*, 857-882.

Grossman, Sanford J. and Hart, Oliver D. (1986), 'The Costs and Benefits of Ownership: A Theory of Vertical and Lateral Integration', **94** *Journal of Political Economy*, 691-719.

Hallwood, Paul C. (1991), 'On Choosing Organizational Arrangements: The Example of Offshore Oil Gathering', **38** *Scottish Journal of Political Economy*, 227-241.

Hart, Oliver D. (1995), *Firms, Contracts, and Financial Structure*, Oxford, Oxford Clarendon Press.

Hart, Oliver D. and Moore, John (1990), 'Property Rights and the Nature of the Firm', **98** *Journal of Political Economy*, 1119-1158.

Hayek, F.A. (1973), *Law, Legislation, and Liberty, vol. 1, Rules and Order*, Chicago, University of Chicago Press.

Heide, J.B. and John, G. (1988), 'The Role of Dependence Balancing in Safeguarding Transaction-Specific Assets', **52** *Journal of Marketing*, 20-35.

Helper, Susan, MacDuffie, John Paul and Sabel, Charles F. (1997), *The Boundaries of the Firm as a Design Problem*, Mimeo, Columbia Law School.

Hennart, Jean-François (1988), 'Upstream Vertical Integration in the Aluminum and Tin Industries', **9** *Journal of Economic Behavior and Organization*, 281-299.

Hennart, Jean-François (1989), 'The Transaction Cost Rationale for Countertrade', **5** *Journal of Law, Economics, and Organization*, 127-153.

Holmström, B. (1979), 'Moral Hazard and Observability', **10** *Bell Journal of Economics*, 74-91.

Holmström, B. and Milgrom, P. (1994), 'The Firm as an Incentive System', **84** *American Economic Review*, 972-991.

Holmström, B. and Tirole, Jean (1989), 'The Theory of the Firm', in Schmalensee, Richard and Willig, Robert (eds), *Handbook of Industrial Organization*, 61-133.

Hubbard, R. Glenn and Weiner, Robert J. (1991), 'Efficient Contracting and Market Power: Evidence from the U.S. Natural Gas Industry', **34** *Journal of Law and Economics*, 25-67.

Jensen, Michael C. (1986), 'Agency Costs of Free Cash Flow, Corporate Finance, and Takeovers', **76** *American Economic Review*, 323-329.

Jensen, Michael C. and Meckling, W. (1976), 'Theory of the Firm: Managerial Behavior, Agency Costs, and Ownership Structure', **3** *Journal of Financial Economics*, 305-360.

Joskow, Paul L. (1985), 'Vertical Integration and Long-Term Contracts: The Case of Coal-Burning Electric Generating Plants', **1** *Journal of Law, Economics, and Organization*, 33-80.

Joskow, Paul L. (1987), 'Contract Duration and Relationship-Specific Investments: Empirical Evidence from Coal Markets', **77** *American Economic Review*, 168-185.

Joskow, Paul L. (1988), 'Price Adjustment in Long-Term Contracts: The Case of Coal', **31** *Journal of Law and Economics*, 47-83.

Joskow, Paul L. (1990), 'The Performance of Long-Term Contracts: Further Evidence from the Coal Markets', **21** *Rand Journal of Economics*, 251-274.

Joskow, Paul L. (1991), 'The Role of Transaction Cost Economics in Antitrust and Public Utility Regulatory Policies', **7** *Journal of Law, Economics, and Organization*, 53-83.

Kenney, Roy W. and Klein, Benjamin (1983), 'The Economics of Block Booking', **26** *Journal of Law and Economics*, 497-540.

Klein, Benjamin, Crawford, Robert A. and Alchian, Armen A. (1978), 'Vertical Integration, Appropriable Rents, and the Competitive Contracting Process', **21** *Journal of Law and Economics*, 297-326.

Klein, Benjamin (1988), 'Vertical Integration as Organized Ownership: The Fisher Body-General Motors Relationship Revisited', **4** *Journal of Law, Economics, and Organization*, 199-213.

Klein, Peter G. and Shelanski, Howard A. (1996), 'Transaction Cost Economics in Practice: Applications and Evidence', **1** *Journal of Market-Focused Management*, 277-296.

Klein, Saul, Frazier, Gary L. and Roth, Victor J. (1990), 'A Transaction Cost Analysis Model of Channel Integration in International Markets', **27** *Journal of Marketing Research*, 196-208.

Kogut, Bruce and Chang, Sea Jin (1991), 'Technological Capabilities and Japanese Foreign Direct Investment in the United States', **73** *Review of Economics and Statistics*, 401-413.

Kreps, David M. (1990), *A Course in Microeconomic Theory*, Princeton, Princeton University Press.

Lafontaine, F. and Masten, Scott E. (1995), 'Franchise Contracting, Organization, and Regulation: Introduction', **2** *Journal of Corporate Finance: Contracting, Governance and Organization*, 1-7.

Langbein, John H. (1987), 'Comparative Civil Procedure and the Style of Complex Contracts', **35** *American Journal of Comparative Law*, 381-394.

Langlois, Richard N. (1992a), *Capabilities and Vertical Disintegration in Process Technology: The Case of Semiconductor Fabrication Equipment*, Working Paper 92-10, Consortium on Competitiveness and Cooperation.

Langlois, Richard N. (1992b), 'External Economies and Economic Progress: The Case of the Microcomputer Industry', **66** *Business History Review*, 1-50.

Langlois, Richard N. and Robertson, Paul L. (1989), 'Explaining Vertical Integration: Lessons from the American Automobile Industry', **49** *Journal of Economic History*, 361-375.

Langlois, Richard N. and Robertson, Paul L. (1995), *Firms, Markets, and Economic Change: A Dynamic Theory of Business Institutions*, London, Routledge.

Levy, Brian and Spiller, Pablo T. (1994), 'The Institutional Foundations of Regulatory Commitment: A Comparative Analysis of Telecommunications Regulation', **10** *Journal of Law, Economics, and Organization*, 201-246.

Levy, David (1985), 'The Transaction Cost Approach to Vertical Integration: An Empirical Examination', **67** *Review of Economics and Statistics*, 438-445.

Lieberman, Marvin B. (1991), 'Determinants of Vertical Integration: An Empirical Test', **39** *Journal of Industrial Economics*, 451-466.

Lucas, Robert E., Jr (1972), 'Expectations and the Neutrality of Money', **4** *Journal of Economic Theory*, 103-124.

MacDonald, James M. (1985), 'Market Exchange or Vertical Integration: An Empirical Analysis', **67** *Review of Economics and Statistics*, 327-331.

MacMillan, Ian C., Hambrick, Donald C. and Pennings, Johannes M. (1986), 'Uncertainty Reduction and the Threat of Supplier Retaliation: Two Views of the Backward Integration Decision', **7** *Organization Studies*, 263-278.

Masten, Scott E. (1984), 'The Organization of Production: Evidence from the Aerospace Industry', **27** *Journal of Law and Economics*, 403-417.

Masten, Scott E. (1994), *Empirical Research in Transaction-cost Economics: Challenges, Progress, Directions*, Mimeo, University of Michigan Business School.

Masten, Scott E. (1996), *Case Studies in Contracting and Organization*, New York, Oxford Press.

Masten, Scott E. and Crocker, Keith J. (1985), 'Efficient Adaptation in Long-Term Contracts: Take-or-Pay Provisions for Natural Gas', **75** *American Economic Review*, 1083-1093.

Masten, Scott E. and Snyder, Edward A. (1993), 'United States versus United Shoe Machinery Corporation: On the Merits', **36** *Journal of Law and Economics*, 33-70.

Masten, Scott E., Meehan, James W., Jr and Snyder, Edward A. (1989), 'Vertical Integration in the U.S. Auto Industry: A Note on the Influence of Specific Assets', **12** *Journal of Economic Behavior and Organization*, 265-273.

Masten, Scott E., Meehan, James W., Jr and Snyder, Edward A. (1991), 'The Costs of Organization', **7** *Journal of Law, Economics, and Organization*, 1-25.

McKelvey, Richard (1976), 'Intransitivities in Multidimensional Voting Models and Some Implications for Agenda Control', **12** *Journal of Economic Theory*, 472-482.

Meese, Alan J. (1997), ''Price Theory and Vertical Restraints: A Misunderstood Relation', **45** *UCLA Law Review*, 143-204.

Menard, Claude (1996), 'On Clusters, Hybrids, and Other Strange Forms: The Case of the French Poultry Industry', **52** *Journal of Institutional and Theoretical Economics*, 154-183.

Milgrom, Paul A. and Roberts, John (1992), *Economics, Organization, and Management*, Englewood Cliffs, NJ, Prentice-Hall.

Monteverde, Kirk and Teece, David J. (1982), 'Supplier Switching Costs and Vertical Integration in the Automobile Industry', **13** *Bell Journal of Economics*, 206-213.

Mueller, Dennis C. (1979), *Public Choice*, Cambridge, Cambridge University Press.

Mueller, Dennis C. (1989), *Public Choice II*, Cambridge, Cambridge University Press.

Mulherin, J. Harold (1986), 'Complexity in Long-Term Contracts: An Analysis of Natural Gas Contractual Provisions', **2** *Journal of Law, Economics, and Organization*, 105-117.

Nee, Victor (1992), 'Organizational Dynamics of Market Transition: Hybrid Forms, Property Rights, and Mixed Economy in China', **37** *Administrative Science Quarterly*, 1-27.

Nelson, Richard R. and Winter, Sidney G. (1982), *An Evolutionary Theory of Economic Change*, Cambridge, MA, Harvard University Press.

North, Douglass C. (1990), *Institutions, Institutional Change and Economic Performance*, Cambridge, Cambridge University Press.

North, Douglass C. (1991), 'Institutions', **5** *Journal of Economic Perspectives*, 97-112.

North, Douglass and Thomas, Robert Paul (1973), *The Rise of the Western World: A New Economic History*, Cambridge, Cambridge University Press.

North, Douglass C. and Weingast, Barry R. (1989), 'Constitution and Commitment: The Evolution of Institutions Governing Public Choice in 17th Century England', **49** *Journal of Economic History*, 803-832.

Norton, Seth W. (1989), 'Franchising, Labor Productivity, and the New Institutional Economics', **145** *Journal of Institutional and Theoretical Economics*, 578-596.

Ordeshook, P.C. (1993), 'Constitutional Stability', **3** *Constitutional Political Economy*, 137-175.

Palay, Thomas M. (1984), 'Comparative Institutional Economics: The Governance of Rail Freight Contracting', **13** *Journal of Legal Studies*, 265-287.

Palay, Thomas M. (1985), 'Avoiding Regulatory Constraints: Contracting Safeguards and the Role of Informal Agreements', **1** *Journal of Law, Economics, and Organization*, 155-176.

Parisi, Francesco (1999), 'Coase Theorem and Transaction Cost Economics in the Law',in J.G. Backhaus, J.G. (ed.), *Elgar Companion to Law and Economics*, Ashgate, Edward Elgar.

Pejovich, Svetozar (1995), *Economic Analysis of Institutions and Systems*, Dordrecht, Kluwer.

Penrose, E.T. (1959), *The Theory of the Growth of the Firm*, Oxford, Oxford University Press.

Pisano, Gary (1990), 'Using Equity Participation to Support Exchange: Evidence from the Biotechnology Industry', **5** *Journal of Law, Economics, and Organization*, 109-126.

Pisano, Gary, Russo, Michael V. and Teece, David J. (1988), 'Joint Ventures and Collaborative Arrangements in the Telecommunications Equipment Industry', in Mowery, David (ed.), *International Collaborative Ventures in U.S. Manufacturing*, Cambridge, MA, Ballinger, 23-70.

Poppo, Laura and Zenger, Todd (1997), 'Testing Alternative Theories of the Firm: Transaction Cost, Knowledge-Based, and Measurement Explanations for Make-or-Buy Decisions in Information Services', **19** *Strategic Management Journal*, 853-877.

Posner, Richard A. (1993), 'The New Institutional Economics Meets Law and Economics', **149** *Journal of Institutional and Theoretical Economics*, 73-87.

Prager, Robin A. (1990), 'Firm Behavior in Franchise Monopoly Markets', **21** *Rand Journal of Economics*, 211-225.

Radner, Roy (1992), 'Hierarchy: The Economics of Managing', **30** *Journal of Economic Literature*, 1382-1415.

Ramseyer, J. Mark (1991), 'Indentured Prostitution in Imperial Japan: Credible Commitments in the Commercial Sex Industry', **7** *Journal of Law, Economics, and Organization*, 89-116.

Riker, William H. (1981), 'Implications from the Disequilibrium of Majority Rule for the Study of Institutions', **74** *American Political Science Review*, 432-447.

Roumasset, James A. and Uy, Marilou (1980), 'Piece Rates, Time Rates, and Teams: Explaining Patterns in the Employment Relation', **1** *Journal of Economic Behavior and Organization*, 343-360.

Rubin, Paul H. (1990), *Managing Business Transactions: Controlling the Cost of Coordinating, Communicating, and Decision Making*, New York, NY, Free Press.

Rumelt, Richard P. (1984), 'Towards a Strategic Theory of the Firm', in Lamb, Robert B. (ed.), *Competitive Strategic Management*, Englewood Cliffs, NJ, Prentice-Hall, 566-570.

Schelling, Thomas C. (1960), *The Strategy of Conflict*, Cambridge, MA, Harvard University Press.

Schotter, Andrew (1981), *The Economic Theory of Social Institutions*, Cambridge, Cambridge University Press.

Selgin, George and White, Lawrence H. (forthcoming), 'A Fiscal Theory of Government's Role in Money', *Economic Inquiry*.

Sharkey, William W. (1982), *The Theory of Natural Monopoly*, Cambridge, Cambridge University Press.

Shelanski, Howard A. and Klein, Peter G. (1995), 'Empirical Research in Transaction Cost Economics: A Review and Assessment', **11** *Journal of Law, Economics, and Organization*, 335-361.

Silverman, Brian S., Nickerson, Jack A. and Freeman, John (1997), 'Profitability, Transactional Alignment, and Organizational Mortality in the U.S. Trucking Industry', **18** *Strategic Management Journal*, 31-52.

Simon, Herbert A. (1991), 'Organizations and Markets', **5** *Journal of Economic Perspectives*, 25-44.

Spiller, Pablo T. (1985), 'On Vertical Mergers', **1** *Journal of Law, Economics, and Organization*, 285-312.

Spulber, Daniel F. (1989), *Regulation and Markets*, Cambridge, MA, MIT Press.

Stuckey, John (1983), *Vertical Integration and Joint Ventures in the Aluminum Industry*, Cambridge, MA, Harvard University Press.

Sugden, Robert (1986), *The Economics of Rights, Cooperation, and Welfare*, Oxford, Basil Blackwell.

Teece, David J. (1980), 'Economies of Scope and the Scope of the Enterprise', **1** *Journal of Economic Behavior and Organization*, 223-247.

Teece, David J. (1982), 'Towards an Economic Theory of the Multi-Product Firm', **3** *Journal of Economic Behavior and Organization*, 39-64.

Teece, David J., Dosi, Giovanni, Rumelt, Richard P. and Winter, Sidney G. (1994), 'Understanding Corporate Coherence: Theory and Evidence', **23** *Journal of Economic Behavior and Organization*, 1-30.

Trakman, Leon E. (1983), *The Law Merchant: The Evolution of Commercial Law*, Littleton, CO, Rothman.

Ullman-Margalit, Edna (1977), *The Emergence of Norms*, Oxford, Oxford Clarendon Press.

Walker, Gordon and Weber, David (1984), 'A Transaction Cost Approach to Make-or-Buy Decisions', **29** *Administrative Science Quarterly*, 373-391.

Walker, Gordon and Weber, David (1987), 'Supplier Competition, Uncertainty and Make-or-Buy Decisions', **30** *Academy of Management Journal*, 589-596.

Wallis, J. and North, Douglass C. (1986), 'Measuring the Transaction Sector in the American Economy, 1870-1970', in Engerman, Stanley L. and Gallman, Robert (eds), *Income and Wealth: Long-Term Factors in American Economic Growth*, Chicago, University of Chicago Press.

Wärnereyd, Karl (1990), 'Conventions: An Evolutionary Approach', **62** *Public Choice*, 155-173.

Weingast, Barry R. (1995), 'The Economic Role of Political Institutions: Federalism, Markets, and Economic Development', **11** *Journal of Law, Economics, and Organization*, 1-31.

Weingast, Barry R. (1996), 'Rational Choice Perspectives on Institutions', in Goodin, Robert E. and Klingemann, Hans-Dieter (eds), *A New Handbook of Political Science*, New York, NY, Oxford University Press.

Werin, Lars and Wijkander, Hans (1992), *Contract Economics*, Cambridge, MA, Blackwell.

Wernerfelt, Birger (1984), 'A Resource-based View of the Firm', **5** *Strategic Management Journal*, 171-180.

Williamson, Oliver E. (1971), 'The Vertical Integration of Production: Market Failure Considerations', **61** *American Economic Review*, 112-123.

Williamson, Oliver E. (1975), *Markets and Hierarchies: Analysis and Antitrust Implications*, New York, NY, Free Press.

Williamson, Oliver E. (1976), 'Franchise Bidding for Natural Monopolies - In General and with Respect to CATV', **7** *Bell Journal of Economics*, 73-104.

Williamson, Oliver E. (1983), 'Credible Commitments: Using Hostages to Support Exchange', **73** *American Economic Review*, 519-540.

Williamson, Oliver E. (1985), *The Economic Institutions of Capitalism*, New York, NY, Free Press.

Williamson, Oliver E. (1988), 'The Economics and Sociology of Organization: Promoting a Dialogue', in Farkas, George and England, Paula (eds), *Industries, Firms, and Jobs: Sociological and Economic Approaches*, New York, Plenum, 159-185.

Williamson, Oliver E. (1990), 'A Comparison of Alternative Approaches to Economic Organization', **146** *Journal of Institutional and Theoretical Economics*, 61-71.

Williamson, Oliver E. (1991a), 'Comparative Economic Organization: The Analysis of Discrete Structural Alternatives', **36** *Administrative Science Quarterly*, 269-296.

Williamson, Oliver E. (1991b), 'Economic Institutions: Spontaneous and Intentional Governance', **7(S)** *Journal of Law, Economics, and Organization*, 159-187.

Williamson, Oliver E. (1991c), 'Strategizing, Economizing, and Economic Organization', **23** *Strategic Management Journal*, 75-94.

Williamson, Oliver E. (1993), 'Transaction Cost Economics Meets Posnerian Law and Economics', **149** *Journal of Institutional and Theoretical Economics*, 99-118.

Williamson, Oliver E. (1996a), 'Economic Organization: The Case for Candor', **21** *Academy of Management Review*, 48-57.

Williamson, Oliver E. (1996b), *The Mechanisms of Governance*, New York, NY, Oxford University Press.

Wilson, James A. (1980), 'Adaptation to Uncertainty and Small Numbers Exchange: The New England Fresh Fish Market', **4** *Bell Journal of Economics*, 491-504.

Witt, Ulrich (1989), 'The Evolution of Economic Institutions as a Propagation Process', **1** *Constitutional Political Economy*, 83-109.

Yarbrough, Beth V. and Yarbrough, Robert M. (1987), 'Institutions for the Governance of Opportunism in International Trade', **3** *Journal of Law, Economics, and Organization*, 129-139.

Zupan, Mark A. (1989), 'Cable Franchise Renewals: Do Incumbent Firms Behave Opportunistically?', **20** *Rand Journal of Economics*, 473-482.

Other References

Arrow, Kenneth J. (1963), 'Uncertainty and the Welfare Economics of Medical Care', **53** *American Economic Review*, 941-73.

Berle, Adolph A. and Means, Gardiner C. (1932), *The Modern Corporation and Private Property*, New York, Macmillan.

Chandler, Alfred D., Jr (1962), *Strategy and Structure: Chapters in the History of the American Industrial Enterprise*, Cambridge, MA, MIT Press.

Denzau, Arthur and Mackay, Robert (1983), 'Gate Keeping and Monopoly Power of Committees', **27** *American Journal of Political Science*, 740-62.

Friedman, Milton (1953), 'The Methodology of Positive Economics', in idem, *Essays in Positive Economics*, Chicago, University of Chicago Press, 3-43.

Gruchy, Allan G. (1972), *Contemporary Economic Thought: The Contribution of Neo-Institutional Economics*, Clifton, NJ, Augustus M. Kelley.

Gruchy, Allan G. (1987), *The Reconstruction of Economics: An Analysis of the Fundamentals of Institutional Economics*, Westport, CT, Greenwood Press.

Hayek, F.A (1937), 'Economics and Knowledge', in idem (1948), *Individualism and Economic Order*, London, Routledge and Kegan Paul, 33-56.

Hayek, F.A. (1945), 'The Use of Knowledge in Society', in idem (1948), *Individualism and Economic Order*, London, Routledge and Kegan Paul, 77-91.

Hayek, F.A. (1967), 'The Results of Human Action but Not of Human Design', in idem, *Studies in Philosophy, Politics, and Economics*, Chicago, University of Chicago Press, 96-105.

Hodgson, Geoffrey M. (1998), 'The Approach of Institutional Economics', **36** *Journal of Economic Literature*, 166-92.

Knight, Frank H. (1921), *Risk, Uncertainty, and Profit,* New York, Hart, Schaffner & Marx.

Langlois, Richard N. (1989), 'What was Wrong with the 'Old' Institutional Economics? (And What is Still Wrong with the 'New'?)', **1** *Review of Political Economy*, 272-300.

Llewellyn, Karl N. (1931), 'What Price Contract? An Essay in Perspective', **40** *Yale Law Review*, 704-51.

Macneil, Ian R. (1974), 'The Many Futures of Contracts', **47** *Southern California Law Review*, 691-816.

Macneil, Ian R. (1978), 'Contracts: Adjustments of Long-Term Economic Relations under Classical, Neoclassical, and Relational Contract Law', **72** *Northwestern University Law Review*, 854-906.

Manne, Henry G. (1965), 'Mergers and the Market for Corporate Control', **73** *Journal of Political Economy*, 110-20.

Menger, Carl (1883), *Untersuchungen über die Methode der Socialwissenschaften und der Politischen Oekonomie insbesondere,* translated as *Investigations into the Method of the Social Sciences with Special Reference to Economics,* New York, New York University Press, 1985.

Mirowski, Phillip A. (1987), 'The Philosophical Basis of Institutional Economics', **21** *Journal of Economic Issues*, 1001-38.

Moe, Terry M. (1989), 'The Political Structure of Agencies', in Chubb, John E. and Peterson, Paul E. (eds), *Can Government Govern?*, Washington, DC, Brookings Institution.

Priest, George L. (1977), 'The Common Law Process and the Selection of Efficient Rules', **6** *Journal of Legal Studies*, 65-82.

Richter, Rudolf (1996), 'Bridging Old and New Institutional Economics: Gustav Schmoller, the Leader of the Younger German Historical Schook, Seen with Neoinstitutionalists' Eyes', **152** *Journal of Institutional and Theoretical Economics*, 567-92.

Robbins, Lionel (1932), *The Nature and Significance of Economic Science,* London, Macmillan.

Roe, Mark (1994), *Strong Managers, Weak Owners: The Political Roots of American Corporate Finance*, Princeton, Princeton University Press.

Rubin, Paul H. (1977), 'Why is the Common Law Efficient?', **6** *Journal of Legal Studies*, 51-63.

Rutherford, Malcolm H. (1983), 'J.R. Commons's Institutional Economics', **17** *Journal of Economic Issues*, 721-44.

Seckler, David W. (1975), *Thorstein Veblen and the Institutionalists: A Study in the Social Philosophy of Economics,* Boulder, CO, Colorado Associated University Press.

Shepsle, Kenneth A. and Weingast, Barry R. (1987), 'The Institutional Foundations of Committee Power', **81** *American Political Science Review*, 85-194.

Simon, Herbert A. (1961) [1947], *Administrative Behavior*, 2nd Ed, New York, Macmillan.

Solove, Ronald L. (1986), 'Alternative Means to Resolve Corporate Disputes: A Survey', **91** *Commercial Law Journal*, 133-140.

Weingast, Barry R. (1994), *Institutions and Political Commitment: A New Political Economy of the American Civil War Era,* manuscript, Stanford University.

Williamson, Oliver E. (1996c), 'Revisiting Legal Realism: The Law, Economics, and Organization Perspective', **5** *Industrial and Corporate Change*, 383-420.

0540
PROPERTY RIGHTS APPROACH

Bibliography Collected by the Editors

Alchian, Armen A. (1961), *Some Economics of Property Rights*, Rand Paper, Rand Corporation.

Alchian, Armen A. (1978), 'Economic Laws and Political Legislation', in Siegan, Bernard H. (ed.), *The Interactions of Economics and the Law*, Lexington, MA, Lexington Books, 139-148.

Alchian, Armen A. and Demsetz, Harold (1973), 'The Property Right Paradigm', **33** *Journal of Economic History*, 16-27.

Arrow, Kenneth J. (1979), 'The Property Rights Doctrine and Demand Revelation under Incomplete Information', in Boskin, Michael J. (ed.), *Economics and Human Welfare: Essays in Honor of Tibor Scitovsky*, New York, Academic Press, 23-39.

Avio, Kenneth L. (1994), 'Aboriginal Property Rights in Canada: A Contractarian Interpretation of R. v. Sparrow', **20** *Canadian Public Policy*, 415-429.

Bajt, Aleksander (1993), 'The Property Rights School: Is Economic Ownership the Missing Link?', **13** *International Review of Law and Economics*, 85-97.

Barzel, Yoram (1974), 'A Theory of Rationing by Waiting', **17** *Journal of Law and Economics*, 73-95.

Barzel, Yoram (1977), 'An Economic Analysis of Slavery', **20** *Journal of Law and Economics*, 87-110.

Barzel, Yoram (1989), *Economic Analysis of Property Rights*, Cambridge, Cambridge University Press, 122 p.

Barzel, Yoram (1994), 'The Capture of Wealth by Monopolists and the Protection of Property Rights', **14** *International Review of Law and Economics*, 393-409.

Benson, Bruce L (1990), *The Enterprise of Law: Justice Without the State*, San Francisco, Pacific Research Institute for Public Policy.

Benson, Bruce L. (1984), 'Rent Seeking from a Property Rights Perspective', **51** *Southern Economic Journal*, 388-400.

Benson, Bruce L. (1986a), 'Boom Towns in the West: Is Profit the Culprit?', **11** *Review of Regional Economics and Business*, 27-38.

Benson, Bruce L. (1986b), 'The Lost Victim and Other Failures of the Public Law Experiment', **9** *Harvard Journal of Law and Public Policy*, 399-427.

Benson, Bruce L. (1991), 'An Evolutionary Contractarian View of Primitive Law: The Institutions and Incentives Arising Under Customary American Indian Law', **5** *Review of Austrian Economics*, 65-89.

Benson, Bruce L. (1992a), 'Customary Indian Law: Two Case Studies', in Anderson, Terry L. (ed.), *Property Rights and Indian Economics*, Rowman and Littlefield Press.

Benson, Bruce L. (1992b), 'The Development of Criminal Law and its Enforcement: Public Interest or Political Transfers', **3** *Journal des Economistes et des Etudes Humaines*, 79-108.

Benson, Bruce L. (1993), 'The Impetus for Recognizing Private Property and Adopting Ethical Behavior in a Market Economy: Natural Law, Government Law, or Evolving Self-Interest', **6** *Review of Austrian Economics*, 43-80.

Benson, Bruce L. (1994a), 'Legal Philosophy', in Boettke, Peter J. (ed.), *The Elgar Companion to Austrian Economics*, London, Edward Elgar, 270-275.

Benson, Bruce L. (1994b), 'Are Public Goods Really Common Pools: Considerations of the Evolution of Policing and Highways in England', **39** *Economic Inquiry*, 249-271.

Benson, Bruce L. (1994c), 'Emerging from the Hobbesian Jungle: Might Takes and Makes Rights', **5** *Constitutional Political Economy*, 129-158. Translated into Spanish and republished (1995) Las Instituciones y Los Derechos de Propiedad al Emerger de la Jungla Hobbesiana: La Fuerza Quita los Reprinted Derechos y los Crea Libertas', 12, 35-75.

Benson, Bruce L. (1995a), 'Competition Among Legal Institutions: Implications for the Evolution of Law', in Gerken, Luden (ed.), *Competition Among Institutions*, London, MacMillan, 153-175.

Benson, Bruce L. (1995b), 'Rights, Entitlements, and Individual Responsibility in the Welfare State', in Karslon, Nils (ed.), *Can the Present Problems of Mature Welfare States Such as Sweden be Solved?*, Stockholm, City University Press, 88-98.

Benson, Bruce L. (1995c), *Toxic Torts by Government*, Independent Policy Report, Oakland, Independent Institute.

Benson, Bruce L. (1996a), 'Restitution in Theory and in Practice', **12** *Journal of Libertarian Studies*, 75-98.

Benson, Bruce L. (1996b), 'Uncertainty, the Race for Property Rights, and Rent Dissipation due to Judicial Changes in Product Liability Tort Law', *Cultural Dynamics*.

Benson, Bruce L. and Wollan, Laurin A., Jr (1989), 'Prison Overcrowding and Judicial Incentives', **3** *Madison Paper Series*, 1-22.

Blümel, Wolfgang, Pethig, Rüdiger and Von Dem Hagen, Oskar (1986), 'The Theory of Public Goods: A Survey of Recent Issues', **142** *Journal of Institutional and Theoretical Economics*, 241 ff.

Böbel, Ingo (1988), *Eigentum, Eigentumsrechte und Institutioneller Wandel* (Property, Property Rights and Institutional Change), Berlin, Springer, 360 p.

Böhm, Stephan (1987), 'Handlungsrechte, Wettbewerb und Privatisierung (Property Rights, Competition and Privatization)', **34** *Wirtschaftspolitische Blätter*, 576-583.

Bottomley, Anthony (1963), 'The Effect of Common Ownership of Land upon Resource Allocation in Tripolitania', **39** *Land Economics*, 91-95.

Brenner, Reuven (1983), *History - the Human Gamble*, Chicago, University of Chicago Press. Reprinted in Spanish edition: *Fondo de Cultura Economics*, Mexico - Spain, 1989.

Brenner, Reuven (1990), 'The Long Road from Serfdom, and How to Shorten it', **17(2)** *Canadian Business Law Journal*, 195-226. Reprinted in Maruyana, M. (ed.), *Management Reform in Eastern and Central Europe*, Aldershot: Dartmouth, 1993, 81-109.

Brenner, Reuven (1991), 'Legal Reforms in the Eastern Bloc: a Precondition to Monetary and Fiscal Policies', in Claassen, E.M. (ed.), *Exchange Rate Policies of the Less Developed Market and Socialist Economies*, 151-174. Reprinted in French in *Journal des Economistes et des Etudes Humaines: Bilingual Journal of Interdisciplinary Studies*, vol. 1, no. 3, October, 1990: 253-277.

Brenner, Reuven (1993), 'From Envy and Distrust to Trust and Ambition', in Baldassari, M. and Mundell, R. (eds), *Building of New Europe*, London, St Martin's Press, 33-59.

Brenner, Reuven (1994), 'The Road from Serfdom: Entrepreneurship and Property Rights Before, During and After Communism', in Kirzner, Israel M. and Rizzo, M. (eds), *Advances in Austrian Economics*, Greenwood, JAI Press, 145-174.

Buhbe, Matthes (1980), *Ökonomische Analyse von Eigentumsrechten - Der Beitrag der economics of property rights zur Theorie der Institutionen* (Economic Analysis of Property Rights - The Contribution of the Property Rights Approach to the Theory of Institutions), Frankfurt am Main, Peter D. Lang, 185 p.

Bydlinski, Franz (1988), *Fundamentale Rechts grundsätze* (Fundamental Principles of Law), New York, Springer Publishers.

Cheung, Steven N.S. (1972), 'The Enforcement of Property Rights in Children, and the Marriage Contract', **82** *Economic Journal*, 641-657.

Clarkson, Kenneth W. (1972), 'Some Implications of Property Rights in Hospital Management', **15** *Journal of Law and Economics*, 363-384.

Coase, Ronald H. (1959), 'The Federal Communications Commission', **2** *Journal of Law and Economics*, 1-40.

Cooter, Robert D. (1993), 'Against Legal Centrism: Review of Robert C. Ellickson's Order Without Law', *California Law Review*, 417 ff.

Copes, Parzival (1984), 'The Market as an Open Access Commons: A Neglected Aspect of Excess Capacity', **132** *De Economist*, 49-60.

Crain, W. Mark and Tollison, Robert D. (1977), 'Attenuated Property Rights and the Market for Governors', **20** *Journal of Law and Economics*, 205-211.

Crain, W. Mark and Zardkoohi, Asghar (1978), 'A Test of the Property-Rights Theory of the Firm: Water Utilities in the United States', **21** *Journal of Law and Economics*, 395-408.

Davies, David G. (1981), 'Property Rights and Economic Behavior in Private and Government Enterprises: The Case of Australia's Banking System', **3** *Research in Law and Economics*, 111-142.

De Alessi, Louis (1980), 'The Economics of Property Rights: A Review of the Evidence', **2** *Research in Law and Economics*, 1-47.

De Alessi, Louis (1983a), 'Property Rights, Transaction Costs, and X-Efficiency: An Essay in Economic Theory', **73** *American Economic Review*, 64-81.

De Alessi, Louis (1983b), 'Property Rights and X-Efficiency: Reply', **73** *American Economic Review*, 843-845.

De Alessi, Louis (1990), 'Form, Substance, and Welfare Comparisons in the Analysis of Institutions', **146** *Journal of Institutional and Theoretical Economics*, 5-23.

De Alessi, Louis and Staaf, Robert J. (1989), 'Property Rights and Choice', in Mercuro, Nicholas (ed.), *Law and Economics*, Boston, Kluwer Academic Publishers, 175-200.

Demsetz, Harold (1966), 'Some Aspects of Property Rights', **9** *Journal of Law and Economics*, 61-70.

Demsetz, Harold (1983), 'The Structure of Ownership and the Theory of the Firm', **26** *Journal of Law and Economics*, 375-390.

Dilorenzo, T.J. (1988), 'Property Rights, Information Costs, and the Economics of Rent Seeking', **144** *Journal of Institutional and Theoretical Economics*, 318-322.

Dnes, Anthony W. (1985), 'Rent Seeking Behaviour and Open Access Fishing', **32(2)** *Scottish Journal of Political Economy*, 159-170.

Dnes, Anthony W. (1989), 'Rent Seeking, Conflict and Property Rights', **36(4)** *Scottish Journal of Political Economy*, 366-374.

Dragun, A.K. (1987), 'Property Rights in Economic Theory', **21** *Journal of Economic Issues*, 859-868.

Eggertsson, Thrainn (1990a), *Economic Behaviour and Institutions*, Cambridge, Cambridge University Press, 385 p.

Eggertsson, Thrainn (1990b), 'The Role of Transaction Costs and Property Rights in Economic Analysis', **34** *European Economic Review*, 450-457.

Elder, Harold W. (1987), 'Property Rights Structures and Criminal Courts: An Analysis of State Criminal Courts', **7** *International Review of Law and Economics*, 21-32.

Epstein, Richard A. (1982), 'Private Property and the Public Domain: The Case of Antitrust', in Pennock, J. Roland and Chapman, John W. (eds), *Nomos XXIV: Ethics, Economics and the Law*, New York, New York University Press, 48-82.

Eschenburg, Rolf (1978), 'Mikroökonomische Aspekte von Property Rights (Micro-economic Aspects of Property Rights)', in Schenk, K.E. (ed.), *Ökonomische Verfügungsrechte und Allokationsmechanismen in Wirtschafsystemen*, Berlin, Duncker and Humblot, 9-27.

Evangelopoulos, Panagiotis (1996), 'E Analyse ton Periousiakon Dikaiomaton kai e Ideologia tes Eleutheres Agoras (Property Rights Analysis and Free-Market Ideology)', **6** *Aissymnetes*.

Evangelopoulos, Panagiotis (1997), *Oikonomike Analyse ton Periousiakon Dikaiomaton kai o Mechanismos tes Agoras* (Economic Analysis of Property Rights and the Market Mechanism), PhD Thesis, University of Athens, Dept. of Economics. Reprinted as monograph: Athens, Libro, 1999

Evangelopoulos, Panagiotis (1998), 'O Kanon tes Pleiopsefias kai o Prosdiorismos ton Dikaiomaton (The Majority Rule and the Stipulation of Rights)', **1** *Episteme kai Koinonia*.

Fezer, Karl-Heinz (1986), 'Aspekte einer Rechtskritik an der economic analysis of law und am property rights approach (Critical Aspects of the Economic Analysis of Law and the Property Rights Approach from a Lawyer's Viewpoint)', **41** *Juristenzeitung*, 817-824.

Fleisher, Arthur A. III, Shughart, William F., II and Tollison, Robert D. (1989), 'Ownership Structure in Professional Sports', **12** *Research in Law and Economics*, 71-75.

Frech, H. Edward III (1975), 'Property Rights and Dynamic Inefficiency of Capitalism: Comment', **83(1)** *Journal of Political Economy*, 209-214.

Frech, H. Edward III (1980a), 'The Property Rights Theory of the Firm and Competitive Markets for Top Decision-Makers', **2** *Research in Law and Economics*, 49-63.

Frech, H. Edward III (1980b), 'Managerial Incentives in Nonproprietary Institutions', **S.1** *Research in Law and Economics*, 46-49.

Frech, H. Edward III and Ginsburg, Paul B. (1981), 'Property Rights and Competition in Health Insurance: Multiple Objectives for Nonprofit Firms', **3** *Research in Law and Economics*, 155-171.

Frey, Bruno S. and Buhofer, Heinz (1988), 'Prisoners and Property Rights', **31** *Journal of Law and Economics*, 19-46.

Furubotn, Eirik G. and Pejovich, Svetozar (1972), 'Property Rights and Economic Theory: A Survey of Recent Literature', **10** *Journal of Economic Literature*, 1137-1162.

Furubotn, Eirik G. and Pejovich, Svetozar (1973), 'Property Rights, Economic Decentralization and the Evolution of the Yugoslav Firm, 1965-1972', **16** *Journal of Law and Economics*, 275-302.

Furubotn, Eirik G. and Pejovich, Svetozar (eds) (1974), *The Economics of Property Rights*, Cambridge, MA, Ballinger, 367 p.

Gäfgen, Gérad (1983), 'Entwicklung und Stand der Theorie der Property Rights. Eine kritische Bestandsaufnahme (Development and Actual Situation of the Property Rights)', in Neumann, M. (ed.), *Ansprache, Eigentums- und Verfügungsrechte*, Berlin, Duncker and Humblot, 43-62.

Gantner, Manfred (1984), 'Schwierigkeiten der Verrechtlichung Ökonomischer Tatbestände (The Difficuly of Transforming Economic Issues into Law)', **31** *Wirtschaftspolitische Blätter*, 423-430.

Gay, David E.R. (1975a), 'Book Review of The Economics of Property Rights, ed. by Furubotn and Pejovich', **42** *Southern Economic Journal*, 162-164.

Gay, David E.R. (1975b), 'Property Rights and Adam Smith', **33** *Review of Social Economy*, 177-179.

Gay, David E.R. (1976), 'Book Review of Henry Manne, The Economics of Legal Relationships', **42** *Southern Economic Journal*, 765-766.

Gay, David E.R. (1978), 'Book Review of Economic Forces at Work, Armen Alchian', **31** *Kyklos*, 504-505.

Gay, David E.R. (1981a), 'Towards a Theory of Entitlements in Comparative Economics', **25** *Rivista Internazionale di Scienze Economiche e Commerciali*, 1021-1028.

Gay, David E.R. (1981b), 'Entitlements and Public Policy', **18** *Social Science Journal*, 87-100.

Gay, David E.R. (1982), 'Book Review of Mercantilism as a Rent-Seeking Society: Economic Regulation in Historical Perspective, Robert B. Ekelund and Robert D. Tollison', **35** *Kyklos*, 732-733.

Gay, David E.R. (1989), 'Viticultural Rent Seeking and Public Policy in Arid Lands', **5** *Forum of the Association for Arid Lands Studies*, 33-40.

Gay, David E.R. (1990), 'A Note on the Deprivatization of the Grand Canyon', **6** *Forum of the Association for Arid Lands Studies*, 41-43.

Gay, David E.R. (1992), 'Teaching Privatization in the Soviet Union: An Experimental Economics Approach', **1** *Classroom Expernomics*, 5-6.

Gay, David E.R. (1994), 'Incentives and Privatization: An Experimental Economics Approach', **22** *Atlantic Economic Journal*, 79 ff.

Gemtos, Petros A. (1991), 'Thesmikes Analyseis sten Oikonomike: E Theoria ton Praxiakon Dikaiomaton (Institutional Analyses in Economics: The Property Rights Theory)', **4** *Aissymnetes*, 27-48.

Goldberg, Victor P. (1986), 'Fishing and Selling', **15** *Journal of Legal Studies*, 173-180.

Gordon, Scott and Stegemann, Klaus (1985), 'The Market as a Commons: Is Catching Customers Like Catching Fish?', **133** *De Economist*, 218-231.

Gotthold, Jürgen (1980), 'Zur ökonomischen 'Theorie des Eigen tums'. Eine kritische Einfuhrung (The Economic Theory of Property - A Critical Introduction)', **144** *Zeitschrift für das gesamte Handels- und Wirtschaftsrecht*, 545-562.

Hafner, Gerhard (1987), *Seerechtliche Verteilung von Nutzungsrechten* (The Assignment of Property Rights on the Sea), New York, Springer Publishers, 533 p.

Hanner, John (1981), 'Governement Response to the Buffalo Hide Trade, 1871-1883', **24** *Journal of Law and Economics*, 239-271.

Hardin, Garrett (1968), 'The Tragedy of the Commons', **162** *Science*, 1243-1248.

Hardin, Garrett and Baden, John A. (eds) (1977), *Managing the Commons*, San Francisco, Freeman, 294 p.

Hesse, Günter (1980), 'Der Property-Rights-Ansatz. Eine ökonomische Theorie der Veränderung des Rechts? (The Property Rights Approach. An Economic Theory of Legal Change?)', **195** *Jahrbuch für Nationalökonomie und Statistik*, 481 ff.

Hesse, Günter (1983), 'Zur Erklärung der Änderung von Handlungsrechten mit Hilfe der ökonomischen Theorie (The Explanation of the Change of Property Rights with Economic Theory)', in Schüller, Alfred (ed.), *Property Rights und ökonomische Theorie*, München, Vahlen, 79-109.

Hutter, Michael (1975), 'The Property Rights Paradigm: A Comment', **188** *Jahrbuch für Nationalökonomie und Statistik*, 552-556.

Hutter, Michael (1979), *Die Gestaltung von Property Rights als Mittel gesellschaftlichwirtschaftlicher Allokation* (The Structure of Property Rights as a Means of Social-Economic Allocation), Göttingen, Vandenhoeck & Ruprecht, 245 p.

Jelic, Ranko (1995), *Drustvena i drzavna svojina* (Social and State Property), Belgrade, Nomos.

Johnsen, D. Bruce (1991), 'Property Rights to Cartel Rents: The Socony-Vacuum Story', **34** *Journal of Law and Economics*, 177-202.

Johnsen, D. Bruce (1992), 'The Incentive Effects of Soft Dollar Brokerage', in Lehn, Kenneth and Kamphuis, Robert (eds), *Modernizing US Securities Regulations: Economic and Legal Perspectives*, 511-519.

Johnsen, D. Bruce (1994), 'Property Rights to Investment Research: The Agency Costs of Soft Dollar Brokerage', **11** *Yale Journal on Regulation*, 75-113.

Johnsen, D. Bruce (1995), 'The Quasi-Rent Structure of Corporate Entreprise: A Transaction Cost Theory', **44** *Emory Law Journal*, 1277 ff.

Johnsen, D. Bruce, Habib, Michel A. and Naik, Narayan Y. (forthcoming), 'Spin-offs and Information', *Journal of Financial Intermediation*.

Jovanovic, Aleksandra (1994), 'Transakcioni Troskovi Privatizacije (Transaction Costs of Privatisation)', **43(9-10)** *Pravni zivot*, 895-905.

Kaulmann, Peter (1987), 'Property rights und Unternehmungstheorie. Stand und Weiterentwicklung der empirischen Forschung (Property Rights and the Theory of the Firm)', **3** *Schriftenreihe Law and Economics*.

Kerber, Wolfgang (1992), 'Innovation, Handlungsrechte und Evolutionärer Marktprozeß (Innovation, Property Rights and Evolutionary Market Process)', in Witt, Ulrich (ed.), *Studien zur Evolutorischen Ökonomik II*, Berlin, 171-195.

Koboldt, Christian (1995), 'Property Rights und Urheberschutz (Property Rights and Copyright)', in Ott, Claus and Schäfer, Hans-Bernd (eds), *Okonomische Analyse der rechtlichen Organisation von Innovationen*, Tübingen, Mohr.

Köhler, Helmut (1980), 'Vertragsrecht und 'Property Rights'- Theorie, Zur Integration Ökonomischer Theorien in das Privatrecht (Contract Law and Property Rights Theory - On the Integration of Economic Theories into Private Law)', **144** *Zeitschrift für das gesamte Handels- und Wirtschaftsrecht*, 589-607.

Krüsselberg, Hans-Günter (1983), 'Property Rights-Theorie und Wohlfartsökonomik (Property Rights Theory and Welfare Economics)', in Schüller, Alfred (ed.), *Property Rights und ökonomische Theorie*, München, Vahlen, 45-75.

Kübler, Friedrich (1983), 'Was leistet die Konzeption der Property Rights für aktuelle Rechtspolitische Probleme? (What is the Use of the Conception of Property Rights for Current Political Problems?)', in Neumann, M. (ed.), *Ansprache, Eigentums- und Verfügungsrechte*, Berlin, Duncker and Humblot, 105-122.

Lehmann, Michael (1983a), 'Eigentum, geistiges Eigentum, gewerbliche Schutzrechte, Property Rights als Wettbewerbsbeschränkungen zur Förderung des Wettbewerbs (Property, Intellectual Property, Commercial Rights of Protection, Property Rights as Restraints of Competition to promote the Competition)', in X (ed.), *Gewerblicher Rechtsschutz und Urheberrecht, InternationalerTeil (Festschrift für E. Ulmer)*, 356-362.

Lehmann, Michael (1983b), 'Patentrecht und Theory der Property Rights, eine ökonomische und juristische Analyse (Patent Law and Property Rights Theory, an Economic and Legal Analysis)', in X (ed.), *Festschrift für R. Franceschelli*, Mailand, 35-51.

Lehn, Kenneth (1982), 'Property Rights, Risk Sharing, and Player Disability in Major League Baseball', **25** *Journal of Law and Economics*, 343-366.

Leibenstein, Harvey (1983), 'Property Rights and X-Efficiency: Comment', **73** *American Economic Review*, 831-842.

Libecap, Gary D. (1986), 'Property Rights in Economic History: Implications for Research', **23** *Explorations in Economic History*, 227-252.

Liebermann, Yehoshua and Syrquin, M. (1983), 'On the Use and Abuse of Rights: An Economic View', **4** *Journal of Economic Behavior and Organization*, 25-40.

Lueck, Dean (1989), 'The Economic Nature of Wildlife Law', **18** *Journal of Legal Studies*, 291-324.

Lunn, John (1985), 'The Roles of Property Rights and Market Power in Appropriating Innovative Output', **14** *Journal of Legal Studies*, 423-433.

Madzar, Ljubomir (1972), *Osnovi Teorije Proizvodnje* (Basics of the Theory of Production), Belgrade, Institut ekonomskih nauka.

Madzar, Ljubomir (1995), *Svojina i Reforma* (Property and Reform), Belgrade, Institut ekonomskih nauka.

Martin, Donald L. (1972), 'Job Property Rights and Job Defections', **15** *Journal of Law and Economics*, 385-410.

Mayhew, Anne (1985), 'Dangers in Using the Idea of Property Rights: Modern Property Rights Theory and the Neo-Classical Trap', **19** *Journal of Economic Issues*, 959-966.

McChesney, Fred S. (1986), 'Government Prohibitions on Volunteer Fire Fighting in Nineteenth-Century America: A Property Rights Perspective', **15** *Journal of Legal Studies*, 69-92.

McCormick, Robert E. and Meiners, Roger E. (1988), 'University Governance: A Property Rights Perspective', **31** *Journal of Law and Economics*, 423-442.

McGee, Robert W. (1994), 'Some Thoughts on the Relationship between Property Rights and Immigration Policy', **42(3)** *Cleveland State Law Review*, 495-508.

McKean, Roland N. (1970), 'Products Liability: Implications of Some Changing Property Rights', **84** *Quarterly Journal of Economics*, 611-626.

Mihajlovic, Kosta (1991), 'Svojina i Efikasnost (Property and Efficiency)', **39(5-6)** *Pravni Zivot*, 561-575.

Miller, Geoffrey P. (1987), 'Economic Efficiency and the Lockean Proviso', **10** *Harvard Journal of Law and Public Policy*, 401 ff.

Mortensen, Dale T. (1982), 'Property Rights and Efficiency in Mating, Racing and Related Games', **72** *American Economic Review*, 968-979.

Nutzinger, Hans G. (1982), 'The Economics of Property Rights - A New Paradigm in Social Science?', in Stigmuller, W. (ed.), *Philosophy of Economics*, Berlin, Springer.

O'Hara, Maureen (1981), 'Property Rights and the Financial Firm', **24** *Journal of Law and Economics*, 317-332.

Ostrom, Elinor (1990), *Governing the Commons. The Evolution of Institutions*, New York, Cambridge University Press.

Parisi, Francesco (1995), 'Private Property and Social Costs', **2(2)** *European Journal of Law and Economics*, 149-173. Reprinted in Posner, Richard A. and Parisi, Francesco (eds), *Law and Economics* 597-622 (Elgar-Ashgate, 1997)

Parisi, Francesco (1998), *A Property-Right Theory of Democratic Voting*, George Mason University Law and Economics Working Paper Series, #98-04.

Pejovich, Svetozar (1982), 'Karl Marx, Property Rights School and the Process of Social Change', **35** *Kyklos*, 383-397.

Pejovich, Svetozar (1984), *Fundamentals of Economics: A Property Rights Approach*, Dallas, Fisher Institute, 258 p.

Pejovich, Svetozar (1990), *The Economics of Property Rights: Towards a Theory*, Dordrecht, Kluwer, 224 p.

Polinsky, A. Mitchell (1979), 'Controlling Externalities and Protecting Entitlements: Property Right, Liability Rule, and Tax-Subsidy Approaches', **8** *Journal of Legal Studies*, 1-48.

Polinsky, A. Mitchell (1980), 'On the Choice Between Property Rules and Liability Rules', **18(2)** *Economic Inquiry*, 233-246.

Polinsky, Mitchell A. (1979), 'Controlling Externalities and Protecting Entitlements: Property Right, Liability Rule, and Tax-Subsidy Approaches', **8** *Journal of Legal Studies*, 1-48.

Polinsky, Mitchell A. (1980), 'On the Choice Between Property Rules and Liability Rules', **18(2)** *Economic Inquiry*, 233-246.

Posin, Daniel Q. (1990), 'The Coase Theorem: If Pigs Could Fly', **37** *Wayne Law Review*, 89-120.

Posin, Daniel Q. (1991), 'Bringing Home the Bacon: A Response to Critics', **38** *Wayne Law Review*, 107 ff.

Posin, Daniel Q. (1995), 'Risk and the Error of the Coase Theorem', **62** *Tennessee Law Review*, 1057-1071.

Posin, Daniel Q. (1996), 'Silicone Breast Implant Litigation and My Father-in-Law: A Neo-Coasean Analysis', **70** *Tulane Law Review*, 2565-2582.

Posin, Daniel Q. (1997), 'The Coase Theorem: Through a Glass Darkly', **61** *Tennessee Law Review*, 868 ff.

Reynolds, R. Larry (1985), 'Institutionally Determined Property Claims', **19** *Journal of Economic Issues*, 941-949.

Richter, Rudolf (1993), 'Ökonomische Theorie des Privateigentums, Thema und Variationen (Economics of Property Rights)', *Jahrbuch für Sozialwissenschaft*.

Rose-Ackerman, Susan (1985), 'Inalienability and the Theory of Property Rights', **85** *Columbia Law Review*, 931-969. Reprinted in Coleman, J. and Lange, J. (eds), New York University Press, Law and Economics, Vol. I, New York, 1992, 421-459.

Rowley, Charles K. and Yarrow, G.K. (1981), 'Property Rights, Regulation and Public Enterprise: The Case of the British Steel Industry 1957-1975', **1** *International Review of Law and Economics*, 63 ff.

Runge, Carlisle Ford (1985), 'The Innovation of Rules and the Structure of Incentives in Open Access Resource', **67** *American Journal of Agricultural Economics*, 368-372.

Ryssdal, Stray A.C. (1995), *Legal Realism and Economics as Behavior - A Scandinavian Look at the Economic Analysis of Law*, Oslo, Juridisk Forlag.

Samuels, Warren J. (1972), 'Welfare Economics, Power, and Property', in Wunderlich, Gene and Gibson, W.L., Jr (eds), *Perspectives of Property*, University Park, PA, Institute for Research on Land and Water Resources, Pennsylvania State University, 61-127.

Schap, David (1988), 'Property Rights and Decision Making in the Soviet Union: Interpreting Soviet Environmental History', **26** *Economic Inquiry*, 389-401.

Schap, David (1989), 'Pricing and Property Rights in Government Enterprises: Some Dynamic Aspects', **11** *Research in Law and Economics*, 113-127.

Schenk, Karl-Ernst (1988), 'Property Rights und Theorie der Institutionen (Property Rights and Theory of Institutions)', *Das Wirtschaftsstudium*.

Schmid, A. Allan (1976), 'The Economics of Property Rights: A Review Article', in Samuels, Warren J. (ed.), *The Chicago School of Political Economy*, East Lansing, MI, Division of Research, Graduate School of Business Administration, Michigan State University, 469-478.

Schmid, A. Allan (1981), 'Predicting the Performance of Alternative Institutions', in Samuels, Warren J. and Schmid, A. Allan (eds), *Law and Economics: An Institutional Perspective*, Boston, Nijhoff, 76-94.

Schmidtchen, Dieter (1983), *Property Rights, Freiheit und Wettbewerbspolitik* (Property Rights, Freedom and Competition Policy), Tübingen, Mohr, 71 p.

Schüller, Alfred (1978), 'Property Rights, Unternehmerische Legitimation und Wirtschaftsordnung. Zum vermögenstheoretischen Ansatz einer allgemeinen Theorie der Unternehmung (Property Rights, Entrepreneurial Legitimation and Economic System. On the Property Rights Approach of a General Theory of the Enterprise)', in Schenk, K.E. (ed.), *Ökonomische Verfügungsrechte und Allokationsmechanismen in Wirtschafsystemen*, Berlin, Duncker and Humblot, 29-87.

Schüller, Alfred (1979), 'Eigentumsrechte, Unternehmenskontrollen und Wettbewerbsordnung (Property Rights, Corporate Control and Competition)', **30** *Ordo: Jahrbuch für die Ordnung von Wirtschaft und Gesellschaft*, 325-364.

Schüller, Alfred (1985), 'Zur Ökonomik der Property Rights (On the Economics of Property Rights)', **14(5)** *Das Wirtschaftsstudium*, 259-265.

Schumann, Joachim (1978), ''Neue Mikroökonomik' und Theorie des Eigentumsrechte. Ansätze zur Ergänzung der mikroökonomischen Theorie (New Microeconomics' and Property Rights Theory. An Introduction to the Completion of Microeconomic Theory)', **7** *Wirtschaftswissenschaftliches Studium*, 307-311.

Schwartz, Pedro (1987), 'The Market and the Metamarket: A Review of the Contributions of the Economic Theory of Property Rights', in Pejovich, Svetozar (ed.), *Socialism: Institutional, Philosophical and Economic*, Dordrecht, Kluwer, 11-32.

Sevic, Zeljko (1995), 'Svojinski oblici i efikasnost funkcionisanja bankarskog sistema (Property Forms and the Banking System Efficiency)', **9** *Pravni zivot*, 647-660.

Smith, Janet Kiholm and Smith, Richard L. (1984), 'State and Local Fiscal Policy: Implications for Property Values and Economic Growth', **12** *Public Finance Quarterly*, 51-76.

Swaney, James A. (1990), 'Common Property, Reciprocity, and Community', **24** *Journal of Economic Issues*, 451-462.

Sweeney, Richard James, Tollison, Robert D. and Willett, Thomas D. (1974), 'Market Failure, the Common-Pool Problem, and Ocean Resource Exploitation', **17** *Journal of Law and Economics*, 179-192.

Teixeira, Pedro Gustavo (1994), 'A questão da protecção dos consumidores nos contratos plurilocalizados (Consumer Protection in International Contracts)', **54** *Revista da Ordem dos Advogados*, 181-343.

Tietzel, Manfred (1981), 'Die Ökonomie Der Property Rights: Ein Überblick (The Economics of Property Rights: A Survey)', **30** *Zeitschrift für Wirtschaftspolitik*, 207-243.

Turnbull, Shann (1991), 'Ownership: Never for Ever', *New Economics and its Writing: History of Political Economy*, 4 ff.

Turnbull, Shann (1997), 'Stakeholder Governance: A cybernetic and property rights analysis', **5(1)** *Corporate Governance: An International Review*, 11-23.

Von Weizsäcker, Carl-Christian (1984), 'Was leistet die Property Rights Theorie für aktuelle wirtschaftspolitische Fragen? (What Brings the Property Rights Theory for Actual Economic Issues?)', in Neumann, M. (ed.), *Ansprache, Eigentums- und Verfügungsrechte*, Berlin, Duncker and Humblot, 123-152.

Williamson, Oliver E. (1990), 'A Comparison of Alternative Approaches to Economic Organization', **146** *Journal of Institutional and Theoretical Economics*, 61-71.

Winiecki, J. (1989), 'Buying Out Property Rights to the Economy from the Ruling Stratum: The Case of Soviet-Type States', **9** *International Review of Law and Economics*, 79-85.

Yang, Xiaokai and Wills, Ian R. (1990), 'A Model Formalizing the Theory of Property Rights', **14** *Journal of Comparative Economics*, 177-198.

0550
GAME THEORY APPLIED TO LAW

Bibliography Collected by the Editors

Aivazian, Varouj A. and Callen, Jeffrey L. (1981), 'The Coase Theorem and the Empty Core', **24** *Journal of Law and Economics*, 175-181.

Aivazian, Varouj A., Callen, Jeffrey L. and Lipnowski, Irwin F. (1988), 'The Coase Theorem and Coalitional Stability', **54** *Economica*, 517-520.

Baird, Douglas G., Gertner, Rober and Picker, Randal C. (1995), *Game Theory and the Law*, Cambridge, MA, Harvard University Press.

Ben-Shahar, Omri (1992), *Strategic Behavior in Judicial Panels*, Discussion Paper, Program in Law and Economics, Harvard Law School, No. 107.

Bonus, Holger (1979), 'Öffentliche Güter, Verführung und Gefangenendilemma (Public Goods, Temptation and the Prisoners' Dilemma)', **10(2)** *List Forum*, 69-102. Reprinted in Grundtexte zur Sozialen Marktwirtschaft, Stuttgart/New York, Gustav Fischer Verlag. 1979/80, pp. 283-305

Bonus, Holger (1980), 'Öffentliche Güter und Gefangenendilemma (Public Gooods and the Prisoners' Dilemma)', in Dettling, W. (ed.), *Die Zähmung des Leviathan. Neue Wege der Ordnungspolitik*, Baden-Baden, Nomos Verlagsgesellschaft, 129-160.

Chang, Howard F. (1997), 'Carrots, Sticks and International Externalities', **17** *International Review of Law and Economics*, 309-324.

Cooter, Robert D., Marks, Stephen V. and Mnookin, Robert H. (1982), 'Bargaining in the Shadow of the Law: A Testable Model of Strategic Behavior', **11** *Journal of Legal Studies*, 225-251. Reprinted in Coleman, Jules and Lange, Jeffrey (eds), *Law and Economics*, Volume 2, New York, University Press, 1992.

Curran, Christopher (1994), 'The Burden of Proof and the Liability Rule for Suppliers of Services in the EEC', **70** *Geneva Papers on Risk and Insurance*, 85-98.

Dana, James D., Jr and Spier, Kathryn E. (1993), 'Expertise and Contingent Fees: The Role of Asymmetric Information in Attorney Compensation', **9** *Journal of Law, Economics, and Organization*, 349-367.

Dana, James D., Jr and Spier, Kathryn E. (1994), 'Designing a Private Industry: Government Auctions with Endogenous Market Structure', **53** *Journal of Public Economics*, 127-147.

Daughety, Andrew F. and Reinganum, Jennifer F. (1993), 'Endogenous Sequencing in Models of Settlement and Litigation', **9** *Journal of Law, Economics, and Organization*, 314-348.

Daughety, Andrew F. and Reinganum, Jennifer F. (1994), 'Settlement Negotiations with Two Sided Asymmetric Information: Model Duality, Information Distribution, and Efficiency', **14** *International Review of Law and Economics*, 283-298.

Daughety, Andrew F. and Reinganum, Jennifer F. (1995a), 'Keeping Society in the Dark: On the Admissibility of Pretrial Negotiations as Evidence in Court', **26** *Rand Journal of Economics*, 203-221.

Daughety, Andrew F. and Reinganum, Jennifer F. (1995b), 'Product Safety: Liability, R&D, and Signaling', **85** *American Economic Review*, 1187-1206.

Davis, Lee N. (1991), *Patenter og Innovationer: Mod et Strategisk Perspektiv (Patenter og Innovationer: Mod et Strategisk Perspektiv.* (Patents andlinnovations: Aiming for a Strategic Perspective)*)*, København, Blytmanns forlag.

Dawid, H. and Feichtinger, G. (1995), *On the Persistence of Corruption/Forschungsbericht*, Research Memorandum, Vienna, Institute for Econometrics, Operation Research and Systems Theory, University of Technology, No. 186.

De Geest, Gerrit (1995), 'Comment: Game Theory versus Law and Economics?', in Bouckaert, Boudewijn and De Geest, Gerrit (eds), *Essays in Law and Economics II: Contract Law, Regulation, and Reflections on Law and Economics*, Antwerpen, Maklu, 287-293.

Eger, Thomas (1996), 'Möglichkeiten und Grenzen des Reputationsmechanismus (Possibilities and Constraints of Reputation Mechanism)', *Wirtschaftspraxis, Verwaltungspraxis, Wirtschaftswissenschaften*, 1-10.

Eidenmüller, Horst (1996), 'Die Banken im Gefangenendilemma, Kooperationspflichten und Akkordstörungsverbot im Sanierungsrecht (The Banks in a Prisoners' Dilemma, Duties to Cooperate in Bankrupty Workouts)', **160** *Zeitschrift für das Gesamte Handels- und Wirtschaftsrecht*, 343-373.

Eidenmüller, Horst (1997), 'Ökonomische und spieltheoretische Grundlagen von Verhandlung/Mediation (Economic and Game Theoretic Foundations of Negotiation and Mediation)', in Breidenbach, S. and Henssler, M. (ed.), *Mediation für Juristen, Konfliktbehandlung ohne gerichtliche Entscheidung*, Köln, Otto Schmidt.

Garcimartin Alférez and Francisco Javier (1996), 'El coste de la ley Helms-Burton para las Empresas Españolas (The Costs of Helms-Burton Rule for Spanish Companies)', *Revista Derecho de los Negocios*, 1 ff.

Hansen, Robert G. and Thomas, Randall S. (1992), 'An Auction - Theoretic Analysis of Corporate Auctioneer's Liability Regimes', **4** *Wisconsin Law Review*.

Hansen, Robert G. and Thomas, Randall S. (1993), 'Auctioning Class Action and Derivative Lawsuits: A Critical Analysis', *Northwestern Law Review*.

Hatzis, Aristides N. (1993), 'Comments on Bertrand Lemmenicier's paper 'Social Justice and its Controversies'', **4** *Journal des Economistes et des Etudes Humaines*, 263-268.

Hay, Bruce L. and Spier, Kathryn E. (1997), 'Burdens of Production in Civil Litigation: An Economic Perspective', **25** *Journal of Legal Studies*.

Huang, Peter H. (1995), 'Strategic Behavior and the Law: A Guide for Legal Scholars to Game Theory and the Law and Other Game Theory Texts', **36** *Jurimetrics Journal of Law, Science and Technology*, 99-114.

Huang, Peter H. and Wu, Ho-Mou (1992), 'Emotional Responses in Litigation', **12** *International Review of Law and Economics*, 31-44.

Huang, Peter H. and Wu, Ho-Mou (1994), 'More Order without More Law: A Theory of Social Norms and Organizational Cultures', **10** *Journal of Law, Economics, and Organization*, 390-406.

Jost, Peter J. (1997), 'Koordinationsverhalten bei Umweltdelikten. Eine spieltheoretische Argumentation (Coordination and Environment Damages)', in Weber, Jürgen (ed.), *Umweltmanagement. Aspekte einer umweltbezogenen Unternehmensführung*, Stuttgart, Schäffer-Poeschel.

Kahan, Marcel (1992), 'Games, Lies and Securities Laws', **67** *New York University Law Review*, 750 ff. Reprinted in **26** *Securities Law Review* 127, 1994.

Kahan, Marcel and Tuckman, Bruce (1993), 'Do Bondholders Lose From Junk Bond Covenant Changes', **66** *Journal of Business*, 499 ff.

Katz, Avery (1988), 'Judicial Decisionmaking and Litigation Expenditure', **8** *International Review of Law and Economics*, 127-143.

Katz, Avery (1990a), 'The Strategic Structure of Offer and Acceptance: Game Theory and the Law of Contract Formation', **89** *Michigan Law Review*, 215-295.

Katz, Avery (1990b), 'Your Terms or Mine: The Duty to Read the Fine Print in Contracts', **21** *Rand Journal of Economics*, 518-537.

Katz, Avery (1996), 'The Economics of Promissory Estoppel in Preliminary Negotiations', **105** *Yale Law Journal*, 1249-1309.

Kerkmeester, Heico (1989), *Recht en Speltheorie: een Economisch Model voor het Ontstaan van Staten en Recht* (Law and Game Theory: an Economic Model for the Emergence of State Organization and Law), Rotterdam, Erasmus University, 212 p.

Kerkmeester, Heico (1995), 'Game Theory as a Method in Law and Economics', in Bouckaert, Boudewijn and De Geest, Gerrit (eds), *Essays in Law and Economics II: Contract Law, Regulation, and Reflections on Law and Economics*, Antwerpen, Maklu, 267-285.

Kerkmeester, Heico (1996), 'Boekbespreking: Baird, D.C., Gertner, R.H. and Picker, R.C., Game Theory and the Law', **25** *Tijdschrift voor Rechtsfilosofie en Rechtstheorie*, 72-75.

Kobayashi, Bruce H. (1992), 'Deterrence with Multiple Defendants: an Explanation for 'Unfair' Plea Bargaining', **23** *Rand Journal of Economics*, 507-515.

Koboldt, Christian (1993), 'Zeitinkonsistenz, Separabilität und Teilspielperfektheit, vom möglichen Segen der 'beschränkten' Rationalität (Time Inconsitstency, Separability, ans Subgame Perfectness, On the Possible Blessing of the 'Bounded' Rationality)', **10** *Homo Oeconomicus*.

Kort, P.M., Feichtinger G., Hartl, R.F. and Haundschmied, J.L. (1995), *Optimal Enforcement Policies (Crackdowns) On a Drug Market*, Working Paper, Maastricht, Tilburg University, Department of Economietrics and CentER.

Krauss, Michael I. (1994), 'La réglementation contre le marché dans le développement de normes (Regulation against the Market in Norms Formation)', **5** *Journal des Economistes et des Etudes Humaines*, 573-599.

Mackaay, Ejan (1988), 'L'ordre spontané comme fondement du droit - un survol des modèles de l'émergence des règles dans la société civile (Spontaneous Order as the Foundation of Law - A Survey of Models of the Emergence of Rules in Civil Society)', **22** *Revue Juridique Themis*, 347-383. Reprinted in **3** *Revue Internationale de Droit Economique*, 247-287.

Mackaay, Ejan (1991), 'Le Droit Saisi par le Jeu (Game-Theory Applied to Law)', *Droit et Société*, 57-81. Reprinted in Ost, François and Van De Kerkhove, Michel (eds), *Le Jeu: un Paradigme pour le Droit*, Paris, Librairie Générale de Droit et de Jurisprudence, 81-110.

Mackaay, Ejan (1992), 'Règle et Décision en Droit (Rule and Decision in Law)', in Bourcier, Danièle and Mackay, Pierre (eds), *Lire le droit - Langue, texte, cognition*, Paris, Librairie Générale de Droit et de Jurisprudence, 41-69.

Parisi, Francesco (1997a), *The Genesis of Liability in Ancient Law*, George Mason University Law and Economics Working Paper Series, No. 97-07.

Parisi, Francesco (1997b), *Rent-Seeking Through Litigation: Adversarial and Inquisitorial Systems Compared*, George Mason University Law and Economics Working Paper Series, No. 97-09.

Png, Ivan Paak-Liang (1983), 'Strategic Behavior in Suit, Settlement and Trial', **14** *Bell Journal of Economics*, 539-550. Reprinted in Levine, D.K. and Lippman, S.A. (eds), *The Economics of Information*, Cheltenham, UK, Edward Elgar.

Png, Ivan Paak-Liang (1987), 'Litigation, Liability, and Incentives for Care', **34** *Journal of Public Economics*, 61-85.

Posner, Eric A. (1998), 'Symbols, Signals, and Social Norms in Politics and the Law', **27** *Journal of Legal Studies*.

Rasmusen, Eric and Ramseyer, Mark J. (1994), 'Cheap Bribes and the Corruption Ban: A Coordination Game Among Rational Legislators', **78** *Public Choice*, 305 ff.

Rasmusen, Eric B., Ramseyer, Mark J. and Wiley, John Shepard, Jr (1991), 'Naked Exclusion', **81** *American Economic Review*, 1137 ff.

Reinganum, Jennifer F. (1988), 'Plea Bargaining and Prosecutorial Discretion', **78** *American Economic Review*, 713-728.

Reinganum, Jennifer F. (1993), 'The Law Enforcement Process and Criminal Choice', **13** *International Review of Law and Economics*, 115-134.

Reinganum, Jennifer F. and Wilde, Louis L. (1986), 'Settlement, Litigation, and the Allocation of Litigation Costs', **17** *Rand Journal of Economics*, 557-566.

Roin, Julie, A. (1995), 'Rethinking Tax Treaties in a Strategic World with Disparate Tax Systems', **81** *Virginia Law Review*, 1753 ff.

Ryssdal, Stray A.C. (1995), *An Economic Analysis of Civil Suits and Appels*, Oslo, Juridisk Forlag.

Sanchirico, Chris William (1997a), 'Evidence Production, Adversarial Process and the Private Instigation of Suits', mimeo, Columbia University Economics Department.

Sanchirico, Chris William (1997b), *Enforcement by Hearing: An Integrated Model of Evidence Production*, mimeo, Columbia University Economics Department.

Sanchirico, Chris William (1997c), 'The Burden of Proof in Civil Litigation: A Simple Model of Mechanism Design', **17** *International Review of Law and Economics*, 431-447.

Schap, David (1986), 'Executive Veto and Informational Strategy: A Structure-Induced Equilibrium Analysis', **30** *American Journal of Political Science*, 755-770.

Schap, David (1988), 'In Search of Efficacious Executive Veto Authority', **58** *Public Choice*, 247-257.

Schap, David (1990), 'Executing Veto and Spending Limitation: Positive Political Economy with Implications for Institutional Choice', **65** *Public Choice*, 239-256.

Schap, David and Carter, John R. (1987), 'Executive Veto, Legislative Override and Structure-Induced Equilibrium', **52** *Public Choice*, 227-244. Reprinted in Rowley, Charles (ed.), *Public Choice Theory*, Edward Elgar, 1993, vol. 3, pp. 47-64.

Schap, David and Carter, John R. (1990), 'Line-Item Veto: Where is Thy Sting?', **4** *Journal of Economic Perspectives*, 103-118.

Schap, David and Daerden, James A. (1994), 'The First Word and the Last Word in the Budgetary Process: A Comparative Institutional Analysis of Proposal and Veto Authorities', **80** *Public Choice*, 35-53.

Schavell, Steven and Spier, Kathryn E. (1996), 'Threats Without Binding Commitment', **5461** National Bureau of Economic Research Working Paper.

Schmidtchen, Dieter and Kirstein, Roland (1997), 'Abkoppelung der Prozeßkosten vom Streitwert? Eine ökonomische Analyse von Reformvorschlägen (Separation of Litigation Costs and the Value of the Case? An Economic Analysis of Reform Proposals)', in Prütting, H. and Rüssmann, H. (eds), *Verfahrensrecht am Ausgang des 20. Jahrhunderts. Festschrift für Gerhard Lüke zum 70. Geburtstag, München 1997*, München, 741-766.

Spier, Kathryn E. (1992a), 'Incomplete Contracts and Signalling', **23** *Rand Journal of Economics*, 432-443.

Spier, Kathryn E. (1992b), 'The Dynamics of Pretrial Negotiation', **59** *Review of Economic Studies*, 93-108.

Spier, Kathryn E. (1994a), 'Settlement Bargaining and the Design of Damage Awards', **10** *Journal of Law, Economics, and Organization*, 84-95.

Spier, Kathryn E. (1994b), 'Pretrial Bargaining and the Design of Fee-Shifting Rules', **25** *Rand Journal of Economics*, 197-214.

Spier, Kathryn E. and Dana, James D., Jr (1993), 'Expertise and Contingent Fees: The Role of Asymmetric Information in Attorney Compensation', **9** *Journal of Law, Economics, and Organization*, 349-367.

Spier, Kathryn E. and Dana, James D., Jr (1994), 'Designing a Private Industry: Government Auctions with Endogenous Market Structure', **53** *Journal of Public Economics*, 127-147.

Spier, Kathryn E. and Spulber, Daniel (1993), 'Pretrial Bargaining and Asymmetric Information: The Mechanism-Design Approach', *mimeo, July 1993*.

Spier, Kathryn E. and Hay, Bruce L. (1996), 'Burdens of Production in Civil Litigation: An Economic Perspective', *Journal of Legal Studies*.

Spier, Kathryn E. and Whinston, Michael (1995), 'On the Efficiency of Privately Stipulated Damages for Breach of Contract: Entry Barriers, Reliance, and Renegotiation', **26** *Rand Journal of Economics*, 180-202.

Spier, Kathryn E. and Shavell, Steven (1996), 'Threats Without Binding Commitment', National Bureau of Economic Research Working Paper.

Spier, Kathryn E. and Sykes, Alan O. (1996), *Capital Structure, Priority Rules, and the Settlement of Civil Claims*, Mimeo, August 1996.

Spier, Kathryn E. and Weinstein, David E. (1995), 'Retaliatory Mechanisms for Eliminating Trade Barriers: Aggressive Unilateralism vs GATT Cooperation', in Chang, Winston W. and Katayama, Seiichi (eds), *Imperfect Competition in International Trade*, Dordrecht, Kluwer Academic Publishers.

Spier, Kathryn E. and Whinston, Michael D. (1995), 'On the Efficiency of Privately Stipulated Damages for Breach of Contract: Entry Barriers, Reliance and Renegotiation', **26** *Rand Journal of Economics*, 180-202.

Stout, Lynn A. (1996), 'Insurance or Gambling? Derivatives Trading in a World of Risk and Uncertainty', **39** *Brookings Review*.

Vracar, K. Stevan (1994), *Preispitivanja pravne metodologije: Nagovestaji drzavno-pravnog integralizma* (Reexamination of the Legal Methodology: Indications of State-Legal Integralism), Belgrade, Naucna knjiga.

Williams, Stephen F. (1973), 'Optimizing Water Use: The Return Flow Issue', **44** *University of Colorado Law Review*, 301-321.

0560
COMPARATIVE LAW AND ECONOMICS

Ugo A. Mattei, Luisa Antoniolli and Andrea Rossato
Università Degli Studi di Trento

Abstract

This chapter aims at providing a definition of this rather new subject, which is situated at the crossroads of two different scholarly traditions, comparative law and economic analysis of the law. Comparative law and economics combines the instruments and methodologies of both these two disciplines because in this way it is possible to better understand the reasons of existing legal rules and institutions and of their evolution. It uses a dynamic approach to law, by focusing on the study of phenomena of legal divergence and convergence. These phenomena may take place within a single legal system, and in this case the analysis of legal formants (a technique created by comparative law) provides the analytical tool for verifying the law in action, which may be hidden behind different formal rules. Interaction may also happen among different legal systems, and we term this latter phenomenon 'legal transplant', which can take place for single rules or institutions or for entire branches of law, and can be determined by different reasons which range from prestige to forced imposition. Economic analysis of law provides further analytical tools that help measure the level and entity of analogy or divergence. Beside the traditional tools of neoclassical economics, useful insights may be gained through the instruments of the new institutional economics, particularly path-dependence, which, through the analysis of the relationship between formal and informal institutions, and of these with organizations, opens new lines of interpretation of legal change.
JEL classification: 0560
Keywords: Comparative Law, Law and Economics, Methodology

1. What is Comparative Law and Economics?

Comparative law and law and economics are well-established legal specialties. The two disciplines may benefit from each other, both having a strong non-state-centric approach to legal analysis. Specifically, comparative law may gain theoretical perspective by using the kind of functional analysis employed in economic analysis of law. Comparative law may proceed a step forward in its target of measuring and understanding analogies and differences among alternative legal patterns by using the tools of what is considered by many scholars the most theoretically advanced social science (Cooter, 1982).

Traditional law and economics is clearly an American product. One of the first applications of comparative law and economics is therefore the translation of such a paradigm to different institutional settings, not only the civil law Mattei and Pardolesi (1991) but also outside of the Western legal tradition (Bussani and Mattei, 1997).

Several factors attest to the existence of an intellectual environment favorable to the reception of law and economics outside the USA: the increasing interest of civilian legal culture for the common law experience and, particularly, for American law (Cooter and Gordley, 1991). This growing interest is due to a multiplicity of factors, the most obvious being the widespread diffusion of the English language which allows access to common law sources; and the appeal of American universities to younger generations of scholars; the introduction by means of the mass media of American cultural models. More generally, it is globalization in the sense of a process of Americanization of the worldwide legal culture that calls for a less parochial approach to the economic analysis of the law.

Within such a favorable environment, law and economics not only comes from the 'right' place but throws in the market of legal ideas all the tremendous prestige of economics, which many scholars regard as the leading social science. Nevertheless, European scholars have not been able so far to develop a European style of law and economics capable of competing in quality with the American one. American intellectual leadership has been complete. The reason for this shortcoming is to be detected in the lack of comparative skills. So far in Europe, the alliance between law and economics on which the very strength of economic analysis of law is grounded has largely failed, and the economic approach has been used more by the lawyers than by the economists (Kirchner, 1991; Finsinger, Hoehn and Pototsching, 1991). Moreover, many lawyers using it are remarkably unaware of the structural nature of their own institutional setting when approached in a comparative perspective (Kirchner, 1991).

Law and economics can be used to build efficient models, which work as uniform terms of comparison for the concrete solutions of the legal institutions analyzed. Such models, although they may introduce unrealistic assumptions (such as zero transaction costs) should be complex enough as not to be simplistic, and may eventually allow the proper measurement of the distance that separates the efficient model from each of the real-world legal system to which it is compared. In such a way the analysis can be completely factual (Cooter and Ulen, 1988).

Since economic models may be used to measure the real impact of a given set of legal signals on the market actors (Prichard, 1988), comparative law and economics, by comparing the law of alternative legal systems with the 'efficient' model offered by economics, conveys the possibility to measure the core of legal system (Schlesinger, 1969), that is the actual analogy (or difference) of the signals they convey to market actors, the assumption being that equal signals will provide similar incentives.

On the other hand, nowadays a strong case is made for the rebirth of 'legal process-style' comparison of alternative legal institutions (Rubin, 1996, p. 1394; Hart and Sachs, 1994). Comparative law may offer to economic analysis a reservoir of institutional alternatives not merely theoretical, but actually tested by legal history (Komesar, 1994; Palmer, 1995). The contribution of comparative law looks particularly promising to law and economics which, until recently, has suffered from a severe American-centric provincialism.

Comparative law and economics is a positive discipline which - from the standpoint of efficiency - 'deals with the transplants that have been made, why and how they were made, and the lessons to be learned from this' (Watson, 1978b, p. 318). Comparative law and economics, on the other hand, may also be considered a practical study which - again from the efficiency point of view - 'deals with the transplants which are appropriate and how they should and can be made' (Watson, 1978b, p. 319). In the language common among law and economics scholars, there may be both a positive and a normative version of comparative law and economics.

1.1 Static and Dynamic Comparative Research

'Comparative law presupposes the existence of a plurality of legal rules and institutions. It studies them in order to establish to what extent they are identical or different' (Sacco, 1991, p. 5).

The comparative analysis of different legal systems shows that there is a need to distinguish between what can be called the 'working rule' and the legal justification given for the application of this rule. The analysis of 'legal formants', that is the different formative elements of a legal rule, has the aim to discover how the 'jurist concerned with the law within a single country examines all of these elements and then eliminates the complications that arise from their multiplicity to arrive at one *working* rule' (Sacco, 1991, p. 22, italics added; Monateri and Sacco, 1998).

Let us consider only two elements involved in a comparative analysis of legal systems: the working rule, that is the rule applied in a given case (traditionally known as law in action) and the legal justifications that are needed in the system to ground the application of this rule. For example: if a patient has suffered damage because of a wrong cure prescribed by a physician we will find, for instance in the USA and in Italy, that the latter must pay to the former a sum of money to restore his loss. But in the USA the judge will find a breach of a duty of care, whereas in Italy a different judge will find a violation of the constitutional right to health, granted by article 32 of the Italian Constitution. The outcome of the case is similar, but the legal justifications for it differ.

Comparative law can be approached within two paradigms: the static and the dynamic analysis. The former is concerned with the comparison of a set of legal formants in two or more legal systems at a given time: it tries to identify differences and analogies within the realm of each legal formants and to understand how each of them contributes in framing the working rule.

Dynamic analysis tries to give account of the mutual interactions between legal systems in the course of history and mainly focuses on legal change.

Given the aim of this entry we will focus mainly on dynamic analysis. The possible result of such an approach can be categorized as follows:

(1) convergence: legal systems starting from different points tend to converge toward similar solutions;
(2) divergence: legal systems moving from similar starting points tend, in the course of time, to reach different legal solutions.

2. Convergence and its Explanations

In comparative law jargon, 'convergence' is defined as the phenomenon of similar solutions reached by different legal systems from different points of departure. Such a convergence may be explained by using both legal transplants and economic efficiency. The general convergence of modern legal systems, despite the large variety of institutional backgrounds, could be explained as a movement towards efficiency. In this case there seem to be a synergy between the efficient model and the prestigious model. Efficiency may be used to evaluate legal transplants. The framing of legal rules may be explained as the outcome of a competitive process. (Mattei, 1997a).

Many different inputs enter what we may call the market of legal culture. Within this market the suppliers meet the needs of the consumers. This process of competition would determine the survival of the most efficient legal doctrine at zero transaction costs. Nevertheless, there are several difficult problems that we must face in order to prevent this simple model from becoming overly simplistic. First, we must consider that in the market of legal culture, suppliers and consumers may be the same. Secondly, the so-called legal tradition, or worse, legal parochialism, may unduly restrict the market and result in failures.

2.1 Legal Transplants

Comparative law has reached an important conclusion in its more recent and sophisticated developments. In most cases, changes in a legal system are due to legal transplants. 'The moving of a rule or a system of law from one country to another' has now been shown to be the most fertile source of legal development since 'most changes in most systems are the result of borrowing' (Watson, 1974, p. 20). Comparative lawyers have been prolific in amassing evidence for this somewhat paradoxical conclusion. Each single legal transplant has its own peculiarities, which make it different from every other. It can be more or less general; more or less confined to a superficial level of the legal system (Watson, 1995).

The attempts to explain legal transplants from one system to another have relied on the largely empty idea of 'prestige'. This shortcoming is due to the fact that comparativists who have been working on legal transplants are less interested in a theoretical explanation of why a legal borrowing happens than in observing its occurrence.

If a transplant happens in a competitive scenario, it is likely that the transplanted rule or doctrine is more efficient than other possible alternatives. Conversely, one could argue that if a doctrine enjoys wide success in the competitive arena of international legal thinking and practice this means that it is more efficient than its alternatives (Mattei, 1994a, 1995a).

In spite of this, the existence of divergences in different legal systems does not mean inefficiency. Indeed, if there is a prima facie case for the efficiency of a legal doctrine on which there is a large agreement within the competitive market of legal theory and practice (Hirsch, 1981), this does not mean that there is just one legal rule efficient for each legal problem. Different legal traditions may develop alternative solutions for the same legal problem which are neutral from the standpoint of efficiency (Rose-Ackerman, 1995).

In many areas of the law, we may find legal change and eventual convergence due to a tendency towards efficiency, which has nothing to do with the so-called prestige of the legal model on which convergence is eventually reached. In the areas of the law where important efficiency concerns are at stake, comparative law and economics can play a crucial role in legal improvement. In its normative dimension it may work as a prestigious support to non-prestigious legal systems which have already reached the efficient solution without having the internal strengths to export it. In its positive dimension it helps to detect these phenomena at work. By using the tools of the comparativists together with those of lawyer's economists we may be able to see if an institutional arrangement, a legal doctrine, or a legal rule of one legal system is more or less efficient than another. We may detect and explain the phenomena of convergence. We may identify those aspects of a given legal system that stand in the way of the reception of an efficient solution. We may be able to foresee long-term efficiency consequences of a given legal arrangement that are impossible to identify if we do not employ comparative methods. By using the comparative approach we can even find a workable answer to the question of what is efficiency. From the point of view of a given legal system, efficient is whatever avoids waste; whatever makes the legal system work better by lowering transaction costs; whatever is considered better by the consumers in the legal marketplace; whatever, in other words, does not pointlessly foreclose the development of a better organized human society; whatever legal arrangement 'they' have that 'we' wish to have because by having it they are better off.

2.2 The Competitive Relationship among Legal Formants

Another explanation of the convergence toward efficiency can be competition among legal formants.

Competition and equilibrium among market actors may well be the key to understanding economics (Stigler, 1987). This concept, however, is virtually unknown to modern lawyers, who presume that the country in which they live has a monopoly on the production of law. Comparative law strikes a hard blow to this view by pointing out the degree to which legal issues are not restrained by national boundaries. Law and economics scholars, who view legal rules as a system of incentives (or implicit prices) rather than as a set of rules enforced by the State, also challenge legal positivism. It is in the area of sources of law that these two non-state-centered approaches seem to better complement one another. Accordingly, a competitive model can accurately describe the relationship between the so-called sources of law (Mattei and Pulitini, 1991). Comparative law and economics considers the law as the product of a competitive process whose outcome may be determined by structural (that is institutional and cultural) constraints of decision making (Cooter and Drexl, 1994; Ulen, 1996). Of course, such constraints, and therefore the outcome of the competition, may well vary from system to system, conferring to different legal formants different degree of authority.

Two major legal theories have developed in Western jurisprudence, which provide conflicting paradigms of legal scholarship: naturalism and positivism. These paradigms, although antithetical, share a common idea, which has remained unchallenged until quite recently. This idea, reinforced by legal positivism, may be referred to most simply as 'the unitary theory of the legal rule'. This theory can be described in terms of a model of hierarchical co-operation: the legislature drafts laws which are applied by courts to concrete situations, possibly with the aid of books and articles written by law professors (Sacco, 1991, 1992b). Of course there may be alternative approaches, as in common law systems. In such an approach the legal rule may be created (or derived) by the courts, again with the cooperation of scholars (or of other courts' precedents) and with the acquiescence of the otherwise powerful legislature.

Lawyers, therefore, had to establish a hierarchy of sources of law to resolve conflicts among them. The assumption was that, once ranked, sources of law would cooperate with each other to provide coherent, unitary legal messages to the community. The basic assumptions of the unitary theory of the law are still shared by the majority of lawyers in both civil and common law systems and are reflected in their terminology and in their disputes.

In recent times, some scholars have developed a theory which, taking into account the transnational nature of law, criticizes the unitary theory of its sources. According to this alternative theory, based on a clear distinction between law and legislation, the legal rule is the result of the interaction of different components, also referred to as 'legal formants' or formative elements (Sacco, 1991).

A legal formant is any legal proposition that affects the solution of a legal problem. For example, rules contained in the writings of legal scholars are legal formants, as well as rules contained in judicial decisions or statutory provisions. Also *obiter dicta*, insofar as they affect the solution of legal problems, may also be considered 'legal formants'. So, too, can administrative regulations, constitutional provisions and even broad definitions contained in codes. Legal propositions that do not contain rules but only definitions or broadly stated principles are legal formants, too. Legal formants, as sources of law, do not have to be (as in traditional theory) mutually coherent, even within the 'professional groups' that elaborate them (scholars, judges, legislators) (Van Caenegem, 1987). Scholars, judges, and legislators represent producers who offer their products (different legal rules conceived to regulate a given relationship) in a more or less competitive market.

Historically, legal systems develop in tremendously complex ways. There are different sets of legal rules not only addressed to different subjects (for example a law for merchants and a law for consumers), but also to the same subject as a result of different transactions (for example administrative agency in its public law v. its private law capacity). This is the product of rather independent, and often competing, legal systems coexisting within the same territory (suffice it to think about arbitration). Legal pluralism is the rule rather than the exception, even after the rise of the modern State. Similar problems of complexity are reinforced because of the multinational interaction of different national legal systems.

Comparative law and economics goes further along this line, addressing the relationship between different formative elements which make any legal rule. Competition rather than hierarchy captures this relationship between sources of authority. Competition is at play either among different legal orders, as among members of the European Union to devise rules of European law or to attract forum shoppers, or between different sources of the law within a given system (Reich, 1992; Antoniolli, 1995, 1996). Of course, these two main patterns do not exclude one another. Applied law is the outcome of a competitive process between 'legal formants'. More generally, law is the synthesis both of exogenous factors, determined by culture, economic structure, and political system, and of endogenous elements. The works of the Austrian school, particularly Hayek's concept of competition with its emphasis on the working of the competitive process rather than the characteristics of competitive equilibrium, is appropriate to describe the formation of the legal rule (Hayek, 1973). From his theory of knowledge, Hayek formulates one of his more fundamental criticisms of perfect competition: knowledge and information, rather than being the basis for, are the *results* of the competitive process. This reverses the causal relationship assumed by traditional economic theory.

Considering the sources of law in competition with each other despite the official hierarchy does not lead us to assume a jurisprudence of 'hunches' due to the staggering variety of the possible outcomes of the competitive process and to the impossibility to predict which legal formant will actually 'win'. Indeed, the result of competition is not less predictable than that of cooperation. It is only more realistic.

Does competition lead to efficient law? It is tempting to conclude that in the long run, within a group of cases, a legal trend may be foreseen as a result of a 'spontaneous order'. It would be even more tempting to say that an 'invisible hand' leads one efficient rule to triumph over all others. Unfortunately, the mentioned complexity of legal systems does not allow us to reach these conclusions (Mattei, 1994a). While in the world of zero transaction costs such evolution towards efficiency could be expected, this is not the case in the real world where institutional and cultural constrains introduce high transaction costs.

2.3 Why Efficiency?

Equity and efficiency are usually perceived as antithetical concepts. An efficient legal solution may not be equitable and an equitable one may not be efficient. Many of the arguments used against law and economics sound like this: law should be concerned with justice and equity; although values may not be costless for a society, lawyers should not be concerned when their pursuit is inefficient.

Comparative law and economics allows us rather original insights on the matter. In using the tools of law and economics together with those of comparative law, the notion of efficiency assumes itself a comparative meaning. An institution, rule or state of the world is never efficient or inefficient in an abstract or absolute way. It may only be so compared with concrete alternatives that may fit better or worse to a given context. The alternative rules, institutions or state of the world may be provided by history, by comparative analysis or by scholarly creativity. Consequently, the notion of efficiency, as used in comparative law and economics, maintains a clearly dynamic meaning, strictly linked with the notion of legal change.

Law is not something that can be understood (as it is usually done in traditional law and economics) as an aggregate of legal rules. It is a much more complex phenomenon that can be understood only by considering a variety of different levels in which a legal proposition appears.

Lawyers are part of the legal system in which they operate in whatever professional capacity they may act in it. When they describe the law, their interpretation is part of the law that they are describing. Law has an important practical dimension. Since the beginning of the Western legal tradition lawyers have been arguing whether law should be more of a theoretical doctrinal enterprise or just a practical business. We can trace this debate to the reaction of the humanists to the bartolists in the fifteenth century (Cannata and Gambaro, 1989). Indeed, the role of lawyers in the Western world can be understood in terms of the continuous interplay of these two different approaches (Berman, 1983). The commitment to doctrine and theory has been the major source of lawyers' legitimacy: they were able to claim they had a neutral approach to problem-solving. The practical aspect of lawyers' work has made them a powerful and influential corporation of hidden law-givers. Since law has a practical dimension it requires an approach somewhat different from that of a purely academic discipline (Gambaro, 1983).

In order to maintain their role in framing legal rules and institutions, lawyers had to find some reason why their opinions about the rules that govern society should count more than anybody else's. They had to legitimize their work. For 900 years, whenever they could not or would not rely on a 'text', they played with the philosophical concepts of equity and justice. In using these concepts, however, they were not worried by or even aware of the many different theoretical notions of equity and justice framed by legal philosophers.

If equity is traditionally a category of legal argument, the same cannot be said for efficiency, which has been marketed only recently as an American product. Seen in terms of the history of ideas, law and economics has grown to be a powerful approach because the discipline has given some strength to the claim that legal scholarship is a science. Indeed, the shift from equity to efficiency brings to the analysis of the law a set of value judgments, which is claimed to be more widely acceptable and less subjective in nature.

The change of focus proposed by law and economics goes right to the heart of the legal discourse. Its agenda is as simple as it is revolutionary: rather than focusing on justice, legal analysis should focus on efficiency. Efficiency should become the key of legal interpretation (Symposium, 1980). Borrowing from the expertise of welfare economics, the economic analysis of law puts the legal discourse through a number of other gyrations: law should not be analyzed as a system of coercion, but as a system of incentives or as a system of implicit pricing. Legal interpretation should not be guided by justice; it should be guided by efficiency (Cooter, 1989). Consequently, lawyers - as opposed to legislators-politicians - should not be concerned with dividing the pie as much as with making it bigger. Their role is not that of helping to cut the slices in a more just way. Issues of distribution should stay outside of the scholarly analysis of lawyers. They are the domain of politics.

Justice is a 'subjective' value, while efficiency is 'objective'. Indeed, there are only a couple of notions of efficiency accepted by the established economic paradigm (Pareto and Kaldor Hicks) and there are as many notions of justice as judging individuals. Reduced to the minimum possible level of value judgment, the efficiency criterion requires lawyers to act in a way that avoids the waste of resources (Mattei, 1994b).

It is easy to observe that the success of law and economics lies in one fundamental epistemological assumption that it has borrowed from economic theory. This assumption is the difference between the world of the *is* and the world of the *ought*, the fact and the value, the positive and the normative levels of the scholarly discourse (Polinsky, 1989; Posner, 1992).

We should first clarify that the word 'positivism' has a number of different meanings (Hovenkamp, 1990). Simplifying the sense more common among lawyers, in which we will use this notion, positivism equates the legal system to what is positive law (that is, binding law) within a given legal order. In this sense, it becomes a State-centric approach to the law, and both law and economics and comparative law can well be considered non-positivistic approaches. Another meaning - that should not be confused with the former, although it shares with it some of the same epistemological assumptions - can be considered fundamental to the very existence of the economic science: in this meaning 'positivism' refers to the paradigm of research that distinguishes between the *is* and the *ought*.

Economics gives to lawyers, with the distinction between the world of the *is* and the world of the *ought*, the possibility of a two steps interpretation, of a more detached look to the legal system. The same is true, and often claimed, of comparative law (Sacco and Gambaro, 1996).

3. Divergence: How to Compare Differences

3.1 The Theory of Property Rights: Rights and Remedies

In order to understand the divergence of legal systems we need some instruments to compare rules and rights that are expressed in different terms in different legal systems. The theory of property rights is usually perceived as a very useful tool in carrying out this task.

A system of property rights is a 'method of assigning to particular individuals the 'authority' to select, for specified goods, any use from an unprohibited class of uses' (Alchian, 1965; Eggertsson, 1990, p. 33).

The literature on the subject usually indicates three categories of property rights: (1) the right to use, transfer or destroy an asset; (2) the right to contract over and gain from an asset; (3) the right to transfer it (Eggertsson, 1990, p. 34).

What gives effect to rights and their consequent desirability and value, are concrete remedial devices (Levmore and Stuntz, 1990). The remedial approach is therefore recommended by comparative law and economics as potentially capable of introducing a degree of measurement to comparative law (Mattei, 1987). Moreover, there is now a sense within the comparativists' community that while the form of the law (in the broad sense of the style of the legal system) is very diversified, its substance may show remarkable phenomena of convergence, at least among systems belonging to the Western legal tradition (LoPucki and Triantis, 1994).

Remedies give value to substantive rights. Each individual is therefore interested in being protected by certain remedies. As only remedies may grant the feasibility of a certain course of action, they may not be granted contemporaneously to conflicting self-interested individuals on the same scarce resource (Levy and Spiller, 1994). One of the two individuals must prevail, and therefore be entitled to a stronger remedy. Accordingly, legal remedies may be analyzed as a scarce resource whose value is a function of that of the resource they permit someone to enjoy.

Different legal systems allocate different bundles of remedies differently when faced with conflicts over scarce resources. The subjective desirability of different combinations of remedies allows for a ranking of different 'property rights' which courts may handle in dealing with externality problems. This degree is a function of the structure of legal remedies supplied by different legal systems, and it is by no means constant. Remedies may be combined among themselves in a large variety of patterns and may be given to protect varying degrees of right-holders' autonomy on the use of different resources (Calabresi and Melamed, 1972; Kaplow and Shavell, 1996). Each legal system (or legal tradition) chooses according to its values (and to the structure of its decisionmakers), which rights are to be valued more and protected as such. Other interests are valued less, and can be redistributed *ex post* by the courts.

In every modern legal experience property rights, in their different forms, carry liabilities with them. Given these liabilities, property rights are not, as a matter of principle, less socially valuable than regulation. The intellectual challenge is to construct a theoretical model of property rights able to take into account this complexity (Mattei, 1997a).

Injunctions (or equivalent remedies such as ostracism or criminal sanctions) are always symptoms of the unlawfulness of the course of action which they enjoin. When there is no injunction, the internalization of the costs of an action is compatible both with lawfulness and with unlawfulness of the course of action, which creates the externality. In other words, it is compatible with any distribution of property rights. Liability rules, on the other hand, are nothing more then an insurance for the entitled share of social welfare. They protect an interest, not a right.

3.2 Property Rights, Liability Rules and the Theory of Transactions Costs

By discussing the historical and comparative law roots of the notion of property rights used in the economic analysis of law (Alchian, 1987), one can examine what may be regarded as the most important difference between comparative law and economics and traditional economic analysis of law. While this approach attempts to account for the different institutional alternatives presented by real-world legal systems, law and economics elaborates its theories on institutional backgrounds which are either abstract natural law models, or which uncritically postulate the modern institutional background of US law (Ajani and Mattei, 1995; Benson, 1989; Benson, 1995).

Comparative law is essentially a historical branch of scholarship which seeks to discern both differences and similarities among alternative legal institutions (Schlesinger, 1988). Its methodology may prove very helpful to law and economics, since it offers a more global perspective on different legal structures and on the evolution of these structure which may shed new light on - and challenge at the same time - certain previously undisputed assumptions of traditional law and economics. As a result, comparative law and economics does not conceive the legal system as a static background for economic analysis able to be captured by a few, never revisited, simplified assumptions. Nor does it assume that the contingencies of the American legal process are the necessary *substratum* for theories concerning the efficiency of law. The legal background represents a dynamic variable which economic analysis of law must reflect in both its positive and in its normative dimension.

The natural law conception of property is an intellectual category which does not exist, and never existed, as 'law in action' in any legal system (Gambaro, Candian and Pozzo, 1992). Using comparative analysis, it is easy to show that applied law only knows more complex forms of property rights based on a mixture of property and liability rules allocated in different ways to different individuals by different institutional agencies in different legal systems (conjunctive property rights).

The idea of property rights which serves as the institutional background for traditional law and economics is that of a bundle of rights that a person has over certain resources. Included in this notion are the enjoyment and transferability of property, and the power to exclude others from it (Demsetz, 1967; Pejovich, 1990). Comparative law and economics questions such assumptions by showing that, due to a historical paradox, law and economics is based on a substantive natural law conception of property rights. This conception, developed by the civil law tradition, was never fully accepted by the common law, and was eventually abandoned by lawyers across the entire Western legal tradition.

Law and economics has maintained the natural law misconception of property. How did this happen? In the cultural milieu of the United States in the 1960s, scholarship was ripe for the merger between law and economics. American lawyers, eager again to use broad theoretical categories, decided to borrow them from economists. Consequently, simplified legal notions that economists have not rediscussed since Adam Smith found their way into legal scholarship. Rather than working within a genuine interdisciplinary effort to develop new legal categories able to reflect the complexity of the institutional system, law and economics borrowed a number of naturalistic legal models. Such models are not only simplistic and unrealistic but also foreign to American common law tradition (Mattei, 1997a)

These assumptions should not be considered necessary components of law and economics. They are the product of accident in the evolution of a scholarly tradition and should be analyzed as such. Comparative law shows that the substantive structure of property rights varies from one legal system to another and never follow the natural law model. Such unawareness may, however, prove dangerous. Comparative law and economics develops the Coasian paradigm by analyzing real-world legal institutions as alternative ways of allocating unavoidable transaction costs.

The notion of property rights suggested by comparative law and economics is at once non-naturalistic and non-positivistic. While it breaks with the former conception, it does not go to the opposite extreme of confining itself within the narrow and contingent boundaries of a single positivist legal system. Taking the comparative approach means offering notions that may be used to understand different patterns of legal organization (Ramseyer, 1989).

Since Coase (1988), we have full knowledge of two alternative models of institutional control of externalities: the Pigouvian model, based on centralized regulations, and the Coasian decentralized model, based on the enforcement of property rights by the courts (Benson, 1991a). Any theory of property rights must take into account the following central point: in the real world there cannot exist a system that deals with externalities using a purely decentralized approach; similarly, there cannot exist a system which deals with externalities in a totally centralized Pigouvian way. This is the consequence of the impossibility of the pure market, as well as of the opposite impossibility of the absence of a market. Property rights and regulation, therefore, serve the same purpose. Their placement in an antithetical structure, an assumption of lawyers, economists, and the law and economics movement, is false (Williamson, 1991).

After Coase, the problem which deserves attention is the allocation of transaction costs which are part of the real world. This allocation is the key to understanding the problem of externalities and to elaborate a realistic conception of property rights. From Coase onward we know that a well-defined system of property rights will take care of externalities because individuals will bargain to reach an efficient result. This wonderful achievement of the Coase theorem has encouraged widespread efforts to use property rights to solve problems of externalities in a variety of situations (Laffont, 1987). The exercise of natural law property rights may impose external costs upon others. Restraints upon these rights are needed to control them. Under the conjunctive conception, obligations, which are needed to restrain external costs, are part of the very idea of property. Consequently, controls upon externalities need not be imposed in opposition to property rights, but may be introduced *ex ante* in the distribution of property rights.

4. An Exercise in Comparative Law and Economics: the Distinction Between Common Law and Civil Law

The lack of comparative understanding within the legal community has created a two-fold problem for law and economics. American law and economics has been remarkably parochial, unable to question the presumed need and immutability of a legal process patterned after the American one. Traditionally, law and economics contributions tend to presume a court system and, more generally, a legal process organized on the American style.

In Europe, the same lack of comparative understanding has prevented committed law and economics scholars from developing original insights capable of shedding new light on the civilian legal process (Mattei and Pardolesi, 1991). Many civilian law and economics scholars have uncritically applied theories which only work in the American scenario to the different background of their legal systems.

More generally, the widespread legal parochialism on both sides of the Atlantic has precluded a distinction between institutional arrangements which are local contingencies incapable of generalization, and deeper levels of legal analysis that can be used in understanding *the law* as a general phenomenon of social organization. The same lack of comparative understanding has, moreover, fueled the false impression that, because of the structure of the civil law tradition, law and economics is less useful as a tool of analysis in Europe than in the United States. The attempt to build models which reflect the complexities of the real world of the law is exactly what comparative law and economics is all about.

The misconception that lawyers introduce into traditional economic analysis of the law may be called the municipal misconception. This misconception stems from the other leading paradigm of jurisprudence in Western law: legal positivism. This is odd, because law and economics may be considered *per se* a remarkably anti-positivistic approach. Lawyers, however, can hardly resist focusing on the legal system they know best (that is, the legal system in which they operate and where they received their legal education). Certain basic institutional arrangements of the legal systems are just presumed to be natural and are never questioned by lawyers trained in that legal system.

Legal positivism equates law with the legal production of the state. Consequently, in its understanding, law exists only as a function of the enforcement mechanisms behind it. This approach is rejected by comparative lawyers who consider a legal problem the same wherever it has to be solved, and the alternative legal systems as possible variables for its solution. It is, however, followed more or less consciously by the majority of lawyers across the legal traditions. Positivism is considered a reaction to natural law. From the perspective of parochialism, however, they push in the same direction.

It is crucial for comparative law and economics to get rid of both of these sets of mute assumptions in order to develop its scholarly paradigm. Indeed, comparative law and economics is neither naturalistic nor positivistic, but struggles to re-introduce a measure of experimentation into the social sciences by comparing the different solutions of legal and social problems adopted in different legal systems. Because of different institutional arrangements and high transaction costs imposed on legal change by legal tradition, the fundamental distribution of powers and the way in which institutional roles are performed in the legal systems cannot be taken for granted either (Damaska, 1986; Shapiro, 1981).

From the comparative law and economics perspective we can see that transaction costs are introduced not only by alternative substantive rules but by different procedural arrangements, remedial devices, legal ideologies, incentives to litigation, and so on; in other words, by all those characteristics, both cultural and institutional, other than substantive rules, that comparativists call the 'style' of the legal system (Ramseyer, 1995). Consequently, comparing transaction costs imposed in the real world by different legal systems introduces the possibility of a measurement and of a more rigorous comparison than otherwise possible. A path is hence open to compare operative rules (or as it was once said, the law in action) rather than mere theoretical descriptions.

Possibly the most fundamental and discussed question in comparative law is the nature of the distinction between common law and civil law. Certainly a gap exists between common law and civil law; such a gap should neither be exaggerated nor underestimated in nature. Comparative law and economics, by borrowing its analytical tools from comparative law, accounts for this gap. At the same time, it borrows from law and economics the tools necessary to bridge it.

In approaching the question of the gap, a dynamic perspective on comparative law is needed (Calabresi, 1982). As a result, we will assume that the dimension of the gap is not fixed, but rather varies in both time and space. Deep structural differences are not, of course, a differently worded statute or regulation, or a supposedly different formalistic reasoning of the courts. Relevant legal process differences include: the way of acquiring information in the legislative process; the different role of public law; structural regulation of class actions; the presence or absence of a jury in the fact-finding process; the completely different system of incentives to sue due to different distribution of the costs of litigation; and the different ways in which courts acquire information (Stein, 1984).

From the timing perspective, the comparative law community agrees that the division between common law and civil law is rooted in the early development of centralized courts of law in England and of academic legal training on the Continent (Baker, 1990). There is also general agreement that, after a peak in the course of the nineteenth century, when the civilian nations codified national systems of law, the significance of the gap has progressively declined.

One of the major issues of law and economics concerns the role of the judge in finding efficient outcomes for legal disputes. Great emphasis is given to the different role of the judge in the common law *vis-à-vis* the civil law (Eisenberg, 1988; Atiyah, 1987). Consequently, it becomes important to scrutinize such difference to see whether it introduces a fundamental limit to the application of law and economics in the civil law.

According to traditional comparative law doctrine, the civil law is mostly a codified system where the role of bureaucratically recruited judges is to interpret and apply a written body of statutes (David and Brierley, 1985; von Mehren and Gordley, 1977). Common law, conversely, consists mostly of case law where technocratic judges are concerned with finding the applicable rule within the body of law made up of legal precedents. If such is the picture of the differences between the two legal traditions, there is no doubt that law and economics, being mainly concerned with efficient judicial decision making, seems at odds with civil law systems where judges limit themselves to mechanically applying the law contained in written codes. If this picture were correct and the judges' role as decision maker in common law and civil law was so different, indeed allocating them the same decision making powers would be very unwise from a legal process perspective. The traditional image of a civil law bureaucratic judge, whose role is not to decide cases in terms of public policy but of a mere interpreter of the political will contained in a statute (the code), has been a widespread commonplace of comparative misunderstanding. This image is opposed to that of a common law judge as the hero of a decentralized system of decision making. This contrast is deepened by arguments about the different value of judicial precedents in the two legal families. Other differences which are frequently cited include a radically different role for legal scholarship, which is allegedly much more authoritative in civil law systems than in common law systems; and the encapsulation of civil law in comprehensive codes (Monateri, 1986). In each of these statements there is some truth (Dawson, 1968), of course, but this does not mean that the consequence of such a background is a radically different legal reasoning which would foreclose the reception of efficiency reasoning in the civil law (Zweigert and Kötz, 1987).

In reality, although it may be true that common law judges are more responsive than their civilian colleagues to policy problems, the aforementioned description is dramatically misleading (Salzberger, 1993; Ramseyer, 1994b), being based on a superficial and outdated image of the differences between the civil law and the common law (Cooter and Ginsburg, 1996). If we consider the role of case law, we find more convergence between modern civil law and common law. In practice, courts in civil law countries make law just as much as courts in common law countries (Gordley, 1994).

5. Comparative Law and Economics and Neo-Institutional Economics

A new fruitful perspective in the study of legal change and legal transplants has been opened to comparative law and economics by recent developments of neoinstitutional economics. Particularly, the idea of path-dependence seems to be a very powerful analytical tool for studying and explaining the evolution of legal systems, where all innovation, be it endogenous or the result of a transplant, depends heavily on the existing institutional framework.

Path-dependent systems are those systems that cannot shake off the effects of past events because small events of a random character, especially those occurring early on the path, influence the selection of one or another among the set of stable equilibria. For this reason *ex ante* predictions of outcomes may not be possible, and consequently it is difficult to foresee future changes. In this situation there is a marked distinction between the notion of *ex ante* efficiency and *ex post* efficiency: the final result may not be the most efficient one in a theoretical world, but it may well be the best achievable in the light of the existing constraints. In other terms, lock-in phenomena, characterized by multiple equilibrium processes and dynamic co-ordination games, may yield Pareto inferior outcomes that tend to be stable (David, 1975). This is a typical result for decentralized decision situations, where a large number of individual agents are linked in a social and informational network; therefore, we may use the term 'network externalities'. In a network context every single decision is taken independently, but the collective behavior is the result of interaction among them. This is also the mechanism at work in the field of social conventions and institutions, where the common knowledge of recurring behavioral patterns directs the decisions of every actor, and therefore it arises expectations on future decisions (Sugden, 1989). The behavioral norm, in its turn, is the result of a chain of small events, and it may well be globally inefficient, especially if the system is numerically small.

Path-dependence shows that the spontaneous evolution of social customs and norms has a great importance in the configuration of historically existing systems and determines their global efficiency (David, 1988). The presence of a network of relationships creates positive feedback mechanisms, since every agent gains by joining a generally shared rule (Arthur, 1988). This mass of a priori beliefs and mutual expectations helps in achieving non-arbitrary solutions in a situation characterized by co-ordination problems, since it channels (in a probabilistic, not deterministic way) behaviors in a predefinite path; precedent, not only in its legal dimension, is an important instrument for decision (Heiner, 1986). In these processes, ideologies (in the sense of commonly shared ideas and values), or 'mentalité' play a very significant role, and therefore any analysis that aims at explaining a social, legal or economic model needs to delve into the dynamics of collective opinion-formation.

The environment in which decisions are taken is crucial, in the sense that it poses constraints and incentives which determine routines of behavior. Those routines lower transaction costs by making choices repetitive, but they also shape reactions to new phenomena, which tend therefore to be path-dependent (Simon, 1986). Ideologies (in the sense of subjective models and theories that explain the world outside) are an important element of every society, since they permit social actors to reach decisions under uncertainty conditions (Hirshleifer, 1987); the bigger the gap between the capacity of choice and the difficulty of picking up one among several alternatives (that is, the complexity of the choice to be made), the greater the role of ideologies, which become key institutions.

Institutions are the rules that govern a society, the ties that define social relationships among people; they shape all kind of exchanges: legal, political, social and economic. Institutions, which can be both formal and informal, reduce uncertainty by defining the range of individual choices, and therefore they reduce transaction costs. Organizations, on the other hand, are all kinds of apparatus, legal, political, social, economic, through which people pursue some kind of shared aims. Organizations work inside a given institutional framework, but at the same time their action influences in a feedback relation the way in which institutions evolve. (North, 1990).

The theory of institutions is based on behavior theory and on transaction costs theory. Transactions costs (Coase, 1960) cover two kinds of costs: those for evaluating the characteristics of the object of the exchange (information and measurement costs) and those for monitoring and ensuring the implementation of the agreements, that is for protecting rights (implementation costs). Production costs, which are the key concept of microeconomic theory, are the sum of transformation costs and transaction costs. The neoclassical model is modified in order to take into consideration transaction costs, by posing asymmetrical information (Akerlof, 1970) and exchanges that are not instant; it therefore requires mechanisms for ensuring complete and correct implementations of the agreements. Institutions are created in order to limit those transaction costs by devising rules that dictate behaviors and by creating incentives and sanctions that render implementation of agreements easier (as for example the role of property law in determining rights and protecting them). Institutions, in short, create the structure in which exchanges take place (North, 1990); the more complex the exchanges (that is the more we move away from the neoclassical model of perfect markets), the more sophisticated and diversified the institutional framework that regulates them. For instance, contracts are generally multidimensional, not instantaneous and incomplete, with significant measurement costs and implementation costs. In a setting of close personal relationships there will be strong incentives to stick to deals and to perform contracts. In more complex and impersonal contexts those bonds tend to become weaker, and different mechanisms are required to ensure implementation, since the drive to opportunistic behaviors is stronger. In this case, the most efficient solution will be to use a third party that controls the correctness of the behaviors and can intervene with sanctions in case of transgression; this new institution will decrease transaction costs for the bargaining parties, but at the same time it will absorb resources for its own management, thereby creating a new kind of transaction costs. All those feature are typical of the structure of the State, which produces public goods like legal rules and bodies for implementing them (judiciary, administrative agencies, and so on).

Institutional change is the mechanism that explains the history of every society, therefore in order to understand historical change we need to focus on institutions (Braudel, 1977). Changes usually happen in an incremental way, and they can move both in an efficient or an inefficient direction, depending on the pre-existing institutional setting and on the kind of incentives they create; the process, therefore, can be defined as path-dependent. The higher transaction costs and the less complete the available information, the more the outcome of evolution will tend to be inefficient. The incremental process of institutional change is attained by marginal adjustments in response to the variation of relative prices (technology, information costs, input factors, and so on) and/or preferences, and it ensures the continuity of systems in spite of their continuous modification. These variations can be determined both by endogenous and exogenous factors and they may start both from the formal and informal institutions. A change of the informal ones is a dispersed process, whereas the modification of formal institutions requires a specific activity by organizations, and therefore greater resources. The change of formal rules implies a sequential adaptation of the informal ties that are related to them, and therefore in the short run a situation of disequilibrium arises, which is then solved by a new equilibrium. History also sometimes experiences discontinuous changes as in the case of revolutions, conquests and calamities, but these are rare events; however, after a strong break there follows a phase where all institutions, especially informal ones, adapt to the new situation, thereby restoring, at least partially, continuity with the pre-existing situation (North, 1990).

Organizations act for the attainment of ends inside an existing institutional framework, and thereby they promote institutional change; the institutional structure orients the process of acquiring knowledge and skills, and this trend is the most important factor of a society's long-term development. These activities require the capacity to build knowledge and to transmit it, and knowledge is mutually dependent from ideology since the level of knowledge determines the conception of the outside world, and this in its turn influences the direction of scientific research. The firm is the type of organization that has been most extensively studied by economists; its existence can be explained by transaction costs: the organization reduces uncertainty in the decision process, and thereby reduces costs (Coase, 1937). As for the firm, the rational and maximizing behavior of all kinds of organizations influences institutional change through the demand of investment for any kind of knowledge, the continuing interaction between activity, knowledge and institutional structure, and the gradual modification of informal bonds. In this dynamic setting, efficiency is not mere allocative efficiency, but rather adaptive efficiency (Pelikan, 1987), which emphasizes the capability to experiment new solutions and to adapt to new conditions. In this sense, trial and error processes performed by a large number of actors in a decentralized structure represent the most efficient model (Hayek, 1960); once more, there is a strong parallel with cultural evolution and evolutionary theory (Boyd and Richardson, 1985).

From a theoretical point of view, the use of a path-dependence model in order to explain legal (economic, social) change places emphasis on causes, rather than on results, since these latter can be explained only by referring to the mechanisms that have shaped the dynamic evolution of the system. This shift of paradigm is new both for lawyers and economists, who have devoted a large part of their analytical efforts in trying to describe a static situation, more than tracing its dynamic evolution and the factors that have determined it. In this sense, path-dependency requires an historical approach, since an accurate description and explanation can only be given in relation to existing systems, with all their peculiar characteristics. Empirical research, with a strong emphasis on timing and circumstances, becomes as important as model-building. This new perspective has both advantages and drawbacks: it is certainly better equipped to explain some complex social phenomena, but on the other hand the characteristics of these systems and the kind of data that are required by this type of analysis make it more difficult to build theoretical models and to make predictions (Crick, 1988). Some efforts in the building of new models and instruments have already been produced in the field of biology and other branches that are referred to as 'sciences of complexity' (Stein, 1989). Nevertheless, social scientists, like lawyers and economists, should be aware that the systems that they study contain volitional agents (that is agents whose actions reflect intentions based on expectations), and therefore they have specific characteristics which are absent in biology or other natural phenomena.

Reality shows an enormous variety of systems, and history does not seem to point to a general trend to evolve towards more efficient solutions. In fact, many systems with very low returns prove to be extremely resistant, and this fact seems to contradict the evolutionary hypothesis as applied to institutions (Alchian, 1950). This enduring inefficiency can be explained by transaction costs and path-dependence: once an institutional framework has been built, it affects the possible evolutionary trends; if the kind of incentives it creates are inefficient, it is very likely that evolution will be inefficient, too (David, 1985).

5.1 Two Examples of Path-dependancy in Law: the HIV Problem and the Organization of the Legal Profession

The possible use of path-dependence for understanding legal change is exemplified by the study of legal reactions in the world to the hemophiliacs with an HIV problem (Mattei, 1997b). This problem struck all legal systems in the same way, since it has required quick and difficult decisions involving different areas, like politics, law, culture and technology. The solutions adopted by several countries (Italy, France, United States, Japan) show that under a situation of distress all legal systems react with path-dependent solutions, that is, solutions that are determined by the institutions and organizations that are already well established. This is also because, by happening simultaneously everywhere and requiring quick reaction, it could not be expected that solutions could circulate easily through transplant; in fact, a major difference in legal transplants runs between those that take place in an incremental and slow way, due mainly to the prestige of the exported model, and those that are the result of single instant decisions, as happens after a revolution (for example the export of Western legal institutions in former Socialist countries) or through forced imposition (for example in former colonial states).

The technical solution to the hemophiliacs with the HIV problem was quickly found by introducing heat treatment techniques in the early 1980s, but the institutional reactions followed different paces and paths. Two sets of elements have been crucial in shaping the outcomes. The first refers to the interplay of formal and informal institutions: the more formal institutions are at odds with informal ones, the less efficient are the results achieved, since informal institutions will resist application of rules that contrast with them. Informal bonds exist in all societies, because they are essential for guaranteeing order in social relationships. Even if their role is clearer in simple societies, it remains crucial also in complex developed societies, which have a strong framework of formal institutions, in the form of moral codes, behavioral norms and implicit conventions. Those informal rules are diffused and dispersed in society, and they create what can be generally termed 'culture', which is the means of transmission through generations of values that shape behaviors through teaching and imitation processes. In societies without a state (Sacco and Gambaro, 1996, pp. 26-27; Sacco, 1996) these kind of ties are very important and stable, since they shape the relationships of a social group that is very homogeneous and closely connected by personal bonds (Colson, 1974). In modern developed societies a general framework of formal institutions is required to manage complexity, but in smaller and more homogeneous sectors within it informal rules can still be essential, as for example in the case of rules of conduct in political parties. The relationship between formal and informal institutions, which form a complex network, is typical of every society and every historical epoch, and it is crucial for understanding the patterns of change; it must be underlined, in any case, that the difference between formal and informal institutions is a matter of degree, moving along a continuum (North, 1990). In the short run, culture determines the choices that are made; in the long run, informal rules may change the institutional framework, and they may even lead to a change of formal rules. The easiness of this transition depends on the existing transaction costs: if the costs for propounding values and ideas are low, they will have a strong push in changing the institutions.

The other element that has influenced the institutional reaction to the HIV problem concerns the prevailing component of every legal system; broadly speaking, legal systems may be grouped according to the prevalence of one of three patterns of law: traditional law, professional law and political law (Mattei, 1997d). The prevailing pattern will determine the legal reaction in the short run, creating a process which is path-dependent, because it is determined by the pre-existing situations. Once more, the time dimension will be crucial, because the lack of time will make it harder to try and transplant a foreign solution, making it much more likely that the existing institutions will be used to perform the new task, as happened in other fields like environmental pollution, car accidents and illegal immigration. In fact, three out of four examined systems reacted in a predictable way: the US with the use of tort law through the judicial system; France and Italy with criminal sanctions and an administrative compensation system, typical of strongly centralized and bureaucratic systems. Only Japan reacted in an unpredictable way, by resorting to tort litigation, instead of the traditional solution of mediation. This outcome is due to the strong opposition of hemophiliacs, who wanted the ruling class to take political responsibility for the HIV problem. The fact that the problem has turned from legal to political explains a revolutionary, not path-dependent reaction (Mattei, 1997b).

The importance of the institutional structure of every legal system can also help to explain the changes undergone by the legal profession in Western countries, which are not explicable on the basis of the traditional distinction between common law and civil law (Mattei, 1997c). We may view the legal profession as an organization that uses the institutional setting to achieve its ends; in this process it is shaped by existing institutions and in its turn it influences the evolution of the institutions themselves. The two existing models of organization for the legal profession are the unitary and the divided bar. As we have mentioned, the dividing line does not run along the civil law/common law distinction (Abel and Lewis, 1988): the analysis of some of the world's paradigmatic systems (USA, England, France and Germany) shows that there is a converging trend towards a unified profession since both England and France, although at a different speed, are moving in that direction, while Germany and the US have always been using this model (Mattei, 1997c). The United States are isolated from the rest of the countries in giving strong incentives to competition and litigation through the use of mechanisms like aggressive advertising and contingent fees. In European countries, on the other hand, legal professions do not push in the sense of stimulating the demand for services, but rather on limiting the supply by rigid control of access to the profession and on avoiding competition by neighboring professions. The effects of endogenous pressures, like the introduction of uniform rules by the European Community, and the push of international competition and the globalization of markets, may well force relevant changes in the future, but the reactions in the short run are bound to be path-dependent.

Endnote

Andrea Rossato authored section 1 to 4, Luisa Antoniolli Deflorian section 5. Ugo Mattei supervised the work and provided most materials.

Bibliography on Comparative Law and Economics (0560)

Adelstein, Richard P. (1981), 'The Plea Bargain in England and America: A Comparative Institutional View', in Burrows, Paul and Veljanovski, Cento G. (eds), *The Economic Approach to Law*, London, Butterworths, 226-252.

Ajani, Gianmaria and Mattei, Ugo (1995), 'Codifying Property Law in the Process of

Transition: some Insights from Comparative Law and Economics', **19** *Hastings International and Comparative Law Review*, 117-137.

Alchian, Armen (1965), 'Some Economics of Property Rights', **30** *Il Politico*, 816-829.

Antoniolli Deflorian, Luisa (1995), 'Il Formante Giurisprudenziale e la Competizione fra il Sistema Communitario e gli Ordinamenti Interni: la Svolta Inefficiente di Faccini Dori (The Judicial Formant and Competition Between the Community Legal System and National Systems: the Inefficient Turn of Faccini Dori)', **13** *Rivista Critica del Diritto Privato*, 735-760.

Antoniolli Deflorian, Luisa (1996), *La Struttura Istituzionale del Nuovo Diritto Commune Europeo: Competizione e Circolazione dei Modelli Giuridici* (The Institutional Structure of the New European Common Law: Competition and Circulation of Legal Models), Trento, Dipartimento di Scienze Giurdiche.

Benson, Bruce L. (1986), 'The Lost Victim and other Failures of the Public Law Experiment', **9** *Harvard Journal of Law and Public Policy*, 399-427.

Benson, Bruce L. (1989), 'Enforcement of Private Property Rights in Primitive Societies: Law Without Government', **9** *Journal of Libertarian Studies*, 1-26.

Benson, Bruce L. (1990a), 'Customary Law with Private Means of Resolving Disputes and Dispensing Justice: A Description of a Modern System of Law and Order without State Coercion', **9** *Journal of Libertarian Studies*, 25-42. Reprinted in 'Law and Order without State Coercion', in Veljanovski, Cento (ed.), *Regulation, Regulators and the Market*, 1991, London, Institute of Economic Affairs, 159-179.

Benson, Bruce L (1990b), *The Enterprise of Law: Justice Without the State*, San Francisco, Pacific Research Institute for Public Policy.

Benson, Bruce L. (1991a), 'Reciprocal Exchange as the Basis for Recognition of Law: Examples from American History', **10** *Journal of Libertarian Studies*, 53-82.

Benson, Bruce L. (1991b), 'An Evolutionary Contractarian View of Primitive Law: The Institutions and Incentives Arising under Customary American Indian Law', **5** *Review of Austrian Economics*, 65-89.

Benson, Bruce L. (1992a), 'Customary Indian Law: Two Case Studies', in Anderson, Terry L. (ed.), *Property Rights and Indian Economics*, Maryland, Rowman and Littlefield Press.

Benson, Bruce L. (1992b), 'The Development of Criminal Law and Its Enforcement: Public Interest or Political Transfers', **3** *Journal des Economistes et des Etudes Humaines*, 79-108.

Benson, Bruce L. (1993), 'The Impetus for Recognizing Private Property and Adopting Ethical Behavior in a Market Economy: Natural Law, Government Law, or Evolving Self-Interest', **6** *Review of Austrian Economics*, 43-80.

Benson, Bruce L. (1994), 'Emerging from the Hobbesian Jungle: Might Takes and Makes Rights', **5** *Constitutional Political Economy*, 129-158. Translated into Spanish and republished (1995), 'Las Instituciones y Los Derechos de Propiedad al Emerger de la Jungla Hobbesiana: La Fuerza Quita los Reprinted Derechos y los Crea Libertas', 12, 35-75.

Benson, Bruce L. (1995), 'Rights, Entitlements, and Individual Responsibility in the Welfare State', in Karslon, Nils (ed.), *Can the Present Problems of Mature Welfare States such as Sweden be Solved?*, Stockholm, City University Press, 88-98.

Benson, Bruce L. (1996), 'Restitution in Theory and in Practice', **12** *Journal of Libertarian Studies*, 75-98.

Brietzke, Paul H. (1994), 'Designing the Legal Frameworks for Markets in Eastern Europe', **7** *Transnational Lawyer*, 35-63.

Burrow, Paul and Veljanovski, Cento G. (eds) (1981), *The Economic Approach to Law*, London, Butterworths.

Buscaglia, Edgardo (1995), 'Judicial Reform in Latin America: The Obstacles Ahead', **4(2)** *Journal of Latin American Affairs*, 8-16.

Buscaglia, Edgardo and Domingo, Pilar (1996), 'Political and Economic Impediments to Judicial Reform in Latin America', in Buscaglia, Edgardo, Ratliff, William and Cooter, Robert (eds), *Law and Economics of Development*, Greenwood, JAI Press.

Bussani, Mauro and Mattei, Ugo (1997), 'Making the Other Path Efficient', in Buscaglia, Edgardo, Ratliff, William and Cooter, Robert, *Law and Economics of Development*, London, JAI Press.

Centner, Terence J. (1995a), 'Adopting Good Samaritan Immunity for Defendants in the Horse Industry', **12** *Agriculture and Human Values*, 69-78.

Centner, Terence J. (1995b), 'The New Equine Liability Statutes', **62** *Tennessee Law Review*, 997-1039.

Centner, Terence J. and Wetzstein, Michael E. (1992), 'Agricultural Pesticide Contamination of Groundwater: Developing a 'Right-to-Spray Law' for Blameless Contamination', **14** *Journal of Agricultural Taxation and Law*, 38-52.

Cooter, Robert D. (1995), 'Law and Unified Social Theory', **22** *Law and Society*, 50-67. Reprinted in Galligan, D.J. (ed.), *Socio-Legal Studies in Context: The Oxford Centre Past and Future*, Blackwell Publishers, Oxford, 50-67.

Cooter, Robert D. and Drexl, Josef (1994), 'The Logic of Power in the Emerging European Constitution: Game Theory and the Division of Powers', **14** *International Review of Law and Economics*, 307-326.

Cooter, Robert D. and Ginsburg, Tom (1996), 'Comparative Judicial Discretion: an Emperical Test of Economic Models', **16** *International Review of Land and Economics*, 295-313.

Cooter, Robert D. and Gordley, James (1991), 'Economic Analysis in Civil Law Countries: Past, Present, Future: Introduction to a Symposium', **11** *International Review of Law and Economics*, 261-263.

Finsinger, Jörg, Hoehn, T. and Pototschnig, A. (1991), 'The Enforcement of Product Liability Rules: A Two-Country Analysis of Court Cases', **11** *International Review of Law and Economics*, 133-148.

Gambaro A., Candian and Pozzo (1992), *Property, Propriété, Eigentum*, Padova, Cedam.

Gordley, James (1984), 'Common Law v. Civil Law: una Distinzione che sta Scomparendo (Common Law v. Civil Law: a Disappearing Difference)', in Cendon, P. (ed.), *Studi in Onore*, Milano, Giuffrè.

Hansmann, Henry B. and Mattei, Ugo (1998), 'The Functions of Trust Law: A Comparative and Economic Analysis', **73** *New York University Law Review*, 434-479.

Hertig, Gerard (1991a), 'Law and Economics in Civil Law Countries: Switzerland', **11** *International Review of Law and Economics*, 293-300.

Hertig, Gerard (1991b), 'The European Community', **11** *International Review of Law and Economics*, 331-342.

Hirsch, Werner Z. (1981), 'Landlord-Tenant Relations Law', in Burrows, Paul and Veljanovski, Cento G. (eds), *The Economic Approach to Law*, London, Butterworths.

Kaplow, Louis and Shavell, Steven (1996), 'Property Rules versus Liability Rules: An

Economic Analysis', **109** *Harvard Law Review*, 713-790.

Kirchner, Christian (1991), 'The Difficult Reception of Law and Economics in Germany', **11** *International Review of Law and Economics*, 227-292.

Komesar, Neil K. (1994), *Imperfect Alternatives: Choosing Institutions in Law, Economics and Public Policy*, Chicago, University of Chicago Press.

Levmore, Saul (1986), 'Rethinking Comparative Law: Variety and Uniformity in Ancient and Modern Tort Law', **31** *Tulane Law Review*, 235-287.

Levmore, Saul (1987), 'Transfusing Tort Law', in Khare, R.S. et al. (eds), *Issues in Compensatory Justice: The Bhopal Accident*, 48-74.

Levmore, Saul and Stuntz, William J. (1990), 'Remedies and Incentives in Private and Public Law: A Comparative Essay', **10** *Wisconsin Law Review*, 483-499.

Levy, Brain and Spiller, Pablo T. (1994), 'The Institutional Foundations of Regulatory Commitment: A Comparative Analysis of Telecommunications Regulation', **10** *Journal of Law, Economics and Organization*, 201-246.

Lopucki, Lynn M. and Triantis, George G. (1994), 'A Systems Approach to Comparing U.S. and Canadian Reorganization of Financially Distressed Companies', **35** *Harvard International Law Journal*, 268-343.

Macey, Jonathan R. and Miller, Geoffrey P. (1995), 'Corporate Governance and Commercial Banking: A Comparative Examination of Germany, Japan and the United States', **48** *Stanford Law Review*, 73-112.

Mattei, Ugo (1987), *Tutela Inibitoria e Tutela Risarcitoria* (Injunctive Relief and Damages), Milano, Giuffrè, 419 p.

Mattei, Ugo (1994a), 'Efficiency in Legal Transplants: An Essay in Comparative Law and Economics', **14** *International Review of Law and Economics*, 3-19.

Mattei, Ugo (1994b), 'Efficiency as Equity Further Steps in Comparative Law and Economics', **18** *Hastings International and Comparative Law Review*, 157-173.

Mattei, Ugo (1994d), 'Dissimilar Form Similar Substance? An Economic Framework for Western Property Law', in Rabello, Alfredo Mordechai (ed.), *European Legal Tradition and Israel*, Jerusalem, Nevo, 197-220.

Mattei, Ugo (1995a), *La proprietà immobiliare* (2nd edn) (Real property), Torino, Giappichelli.

Mattei, Ugo (1995b), 'The Comparative Law and Economics of Penalty Clauses', **43** *American Journal of Law and Economics*, 427-445.

Mattei, Ugo (1997a), *Comparative Law and Economics*, Ann Arbor, MI, University of Michigan Press.

Mattei, Ugo (1997b), 'Legal Systems in Distress. HIV Contaminated Blood, Path Dependency and Legal Change', Olin Law and Economics Working Papers, Boalt Hall, U.C. Berkely.

Mattei, Ugo (1997c), 'The Legal Profession as an Organisation. Understanding Changes in Common Law and Civil Law', *Olin Law and Economics Working Papers*, Boalt Hall, U.C. Berkely.

Mattei, Ugo (1997d), 'Three Patterns of Law: Taxonomy and Change in the World's Legal Systems', **45** *American Journal of Comparative Law*, 5-44.

Mattei, Ugo (1998), 'Fact and Value in the Economic Approach to Legal Interpretation: Some Questions to Professors Derrida, Ferraris and Vattimo', Discussion Paper presented at the seminar: Law, Justice and Interpretation, Università di Trento, in Bussani, M., Mauro, M. and Ferraris, Maurizio (eds), *Droit, Justice, Interpretation*, Bari-Roma, Latera.

Mattei, Ugo and Pardolesi, Roberto (1991), 'Law and Economics in Civil Law Countries: A Comparative Approach', **11** *International Review of Law and Economics*, 265-275.

Mattei, Ugo and Pulitini, Francesco (1991), 'A Competitive Model of Legal Rules', in Breton, Galeotti and Salmon, Wintrobe (eds), *The Competitive State*, Dordrecht, Kluwer.

Moller, Michael and Nielsen, Niels Chr. (1994), 'Okonomers og juristers syn på arv (Economist's and Lawyer's View of Inheritance)', in Lynge Andersen, Lennart and Mogelvang-Hansen, Peter (eds), G.E.C. Gad.

Ota, Shozo (1991), 'Law and Economics in Japan: Hatching Stage', **11** *International Review of Law and Economics*, 301-308.

Palmer, Matthew S.R. (1995), 'Toward an Economics of Comparative Political Organization: Examining Ministerial Responsibility', **11** *Journal of Law, Economics, and Organization*, 164-188.

Parisi, Francesco (1994) , 'Alterum non Laedere: An Intellectual History of Civil Liability', **39** *American Journal of Jurisprudence*, 317-351.

Parisi, Francesco (1999), 'Rent-Seeking Through Litigation: Adversarial and Inquisitorial Systems Compared', International Review of Law and Economics, forthcoming.

Parisi, Francesco and Frezza, Giampaolo (1999), 'Family Law and Successions' in U. Mattei (ed.), *Introduction to Italian Law,* Boston, Kluwer Law International.

Parisi, Francesco and Frezza, Giampaolo (1999), 'Il Concorso di Colpa: Analisi Economico-Comparata (Parte II)', in *Rivista Trimestrale di Diritto e Procedura Civile* forthcoming.

Pastor, Santos (1991), 'Law and Economics in Spain', **11** *International Review of Law and Economics*, 309-317.

Prichard, J. Robert S. (1988), 'A Systematic Approach to Comparative Law: The Effect of Cost, Fee and Financing Rules on the Development of the Substantive Law', **17** *Journal of Legal Studies*, 451-475.

Ramseyer, J. Mark (1986), 'Lawyers, Foreign Lawyers, and Lawyer-Substitutes: The Market for Regulation in Japan', **27** *Harvard International Law Journal*, 499-986.

Ramseyer, J. Mark (1987), 'Takeovers in Japan: Opportunism, Ideology and Corporate Control', **35** *UCLA Law Review*, 1-64.

Ramseyer, J. Mark (1989), 'Water Law in Imperial Japan: Public Goods, Private Claims, and Legal Convergence', **18** *Journal of Legal Studies*, 51-77.

Ramseyer, J. Mark (1991a), 'Indentured Prostitution in Imperial Japan: Credible Commitments in the Commercial Sex Industry', **7** *Journal of Law, Economics, and Organization*, 89-116.

Ramseyer, J. Mark (1991b), 'Legal Rules in Repeated Deals: Banking in the Shadow of Defection in Japan', **20** *Journal of Legal Studies*, 91 ff.

Ramseyer, J. Mark (1993a), 'Columbian Cartel Launches Bid for Japanese Firms', **102** *Yale Law Journal*, 2005 ff.

Ramseyer, Mark J. (1993b), *Credibly Committing to Efficiency Wages: Cotton Spinning Cartels in Imperial Japan*, University of Chicago Law School Roundtable.

Ramseyer, J. Mark (1994a), 'Explicit Reasons for Implicit Contracts: The Legal Logic to the Japanese Main Bank System', in Masahiko, Aoki and Patrick, Hugh T. (eds), *The Japanese Main Bank System: Its Relevance For Developing and Transforming Economies*, Oxford, Oxford University Press, 231 ff.

Ramseyer, J. Mark (1994b), 'The Puzzling (In)Dependence of Courts: A Comparative Approach', **23** *Journal of Legal Studies*, 721-747.

Ramseyer, J. Mark (1995), 'The Market for Children: Evidence from Early Modern Japan', **11** *Journal of Law, Economics, and Organization*, 27 ff.

Ramseyer, J. Mark (1996a), 'Products Liability Through Private Ordering: Notes on A Japanese Experiment', **144** *University of Pennsylvania Law Review*, 1823-1840.

Ramseyer, J. Mark (1996b), *Odd Markets in Japanese History: Law and Economic Growth*, New York, Cambridge University Press.

Ramseyer, J. Mark and Rosenbluth, Frances McCall (1993), *Japan's Political Marketplace*, Cambridge, MA, Harvard University Press.

Ramseyer, J. Mark and Nakazato, Minoru (1989), 'The Rational Litigant: Settlement Amounts and Verdict Rates in Japan', **18** *Journal of Legal Studies*, 263 ff.

Rasmussen, David W. and Benson, Bruce L. (eds) (1994), *The Economic Anatomy of a Drug War: Criminal Justice in the Commons*, Lanham, MD, Rowman and Littlefield.

Reich, Norbert (1992), 'Competition between Legal Orders: A New Paradigm of EC Law', **29** *Common Market Law Review*, 861-896.

Rose-Ackerman, Susan (1995), *Controlling Environmental Policy: The Limits of Public Law in Germany and The United States*, New Haven, Yale University Press.

Rubin, Edward L. (1996), 'The New Legal Process, the Synthesis of Discourse and the Microanalysis of Institutions', **109** *Harvard Law Review*, 1393 ff.

Rudden, Bernard (1987), 'Economic Theory v. Property Law: The Numerus Clausus Problem', in Eekelaar, John and Bell, John (eds), *Oxford Essays in Jurisprudence, Third Series*, Oxford, Oxford Clarendon Press, 239 ff.

Salzberger, Eli M. (1993), 'A Positive Analysis of the Doctrine of Separation of Powers, or: Why do we have an Independent Judiciary?', **13** *International Review of Law and Economics*, 349-379.

Sinden, J.A. (1994), 'Learning to Love Japan: Social Norms and Market Incentives', **31** *University of San Diego Law Review*, 263 ff.

Skogh, Gorajn (1991), 'Law and Economics in Sweden', **11** *International Review of Law and Economics*, 319-324.

Turnbull, Shann (1997), *Evolution of Business and the Corporate Structure*, Corporate Directors' Diploma Course, University of New England, Armidale, Australia, Topic 1.1.

Ulen, Thomas S. (1996), 'Comparative Law and Economics of Federalism', **2** *Cardozo Electronic Law Bulletin*, http://www.gelso.unitn.it/card-adm/Comparative/Ulen-1996/ulen1.htm.

Watson, Alan (1974), *Legal Transplants: An Approach to Comparative Law*, Charlottesville, VA, University Press of Virginia.

Watson, Alan (1978a), *Society and Legal Change*, Cambridge, Cambridge University Press.

Weigel, Wolfgang (1991), 'Prospects for Law and Economics in Civil Law Countries: Austria', **11** *International Review of Law and Economics*, 325-329.

Williams, Philip L. (1994), 'The Exercise of Market Power: Its Treatment under the Australian and New Zealand Statutes', **9** *Review of Industrial Organization*, 607-626.

Other References

Abel, Richard L. and Lewis, Philip S.C. (eds) (1988-89, 3 vols; 1995, abridged updated edition), *Lawyers in Society*, Berkeley, University of California Press.

Agostini, Eric (1988), *Droit Comparé* (Comparative Law), Paris, Presses Universitaires de

France (PUF).

Ajani, Gianmaria (1991), 'The Soviet Experience with Codification: Theoretical and Comparative Perspectives' in Buxbaum, Richard M.and Hendley, Kathryn (eds), *The Soviet Sobranie of Law,* Berkeley, International and Area Studies, University of California at Berkeley.

Ajani, Gianmaria (1995),'By Chance and Prestige: Legal Transplants in Russia and Eastern Europe', **43** *American Journal of Comparative Law,* 93-117.

Akerlof, George A. (1970), 'The Market for Lemons: Qualitative Uncertainty and the Market Mechanism', **84** *Quarterly Journal of Economics*, 488-500.

Alchian, Armen A. (1950), 'Uncertainty, Evolution and Economic Theory', **58** *Journal of Political Economy*, 211-221.

Alchian, Armen A. (1987), 'Property', *The New Pagrave - A Dictionary of Economics*, London, Macmillan.

Arthur, W.B. (1988), 'Self-reinforcing Mechanisms in Economics', in Anderson, Philip, Arrow, Kenneth and Pines, David, *The Economy as an Evolving Complex System*, Reading, MA, Addison Wesley.

Atiyah, Patrick S. (1987), 'Common Law', *The New Palgrave - A Dictionary of Economics*, London, Macmillan.

Baker, John Hamilton (1990), *An Introduction to English Legal History,* 2nd edn, London, Butterworths.

Berman, Harold Joseph (1983) *Law and Revolution: The Formation of the Western Legal Tradition*, Cambridge, MA, Harvard University Press.

Boyd, Robert and Richardson, Peter J. (1985), *Culture and the Evolutionary Process*, Chicago, University of Chicago Press.

Braudel, Fernand (1977), *Afterthoughts on Material Civilization and Capitalism*, Baltimore, Johns Hopkins University Press.

Calabresi, Guido (1961), 'Some Thoughts about Risk Distribution and the Law of Torts', **70** *Yale Law Journal*, 499-553.

Calabresi, Guido (1970), *The Cost of Accidents: A Legal and Economic Analysis*, New Haven, Conn., Yale University Press.

Calabresi, Guido (1982), *A Common Law for the Age of Statutes,* Cambridge, MA, Harvard University Press.

Calabresi, Guido (1991), 'The Pointlessness of Pareto. Carrying Coase Further', **100** *Yale Law Joural*, 1211-1237.

Calabresi, Guido and Melamed, D. (1972), 'Property Rules, Liability Rules, Inalienability: One View of the Cathedral', **85** *Harvard Law Review*, 1089-1128.

Cannata, Carlo Augusto and Gambaro, Antonio (1989), *Lineamenti di storia della giurisprudenza europea* (Elements of History of European Jurisprudence), 4th edn, Torino, Giappichelli.

Castan, Tobenas and Don, Jose (1988), 'Contemporary Legal Systems of the Western World', **25** *Comparative Juridical Review*, 105-171.

Cheshire, Geoffrey Chevalier and Burn, Edward Hector (1988), *Modern Law of Real Property*, 14th edn, London, Butterworths.

Cheung, Steven N.S. (1991), 'Common Property Rights', *The New Palgrave - The World of Economics*, London, Macmillan.

Coase, Ronald (1937), 'The Nature of the Firm', **4** *Economica*, 386-405.

Coase, Ronald ([1960] 1988), 'The Problem of Social Cost', **3** *Journal Law and Economics*, 1-44, (1988), *The Firm, the Market and the Law*, Chicago, Chicago University Press.

Colson, Elisabeth (1974), *Tradition and Contract: The Problem of Order*, Chicago, Adeline.

Cooter, Robert (1982), 'Law and the Imperialism of Economics: an Introduction to the Economic Analysis of Law and a Review of the Major Books', **29** *University of California Los Angeles Law Review*, 1260-1269

Cooter, Robert (1982a), 'The Cost of Coase', **11** *Journal of Legal Studies*, 1-33.

Cooter, Robert (1987), 'The Coase Theorem', *The New Palgrave - A Dictionary Of Economics*, London, Macmillan.

Cooter, Robert (1989), 'The Best Right Laws. Value Foundations of the Economic Analysis of Law', **64** *Notre Dame Law Review*, 817-837.

Cooter, Robert and Ulen, Thomas (1988), *Law and Economics*, Glenview, Ill, Scott and Foresman.

Crick, Francis (1988), *What Mad Pursuit?*, New York.

Damaska, Mirjan R. (1986), *The Faces of Justice and State Authority*, New Haven, Yale University Press.

David, Paul A. (1985), 'Clio and the Economics of QWERTY', **75** *American Economic Review*, 332-337.

David, Paul A. (1988), 'Path-Dependence: Putting the Past into the Future of Economics', Institute for Mathematical Studies in the Social Sciences, Technical Report 533, Stanford University.

David, Paul A. (1975), *Technical Choice, Innovation and Economic Growth: Essays on American and British Experience in the Nineteenth Century*, Cambridge, Cambridge University Press.

David, René (ed.) (1971), *Sources of Law, International Encyclopedia of Comparative Law*, Tuebingen, Mohr; Den Haag, Nijhoff.

David, René and Brierley, John E.C. (1985), *Major Legal Systems in the World Today*, 3rd edn, London, Stevens.

Dawson, John Philip (1968), *The Oracles of the Law*, Westport, Conn.: Greenwood.

Demsetz, Harold (1967), 'Toward a Theory of Property Rights', **57** *American Economic Review*, 347-359.

Dias, C.J. et al. (eds) (1981), *Lawyers in the Third World: Comparative and Developmental Perspective*, Uppsala: Scandinavian Institute of African Studies; New York, International Center for Law in Development.

Dworkin, Ronald M. (1978), *Taking Rights Seriously*, Cambridge, MA, Harvard University Press.

Eggertsson, Thrainn (1990), *Economic Behavior and Institution*, Cambridge, Cambridge University Press.

Eisenberg, Melvin Aron (1988), *The Nature of the Common Law*, Cambridge, MA, Harvard University Press.

Epstein, Richard A. (1985), *Takings: Private Property and the Power of Eminent Domain*, Cambridge, MA, Harvard University Press.

Epstein, Richard A. (1986), 'Past and Future: The Temporal Dimension in the Law of Property', **64** *Washington University Law Quarterly*, 667-722.

Eskridge, William N. and Frickey, Philip P. (1994), 'The Making of the Legal Process', **107** *Harvard Law Review*, 2031- 2055.

Friedman, David (1987), 'Law and Economics', *The New Palgrave - A Dictionary of Economics*, London, Macmillan.

Gambaro, Antonio (1983), 'Il Succeso del Giurista', **5** *Foro Italiano*, 85-93.

Gambaro, Antonio (1992), 'Property', in Gambaro, Antonio et al. (1992), *Property, Propriété, Eigentum*, Padova, CEDAM.

Gambaro, Antonio (1994), 'Codes and Constitutions in Civil Law', in Rabello, Alfredo Mordechai (ed.), *European Legal Tradition and Israel*, Jerusalem, Nevo.

Gely, Rafael and Spiller, Pablo T. (1990), 'A Rational Choice Theory of Supreme Court Statutory Decisions with Applications to the State Farm anf Grove City Cases', **6** *Journal of Law, Economics and Organization*, 263-300.

Gilmore, Grant (1977), *The Ages of American Law*, New Haven: Yale University Press.

Glendon, Mary Ann, Gordon, Michael Wallace and Osakwe, Christopher (1994), *Comparative Legal Traditions*, 2nd edn, St Paul, Minn., West Publishing.

Gordley, James (1991), *The Philosophical Origin of Modern Contract Doctrine*, Oxford, Clarendon.

Gordley, James (1993), 'Common Law and Civil Law', **3** *Zeitschrift für Europäisches Privatrecht*, 498 ff.

Gordley, James (1994), 'Common Law versus Civil Law: una Distinzione che sta Scomparendo (Common Law versus Civil Law: a Disappearing Difference), in Cendon, P. (ed.), *Studi in Onore di Rodolfo Sacco*, Milano, Giuffrè.

Gordley, James and Mattei, Ugo (1996), 'Protecting Possession', **44** *American Journal of Comparative Law*.

Gorla, Gino (1981), *Diritto Comparato e Diritto Comune Europeo* (Comparative Law and European Common Law), Milano, Giuffrè.

Grande, Elisabetta (ed.) (1995), *Transplants, Innovation and Legal Tradition in the Horn of Africa*, Torino: Harmattan.

Graziadei, Michele and Rudden, Bernard (1992), 'Il Diritto Inglese dei Beni ed il Trust: Dalle Res al Fund (The English Law on Goods and the Trust: from Res to Fund)', *Quadrimestre* 458

Hart, Henry M. and Sachs, Albert M. ([1958] 1994), *The Legal Process. Basic Problems in the Making and Application of Law*, edited by W.M. Eskridge and P.P. Frickey, Westbury, NY.

Hart, Herbert Lionel A. (1961), *The Concept of Law*, Oxford, Clarendon.

Hayek, Friedrich A. (1960), *The Constitution of Liberty*, Chicago, University of Chicago Press.

Hayek, Friedrich A. (1973), *Law, Legislation and Liberty*, Chicago, University of Chicago Press.

Heiner, Ronald (1986), 'Imperfect Decisions and the Law: On the Evolution of Legal Precedent and Rules', **15** *Journal Legal Studies*, 227-262.

Hirshleifer, Jack (1987), *Economic Behavior in Adversity*, Chicago, Chicago University Press.

Horn, Norbert, Kotz, Hein and Leser, Hans G., translated by Weir, Tony (1982), *German Private and Commercial Law. An Introduction*, Oxford, Clarendon Press.

Horwitz, Morton J. (1992), *The Transformation of American Law 1870-1960, The Crisis of Legal Hortodoxy*, Oxford, Oxford University Press.

Hovenkamp, Herbert (1990), 'Positivism in Law and Economics', **78** *California Law Review*, 815-852.

Laffont, J.J (1987), 'Externalities', *The New Palgrave - A Dictionary of Economics*, London, Macmillan.

Lawson, Frederick Henry and Rudden, Bernard (1984), *An Introduction to the Law of Property*, Oxford, Clarendon Press.

Legrand, Pierre (1995), 'Strange Power of Words: Codification Situated', **9** *Tulane European and Civil Law Forum*, 1 ff.

Lupoi, Maurizio (1994), *Introduzione ai Trusts* (An Introduction to the Law of Trusts), Milano: Giuffrè.

Malloy, R.P. Evensky, J. (eds) (1994), *Adam Smith and the Philosophy of Law and Economics*, Dordrecht, Kluwer.

Manne, Henry J. (1977), *The Economics of Legal Relationship, Readings in the Theory of Property Rights,* St Paul, West Publishing.

Mattei, Ugo (1988), *Stare Decisis*, Milano, Giuffrè.

Mattei, Ugo (1994e), *Common Law: Il Diritto Anglo-Americano* (Common Law: Anglo-American Law), Torino, UTET.

Mattei, Ugo (1994f), 'Why the Wind Changed: Intellectual Leadership in Western Law', **42** *American Journal of Comparative Law*, 195-218.

Mattei, Ugo (1994g), 'Verso una Tripartizione non Eurocentrica dei Sistemi Giuridici (Towards a non-Eurocentric Tripartition of Legal Systems), in *Studi in memoria di Gino Gorla*'.

Merryman, John Henry (1969), *The Civil Law Tradition: An Introduction to the Legal Systems of Western Europe and Latin America*, Stanford, Stanford University Press.

Michelman, Frank I. (1971), 'Pollution as a Tort: A Non-accidental Perspective on Calabresi's Costs', **80** *Yale Law Journal*, 647-686.

Milsom, Stroud Francis Charles (1969), *Historical Foundations of the Common Law*, London, Butterworths.

Monateri, Pier Giuseppe (1986), *Legal Doctrine as a Source of Law: A Transnational Factor and a Historical Paradox*, Italian National Reports, 12 Congress of the International Academy of Comparative Law, Milano, Giuffrè.

Monateri, Pier Giuseppe (1984), *La Sineddoche* (The Synecdoche), Milano, Giuffrè.

Monateri, Pier Giuseppe, Sacco, Rodolfo (1998), 'Legal Formants', in *The New Palgrave - A Dictionary of Economics*, London, Macmillan.

Nader, Laura (1967), 'The Anthropological Study of Law', **67** *American Anthropologist*, 3 ff.

North, Douglass C. (1990), *Institutions, Institutional Change and Economic Performance*, Cambridge, Cambridge University Press.

North, Douglass C. (1994), *Istitutuzioni, Cambiamento Istituzionale, Evoluzione dell'Economia* (Institutions, Institutional Change and Economic Performance), Bologna, Il Mulino.

Pejovic, Svetozar (1990), *The Economics of Property Rights: Towards A Theory of Comparative Systems*, Dordrecht, Kluwer.

Pelikan, P. (1987), 'The Formation of Incentive Mechanisms in Different Economic Systems', in Hedlund Stefan (ed.), *Incentives in Economic Systems*, New York, New York University Press.

Pigou, Arthur C. (1960), *The Economics of Welfare*, 4th edn, New York, NY, Macmillan.

Pizzorusso, Alessandro and Capotorti, Francesco (1988), *Law in the Making: A Comparative Survey*, Berlin, Springer.

Polinsky, A. Mitchell (1989), *An Introduction to Law and Economics*, 2nd edn, Boston, MA, Little, Brown.

Posner, Richard (1992), *Economic Analysis of the Law*, 4th edn, Boston, MA, Little, Brown.

Prosser, William Lloyd and Keeton, W. Page (1984), *The Law of Torts*, 5th edn, St Paul, Minn., West.

Rabello, Alfredo Mordechai (ed.) (1994), *European Legal Tradition and Israel*, Jerusalem, Nevo.

Rebuffa, Giorgio (1981), 'Analisi giuridica ed analisi economica (Legal analysis and economic analysis)', in Tarello, Giovanni (1981), *Materiali per una Storia della Cultura Giuridica* (Materials for a History of Legal Culture), Bologna, Il Mulino.

Reyntjens, Filip (1991), 'Note sur l'Utilité d'Introduire un Système Juridique "Pluraliste" dans la Macro-Comparaison des Droits (Note on the Utility of Introducing a "Pluralist" Legal System in the Macro-Comparison of Law)', *Revue du Droit International et Droit Comparé*, 41.

Rouland, Norbert (1988), *Anthropologie Juridique* (Legal Anthropology), Paris, Presses Universitaires de France.

Rudden, Bernard (1994), 'Things as Thing and Things as Wealth', **14** *Oxford Journal of Legal Studies*, 81-97.

Sacco, Rodolfo (1974), 'Les Buts et les Méthodes de la Comparaison du Droit (Aims and Methods of Comparative law)', in X (ed.), *Rapports Nationaux Italiens au IX Congrès de Droit Comparé*, Teheran, Milano, Giuffrè.

Sacco, Rodolfo (1991), 'Legal Formants, A Dynamic Approach to Comparative Law', **39** *American Journal of Comparative Law*, 1-39; 343-401

Sacco, Rodolfo (1992a), 'The Uniformization of Private Law', in Pizzorusso, Alessandro (ed.), *Italian Studies in Law 1*.

Sacco, Rodolfo (1992b), *Introduzione al Diritto Comparato* (Introduction to Comparative Law) Torino, UTET.

Sacco, Rodolfo (1996), *Diritto dei Paesi Africani* (Law of African Countries), Torino: UTET.

Sacco, Rodolfo and Gambaro, Antonio (1996), *Sistemi Giuridici Comparati* (Comparative Legal Systems), Torino, UTET.

Schlesinger, Rudolf B. (1969), *Formation of Contract. A Study into the Common Core of Legal Systems*, Dobbs Ferry, Oceana.

Schlesinger, Rudolf B. et al. (1988), *Comparative Law: Cases, Texts, Materials*, 5th edn, Mineola, Foundation.

Schuck, Peter H. (1991), *Tort Law and the Public Interest*, New York, Norton.

Shapiro, Martin M. (1981), *Courts: A Comparative and Political Analysis,* Chicago, University of Chicago Press.

Simmonds, N.E. (1987), 'Natural Law', in *The New Palgrave - A Dictionary of Economics*, London, Macmillan.

Simon, Herbert (1986), 'Rationality in Psychology and Economics', in Hogarth, R.M. and Reder, M.W. (eds), 'The Behavioral Foundations of Economic Theory', **59** *Journal of Business* (supplement), 209-224.

Simpson, Alfred William Brian (1987), *A History of the Common Law of Contract*, Oxford: Clarendon.

Smith, Adam (1981a), *Lectures on Jurisprudence*, edited by R.L. Mek, D.D. Raphael and P.G. Stein, Indianapolis, Liberty Classics.

Smith, Adam (1981b), *An Inquiry into the Nature and Causes of the Wealth of Nations* edited by R.H. Campbell and A.S. Skinner, Indianapolis, Liberty Classics.

Sonneveldt, Frans and van Mens, Herrie L. (eds) (1992), *The Trust. Bridge or Abyss Between Common Law and Civil Law Jurisdictions?*, Deventer; Boston, Kluwer.

Stein, Daniel L. (1989), *Lectures in the Sciences of Complexity*, Redwood City, CA, Addison Wesley.

Stein, Peter (1984), *Legal Institutions: the Development of Dispute Settlement,* London, Butterworths.

Stein, Peter and Shand, John (1974), *Legal Values in Western Society,* Edinburgh, Edinburgh University Press.

Stigler, George (1987), 'Competition', *The New Palgrave: A Dictionary of Economics,* London, Macmillan.

Sugden, R. (1989), 'Spontaneous Order', **3** *Journal of Economic Perspectives*, 85-98.

Symposium (1993), 'Selecting Minds', **41** *American Journal of Comparative Law*, 351-499.

Symposium (1980), 'Efficiency as Legal Concern', **8** *Hofstra Law Review*, 485-770.

Symposium (1987), 'Economists on the Bench', **50** *Law and Contemporary Problems*, 1-286.

Symposium (1989), 'Post-Chicago Law and Economics', **65** *Chicago-Kent Law Review*, 23-191.

Symposium (1996), 'Law, Economics and Norms', **144** *University of Pennsylvania Law Review*.

Van Caenegem, Raoul Charles (1987), *Judges, Legislators and Professors: Chapters in European Legal History,* Cambridge, Cambridge University Press, 1643-2339.

Vanderlinden, Jacques (1982), 'A Propos des Familles de Droits en Droit Civil Comparé', in X. (ed.), *Hommages á R. Dekkers*, Bruxelles, Bruylant, 363 ff.

Varga, Csaba (1991), *Codification as a Socio-Historical Phenomenon*, Budapest: Akadémiai Kiado.

Vining, Joseph (1984), *Legal Identity: The Coming Age of the Public Law*, New Haven, Yale University Press.

Von Mehren, Arthur Taylor and Gordley, James (1977), *The Civil Law System: An Introduction to the Comparative Study of Law,* 2nd edn, Boston, Little Brown.

Watson, Alan (1978b), 'Comparative Law and Legal Change', **313** *Cambridge Law Journal*, 318 ff.

Watson, Alan (1993), *Legal Transplants: An Approach to Comparative Law,* 2nd edn, Athens, University of Georgia Press.

Watson, Alan (1995), 'From Legal Transplants to Legal Formants', **43** *American Journal of Comparative Law*, 469-476.

White, J.B. (1987), 'Economics and Law: Two Cultures in Tension', **54** *Tennessee Law Review*, 161-202.

Wiegand, Wolfgang (1991), 'Reception of American Law in Europe', **39** *American Journal of Comparative* Law, 229-248.

Williamson, Oliver E. (1991), 'Economic Institutions: Spontaneous and Intentional Governance', **7** *Journal of Law, Economics and Organization*, 159-187.

Zweigert, Konrad and Kötz, Hein (1998), *An Introduction to Comparative Law,* 3rd edn (translated from the German by Weir, Tony), Oxford, Clarendon.

0570
EXPERIMENTAL LAW AND ECONOMICS

Richard H. McAdams
Professor of Law, Boston University School of Law

Abstract

This chapter reviews experimental economics research relevant to law and economics. The introduction includes a brief discussion of experimental methodology and a survey of the categories of economics experiments relevant to law and economics, with citations to other reviews and compilations. The bulk of the chapter reviews two series of economics experiments designed to test theoretical claims of law and economics: those relating to the Coase theorem and those relating to pre-trial bargaining and settlement.
JEL classification: C90, C91, C92
Keywords: Experiment, Methodology, Coase, Bargaining, Settlement

A. Introduction

1. Introduction

The laboratory experiment is a time-honored tool for empirical inquiry. Although some economists have always made use of the technique (see Roth, 1993), historically, most relied on field research. In recent years, however, the pace of economic experimentation has greatly accelerated. 'From the early 1970s the number of papers has grown from two or three per year to numbers approximating 100 per year. The number of researchers has grown from a small handful in the early 1970s to hundreds' (Plott, 1991, p. 901). Economists use experiments, by themselves or in combination with field observation, to test existing theories, investigate puzzling phenomena - sometimes unguided by theory - and to evaluate policies, private or public. (See Roth, 1987b, p. 2; Roth, 1986).

Thus, when Elizabeth Hoffman and Matthew Spitzer first introduced the idea of experimental *law and* economics, they did so by reviewing a substantial portion of the extant experimental literature for its possible application to law (see Hoffman and Spitzer, 1985b); Hoffman, 1985). Today, however, the body of experimental economics is too vast for a short review, yet most of it remains relevant to law and economics. Several books provide useful introductions, including Roth (1987b), Thaler (1992), Davis and Holt (1993), Kagel and Roth

(1995a), and, as does a web site maintained by Roth.

This chapter reviews experimental law and economics in the following order. Section 2 discusses experimental methodology. Section 3 reviews six categories of experimental economics and briefly comments on their relevance to law. The remainder of the article reviews experiments that directly test propositions of law and economics. Section 4 describes the few law and economics experiments concerning individual decision making under conditions of no bargaining. Sections 5-6 discuss law and economics experiments relevant to the Coase Theorem. Sections 7-10 discuss law and economics experiments relevant to pre-trial bargaining and settlement. Section 11 concludes.

2. Experimental Methodology

The essence of a true experiment is random assignment: by randomly placing subjects in groups exposed to different experimental and control conditions, the researcher can control the effect of variables other than the ones he or she seeks to study (see Zeisel, 1973, p. 107). By focusing only on the variables a particular theory makes relevant, experiments have the potential for strong internal validity and provide the most favorable setting for testing a theory. If the theory fails to predict the relationship between variables in a pristine laboratory environment, there are strong grounds to reject it (see Plott, 1991, p. 905; Wilde, 1981, p. 143). Another methodological advantage to experiments is replication. Anomalous findings in the field may be dismissed as measurement error, but unexpected experimental findings often prompt others to repeat the experiment. Replicated 'anomalies' demonstrate the need for revising existing theory.

A constant methodological concern, however, is an experiment's 'parallelism' or 'external validity' - the degree to which the results may be generalized to populations and behavior outside the experiment (see Smith, 1982). The artificiality of the laboratory poses some inherent risk in this regard. Wilde (1981, p. 142) contends, however, that, properly constructed, the experiment creates 'a small-scale microeconomic environment in which real economic agents make real economic decisions'. In other words, in these experiments, the laboratory *contains* a market. 'Since the laboratory economies are real, the general principles and models that exist in the literature should be expected to apply with the same force to these laboratory economies as to those economies found in the field' (Plott, 1991, p. 905). Of course, some differences remain. Laboratory markets are often populated only by students. Moreover, the experimenter's presence and observation may affect these (or any) subjects differently than does the presence or observation of other actors in real world markets.

The idea of creating a market in the laboratory helps to distinguish experimental economics from a similar experimental literature in social and cognitive psychology. Psychological experiments are often quite relevant to economic theory and some experiments in one discipline are inspired by experiments in the other (see Rabin, 1998; Thaler, 1991, 1992). But besides differences in the kind of questions each discipline finds interesting, there is a methodological difference. Psychologists tend to ask their subjects questions. Typically, the psychologist records the answers of subjects exposed to different experimental conditions but rewards them all the same (including sometimes not at all). (See Smith, 1989, pp. 162-167, 1991, pp. 878-887).

By contrast, economic experimenters employ conditions that create different incentives for behavior and then observe how subjects react. Typically, creating market incentives involves differential rewards of subjects, that is, letting the subjects know the size of the payment they receive depends on the outcome of decisions they make in the experiment. These two methods often produce different results as verbal behavior diverges from non-verbal (sometimes called 'actual') behavior. (See Smith, ibid). As Vernon Smith observes, the difference is itself interesting and researchers should address 'the gap between evidence concerning how people think about economic questions and evidence concerning how people behave in experimental markets' (Smith, 1989, p. 163). But a concern with actual behavior (so understood) continues to characterize economic experiments.

For further methodological discussion, see Roth (1988, 1994) and Thaler (1991, pp. 189-195).

3. Categories of Economics Experiments Relevant to Law

The experimental economics literature intersects law and economics at many points. Categorizing the literature is difficult because a series of experiments is typically relevant to a number of economic topics. Combining the comprehensive reviews in Davis and Holt (1993) and Kagel and Roth (1995), I observe six (somewhat overlapping) primary categories of experimental economics research relevant to legal research: (1) individual decision making; (2) collective action (public goods) and coordination problems; (3) bargaining; (4) auctions; (5) industrial organization; and (6) experimental asset markets (asymmetric information).

Individual Decision Making

In one sense, all economic experiments investigate how individuals make decisions, but most of the experiments have the individual interact with others in a market or bargaining situation. A narrower subset of experiments focus on individual choice in relative isolation, usually to study decision making under conditions of risk or uncertainty. These experiments reveal various failures in expected utility theory, cognitive errors and biases. For reviews, see Camerer (1995), Davis and Holt (1993, pp. 435-504); Thaler and Tversky (1992).

The nature of individual decision making is obviously important to legal analysis. Consider two examples. First, Hoffman and Spitzer (1993), survey the extensive economic literature on the difference in willingness to pay and willingness to accept, finding the deviation relevant to the choice between property and liability rules (pp. 104-112). This subject is perhaps the topic of greatest overlap with psychological experiments. For examples, see Korobkin (1998) and Rachlinski and Jourden (1998).

Second, the quality of decision making under risk is relevant to virtually any area of law. Hasen (1990), for example, finds one area of this research - 'framing' effects - relevant to the rules governing products liability and contracts of adhesion. A separate issue is how differences in risk-preferences might affect legal analysis. Block and Gerety (1995) report an experiment showing that students are more risk averse than prisoners. Relative to one another, students were deterred more by increases in the severity of punishment, while prisoners were more sensitive to changes in the certainty. Brinig (1995a, 1995b) reports experimental data on the link between gender and risk aversion and considers how a gender gap in risk preference could be relevant to divorce law.

Collective Action (Public Goods) and Coordination Problems

Economic experiments test the predictions of game theory concerning public goods and coordination problems. The public goods experiments discover more cooperation and less free riding than game theory predicts; the experiments begin to identify the conditions that produce these results. For reviews, see Davis and Holt (1993, pp. 317-80); Ledyard (1995) and Roth (1995a, pp. 26-35). The coordination experiments study adaptive learning and the emergence of equilibria in games with multiple equilibria. For a review, see Ochs (1995).

These results matter greatly to law because state action is often justified by the need to subsidize public goods or to establish efficient equilibria. Conversely, antitrust law is concerned with the conditions under which firms will constrain free riding and cooperate on price and other matters. Similarly, McAdams (1995, pp. 1011-1017) relies on the public goods/collective action problem experiments in predicting the resiliency of cartel-like behavior by racial groups.

Bargaining

Bargaining experiments test how frequently individuals will reach agreement and how frequently the agreement will be efficient. For reviews, see Davis and Holt (1993, pp. 241-275) and Roth (1995b). This subject is the matter at issue in the Coase Theorem and of great relevance when choosing between liability and property rules. See Hoffman and Spitzer (1985, pp. 1009-1013). Bargaining experiments are also relevant to predicting settlement of litigation and selecting default rules in contract.

Auctions
Auction experiments isolate the conditions that facilitate and hinder competitive pricing. For reviews, see Davis and Holt (1993, pp. 125-172, 275-305) and Kagel (1995). Competitive pricing is an obvious concern of antitrust law. In addition, these experiments reveal 'incentive-compatible' means of measuring the demand for public goods - a matter relevant to efficient regulation and taxation (see Hoffman and Spitzer, 1985, pp. 1002-1009, 1015-1020). Auction experiments are also relevant to public contract law, by which the government seeks to structure competitive bidding to obtain competitive prices. See, for example, Ayres and Cramton (1996); Marshall, Meurer and Richard (1991).

Industrial Organization
Experiments in industrial organization reveal how different institutions and industrial structures facilitate competition or collusion, central issues for antitrust and consumer protection law. For reviews, see Davis and Holt (1993, pp. 173-240) and Holt (1995). Experimental markets also reveal the number of informed 'shoppers' and the level of warranty enforcement necessary to ensure competitive pricing, a subject of obvious import for consumer protection law, contracts and antitrust (see Hoffman and Spitzer, 1985b, pp. 1021-1023).

Experimental Asset Markets (Asymmetric Information)
Experimental asset markets test the predictions of the rational expectations model, including the effect that asymmetric information, suspensions in trade, limitations on price changes and method of compensating traders have on the formation of equilibria. For reviews, see Davis and Holt (1993, pp. 381-433) and Sunder (1995). These matters are of obvious concern to the regulation of securities.

4. Law and Economics Experiments: Individual Decision Making

Many law and economics scholars have begun to apply the data from economic (and other) experiments to the economic analysis of law. The applications grow increasingly common. For an illustrative example, see Jolls, Sunstein and Thaler (1998). Law and economics scholars have also contributed directly to this literature by conducting experiments themselves. Two series of law and economics experiments deserve extended attention, which begins in the next section: (1) experiments relating to the Coase Theorem, that is, that concern bargaining around legal entitlements; and (2) experiments relating to pre-trial bargaining and settlement. These bargaining experiments merit review because they were designed to test theoretical propositions of law and economics and because they have reached a critical mass.

One other type of law and economics experiment deserves mention because it tests law and economics propositions but, unfortunately, has *not* reached a critical mass. Lewis Kornhauser's and Andrew Schotter's experiments study individual decision making (rather than bargaining) under different legal rules. In experiments modeling one-person accidents (see Kornhauser and Schotter, 1990), the subjects decided how much to spend to affect the probability of an accident. The subjects made this decision knowing that they would have to compensate for the harm of any accident according to either a negligence or strict liability standard. Kornhauser and Schotter found that the two standards unexpectedly produced different levels of care: strict liability initially produced overprecaution followed by underprecaution, while negligence produced a more optimal level of care. In Kornhauser and Schotter (1992) they modeled two-person accidents, where the care of both subjects affected the probability of an accident, but where subjects chose their care level without bargaining with the other. The results were largely consistent with predictions of tort theory, except that negligence with contributory negligence achieved greater efficiency than a simple negligence rule.

This type of experimental design is obviously important. According to economic theory, where transaction costs prevent bargaining, legal rules will affect individual behavior. Experiments can test whether, in these circumstances, particular legal rules have the predicted effect. Nonetheless, with the exception of Kornhauser and Schotter, law and economics experiments focus exclusively on bargaining behavior, as will the remainder of this article.

B. Experiments Relating to the Coase Theorem

5. When will Bargaining around Legal Entitlements Produce the Efficient Outcome?

5.1 Experiments Relating to the Coase Theorem: Introduction

A number of experiments purport to 'test' the Coase Theorem. Yet even stating the Coase Theorem is a matter of some controversy; there are various interpretations, a few of which seem unfalsifiable. For example, see Donohue (1989), Ellickson (1989) and Lindgren (1990). Thus, rather than discuss whether these experiments 'prove' or 'disprove' the Theorem, I will simply address how their findings relate to certain questions that are widely acknowledged to be important for legal analysis: When will parties bargain around legal entitlements? How often they will reach the efficient outcome by doing so? And given such bargaining, will the allocation of legal entitlements affect the distribution of wealth? The experiments relating to the Coase Theorem begin to answer these questions by identifying (a) the conditions under which bargaining achieves an efficient outcome regardless of legal entitlement and (b) the conditions under which legal entitlements affect the distribution of wealth. Roth (1995b, pp. 292-293) notes that

> most of the evidence [generated by economists] suggests that disagreements and costly delays are pervasive even when it is evident that there are gains to be had from agreement. ... [E]xperimental evidence suggests that disagreements are pervasive even in situations ... that eliminate the most obvious potential sources of incomplete information.

Forsythe, Kennan and Sopher (1991, p. 267), for example, review experiments resulting in a substantial range of inefficient outcomes. But most of this evidence arises from experiments where the bargaining is anonymous; researchers have often sought to exclude 'volatile' social influences in order to test certain baseline predictions of game theory see (Roth, 1995b, p. 303). For legal analysis, however, the bargaining of interest is usually face-to-face. We cannot assume that anonymous and public bargaining produce the same level of efficient agreement. Indeed, Radner and Schotter (1989) and Roth (1995b, pp. 296-298) find that face-to-face bargaining produces greater efficiency. Against this background, law and economics scholars have sought to determine how frequently parties will, through face-to-face bargaining, reach an efficient outcome, even when that outcome requires one party to 'sell' its legal entitlement.

5.2 Hoffman and Spitzer

In this regard, Elizabeth Hoffman and Matthew Spitzer have conducted a series of experiments that are perhaps the best known in law and economics. The series is based on a design introduced in the initial article (see Hoffman and Spitzer, 1982). First, two subjects (students) were designated as A or B and one of them was selected - by coin flip - to be the 'controller'. The controller was granted the power to select a number from a chart that indicated the number of dollars that A and B would then receive. For example, in one experimental condition, the payoff schedule was as follows (p. 86):

Number	A's Payoff ($)	B's Payoff ($)
0	0.00	12.00
1	4.00	10.00

Number	A's Payoff ($)	B's Payoff ($)
2	6.00	6.00
3	8.00	4.00
4	9.00	2.00
5	10.00	1.00
6	11.00	0.00

Note that, without the *possibility* of bargaining, the conventional prediction is that A would choose number 6 and B would choose number 0. But Hoffman and Spitzer explicitly provided for bargaining. Subjects A and B were placed in a room together, each was given the entire payoff schedule, and the instructions informed them that the non-controller 'may attempt to influence the controller to reach a mutually acceptable joint decision' and 'may offer to pay part of all of his or her earnings to the controller' (p. 83). In addition, Hoffman and Spitzer provided in the instructions an 'agreement form' and indicated that, if the parties used the form to reallocate part of one party's payoff to the other party, the experimenters would pay the subjects according to their agreement (p. 84). With the possibility of bargaining, the prediction is that, regardless of who the controller is, A and B will agree to choose and split the largest joint payoff, number 1.

In this experimental condition, Hoffman and Spitzer (1982, p. 92) found that nearly all (23 of 24) of the pairs did bargain to the point of their highest joint return. They did not actually demonstrate that the bargaining *produced* these optimal outcomes because they did not include a control in which bargaining was not permitted. Harrison and McKee (1985), however, provide exactly such a test using a very similar design except without permitting side payments. In none of twelve such decisions did the parties choose the joint profit maximum (p. 664). By contrast, and confirming Hoffman and Spitzer, Harrison and McKee (p. 664) found that when side payments were permitted, the overwhelming majority of pairs agreed on the optimal outcome. With a controller rule like Hoffman and Spitzer's, 88 percent (15 of 17) reached that outcome; with a joint controller rule where the parties risked a poor outcome if they failed to agree, they reached the optimal result in 97 percent of the decisions (33 of 34). Thus, there is experimental support for the proposition that, under certain conditions, face-to-face bargaining can induce nearly all parties to reach an optimal outcome they would otherwise not achieve.

Hoffman and Spitzer's (1982) initial experiment contained several other conditions, each of which presented a less favorable or at least different setting for bargaining. Their subsequent experiments also introduced new features designed to make bargaining more difficult. In most cases, the parties still bargained to the optimal joint outcome.

For example, in one condition of the initial experiment, they provided each party with incomplete information: subjects were shown the schedule for their own payoffs only, though they were allowed to share information during bargaining. Hoffman and Spitzer (1982, p. 92) found that nearly all (19 of 20) of the pairs still bargained to reach their highest joint return. In addition, over 90 percent (27 of 29) of 3-person groups with full information reached the jointly optimal outcome. With limited information, 3-person groups with one controller almost always (19 or 21) agreed to the jointly optimal outcome. But limited information did impede such agreements when Hoffman and Spitzer created a more complex 3-person arrangement with limited information and *two* 'joint controllers' - in which the lowest number selected by either controller would dictate the monetary payoffs. These groups agreed on the optimal outcome in only 60 percent of the cases (9 of 15).

In a later experiment, Hoffman and Spitzer (1985a) manipulated the mechanism of determining which subject was the 'controller'. They used a simple coin flip (the original means) and a game in which the winner was controller, each with and without a statement that the winner had thereby 'earned' the right to be controller. The subjects still made the optimal agreement over 90 percent of the time (p. 275). Hoffman and Spitzer (1986) used the basic design for groups of three, four, ten, and twenty, with full or limited information and single or joint controllers, making single or sequential decisions. The prior result held: of 445 experimental decisions, '93 percent . . . chose the profit-maximizing outcome; 98 percent of the ten- and twenty-subject decisions chose it. Efficiency [was] somewhat lower (91 percent) with limited than with full information (94 percent), but - critically - it is at least 90 percent for all but a few experimental treatments' (p. 156). Hoffman and Spitzer concluded that their data justifies a presumption in favor of the Coase Theorem - by which they mean that parties will bargain around legal entitlements to reach efficient outcomes - in 'a substantial class of disputes' such as neighborhood nuisances involving dog kennels or funeral parlors (p. 162).

5.3 Other Experiments on Coasean Bargaining and Efficiency

Coursey, Hoffman and Spitzer (1987) introduced a new complication by having the subjects bargain over more than monetary payments. To introduce an item that could affect the 'dignity' of a subject, they made part of the 'payoff' that subject A, but not B, might have to hold in his or her mouth for 20 seconds an ounce of a 'very bitter-tasting and unpleasant substance,' sucrose octa-acetate

(SOA) (p. 223). The payoff sheet provided (p. 248):

Number	A's Payoff ($)	A Tastes?	B's Payoff ($)
1	10	No	0
2	10	Yes	20

Coursey et al. (1987) believed that number 2 was the joint-profit-maximizing outcome (p. 225) because a separate bidding experiment had shown that the average value placed on avoiding the required taste of SOA was $4. Even if this result were rejected in favor of survey data, the absolute maximum value for avoiding the taste is $15 (p. 223). Coursey et al. (1987) described the taste of SOA to all subjects but manipulated information according to who was allowed to sample the SOA prior to bargaining: A and B, A only, B only, or neither. In the end, none of the variations affected the success of bargaining to reach the optimal outcome: when B was the controller, he or she selected number 2 in every case (22 of 22); when A was the controller, he or she selected number 2 almost 90 percent of the time (16 of 18) (1987) (p. 227). Thus, Coursey et al. (1987), conclude that even when parties in the real world face physically unpleasant externalities like loud noises or foul odors, their data suggests that parties are very likely to bargain to the optimal result regardless of legal entitlements.

Schwab (1988) obtained somewhat contrary results using a very different experimental design. Schwab created a bargaining scenario for students in a labor law course and an industrial and labor relations course. Subjects were not paid but their performance was a factor in their grade. Schwab provided the subjects with a preference sheet allocating points for bargaining outcomes along four dimensions: hourly wage, number of vacation days, noise reduction, and the right of the firm to transfer work to its nonunion plant during the contract term (the 'relocation clause'). Subjects were only told their own preferences; they were permitted to reveal their preferences orally but forbidden from disclosing their preference sheet. The point allocations for each side left room for substantial cooperative gains.

Schwab distinguishes two issues I have been discussing together: whether the contracts achieved all possible cooperative gains and whether a legal entitlement affected the amount of cooperative gains achieved. As to the first, he rejects what he terms the 'strong efficiency hypothesis' because only '20 percent of the contracts were fully efficient' (p. 251). Of 108 contracts, all included the efficient noise reduction clause and all but three contracts included a wage that fell within the cooperative range (p. 251 n.38). But only 31 percent (33) required a sufficient number of vacation days to exhaust the potential cooperative gain and only 65 percent (70) included the efficient relocation clause. Nonetheless, Schwab confirms what he terms the 'weak efficiency hypothesis'. For the relocation term, Schwab had created varying contract presumptions, specifying that, unless otherwise agreed, the company either could or could not relocate. Regardless of condition, there was no statistically significant difference in the number of contracts requiring the company to stay or in the number of contracts reaching the optimal result for this issue, which varied across contracts within each condition (p. 252). Thus, the parties achieved roughly the same less-than-perfect level of efficiency regardless of how the legal entitlement was allocated.

Because there are many differences between Schwab's experiment and the Hoffman and Spitzer design, it is not possible, without additional work, to specify which conditions produced the different rates of efficient contracts. Perhaps Schwab's results apply to complex bargaining over a set of issues while the earlier experiments are valid for bargaining over an single issue. Or, possibly, Schwab failed to induce the subjects to put forth enough effort because he did not pay them for their efforts. Perhaps, however, the Hoffman and Spitzer design is flawed because it remains abstracted from actual legal entitlements: (i) the 'controller' subjects are never told that the *law* gives them the right to select the control number, and (ii) the non-controller subject is never told that he or she suffers from an externality *caused* (in part) by the controller. If these omissions are important, Schwab's experiment may have elicited typical emotional reactions that impede bargaining, while Hoffman and Spitzer's design did not. To use one of Hoffman and Spitzer's examples, it would be interesting to employ their design, but to inform the subjects that, for purposes of the experiment, they should assume that one of them owns a noisy, smelly dog kennel and the other owns a nearby residence, and that the law entitles one of them to select unilaterally the level of kennel operations.

Admittedly, Hoffman and Spitzer found similar results (concerning efficiency) when subjects were told one of them 'earned' the right to be controller by defeating the other subject in a simple game. But perhaps parties bargain differently if they are told - as Schwab's subjects were - that the source of their entitlements is legal. Hoffman and Spitzer also used SOA to test whether subjects would bargain over matters affecting their dignity. But the abstract experimental design does not make it appear that one subject (rather than the experimenter) is *causing* or threatening to cause the other to taste SOA. Providing a real world factual scenario - where a kennel owner causes the neighbor to smell something unpleasant - might invoke a different or stronger set of emotions and impede bargaining.

Of course, Schwab's results confirm Hoffman and Spitzer on the claim that legal entitlements will not affect the degree to which people bargain to the efficient result. But the experiments do not yet justify Hoffman and Spitzer's claim for a factual presumption that parties will bargain around legal entitlements. What their experiments appear to demonstrate is that, if potential bargainers are (i) enticed by money or grades to meet together in a room and (ii) invited to bargain, then the initial assignment of entitlements will not affect the percentage of efficient agreements they create. Hoffman and Spitzer generalize from this data to predict how people in the real world will react to externalities. Yet many individuals may never consider offering to sell or buy a legal entitlement that is not explicitly a market good. The neighbor of the dog kennel may not - without the kind of prompting provided in the experiment - consider offering the kennel owner money to limit the noise or smell of his operations. In addition, when individuals are interested in bargaining - and especially when large groups are involved - a crucial barrier may be the cost of gathering the parties together at a single place and time. Indeed, one strategy of hard bargaining is to pretend to be uninterested in even meeting with the other side. However compelling the experiments are for demonstrating what happens after parties meet for the purpose of bargaining, they do not provide evidence that parties in the real world will get that far.

In sum, even though this area is one of the richest for experimental work, these experiments only begin to identify the conditions under which face-to-face bargaining will achieve an efficient outcome.

6. When will Legal Entitlements Affect Wealth Distribution?

6.1 Coasean Bargaining and the Distribution of Wealth

If individuals will bargain around legal entitlements, the law may not affect allocative efficiency. But law may still affect the distribution if legal entitlements work to enrich those who can sell them. On this score, the first Hoffman and Spitzer study found a surprising result. Hoffman and Spitzer (1982, pp. 92-95) found that significant numbers of controllers 'shared' the maximum payoff equally or nearly equally. The standard prediction would be that a controller would demand at least his individual maxima - what he could get without cooperation. But more controllers evenly split the payoff than received at least their individual maxima. Over half of the 114 bargains resulted in a division within one dollar of an even split. Thus, subjects did not exploit the potential monetary gain from being the controller. This finding suggests that the entitlement affects wealth less than is expected.

Subsequent experiments retested this result. Hoffman and Spitzer (1985a) proposed that the arbitrary means of selecting the controller - a coin flip - caused many subjects to believe that the 'fair' distribution was an even split. Thus, they reran the experiment using four different means of selecting a controller: (1) Some subjects played a game and the winner was controller; researchers told the subjects the winner had 'earned' that right. (2) Some controllers were selected by a coin flip and told that the winner 'earned' the right. The remaining controllers were selected by winning (3) the game or (4) a coin flip, but with no statement. In the latter two conditions, with no 'moral authority' statement, 61 percent of the bargains resulted in nearly even splits (p. 275). Conversely, in the first condition, with the game plus 'moral authority,' only 32 percent were nearly even splits. The second condition fell in between: 50 percent nearly even splits (p. 277). Further analysis revealed that the 'moral authority' statement significantly affected the allocation; the method of selection was also weakly significant (p. 280).

Hoffman and Spitzer speculate about the significance of these interesting findings. But they do not acknowledge the potential limitation the results have for the design of their experiment: fairness might be a restraint on bargaining. If individuals react strongly to the perceived fairness of the situation - if they are willing to sacrifice money in order to achieve a fair outcome - then they might refuse to consent to a bargain that produced an unfair result, even if it constituted the joint maximum payoff. Perhaps an individual would think it 'unfair' for a polluter to benefit by being paid to refrain from exercising its legal entitlement to pollute. As stated above, one cannot confidently predict that parties will bargain around legal entitlements in the real world unless the experiment has attempted to elicit all the responses - including, potentially, fairness concerns - that might inhibit bargaining. Yet the Hoffman and Spitzer design, though it elicits such fairness concerns in the distribution of the payoff, seems too abstract to test fairness as a constraint on bargaining. For a more general discussion of fairness in experiments, see Roth (1995b, pp. 270-274, 279-281).

Perhaps the concern is overstated. In the similar experiment by Harrison and McKee (1985), researchers used a coin flip to select the controller, but their experiment provided different explanations for the payoff sharing in these experiments. First, they found that altruistic payoff divisions declined as the stakes increased (p. 662). Increasing the available surplus from $1 to $2 decreased such divisions from 60 percent (9 of 15) to 11 percent (1 of 9). Second, 'learning' decreased altruistic payoff divisions (p. 665). Harrison and McKee created a condition involving 'joint property rights', where both parties must agree to the number or they receive either a random payoff or a payoff of zero. When subjects 'trained' under this condition were then given the power of a unilateral controller, they received at least their individual maxima payoff in 76.5 percent (13 of 17) of the bargains.

With these manipulations, the legal entitlements *did* affect the distribution of wealth, almost as much as theory predicts. But there is one situation where economic theory does not expect an entitlement to affect distribution: where it merely states a presumption. Nonetheless, Schwab (1988) found that a waivable contractual presumption did affect distribution. In his collective bargaining experiment, Schwab specified in one condition that, unless otherwise agreed, the company could relocate; in the other condition, the presumption was against relocation. The subjects often bargained around this presumption when it was efficient to do so. But union negotiators obtained significantly better overall contracts when the presumption favored them, while management did significantly worse. '[B]argainers ... acted as if they must purchase the right when the legal presumption favored the other party and thus were in a weaker bargaining position' (p. 255).

In sum, the experimental results are difficult to explain. Though legal entitlements can be made to affect distribution in the anticipated direction, there remain some instances where they have far less effect than expected. And a mere contractual presumption unexpectedly appears to affect the distribution of wealth.

C. Experiments Relating to Pre-Trial Bargaining and Settlement

7. Pre-Trial Bargaining and Settlement: Introduction

Law and economics scholars have also used experiments to investigate pre-trial bargaining and settlement. Along with empirical studies of litigation, the accumulated evidence is beginning to have some effect on the theoretical models describing the decision to proceed to trial. Settlement models are also affected by psychology experiments on the subject. For example, see Korobkin and Guthrie (1997).

As a preliminary matter, note that the Coase Theorem experiments reviewed above (and bargaining experiments generally) are relevant to the settlement of litigation. Both involve bargaining with potential cooperative surplus. The Hoffman and Spitzer design is sufficiently abstract to encompass litigation settlement, if one imagines the controller - whether A or B - as a plaintiff who can, by going to trial, obtain a judgment equal to the maximum payoff available to him or her on the payoff schedule. The joint maximum represents the settlement alternative, larger than any non-cooperative outcome because it avoids the costs of trial. If so, the results are encouraging because litigation is a context in which parties, or their agents, usually contemplate a bargaining solution. Nonetheless, the limitations of the Coase Theorem experiments are significant, most notably because they do not model the risks involved in the outcome of litigation.

8. Coursey and Stanley

Settlement experiments focus on bargaining under conditions of risk. Don Coursey and Linda Stanley tested economic predictions about settlements rates under different rules for assessing litigation costs: (1) the American rule, where each party bears it own costs; (2) the British rule, where the loser pays both sides' costs; and (3) a modified version of Rule 68 of the Federal Rules of Civil Procedure where a plaintiff pays both sides' costs if he or she does no better at trial than the defendant's final settlement offer and otherwise each side pays his or her own costs (see Coursey and Stanley, 1988). Coursey and Stanley had pairs of subjects (students) anonymously bargain to divide 100 tokens, each to be redeemed at the end of the experiment. Absent agreement, a random draw provided a number representing the trial outcome according to a probability distribution the subjects were given. Trial costs were represented by 40 tokens which were taken from one or both subjects according to one of the three cost rules being tested. Coursey and Stanley found that the modified Rule 68 and the British rule produced more settlements than the American Rule. In addition, settlements under the modified Rule 68 were more favorable to the defendant than settlements under the American Rule, while the British rule settlements favored the defendant more than the American rule only when the probability of plaintiff success was less than 50 percent (pp. 174-175).

In a subsequent experiment using a similar design, Stanley and Coursey (1990) tested certain implications of the 'Priest-Klein hypothesis'. George Priest and Benjamin Klein attempt to explain why litigants sometimes fail to settle even though proceeding to trial imposes significant costs on each (given the American rule) (see Priest and Klein, 1984; Priest, 1985). They propose that each side, using imperfect information, estimates the value of the case with error. When the plaintiff overestimates and/or the defendant underestimates the trial result, there is no settlement range and the parties proceed to trial. If so, as parties gain more information about the suit, their error range should decline, and so should the probability of trial. Stanley and Coursey (1990) confirmed this result. They had the color of a chip randomly drawn from an urn determine the 'trial outcome'. When they permitted the subjects to sample larger numbers of chips from that urn, to determine more accurately the likely trial outcome, the settlement rate increased. The Priest-Klein model also implies that the settlement rate would increase as the cost of trial increased, thereby creating greater benefits to avoiding trial. Yet Stanley and Coursey failed to find support for this prediction.

9. Loewenstein and Babcock

Another study provides a possible explanation for this latter finding. Loewenstein et al. (1993) created a highly realistic settlement scenario. They provided subjects (all students) with 27 pages of testimony from an actual accident case. They assigned pairs to the roles of plaintiff and defendant and provided a half-hour for them to bargain over a settlement. Besides the fixed fee paid to each subject, the experimenters provided the defendant \$10 and explained that defendant would have to pay \$1 of that amount for every \$10,000 the plaintiff was awarded in settlement or by trial. The subjects were told the trial award was based on the valuation provided for the experiment by a judge; they were not told the amount, which was \$30,560. If the parties failed to reach agreement, the plaintiff was awarded this amount; the parties also had to pay litigation costs, which were specified in advance but varied across subjects. Before negotiations began, however, the subjects wrote down their estimate of what the judge would award and what would be 'fair'. They were informed that these estimates would not be shown to the other side.

Loewenstein et al., confirm the unexpected finding of Stanley and Coursey: differing levels and distributions of litigation costs did not significantly affect the frequency of settlement (pp. 149-150; 152). The focus of Loewenstein et al., however, was the relevance of two other factors to settlement. (1) Psychology evidence suggests that an 'egocentric' or self-serving bias causes individuals to interpret facts in ways that further their interests or self-image. (2) Economic evidence suggests that individuals are motivated, in part, by a concern for fairness. The first point suggests that the estimation errors regarding the outcome of a trial are *not* - as the Priest-Klein model suggests - random, but that each side tends to overestimate its chances of prevailing. The second point suggests that parties will be less influenced by factors not relevant to assessing fairness. Finally, given bias, a party is likely to view as 'fair' an outcome relatively favorable to his or her interests.

The results confirm the importance of these factors. First, even though the parties had (and knew they had) identical information about the suit, Loewenstein et al., found that their estimates for the case were significantly different: 'Plaintiffs' predictions of the judge's award, on average, were \$14,527 higher than defendants'. Mean plaintiffs' fair-settlement values were \$17,709 higher than defendants'' (p. 150). These differences disconfirm the Priest-Klein assumption that errors are randomly distributed. Second, the difference in fairness assessments were slightly better predictors of settlement than the difference in the predictions of the judge's award (pp. 152-153). This finding supports the importance of perceived fairness to settlement and may explain why litigation costs were surprisingly unimportant: because individuals based their assessments of fairness only on the merits of the case (p. 154).

A similar study by the same authors, Babcock et al. (1995), provides striking confirmation of the effect of egocentric bias on settlement. The researchers had the subjects (graduate students in business, law and public policy) bargain over settlement as above, but manipulated the order in which subjects read the case material and received their assigned role. When the roles of plaintiff and defendant were assigned after the subjects read the case materials, they settled 94 percent of the time. When the roles were assigned *before* the subjects read the materials, the settlement rate fell to 72 percent, a highly significant difference (p. 1339). The parties differed in their assessments of the fair settlement and their predictions of the judge's award, only when they were assigned their roles before reading the case material (p. 1340). Thus, parties appear to interpret information egoistically when they have a stake in the subject matter of the information at the time they receive it. The mutual bias decreases settlement. The authors suggest, contrary to most analyses, that increasing the information each side has about the dispute may therefore *decrease* the probability of settlement (p. 1342).

More generally, the importance of these studies is to suggest that simpler experiments, like that of Coursey and Stanley (1988), may fail to capture some important dynamics of settlement by abstracting away from the complexities of a lawsuit. The simple bargaining game Coursey and Stanley use is, in their words, 'devoid of any similarities to real world legal processes' (p. 167). Yet a fair test of the egocentric bias hypothesis may require a realistically complex set of facts to permit different parties to reach different conclusions about the expected outcome. And a fair test of the fairness hypothesis may require a set of facts that, for many subjects, raise fairness concerns. Of course, complexity imposes costs of its own. The point is not that we cannot learn further from simple experiments testing how very narrow factors affect settlement, but that we cannot fully generalize the results of such experiments until after the findings are confirmed in more realistic settings.

10. Other Experiments on Pre-Trial Bargaining and Settlement

More recent studies continue to use very simple bargaining games to study pre-trial negotiation and settlement. Thomas (1995) created a settlement game with monetary payoffs. He gave the subjects (students) an estimate of the expected outcome of trial along with a range of error uniformly distributed around the estimate. He found support for the Priest-Klein claim that 'disputes close to the decision standard' - meaning where the defendant's conduct is just above or below the level at which liability is imposed - 'go to trial at a higher rate than do other disputes'. He could not confirm a second claim, however, that the 'improvements in the ability of parties to evaluate information increase the settlement rate', though the coefficient for error had the expected sign (p. 219).

Croson and Mnookin (1997) conducted an experiment to test the claim of Gilson and Mnookin (1994) that parties to a lawsuit can achieve gains by employing lawyers as agents. The claim is that lawyers develop reputations for conducting litigation either in a highly contentious and costly manner - as 'gladiators' - or a cooperative mode - as 'cooperators'. If parties who do not trust each other choose cooperative agents, they may lower the joint costs of conducting the litigation. To test the idea, Croson and Mnookin ran modified prisoners' dilemma games in which subjects (law students) chose one or the other type of lawyer (or a third type without a reputation) to represent them for 10 rounds. In the 'litigation game', the dominant strategy was to select a gladiator, which most subjects did. But in the 'prelitigation game', a subject could change his or her lawyer if, but only if, he or she had selected a cooperator for the prior round but the opponent had selected a gladiator. For this game, there are two Nash equilibria - two cooperators or two defectors. The result was that 76 percent of subjects employed cooperators in the prelitigation game as opposed to 17.5 percent in the litigation game (p. 341). Generalizing the result is difficult, however, since litigants in the real world are able to switch *from*, as well as to, gladiators.

In sum, the experiments on litigation settlement are not yet sufficiently plentiful to allow strong generalizations. As with experiments on Coasean bargaining, there is some indication - not yet proved or disproved - that the process of negotiation may be affected by the factual nature of what is being negotiated.

D. Conclusion

Experimentation is still relatively new to economics and even more novel for law and economics. Kagel and Roth (1995) and Davis and Holt (1993) comprehensively review the experimental economics literature, virtually all of which is relevant to law. Two series of bargaining experiments directly test claims of law and economics theory: experiments related to the Coase theorem and to pre-trial settlement. Both are still fairly undeveloped, leaving open a great need for further work merely to resolve the different results of existing experiments. Such work could be very fruitful as experimentation remains a powerful tool for testing and refining theory.

Acknowledgments

A number of people assisted me by commenting on an earlier draft or discussing the experimental economics literature, or both. I thank Rachel Croson, Lewis Kornhauser, Jim Lindgren, Anna Marshall, Stewart Schwab, and an anonymous referee.

Bibliography on Experimental Law and Economics (0570)

Ashenfelter, Orley, Currie, Janet, Farber, Henry S. and Spiegel, Matthew (1992), 'An Experimental Comparison of Dispute Rates in Alternative Arbitration Systems', **60** *Econometrica*, 1407-1433.

Babcock, Linda, Loewenstein, George, Issacharoff, Samuel and Camerer, Colin F. (1995), 'Biased Judgments of Fairness in Bargaining', **85** *American Economic Review*, 1337 ff.

Block, Michael K. and Gerety, Vernon E. (1995), 'Some Experimental Evidence on Differences between Student and Prisoner Reactions to Monetary Penalties and Risk', **24** *Journal of Legal Studies*, 123-138.

Brinig, Margaret F. (1995a), 'Does Mediation Systematically Disadvantage Women?', **2** *William and Mary Journal of Women and the Law*, 1-34.

Brinig, Margaret F. (1995b), 'Why Can't a Woman be More Like a Man? or Do Gender Differences Affect Choice?', in Simon, Rita J. (ed.), *Neither Victim nor Enemy*, Lanham, MD, University Press of America, 29-59.

Camerer, Colin (1995), 'Individual Decision Making', in Kagel, John H. and Roth, Alvin E. (eds), *The Handbook of Experimental Economics*, Princeton, Princeton University Press, 587-703.

Coursey, Don L. and Stanley, Linda R. (1988), 'Pretrial Bargaining Behavior within the Shadow of the Law: Theory and Experimental Evidence', **8** *International Review of Law and Economics*, 161-179.

Coursey, Don L., Hoffman, Elizabeth and Spitzer, Matthew L. (1987), 'Fear and Loathing in the Coase Theorem: Experimental Tests Involving Physical Discomfort', **16** *Journal of Legal Studies*, 217-248.

Coursey, Don L., Isaac, R. Mark and Smith, Vernon L. (1984), 'Natural Monopoly and Contested Markets: Some Experimental Results', **27** *Journal of Law and Economics*, 91-113.

Crafton, Steven M. and Brinig, Margaret F. (1994), *Quantitative Methods for Lawyers*, Durham, NC, Carolina Academic Press.

Croson, Rachel and Mnookin, Robert H. (1997), 'Does Disputing Through Agents Enhance Cooperation? Experimental Evidence', **26** *Journal of Legal Studies*, 331-345.

Davis, Douglas and Holt, Charles A. (1993), *Experimental Economics*, Princeton, Princeton University Press.

Dutta, Shantanu and John, George (1995), 'Combining Lab Experiments and Industry Data in Transaction Cost Analysis: The Case of Competition as a Safeguard', **11** *Journal of Law, Economics and Organization*, 87-111.

Forsythe, Robert, Kennan, John and Sopher, Barry (1991), 'An Experimental Analysis of Bargaining and Strikes with One-sided Private Information', **81** *American Economic

Review, 253-278.

Gay, David E.R. (1992), 'Teaching Privatization in the Soviet Union: An Experimental Economics Approach', **1** *Classroom Expernomics*, 5-6.

Harrison, Glenn W. and McKee, Michael (1985), 'Experimental Evaluation of the Coase Theorem', **28** *Journal of Law and Economics*, 653-670.

Harrison, Glenn W., Hoffman, Elizabeth, Rustrom, E.E. and Spitzer, Matthew L. (1987), 'Coasian Solutions to the Externality Problem in Experimental Markets', **97** *Economic Journal*, 388-402.

Hoffman, Elizabeth (1985), 'Bibliography of Work on Experimental Economicsa', **85** *Columbia Law Review*, 1025-1035.

Hoffman, Elizabeth and Spitzer, Matthew L. (1982), 'The Coase Theorem: Some Experimental Tests', **25** *Journal of Law and Economics*, 73-98.

Hoffman, Elizabeth and Spitzer, Matthew L. (1985a), 'Entitlements, Rights, and Fairness: An Experimental Examination of Subjects' Concepts of Distributive Justice', **14** *Journal of Legal Studies*, 259-297.

Hoffman, Elizabeth and Spitzer, Matthew L. (1985b), 'Experimental Law and Economics: An Introduction', **85** *Columbia Law Review*, 991-1024.

Hoffman, Elizabeth and Spitzer, Matthew L. (1986), 'Experimental Tests of the Coase Theorem with Large Bargaining Groups', **15** *Journal of Legal Studies*, 149-171.

Hoffman, Elizabeth and Spitzer, Matthew L. (1993), 'Willingness to Pay vs. Willingness to Accept: Legal and Economic Implications', **71** *Washington University Law Quarterly*, 59-114.

Hoffman, E., McCabe, Kevin A., Shachat, K. and Smith, V.K. (1994), 'Preferences, Property Rights and Anonymity in Bargaining Games', **7** *Games and Economic Behavior*, 346-380.

Holt, Charles A. (1989), 'The Exercise of Market Power in Laboratory Experiments', **32S** *Journal of Law and Economics*, 107-130.

Holt, Charles A. (1995), 'Industrial Organizations: A Survey of Laboratory Research', in Kagel, John H. and Roth, Alvin E. (eds), *The Handbook of Experimental Economics*, Princeton, Princeton University Press, 349-444.

Kagel, John H. (1995), 'Auctions: A Survey of Experimental Research', in Kagel, John H. and Roth, Alvin E. (eds), *The Handbook of Experimental Economics*, Princeton, Princeton University Press, 501-586.

Kagel, John H. and Roth, Alvin E. (eds) (1995), *Handbook of Experimental Economics*, Princeton, Princeton University Press.

Kelman, Mark G. (1985), 'Comment on Hoffman and Spitzer's Experimental Law and Economics', **85** *Columbia Law Review*, 1037-1047.

Kornhauser, Lewis A. and Schotter, Andrew (1990), 'An Experimental Study of Single-Actor Accidents', **19** *Journal of Legal Studies*, 203-233.

Kornhauser, Lewis A. and Schotter, Andrew (1992), *An Experimental Study of Two-Actor Accidents*, C.V. Starr Center for Applied Economics, Research Report, No. 92-57.

Ledyard, John O. (1995), 'Public Goods: A Survey of Experimental Research', in Kagel, John H. and Roth, Alvin E. (eds), *The Handbook of Experimental Economics*, Princeton, Princeton University Press, 111-194.

Loewenstein, George, Issacharoff, Samuel, Camerer, Colin and Babcock, Linda (1993), 'Self-Serving Assessments of Fairness and Pretrial Bargaining', **22** *Journal of Legal Studies*, 135-159.

McCabe, Kevin A., Rassenti, Stephen J. and Smith, Vernon L. (1991), 'Experimental Research on Deregulated Markets for Natural Gas Pipeline and Electric Power Transmission Networks', **13** *Research in Law and Economics*, 161-189.

Ochs, Jack (1995), 'Coordination Problems', in Kagel, John H. and Roth, Alvin E. (eds), *The Handbook of Experimental Economics*, Princeton, Princeton University Press, 195-251.

Plott, Charles R. (1991), 'Will Economics Become an Experimental Science?', **57** *Southern Economic Journal*, 901-919.

Rabin, Matthew (1998), 'Psychology and Economics', **36** *Journal of Economic Literature*, 11-46.

Radner, Roy and Schotter, Andrew (1989), 'The Sealed Bid Mechanisms: An Experimental Study', **48** *Journal of Economic Theory*, 179-220.

Roth, Alvin E. (web), *Web Page on Game Theory and Experimental Economics*, at http://www.pitt.edu:81/~alroth.html.

Roth, Alvin E. (1986), 'Laboratory Experimentation in Economics', **2** *Economics and Philosophy*, 245-273.

Roth, Alvin E. (1987a), 'Introduction and Overview', in Roth, Alvin E. (ed.), *Laboratory Experimentation in Economics: Six Points of View*, Cambridge, Cambridge University Press, 1-13.

Roth, Alvin E. (ed.) (1987b), *Laboratory Experimentation in Economics: Six Points of View*, Cambridge, Cambridge University Press.

Roth, Alvin E. (1988), 'Laboratory Experimentation in Economics: A Methodological Overview', **89** *Economics Journal*, 974 ff.

Roth, Alvin E. (1993), 'The Early History of Experimental Economics', **15** *Journal of the History of Economic Thought*, 184-209.

Roth, Alvin E. (1994), 'Let's Keep the Con Out of Experimental Econ.: A Methodological Note', **19S** *Empirical Economics*, 279-289.

Roth, Alvin E. (1995a), 'Introduction to Experimental Economics', in Kagel, John H. and Roth, Alvin E. (eds), *The Handbook of Experimental Economics*, Princeton, Princeton University Press, 3-109.

Roth, Alvin E. (1995b), 'Bargaining Experiments', in Kagel, John H. and Roth, Alvin E. (eds), *The Handbook of Experimental Economics*, Princeton, Princeton University Press, 253-348.

Schwab, Stewart (1988), 'A Coasean Experiment on Contract Presumptions', **17** *Journal of Legal Studies*, 237-268.

Shelanski, H. and Klein, Peter G. (1995), 'Empirical Research in Transaction Cost Economics: A Review and Assessment', **11** *Journal of Law, Economics, and Organization* in Frech, H.E. (ed.), *Regulating Doctors' Fees: Competition, Benefits, and Controls under Medicare*, Washington, DC, American Enterprise Institute, 335 ff.

Shogren, Jason F. (1992), 'An Experiment on Coasian Bargaining Over Ex Ante Lotteries and Ex Post Rewards', **17S** *Journal of Economic Behavior and Organization*, 153-169.

Smith, Vernon (1982), 'Microeconomic Systems as an Experimental Science', **72** *American Economic Review*, 923 ff.

Smith, Vernon (1989), 'Theory, Experiment and Economics', **3** *Journal of Economic Perspectives*, 151-169.

Smith, Vernon (1991), 'Rational Choice: The Contrast between Economics and Psychology', **99** *Journal of Political Economy*, 877-897.

Stake, Jeffrey E. (1995), 'Loss Aversion and Involuntary Transfers of Title', in Malloy, Robin P. and Braun, Christopher K. (eds), *Law and Economics: New and Critical Perspectives*, New York, Peter Lang, 331-360.

Stanley, Linda R. and Coursey, Don L. (1990), 'Empirical Evidence on the Selection Hypothesis and the Decision to Litigate or Settle', **19** *Journal of Legal Studies*, 145 ff.

Sunder, Shyam (1995), 'Experimental Asset Markets: A Survey', in Kagel, John H. and Roth, Alvin E. (eds), *The Handbook of Experimental Economics*, Princeton, Princeton University Press, 445-500.

Thaler, Richard H. (1991), *Quasi Rational Economics*, New York, Russel Sage Foundation.

Thaler, Richard H. (1992), *The Winner's Curse: Paradoxes and Anomalies of Economic Life*, Princeton, Princeton University Press.

Thaler, Richard H. and Tversky, Amos (1992), 'Preference Reversals', in Thaler, Richard, *The Winner's Curse: Paradoxes and Anomalies of Economic Life*, Princeton, Princeton University Press, 79-91.

Thomas, Robert E. (1995), 'The Trial Selection Hypothesis without the 50 Percent Rule: Some Experimental Evidence', **24** *Journal of Legal Studies*, 209-228.

Wilde, Louis L. (1981), 'On the Use of Laboratory Experiments in Economics', in Pitt, Joseph C. (ed.), *Philosophy in Economics*, Boston, D. Reidel, 137-148.

Wittman, Donald A., Friedman, Daniel, Crevier, S. and Braskin A. (1997), 'Learning Liability Rules', **25** *Journal of Legal Studies*.

Zeisel, Hans (1973), 'Reflections on Experimental Techniques in the Law', **2** *Journal of Legal Studies*, 107-124.

Other References

Ayres, Ian and Cramton, Peter (1996), 'Deficit Reduction Through Diversity: How Affirmative Action at the FCC Increased Auction Competition', **48** *Stanford Law Review*, 761-814.

Donohue, John J., III (1989), 'Diverting the Coasean River: Incentive Schemes to Reduce Unemployment Spells', **99** *Yale Law Journal*, 549-609.

Ellickson, Robert C. (1989), 'The Case for Coase and against "Coaseanism"', **99** *Yale Law Journal*, 611-630.

Gilson, Ronald J. and Mnookin, Robert H. (1994), 'Disputing through Agents: Cooperation and Conflict between Lawyers in Litigation', **94** *Columbia Law Review*, 509-566.

Hasen, Richard L. (1990), 'Efficiency Under Informal Asymmetry; The Effect of Framing on Legal Rules', **38** *UCLA Law Review*, 391-438.

Jolls, Christine, Sunstein, Cass. R. and Thaler, Richard (1998), 'A Behavioral Approach to Law and Economics', **50** *Stanford Law Review*, 1471-1550.

Korobkin, Russell (1998), 'The Status Quo Bias and Contract Default Rules', **83** *Cornell Law Review*, 608-687.

Korobkin, Russell and Guthrie, Chris (1997), 'Psychology, Economics, and Settlement: A New Look at the Role of the Lawyer', **76** *Texas Law Review*, 77-141.

Lindgren, James (1990), ''Ol' Man River ... He Keeps on Rollin' Along': A Reply to Donohue's 'Diverting the Coasean River'', **78** *Georgetown Law Journal*, 577-591.

Marshall, Robert C., Meurer, Michael J. and Richard, Jean-Francois (1991), 'The Private Attorney General Meets Public Contract Law: Procurement Oversight by Protest', **20** *Hofstra Law Review*, 1-71.

McAdams, Richard H. (1995), 'Cooperation and Conflict: The Economics of Group Status Production and Race Discrimination', **108** *Harvard Law Review*, 1003-1084.

Priest, George L. (1985), 'Reexamining the Selection Hypothesis: Learning from Wittman's Mistakes', **14** *Journal of Legal Studies*, 215-243.

Priest, George L. and Klein, Benjamin (1984), 'The Selection of Disputes for Litigation', **13** *Journal of Legal Studies*, 1-55.

Rachlinski, Jeffrey J. and Jourden, Forest (1998), 'Remedies and the Psychology of Ownership', **51** *Vanderbilt Law Review*.

0580
LAW AND ECONOMICS OF DEVELOPMENT

Edgardo Buscaglia
Hoover Institute, Stanford University

Abstract

This chapter provides a review of the main channels through which legal systems affect economic development. High costs for determining property rights are still common in most developing countries. Confiscations; multiple, high and unanticipated taxation applied to the same bundle of property rights again and again; unclear definition of contractual obligations; inconsistent application of the laws coupled with corruption, and ad hoc regulations make property rights more insecure and have also caused increased transaction costs within the marketplace. This institutional instability increases the discount rate applied to social interactions in future periods, thereby hampering investments, savings and the consumption of durable goods.

This chapter approaches the main substantive and procedural legal factors that nations need to address in order to promote economic growth and development. The substantive legal requirements for economic development are analyzed here by identifying the efficiency enhancing sources of legal norms (that is, bottom-up formalization of legal norms, legal transplants and legal integration). Economic growth and social development are also affected by legal procedures and the mechanisms through which norms are enforced and interpreted by the court system and alternative dispute resolution mechanisms. This chapter also identifies how corruption and the lack of efficiency and effectiveness found in dysfunctional court systems affect investment and economic development.
JEL classification: K00, O54
Keywords: Law and Economics, Development, Judiciary, Research

1. Introduction

To what degree does law promote economic development? To what extent does creating wealth through the accumulation of human and nonhuman capital require a set of rules securing property rights, governing civil and commercial relationships, and making the exercise of the state's power more predictable? To what extent might economic growth be affected if rules are clearly defined, made public, and applied in a consistent manner? To what extent are investment projects affected by mechanisms to resolve conflicts based on the binding decisions of an independent judiciary and procedures to change the rules when change is needed? Measuring the extent of the impact of the law is an empirical inquiry. The answers to these questions represent the new frontier in law and economics. In most less developed countries, uncertainty related to the application of the law due to discretionary power and an inefficient administration of justice are affecting trade and investment by increasing transactions costs and fostering corruption. Observations and logical truths are abundant, yet the empirical verification of these logical truths seems to be scarce.

The first part of this chapter approaches the main substantive legal factors that nations need to address in order to promote economic growth and development. This first part will address the substantive legal requirements for economic development by identifying the main efficiency-enhancing sources of legal norms (that is, bottom-up formalization of legal norms; legal transplants and legal integration). I examine the impact of legal transplants on economic efficiency and demonstrate this by reviewing the transplantation of trade-related intellectual property laws in Latin America. Also examined is the incorporation of efficiency-enhancing legal doctrines through economic integration and a jurimetric case study of trade agreements in South America. Finally, this part of the chapter analyzes the impact of laws on organizational structures.

The second part of this chapter addresses the procedural aspects of the law and economics of development. I first address the role of the judiciary and its impact on economic development. Also presented is a case study providing an economic and inferential analysis of the court systems in Latin America. Finally, the chapter provides an account of the symptoms of a dysfunctional court system (that is, inefficiency, ineffectiveness and corruption) and examines the impact of these institutional symptoms on economic development.

The conclusion to this chapter defines the scope of the field and possible future areas of research.

The process of economic transformation through deregulation and the privatization of the means of production in many developing countries coupled with intensified international trade of complex goods and services requires a legal framework with clear rules for economic interaction. The magnitude of the economic transformation experienced by many developing countries in recent years involves increasingly complicated contractual relationships among savers, producers, investors and customers. This process of growth needs a system of rules able to enhance risk management in a increasingly complex economy. Legal, judicial and alternative dispute resolution systems are potential institutional improvements in how society deals with higher social complexity and increasing risks generated by human interactions. The clear identification and specification of these improved mechanisms is the first problem waiting to be solved by the economic analysis of law in developing countries.

A modern market economy requires laws that are able constantly to redefine rights and market relationships when new forms of corporate structure emerge; to provide ever-changing determinations of contractual obligations, and extend them to new forms of financial instruments, tangible and intangible property; to redefine and enforce the rights of victims of new technologies and activities while protecting the environment from newly emerging risks. These are only some examples of the tremendous flexibility that the legal and judicial systems require in order to adapt the laws to a dynamic economic system. As Cooter (1996a, pp. 2-3) states in his pioneering piece, 'if economic law is poorly adapted to the economy, expectations conflict, cooperating is difficult, and disputes consume resources. Conversely, if economic law is adapted to the economy, people cooperate with each other, harmonize their expectations, and use resources efficiently and creatively'. If public institutions are defective and political conditions too unstable, private contractual arrangements will also become riskier and negatively affect private investment. In short, the formation of larger markets and the possibility of longer-term contracts, both necessary conditions for economic growth, are hampered by an unclear or undefined system of legal rules and inconsistent application and interpretation of those rules. The application of the economic analysis of law to development issues sponsors a clear and consistent definition and enforcement of the conditions of ownership in developing countries undergoing transformations. As Orr and Ulen (1993, p. 3) argue,

> a government that credibly commits itself to upholding rights of property and contract enforcement not only provides a basis whereby partners in economic transactions can trust each other; it also reinforces the hope that the government itself can be trusted to transact honorably and to meet its contractual obligations.

Yet high costs for determining property rights are still common in most developing countries. Confiscations and multiple, high and unanticipated taxation applied to the same bundle of property rights again and again, unclear definition of contractual obligations, inconsistent application of the laws coupled with corruption, and ad hoc regulations have all made property rights more insecure and have also caused increased transaction costs within the marketplace. This institutional instability increases the discount rate applied to social interactions in future periods, thereby hampering investments, savings, and the consumption of durable goods. The most interesting question then remains: What are the structures of the most effective legal and judicial mechanisms that would be able to interpret and translate those social norms into laws in less developed countries?

The economic analysis of the law in developing countries represents an attempt to identify changes in laws, regulations and enforcement mechanisms that, within the legal tradition of each country, would be able to enhance economic efficiency and improve equity. Edmund Kitch (1983) argues that law and economics focuses on the study of the impact of a system of rewards and penalties that affect individual behavior. These rewards and penalties are defined by laws, regulations, doctrines, court cases, social norms, and so on. The central goal of law and economics is then to analyze the individuals' and firms' maximizing behavior within a system of rules in order to identify the effects of laws. In this sense, law and economics follows a methodology compatible with a legal realism and within an elaborate framework of analysis provided by microeconomic theory. In this context, I will analyze how legal doctrines are not hermetically sealed, self contained, or even self sustaining. I will follow a legal realism found in law and economics where the law cannot be understood apart from its social context. Thus, an understanding of how to enhance a more efficient social order through legal reform will be attained through an empirical study of human behavior.

A. Substantive Aspects of the Law and Economics of Development

2. Efficiency and the Source of Legal Norms

One recently emergent line of research in the law and economics of development literature concentrates on the microeconomic foundations of the sources of those rules that will allow the law and its enforcement mechanisms to adapt to a modern economy and, by adapting, foster economic growth. This topic is explored by Cooter (1996a) who argues that efficiency is enhanced by a 'bottom up' process of capturing social norms that are already in place as 'informally' relevant in human interaction. Norms are understood here as coordinating mechanisms for social interaction. This decentralized approach to lawmaking stands in sharp contrast to the centralization proposed by the first law and development movement that during the 1960s and 1970s proposed a clear centralization and 'modernization' of the laws through transplants. The most important works in this first movement can be ascribed to Trubek (1972), Galanter (1974), Seidman (1978), and who sponsored a comprehensive, centralized, and top-down legislative reform aimed at modernizing the public and private dimensions of the law.

There are four legal traditions relevant in this century: civil law, common law, administrative law and socialist law. Eastern Europe and China have slowly shifted from a socialist legal system characterized by the production of centralized public rules to prerevolutionary private civil law. The common or judge-made law sustained by *stare decisis* has suffered from the significant expansion of administrative law. In this scenario, administrative law, as the framework establishing the rules to be followed in the relationship between the state and private individuals, has been the byproduct of the expansion of the government role in western societies. Therefore, these legal traditions are in a constant state of flux.

The civil law systems are currently facing a choice between either legalizing and enforcing social norms in a bottom-up approach by following the policy prescriptions of Hayek (1973) or creating regulations in a centralized top-down manner. For example, the civil code can either capture the norms of local and international business communities or simply impose rules on a top-down approach. One of the most important dilemmas facing developing countries in their current legal evolution is the choice between centralized law versus decentralized law-making capabilities. Following Hayek (1973), one could argue that the higher information constraints that are the product of added social complexity require public policy to decentralize law-making by capturing norms and thus reducing market transaction costs. As Cooter (1996a, p. 148) states, 'efficiency requires the enforcement of customs in business communities to become more important relative to the regulation of business'. As he (p. 154) also argues, 'customs arise when external effects align with incentives for signaling'. From this perspective, the irrelevance of the laws enacted by parliaments in many countries must be understood as a reflection of the lack of links between the essence of what the law stipulates and the social norms followed by people and businesses in their daily life. When regulations or laws show this lack of compatibility, the costs of complying and enforcing the law become higher. These are the so-called 'bad laws' mentioned by de Soto (1989) in his path-breaking work in which he identifies a deficient rule by comparing the approximate transaction cost of complying with the law against the transaction cost of following the social norm within an informal market. In de Soto's work one can observe that these higher transaction costs are rooted in the drive of governments to centralize lawmaking without regard to the true social practices followed by people. Only when the laws and regulations reflect these practices will the transaction costs of the social interactions affected decline and a movement towards efficiency occur. From de Soto's (1996a) perspective, the size of many informal sectors around the globe is intimately related to the way laws and regulations fail to capture the social practices followed by society.

By following the pioneering studies by Cooter (1994, 1996a) and Mattei (1993) we could argue that the laws generating obedience are the ones truly compatible with the ethical code prevailing in society. Individuals in social frameworks seek the kind of predictability that will tend to increase their capacity to generate wealth through their interactions. The state of nature or 'grab what you can' is not a priori desirable or compatible with long-term survival under a 'veil of ignorance'. Different levels of concentration of political and economic power may be compatible with predictable rules of the game. Yet for all levels of concentration of political and economic power, the social norms and values supporting the prevailing and predictable rules of political and economic interaction would tend to enhance allocative and productive efficiency by reducing transaction costs of interacting. In this scenario, civil society's norms will be found by public institutions and transformed into formalized legal rights and obligations.

One could here extend Cooter's analysis and state that, in order to enhance efficiency, politics must follow not just the market but also the non-market social norms. In a more comprehensive fashion, civil society's market and non-market rules for social interaction provide a law-making guide for the legislature and the judiciary. By making laws familiar to the individual, the transaction costs of human interactions decrease and allow society to achieve efficiency in its market and non-market activities. The evolution of intellectual property laws in developing countries, described in the next section, provides a good example of how legal transplants provided a channel through which national laws started to capture business practices and social norms.

3. Legal Transplants and Economic Efficiency

Let us now address the economic analysis of efficiency-enhancing substantive legal reform in developing countries. There are two main choices for a developing country when selecting the source of its laws. A country can adopt a law from within its own institutional mechanisms, or it can transplant rules from outside its political-legal zone of dominance. A key need in the economic analysis of the law is to determine a framework for predicting which of the two options is the most efficiency-enhancing alternative. Watson (1978a) has shown that most legal reforms are due to transplants. Therefore, we should also explain why, from an international pool of laws available for transplant, certain rules and institutions are commonly used while others are rejected. For example, why is it that some countries adopt the same rules to protect intellectual property? In more general terms, we should also explain why some countries adopt civil law as opposed to common law systems, or separation of powers as opposed to parliamentary systems. As Mattei (1994) and Ulen (1996) pointed out, one reason could be simply 'prestige'. Yet they point out that prestige is not a measurable variable and, thus, it is difficult to verify the hypothesis in a scientific manner. Microeconomic theory, on the other hand, can provide a justification for the transplant by testing if the legal rules transplanted are also the most efficient ones. In other words, an intertemporal cost-benefit analysis may provide an explanation of why some legal rules and systems are adopted and others rejected. Within this scenario, Eggertson (1990) and Ulen (1997) point out that the economic efficiency hypothesis proposes that different legal systems may compute the costs and benefits of legal rules for the same situation differently because real economic factors (such as resource endowments and tastes) are different across regions and nations. At the same time, it is also true that legal reforms are subject to the political supply and demand given by vested interests. That is, professional interests which may be threatened by any profound alteration in the legal system as it exists and from which they have benefited. To a large extent, the successful implementation of any reform depends on these agents, ultimately responsible for effective law-enforcement.

4. Case Study: Intellectual Property Laws in Developing Countries

Buscaglia and Ulen (1994) apply the above cost-benefit approach to transplants to the recent adoption of intellectual property laws under the GATT umbrella. Recent empirical studies conducted by Foray and Freeman (1993) show that in order to ensure a 'catching-up' growth process, developing countries need to expand the size of their domestic savings and human capital pools through the application of clear laws and consistent enforcement. The observed differences in wealth among countries has always captured the attention of scholars in many fields. Lucas (1988) describes the powerful effects of technological change and the need to enhance technological learning in the process of economic development. Yet 'catching-up' is a process that depends on much more than just technological change, understood as increasing the incorporation of new technologies into the production capacity of firms. Bell and Pavitt (1993) bring to our attention the importance of technological learning, defined as an increase in the resources needed for generating and managing technical change. In this context, what needs to be addressed is not just the lack of industrial capacity or technical change but also the dearth of technological capability as the most basic and acute deficiency in most less developed countries (LDCs). Technological learning, however, requires a deeper transformation in a society than technological change does. Technological learning implies the building of institutions and skills capable of generating technical change in the future. It is at this deeper level that, for example, the intellectual property framework will affect future technical change.

The increasing permeability of national frontiers subject to international trade and ideas is of such magnitude that it has forced national authorities to reconsider the legal foundation of intellectual property rights. The Paris and Berne Conventions provided a legal framework for more than a century containing two main doctrines. The doctrine known as 'territoriality' sustaining that property rights are to be honored according to each state's rules; and the doctrine of 'independence' establishing that granting property rights within one state did not force other states to grant the same rights. These two doctrines have become irrelevant under the new order emerging after the Uruguay Round. Under the supervision of the newly created World Trade Organization, the harmony or uniformity of laws has been sought as the ideal way to encourage the international flow of goods and services. This new framework has solidified the view that the justification for granting intellectual property rights, such as a patent, is based on social norms required by the need to exchange benefits between society and the innovator. The innovator receives a monopolistic return from an investment in order for society to be able to benefit from an incremental diffusion in knowledge that otherwise would have been kept as a secret.

The international enforcement of intellectual property rights experienced a drastic evolution during the past three decades. For more than a century, the international intellectual property regime was governed by the Paris and Berne Conventions which provided ample scope for cooperation but at the same time left to national legislation to define the main aspects of intellectual property rights. After World War II, a concern with the balance between the rights of the author and the benefits of diffusing knowledge to less-developed countries (LDCs) as fast as possible challenged the norm based on the aforementioned exchange of benefits between society and the innovator. The need for rapid industrialization and vast improvements in technologies were justifications for LDC governments to impose requirements limiting the rights and benefits of innovators. Two typical examples of limitations to the rights of innovators occurred in most LDCs when: (a) a patent can only be granted if the intellectual property is worked and exploited within the national frontiers of a country (a working requirement); and (b) the terms and royalties for licenses of intellectual property can be determined by the government in the absence of agreement by the innovator (compulsory licensing). Under these two types of restrictions, LDC governments abandoned the formula of exchange based on monopoly for diffusion and replaced it with an approach based on granting intellectual property rights in exchange for foreign direct investment. Difficult problems remained, however. Common features of many legal systems in LDCs show intellectual property rights subject to inconsistent coverage, uncertain terms of protection, arbitrary transferability, compulsory licensing regimes and inadequate enforcement. The national character of this type of legislation, however, has been increasingly called into question by industrialized countries. The advanced economies' challenge to the old legal order can be explained by drastic changes in business practices and norms of behavior. More specifically, the need for legal reforms were caused by the technological breakthroughs of the 1970s and the subsequent revolutionary impact of microelectronics, biological inventions, computer software and other high technology sectors. These sectors required increasing investments in research and development paid by businesses from those industrialized countries mainly responsible for the production of these knowledge-intensive products. Under this scenario, international trade of knowledge-intensive products gained relevance as a proportion of each developed countries' exports and national production.

5. Trade-Related Intellectual Property Rights

The new reality shows that the United States (US), the European Union (EU) and Japan are increasingly dependent for their competitiveness on their ability to protect the value inherent in intellectual property. At the same time, most of the LDCs are extremely dependent on exports to advanced economies. Many of these LDC exports benefit from the Generalized System of Preferences (GSP) granted by the European Union and the United States, whereby special lower tariffs or preferences are applied to designated LDC exports. This mutual dependence made it possible for advanced and developing economies to start bilateral negotiations with a potential for mutually beneficial agreements in order to find a solution to the lack of protection of intellectual property rights. The 'stick' in these negotiations was provided by the threat of loss of access to the United States and European markets through the cancellation of GSP benefits. But foreign pressure is not the only force that is able to explain legal reforms in LDCs.

Since 1995 and under the World Trade Organization (WTO) supervision, many less-developed countries have adopted trade-related intellectual property rights (TRIPs) that are more compatible with the American and European minimum standards of protection. Some may even classify these legal reforms as 'transplants'. As part of the GATT framework, the WTO will (a) finally enforce a set of internationally recognized standards for the protection of intellectual property rights for incorporation into national laws; and (b) develop a consultation and dispute settlement mechanism for overseeing the implementation of the international norms and resolve any government to government disputes regarding the interpretation of such norms.

Primo-Braga (1990a) observes that modern intellectual property rules have not been applied or enforced by governments in developing countries even when the benefits of such rules are widely recognized by local business interests and by the countries generating the essential technologies needed for development. However, the forces explaining this pre-GATT inertia or the causes behind the current emergence of a region-wide intellectual property reform throughout Latin America have been overlooked. This oversight is explained by the failure to recognize how the costs and benefits of legal reform operate on a different time frame. More specifically, the costs of legal reform are seen by politicians in less developed countries as a short-term liability hampering their chances for reelection. On the other hand, the benefits of defining and enforcing intellectual property rights are perceived as more distant and less tangible.

As stated in Buscaglia and Ulen (1994, p. 159), legal reforms in developing countries must be seen as the joint effect of local political conditions and foreign economic pressures. These two forces explain the international legal convergence observed in the intellectual property arena. As stated above, the foreign economic pressures to reform intellectual property laws arise particularly because an increasing proportion of imports to Latin America consist of information-intensive goods and services. From a domestic policy perspective, the movement toward intellectual property reform corresponds with the complete failure of the import substitution approach to development. From the early 1930s until the late 1980s, most developing countries encouraged domestic (import substitution) manufacturing investment, suppressed agricultural prices and expanded the size of their public sector enterprises while attempting to stimulate savings and investment through taxation and credit allocated by the public sector. The prevailing view, represented in Prebisch (1950), was that a shortage of domestic physical capital was the key impediment to development. Import substitution industries grew behind protective walls based on subsidies and tariffs in a *milieu* where many other determinants of the rate of economic growth, such as investment in human capital and the role of microeconomic incentives, were completely ignored by policymakers. Protection of import substitution industries allowed domestic prices and costs to far exceed international prices and created little incentive for efficiency. These protected industries produced substitutes for imports but usually depended on the import of raw materials and technology. Import demand grew rapidly as these firms imported capital goods to accelerate investment. The anti-export bias, combined with the import-substitution program, caused a scarcity of foreign exchange and this, in turn, created a structural barrier to the investment in expensive first-rate technologies. Within this environment protected from international trade, however, firms could still survive investing in second-rate technologies. As described in Buscaglia (1993) this approach to development came to an end during the international debt crisis of the 1980s when developing countries' policymakers realized that internal markets and import substitution were not enough to assure sustainable growth. The demise of the import-substitution model left most developing countries with no other option for economic growth than to eliminate trade barriers and promote competitive exports through the incorporation of world-class technologies. As a result of these foreign and domestic pressures, LDCs were forced to reconsider many of their legal institutions, including their national intellectual property laws. In this context, the international economic and political environment described here has produced a convergence of LDC laws towards the intellectual property legal frameworks prevailing in nations generating standard technologies.

6. Legal Transplants and Economic Integration

Legal transplants are a key main source of trade-related legal changes in developing countries. Most LDCs have chosen an export-led approach to economic growth and they are also eager to attract much needed foreign direct investment (FDI). In order to enhance trade openness abroad and at the same time attract foreign investment to their domestic markets, they must provide a more stable environment in which to do business. Therefore, competitive pressures arise on LDCs to harmonize their legal systems with those in countries exporting capital by incorporating foreign legal frameworks that developed-country firms perceive to enhance their productive efficiency.

A central topic to be addressed in law and economics of development must focus on the study of what are the main economic factors explaining the formation of legal transplants and legal integrations that tend to enhance productive efficiency. As stated in Ulen (1996, p. 9), 'Law and Economics has been one of the most important and productive innovations in legal scholarship of the twentieth century. Yet its contributions to the issues of constitutional law, including federalism, are relatively modest'. From this perspective, we could add that the attention paid to the analysis of legal and economic integration have also been insufficient.

The mechanisms through which parliaments and the judiciary in civil law countries would capture and translate these norms into law would require an identification of those practices that have become standard in business communities and a required justification of how those practices create efficiency-compatible incentives. The efficiency aspects of these practices must be analyzed with the aid of the theoretical and empirical tools used by economists. For example, this approach to law-making could use empirical techniques within the so-called jurimetric framework of analysis. In this way, the economic impact of legal reforms could be captured through the use of parametric and non-parametric techniques. Relatively few empirical studies have been advanced in law and economics and even fewer within the economic analysis of development. Yet studies by Long and Buscaglia (1997), Cooter and Ginsburg (1996) and Buscaglia and Guerrero (1995) have clearly shown the great advantages of applying statistical techniques to the economic analysis of the law. Without any doubt, jurimetrics represents a real frontier in the law and economics of development. The potential to rationalize public policymaking with the help of jurimetric techniques represents a clear improvement in the analysis of the economic impact of legal reforms proposed in all developing countries.

Many may argue that civil law systems would tend to reject the economic analysis of their laws. Yet, quoting Cooter (1996a, p. 145),

> Judges allegedly make law in civil law systems by interpreting codes, not finding social norms. Compared to common law countries, the codifiers in civil law countries apparently have more influence and the judges allegedly have less influence. Interpreting some codes, however, looks a lot like finding social norms. Comparative lawyers, consequently, debate whether the apparent differences in the two systems are real or illusory

From this perspective, one could argue that civil law systems have the capacity to react to efficiency forces as much as common law systems do. Moreover, it may come as a surprise to many sponsoring a centralized legal system that the civil law originally evolved as a common law system. In Watson (1978a) we can find an excellent account of this evolution. Let us not forget that, before the nineteenth century, the European *ius commune* was based on the judge's interpretation of Roman law within the local norms and practices. The centralization of law making through legislatures aimed at replacing laws based on social norms, practiced by people and found by judges, with what Cooter (1996a) calls 'rational' rules that were 'designed' to engineer a better way of life for society. The judge was supposed to only interpret laws generated by legislatures and not find norms. The interpretation of norms, however, was also subject to an implicit and subtle application of social norms as inputs in the opinions of judges. Yet, this post Napoleonic framework took away power from the judicial branch and made it more dependent.

The formation of trading blocks can be analyzed with the same tools that law and economics has applied to the analysis of federalism. This approach focuses on identifying and measuring the benefits *versus* the costs of generating added political and economic integration. Long and Buscaglia (1997) recently advanced empirical research in this area. It is useful to present a summary of this empirical study on economic integration below. The methodology used in this piece provides an alternative research path where the links between the existence of legal transplants and economic structures can be explored and discussed in future studies.

Developing nations are currently facing a unique opportunity created by global free trade, the continuous decline in transportation and communication costs coupled with the unprecedented availability of generic applied knowledge and the expanding flows of international financial investments. However, many of these countries lack the institutional capability to create or absorb the applied knowledge aforementioned. Legal and economic reforms that are currently occurring in LDCs are, in some cases, strengthening the foundations for economic growth. In all cases, these legal and economic reforms are based on strategies aimed at giving domestic producers a more important role in the development of their economies.

During the 1980s, increasing competition and volatility in world markets have induced industrialized and developing countries alike to cluster together in regional economic blocs. This trend was spurred by three additional main factors: (i) technological innovations in transportation and communications have expanded the relevant size of the markets for an increasing number of goods and services; (ii) the overall economic slowdown in world trade during the period 1988-92, accelerated by the collapse of the Communist regimes; and (iii) the near failure of the multilateral trade negotiations sponsored by GATT at the Uruguay Round. In turn, the near-breakdown in multilateral trade negotiations served to create an environment compatible with bilateral and regional accords.

7. Legal Integration and Economic Development

Legal integration is another main external source of legal changes that have an impact on efficiency in many developing countries. Of central interest, in our analysis, is why governments choose some strategies over others in pursuing legal/economic integration. Long and Buscaglia (1997) propose that a successful legal/economic integration is a function of the convergence of three broad conditions: (1) the compatibility of political systems; (2) the public sector's expectation of gains from liberalizing international trade; and (3) the private sector's expectation of gains from regionalizing production, transferring capital and technology and harmonizing trade-related rules. Some or all of these factors are key driving forces behind the main trade agreements within the western hemisphere, Europe and Asia: the North American Free Trade Agreement (NAFTA) of the United States, Canada and Mexico; the Andean Pact involving Bolivia, Colombia, Ecuador, Peru and Venezuela; and the Common Market of the South (MERCOSUR) covering Argentina, Brazil, Chile, Paraguay and Uruguay, the European Union and the Asian Economic bloc. As a case study, the empirical study summarized below concentrates on providing an empirical verification of the above third condition in Latin America.

The ongoing Latin American economic transformation has created a need for new and major legal developments. Yet, what are the main economic forces explaining the drive to integrate throughout Latin America's economic history? A jurimetric analysis in Long and Buscaglia (1997) shows that growth in international intra-sectoral trade comes hand-in-hand with the private sector's growing demand for the harmonization of trade-related laws. In addition to the legal issues mentioned above, harmonization does occur in many other areas. A survey of the legal history of economic integration reveals that harmonization occurs in specific areas such as banking, insurance, securities, liberal professions, international securities exchange regulations and transport. We see that the future of hemispheric integration and trade processes necessarily entails the deepening and development of these legal areas. However, Latin American economic history has been littered with the hulls of shipwrecked trade agreements seeking legal integration. Yet, the compatibility in the evolutionary natures of two or more legal systems has to be introduced as a factor that will affect the need and feasibility of legal integrations. Moreover, the empirical review of patterns of trade in Long and Buscaglia (1997, pp. 10-12) shows that this legal compatibility is driven by international similarities in economic structures.

Table 1 aims at associating legal agreements seeking harmonization in trade-related rules with other economic factors such as the number of high growth non-agricultural trade-related sectors of the economy of selected LDCs. A review of Table 1 below shows that there exists a strong association between the emergence of high growth (above 5 percent annual growth in sales) non-agricultural sectors (that is, changes in economic structure) and the number of legal amendments in the commercial codes on the one hand and the drive of a country to harmonize its legal system through international trade-related agreements on the other. For example, we observe that Argentina and Brazil who possess the most dynamic economies during the period 1850-1990 (with 16 and 14 new non-agricultural trade-related sectors respectively) are also the countries with the largest number of amendments to their commercial codes and with the largest number of trade-related legal treaties signed (that is, 31 for Argentina and 35 for Brazil). As expected, more complex economic systems (that is, a larger number of high growth new trade-related sectors) experience more complexity in their legal systems by undertaking more amendments in their commercial codes. At the same time, Table 1 shows that dynamic economies are also more likely to harmonize their legal systems through international legal agreements.

Table 1
Legal Changes vs. Economic Structure During 1850-1990

Country	No. of Amendments in Commercial Codes	No. of Trade Related Non-Agricultural Sectors	No. of International Legal Agreements
Argentina	515	16	31
Bolivia	19	1	3
Brazil	521	14	35
Chile	467	11	25

Colombia	9	0	7
Ecuador	14	1	6
Peru	56	0	12
Uruguay	12	1	5
Venezuela	5	2	1

Table 2 shows a clear pattern where the region's most dynamic economies are also the ones that are more likely to enter into international legal agreements with each other involving harmonization of private law. One can argue that as an increasing number of business exchanges occur in countries with overlapping growing trade-related sectors, their need for legal harmonization will tend to increase. This explains why in Table 2 we observe that most attempts to harmonize legal frameworks have mainly involved countries such as Argentina, Brazil and Chile. These countries all experienced growth in the most dynamic trade-related sectors (for example, agro-manufacturing, minerals, steel, financial services, transportation and energy).

Table 2
Matrix of Inter-Country Legal Agreements
Covering Commercial Areas

	Arg.	Bra.	Bol.	Ch.	Col.	Ec.	Peru	Urug.	Ven.
Argentina	0	14	1	10	2	1	2	1	0
Brazil	14	0	2	7	3	2	4	2	1
Bolivia	1	2	0	0	0	0	0	0	0
Chile	10	7	0	0	2	1	3	1	1
Colombia	2	3	0	2	0	0	0	0	0
Ecuador	1	2	0	1	0	0	2	0	0
Peru	2	4	0	3	0	2	0	0	1
Uruguay	1	2	0	1	0	0	0	0	1
Venezuela	0	1	0	1	0	0	1	1	0

8. Inferential Jurimetric Analysis of Legal Integration

Based on the evidence found in Table 1 and Table 2 taken from Long and Buscaglia (1997), we can assert that many Latin American experiments aimed at legal harmonization may have failed to produce substantive results due to a lack of private sector lobbying pushing for compatible legal solutions addressing trade issues. More specifically, countries with overlapping dynamic trade-related sectors (that is, experiencing a higher proportion of intra-sectoral international exchanges as a proportion of total trade) will at the same time possess private sectors demanding compatible legal frameworks within the areas affecting their products. This also explains the push for intellectual property and competition reforms and harmonization of rules among Argentina, Brazil and Chile. In this context, imagine two types of countries hoping to harmonize their commercial laws: countries where private commercial laws are not far from their evolutionary base and where no dynamic trade-related non-agricultural sectors producing information-intensive products exist (for example, Bolivia, Colombia, Uruguay) and, in contrast, countries with relatively evolved commercial legal systems and with a high proportion of their trade concentrated on dynamic sectors (such as Argentina, Brazil, Chile). The quantitative evidence (Tables 1 and 2) and the analysis advanced above would predict that legal harmonization between these two types of countries will have less chances of success. In these cases, the private sectors within each of these types of countries will demand different kinds of commercial legal frameworks. As a result, integration will be more difficult. For example, one can observe that private sector firms in Bolivia importing Brazilian computer software and hardware, compact disks, or movies, do not have an incentive to lobby for the enactment of intellectual property, government procurement, or competition laws compatible with the needs and interests of the Brazilian firms exporting these products to Bolivia. Figure 1 shows that the main drive to harmonize trade-related laws was concentrated among those countries experiencing high levels of international intra-sectoral trade. For example, we see that Brazil and Argentina with 35 and 31 trade-related legal agreements, respectively, are also the countries with the highest level of intra-sectoral trade.

Clearly, Argentina, Brazil and Chile are the countries with the highest levels of intra-sectoral trade as a proportion of their total trade that, according to our argument, also possess the most dynamic private sectors lobbying for legal integration. The number of legal agreements attached to each of these three countries during the period 1890-1990 clearly support our claim. In fact, those industries involved in intra-sectoral trade within MERCOSUR were the main forces lobbying for legal harmonization of standards and regulations. Let us note that intra-sectoral trade within MERCOSUR grew at an unprecedented rate after tariffs were first reduced in 1988 as part of the ABIP Treaty. The relative importance of intra-sectoral trade between Argentina and Brazil increased from 19.2 to 39 percent of total exports in Argentina and from 5.3 to 23.8 percent in Brazil. These industries included the automobile, energy, steel. pharmaceutical, mineral and textile sectors.

Figure 1
Legal Treaties vs. Avarage Sectoral Trade: 1890-1990

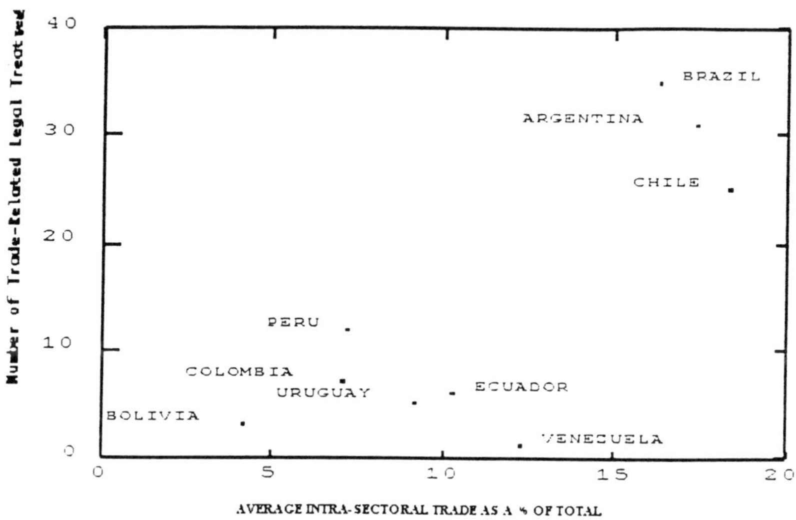

One could also claim that the relatively larger countries (Argentina and Brazil), due to the larger stakes in trade and their larger GDP, will seek to determine a specific type of legal harmony with their main trade partners through legal agreements. On the other hand, smaller countries in Latin America (for example, Uruguay and Ecuador) will just 'free ride' by transplanting legal frameworks to their own environment. A regression analysis covering the variables aforementioned will test this and the above claims. We can see in Table 3 below that the number of legal agreements during the period 1890-1990 in the twenty countries surveyed is our dependent variable. The number of amendments to the commercial codes (AMEND), the number of non-agricultural trade-related sectors (NO_TRNA) and the average intra-sectoral trade as a proportion of total trade (AV_INTRA) are all predictors. These are all variables that help to predict the drive to harmonize legal frameworks within Latin America during the period 1850-1990. As we can see, all these explanatory variables are significant at the 5 percent level. On the other hand, the relative size of the GDP (%GDP/T.GDP) is not a significant variable. In other words, relative size does not explain the drive to harmonize legal frameworks. Finally, we see that 62.7 percent of the variability in our dependent variable is explained by the independent variables included.

Table 3
Multiple Regression Analysis

DEP VAR:NO_LEGAG N: 20 MULTIPLE R: 0.792
SQUARED MULTIPLE R: 0.627 STANDARD ERROR OF ESTIMATE: 2.04

Variable	Coefficient	Std	Error Tolerance	T	P (2-tail)
CONSTANT	146	12	0	1216	0
AMEND	10	1	95	749	2
NO TRNA	43	5	95	861	0
AV INTRA	72	23	99	316	0
%GDP/T.GDP	5	15	86	33	34

9. The Impact of Laws on Organizational Structures

The impact of substantive norms on productive efficiency needs to be assessed by identifying the type or organizational structures that would emerge under different sets of legal rules. The full identification of the implicit price transmitted by institutions to firms and individuals, on the one hand; and the specification of the institutional structure needed to attain allocative and productive efficiency on the other, are two areas where law and economics possesses a comparative advantage with respect to other social sciences. Thus, the works presented in this field cover a positive and a normative approach to the economic analysis of the law. Douglass North (1990) has already pointed at the relationship between the property rights framework, transaction costs and economic growth. Moreover, the study of market and non-market behavior reacting to implicit prices established through laws falls within the best tradition of the University of Chicago approach to law and economics. Yet other approaches need to be incorporated into the legal and economic study of development, such as the study of the behavior of organizations and their economic environment proposed by Oliver Williamson (1991) and the analysis of the factors related to intermediate organizations with the potential to hamper economic growth described by Mancur Olson (1982, 1993). In short, the understanding of how laws have an impact on market and organizational structures also need to be the focus of attention of development economists in search of answers explaining the lack of international convergence in economic growth rates.

Coase (1960) has shown that transaction costs determine the nature and organization of economic activity and the distribution of income. One interesting aspect to be addressed in development studies are the changes in legal rules and their enforcement mechanisms that are needed to promote the existence of public and private organizations in which their members' increase in wealth position is compatible with attaining the goals of the organization and improving the overall wealth of society. In this scenario, behavioral patterns such as low factor productivity incentives and corruption (that is, a transfer of wealth caused by the use of public office for private benefit) can be understood as symptoms of organizational defects explained by systems where individuals perceive that their wellbeing does not go hand in hand with the wellbeing of the organization in particular and society in general. In this scenario, a pattern of defective organizational structures hampers the creation of wealth and economic growth.

There are specific key variables whose dynamic interplay determine the performance of all organizations. These key variables correspond to the following two main areas: (a) the internal organization of an economic or political unit that includes the internal structures and arrangements between the principal and the agents by which the owner causes the managers to act for the goals set by the owner; and (b) external incentives that are composed of all those variables relating primarily to market factors that, although not under the control of the principals, discipline the agents and principals in performance. The past eight years of economic and political reforms across eastern Europe, Latin America and Africa have made it clear to those working on public policy reforms that the social and economic development of nations require newly designed organizations that are able to harmonize the incentive to create private wealth with the progress of society in general. This amounts to an invisible hand within the organization that can be explained by its own structure.

The links between the impact of private and public law on organizational structures in developing countries has not been explored until recently. The work advanced by Trebilcock (1997) goes into the main links between the quality of public sector governance, organizational structures and the economic progress of nations. This work covers the relationship between the nature of a political system and its economic performance. Subsequently, it answers two main questions: (i) what type of institutions are most conducive to economic development and (ii) what factors or conditions encourage or alternatively impede the adoption of efficient institutions.

The research conducted by de Soto (1989, 1996a) follows an original examination of the property rights framework in developing countries, in this case Peru and describes the way in which the lack of predictable property rights rules have affected the structure of private firms, investment and economic growth. De Soto's historical analysis provides a decisive link between ownership rules and the complexity in the pattern of market transactions. Clearly, his analysis provides answers to key questions through the use of the economic theory of property. First, de Soto asks what should be privately owned in an environment where state ownership has been the norm until recently; and second, how should property rights be enforced in order to assure a compatibility between social norms and written law. In this scenario, de Soto requires this compatibility in order to assure that the law will be followed by the average citizen. In this context, he stresses the fact that in the absence of clear and enforced legal rules, people will substitute clear and enforceable customs and norms for the collectively enforced set of legal rules. As stated in Buscaglia and Ratliff (1997), from an economic standpoint, regionally-determined bubbles of customary systems may not be as efficient as a bottom-up collectively enforced set of legal rules.

B. Procedural Aspects of the Law and Economic Development

10. The Judiciary and Economic Development

As developing countries continue their process of economic reforms, the need for a well functioning judiciary becomes increasingly evident. Yet, the empirical dimension of the economic analysis of legal procedures is in its infancy. As stated in Buscaglia and Domingo (1996), democratization, growing urbanization and the adoption of market reforms have all created additional demands for court services throughout the region. These three factors have increased the complexity of social interactions, thereby making the enhancement of the judiciary's conflict-resolution capabilities even more necessary. In addition, the shift of most economic transactions toward the market domain and away from the public administrative sphere of the state has created an unprecedented increase in private sector demand for an improved definition of rights and obligations.

The judiciary is a key element of economic development. The judicial system includes all the mechanisms needed to interpret and apply the laws and regulations. More importantly, the judiciary is the main link through which the economic impact of the legal system can be identified. The productive role of the judicial sector within the economic system consists of resolving conflicts by providing the substantive and procedural structure to facilitate the exchange of rights to physical and intangible assets. Judiciaries in most developing countries, however, suffer from increasing backlogs, delay and corruption. As shown in many Gallup polls, this has generated complete distrust of the system by the private sector and the public in general. Moreover, the judiciary can also affect the behavior of private investment. Lack of access to an equitable and efficient judicial system creates added uncertainty and hampers the realization of beneficial transactions. In the absence of an impartial and efficient judiciary, the performance of mutually beneficial transactions depends upon the presence of pre-existing reputation and repeated transactions among parties. This requirement excludes many potentially beneficial transactions involving previously unfamiliar parties or startup businesses from occurring.

Legal principles supporting the prevailing economic systems in many developing countries are nominally based on the freedom to exercise individual property rights. But legislation is meaningless without an effective judicial system to interpret it. Consistent interpretation and application of the laws by courts provides a stable institutional environment in which the long-term consequences of economic decisions can be assessed by businesses and the public. In this context, an ideal judicial system is composed of institutions capable of applying and interpreting laws equitably and efficiently. Under most of the judicial systems in Latin America, however, laws are not subject to predictable interpretation. This uncertainty, coupled with delays in resolving cases, further increases the costs of access to justice and doing business.

11. Judicial Systems in Developing Countries

The belief that the judicial sector in Latin America is ill-prepared to foster private sector development within a market system is growing. Business surveys conducted by the World Bank (1993) indicate that the judicial system is considered to be among the top ten significant constraints to private sector development. Basic elements that constitute an efficient judicial system are missing: relatively predictable outcomes within the courts; accessibility of the courts by the population, regardless of income level; reasonable time to disposition; and adequate court-provided remedies. Increasing delays, backlogs and the uncertainty associated with expected court outcomes have diminished the quality of justice throughout the region. The judiciary is faced with several obstacles, including a dysfunctional administration of justice, lack of transparency and a perception of corruption.

As an example found in Buscaglia (1995), Table 4 presents country comparisons in the monthly percentage changes in delays and backlogs in federal jurisdictions of selected Latin American countries that have reliable data. Average changes, in monthly terms, for the period 1983-93 show a pronounced deterioration compared to the period 1973-82, which helps explain the public's dissatisfaction with judicial systems throughout the region.

Table 4
Change in Delay and Backlogs in Latin American Courts, 1973-93

	% Change in Median Delay		% Change in Backlogs	
Country	1973-82	1983-93	1973-82	1983-93
Argentina	167	478	92	479
Brazil	23	391	22	197
Chile	84	111	121	294
Colombia	34	278	91	281
Mexico	N/A	N/A	72	341
Venezuela	31	483	118	513

Sources: Supreme Court Bureau of Statistics for respective countries.

This data may also explain the results from a recent survey of the region's judicial systems conducted by the World Economic Forum (1993) that shows the majority of court users are 'not inclined' to bring disputes to court because they perceive the system as slow, uncertain and costly, or of 'poor quality'. Lack of confidence in the administration of justice is more pronounced among small economic units and low-income families.

One of the main premises within the economic analysis of the law is that institutions transmit implicit prices. An empirical analysis of legal procedures must identify the extent to which the prices imposed by legal procedures change the court users' behavior. The following example given in Buscaglia (1996a) provides an option for future research. In this example, the court system can increase the cost of resolving disputes when times to disposition increase. Figures 2 and 3 apply to the Civil Courts in Ecuador and Argentina. These graphs clearly show that the yearly percentage growth in the times to dispositions faced by the general public (measured on the horizontal axis) have been increasing in both countries since 1984. The median percentage increase in the times to disposition have been pronounced during the period 1984-94.

This clearly represents an increase in the average costs of litigation. We observe that the public reacts to this increase in costs by decreasing their filings per capita. This price effect explains the decrease in the average filings per court after discounting for changes in the number of courts, forms of case termination and for economic and population growths within the Federal District in Argentina and Quito in Ecuador. We can then interpret this graph as an expression of the effects of the increase in the implicit price imposed by the growing times to disposition faced by the general public. People react to this added cost by reducing their filings and not redressing their grievances within the court system. Our results also confirm the account of the informal courts of justice given by de Soto (1989) in Peru where people quit the formal court system and resolve their disputes within neighborhood councils.

A judicial crisis is also identified with precision for the first time in the literature in Buscaglia (1996a) and Buscaglia, Ratliff and Dakolias (1995) by using the quantitative measures based on growth rates in times to disposition and growth rates in filings per court. Specifically, a judicial crisis begins at the point where backlogs, delays and payoffs increase the cost (implicit or explicit) of accessing the system. When costs become too high, people start restricting their use of the judiciary, as we also see in Figures 2 and 3 below. By examining these graphs, we see that the points of inflexion show when a judicial crisis - more specifically, the judicial crises occurring in Ecuador in 1986 and in Argentina in 1985 - starts. Let us note that the collapse of the Latin American judiciaries takes place under the complete absence of legally enforced alternative dispute resolution mechanisms (for example arbitration or mediation).

Figure 2
Ecuador's Civil Cases: 1984-1994

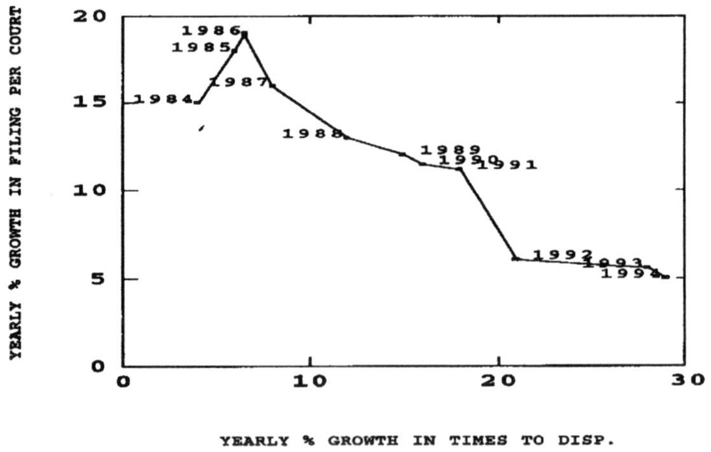

Figure 3
Argentina's Civil Cases: 1984-1994

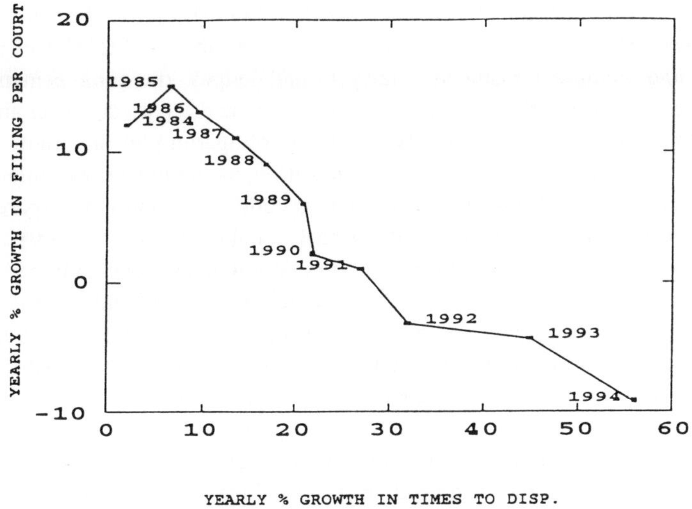

12. Economic and Inferential Analysis of the Courts

The enhancement of the capability of the courts to satisfy the demand for dispositions is one of the most challenging and important aspects of judicial reform. Almost everywhere in Latin America, courts are unable to supply enough services to satisfy the current demand. The lack of ability to satisfy this demand manifests itself through the increasing backlogs and time delays observed in Table 1. These delays are usually ascribed to lack of resources or procedural defects. For example, it is often argued that many countries in Latin America provide inadequate budgets to the courts, which impedes the judiciary from sustaining even the minimal needs to ensure the public's access to justice. It is also believed that inadequate budgets perpetuate the dependence of the judiciary, generate corruption among court personnel and prevent the judiciary from attracting well-qualified judges and support staff. In this context, many judges and legal scholars argue that the judiciary must have a separate budget subject to its control and management. The jurimetric analysis in Buscaglia and Ulen (1997) provides a statistical framework within which those key variables affecting the times to disposition are identified through non-parametric techniques.

If the judiciary is to provide the impartiality and efficiency necessary for public trust, a well defined program for judicial reform needs to address the major causes of deterioration in the quality of court services. This reform effort must address the root political, economic and legal causes of an inefficient and inequitable judiciary and not simply deal with its symptoms. Basic elements of judicial reform must include improvements in the administration of the courts and case management practices; the redefinition and/or expansion of legal education programs and training for students, lawyers and judges; the enhancement of public access to justice through legal aid programs and legal education aimed at fomenting public awareness of its rights and obligations in the courts; the availability of ADR mechanisms, such as arbitration, mediation and conciliation; the existence of judicial independence (that is, budget autonomy, transparency of the appointment process and job security) coupled with a transparent disciplinary system for court officers; and the adoption of procedural reforms, where necessary. Each component is an integral part of judicial reform as a whole. It is unrealistic, however, to think that all the components can be dealt with at once. Stages of action must be planned with consideration given to the costs and benefits of reform as perceived by the judiciary.

Some countries in Latin America have proposed allotting a pre-specified proportion of the government's budget to the judiciary as a way to address the low-salary problem but also as a mechanism to reduce times to disposition and backlogs. However, a country-by-country approach is always required. International differences in procedural requirements, substantive law and cultural legal history mean that the resources needed by courts in commercial jurisdictions to produce a certain type and quantity of services (for example, 1000 bankruptcy rulings) will greatly vary among countries. This means that 3 percent of the government budget devoted to the judiciary in one country may have a very different impact on times to disposition than the same amount devoted to the courts in another country. Therefore, it is doubtful that a higher fixed proportion of the government's budget would necessarily improve the functioning of the judicial system.

Based on these figures and the times to disposition in Figure 1, there is no proven significant international correlation between judicial efficiency (measured in terms of backlogs and times to disposition) and size of the government budget allocated to the courts. Figure 4 clearly demonstrates this lack of correlation within Latin America. The country-specific average percentage changes in the median times to disposition are measured on the vertical axis with a two-year lag after the average percentage changes in real spending devoted to the judiciary (measured on the horizontal axis) are introduced. The changes in real spending are adjusted for population and economic growth in each of the countries considered. These measurements are applied to the civil jurisdictions in each country. As we can see, countries with the largest changes in spending are not usually those experiencing the lowest times to disposition. For example, Brazil and Chile are clear examples of this lack of correlation.

Figure 4
Judicial Efficiency and Allocated Budget

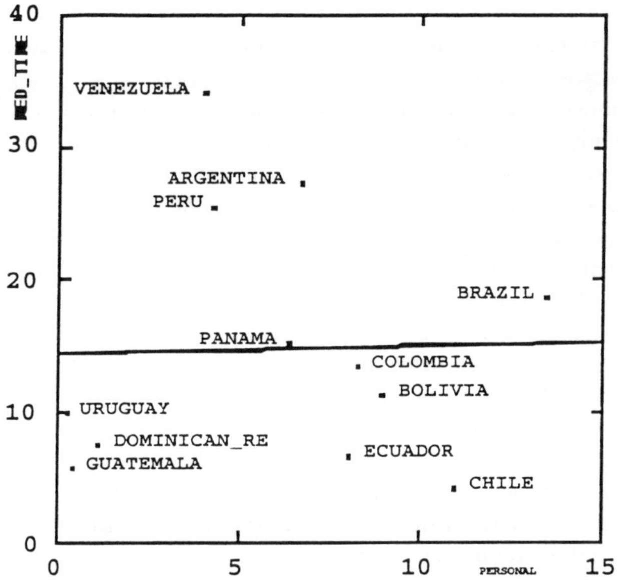

The reason for this lack of correlation lies in the fact that, on the one hand, additional resources (personnel and capital) initially reduce backlogs and delay due to improvements in court productivity. But after our two-year lag, a better endowed judiciary starts attracting additional demand (filings per court) from citizens and businesses that otherwise would be reluctant to use the courts due to the previously high litigation costs. The joint effects of both forces make it difficult to determine the consequences of adding or subtracting resources devoted to the judiciary. It is therefore much more sensible to implement a budgetary mechanism where courts can request funds based on projected increases in filings within each subject matter and geographical jurisdiction.

The enhancement of the courts' capacity to satisfy the demand for dispositions is one of the most challenging and important aspects of judicial reform. Everywhere in Latin America courts are unable to perform their basic function as mechanisms for the interpretation and application of the law. The inability to satisfy this demand manifests itself in increasing backlogs and time delays observed throughout the region. These delays are due, in part, to the lack of resources or, in many cases, to procedural defects. Other reasons are the lack of legal training, the absence of an active case management style, or an excessive administrative burden falling on judges. For example, Buscaglia, Ratliff and Dakolias (1995) found that approximately 70 percent of Argentine judges' time is spent on nonadjudicative tasks. The same administrative duties occupy 65 and 69 percent of available judicial time in Brazil and Peru, respectively.

13. Corruption and Institutional Inertia: Causes and Consequences

The development of an economic theory of judicial and procedural reform is in its infancy. Only by defining the factors enhancing or hampering judicial reform can we propose policy prescriptions for the modernization of the judiciary. In this context, we must take into account not only the present and future costs and benefits of reforms to society, but also the changes in present and future individual benefits (rents) as perceived by court officers in particular and government officials in general. We need to examine two elements of judicial reform implementation. First, the causes of institutional inertia that impede much needed court reforms need to be identified. Second, we also need to ask why reforms occur in some places but not in others by identifying the costs and benefits of implementing judicial reforms, as perceived by members of the court. Nevertheless, one key question remains: Why are the very judicial reforms that would eventually benefit most segments of society often resisted and delayed by the judiciary? The answer stems from the institutional inertia observed during the implementation of judicial reforms.

There is a widespread perception in Latin America that government officials use the courts as rent-seeking mechanisms. We can here identify substantive, procedural and organizational factors explaining the increasing presence of corrupt activities within the courts. Let us first point at the lack of consistency found in the jurisprudence that gives judges discretionary power to decide cases within a wide range of possibilities. The lack of a computer system that would permit judges and lawyers to monitor the latest decisions and to detect doctrinal inconsistencies adds to the persistence of irregularities and corrupt practices. Moreover, poorly trained judges in an overburdened legal system are also susceptible to corrupt influences and create an environment where the rule of law cannot be guaranteed. From a procedural standpoint, ex parte communication is permitted and common practice in most Latin American countries where judges can spend a good part of the day meeting lawyers and parties separately. Such communication creates incentives for corrupt behavior and lack of accountability within the courts. A second procedural element contributing to the existence of corruption has to do with the lack of standards applied to the times to disposition experienced by each type of case. Lack of time standards coupled with court delay allow court personnel to 'charge a price' for speeding the procedure. From an organizational perspective, the concentration of power given by the multiple roles assumed by a typical judge (that is, in most courts the judge is responsible for strategic planning, managing personnel, administering resources, budgetary control and planning and adjudicating cases) create incentives for corrupt behavior due to the lack of external and internal organizational control mechanisms. Addressing these substantive, procedural and organizational factors is a necessary condition to eradicate corruption within the court systems.

If the judicial sector and other members of the government use the courts for rent-seeking purposes, then it should not be surprising to find members of the bench and their clerks blocking efficiency-enhancing judicial reforms. In this context, court reforms promoting uniformity, transparency and accountability in the process of enforcing laws would necessarily diminish the courts' capacity to extract rents, in the form of illicit payments from the private sector.

Previous studies argue that judicial inertia in enacting reform stems from the long-term nature of the benefits of reform, such as added economic growth or investment. These benefits cannot be directly captured in the short term by potential reformers within the government. Contrast the long-term nature of these benefits with the short-term nature of the main costs of reform, notably a perceived decrease in rents to the courts (for example, explicit payoffs and other informal inducements provided to court officers). This asymmetry between short-term costs and long-term benefits tends to block judicial reforms and explains why court reforms, which eventually benefit most segments of society, are often resisted and delayed. Reform sequencing, then, must ensure that short-term benefits compensate for loss of rents by court officers responsible for implementing the changes. That is, initial reforms should allow for short-term benefits for court officers. In turn, court reform proposals generating longer-term benefits to the judiciary need to be implemented in later stages of the reform process.

Additional forces also enhance the judicial reform process. We usually observe that periods of judicial crisis come hand-in-hand with a general consensus to reform the court system. As stated above, a judicial crisis begins at the point where backlogs, delays and payoffs increase the cost (implicit or explicit) of accessing the system. When costs become too high, people restrict their use of the judiciary, as shown in Figures 2 and 3 above, to the point where the capacity of the courts to extract rents will diminish. At that point members of the court and governments embrace judicial reforms in order to recover their prestige and rent seeking capacity. The judiciary would more likely be willing to conduct deeper court reforms during a crisis as long as reform proposals contain sources of short-term benefits, such as greater administrative power of lower courts, judicial independence and increased court resources.

It comes as no surprise, then, that those Latin American countries undertaking judicial reforms have all experienced a deep crisis as characterized above - that is, sharp decreases in average filings per civil court. Important judicial reforms are being implemented in Ecuador, Mexico and Venezuela. In each of these three cases, additional short-term benefits guaranteed the political support of key magistrates who were willing to discuss judicial reform proposals only after a deep crisis diminished their capacity to serve the public. These benefits included generous early retirement packages, promotions for judges and support staff, new buildings and expanded budgets. Nevertheless, to ensure lasting judicial reform, short-term benefits must be channeled through institutional mechanisms capable of sustaining reform. The best institutional scenario is one in which judicial reforms are the byproduct of a consensus involving the judiciary and at least one of the other two branches of power, the legislative and executive branches. Additionally, the political leverage of expected winners from reform should counteract the activities of potential rent-losers.

14. The Social Impact of Corruption

In short, according to Buscaglia, Ratliff and Dakolias (1995, pp. 34-36), two counteracting forces explain why many developing-country governments have failed to provide an efficient judicial sector compatible with a market economy. On the one hand, efficiency-enhancing institutional change accounts for the actual reform and institutional transformation of Latin American judiciaries, while on the other hand, issues related to corruption within the courts account for institutional inertia in enacting judicial reform. Then, the nature of the relationship between a society, its legal rules and its judicial sector can be explained in terms of political rent-seeking activities and economic efficiency arguments. These two influences can also contribute to the understanding of the legal and judicial development of a nation.

Before a judicial crisis strikes, however, corruption runs rampant within the judiciary. In all cases one can observe that corruption generates immediate positive results for the individual court-user who is *willing and able* to pay the bribe. Nevertheless, the widespread effects of corruption on the overall social system are extremely pernicious. Those court-users who are not able or willing to supply illicit incentives will be excluded from the provision of a supposedly 'public good' (that is, court services) that in reality corruption transforms into a private good subject to an uncertain price. Even though corruption may remove red tape for those who are able to pay the bribe, the judicial system becomes inequitable in the perception of all of those who are excluded from the system. This sense of inequity has a long-term effect on social interaction. A corrupt judiciary promotes an inequitable social system where the allocation of resources subject to adjudication is less correlated to rights and obligations and more directly determined by the initial endowment of resources held by the court-user.

Buscaglia (1996a) shows that a 'perceived' inequitable allocation of resources hampers the productive incentives of those who are excluded from the provision of basic public goods, such as court services. One may initially think that, by eliminating bureaucratic red tape, the payment of a bribe can also enhance economic efficiency. However, this is a fallacy. As in a typical prisoner dilemma, corruption may benefit the individual who is *able and willing* to supply the bribe. However, the macro-social environment is negatively affected by a diminishing economic productivity over time caused by the general perception that the allocation of resources is determined by corrupt practices and therefore is inherently inequitable. In this respect, present corruption decreases future productivity, thereby reducing dynamic efficiency (that is, the present value of future national income). From this perspective, a more efficient public court system coupled with available ADR mechanisms provided by the private sector can foster the necessary balance between equity and efficiency in the provision of justice - a balance that is notably lacking throughout Latin America. Even more so, judicial reform programs must also address the lack of court access afforded to low-income segments of the population. Court reform increases efficiency and reduces these barriers to low-income segments, thereby contributing to the stabilization of democracy in Latin America.

C. Conclusion

15. Scope of the Field

As a body of knowledge within the social sciences, the economic analysis of the law certainly needs to reinforce its power to verify claims based on observations. Here, of course, we would depart from the Austrian School's tradition of limiting itself to the identification of logical truths in the study of human action and interaction and side with a legal realism which allows to develop a more structured public policy in the legal realm. In no other area is the development of a 'tool kit' of empirical capabilities more necessary than in the legal and economic study of development.

We have approached law and economics of development in this chapter by covering the main theoretical and empirical scholarly work identifying the substantive sources of efficiency-enhancing legal doctrines (that is, bottom-up approach to law making, legal transplants and legal integration) in less developed countries. We have also discussed the main procedural requirements needed to sustain an economic system based on impersonal exchange (a judicial sector with alternative dispute resolution mechanisms) while also exploring some of the main symptoms of a dysfunctional judiciary (corruption and lack of efficiency in the courts).

16. Future Research Path

The measurability of the price matrix set by institutional frameworks relates, of course, to achieving efficiency in consumption and production through much needed reforms in private and public law. Yet these legal reforms and their impact on efficiency must also connect to the issue of fostering political stability through a widespread perception of equity within the members of society. This brings us to one of the most important areas of law and economics to be developed in future studies: the links between legal reform, efficiency and equity. Economists tend to shy away from the microeconomic study of 'ethics'. Yet, as Cooter's (1996b) study has shown, the rigorous microeconomic analysis of the compatibility between equity and efficiency is real and useful. As demonstrated in Alesina et al. (1992), developing countries face a social environment in which a vast proportion of their population lives under material conditions incompatible with social and political stability. Paying close attention to the links between legal reforms and efficiency is only one step in the right direction.. From all those possible 'efficiency' scenarios one could argue that the economic analysis of the law needs to provide a framework within which one can select among the many efficiency-enhancing legal institutions and rules that would foster a perception of equity among the population. From this perspective, as stated in Buscaglia (1996a) a perception of a level playing field can be traced to the individual's incentives to enhance its own productivity within the economic system. At this point in time, there is much more scholarship to be offered in this area.

Acknowledgments

The comments of three anonymous referees are gratefully acknowledged. The author is also grateful for the outstanding research assistance of Brian Johnson, Shawn McMahon and Paulina Sierra Samano. The usual disclaimers apply.

Bibliography on Law and Economics of Development (0580)

Alesino, Alberto, Ozler, Sule, Roubini, Nouriel and Sweagel, Phillip (1992), 'Political Instability and Economic Growth', **4173** NBER Working Paper.

Andvig, Jens C. and Moene, Karl Ove (1990), 'How Corruption May Corrupt', **13** *Journal of Economic Behavior and Organization*, 63-76.

Arantes, Peter, Gellhorn, Ernest A. and Robinson, Glen O. (1983), 'A Theory of Legislative Delegation', **68** *Cornell Law Review*, 23-56.

Axelrod, R. (1981), 'The Emergence of Cooperation Among Egoists', **75** *American Political Science Review*, 306-318.

Axelrod, Robert (1984), *The Evolution of Cooperation*, New York, Basic Books.

Backhaus, Jürgen G. (1996), 'An Economic Analysis of Constitutional Law', in Buscaglia, Edgardo, Ratliff, William and Cooter, Robert (eds), *Law and Economics of Development*, JAI Press.

Bardhan, Pranab K. (1989), 'The New Institutional Economics and Development Theory: A Brief Critical Assessment', **17(9)** *World Development*, 1389-1395.

Barragan, Julia (1994), *Como se Hacen Las Leyes*, Venezuela, Caracas, Editorial Planeta.

Barton, John (1996), 'The Economic and Legal Context of Contemporary Technology Transfer', in Buscaglia, Edgardo, Ratliff, William and Cooter, Robert (eds), *Law and Economics of Development*, JAI Press.

Barzel, Yoram (1990), *Economic Analysis of Property Rights*, New York, Cambridge University Press.

Becker, Gary S. (1976), *The Economic Approach to Human Behavior*, Chicago, University of Chicago Press, 314 p.

Becker, Gary S. (1983), 'A Theory of Competition among Pressure Groups for Political Influence', **98** *Quarterly Journal of Economics*, 371-383.

Bell, Martin and Pavitt, Keith (1993), 'Technological Accumulation and Industrial Growth: Contrasts Between Developed and Developing Countires', **2** *Industrial and Corporate Change*, 157-210.

Benson, Bruce L. (1984), 'Rent Seeking from a Property Rights Perspective', **34** *Southern Economic Journal*, 345-378.

Birch, Melissa and Primo-Braga, Carlos Alberto (1992), 'Regulation in Latin America: Prospects for the 1990s', in, *Texas Papers on Latin America 93-08*, Illinois, Latin America 2000 Conference, University of Illinois, Urbana-Champaign, Illinois.

Boyd, James (1996), 'Environmental Liability Reform and Privatization in Central and Eastern Europe', **3** *European Journal of Law and Economics*.

Brenner, Reuven (1994), *Labyrinths of Prosperity*, Ann Arbor, MI, University of Michigan Press.

Bromley, Daniel W. (1989), 'Property Relations and Economic Development: The Other Land Reform', **17** *World Development*, 867-877.

Bromley, Daniel W. (1993), 'Reconstituting Economic Systems: Institutions in National Economic Development', **11** *Development Policy Review*, 131-151.

Bromley, Daniel W. (1994), 'The Enclosure Movement Revisited: The South African Commons', **28** *Journal of Economic Issues*, 357-365.

Burke, John J.A. (1996), 'The Economic Basis of Law as Demonstrated by the Reformation of NIS Legal Systems', **18** *Loyola of Los Angeles International and Comparative Law Journal*, 207 ff.

Buscaglia, Edgardo (1993), *Law, Technological Progress and Economic Development*, California, Stanford University Press, Hoover Institution, International Studies Program, Stanford.

Buscaglia, Edgardo (1994), 'Legal and Economic Development: The Missing Links', **35** *Journal of Inter-American Studies and World Affairs*, 153-169.

Buscaglia, Edgardo (1995), 'Judicial Reform in Latin America: The Obstacles Ahead', **4** *Journal of Latin American Affairs*, 8-16.

Buscaglia, Edgardo (1996a), *Legal and Economic Integration in Latin America: The Lessons of MERCOSUR*, Paper Presented at the Comparative Law and Economics Meeting in Siena, Italy May 13-14.

Buscaglia, Edgardo (1996b), 'Factores Economicos que Explican la Integracion Legal en Latinoamerica: El Caso de MERCOSUR', in *Contribuciones*, Argentina, Buenos Aires, Konrad Adenauer Foundation.

Buscaglia, Edgardo (1997a), 'An Economic Analysis of Corrupt Practices within the Judiciary in Latin America', in, *Law and Economics V*, Deventer, Kluwer Press.

Buscaglia, Edgardo (1997b), 'Introduction', in Buscaglia, Edgardo, Ratliff, William and Cooter, Robert (eds), *Law and Economics of Development*, JAI Press.

Buscaglia, Edgardo and Domingo, Pilar (1996), 'Political and Economic Impediments to Judicial Reform in Latin America', in Buscaglia, Edgardo, Ratliff, William and Cooter, Robert (eds), *Law and Economics of Development*, JAI Press.

Buscaglia, Edgardo and Guerrero, Jose Luis (1995), 'Quantitative Analysis of Counterfeiting Activities in Developing Countries in the Pre-GATT Period', **35** *Jurimetrics Journal*, 221-241.

Buscaglia, Edgardo and Long, Clarisa (1997), *Essays in Public Policy*, Stanford, CA, Hoover Institution, Stanford University.

Buscaglia, Edgardo and Ratliff, William (1997), 'Judicial Reform in Latin America: A Condition for Economic Development', in Buscaglia, Edgardo, Ratliff, William and Cooter, Robert (eds), *Law and Economics of Development*, JAI Press.

Buscaglia, Edgardo and Ulen, Thomas S. (1994), *A Comparative Analysis of the Intellectual Property Law in Argentina within the GATT Framework*, Paper Presented at the 1994 Annual Meetings of the American Law and Economics Association, Stanford University, May 13-15.

Buscaglia, Edgardo and Ulen, Thomas (1997), 'A Quantitative Assessment of the Efficiency of the Judicial Sector in Latin America', **17** *International Review of Law and Economics*, 275-291.

Buscaglia, Edgardo, Ratliff, William and Dakolias, Maria (1995), *Judicial Reform in Latin America: A Framework for National Development, Essays in Policy Studies*, Stanford, CA, Stanford University Press.

Buscaglia, Edgardo, Ratliff, William and Dakolias, Maria (1997), 'Judicial Reform in Latin America: A Framework for National Development', in *Essays in Policy Studies*, Stanford, CA, Stanford University Press.

Bussani, Mauro and Mattei, Ugo (1996), 'Making the Other Path Efficient: Economic Analysis and Tort Law in Less Developed Countries', in Buscaglia, Edgardo, Ratliff, William and Cooter, Robert (eds), *Law and Economics of Development*, JAI Press.

Cabrillo, Francisco (1994), 'Industrialización y Derecho de daños en la España del siglo XIX (Industrialization and Tort Law in XIXth Century Spain)', **12** *Revista de Historia Económica*, 591-609.

Cadwell, Charles (1995), 'Implementing Legal Reform in Transition Economies', *Paper Presented at the American Law and Economies Association Annual Meeting at the University of California at Berkeley, May 13-14*.

Calabresi, Guido (1961), 'Some Thoughts on Risk Distribution and the Law of Torts', **70** *Yale Law Journal*, 35-46.

Capelletti, Mauro (1989), *The Judicial Process in Comparative Perspective*, Oxford, Clarendon Press.

Carbonetto, Daniel, Hoyle, Jenny and Tueros, Mario (1988), *Lima: Sector Informal I*, Lima: Centros de Estudios para el Desarrollo y la Participacion (CEDEP), Lima, Peru.

Carino, Ledivina V. (ed.) (1986), *Bureaucratic Corruption in Asia: Causes, Consequences and Controls*, Quezon City, Philippines, JMC Press.

Carvallho, Jose L. (1994), *Private Sector Development and Property Rights in Latin America*, Washington, DC, World Bank, Latin America Technical Department.

Clagett, Helen (1952), *The Administration of Justice in Latin America*, Dobbs-Ferry, NY, Oceana Publications.

Coase, Ronald H. (1960), 'The Problem of Social Cost', **3** *Journal of Law and Economics*, 1-44. Reprinted in Ackermann, Bruce A. (ed.), *Economic Foundations of Property Law*, Boston, Little Brown, 1975, 17-22. Reprinted in Medema, Steven G. (ed.),*The Legacy of Ronald Coase in Economic Analysis*, Vol.2, Aldershot, Edward Elgar Publishing, 1995, 5-48. Reprinted in Coase, Ronald H., *The Firm, the Market and the Law*, Chicago, University of Chicago Press, 1988.

Coase, Ronald H. (1991), 'The Institutional Structure of Production', in Coase, Ronald H. (ed.), *Essays on Economics and Economists*, Chicago, IL, University of Chicago Press.

Coelho, Philip R.P. (1985), 'An Examination into the Causes of Economic Growth', **7** *Research in Law and Economics*, 89-116.

Cooter, Robert (1994), 'Structural Adjudication and the New Law Merchant: A Model of Decentralized Law', **14** *International Review of Law and Economics*, 215-231.

Cooter, Robert D. (1989), 'The Best Right Laws: Value Foundations of the Economic Analysis of Law', **64** *Notre Dame Law Review*, 816-819.

Cooter, Robert D. (1991), 'Inventing Market Property: The Land Courts of Papua New Guinea', **25** *Law and Society Review*, 759-801.

Cooter, Robert D. (1996a), 'Decentralized Law for a Complex Economy: The Structural Approach to Adjudicating the New Law Merchant', **144** *University of Pennsylvania Law Review*, 1643-1696.

Cooter, Robert D. (1996b), 'The Theory of Market Modernization of Law', **16** *International Review of Law and Economics*, 141-172.

Cooter, Robert D. and Ginsburg, Tom (1996), 'Comparative Judicial Discretion: An Empirical Test of Economic Models', Working Paper No 95-1, Program in Law and Economics, Working Paper Series, School of Law, University of California at Berkeley.

Cooter, Robert D. and Gordley, James (1991), 'Economic Analysis in Civil Law Countries: Past, Present, Future - Introduction to a Symposium', **11** *International Review of Law and Economics*, 261-263.

Cooter, Robert D. and Kornhauser, Lewis A. (1980), 'Can Litigation Improve the Law without the Help of Judges', **9** *Journal of Legal Studies*, 139-163.

Cooter, Robert D. and Ulen, Thomas S. (1988), *Law and Economics*, Glenview, IL, Scott, Foresman and Company.

Cowell, Frank A. (1990), *Cheating the Government: The Economics of Evasion*, Cambridge, MIT Press, 267 p.

David, René and Brierley, John E.C. (1985), *Major Legal Systems in the World Today, 3rd Edition*, New York, The Free Press.

Dawson, John P. (1968), *The Oracles of the Law*, Ann Arbor, MI, University of Michigan Press.

De Meza, David and Gould, J.R. (1992), 'The Social Efficiency of Private Decision to Enforce Property Rights', **100** *Journal of Political Economy*, 561-580.

de Soto, Hernando (1989), *The Other Path*, New York, Harper and Row.

de Soto, Hernando (1996a), 'Property Rights and Economic Progress in Developing Countries: The Peruvian Experience', in Buscaglia, Edgardo, Ratliff, William and Cooter, Robert (eds), *Law and Economics of Development*, JAI Press.

de Soto, Hernando (1996b), 'Preface', in Buscaglia, Edgardo, Ratliff, William and Cooter, Robert (eds), *Law and Economics of Development*, JAI Press.

Dezalay, Yves and Garth, Bryant G. (1995), 'Merchants of Law as Mortal Entrepreneurs: Constructing International Justice from the Competition for Trasnational Business Disputes', **29** *Law and Society Review*, 27-64.

Dolinger, Jacod and Rosen, Keith (1992), *A Panorama of Brazilian Law*, North-South Center and Editora Explanada Ltd.

Douglas, Mary (1986), *How Institutions Think*, Syracuse, NY, Syracuse University Press.

Eggertsson, Thrainn (1990), *Economic Behaviour and Institutions*, Cambridge, Cambridge University Press, 385 p.

Eisenberg, Melvin Aron (1988), *The Nature of the Common Law*, Cambridge, MA, Harvard University Press, 204 p.

Elliott, E. Donald, Ackerman, Bruce A. and Millian, John (1985), 'Toward a Theory of Statutory Evolution: The Federalization of Environmental Law', **1** *Journal of Law, Economics and Organization*, 313-340.

Emiola, Akintude (1987), *Nigerian Labor Law*, 2nd edn, Ethiope Publishing Company.

Farber, Daniel A. and Frickey, Philip P. (1991), *Law and Public Choice: A Critical Introduction*, Chicago, IL, University of Chicago Press, 159 p.

Fiorina, M. (1982), 'Legislative Choice of Regulatory Forms: Legal Process or Administrative Proces?', **39** *Public Choice*, 33 ff.

Fleisig, Heywood (1994), *Law. Legal Procedure and the Economic Value of Collateral: The Case of Bolivia*, Washington, DC, World Bank, Private Sector Development Department.

Foray, Dominique and Freeman, Christopher (eds) (1993), *Technology and the Wealth of Nations*, Stanford, CA, Stanford University Press, 23-34.

Galanter, Michael (1974), 'Why Haves' Come Out Ahead: Speculation on the Limits of Legal Change', **9** *Law and Society Review*, 95 ff.

Garland, David (1990), *Punishment in Modern Society: A Study in Social Theory*, Chicago, IL, University of Chicago Press.

Gil Diaz, Francisco and Fernandez, Arturo (1991), 'Del Desarrollo Institutcional al progreso Economico (Institutional Development and Economic Progress)', in Gil Diaz, Francisco and Fernandez, Arturo (eds), *El Efecto de la Regulacionen Algunos de los Sectores de la Economia Mexican, Fondo de Cultura Economica*, Instituto Technologica Autonomo de Mexico/ and Centro Internacional para el Desarrollo Economico, 134-189.

Goodman, M. (1978), 'An Economic Theory of the Evolution of the Common Law', **7** *Journal of Legal Studies*, 393 ff.

Gould, David J. (1980), *Bureacratic Corruption and Underdevelopment in the Third World: The Case of Zaire*, New York, Pergamon Press.

Gould, David J. and Amaro Reyes, Jose A. (1983), 'The Effects of Corruption on Administrative Performance: Illustrations from Developing Countries', World Bank Staff Working Paper No 580, Management and Development Series, Washington DC: The World Bank.

Granado del, Juan Javier (1996), *Legis Imperium*, Bolivia, La Paz, Fondo Editorial de la Univesidad Iberoamericana.

Guasch, Luis and Spiller, Pablo T. (1994), *Regulation and Private Sector Development in Latin America*, Washington, DC, World Bank, Latin America Technical Department.

Hachette, Dominique and Luders, Rolf (1993), *Privatization in Chile: An Economic Analysis*, San Francisco, CA, ICS Press.

Hansmann, Henry B. and Mattei, Ugo (1994), 'The Comparrative Law and Economics of Trusts', Paper Presented at CLEF at Geneva, Switzerland.

Hayashida, Seimei (1992a), 'Ho ha Keizaidearu (Law is Economics)', **42** *Hokudai Hogaku Ronshu* (Hokkaido Law Review), 1369-1412.

Hayashida, Seimei (1992b), 'Ho to Keizai, Keizaibunseki, Hihan to Paradaimu (Law and Economics, Economic Analysis, Its Critique and Paradigm)', **42** *Hokudai Hogaku Ronshu* (Hokkaido Law Review), 905-956. Part 2, 1234-1272.

Hayek, Friedrich A. (1973), *Law, Legislation and Liberty*, Chicago, University of Chicago Press.

Hirshleifer, Jack (1982), 'Evolutionary Models in Law and Economics', *Research in Law and Economics*.

Hirshleifer, Jack and Coll Martinez, Juan Carlos (1988), 'What Strategies can Support the Evolutionary Emergence of Cooperation?', **32** *Journal of Conflict Resolution*, 367-398.

Huanca Ayaviri, Felix (1995), *Analisis Economico del Derecho*, Bolivia, La Paz, Fondo Editorial de la Universidad Iberoamericana.

Huntington, Samuel (1979), 'Modernization and Corruption', in Ekpo (ed.), *Monday, Bureaucratic Corruption in Sub-Saharan Africa: Towards a Search for Causes and Consequences*, Washington, DC, University Press of America.

Inman, Richard (1990), *Markets, Government and the 'New' Political Economy*, Cambridge, MA, The MIT Press.

James, William Roden (1973), *Modern Land Law in Nigeria*, Nigeria, University of Ife Press.

Karst, Kenneth L. (1966), *Latin American Legal Institutions: Problems for Comparative Study*, Los Angeles, UCLA Latin American Center.

Karst, Kenneth L. and Rosen, Keith (1975), *Law and Development in Latin America*, Berkeley, University of California Press.

Kikeri, Sunita, Nellis, John and Shirley, Mary (1992), *Privatization: The Lessons of Experience*, Washington, DC, The World Bank.

Kirchner, Christian (1991), 'The Difficult Reception of Law and Economics in Germany', **11** *International Review of Law and Economics*, 277-292.

Kitch, Edmund W. (1983), 'Intellectual Foundations of Law and Economics', **33** *Journal of Legal Education*, 183-209.

Klitgaard, Robert (1988), *Controlling Corruption*, Berkeley, University of California Press, 220 p.

Klitgaard, Robert (1991), *Adjusting to Reality: Beyond State versus Market in Economic Development*, San Francisco, CA, ICS Press.

Kornhauser, Lewis A. (1984), 'The Great Image of Authority', **36** *Stanford Law Review*, 349-389.

Larson, Bruce A. and Bromley, Daniel W. (1990), 'Property Rights, Externalities and Resource Degradation: Locating the Tragedy', **33** *Journal of Development Economics*, 235-362.

Leff, Arthur A. (1974), 'Economic Analysis of Law: Some Realism About Nominalism', **60** *Virginia Law Review*, 78 ff.

Leoni, Bruno (1991), *Freedom and the Law*, Indianapolis, Liberty Fund.

Long, Clarisa and Buscaglia, Edgardo (1997), 'A Quantitative Analysis of the Legal and Economic Integration in Latin America', in Buscaglia, Edgardo, Ratliff, William and Cooter, Robert (eds), *Law and Economics of Development*, JAI Press.

Lucas, Robert E. (1988), 'On the Mechanics of Economic Development', **22** *Journal of Monetary Economics*, 248-257.

Makgetla, Neva and Seidman, Robert B. (1989), 'The Applicability of Law and Economics to Policymaking in the Third World', **23** *Journal of Economic Issues*, 35-77.

Malloy, Robin Paul (1986), 'Equating Human Rights and Property Rights. the Need for a Moral Judgment in an Economic Analysis of Law and Social Policy', **163** *Ohio State Law Journal*, 78-89.

Marasinghe, M.L. (1984), 'Towards a Third World Perspective of Jurisprudence', in Marasingue, M.L. and Conklin, W.E. (eds), *Essays on Third World Perspective in Jurisprudence*, Singapore, Malaysian Law Journal PTE, Ltd.

Margadant, Guillermo Floris (1983), *An Introduction to the History of Mexican Law*, Dobbs-Ferry, NY, Oceana Publications.

Martinez, Gabriel (1997), 'Competition Policy and Deregulation in Mexico in the late 1990s', in Buscaglia, Edgardo, Ratliff, William and Cooter, Robert (eds), *Law and Economics of Development*, JAI Press.

Mathews, R.C.O. (1986), 'The Economics of Institutions and the Source of Growth', **69** *Economic Journal*.

Mattei, Ugo (1993), 'Law and Economics in Civil Law Countires: A Comparative Approach', **14** *International Review of Law and Economics*, 265-275.

Mattei, Ugo (1994), 'Efficiency in Legal Transplants: An Essay in Comparative Law and Economics', **14** *International Review of Law and Economics*, 245 ff.

Mattei, Ugo and Pardolesi, Roberto (1991), 'Law and Economics in Civil Law Countries: A Comparative Approach', **11** *International Review of Law and Economics*, 265-275.

Mattick, Ross (1992), 'Agrarian Reform in West Bengal: The End of an Illusion', **20(5)** *World Development*, 735-750.

Mauro, Paolo (1995), 'Corruption and Growth', **111** *Quarterly Journal of Economics*, 681-711.

McGee, Robert W. (1992), *The Market Solution to Economic Development in Eastern Europe*, The Edwin Mellen Press, 320 p.

McKinnon, Ronald I. (1991), *Lessons of Economic Liberalization: Financial Control in the Transition to a Market Economy*, Baltimore, MD, John Hopkins University Press.

Mercuro, Nicholas and Ryan, Timothy P. (1984), *Law, Economics and Public Policy*, Greenwood, JAI Press.

Merryman, John Henry (1985), *The Civil Law Tradition*, Stanford, CA, Stanford University Press.

Merryman, John Henry and Clark, David (1978), *Comparative Law: Western European and Latin American Legal Systems-Cases and Meterials*, Indianapolis, Bobbs-Merrill.

Milgrom, Paul R. and Roberts, John (1988), 'An Economic Approach to Influence Activities in Organizations', **94** *American Journal of Sociology, supplement.*

Myrdal, Gunnar (1989), 'Corruption as a Hindrance to Modernization in South Asia', in Heidenheimer, Arnold J., Jophnson, Michael and Le Vine, Victor (eds), *Political Corruption: A Handbook*, New Brunswick, NJ, Transaction Press, 406-407.

North, Douglass (1981), *Sturcture and Change in Economic History*, New York, W.W. Norton.

North, Douglass (1987), 'Institutions, Transaction Costs and Economic Growth', **25** *Economic Inquiry*, 456-489.

North, Douglass (1990), *Institutions, Institutional Change and Economic Growth Performance*, Cambridge, Cambridge University Press.

North, Douglass (1991), 'Institutions', **5(1)** *Journal of Economic Perspectives*.

Nozick, Robert (1974), *Anarchy, State and Utopia*, New York, Basic Books.

Ogus, Anthony I. (1995), 'Economics and Law Reform: Thirty Years of Law Commission Endeavor', **11** *Law Quarterly Review*, 407-420.

Olson, Mancur (1965), *The Logic of Collective Action: Public Goods and the Theory of Groups*, Cambridge, MA, Harvard University Press, 186 p.

Olson, Mancur (1982), *The Rise and Decline of Nations*, New haven, Yale University Press.

Olson, Mancur (1993), 'Dictatorship, Democracy and Development', **87** *American Political Science Review*, 567-576.

Orr, Daniel and Ulen Thomas S. (1993), 'The Role of Trust and the Law in Privatization', **33** *Quarterly Review of Economics and Finance*, 135-155.

Ostrom, Elnor (1990), *Governing the Commons: The Evolution of Institutions for Collective Action*, Cambridge, Cambridge University Press.

Ott, Claus and Schäfer, Hans-Bernd (1991), 'Emergence and Construction of Efficient Rules in the Legal System of German Civil Law', Paper Presented at the European Law and Economics Association.

Paredes, Ricardo (1997), 'Jurisprudence of the Antitrust Commissions in Chile', in Buscaglia, Edgardo, Ratliff, William and Cooter, Robert (eds), *Law and Economics of Development*, JAI Press.

Pator, Santos (1989), *Economia y Sistema Juridico. Una Introduccion al Analisis Economico del Derecho* (Introduction to Economic Analysis of Law), Madrid, Tecnos.

Pinheiro, Neto (1990), *Consumer Protection in Brazil*, Sao Paolo, Advogados.

Posner, Richard A. (1980), 'A Theory of Primitive Society, with Special Reference to Law', **23** *Journal of Law and Economics*, 1-25.

Posner, Richard A. (1992), *Economic Analysis of Law, 4th edn*, Boston, Little Brown and Company.

Prebisch, Raul (1950), *The Economic Development of Latin America and its Principal Problems*, New York, Lake Success, United Nations.

Priest, George L. (1987), 'Measuring Legal Change', **3** *Journal of Law, Economics and Organization*, 193-225.

Primo-Braga, Carlos Alberto (1990a), 'The Developing Country Case for or Against Intellectual Property Protection', in *Strengthening Protection of Intellctual Property in Developing Countries*, Washinton DC, The World Bank, 69-87.

Primo-Barga, Carlos Alberto (1990b), *Strengthening Protection of Intellectual Property in Developing Countries*, Washington, DC, The World Bank.

Ramseyer, J. Mark (1989), 'Water Law in Imperial Japan: Public Goods, Private Claims and Legal Convergence', **18** *Journal of Legal Studies*, 51-77.

Ramseyer, J. Mark and Rosenbluth, Frances M. (1995), *The Politics of Oligarchy: Institutional Choice In Imperial Japan*, New York: Cambridge University Press.

Rapp, Richard Tilden and Rozek, Richard P. (1990), 'Benefits and Costs of Intellectual Property Protection in Developing Countries', **24** *Journal of World Trade*, 75-102. Reprinted in 'How Property Protection Fuels Economies', **3** *Les Nouvelles*, 1992.

Ratliff, William and Rosenbluth, Frances M. (1997), 'Judicial Reform: The Neglected Priority in Latin America', in Rich, Paul and de los Reyes, Guillermo (eds), *The Annals of the American Academy of Political and Social Science*, London, Sage Press.

Rawls, John (1971), *A Theory of Justice*, Cambridge, MA, Harvard University Press.

Reuven, Brenner (1980), 'Economics: An Imperialistic Science?', **9** *Journal of Legal Studies*, 184 ff.

Roemer andrès (1989), *Evaluacion Juridica, Finmanciera, y Economicade la Camaronicultura en Mexico*, Instituto Tecnologico Autonomo de Mexico.

Roemer andrès (1993), *Introduccion al Analisis Economico del Derecho*, Mexico City, Fondo de Cultura Economica.

Rose-Ackerman, Susan (1978), *Corruption: A Study in Political Economy*, New York, Academic Press. Reprinted as 'Problem Der Ökonomischen Theorie', in Fleck, C. and Helmut Kuzmics (eds), Korruption: Zur Soziologie.

Rose-Ackerman, Susan (1980), 'Risktaking and Reelection: Does Federalism Promote Innovation?', **89** *Journal of Legal Studies*, 593-616.

Rose-Ackerman, Susan (1981a), 'Does Federalism Matter: Political Choice in a Federal Republic', **89** *Journal of political Economy*, 347 ff.

Rose-Ackerman, Susan (1981b), 'Does Federalism Matter?: Political Choice in a Federal Republic', **89** *Journal of Political Economy*, 152-165.

Rose-Ackerman, Susan (1986), 'Reforming Public Bureaucracy through Economic Incentives?', **2** *Journal of Law, Economics and Organization*, 131 ff.

Rosenn, Keith S. (1984), 'Brazil's Legal Culture: The Jeto Revisited', **1** *Florida International Law Journal*.

Rubin, Edward L. (1996), 'The New Legal Process, the synthesis of Discourse and the Microanalysis of Institutions', **109** *Harvard Law Review*, 1393 ff.

Rubin, Paul H. (1993), 'Growing a Legal System, with Special Reference to the Post-Communist Economies' Center for International Reform and the Informal Sector', Working Paper No 63.

Saharay, H.K. (1988), *Labor and Social Laws in India*, Eastern Law House.

Santhanam Committee (1994), *Report by the Committee on Prevention of Corruption*, Government of India, Ministry of Home Affairs.

Schlesinger, Rudolf B. (1959), 'Common Law and Civil Law-Comparison of Methods and Sources', in, *Comparitive Law Cases, Texts and Materials*, Foundation Press.

Seidman, Ann and Seidman, Robert B. (1996), 'Drafting Legislation for Development: Lessons from a Chinese Project', **44** *American Journal of Comparative Law*, 1 ff.

Seidman, Robert B. (1978), *State, Law and Development*, New York, St Martin's Press.

Shleifer, Andrei (1994), 'Establishing Property Rights', in, *Proceedings of the World Bank at the Annual Conference on Development Economics*, Washington, DC, The World Bank.

Shleifer Andrei and Vishny, Robert W. (1993), 'Corruption', **108** *Quarterly Journal of Economics*, 599-617.

Simpson, Alfred William Brian (1975), *A History of Common Law of Contract*, Oxford, Clarendon Press.

Sjaastad, Espen and Bromley, Daniel W. (1997), 'Indigenous Land Rights in Sub-Saharan Africa: Appropriation, Security and Investment Demand', **25** *World Development*, 549-562.

Stone, Andrew, Levy, Brian and Paredes, Ricardo (1992), 'Public Institutions and Private Transactions: The Legal and Regulatory Environment for Business Transactions in

Brazil and Chile', *Policy Research Working Paper Series 891*, World Bank: Country Economics Department, Washington DC.

Swallow, Brent and Bromley, Daniel W. (1994), 'Co-Management or No Management: The Prospects for Internal Governance of Common Property Regimes through Dynamic Contracts', **22** *Oxford Agrarian Studies*, 3-16.

Swallow, Brent and Bromley, Daniel W. (1995), 'Institutions, Governance and Incentives in Common Property Regimes for African Rangelands', **6** *Environmental and Resource Economics*, 99-118.

Tokman, Victor (1989), 'Policies for a Heterogeneous Informal Sector in Latin America', **17** *World Development*, 1067-1076.

Tokman, Victor (1992), *Beyond Regulation: The Informal Economy in Latin America*, Boulder, CO, Lynne Rienner.

Trebilcock, Michael J. (1983), 'The Prospects of 'Law and Economics': A Canadian Perspective', **33** *Journal of Legal Education*, 288-290.

Trebilcock, Michael J. (1997), 'What Makes Poor Countries Poor?: The Role of Institutional Capital in Economic Development', in Buscaglia, Edgardo, Ratliff, William and Cooter, Robert (eds), *Law and Economics of Development*, JAI Press.

Trubek, E. (1972), 'Towards a Social Theory of Law: 'An Essay on the Study of Law and Development', **82** *Yale Law Journal*, 1 ff.

Ulen, Thomas S. (1996), 'The Comparative Law and Economics of Federalism', Paper Presented at the Comparative Law and Economics of Legal Integration Conference in Siena, Italy, May 13-14.

Ulen, Thomas (1997), 'Law's Contributions to Economic Growth', in Buscaglia, Edgardo, Ratliff, William and Cooter, Robert (eds), *Law and Economics of Development*, JAI Press.

Uvieshara, E.E. (1976), *Trade Union Law in Nigeria*, Benin City, Ethiope Publishing Company.

Van Den Bergh, Roger (1992), 'Law and Economics in Europe: Present State and Future Prospects', in Bouckaert, Boudewijn and De Geest, Gerrit (eds), *Bibliography of Law and Economics*, Deventer, Kluwer Academic Publishers.

Van den Brink, Rogier, Chavas, Jean-Paul and Bromley, Daniel W. (1995), 'The Economics of Cain and Abel: Agro-Pastoral Property Rights in the Sahel', **31** *Journal of Development Studies*, 373-399.

Watson, Alan (1974), *Legal Transplants: An Approach to Comparative Law*, Cambridge, MA, Harvard University Press.

Watson, Alan (1978a), 'Comparative Law and Legal Change', **313** *Columbia Law Journal*, 45-67.

Watson, Alan (1978b), *Society and Legal Change*, Cambridge, Cambridge University Press.

White, Eduardo (1975), *Control of Restrictive Practices in Latin America*, New York, Viking Press.

Williamson, Oliver E. (1991), 'Intellectual Foundations: The Need for a Broader View', **33** *Journal of Legal Education*, 210-216.

Wilson, James Q. (1989), *Bureaucracy: What Government Agencies Do and Why they Do It*, New York, Basic Books.

World Bank (1993), *Ecuador: Constraints to Private Sector Development*, Washington, DC, The World Bank, Trade, Finance and Private Sector Development Division, LAC Country Department IV.

World Economic Forum (1993), *World Competitiveness Report*, Baltimore, MD, John Hopkins University Press.

X (1990), Pinheiro Neto, Sao Paulo: Advogados.

X (1991), *Consumer Protection Law in India*, Bombay, N.M. Tripathi Pvt. Ltd.

Xue-Lascoux, Zhiqun and Bromley, Daniel W. (1996), 'Necessity and Purpose in Chinese Agriculture: 1949-95'', **24** *Oxford Development Studies*, 261-280.

Ziskind, David (1987), *Labor Provisions in African Constitutions*, Los Angeles, Litlaw Foundation.

0610
PUBLIC CHOICE, CONSTITUTIONAL POLITICAL ECONOMY AND LAW AND ECONOMICS

Ludwig Van den Hauwe
Brussels, Belgium

Abstract

The various subdisciplines within the emerging 'new institutionalism' in economics all draw special attention to the legal-political constraints within which economic and political agents choose and therefore represent a return of economics to its appropriate legal foundations. By changing the name of his research programme to constitutional political economy Buchanan distanced himself from those parts of the public choice literature that remained too close to the traditional welfare economics approach. This chapter draws lessons for law and economics from recent developments in the re-emerging field of constitutional political economy. CPE compares alternative sets of institutional arrangements, in markets and the polity, and their outcomes, using 'democratic consent' as an internal standard of comparison. The chapter discusses the methodological foundation of the CPE approach, presents Buchanan's reconstruction of the Coase theorem along subjectivist-contractarian lines and gives an overview of recent contributions to the literature.
JEL classification: B41, D70, H10
Keywords: Constitutional Economics, Constitutional Political Economy, Public Choice, James M. Buchanan, Methodological Foundation

A. The Manifold Legacy of Adam Smith

1. Introduction

As the title of this chapter suggests, the new law and economics movement on the one hand and the now rapidly emerging field of constitutional political economy - as well as the somewhat older public choice branch of economics from which it emerged - on the other hand, are research traditions that are in some respects genuinely related. In other respects the differences between them are sufficiently important, however, to warrant a more or less detailed discussion.

Both exemplify the 'extension' of economics beyond its traditional boundaries - from market to non market behaviour - and both belong to a set of subdisciplines that draw special attention to the legal-political constraints within which economic and political agents operate. Both constitute complemental facets of the emerging 'new institutionalism' in economics.

Both may have drawn substantial inspiration from the encompassing theoretical perspective and the reformist attitude that were characteristic of Adam Smith's approach. Indeed, CPE can be considered to be an important component of a more general revival of the classical emphasis, particularly as represented in the works of Adam Smith. Among the various approaches to the new economic institutionalism, constitutional economics is probably the one that comes closest to what in Adam Smith's time was called 'moral philosophy'. It seeks to bring closer together again the economic, social, political, philosophical and legal perspectives that were once part of the study of moral philosophy, and which the process of specialization in modern academia has fragmented into separate fields. Buchanan's constitutional economics is the modern-day counterpart to what Smith called 'the science of legislation', an academic enterprise that is concerned with a comparison of the working properties of alternative sets of rules, and ultimately aims at guiding our efforts to improve the social order in which we live by improving 'the rules of the game'.

On the other hand, Coase, in his 1991 Nobel Memorial Lecture (Coase 1992, p. 713), made the claim that during the two centuries since the publication of *The Wealth of Nations*, the main activity of economists - including, by implication, a very substantial part of his own work - had been to fill the gaps in Adam Smith's system, to correct his errors, and to make his analysis vastly more exact.

The new law and economics field is usually said to have started in the early 1960s, when Guido Calabresi's first article on torts and Ronald Coase's article on social cost were published (Calabresi 1961; Coase 1960). Coase's article was without any doubt the more significant for the long-run development of the new law and economics field.

Modern public choice - or the economics of politics - is usually said to have been founded by such classics as Black (1958) - following earlier papers published in the late 1940s and early 1950s - Arrow (1951), Downs (1957) and the precursory inquiries in Schumpeter (1942) - though elements of public choice analysis can already be found in the work of Pareto (see Backhaus, 1978). The major breakthrough, however, came with Buchanan and Tullock (1962). *The Calculus of Consent* was a seminal work in several respects. The public choice perspective is usually characterized as combining two distinct elements: the extension of the economist's model of utility-maximizing behaviour to political choice and the conceptualization of 'politics as exchange'. The Calculus was the first book that integrated these two elements into a coherent, logical structure. Moreover, the Calculus differed from the precursory works in that it embodied justificatory argument. It sought to outline, at least in very general terms, the conditions that must be present for an individual to find it advantageous to enter into a political entity with constitutionally delineated ranges of activity or to acquiesce in membership in a historically existing polity. It was recognized that, if one remains within the presuppositions of methodological individualism, the state or the polity must ultimately be justified in terms of its potential for satisfying individuals' desires (see also Buchanan, 1987, p. 133).

Furthermore, *The Calculus of Consent* confronted the market failure presumption of the new welfare economics by demonstrating that the problems associated with markets were ubiquitous, indeed entered into the calculus of political consent arguably with far greater significance because of the indivisibility of collective action (Rowley, 1993, p. xiii; Goetz, 1991, p. 10). The market failure concepts were applied evenhandedly to the alternative institutional arrangements, especially those of political control, and for the first time various policy arguments could benefit from a consistent and balanced approach.

Finally, the Calculus contained the germs of the recent developement of the research programme of constitutional political economy. It seems that Tullock's complaint about the lack of further research along the lines suggested in the Calculus was premature (Tullock, 1987, p. 139). The boundary between public choice, in its non-constitutional aspects of inquiry, and constitutional political economy may seem somewhat fuzzy. It is generally considered that public choice, in which attention is concentrated on analyses of alternative political choice structures and on behaviour within those structures is, through its focus on predictive models of political interactions, a preliminary but necessary stage to the more general constitutional inquiry.

On the other hand, law and economics remains somewhat closer to orthodox economic theory than either constitutional economics or public choice. The standard efficiency norm remains central to the law and economics subdiscipline, both as an explanatory benchmark and as a normative ideal.

The complex relationships between law and economics and public choice were carefully analysed in (Rowley, 1989). A masterly survey of the public choice literature is contained in Mueller (1989). Equally recommendable is Rowley's (1994) essay on 'Public choice economics' in Boettke (1994). In the present chapter we propose to draw some lessons for law and economics from recent developments in the re-emerging field of constitutional political economy.

At a time of major worldwide constitutional change, it will come as no surprise that the focus of public choice discussion is shifting away from ordinary political choices to the institutional-constitutional structure within which politics takes place.

2. Leading Journal

The leading journal of the sub-discipline is *Constitutional Political Economy.* Some preliminary and intuitive understanding of what CPE is all about can be gained from explaining the logic behind the logo of the journal, which is drawn from Greek mythology. CPEs logo is a representation of the familiar Homeric account of how Ulysses heard the Sirens singing, and survived (see Brennan and Kliemt, 1990). Ulysses wanted to hear the exquisite voices of the Sirens. He was passing close by and, in principle, there was nothing to prevent him from listening to them while continuing his journey. However, he recognized that the power of these voices was such that he would steer the ship ever closer to the rocks where the Sirens were located. The ship would be wrecked and he would be unable to continue his journey.

Formally, Ulysses faced a problem of time inconsistency in his optimal plan. His optimal plan was to listen to the Sirens and then continue his journey. But this was time inconsistent, because once he had embarked on the plan by listening to the Sirens he would not be able to implement the later part of the plan, the rest of his journey. By contrast, a time consistent optimal plan is one that specifies a sequence of actions (*At*, *At*+1, *A*t+2 and so on), one for each moment in time (*T*, *T*+1, *T*+2 and so on), which enjoys the property that the individual will actually choose in each time period the action specified by the plan. Thus, when *T*+1 occurs, having undertaken *At* in *T*, the individual will still choose *At*+1 as the best action rather than some other, and so on.

The time-inconsistency arises because the Sirens affect Ulysses' preferences. His perception of the best action changes in the middle of the plan and this leads him to deviate from the original version. Ulysses implemented his optimal plan by denying himself freedom at the later stage of the plan. Having instructed his men to tie him to the mast and to ignore any orders to do anything other than sail past the rocks, he told them to plug their ears and row.

Thus, Ulysses established for himself a private constitution, a set of more or less binding rules that constrained his future choices. By exploiting elements of his natural and social environment, Ulysses was able to subvert certain inclinations of his future self, inclinations that he knew would be destructive to his overall interests but which would nevertheless prove irresistible when they arose.

Though the theory of private constitution is a - small - part of the domain of constitutional political economy (Buchanan, 1990, p. 3), the principal issue for constitutional political economy is that of forming a mutually agreeable constitution for social arrangements among a community of persons. Ulysses is therefore to be seen not merely as a single actor but more particularly as representing society as a whole, and the mast and rope are to be identified as the rules by which ordered society is governed.

As Brennan and Kliemt (1990, p. 125) point out, some care must be taken in interpreting any such image. Following the individualist methodology, 'social action' must be decomposed into the actions of the individuals of whom society is made up. The exercise of social binding, specifically, must be seen as an intrinsically multilateral activity. Each agrees to a set of rules and procedures because this is the price each must pay to restrict the conduct of others. 'Weakness of the social will' will arise precisely because it is opportunistically rational for any individual to depart from the collectively agreed rules and procedures.

Moreover, in the setting with which CPE is concerned, there is no external technology available that is totally effective or not excessively costly. The tools of enforcement and maintenance must themselves be socially constructed. Human beings are not bound by nature to pursue rules: they are endowed with the capacity to deviate from rules if it is profitable to do so. Accordingly, we must search out rules which so order individuals' behaviour that it is individually profitable for most people to keep and enforce those rules most of the time. The gains from violation should not be too great. The analysis of the kind of rules and the associated institutional apparatus that exhibit these properties represents a centrepiece of constitutional political economy as an area of inquiry.

As far as dynamic choice theory in the strict sense is concerned, mention must certainly be made of the promising and in-depth analysis of the problem of dynamic consistency offered in McClennen (1990a). McClennen develops his argument in the context of a critical examination of the principles that constitute the cornerstone of the modern theory of expected utility and subjective probability: the weak ordering and the independence principles. McClennen argues for an alternative to the myopic and sophisticated approaches to the problem of dynamic consistency: the theory of resolute choice. The resolute chooser achieves dynamic consistency by regimenting ex post choice to his ex ante evaluation of plans, thus achieving a 'cooperative arrangement' between his present self and his relevant future selves that satisfies the principle of intrapersonal optimality. Technically speaking, resolute choice characterizes a commitment to dynamic consistency

(DC) and normal-form/extensive-form coincidence (NEC) at the expense of separability (SEP). Reference should also be made to McClennen (1993).

The problem of time inconsistency is addressed formally in Klein (1990).

B. The Theoretical Foundations of Constitutional Political Economy

3. Constitutional and Sub-Constitutional Choice

One solution to the problem of defining 'constitutional political economy' would consist of characterizing it simply as 'the economic analysis of constitutional law' (see Backhaus, 1995). The examination of real-world constitutions using the perspective of modern constitutional political economy is certainly an interesting exercise and can provide a kind of test for the usefulness of the CPE approach. In addition to Backhaus (1995), reference should be made to several case studies. Holcombe (1991) analyses the role of constitutional rules as constraints on government using three United States constitutions: the Articles of Confederation (1781), the Constitution of the United States and the Confederate Constitution. Brennan and Pardo (1991) examine the Spanish Constitution (1978). Sobel (1994) analyses the evolution of two international constitutions: the League of Nations Covenant and the United Nations Charter. However, the aforesaid definitional strategy may tend to be somewhat misleading. The use of the term 'constitutional' in the self-description of the subdiscipline is largely metaphorical.

CPE as a scientific subdiscipline is characterized by a particular kind of orientation in social analysis. Whereas orthodox economic analysis attempts to explain the choices of economic agents, their interactions with one another, and the results of these interactions, within the existing legal-institutional-constitutional structure of the polity, constitutional economic analysis attempts to explain the working properties of alternative sets of legal-institutional-constitutional rules that constrain the choices and activities of economic and political agents. The emphasis is on the rules that define the framework within which the ordinary choices of economic and political agents are made. Thus, CPE involves a 'higher' level of inquiry than orthodox economics. CPE examines the choice of constraints as opposed to the choice within constraints.

A preliminary example can be drawn from the theory of 'market failure'. We know that under some conditions, and given the legal order of the protective state (the protection of property and the enforcement of contracts), 'markets fail' when evaluated against idealized 'efficiency' criteria. But in examining allocative institutions, the economist should ask 'As compared to what?' (Goetz, 1991, p. 10). We know today that 'politics fails' when evaluated by the same criteria. The analysis and comparison of the working properties of underlying sets of rules or constraints constitutes the domain of constitutional economics.

A market is always a system of social interaction characterized by a specific institutional framework, that is, by a set of rules defining certain restrictions on the behaviour of the market participants. 'Market failure' arguments sometimes tend to ignore that the rules upon which a market is based may well be variable and that an adjustment in these rules is possibly a better way to deal with alleged shortcomings than to replace market forces by a political mechanism.

When it is said that the rules upon which a market is based may well be variable, this should not be misunderstood. It means that the rules can be varied at the level of constitutional choice. At the level of sub-constitutional (or post-constitutional) choice, the rules are parameters: they are items that single economic entities cannot adjust and, indeed, must adjust to. Coase's (1960) tradable property rights are not really rules as the constitutional economist defines them. Coase's tale was about *trading* defined rights, about private rearrangements of rights within a given legal structure, not about *redefining* the rights that the market participants hold. We will take a closer look at Coase's contribution in the next section.

Elementary to any constitutional analysis is therefore the explicit recognition of a notion of hierarchy. Any constitutional analysis will distinguish between at least two levels of choice - constitutional choice and sub-constitutional (or non-constitutional) choice - and correspondingly also between constitutional and sub-constitutional preferences. Constitutional choices are choices among alternative rules (constraints). Sub-constitutional choices are among alternative strategies available within rules (constraints), such as ordinary market choices.

4. Methodological Individualism

Only individuals choose and act. CPE is informed by an explicit methodological individualism (Buchanan, 1990, p. 13). Whatever phenomena at the social aggregate level we seek to explain, we ought to show how they result from the actions and interactions of individual human beings who, separately and jointly, pursue their interests as they see them, based on their own understanding of the world around them (Vanberg, 1994, p. 1). An aggregative result that is observed but which cannot, somehow, be factored down and explained by the choices of individuals, stands as a challenge to the scholar rather than as some demonstration of non-individualistic organic unity.

5. Homo Economicus

Orthodox public choice models usually contain the postulate of homo economicus: they go beyond the logical presuppositions of individualism to incorporate non-tautological models of individual utility maximization. Individuals are assumed to seek their own interests, which are defined so as to retain operational content. It is increasingly recognized, however, that at least a part of the traditional public choice emphasis has been wrongly placed. Thus the emphasis is shifted away from the motivational postulates for political actors to the incentive structures of politics. In Buchanan (1993a, p. 69) it is argued that the seminal Alchian (1950) analysis of the market's analogue to evolutionary selection can be extended to politics in relatively straightforward fashion, the difference between the two evolutionary models lying in the compatibility with overall efficiency. The structure of the politics in which politicians act requires them to act contrary to public interests if they are to survive at all. For the constitutional economist the relevant question then becomes: 'How can Constitutions be Designed so that Politicians who Seek to Serve "Public Interest" can Survive and Prosper?' (Buchanan, 1993b).

6. Normative Individualism

The whole exercise of CPE is ultimately aimed at offering guidance to those who participate in the discussion of constitutional change. In other words, constitutional economics is meant to offer a potential for normative advice in constitutional matters and to provide a normative framework for comparative institutional analysis. As a normative enterprise, CPE is informed by normative individualism: the presumption that the evaluations of the persons involved, their interests and values, provide the relevant criterion against which the merits of alternative sets of rules are to be judged.

7. Excursion: The Wicksellian Ancestry

The distinguishing feature of the Buchanan and Tullock (1962) approach to the study of political institutions from a normative viewpoint was to treat the political process by which individuals advance their interests as one of exchange. In adding this second element - 'politics as exchange' - to the utility maximizing models for individual choice behaviour in politics, they were directly influenced by the great work of Knut Wicksell.

CPE could be characterized as 'Wicksellian' political economy. Wicksell's influence is discussed in Wagner (1988). In his basic work on fiscal theory Wicksell (1896) called attention to the significance of the rules within which choices are made by political agents, and he recognized that efforts at reform must be directed toward changes in the rules for making decisions rather than toward modifying expected results through influence on the behaviour of the actors.

In order to take these steps, Wicksell needed some criterion by which the possible efficacy of a proposed change in rules could be judged. He introduced the now-familiar (near to) unanimity or consensus test. Thus for Wicksell 'the consent of the governed' was the point of departure for the evaluation of government activities.

This 'Wicksellian' idea has had considerable influence on Buchanan's approach. According to Buchanan, politics must be understood in terms of the model of market exchange. Thus, the political proces is conceptualized as one of mutually beneficial exchange. It is for this reason that he is drawn to unanimity as a collective decision rule. Since the choice among rules is more a social choice than an exchange, the form of voluntary exchange is political consent. Through the emphasis on 'consent' or 'agreement' as a normative yardstick, the research program of CPE became closely related to the contractarian tradition in political philosophy. As Buchanan sees it, contractarian political institutions typically exhibit three attributes. Central to the contractarian vision of the political process is the place of the individual. Individuals' own - and necessarily subjective - evaluations, their interests and values constitute the relevant benchmark against which the efficiency or desirability of alternative rule-regimes or institutions are to be judged. Contractarianism complies with this criterion by according each individual equal treatment at the constitutional stage. The unanimity rule serves to protect the individuals' rights and thereby ensures that those rules and institutions that become imbedded in the constitution will also treat individuals equally and impartially. Second, there is the fundamental distinction between actions taken within the constitutional rules, and changes in the rules themselves. The latter are to occur only at the constitutional stage and ideally are made using the unanimity rule. The image of political activity as a two-stage process, first developed in *The Calculus of Consent*, has recurred in many of Buchanan's later writings as a sort of normative benchmark or yardstick by which to measure the quality of a community's political institutions. Third, actions taken in the second stage of the political process should be effectively constrained by the rules written in the first, constitutional stage, and this is true not only for the individual citizen, but also for the elected representatives, and the bureaucrats and jurists who administer the system.

Recapitulating and summarizing, we can say that the two most important aspects of Buchanan's position are his emphasis on 'rules of the game' and his analysis of efficiency as involving consent. At the most fundamental level of constitutional choice, consent serves as the basis of justification. It provides the ultimate criterion of efficiency. Unlike other economists who have emphasized either the efficiency or rationality of rules, Buchanan is concerned exclusively with whether or not people consent to them.

It should be noted that Buchanan and traditional economic analysts develop the relationship between autonomy and efficiency in exactly opposite ways (Coleman, 1990, p. 141). Traditional economists believe that efficiency can be defined as a property of social states independent of the process of voluntary exchange. For example, the perfectly competitive market is efficient, but the outcome of the prisoner's dilemma is not. And given the logic of the relevant concepts - especially Pareto superiority - it follows logically that people would consent to efficient rules. Consent follows from efficiency. Buchanan puts the matter exactly the opposite way. What people consent to is efficient. Efficiency follows from consent.

In contrast with Paretian 'optimum resource allocation', a situation of 'Wicksellian efficiency' will be characterized by the fact that citizens are satisfied that the existing system of rules, institutions and policies of their society is free from improper coercion (Wiseman, 1990, p. 110).

The Wicksellian criterion of social efficiency focuses on subjective choice processes, in marked contrast to the Paretion optimality condition of neoclassical welfare economics, which permits an external observer to use individual utility as an objective measure of welfare. Social efficiency is too complex a notion to be reduced to a set of technical propositions concerning resource-use. Efficiency is not a property of social states that could be specified or defined independently of the actions of individuals and the process of voluntary exchange.

The limitations of conventional Pareto criteria in assessing efficiency are also discussed by De Alessi (1992).

However, Wicksell did not move beyond the development of criteria for evaluating policy alternatives one at a time.

Buchanan and Tullock (1962) operationalized Wicksell's (1896) insights and extended the applicability of the unanimity or consensus criterion from the level of particular proposals to the level of rules - to constitutional rather than post-constitutional or in-period choices.[*]

For Buchanan and Tullock (1962, Chapter 6) constitutional design was a matter of determining which voting rule or choice mechanism would be specified by the constitution for each state activity. The best public decision rule for each activity was the one that minimized interdependence costs. It was specified that the representative individual perceived interdependence costs for an activity as the sum of the anticipated external costs levied on that individual if not part of the decision set, and the anticipated decision making costs experienced by the individual if part of the decision set. External costs arise because some individuals cash in the benefits of collective decisions but shift the costs to other individuals. The group forces an individual to contribute to collective action that is not wanted by that individual (at that price). From the point of view of the individual in question, external costs are the result of wrong decisions. The higher the percentage required for a group decision, the lower the chance of wrong decisions being made, so that the corresponding curve will show a declining trend. Decision-making costs are the individual investment of time and energy in the process of negotiation, expressed in money value. The closer the requirement of unanimity comes to being met, the higher the decision costs will be because, among other reasons, strategic behaviour of individuals becomes more profitable. The corresponding curve therefore has a rising trend. The sum of both external costs and decision costs was shown to have a unique minimum somewhere between the extremes of individual rule and unanimity rule, the exact position depending on relative external and decision costs.

The shift of the Wicksellian criterion to the constitutional stage of choice has some remarkable consequences. It becomes conceivable to allow for the possibility that preferred and agreed-on decision rules might embody sizable departures from the unanimity limit, including simple majority voting in some cases and even less than majority voting in others (Buchanan, 1987, p. 135). The constitutional calculus suggests that both the costs of reaching decisions under different rules and the importance of the decisions are relevant. Since both of these elements vary, the preferred rule will not be uniform over all ranges of potential political action. The in period Wicksellian criterion may remain valid as a measure of the particularized efficiency of the single decision examined. But the in period violation of the criterion does not imply the inefficiency of the rule as long as the latter is itself selected by a constitutional rule of unanimity.

As a consequence, while it was recognized that unanimity and not majority rule is the pivot of constitutional democracy, it was equally demonstrated that 'at best, majority rule should be viewed as one among many practical expedients made necessary by the costs of securing widespread agreement on political issues when individual and group interests diverge' (Buchanan and Tullock, 1962, p. 96).

The appropriate degree of inclusiveness of the collective decision-making rule - for example qualified majority rule - as an instrument to cope with perverse forms of uncertainty about the incidence of collective decisions is discussed in Pinto Barbosa (1994).

8. The Rent Seeking Trap

It has become common to model the choice situation at the constitutional as well as the post-constitutional stage with potentially conflicting interests between rational persons as a classic Prisoner's Dilemma (Wagner and Gwartney 1988, p. 32; Buchanan, 1993b, p. 2). The Prisoner's Dilemma game depicts a situation in which private interests and the search for individual gain, when generalized, become the source of mutually harmful results. In other words, private interests cannot be generalized without losses. But what can be generalized (moral codes) does not obey private motivations. Conflicting interests are clearly involved, since everybody wants to be the only defector.

<table>
<tr><th colspan="4">Classic Prisoner's Dilemma</th></tr>
<tr><td colspan="2" rowspan="2"></td><td colspan="2">B</td></tr>
<tr><td>C</td><td>D</td></tr>
<tr><td rowspan="2">A</td><td>C</td><td>3,3</td><td>1,4</td></tr>
<tr><td>D</td><td>4,1</td><td>2,2</td></tr>
</table>

In 'generalized Prisoner's Dilemma situations', that is, social constellations under which individuals, in separate and rational pursuit of their own interests, unintentionally but systematically contribute to an overall outcome that is undesirable for all of them (or in any case less desirable than some alternative outcome that could be realized by concerted, organized action) there is a possible potential for mutual gains by collective action (collective organization).

In this way the constitution is essentially a contract intended to secure mutual gains from social cooperation and to avoid the dominant defective strategy in the Prisoner's Dilemma game which leads to a socially inefficient Nash equilibrium solution. Since the mutual gains from social cooperation constitute a public good, the maintenance of the constitutional contract gives rise to a problem that will not resolve itself naturally.

Even when it is supposed that agreement on appropriate rules can be achieved at the stage of constitutional contract formation, it should be recognized that individuals and interest groups inevitably will attempt to engage in post-contractual opportunism (problem of constitutional maintenance). Therefore the agreement, once achieved, must be enforceable. This opportunism takes several forms. First, each individual may have an incentive to defect from the cooperative agreement after it has been concluded (compliance or unilateral defection problem). Whether or not it is rational for persons to comply with rules that they constitutionally may agree on is a matter of contingent, factual circumstances. It depends on whether or not the constraints that persons face after the agreement, that is post-constitutionally, make it rational for them to comply with previously agreed-on rules. As Vanberg has pointed out repeatedly, their constitutional interests and their compliance interests are not necessarily in congruence (Vanberg, 1994, passim, for example, pp. 21-23).

A second form of post-contractual opportunism consists of rent seeking and special interest plundering, which ultimately reduce the value of post-contractual cooperation and undermine the constitution itself. Groups of individuals have an incentive to seek and capture the instruments of state power and to use them as vehicles to enrich themselves in ways that are unattainable for private citizens.

Rent-seeking is a term used by economists to describe actions taken by individuals and groups to alter public policy in order to gain personal advantage at the expense of others.

The incentive to engage in rent-seeking activities is directly proportional to the ease with which the political process can be used for personal (or interest group) gain at the expense of others. In other words, distributional politics is viable and tends to become dominant to the extent that differential treatment is constitutionally permissible (Buchanan, 1993b, p. 6).

Tullock (1959) had already shown that under any voting system which requires less than unanimous approval to implement policies, majority coalitions of interest groups will seek to obtain public provision of special interest projects. A few years later Tullock (1967) independently published his innovative ideas on what came to be called rent-seeking, which he argued entailed social costs. The latter were called 'rent-seeking costs' or, by some, 'Tullock Costs'. Tullock Costs have been re-analysed recently by Spindler (1990).

The dominant strategy for any organized interest group in a majoritarian polity is to lobby for policies which provide large benefits to its members and disperse the costs over everyone else. This tendency exists even in liberal democracies. Through implicit vote-trading, a coalition of interest groups, comprising a bare majority of voters, can get all or at least most of their favoured projects approved for public provision. Under certain conditions, the total costs of these projects can exceed their total benefits, while cost spreading through the 'fisc' induces a rational ignorance of this process on the part of the disadvantaged majority. On the other hand, the asymmetric distribution of cooperative benefits leads subgroups of the collective to invest energy in the struggle for access to the government's coercive power. But the effort may turn out to cost more than it is worth and the end result will be that the collective's loss purchases the subgroup's gain (Schmidtz, 1991, p. 91).

Buchanan and Lee (1991) demonstrate that the gains from politically generated restrictions on markets, even to organized producing interests, are more apparent than real. The analysis demonstrates that under plausibly realistic assumptions concerning coalition sizes, excess burdens, organizational costs and rent seeking outlay, a genuine utility-maximizing calculus may dictate support for constitutional prohibition of all market restrictions, by all members of the polity, including those producer interests that might be considered to be potentially identifiable beneficiaries of cartelization.

Principal-agent theory has been used to examine the rent-seeking problem (Anderson and Hill, 1986; Merville and Osborne, 1990). The principal, also the citizen, grants the agent (the government) the power of coercion. In exchange, the agent supplies the principal with public goods. Since the capitalized value of public assets is owned collectively, public-good outputs of the government are like communal resources with widely diffused benefits. It soon becomes evident to vote-maximizing agents or legislators that they can maximize their political support by significantly reducing the provision of public goods to the population at large in favor of greater transfers to interest groups. These transfers are financed by general tax collections and provide concentrated benefits to designated groups. Such collusion between agents and special interest groups will invariably lead to the development of a Leviathan state.

Merville and Osborne (1990) use agency theory to demonstrate formally that, in majority-rule political systems, coalitions of minority factions will induce politicians to systematically break the constitutional contract in order to supply special interest projects. Unlike contracts in private markets, political contracts are much more susceptible to this kind of opportunism.

Is the rent-seeking trap inescapable? A serious consideration of this question will take us a long way to the understanding of constitutional political economy.

By far the most important problem with respect to ensuring the self-enforcing character of a constitutional contract is that it must successfully constrain the power of the Leviathan state itself. Whereas Brennan and Buchanan (1980) endow Leviathan with the objective of revenue maximization, La Manna and Slomp (1994) argue that Hobbes's political construct envisages a sovereign-principal who devises rules and incentives to induce his subjects-agents to contribute to his own preservation and glory. Leviathan is a glory seeker instead of a revenue maximizer.

Generally speaking substantive constraints on government have been dismissed as ineffective precisely because of the wide latitude they allow for reinterpretation. Wagner and Gwartney (1988, pp. 44-49) make a strong case for procedural rules designed to uphold decentralization of governmental powers and to prevent the formation of legislative coalitions. Procedural rules will provide more effective mechanisms for self-enforcement than will substantive restraints on government. In their view, the weakness of substantive restraints derives from the politicization of the Supreme Court and the ease with which legislatures can find alternative ways to implement any given policy. They propose procedural rules requiring larger legislative majorities for legislative action at higher levels of government, thereby diffusing the power of the state to regional and local governments.

Several other 'solutions' have been proposed in the literature.

9. Judicial Independence

Does independence of the judiciary serve the long-term public good? The traditional view of the purpose of judicial independence has been attacked as naive by law and economics and public choice scholars. Unlike many legal contracts, it is argued, there is no third-party enforcer, external to the contract, who can ensure that defectors are caught and forced to comply with the terms of the agreement. Though many countries have a nominally independent Supreme Court whose purpose is to enforce the constitution, the Supreme Court can only do this imperfectly in most cases, because the judges themselves are not totally immune from political pressure by groups wishing to subvert the original intent of the constitution. Thus, given the unreliability of third-party enforcement, and given the strong individual incentives to defect from social cooperation, the constitutional contract should somehow be self-enforcing if it is to be maintained.

The interest group theory first advanced by Landes and Posner (1975) makes the independent judiciary an integral part of the system of rent-seeking engineered by Congress. However, the debate goes on. A very detailed criticism of the Landes-Posner theory is contained in Boudreaux and Pritchard (1994). They argue that the Landes-Posner theory is seriously deficient and conclude that the United States federal judiciary is truly independent of Congress and the President, and that this independence was designed by the Constitution's framers as a means of furthering sound government.

Blankart (1994) compares the legal rules for private clubs with the constitutions of representative governments. A nearly perfect laboratory case for a club government can be found in the example of Switzerland. The Swiss do not have a constitutional court, but have developed instead a system of popular voting rights serving as a substitute for a judicial review by a constitutional court. Though this system does not work perfectly, it has relative advantages in comparison to constitutional courts, which often tend to become political decisionmakers thereby circumventing the control of citizens-as-principals.

Moser (1994) carefully analyses the contribution of the Swiss and the US constitutions to protect economic liberties, and compares the different strategies that both constitutions rely on to achieve this goal. It is argued that the substantial constitutional changes that did occur in both countries followed strikingly similar patterns: the constitutional protection of economic liberties was eroded in both countries, especially as far as federal legislation is concerned, due to changes in the interpretation of the constitution through the courts, or by formal amendment. Tucker (1992) looks at the impact and the judicial philosophy of the now dominating Conservative group of justices on the Supreme Court. Rowley (1992) examines the erosion of the economic liberties of US citizens with special reference to the takings-clause provisions of the Fifth Amendment. It is noticed that the Court changed direction during the late 1980s as justices appointed by Presidents Reagan and Bush gained ascendancy.

10. A Rule of Law in Politics

According to Buchanan (1993b) the direction of constitutional reform is obvious. If, somehow, the potential for differential treatment is reduced, so will be the inducement to rent-seeking behaviour. The off-diagonal solutions should simply be made impossible to achieve by the introduction of some rule or norm that prevents participants from acting or being acted upon differently, one from the other.

If the off-diagonal attractors are eliminated, then the players operate with the following reduced matrix:

		B	
		C	D
A	C	3,3	X
	D	X	2,2

Thus the constitutional reform measure modifies the original Prisoner's Dilemma game into a reduced setting in which each player, as a member of a political coalition, knows that any choice of an action or strategy must involve the same treatment of all players or constituencies (Buchanan, 1993b, p. 3).

If and to the extent that differential treatment is replaced with equal treatment, or with the principle of generality in politics - analogous to that present in an idealized version of the rule of law - mutual exploitation will be avoided and politicians who seek to serve the 'public interest' will survive and prosper (Buchanan, 1993b, p. 6). Therefore it seems at least conceivable that rational persons, at the stage of entering into the agreement, may recognize the 'rent-seeking trap' and engage in concerted efforts to escape.

However, in the hypothetical matrix construction above, the interaction was in fact assumed to occur in a state of nature, with each person holding equal prospects for membership in the majority and minority coalitions. This means that membership was assumed to be symmetrical among all participants. But this assumption may turn out to be too heroic with respect to real world settings.

The prospects may differ among persons and groups of persons so as to create divergences in interests which may become a source of disagreement. Thus the question remains whether it is possible to modify the constitutional choice setting so as to reconcile such possible divergences. It appears that, at least from the perspective of potentially-conflicting interests among constituencies, the general problem of constitutional efficiency and survivability does not resolve itself naturally.

11. Veil of Uncertainty and/or Ignorance Versus the Availability of Exit Options

Is it possible to specify the conditons under which constitutional agreement may be facilitated in real, non-hypothetical choice situations? Is it possible to modify the constitutional choice setting so as to reconcile divergences in interests?

In this respect, two lines of reasoning have been pursued in the contractarian and neo- contractarian literature.

The first line of argument focuses attention on the need for a 'veil of uncertainty and/or ignorance' as a precondition for an efficient constitution. Buchanan and Tullock (1962) had to present a convincing positive argument that unanimous consent at the constitutional level was possible at all. How can agreement be achieved on rules among persons with potentially conflicting constitutional interests? Buchanan and Tullock's (1962) characteristic way of approaching this issue consists of emphasizing the uncertainty confronting all individuals taking part in constitutional deliberations. The existence of 'a veil of uncertainty' induces individual participants in a constitutional process to prefer rules that do not systematically favour any particular subset of citizens.

The proposed remedy involves the introduction of some means of insuring a person's inability to foresee reliably their future particularized interests, as these may be affected by different rules, thereby inducing persons to make constitutional choices on some assessment of the general working properties of alternative rules, and divorced from particularized interests. Thus, agreement is facilitated by whatever increases a person's uncertainty about the particular effects that alternative rules can be expected to have on them. In fact the assumption of a 'veil of uncertainty' was also hidden in Buchanan (1993b), discussed above.

Buchanan's approach has affinities with John Rawls's (1971) construction, who utilizes the veil of ignorance along with the fairness criterion to derive principles of justice that emerge from a conceptual agreement at a stage prior to the selection of a political constitution. Thus in Rawls's construction the prospect of agreement is secured by defining certain 'ideal' conditions under which constitutional choices are hypothetically made. The choosers are assumed to be placed behind a 'veil of ignorance', that makes it impossible for them to know anything specific about how they will be personally affected by alternative rules. Ignorant about their prospective specific interests in particular outcomes, they are induced to judge rules 'impartially'. Potential conflict in constitutional interests is not eliminated, but the veil of ignorance transforms potential interpersonal conflicts into intrapersonal ones (Vanberg, 1994, p. 170).

However, the constitutionalist notion of a veil of uncertainty is not very operational. It is not clear how genuine uncertainty could be achieved in real-world constitution formation. Moreover, in certain parts of the rent-seeking literature there is a certain tendency to suggest that conflicts of interest are no less characteristic for choices among rules at the constitutional stage than for choices within rules and that therefore the idea of some genuine constitutional agreement is a mere illusion when placed in a real-world context. This view seems to be espoused by, for example, Sutter (1995).

Therefore, it has been argued that the availability of exit options can ensure a competitive setting for participants in constitutional deliberations and can even substitute for a veil of uncertainty. This condition for efficiency can be given operational substance in processes of real-world constitution formation (Lowenberg and Yu, 1992).

In order to produce an efficient social contract or constitution, deliberations must be carried out in a competitive 'constitutional environment'. This condition is satisfied if an exit option exists for each contracting party. As will be argued later on, this conclusion is quite consistent with the Wicksell-Buchanan-Vanberg contractarian consensus test. Only in a competitive setting does unanimous agreement acquire operational substance (normative content).

The notion of exit has thus been invoked to give more operational substance to the concept of voluntary agreement. It is derived from Hirschman's (1970) classic distinction between exit and voice. Exit (and entry) is an important means by which individuals are able to express their preferences, and is precisely the method through which preferences are revealed in competitive markets for private goods.

An exit option introduces an element of market-like competition into the contracting process, which limits the ability of any party to wield power over another party. It is not even necessary that this exit option be exercised, since merely the threat of its use should be enough to restrain rent appropriation. The scope for opportunism is effectively constrained by competition, actual or potential.

Furthermore, it is argued that exit options can help to solve the constitutional maintenance problem by establishing a competitive environment for post-constitutional political and market exchange (Lowenberg and Yu, 1992).

12. Federalism, Once Again

The strengthening of regional and local government relative to national government has been advocated by many scholars as an effective way to restrain the growth of legislative redistribution. The existence of separate jurisdictions with some protected powers within a constitutional federation inhibits coercive behaviour by the government. Such an arrangement facilitates migration at low cost between federal sub-regions and thereby enhances competition between these sub-regions. The resulting mobility forces competitive governmental units to supply public goods in preferred quantities and to 'price' them broadly in line with relative marginal evaluations.

The foregoing is related to the Tiebout effect (Tiebout, 1956), which says that individuals will sort themselves across communities in accordance with their preferences for the packages of taxes and public goods provided in each community. The ability of the owners of property rights to move to competing jurisdictions protects them from potential rent appropriation by a coercive government. Therefore, it is argued, a federalist constitution can effectively constrain the power of the state. In a federal system, citizens seeking political relief can vote with their feet.

The preceding paragraphs suggest that post-contractual exit opportunities might be characterized in terms of Tiebout competition between different political groupings. If the constitution permits mobility and political plurality, it will help establish and maintain a competitive political postconstitutional environment.

The unifying theme in the preceding approach to constitution formation and maintenance is generally that of exit (or entry).

C. Outline of a Reconstruction of the Coase Theorem from a Subjectivist-Contractarian Perspective

13. Buchanan on the Irrelevance of Transaction Costs

One way to interpret the Coase (1960) analysis consists of seeing it as a contribution to the externality literature, though Coase would presumably object to any use of the term 'externality'. Put in externality language, Coase was essentially arguing that all Pareto-relevant externalities would tend to be eliminated in the process of free exchange contract among affected parties (Buchanan and Stubblebine, 1962).

According to Buchanan (1984) Coase did not like the Buchanan-Stubblebine externality paper and Buchanan conjectures that Coase's objection may have stemmed from a certain 'ambiguity in perspective' (Buchanan, 1984, p. 11, footnote 6).

The 'ambiguity in perspective' Buchanan refers to is related to the fact that there are two profoundly different conceptions of competition and the competitive process. In the objectivist perspective, there is an efficient allocation of resources independently of any process through which it is generated. From this supposition, it follows that institutional arrangements can be directly evaluated in terms of their relative success or failure in attaining the desired pattern of resource use. Normative argument in support of competitive institutions emerges, in this perspective, only because such institutions tend to be relatively superior 'devices', 'instruments', or 'mechanisms' in generating independently derived results. Where competitive institutions do not seem to exist, as defined by some independently derived structural criteria (for example, the number of firms in an industry, concentration ratios, and so on), there emerges a normative argument for direct intervention with the voluntary exchange process as a means of moving results toward the externally derived allocative norm or ideal.

In the subjectivist-contractarian perspective, 'efficiency' cannot be said to exist except as determined by the process through which results are generated, and criteria for evaluating patterns of results must be applied only to processes. In this perspective, voluntary exchanges among persons, within a competitive constraints structure, generate efficient resource usage which is determined only as the exchanges are made. Competitive institutions in this perspective are not instruments to be used to generate efficiency. They are, instead, possible structures, possible rules or sets of rules, that may emerge from generalized agreement. The role of the political order, of law or government, is to facilitate agreement on institutional arrangements, and to police rights assigned under such agreements.

In Buchanan (1984) it is argued that Coase, despite his own earlier contribution to what can be called the subjectivist theory of opportunity cost (see Buchanan, 1969, pp. 26-29; Coase, 1960) presented his argument - through a series of hypothetical and historical examples - largely in terms of presumably objectively-measurable and independently-determined harm and benefit relationships. It is suggested that Coase was, indeed, applying outcome criteria for allocative efficiency to results of the exchange process rather than limiting his attention to the process itself. Therefore the whole analysis becomes vulnerable to the critique mounted by Cooter (1982) and others who suggest that the Coase theorem fails in non-competitive settings. Small-number bargaining settings will necessarily fail to guarantee efficiency due to the presence of incentives for strategic behaviour, independently of any communication-information failures. In large-number settings, all parties may have free-rider motivations. In both of the latter cases, interpreted in terms of satisfying outcome criteria for efficiency, free exchange and contract among parties do not necessarily generate an allocation of resources to their most highly valued uses. 'Externalities' that are Pareto-relevant may remain in full trading equilibrium. Parties to potential exchanges who are rational maximizers of expected utilities may fail to reach the presumed objectifiable Pareto efficiency frontier. However, Buchanan contends that if the whole Coase analysis is interpreted in subjectivist-contractarian terms, the critique can be shown to be without substance.

Buchanan (1984) is an explicit attempt to re-interpret the Coase (1960) theorem along consistent subjectivist-contractarian (or, if preferred, Austrian-Wicksellian) lines.

If there is no objective criterion for resource use that can be applied to outcomes, as a means of indirectly testing the efficacy of the exchange process, then as long as exchange remains open and as long as force and fraud are not observed, that upon which agreement is reached is, by definition, that which can be classified to be efficient. The Coase theorem thus seems to become a tautology. How could, in this construction, inefficiency conceivably emerge? Is that which is always necessarily efficient?

Of course it is not. Already in Buchanan (1959) it was suggested that agreement is the only ultimate test for efficiency, but that the test does not need to be confined in application to the allocative results or outcomes generated under explicitly existing or defined institutional-structural rules. The agreement test for efficiency may be elevated or moved upward to the stage of institutions or rules, as such.

The proper role for the normative political economist is that of discovering potential rules changes that might yield general benefits and then presenting these changes as hypotheses subject to the Wicksellian contractual-consensus test. If, when presented with a suggested change in rules, agreement among all potentially interacting parties is forthcoming, the hypothesis is corroborated. The previously existing rule is proven to be inefficient. Agreement on a change in the rules within which exchanges are allowed to take place is a signal that patterns of outcomes reached or predicted under the previously-existing set of rules are less preferred or valued than the patterns expected to be generated under the rule-as-changed. Hence, the new rule is deemed more efficient than the old. If disagreement emerges on the proposed rules change, the hypothesis is falsified. The existing rule is classified as Pareto-efficient. And, given this institutional setting, any outcomes attained under free and open exchange processes are to be classified as efficient.

Let us consider as an example the classic externality case from welfare economics, the setting in which ordinary economic activity within well defined legal rights imposes noncompensated damages on a sufficiently large number of persons so as to insure failure of a bargained solution due to free-rider motivation. The 'uncorrected' outcomes in this setting should still be classified as 'efficient' as long as all members of the relevant community remain free to make intervening offers and bids to those traders whose activity is alleged to generate the spillover harms. The institutional structure may not be efficient, however. The political economist may hypothesize that general agreement can be secured on some change in institutional structure and that explicit political or governmental decision rules may come to be accepted by all parties as being preferred to the decision rules of the market. Even though the outcomes reached may still be classified to be 'efficient' - *given* the assignment of rights, and *given* the institution of exchange - the institution of voluntary exchange, as ordinarily understood, may not, in this case, be efficient. This implication may sound somewhat paradoxical but for the subjectivist-contractarian it creates no difficulty since he does not acknowledge the uniqueness of the resource allocation that is properly classified to be efficient: it depends necessarily on the institutional structure within which resource utilization-valuation decisions are made.

There is a second seeming paradox. That political-governmental decision rule upon which agreement is reached may not require consent of all parties to reach particular outcomes, either explicitly or implicitly. The efficient decision rule may be such that specific outcomes need not meet the consensus test. The analysis contained in Buchanan and Tullock (1962), which is essentially an analysis of the choice among political decision-making rules had highlighted the fact that the costs of reaching agreement increase significantly as the size of the group required to agree is expanded. However, this situation need not imply that the unanimity principle for constitutional changes is inapplicable. The members of the group may be observed to agree on changes in the rules that produce results which, when classified by the orthodox Pareto criterion, are clearly 'nonoptimal'. In other words, 'optimal rules' may generate results that may be classified as nonoptimal.

With majority rule, or any less than unanimity rule, for political-governmental decisions, the decision structure can itself be efficient while at the same time the particular outcomes attained under the structure are to be presumed inefficient, at least in some situations, for those who are directly coerced. Buchanan believes that to introduce 'transactions costs' as a barrier to the attainment of efficiency confuses rather than clarifies the complex set of issues involved. The several so-called transaction costs barriers to efficiency in resource allocation - information and communication constraints, free rider constraints, strategic behaviour ... - can be more appropriately analysed in the context of hypotheses about institutional reform (Buchanan, 1984, p. 23).

D. Refinements and Applications: A Survey of Contributions

14. Foundational Explorations

One of the major discussions in contemporary institutional economics concerns the relation between rationality and rule following. The problem is akin to what philosophers will recognize as an unresolved issue in the history of ethics. As several authors have recognized, the problem was posed at the very beginning of the history of philosophizing about the justification of moral rules, in Plato's Republic (McClennen, 1990a, p. 262). In Plato (1992, pp. 34-35, Book II, sec. 359) Glaucon challenged Socrates to prove that being just is rational even if we suppose that the material rewards of being just accrue exclusively to the unjust. The story of the ring of Gyges seems to drive a wedge between the concept of rational choice and that of choice that respects the usual kinds of moral constraints. In the language of public goods theory, the challenge is to show that when the material payoff of being just is a public good - enjoyed by everyone but its producers - there is nevertheless a hidden private benefit that makes it rational to produce this public good (Schmidtz, 1991, p. 165).

There appears to be an essential tension between the notion of rational, self interested behaviour - as postulated in economics - and the notion of a viable moral order. In the relevant literature this problem is referred to as the 'Hobbesian problem of social order' or simply the 'Hobbesian problem'.

Vanberg (1993, 1994) presents an interpretation of the rational choice and rule-following perspectives which allow their consistent integration into a common theoretical framework. Hayek had already argued that man is 'as much a rule-following animal as a purpose-seeking one' (Hayek, 1973, p. 11). Generally speaking, Vanberg's program can be characterized as a systematic and transdisciplinary integration of J.M. Buchanan's contractarian perspective with F.A. Hayek's evolutionary approach, making use of insights from a wide range of fields. The contractarian element in Hayek's thought has also been identified by Sugden (1993a). The contrast between Hayek's and Buchanan's systems of ideas is highlighted by, for example, Gray (1990).

Vanberg (1993a, p. 187) distinguishes maximizing and adaptive forms of rationality and argues that an evolutionary perspective using the concept of adaptive rationality 'may help to systematically account for observed behavioral tendencies which appear to defy explanation in standard rationality terms'. This argument is related to Hayek's notion that rule following is a response to humankind's imperfect understanding of their environment. Rules are not chosen as a result of a full rational appraisal but can best be seen as more or less reasonable adaptations to a complex world and not necessarily as optimal in their functioning.

On one occasion, Vanberg argues that rule-following behaviour, while relatively unresponsive to variations in particular situational circumstances, 'is quite compatible with choice and 'calculation' at the rule level' (Vanberg, 1994, pp. 16-17), thus suggesting that the problem can be thought of in terms of a rational maximizing choice on a metalevel. However, if maximizing itself is subject to, say, information costs, the choice of rule cannot be seen in optimizing terms. There seems to be no alternative to separating the concept of rationality from the notion of optimization. In this way Simon distinguished procedural from substantive rationality (Simon, 1976). Simon argued that the orthodox neoclassical concept of rationality as maximizing implies an unrealistic view of man's cognitive abilities, of his access to information and his computational capacities. The alternative concept of rationality which Simon proposes, namely that of bounded, procedural or adaptive rationality, is in essence a theory of behavioural learning, a theory which seeks to understand a person's current behaviour in terms of his or her past experience. Simon's theory of human decision making views an actor's choice-behaviour as based on a repertoire of behavioural patterns, routines or programmes.

An extension of the bounded rationality problem has been provided by Ronald Heiner (1983, 1990, among others). Formal economics is a theory of perfect choice that assumes agents always make best decisions based on available information. The latter may itself be inaccurate or incomplete, but no further imperfection enters into the analysis about the agents' ability to decide optimally. In a sequence of articles, Heiner has made an effort to develop a theory of imperfect choice which provides an argument for why rational, but imperfect agents may profit from following rules instead of attempting to maximize advantage on a case-by-case basis.

Heiner's argument is that there is often a gap between an agent's competence at problem solving and the difficulty of the decision problem faced. Given such a 'C-D gap', which will tend to exist in complex decision problems, agents will be subject to unpredictable errors and mistakes in selecting the most preferred alternative. The extent of these errors possibly means that an agent will do better by following a simple rule rather than by attempting to maximize in each case. Heiner's analysis implies that imperfect agents benefit from being governed by rules adapted only to recurrent situations and from ignoring relevant, even costlessly available information. The Heiner (1990, pp. 39-40) analysis also suggests a basic tradeoff between reaching initial agreement over constitutional rules and the stability of future compliance to them once they are put into practical application. There is a basic tradeoff between ignorance and uncertainty that promote consensus over ex ante rules (that is, before anyone has had any actual experience living under them), and the reliability of any such advance agreement in avoiding rules that turn out destabilizing ex post due to errors that are self-recognized through the very ongoing experience generated by following the rules.

Thus, maintaining allegiance to previously agreed social rules can be a far more difficult challenge than reaching initial agreement about which rules to begin following - especially if the initial agreement was achieved under a veil of ignorance about the practical consequences of applying rules to future conditions.

15. Contractarianism and Evolutionism

In the modern research programme of Constitutional Political Economy two strands of thought are systematically interwoven: a subjectivist-contractarian strand of Austrian-Wicksellian origin, on the one hand, and an evolutionistic strand, which essentially works out the implications that follow from Popperian evolutionary epistemology for the issues of socio- economic-political organization.

For recent discussions of contractarianism, and apart from Buchanan's and Vanberg's own contributions, reference is made to Binmore (1990), Hardin (1990), Mueller (1990) and Sugden (1990). Coleman (1990) contains a valuable comparison of Buchanan's form of contractarianism with that of the philosophers John Rawls and David Gauthier. Sugden (1993a) outlines a procedural or contractarian formulation of rights. Gaus (1991) sketches an account of political authority and democracy that depicts them as responses to our moral disagreements and our inability to rationally resolve them on their merits.

The constitutional contract is often interpreted as a device to overcome the hypothetical state of anarchy (see, for example, Buchanan, 1975). How can, in a pre-constitutional setting that lacks any institutional forms, a unanimous agreement on the rules and the agency enforcing the rules be imagined to emerge? Witt (1992) conceptualizes the problem in game theoretic terms and explores the logical basis of the dilemma that turns up in this context. While the protective agency has to be endowed with sufficiently powerful coercive means to prevent anyone breaking the social contract, this concentration of power may itself induce a violation by making the protective agency usurp its power.

The implications of subjectivism are equally remarkable. Traditionally, the subjectivists par excellence within economics were the Austrians. Vanberg (1994, Chap. 13) has consistently worked out the implications of subjectivism for the theory of organized, collective action. The normative focus is shifted from endstates or outcomes, as such, to the process through which these outcomes or endstates emerge. The relevant question becomes whether the process by which outcomes and endstates are brought about can reasonably be assumed to reflect the preferences of the individuals concerned, as revealed in their actual choice behaviour. Thus the approach is incompatible with criteria that - as is true for Benthamite utilitarianism - are individualistic in the sense of measuring the goodness of social matters in terms of individual utilities, but do so without reference to individuals' choices. It can be characterized as choice-individualism, as opposed to the utility-individualism that underlies the whole tradition of the concept of a social welfare function.

Vanberg clearly recognizes that the true problem with the agreement criterion is not that it is too demanding but, instead, that it has too little normative content. A criterion needs to be specified which allows one to distinguish between constraints that are judged to render the respective individual choices involuntary, and those that do not. His analysis reaches the conclusion that a consistent normative-individualist approach needs to rely on a combined and simultaneous application of a purely procedural, rule oriented, as well as a substantive, avoidance/exit-cost criterion. The avoidance/exit cost perspective arguably provides a more operational specification of the contractarian norm than the notion of a hypothetical contract to which Buchanan (1975, 1977) as well as Rawls (1971) appeal. The exit perspective is consistently followed by, for example, Lowenberg and Yu (1992) and Mbaku (1995).

The evolutionistic strand of thought in fact consists of a complex set of more or less interrelated theses some of which are more controversial than others. The least problematical ingredient is reflected in the idea, related to Hayek's 'limits of reason' insight, that, in the realm of rules and institutions no less than in other areas, we can never know ex ante what the best solutions to our problems will be, if alone - as Popper has pointed out in his critique of historicism - because we cannot know today what we will know tomorrow. In fact, we cannot know ex ante what our future problems will be. Therefore, we need to rely at least to some extent on the explorative potential of open ended, competitive processes and on the kind of experience that accumulates in trial and error learning. But there is no reason to expect that what survives necessarily coincides with what is desirable in the sense of being responsive to the interests and preferences of the persons involved. It would seem entirely unfounded to expect an unqualified evolutionary process generally to produce such favourable conditions. On the other hand, a recognition of 'the limits of our reason' should not imply that we cannot say something about the kinds of conditions and process-characteristics that enhance responsiveness to the interests and preferences of the persons involved. Indeed, creating and maintaining such conditions has to be the primary task for deliberate constitutional design. There is room for both evolutionary learning and constructive design, not only as compatible, but also as indispensible and complementary elements of an appropriate socio-economic-political order. This insight leads Vanberg to develop the notion of 'constitutionally-constrained evolution (or competition)', a combination of deliberate design and evolutionary learning: the design of a framework of meta rules - the idea of a meta constitution - within which efforts in constitutional construction are subject to a kind of evolutionary competition that promises to make selections in favour of rules that serve the interests of the respective constituencies. The programme culminates in a theory of institutional competition among jurisdictions viewed as a knowledge-creating discovery process (Vanberg, 1994, p. 284; Vanberg and Kerber, 1994).

Institutional competition has been analysed from a variety of perspectives. Wiseman (1990) argues that analysis of voice and exit dimensions of a fiscal constitution is a means of appraising the efficiency of social arrangements. Marlow (1992) argues that one's view toward the design of voice and exit options is affected by one's perception of the appropriate size of government. It is recognized that the design of voice and exit options in the fiscal constitution exerts a predictable influence on policy. Sinn (1992) analyses competition among governments on the basis of a model that views countries as clubs.

Evolutionary themes are further explored in the following contributions. Parisi (1995) contains a sophisticated outline of a theory of spontaneous law. Wohlgemuth (1995) contrasts the neoclassical and the market process conceptions of economic and political competition and develops an alternative agenda for many fields of public choice. Gruner (1995) examines evolutionary stability of social norms in a formal socioeconomic equilibrium model. The institutional evolution of the Icelandic Commonwealth (930-1264 AD) is discussed in Solvason (1993).

It has almost become a commonplace to state that game-theoretic notions and approaches capture essential elements of the evolutionary paradigm. Most of the arguments can be related to repeated coordination (Warneryd, 1990), Prisoner's Dilemma (see Axelrod, 1984) or hawk dove (Sugden, 1989) games. Generally speaking, the extension of the market analogy to the constitutional level, that is, to the rules and institutions within which market coordination takes place, is not corroborated by the game-theoretic analysis of invisible-hand processes. This analysis does not warrant the conclusion that invisible-hand processes will operate to generate efficient results, except under a highly restrictive set of conditions. This point is illustrated by, for example, Warneryd (1990). Warneryd discusses the evolutionary game theoretical approach to the emergence of conventions, that is, institutions that solve recurrent coordination problems. It is argued that conventions may be said to minimize transaction costs, but that they need not be efficient.

16. Compliance, Renegotiation, Secession

Constitutional preferences, like any other preferences, can be assumed to embody two conceptually distinct components, an interest-component and a theory-component. Rational actors will have reasons to be concerned, not only about the interest dimension, but also about the theory dimension in constitutional choice.

Both concerns have certain implications for the kinds of 'procedural constraints' that can be expected to facilitate actual agreement, implications that need not be in perfect accordance.

So far as the interest dimension is concerned, it has been a central tenet of constitutional political economy at least since Buchanan and Tullock (1962) that constitutional deliberations must take place behind a veil of uncertainty in order for a constitution to be efficient. The prospects for reaching constitutional agreement are enhanced by whatever tends to increase persons' uncertainty about the particular effects that alternative rules can be expected to have on them, that is, by whatever tends to thicken the veil. The veil notion can be seen as a summary label for factors that, by increasing uncertainty, tend to alleviate potential conflicts in constitutional interests.

It should be noted that potential knowledge-based disagreement obviously requires the opposite cure. The prospects of agreement on desirable or efficient rules and the prospects for adopting such rules are enhanced, not by creating uncertainty, but, on the contrary, by raising the level of mutually-shared information and knowledge on the general working properties of alternative rules. The Buchanan-Tullock 'veil of uncertainty' and the Rawlsian 'veil of ignorance' are assumed to render persons uncertain or ignorant about their particularized interests while not inhibiting their capability accurately to anticipate the general effects of potential alternative rules. In other words, their constitutional theories are supposed to be perfect and non-controversial. Informational problems with regard to the general working properties of rules do not exist.

This section is concerned with the interest dimension, that is, with the difficulties involved in any attempt to achieve agreement on rules among persons with potentially-conflicting constitutional interests. Moreover, once agreement has been achieved, the agreement must be enforceable because each individual has a subsequent incentive to defect from the cooperative agreement.

It is recalled that in the contractarian and neo-contractarian literature two lines of reasoning have been pursued which focus central attention on the interest-component in constitutional choice with a view toward modification of the constitutional choice setting so as to reconcile potential divergences. Both are concerned with the general problem of constitutional efficiency and survivability.

The first line of argument, which is discussed in this section, focuses attention on the need for a 'veil of uncertainty' as a precondition for an efficient constitution. The second line of argument adopts an exit (entry) perspective.

Though Rawls's idea of constitutional choice 'behind the veil of ignorance' and Buchanan's notion of 'conceptual agreement' cannot be expected to provide a workable criterion upon which actual normative judgements on existing social arrangements could be based, they do serve a useful heuristic function by directing attention to the question of whether - based on our general understanding of the nature of human choice - it can be plausibly assumed that some existing set of rules could have been voluntarily agreed upon by all participants at some original stage of decision.

A notion that is typically used in this respect in contractarian theories is *fairness*. Fairness can be induced by two independent factors: (1)

uncertainty, as has been indicated already, and (2) the concern for stability, which will be discussed below.

In real-world settings persons are typically not totally ignorant about their particular constitutional interests. But they are not perfectly certain about these interests either. They typically find themselves behind a veil of uncertainty that prevents them from accurately anticipating the particular ways in which they will be affected by the prospective working properties of alternative rules.

The veil's thickness may vary, depending on certain characteristics of the actual choice situation. As the veil's thickness increases so will the prospect of achieving agreement. The variables that affect the veil's thickness can to some extent be manipulated and rational actors can take deliberate measures designed to put themselves behind a thicker veil, thereby enhancing the prospects of realizing potential gains from constitutional agreement.

In this respect the following observations are made. The degree of uncertainty is, in part, a function of the sort of rules that are under consideration. The essential dimensions here are the generality and the durability of rules. The more general rules are and the longer the period over which they are expected to be in effect, the less certainty persons can have about the particular ways in which alternative rules will affect them. They will therefore be induced to adopt a more impartial perspective and, consequently, they will be more likely to reach agreement. The veil of uncertainty works by moderating the differences among identifiable constitutional interests, thus inducing fairness or impartiality and facilitating agreement in constitutional choice.

There is an additional factor through which fairness can be induced, independent from the uncertainty factor, but working in the same direction. This factor is the concern for stability. The possibility of realizing gains by operating under constitutional constraints is not just a matter of securing some initial agreement; it is also a matter of a sufficient level of ongoing agreement, of continuing acquiescence in an ongoing co-operative arrangement. Stability refers to the viability of a constitutional arrangement over time. Rational actors can be expected to take considerations of stability into account when engaging in constitutional choice. To the extent that fairness and stability are interrelated, the concern for stability will induce a concern for fairness or impartiality even in persons who may be perfectly aware of the particular effects that alternative rules will have on them. It is not the uncertainty about one's own particular position that will induce impartiality, but the anticipation that a constitutional arrangement is unlikely to be stable if it is only designed to serve one's own particular interests.

How precisely are stability and fairness interrelated? Two aspects of the stability problem should be distinguished. They are not always sufficiently separated in discussions on the issue: the compliance problem and the renegotiation problem.

First, in order for a constitutional arrangement to be stable over time it has to command a sufficient level of compliance. However, compliance with rules is certainly not a direct function of their fairness. The fact that rules are perceived as fair by the relevant group of persons does not, *per se*, guarantee a willingness to comply with those rules. The compliance problem results from the fact that there may be potential gains from defecting. Whether such gains exist or not is not *per se* dependent on the fairness properties of the arrangement. To the extent that such gains exist, a compliance or unilateral defection problem is present even with perfectly fair rules.

Second, constitutional arrangements should also command a sufficient level of ongoing agreement. A constitutional agreement that favours particular interests may be achievable under 'suitable' conditions, but such agreement can be expected to be less robust with regard to potential changes in circumstances than fair arrangements. Unfair arrangements may tend to give rise to the renegotiation problem. It is especially with regard to renegotiation rather than with regard to compliance that the concern for stability can be expected to induce a concern for fairness. There is a much more direct relation between the fairness issue and renegotiation than there is between fairness of rules and compliance with rules.

For further discussion on the foregoing and related issues, reference is made to the following contributions.

Several fundamental issues relating to the problem of constitutional stability are discussed in Ordeshook (1992). Twight (1992) assesses the extent to which consensuality is likely to characterize the process of constitutional revision. Theoretical and empirical grounds are provided for concluding that non-consensual constitutional revision is often the rule rather than the exception. The endogeneity of politically relevant transaction costs and their manipulation by self-interested political actors in a post-constitutional environment are central to the analysis. The theory of constitutional maintenance is equally examined in Niskanen (1990).

Constitutional renegotiation may end in impasse. Young (1994) examines the political economy of secession. Special reference is made to the case of Quebec. The author explains why secessionist movements have not been successful in industrialized welfare states, even when the structural preconditions are largely present, as in cases like Scotland and Belgium. A formal analysis of constitutional secession clauses using game theory is made in Chen and Ordeshook (1994).

17. The Common Law and its 'Efficiency'

Buchanan (1977) criticized Posner (1972) for its failure to make the vital distinction between the two functional roles in which lawyers may find themselves: Posner appears to offer potential advice and counsel to future judges and legislators alike. But, recalls Buchanan, the judge should not change the basic law because by such behaviour he would be explicitly abandoning the role of jurist for that of legislator. In his role of jurist he should enforce existing law instead of enacting new legislation. Buchanan referred explicitly to Leoni's (1961) distinction between law and legislation. It follows from Buchanan's argument that there is no justification at all for a judicial introduction of the putative efficiency norm, presumably to be imposed independently of the political process. This view is implied by the adoption of the subjectivist-contractarian consensus or unanimity rule as a benchmark for efficiency. The normative economist can advance alternative sets of rules as a hypothesis to be tested in the political exchange process, but he should never be allowed to take the arrogant stance of suggesting that this or that set of institutions is or is not more efficient.

In a similar vein De Alessi and Staaf (1991) argue that the law and economics view of the common law as an efficient process that promotes the evolution of efficient rules through an auction-like mechanism is flawed because it fails to cope with the problem of aggregating preferences. They argue that the belief that the efficiency of the common law is enhanced by assigning disputed rights so as to lower transaction costs is also flawed. The common law provides a form of unanimity by allowing individuals to contract around the rule and provides order by maintaining transitivity, through the use of precedent, in the application of the rule to new situations.

Aranson (1992) highlights another problem: in the neoclassical approach to law and economics, the common law judges, in rendering decisions that maximize wealth, are placed in the position of calculators of comparative values. However, this task confronts the courts with an insoluble economic calculation problem, analogous to the problem faced by central economic planners. Therefore, courts should prefer to stay as close by as they can to a rights-based jurisprudence.

Wagner (1992) argues that social processes regarding the formation of rules should be assessed in terms of their ability to provide a framework of stable rules guaranteeing the stability of expectations and allowing people to plan their economic activities. The dichotomy between statutory and common law is overdrawn, because both derive from the same source in a setting where there are no longer polycentric sources of competing authority, since the contemporary nation-state - presumably Wagner has the United States of

America in mind - has the capacity to absorb all alternative sources of authority into itself.

More radically Benson (1992b) argues that the government-backed common law system is more likely to adopt inefficient rules than a genuine customary law system. Though he recognizes that much of common law was simply a codification of the basic norms common to Anglo-Saxon society, Benson recalls that common law was also royal law and that even during its earliest periods of development some aspects of it were legislated and imposed by authoritarian kings. Furthermore, when a government's judges make new law through precedent, it becomes enforceable law for everyone in the society whether it is a mutually beneficial law or not. Common law precedents are backed by the coercive power of the state and, therefore they take on the same authority as statute law.

Yandle (1991) develops a vision of the Common Law as an 'organic' Constitution, reflecting evolved social norms, a result that causes ordinary people to accept the authority of judges.

18. Studies in the History of Ideas

There now is a fair number of review articles on Buchanan's thought. Besides those already mentioned, reference can be made to Brennan (1987, 1990), Congleton (1988) and Yeager (1990).

In Germany, institutional analysis has a long and autonomous tradition, which has not been given proper international recognition. This applies especially to the neoliberal Ordnungstheorie, of which Walter Eucken is generally acknowledged to be the leading representative. Leipold (1990) examines the methodological and theoretical similarities and differences between Eucken's Ordnungstheorie and Buchanan's Constitutional Economics. Though there is no tradition of pluralism in German history, some German thinkers developed ideas which came remarkably close to later English and American pluralists. This development, particularly as exemplified in the work of Georg Beseler, Otto Gierke and later Hugo Preuss, is dealt with in Dreyer (1993).

Aranson (1991) argues for the coherence of Calhoun's political thought, when read in the light of modern public choice theory and contrary to earlier interpretations.

Madison's constitutional political economy is carefully examined in Dorn (1991). James Madison was instrumental in the design, ratification, and implementation of the American Constitution. He also was the major force behind the Bill of Rights. It is in the light of these accomplishments that Madison has been called 'The Founding Father'. Because he focused on the rules or principles of a liberal order rather than on the outcomes, James Madison can properly be viewed as a pioneering constitutional political economist. Drawing on the political theory of Locke and the economic theory of Smith, Madison successfully combined the two to form a coherent theory of constitutional economics. Adopting a self-interest postulate, he showed that social and economic order are best achieved by allowing open competition to prevail under a rule of law protecting private property and freedom of contract. Thus, he clearly recognized the close relation between political order and economic order, and he anticipated many of the themes in the public choice/constitutional economics literature.

One of the insights of Madison and other framers of the US constitution was that a bicameral legislature might function as a device to limit the power of legislative coalitions. The idea was that each house would be elected differently and consequently would represent different interests. The requirement of a simultaneous majority in both houses in order for legislation to be enacted would then guarantee a broad social consensus. It should be noted that the differences between the two chambers have been eroded subsequently. However, the argument for bicameral legislatures on efficiency grounds and the urge that the two houses be elected by radically different methods, was at the theoretical level revived in this century by Tullock (see Buchanan and Tullock, 1962, Chap. 16, written by Tullock; see also Tullock, 1987).

Elazar (1991) argues that the work of an early political scientist, Johannes Althusius, who developed his theory of the polity on the eve of the modern epoch at the end of the sixteenth century, offers an important starting point for building a postmodern theory of political and social organization. Althusius (1991) is a collection of excerpts from his Politica Methodice Digesta (1603/1614).

Sir Edward Coke's role as a constitutional entrepreneur in seventeenth-Century England is highlighted in Yandle (1993).

19. Variations on Hayekian Themes

Constitutional political economy shares much of the spirit of Hayek's inquiry into the interrelation between the order of rules and the order of actions, and of his message that changes in the order of rules are the principal means by which we can hope to improve the socio-economic- political order under which we live (Vanberg, 1994, passim). It will come as no surprise, then, that several contributions elaborate explicitly on Hayekian themes. Buchanan's personal recollections of F.A. Hayek are set out in Buchanan (1992).

Streit (1993) brings out clearly how Hayek's approach to the social sciences, especially to economics, is rooted in his epistemological position, particularly as he set it out in Hayek (1952). Butos and Koppl (1993) outline a theory of expectations based on Hayek's cognitive theory. The central tenet of the theory, which is intended to have both policy implications and testable empirical content, is that economic expectations will serve as reliable guides to action only when certain 'filtering conditions', that is certain constitutional constraints such as the atomicity of the market process and the stability of the rules governing that process are satisfied. A failure of either condition creates a loose 'system constraint' and thus a loose link between environment and expectation, as the theory of 'big players' illustrates. Big players, of which central bankers are a prototypical example, introduce a wedge between epistemic knowledge and social reality. The theory highlights the connection between the choice of constraints and its epistemic consequences. The big player theory also suggests a possible direction for future empirical work in a Hayekian tradition. Within the adopted framework 'neoclassical' economics and 'radical Keynesianism' may be seen in a sense as limiting cases. When certain filtering conditions are in place, the results of the market process may be described by 'neoclassical' models of rational maximizing and action will seem predictable at least at some aggregate level. To the extent that these conditions fail, the market process will be influenced by animal spirits and the like and action will seem unpredictable to the observing economist. Thus the evolutionary logic of Hayekian economics provides the general theoretical foundations for special empirical theories, such as the big player theory, which may identify the precise causes and consequences of observed deviation from the neoclassical model.

It is to be regretted that the recently developing literature on, say, monetary constitutionalism has largely failed to incorporate these Hayekian insights. Recent events in the European Monetary System on the one hand, and monetary disintegration in the former Soviet Union on the other, have revived interest in the question of how to design and choose a monetary regime that ensures monetary stability for both parts of Europe. Even among economists who are otherwise considered staunch advocates of laissez-faire policy, money is still regarded as the prime and uncontroversial example of a good that has to be provided by government. Buchanan (1962), accepting the premise that money is a public good that can only be provided by government, derives its optimal properties from a constitutional perspective. In the same vein Spinelli and Masciandaro (1993) argue for a constitutionalization of the target of monetary stability in Italy.

Hefeker (1995) has argued that the objective of monetary stability can be achieved either by complete monetary union or by currency competition and that both regimes may be viable solutions depending on the circumstances.

His paper makes the case for monetary union in Western Europe, even though he recognizes that monetary union is no alternative for Eastern Europe and the former Soviet Union.

We believe that the critical examination and evaluation of the properties of alternative monetary regimes constitutes one of the most interesting and exciting lines of future research within the field of constitutional economics.

Choi (1993) offers a critical evaluation of Hayek's 'atavism of social justice' thesis, suggesting an alternative explanation for the widespread demands for social justice in contemporary society, based on the analysis of the nature of entrepreneurship and its tendency to incite envy.

Tuerck (1995) re-interprets Hayek's theory of mind in the light of contemporary philosophy of artificial intelligence.

20. Towards a Constitutional Economics of the Firm

Vanberg (1992a) compares four theoretical approaches to the study of organizations that can be identified in the relevant literature: the goal paradigm, the exchange paradigm, the nexus of contracts paradigm, and the constitutional paradigm. It is argued that the latter provides the more fruitful theoretical perspective in that it reconciles an individualist methodology with an account of organizations as corporate actors, as units of collective action.

In search of a more decisive argument in the controversy concerning alternative forms of ownership of firms and allocation of capital, Pelikan (1993) complements and qualifies the standard incentive argument by an argument considering a less well explored factor: the competence with which firms are organized and managed. Alternative forms of ownership of firms are assessed according to their impact on this competence. The general conclusion is that private and tradable ownership of firms is a necessary condition for efficiency of supply. The competence argument strengthens the neoliberal defence of private ownership and market competition. It is in allocating the authority to organize supply to agents of high relevant competence, and in demoting from this authority agents of low competence, that private and tradable ownership of firms is shown to have its decisive comparative advantage.

Kiser (1994) rationalizes public enterprise by analysing the constitutional choice between private and public ownership of production arrangements. Arguing that results depend on who does the choosing, the article compares choices by self-governing citizens with choices by self- directed governmental officials. The resulting institutional theory identifies four conditions that cause citizens to favour public over private ownership: natural monopoly, output and process invisibilities, the production of consumer necessities, potential producer moral hazard. None of the conditions refers to the standard concept of economic efficiency, which guides most economic comparisons of public and private enterprise.

Langlois (1995) argues that Hayek's theory of spontaneous order can in fact include the case of such apparently purposive and extramarket forms as the business firm. In other words, Hayek's theory of the market as a spontaneous order has implications for the theory of the firm that the mainstream Coasean approach has yet fully to absorb. Langlois picks up a number of suggestions in Hayek's evolutionary theory of social institutions and uses them to draw a picture of the firm that is somewhat different from that drawn by neoclassical transaction-cost analysis. In the Hayekian picture, firms and markets are both systems of rules of conduct. Both are systems for economizing on knowledge in the face of economic change, albeit quite different kinds of knowledge and change. Moreover, there is a sense in which the firm exists not in order to centralize control over knowledge but - like the market - precisely to decentralize the use of knowledge. In the end, it is argued that the firm is no model for political planning for one very simple reason: the firm does not plan.

Adelstein (1991) draws upon the contractarian distinction between constitutional and operational levels of personal choice and an evolutionary analysis of the growth of firms to illuminate the complex issues surrounding the emergence of large-scale economic organization in the United States in the years since 1870.

21. Redistribution

There have been two recent attempts to provide a rationale for redistribution within the scope of constitutional political economy. Kliemt (1993b) argues that redistribution can be institutionalized at the constitutional level to attain a 'minimum welfare state' without violating basic principles or incurring risks beyond those that are present in the minimal state itself. Wessels (1993) describes a situation in which individuals may unanimously agree to transfer income at the constitutional stage on the grounds that redistribution provides income insurance. Both are criticized, invoking the usual arguments, by Pasour (1994).

22. European Integration

Streit and Mussler (1994) analyse the changes in the economic constitution of the European Community since its foundation in 1958. It is argued that as far as the economic constitution is concerned, the Treaty of Maastricht is dominated by traits which are characteristic of modern welfare states. The editors of *Constitutional Political Economy* took Vibert (1995) as a starting point to devote the 1996 Vol. 7 No. 4 issue of their journal to the theme *Europe: A Constitution for the Millennium.* This special issue includes articles by Blankart (1996, pp. 257-265), Buchanan (1996, pp. 253-256), Frey (1996, pp. 267-279), Holcombe (1996, pp. 281-291), Mueller (1996, pp. 293-302), Ostrom (1996, pp. 303-308), Sobel (1996, pp. 309-316) and Vaubel 1996, (pp. 317-324).

23. Other and Related Subjects

A constitutional approach to international private law is contained in Schmidtchen and Schmidt-Trenz (1990). Constitutional issues concerning transition in Eastern Europe and the former Soviet Republics are discussed in Sunstein (1991), Apolte (1995) and Ordeshook and Shvetsova (1995). Brunetti and Weder (1994) argue that establishing strategies for the control of state discretionary power is a crucial precondition for overcoming credibility problems and generating long-term economic growth in less developed countries. Kratochwil (1992) suggests an alternative approach to the study of international politics. A critical examination of the Clean Water Act from a constitutional perspective is contained in Meiners and Yandle (1992). Pauly (1994) examines the concept that social insurance for medical care may represent a kind of constitutional choice.

Kuran (1993) argues that public opinion breeds tyranny by forcing individuals to refrain from voicing their genuine thoughts and feelings. Several devices to cope with the emergence and persistence of certain social taboos are discussed. Lipford (1992) applies constitutional economics to the constitutions and rules that govern seven of the eight largest US Christian denominations. A positive theory of economic fairness is constructed in Isaac, Mathieu and Zajac (1991). Public debt repudiation is analysed, using Jefferson's model in Gunter (1991).

E. Conclusions

Throughout the writing of the present article we constantly had in mind the editors' aim of providing the readers of the Encyclopedia of Law and Economics with a well-informed overview of the existing literature. Some readers may find that our strategy of favouring 'comprehensiveness' at the expense of 'structure' has to some degree distracted from the flow of argument. However, we are reasonably confident that the unifying theme underlying the whole will be clear. The various subdisciplines of Public Choice, Law and Economics, Constitutional Political Economy and others all represent, as opposed to the independence-isolation of economics, a return of economics to its appropriate legal foundations. But this theme only loosely connects the subparts and sections of this article. In fact the four subparts and even most of the subsections can be read largely independently. This can only add to the reader's convenience

Admittedly, and strictly from the title, the public choice element was somewhat neglected, relative to the constitutional political economy element. This bias is explained by our own priorities, but only in part. It was Buchanan himself who in the 1980s changed the name of his research program to *constitutional economics*. Early on, Buchanan had made it clear that he regarded the traditional approach to economic policy advice based on welfare economics as a scientifically flawed and politically alarming development. Welfare economics draws its conclusions from a comparison of the working properties of *real* markets with *idealized* criteria. Then, confronted with the inefficiencies of reality compared to the idealized model, the market failure approach proceeds to suggest alternative measures which consist in *real* government interventions which are *assumed* to eliminate the inefficiencies. Thus, welfare economics runs the danger of becoming a 'nirvana approach' (Demsetz, 1969), meaning that it fails to identify the relevant alternatives for drawing its conclusions. First, in judging the real economy in order to arrive at policy advice, the relevant alternative is not an idealized market but 'another' real economy, one that would emerge under a different set of constraints. This means one has to compare alternative institutional arrangements, in markets and the polity, and their outcomes. Second, such a comparison requires a criterion that is equally apt in evaluating the economic as well as the political order, that is a non-ideal, internal standard of comparison. For Buchanan, democratic consent provides this kind of criterion (Pies, 1996, p. 26).

Despite its general direction towards a comparison of alternative institutional arrangements, large parts of the public choice literature seem like an empirically oriented welfare economic analysis of the political sector and use the welfare-economic concept of normative efficiency as a benchmark, thus more or less duplicating the 'nirvana approach'. The term 'constitutional economics' clearly distanced Buchanan's paradigm from those parts of the public choice literature that make welfare economic efficiency the measure of all things. The term more adequately describes the topic of his institutional, rules-directed analyses.

Bibliography on Public Choice, Constitutional Political Economy, and Law and Economics (0610)

Adelstein, Richard P. (1991), 'Deciding for Bigness: Constitutional Choice and the Growth of Firms', **2** *Constitutional Political Economy*, 7-30.

Althusius, Johannes (1991), 'An Early Contractarian Constitutionalist (Excerpts from his Politica Methodice Digesta)', **2** *Constitutional Political Economy*, 209-223.

Anderson, Gary M. and Tollison, Robert D. (1992), 'Morality and Monopoly: The Constitutional Political Economy of Religious Rules', **12** *Cato Journal*, 373-392.

Anderson, Terry L. and Hill, Peter J. (1986), 'Constraining the Transfer Society: Constitutional and Moral Dimensions', **6** *Cato Journal*, 317-341.

Apolte, T. (1995), 'Democracy, Dictatorship, and Transformation: A Proposal for a Constitution-Guided Systematic Change in Formerly Soviet Republics', **6** *Constitutional Political Economy*, 5-20.

Aranson, Peter H. (1991), 'Calhoun's Constitutional Economics', **2** *Constitutional Political Economy*, 31-52.

Aranson, Peter H. (1992), 'The Common Law as Central Economic Planning', **3** *Constitutional Political Economy*, 289-319.

Arantes, Peter, Gellhorn, Ernest A. and Robinson, Glen O. (1983), 'A Theory of Legislative Delegation', **68** *Cornell Law Review*, 23-56.

Arrow, Kenneth J. (1951), *Social Choice and Individual Values*, New York, John Wiley and Sons.

Axelrod, Robert (1984), *The Evolution of Cooperation*, New York, Basic Books.

Backhaus, Jürgen G. (1978), 'Pareto on Public Choice', **33** *Public Choice*, 5-17.

Backhaus, Jürgen G. (1995), *An Economic Analysis of Constitutional Law, research memorandum*, Maastricht, University of Limburg.

Backhaus, Jürgen G. (1996), 'An Economic Analysis of Constitutional Law', in Buscaglia, Edgardo, Ratliff, William and Cooter, Robert (eds), *Law and Economics of Development*, Greenwood, JAI Press.

Baird, Charles W. (1989), 'James Buchanan and the Austrians: The Common Ground', *Cato Journal*, 201 ff.

Barnes, David W. and Stout, Lynn A. (1992), *Economics of Constitutional Law and Public Choice*, St Paul's West Publishing Company.

Becker, Gary S. (1983), 'A Theory of Competition among Pressure Groups for Political Influence', **98** *Quarterly Journal of Economics*, 371-383.

Ben-Shahar, O. (1992), 'Strategic Behavior in Judicial Panels', Discussion Paper No. 107, Program in Law and Economics, Harvard Law School.

Benson, Bruce L. (1981a), 'Why are Congressional Committees Dominated by "High Demand" Legislators?', **48** *Southern Economic Journal*, 68-77.

Benson, Bruce L. (1981b), 'A Note on Corruption of Public Officials: The Black Market for Property Rights', **5** *Journal of Libertarian Studies*, 305-311.

Benson, Bruce L. (1983a), 'High Demand Legislative Committees and Bureaucratic Output', **11** *Public Finance Quarterly*, 259-281.

Benson, Bruce L. (1983b), 'The Economic Theory of Regulation as an Explanation of Policies Toward Bank Mergers and Holding Company Acquisitions', **28** *Antitrust Bulletin*, 839-862.

Benson, Bruce L. (1984a), 'Rent Seeking as a Justification for Privatization', **7** *Journal of Contemporary Studies*, 5-12.

Benson, Bruce L. (1984b), 'Rent Seeking from a Property Rights Perspective', **51** *Southern Economic Journal*, 388-400.

Benson, Bruce L. (1988a), 'An Institutional Explanation for Corruption of Criminal Justice Officials', **8** *Cato Journal*, 139-163.

Benson, Bruce L. (1988b), 'Corruption in Law Enforcement: One Consequence of 'The Tragedy of the Commons' Arising with Public Allocation Processes', **8** *International Review of Law and Economics*, 73-84.

Benson, Bruce L. (1989), 'Further Thoughts on Rent Seeking, Bureaucratic Output, and the Price of Complements', **63** *Public Choice*, 279-281.

Benson, Bruce L. (1991), 'An Evolutionary Contractarian View of Primitive Law: The Institutions and Incentives Arising Under Customary American Indian Law', **5** *Review of Austrian Economics*, 65-89.

Benson, Bruce L. (1992a), 'The Development of Criminal Law and its Enforcement: Public Interest or Political Transfers', **3** *Journal des Economistes et des Etudes Humaines*, 79-108.

Benson, Bruce L. (1992b), 'Customary Law as a Social Contract: International Commercial Law', **2** *Constitutional Political Economy*, 1-27.

Benson, Bruce L. (1994), 'Third Thoughts on Contracting Out', **11** *Journal of Libertarian Studies*, 44-78.

Benson, Bruce L. (1995), 'Toxic Torts by Government', in *Independent Policy Report*, Oakland, Independent Institute.

Benson, Bruce L. and Baden, John (1985), 'The Political Economy of Government Corruption: The Logic of Underground Government', **14** *Journal of Legal Studies*, 391-410.

Benson, Bruce L. and Faminow, Merle D. (1984), 'Rent Seeking and Supply Management in Canada', **32** *Canadian Journal of Agricultural Economics*, 548-558.

Benson, Bruce L. and Faminow, Merle D. (1986), 'Regulatory Transfers in Canadian-American Agriculture: The Case of Supply Management', **6** *Cato Journal*, 271-294.

Benson, Bruce L. and Greenhut, Melvin L. (1986), 'Interest Groups, Bureaucrats and Antitrust: An Explanation of the Antitrust Paradox', in Grieson, Ronald E. (ed.), *Antitrust and Regulation*, Lexington, MA, Lexington Books, 53-90.

Benson, Bruce L. and Johnson, Ronald N. (1986), 'Capital Formation and Interstate Tax Competition', in Lee, Dwight (ed.), *Taxation and the Deficit Economy: Fiscal Policy and Capital Formation in the United States*, Cambridge, MA, Ballinger Press, 407-436.

Benson, Bruce L. and Johnson, Ronald N. (1986), 'The Lagged Impact of State and Local Taxes on Economic Activity and Political Behavior', **24** *Economic Inquiry*, 389-402.

Benson, Bruce L. and Mitchell, Jean (1988), 'Rent Seekers Who Demand Government Production: Bureaucratic Output and the Price of Complements', **56** *Public Choice*, 3-16.

Benson, Bruce L., Greenhut, Melvin L. and Holcombe, Randall (1987), 'Interest Groups and the Antitrust Paradox', **6** *Cato Journal*, 801-817.

Benson, Bruce L., Kim, Iljoong and Rasmussen, David W. (1994), 'Estimating Deterrence Effects: A Public Choice Perspective on the Economics of Crime Literature', **61** *Southern Economic Journal*, 161-168.

Benson, Bruce L., Rasmussen, David W. and Sollars, David L. (1995), 'Police Bureaucrats, Their Incentives, and the War on Drugs', **83** *Public Choice*, 21-45.

Bergstrom, John C. and Centner, Terence J. (1989), 'Agricultural Nuisances and Right to Farm Laws', **19** *Review of Regional Studies*, 23-30.

Binmore, Ken (1990), 'Evolution and Utilitarianism: Social Contract III', **1** *Constitutional Political Economy*, 1-26.

Black, D. (1958), *The Theory of Committees and Elections*, Cambridge, Cambridge University Press.

Blankart, Charles B. (1994), 'Club Governments versus Representative Governments', **5** *Constitutional Political Economy*, 273-285.

Blankart, Charles B. (1996), 'The European Union's Debt Question: A Conceptual Viewpoint', **7** *Constitutional Political Economy*, 257-265.

Boettke, Peter (ed.) (1994), *The Elgar Companion to Austrian Economics*, Brookfield, Edward Elgar.

Boudreaux, D.J. and Pritchard, A.C. (1994), 'Reassessing the Role of the Independent Judiciary in Enforcing Interest-Group Bargains', **5** *Constitutional Political Economy*, 1-21.

Brennan, Geoffrey (1987), 'The Buchanan Contribution', **45** *Finanzarchiv*, 1-24.

Brennan, Geoffrey (1990), 'James Buchanan's Public Economics: One Proposition, Two Speculations and Three Queries', **1** *Constitutional Political Economy*, 113-133.

Brennan, G. and Buchanan, James M. (1980), *The Power to Tax: Analytical Foundations of a Fiscal Constitution*, Cambridge, Cambridge University Press.

Brennan, G. and Hamlin, A (1995), 'Economizing on Virtue', **6** *Constitutional Political Economy*, 35-56.

Brennan, Geoffrey and Kliemt, Hartmut (1990), 'Logo Logic', **1** *Constitutional Political Economy*, 125-127.

Brennan, Geoffrey and Pardo, Jose Casas (1991), 'A Reading of the Spanish Constitution (1978)', **2** *Constitutional Political Economy*, 53-79.

Brinig, Margaret F. (1992), 'Politics, Economics and the McCarren Ferguson Act', **73** *Public Choice*, 371-383.

Brinig, Margaret F. (1993), 'The Law and Economics of No-Fault Divorce', **27** *Family Law Quarterly*, 453-470.

Brinig, Margaret F. (1995), 'Through a Glass Darkly, a Review of Neil Komesar's Imperfect Alternatives', **78** *Public Choice*, 190-194.

Brinig, Margaret F., Holcombe, Randall G. and Schwartzstein, Linda A. (1993), 'Public Choice and Lobbying Regulation', **74** *Public Choice*, 377-384.

Brooks, Michael (1997), 'Some Reflections on The Calculus of Consent', **8** *Constitutional Political Economy*, 3-13.

Brunetti, Aymo and Weder, Beatrice (1994), 'Political Credibility and Economic Growth in Less Developed Countries', **5** *Constitutional Political Economy*, 23-43.

Buchanan, James M. (1959), 'Positive Economics, Welfare Economics, and Political Economy', **2** *Journal of Law and Economics*, 124-138.

Buchanan, James M. (1962), 'Predictability: The Criterion of Monetary Constitutions', in Yeager, L.B. (ed.), *In search of a Monetary Constitution*, Cambridge, MA, Harvard University Press, 155-183.

Buchanan, James M. (1975), *The Limits of Liberty*, Chicago, IL, University of Chicago Press.

Buchanan, James M. (1977), 'Good Economics - Bad Law', *Freedom in Constitutional Contract,* Chapter 3, Texas, A&M University, 40-49.

Buchanan, James M. (1984), 'Rights, Efficiency, and Exchange: The Irrelevance of Transactions Cost', in Neumann, M. (ed.), *Ansprache, Eigentums- und Verfügungsrechte*, Berlin, Duncker and Humblot, 9-24. Reprinted in Medema, S.G. (ed.) (1995), *The Legacy of Ronald Coase in Economic Analysis,* Volume II, Chapter 8, Aldershot, Edward Elgar, 175-190.

Buchanan, James M. (1987), 'Justification of the Compound Republic: The Calculus in Retrospect', **7** *Cato Journal*, 305-312. Reprinted in Gwartney, J.D. and Wagner, R.E. (eds) (1988), *Public Choice and Constitutional Economics*, London, JAI Press, 131-137.

Buchanan, James M. (1990), 'The Domain of Constitutional Economics', **1** *Constitutional Political Economy*, 1-18.

Buchanan, James M. (1991a), 'Jack Wiseman: A Personal Appreciation', **2** *Constitutional Political Economy*, 1-6.

Buchanan, James M. (1991b), 'The Domain of Constitutional Political Economy', in Buchanan, James M. (ed.), *The Economics and Ethics of Constitutional Order*, Ann Arbor, MI, University of Michigan Press, 3-18.

Buchanan, James M. (1992), 'I Did Not Call Him "Fritz": Personal Recollections of Professor F. A. v. Hayek', **3** *Constitutional Political Economy*, 129-135.

Buchanan, James M. (1993a), 'Public Choice after Socialism', **77** *Public Choice*, 67-74.

Buchanan, James M. (1993b), 'How can Constitutions be Designed so that Politicians who Seek to Serve "Public Interest" can Survive and Prosper?', **4** *Constitutional Political Economy*, 1-6.

Buchanan, James M. (1996), 'Europe as Social Reality', **7** *Constitutional Political Economy*, 253-256.

Buchanan, James M. and Lee, Dwight R. (1991), 'Cartels, Coalitions, and Constitutional Politics', **2** *Constitutional Political Economy*, 139-161.

Buchanan, James M. and Stubblebine, Wm.C. (1962), 'Externality', **29** *Economica*, 371-384.

Buchanan, James M. and Tullock, Gordon (1962), *The Calculus of Consent: Logical Foundations of Constitutional Democracy*, Ann Arbor, MI, University of Michigan Press.

Butler, Henry N. and Ribstein, Larry E. (1990), 'Opting Out of Fiduciary Duties: A Response to the Anti-Contractarians', **65** *Washington Law Review*, 1 ff.

Butler, Henry N. and Ribstein, Larry E. (1994), 'Corporate Governance Speech and the First Amendment', **43** *University of Kansas Law Review*, 163 ff.

Butos, William N. and Koppl, Roger G. (1993), 'Hayekian Expectations: Theory and Empirical Applications', **4** *Constitutional Political Economy*, 303-329.

Centner, Terence J. (1985), 'Cooperatives: A Search for Equitable Relief from the Equity Redemption Problem', **8** *Journal of Agricultural Taxation and Law*, 120-144.

Centner, Terence J. (1993), 'Circumscribing the Reduction of Open Space by Scattered Development: Incorporating A German Concept in American Right-to-Farm Laws', **8** *Journal of Land Use and Environmental Law*, 307-324.

Centner, Terence J. (1994), 'Preserving Rural-Urban Fringe Areas and Enhancing the Rural Environment: Looking at Selected German Institutional Responses', **12** *Arizona Journal of International and Comparative Law*, 27-44.

Centner, Terence J. (1995a), 'Adopting Good Samaritan Immunity for Defendants in the Horse Industry', **12** *Agriculture and Human Values*, 69-78.

Centner, Terence J. (1995b), 'The New Equine Liability Statutes', **62** *Tennessee Law Review*, 997-1039.

Chapman, Bruce (1982), 'Individual Rights, Good Consequences, and the Theory of Social Choice', **12** *Journal for the Theory of Social Behavior*, 317-328.

Chapman, Bruce (1983), 'Rights as Constraints: Nozick vs Sen', **15** *Theory and Decision*, 1-10.

Chapman, Bruce (1987), 'Pensions, Sex Discrimination, and the Value of Life after Death', **7** *International Review of Law and Economics*, 193-214.

Chen, Yan and Ordeshook, Peter C. (1994), 'Constitutional Secession Clauses', **5** *Constitutional Political Economy*, 45-60.

Choi, Young Back (1993), 'Entrepreneurship and Envy', **4** *Constitutional Political Economy*, 331-347.

Coase, Ronald H. (1960), 'The Problem of Social Cost', **3** *Journal of Law and Economics*, 1-44. Reprinted in Coase, Ronald H., *The Firm, the Market and the Law*, Chicago, University of Chicago Press, 1988.

Coleman, James S. (1991), 'Natural Persons, Corporate Actors, and Constitutions', **2** *Constitutional Political Economy*, 81-106.

Coleman, Jules L. (1990), 'Constitutional Contractarianism', **1** *Constitutional Political Economy*, 135-148.

Congleton, Roger D. (1988), 'An Overview of the Contractarian Public Finance of James Buchanan', **16** *Public Finance Quarterly*, 131-157.

Cooter, Robert D. (1985), 'Unity in Torts, Contracts and Property: The Model of Precaution', **73** *California Law Review*, 1-51. Reprinted in Goldberg, Victor (ed.), *Readings in the Economics of Contract Law*, Cambridge University Press, 1989. Reprinted in Medema, Steven G. (ed.), *The Legacy of Ronald Coase in Economic Analysis*. Reprinted in Craswell, Richard and Schwartz, Alan (eds), *Readings in Contract Law*.

Cooter, Robert D. (1994), 'Market Affirmative Action', **31** *San Diego Law Review*, 133-168.

Cooter, Robert D. and Ulen, Thomas S. (1988), *Law and Economics*, New York, Harper Collins Publishers.

De Alessi, Louis (1992), 'Efficiency Criteria for Optimal Laws: Objective Standards or Value Judgements?', **3** *Constitutional Political Economy*, 321-342.

De Alessi, Louis and Staaf, Robert J. (1991), 'The Common Law Process: Efficiency or Order?', **2** *Constitutional Political Economy*, 107-126.

de Figueiredo, John M. and Teece, David, J. (1996), 'Mitigating Procurement Hazards in the Context of Innovation', **5** *Industrial and Corporate Change*, 537-559.

de Figueiredo, John M. and Tiller, Emerson H. (1996), 'Congressional Control of the Courts: A Theoretical and Empirical Analysis of Expansion of the Federal Judiciary', **39** *Journal of Law and Economics*, 435-462.

Dnes, Antony W. (1988), 'Rent Seeking, Entrepreneurship, Subjectivism and Property Rights: A Comment', **144** *Journal of Institutional and Theoretical Economics*, 891-893.

Dnes, Antony W. (1989), 'Rent Seeking, Conflict and Property Rights', **36** *Scottish Journal of Political Economy*, 366-374.

Dorn, James A. (1991), 'Madison's Constitutional Political Economy: Principles for a Liberal Order', **2** *Constitutional Political Economy*, 163-186.

Downs, A. (1957), *An Economic Analysis of Democracy*, New York, Harper and Row.

Dreyer, M. (1993), 'German Roots of the Theory of Pluralism', **4** *Constitutional Political Economy*, 7-39.

Dwight, Lee (1997), 'Dennis C. Mueller: Constitutional Democracy (Book Review)', **8** *Constitutional Political Economy*, 165-167.

Eichenberger, Reiner (1994), 'The Benefits of Federalism and the Risk of Overcentralization', **47(3)** *Kyklos*, 403-420.

Elazar, Daniel J. (1991), 'The Multifaceted Covenant: The Biblical Approach to the Problem of Organizations, Constitutions, and Liberty as Reflected in the Thought of Johannes Althusius', **2** *Constitutional Political Economy*, 187-208.

Elhauge, Einer Richard (1991), 'Does Interest Group Theory Justify More Intrusive Judicial Review?', **101** *Yale Law Journal*, 31 ff.

Elhauge, Einer Richard (1996), 'Are Term Limits Undemocratic', **63** *University of Chicago Law Review*.

Farber, Daniel A. and Frickey, Philip P. (1991), *Law and Public Choice: A Critical Introduction*, Chicago, IL, University of Chicago Press, 159 p.

Fischel, William A. (1979), 'Determinants of Voting on Environmental Quality: A Study of a New Hampshire Pulp Mill Referendum', **6** *Journal of Environmental Economics and Management*, 107-118.

Fischel, William A. (1980), 'Zoning and Land Use Reform: A Property Rights Perspective', **1** *Virginia Journal of Natural Resources Law*, 69-93.

Fischel, William A. (1992), 'Property Taxation and the Tiebout Model: Evidence for the Benefit View from Zoning and Voting', **30** *Journal of Economic Literature*, 163-169.

Fischel, William A. (1996), 'The Political Economy of Just Compensation: Lessons from the Military Draft for the Takings Issue', **19** *Harvard Journal of Law and Public Policy*.

Fischel, William A. and Campbell, Colin D. (1996), 'Preferences for School Finance Systems: Voters versus Judges', **49** *National Tax Journal*, 1-15.

Fishel, William A. and Shapiro, Perry (1988), 'Takings, Insurance and Michelman: Comments on Economic Interpretations of 'Just Compensation' Law', **17** *Journal of Legal Studies*, 269-293. Reprinted in Ellickson, Robert, Rose, Carol and Ackerman, Bruce (eds), *Perspectives on Property Law*, 2nd edn, 514-530, Boston, Little Brown, 1995.

Fischel, William A. and Shapiro, Perry (1989), 'A Constitutional Choice Model of Compensation for Takings', **9** *International Review of Law and Economics*, 115-128.

Frech, H. Edward III (1972), 'The Public Choice Theory of Murray N. Rothbard: A Modern Anarchist', **14** *Public Choice*, 143-154.

Frech, H. Edward III, Deacon, Rovert, Decanio, Stephen J. and Johnson, Bruce M. (1990), *Taxing Energy: Oil Severence Taxation and the Economy*, New York, Holmes and Meyer.

Frey, Bruno S. (1990), 'From Paradoxes to Social Rules, or: How Economics Repeats Itself', **1** *Constitutional Political Economy*, 27-34.

Frey, Bruno S. (1996), 'A Directly Democratic and Federal Europe', **7** *Constitutional Political Economy*, 267-279.

Garcia Villarejo, Salinas, Avelino and Sánchez, Javier (1993), *Manual de Hacienda Pública general y de España* (Public Treasury Manual), Madrid, Tecnos.

Garcia Viñuela, Enrique (1996a), 'Financing Political Parties: A Public Choice Approvach', *Economia delle Scelte Pubbliche*, 2-3.

Garcia Viñuela, Enrique (1996b), 'La Financiación de los Partidos Políticos: un Enfoque de Elección Pública (Financing Political Parties: A Public Choice Approach)', **92** *Revista de Estudios Políticos*.

Garcia Viñuela, Enrique (1996c), 'Una nota sobre la Teoría del Estado de Anthony de Jasay (A Note on Anthony de Jasay's Theory of the State)', **136** *Hacienda Pública Española*.

Garcia Viñuela, Enique and Vazquez Vega, Pablo (1996a), 'Financing the Political Parties: A Public Choice Approach', **2-3** *Ecomonia delle Scette Pubbliche*, 139-153.

Garcia Viñuela, Enrique and Vazquez Vega, Pablo (1996b), 'La Financiación de los Partidos Politicos. Un Enfoque de Elección Pública (Financing Political Parties: A Public Choice Approach)', **92** *Revista de Estudios Políticos*.

Gaus, Gerald F. (1991), 'Public Justification and Democratic Adjudication', **2** *Constitutional Political Economy*, 251-281.

Goetz, C.J. (1991), 'Uncommon Common-sense vs. Conventional Wisdom: The Virginia School of Economics', Prepared for the Seventh Annual Lecture in the Virginia Political Economy.

Goldberg, Victor P. (1974), 'Public Choice - Property Rights', **8** *Journal of Economic Issues*, 555-579. Reprinted in Samuels (ed.), *Methodology of Economic Thought*, New Brunswick, NJ, Transaction Books, 1978.

Goldberg, Victor P. (1977), 'On Positive Theories of Redistribution', **11** *Journal of Economic Issues*, 119-132.

Goldberg, Victor P. (1982), 'Peltzman on Regulation and Politics', **39** *Public Choice*, 291-297.

Goldberg, Victor P. (1988), 'Clarifying the Record: A Comment', **144** *Journal of Institutional and Theoretical Economics*, 885-888.

Goldberg, Victor P. and Olmstead, Alan L. (1975), 'Institutional Change and American Economic Growth - A Critique of Davis and North', **12** *Explorations in Economic History*, 193-210.

Gray, John H. (1990), 'Buchanan on Liberty', **1** *Constitutional Political Economy*, 149-168.

Greenhut, Melvin L. and Benson, Bruce L. (1989), *American Antitrust Law in Theory and in Practice*, Aldershot, Avebury.

Gruner, Hans Peter (1995), 'Evolutionary Stability of Social Norms in a Socioeconomic Equilibrium Model', **6** *Constitutional Political Economy*, 233-245.

Gunter, Frank R. (1991), 'Thomas Jefferson on the Repudiation of Public Debt', **2** *Constitutional Political Economy*, 283-301.

Hardin, Russell (1990), 'Contractarianism: Wistful Thinking', **1** *Constitutional Political Economy*, 35-52.

Hasen, Richard L. (1993), 'An Enriched Economic Model of Political Patronage and Campaign Contributions: Revising Supreme Court Jurisprudence', **14** *Cardozo Law Review*, 1311 ff.

Hasen, Richard L. (1996a), 'Voting Without Law?', **144** *University of Pennsylvania Law Review*, 2135 ff.

Hasen, Richard L. (1996b), 'Clipping Coupons for Democracy: An Egalitarian/Public Choice Defense of Campaign Finance Vouchers', **84** *California Law Review*, 1 ff.

Hefeker, Carsten (1995), 'Monetary Union or Currency Competition? Currency Arrangements for Monetary Stability in East and West', **6** *Constitutional Political Economy*, 57-69.

Heiner, Ronald A. (1983), 'The Origin of Predictable Behavior', **73** *American Economic Review*, 560-595.

Heiner, Ronald A. (1990), 'Rule-Governed Behavior in Evolution and Human Society', **1** *Constitutional Political Economy*, 19-46.

Hirschman, Albert O. (1970), *Exit, Voice and Loyalty*, Cambridge, MA, Harvard University Press.

Holcombe, Randall G. (1991), 'Constitutions as Constraints: A Case Study of Three American Constitutions', **2** *Constitutional Political Economy*, 303-328.

Holcombe, Randall G. (1996), 'Vibert's Vision: Constitutional Theory in Search of a Constitution', **7** *Constitutional Political Economy*, 281-291.

Isaac, R. Mark, Mathieu, Deborah and Zajac, Edward E. (1991), 'Institutional Framing and Perceptions of Fairness', **2** *Constitutional Political Economy*, 329-370.

Kiser, Larry L. (1994), 'A Constitutional Theory of Public Enterprise', **5** *Constitutional Political Economy*, 287-306.

Klein, Daniel B. (1990), 'The Microfoundations of Rules vs. Discretion', **1** *Constitutional Political Economy*, 1-19.

Kliemt, Hartmut (1993a), 'Constitutional Commitments', **12** *Jahrbuch für Neue Politische Ökonomie*, 145-173.

Kliemt, Hartmut (1993b), 'On Justifying a Minimum Welfare State', **4** *Constitutional Political Economy*, 159-172.

Kliemt, Hartmut (1995), 'Rule of Law and the Welfare State', **56** *Philosophica*, 121-132.

Kratochwil, Friedrich (1992), 'International Order and Individual Liberty: A Critical Examination of "Realism" as a Theory of International Politics', **3** *Constitutional Political Economy*, 29-50.

Kuran, Timur (1993), 'Mitigating the Tyranny of Public Opinion: Anonymous Discourse and the Ethic of Sincerity', **4** *Constitutional Political Economy*, 41-78.

Kurz, Heinz D. (ed.) (1993), *United Germany and the new Europe*, Aldershot, Elgar, 333 p.

La Manna, Manfredi M.A. and Slomp, Gabriella (1994), 'Leviathan: Revenue Maximizer or Glory Seeker?', **5** *Constitutional Political Economy*, 159-172.

Langlois, Richard N. (1995), 'Do Firms Plan?', **6** *Constitutional Political Economy*, 247-261.

Leipold, Helmut (1990), 'Neoliberal Ordnungstheorie and Constitutional Economics: A Comparison between Eucken and Buchanan', **1** *Constitutional Political Economy*, 47-65.

Levmore, Saul (1989), 'Parliamentary Law, Majority Decisionmaking, and the Voting Paradox', **75** *Virginia Law Review*, 971-1044.

Levmore, Saul (1996), 'Coalitions and Quakes: Disaster Relief and its Prevention', **3** *University of Chicago Law School Roundtable*, 1-34.

Lingle, Christopher (1991), 'Constitutional Political Economy and Analysis of Reform Alternatives for Post Apartheid South Africa', **15** *Journal for Studies in Economics and Econometrics*, 31-41.

Lipford, Jody (1992), 'Organizational Reputation and Constitutional Constraints: An Application to Religious Denominations', **3** *Constitutional Political Economy*, 343-357.

Livingston, Marie Leigh (1987), 'Evaluating the Performance of Environmental Policy: Contributions of Neoclassical, Public Choice, and Institutional Models', **21** *Journal of Economic Issues*, 281-294.

Lowenberg, Anton D. and Yu, Ben T. (1992), 'Efficient Constitution Formation and Maintenance: The Role of "Exit"', **3** *Constitutional Political Economy*, 51-72.

Manning, Richard L., Elhauge, Einer and Lott, John R., Jr (1996), 'How Term Limits Enhance the Expression of Democratic Preferences', **5** *Supreme Court Economic Review*.

Marlow, Michael L. (1992), 'Intergovernmental Competition, Voice and Exit Options and the Design of Fiscal Structure', **3** *Constitutional Political Economy*, 73-88.

Marlow, Michael L., Orzechowski, William P. (1997), 'The Separation of Spending from Taxation: Implications for Collective Choices', **8** *Constitutional Political Economy*, 151-163.

Mbaku, John Mukum (1995), 'Preparing Africa for the Twenty-first Century: Lessons from Constitutional Economics', **6** *Constitutional Political Economy*, 139-160.

McClennen, Edward F. (1990a), *Rationality and Dynamic Choice: Foundational Explorations*, Cambridge, Cambridge University Press.

McClennen, Edward F. (1990b), 'Foundational Explorations for a Normative Theory of Political Economy', **1** *Constitutional Political Economy*, 67-99.

McClennen, Edward F. (1993), 'Rationality, Constitutions, and the Ethics of Rules', **4** *Constitutional Political Economy*, 173-210.

Medema, Steven G. (1991), 'Another Look at the Problem of Rent Seeking', **25** *Journal of Economic Issues*, 1049-1065.

Meiners, Roger E. and Yandle, Bruce (1992), 'Constitutional Choice for the Control of Water Pollution', **3** *Constitutional Political Economy*, 359-380.

Merville, Larry J. and Osborne, Dale K. (1990), 'Constitutional Democracy and the Theory of Agency', **1** *Constitutional Political Economy*, 21-47.

Miller, Geoffrey P. (1994), 'Politics of Deposit Insurance Reform: The Case of Argentina, Federal Reserve Bank of Chicago, Proceedings of A Conference on Bank Structure and Competition' republished as 'Políticas de Reforma de Seguro de Depósito. El Caso de la Argentina', in *Revista de Derecho Bancario y de la Actividad Financiera*, Año 4, Enero-diciembre 1994, No. 19/24, at 221-239, **473** *Argentine Journal*.

Miller, Geoffrey P. and Macey, Jonathan R. (1987), 'Toward an Interest Group Theory of Delaware Corporate Law', **65** *Texas Law Review*, 469 ff.

Mitchell, W.C. (1988), 'Virginia, Rochester and Bloomington: Twenty-five Years of Public Choice and Political Science', **56** *Public Choice*, 101-119.

Moser, Peter (1994), 'Constitutional Protection of Economic Rights: The Swiss and U.S. Experience in Comparison', **5** *Constitutional Political Economy*, 61-79.

Mueller, Dennis C. (1989), *Public Choice II*, Cambridge, Cambridge University Press, 518 p.

Mueller, Dennis C. (1990), 'James M. Buchanan: Economist cum Contractarian', **1** *Constitutional Political Economy*, 169-196.

Mueller, Dennis C. (1996), 'Constitutional Quandaries in Europe', **7** *Constitutional Political Economy*, 293-302.

Niskanen, William A. (1990), 'Conditions Affecting the Survival of Constitutional Rules', **1** *Constitutional Political Economy*, 53-62.

Ordeshook, Peter C. (1992), 'Constitutional Stability', **3** *Constitutional Political Economy*, 137-175.

Ordeshook, P.C. and Shvetsova, O. (1995), 'If Hamilton and Madison were Merely Lucky, What Hope is there for Russian Federalism?', **6** *Constitutional Political Economy*, 107-126.

Ostrom, Vincent (1996), 'Faustian Bargains', **7** *Constitutional Political Economy*, 303-308.

Parisi, Francesco (1995), 'Toward a Theory of Spontaneous Law', **6** *Constitutional Political Economy*, 211-231.

Pasour, E.C., Jr (1994), 'Redistribution and Constitutional Political Economy', **5** *Constitutional Political Economy*, 81-98.

Pauly, Mark V. (1994), 'Avoiding the Mistreatment of Bad Risks in a Democracy: Universal Health Insurance from a Constitutional Perspective', **5** *Constitutional Political Economy*, 307-318.

Pelikan, Pavel (1993), 'Ownership of Firms and Efficiency: The Competence Argument', **4** *Constitutional Political Economy*, 349-392.

Pies, Ingo (1996), 'Public Choice versus Constitutional Economics: A Methodological Interpretation of the Buchanan Research Program', **7** *Constitutional Political Economy*, 21-34.

Pinto Barbosa, A.S. (1994), 'Manipulating Uncertainty', **5** *Constitutional Political Economy*, 255-271.

Posner, Eric (1997), 'The Political Economy of the Bankruptcy Reform Act of 1978', **96** *Michigan Law Review*.

Puy Fraga, Pedro (1987), 'El Programa de la Economía Constitucional: Una Síntesis (The Constitutional Economics Program: an Abstract)', **192** *Revista de Derecho Financiero y Hacienda Pública*, 1181-1194.

Puy Fraga, Pedro (1991), 'Contractualismo y Justicia (Contractualism and Justice)', in M. Otero, C. Rovira y M. Segura (Coords), *Problemas de la Ciencia Jurídica. Homenaje a Francisco Puy Muñoz*, Santiago, Servicio de Publicacións da Universidade de Santiago de Compostela, 269-289.

Puy Fraga, Pedro (1993), *Análisis Económico del Derecho y la Política* (Economic Analysis of Law and Politics), Santiago de Compostela, Fundación Alfredo Brañas, 224 p.

Puy Fraga, Pedro (1994), 'Elección Pública y Estado del Bienestar (Public Choice and Welfare State)', in Luis Caramés (ed.), *La Crisis del Estado del Bienestar*, Santiago de Compostela, Asociación Galega de Estudios de Economía do Sector Público, 481-506.

Puy Fraga, Pedro (1995a), 'Democracia Representativa e Reforma Constitucional (Representative Democracy and Constitutional Reform)', in Leiceaga, Fernández, Rodríguez, Jordán, Iglesias, E. López and Deza, X. Vence (eds), *Estudos en Homenaxe ó Profesor Xose Manuel Beiras Torrado*, Universidade de Santiago de Compostela, 141-161.

Puy Fraga, Pedro (1995b), 'Economía y Política en Yugoslavia (1945-1990): el Fracaso de un Experimento de Organización Económica y Social', in *Economics and Politics in Jugoslavia (1945-1990): A Failed Experiment of Social and Economic Organization; La crisis de los Balcanes, monografías del CESEDEN*, Madrid, Ministerio de Defensa, 115-136.

Puy Fraga, Pedro (1995c), *Economía en Broma y en Serio* (Economics for Fun and Serious), Madrid, Minerva, Fundación Alfredo Brañas, 163 p.

Puy Fraga, Pedro (1995d), *Economía constitucional y Constitución española de 1978* (Constitutional Political Economy and The Spanish Constitution of 1978), Santiago de Compostela, edición en microficha, Servicio de Publicaciones da Universidade de Santiago de Compostela.

Ramseyer, J. Mark (1994), 'The Puzzling (In)Dependence of Courts: A Comparative Approach', **23** *Journal of Legal Studies*, 721-747.

Ramseyer, J. Mark and Rosenbluth, Frances McCall (1993), *Japan's Political Marketplace*, Cambridge, MA, Harvard University Press.

Ramseyer, J. Mark and Rosenbluth, Frances M. (1995), *The Politics of Oligarchy: Institutional Choice in Imperial Japan*, New York, Cambridge University Press.

Rasmusen, Eric and Ramseyer, J. Mark (1994), 'Cheap Bribes and the Corruption Ban: A Coordination Game Among Rational Legislators', **78** *Public Choice*, 305 ff.

Rasmussen, David W. and Benson, Bruce L. (eds) (1994), *The Economic Anatomy of a Drug War: Criminal Justice in the Commons*, Lanham, MD, Rowman and Littlefield.

Rawls, John (1971), *A Theory of Justice*, Cambridge, MA, Harvard University Press.

Ribstein, Larry E. (1992a), 'Efficiency, Regulation and Competition: A Comment on Easterbrook and Fischel', **87** *Northwestern University Law Review*, 254 ff.

Ribstein, Larry E. (1992b), 'Corporate Political Speech', **49** *Washington and Lee Law Review*, 109 ff.

Ribstein, Larry E. (1993), 'The Mandatory Rules of the ALI Code', **61** *George Washington Law Review*, 984 ff.

Ribstein, Larry E. (1995), 'The Constitutional Conception of the Corporation', **4** *Supreme Court Economic Review*, 95 ff.

Roin, Julie, A. (1988), 'United they Stand, Divided They Fall: Public Choice Theory and the Tax Code', **74** *Cornell Law Review*, 62-134.

Rose-Ackerman, Susan (1992), *Rethinking The Progressive Agenda: The Reform of The American Regulatory State*, New York, Free Press, 1992.

Rowley, Charles K. (1989), 'Public Choice and the Economic Analysis of Law', in Mercuro, Nicholas (ed.), *Law and Economics*, Boston, Kluwer Academic Publishers, 123-174.

Rowley, Charles K. (1992), 'The Supreme Court and Takings Judgments: Constitutional Political Economy versus Public Choice', in Mercuro, Nicholas (ed.), *Taking*

Property and Just Compensation: Law and Economics Perspectives of the Takings Issue, Boston, Kluwer Academic Publishers, 79-124.

Rowley, Charles K. (1993), 'Introduction', in Rowley, Charles K. (ed.), *Public Choice Theory Volume I, The International Library of Critcal Writings in Economics*, Aldershot, Edward Elgar, ix-xxix.

Rowley, Charles K. (1994), 'Public Choice Economics', in Boettke, Peter, *The Elgar Companion to Austrian Economics*, Brookfield, VT, Edward Elgar, 285-293.

Rubin, Paul H. (1975), 'On the Form of Special Interest Legislation', *Public Choice*, 75-90.

Rubin, Paul H. (1979), 'Public Interest Lobbies: Membership and Influence', *Public Choice*, 45-54.

Rubin, Paul H. and Kau, James B. (1978), 'Voting on Minimum Wages: A Time Series Analysis', *Journal of Political Economy*, 337-342.

Rubin, Paul H. and Kau, James B. (1981), 'The Impact of Labor Unions on the Passage of Economic Legislation', *Journal of Labor Economics*, 133-145.

Rubin, Paul H. and Kau, James B. (1993), 'Ideology, Voting and Shirking', *Public Choice*, 151-172.

Rubin, Paul H., Kau, James B. and Keenan, Donald C. (1982), 'A General Equilibrium Model of Congressional Voting', *Quarterly Journal of Economics*, 271-294.

Ruiter, Dick W.P. (1994), 'Economic and Legal Institutionalism: What can they Learn from Each Other?', **5** *Constitutional Political Economy*, 99-115.

Ruiz-Huerta Carbonell, Jesús (1992), 'Vigencia y Operatividad del Principio de la no Confiscatoriedad de los Tributos en el Ordenamiento Español (The Principle of Non Confiscation of Taxes: Enforcement in Spain)', **64** *Revista Crónica Tributaria.*

Ruiz-Huerta Carbonell, Jesús (1994), 'The Dimension, Effectiveness and Effciency of Public Expenditure', in, Wildavsky, Aaron and Zapico-Goni, Eduardo (eds), *National Budgeting for Economic and Monetary Union*, European Institute of Public Administration, 195-199.

Ruiz-Huerta Carbonell, Jesús (1995), *Las Rentas de las Personas Mayores* (Eldest Citizens' Income), SECOT.

Ruiz-Huerta Carbonell, Jesús and Giménez, Antonio (eds) (1993), *Estructura Institucional y Gestión del Gasto Público en Algunos Paises de la OCDE* (Institutuional Structure and Managment of Public Expenditure in Some Countries), Estudios de Hacienda Pública, Instituto de Estudios Fiscales.

Ruiz-Huerta Carbonell, Jesús, Alvarez, Jesús, Ayala, Luis, Iriondo, Iñaki, Martinez, Rosa and Palacios, Juan Ignacio (1995), 'La Distribución Funcional y Personal de la Renta en España (Functional and Personal Distribution of Income in Spain)', *Premio de Investagión 1995 del Consejo Económico y Social.*

Ryssdal, Stray A.C. (1995), *Legal Realism and Economics as Behavior - A Scandinavian Look at the Economic Analysis of Law*, Oslo, Juridisk Forlag AS, Nerenius & Santérus Förlag AB Gad Jura AS.

Salinas, Javier (1980), 'Traducción e Introducción a la Versión Española (The Calculation of Consensus)', in Buchanan, J.M. and Tullock, G., *El Cálculo del Consenso*, Madrid, Ed. Espasa Calpe.

Salinas, Javier (1991), *Economía Política del Federalismo Fiscal Español* (Political Economy of the Spanish Fiscal Federalism), Madrid, Instituto de Estudios Fiscales.

Salinas, Javier (1993), *Economía Política Constitucional de los Presupuestos Públicos* (Constitutional Political Economy of the Budget), Madrid, Tecnos.

Salinas, Javier (1995), 'Economía Constitucional de la Descentralización del Sector Público en España (Constitutional Economy of Descentralization of the Spanish Public Sector)', in Capítulo del libro, *La Financiación de las Comunidades Autonomas, Análisis y Orientación desde la Teoría del Federalismo Fiscal*, Valladolid, Consejeria de Economía, Junta de Castilla y León, 29-54.

Salinas, Javier (1996), 'Economía Constitucional de la Política Fiscal Española y la Convergencia Europea (Constitutional Economy of Spanish Tax Policy and European Covergence)', in *Proceedings, XVIII Jornadas de la Dirección General del Servicio Juridico del Estado sobre la Constitución Española y el Ordenamiento Comunitario Europeo*, Madrid, Ministerio de Justicia.

Sanjiao Otero, Francisco Javier (1991), 'Una Aproximación al Estudio de los Ciclos Político Económicos (Political-Economic Cycles)', in X (ed.), *Estudios en Homenaje al Prof. Carlos G. Otero Diaz*, Universidade de Santiago de Compostela, 657-673.

Sanjiao Otero, Francisco Javier (1993), 'Decisións Políticas e Ciclos Económicos (Political Decisions and Economic Cycles)', in, *Análisis Económico del Derecho y de la Política*, Fundación Alfredo Brañas, 173-190.

Schap, David (1985), 'X-Inefficiency in a Rent-Seeking Society - A Graphical Analysis', **25** *Quarterly Review of Economics and Business*, 19-27.

Schap, David (1986a), 'Executive Veto and Informational Strategy: A Structure-Induced Equilibrium Analysis', **30** *American Journal of Political Science*, 755-770.

Schap, David (1986b), *Municipal Ownership in the Electric Utility Industry: A Centennial View*, New York, Praeger Publishers.

Schap, David (1988a), 'Property Rights and Decision Making in the Soviet Union: Interpreting Soviet Environmental History', **26** *Economic Inquiry*, 389-401.

Schap, David (1988b), 'In Search of Efficacious Executive Veto Authority', **58** *Public Choice*, 247-257.

Schap, David (1989), 'Pricing and Property Rights in Government Enterprises: Some Dynamic Aspects', **11** *Research in Law and Economics*, 113-127.

Schap, David (1990), 'Executing Veto and Spending Limitation: Positive Political Economy with Implications for Institutional Choice', **65** *Public Choice*, 239-256.

Schap, David and Carter, John R. (1987), 'Executive Veto, Legislative Override and Structure-Induced Equilibrium', **52** *Public Choice*, 227-244. Reprinted in Rowley, Charles (ed.), *Public Choice Theory*, Edward Elgar, 1993, vol. 3, 47-64.

Schap, David and Carter, John R. (1990), 'Line-Item Veto: Where is Thy Sting?', **4** *Journal of Economic Perspectives*, 103-118.

Schap, David and Daerden, James A. (1994), 'The First Word and the Last Word in the Budgetary Process: A Comparative Institutional Analysis of Proposal and Veto Authorities', **80** *Public Choice*, 35-53.

Schap, David and Dimasi, Joseph A. (1985), 'The Appropriate Specification of Constant Elasticity Demand Functions', **2** *Social Choice and Welfare*, 89-94.

Schmidtchen, Dieter and Schmidt Trenz, Hans Jorg (1990), 'The Division of Labor Is Limited by the Extent of the Law: A Constitutional Approach to International Private Law', **1** *Constitutional Political Economy*, 49-71.

Schmidtz, David (1991), *The Limits of Government*, Boulder, CO, Westview Press.

Schumpeter, Jospeh A. (1942), *Capitalism, Socialism, and Democracy*, New York, Harper and Row.

Schwartzstein, Linda A. (1991), 'Bureaucracy Unbounded: The Lack of Effective Constraints on the Judicial Process', **35** *St Louis University Law Journal*, 597 ff.

Shaviro, Daniel N. (1990), 'Beyond Public Choice and Public Interest: A Study of the Legislative Process As Illustrated by Tax Legislation in the 1980s', **139** *University of Pennsylvania Law Review*, 1-123.

Shaviro, Daniel N. (1997), *Do Deficits Matter?*, Chicago, University of Chicago Press.

Simon, Herbert A. (1976), 'From Substantive to Procedural Rationality', in Latsis, S.J. (ed.), *Method and Appraisal in Economics*, Cambridge, Cambridge University Press, 129-148.

Sinn, Stefan (1992), 'The Taming of Leviathan: Competition Among Governments', **3** *Constitutional Political Economy*, 177-196.

Sobel, Russell S. (1994), 'The League of Nations Covenant and the United Nations Charter: An Analysis of Two International Constitutions', **5** *Constitutional Political Economy*, 173-192.

Sobel, Russell S. (1996), 'Vibert's European Union: A United Nations or a United States?', **7** *Constitutional Political Economy*, 309-316.

Solvason, Birgir T.R. (1993), 'Institutional Evolution in the Icelandic Commonwealth', **4** *Constitutional Political Economy*, 97-125.

Spence, David B. (1997), 'Administrative Law and Agency Policymaking: Rethinking the Positive Theory of Political Control', **14** *Yale Journal on Regulation*.

Spindler, Z.A. (1990), 'Constitutional Design for a Rent Seeking Society: Voting Rule Choice', **1** *Constitutional Political Economy*, 73-82.

Spinelli, Franco and Masciandaro, Donato (1993), 'Towards Monetary Constitutionalism in Italy: With a Rehearing of the Debate for the Drawing up of the Present Constitution', **4** *Constitutional Political Economy*, 211-222.

Stout, Lynn A. (1992), 'Strict Scrutiny and Social Choice: An Economic Inquiry into Fundamental Rights and Suspect Classifications', **80** *Georgetown Law Journal*, 1787-ff.

Stout, Lynn A. (1993), 'Poverty and Failure in the Market for Human Capital', **81** *Georgetown Law Journal*, 1947 ff.

Stout, Lynn A. and Barnes, David D. (1992), *Cases and Materials on Law and Economics*, St Paul's West Publishing Company.

Stout, Lynn A. and Barnes, David D. (1992), *Economics of Constitutional Law and Public Choice*, St Paul's West Publishing Company.

Streit, Manfred E. (1993), 'Cognition, Competition, and Catallaxy: In Memory of Friedrich August von Hayek', **4** *Constitutional Political Economy*, 223-262.

Streit, Manfred E. and Mussler, Werner (1994), 'The Economic Constitution of the European Community: From Rome to Maastricht', **5** *Constitutional Political Economy*, 319-353.

Streit, Manfred E. and Voigt, Stefan (1993), 'The Economics of Conflict Resolution in International Trade', in Friedmann, D. and Mestmäcker, E.J. (eds), *Conflict Resolution in International Trade*, Baden-Baden: Nomos, 39-77.

Streit, Manfred E. and Voigt, Stefan (1996), 'Toward Ever Closer Union - Or Ever Larger? Or Both? Entry to the European Union from the Perspective of

Constitutional Economics', **16** *International Review of Law and Economics*, 385-388.

Sugden, Robert (1989), 'Spontaneous Order', **3** *Journal of Economic Perspectives*, 85-97.

Sugden, Robert (1990), 'Rules for Choosing among Public Goods: A Contractarian Approach', **1** *Constitutional Political Economy*, 63-82.

Sugden, Robert (1993a), 'Normative Judgments and Spontaneous Order: The Contractarian Element in Hayek's Thought', **4** *Constitutional Political Economy*, 393-424.

Sugden, Robert (1993b), 'Rights: Why Do They Matter, and to Whom?', **4** *Constitutional Political Economy*, 127-152.

Sunstein, Cass R. (1991), 'Constitutionalism, Prosperity, Democracy: Transition in Eastern Europe', **2** *Constitutional Political Economy*, 371-394.

Sutter, Daniel (1995), 'Constitutional Politics Within the Interest-Group Model', **6** *Constitutional Political Economy*, 127-137.

Sutter, Daniël (1997), 'Enforcing Constitutional Constraints', **8** *Constitutional Political Economy*, 139-150.

Svendsen, Gert Tinggaard (1995), 'Den Stationære Bandit - og Lobbyisme (The Stationary Bandit and Lobbyism)', **3** *Okonomi & Politik*, 24-31.

Thorbecke, Willem (1995), 'Free Trade versus Managed Trade: A Constitutional Political Economy Perspective', **151** *Journal of Institutional and Theoretical Economics*, 373-389.

Tiebout, Charles M. (1956), 'A Pure Theory of Local Government Expenditures', **64** *Journal of Political Economy*, 416-424. Reprinted in Cowen, T. (ed.) (1992), *Public Goods and Market Failures*, Chapter 9, London, Transaction Publishers.

Tucker, David F.B. (1992), 'Conservatives on the Supreme Court', **3** *Constitutional Political Economy*, 197-222.

Tuerck, David G. (1995), 'Economics as Mechanism: The Mind as Machine in Hayek's Sensory Order', **6** *Constitutional Political Economy*, 281-292.

Tullock, Gordon (1959), 'Problems of Majority Voting', **67** *Journal of Political Economy*, 571-579.

Tullock, Gordon (1967), 'The Welfare Costs of Tariffs, Monopolies and Theft', **5** *Western Economic Review*, 224-232.

Tullock, Gordon (1987), 'The Calculus: Postscript after 25 Years', **7(2)** *Cato Journal*, 313-321. Reprinted in: Gwartney, J.D. and Wagner, R.E. (eds) (1988), *Public Choice and Constitutional Economics*, Greenwood, JAI Press Inc., 139-147.

Turnbull, Shann (1973), 'Eliminating Foreign Ownership, Growth', **26** *Committee for the Economic Development of Australia, Melbourne*, 1-13.

Turnbull, Shann (1974a), 'Making the Securities Industry a Growth Business', **Feb.** *Australian Stock Exchange Journal*, 34-40.

Turnbull, Shann (1974b), 'Controlling World Corporations', **1** *Jassa, Australian Society of Security Analysts*, 21-25.

Turnbull, Shann (1975), 'Fading Out with a Profit-Planned Corporate Obsolescence', **55** *The Canadian Forum, Toronto*, 14-16.

Turnbull, Shann (1985), 'Trusteeship as a Technique for Sustainable Industrialisation', in Gandhi Marg (ed.), *Gandhi Peace Foundation*, New Delhi, 7:8&9, 634-643.

Turnbull, Shann (1991), 'Ownership: Never for Ever', *New Economics, Newsletter of the New Economics Foundation*, Issue nineteen/autumm, London, 4-0.

Twight, Charlotte (1992), 'Constitutional Renegotiation: Impediments to Consensual Revision', **3** *Constitutional Political Economy*, 89-112.

Vanberg, Viktor J. (1992a), 'Organizations as Constitutional Systems', **3** *Constitutional Political Economy*, 223-253.

Vanberg, Viktor J. (1992b), 'A Constitutional Political Economy Perspective on International Trade', **43** *Ordo: Jahrbuch für die Ordnung von Wirtschaft und Gesellschaft*, 375-392.

Vanberg, Viktor J. (1993a), 'Rational Choice, Rule-Following and Institutions, an Evolutionary Perspective', in Maki, Gustafsson and Knudsen (eds), *Rationality, Institutions and Economic Methodology*, London, Routledge, (Chapter 7) 171-200.

Vanberg, Viktor J. (1993b), 'Constitutionally Constrained and Safe-guarded Competition in Markets and Politics with Reference to a European Constitution', **4** *Journal des Economistes et des Etudes Humaines*, 3-27.

Vanberg, Viktor J. (1994), *Rules and Choice in Economics*, London and New York, Routledge, 310 p.

Vanberg, Viktor J. (1997), 'Institutional Evolution through Purposeful Selection: The Constitutional Economics of John R. Commons', **8** *Constitutional Political Economy*, 105-122.

Vanberg, Viktor J. and Kerber, Wolfgang (1994), 'Institutional Competition among Jurisdictions: An Evolutionary Approach', **5** *Constitutional Political Economy*, 193-219.

Vaubel, Roland (1996), 'The Constitutional Future of the European Union', **7** *Constitutional Political Economy*, 317-324.

Vazquez Vega, Pablo (1992), *Análisis Económico de las Organizaciones Internacionales* (Economic Analysis of International Organizations), Universidad Complutense.

Vibert, Frank (1995), *Europe: A Constitution for the Millenium*, Dartmouth, Aldershot.

Voigt, Stefan (1993), 'On the Internal Consistency of Hayek's Evolutionary Oriented Constitutional Economics - Some General Remarks', **3** *Journal des Economistes et des Etudes Humaines*, 461-476.

Voigt, Stefan (1994), 'European Political Union - An Appropriate Example for Applying Constitutional Economics to Real-Life Problems? A Note on an Article by James M. Buchanan', **45** *ORDO*, 273-286.

Voigt, Stefan (1996), 'Pure Eclectism - The Tool Kit of the Constitutional Economist', **7** *Constitutional Political Economy*, 177-196.

Voigt, Stefan (1997), 'Positive Constitutional Economics - A Survey', **90** *Public Choice*, 11-53.

Wagner, Richard E. (1988), 'The Calculus of Consent: A Wicksellian Retrospective', **56** *Public Choice*, 153-166.

Wagner, Richard E. (1992), 'Crafting Social Rules: Common Law vs. Statute Law, Once Again', **3** *Constitutional Political Economy*, 381-397.

Wagner, Richard E. and Gwartney, James D. (1988), *Public Choice and Constitutional Economics*, JAI Press Inc..

Warneryd, Karl (1990), 'Conventions: An Evolutionary Approach', **1** *Constitutional Political Economy*, 83-107.

Wessels, Joachim H. (1993), 'Redistribution from a Constitutional Perspective', **4** *Constitutional Political Economy*, 425-448.

Wicksell, Knut (1896), *Finanztheoretische Untersuchungen*, Jena, Gustav Fischer, 76-159.

Wicksell, Knut (1988), 'A New Principle of Just Taxation', Reprinted in Gwartney, J.D. and Wagner, R.E. (eds) (1988), *Public Choice and Constitutional Economics*, Chapter 5, 117-130.

Wiseman, Jack (1990), 'Principles of Political Economy: An Outline Proposal, Illustrated by Application to Fiscal Federalism', **1** *Constitutional Political Economy*, 101-124.

Witt, Ulrich (1992), 'The Emergence of a Protective Agency and the Constitutional Dilemma', **3** *Constitutional Political Economy*, 255-266.

Wittman, Donald A. (1991), 'Nations and States: Mergers and Acquisitions; Dissolutions and Divorce', **81** *American Economic Review. Papers and Proceedings*, 126-129.

Wohlgemuth, M. (1995a), 'Economic and Political Competition in Neoclassical and Evolutionary Perspective', **6** *Constitutional Political Economy*, 71-96.

Wohlgemuth, Michael (1995b), 'Economic and Political Competition in Neoclassical and Evolutionary Perspective', **6** *Constitutional Political Economy*, 71-96.

Yandle, Bruce (1991), 'Organic Constitutions and Common Law', **2** *Constitutional Political Economy*, 225-241.

Yandle, Bruce (1993), 'Sir Edward Coke and the Struggle for a New Constitutional Order', **4** *Constitutional Political Economy*, 263-285.

Yandle, Bruce (1997), 'Charles K. Rowley: The Political Economy of the Minimal State', **8** *Constitutional Political Economy*, 93-95.

Yeager, Leland B. (1990), 'Buchanan on Scope and Method', **1** *Constitutional Political Economy*, 197-220.

Young, Robert A. (1994), 'The Political Economy of Secession: The Case of Quebec', **5** *Constitutional Political Economy*, 221-245.

Other References

Alchian, Armen A. (1950), 'Uncertainty, Evolution and Economic Theory', **58** *Journal of Political Economy*, 211-221. Reprinted in: Alchian, Armen A., *Economic Forces at Work*, 1977, Indianapolis, LibertyPress, Chapter 1.

Buchanan, James M. (1969), *Cost and Choice*, Chicago: The University of Chicago Press.

Calabresi, Guido (1961), 'Some Thoughts on Risk Distribution and the Law of Torts', **70** *Yale Law Journal*, 499-553.

Coase, Ronald H. (1992), 'The Institutional Structure of Production', **82** *American Economic Review*, 713-719.

Cooter, Robert D. (1982), 'The Cost of Coase', **11** *Journal of Legal Studies*, 1-34.

Demsetz, Harold (1969), 'Information and Efficiency: Another Viewpoint', **12** *Journal of Law and Economics* , 1-22.

Hayek, Friedrich A. (1952), *The Sensory Order*, Chicago, University of Chicago Press.

Hayek, Friedrich A. (1973), *Rules and Order*, London, Routledge.

Landes, William M. and Posner, Richard A. (1975), 'The Independent Judiciary in an Interest-Group Perspective', **18** *Journal of Law and Economics*, 875-901.

Leoni, Bruno (1961), *Freedom and the Law*, Princeton, D. Van Nostrand.

Plato (1992), *The Republic*, London, David Campbell.
Posner, Richard A. (1972), *Economic Analysis of Law*, Boston, Little Brown.

0620
LAW AND MACROECONOMICS

Richard L. Gordon
Professor of Mineral Economics, Pennsylvania State University

Abstract

This chapter argues that imperfections in the working of individual (nonfinancial) markets are not a clear source of macroeconomic instability and that better regulation of these markets is not the way to stabilize the economy. Improvement here means both increased surveillance and removing government-fostered deficiencies. The basic arguments are (1) the long-standing disarray that distinguishes macroeconomics from microeconomics greatly increased starting in the 1970s, (2) great dispute exists over the workability of different 'classic' macroeconomic measures, (3) despite at least seven decades of advocacy of microeconomic measures for macroeconomic goals, no defensible case exists, (4) support for microeconomic measures rests on a belief in a high degree of market failure about which microeconomists have become more skeptical, (5) these weaknesses imply that no clear macroeconomic benefits offset the microeconomic drawbacks of regulations of individual markets, and (6) extensive deregulation would produce substantial microeconomic and macroeconomic benefits, but the microeconomic case is much stronger.
JEL classification: K00, E00
Keywords: Macroeconomics, Keynes, Law and Economics

1. Introduction

This chapter examines contentions that imperfections in the working of individual (nonfinancial) markets are a source of macroeconomic instability and that better regulation of these markets is the most feasible way to offset these imperfections. Improvement here means both increased surveillance and removing government-fostered deficiencies. The overriding theme is the approach has little support.

The basic arguments are (1) the long-standing disarray that distinguishes macroeconomics from microeconomics greatly increased starting in the 1970s, (2) great dispute exists over the workability of different 'classic' macroeconomic measures, (3) despite at least seven decades of advocacy of microeconomic measures for macroeconomic goals, no defensible case exists, (4) support for microeconomic measures rests on a belief in a high degree of market failure about which microeconomists have become more skeptical, (5) these weaknesses imply that no clear macroeconomic benefits offset the microeconomic drawbacks of regulations of individual markets, and (6) extensive deregulation would produce substantial microeconomic and macroeconomic benefits, but the microeconomic case is much stronger.

Dealing with these points requires much effort. The prior two paragraphs not only make sweeping assertions, but use numerous ambiguous terms. The article then seeks to undertake four tasks. (1) The terms are clarified. (2) Selected parts of the debates over macroeconomics are reviewed. As the literature review below seeks to suggest, the chapter necessarily cannot even fully cover every idea encountered. Choice is limited to those that seem more relevant. Others can (and indeed in the refereeing process did) stress different viewpoints. (3) The microeconomics of market behavior are sketched. (4) Perspective is provided on the history of proposals to use microeconomic policies to secure macroeconomic goals.

2. The Nature of Macroeconomics Recalled

While economists occasionally use the term macroeconomics to describe any highly aggregative analysis, the more usual concepts relate to economy-wide instabilities, particularly in unemployment rates but also involving inflation and balance of payments problems. This clearly is the stress of the many macroeconomics texts. Since the rise of extensive formal studies of macroeconomics, the traditional concerns with the allocation of resources in markets became microeconomics.

Actually, both branches deal with the total economy. Macro concentrates on how the combined behavior produces instabilities. Micro stresses how well each component of the economy performs the task of making useful goods available to consumers.

Nothing in economics is neat, and this is true of the borders between macro and microeconomics. The banking system is both a micro and a macro concern. The role of banks in money supply is a basic concern of macroeconomics. The role of banks in serving individuals involves employing the standard tools of microeconomics. In practice, a further fuzzing arises from conventions adopted in standard texts. Economic growth, at least as conventionally modeled, is clearly a microeconomic problem, and any correction is by policies affecting individual markets. To be sure, more applied discussions recognize the impacts of alternative government tax and spending policies. For example, US political debates present, albeit in the overly loose fashion necessarily adopted in political debates, a choice between a Democratic model focusing on growth promoting government spending and a Republican view focused on making more money available for private sector investment. Conventionally, micro texts at both the advanced undergraduate and graduate level ignore economic growth. (A major exception is Mas-Colell, Whinston and Green, 1995). Macro texts, in contrast, typically cover growth.

Unemployment is central because it is harder to explain or correct than inflation and balance of payments problems. The basic causes and cures of the last two were established by the eighteenth century (as in David Hume's essays that relate to economics). In contrast, neither what causes unemployment nor what if anything can be done about it is well determined. Many explanations exists, but all have severe (and widely examined) drawbacks. This chapter argues that indeed these defects are so severe that any public policies must assume that they are dealing with a mysterious disease whose origin and untreated response are unknown.

What is most important here is that macroeconomics concentrates on monetary and fiscal policy. Increasing or decreasing control of individual nonfinancial markets has a decidedly secondary role. Macroeconomic theorists who contend that problems in nonfinancial markets or in their regulation are the main cause of instability often do not advocate cures involving directly altering control of these markets. One has to resort to nonconformist writings to find strong arguments for regulatory approaches to instability. Kelman's (1993) effort to examine the issue tries valiantly to find good rationales but only identifies drawbacks.

3. The Tools to Consider

The central policy distinction made here is between the monetary and fiscal policies that are the focus of traditional macroeconomics and regulatory initiatives. Monetary policy relates to control by various means of the supply of money in the economy. (Such financial innovations as mutual funds that invest in short-term securities and allow owners to withdraw funds by writing checks and credit and debit cards have increased the always difficult problem of distinguishing money from other financial assets. This problem is not relevant here.) Fiscal policy relates to the effects of government tax and spending policy.

Regulation here means those government policies that control the behavior of individual firms and households in the economy. The concept considered here is somewhat broader than that used in other discussions of regulation. In particular, a key element proves government policies governing the compensation and rights of workers and the treatment of trade unions. 'Regulatory' economists tend to leave most of these issues to labor economists. Stress is on good market controls; the only labor policies treated are health and safety regulation. Regulatory policies are the focus of many articles in this encyclopedia. For that reason and because of space limitations, I neither delineate in detail nor evaluate the microeconomic problems of such policies.

The formidable difficulties of producing predictable results from such policies is taken as proved elsewhere.

A more critical consideration is that the scope of proposed regulations may be greater when macroeconomic considerations are added to microeconomic concerns. The macroeconomics literature talks of incomes policy that involves controls of prices and wages throughout the economy. Microeconomic practice emphasizes concentrating on sectors in which monopoly power exists or markets fail to internalize all costs. This distinction can be interpreted in at least three different ways. First, the two arguments may be equivalent ways of stating the same view; economywide may really only mean monopoly sectors. Second, macroeconomists may see more monopoly than do microeconomists. Third, macroeconomists may feel that many sectors that cause no microeconomic problems are macroeconomic threats. Some indications arise that enthusiasts of wage and price controls, in fact, see a greater prevalence of extensive monopoly power than do microeconomists specializing on monopoly problems.

4. An Overview of the Macroeconomic Policy Debates

Stress here is on conflict between 'Keynesians' and classical economists. Both approaches encompass many different, often mutually incompatible specific analyses. For present purposes, examples of each position that seemed most germane are presented. The Keynesian position is identified with the view that real economies have features that produce large, undesired, and undesirable instability *and* that feasible 'active' public policies exist to improve on unregulated performance. Active means closely viewing economic behavior and reacting to it.

The classical position involves numerous criticisms of the Keynesian outlook. In particular, an influential new classical group of macroeconomists has dramatically expanded the demonstration of the impediments to successful government programs to stabilize the economy. A key unfluence on acceptance of the case is rejection by economists from all viewpoints of the 1930s belief that deep extended depressions are an ever present danger. The arguments are not conclusive. However, they have enough plausibility that serious consideration must be given the possibility that feasible active policies are ill-defined, if not nonexistent.

Even if this conclusion is rejected, it still can be inferred that whatever is done must be limited by implementation problems. Behind the bitter debates may only be a minor quarrel about exactly how *small* is the scope for action. The analysis here focuses on this narrowing of the ambitions of active monetary and fiscal policy from the more ambitious proposals of the 1936 to 1968 period. To the extent they support anything, modern Keynesians advocate restrained intervention that has been called coarse tuning (Lindbeck, 1993, p. 154) (in obvious response to the excessive prior claims that one could fine tune the economy). Much effort was devoted to arguing that active policies were desirable without indicating whether the activism significantly differed from following policy rules. Attention turns to arguing that, given these limitations and the widely known microeconomic drawbacks, increased regulation of nonfinancial markets is not an attractive alternative stabilization policy.

Unfortunately, reasonably treating these supposedly limited questions requires examination of most of the thorniest issues of both macroeconomics and microeconomics. In particular, the proposition that regulating individual markets is a desirable macroeconomic policy presumes that actual economies are best described by theories of imperfect markets. Acceptance of the empirical relevance of such theories, moreover, does not suffice to justify market regulation. It must also be shown that such regulation is a desirable way to offset the effects of market imperfections. In particular, the intervention must reduce unemployment and not produce other effects, such as increased inflation or undesirable impacts on the regulated markets, that cause harms that outweigh the employment benefits.

The issues have been major concerns in economics for nearly seven decades. All of the key questions remain unresolved and indeed often not even clearly raised. The characteristics, causes and cures of economic instability and how best to analyze them are all bitterly debated. A growing stress on theoretic prowess may have caused analysts inadequately to consider the empirical relevance of the theories. At least three issues arise about macroeconomics. The first is what comprises the theoretically sound models of instability. The second is which of these models best explains reality. The issue about theory choice stressed here is whether market imperfections are the primary causes of economic instability. It must be shown that the theoretically possible alternative mechanism prevails in practice.

The third concern stressed here is what the realistic models say about the correctability of behavior. They must show that the characteristics of the economy also allow effective stabilization policy.

5. Viewpoints

The combination of possible viewpoints produces a mass of alternative positions about problems, solutions, and the best ways to analyze them. Even without considering the many variant positions on how to analyze the issues, at least five policy postures can be delineated. Several different ways exist to reach each of the policy outlooks. Given the underlying complexity, the categories are devised as epitomes to make the discussion manageable. (The classification initially was designed to recognize distinctions made by Kelman, 1993, and overcome their drawbacks, particularly his failing to distinguish between the two radically different branches of new classical economics.) The classification is among traditional Keynesians, microinterventionists, deregulators, microkibbitzers (or Kennedy Keynesians), and skeptics about intervention.

To examine alternative routes to these policy postures, the valuable ambitious survey by Snowdon, Vane and Wynarczk (1995) distinguishes among classical Keynesians, new Keynesians, post Keynesians, monetarists, market clearing classicists, real business cycle advocates, and Austrians. As discussed below, the last four each develop somewhat different cases against active stabilization policy.

The position associated here with Keynesians, as noted, is that active monetary and fiscal policy is effective and preferable as an anti-unemployment tool. This certainly is the classical Keynesian position, and a large part of new Keynesian economics is devoted to defending against new classical criticism. Some post-Keynesian economists advocate wage and price controls.

Monetary and fiscal policy can take many forms. Thus, general approval of active stabilization involves support of many different specific practices. What is feasible is ill-discussed. The present treatment stresses the problems of any forms of activism and does not examine exactly what might be feasible. For reasons discussed below, labeling these views Keynesian is common but not necessarily universal.

The microinterventionists and deregulators believe that better government supervision of individual firms throughout the economy can contribute to reducing unemployment or at least allow the reduction to occur with less inflation than if only monetary and fiscal policy are used. Microinteventionists believe that unemployment is a serious problem originating from inherent market frictions *and* most appropriately cured by *increasing* regulation of individual markets. Deregulators, who tend to doubt the severity of economic instability, see government as creating the critical barriers to good performance and want to *decrease* regulation.

The increased regulation outlook had its height in the 1930s. The extensive thrashing about for explanation of the profound economic collapse in that decade produced many theories. A number stressed the role of rigidities in the economy. The supporters differed considerably in what they proposed. Suggestions were then made for either extensive national economic planning to regulate private market behavior or radically restructuring the economy by vigorous application of US antitrust laws (see below). Some of the advocates survived long after World War Two but attracted little intellectual support. Politicians, to be sure, have acted on acceptance of the belief. In contrast, the overregulation thesis is largely noted in passing by the most avid antigovernment economists. (Kelman gives the macroeconomic elements of these arguments greater prominence than they ever have secured in the economic literature.)

The failure of massive depressions to emerge since World War Two lessened, but did not eliminate, concerns. The question of whether more directly confronting market or government imperfections was an effective strategy persisted but never dominated. Support for such measures was limited.

At least two episodes arose in the United States. They were inspired largely by the persistent problems of taming inflation generated by the Korean and Viet Nam wars. Towards the end of the Eisenhower presidency, much discussion arose of cost inflation. The Kennedy administration devised a response, but it was the alternative option discussed next. The Nixon administration was enduring inflationary problems reflecting lingering effects of the Viet Nam War and then was hit with the 1973-74 oil price shocks. The administration adopted first a set of general price controls and then initiated what proved an extended concentration on regulating energy for many reasons including alleged macroeconomic benefits. The much explored energy experience (see Bradley's massive 1995 effort to sum up the experience) illustrated the severe microeconomic problems that can arise.

Many of those involved during the 1980s in developing more acceptable theories of how rigidities cause economic instability are cautious about making policy suggestions. The point is made in the editors' introduction to Mankiw and Romer's anthology of US writings developing such models. One author in Mankiw and Romer (Bryant, 1983, vol. 2, p. 28) notes 'almost anything can be modeled as optimizing behavior'. The Winter 1993 issue of the *Journal of Economic Perspectives* had a symposium on the work in which the new Keynesians Romer, Greenwald and Stiglitz, a leading old Keynesian, Tobin, and a new classical economist, King all express reservations about the empirical relevance of the theories. Robert J. Gordon (1990) (from a distinguished family of economists to which I am not related) has separately discussed the drawbacks. All sides argue that it is still not established what rigidities are most critical and how they operate. Thus, the latest work on imperfections at most is the basis for eventual development of policy advice.

When John F. Kennedy was elected, his official and unofficial economic advisors adopted a compromise between Keynesianism and microintervention. Recognizing the drawbacks of explicit controls, the advisers proposed a halfway house approach of wage-price guideposts to indicate to industry what would be noninflationary wage and price changes. Estimates were provided of the rates of wage and price increases consistent with overall price stability. Industry and trade unions were exhorted to keep wage and price changes within these guideposts. This was a curious, justly largely forgotten episode since economic analysis tends to scorn reliance on unenforceable pressures. Indeed, the only reason that this approach is mentioned is that Mankiw and Romer included a paper by Okun advocating among other things a return to guideposts (and proving a link, badly missing elsewhere in the anthology, to precursor work from 1935 to 1970).

6. The Skeptics

The skeptical view stressed here is that high unemployment is transitory, of ill-understood origins, and cannot be alleviated by public policy. Skepticism, as discussed below, involves various challenges to belief that instability is correctable. Objections are both theoretical and practical. It is argued that theories stressing instability have questionable theoretic basis and little empirical relevance. Another contention is that instabilities are so difficult to recognize and so transitory and policy responses are so slow and variable that intervention is likely to be harmful.

Skepticism, as treated here, is an extension of the Milton Friedman position and its development by the macroeconomists using, among other things, the assumption of rational expectations. That last assumption is compatible with many different further premises; the new classics initially concentrated on models in which policy ineffectiveness is likely. The main difference of the present discussion is its greater stress on the absence of a convincing explanation for the causes of unemployment.

The absence of such an explanation strengthens skepticism. Thus, this article stresses the defects of business cycle theories with a clear message of any type on both causes and policies. I read Friedman as saying only that passive monetary is the least worst available alternative. The wildly implausible idea that all problems will vanish under a monetary rule has its supporters, but Friedman does not seem one of them. Similarly, I note with no enthusiasm efforts of real business cycle theorists to suggest business fluctuations are not a policy issue because they arise from voluntary changes in the willingness to work.

7. The Rise of Macroeconomics

Historically economics concentrated on attainment of efficiency in the marketplace. Disturbances such as unemployment, inflation and problems with international balances of payments were considered secondary. Textbooks prior to the end of World War Two I hardly mentioned the issues. Writings existed, but they apparently commanded limited attention. (The impression about earlier textbooks is based on sampling made over many years. Here, Samuelson's complaints (for example 1977, p. 770) that the issues were ignored when he was an undergraduate in the 1930s should be contrasted with the mass of material cited in Haberler's *Prosperity and Depression*.) The persistence of massive unemployment in North America and Europe in the 1930s shattered the prevailing beliefs. Economists struggled to devise better explanations of economic instability. The result of all this was the emergence of macroeconomics.

The new realm of macroeconomics was dominated for a long time by models inspired by the work of John Maynard Keynes in the *General Theory of*

Employment, Interest, and Money. Keynes presented an exposition on the causes of instability (or at least of a depression as prolonged as that in the 1930s) that secured wide acceptance as the needed answer. Given the ambiguity of Keynes's work and the need to deal with circumstances radically different from those of the 1930s, enormous explanation, refinement and revision have occurred.

Keynes-inspired economics has at least three major components - a framework for analyzing economic instability, a vision about the nature of the instability, and views on stabilization prospects given the instability. Much controversy appropriately arises about what is the correct view of each area. A more unusual aspect of the debate is the preoccupation about whether a given interpretation is one advocated by Keynes. This contrasts with the excessively short memory of many microeconomists who often write as if general equilibrium theory leaped from Walras to Arrow and Debreu without the intermediate assistance of even Hicks and Samuelson. For most purposes, the debate about interpreting Keynes is a distraction from the fundamental questions about what is the most useful way to model the economy.

The difficulty of determining what Keynes meant arises from the loose, often ambiguous, exposition in the *General Theory*. Examining the mass of Keynes's other writings apparently increases the uncertainty about his beliefs. Similarly, those who differ with some possibly quite substantial part of the Keynesian position as defined here may or may not still identify themselves as a Keynesian in a looser sense.

The greatest consensus exists about the basic analytic framework. That used generally is an extension of J.R. Hicks's pioneering 1937 effort to provide a systematic formulation of what Keynes meant. The accord, however, consists only of agreement to employ a few equations dealing with, among other things, the supply and demand for four goods - production as a whole, labor, money and an interest bearing security.

Considerable variation prevails in the specification of equations in different theoretic exercises. In many cases, these alternatives are presented as one providing a superior view of actual economic conditions. Others are simply efforts to test the sensitivity of results to the assumptions. (Hicks's version of Keynes was one of the earliest to argue that the *General Theory* did not assume imperfect competition. Hicks concentrates on differences between Keynes and the classics about the sensitivity to interest rates and the level of income of demands for money and investment goods and the supply of savings. The labor and good production market are absent from Hicks's models but appear in Modigliani's widely cited 1944 effort to summarize the debate.)

As discussed more fully below, many macroeconomics models of persistent unemployment long have assumed some departure from the (idealized) assumptions of the microeconomic theory of competitive markets. Some observers, notably Patinkin (1965), correctly argue that this approach trivializes and misrepresents Keynes and thus that an alternative view of Keynes was needed. (Patinkin makes this case tacitly.) The implications of major departures from the core assumptions of the theory of competitive markets are too obvious to justify terming the consideration of imperfections a revolution. The attacks on classical economics in *General Theory* are deemed to suggest flaws in the old analysis less obvious than neglect of market imperfections.

Patinkin focused on an issue that then and now traditional theory cannot treat, the speed of adjustment. He suggested that this adjustment might be too slow, where too slow means slow enough that governmental intervention could effectively speed the process. This viewpoint, however, has received few adherents. Economic rigidity models of various forms discussed below remain the mainstay of theories of persistent unemployment. Keynes's exposition is too fuzzy to resolve definitely whether he postulated a more subtle problem, overstated the newness of his theory, or both. Validating Patinkin's view of Keynes or the similar contentions of Clower (1965) and Leijonhufvud (1968) is not feasible or essential. The observation that the implications of market imperfections is (better) treated by classical economics remains valid whatever Keynes believed.

Haberler's (1958) study of economic instability largely written before the appearance of the *General Theory* anticipates the concern over stress on market imperfections: 'It might therefore just as well be maintained that rigidity of our economic system, or its financial or monetary organisation, or particular features of the latter, are the causes of the cycle as that inventions or crop changes or changes in demand are responsible' (p. 6).

By itself, this debate over what comprises the most relevant macroeconomic models and how consistent that model is with that of Keynes could be and often is a mere intellectual exercise. The germane concern is about the practical implications of whatever is the right model. In particular, the central issue is whether the characteristics of actual macroeconomics justify and permit effective countercyclical policies.

8. Alternative Views on the Stability Problem

While many different models exist, the number of possible outcomes is limited. The basic possibilities are stagnation (unemployment that inspires no market generated corrections), a business cycle sufficiently prolonged that public policy can lessen its impacts, and a business cycle so transitory that public policy cannot lessen the impacts. Feasibility depends upon the comparative length of the cycle and of policy response.

The stagnation idea was one that arose in the depression of the 1930s and died with the boom after World War Two. Whatever Keynes believed, some of those whom Keynes inspired initially argued that unemployment was chronic. The original Keynesian approach, therefore, stressed the existence of inherently correctable persistent demand deficiencies in the economy. Fears of massive persistent unemployment faded and with them interest in equally massive and slow moving programs of government spending.

The alternative view that temporary periods of unemployment, the problem often called the business cycle, arise now predominates. The 'Keynesian' position is that public policy can fruitfully counteract these transitory downturns. The 'classical' approach stressed here is essentially an attack on the legitimacy of this extension to short recessions of claims plausible to persistent depressions. (In fact, such concerns have been raised within the Keynesian traditions, see Phillips, 1950, 1954, 1956 and Allen, 1956.)

Inflation proved a more persistent problem than many Keynesians (but not Keynes himself) expected. Reflecting these changes, Keynesian economics greatly altered its focus from 1936 to its 'crisis' in the 1970s. The revised belief was that the fluctuations that did occur had characteristics that should and could be counteracted by active government policies. The initial successes in the 1960s produced faith (indeed in the worst cases arrogance) that this view had been vindicated.

9. The Return of Classical Macroeconomics

During the years immediately after World War Two, only a few economists, most notably Milton Friedman, argued that the problems and the ability to deal with them had been overstated. To be sure, there were a substantial number of older economists, of whom Haberler is an example, who were unimpressed by Keynes's analysis when it appeared and never recanted. Paul Samuelson's fascination (for example 1977, p. 878) with Kuhn's concept of scientific revolutions undoubtedly involved appreciation of Kuhn's concept of a recalcitrant old guard who refused to recognize the truth. Long before Kuhn provided supporting rationales, the Keynesians were quite successful at dismissing older critics as obdurate. The revival of more classical approaches implies the dismissals may have been premature. The old school lived to see their earlier doubts gain support that attracted new disciples. Snowdon, Vane and Wynarczk (1995, p. 21) suggest that indeed Kuhn's analysis is generally inappropriate for economics because no outlooks are abandoned.

Stagflation (high unemployment, inflation, and slow growth) in the 1970s caused greater attention to Friedman's views. A group of economists termed the new classical economists developed models that raised the possibility that Friedman's criticisms understated the drawbacks of intervention.

Friedman and similar critics stress the existence of long and unknown lags in the recognition of problems, design of response, and reaction to the response. Given all these lags, active public policy cannot clearly produce improvement and might even be harmful. This position has been enormously influential. Many fully accept the arguments. More importantly, those who defend active stabilization policy advocate actions far less ambitious than those proposed in the 1960s.

After the disastrous performance in the 1970s, Friedman's argument that instability was not necessarily inherent and definitely was not correctable received increased attention. This encouraged economists too young to be influenced by the experiences of the 1930s to examine what lay behind the earlier beliefs. In particular, economists such as Lucas and Sargent developed an alternative, more formal analysis to deal with Friedman's assertions. (At least three major anthologies are available on new classical economics: Lucas and Sargent, 1981, a large collection of pieces by many writers who deal with economics principles, statistical techniques, and empirical evidence; Lucas, 1981a, a collection of work authored or co-authored by Lucas; and Miller, 1994, a collection stressing later work, all associated with the Federal Reserve Bank of Minneapolis.) The new analysis showed that under some conditions intervention was totally ineffective.

10. Market Clearing Rational Expectations Models

Since this result depended on introducing expectations into macroeconomic models and the developers relied specifically on a theory of expectations developed by Richard Muth, one name given the application to macroeconomics was based on the term 'rational expectations' which Muth used to describe his approach.

Since the theory also insisted that it should be assumed that markets clear rapidly, the alternative name of market clearing macroeconomics was also used. The meaning of market clearing used by the group seems widely misunderstood. Lucas's formulation seems to indicate nothing more than an analytic strategy (1981a, p. 226). He felt that assuming perpetual disequilibrium was too permissive. However, he adds that equilibrium states are not always desirable. One way of interpreting him is by recalling Alfred Marshall's period analysis. In Marshall, markets always clear but not all the ultimately desirable responses are made immediately. Reality consists of a successions of ever better adjustments to underlying conditions. Nevertheless, the new classical economists tend to see a rapid full adjustment.

Finally, the approach was dubbed new classical since it in many ways suggested that classical competitive theory was still the most practically relevant model. One of the critical ways was to assert that prior models lacked 'microfoundations'. By this was meant that no plausible microeconomic theories existed to justify many parts of the prior interventionist macroeconomic models. This applied at least to the assumptions about expectations, the specification of equations in econometric models of the economy, and the assertions of price rigidities.

In the most dramatic applications, the approach showed cases in which active policy would be ineffective. (Lucas's work provided a starting point, but the fullest developments were in papers in Lucas and Sargent, notably those authored by Sargent and Wallace.) These new classical economists contended that Keynesian arguments, particularly those associated with the Lipsey (1960) and Samuelson and Solow (1960) developments of Phillips's 1958 analysis of an inflation unemployment trade-off, depended on assuming that the public was irredeemably stupid. The new classical economists argued that, if the public anticipated that monetary expansion would occur, they would neutralize its output effects by inflating prices by the amount of the monetary expansion. The result is an immediate consequence of the key assumptions of competitive markets that adjust slowly but not interminably and of decision makers capable of anticipating public policy. The essence of the case is that the models assume enough flexibility in the economy to rule out any output of monetary expansion except that resulting from failure to anticipate.

Another key contention was that statistical analysis could not establish which theory was correct. The new classical argument was extended to remind macroeconomists of the classic econometric problem of observational equivalence (see, for example, Sargent, 1976b). In many cases including those of concern here, observable behavior can be consistent with many radically different theories. (The basic idea is that we only observe the interaction of supply and demand. An approach called identification is used to move backward from the observed results to determining the equations that produced the equilibrium. However, models tend to be overidentified, that is, consistent with an infinite number of conditions.)

The new classicists also adopt Friedman's concerns about the enormous data needs for successful stabilization. Much effort has been devoted to showing the imperfection of the models and how to develop models in which active stabilization works. This seems an inadequate response. The new classicists are challenging the empirical validity of faith in active instability. A response must include convincing factual evidence to the contrary.

While the new classical economists described their work as supporting Friedman's arguments, he was not pleased. He joined many Keynesians with concerns over the allegedly high degree of rationality assumed (see his comments to Snowdon, Vane and Wynarczk, 1995, p. 175). He felt that his arguments were more plausible than the assumptions of rationality made by the new classical economists. These complaints may exaggerate the differences. Friedman had suggested the idea that real effects of monetary policy were possible only if people were temporarily fooled.

The new classical economists made the sensible extension of specifying what was required to eliminate surprise. The analysis leaves some room for temporary surprise. More critically, however, the approach at least implicitly warns that *all* theories of the business cycle, particularly the monetary, rely to various degrees on the assumption of transitory, potentially ultimately correctable confusion over what the monetary authorities are doing. Lucas himself relies on such a lag. The minimum contribution of a rational expectations benchmark is warning that the magnitude and duration of effects depends upon precisely what economic analysis cannot treat, the precise degree to which reality differs from idealized conditions.

A further implication is that, as is surely true in 1997, after decades of active monetary policy the private sector will better understand and anticipate the actions of the monetary authorities. In short, monetary policy can create disturbances, but their nature is too unclear and so subject to eventual erosion to permit counteraction. Attacks on rationality, moreover, have overstated what one must know. What is involved is knowledge about what the monetary authorities are doing and what it implies. The leading newspapers and television networks have managed to grasp such information.

Houthakker's (1957) research on the operation of futures markets suggested that the few full-time professionals with knowledge of market conditions dominated the markets and made them efficient. (This is an implicit application of Hayek's arguments about how markets economize on knowledge acquisition.) Similar specialists could operate in other markets to ensure they two were guided by the best possible knowledge.

11. Further Challenges

Friedman in collaboration with Anna Schwartz (1963, 1982) added another element to the anti-intervention case. They examined the monetary record in first the United States and then the United Kingdom and observed a high correlation between money supply movements and economic instability. They concluded that monetary policy seemed the cause rather than merely reacting. A major part of the analysis was a detailed description of policies before and during the great depression. The review led them to attribute the depression to overly aggressive monetary restriction in the late 1920s and failure to expand money in the 1930s by the US Federal Reserve Board. Two leading subsequent commentators, Kindleberger (1986) and Temin (1989), disputed Friedman and Schwartz's explanation of why the Federal Reserve acted improperly but agreed that bad monetary policy was the critical cause. A symposium in the Spring 1993 *Journal of Economic Perspectives* (C. Romer, Margo, Calomiris and Temin) reinforced this viewpoint.

These conclusions dispute the central premise of Keynesian economics stressing inherent, correctable instability in the economy. Clearly, as Friedman and Schwartz know, strong associations simply suggest linkages. Ultimately, we rely on our judgments about the plausibility of different explanations. If Friedman and Schwartz are right, the Keynesians identified the disease (bad policy) as the cure. This is an ultraclassical (almost Austrian) conclusion that in macroeconomics as well as microeconomics government is better thought of as a threat than as an all knowing benevolent force. This, in turn, hits at a main weakness of the neoclassical synthesis, the inconsistencies between its views of government in microeconomics as opposed to macroeconomics. It is possible that macroeconomic problems are so much more serious or more tractable that government can be trusted more in macroeconomics than in microeconomics. It also is possible that the drawbacks that arise in microeconomic problems also occur in macroeconomics. These conclusions become muted but still relevant if less classical explanations are more valid. We are left with concerns that, as already noted, all responsible observers share, about the severe limits to active intervention.

12. Real Business Cycles

Some new classical economists, as noted, responded to discontent with the explanations given of business cycles by proposing new real (in the economic sense of non-monetary) theories of the business cycle in which variations in employment were voluntary responses to changing market conditions such as sudden changes in the productivity of the economy. This is a very different approach that, if valid, would be the ultimate challenge to Keynesian economics. Countercyclical policy would be interfering with efficient behavior.

Real business cycle theory to date is severely (and properly) criticized because it is as unconvincing as all the prior simple explanations. In particular, no plausible justifications were provided for belief in developments that would inspire massive but temporary voluntary decisions of some workers to stop working. (Even the advocates recognize the difficulty of identifying real phenomena that explain historical experience. The summer 1989 issue of *The Journal of Economic Perspectives* presents papers by Plosser, a developer, and Mankiw, a skeptic.)

Snowdon, Vane and Wynarczk note the thread in real business cycle analysis that emphasizes the cycles are random deviations from trends. The discussion fails to cite Slutsky's classic paper that deals with possibility that by its nature economic evolution will have random deviations from trends. This earlier work relies on the broad view that the complex processes involved cannot be expected to operate smoothly. This seems more satisfactory than the view that the unevenness has a cause.

13. The State of Policy

New classical economics, Austrian economics, and Friedman all effectively argue that Adam Smith's concerns about the difficulties in determining the public good applies as much to stabilizing the whole economy as to regulating individual markets. 'Keynesian' belief in the opposite presumption is challenged to provide a convincing counterargument.

The arguments were essentially a formalization of a key tacit premise in macroeconomics. It was an act of judgment, heavily influenced by the great depression, that stabilization policy was needed. Keynesian economics and the broader neoclassical synthesis in which it was embedded effectively argued that the dangers of unemployment were so severe and readily correctable that it was obvious that economists should suspend their traditional distrust of intervention. The continuation of this approach after 1945 involved a giant leap that was never well justified. What was true for a chronic depression was clearly less justified for a world of milder business cycles.

As long as the policy seemed to work, it escaped challenge. Leaps of faith seemed good enough. Once the program faltered, economists felt emboldened to restate the traditional doubts about intervention. These new classicists challenged the prevailing evaluation criteria by suggesting many reasons why this approach was suspect.

Given the strong commitment among macroeconomists to active stabilization policy, these views have been resisted vigorously. Stress is on complaints that the models assume an implausibly high degree of rationality, postulate unrealistically well functioning markets, and inadequately explain the business cycle. A striking contrast between the new classical and new Keynesian analyses is that the former involved extensive consideration of the theory and practice of statistical testing of hypotheses while the latter concentrates on pure theorizing. As suggested above, these complaints inadequately consider whether the flaws suffice to justify active stabilization policy. As discussed below, to date, the most that the Keynesians can claim is that such justification *might* exist. Thus, the attacks on new classical economics seem incomplete.

The Keynesians might have explicitly countered with what they seem to believe, that the risks of inaction were too great to allow reliance on simple rules. Probably because they recognize that the new classical economics also warns that action also poses possibly greater dangers, Keynesians have tried to refute the criticisms.

Unfortunately, the situation precludes a conclusive resolution. The situation is standard in economic policy debates. We have two radically different judgments of what constitutes the prudent strategy. One side is concerned with the perils of inaction and urges continued effort. The other side concentrates on the evils of intervention and urges radically altered less intrusive controls. This obviously cannot be settled here. What is critical is that the doubts are sufficient to justify restraint about adopting radical new measures.

14. Confronting Cyclicality

Keynesian and other widely used macroeconomic models have a flaw of dealing only with equilibrium at a specific moment. A long tradition has at least tacitly recognized that this approach ignores the expansion of the economy and the variations in expansions traditionally termed business cycles. Early Keynesians expressed their recognition by developing models explicitly treating cycles. More classical economists directly attacked neglect of cyclicality as a fatal flaw of Keynesian economics.

In its most general and useful sense, the business cycle idea suggests that increased unemployment occurs in an ever-changing economy and that economy may spontaneously generate measures to eliminate the unemployment. To understand the debate, we must recall now abandoned work in economics.

Staring in the 1930s, various economists, most notably the very young Paul Samuelson, tried to devise macroeconomic models that accounted for these cyclical forces. Samuelson and those who followed him concentrated on the existing theory most readily reduced to a manageable model. In particular, he treated an accelerator model in which investment depended on the most recent change in national output. (By modern standards, this is a hopelessly naive model since it ignore anticipations.) This effort reached a dead-end in the 1950s (see Allen, 1956). The models had become unmanageable long before they produced a plausible analysis of cyclicality. Macroeconomists abandoned not only the development but also the recollection of cyclical analysis. In the process of abandoning this approach, a critical insight was weakened. Studies, particularly those of Phillips (1950, 1954, 1956, 1957), of stabilization policies in a cyclical economy showed the difficulty of producing desirable results in a steadily moving economy. A basic problem of any interventionist strategy is that long effort has failed to produce a convincing analysis of cyclicality. It can be argued that the analysts have lost sight of the difficulties involved.

Cycle theory was followed by steady-state growth theory that traced the effects of steady increases in the ability to produce. Here too, the difficulties of analyzing complex cases long hindered progress; some signs of revival have arisen but are treated here. However, the pioneering models in this realm are widely cited in later macroeconomic models.

Shortly after the appearance of the *General Theory*, the League of Nations published a survey of business cycle economics. The review was by Gottfried Haberler, an Austrian trained economist long associated (particularly in his long career after the book was published) with anti-intervention views on the economy. (Haberler revised the book twice for the League and finally in 1957 the Harvard University Press issued a fourth edition. The last is used here. According to that edition, every edition had two main parts, the survey of different theories and a 'Synthetic Exposition Relating to the Nature and Causes of Business Cycles'. The fourth edition omitted much material from earlier editions, retained a chapter on Keynes added to the second edition, and added reprinted of later articles.) The discussion provides a richer view of proposed explanations and their drawbacks than appears in subsequent work.

Haberler begins by discussing the problems of explanation. He suggests, for example, that some supposedly single-cause models at least tacitly postulate additional influences. Supply or demand shock-based models make presumptions about the adaptability of the economy and particularly the monetary system to shocks. Monetary theories may implicitly concern the response of the monetary authorities to external forces. His basic posture is that the theories are at best incomplete and often indefensible. Subsequent work has neither added plausible new explanations nor overcome the severe deficiencies of prior concepts.

15. The Causes Considered

Haberler's survey of views distinguishes several categories of causes - purely monetary theory (nonmonetary, monetary, and demand change), overinvestment theories, changes in costs, horizontal maladjustments, overindebtedness, underconsumption, psychology and harvests. However, over half his discussion of explanations is devoted to overinvestment.

Haberler's monetary theory is devoted entirely to the views of R.W. Hawtrey. The latter's theory holds that business cycles are due entirely to unwise fluctuations in the money supply. Emphasis is on the effects on real interest rates. (This is a stronger and thus less convincing argument against active monetary policy that the later view of Milton Friedman that stable growth has better effects than active monetary management. Hawtrey as interpreted by Haberler argues that active monetary policy is cause rather than cure or aggravating force.) As proves true of many of the models discussed, this theory involves precisely the dependence on failures of anticipation about which the rational expectations approach warns.

The alternatives to a purely monetary approach tend to involve a generic problem of imbalances among supplies, demands and prices. Haberler's discussion of specific theories thus often expands upon his initial warning that whatever problem a given theorist stresses, the analysis typically involves the interaction of several forces.

Monetary overinvestment theories such as Wicksell's (and Hayek's as epitomized by Snowdon, Vane and Wynarczk) differ from Hawtrey's 'pure' monetary theory by stressing the influence on investment of changes in real interest rates. Haberler starts his review of nonmonetary overinvestment theories by noting that the lack of explicit consideration of money is a flaw. The theorists 'are compelled to assume an elastic currency or credit supply in order to prove what they wish to demonstrate' (p. 73).

Haberler then turns to a central ideal in business cycle theory, the acceleration principle, used in Samuelson's model (1966, vol. 2, pp. 1107-1124) and its extensions. This theory builds on the fact that investment either replaces retired capital goods or adds to productive capacity. A simple rule is that investment to add new capacity is proportional to the change in output in the recent past. While the level of economic output changes slowly, the changes and thus investment can move radically. Haberler ends his discussion of qualifications to the theory with consideration of expectations. He notes 'any investment, directly or indirectly is looking forward to, and is made in the expectation of, a future demand for consumers goods' (p. 97). His concern is more qualified than that of the 1970s. Haberler talks only of 'types of investment which look forward to their utilisation to a very distant future' (p. 98).

The cost change theory that Haberler stresses is that as a boom proceeds, firms start operating on a steeply rising portion of their cost curves. Haberler recognizes that this would not be problematic unless real wages and prices failed to adjust to these changes. Horizontal maladjustments are the lack of correspondence between demand and supply in goods and factor markets. According to Haberler (1957, p. 115), the overindebtedness theory is most satisfactory in warning that existing debt hinders response to downturns and less satisfactory in suggesting that the rise in burdens restrain activity and produce downturns. The financial organization explanation is that valuing financial assets in nominal money reduces price flexibility.

Haberler views overconsumption as a grab-bag of illformulated, often invalid theories. The valid theories, moreover, are often restatements of theories best classified under his other categories. He indicates that many theories involve economically unsound ideas that consumption is inherently unable to expand as rapidly as productive capacity. Haberler indicates that valid theories involve short-run imbalances among consumption, savings, investment and productive capacity. In some of these models, stress is on income distribution effects. A shift of income from wages to profits undesirably reduces consumption.

Haberler views psychological theories as attempting to postulate swings arising from optimism and pessimism distinct from the fluctuations observed in other theories. Haberler notes the difficulties of distinguishing these effects but does not deny their existence.

As suggested above, Haberler's leaves us with many ideas and no clear way to determine whether any of those that are theoretically sound are empirically relevant. In short, he documents the case that a satisfactory explanation is unavailable. It is argued above that little progress has been made in the last six decades at overcoming these problems.

16. Imperfect Competition and Unemployment: The Microeconomic Background

One critical controversy in macroeconomics centers on whether the traditional flexible competitive market outlook or alternative imperfect market or defective governments models best describe actual economies. The macroeconomic debates are echoes of the microeconomic debate over what is the empirically most valid model of the economy. Since the relevance of the associated macroeconomic models depends on the underlying microeconomic work, the nature of the latter must be considered.

The history of the microeconomics of imperfect markets is convoluted. A particular concern is that theory and practice may have radically diverged. The case for regulating markets arose in ill-formulated work in the 1930s. Means (1939, 1972) became the quintessence of the process due to his long-standing, diverse and often discussed efforts. His most persistent idea was that industrial prices were excessively rigid. This view was, in typical Means fashion, derived solely from observation of data. Reaction to arguments lacking either theoretic basis or proper skepticism about the problems of data interpretation clearly were a major inspiration for Edward S. Mason's efforts to encourage sounder work on the issues (as is clearly shown in the germane articles in the anthology of his writings (1957) and in his later (1982) essay reflecting on economics at Harvard in the 1930s).

The results were development of both sounder theories and better empirical analyses. The theory has produced an overwhelming number of models. By sheer count, those models that postulate market imperfections seem to dominate. Even the term is loaded in this direction. Imperfect, in practice, means a departure from the idealized assumptions used in general equilibrium models that are the primary tools of modern economic theory. However, the essence of models is deliberate simplification. Reality thus is more complex than the model. Theorists often fail to consider how these complications alter what is optimal. In addition to the attention to market failure, important work has been done on developing models suggesting the microeconomic drawbacks of regulation, government failure.

An important aspect of the evolution was the emergence starting in the 1970s (and still continuing) of theories inspired by the formalism of post World War Two economic theories. This new work displays both the strengths and weaknesses of formalism. The inadequate microfoundations displayed by those like Means have been banished. However, theory only establishes what might happen. Empirical verification is needed to determine the practical relevance of alternative visions. A tendency exists relentlessly to follow every idea without concern about relevance. The emphases in the theorizing seem better explained by the greater ease with which market imperfections can be analyzed.

The literature is too vast to treat adequately here. Among the more important overviews are the essays in Schmalensee and Willig, the treatises by Tirole, Krouse, and Spulber (who uniquely does reflect on the limits to applications), and the texts by Scherer and Ross (1990) and by Carlton and Perloff (1994). The critiques of Schmalensee and Willig by Peltzman (1991), Fisher (1991), and Klevorick (1991) all reflect the concern expressed here over inadequate consideration of empirical relevance. This, in turn, reflects a broader discord about the practical importance of monopoly that these critiques neglect.

Applied economics and even public policy has moved towards discontent with regulation that is so widespread that its nature can only be sketched here. Both regulation of individual markets and the efforts to use broad 'antitrust' policies to regulate competition are under severe challenge.

With antitrust, the 'moderate' position is that long-standing proposals massively to restructure industry lack justification for action and that policies over mergers, price fixing, and other trade practices must be administered with greater concern for promoting competition. Bork, 1978, and Posner, 1976, in their books on antitrust state well all but the first of these points. The best indicator of what has happened with restructuring is the lack of efforts since the late 1960s to promote the approach.) However, the Chicago position on flawed regulation has regularly led to conclusions that satisfactory administration is intrinsically impossible. Failure to apply this proposition to antitrust invited and ultimately received challenge (see McChesney and Shughard, 1995).

The views on more specialized policies ranges from condemnation (for example, for most agricultural, transportation, and energy intervention) to desires for radical reform (for example, for environmental regulation). The challenges involve a mixture of skepticism over both whether any of the market imperfections cause significant problems and whether public policy can make things better. No one book can do all this justice, but Viscusci, Vernon and Harrington (1995) covers much of the critical ground from a careful analytic view. The Cato Institute, a vigorous advocate of limited government, prepares more sweeping but much less analytic surveys of interventions that seem unsound.

One polar extreme is the Chicago position that monopoly is rare and transitory unless supported by government policy. Some economists (for example, Scherer and Ross, 1990, p. 541, talk of Chicago being 'fervent in advancing simplistic theories of economic behavior' and Bresnahan in his comments in Fisher, 1991, p. 227, talks of 'the too-hasty Chicago consensus') profess scorn for this outlook. However, this does not produce great concern over monopoly or enthusiasm for regulation. Scherer and Ross's attacks on Chicago, for example, preface sections absent from earlier versions extensively discussing previously neglected Chicago arguments.

The point here is that the ability of market regulation to accomplish anything is under severe challenge. Thus, a case for regulating on macroeconomic grounds must overcome three problems - (1) proving possible imperfections exist, (2) showing that they have important macroeconomic effects, and (3) devising workable policies to overcome the problem.

17. The Effort at Application

The case here is that work to date falls far short of fulfilling the requirements just set. It is suggested that all that has been done yet is produce theories that show how imperfections might produce major macroeconomic effects. Empirical verification has not been provided. Moreover, considerable evidence exists that even the developers of the theory are concerned about this limitation.

Stress here is on a group of US economists who have termed themselves new Keynesians and Europeans who have emphasized labor market imperfection issues. New Keynesian analysis is the effort of a newer generation of economists to evaluate the attacks on the Keynesian faith of the leading academics (notably Samuelson in his textbook and Tobin in his extensive writings on macroeconomics) of the immediate post-World War Two years. US new Keynesians come from leading universities, particularly those in the forefront of advancing the Keynesian revolution, and publish in the major long established journals.

The focus is governed by the high accessibility of the work, particularly in the Mankiw and Romer anthology noted above. The term new Keynesian might suggest that active macroeconomic is feasible. However, even the advocates of the concepts are more cautious. They admit that the work only suggests arguments that might lead to revival of belief in active monetary and fiscal policy. Mankiw and Romer (in their introduction) add that some of the developers of the models reach the new classical conclusion that it is infeasible in practice to implement such policies.

Whatever their influence on microeconomics, the models of imperfect markets were seized upon (in many cases by their developers such as Carlton, Stiglitz and Shapiro, all also contributors to Schmalensee and Willig) in the 1980s as the basis of more sophisticated models of the macroeconomics implications of violations of core assumptions. In the process, newer forms of disfunction were discovered (see below).

This methodology can be contrasted with the older post-Keynesian movement. As one proponent of the group (Sawyer, 1991, p. 202) notes, the term post Keynesian evolved from a umbrella for all reviews of Keynes to a description of a specific approach to macroeconomics that includes concern over the impacts of market imperfections. The post Keynesians, however, seem to revel in unorthodoxy and separation from the rest of the macroeconomics profession (see Snowdon, Vane and Wynarczk, 1995, pp. 367-380).

18. New Keynesian Models

New Keynesian economics is a collection of more traditional analyses of market imperfections. Many, but probably not all, of the proponents sought to refute the new classical approach. Stress was on models with sound microeconomic bases in which instability was inherent. Usually, these models provide microeconomic justifications for assuming good or factor price rigidities that lead to persistent unemployment. However, the models include some with characteristics that can preclude the existence, uniqueness, or stability of equilibrium. The details are not critical here. Bryant's observation strongly holds. With enough assumptions about market imperfections, theorists can develop models that inevitably lead to persistent unemployment. Mankiw and Romer divide the contributions into seven parts - costs of price change, the role of contracts, good market monopoly, 'coordination failures', labor market behavior, imperfect credit markets and cyclical behavior of the goods markets.

Costs of price changes, infelicitously termed menu costs by Mankiw (Chapter 1 in Mankiw and Romer, 1991), are the expenses of making, reporting and implementing a price change. (Except as noted, all the ideas presented here come from Mankiw and Romer and the attacks on them come from the articles noted above.) As pioneering work by Barro (1972) (a new classical economist) showed, when price changing is expensive, it is no longer optimal to respond instantaneously to price changes. The price change should occur only when the transaction costs are repaid by higher profits from operations. Between price changes, the price should be a (time-weighted) average of the prices that would clear the market under flexible pricing. A series of articles (for example, Mankiw and Akerloff and Yellen, 1985 - chapter 2 in Mankiw and Romer) examined how pursuit of such policies might increase macroeconomic instability by inadequately responding to changing market conditions.

As is standard in this literature, doubts have been raised about the theoretical and empirical plausibility of the models (see the articles noted above and Snowdon, Vane and Wynarczk). Even the menu metaphor is viewed skeptically. It is pointed out that announcing price changes often is cheap. Cheap changes such as scribbled entries or mimeographed inserts were possible long ago - for example, when I worked in my father's restaurant in the 1950s; modern technology allows cheap production of formal looking updates. The new Keynesian literature often cites an unpublished study that recognized that the large US mail order retailers issue new catalogs far more often than they change prices. It is suggested that better explanations must be provided about why frequent price changes are undesirable.

Another concern is that reliance on long-term contracts can be destabilizing. Those presenting such models clearly recognize that the problem with such contracts is that they inevitably involve incorrect specification of future economic conditions. The first work in this realm took the existence of contracts as given, and only later was a transaction cost justification developed. The theories stress the difficulties of changing contracts. Stanley Fischer's 1977 article (chapter 7 in Mankiw and Romer and also in Lucas and Sargent) on the subject examines the role of adjustment clauses in contracts but only notes that the 'right' clause would be more complex than those actually chosen. This seems too pessimistic. Actual contracts have explicit provisions to increase response to changing conditions. Bad contracts are renegotiated. (This criticism emerged from my experiences with energy contracts rather than from the literature.)

Another type of model simply considers the macroeconomic consequences of oligopoly. Most of these models examine how with monopoly labor supply, macroeconomic policy can offset the supply restriction and expand output. Examples are noted below.

Another, particularly complex, family of models deals with what are termed coordination failures. These involve situations in which the characteristics of the economy produce multiple equilibriums, the free market choice may not be optimal, and public policy can move the economy to a more efficient equilibrium. An article (Cooper and John, chapter 16 in Mankiw and Romer) synthesizing the work suggests that the problem is best viewed of one of an economy operating under the principles of the noncooperative games so beloved by new industrial organization theorists. At a minimum, this raises the problem, on which the game theorists have lavished much attention, that noncooperative behavior is not good for the decision makers and should be (but not necessarily is) abandoned when interactions regularly reoccur. Those skeptical of game theory would argue that its microeconomic limitations make it a poor basis for macroeconomics.

Another area is alternative labor market models that postulate conditions under which wages should be less flexible than traditional theory seems to suggests or reexamine the nature of unemployment. American new (and old) Keynesians focus on such ideas as efficiency wages that postulate that effort is increased by paying higher wages. A European alternative due to Lindbeck and Snower (1988) is of a conflict between insiders (the already employed) and outsiders (those not employed). Without unionization the insiders have the advantages of training, experience, and ability to 'harass' newcomers. Unionization furthers insiders' advantages. Another European analysis by Layard, Nickell and Jackel (1991) relies on less traditional concepts such as mark-up prices. As discussed below, these European analyses have a much heavier policy content than models in Mankiw and Romer.

Attention also is given to why capital markets may be imperfect. Another form of imperfection involves the alleged cyclicality examined by Haberler in the relationship between price and marginal cost.

Two eminent older Keynesians, Hahn and Solow (1995) produced another, much less successful, effort to revitalize the case for intervention. They only use theoretical models (which are less transparent than those in Mankiw and Romer). Thus, Hahn and Solow too are subject to the prior criticism of inadequate testing. They conclude, 'But whatever the answer, imperfect information is not of itself an argument for inaction' (p. 152). This seems at best an ex cathedra argument for supporting active policy. It does not even address the question of how much activity is feasible. Their case, moreover, is not helped by the strategy employed. The bulk of their book develops a series of difficult-to-comprehend models in which instability arises and can be cured by the right policy. These models have the drawbacks of lack of clear difference in substance between those in Mankiw and Romer and considerably lesser clarity.

Snowdon, Vane and Wynarczyk's survey of the work notes the work 'has been, until recently heavily biased towards theoretical developments (p. 328), 'yielded numerous elegant theories which are often unrelated' (p. 328), and has not produced uniform policy conclusions (p. 326). On the last, Snowdon, Vane and Wynarczyk add that '*most*' new Keynesians see a need for government actions for 'coarse-tuning - policies designed to offset or avoid serious macro level problems' (p. 326). (Coarse tuning was Lindbeck's term for limited intervention, 1993, p. 154.) At least as defined by Mankiw and Romer, the new Keynesians are necessarily too diverse to form a clear approach. At least two of those included in Mankiw and Romer, Solow and Okun, are veteran traditional Keynesians. At least two others, Hall and Taylor, are skeptical about intervention.

The new Keynesians have only demonstrated something that the new classicists never attacked, the existence of more theoretically sound models of market imperfections that cause economic instability. In the worst cases, the success of active intervention depends upon knowing what model characterizes the economy. At best, the theories have established that in principle rational expectations need not by themselves render policy ineffective. The nature and correctability of actual economic instability remain where they always have been, uncertain and controversial.

19. The Policy Failure Alternative

A curiosity here is that so little attention has been given to the possibility that bad regulation is a major cause of instability. Aspects of a bad policy model were (a secondary) part of the early classical approach to instability and at least one new theory revives this approach. The traditional arguments noted how trade union insistence on rigid nominal wages was the major barrier to effective macroeconomic adjustment. Union success was blamed on the willingness of governments to support union activity. While many expressions of this view appeared, that from Mises (1966, pp. 769-779) seems to be the only one still widely available.

This is not a central point of Austrian macroeconomics. The epitomes both by Mises (1966, pp. 538-586) and by Snowdon, Vane and Wynarczk suggest that the crux is a monetary theory involving uneven receipt of the increased money supply that produces incorrect perceptions and distortions in the behavior of real variables. Mises (p. 580) talks of 'the futile attempts to explain the cyclical fluctuations by a nonmonetary doctrine', Snowdon, Vane and Wynarczk (p. 363) view wage and rigidity arguments as elements added on to explain the severity of the great depression. It is presumably the existence of such views that caused

Patinkin to criticize interpreting Keynes as postulating only market imperfections.

Among the newer work, only the European models stressing labor market defects have a strong government failure component. The microeconomic defects of regulation are clear. Skepticism about macroeconomic explanation implies that one cannot and thus should not add macroeconomic justifications to deregulation. However, glimmers of concern do arise. Snowdon, Vane, and Wynarczyk (p. 327) note that the insider-outsider approach produced numerous suggestions to increase labor market flexibility. These include easing up on existing policies such as job security legislation, laws encouraging unionization, and unemployment insurance. However, new programs are proposed to retrain, increase labor mobility particularly by making the housing market function better (without discussing whether this means more aid or removal of government controls), and profit sharing. Lindbeck and Snower (1988, pp. 260-268), Lindbeck (1993, pp. 150-169), and Layard, Nickell, and Jackman all examine some of these alternatives.

Goff (1996) has surveyed the role of regulation in the US economy and attempted to measure its impact. Such a process is hindered by lack of a clear measure of the extent of regulation. Goff, therefore, employed a standard method for dealing with the problem, statistically generating an artificial measure, that is, the weighted function of observable indicators such as that perennial - the size of *The Federal Register*, the US government's report on its new proposed and adopted regulations, the budgets of regulatory agencies, the ratio of lawyers to engineers and scientists in industry, litigation and state government employment. Given this index, Goff seeks to test whether changes in regulation affected performance. His tests are avowedly simple. He examines the association between changes in the trend in key measures of macroeconomic activity are correlated with increasing regulation. He is well aware that other forces may be at work, but at the simple level at which he worked, he can only introduce two alternative variables, oil prices and non-defense government spending. In any case, he concludes that regulation reduced growth in gross national (sic) product by 0.9 percentage points.

20. Conclusions

The present discussion has argued that considerable debate prevails in macroeconomics about the nature of economic instability and whether governments can act to counteract them. The policies advocated range from ones that heavily limit government flexibility to those that encourage extensive action including and possibly centering on regulation of individual industries. What seems to be the 'moderate' position at the end of the twentieth century is that governments should cautiously alter monetary and fiscal policy in response to changing circumstances. Caution is the minimum response necessitated by new classical criticisms. Market regulation remains suspect by both new classicists and the believers in the neoclassical synthesis. This suspicion arises from the presence of much evidence of the drawbacks of regulation and the absence of evidence that regulation is stabilizing. Efforts over six decades have only strengthened these doubts.

21. Background to the Chapter

The author is a specialist in applied microeconomics who examines macroeconomics mainly to determine its relevance to efforts to justify control of individual markets on macroeconomic grounds. My research activity is devoted entirely to study of markets and their regulation. This article is heavily influenced by the universal occurrence of severe government failure in everything that I have studied. My teaching included a long period teaching a graduate theory course. All this has required persistent examination of the literature in microeconomic theory. I have reviewed macroeconomics to evaluate proposals to regulate energy markets in the interest of macroeconomic stability. Prior writings that caused the invitation to write this article were inspired by recognition that energy economists were accepting macroeconomic arguments for intervention that were not well supported in the macroeconomic literature.

I am Professor Emeritus of Mineral Economics, College of Earth and Mineral Sciences, The Pennsylvania State University, University Park Pa, 16802. Since I was born in 1934, I am too young to have first hand knowledge of the 1930s, but old enough to be aware of prior work inadequately considered by the new Keynesians and their inspirations among the new industrial organization theorists.

My examination of literature, in any case, is selective. This article extends research undertaken for my 1994 book, *Regulation and Economic Analysis*. My starting points were the then current editions of several undergraduate texts in macroeconomics, the very advanced survey by Blanchard and Fischer, and four anthologies noted in the text of major articles on macroeconomic. This suggested much additional reading including a return to some old favorites remaining in my personal library. This reading has unearthed far more references than can readily be mastered. A referee alerted me to a particularly valuable survey of the work (Snowdon, Vane and Wynarczyk) and European work on imperfect labor markets.

22. Bibliographic Note

Thousands of books and articles on these issues have appeared. The books include many comprehensive textbooks and a few more specialized surveys.

Despite their mass, no single book fully covers all the issues or adequately cites the literature.

The articles appear in the many journals directed at professional economists, the various periodicals produced by banks, particularly the regional Federal Reserve Banks in the United States, and symposium volumes originating from among others again the regional Federal Reserve Banks and research institutes such as Brookings and the National Bureau of Economic Research. Numerous anthologies, some devoted to a topic and others to a specific author, have appeared. Some major articles have multiple incarnations. Among the participants in the debates for whom anthologies of relevant writings exist are Keynes, Hicks, Samuelson, Tobin, Friedman and Lucas.

Each item consulted adds references to more publications. The listings here are deliberately limited. I have selected anthologies, texts and treatises that collectively include or discuss a large part of macroeconomics from the 1930 to the 1990s. Much of the material contained is not explicitly cited. Thus, while some classics are not listed, they often are contained in what is cited. Another limitation is that no pretense was made exhaustively to examine the many texts designed for the second (in US academic jargon, intermediate) undergraduate course in macroeconomic theory. My citations of texts consist of two long extant ones that are frequently cited and one, recommended by a colleague, that I found a good alternative; the citations whenever possible are to the latest edition of which I was aware rather than to the edition actually examined.

In the process of preparing my 1994 book, I began compiling a master bibliography of works cited in summary volumes on microeconomics and macroeconomics consulted. Part of the effort was to overcome the irritating failure of many authors to provide an integrated bibliography. My bibliography became unmanageably massive as I extended its reach. The germane literature in macroeconomics alone is too extensive to treat adequately and the literature on modern industrial organization, while smaller, is still overwhelming.

The books cited here include anthologies that contain at a minimum important parts of the literature and at their best helpful guides to the rest of the literature. Miller alone of these books has a unified bibliography. Mankiw and Romer have an extensive bibliography (broken into separate parts by topic areas), but it falls far short of presenting everything cited in the book. Among surveys, Snowdon, Vane and Wynarczk uniquely provides a unified and extensive bibliography. Blanchard and Fischer prepare separate bibliographies for each chapter. Even when a bibliography exists, it does not necessarily provide all the critical information. In particular, often the reprinting in anthologies is not noted. Generally, I have provided both the original citation and at least one of the reprints of which I was aware for articles. However, I have not attempted to examine every writer's collected works. The main exception is Samuelson. So much of what is cited comes from inaccessible original sources such as symposium volumes that his collected works are the best source.

Bibliography on Law and Macroeconomics (0620)

Akerlof, George A. and Yellen, Janet L. (1985), 'A Near-Rational Model of the Business Cycle with Wage and Price Inertia', **100** *Quarterly Journal of Economics*, supplement, 176-213. Reprinted in Mankiw and Romer (1991), vol. 1, 43-58.

Allen, R.G.D. (1956), *Mathematical Economics*, London, Macmillan and Co. and New York, St Martin's Press

Bain, Joe S. (1956), *Barriers to New Competition: Their Character and Consequences in Manufacturing Industries*, Cambridge, MA, Harvard University Press.

Bain, Joe S. (1968), *Industrial Organization*, 2nd edn, New York, John S. Wiley & Sons.

Barro, Robert J. (1972), 'A Theory of Monopolistic Price Adjustment', **39** *Review of Economic Studies*, (January), 17-26.

Blanchard, Olivier Jean, and Fischer, Stanley (1989), *Lectures on Macroeconomics*, Cambridge , MA, The MIT Press.

Bork, Robert H. (1978), *The Antitrust Paradox, a Policy at War with Itself*, New York, Basic Books.

Bradley, Robert L., Jr. (1995), *Oil, Gas and Government.: The U.S. Experience*, Lanham, Rowman & Littlefield.

Bryant, John B. (1983), 'A Simple Rational-Expectations Keynes-Type Model', **98** *Quarterly Journal of Economics*, (August), 525-528. Reprinted in Mankiw and Romer (1991), vol. 2, 25-29.

Burstein, M. L. (1963), *Money*, Cambridge, MA, Schenkman Publishing.

Calomiris, Charles. W. (1993), 'Financial Factors in the Great Depression', **7** *Journal of Economic Perspectives*, (Spring), 61-85.

Carlton, Dennis W. and Perloff, Jeffrey M. (1994), *Modern Industrial Organization*, 2nd edn, New York, Harper Collins.

Cato Institute (1997), *Cato Handbook for Congress: 105th Congress*, Washington, DC, The Cato Institute.

Clower, Robert W. (1965), 'The Keynesian Counter Revolution: An Appraisal', in Hahn, Frank and Brechling, F. (eds), *The Theory of Interest Rates*, London, Macmillan. Excerpted in Clower (ed.) (1969), 270-297.

Clower, Robert (ed.) (1969), *Monetary Theory*, Harmondsworth, Penguin Books.

Dornbusch, Rudiger and Fischer, Stanley (1993), *Macroeconomics*, 6th edn, New York, McGraw-Hill Book Company.

Fellner, William and Haley, Bernard F. (eds) (1951), *Readings in the Theory of Income Distribution*, Philadelphia, Blakiston.

Fischer, Stanley (1977), 'Long Term Contracts, Rational Expectations, and the Optimal Money Supply', **85** *Journal of Political Economy*, (February), 191-206. Reprinted in Lucas and Sargent (1981), 261-275 and in Mankiw and Romer (1991), vol. 1, 216-231.

Fisher, Franklin M. (1991), 'Organizing Industrial Organization: Reflections on the *Handbook of Industrial Organization*', *Brookings Papers on Economic Activity: Microeconomics 1991*, 201-240. (Comments, 226-238)

Friedman, Milton (1948), 'A Monetary and Fiscal Framework for Economic Stability', **38** *American Economic Review,* (June), 245-264. Reprinted in Friedman (1953), 117-156 and in Lutz and Mints (1951), 369-393.

Friedman, Milton (1953), *Essays in Positive Economics*, Chicago, University of Chicago Press.

Friedman, Milton (1956),'The Quantity Theory of Money: A Restatement', in Milton Friedman (ed.), *Studies in the Quantity Theory of Money*, Chicago, University of Chicago Press. Reprinted in Friedman (1969), 51-67 and Friedman (1987), 285-303.

Friedman, Milton (1968), 'The Role of Monetary Policy', **58** *American Economic Review*, (March), 1-17. Reprinted in Friedman (1987), 387-403.

Friedman, Milton (1969), *The Optimum Quantity of Money and Other Essays*, Chicago, Aldine.

Friedman, Milton (1970), 'A Theoretical Framework for Monetary Analysis', **78** *Journal of Political Economy*, (March/April). Reprinted in Gordon, Robert J. (ed.), *Milton Friedman's Monetary Framework*, Chicago, University of Chicago Press.

Friedman, Milton (Leube, Kurt R., ed.) (1987), *The Essence of Friedman*, Stanford, Hoover Institution Stanford University.

Friedman, Milton and Schwartz, Anna J. (1963), *A Monetary History of the United States, 1867-1960*, Princeton, Princeton University Press.

Friedman, Milton and Schwartz, Anna J. (1982), *Monetary Trends in the United States and the United Kingdom*, Chicago, University of Chicago Press.

Fudenberg, Drew and Tirole, Jean (1991), *Game Theory*, Cambridge, MA, The MIT Press.

Goff, Brian (1996), *Regulation and Macroeconomic Performance*, Boston, Kluwer Academic Publishers.

Gordon, Richard L. (1994), *Regulation and Economic Analysis, A Critique over Two Centuries*, Boston and Dordrecht, Kluwer Academic Publishing.

Gordon, Robert Aaron, and Klein, L.R. (eds) (1965), *Readings in Business Cycles*, Homewood, Richard D. Irwin.

Gordon, Robert J. (1990), 'What is New-Keynesian Economics?', **28** *Journal of Economic Literature*, (September), 1125-1171.

Gordon, Robert J. (1993), *Macroeconomics*, 6th edn, Glenview, Scott-Foresman.

Greenwald, Bruce and Stiglitz, Joseph (1993), 'New and Old Keynesians', **7** *Journal of Economic Perspectives*, (Winter), 23-44.

Haberler, Gottfried (ed.) (1944), *Readings in Business Cycle Theory*, Homewood, Richard D. Irwin.

Haberler, Gottfried (1957), *Prosperity and Depression: A Theoretical Analysis of Cyclical Movements*, new and revised (fourth) edition, Cambridge, MA, Harvard University Press, 1964. (First three editions 1937, 1939, and 1941 Geneva, League of Nations.

Hahn, Frank and Solow, Robert M. (1995), *A Critical Essay in Modern Macroeconomic Theory*, Cambridge, MA, The MIT Press.

Hayek, Friedrich A. (1945). 'The Uses of Knowledge in Society', **35** *American Economic Review*, (September), 519-530. Reprinted in Hayek (1948), 77-91 and Hayek (1984), 211-224.

Hayek, Friedrich A. (1948), *Individualism and Economic Order*, Chicago, Ill., University of Chicago Press.

Hayek, Friedrich A. (Nishiyama, Chiaki and Leube, Kurt R., eds) (1984), *The Essence of Hayek*, Stanford, Hoover Institution Stanford University.

Hicks, John R. (1937), 'Mr. Keynes and the Classics', **5** *Econometrica*, (April), 147-159. Reprinted in Fellner and Haley (1951), 461-476 and Hicks, J.R. (1982), *Money Interest and Wages, Collected Essays on Economic Theory*, vol. II, Cambridge, MA, Harvard University Press and Oxford, Basil Blackwell, 100-115.

Hicks, J.R. (1950), *A Contribution to the Theory of the Trade Cycle*, Oxford, Oxford University Press.

Houthakker, H.S. (1957), 'Can Speculators Forecast Prices?', **39** *The Review of Economics and Statistics*, (May), 143-151.

Hume, David (1985), *Essays: Moral, Political, and Literary*, Indianapolis, Liberty Classics.

Kelman, Mark (1993), 'Could Lawyers Stop Recessions? Speculations on Law and Macroeconomics', **45** *Stanford Law Review*, (May), 1215-1310.

Keynes, John Maynard (1936), *The General Theory of Employment, Interest and Money*, New York, Harcourt Brace and London, Macmillan and Company. (Available in the Royal Economics Society collected works series.)

Kindleberger, Charles P. (1986), *The World in Depression, 1929-1939*, Berkeley, University of California Press.

King, Robert G. (1993), 'Will the New Keynesian Macroeconomics Resurrect the IS-LM Model?', **7** *Journal of Economic Perspectives*, (Winter), 67-82.

Klevorick, Alvin K. (1991), 'Directions and Trends in Industrial Economics: A Review Essay on the *Handbook of Industrial Organization*', in *Brookings Papers on Economic Activity: Microeconomics 1991*, 241-280 (Comments, 265-279).

Kreps, David M. (1990), *A Course in Microeconomic Theory*, Princeton, Princeton University Press.

Krouse, Clement G. (1990), *Theory of Industrial Competition*, Cambridge, MA, Basil Blackwell.

Kuhn, Thomas (1970), *The Structure of Scientific Revolutions*, 2nd edn, enlarged, Chicago, University of Chicago Press.

Layard, Richard, Nickell, Stephen and Jackman, R. (1991), *Unemployment: Macroeconomic Performance and the Labor Market*, Oxford, Oxford University Press.

Leijonhufvud, Axel (1968), *On Keynesian Economics and the Economics of Keynes, A Study in Monetary Theory*, New York, Oxford University Press.

Lindbeck, Assar (1993), *Unemployment and Macroeconomics*, Cambridge, MA, The MIT Press

Lindbeck, Assar and Snower, Dennis (1988), *The Insider-Outsider Theory of Employment and Unemployment*, Cambridge, MA, The MIT Press.

Lipsey, Richard G. (1960), 'The Relationship between Unemployment and the Rate of Change of Money Wages in the United Kingdom 1862-1957: A Further Analysis', **27** *Economica*, (February), 1-31. Reprinted in Gordon and Klein (1965), 457-487.

Lucas, Robert, E., Jr (1972a), 'Econometric Testing of the Natural Rate Hypothesis', in Eckstein, Otto (ed.), *The Econometrics of Price Determination Conference*, Washington, DC, U.S. Federal Reserve System Board of Governors, 50-59. Reprinted in Lucas (1981), 90-103.

Lucas, Robert, E., Jr (1972b), 'Expectations and the Neutrality of Money', **4:2** *Journal of Economic Theory*, (April), 103-124. Reprinted in Lucas (1981), 66-89.

Lucas, Robert E., Jr (1973), 'Some International Evidence on Output-Inflation Tradeoffs',**63** *American Economic Review*, (June), 326-334. Reprinted in Lucas (1981), 131-145.

Lucas, Robert E., Jr (1975), 'An Equilibrium Model of the Business Cycle', **83** *Journal of Political Economy*, (December), 1113-1144. Reprinted in Lucas (1981), 179-214.

Lucas, Robert E., Jr (1976), 'Econometric Policy Evaluation: A Critique', in Brunner, Karl and Meltzer, Allan (eds), *The Phillips Curve and Labor Markets*, *Carnegie-Rochester Conference Series on Public Policy*, vol. 1, 19-46. Reprinted in Lucas (1981), 104-130.

Lucas, Robert E., Jr (1977), 'Understanding Business Cycles', in Brunner, Karl and Meltzer, Allan (eds), *Stabilization of the Domestic and International Economy*, *Carnegie-Rochester Conference Series on Public Policy*, 7-29. Reprinted in Lucas, (1981), 215-239.

Lucas, Robert E., Jr (1981a), *Studies in Business Cycle Theory*, Cambridge, MA, The MIT Press.

Lucas, Robert E., Jr (1981b), 'Tobin and Monetarism: A Review Article', **19** *Journal of Economic Literature*, (June), 558-567.

Lucas, Robert E., Jr (1987), *Models of Business Cycles*, Oxford, Basil Blackwell.

Lucas, Robert E., Jr and Sargent, Thomas J. (eds) (1981), *Rational Expectations and Practice*, Minneapolis, Minn., University of Minnesota Press.

Lutz, Friedrich A. and Mints, Lloyd W. (eds) (1951), *Readings in Monetary Theory*, Philadelphia, Blakiston (subsequently Homewood, Richard D. Irwin).

McChesney, Fred S. and Shughard, William F., II (eds) (1995), *The Causes and Consequences of Antitrust*, Chicago, University of Chicago Press.

Mankiw, N. Gregory (1985), 'Small Menu Costs and Large Business Cycles: A Macroeconomic Model of Monopoly', **100** *Quarterly Journal of Economics*, (May), 529-537. Reprinted in Mankiw and Romer (1991), vol. 1, 29-42.

Mankiw, N. Gregory (1989), 'Real Business Cycles: A New Keynesian Perspective', **3** *Journal of Economic Perspectives*, (Summer), 79-90.

Mankiw, N. Gregory (1990), 'A Quick Refresher Course in Macroeconomics', **28** *Journal of Economic Literature*, (December), 1645-1660.

Mankiw, N. Gregory and Romer, David (eds) (1991), *New Keynesian Economics*, 2 vol., Cambridge, MA, The MIT Press.

Margo, Robert A. (1993), 'Employment and Unemployment in the 1930s', **7** *Journal of Economic Perspectives*, (Spring), 41-59.

Mas-Colell, Andreu, Whinston, Michael D. and Green, Jerry R. (1995), *Microeconomic Theory*, New York, Oxford University Press.

Mason, Edward S. (1957), *Economic Concentration and the Monopoly Problem*. Cambridge, MA, Harvard University Press.

Mason, Edward S. (1982), 'The Harvard Department of Economics from the Beginning to World War II', **97** *Quarterly Journal of Economics*, (August), 383-433.

Means, Gardiner (1939), *The Structure of the American Economy*, Washington, National Resources Council.

Means, Gardiner (1972), 'The Administered-Price Thesis Reconfirmed', **62** *American Economic Review*, (June), 292-306.

Miller, J. Preston (ed.) (1994), *The Rational Expectations Revolution: Readings from the Front Line*, Cambridge, MA, The MIT Press.

Mises, Ludwig von (1966), *Human Action: A Treatise on Economics*. 3rd rev. edn, Chicago, Henry Regnery Company. (Now published by Contemporary Books Inc., Chicago)

Modigliani, Franco (1944), 'Liquidity Preference and the Theory of Interest and Money', **12** *Econometrica*, (January), 45-88. Reprinted in Lutz and Mints (1951), 186-239.

Okun, Arthur (1975), 'Inflation: Its Mechanics and Welfare Costs', *Brookings Papers on Economic Activity* #2, 351-401. Reprinted in Mankiw and Romer (1991), vol. 2, 327-375.

Patinkin, Don (1965), *Money, Interest and Prices*, 2nd edn, New York, Harper and Row. (Available minus appendixes from MIT Press)

Peltzman, Sam (1991), '*The Handbook of Industrial Organization*: A Review Article', **99** *Journal of Political Economy*, 201-217.

Phillips, A.W. (1950), 'Mechanical Models in Economic Dynamics', **17** *Economica* NS, (#67 August), 283-305.

Phillips, A.W. (1954), 'Stabilization Policy in a Closed Economy', **64** *Economic Journal*, (June), 290-323.

Phillips, A.W. (1956), 'Some Notes on the Estimation of the Time-Forms of Reactions in Interdependent Dynamic Systems', **23** *Economica* NS, (#90 May), 99-113.

Phillips, A.W. (1957), 'Stabilization Policy and the Time Form of Lagged Responses', **47** *Economic Journal*, (June), 265-277. Reprinted in Gordon and Klein (1965), 66-79.

Phillips, A.W. (1958), 'The Relation Between Unemployment and the Rate of Change of Money Wage Rates in the United Kingdom, 1861-1957', **25** *Economica* NS, (Issue # 100 November), 283-299.

Plosser, Charles L. (1989), 'Understanding Real Business Cycles', **3** *Journal of Economic Perspectives*, (Summer), 51-77.

Posner, Richard A. (1976). *Antitrust Law, An Economic Perspective*, Chicago, University of Chicago Press.

Romer, Christina D. (1993), 'The Nation in Depression', **7** *Journal of Economic Perspectives*, (Spring), 19-39.

Romer, David (1993), 'The New Keynesian Synthesis', **7** *Journal of Economic Perspectives*, (Winter), 5-22.

Samuelson, Paul A. (1939), 'Interactions between the Multiplier Analysis and the Principle of Acceleration', **21** *Review of Economic Statistics*, (May), 75-78. Reprinted in Haberler (1944), 261-269 and Samuelson (1966), vol. 2, 1107-1110.

Samuelson, Paul A. (Stiglitz, Joseph E., ed.) (1966), *The Collected Scientific Papers of Paul A. Samuelson*, , 2 vols, Cambridge, MA, The MIT Press.

Samuelson, Paul A. (Merton, Robert C., ed.) (1972), *The Collected Scientific Papers of Paul A. Samuelson*, , vol. 3, Cambridge, MA, The MIT Press.

Samuelson, Paul A. (Nagatani, Hiroaki and Crowley, Kate, eds) (1977), *The Collected Scientific Papers of Paul A. Samuelson*, vol. 4, Cambridge, MA, The MIT Press.

Samuelson, Paul A. (Crowley, Kate, ed.) (1986), *The Collected Scientific Papers of Paul A. Samuelson*, vol. 5, Cambridge, MA, The MIT Press.

Samuelson, Paul A. and Solow, Robert M. (1960), 'Analytic Aspects of Antiinflation Policy', **50** *American Economic Review Papers and Proceedings*, (May), 177-194. Reprinted in Samuelson (1966), vol. 2, 1336-1353.

Sargent, Thomas J. (1973), 'Rational Expectations, the Real Rate of Interest and the Natural Rate of Unemployment', *Brookings Papers on Economic Activity*, 429-480. Reprinted in Lucas and Sargent (1981), 159-198.

Sargent, Thomas J. (1976a), 'A Classical Macroeconomic Model for the United States', **84** *Journal of Political Economy*, 207-237. Reprinted in Lucas and Sargent (1981), 521-551.

Sargent, Thomas J. (1976b), 'The Observational Equivalence of Natural and Unnatural Rate Theories of Macroeconomics', **84** *Journal of Political Economy*, 631-640. Reprinted in Lucas and Sargent (1981), 553-562.

Sargent, Thomas and Wallace, Neil (1975), '"Rational Expectations", The Optimal Monetary Instrument and the Optimal Money Supply Rule', **83** *Journal of Political Economy*, (April), 241-254. Reprinted in Lucas and Sargent (1981), 215-228.

Sargent, Thomas and Wallace, Neil (1976), 'Rational Expectations and the Theory of Economic Policy', **2** *Journal of Monetary Economics* (previously Federal Reserve Bank of Minneapolis Studies in Monetary Economics 2). Reprinted in Lucas and Sargent (1981), 199-213.

Sawyer, Malcolm C. (1991), 'Post-Keynesian Macroeconomics', in Greenaway, David, Blarney, Michael and Stewart, Ian (eds), *Companion to Contemporary Economics*, London, Routledge, 184-206.

Scherer, F.M. and Ross, David (1990), *Industrial Market Structure and Economic Performance*, 3rd edn Boston, Houghton-Mifflin Co.

Schmalensee, Richard and Willig, Robert D. (eds) (1989), *Handbook of Industrial Organization*, 2 vols, Amsterdam, North-Holland (Elsevier).

Slutsky, Eugen (1937), 'The Summation of Random Causes as the Source of Cyclic Processes', **5** *Econometrica*, (April), 105-146.

Smithies, Arthur and Butters, J. Keith (eds) (1955), *Readings in Fiscal Policy*, Homewood, Richard D. Irwin.

Snowdon, Brian, Vane, Howard, and Wynarczyk, Peter (1995), *A Modern Guide to Macroeconomics: An Introduction to Competing Schools of Thought*, Aldershot, Edward Elgar.

Spulber, Daniel F. (1989), *Regulation and Markets*, Cambridge, MA, The MIT Press.

Stadler, George W. (1994), 'Real Business Cycles', **32** *Journal of Economic Literature*, (December), 1750-1783.

Stigler, George J. (1988a), *Memoirs of an Unregulated Economist*, New York, Basic Books.

Stigler, George J. (ed.) (1988b), *Chicago Studies in Political Economy*, Chicago, University of Chicago Press.

Temin, Peter (1989), *Lessons from the Great Depression: The Lionel Robbins Lectures for 1989*, Cambridge, MA, The MIT Press.

Temin, Peter (1993), 'Transmission of the Great Depression', **7** *Journal of Economic Perspectives*, 87-102.

Tirole, Jean (1988), *The Theory of Industrial Organization*, Cambridge, MA, The MIT Press.

Tobin, James (1993), 'Price Flexibility and Output Stability: An Old Keynesian View', **7** *Journal of Economic Perspectives*, 45-65.

Viscusi, W. Kip, Vernon, John M. and Harrington, Joseph E., Jr (1995), *Economics of Regulation and Antitrust*, Cambridge, MA, The MIT Press.

Woglom, Geoffrey (1988), *Modern Macroeconomics*, Glenview, Scott, Foresman.

0630
OTHER SOCIOLOGICAL APPROACHES

Ian R. Macneil
Wigmore Professor of Law
Northwestern University

Abstract

The following aspects of law and economics important to understanding comparisons to be made to other sociological approaches are set out: (1) the fundaments of economic behavior; (2) the many worlds of law and economics; (3) the unity of law and economics; and (4) Posnerian law and economics. Other sociological approaches to law, particularly American, are described: (1) case-law research as a sociological approach to law; (2) approaches based on particular theories; (3) empirical sociological approaches generally and as compared with law and economics, particularly Posnerian law and economics; and (4) empiricism as the meeting ground between law and economics and other sociological approaches, a meeting ground in which empirical product rather than competing theories may be the most important aspect. Finally, the positions of law and economics and other sociological approaches as competitors are explored
JEL classification: K00
Keywords: Case-Law, Empirical, Law and Economics, Posner, Sociology

1. Introduction

Any comparison between law and economics and other sociological approaches is complicated by the fact that there is neither a single law and economics approach nor a single noneconomic sociological approach to law. Moreover, when law and economics takes a serious empirical turn it may for all practical purposes be indistinguishable from empirical noneconomic sociology (see Sections 10 and 11). To deal with these problems of diversity and to make comparison feasible in the small compass of this part, I shall focus on what may be called the Posnerian approach to law and economics (see Section 5). (There is a danger in this, as it is all too easy improperly to equate law and economics with the Chicago School, and particularly Posnerian, economics, see Donohue, 1997. There is, however, no intention of doing so here.) On the sociological side I shall range somewhat more broadly (see Section B).

Part A treats a number of aspects of law and economics important to the comparisons to be made to other sociological approaches: (1) the fundaments of economic behavior; (2) the many worlds of law and economics; (3) the unity of law and economics; and (4) Posnerian law and economics.

Part B describes other American sociological approaches to law: (1) case-law research as a sociological approach to law; (2) approaches based on particular theories; (3) empirical sociological approaches generally and as compared with law and economics; and (4) empiricism as the meeting ground.

Finally, Part C considers law and economics and other sociological approaches as competitors.

A. Law and Economics

2. The Fundaments of Economic Behavior

To understand law and economics it is essential to understand what its practitioners mean by economic behavior.

First, economic behavior is the behavior of individuals, not collective behavior as such. Second, it is behavior that individuals choose from among available alternatives. It is thus distinguishable from behavior over which an individual literally has no control at the time it occurs, as for example where an person with an unfastened seatbelt is thrown against a windshield in a head-on automobile accident. Third and finally, it is behavior an individual chooses by somehow assessing (by no means necessarily consciously) that the benefit of the behavior to the individual exceeds its costs. The latter aspect is so vital to economics that economists have sanctified it by adding an appealing adjective, *rational*.

This adjective is not intended in economics to mean reasonable - it's ordinary usage - and its meaning in law and economics is unclear. (Ronald Coase, 1993, p. 98, cautions against 'any economic concept that includes the word "rational"'.) Nonetheless, its repeated use by economists has led to such analysis being called rational choice theory. (It is by no means clear what this third element - with or without an adjective - adds to the second. When an individual chooses to behave in a specified manner, no matter how self-destructive, bizarre, or even utterly mad that behavior may appear to others, the individual obviously at that instant perceives the benefits as exceeding the costs. Only *un*chosen behavior, that is, beyond any control by the individual, could be otherwise.)

It is also important to point out what law and economists typically do *not* mean by economic behavior. *Economic* is not limited to matters relating to the production, distribution and consumption of material goods and services, the common usage of the term. Typical law and economists most emphatically do not mean that economic analysis is possible only of behavior relating to material matters. Thus, as used in law and economics, no one, economist or otherwise, can gainsay that rational choice theory *can* be applied to *any* subject about which people make choices. Failure to recognize this can lead to confusion and misplaced criticism of law and economics (see Cotterell, 1995, particularly pp. 347-348, 357 n.2). To avoid such confusion *economics* is here limited to mean rational choice theory, and never used in its common-usage sense.

One of the many consequences of these characteristics of rational choice theory is that it cannot recognize *within its theoretical structure* any kind of relationship among people other than that of competition. Thus the model epitomizes Mrs Thatcher's alleged dictum, 'There is no society, only individuals'. (This is not to say, of course, that the model cannot be or is not used to analyze behavior in what even law and economists - but only while stepping outside their model - would recognize as relationships, including those in which they recognize altruistic elements. Again, of course, the model can also be used to analyze an individual's choice among his or her own competing desires, desires which may impinge differentially on relations with others. This is not, however, a recognition of relations *within the theoretical structure of the model*, such as is typically found in other sociological approaches.)

3. The Many Worlds of Law and Economics

In spite of the dominance of rational choice theory, any given work in law and economics may differ from another in at least any of the following somewhat overlapping respects:

a. Normativism and positivism: ranging from insistence that economic analysis is nothing but positivist prediction to full recognition that it is necessarily normative from start to finish.
b. Objective of analysis: determining (1) Pareto-superior positions, (2) Kaldor-Hicks efficiency, (3) wealth maximization, (4) distributional effects, or (5) some combination.
c. Rational behavior: meaning of:
   (1) Nature: ranging from *any* chosen behavior to requiring inclusion of varying degrees of knowledge, thoughtfulness, and reasonableness (rationality in the usual sense of the word) in the behavior;
   (2) Consistency of behavior: varying assumptions of consistency of behavior over time;
   (3) Boundedness: accepting or not recognizing boundedness of rationality;
   (4) Consistency of use of the term throughout the work in question.
d. Transaction costs: recognition and assessment of impact: (1) ignored, (2) recognized but explicitly excluded, (3) analyzed as supplemental to

theoretical analysis, (4) entire focus on transaction costs, (5) treatment ranging from casual to systematic empiricism.

e. Relations, recognition as such: ranging from no recognition of relations other than competition among individuals to primary focus on relations in the institutional school of law and economics (see Section 2).
f. Empiricism: ranging from entirely theoretical to heavily empirical.
g. Distributional effects: (1) ignored, (2) recognized but explicitly excluded on varying grounds, such as ceteris paribus, unimportance, or on the grounds that they should be dealt with apart from the subject being analyzed, for example through general taxation and welfare, (3) treated as essential aspect of analysis.
h. Individualism: attitudes towards: ranging from strongly individualistic to a variety of non-individualistic positions.
i. Market-solutions: attitudes towards: ranging from pro-market to neutral to anti-market (the latter being rare).
j. Politico-legal goals: ranging widely over the political spectrum with varying ranges of obscurity and clarity.
k. Power: from ignoring to considering power either as a benefit individuals seek that affects choices or as a social subject requiring analysis per se.

Some of the diversity of these many worlds is shown by De Geest (1995), who, however, suggests a unity greater than that perceived by the authors of this part.

4. The Unity of Law and Economics

In spite of the foregoing, three factors bring considerable unity to law and economics.

First is the centrality of rational choice theory (see Section 2) with its foundation in the individual. Second, the field remains an area dominated by theoretical and deductive, rather than empirical and inductive, analysis, although the latter seems to be growing in importance. See Donohue (1997); Shelanski and Klein (1995). Third, at least in the United States, there is a dominant school of law and economics, epitomized by the work of Richard Posner (see generally Posner, 1992), to which I now turn.

5. Posnerian Law and Economics

The Posnerian school falls at the following locations on the spectra set out in Subsection 3:

a. Normativism and positivism: focuses on allegedly positive prediction and typically claims great formal predictive power, even as it fails to recognize limitations in rational choice theory that require empirical rather than formal proof of conclusions;
b. Objective of analysis: seeks to promote efficiency and wealth maximization;
c. Rational behavior: meaning of: is often unclear on the operational meaning of rationality;
d. Transaction costs: treatment is often cursory and may be inconsistent with the Coase theorem as now generally understood;
e. Relations, recognition as such: rejects any idea of relations, other than those of competition among individuals (see Section 2.);
f. Empiricism: empirical work may or may not be done, as it is unnecessary in light of claims to positive prediction by the theoretical model;
g. Distributional effects: treats distributional effects as beyond the pale; (Posner himself has dealt at considerable length with distributional issues such as measuring inequality, redistribution through liability rules, and taxation, see Posner, 1992, pp. 455-515. Nonetheless it is difficult to find Posnerian analyses of particular subjects where treatment of distributional issues goes beyond, at most, a slighting acknowledgement that the only justification for ignoring the result produced by rational choice theory would be to redistribute wealth.)
h. Individualism: attitudes towards: has a strong individualist bias, including large organizations within the concept of individuals except when analyzing internal operations of an organization.
i. Market-solutions: attitudes towards: favors market-solutions; opposes not only government regulation but also any social governance other than that of competing individuals;
j. Politico-legal goals: is often accused of right wing political biases. To paraphrase Posner: 'Suspicion persists that [law and economics] owes a lot more to visceral [right]-wing political preferences than to any body of theory.' (Posner, 1995, p. 269);
k. Power: ignores power either as a benefit individuals seek that affects choices or as a social subject requiring analysis per se.

B. Other Sociological Approaches

For an extensive treatment of law and the social sciences see Lipson and Wheeler (1986); respecting law and sociology see Arnaud et al. (1993).

6. Introduction

In contrast to rational choice theory, noneconomic sociological approaches treat collective behavior or relationships rather than focusing on individuals as such. They may or may not pay much attention to choice, viewed either individually or collectively. They may or may not pay much attention to the idea of benefits and costs in choosing. And they may or may not pay much attention either to vague concepts of rationality as found in economic analysis or to rationality in the ordinary sense of reasonableness.

Given their social orientation, noneconomic sociological approaches often recognize and focus heavily on social, as distinguished from individualistic, concepts. Thus, for example, in his excellent article comparing law and economics and sociological approaches to law, Cotterell mentions among others such concepts as: law, social change, legal relationships, social relationships, solidarity, general social trends, enduring patterns, mediating forces, culture, broad movements, legal modernity and more specifically, 'power and governmentality,' (Foucault), 'self-referential systems of communication' (Luhmann), 'the "life world" and the public sphere' (Habermas), and other concepts developed by such diverse scholars as Marx, Tönnies, Durkheim, Weber, Parsons, Neumann and Unger (Cotterell 1995). Althusser, Gramsci and Gurvitch would have been worthy additions to this list.

Like economics, sociology means many things, and a wide variety of sociological approaches to law other than law and economics exist, far more indeed than in the world of law and economics itself. (These include law and anthropology, untreated here only because it has its own treatment in 0640. As Cotterell says, '[In] address[ing] the complexities of law's relations to culture ... it seems that no useful line can now be drawn between anthropological and sociological research' (Cotterell, 1995, p. 350). For example, Roscoe Pound advanced the idea of sociological jurisprudence early in this century, and that concept has been important to the study of law ever since. Even legal philosophers one does not usually think of in such terms may consider themselves sociological. For example, as Posner (1995, p. 279, n. 2) points out, H.L.A. Hart described his *The Concept of Law* as 'an essay in descriptive sociology'. Jurisprudence, sociological or otherwise, is not, however, what is generally meant by law and sociology, and I shall address it no further. (We thus omit consideration of such important works as Black, 1989.) Instead, from among the many possibilities in this complex world of law and sociology, focus here is on three kinds of sociological approaches to law: case-law research, particular-theory approaches, and empiricism with little or no theoretical base.

7. Case-law Research as a Sociological Approach to Law

The term 'case-law research' is used here to mean research aimed at finding out what judicial and/or administrative decision-makers have done respecting particular issues. (Case-law research may be and often is, of course, conducted in connection with more formal approaches of various kinds, such as law and economics and various critical theories. The discussion following is limited largely to case-law research not so connected, although much of what is said applies to such instances as well.)

It is seldom, if ever, recognized in academia that - at least as conducted in the United States - ordinary case-law research is a form of sociological study of law. This omission calls for explanation given that such research is by far the most common form of American legal study - both within and without the academy. In spite of the proliferation of academic and quasi-academic journals it may safely be assumed that the majority of such research is done in the day-to-day world of lawyers and judges, administrators and legislators, and their various staff members. Nonetheless, even with the exclusion of such work of the real world, academic case-law research, that in law reviews, other legal periodicals, and monographs of various kinds overwhelms in volume all the more formal scholarly approaches put together.

In the light of this dominance, it is worth pausing to consider what case-law research is in the American context, what are its advantages and disadvantages as a form of sociology, and the general ignoring of such work as a sociological approach.

Nature of American Case-Law Research

The vast bulk of American case-law research focuses on opinions of appellate federal and state courts, although there are important exceptions, particularly where the law is much involved with administrative agencies, as in taxation, various kinds of regulation and government procurement.

The day has long since passed, if it ever really existed, when researchers into American case-law thought they would find Langdellian scientific principles operating in the cases. (There is, of course, an important exception, namely researchers who hold to some theory such as the implementation of principles of efficiency by common law courts or particular theories of oppression characterizing various critical approaches.) The Realist movement, if it did nothing else, legitimized examining cases to see what the courts really were doing, rather than just what they were saying, in laying down the rules of law. (One should properly say re-legitimizing following the long post-Civil War period of relative dominance of the formal style, see Llewellyn, 1960. This is not to say that in such research logic-chopping based exclusively on words is not only commonplace, but probably a good deal more common than more purposive analyses. Nonetheless, the better work - whether of practitioner, bench or academic - never slights the latter.

Case-law research of this kind is what Twining (1974) has called a 'method of detail'. And it is often, although by no means always, also a kind of 'thick description' (Geertz, 1973, ch. 1), as summarized by Cotterell (1995, p. 350):

> Thick description moves social interpretation away from a search for abstractions that attempt to explain complex patterns of actions in terms of a minimum of rationally organized principles related to a general theory. It seeks rather a portrayal of complexity in all its ambiguity and richness. Geertz remarks that the study of mankind often involves substituting complex pictures of social phenomena for simple ones while trying to keep the persuasive character of the earlier simpler ones. (Geertz, 1973, pp. 33-34)

The work of Childres and Spitz (1972) on the parol evidence rule illustrates how purposive case-law analysis can result in thick description, as does Feinman (1995). Childres and Spitz examined a large sample of cases applying a rule stated by the courts as unitary. From the facts of the cases, as distinct from the words of the opinions, Childres and Spitz concluded that in fact there were three markedly different rules, depending upon whether the contract in question was a formal contract, an informal contract, or involved an abuse of the bargaining process. (In quite rare instances work of this kind purports to apply statistical principles.)

An important characteristic of the bulk of case-law research is that it is atheoretical. The researcher typically is interested in finding out what is going on and then drawing various conclusions respecting such things as what the law is in terms of formal rules (favorite of law students), what it is in terms of actual application, what policies are or are not being implemented, and how all these things might be changed for the better as the particular researcher views the world. (Only when the research is conducted in the context of a particular theory, for example law and economics, can it be said to be theoretical in nature.)

Case-law Research as Factual rather than Legal Research

The great bulk of case-law research is aimed at enhancing knowledge about the law itself (for whatever purpose). Nonetheless it can be and is conducted for the purpose of learning about party behavior as such. Among many possible examples outside the field of criminology are Frasco (1991) (survey of exclusive dealing and tie-in cases to ascertain motivations for such contracts) and Kaufmann and Stern (1988) (the perception of relational exchange norms in commercial litigation; database is trial court records). (Legal historians, who often do not consider their work a sociological approach nonetheless often rely on case-law research to learn about society itself.) A great deal of legal history is of this nature (see Wahl, 1998, for a survey of all of the nearly 11,000 Southern appellate cases involving slavery). The two motivations for research can easily merge in light of the impact of law on party behavior, as Mnookin and Kornhauser's (1979) phrase 'bargaining in the shadow of the law' suggests.

Limitations of Case-Law Research as Sociology

Most case-law research is casual in the sense that it is neither exhaustive of all the cases on a given subject nor a statistical sampling of all such cases. (Studies of the kind mentioned in the preceding paragraph tend to be exceptions.) Rather the selection is likely to be made on the basis of hierarchical importance of the courts or agencies rendering the decisions, often with jurisdictional and/or geographical considerations in mind. Casual does not, however, mean lacking in thoroughness, as to which the work varies greatly.

In addition, the formulation of just what constitutes the 'given subject' is generally far less stringent than is expected in formal sociological approaches.

The most important limitation of all is the pathological nature of cases. Invariably they concern situations where not only have things gone wrong, but they have gone wrong so seriously that the resulting conflicts were not settled without litigation, and generally were not settled even after at least one court or agency had rendered a decision. Moreover, the 'facts' of cases are not the facts of the situation giving rise to them, but those facts strained through and distorted by the highly adversarial processes of the legal system. Thus study of cases presents a highly solipsistic and distorted view of both the general social circumstances being examined and the particular facts of each case.

Finally, those who believe that some theoretical base is essential to worthwhile legal research will see atheoretical case-law research as useless. Those who believe further that a particular theoretical base is essential to understanding law and advocating legal policy will likely see atheoretical case-law research as harmful for obscuring the truth.

The Non-Recognition of Case-Law Research as a Sociological Approach to Law

There are probably many reasons why case-law research is seldom if ever recognized as a sociological approach to law. Most, if not all, of the limitations described above make it far less systematic and and aimed at truth-seeking than a word such as sociology generally suggests. Moreover academic case-law research likely is tainted in many minds by the similarity of its basic techniques to case-law research in the real world of the law. The latter is always highly instrumental and typically highly adversarial, neither characteristic being appropriate to a scholarly investigation in the traditional sense. Finally, for all its factual orientation, case-law nonetheless generates general rules. Case-law research thus can be - and, where formality dominates the law, is likely to be -

nothing more than a way of distilling general rules, as the maddening habits of most law students bring home to every American law teacher. To the degree this is true, case-law research is no more sociology that would be reading a civil code.

The consequences of non-recognition of case-law research as part of the world of law and sociology are quite serious. Probably the most important is the exclusion of a vast body of information as being essentially unworthy in systematic sociological investigation. Nonetheless, flawed though it is, information derived from case-law research is far from useless. This is particularly so because of the close relation between academic case-law research and that in the real world of the law. Another consequence is that such non-recognition exacerbates the separation of academic scholarly work from the work of the legal profession and legal institutions (see Edwards, 1992). Yet another is that it distorts the perceptions of the relationships between competing approaches to the law (see Section 5). Closely related to this is the present day derogation of such work in American law schools. Even the highest quality of original but straightforward case-law research is unlikely to yield tenure in elite American law schools, or perhaps even to generate summer-research grants.

8. Approaches Based on Particular Theories

Professor Cotterell has described sociology of law as 'the effort to develop systematic, empirically oriented, theoretically guided knowledge of law as a social phenomenon' (Cotterell, 1995, p.347). Except that the empirical orientation is often quite thin, this is an accurate description of some sociological approaches to law, hereafter called theory-driven. (Relatively non-theoretical empirical sociological approaches, see Section 9, do not, of course, fit this description.)

Such approaches are like law and economics in that they are based on particular theories. Marxian analysis, now in considerable eclipse, is perhaps the first to come to mind. But of the five examples Richard Posner recently gave of sociology of law being done 'under other names' in the United States (Posner, 1995, p. 265) four - critical legal studies, critical race theory, feminist jurisprudence, and gay and lesbian studies - are theory-driven. (Regarding critical legal studies see Kelman, 1987; critical race theory: Crenshaw et al., 1995; Delgado and Stefancic, 1993; feminist jurisprudence: Decoste, Munro and MacPherson, 1991; George and McGlamery, 1991; Symposium, 1993; gay and lesbian studies: Arriola, 1994; Eskridge, 1994; Robson, 1992; Robson and Duberman, 1997.) Such theory-driven sociology of law is particularly prevalent in Europe. Van Loon, Delrue and van Wambeke (1995, p. 380), for example, note that 'a lot of the European sociologists of law (of course, also with exceptions) strive for a major theoretical image'. (For examples see Section 6.)

Again like law and economics, in such theory-driven approaches the positive truth of the basic theory, if any is claimed, is assumed rather than proved empirically. Indeed, it is in the nature of such theories that they cannot be proved empirically in anything remotely close to scientific proof. (Many if not most rational choice theorists would probably argue that the positive nature of rational choice theory has been proved repeatedly, and needs no further proof. But what in fact has been proved repeatedly is that - at best - with proper empirical bases it can produce relatively positive conclusions respecting particular applications. Even so, as suggested in Section 10, it is probably the empirical base that supplies whatever positivism exists, rather than the theory.)

These theory-driven sociological approaches, at least American versions, tend to be also like law and economics in that systematic empirical work is likely to be thin on the ground. For example, critical empirical studies seem to_come more from individuals like Richard Abel (1989, Abel and Lewis, 1988-89), who is related to the critical legal studies movement than from those commonly viewed as at its center, such as Duncan Kennedy, Mark Tushnet or Roberto Unger (to the extent it can be said to have a center).

Nonetheless, these theory-driven sociological approaches differ from law and economics in a number of respects.

First, their analysis is almost always founded less on individual behavior than on behavior of groups identified by such factors as class (in the case of Marxian analysis and often critical legal studies), race, gender, and sexual orientation.

Second, the focus of analysis is typically on power relations in which power respecting material affairs as such - the principal focus of law and economics - may or may not be a principal concern. Power respecting ideology and culture-formation are of particular interest to many scholars of theory-driven sociological approaches.

Third, within particular subject areas competing theories exist, thereby multiplying diversity of approaches.

Fourth, although all these theory-driven sociological approaches are related, at least in the United States, to groupings with significant socio-political power in the nonacademic world, at the present time they all remain relatively marginal in American law schools. Their heaviest impact in the latter is probably collectively in terms of fostering academic atmospheres which may, for lack of a better description, be described as 'politically correct'. In particular, neither collectively nor separately have they achieved the power position, at least in American law schools, of the law and economics movement.

The foregoing non-mainstream attribute is related to a fifth characteristic: these approaches are all related to particular social causes. (One need not, however, go as far as Posner, 1995, p. 269, who said: 'Suspicion persists that critical legal studies owes a lot more to visceral left-wing political preferences than to any body of theory'.) None of the causes they represent have, however, been able to achieve more than limited acceptance either within or without academia as compared to the prevailing socioeconomic patterns of modern capitalist-consumer society. To a degree this is true also of law and economics. The latter has nonetheless been markedly more successful in achieving standing and power for its advocates, at least in American law schools, than have all the theory-driven sociological approaches combined.

9. Empirical Sociological Approaches-General

Van Loon, Delrue and van Wambeke (1995, p. 380) have pointed to the 'greater emphasis on induction, on empiricism, and on methodology in the United States' compared with Europe. They went on: 'The American scholars - of course, with exceptions - tend to build theory inductively, from the bottom up, driven_by data, policy concerns and empirical observations.' (see also Posner, 1995, pp. 272-273). Van Loon's word *theory* needs to be treated gingerly. The *theory* produced by or related to such work, in America at least, is not macrotheory of the type I have called theory-driven law and sociology. Rather it tends, at most, to be what Cotterell calls middle-range theory, usually concerned 'with analyzing the causal effects of legal change on wider social change or with specifying the social mechanisms by which law can bring about or hinder social change' Cotterell (1995, p. 352).

Rubin has made these points more specifically in terms of a particular field, contracts:

> American sociology tends to be heavily empirical, but law schools lack the intellectual infrastructure to carry out sustained empirical research. Unlike economics, no dominant theoretical approach has emerged in sociology, and the theories of America's leading theoreticians such as Talcott Parsons and Herbert Garfinkel proved difficult for contracts scholars lacking sociological training to apply. The same is true for German social theory, which may represent a more promising approach. While jurisprudence has been receptive to Habermas and Gadamer, contract scholarship has tended to overlook the more applicable work of their contemporaries such as Niklas Luhmann, Gunther Teubner, and Claus Offe. The result, once again, was the delayed development of a theory for understanding and evaluating the contractual process itself, as opposed to the judicial rules that are applied when that process goes awry. (Rubin, 1995, pp. 113-114)

Before proceeding, the obvious should be noted: theory-driven and empirical approaches as I have used the terms are not watertight compartments. To whatever degree there is serious empirical work they can easily overlap. Richard Abel has already been mentioned as an example of a theory-influenced (driven may be too strong a word in this case) scholar doing extensive empirical work. On the other hand, van Loon and his colleagues, who appear more in the American mode as they describe their work in van Loon and Langerwerf (1990), van Loon and Wouters (1992), nonetheless relate it to Durkheim and Weber (van Loon, Delrue, and van Wambeke, 1995, pp. 382-384)

American sociology of law is related historically to the American Legal Realist movement, which may be summarized by the words in 1926 of Charles E. Clark and Robert M. Hutchins quoted in Schlegel (1980, p. 459): 'We regard the facts as the prerequisite of reform'. The strongholds of that movement were Yale Law School and to a lesser extent, Columbia Law School (see generally Schlegel, 1995). More recently the University of Wisconsin Law School is often considered the center of law and sociology, although the American Bar Foundation is a very important non-law school center. The realist movement is often thought to be dead. It is, however, difficult to understand exactly what that means when present-day names like Lisa Bernstein, Howard Erlanger, Lawrence Friedman, Mark Galanter, John Heinz, Willard Hurst, Richard Lempert, Stewart Macaulay, Robert Mnookin, Ralph Nader, H. Laurence Ross, David Trubek, William Whitford and David Wilkins, to mention a few, are considered. Although law and society is a broader concept than law and sociology, all elements of the law and society movement are, in a sense, realist (see Friedman, 1986).

Oddly enough, criminology, which is a major if not the major area of mainstream academic sociology and law, is less likely to come to mind. This seems to be because the subject has never established a significant foothold in the curriculum of American law schools. For example, the leading list of American law school teachers by subjects contains headings for Criminal Justice and Criminal Procedure (AALS, 1995, pp. 1077-1091), but none for Criminology. So too, names like Morris, Zimring and Jacobs, and their related criminology centers, appear in the AALS Directory, but not as teachers of criminology (AALS, 1995, pp. 691, 989, 529). (Stanton Wheeler at Yale Law School is, however, an exception.) This is in sharp contrast with the comparable list in the United Kingdom, where the list of teachers with a particular interest in Criminology is larger than for either Criminal Justice or Criminal Procedure, although smaller than for Criminal Law (SPTL, 1996, pp. 129-130). (Penology and Sentencing add quite a few more names to Criminology. The comparison between Britain and the United States is rough, because the SPTL lists research interests rather than subjects taught. See, however, SLSA (1996, pp. 282-283, 306) which shows both research and teaching interests, with about two and half times as many members listing criminology in the latter category as in the former.)

As with law and economics the empiricism of other sociological approaches may range from the most casual to the most systematic. The more systematic it is the more it is likely to be recognized as a sociological approach.

10. Empirical Sociological Approaches - Comparison with Posnerian Law and Economics

Like all noneconomic sociological approaches, empirical approaches focus on collective behavior rather than on individual behavior as such, and are thus sharply different from Posnernian law and economics. Beyond that, the eclectic nature of empirical sociological approaches limits comparison to generalities of the following kinds.

a. Normativism and positivism: The very nature of the complexities examined and the obvious limitations of the investigative techniques available render ludicrous any claims to the kinds of genuine positivism claimed for Posnerian law and economics. The most that can ever reasonably be claimed is to have made a heavily persuasive case for the existence of particular facts, causes, desirable routes of change, and the like.
b. Objective of analysis: The objective is to ascertain the social facts seen by the researcher as pertinent to the subject of investigation as defined by the researcher. Thus maximization of wealth as defined by the economic model, the goal of Posnernian law and economics, may (unlikely) or may not be the goal sought by the researcher, and if it is is almost sure to be but one of many.
c. Rational behavior: meaning of: To whatever extent, generally very limited, the noneconomic researcher is concerned with rational choice theory, *rational* means what it means in the theory. As was seen in Section 2, however, the word has many meanings in economics. The obfuscation of the term as used in economics is likely to be exacerbated when used by noneconomic sociologists on account of their tendency to conceive of economics as limited to material human affairs. Thus the word can in their hands, but probably does not, have the same meaning as in Posnernian law and economics. Thus noneconomic use of *rational* is likely to refer to reasonableness, its common meaning among everyone except economists.
d. Transaction costs: recognition and assessment of impact: Noneconomic sociological approaches in a sense treat nothing but transaction costs. The phrase ‘transaction costs’ postulates, however, at least relatively discrete transactions as the focus of analysis. It is itself a markedly discrete way of

thinking about the way exchange occurs in relations (see Macneil, 1981). Thus noneconomic empirical sociological approaches deal with transaction costs. Unlike Posnernian law and economics, such treatment is typically from relational perspectives, and quite likely occurs without calling the subject studied 'transaction costs.'

e. Relations, recognition as such: Noneconomic sociological approaches by definition focus on relations of all kinds and are thus antithetical to Posnernian law and economics with its focus on individuals whose only relationship is competitive.
f. Empiricism: This is the core of this approach, and is in sharp contrast to Posnernian law and economics, where it is typically slighted.
g. Distributional effects: Likely to be considered where viewed as pertinent and significant to the subject, and thus once again sharply at odds with Posnernian law and economics.
h. Individualism: attitudes towards: Nothing in the nature of empirical noneconomic approaches favors or disfavors individualism, and it is thus theoretically more neutral than Posnernian law and economics on this score. But see the discussion of attitudes towards market-solutions below; similar things could be said about individualism.
   Noneconomic empirical sociologists are less likely than Posnerians to consider large organizations to be individuals for the purpose of investigation.
i. Market-solutions: attitudes towards: Nothing in the empirical approach as such favors either market or nonmarket solutions, and it is thus theoretically more neutral than Posnernian law and economics on this score. Nonetheless empiricists with a strong bent towards market solutions are likely to end up in the law and economics camp, empirical side, rather than in noneconomic sociology. This is particularly so of American legal educators, given the power in American law schools of law and economics, especially Posnernian law and economics, see Posner (1995). Thus American empirical sociological approaches are more likely to be conducted by individuals who range from having relatively neutral views about market-solutions to those who heavily favor governmental and other regulatory solutions.
j. Politico-legal goals: There is nothing in the nature of noneconomic empirical sociological approaches that precludes right wing political biases. Nonetheless, in the American context at least, those engaging in such approaches are probably generally thought of as political liberals ranging from middle to leftish, but not radicals in the various critical camps mentioned in Section 8.
k. Power: In contrast to Posnernian law and economics, power may be recognized as an important factor either explicitly or implicitly.

11. Empirical Studies: the Meeting Ground

Empirical work apart from case-law research has been mentioned respecting all three of the major sociological approaches treated in this part: law and economics, other theory-driven sociology, and other nontheory-driven empirical sociology. (This is not to suggest that *any* social investigation can ever be free of ideology and unexpressed theories.)

Empirical work is where all approaches can meet in equal competition. Or to put it in another way, where empirical work is a central focus of study the approach behind it may be singularly unimportant. Consider, for example, Ellickson's investigation of the ways in which farmers and ranchers in Shasta County, California work out animal trespass disputes. Ellickson used social science methods in his study, focusing on a local case study (a narrow but deep wedge of location and time), gathering demographic and documentary evidence, and conducting extensive field interviews with a range of participants. He then used this finely detailed, highly localized data as a basis for theorizing about a broader slice of reality (Larson , 1995, p. 229, citing Ellickson, 1986, pp. 627-628; see also Ellickson, 1991).

'Ellickson concluded that high transaction costs were such a barrier to legal recourse that neighbors instead had worked out their problems in a neighborly fashion, developing a set of customary norms that became their "Order Without Law"' Larson (1995, p. 232 n. 278). As noted, this investigation was conducted in terms of transaction costs by its author, a devoted law and economist. See Ellickson (1993). Moreover, he keyed his work to Coase's theory about social costs, Coase (1960), a Posnerian Bible until Coase explained what he really meant: what matters is not what happens theoretically when there are no transaction costs, but what happens in reality when there are. Coase (1993).

To those of genuinely empirical bent, what counts about Ellickson's Shasta County study is not its origin in the mind of a law and economist or what it may or may not show about rational choice theory. What matters is the quality of his empirical work and the knowledge of human behavior that can be derived therefrom.

This is equally true of sociologists proceeding from other viewpoints. To those of genuinely empirical bent, what counts about the studies of van Loon, Delrue and van Wambeke of litigation, for example, is not their origin in the minds of Weberian-Durkheimians or what they may show about Weberian-Durkheimian theory. What counts is the quality of their empirical work and the knowledge of human behavior that can be derived therefrom.

Various authors have talked about the coming together of law and economics and sociology - Campbell (1996), De Geest (1995), Posner (1995) - as well as economics and sociology more generally - Baron and Hannan (1994). Posner, for example, urges 'the erasure of the remaining disciplinary boundaries that are retarding the complete merger of sociology with the other scholarly disciplines that study law' (Posner, p. 266).

If such a merger is in prospect the question is *how* they come together, and here there are great variations. It is clear enough that Posner means a merger along the lines of the Norman conquest of the Anglo-Saxons, with Posnerian law and economics in the role of the Normans. (Just as Norman England was a merger and not genocide, so too Posner would leave something of noneconomic sociology intact, such as the impact of social class on economically inexplicable behavior, see (Posner, 1995, p. 278.) De Geest, on the other hand, sees law and economics as already a combination of economics, sociology, psychology and other sciences, a pattern very much at odds with Posnerian law and economics.

I too see a possible merger in the offing, one closer to De Geest's than to Posner's position. What is suggested here is that empirical studies of law themselves may be in the process of establishing a field of study that essentially transcends the economic and noneconomic boundaries. In that field the competition will be over empirical quality with theoretical approaches playing only a secondary role. Out of such an eclectic body of research could come an eclectic social science in which a wide variety of theories all were viewed as valuable analytical tools, but with none having a monopoly on whatever limited positivism is possible in social investigation. For a suggestion of a merger along somewhat similar lines relating to crime, see Panther (1995, pp. 372-375).

C. Standing in the Competition of Law and Economics and Other Sociological Approaches

There can be little doubt that much competition exists among the proponents of these various approaches for prominence in the study of law. Richard Posner has proclaimed more or less total victory in this competition for law and economics, at least insofar as American legal studies are concerned (Posner, 1995).

12. Victory?

It would be foolish to deny that law and economics has become the most powerful single monofocused discipline in American legal studies. Nonetheless, the victory is neither as complete nor as satisfactory from a Posnerian standpoint as might appear from reading Posner's account. Before taking up more serious aspects, it might be noted that although Posner professed to be unaware that sociology of law is commonly taught in American law schools (Posner, 1995, p. 275), half again as many names are listed as teaching Law and the Social Sciences as Law and Economics in AALS (1995, pp. 1153-1154, 1158-1160). It is true that the former category is a potpourri. It even includes some teachers, for example, Guido Calabresi, who prefer their law and economics teaching to be so categorized rather than under the more specialized heading. Nonetheless, a riffle through the entries for some of the teachers so listed suggests that some form or aspect of law and sociology is taught in American law schools a good deal more than Posner suggests. (In terms of expression of law teacher interests the picture in Britain is dramatically opposite from Posner's view. Only 5 law teachers identify an interest in law and economics, compared to 14 for sociology of law and 7 for socio-legal studies. SPTL (1996, pp. 130, 135, 136).) I turn now to more significant tests of success.

First, when academic case-law research of the type described in Section 7 is counted as a noneconomic sociological approach, law and economics falls into a very distant second place. Moreover, academic case-law research has a mighty sibling in the day-to-day work of bench and bar. Although law and economics may dominate a few areas of legal practice, most notably antitrust and restrictive practices, and may, as Posner claims, have had an effect on the deregulatory movement, it is a long, long way from dominating or even playing a major role in most areas of the law. There are undoubtedly a growing number of judges relatively literate in law and economics. That does not, however, mean that they are necessarily converts who view economic analysis as a primary, much less the primary, tool of their trade. (For a critical discussion of the relationship between theoretical studies like law and economics and the legal profession, see Edwards, 1992.)

Second, as noted in Section 3, there are many worlds of law and economics, a field not originated by Posner. Nor, in spite of Posner's prolific work and the dominance of Posnerian thinking, by any stretch of the imagination has Posnerian law and economics ever occupied the entire field of law and economics. Furthermore, even apart from its diverse origins, the centrifugal forces afflicting any maturing ideology seem to be well and truly loose in law and economics. Moreover, other theories, in particular game theory, have come muscling into law and economics. Game theory proceeds from the individualistic benefit/cost concept as does law and economics. Nonetheless, game theory, with its stress on asymmetric information and strategic behavior, brings uncertainties to the picture utterly inconsistent with the kinds of claims to positivism often made on behalf of law and economics. ('[T]he strong predictions of the price theoretic models quickly degenerate into a fragmented array of models whose predictions are highly dependent on the nature of the initial assumptions', Donohue, 1997).

An illustration of the centrifugal forces affecting law and economics comes from the institutional school of which Oliver Williamson is the leading voice.

Williamson responded to Posner's analysis of that school (Posner, 1993), in the following manner:

> Posner (1) has not understood the Coasian message (or does not like what he hears), (2) misconstrues transaction costs economics, (3) misconstrues game theory, (4) has a truncated understanding of bounded rationality, the economics of information, and maximizing, and (5) mischaracterizes empirical research in transaction cost economics. (Williamson, 1993b, p. 99, replying to Posner's attack on Williamson, 1993a. Such comments hardly augur well for a unified law and economics under the Posnerian banner)

The presence of these forces swirling around Posnerian law and economics goes blithely unrecognized in Posner's mention of Guido Calabresi as one of the six law and economics academics on the federal Courts of Appeal (Posner, 1995, p. 281, n. 30). Calabresi, who with Coase has legitimate claim to be the co-founder of law and economics, never has been in the Posnerian school. Moreover, four years before this citation of his name appeared, Calabresi specifically and vigorously rejected several of the most fundamental principles underlying Posnerian law and economics (Calabresi, 1991).

Given these divergent forces, whatever claim may be made for a victory of economic analysis over other sociological approaches does not, as Posner clearly would like us to think, support a claim of such victory for Posnerian law and economics.

Third, and perhaps most important respecting any claim of a Posnerian victory, is the impact of empiricism on the relationship between law and economics and other sociological approaches. As suggested in Section 11, what matters about empirical work is its quality, not the particular intellectual camp from whence it comes, for example, Ellickson's Shasta County study (Ellickson, 1986). Ellickson analyzed the outcome from the standpoint of transaction cost economics. The social facts as found by Ellickson, however, equally vindicate relational contract theory in which transaction costs are viewed as too narrow a social concept (Macneil, 1981). Thus, in terms of the empirical work itself, Ellickson's work is just as much a part of the noneconomic sociological approach of relational contract as it is a part of law and economics. Ellickson's fine work turns out not to be victory of law and economics over a noneconomic sociological approach, but a victory for empiricism.

The dangers to Posnerian orthodoxy, or even to the minimum of economics orthodoxy, of high quality empirical work by law and economists should be obvious. Such work focusing on transaction costs, and/or taking into adequate account assymetric information and the possibilities of strategic bargaining, may come perilously close to demonstrating the validity of noneconomic approaches with their emphasis on complex social worlds. It could thus lead to what Posner

(1995, p. 266) called an 'erasure of the remaining disciplinary boundaries'. A merger of law and economics and other sociological approaches at the empirical level with theory being very much of secondary importance is not, however, the erasure Posner had in mind. His was an erasure of disciplinary boundaries whereby rational choice theory would take over the world. (Not surprisingly he denies this in idem. pp. 277-279.)

13. The Causes of the Relative Success of Law and Economics in America

Posner attributes his claimed victory of law and economics to the following: Max Weber's bequest to sociology of a 'useless methodology', idem. pp. 267-268); insofar as criminology is concerned 'a discredited approach to criminality and its control' (p. 270); the 'lack of theoretical and empirical [sic!] ambition' of American sociology of law compared with law and economics (p. 272); a lack of normative punch compared to law and economics (p. 273); the failure of law and sociology 'to retool with the methods of a rival discipline', that is, law and economics (p. 274), prevented by such factors as the 'left-liberal bent' of law and sociologists who perceive law and economics as being 'politically conservative', reluctance to accept the 'knowledge-claims' of other disciplines, and professional envy (pp. 274-275).

Whatever one may think of the merits of Posner's factors purporting to foster the relative success of law and economics included, his list is far from complete. Other factors are not only important, but might well be thought to be substantially more important than those listed.

Perhaps the most important factor Posner omits is the political climate developing in America (and elsewhere) as law and economics was getting its foothold in American law schools. Reactions against the State from right and left achieved national prominence with the Republican nomination of Barry Goldwater in 1964 and the anti-war movement of the late 1960s and early 1970s. Opposition to the bureaucratic welfare state legacies of the New Deal, Fair Deal, and Great Society increased during the period until it culminated in the presidency of Ronald Reagan in 1980. Anti-regulation, pro-market positions such as those of Alfred Kahn respecting the airlines became politically respectable in a way that they had not been since the days of the Hoover administration. Nor was this confined to the far right or even the right. On the international scene the liberal establishment, heavily eastern and Republican, long had been supporters of free trade. It is hardly surprising that law and economics, particularly of the ideological Posnerian variety, thrived in such an atmosphere. Nor is it surprising that sociological approaches more likely to be neutral or favorable towards regulation were less likely to thrive. (Interestingly enough, Mrs Thatcher's 1979 triumph seems to have largely failed to produce a similar pattern in British academia; perhaps this in part reflected that, unlike Ronald Reagan, she never enjoyed the support of much more than 40 percent of the electorate.)

Even the most casual observation of American law schools, particularly the more elite law schools, reveals how responsive their curricula and research are to what is going on in the outside world. The 1940s saw a proliferation of law school activity in areas like labor law (collective bargaining and unfair labor practices) and administrative law reflecting the the New Deal. Comparative and public international law blossomed in the postwar Cold War era with America's new world role. Law and poverty and civil rights courses came with the Lyndon Johnson's Great Society. Courses and studies relating in a wide variety of ways to international trade have blossomed as its importance to the American economy have become more and more widely recognized. It is hardly surprising that a market-oriented and often right-wing subject like law and economics thrived in the 1970s and thereafter. Indeed it would have been simply amazing had it not.

A second factor in the relative success of law and economics undoubtedly has to do with the speed and simplicity of effort required for various kinds of intellectual work. For example, case-law research and empirical studies based on published statistical information can be done in a library with far greater speed and simplicity of effort than empirical studies can be done in the field. This is almost certainly the primary reason that the empirical studies envisioned by the early American realists, and sometimes conducted on a pilot basis, caught on in American law schools only to a extremely limited degree. Theoretical law and economics can in turn be done with far greater speed and simplicity of effort than can be case-law and other library-based research.

None of the foregoing is to make any judgment whatever about the intellectual challenge or difficulty of the different kinds of enterprise. It is simply that most thought-experiments based on hypothetical situations can typically be done faster than activities requiring fact-gathering, and that library fact-gathering can typically be done faster than field fact-gathering. Thus theoretical law and economics is in cost terms at a significant advantage in competition with case-law research. It is at an even greater advantage in competition with empirical approaches, particularly field studies. In an academic world increasingly focussed on publish-or-perish this has made law and economics singularly attractive to those with real or imagined ability to carry out such analysis. This is especially true in any law school where article-counting is an important aspect of promotion and tenure.

The big challenge to law and economics on this score will come to whatever degree it shifts towards empiricism and particularly towards the more time-intensive forms of field study such as that of Ellickson in Shasta County. To whatever degree law and economics shifts in this direction its competitive advantage will tend to disappear.

A third important factor in the relative success of the law and economics movement has been its considerable financing from sources with pro-market, and often right-wing, ideologies, of which the Olin Foundation stands out. This financing included particularly a major effort to proselytize law teachers. Starting in the late 1960s Henry Manne, a Chicago School enthusiast, organized a well-financed and most attractive summer program, first at the University of Rochester and later at the University of Miami. A very substantial number of law teachers were both taught the basics of law and economics and propagandized about its merits by this program. (It was nicknamed Pareto in the Pines and after its move south, Pareto in the Palms.) Manne continued such well-funded programs and others after moving to Emory University in 1980 and later founding a law and economics law school at George Mason University. Nothing on a remotely comparable scale has ever been available to provide financial support for noneconomic sociological training and propaganda.

D. Conclusion

In conclusion, the great and probably unbridgeable gulf between various other sociological approaches and Posnerian law and economics is much smaller respecting other varieties of law and economics, particularly institutional law and economics. These smaller gaps are likely to become smaller yet to whatever extent both law and economics and other sociological approaches move in the direction of empirical studies.

Acknowledgements

I am indebted to Jane E. Larson for reviewing the manuscript and making many helpful comments, including her point concerning legal historians and case-law research in Section 7, as well as for supplying references, particularly for the theory-driven sociological approaches mentioned in Section 8. The following also very kindly brought to my attention a number of important bibliographical items: David A. Campbell, John J. Donohue III, August 16, 1999 and Patrick J. Kaufmann. Finally I am everlastingly indebted to my wife Nancy for helping me work through problems relating to the many weaknesses of rational choice theory, with the result that I decided to limit the critique here to its Posnerian variant.

Bibliography on Other Sociological Approaches (0630)

Abel, Richard L. (1989), *American Lawyers*, New York, NY, Oxford University Press.

Abel, Richard L. and Lewis, Phillip S.C. (1988-89), *Lawyers in Society*, 3 vols, Berkeley, CA, University of California Press.

Arnaud, André-Jean, et al. (1993), *Dictionaire Encylopédique de Théorie et de Sociologie du Droit*, Paris, Libraire Générale de Droit et de Jurisprudence.

Arriola, Elvia R. (1994), 'Gendered Inequality: Lesbians, Gays and Feminist Legal Theory', **9** *Berkeley Women's Law Journal*, 103 ff.

Association of American Law Schools (AALS) (1995), *The AALS Directory of Law Teachers 1995-96*, St Paul, MN, West Publishing Company.

Baron, James N. And Hannan, Michael T. (1994), 'The Impact of Economics on Contemporary Sociology', **32** *Journal of Economic Literature*, 1111-1146.

Black, Donald (1989), *Sociological Justice*, New York, NY, Oxford University Press

Calabresi, Guido (1991), 'The Pointlessness of Pareto: Carrying Coase Further', **100** *Yale Law Journal*, 1211-1237

Campbell, David A. (1996), 'On What is Valuable in Law and Economics', **8** *Otago Law Review*, 489-514

Campbell, David A. (1997), Law and Economics and its Relationship to Sociology, in Tomasic, R., *The Sociology of Law*, 2nd edn, London, Sage

Childres, Robert and Spitz, Steven J. (1972), 'Status in the Law of Contracts', **47** *New York University Law Review*, 1-31.

Coase, Ronald (1960), 'The Problem of Social Cost', **3** *Journal of Law and Economics*, 1-44

Coase, Ronald (1993), 'Coase on Posner on Coase', **149** *Journal of Institutional and Theoretical Economics*, 96-98.

Cotterell, Roger (1995), 'Sociological Interpretations of Legal Development', **2** *European Journal of Law and Economics*, 347-359.

Crenshaw, Kimberle Williams, Gotanda, Neil, Peller, Gary and Thomas, Kendall (1995), *Critical Race Theory: The Key Writings that Formed the Movement*, New York, NY, The New Press.

Decoste, F.C., Munro, K.M. and MacPherson, Lillian (1991), *Feminist Legal Literature: An Annotated Bibliography,* New York, Garland Pub.

De Geest, Gerrit (1995), 'Toward an Integration of Economic and Sociological Approaches?', **2** *European Journal of Law and Economics*, 301-308.

Delgado, Richard, and Stefancic, Jean (1993), 'Critical Race Theory: An Annotated Bibliography', **79** *Virigina Law Review*, 461

Donohue, John J. III (1997), *The Path of Law and Economics*, forthcoming.

Edwards, Harry T. (1992), 'The Growing Disjunction between Legal Education and the Legal Profession', **91** *Michigan Law Review*, 34-78.

Ellickson, Robert C. (1986), 'Of Coase and Cattle: Dispute Resolution Among Neighbors in Shasta County', **38** *Stanford Law Review*, 623-680

Ellickson, Robert C. (1991), *Order Without Law: How Neighbors Settle Disputes*, Cambridge, MA, Harvard University Press.

Ellickson, Robert C. (1993), 'Property in Land', **102** *Yale Law Journal*, 1315-1400.

Eskridge, William N. (1994), 'Gaylegal Narratives', **40** *Stanford Law Review*, 607.

Feinman, Jay M. (1995), *Economic Negligence, Liability of Professionals and Businesses to Third Parties for Economic Loss*, Boston, MA, Little, Brown & Co.

Friedman, Lawrence M. (1986), 'The Law and Society Movement', **38** *Stanford Law Review*, 763-780

Frasco, Gregg, (1991), *Exclusive Dealing: A Comprehensive Case Study*, Lanham, MD, University Press of America.

Geertz, Clifford (1973), *The Interpretation of Cultures: Selected Essays*, New York, NY Basic Books.

George, Paul M. and McGlamery, Susan (1991), 'Women and Legal Scholarship: A Bibliography', **77** *Iowa Law Review*, 87 ff.

Holzhauer, Rudi W. and Teijl, Rob (1995), 'Comment on Francis van Loon, Stephane Delrue, and Wim van Wambeke, "Sociological Research on Litigation: Perspectives and Examples"', **2** *European Journal of Law and Economics*, 387-392.

Kaufmann, Patrick J. and Stern, Louis W. (1988), 'Relational Exchange Norms, Perceptions of Unfairness and Retained Hostility in Commercial Litigation', **32** *Journal of Conflict Resolution*, 534-552.

Kelman, Mark (1987), *A Guide to Critical Legal Studies*, Cambridge, MA, Harvard University Press.

Larson, Jane E. (1995), 'Free Markets Deep in the Heart of Texas', **84** *Georgetown Law Journal*, 179-260.

Lipson, Leon and Wheeler, Stanton (eds) (1986), *Law and the Social Sciences*, New York, NY, Russell Sage Foundation.

Llewellyn, Karl N. (1960), *The Common Law Tradition: Deciding Appeals*, Boston, MA, Little Brown.

Macneil, Ian R. (1981), 'Economic Analysis of Contractual Relations: Its Shortfalls and the Need for a "Rich Classificatory Apparatus"', **75** *Northwestern University Law Review*, 1018-1063.

Mnookin, Robert H. and Kornhauser, Lewis A. (1979), 'Bargaining in the Shadow of the Law: The Case of Divorce', **88** *Yale Law Journal*, 950-997.

Panther, Stephan M. (1995), 'The Economics of Crime and Criminal Law: An Antithesis to Sociological Theories?', **2** *European Journal of Law and Economics*, 365-378.

Posner, Richard A. (1992), *Economic Analysis of Law*, 4th edn, Boston, MA, Little Brown.

Posner, Richard A. (1993), 'The New Institutional Economics Meets Law and Economics', **149** *Journal of Institutional and Theoretical Economics*, 73-87.

Posner, Richard A. (1995), 'The Sociology of the Sociology of Law: A View from Economics', **2** *European Journal of Law and Economics*, 265-284.

Robson, Ruthan (1992), *Lesbian (Out)law: Survival Under the Rule of Law*, Ithaca, NY, Firebrand Books.

Robson, Ruthan and Duberman, Martin (eds) (1997), *Gay Men, Lesbians, and the Law*, New York, NY, Chelsea House.

Rubin, Edward L. (1995), 'The Nonjudicial Life of Contract: Beyond the Shadow of the Law', **90** *Northwestern University Law Review*, 107-131.

Schlegel, John Henry (1995), *American Legal Realism and Empirical Social Science*, Chapel Hill, NC, University of North Carolina Press.

Schlegel, John Henry (1980), 'American Legal Realism and Empirical Social Science: From the Yale Experience', **28** *Buffalo Law Review*, 459-586.

Shelanski, Howard A. and Klein, Peter G. (1995), 'Empirical Research in Transaction Cost Economics: A Review and Assessment', **11** *Journal of Law, Economics and Organization*, 335-361.

Society of Public Teachers of Law (SPTL) (1996), *Directory of Members 1997*, Butterworths.

Socio-Legal Studies Association (SLSA) (1996), *Directory of Members 1996*, Butterworths.

Symposium (1993), 'Can Feminists Use the Law to Effect Social Change in the 1990s?', **87** *Northwestern University Law Review*, 1252.

Twining, William L. (1974), 'Law and Social Science: The Method of Detail', *New Society*, June 27, 1974, 758-761.

van Loon, Francis and Langerwerf, Etienne (1990), 'Socioeconomic Development and the Evolution of Litigation Rates of Civil Courts in Belgium, 1835-1980', **24** *Law and Society Review*, 285-298.

van Loon, Francis and Wouters, Yolande (1992), 'Civil Litigation in Belgium: The Reconstruction of the Pyramid of Legal Disputes: A Preliminary Report', **20-21** *Droit et Société*, 199-210.

van Loon, Francis, Delrue, Stephane and Van Wambeke, Wim (1995), 'Sociological Research on Litigation: Perspectives and Examples, **2** *European Journal of Law and Economics*, 379-385.

Wahl, Jenny Bourne (1998), *The Bondsman's Burden: An Economic Analysis of the Common Law of Southern Slavery*, Cambridge, Cambridge University Press.

Williamson, Oliver E. (1993a), 'The Evolving Science of Organization', **149** *Journal of Institutional and Theoretical Economics*, 36-63.

Williamson, Oliver E. (1993b), 'Transaction Cost Economics Meets Posnerian Law and Economics', **149** *Journal of Institutional and Theoretical Economics*, 99-118.

0640
THE LAW AND ECONOMICS OF ANTHROPOLOGY

Robert Cooter
University of California at Berkeley

Abstract

I briefly review the classics of legal anthropology and discuss the economic analysis relevant to it.
JEL classification: K00
Keywords: Law, Economics, Anthropology, Property, Social Norms

'Just look along the road, and tell me if you can see either of [the messengers].'
'I see nobody on the road,' said Alice.
'I only wish *I* had such eyes,' the King remarked in a fretful tone. 'To be able to see Nobody! And at that distance too! Why, it's as much as *I* can do to see real people, by this light!' (Lewis Carroll's *Through the Looking-Glass*, Chapter 7)

As a rule of thumb, an academic subject exists when someone teaches it regularly at a major university. By this standard, the subject of law, economics and anthropology does not exist. A review essay requires eyes that the King attributed to Alice. In contrast, legal anthropology exists and so does the economic analysis of law. I will offer some remarks on how these two subjects relate to each other.

1. Legal Anthropology

Legal anthropology is a small subject that is taught in a few universities, especially in America (Kuppe and Potz, 1994). I recently asked teachers of law and anthropology at major American universities to send me the reading lists for their classes. The readings were 'all over the map' both literally and figuratively. The struggle in anthropology over the subject's identity has infected law and anthropology. Some strands in modern anthropology, such as symbolic anthropology (Geertz, 1983), have no apparent relationship to the economic analysis of law. Others, such as economic anthropology (Dalton, 1967; Plattner, 1989) and anthropological materialism (Harris, 1968), have a modest relationship to the economic analysis of law. In general, the analytical techniques used in the economic analysis of law are not understood or appreciated by anthropologists.

Reviewing the different strands of anthropological thought is a difficult task (Ortner, 1984) and relating them to the economic analysis of law in a brief article is impossible. I will attempt something more limited and modest. My main aim is to describe for law and economics scholars their subject's frontier with anthropology. Legal anthropology has a small, classical literature, which I will describe briefly. Then I will review in more detail the aspects of the economic analysis of law that relate to classical concerns of anthropology.

Legal anthropology developed its classical literature (Conley and O'Barr, 1993) in the twentieth century when anthropology books and monographs devoted to law first appeared. Malinowski (1926), who first conducted systematic field research on tribal law, debunked the myth that tribal law consists of strict prohibitions and harsh punishments resembling criminal law. Instead, he observed an elaborate system of compensation in Polynesia for harm done to others, resembling the modern law of property and torts, but without anything similar to formal courts. He commented on the usefulness of such a system and tried to explain how it worked .

Llewellyn and Hoebel (1941) interviewed Cheyenne Indians in the 1920s and reconstructed their legal order as it existed in the 1860s before conquest and subjugation. This study applied the 'case method' of the common law to tribal law, thus minimizing the distinctiveness of techniques required in legal anthropology. The 'cases' consist of memories, stories and myths about law and government. As practiced by Llewellyn and Hoebel, the 'case method' explores the purposes and uses of political practice and law, which makes legal realism resemble functionalism.

Bohannan (1957) observed disputes in the customary courts ('moots') of the Tiv in colonial Nigeria. Like Llewellyn and Hoebel, he analyzed cases, but in greater detail and subtlety, revealing the cultural obstacles to understanding exotic legal systems. Bohannan's concern over objectivity and neutrality in comparing cultures anticipates recent methodological discussion in anthropology. Gluckman (1965) provided the same kind of in-depth study of the legal culture of another African group, the Barotse. Pospisil (1958) extended this tradition by attempting something resembling a codification of the customary law of a group in New Guinea who lived in the 1950s under limited Dutch legal control.

The small, classical literature aimed at describing aspects of tribal law that the modern state had not changed or distorted. More recent studies in this tradition explicitly concern the way custom responds to state and market (Collier, 1973; Moore, 1986; (Nader, 1990; Sierra, 1995), including the attempts of subordinate peoples to secure themselves against exploitation (Nader, 1990; Comaroff and Roberts, 1981). Whereas the classical literature concerned tribes, modern studies in legal anthropology often concern formal, non-western legal systems, such as Islamic or Buddhist law (Fikentscher, 1995), thus effacing the distinction between legal anthropology and comparative law. Contemporary anthropologists have also developed an interest in the way contemporary customs interact with modern law in countries like the US (Greenhouse, 1986).

2. Economic Analysis

I now turn to the smattering of articles on anthropology that fit within the modern law and economics movement. In an earlier review Brenner (1983), stresses population growth as the destabilizing influence that causes innovation and economic development in tribes. Only a few papers in law and economics concern law among tribal people. Perhaps the most discussed is the paper by Demsetz (1967) which proposes a simple theory of the origins of property. Demsetz reasoned that private property emerges from a prior rule permitting open access to resources, and this event should occur at the point in history when the benefits of the change exceed the costs. He observed that when everyone has open access to a resource, over-exploitation produces a dead-weight loss, as with over-fishing on the high seas. In contrast, private ownership can eliminate this dead-weight loss, but, unlike open-access, private property requires costly definition and enforcement of ownership rights. So Demsetz predicts that privatization will occur when the dead-weight loss of open access exceeds the transaction costs of exclusion by private property rights.

For evidence in favor of this theory, Demsetz relies upon secondary sources, notably concerning the fur trade among North American Indian tribes. More careful examination proves that Demsetz got some important facts wrong. Tribal people live among kin with extensive, complicated obligations to each other, including obligations about using land. These obligations create a very different legal regime from open access. So the characteristic movement in tribal property law is not from open access to private ownership. Rather, new customary rights in property continually evolve from old customary rights in property (Cooter, 1991). Tradition persists by continually inventing new things.

Economists often contrast individual and group ownership, but these labels are too imprecise to fit customary law. Research on property rights has revealed variety and detail in the political arrangements by which small groups manage their assets (Eggertsson, 1992; Ellickson, 1993; McCloskey, 1975a, 1975b; Ostrom, 1990). Even without individual ownership, small groups of people living intimate lives seldom suffer the political paralysis that causes deadweight losses like the infamous tragedy of the commons.

Note that the Demsetz paper reveals a characteristic weakness of anthropological work among law and economics scholars: they lack intuition because they have never done field research. For an early exception in property law, see Trebilcock (1981).

In another paper with high ambition, Posner (1980) interprets the behavior of tribes as a response to missing insurance markets. The combination of the hazards of primitive life and the absence of insurance, according to this view, causes people to form long-run relationships and redistribute wealth. Like Demsetz, this paper contributes to anthropology by raising the level of generality in formulating familiar trade-offs.

Risk-reduction is important to cases where customary law allows relatively open access to a resource, such as summer grazing land in Mongolia. Variations in weather impose risks on people living off the land. A customary rule of open access enables people to relocate quickly from one micro-climate to another, thus reducing climatic risk (Cooter, 1995; McCloskey, 1976; Nugent and Sanchez, 1993). Open-access, however, discourages investments to improve the land. So the trade-off is between dead-weight loss and risk-spreading, not the trade-off between dead-weight loss and transaction costs of exclusion as proposed by Demsetz.

3. Social Norms

As explained, legal anthropology especially concerns customary law. Proponents of legal decentralization typically admire custom because it arises spontaneously, outside the state (Hayek, 1976; Leoni, 1991). The informality of social norms obscures their operation and causes observers to under-estimate their importance relative to formal law. Modern business is often conducted in rational ignorance of the law (Macaulay, 1963). Informal law plays an especially important role in basic markets where state enforcement of contracts fails, as in capital markets in developing countries (Winn, 1994). Over-zealous regulation forces informal law to operate in opposition to formal law, which impairs economics development (De Soto, 1989).

In recent years, economic theories have corrected the tradition of underestimating informal norms. The analysis of social norms has become central to the law and economics agenda, especially after Ellickson's research on liability for straying cattle framed legal decentralization in terms of the Coase Theorem (Ellickson, 1991). Two bodies of theory are joined in the economic analysis of social norms. First, game theory has been adapted to the specific circumstances in which social norms direct behavior (Ullmann-Margalit, 1977; Taylor, 1987). Second, competition among social norms resembles competition in evolutionary biology, so the application of game theory to evolutionary biology provides models for understanding social norms (Hirshleifer, 1987; Frank, 1988; Gruter, 1991; Gruter and Masters, 1992).

The economic analysis of social norms, such as the customary law of property or customary obligations of redistribution, draw upon a fundamental result in game theory: one-shot games with inefficient solutions, such as prisoner's dilemma, often have efficient solutions when repeated between the same players (Fudenberg and Maskin, 1986). This generalization grounds the utilitarianism of small groups, by which I mean the tendency to create efficient rules for cooperation within small groups. Kinship provides a framework for repeated interaction among the same people. Consequently, game theory predicts that kin groups such as tribes can solve problems of internal cooperation without relying upon state law. Landa has used this result to study groups of Chinese traders (Landa, 1981).

Kinship, however, is not the only basis for dense social networks in intimate societies. Much like kinship, trade organizations can provide a framework for repeated interaction (Cooter and Landa, 1984). Historical institutions such as the medieval law merchant can be understand in this light (Milgrom, North and Weingast, 1990; Greif, 1993). Bernstein has demonstrated this fact in careful, detailed studies of modern diamond exchanges (Bernstein, 1992) and commodity trading associations (Bernstein, 1996). Social groups, in which people have repeated transactions with each other, must be distinguished from social categories by which people are classified. Unlike social groups, people who fall in the same social category might not have ties to each other, so they may have inefficient interactions (Posner, 1995).

I have reviewed various economic studies of social norms. The economic analysis of social norms requires a comprehensive vision, but none has emerged as yet. According to one approach, law should ideally correct failures in the 'market for social norms', rather like regulations should ideally correct failures in the market for commodities (Cooter, 1994). This approach requires an analysis of the incentive structures in society that cause the evolution of efficient social norms, and, conversely, the incentive structures that cause social norms to fail. The application of game theory to customary forms of discrimination suggests an important kind of failure (Akerlof, 1980, 1985; McAdams, 1995; Posner, 1996). A thorough development of a theory of the evolution of social norms would provide the foundation for a theory of adjudication, especially in the area of common law.

4. Conclusion

I organized my description of the law and economics of anthropology in terms of these underlying ideas: property, long-run relationships and social norms. Now I need to mention some loose ends that do not fit my categories. First, some law and economics scholars have examined issues concerning American Indians (McChesney, 1990; Cornell and Kalt, 1993; Anderson and McChesney, 1994). Second, some studies in comparative law and economics have an anthropological flavor (Kuran, 1995). Finally, a few brave scholars have attempted to cross the deep divide between meaning and behavior in social science by using the tools of law and economics to interpret stories and parables from the Bible (Levmore, 1995; Miller, 1994, 1995, 1996a), or by trying to adapt the rigorous individualism of economics to encompass a theory of culture (Audain, 1995). These papers parallel the strong turn towards interpretivism in anthropology in general (Geertz, 1983) and in legal anthropology in particular, which stresses the distortion of the *meaning* of law as a consequence of political domination (Comaroff, 1992; Williams, 1994).

Finally, I want to conclude by remarking on the interaction between anthropology and economics. In anthropology as in politics, the confidence of colonialism dissipated into the self-doubt of post-colonialism. Economics, in contrast, retains its brash self-confidence. Given these facts, some anthropologists associate economics imperialism with the mentality of political colonialism. Abandoning such ideological conceptions would create a better atmosphere for anthropology and economics to learn from each other. The economic analysis of legal anthropology remains more aspiration than reality. Economists believe correctly that they can bring more systematic analysis to a range of topics in anthropology. Adapting economic theory to new institutions and cultures, however, requires careful field research. Without a commitment to field research, economic theory remains too remote from its object of study to convince anthropologists immersed in other cultures.

Bibliography on the Law and Economics of Anthropology (0640)

Akerlof, George A. (1980), 'A Theory of Social Custom, of Which Unemployment may be one Consequence', **94** *Quarterly Journal of Economics*, 719-775.

Akerlof, George A. (1985), 'Discriminatory, Status-based Wages among Tradition Oriented, Stochastically Trading Coconut Producers', **93** *Journal of Political Economy*, 265-276.

Anderson, Terry L. and McChesney, Fred S. (1994), 'Raid or Trade? An Economic Model of India-White Relations', **37** *Law and Economics*, 39-74.

Audain, Linz (1995), 'Critical Cultural Law and Economics, the Culture of Deindividualization, the Paradox of Blackness', **70** *Indiana Law Review*, 709 ff.

Bernstein, Lisa (1992), 'Opting Out of the Legal System: Extralegal Contractual Relations in the Diamond Industry', **21** *Journal of Legal Studies*, 115-157.

Bernstein, Lisa (1996), 'Merchant Law in a Merchant Court: Rethinking the Code's Search for Immanent Business Norms', **114** *University of Pennsylvania Law Review*, 1643-1696.

Bohannan, Paul (1957), *Justice and Judgement Among the Tiv*, London.

Brenner, Reuven (1983), 'Trust, Population, and Wealth; or, Why did Cain Kill Abel?', in *History - the Human Gamble*, Chicago, IL, University of Chicago Press, 62-104. Reprinted in Spanish edition: Fondo de Cultura Economics, Mexico - Spain, 1989.

Collier, Jane (1973), *Law and Social Change in Zinacantan*, Stanford, CA, Stanford University Press.

Comaroff, John L. (1992), *The Discourse of Rights in Colonial South Africa: Subjectivity, Sovereignty, Modernity*, Vol. I (with J. Comaroff), Chicago, IL, University of Chicago Press.

Comaroff, John L. and Roberts, Simon (1981), *Rules and Processes: The Cultural Logic of Dispute in an African Context*, Chicago, IL, University of Chicago Press.

Conley, John M. and O'Barr, William M. (1993), 'Legal Anthropology Comes Home: A Brief History of the Ethnographic Study of Law', **27** *Loyola Law Review*, 41-64.

Cooter, Robert D. (1991), 'Inventing Market Property: The Land Courts of Papua New Guinea', **25** *Law and Society Review*, 759-801.

Cooter, Robert D. (1994), 'Structural Adjudication and the New Law Merchant: A Model of Decentralized Law', **14** *International Review of Law and Economics*, 215-231.

Cooter, Robert D. (1995), 'Mongolia: Avoiding Tragedy in the World's Largest Commons', *Olin Working Paper in Law and Economics*, Boalt Hall School of Law, Berkeley.

Cooter, Robert D. and Landa, Janet T. (1984), 'Personal versus Impersonal Trade: The Size of Trading Groups and Contract Law', **4** *International Review of Law and Economics*, 15-22.

Cornell, Stephen and Kalt, Joseph P. (1993), 'Where does Economic Development Really Come From? Constitutional Rule Among the Modern Sioux and Apache', **93** *Faculty Research Working Papers*, John F. Kennedy School of Government, Harvard University, 30 ff.

Dalton, George (1967), *Tribal and Peasant Economies*, Austin, University of Texas Press.

De Soto, Hernando (1989), *The Other Path*, New York, Harper and Row.

Demsetz, Harold (1967), 'Toward a Theory of Property Rights', **62** *American Economic Review*, 347-359.

Eggertsson, Thrainn (1992), 'Analyzing Institutional Successes and Failures: A Millenium of Common Mountain Pastures in Iceland', **12** *International Review of Law and Economics*, 423-437.

Ellickson, Robert C. (1991), *Order Without Law: How Neighbors Settle Disputes*, Cambridge, MA, Harvard University Press.

Ellickson, Robert C. (1993), 'Property in Land', *Yale Law Journal*.

Fikentscher, Wolfgang (1995), *Modes of Thought: A Study in the Anthropology of Law and Religion*, Tubingen, J.C.B. Mohr (Paul Siebeck).

Frank, Robert H. (1988), *Passions Within Reason: The Strategic Role of the Emotions*.

Fudenberg, Drew and Maskin, Eric (1986), 'The Folk Theorem in Repeated Games with Discounting or with Incomplete Information', **54** *Econometrica*, 533-554.

Geertz, Clifford (1983), 'The Way We Think Now: Toward an Ethnography of Modern Thought', *Local Knowledge*.

Gluckman, Max (1965), *The Ideas in Barotse Juriprudence*, New Haven, Yale University Press.

Greenhouse, Carol J. (1986), *Praying for Justice: Faith, Order, and Community in an American Town*, NY, Cornell Univesity Press.

Greif, Avner (1993), 'Contract Enforceability and Economic Institutions in Early Trade: The Maghiribi Trader's Coation', **83** *American Economic Review*, 525-548.

Gruter, Magaret (1991), *Law and the Mind: Biological Origins of Human Behavior*, Newbury Park, California, Sage.

Gruter, Magaret and Masters, Roger (1992), *The Sense of Justice: Biological Foundations of Law*, Newbury Park, California, Sage.

Harris, M. (1968), *The Rise of Anthropological Theory*, New York.

Hayek, Friedrich A. von (1976), *Planning and the Rule of Law*, Chicago, University of Chicago Press.

Hirshleifer, Jack (1987), 'Evolutionary Models in Economics and Law: Cooperation versus Conflict Stategies', **9** *Economic Behavior in Adversity*.

Kuppe, Rene and Potz, Richard (1994), *Law and Anthropology: International Yearbook for Legal Anthropology*, Dordrecht/Boston/London, Martinus Nijhoff Publishers.

Kuran, Timur (1995), 'Islamic Economics and the Islamic Subeconomy', **9** *Journal of Economic Perspectives*, 155-173.

Landa, Janet T. (1981), 'A Theory of the Ethnically Homogeneous Middleman Group: An Institutional Alternative to Contract Law', **10** *Journal of Legal Studies*, 349-362.

Leoni, Bruno (1991), *Freedom and the Law*, Indianapolis, Liberty Fund.

Levmore, Saul (1995), 'Rethinking Group Responsibility and Strategic Threats in Biblical Text and Modern Law', **71** *Chicago-Kent Law Review*, 85 ff.

Llewellyn, Karl N. and Hoebel, Adamson E. (1941), *The Cheyenne Way: Conflict and Case Law in Primitive Jurisprudence*, University of Oklahoma Press.

Macaulay, Stewart (1963), 'Non-Contractual Relations in Business: A Preliminary Study', **25** *American Sociological Review*, 55-70. Reprinted in Goldberg, Victor P. (ed.), *Readings in the Economics of Contract Law*, Cambridge, Cambridge University Press, 1989, 4-15.

Malinowski, Bonislaw (1926), *Crime and Custom in Savage Society*, New York.

McAdams, Richard H. (1995), 'Cooperation and Conflict: The Economics of Group Status Production and Race Discrimination', *Harvard Law Review*.

McChesney, Fred S. (1990), 'Government as Definer of Property Rights: Indian Land Ownership, Ethnic Externalities, and Bureaucratic Budgets', **19** *Journal of Legal Studies*, 297-335.

McCloskey, D.N. (1975a), 'The Economics of Enclosure', in Parker, W.N. and Jones, E.L. (eds), *European Peasants and Their Markets*, ASIN.

McCloskey, D.N. (1975b), 'The Persistence of English Common Fields', in Parker, W.N. and Jones, E.L. (eds), *European Peasants and Their Markets*, ASIN.

McCloskey, Donald N. (1976), 'English Open Fields as Behavior Towards Risk', in Unselding, Paul (ed.), *Research in Economic History 1*, Greenwich, CT, JAI Press.

Milgrom, Paul R., North, D. and Weingast, B. (1990), 'The Role of Institutions in the Revival of Trade: The Law Merchant, Private Judges, and the Champagne Fairs', **2** *Economic and Politics*, 1-23.

Miller, Geoffrey P. (1992), 'The Culture of Capital: Comments on Conley and O'Barr', **71** *North Carolina Law Review*, 201 ff.

Miller, Geoffrey P. (1993a), 'Ritual and Regulation: A Legal Economic Interpretation of Selected Biblical Texts', **22** *Journal of Legal Studies*, 477-501.

Miller, Geoffrey P. (1993b), 'Contracts of Genesis', **22** *Journal of Legal Studies*, 15-45.

Miller, Geoffrey P. (1994), 'The Legal-Economic Analysis of Comparative Civil Procedure, the Legal-Economic Approach to Biblical Interpretation', **150** *American Journal of Comparative Law Journal of Institutional and Theoretical Economics*, 755 ff.

Miller, Geoffrey P. (1995), 'Verbal Feud in the Hebrew Bible: Judges 3:12-30 and 19-21', *Journal of Near Eastern Studies*.

Miller, Geoffrey P. (1996a), 'Ancient Law: the New Learning (tentative title) (1996) Constitutionalist: A Legal-Economic Interpretation of Exodus 17:8-16 and Related Texts', **70** *Chicago-Kent Law Review*, 1829 ff. To be republished in Lindgren, James, Miller, Geoffrey et al. (eds).

Miller, Geoffrey P. (1996b), 'The Song of Deborah: A Legal-Economic Analysis', **144** *University of Pennsylvania Law Review*, 2293 ff.

Moore, Sally Falk (1986), *Social Facts and Fabrications: Customary Law in Kilimanjaro 1880-1980*, New York, Cambridge University Press.

Nader, Laura (1990), *Harmony Ideology: Justice and Control in a Zapotec Mountain Village*, Stanford, CA, Stanford University Press.

Nugent, Jeffrey B. and Nical Sanchez (1993), 'Tribes, Chiefs, and Transhumance: A Comparative Institutional Analysis', **87** *Economic Development and Cultural Change*, 113 ff.

Ortner, Sherry (1984), 'Theory in Anthropology Since the Sixties', **26** *Comparative Studies in Society and History*, 125-166.

Ostrom, Elinor (1990), *Governing the Commons: Evolution of Institutions for Collective Action*, Cambridge, Cambridge University Press.

Plattner, Stuart (1989), *Economic Anthropology*, Stanford, Hoover Institute Press, Stanford University.

Posner, Eric A. (1995), 'The Regulation of Groups: The Influence of Legal and Nonlegal Santions on Collective Action', **63** *University of Chicago Law Review*, 113-197.

Posner, Eric A. (1996), 'Law, Economics and Inefficient Norms', **145** *University of Pennsylvania Law Review*, 1697-1744.

Posner, Richard A. (1980), 'A Theory of Primitive Society, with Special Reference to Law', **23** *Journal of Law and Economics*, 1-25.

Pospisil (1958), *Kapauku Papuans and Their Law*, New Haven, Published for the Dept. of Anthropology, Yale University.

Sierra, Maria Teresa (1995), 'Indian Rights and Customary Law in Mexico: A Study of the Nahuas in the Sierra de Puebla', **29** *Law and Society Review*, 227-254.

Taylor, Michael (1987), *The Possibility of Cooperation*, Cambridge, Cambridge University Press.

Trebilcock, Michael J. (1981), 'Communal Property Rights: The Papua New Guinea Experience', *University of Toronto Law Journal*.

Ullman-Margalit, Edna (1977), *The Emergence of Norms*, Oxford, Clarendon Press.

Williams, Robert, A., Jr (1994), 'Linking Arms Together: Multicultural Constitutionalism in a North American Indigenous Vision of Law and Peace', **82** *California Law Review*, 981-1049.

Winn, Jane Kaufman (1994), 'Informal Financial Practices of Small Business in Taiwan', **28** *Law and Society Review*, 193-241.

0650
NEW ECONOMIC HISTORY AND LAW AND ECONOMICS

Alexander J. Field
Professor of Economics at Santa Clara University

Abstract

This chapter reviews the contributions of the new economic history in light of their relationship to the study of law and economics. After reviewing the progress of the subdiscipline over the past century, and comparing the approaches of new and old economic historians, the chapter provides an overview of some of the most important controversies in the field and offers a bibliography with references to the relevant literature.
JEL classification: K0, N0.
Keywords: New Economic History, Law and Economics, German Historical School

1. Introduction

The purpose of this chapter is to give readers a broad overview of the new economic history and its relationship to the study of law and economics. The emphasis is not primarily on contributions specifically concerned with law and institutional structure as explananda per se - such matters are treated elsewhere in these volumes. Rather the focus is on what the field of the new economic history is, what its relationship is to the 'old economic history', and how its methodology and concerns relate to those of the economics discipline on the one hand and the study of law and economics on the other.

To understand the relationship between law and economics and the new economic history, it is important to understand what the new economic history is (or was, since it is hardly new anymore) and what it reacted against. Economic history began its life as a specialized social science subdiscipline with close links to legal and institutional scholarship, and considerable shared interest in documenting rule variation and its independent causal influence on economic life. Receptivity to that methodological stance waned during the heyday of the new economic history, although there is evidence in recent years that it is beginning to wax again.

The new economic history was born in the United States in the late 1950s and early 1960s, and has subsequently come to have increasing influence in Europe and the rest of the world as well. Prior to the late 1950s scholarship in the area of economic history had a strong institutional, legal, and arguably statistical focus, but was largely agnostic when it came to the desirability of applying formal economic theory to historical inquiry. Attitudes toward theory changed with the advent of the new economic history, and with these came differences in how old and new economic historians defined their tasks. A strand of continuity over the last century has been a subject of concern in the history of growth and development. In this context, economic history is distinguishable from the history of economic thought, a branch of intellectual history.

2. The Legacy of the German Historical School

The first professor of economic history in the United States, William J. Ashley, assumed his position at Harvard University in 1892, seven years after the founding of the American Economic Association and eight years after the establishment of the American Historical Association. The initial memberships of both of these associations were heavily influenced by ideals and scholarship developing within German universities, which led the world in doctoral instruction at the end of the nineteenth century. Indeed, up until the 1880s it was impossible to obtain a PhD in the United States; the first American programs were established at Johns Hopkins University and Clark University at the end of the century.

The German tradition of economic scholarship, associated with such scholars as Wilhelm Roscher, Gustav von Schmoller, Karl Knies and Werner Sombart, emphasized inductive generalizations reached through the careful study of primary materials, and defined itself in opposition to the more abstract deductive approach popularized in England by David Ricardo and others. German economic scholarship was dynamic and developmental, in that it sought to delineate and understand how economic categories changed and evolved over time, leading to various 'stage' theories, or at least typologies of economic progress. The ambitions of German historical economists were hardly modest: they looked forward to a victory over the English approach as complete as had been Adam Smith's over Mercantilist doctrine (Gay, 1941, p. 10).

This ambition was overreaching, a conclusion announced as early as 1901 by Thorstein Veblen and affirmed consistently by scholars thereafter (Veblen, 1901). Neither the extensive description of legal and institutional environments nor the development of stage theories of economic development would halt the elaboration, development and growing influence of partial and general equilibrium analysis known generically as neoclassical economics. But the failure of the historical school to supplant economic theory led many economists to dismiss its concerns, in particular the emphasis on description of the institutional and cultural context within which economic activity takes place as a starting point for static economic analysis, and the focus on the *process* of economic growth and development - the how and why of institutional change over time and its consequences - as of limited relevance to economic inquiry. Specialized scholars in economic history rejected, and continue by and large to reject, this view. But the drift away from the German tradition within US economics departments left a major unanswered question: what was to be the role of legal and institutional scholarship and more particularly what were economic historians supposed to do within economics departments? This question has been finessed during the twentieth century, and remains with us today. In England and Europe, on the other hand, it was largely resolved politically, although not intellectually, through the establishment of separate departments of economic history.

The finessing began with the first US appointment in the field. When Ashley migrated from England to assume the first American chair in economic history, he took pains to distance himself from the German tradition by rejecting any ambition to supplant economic theory. In exchange, he asked that the study of economic history in economics departments 'be let alone'. Thus was a truce declared. He proposed an historic division of labor within economics departments, with economists concerned with static analysis within existing institutional structures, and economic historians assuming the tasks not only of documenting the historical trajectories of development, but also of describing institutional structure, documenting its changes across time and space and considering its impact on economic growth. The position of economic history *vis à vis* historical scholarship was reaffirmed by Ashley's successor at Harvard, Edwin Gay, in his presidential lecture inaugurating the Economic History Association in 1940. Gay, a student of Schmoller, who had in turn been a student of Roscher, candidly reiterated the view that 'the full hopes of the historical economists have not been realized and are not realizable' (Gay, 1941, p. 13).

But the rejection of the 'full hopes' of the German school did not mean for Ashley or for Gay that economic historians in the United States rejected wholesale its concerns or methods. The most important area of continuity between the German and English traditions in Europe and indeed between the old and new economic history in the United States has been a subject concerned with the process of economic growth and development. A key difference between old and new economic history, we shall see, has been the role allotted to legal and institutional structure as independent factors accounting for variations in economic performance over time. For old economic historians that role was much larger, which is why, for them, delineation of structure was the starting point (although not, in principle, the ending point) for analysis.

One can appreciate the old economic history perspective on the tasks of economic history in this excerpt from a paper published in 1913 by Guy Callender in the *American Historical Review*. Callender, then professor of economic history at Yale, began by contrasting the lack of interest in economic history he experienced that year at the annual meeting of the American Economic Association with that displayed by historians at their conclave. He noted that relative interest levels in the two disciplines appeared to have reversed over the previous two decades and went on to reaffirm the indebtedness of economic history to the German historical tradition, as well as the primacy of institutional analysis as the starting point for economic inquiry: 'economic history owes its existence to [the historical school] ... Economic science ought to be primarily a theory of development and not merely an explanation of the way in which human beings produce wealth and share it as income under a given set of social conditions'.

Callender's vision of economic history as a fundamentally empirical science, concerned with growth and development, recognizing that institutions have consequences for economic performance and may change over time in ways we should try and understand, is a statement of the tasks of economic history that continues to have relevance today. But only parts of it would have found favor at the height of the new economic history revolution. Although new economic historians were as concerned as was Callender with understanding growth and development, institutional variation was *not* the first thing they turned to in accounting for it.

A second arguable area of continuity among old and new economic history has been an emphasis on the use of statistics to measure economically important magnitudes. Sir John Clapham, in his inaugural lecture for the first chair in economic history at Cambridge University in England proclaimed it 'the obvious business of an economic historian to be a measurer above other historians' (cited in McCloskey, 1987, p. 41; from Clapham 1930, p. 68), and most new economic historians would embrace the sentiment. The continuity is arguable, however, because old economic historians' interest in statistics was often limited to documenting the historical record.

New economic historians have been interested in doing more than just clarifying the record per se: they have yearned to verify conjectures, to 'test hypotheses'. New economic historians have been more likely to say, 'well, if this is true, then that must be true. Let's go look at the data and see if it is.' They have also been armed with more powerful statistical techniques - in particular multiple regression - and much cheaper computational tools than were available to their predecessors. And they have approached with enthusiasm the task of teasing out relationships and possible causal connections from the experiments provided by history in what of course has had to remain a nonexperimental science.

Another reason the continuity is arguable is that in the first half of the twentieth century the most dedicated analyzers of quantitative historical data were not economic historians per se but rather students of business cycles associated with the National Bureau of Economic Research. Wesley Mitchell, Arthur Burns and Simon Kuznets were certainly sympathetic to the study of economic history, but it was not their primary professional identification. This anomaly led Carter Goodrich to wonder, on the eve (or morning?) of the revolution in 1960, whether economic history [was] 'one subject or two?' He commented that 'the study of business cycles and conventional economic history are for the most part carried on in separate compartments' and that 'twice during the present century ... a vigorous body of research concerned with economic changes over time [has] developed largely in isolation from conventional economic history'. (The first was the study of business cycles, the second the resurgence in the 1950s in interest in economic growth.) 'In each case the new work was quantitative in method, and the result was the phenomenon of two separate bodies of scholarship - the one written in prose and calling itself economic history, the other written mainly in figures and calling itself by another name' (Goodrich, 1960, p. 531).

Goodrich concluded by asking plaintively whether 'If these are tasks that can be done better by scholars operating under another banner, is there any remaining purpose for us to serve?' The partial isolation of the field from work relevant to its main concerns was something that new economic historians wished to remedy, and it is one area in which there has been partial success.

A final area of continuity between the German and English/American traditions was in the commitment to describing and communicating to students the important and essential features of legal and institutional environments, even as this commitment received less and less affirmation from mainstream economists. Here one finds the weakest link between old and new economic history - a point of obvious relevance to scholars in the law and economics area. Both old and new historians have sought to understand and explain growth. Old economic historians, and institutional economists such as John R. Commons, were interested in institutions, not so much in and of themselves, as for the insight they might offer into variations in economic performance. Nevertheless, for old economic historians, one started with the institutions, and in that sense they were primary (Redlich, 1965, p. 482).

3. The Committee for Research in Economic History and the Founding of the Economic History Association

It is fair to say that throughout the first four decades of the twentieth century, American scholarship proceeded very much in the shadow of Europe. The outbreak of the World War Two in Europe created conditions under which the modern American university would blossom, both because of the interruptions of contacts and scholarly materials from overseas and because of the exodus of scholars (and scholars to be) from the war-torn continent. The latter migration, which brought to the United States such luminaries as Alexander Gerschenkron and Simon Kuznets, enriched economic history in the United States as it did other scholarly fields, and the increased difficulty of maintaining scholarly contact with Europe helped lead to the establishment in 1940 of a US based Economic History Association (EHA).

Although an Economic History Society (EHS) had existed in England since 1926, and been supported by American scholars, there were concerns that the EHS was partial to European topics and thus intermittent pressures for a new association on the western side of the Atlantic. The war catalyzed these concerns, and the establishment of the EHA along with its journal, the *Journal of Economic History*, announced and ratified at meetings of both the American Economics and the American Historical Associations in 1940, fleshed out the thesis against which the antithesis of the new economic history would be opposed (Lamoreaux, 1998).

Two other developments should be noted in order fully to appreciate the historical setting in the United States in the late 1950s and early 1960s, within which the new economic history strode brashly forward. The first was the establishment, also in 1940, with Rockefeller Foundation support, of the Committee on Research in Economic History, administered for the first 10 years through the Social Science Research Council, and incorporated separately thereafter. (The other, dealt with subsequently, was the rapid growth after 1957 of the American university system, the consequence of demographic trends and the launching of Sputnik.) The purpose of the Rockefeller grant was quite simply 'to develop the field of economic history.' To do this the committee supported studies of the role of government and its relationship to economic development, of entrepreneurship within the private sector, of the banking system and its role in mobilizing capital and facilitating interregional and intersectoral intermediation, and of historical statistics (Cole, 1953, p. 79).

The latter initiative is probably least well known yet illustrates how interest in statistical data does represent at least a weak strand of continuity between the concerns of the old and new economic history. CREH funding partially supported the preparation of the first edition of *Historical Statistics of the United States*, published by the Federal government's Bureau of the Census in 1949 (Cole, 1953). This publication and its successors both reflect and have served as a starting point for much research in US economic history, providing authoritative statistical series extending far beyond those available in current editions of the *Statistical Abstract of the United States* or *Economic Report of the President*. A second edition of *Historical Statistics* appeared in 1960, with data through 1957, and a Bicentennial edition in 1975, with data through 1970. A new 'millennial' edition is now under preparation by a consortium of economic scholars in universities (because of budget cutbacks the United States Census Bureau has been unwilling to fund a revision) and is scheduled to be published in both print and electronic editions by Cambridge University Press in the year 2000.

The other CREH initiatives, particularly those in the areas of institutional structure, strengthened 'old economic history' traditions that new economic historians would enthusiastically reject. The committee's grants in the institutional area reflected a view that governments of American states had, in the early history of the republic, played an influential role in fostering economic development and that the increased federal role evident in the New Deal should be understood as a change in the locus of regulatory influence and government action to improve economic performance, not wholesale abandonment of a laissez faire past. CREH funding supported the well-known works by Oscar and Mary Handlin on the role of government in Massachusetts (Handlin and Handlin, 1969), as well as Louis Hartz's 1955 treatise on government in Pennsylvania, *The Liberal Tradition in America.* Less familiar are CREH funded studies of Georgia (Heath, 1954) and Missouri (Primm, 1954).

The intellectual framework underlying these grants was the 'old economic history' belief in the need for an intellectual division of labor between scholars who would describe the institutional setting within which economic activity (and the processes that led to its change over time) took place, and those who would model and study behavior within such settings. The position of economic historians within economics departments had traditionally reflected this division of labor, but it was and continued to be an awkward division because the intellectual tools needed to do the former well were different from those required to excel at the latter. Analyzing economic behavior within an institutional framework required tools of great analytical sophistication whereas studies of an evolving institutional environment required sensitivity to context, nuance and skills in the interpretation of documentary materials, all more likely to be found in humanities as opposed to mathematics or statistics departments.

It was this divergence of traditions and methodologies, particularly with respect to the use of formal economic theory in historical analysis, that the new economic historians would ultimately try to bridge. Fogel (1965, p. 95) argued in 1965 that 'the new economic history represents a reunification of economic history with economic theory and thus brings to an end the century old split between these two branches of economics'. The new economic historians possessed stronger training in statistical methods and econometrics than did their predecessors. But the emphasis on the use of statistics for measurement was not, as has been noted, entirely new. In that sense the term Cliometrics (from Clio, the muse of history), sometimes used synonymously for the new economic history, is misleading to the extent that it focuses on a less fundamental methodological initiative.

The more fundamental departure involved the selfconscious use of formal economic theory to model historical questions and, in so doing, identify empirically measurable magnitudes of interest and what might reasonably be inferred from them (McCloskey, 1978, p. 15). But the precise extent to which the revolution represented a rejection or abandonment of the historical division of labor announced by Ashley was always unclear. From the standpoint of law and economics - and the future of historical economics - the big and unanswered question remained: what was to be the role of legal and other institutions in the study of economic history, or, for that matter, economics? New economic historians dealt with the issue, with one or two notable exceptions, largely by ignoring it.

It was perhaps not coincidental that neither the Handlins nor Hartz had doctorates in economics or resided in economics departments (Oscar Handlin was in History and Hartz in the Government department, both at Harvard). Indeed, by the late 1940s, it was rare to find individuals within economics departments who had the background or interest to conduct such studies. The studies of the state's role in economic development were conducted by scholars outside of economics, scholars frankly more attuned to the historical analysis of the particular than were most economists by this time.

A second main CREH initiative, however, addressed private action within the governmental structures that Hartz and the Handlins were examining. This led to the establishment at Harvard in 1948 of a Center for Entrepreneurial History, an effort reflecting a Schumpeterian view that the driving economic forces within the private sector (circumscribed by legal, cultural and institutional structures) was the entrepreneur. Philosophically, this represented an extension, in a sense, of the 'great man' tradition of political and diplomatic history to economic history. The actual role played by Schumpeter in this center is unclear. He commented extensively on Cole's 1946 proposal for such a center in an essay published in part in the *Journal of Economic History* in 1947 as 'The Creative Response in Economic History' and in full in a recent edited collection of papers by Richard Swedberg (Swedberg, 1991, pp. 406-428). But Schumpeter spent most of the last years of his life (he died in 1950) at work on his monumental *History of Economic Analysis*.

In spite of Schumpeter's presence and legacy in the department, this initiative did not find more fertile intellectual ground within the Harvard department than had the state institutional studies. The methods used to study entrepreneurs were not those favored by the developing 'science' of economics, and most found it hard to see how a doctorate in the field was of much help in pursuing such studies. Finding little to assist them analytically or theoretically within economic theory, entrepreneurial historians turned to other disciplines, such as social psychology, for inspiration (McClelland et al., 1953). Thus the two main CREH initiatives had relatively little influence on scholars interested in historical economics who also had some systematic exposure to formal economics.

Establishment of the Research Center in Entrepreneurial History did, however, lead to the establishment of a second American journal in the area, *Explorations in Entrepreneurial History*, a journal that would be renamed *Explorations in Economic History* in 1969, presumably to distance itself somewhat from its intellectual origins and broaden its appeal. (A third American outlet, an annual, *Research in Economic History*, began publication in 1979.)

The final factors reinforcing the growth of the new economic history were US demographic trends and the launching in October of 1957 of Sputnik. The Soviet scientific and propaganda triumph led to a great deal of national soul searching and a substantial increase of US funding for scientific, including social scientific research. Although the baby boom in the US peaked in that year, the enormous number of children born after World War Two and their eventual demands for higher education, contributed, along with Sputnik, to a golden age for American academicians between 1957 and 1969. These were years of great expansion in the capacity of the American University system as undergraduate enrollments soared and faculty shortages developed. New and expanded graduate training programs designed to address these shortages served in the short run only to worsen them as they added their own demand for new faculty to an already undersupplied pool (the phenomenon can be understood in economic terms as a capital stock adjustment phenomenon). The real income of scholars and funds available for research increased over these years until the expanded graduate programs eventually flooded the faculty market as the 1970s began, and the macroeconomic legacy of the Vietnam war led to more moderate levels of support for scientific research (Field, 1987a).

4. The New Economic History - Goals and Agenda

The new economic history defined itself and made its greatest impact during these golden years. What the insurgents promised was an extension of the revolution in method then sweeping the economics profession as a whole, a revolution that emphasized much greater use of analytical, mathematical and statistical methods, to economic history. The old intellectual guideposts were vigorously attacked. In particular, two pillars of the CREH initiatives and the traditional economic history - (1) the emphasis on description of institutional or legal structures as the first step in understanding the process of development and (2) the study of entrepreneurial behavior within those structures - was, if not rejected, at least very substantially reduced in the attention devoted to it.

First, the causal importance of entrepreneurial choice, vision, and action was downplayed. As William Parker put it, in discussing how rational businesspeople had responded to the changes in prices resulting from technological change, capital accumulation, demographic growth and the expansion of natural resources, 'there is not much room here for good and bad entrepreneurs' (Parker, 1971, p. 6). As a consequence of such attitudes, students of entrepreneurial history felt themselves increasingly less welcome within the Economic History Association (Lamoreaux, 1998).

Gone also was much reverence for studies of evolving institutional structures, such as those by Hartz and the Handlins, with their implicit assumption that politics and public policy choices mattered because they influenced the environment within which economic activity took place. Fishlow and Fogel (1971, p. 18) argued that the shift to an explicit concern with long run economic growth and development meant an 'inevitable shift of focus from earlier writing in which the description of the institutional structure was the central objective'. In principle the concern of old economic historians with institutions was instrumental - the ultimate purpose was, or should have been, to shed light on economic performance. In practice, Fishlow and Fogel's implicit criticism is probably fair: scholars did end up focussing centrally on description of the institutional structures, spending less time articulating clearly what their impact was on performance. In any event, instead of entrepreneurs and institutions, much greater emphasis was now placed on technological and demographic change and their consequences, worked out and understood within the analytical framework provided by formal economic theory. Such a framework could, of course, be used to explore the consequences of variation in rule structures, but such issues were less frequently explored.

Why did the new economic history give law and institutions so little intellectual shelf space? Some scholars were influenced by residual Marxian views that the forces of production (technology) ultimately influenced the relations of production (institutions, culture). Thus it was deemed less important to study the evolution of institutions per se - since ultimately they were epiphenomenal. It was far better to go right to the source: the technological and demographic prime movers of history. Ironically, these residual Marxian tendencies often dovetailed conveniently with a conservative approach to public policy issues, in the sense that at one level, institutions did not matter all that much and therefore it was not worth spending a great deal of time studying them or exploring the consequences of changes or variation in them (Field, 1991, pp. 2-4).

In some instances this view was supported by careless interpretations of the 'Coase theorem' (Field, 1991, pp. 10-16). Coase, of course, never developed his analysis as a theorem - this language, common in economic discourse, itself reflected the encroachment within economics departments of the culture and language of mathematics departments - but his articles did suggest that, *assuming there were no transactions costs*, the initial assignment of economic rights should not affect the ultimate economic disposition of a resource. Coase's analysis was microeconomic, and it is not clear he ever intended it to apply at the level of macroinstitutional structure. He admitted that the institution of slavery probably did affect the disposition of resources - for example, black labor in the New World - but took this to be the exception, rather than the rule. For older economic historians, and those interested in general in the consequences of institutional change and variation, the impact of an institution such as slavery on the regional and sectoral distribution of inputs is, of course, the rule rather than the exception. Moreover, transactions costs do exist, and consequently some institutional rules are superior - more efficient - than others, in the sense that they economize on transactions costs or allow risk to be borne by parties who are better situated to do so. That indeed, is the insight that underlies much recent law and economic literature, and represents a productive way in which law and economics scholars have tried to make endogenous the 'choice' of legal rules.

Coase's position on the role of legal institutions as exogenous determinants of performance remains, however, ambiguous. In a 1997 retrospective, the law and economics scholar William M. Landes wrote that he (Landes)

> was genuinely interested in explaining legal rules and doctrine from an economic perspective. Coase was not. He believed that knowledge of law and legal institutions was valuable because it helped one understand how explicit markets truly worked ... (Landes, 1997)

That sentiment, of course, would place Coase squarely in the intellectual traditions represented by old economic history.

For whatever reasons, new economic historians were, on balance, less interested in legal, political and constitutional issues, particularly at the macro level. Either such issues were ignored, on the grounds that for the regions and time periods under investigation such conditions were relatively stable, or had variations whose effects were swamped by variations in other (technological or demographic) variables; or attempts were made to explain change with reference to technological and demographic models which did not in turn make reference to institutions as givens within the explanatory model. One of the most ambitious attempts along these lines was that by North and Thomas, which attempted to account for eight centuries of European development in 158 pages, trying to appeal only to technological and demographic variables, and avoid reference to 'ad hoc' political or institutional conditions or changes as causal factors in their own right (North and Thomas, 1973; Field, 1981).

Why this aversion to explicitly recognizing institutional factors as both consequential and in part exogenous? Probably because there was a sense that to do so was to allow the camel's nose under the tent, to take the first step down the slippery slope of adhocery whereby the methodology and concerns of the old economic history would reintroduce themselves. If one analyzes the North and Thomas argument carefully, however, one finds that they are in fact, and scarcely surprisingly, forced to violate their methodological strictures in order to tell their story. In subsequent works North appears to acknowledge this, by explicitly discussing the impact on behavior of such factors as ideology (North, 1981, 1990) but the underlying methodologically individualist research program persists.

Having rejected or drastically downplayed the old economic history's concerns with entrepreneurship and institutions, the revolutionaries levied a more general methodological criticism. Rightly or wrongly, they stigmatized their older colleagues as having been satisfied with general and vague qualitative statements about causal factors in economic growth. Cliometricians insisted that explanatory hypotheses be explicitly set forth and that scholars go beyond the simple qualitative statement that something mattered, to exploring exactly how much it mattered. For example, Robert Fogel and Albert Fishlow rejected the argument by W.W. Rostow and others that the railroad was 'critical' or 'indispensable' for nineteenth century American economic development on the grounds that one could not attach economic magnitudes to these qualitative evaluations (Fogel, 1964; Fishlow, 1965a). They explored the indispensability thesis about American railroads using a 'counterfactual methodology' by asking how much lower would have been GNP if the railroad had not been developed, in one case in 1859, in the other in 1890. The difference between GNP as it was in actuality and what it would have been in the absence of the railroad represents the 'social savings' of the innovation.

Historians objected strongly to the counterfactual methodology but, as noted, the charge that previous students of historical economics had been uninterested in measurement is unfair. What was true was that more conscious theorizing now made it possible to tease out new and intriguing inferences from quantitative data, and helped direct researchers towards particular (and sometimes different) magnitudes. In retrospect, the indictment of old economic historians as uninterested in measurement and prone to set forth casual, qualitative and empirically unsubstantiated causal hypotheses could with rather more justification have been levied at many of the mathematical theorists then coming to dominate economic departments.

Is this entirely coincidental? If one takes the *methodenstreit* of the early 1960s at face value, it concerns how theoretically self conscious economic history should be. But perhaps old economic historians were merely stalking horses in a struggle as much within economics itself as to how empirically and historically focused the larger discipline would be. This is a speculative hypothesis, and the evidence supporting it inconclusive. McCloskey, writing in 1976, did not think this was so - (s)he felt that the attack on old economic history - certainly a far weaker adversary than those gradually importing math department values into economics departments, represented a political error, a failure by 'economic imperialists' to insure sufficient levels of domestic support (McCloskey, 1976, p. 438). It was easier to beat up on the old economic historians, but perhaps not wiser in the longer run. McCloskey also studied the percentage of column inches devoted to economic history in the main general interest economic journals in the United States (*American Economic Review*, *Quarterly Journal of Economics*, *Journal of Political Economy*) and found a significant downward shift between the periods 1925-44 and 1945-74; there is little evidence that this trend has been reversed in the last quarter century. Callender, of course, was already bemoaning this neglect in 1913.

Certainly Douglass North's comment in 1965 displays little ambivalence about who the heroes were:

> In summary, it is my conviction that we need to sweep out the door a good deal of the old economic history, to improve the quality of the new economic history, and it is incumbent upon economists to cast a skeptical eye upon the research produced by their economic history colleagues to see that it lives up to standards which they would expect in other areas of economics. (North, 1965, p. 91)

The irony is that comments such as those of North have, on balance, fostered neither hostility toward economic history nor a critical perspective on its practice. Rather they run the danger of feeding indifference. Such indifference impoverishes economic analysis as a whole, but its prevalence is not entirely the fault of mainstream economists. Both economics and economic history might well have been healthier had a different course been pursued by the revolutionaries, had they not embraced so uncritically the potential of neoclassical economic theory to illuminate historical inquiry. As McCloskey noted, 'The days are passing when the social sciences bridged the two cultures, literary and scientific, and economics burned the bridge long ago' (McCloskey, 1976, p. 439).

In general, economic theorists have actually been less enthusiastic about the power of their tools to illuminate historical inquiry (in some cases the skepticism seems to spill over to contemporary data as well) than have been new economic historians. Simon Kuznets summarized discussion of a variety of methods papers at the 1957 EHA annual meetings and noted, somewhat surprisingly, that

> Three theorists on a panel were 'rather skeptical of the value of greater integration of economic theory and economic history' …. On the other hand, at least some of the panel discussants and Gerschenkron from the floor, appeared to feel a greater need for reliance (in economic history) on economic theory... it did seem as if almost all economic theorists participating in the discussion were doubtful of the value of theory in work on economic history, while at least some economic historians felt that it [was] needed. (Kuznets, 1957, p. 550)

One detects a similar reticence on the part of theorists at a 1984 AEA session to propagandize too highly for the value of their tools in historical inquiry (Solow, 1985, p. 328).

5. Economic History, Douglass North and the Nobel Prize

The Nobel prize in economics was first awarded in 1969, and a review of recipients with work touching on economic history, law and economics, and their relationship provides perspective on the recent evolution of these disciplines. Simon Kuznets was the first of five honorees with such connections. Although Kuznets, who received the award in 1971, did not consider himself primarily a new economic historian, he trained many of its pioneers (such as Robert Fogel and Stanley Engerman) and his development of national income accounting reflected the new economic history's passion for measurement. Kuznets' work laid the foundation for modern empirical macroeconomics and macroeconomic history, even though, as noted by Goodrich above, the National Bureau tradition proceeded largely independently from economic history.

Five years later (1976) Milton Friedman received the award. From the standpoint of economic history, his greatest contribution has been in the area of monetary history, in particular the monumental 1963 work coauthored with Anna Schwartz, *A Monetary History of the United States* (Friedman and Schwartz, 1963). Friedman's work, and the reaction to it, played an important role in seating the study of cyclical macroeconomic phenomena squarely within the purview of economic history. Part of the success here, however, is attributable to a shift toward a more contemporary focus on policy issues by the National Bureau under the leadership of Martin Feldstein, with the consequence that historical studies of business cycles no longer play as central a role in the Bureau's agenda.

Fifteen years later, in 1991, Ronald Coase won the prize. Coase is a pivotal figure in the development of industrial organization as well as law and economics, and his contributions are discussed in detail elsewhere in these volumes. To the extent that economic historians have developed a more sophisticated approach to economic and legal institutions, his ideas have been important. Yet for reasons having to do with the sociology of the profession, his overall influence on economic history has been curiously weak. This is because scholars who start out self-identifying as economic historians, but become interested and proficient in a 'Coasian' type of analysis, generally begin publishing in law reviews or law and economics journals. There is little bias against an historical perspective in law; indeed one might argue that such a perspective is essential, and thus the barriers to exit in this direction are weak.

Finally, in 1993, two pioneers of the new economic history, Robert Fogel and Douglass North, received the prize. Fogel was a central player in two of the defining intellectual debates of the Cliometrics revolution, the study of how indispensable were the American railroads and, in a book coauthored with Stanley Engerman in 1974, *Time on the Cross*, the economics of slavery. This latter work, which attempted to turn upside down much received wisdom about how efficient the slave plantation system had been, and how well slaves were housed, fed, clothed and treated, engendered enormous controversy within the profession. In the last two decades, Fogel has pioneered in the use of historical demographic data to study variations and changes in the standard of living.

Douglass North made important empirical contributions to the economic history of the antebellum period, in particular his study of the US as an export-led economy from 1790 to 1860 (North, 1961). But his greatest professional success has been in trying to fill the gap left by the new economic history's attack on the older legal/institutional tradition. For many scholars outside of the profession, North *is* the new economic history. But there is a real question as to how central North's institutional work is to the new economic history or what exactly law and economics scholars should draw from it. How to reintegrate institutions with historical analysis without reembracing the 'errors' of the old economic history? As noted, in his 1973 work with Robert Paul Thomas, instead of making the study of the institutional framework the starting point of analysis, North struggled bravely to avoid appeals to ad hoc explanations, and instead to develop endogenous theories of institutions: that is, August 17, 1999 theories that would explain within a general (not historical or case-specific) framework, how and why institutions varied over time and space. The problem with such an approach is this. If we take the fundamental task of economic history to be understanding and explaining economic performance over time, then an interest in institutions - by old or new economic historians - is ultimately relevant only to the degree that it can shed light on such performance. To the extent that institutions are made endogenous - determined within the context of a general theory by more fundamental factors such as technology or demography, they cannot play an independent role in accounting for variation in performance.

These are the dimensions of the intellectual box that North - and scholars in many other disciplines - have struggled mightily to escape from. In a 1971 book coauthored with Lance Davis, Davis and North were willing to take the initial constitutional setup as given, but then went on to describe how private groups motivated by self interest seized profitable opportunities to make institutional innovations. Ex post one can certainly find many cases where such a perspective makes good narrative history. But whether Davis and North actually succeed in developing a general theory, an 'explanatory framework' that leads to refutable hypotheses, remains questionable. This was the view of Olmstead and Goldberg (1975), who also pointed out that many of the factors (such as public opinion) that North and Davis took as exogenous environmental factors, could in fact also be affected by expenditures of resources by private groups.

In the previously discussed *The Rise of the Western World*, coauthored with Robert Paul Thomas (North and Thomas, 1973), North tried to make endogenous the entire institutional structure of Western Europe, accounting for the breakdown of feudalism and the rise of modern economic and political institutions with reference only to more fundamental factors, such as demographic change and, to a lesser degree, new technology. The key component of their analysis is the labor to land ratio, whose rise, caused by population growth, is supposed to account for the demise of feudalism. But feudalism in western Europe broke down both as population rose, prior to the Black Death, and when population fell, after the plague. Moreover, falling population appears to have been associated with a recrudescence of feudalism in Eastern Europe, and it was precisely the scarcity of labor that Evsey Domar has used to explain the initiation and persistence of coerced labor regimes, both in Eastern Europe, and in the American South (Domar, 1970). Looked at objectively, one extracts from the work a theory that says that rising labor to land ratios lead to breakdowns of coerced labor regimes, except when they do not.

In later work, North (1981, 1990) has made valiant attempts to respond to such criticisms, but as one reads his contributions, one cannot help but continue to ask how much of the 'explanation' represents ex post rationalization for what has happened. One continues to be troubled by the paucity of testable hypotheses, as compared, for example, with his earlier empirical studies of the US as a (cotton) export led economy prior to the Civil War (North, 1961). That theory generated predictions that other scholars such as Fishlow (1965b) could then test (in a way not favorable to the North hypothesis) but in the process our understanding of antebellum economic history advanced.

Northian institutional economic history tends to be neither quantitatively empirical nor, because of its sweep, informed by detailed knowledge of law in its particulars. In contrast, scholars in the law and economics area *must* possess such understanding. In the United States, a minimum familiarity with the law of property, contracts, civil procedure and torts (at least at the level it is taught in a typical first year law school curriculum) as well as some Constitutional Law is in general a precondition for success in the field. Particularly in countries with an Anglo Saxon tradition, legal research and historical archival research have important similarities: the role of precedent (stare decisis) means that history matters (although in legal research the 'archives' are more likely to be computer searchable).

Legal scholarship, in general, has a solid grounding in the history and historiography of the law, as reflected for example in the enormous footnote apparatus of a typical law review article. Empirical economics and economic history, in general, have a firm grounding in the statistical record. Northian institutional economic history, written almost exclusively from secondary sources, often lacks much of either. Armchair economic theorists, and North, have a fondness for 'stylized facts' but stylized facts are sometimes simply wrong, and someone has to be responsible for trying to ensure that the generalizations are reasonable. It falls to economic (and legal) historians to be at least as concerned with accurately characterizing the stylized facts as explaining them.

North, as we have seen, has been a continuing proponent of revitalizing economic history through the introduction of the perspectives of economic theory, and the urge to generalize in his work often militates against detailed immersion in the particulars of a topic. But importing even a little bit of the attitude toward data of theoretical economists into historical, let alone legal or institutional scholarship, creates real problems. In an effort which has been relatively exceptional in recent years, however, Wallis and North (1986) did try empirically to estimate the size of the transactions economy: that part of economic activity devoted to negotiating and transactions among individuals, as opposed simply to producing the goods or nontransactions services (like haircuts).

In reflecting on North's contributions, one is struck by the extent to which the interface between law and economics and economic history might benefit from more contributions such as McCurdy (1978). This article, although published in the *Journal of Economic History*, displays the legal historian's knowledge of constitutional and statutory law and attention to detail sometimes lacking in North's grand excursions. I mention McCurdy's article first because it is relatively obscure and second because it deals with private actions to achieve institutional change - in this case those of American corporations such as Singer to eliminate state created obstacles to interstate trade, and in so doing help forge a national market. Such actions in response to opportunities for gain are of course the main subject of Davis and North.

When all is said and done, however, North deserves credit for the indefatigable way in which he has worked successfully to reinject a concern with legal and institutional arrangement back in to the new economic history. What can law and economics scholars learn from North's sweeping forays into institutional and economic history? Probably not too much about law and economics. But his work can open up for them a better understanding of the broad macroeconomic concerns about growth and development that are second nature to practicing economic historians and remain at the core of the discipline. Interested readers should consult North's numerous publications (see bibliography) as well as surveys such as Libecap, (1978, 1986).

Returning to Fogel, the publication of *Time on the Cross* in 1974 engendered enormous publicity and an equally massive intellectual reaction (see David et al., 1976). Looking back from the perspective of the late 1990s, the controversy over slavery in the 1970s, which continued a conversation begun by Conrad and Meyer in 1958, was in a very real sense the beginning of the end of the new economic history as a revolutionary movement (Conrad and Meyer, 1958). There have been few contributions in the last two decades that have engendered anywhere near as much heat, with the possible exception of relatively recent work on technological lock-in (Arthur 1994; David, 1985).

This reduction in heat has not been entirely regrettable. Some of the criticisms of the old economic history evidenced more bluster than substance, and when the dust settled and these critiques were subject to more dispassionate analysis, were found to have weak intellectual foundations. Although there were a few more displays of revolutionary rhetoric in the late 1970s, the field began to exhibit more intellectual maturity. The sense of superiority that economic historians trained as economists maintained *vis à vis* their colleagues trained as historians began to weaken, and a rapprochement of sorts took place at least with those historians who remained active in the Economic History Association because of their interest in the application of social science methods to history.

Although mathematical symbols and econometric results continue to appear frequently within the pages of economic history articles, text and narrative hold their own as important parts of the exercise in persuasion. And so an uneasy methodological truce has been reestablished, with economic history in the late twentieth century perhaps now poised to provide object lessons both to historians and to economists about how to conduct empirically based, analytically sophisticated inquiries into social phenomena.

But the fundamental issue of the role of legal and institutional analysis within economics and the role of economic historians in addressing such phenomena remains unresolved. The finesses simply have not been successful. Perhaps the scholar who came closest to striking the right balance in recent decades was Jonathan Hughes. Hughes, although a new economic historian, was always something of a maverick, publishing entrepreneurial history when it was no longer fashionable, and, when it was no longer fashionable, continuing to treat the institutional environment as consequential and at least partially exogenous, and thus deserving of detailed attention in its own right (Hughes, 1966, 1977). His approach to institutions can also be appreciated by reading the first sections of his textbook (Hughes, 1990).

6. What have been the Contributions of the New Economic History in Recent Decades?

The best current overview of the contributions of the new economic history to the economic history in the United States is Atack and Pasell (1994). This is the second edition of a volume that appeared first in 1979 as Lee and Passell. The second edition is more comprehensive and balanced; the first, for example, devoted almost a third of its text to slavery, reflecting the extent to which that topic dominated discussion in the 1970s. For a survey of the state of the art in economic history circa 1972, readers should consult Davis, Easterlin and Parker, 1972. For a textbook on American topics with a somewhat more chronological approach, see Hughes (1990). Although this essay focuses largely on American topics, readers interested in what the new economic history has accomplished for the historiography of British growth should consult Floud and McCloskey (1994). For a modern survey of the role of technological change in economic development, see Mokyr (1990). For membership lists, online book reviews, sample syllabi, discussion groups, and more, consult the website maintained by the Cliometrics society at http://cs.muohio.edu. The Cliometrics association also publishes a newsletter, which in recent years has printed interviews with new economic history pioneers.

Identifying the significant post-slavery controversy developments in US economic history is difficult. Southern agriculture has continued to figure, with important books by Ransom and Sutch (1977) and Wright (1978, 1986). Ransom and Sutch (1977) and Wright (1986) both focus on the post bellum period, as do Alston and Ferrie (1985). The greater interest in post Civil War topics was reinforced by the publication in 1977 of Alfred Chandler's *The Visible Hand.* The book was influential not only because of its masterful reinterpretation of the dependence of the rise of the modern business enterprise on new communication and transportation technologies (the telegraph and the railroad), not only for the stimulus it has given to the study of post Civil War topics, but also because it was significant in reintegrating the sophisticated study of business history into the agenda of economic history (Field, 1987a; Temin, 1991; Lamoreaux and Raff, 1995; Lamoreaux, Raff and Temin, 1998).

The 1980s also saw an emphasis on the systematic analysis of height by age data to shed new light on variations in standards of living across time and space. This has been part of a broader increase in the interests of new economic historians in historical demography (Steckel, 1995). Another notable development has been increased interest in the phenomenon of technological lock-in - the idea that economies might be subject to technological hysterisis and thus path-dependent. The argument is that accidents of the past can matter, determining everything from the shape of a dollar bill to our dependence on internal rather than external combustion (steam) engines for road transport (David, 1985; Arthur, 1994). While this literature has developed largely out of an interest in technological trajectories, it has great potential relevance for the study of legal structure and institutions. Indeed, since there is broader variation in legal structures at moments in time than there is in technological practice, lock-in effects might be more significant in the analysis of law than in technology per se. This is largely an unexplored area (Field, 1991), however, and the empirical significance of technological lock-in remains under debate (Liebowitz and Margolis, 1990), although it has figured heavily in the 1998 Department of Justice antitrust proceeedings against the Microsoft corporation.

Other major trends in the 1980s and 1990s have included an emphasis on what might be called applied labor economics using older data - with analysis applied to everything from the traffic in indentured servants in the colonial period (Galenson, 1981) to the earnings of women (Goldin, 1990). But macroeconomics has not been entirely eclipsed, particularly in studies of the Great Depression. Its history remains in an unsettled state, but not for want of attention, with a new international perspective (Eichengreen, 1992; Temin, 1989), which emphasizes the deflationary consequences of failure to abandon gold as well as new work by Field (1992) and Romer (1992) exploring internal reasons why the depression in the United States was so long and a number of contributions focusing on the role of financial structure (see Calomiris, 1993 for a review of recent research on financial aspects of the downturn).

In other work Romer has questioned the conventional wisdom that the post-World War Two period has in fact been less volatile than prior periods. Romer's methodology was thought provoking, but the contribution is notable also because it signals the degree to which, whether on the microeconomic or macroeconomic side, the great unexplored frontier for economic historians lies in the post-World War Two period. It is symptomatic that the Atack and Passell survey stops in 1940, and the postwar sections in standard economic history texts tend to be relatively weak. When the new economic history began in the late 1950s, the end of the World War Two was barely a decade in the past, and consequently it was hard to think of the postwar period in historical terms. More than half a century has now elapsed since 1945, a half century that will benefit in the future from the detailed attentions of economic historians. Such work will likely cause us increasingly to rethink interpretations of prior periods.

7. Conclusion

Scholars in law and economics should read economic history not so much because of what it will teach them about law, but because of what it can teach them about economies. In spite of all the methodological writing about the differences between old and new economic history, one constant throughout the century during which the subdiscipline of economic history has had a distinct existence has been an empirical concern with the process of economic growth and development. This theme unifies the practitioners of the German historical school, with their tastes for inductively developing stage theories of growth, through the old economic history up through and continuing with the new economic history. The general understanding of the trajectories of growth and development, and the creative use of the framework of economic theory to account for these are valuable complements to the knowledge base typically possessed by the law and economics scholar. So too is the consistent approach to data and measurement - particularly because the study of law and economics, with the possible exception of studies of criminal law, is not in general empirically quantitative.

The contributions of the new economic history to legal analysis per se are less clear, with the possible exception of recent work on lock in. First of all, law and economics scholars will already be familiar with much of it, because individuals who may have begun in economic history have mastered the body of knowledge possessed by law and economic scholars and have consequently published in *Journal of Law and Economics* or various Law Reviews. A search of the Econ Lit database (published for the American Economic Association by Silver Platter) for economic history and law brings up over a thouand citations, but most of them are *not* in economic history journals.

Law and economics researchers interested in institutional and legal structure per se may actually find more of interest in the writings of old economic historians. But for economic historians, the interest in law and institutions has, at least in principle, always been instrumental - the payoff comes in understanding how variation in such structures may affect performance. Naturally, time in the classroom and time in the library is limited and old economic historians can be faulted for sometimes appearing to lose steam after describing the changing institutional structure, perhaps assuming that the connections with economic performance were obvious. They are not. On the other hand, new economic historians have often ignored the institutional structure or tried to make it endogenous. It is in understanding the links between legal and institutional structure and performance that lie the greatest challenges to scholars in law and economics and economic history.

Acknowledgments

I would like to thank Peter Temin, Gavin Wright and an anonymous referee for their helpful comments.

Bibliography on New Economics History and Law and Economics (0650)

Because a comprehensive list of references to specific contributions in the new economic history would be far too extensive for this collection, I focus on some main contributions which will give the reader a sense of the contributions, as well as a selection of survey and evaluative pieces that help to provide an overview.

Alston, Lee J. and Ferrie, Joseph P. (1985), 'Labor Costs, Paternalism and Loyalty in Southern Agriculture: A Constraint on the Growth of the Welfare State', **45** *Journal of Economic History*, 95-117.

Arthur, Brain (1994), *Increasing Returns and Path Dependence in the Economy*, Ann Arbor, University of Michigan Press.

Ashley, W.J. (1893), 'On the Study of Economic History', **17** *Quarterly Journal of Economics*.

Ashton, T.S. (1946), 'The Relation of Economic History to Economic Theory', *Economica* NS May 1946, reprinted in the Study of Economic History, edited by N.B. Harte, London, Frank Cass, 1971, 161-80

Atack, Jeremy and Passell, Peter (1994), *A New Economic View of American History*, 2nd edn, New York, W.W. Norton.

Callender, Guy S. (1913), 'The Position of American Economic History', **19** *American Historical Review,* 80-97.

Calomiris, Charles (1993), 'Financial Factors in the Great Depression', **7** *Journal of Economic Perspectives*, 61-85.

Chandler, Alfred (1977), *The Visible Hand: The Managerial Revolution in American Business*, Cambridge, Harvard University Press.

Clapham, J.H. (1930), 'Economic History as a Discipline', **V** *Encyclopedia of the Social Sciences*, New York, Macmillan.

Cochran, Thomas C. (1959), 'Recent Contributions to Economic History: The United States, The Twentieth Century', **19** *Journal of Economic History*, 64-75.

Cole, Arthur H. (1953), 'Committee on Research in Economic History: A Description of its Purposes, Activities, and Organization', **13** *Journal of Economic History*, 79-87.

Conrad, Alfred and Meyer, John (1958), 'The Economics if Slavery in the Antebellum South', **66** *Journal of Political Economy*.

David, Paul A. (1985), 'Clio and the Economics of QWERTY', **75** *American Economic Review*, 332-337.

David, Paul A. et al. (1976), *Reckoning with Slavery : A Critical Study in the Quantitative History of American Negro Slavery*, Oxford, Oxford University Press.

Davis, Lance E. and North, Douglass C. (1971), *Institutional Change and American Economic Growth*, Cambridge, Cambridge University Press.

Davis, Lance E., Easterlin, Richard and Parker, William (1972), *American Economic History: An Economists' History of the United States*, New York, Harper and Row.

Domar, Evsey (1970), 'The Causes of Slavery and Serfdom, A Hypothesis', **30** *Journal of Economic History*, 18-32.

Eichengreen, Barry (1992), *Golden Fetters: The Gold Standard and the Great Depression, 1919-1939*, New York, Oxford University Press.

Engerman, Stanley L. (1992), 'Coerced and Free Labor: Property Rights and the Development of the Labor Force', **29** *Explorations in Economic History*, 1-29.

Field, Alexander J. (1981), 'The Problem with Neoclassical Institutional Economics: A Critique with Reference to the North-Thomas Model of Pre-1500 Europe', **18** *Explorations in Economic History*, 174-198.

Field, Alexander J. (1987a), 'The Future of Economic History', in Field, A.J. (ed.), *The Future of Economic History*, Boston, Kluwer-Nijhoff.

Field, Alexander J. (1987b), 'Modern Business Innovation as a Capital Saving Innovation', **47** *Journal of Economic History*, 473-485.

Field, Alexander J. (1991), 'Do Legal Systems Matter?', **28** *Explorations in Economic History*, 1-35.

Field, Alexander J. (1992), 'Uncontrolled Land Development and the Duration of the Depression in the United States', **52** *Journal of Economic History*, 785-805.

Fishlow, Albert (1965a), *American Railroads and the Transformation of the Antebellum Economy*, Cambridge, Harvard University Press.

Fishlow, Albert (1965b), 'Antebellum Interregional Trade Reconsidered', in Andreano, Ralph (ed.), *New Views in American Economic Development*, Cambridge, Harvard University Press.

Fishlow, Albert and Fogel, Robert, (1971), 'Quantitative Economic History: An Interim Evaluation - Past Trends and Present Tendencies', **31** *Journal of Economic History*, 15-42.

Floud, Roderick (1994), *The Economic History of Britain Since 1700* , 2nd edn, Cambridge, Cambridge University Press.

Floud, Roderick and McCloskey, Donald (1994), *The Economic History of Britain Since 1700*, 2nd edn, Cambridge, Cambridge University Press.

Fogel, Robert, William (1964), *Railroads and American Economic Growth: Essays in Econometric History*, Baltimore, Johns Hopkins University Press.

Fogel, Robert, William (1965), 'The Reunification of Economic History with Economic Theory', **55** *American Economic Review*, 92-98.

Fogel, Robert, William and Stanley Engerman (1974), *Time on the Cross: The Economics of American Negro Slavery*, Boston, Little Brown.

Friedman, Milton and Schwartz, Anna J. (1963), *A Monetary History of the United States, 1867-1960*, Princeton, Princeton University Press.

Galenson, David (1981), *White Servitude in colonial America: An Economic Analysis*, Cambridge, Cambridge University Press.

Gay, Edwin F. (1941) 'The Task of Economic History', **1** *Journal of Economic History*, 9-16.

Goldin, Claudia, Dale (1990), *Understanding the Gender Gap: An Economic History of American Women*, New York, Oxford University Press.

Goodrich, Carter (1959), 'Recent Contributions to Economic History: The United States, 1789-1860', **19** *Journal of Economic History*, 25-43.

Goodrich, Carter (1960), 'Economic History: One Field or Two?', **20** *Journal of Economic History*, 531-538.

Gras, N.S.B. (1930), 'Economic History in the United States', *Encyclopedia of the Social Sciences*, New York, Macmillan.

Handlin, Oscar and Handlin, Mary Flug (1969), *Commonwealth: A Study of the Role of Government in the American Economy: Massachusetts, 1774-186* (rev. edn), Cambridge, MA, Belknap Press of Harvard University Press.

Heath, Milton Sydney (1954), *Constructive Liberalism, the Role of the State in Economic Developments in Georgia to 1860*, Cambridge, Harvard University Press.

Heaton, Herbert (1941), 'The Early History of the Economic History Association', **1** *Journal of Economic History*, 107-109.

Higgs, Robert (1985), 'Crisis, Bigger Government, and Ideological Change: Two Hypotheses on the Ratchet Phenomenon', **22** *Explorations in Economic History*, 1-28.

Hughes, Jonathan (1966), *The Vital Few; American Economic Progress and its Protagonists*, Boston, Houghton Mifflin.

Hughes, Jonathan (1977), *The Governmental Habit: Economic Controls from Colonial Times to the Present*, New York, Basic Books.

Hughes, Jonathan (1990), *American Economic History*, 3rd edn, Glenview, Scott Foresman.

Kuznets, Simon (1941), 'Statistics and Economic History', **1** *Journal of Economic History*.

Kuznets, Simon (1957), 'Summary of Discussion and Postscript', **17** *Journal of Economic History*, 545-553.

Lamoreaux, Naomi (1998), 'Economic History and the Cliometric Revolution', in Molho, Anthony and Wood, Gordon (eds), *Imagined Histories: American Historians Interpret the Past*, Princeton, Princeton University Press.

Lamoreaux, Naomi and Raff, Daniel M.G. (1995), *Information and Coordination: Historical Perspectives on the Organization of Enterprise*, Chicago, University of Chicago Press.

Lamoreaux, Naomi, Raff, Daniel M.G. and Temin, Peter (1998), *Learning by Doing in Markets, Firms and Countries*, Chicago, University of Chicago Press.

Landes, William (1997), 'The Art of Law and Economics: An Autobiographical Essay', *American Economist*, 31-42.

Lee, Susan and Passell, Peter (1979), *A New Economic View of American History*, New York, W.W. Norton.

Libecap, Gary D. (1978), 'Economic Variables and the Development of the Law', **38** *Journal of Economic History*, 338-362.

Libecap, Gary D. (1986), 'Property Rights in Economic History: Implications for Research', **23** *Explorations in Economic History*, 227-252.

Liebowitz, Stanley J. and Margolis, Stephen E. (1990), 'The Fable of the Keys', **31** *Journal of Law and Economics*, 1-25.

McClelland, David C. et al. (1953), *The Achievement Motive*, New York, Appleton-Century-Crofts.

McCloskey, D.N. (1976), 'Does the Past Have Useful Economics?', **14** *Journal of Economic Literature*, 434-461.

McCloskey, D.N. (1978), 'The Achievements of the Cliometric School', **38** *Journal of Economic History*, 13-28.

McCloskey, D.N. (1987), *Econometric History*, London, Macmillan.

McCurdy, Charles W. (1978), 'American Law and the Marketing Structure of the Large Corporation, 1875-1890', **38** *Journal of Economic History*, 631-649.

Mokyr, Joel (1990), *The Lever of Riches: Technological Creativity and Economic Progress*, Oxford, Oxford University Press.

North, Douglass C. (1961), *The Economic Growth of the United States, 1790-1860*, Englewood Clifffs, Prentice Hall.

North, Douglass C. (1965), 'The State of Economic History', **55** *American Economic Review*, 86-91.

North, Douglass C. and Lance Davis (1971), *Institutional Change and American Economic Growth*, Cambridge, Cambridge University Press.

North, Douglass C. (1981), *Structure and Change in Economic History*, New York, Norton.

North, Douglass C. (1990), *Institutions, Institutional Change and Economic Performance*, Cambridge, Cambridge University Press.

North, Douglass C. and Thomas, Robert Paul (1973), *The Rise of the Western World*, Cambridge, Cambridge University Press.

North, Douglass C. and Weingast, Barry (1989), 'Constitutions and Commitment: Evolution of Institutions Governing Public Choice', **49** *Journal of Economic History*, 803-832.

Olmstead, Alan and Goldberg, Victor P. (1975), 'Institutional Change and American Economic Growth', **12** *Explorations in Economic History*, 193-210.

Parker, William (1971), 'From Old to New to Old in Economic History', **31** *Journal of Economic History*, 3-14.

Primm, James Neal (1954), *Economic Policy in the Development of a Western State, Missouri, 1920-1860*, Cambridge, Harvard University Press.

Ransom, Roger and Sutch, Richard (1977), *One Kind of Freedom: The Economic Consequences of Emancipation*, Cambridge, Cambridge University Press.

Redlich, Fritz (1965), 'New and Traditional Approaches to Economic History and their Interdependence', **25** *Journal of Economic History*, 480-495.

Romer, Christina (1986), 'Is the Stabilization of the Postwar Economy a Figment of the Data?', **76** *American Economic Review*, 314-334.

Romer, Christina (1992), 'What Ended the Great Depression?', **52** *Journal of Economic History*, 757-784.

Solow, Robert (1985), 'Economic History and Economics', **75** *American Economic Review*, 328-331.

Temin, Peter (1969), *The Jacksonian Economy*, New York, W.W. Norton.

Temin, Peter (1989), *Lessons from the Great Depression*, Cambridge, MIT Press.

Temin, Peter (ed.) (1991), *Inside the Business Enterprise: Historical Perspectives on the Use of Information*, Chicago, University of Chicago Press.

Umbeck, John (1977), 'The California Gold Rush: A Study of Emerging Property Rights', **14** *Explorations in Economic History*, 197-226.

Usher, Abbot Payson (1949), 'The Significance of Modern Empiricism for History and Economics', **9** *Journal of Economic History*, 137-155.

Steckel, Richard (1995), 'Stature and the Standard of Living', **33** *Journal of Economic Literature*, 1903-1940.

Swedberg, Richard (ed.) (1991), *Joseph A. Schumpeter: The Economics and Sociology of Capitalism*, Princeton, Princeton University Press.

Veblen, Thorstein (1901), 'Gustav Schmoller's Economics', **16** *Quarterly Journal of Economics*, 69-93.

Wallis, John, Joseph and North, Douglass C. (1986), 'Measuring the Transactions Sector in the American Economy, 1870-1970', in Engerman , Stanleyand Gallman, Robert E. (eds), *Long Term Factors in American Economic Growth*, Chicago, University of Chicago Press, 95-148.

Whaples, Robert (1995), 'Where is there Consensus among American Economic Historians?' **55** *Journal of Economic History*, 139-154.

Wright, Gavin (1978), *The Political Economy of the Cotton South: Households, Markets, and Wealth in the Nineteenth Century*, New York, Norton.

Wright, Gavin (1986), *Old South, New South: Revolutions in the Southern Economy since The Civil War*, New York, Basic Books.

0660
CRITICAL LEGAL STUDIES

Wayne Eastman
Rutgers University, Graduate School of Management

Abstract

This chapter focuses on the relationship between critical legal studies as an intellectual movement in American law schools, and law and economics, in both Chicago and other forms. The critical legal studies critique of law and economics can reasonably be understood as an effort to foster alternative, radical approaches to law and economics that acknowledge and proceed from politically-charged contradictions within the discipline. The intellectual engagement between critical legal studies and law and economics over the last twenty years has not mediated the contradiction between the critical legal studies and law and economics views of law.
JEL classification: K00
Keywords: Critical Legal Studies, Ideology, Rhetoric, Law and Economics.

1. The Institutional and Political Context

In the 1970s, just as the Chicago school of law and economics (0200, 0500) was moving beyond the relatively narrow doctrinal areas in which it had earlier been cabined, another movement, antithetical to the free market conservatism of the Chicago school and the kindred though distinct Virginia school (0610), arose in American law schools. This movement, critical legal studies (CLS), was launched as a theoretical school in substantial part through writings by Roberto Unger (1975) and Duncan Kennedy (1976, 1979) of Harvard Law School, and was institutionalized through the Conference on Critical Legal Studies, begun in 1977.

CLS drew much of its inspiration and many of its adherents from the rise in the 1960s in the United States and Europe of an egalitarian, anti-statist New Left politics. Though partisans of both the Chicago school and CLS tended to share a jaundiced view of the liberal centrist, New Deal/Great Society, 'welfare/warfare' state, their diagnoses of what was wrong with that state and the social order in which it was embedded were profoundly different. Where Chicago school academics saw inattention to the price mechanism and upheld an idealized common law that harkened back to the visions of late nineteenth-century laissez-faire legal theorists, CLS academics saw a troubling adherence to routine, hierarchy, and rationalized violence in the liberal order.

The sharply different political visions of CLS and Chicago law and economics, along with differences in cultural politics between typical partisans of the movements, reflected in matters such as hairstyle and dress, did not in themselves determine that there would be intellectual engagement between CLS and law and economics. But they foreshadowed that any engagement would likely be a conflictual one, and that once CLS arose as a distinct and assertive movement, the publication of an early article on legal form by Duncan Kennedy (1973) in the then-new Chicago school Journal of Legal Studies (0100) would not be followed by further articles by CLS advocates in the law and economics journals.

Beyond the general political divisions between them, the shared jurisprudential ambition of both CLS and Chicago law and economics to decode and translate the law according to their own distinctive methodologies - to, as it were, provide a Rosetta Stone for law - has been a crucial additional factor that has led to persistent conflict between CLS and law and economics. That conflict can be traced back to the underlying tension between the law and economics commitment to understanding law centrally in terms of economics and the CLS commitment to understanding law centrally in terms of politically-charged, deep-rooted yet also contingent patterns of contradiction.

This chapter essay will focus on the relationship between CLS as an intellectual movement in American law schools, one with the general approach to interpreting law noted above, and law and economics, in both Chicago and other forms. It does not deal with critical or leftist legal academic movements in general, such as Law and Society, that may have some interest in law and economics; nor does it deal with European scholarship that denominates itself as critical and that has some relationship to American CLS, but that is more closely connected outside the UK to a European tradition of contrasting formal approaches to social, or welfare state, approaches to law (see, for example, Wilhemsson, 1993 on critical contract law) and in the UK to a class-oriented analysis drawing on Marxism (see, for example, Fitzpatrick and Hunt, 1987).

The intellectual engagement between CLS and law and economics over the last twenty years has not mediated the contradiction between the CLS and law and economics views of law. At least two major reasons for the impasse can be offered. First, the engagement has overwhelmingly consisted of CLS analyses of law and economics, and the relative absence of back-and-forth exchange has made change in the terms of the debate difficult. Second, there has been a question as to whether advocates of law and economics and CLS believe there is any substantial value in appropriating at least some aspects of the other movement's approach; in the absence of such a belief, attempts from either CLS or law and economics to mediate the basic tension between the movements are unlikely.

The relative dearth of law and economics attention to CLS can be taken as reflective of law and economics supporters by and large viewing CLS as a movement that, whatever its merits as jurisprudence, has little or nothing to contribute to the law and economics project of relating economic reasoning to law. On the CLS side, the situation has been more complex. To interpret the CLS treatment of law and economics as a justification for a dismissive stance toward the genre by the legal left is oversimple, since that interpretation misses the substantial degree of attraction to as well as repulsion from law and economics in CLS work.

The two major figures in the CLS engagement with law and economics, Duncan Kennedy and Mark Kelman, have been substantially involved in doing what can be termed 'CLS law and economics', that is, law and economics from a CLS perspective (Kelman, 1979a, 1991a, 1993; Kennedy, 1987, 1992, 1994), as well as in critically analyzing non-CLS law and economics (Kelman, 1979a, 1979b, 1980, 1983, 1984, 1985, 1987a, 1987b, 1988; Kennedy, 1981a, 1981b, 1982, 1985; Kennedy and Michelman, 1980). Nevertheless, their work, especially their more theoretically aggressive work, and that of other CLS supporters has been more widely viewed as a powerful criticism of prevailing assumptions and practices in law and economics than as a charter for an alternative, radical law and economics. Though Kennedy's and Kelman's own practice contains an implicit defense of the value of doing radical law and economics and suggests certain contours that it can take, CLS law and economics is at this point a developing rather than a fully developed genre. Its future prospects will depend in part on whether CLS supporters can provide a persuasive rationale for how CLS analysis can aid in doing law and economics, as well as more examples of CLS law and economics.

2. The CLS Critique of Law and Economics: An Overview

The major theme in CLS analysis of law and economics, which is closely parallel to the major theme in CLS analysis of law more generally, can be readily summarized: law and economics, though typically couched as an apolitical, technical exercise, is in fact an intensely political project. Arguments in law and economics both rely upon and themselves embody controversial political judgments. Law and economics argument, like legal argument, is ideological; both genres are structured by intractable though not immutable political contradictions. The dream of a meaningful technical efficiency discourse purged of political contradiction is a chimerical nightmare, both because it is false and because adherence to it tends to move political argument rightward to a band between pragmatic, technocratic centrism and free-market libertarianism. (How this rightward tendency operates and whether it is potentially reversible in a revised law and economics are matters as to which there is no discernible consensus in CLS scholarship, in contrast to the consensus prevailing on the political nature of law and economics.) The central CLS theme of politics repressed and regained - which implicitly and sometimes explicitly relies on the idea of an awakening, an opening of argument to radical political possibilities (Kelman, 1987a, 294-95) - is present both in early and in more recent and contemporary CLS work on law and economics. Significant subthemes of the CLS critique of law and economics as political that have also persisted over time and that will be examined in this chapter include questioning the coherence of the notion of efficiency; questioning the scientific and logistic pretentions of law and economics rhetoric; and criticizing the Coase Theorem and transaction costs analysis.

One qualification to the general point that CLS analysis of law and economics parallels CLS analysis of law should be noted. In contrast to certain Marxist and other traditional leftist critiques that stress the function of law in upholding a coherent set of ruling-class interests, CLS has consistently emphasized the presence of multiple, contradictory strands within law. The Gramscian ideological hegemony that some CLS scholarship has seen as upheld and constituted through law is itself a field of contradiction, rather than a coherent articulation of a single set of ruling-class values. In thinking about law and economics, though, CLS supporters have sometimes been drawn toward viewing the genre as univocal and unambivalent, in a way that contrasts with the general CLS method of identifying contradiction in law and that in effect adopts (from an unfriendly perspective) the Chicago school's vision of law and economics as a genre that avoids the intractable political divides that attend law. How CLS views law and economics is consequential for CLS in the following way: an understanding of law and economics as a univocal instantiation of a particular set of values, especially conservative ones, is likely to rationalize disengagement from economics by the legal left. At any rate, such an understanding is less likely to foster CLS involvement in law and economics than an understanding of law and economics as an active field of ideological contestation, especially one that allows for the expression of radical as well as liberal politics.

3. Leaders in the CLS Engagement with law and economics

Just as the vitality of Chicago law and economics as a mainstream, politically conservative academic movement has depended significantly upon the organizing energy and intellectual ambition of Richard Posner, the vitality of CLS as a dissenting, radical academic movement has in large part been a product of the organizing energy and intellectual ambition of Duncan Kennedy. Before going to law school, Kennedy studied economics as an undergraduate and graduate student, and this biographical detail has shaped both his work and, through him, the direction of CLS. Even work by Kennedy that is not primarily concerned with law and economics, such as his analysis of how contract law is structured by a persistent tension between individualism and altruism that plays out in the form as well as the content of legal directives (1976), is marked by an attention to law and economics (see, for example, Kennedy, 1976, pp. 1746-51, describing laissez-faire and the altruist case against it, and pp. 1762-64, arguing that transaction costs analysis does not provide an objective basis for legal decisions). Both because of Kennedy's role in CLS in intellectually inspiring others' work and because of his own extensive body of law and economics work, which not only makes fundamental criticisms of mainstream approaches to law and economics but also includes a diverse group of articles in which he does law and economics from a CLS perspective, Kennedy has been the central figure in the CLS engagement with law and economics.

The second major figure in doing work that brings CLS and law and economics together has been Mark Kelman of Stanford Law School. Where Kennedy has written on a wide variety of legal topics in addition to law and economics, Kelman has devoted himself centrally to analyzing and doing law and economics, and his work over the years shows a close involvement with mainstream law and economics and economics literature. His 'A Guide to Critical Legal Studies' (1987a) contains an analysis of law and economics that is the clearest, most thoroughly worked out effort within the CLS literature to relate the critique of law and economics to the CLS critique of law more generally. In that work, Kelman contends that Chicago school law and economics represents an effort to repress intractable contradiction in liberal legal thought by unreflectively elevating certain privileged positions or poles, notably individualism and value subjectivity, over their polar opposites, altruism and value objectivity. These opposite positions are also subordinated, but less thoroughly so, Kelman suggests, in mainstream legal argument and in non-Chicago law and economics work, such as Calabresi's (1970), whose less monolithic repression of contradiction makes it less representative of law and economics as an intellectual genre than Chicago work.

Kelman's image of law and economics in 'A Guide to CLS' as pervaded at a deep level by a Chicago ideology that fails to acknowledge contradiction and strives for a unified, gapless view of the world might be taken as a brief against radical or even liberal involvement in the genre. Given among other things Kelman's own extensive involvement in doing law and economics and the possibility of splitting open a gapless law and economics discourse into one more obviously laden with contradiction, that is hardly an inevitable interpretation of Kelman's thesis. Nevertheless, his analysis in 'A Guide to CLS' and certain of his other work (see, for example, Kelman, 1984) suggests an ambivalence about law and economics that is illustrative of a dilemma that has faced CLS supporters over the years, one that has often been misunderstood by those outside CLS. CLS as a movement has been devoted to rather than deprecatory of contradiction; given that perspective, discourses laden with profound internal contradiction are fine to participate in, contrary to mischaracterizations of CLS as supporting withdrawal from legal discourse because of its internal contradictions. Rather, the problem for CLS in regard to law and economics and particular subgenres of law and economics, such as efficiency arguments, lies with how to open up to contradiction discourses whose premises or rhetorical conventions are, or are perceived to be, structured so as to shut contradiction out.

4. The Incoherence of Efficiency

In modern law and economics (and economics more generally), efficiency is the central concept, the means by which normative evaluation and technical, value-free analysis are reconciled and brought together. That is, efficiency is the master device for mediating the fact-value antinomy (Unger, 1975) that pervades the social order in which law and economics is embedded. This CLS understanding of the linchpin role of efficiency in contemporary economic argument, which is differently expressed but hardly different in substance from that within mainstream law and economics, has naturally led to CLS scholarship that critically analyzes the notion of efficiency. The CLS article that focuses most directly and thoroughly on that theme is Duncan Kennedy's 'Cost-Benefit Analysis of Entitlement Problems' (1981a); early work of Kelman's on the Coase Theorem (1979b, 1980) and ambivalence and regret in consumers (1979a) makes related points, and complements and extends the discussion in 'Cost-Benefit Analysis' of some topics, such as offer-asking price disparities.

Kennedy's general claim in 'Cost-Benefit Analysis' is that efficiency claims lack the objectivity, coherence and autonomy from political value judgments that liberal law and economics (and presumably conservative law and economics as well, which he does not focus on) demands from them. After an historical review contending that efficiency arguments based on internalizing externalities became the mainstay of postwar liberal law reform movements in areas such as products liability, he describes how liberal law and economics responded creatively to Coase's criticism of Pigou's externalities analysis by broadening externalities to include psychic costs (such as unhappiness of New Jersey suburbanites at the destruction of Alaskan wilderness) that high transaction costs prevented from being recognized, but that should be recognized under liberal law and economics' version of Coasean analysis. Kennedy goes on to argue that proponents of liberal law and economics have switched among different plausible methods of valuing entitlements in an ad hoc fashion that serves liberal policy goals but vitiates efficiency as a neutral, apolitical criterion. Consumers ask much more to give up a right than they will offer to obtain a monetarily equal right; it is not wrong to use high values to measure externalities, but any set of prices one uses involves a political judgment (see also Baker, 1975). He makes further arguments that the hope to achieve a determinate liberal efficiency calculus falls victim as well to problems of totalitarianism (that is, overcoming externalities and transaction costs entails an overweening state apparatus), wealth effects (that is, valuations and thus the efficiency calculus are distorted by wealth), and multiple equilibria (that is, determinate efficiency analyses break down when bargaining is allowed on all topics, rather than just one or a few).

In 'Cost-Benefit Analysis', Kennedy does not criticize the political values of the practitioners of liberal law and economics (who as identified by Kennedy include a writer also identified with CLS, Thomas Heller, 1976, and another, Frank Michelman, who co-authored an important law and economics article with Kennedy (Kennedy and Michelman, 1980)). As Kennedy articulates it, his dispute with liberal law and economics is a formal one, based on his disagreement with liberal law and economics' reliance on efficiency claims that conceal the political, value-laden nature nature of the choices that liberal law and economics supporters argue for. In a conclusion that in a sense reverses that of his earlier 'Form and Substance' in which he argued that the enterprise of liberal law reformers such as Skelly Wright should be wished 'what success is possible short of the overcoming of its contradictions' (Kennedy, 1976, p. 1778), in 'Cost-Benefit Analysis' Kennedy gives an equivocal, highly skeptical answer to the question of whether there is any role at all for efficiency in law and economics analysis: Coasean transaction costs analysis fails to increase the normative bite of economics, and the possibility of applying a technical efficiency criterion successfully is just as implausible, even absurd, as it was in the days of pre-Coasean welfare economics (1981a, pp. 444-45).

A noteworthy point about the early CLS critique of efficiency that is epitomized in 'Cost-Benefit Analysis' is the relatively limited, technical nature of the claim that efficiency is incoherent. In contrast to domains such as contract law, in which Kennedy and other CLS scholars traced out persistent, deep-seated conflict between different political visions, the incoherence of efficiency is presented in 'Cost-Benefit Analysis' in terms of offer-asking price disparities and wealth effects rather than of fundamental value contradictions inhering within the prevailing rhetoric of efficiency. 'Cost-Benefit Analysis' and the succeeding articles that criticize and defend Kennedy's arguments about the inability of efficiency discourse to provide determinate, apolitical conclusions on policy questions (see especially Carlson, 1986; Kelman, 1987b; Markovits, 1984) make an implicit choice to evaluate efficiency rhetoric on the basis of whether it can live up to a promise to provide determinate answers to policy questions. Though this way of evaluating efficiency accords with a significant strain in CLS that condemns rhetoric that makes false claims of determinacy and objectivity, it could be taken to imply the conclusion that efficiency rhetoric would be more worthwhile to deploy by CLS lights if it were possible to purge it of its incoherence. But that conclusion is exactly backward. Instead, the objection in early CLS work to the deployment of the rhetoric of efficiency in law and economics is explicable if it is seen in terms of a belief that efficiency arguments were too circumscribed by their premises and too lacking in expressible political contradictions to be of significant value. (Other beliefs defensible at the time, and arguably still, may well of course have motivated CLS reluctance to deploy efficiency arguments, including a belief, suggested in the conclusion to 'Cost-Benefit Analysis' that efficiency analysis overall serves as a brake on reformist enthusiasm by postulating an efficiency-equity tradeoff, and a concomitant belief, pursued in later work by Kennedy (1982, 1987), and discussed in the section of this chapter on CLS law and economics, that CLS work in law and economics should eschew efficiency arguments in favor of distributional arguments.) What could make efficiency discourse worth deploying from a CLS perspective - and what certain recent CLS or CLS-like scholarship has reflected - is an understanding of efficiency as ridden with internal, politically-fraught contradiction.

The best-articulated recent working out of what could be described as a developing CLS position that efficiency discourse contains within it different models that are in serious political tension with one another and that have quite different, though not determinate, implications for law, is contained in Bill Bratton's 'Game Theory and the Restoration of Honor to Corporate Law's Duty of Loyalty' (1995). (Bratton, 1989a, describing different economic approaches to the firm, foreshadows some of these themes.) In his 1995 article, Bratton compares Jensen and Meckling's contractual, agency-theory view of the firm to Kreps' game-theoretic view of the firm, in which cooperative outcomes depend on at least the possibility of honorable behavior, and argues that Kreps' approach could (and, he suggests, should) lead to corporate law more supportive of the duty of loyalty than 1980s decisions influenced by the Jensen and Meckling model. Though Bratton's article is less insistent about the irrefragibility of contradiction than CLS scholarship has traditionally been, his is very much an argument about repressed internal political tension within the notion of efficiency, and as such (respecting that Bratton in the article does not identify his analysis with CLS) constitutes a significant contemporary CLS contribution to the critique of law and economics.

Another recent article, 'How Coasean Bargaining Entails a Prisoners' Dilemma' (Eastman, 1996b), is also structured in part around the notion of politically significant contradiction within efficiency discourse. The formal claim is that there is an equivalence between two stories, the Prisoners' Dilemma and

Coasean bargaining to achieve a surplus, that are generally seen as having very different meanings; the substantive claim is that efficiency discourse operates to repress awareness of contradiction by setting up two different stories with presumably different logical groundings, although these logical twists are actually the same. Though the article's focus on the formal link between Coasean bargaining and the Prisoners' Dilemma suggests that its objective is the traditional CLS one of debunking scientic pretension in law and economics, the overall argument, like that in Bratton's article, assumes and operates from the premise that there are meaningful political contradictions within the efficiency idea.

In developing further CLS analyses of contradictions within efficiency, there is relevant material to be drawn from Kelman's early arguments about psychological division in 'Choice and Utility' (1979a). Kelman's strategy was to debunk neoclassical theory that overlooked ambivalence and regret, but one could now point to economic approaches advanced since 1979, such as regret theory, that incorporate at least part of his argument and that are in politically-salient tension with subjective expected utility theory. Or (riskily for noneconomists, but CLS scholars accustomed to taking intellectual risks should not, one trusts, be paralyzed by this one) one could propose new law and economics models that are at least plausible in the terms of efficiency discourse and are also in self-conscious political tension with other, prevailing models.

Another significant source for the developing CLS argument about persistent contradiction within efficiency comes from work by mainstream law and economics scholars that has arguably though not necessarily been influenced by CLS. Cooter (1982) notes the sharp contrast between the optimistic Coase Theorem and a pessimistic 'Hobbes Theorem' that assumes strategic behavior will block desirable bargains. Neither approach to achieving efficiency is analytically preferable; rather, as Cooter notes, values and assumptions about human nature are at stake in any effort to mediate between them. A similar, somewhat broader point, is made by Hovenkamp (1992), who analyzes the inconsistent views of human nature and 'rationality' in the Coase Theorem, price theory, and Arrow's Theorem/social choice theory, which all enjoy high standing within orthodox efficiency analysis despite their contradictory features. Ian Ayres makes good observations on the politically significant contrast between game theory and price theory as approaches to efficiency, and the likely political correlates of the ascendancy of game theory (Ayres, 1990). Ayres' own game theoretic work, though it avoids assertive claims about contradiction, persistently deploys efficiency arguments in a fashion that flips Chicago orthodoxy. For example, Ayres and Talley (1995) argue that liability rules generate higher welfare than property rules under certain assumptions, an argument that flips the Chicago law and economics case for property rules in low transaction cost situations. Interestingly, Louis Kaplow's and Stephen Shavell's response to Ayres and Talley is an indeterminacy argument that leaves the original Chicago claim undefended; the articles together suggest the space that has opened up in law and economics efficiency arguments for flipping and indeterminacy exercises that CLS scholars should be interested in carrying out and opening to radical as well as liberal politics.

5. The Coase Theorem

Coasean analysis points out that externalities do not in and of themselves warrant regulation, given the possibility that the parties can reach an efficient outcome through bargaining. A major liberal law and economics response to that point, essentially the one criticized by Kennedy in 'Cost-Benefit Analysis', has been to stress the pervasiveness of transaction costs. This liberal response, plausible as it is in terms of Coase's argument, gives significant ground to the Chicago, anti-regulatory position: compared to the Pigouvian externalities framework, the externalities plus transaction costs framework requires an additional layer of justification for legal intervention, since the mere existence of externalities is no longer a sufficient warrant to regulate.

Since transaction cost analysis as a replacement for Pigouvian externalities analysis entailed a significant though indeterminate conservative, anti-regulatory shift in presumptions, the general reluctance within CLS to jump on board the Coasean bandwagon is entirely explicable. The transition from Pigou's framework to Coase's involved a shift of the ideological playing field toward the libertarian, Chicago right, and CLS as a left-of-center academic movement has had good reason to contest that shift, rather than simply play according to the new, Coasean rhetoric, as liberal law and economics was doing. Opting out of law and economics efficiency rhetoric, which CLS verged on doing in the early 1980s, can be seen as one response to the problem of a rightward shift in efficiency analysis. A second CLS response has been to develop arguments that Coase's analysis was wrong, or should be interpreted in a different way.

The initial major CLS work on the Coase Theorem was by Kelman (1979b, 1980, 1985). Kelman (1979b) makes a multi-pronged attack on the Theorem that criticizes both its empirical plausibility and its normative implications. First, because the amount that consumers want to give up an entitlement is likely to be much higher than the amount they will pay to obtain an entitlement they do not have, the Coase Theorem proposition that under zero transaction costs the same efficient pattern of activity will take place regardless of the legal rules in effect is likely to be wrong in practice. If neighbors have an initial entitlement to be free of pollution, it is unlikely the manufacturer will be able to buy them out; on the other hand, if the manufacturer has the initial entitlement to pollute, it is much less likely, even with costless bargaining, that the neighbors will value freedom from pollution enough to bribe the manaufacturer not to pollute. Second, the Theorem 'works' (that is, is counterintuitive rather than simply a truism) because it points out typically unsuspected opportunities to bargain, such as between the rancher and the farmer in Coase's original example. Kelman criticizes the Theorem's implicit support for making bargaining ubiquitous in strong terms: 'The real substantive vision of the Coase Theorem, its real cultural 'contribution', is to a particular worldview that seems to me both a distorted 'description' and a horrifying covert ideal' (Kelman, 1985, p. 1046).

In contrast, Schlag (1986) describes the Coase Theorem not as a charter for bargaining and commodification but rather as a potentially radical vehicle for the critique of legal concepts; he suggests that this critique can begin by substituting 'conceptualization' for 'choice of liability rule' in statements of the Theorem. His second take on the Theorem, and the transaction costs analysis associated with it, is less optimistic; he argues that transaction costs analysis has fallen prey to the same limitations and rigidities that were criticized by Coase in Pigouvian externalities analysis (Schlag, 1989).

Recently Eastman (1996a) has translated the Coase Theorem into game-theoretic terms. He argues that what distinguishes the Theorem from standard game-theoretic analyses is a Coasean assumption of payoff mutability, under which people engage in promises and threats in an effort to enhance their positions. Understanding the Coase Theorem in terms of this 'everything is up for grabs' assumption leads to quite different implications for law than those associated with standard interpretations of the Theorem. While the conventional wisdom associated with the Theorem supports bargaining and worries only about strategic behavior as an obstacle to desirable agreements, the game-theoretic understanding points out the significance of undesirable threat bargaining, and suggests a potential value for legal regulation that inhibits opportunities for threat bargaining.

6. The Critique of Law and Economics Rhetoric

CLS scholarship from its inception has had a distinctive concern with the form in which academic and judicial arguments are made. In law and economics, that CLS concern has focused on arguments and interpretations that are ideological but are made in a fashion that suggests they are scientifically grounded in foundational logic or hard data. Through unmasking claims to scientific status, CLS advocates have hoped to bring political division to the discipline's surface and possibly to move liberals to the left.

Kennedy's first major published article on law and economics, 'Are Property and Contract Efficient?', written with Frank Michelman (Kennedy and

Michelman, 1980), a Harvard colleague of Kennedy's sympathetic to but not affiliated with CLS, is a central work in the critique of law and economics rhetoric. The basic point of the article is straightforward: arguments for the efficiency of private property (or alternatives to private property, such as the state of nature or forced sharing), and parallel arguments for the efficiency of free contract (or alternatives to contract), need to be made on a contextual, empirical basis. The efficiency of property or contract does not logically follow from the assumption that people are rational satisfiers of their desires. The authors modestly present their argument as one that should not surprise economically-sophisticated readers, describing the succession of efficiency arguments they debunk as mistakes, or 'traps for the unwary'.

The major arguments for the efficiency of private property over forced sharing or the state of nature that Kennedy and Michelman attack in their role as trap-shooters are briefly summarized below, along with the article's rebuttals:

1. 'Security increases production' - not necessarily, since people may work more if outcomes are uncertain; a state of nature or forced sharing might go along with an order under which there would be more rather than less industry.
2. Theft is inefficient - under private property, transaction costs may inhibit efficient transfers that would take place in a state of nature; there is no prior guarantee that private property will lead to more efficient transactions.
3. Private property reduces uncertainty - not necessarily; it all depends on whose uncertainty we are talking about, since more certainty for one party entails less certainty for another, as Hohfeldian analysis demonstrates.
4. Private property aids coordination - not necessarily, since private property is highly vulnerable to strategic behavior and associated prisoners' dilemmas that might be averted under forced sharing, or by a strong hand arising out of a state of nature.
5. Private property leads to an optimum work-leisure tradeoff - the tradeoff will vary according to the parties' initial entitlements, but there is no basis for imputing inefficiency to state of nature or forced sharing tradeoffs relative to private property tradeoffs.

Given the stark oppositions Kennedy and Michelman employ (for example, between 'private property' and 'forced sharing for needs', their article has a radical flavor, rather than the liberal flavor that would have been created by an argument that there is no necessary inefficiency associated with, say, Swedish social democracy compared to the less egalitarian American order. But because they do not challenge the efficiency criterion as incoherent and necessarily beset by political tensions, their article can be and has been (Kelman, 1987a) characterized as a criticism of an unwarranted conservative tilt in law and economics rather than as a CLS argument.

Even allowing for the article's acceptance of the efficiency criterion, though, there is a significant sense in which it can and should be regarded as a major contribution to the CLS critique of law and economics. The basic point of the article is a claim about indeterminacy, specifically about the indeterminacy of the relationship between efficiency and institutional arrangements. This point resonates in CLS terms in a way that it does not in the terms of liberal or conservative law and economics. In a variety of domains apart from the critique of law and economics, CLS supporters have contended that mainstream legal argument unwarrantedly asserts or implies that there is a determinate, foundational link between logic and policy; sometimes CLS supporters have tried to tie their arguments to philosophical critiques of foundationalism (see, for example, Peller, 1985; Singer, 1984). Liberal law and economics, it would seem, lacks the distinctive interest in this issue of rhetorical form that CLS has had. Of all the critical works on law and economics, Kennedy and Michelman's article stands out as the one that is most clearly organized around the indeterminacy theme. Though it is quite right that the article's indeterminacy claims can be seen, as the authors suggest, as simply upholding economic conventional wisdom, the indeterminacy claims also serve as a criticism of law and economics rhetoric that implies a logic-based, determinate, efficiency foundation for some version of market capitalism. In that sense, Kennedy and Michelman's article is arguably the single one in the critique of law and economics that has the sharpest connection to the general CLS criticism of mainstream legal rhetoric; one's reaction to the article's basic indeterminacy theme is an excellent test for gauging one's overall reaction to the CLS critique of law and economics.

The CLS critique of law and economics rhetoric invites questions as to whether the desired outcome is an abandonment of law and economics, a modification of law and economics rhetoric in order to make it more politically candid and less scientistic, or a sort of public advisory system about the hazards of law and economics, along the lines of the small craft warnings issued by the Coast Guard. The second alternative seems to be the preferred one among CLS supporters. For example, in the work of Mark Kelman (see especially Kelman, 1984, 1991a), one senses that the aim is modifying law and economics rhetoric rather than extirpating the genre (or simply advising its consumers), given Kelman's own work in law and economics as well as his disagreement with those on the left who wish to ignore economic arguments (Kelman,1991b). Similarly, in a recent article that presents alternative versions of the Prisoners' Dilemma, the Coase Theorem, and price theory in the course of criticizing false determinacy in law and economics rhetoric and making a case for internal contradiction in efficiency claims, Eastman (1996c) endorses what amounts to a 'mend it, don't end it' attitude to law and economics that supports the telling of heterodox law and economics stories rather than abandonment of the genre.

To the extent CLS scholarship comes down in favor of the use of law and economics in some form, there is an issue, which CLS work to date has not dwelt on, as to the basis on which one might justify that stance. Kennedy (1992, p. 1314) makes a brief, ambivalent defense of the rhetoric of cost/benefit analysis: 'It is more "authentic" for me, than the voice of role-reversed male sensitivity ... This is so even though I am constituted in ways I don't like, and think are dangerous, by this very language ("it" speaks "me") and wish it were a different, better vehicle.' One can, as Eastman (1996c) does, simply rationalize law and economics as a storytelling project that is not necessarily worse than other, less logistic, types of storytelling. But this elides the issue, a sensitive one on the (post)modern, self-consciously non-foundationalist left, of whether one believes that through the logistic storytelling of law and economics one is discovering things about how the world works, or at least about how certain human communities organize their concepts. The issue is not significant to the extent CLS is not engaged in doing law and economics, but becomes a probably unavoidable, if perhaps annoying, issue for a philosophically-reflective CLS movement, some of whose supporters are committed to some kind of law and economics.

7. CLS Law and Economics: 'The Distributive Turn' and 'The Ideological Turn'

Instead of making general arguments aimed at justifying CLS participation in law and economics, the leading figures in the CLS involvement with law and economics, Kennedy and Kelman, have done law and economics without extensive elaboration of their reasons. CLS law and economics as embodied in their work has spanned a wide gamut formally, ranging from technical analyses employing price theory (Kennedy, 1987) to relatively nontechnical arguments (Kennedy, 1992). But it is not patternless. Two main tendencies can be identified in their critical law and economics: (1) 'the distributive turn' - that is, analyses of the distributional consequences of contractual terms and legal rules and strategies (Kennedy, 1982, 1987, 1994); and (2) 'the ideological turn' - that is, work that may make cost-benefit or efficiency arguments in a fashion paralleling that in liberal law and economics, but with an overt specification of the ideological context and purpose of the arguments (Kelman, 1979b, 1991a, 1993; Kennedy, 1992; Kennedy and Specht, 1994). Of the two, the distributive turn has been the better articulated as a method (particularly in Kennedy, 1982, 1987). But the ideological turn, though currently less realized methodologically, is also a significant element in certain CLS law and economics, and is likely to assume increasing significance to the extent CLS scholarship further develops the analysis of internal contradictions within efficiency discourse and deploys efficiency arguments.

As a technical method, the distributive approach as carried out in Kennedy (1987) employs conventional price theoretic analysis for purposes of analyzing distributional consequences, thus flipping the mainstream preference for analyzing efficiency consequences. The basic idea in Kennedy's article is that selective intervention to enforce the warranty of habitability (selective in that it focuses on periods when landlords in declining neighborhoods would otherwise 'milk' their properties by ending maintenance, even though the property remains profitable enough to maintain), can redistribute income to tenants without reducing the supply of low income housing. Because the technical apparatus employed by Kennedy is that of neoclassical price theory, his method is well-suited to being adopted or adapted by non-CLS law and economics scholars. A potentially promising channel for future development of the distributive turn in CLS law and economics lies in the deployment of game theory rather than, or along with, price theory. The opportunities price theory alone offers for CLS are arguably constrained by its built-in opposition between distributional and efficiency analyses; the overt, surfaced quality of this opposition within the mainstream to some extent defangs a CLS project of surfacing contradiction, though it does not vitiate the value of work that upholds the subordinated, distributional part of price-theoretic analysis.

The turn toward highlighting the ideological context and nature of the law and economics arguments one makes is seen in law and econmics work by Kelman that could otherwise be plausibly classified as liberal law and economics. For instance, his analysis of concepts of discrimination (1991a) has a central logical nub (that even 'unbiased' tests that predict the job performance of blacks and whites equally well may result in substantially higher proportions of blacks who could do the job successfully not getting hired) that could reasonably be viewed as liberal law and economics. But Kelman's analysis of that point is embedded in a lengthy analysis of the ideological correlates of different approaches to understanding discrimination. His logicizing of different stories of discrimination is law and economics; his placing all these stories, in their logicized as well as their initial forms, in ideological context is CLS, and makes the overall project of the article one in CLS law and economics. The combination of logicizing and ideological analysis makes the article quite complex, more so than either mainstream law and econmics that ignores the ideological content of the arguments it makes or critical literature that eschews law and economics logicizing. This complexity is arguably a major virtue of CLS law and economics that takes the ideological turn; it will require some adjustment for academic readers accustomed to established forms of law and economics and CLS.

The structural complexity of CLS law and economics that places its arguments in ideological context is also shown in Kennedy's 'Sexy Dressing' (Kennedy, 1992), which makes a cost-benefit argument that men have an erotic self-interest in fighting the sexual abuse of women. Here, Kennedy combines Calabresian, Posnerian law and economics with Saussurian structuralism, postmodern pro-sex feminism, simultaneously self-critical and self-justifying 'straight white male middle class radical' introspection, and close reading of many fashion magazines. The resulting article is a sufficiently complex brew to make any suggestion for further complexifying it, or work drawing upon it, seem counterintuitive, even outright wrong. But in terms of CLS law and economics there is a plausible case for heightening the formality of the law and economics argument in ambitious articles like 'Sexy Dressing'. Doing so would not only tend to stretch the boundaries of law and economics but also might heighten tensions that ideologically-reflective CLS law and economics plays off of and tries to accentuate. 'Sexy Dressing', in this view, should not be seen as a non-law and economics article with minor law and economics window dressing, or as a sui generis effort unsuitable for emulation by anyone without command of all the elements in Kennedy's eclectic theoretical toolkit. Rather, the article can serve as a template for future CLS law and economics projects, ones that may well complexify or 'tech up' their law and economics to a greater extent than Kennedy chose to in his article.

8. Additional Themes in the CLS Engagement with Law and Economics: Historical, Philosophical, and Discipline-Specific Work

CLS work relating to law and economics is by no means limited to the broad subjects treated thus far. Although this review essay focuses on themes in CLS scholarship on law and economics that cut across particular areas of law, arguably the most significant work in terms of the long-term viability of the CLS engagement with law and economics is discipline-specific work in corporate law, labor law, housing law and other areas.

An area in which a substantial body of CLS law and economics has developed is housing law and policy (Aoki, 1993; Ford, 1994; Fox, 1991; Keller, 1988; Kennedy, 1987, 1994; Kennedy and Specht, 1994; Kinning, 1993; Kolodney, 1991; McUsic, 1988). That work has considerable diversity in approach, ranging as it does from Kolodney's use of tipping models to analyze gentrification (1991) to Kinning's empirical survey of selective code enforcement in Minneapolis (1993) to Keller's proposal for a tort remedy for breaches of landlord duty (1988) to Ford's mixture of economic analysis, critical legal theory, critical race theory, and aspirational proposals for combatting segregation (1994). But for all these differences in approach, the housing literature constitutes a collective whole that is identifiably CLS law and economics in its simultaneous commitment to economic analysis and to critical analysis of the politics of law.

Although housing law stands out for its overall body of CLS law and economics, there are other areas of law in which CLS scholarship has fruitfully engaged law and economics, among them antitrust (Peritz 1984, 1989, 1990), debtor-creditor (Carlson, 1992, 1994), labor and employment (Klare, 1988; Stone, 1991), contract (Kennedy, 1976, 1982), discrimination (Kelman, 1991a), critical race theory (Audain, 1995), transitional economies (Alexander, 1994; David Kennedy, 1991), property (Alexander, 1982), tort (Kennedy, 1982; Kelman, 1988), international law (David Kennedy, 1994), and tax (Heller, 1979). Also worthy of note is work that, although done by writers not necessarily identified with CLS, applies a critical approach of identifying contradiction and parsing the politics of legal and economic argument: Bratton's work in corporate law (Bratton 1984, 1989a, 1989b, 1995) is especially noteworthy in this regard, and one could also note Millon's (1990) work on corporate law and Harrison's (1995) on contract law. A final category of work worth noting is scholarship by certain founding figures in CLS whose interests were centered around the application of social science to law, not through law and economics but through empirical sociology in the radical Weberian tradition (see, for example, Richard Abel, 1982, on tort law and David Trubek, 1984 on the use of empirical methods in CLS). Though their work is more in keeping with the Law and Society movement than with CLS as it developed through the theorizing of Unger and Kennedy, some work in this line, such as Trubek's, deals with both CLS and social science, if not law and economics in particular.

A considerable amount of CLS scholarship is historical, and some of that work deals with law and economics. For example, in 'Essays on the Fetishism of Commodities' (1985), Kennedy carries out an historical analysis of the role of law in classical economics, Marx's discussion of commodity fetishism and neoclassical economics and argues that a realist understanding of law destabilizes the sense of law as a coherent block that appears in classical economics, in Marx's response to it, and in neoclassical economics' effort to overcome and partially acknowledge Marx's critique. In a more contemporary context, Bratton (1989a) provides an historical examination of theories of the firm.

Finally, some CLS scholars, such as Unger, have had a particular concern with philosophy, or with the work of particular philosophers. On occasion, such concerns have intersected with the analysis of law and economics in CLS work. Work by David Carlson criticizing Chicago work on bankruptcy in the course of analyzing Rawls' political philosophy, and arguing that the notion of the perfect market embodies in Derridean terms an incoherent philosophy of presence that both presupposes and negates the idea of an opportunity cost (Carlson, 1993), exemplify this intersection. A further subtheme in the CLS critique of law and economics that is to some degree related to the concern with analyzing the work of particular philosophers involves personalizing the critique, by focusing specifically on the work of Richard Posner (see, for example, Balkin, 1987; Minda,

1978; for a good example of such work by an author less identified with CLS, see also West, 1986).

9. Carrying the CLS Critique Forward: The Ideological Structuring of Economic Argument

CLS scholarship has focused its attention on law and economics, instead of the economic discourse from which law and economics draws. One can certainly understand the reasons that have led legal critics to engage in a critique of the work of legal economists such as Posner rather than of economists more generally. But given that economics, for all the formidable and specialized analytical talent of many in the discipline, operates under social scientific rhetorical constraints that inhibit the critical analysis of how economic arguments are constructed and achieve their effects, there is a significant gap that CLS can help fill. The critique of law and economics is also the critique of economics, and there is a relative openness in law reviews, much of it won by CLS efforts over the years, to the kind of serious critical analysis of patterns of argument that is not currently cognizable within the conventions of social science publication. What follows are preliminary observations on the kind of critique of economic argument that CLS is particularly qualified to make. These observations are followed by an analysis of the contents of a recent issue of the *American Economic Review*, designed to show how a critical theory of the ideological structuring of economic argument can be hooked up to current practice in the field. Finally, the analysis of the ideological nature of economic discourse will be drawn on for a brief 'how to' guide for creating critical law and economics.

On economic arguments: A starting point of CLS theory on this point is that economic discourse is ideological. What does that mean? Just as legal discourse is largely constituted by liberal and conservative argument bites, economic discourse largely consists of similar ideological argument bites, more logically elaborate than in law, that are associated with economic models. 'Public goods', 'externalities', and 'underconsumption' are a few terms evoking argument bites and models that are typically though by no means necessarily liberal ('asymmetric information', 'adverse selection' and 'relational contracting' are others); 'rational expectations', 'monetarism' and 'supply side' evoke typically conservative argument bites/models (also 'transaction costs', 'Coase Theorem' 'contract law').

How does economic argument work? One tries to make a connection between analytical logic and a real world situation. Typically, what makes the connection interesting is that it has ideological, liberal-conservative significance. Empirical economics is also ideological; what makes an empirical study work is that it suggests - and it may do so allusively rather than dogmatically - a moral about the way the world works.

Both legal argument and economic argument involve issues of methodological or stylistic politics as well as issues of substantive politics. In law, many cases involve politics at the level of form or style - for example, in deciding whether to use a standard or a rule. In economics, similar formal choices exist as to type of analysis on conducts - say game theory vs. supply-demand analysis - and as to level of technicality.

In one type of legal argument, one tries to rationalize a field, such as First Amendment law, by providing a theoretical rationale for deciding cases in a certain way - for example, the government must not restrict speech based on the notion that one way of seeking the good is superior to another way. Here legal argument is ideological in a way that is closely parallel to the way economic argument is ideological. Talent in making legal arguments to rationalize a field involves the ability to convert a politically significant analytical framework into something that can be plugged into a variety of real world situations. Similarly, economic models can potentially be applied to a wide array of circumstances; talent in making economic arguments in part involves the ability to see how the logic of certain models can have a home in novel contexts.

10. An Example of the Ideological Structuring of Economic Argument: Articles in an Issue of *American Economic Review*

The CLS understanding of economic argument as ideological should be justifiable in relation to specific cases. What follows is an examination of all the articles in a recent issue of a leading American economics journal, carried out in some detail for one article and more briefly for the remaining thirteen. (The reader who wants exposition of the general CLS position on law and economics rather than a fairly detailed empirical case for its plausibility may wish to skim or skip this section.) Apart from whatever value the examination of these articles may have in informally testing the CLS proposition that argument in economics is ideological, another purpose of the examination of the articles conducted here is to suggest potential ways to create law and economics in general and CLS law and economics in particular.

'Rat Race Redux: Adverse Selection in the Determination of Work Hours in Law Firms' (1996), the first article in the issue in question, shows how suboptimal 'rat race' equilibria with excessively high hours can develop as a result of partners using hours worked as an indicator of how associates will behave if they become partners. The article uses an adverse selection model with two imperfectly observable types of lawyers - long-hours workers and short-hours workers - to show how employers' desire to differentiate between long- and short-hours workers can lead to inefficiently high hours equilibria. Maximum hours laws can break the inefficient separating equilibrium and lead to an efficient equilibrium.

The authors note how Akerlof originally set up a rat race equilibrium in a highly unrealistic fashion that might have created the impression that such a situation is an impractical oddity. Their model, on the other hand, is clearly one that is designed to be significant in real-world terms:

> Rat race equilibria reduce access to powerful positions for those unwilling to tolerate excessive work hours early in their careers. This selection process may have the effect, although not the intent, of keeping a disproportionate number of qualified women out of leadership positions in business and professional organizations. (p. 347)

Adverse selection models have grown enough in influence and recognition to be applied in a context that gives them a sharper left/liberal edge, as in 'Rat Race Redux', which makes an argument with a conclusion parallel to Schor's in *The Overworked American* (Schor, 1991). Compare the early use of adverse selection to defend lemon disclosure laws in the used car market - here the model was being used in a more politically innocuous, centrist fashion. Akerlof's expressing his rat race equilibrium in an unrealistic fashion was quite possibly related to the existence of a centrist consensus that the issue of high professional-managerial work hours was not one to be taken seriously. 'Rat Race Redux', which does take the issue seriously, challenges that centrist consensus.

In thinking about the development of adverse selection models from Akerlof to 'Rat Race Redux', one sees a rational basis for the intuition that novel as opposed to accepted high-tech methods in economics may well have a centrist, nonradical cast. To introduce a new high-tech model on behalf of a way of thinking about the world that is not already familiar to readers is to court bafflement. Tech 'works' - produces a nod and a sense of 'aha' insight on the reader's part - by linking up a more or less recondite, intricate and aesthetically pleasing set of logical/mathematical operations with a real world phenomenon. But if the author's attitude toward the real world phenomenon is itself recondite and counterintuitive, the result of combining that attitude with unfamiliar high tech may well be confusing at best and incomprehensible at worst. A genre of CLS law and economics that creates new technology would be a very fine thing indeed to have. But a more plausible direction for CLS law and economics involves turning technology that is already recognizable from its use on behalf of centrist conclusions to more radical ends, as 'Rat Race Redux' ably does.

In 'Rat Race Redux' as with economic arguments in general, the tech can be flipped. Instead of the article's overwork equilibria, what about an underwork equilibrium? Suppose the partners in a law firm believe that success depends on identifying future partners who will fit in well into their white shoe club, and weeding out associates who will not. Type 1 attorneys are the 'clubbable' ones, while Type 2 are the overly aggressive, 'unclubbable' ones, who generate more short-term billings from their high hours, but who are not desirable as rainmakers or future members of the partnership. Of course, knowing the partners' preferences, Type 2 associates have an incentive to disguise their status by not working longer hours. But by establishing a firm culture with a sufficiently white shoe atmosphere and low work hours ceilings, the partners can drive out the Type 2 attorneys by making the firm an uncomfortable place for them to work. The result is an inefficient underwork equilibrium.

Readers may differ in their evaluation of the relative plausibility of the 'Rat Race' and 'Reverse Rat Race' stories. In my view, the authors' rat race story seems like a much convincing evocation of contemporary Wall Street law firms than the flipped story, but that is of course not a matter of the logic of adverse selection tilting one way or another but of contingent, empirical factors. The point here is not to insist on one story or the other, but to support the critical intuition that the logical apparatus of the adverse selection model does not in itself carry the day for a particular political moral.

'Rat Race Redux' illustrates the complexities of telling an economic story that resonates in critical terms. The article accomplishes the considerable feat of telling a clever story with a potentially radical moral while using standard economic assumptions. But in relation to the adverse selection model, the lower work preference attorneys whom the partners are trying to ferret out are like the lemons in Akerlof's used-car story - not people one necessarily feels empathy or support for. The adverse selection story of 'Rat Race Redux' is technically prettier than the simpler, 'keeping up with the Joneses' Prisoners' Dilemma story of competition for material goods leading people to work excessively long hours that Schor (1991) tells. But Schor's Dilemma story accords more readily with the spirit of the case for reducing work hours than the adverse selection story of attorneys trying to disguise their low work hours preferences. Both stories are good liberal law and economics stories that can be made radical by being told with attention to thir ideological context; whether one values the greater technical elegance of the 'Rat Race Redux' adverse selection argument or the closer connection to critical feeling in the Overworked American Prisoners' Dilemma argument is a matter of aesthetic and political judgment.

The CLS law and economics analysis just carried out for 'Rat Race Redux' can be compressed into a brief description of the article's story, its ideology, its legal implications, and possibilities for reversing or flipping the story's moral. What follows is a concise analysis of 'Rat Race Redux' and of all the remaining papers in the issue of AER in which in appears.

(1) Rat Race Redux: Adverse Selection in the Determination of Work Hours in Law Firms, Renee M. Landers, James B. Rebitzer and Lowell J. Taylor, AER, Vol. 86 (1996): 329-348.
The story: Adverse selection/asymmetric information. Adverse selection may lead to an inefficiently high number of hours worked, with firms setting a very high hours standard to drive out asssociates who pretend to be interested in working long hours to win the favor of partners.
The story's ideology: Liberal/radical.
Legal implications: Cut work hours.
Possibilities for flipping the model: Adverse selection may lead to an inefficiently low level of hours worked, given an incentive of associates to pretend to be 'clubbable' to win the favor of partners.

(2) Veblen Effects in a Theory of Conspicuous Consumption, Laurie Simon Bagwell and B. Douglas Bernheim, AER, Vol. 86 (1996): 349-373.
The story: Signalling/asymmetric information. Given certain assumptions about demand for luxury goods by lower income and high income households, a desire to signal wealth can produce willingness to pay a high price for a good that is identical in quality to a lowèr price good (that is, a 'Veblen effect'). Excise taxes on such a luxury good are nondistortionary taxes on pure profit.
The story's ideology: Liberal.
Legal implications: Tax luxury goods.
Possibilities for flipping the model: The argument here flips itself in a sense, in that the authors discuss how the presence of Veblen effects depends on empirical assumptions about luxury and budget goods. This type of flipping, though, leaves the overall politics of the model unscathed. That is, by employing a model that assumes the significance of status concerns in motivating people, the article's perspective accords well with liberal skepticism about the value of material acquisitiveness; noting that the Veblen effects are empirically contingent does not flip the model's politics. One way to produce a flipped, conservative version of this article would involve setting up an analytical model that overall embodies conservative skepticism about liberal values (a public choice model might be good for that purpose) and then going through the technical hoops to show how how, based on certain plausible assumptions about the shape of functions, a particular inefficiency will be generated.

(3) The Gender Gap, Fertility, and Growth, Oded Galil and David N. Weil, AER, Vol. 86 (1996): 374-387.
The story: Assuming that men have an advantage in 'brawn' while the sexes are equal in 'brains', an increase in capital per worker will raise women's relative wages, which in turn will decrease fertility, which in turn will increase capital per

worker. Thus, a positive feedback loop exists; further, technology is a way to escape high fertility/low capital equilibria.
The story's ideology: Conservative.
Legal implications: The gender gap will likely narrow without legal intervention, which reduces the case for such intervention.
Possibilities for flipping the model: The optimistic invisible hand story of increasing growth and gender equality that is told here depends on a model that employs a simple 'brains' vs. 'brawn' dichotomy. Alternative models that employ different dichotomies - for example, models in which higher capital levels increase returns to very high levels of work hours as opposed to moderate hours, or to mathematical as opposed to verbal skills - could be used to suggest that economic growth without legal and political activism by and for women is likely to generate an increasing rather than a diminishing gender gap.

(4) The Timing and Incidence of Exploratory Drilling in Offshore Wildcat Tracts, Kenneth Hendricks and Robert H. Porter, AER, Vol. 86 (1996): 388-407.
The story: Free rider effect/asymmetric information. Holders of oil leases face a free rider problem, in that the outcome of one's neighbor's drilling provides useful information. An empirical study indicates that many tracts are drilled toward the end of the lease period, suggesting that companies are often unsuccessful in cooperating to solve the free rider problem.
The story's ideology: Liberal.
Legal implications: Although the authors do not give policy implications, one can infer that it might be a good idea for the government to require winning bidders to drill (assuming the free-rider behavior here is socially undesirable).
Possibilities for flipping the model: Since this is an empirical study, flipping does not work in the same way here as it does with theoretical papers. One could reinterpret the results to emphasize that leaseholders most of the time avoid a 'war of attrition' in which they wait to see what others do, and thus bill the study as supportive of a conservative position that free rider inefficiencies can be resolved without outside intervention, rather than a liberal position that free rider market failures are widespread.

(5) The Swing Voter's Curse, Timothy J. Fedderson and Wolfgang Posendorfer, AER, Vol. 86 (1996): 408-424.
The story: Winner's curse/asymmetric information. Abstention from voting can be rational for less-informed voters, because they have an interest in allowing voters who know which candidate is preferable to control the result.
The story's ideology: Conservative.
Legal implications: Efforts to create higher turnout through, for example, mandatory voting laws are misconceived, as are efforts to reduce the difference

in turnout in the US between more educated and less educated people.
Possibilities for flipping the model: The article uses the winner's curse apparatus in a way that lends implicit support to a traditionalist conservative belief in the superior qualifications of some voters to decide elections. (The model also upholds a centrist, 'ticket-splitting' view of politics by postulating two classes of voters: independents who are sensitive to the state of the world and partisans who are not.) The contrary liberal argument about abstention (which is probably more orthodox than the article's conservative argument, at least among policy intellectuals) is a free-rider claim about an individually 'rational' incentive to abstain that is collectively undesirable. This liberal argument supports voluntary or mandatory measures to increase turnout, and can be given a sharper edge by combining it with an argument that the substantial social class disparity in abstention in the US is a 'rational' response to class bias in the US political system, rather than to deference by the less educated to the superior judgments of the more educated.

(6) How do Senators Vote? Disentangling the Role of Voter Peferences, Party Affiliation, and Senator Ideology, Steven D. Levitt, AER, Vol. 86 (1996): 425-441.
The story: The liberalism or conservatism of senatorial voting, as measured by ADA score, is more dependent on the senator's own ideology than on other factors such as party affiliation and degree of constituency liberalism.
The story's ideology: Unclear.
Legal implications: Unclear.
Possibilities for flipping the model: This is a methodological article that studies liberal-conservative politics but does not itself have a clear liberal-conservative significance. The model assumes that the senator's ideology is the residual influence, which is certainly debatable - what about error in measuring other variables, or unmeasured potential influences such as the economic interests of the senator's constituency? But the article's modeling of the centrality of ideology does not have a clear methodological politics; the model could accord either with a new left/CLS belief in the value as well as the inevitability of ideology and ideological debate, or with a new right/public choice belief in representatives' ideology as rent-seeking.

(7) Revenue Effects and Information Processing in English Common Value Auctions, Dan Levin, John H. Kagel and Jean-Francois Richard, AER, Vol. 86 (1996): 442-460
The story: Behavioral economics/winner's curse/auction theory. Theoretically, one would expect English common value auctions in which the high bidder wins at the second highest price to raise more revenue than first price, sealed bid auctions, because bidders can use other bidders' behavior to help them avoid

winner's curse problems. Experimentally, though, sealed bid auctions raise more revenue from inexperienced bidders, who suffer from the winner's curse; for experienced bidders, English auctions did increase revenue.
The story's ideology: Liberal.
Legal implications: The recommendation for the government to use English auctions to maximize revenue does not necessarily apply when bidders are inexperienced.
Possibilities for flipping the model: Behavioral economics typically deals with whether people do or do not conform to 'rational choice' predictions in practice. Articles such as this one that show people acting 'irrationally' are not politically clear-cut. This empirical study has been classified as having a liberal politics, both because a finding that people do not actually act in accord with 'rational choice' predictions helps undermine one of the tenets of free-market ideology, and because the authors here were sympathetic in their attitude toward the heuristic their experimental subjects used as a substitute for maximizing. At the same time, the study, like much behavioral economics, has potential to be understood in a conservative fashion as a how-to manual on how to take advantage of people whose behavior does not accord with 'rational choice.'

(8) Avoidable Cost: Ride a Double Auction Roller Coaster, Mark H. Van Boening and Nathaniel Wilcox, AER, Vol. 86 (1996): 461-477.
The story: Double auction markets such as those employed on stock exchanges are usually supported as efficient, but in a situation characterized by high 'avoidable costs' (that is, high costs for any level of production above zero, as with flying a plane), experiments indicate that double auctions may well be inefficient. There, cooperative institutions may well have a role in creating efficient outcomes.
The story's ideology: Liberal.
Legal implications: For regulators to impose double auction markets is not necessarily a good idea; sometimes cooperative institutions may work better.
Possibilities for flipping the model: Although the overall point about the failure of a competitive market is a liberal one, in the regulatory context the message may be opposed to certain antitrust initiatives assocated with political liberals. More broadly, the conservative flip on this type of experimental economic work would involve looking at an institutional situation in which the prevailing (liberal) assumption is that free-rider problems or other market failures will prevent an efficient solution from being achieved in the absence of regulation, and showing experimentally that, at least in a significant category of these situations, efficient solutions will in fact be reached without regulation.

(9) Holdups, Standard Breach Remedies, and Optimal Investment, Aaron S. Edlin and Stefan Reichelstein, AER, Vol. 86 (1996): 478-501.

The story: The law and economics literature contains both arguments that contracting parties will *under*invest because their relationship-specific investments will be subject to opportunism and that they will *over*invest because an expectation measure of damages will compensate them for inefficient investment. For the parties, the solution to the investment problem is to specify a quantity at which the opportunism tax on investment is balanced by the breach subsidy to investment. For the legal system, both expectation damages and specific performance will lead to efficient outcomes when only one party makes relationship-specific investments; only specific performance is efficient when both parties do so.

The story's ideology: Conservative.

Legal implications: If possible, grant specific performance when both parties make relationship-specific investments.

Possibilities for flipping the model: The story here has been classified as conservative because the contemporary liberal position on contractual opportunism and regard for the other's welfare seems to rely centrally on notions of moral standards, such as good faith and promissory estoppel, and status, such as inequality in bargaining power and unconscionability, that the model eschews in favor of apparently nonevaluative, nonstatus-based decision making rules. At the same time, the story's recommendation of specific performance by itself could be either liberal or conservative, depending on factors such as the status of the parties that the model abstracts from. Also, at a general level, a political preference for specific performance over expectation goes along with liberal doubts about the effectiveness of markets; the combination of all these factors, along with certain differences between the political center in legal and economic discourse (the failure of the model to consider value-oriented alternatives to rule-based decision -making, which makes it right of center in relation to law, does not necessarily do so in relation to economics) makes the politics of the model complex, though fair to classify in the final analysis as conservative. One way to flip this model into a liberal one would be to begin from a set of assumptions under which opportunism and lack of regard for the other's welfare will generate inefficient results absent particularized, status-conscious legal strategies. Another, critical approach to flipping the story would be to structure a model in which the assumptions lead to no efficient solution being available either through the parties' negotiation or through regulation.

(10) Employee Buyout in a Bargaining Game with Asymmetric Information, Avner Ben-Neur and Byoung Jun, AER, Vol. 86 (1996): 502-523.
The story: Asymmetric information/signalling. Employees who do not know the true profitability of a firm can make offers to buy the firm as well as wage demands; unprofitable owners will agree to sell, while profitable ones will prefer to meet the wage demands.
The story's ideology: Liberal.
Legal implications: The expansion of negotiations between employers and employees from wages only to employee ownership (and by extension, from wages to other typically unnegotiated subjects) enhances efficiency by providing opportunites for overcoming asymmetric information problems.
Possibilities for flipping the model: A conservative flip: Suppose the employees have private information about their likely future contributions to the firm; the employer allows 'profitable' and 'unprofitable' employees to signal their status by telling all employees they are subject to downsizing and allowing them all to quit with a bit of severance pay, as well as by making a wage offer. The general point in flipping the liberal, potentially radical, model presented in the article is that the additional subjects that are placed on the table to facilitate efficiency-enhancing signalling need not be subjects that accord with a liberal (or radical) reformist agenda; they may be instead be subjects like mass termination of employees that accord better with a conservative politics.

(11) Aggregation Without Separability: A Generalized Composite Commodity Theorem, Arthur Lewbel, AER, Vol. 86 (1996): 524-543.
The story: A methodological piece that focuses on technical assumptions underlying the construction of price indices.
The story's ideology: Unclear. The story lacked the ideologically significant punchline that nearly all the other articles had. Certainly the general topic of price indices and inflation is a politically sensitive one, and there may be a hidden moral that escaped this reviewer's attention.
Legal implications: Unclear.
Possibilities for flipping the model: Unclear. For one with a closer sense of different schools within econometrics, the article would quite possibly embody a methodological politics (just as a law review article that apparently eschews substantive political storytelling in favor of a focus on methodological or procedural matters embodies some kind of politics of form), and possibilities for flipping would accordingly present themselves.

(12) Voluntary Export Restraints, Antidumping Procedure and Domestic Politics, B. Peter Rosendorff, AER, Vol. 86 (1996): 544-561.
The story: Signalling. Anti-dumping legislation leads to inefficient voluntary export restraints as the outcome of a game in which actions on anti-dumping

petitions signal the desire of governments for voluntary export restraints by foreign producers. Given the median voter theorem and widely dispersed stock ownership, governments may well value firm profits more than tariff revenues, while at the same time asserting a rhetorical commitment to free trade.
The story's ideology: Conservative.
Legal implications: Anti-dumping laws are undesirable.
Possibilities for flipping the model: Here, the signalling model relies on assumptions that welfare is lowered by tariffs and voluntary export restraints; given that, the pro-free trade politics of the story are both transparent and readily flipped by making different assumptions.

(13) Entry, Exit, Growth, and Innovation over the Product Life Cycle, Steven Klepper, AER, Vol. 86 (1996): 562-583.
The story: The idea is to explain a pattern in which product markets are characterized by an initial phase with innovative products and competing designs to a later stage in which a dominant design emerges, market shares stabilize, and larger firms predominate. The model assumes that the ability to appropriate returns from process R&D (that is, production-oriented rather than new product-oriented R&D) depends on firm size, which leads to large firms and a shutout of new entrants.
The story's ideology: Conservative.
Legal implications: An anti-regulation, hands-off message is the logical accompaniment of this type of economic storytelling.
Possibilities for flipping the model: This is economics in the conservative genre of providing a more or less sunny explanation of why things are the way they are, or at least seem to be. The corresponding liberal genre would explain the product life cycle in a less sunny fashion, perhaps by using monopoly power rather than process R&D as the driving assumption in the model. Either way, the aesthetics of the exercise depend on whether the particular simple conditions of the model seem to determine the situation in a persuasive, interesting fashion.

(14) Heterogeneity, Stratification, and Growth: Macroeconomic Implications of Community Structure and School Finance, Roland Benabou, AER, Vol. 86 (1996): 584-609.
The story: Sorting families homogeneously in schooling minimizes the costs of existing heterogeneity, but integration reduces heterogeneity faster, thus reducing growth in the short term but raising it in the long term.
The story's ideology: Liberal.
Legal implications: Integrate and equalize. Specifically, avoid stratification in schooling through school finance reform, and state rather than private or local control of schools.
Possibilities for flipping the model: The liberal heart of the story - the long-term

positive effects of socioeconomic (and by extension racial and ethnic) integration overriding the short-term negative effects - depends on the assumptions made in the model about economic heterogeneity and its negative effects. To tell a conservative story, switch the negative assumptions about heterogeneity. To tell a radical story about, say, the superiority of raising children in kibbutzes rather than in individual homes, only a small tweaking of the model would be necessary.

11. Law and Economics: A Critical How-To

A theoretical law and economics story may begin with a logical puzzle or it may begin with a question about a rule, an institution or people's actions. But whether the initial kernel is a 'real world' situation or a logical model, the point of the storytelling exercise, as suggested by the foregoing review of current economic articles, is to hook up logic with some significant situation in a politically significant fashion. Or, to put the how-to process for doing law and economics in outline form:

1. Start with either a juicy logical twist *or* some significant real-world situation.
2. Now connect up your starting point to a real-world situation, if you started with logic, or to a neat logical point, if you started with a situation.
3. Make sure there's something politically significant - that is, ideologically pointed - in the connection you make.

Since the linking of logic, situation, and moral in law and economics storytelling/model building involves a substantial degree of creativity, it is not possible to produce a law and economics story in the same way that one can produce results using the formula for quadratic equations. A major premise of CLS law and economics is that one has a high level of freedom in hooking up logical models and salient real world situations. That freedom to choose a particular phenomenon out of all the ones in the world to which the model might be applicable makes hash out of any claim that the logic has now been shown to have determinate real-world implications. The inventive researcher trying to think of an application for the model is in effect rummaging through a huge number of potential real-world situations, very likely without being aware of how many she is implicitly considering and rejecting. When she finds a phenomenon for which there is a feeling of match or fit, the connection she draws between the logic and the phenomenon may be convincing to her and to her readers. But she has not proven that the connection is something other than fortuitous, and she and her readers, no matter how plausible they find the connection, should carry more than a twinge of doubt about it, given the uncontrolled way in which models are linked to phenomena in law and economics.

More doubts are in order. Even if one believes there is a truly pretty and convincing connection between a particular logical twist and a particular phenomenon, one has not shown that the logic is the driver of the phenomenon. What one has shown by mapping logic onto phenomenon is a connection, an analogy of sorts. One has not shown causality. It is just as plausible - more plausible in most circumstances in law and economics - to view the link between logic and phenomenon not in terms of an underlying, causally prior mathematical substrate of the phenomenon, but in causally agnostic terms. Discovering that logical twist A has a pleasing, powerful correspondence to a particular facet of the world does not show that that facet is determined by the logic. When one discovers a pleasing, powerful connection between a legal category and a phenomenon, one is, as a participant in the culture of modern 'legal science', skeptical about any claim that the legal category somehow captures or causes the situation; rather, one is likely to believe, in keeping with the arguments of antiformalist critics in law, that the sense of connection or correspondence between legal models and phenomena reflects socially and politically contingent states of consciousness rather than the causal efficacy of legal categories. A similar caution, rather than an overexuberant sense of economic reason as laying bare the logic of the world's workings, would seem to be advisable in economics in general and in law and economics in particular.

A how-to approach to creating law and economics stories that reflects CLS assumptions about the ideological, contested, and indeterminate nature of law and economics arguments is of course not uniquely the property of those who want to tell critical rather than other kinds of stories. But there is at least some reason to believe that understanding law and economics as a process of ideological storytelling is more empowering for CLS law and economics than it is for, say, Chicago law and economics. A group of law and economics practitioners who can candidly talk about how to put together and flip ideological law and economics can arguably do a better job at it than those whose rhetorical conventions make that kind of discussion taboo, at least in public. To be sure, there is the counterclaim that CLS law and economics, at least if it takes the ideological turn of exposing the politics of its own arguments and even considering how they could be flipped, is shooting itself in the foot compared to law and economics that represses at every turn its status as ideology. But it could also be the case that politically-reflective CLS law and economics such as Kelman (1993) and Kennedy (1992) might over time benefit in the marketplace of ideas from the way it can make other versions of law and economics seem simplistic.

12. Conclusion

The CLS critique of law and economics can reasonably be understood as an effort to foster alternative, radical approaches to law and economics that acknowledge and proceed from politically-charged contradictions within the discipline. Thus understood, the relative lack of engagement of much of the legal left with economics becomes a sign of loss rather than victory for the CLS critique. At the same time, though, the growth of a larger and more politically diverse law and economics movement becomes interpretable as a success, one that may be related in part to CLS denunciations of the right-wing tilt in the Posnerian, Coasean version of law and economics. Though CLS attacks on ideological tilt in law and economics have not made for amicable relations between the movements, the CLS critique has likely enhanced the viability of liberal law and economics. Liberal dissent from Chicago orthodoxy has been easier to take by comparison with the more fundamental CLS critique, and the rise of liberal law and economics in the law reviews has enhanced the academic credibility of a movement under attack as right-wing ideology. Nor was the opening to liberalism especially threatening to conservatives if liberal law and economics could be contained, as it has been thus far in the US, within the framework of continuing conservative control of the major journals and professional association in the discipline.

Given the predominant role of Chicago, law and economics over the last twenty years has helped move law in the US to the right. But in the future, law and economics may well help move economics to the left. The law and economics project can certainly operate in the direction of making legal argument more purportedly scientific and value-free, but it also inherently has the potential to tip in the direction of making economics a more overt domain of logicized ideological argument. The politics of such a tipping are themselves contingent, but there is a major future risk for the right in the contemporary burgeoning of law and economics that, in the US, has been one of the right's great intellectual triumphs.

As for CLS: the movement's identity has always been as a counterhegemonic, dissenting one, and there is no likelihood of that stance changing. But especially given the continued rise of law and economics, a counterhegemonic, dissenting CLS involvement in the discipline as critics and also as participants is both likely and called for. Legal leftist ambivalence about employing 'the master's tools' of technical economic analysis can and should be overcome, aided by the realization that such tools are not the predetermined property of the liberal center and the right but are available for deployment on behalf of more radical visions.

Bibliography on Critical Legal Studies (0660)

Abel, Richard L. (1982), 'A Socialist Approach to Risk', **41** *Maryland Law Review*, 695 ff.

Alexander, Gregory S. (1982), 'The Concept of Property in Private and Constitutional Law: The Ideology of the Scientific Turn in Legal Analysis', **82** *Columbia Law Review*, 1545-1599.

Alexander, Gregory S. (1988), 'Takings, Narratives and Power', **88** *Columbia Law Review*, 1752 ff.

Alexander, Gregory S. (1997), *Commodity and Propriety: Competing Visions of Property in American Legal Thought, 1776-1970*, Chicago, University of Chicago Press.

Alexander, Gregory S. (ed.) (1994), *A Fourth Way?: Privatization, Property, and the Emergence of New Market Economies*, New York, Routledge.

Aoki, Keith (1993), 'Race, Space and Place: The Relation Between Architectual Modernism, Post-Modernism, Urban Planning and Gentrification', **22** *Fordham Urban Law Journal*, 699 ff.

Audain, Linz (1992), 'Ctritical Legal Studies, Feminism, Law and Economics, and the Veil of Intellectual Tolerance: A Tentative Plea for Cross-Jurisprudential Dialogue', **20** *Hofstra Law Review*, 1017 ff.

Audain, Linz (1995), 'Critical Cultural Law and Economics, the Culture of Deindividualization, the Paradox of Blackness', **70** *Indiana Law Journal*, 711 ff.

Baker, C. Edwin (1975), 'The Ideology of the Economic Analysis of Law', **5** *Philosophy and Public Affairs*, 3-48.

Baker, Tom (1996), 'On the Genealogy of Moral Hazard', **75** *Texas Law Review*, 237-292.

Balkin, J.M. (1986), 'Learning Nothing and Forgetting Nothing: Richard Epstein and the Takings Clause', **18** *Urban Law*, 707 ff.

Balkin, J.M. (1987), 'Too Good to be True: The Positive Economic Theory of Law', **87** *Columbia Law Review*, 1447 ff.

Black, Kreider and Sullivan, C.L.S. (1988), *Economic Realism and the Theory of the Firm*, Miami.

Bratton, William W., Jr (1984), 'The Interpretation of Contracts Governing Corporate Debt Relationships', **5** *Cardozo Law Review*, 371 ff.

Bratton, William W., Jr (1989a), 'Corporate Debt Relationships: Legal Theory in a Time of Restructuring', **1989** *Duke Law Journal*, 92 ff.

Bratton, William W., Jr (1989b), 'The New Economic Theory of the Firm: Critical Perspectives from History', **41** *Stanford Law Review*, 1471-1527.

Bratton, William W., Jr (1992), 'The Economic Structure of the Post-Contractual Corporation', **87** *Northwestern Law Review*, 180 ff.

Bratton, William W., Jr (1995), 'Game Theory and the Restoration of Honor to Corporate Law's Duty of Loyalty', in Mitchell, Lawrence E. (ed.), *Progressive Corporation Law*, Boulder, Westview Press.

Carlson, David Gray (1986), 'Reforming the Efficiency Criterion: Comments on Some Recent Suggestions', **8** *Cardozo Law Review*, 39 ff.

Carlson, David Gray (1992), 'Bankruptcy Theory and the Creditors' Bargain', **61** *University of Cincinnati Law Review*, 453 ff.

Carlson, David Gray (1993), 'On the Margins of Microeconomics', **14** *Cardozo Law Review*, 1867 ff.

Carlson, David Gray (1994), 'The Politics of Article 9: On the Efficiency of Secured

Lending', **80** *Virginia Law Review*, 2179 ff.

Culp, Jerome M. (1987), 'Judex Economicus', **50(4)** *Law and Contemporary Problems*, 95-140.

Curran, William J. III (1987a), 'Beyond Economic Concepts and Categories: A Democratic Refiguration of Antitrust Law', **31** *St Louis University Law Journal*, 349-378.

Curran, William J. III (1987b), 'Antitrust and the Rule of Reason', **28** *St Louis University Law Journal*, 745 ff.

Eastman, Wayne (1996a), '"Everything's Up for Grabs": The Coasean Story in Game-Theoretic Terms', **31** *New England Law Review*.

Eastman, Wayne (1996b), 'How Coasean Bargaining Entails a Prisoners' Dilemma', **72** *Notre Dame Law Review*, 89 ff.

Eastman, Wayne (1996c), 'Telling Alternative Stories: Heterodox Versions of the Prisoners' Dilemma, the Coase Theorem and Supply-Demand Equilibrium', **29** *Connecticut Law Review*, 727 ff.

Feinman, Jay M. (1988), 'Practical Legal Studies and Critical Legal Studies', **87(3)** *Michigan Law Review*, 724-731.

Fitzpatrick, Peter and Hunt, Alan (eds) (1987), *Critical Legal Studies*, Oxford, Oxford University Press.

Ford, Richard (1994), 'The Boundaries of Race: Political Geography in Legal Analysis', **107** *Harvard Law Review*, 1843 ff.

Fox, Rachel (1991), 'The Selling Out of Mount Laurel: Regional Contribution Agreements in New Jersey's Fair Housing Act', **16** *Fordham Urban Law Journal*, 507 ff.

Georgakopoulos, Nikos L. (1995), 'Peri Tmematikou Daneismou apo ten Amerikanike Nomike Skepse (On the Piecemeal Borrowing from the American Legal Thought)', **43** *Nomiko Vema*, 799-807.

Grady, Mark F. (1995), 'Politicization of Commodities: The Case of Cadaveric Organs', **20** *Journal of Corporate Law*, 51 ff.

Hager, Mark (1991), 'Posner's Juris. of Class.', **41** *American Law Review*, 7 ff.

Harrison, Jeffrey L. (1986), 'Egoism, Altruism, and Market Illusions: the Limits of Law and Economics', **33** *UCLA Law Review*, 1309-1363.

Harrison, Jeffrey L. (1995), 'Class, Entitlement and Contract', in Malloy, Robin P. and Braun, Christopher K. (eds), *Law and Economics: New and Critical Perspectives*, New York, Peter Lang.

Heller, Thomas C. (1976), 'The Importance of Normative Decision-Making: The Limitations of Legal Economics as a Basis for Liberal Jurisprudence - As Illustrated by the Regulation of Vacation Home Development', *Wisconsin Law Review*, 385 ff.

Heller, Thomas C. (1979), 'Is the Charitable Exemption from Property Taxes an Easy Case? General Concerns about Legal Economics and Jurisprudence', in Rubinfeld, Daniel L. (ed.), *Essays on the Law and Economics of Local Governments*, Washington, D.C.: The Urban Institute.

Honoroff, Bradley (1983), 'Reflections on Richard Posner', **18** *CR-CL*, 287 ff.

Horwitz, Morton J. (1976), 'The Legacy of 1776 in Legal and Economic Thought', **19** *Journal of Law and Economics*, 621 ff.

Horwitz, Morton J. (1980), 'Law and Economics: Science or Politics?', **8** *Hofstra Law Review*, 905-912.

Keller, Susan (1988), 'Does the Roof have to Cave In?: The Landlord/Tenant Power Relationship and the Intentional Infliction of Emotional Distress', **9** *Cardozo Law*

Review, 1663 ff.

Kelman, Mark G. (1979a), 'Choice and Utility', *Wisconsin Law Review*, 769-797.

Kelman, Mark G. (1979b), 'Consumption Theory, Production Theory and Ideology in the Coase Theorem', **52** *Southern California Law Review*, 669-698.

Kelman, Mark G. (1980), 'Spitzer and Hoffman on Coase: A Brief Rejoinder', **53** *Southern California Law Review*, 1215-1223.

Kelman, Mark G. (1983), 'Misunderstanding Social Life: A Critique of the Core Premises of "Law and Economics"', **33** *Journal of Legal Education*, 274-284.

Kelman, Mark G. (1984), 'Trashing', **36** *Stanford Law Review*, 293-348.

Kelman, Mark G. (1985), 'Comment on Hoffman and Spitzer's Experimental Law and Economics', **85** *Columbia Law Review*, 1037-1047.

Kelman, Mark G. (1986), 'Taking Takings Seriously: An Essay for Centrists', **74** *California Law Review*, 1829 ff.

Kelman, Mark G. (1987a), *A Guide to Critical Legal Studies*, Cambridge, MA, Harvard University Press.

Kelman, Mark G. (1987b), 'The Necessary Myth of Objective Causation Judgments in Liberal Political Theory', **63** *Chicago-Kent Law Review*, 579-637.

Kelman, Mark G. (1988), 'On Democracy-Bashing: A Skeptical Look at the Theoretical and "Empirical" Practice of the Public Choice Movement', **74** *Virginia Law Review*, 199-273.

Kelman, Mark G. (1991a), 'Concepts of Discrimination in "General Ability" Job Testing', **104** *Harvard Law Review*, 1157 ff.

Kelman, Mark G. (1991b), 'Emerging Centrist Liberalism', **43** *Florida Law Review*, 417 ff.

Kelman, Mark G. (1993), 'Could Lawyers Stop Recessions?: Speculations on Law and Macroeconomics', **45** *Stanford Law Review*, 1215 ff.

Kennedy, David (1991), 'Turning to Market Democracy: A Tale of Two Architectures', **32** *Harvard International Law Journal*, 373 ff.

Kennedy, David (1994), 'The International Style in Postwar Law and Policy: John Jackson and the Field of International Economic Law', *Utah Law Review*, 7 ff.

Kennedy, Duncan (1973), 'Legal Formality', **2** *Journal of Legal Studies*, 351-398.

Kennedy, Duncan (1976), 'Form and Substance in Private Law Adjudication', **89** *Harvard Law Review*, 1685-1778. Reprinted in Kronman, Anthony T. and Posner, Richard A. (eds), *The Economics of Contract Law*, Boston, Little Brown, 1979, 100-107.

Kennedy, Duncan (1979), 'The Structure of Blackstone's Commentaries', **28** *Buffalo Law Review*, 205 ff.

Kennedy, Duncan (1981a), 'Cost-Benefit Analysis of Entitlement Problems: A Critique', **33** *Stanford Law Review*, 387-445.

Kennedy, Duncan (1981b), 'Cost-Reduction Theory as Legitimation', **90** *Yale Law Journal*, 1275-1283.

Kennedy, Duncan (1982), 'Distributive and Paternalist Motives in Contract and Tort Law, with Special Reference to Compulsory Terms and Unequal Bargaining Power', **41** *Maryland Law Review*, 563 ff.

Kennedy, Duncan (1985), 'The Role of Law in Economic Thought: Essays on the Fetishism of Commodities', **34** *American University Law Review*, 939 ff.

Kennedy, Duncan (1987), 'The Effect of the Warranty of Habitability on Low Income Housing: "Milking" and Class Violence', **15** *Florida State University Law Review*, 485 ff.

Kennedy, Duncan (1991), 'The Stakes of Law, or Hale and Foucault!', **15** *Legal Studies*, 327 ff.

Kennedy, Duncan (1992), 'Sexy Dressing', **26** *New England Law Review*, 1309 ff. *Sexy Dressing*, Cambridge, MA: Harvard University Press (1994b)

Kennedy, Duncan (1994), 'Neither the Market Nor the State: Housing Privatization Issues', in Alexander, Gregory S. (ed.), *A Fourth Way?: Privatization, Property, and the Emergence of New Market Economies*, New York: Routledge.

Kennedy, Duncan and Michelman, Frank I. (1980), 'Are Property and Contract Efficient?', **8** *Hofstra Law Review*, 711 ff.

Kennedy, Duncan and Specht, Leopold (1994), 'Housing Cooperatives as a Mode of Privatization', in Alexander, Gregory S. (ed.), *A Fourth Way?: Privatization, Property, and the Emergence of New Market Economies*, New York: Routledge.

Kinning, Robin (1993), 'Selective Housing Code Enforcement and Low-Income Housing Policy: Minneapolis Case Study', **21** *Fordham Urban Law Journal*, 159 ff.

Klare, Karl (1988), 'Workplace Democracy and Market Reconstruction: An Agenda for Legal Reform', **38** *Catholic University Law Review*, 1 ff.

Kolodney, Lawrence K. (1991), 'Eviction Free Zones: The Economics of Legal Bricolage in the Fight Against Displacement', **18** *Fordham Urban Law Journal*, 502 ff.

Levinson, Sanford (1991), 'Strolling Down the Path of the Law (and Toward Critical Legal Studies?): The Jurisprudence of Richard Posner' (Book Review of the Problems of Jurisprudence), **91** *Columbia Law Review*, 1221-1252.

McUsic, Molly (1988), 'Note, Reassessing Rent Control: Its Economic Impact in a Gentrifying Housing Market', **101** *Harvard Law Review*, 1835 ff.

Millon, David (1990), 'Theories of the Corporation', *Duke Law Journal*, 201 ff.

Minda, Gary (1978), 'The Lawyer-Economist at Chicago: Richard A. Posner and the Economic Analysis of Law', **39** *Ohio State Law Journal*, 439 ff.

Minda, Gary (1989), 'The Law and Economics and Critical Legal Studies Movement in American Law', in Mercuro, Nicholas (ed.), *Law and Economics*, Boston, Kluwer Academic Publishers, 87-122.

Peller, Gary (1985), 'The Metaphysics of American Law', **73** *California Law Review*, 1151 ff.

Peritz, Rudolph J. (1984), 'The Predicament of Antitrust Jurisprudence: Economics and the Monopolization of Price Discrimination', *Duke Law Journal*, 1205-1295.

Peritz, Rudolph J. (1989), 'The 'Rule of Reason' in Antitrust Law: Property Logic in Restraint of Competition', **40** *Hastings Law Journal*, 285-342.

Peritz, Rudolph J. (1990), 'A Counter-History of Antitrust Law', *Duke Law Journal*, 263 ff.

Schlag, Pierre (1986), 'An Appreciative Comment on Coase's the Problem of Social Cost: A View from the Left', *Wisconsin Law Review*, 919-962.

Schlag, Pierre (1989), 'The Problem of Transaction Costs', **62** *Southern California Law Review*, 1661-1699.

Schwartzstein, Linda A. (1992), 'Austrian Economics and the Current Debate between Critical Legal Studies and Law and Economics', **20** *Hofstra Law Review*, 1105 ff.

Singer, Joseph W. (1984), 'The Player and the Cards: Nihilism and Legal Theory', **94** *Yale Law Journal*, 1 ff.

Spann, Girardeau A. (1988), 'A Critical Legal Studies Perspective on Contract Law and Practice', *Annual Survey of American Law*, 223-292.

Stone, Katherine Van Wezel (1991), 'Employees as Stakeholders Under State Nonshareholder Constituency Statutes', **21** *Stetson Law Review*, 45 ff.
Trubek, David (1984), 'Where the Action is: Critical Legal Studies and Empiricism', **36** *Stanford Law Review*, 575 ff.
Tushnet, Mark (1991), 'Critical Legal Studies: A Political History', **100(5)** *Yale Law Journal*, 1515-1544.
Unger, Roberto Mangabeira (1975), *Knowledge and Politics*, New York, Free Press.
Van Wezel Stone, Katherine (1991), 'Employees as Stakeholders Under State Nonshareholder Constituency Statutes', **21** *Stetson Law Review*, 45 ff.
Vracar, K. Stevan (1994), *Preispitivanja pravne metodologije: Nagovestaji drzavno-pravnog integralizma* (Reexamination of the Legal Methodology: Indications of State-Legal Integralism), Belgrade, Naucna knjiga.
West, Robin (1986), 'Submission, Choice, and Ethics: A Rejoinder to Judge Posner', **99** *Harvard Law Review*, 1449-1456.
West, Robin (1989), *Taking Preferences Seriously*, Tulane.
Wilhelmsson, Thomas (ed.) (1993), *Perspectives of Critical Contract Law*, Aldershot, Dartmouth.

Other References

American Economic Review (1996), **86(2)** (all articles).
Ayres, Ian (1990), 'Playing Games with the Law', **42** *Stanford Law Review*, 1291 ff.
Ayres, Ian and Talley, Eric (1995), 'Solomonic Bargaining: Dividing a Legal Entitlement to Facilitate Coasean Trade', **104** *Yale Law Journal*, 1027 ff.
Calabresi, Guido (1970), *The Cost of Accidents: A Legal and Economic Analysis*, New Haven, CT, Yale University Press.
Cooter, Robert (1982), 'The Cost of Coase', **11** *Journal of Legal Studies*, 1 ff.
Hovenkamp, Herbert (1992), 'Rationality in Law and Economics', **60** *George Washington Law Review*, 293 ff.
Markovits, Richard S. (1984), 'Duncan's Do-nots: Cost-Benefit Analysis and the Determination of Legal Entitlements', **36** *Stanford Law Review*, 1169 ff.
Schor, Juliet (1991), *The Overworked American*, New York, Basic Books.
Posner, Richard A. (1972), *The Economic Analysis of Law*, Boston, Little Brown.

0710
RATIONAL CHOICE THEORY IN LAW AND ECONOMICS

Thomas S. Ulen

Alumni Distinguished Professor of Law, College of Law, University of Illinois at Urbana-Champaign and Professor, University of Illinois Institute of Government and Public Affairs

Abstract

The great appeal of law and economics has been its use of a coherent theory of human decision making (rational choice theory) to examine legal rules and institutions. While the innovations and accomplishments of that theory in the analysis of the law have been many and important, there has been a great deal of dissatisfaction among more traditional legal scholars with the rational-choice foundation of law and economics. This chapter, first, explains rational choice theory and its importance in the economic analysis of law; second, summarizes some of the literature from economics, cognitive psychology, and other disciplines that have been critical of rational choice theory; and, third, speculates on the impact of those criticisms on the economic analysis of law.

JEL classification: K00

Keywords: Rationality, Bargaining, Human Decision Making, Methodological Criticism

1. Introduction

When law and economics was a new field in the legal curriculum and just becoming a regular part of academic legal discourse, the use of microeconomic theory to discuss traditional legal topics aroused interest but also suspicion and hostility. Prominent among the reasons for this suspicion and hostility was the feeling that the economist's account of human decision making - rational choice theory - was so deeply flawed that conclusions derived from that account ought to be taken with a very large grain of salt, if not rejected outright. To take one example, the economic theory of the decision to commit a crime asserted that the potential criminal evaluated the expected costs and expected benefits of the criminal act and committed the crime only if the expected benefits exceeded the expected costs.

Many traditional legal scholars, judges and practitioners to whom such examples of law and economics were given felt that the root of their unhappiness with the conclusions of the new discipline lay with the economist's contention that all decisions (like that to commit a crime) are the result of rational deliberation. The rational utility- or profit-maximizers of microeconomic theory seemed to bear very little correlation to the flesh-and-blood human beings with whom the law dealt. Therefore, to the extent that law and economics used rational choice theory as its principal theory of human decision making, the field had a difficult time in convincing traditional legal scholars that it should be taken seriously.

In this chapter I first describe the rational choice model of decision making and then give some examples of the use of that theory in law and economics. Next I describe some criticisms of rational choice theory that have been made principally by cognitive and social psychologists. And finally, I speculate on the implications of these criticisms for the economic analysis of law.

A. Rational Choice Theory

Rational choice theory is at the heart of modern economic theory and in the disciplines contiguous to economics, such as some parts of political science, decision theory, sociology, history and law, that have adopted the theory as their model of decision making. In this section I define rational choice, show how it is used in economics and describe its use in other disciplines and suggest why traditional scholars in those other disciplines find problems with rational choice theory.

2. Definitions of Rational Choice

There is no widely accepted definition of rational choice theory, but there are two important senses in which the term is used. The first is an informal sense: choice is said to be rational when it is deliberative and consistent. The decision maker has thought about what he or she will do and can give a reasoned justification for the choice. And taking choices over time or focusing on their choices about particular things, such as food or class choices in college, one expects rationality to lead to consistent (and relatively stable) choices. That is, one expects that there will be no wild and inexplicable swings in the objects of their choices and that the means chosen to effectuate the goals of the decision maker will be reasonably well-suited to the attainment of those goals (Nozick, 1993)

Like many informal definitions this one is highly imprecise. Indeed, because almost all action would seem to be deliberative and consistent, this informal definition does not seem to allow us to distinguish rational from irrational action. Everything confirms the definition and nothing refutes it.

The second sense in which the profession uses "rational choice" is more formal: consumers have transitive preferences and seek to maximize the utility that they derive from those preferences, subject to various constraints. Transitive preferences are those for which, if some good or bundle of goods denoted *A* is preferred to another good or bundle of goods denoted *B* and *B* is preferred to a third good or bundle of goods denoted *C*, then it must be the case that *A* is preferred to *C*. By contrast, if it were the case that *A* were preferred to *B*, *B* were preferred to *C* and *C* were preferred to *A*, we would find that distinctly odd - indeed, irrational. Similarly unobjectionable is the assumption that the decision maker seeks to maximize utility subject to various constraints (such as those imposed by income, time, cognitive resources and the like). Most economists find this more formal sense of rational choice to be so obvious that they never doubt it and are puzzled by those who do. (For a discussion of other formal conditions on rational choice, see Plous, 1993, pp. 80-82.)

However obvious the formal sense of rational choice may be to economists and to those in other disciplines who have adopted it as their model of human decision making, the formal sense has not been without its critics. Two such criticisms are worth noting here. First, some have said that the formal notion of rational choice is as tautological as the informal sense. That is, there is no, or almost no, behavior that refutes the formal sense of rationality. All behavior may be said to be directed at utility maximization (who would ever do otherwise?) and all preferences can be said to be transitive. For instance, one might explain many instances of seemingly intransitive preferences as being the result of a change in preferences over time. Second, one can show some inconsistencies or puzzles in the notion of transitive preferences. Suppose that we have asked a subject how he feels about a teaspoonful of sugar. Now we add a grain of sugar to that spoonful. If the subject likes sugar, he should presumably prefer the augmented spoonful to the original on the theory that more is better. (If he does not like sugar, then he should prefer the original spoonful.) However, it is likely to be the case that the subject cannot distinguish the spoonful with one more grain of sugar from the original spoonful. If so, he may say that he is indifferent between the two. (This confusion between "more is better" and indifference is itself puzzling, but set that puzzle to one side.) If we continue to add grains of sugar to the original spoonful and ask the subject each time we do so how he compares the augmented with the previous spoonful, he will probably continue to say that he cannot distinguish and is, therefore, indifferent. But ultimately the grains of sugar will add up to something substantially greater than the original spoonful. So, even though the subject will have contended that each successive spoonful was just as good as the original so that, by transitivity, the final heaping spoonful should be indifferent to the first, the subject is almost certain to prefer the heaping spoonful to the original teaspoonful.

3. The Uses of Rational Choice Theory in Economics

These problems notwithstanding, economists have found rational choice theory to be a very useful model for forming hypotheses about market behavior. There are five principal reasons for this. First, the theory allows economists to make predictions about economic behavior and, by and large, those predictions are borne out by the empirical evidence. For example, rational choice theory predicts and empirical work confirms, that when the wage rate rises, all other things held equal, the supply of labor increases and the demand for labor decreases; when the price of alcohol rises, relative to that of other goods and services, the quantity demanded goes down (if not by much); when the price of a good or service rises, again, relative to that of other goods and services, productive effort tends to shift into the supply of that good or service; and when the price of an input rises relative to that of its substitutes, producers tend to use less of that input and relatively more of the substitutes. These sorts of results are so widespread, so familiar to professional economists and so central to the tenability of modern microeconomic theory that it is not surprising that rational choice theory forms such an important part of the canon of modern microeconomics.

Second, whenever there are seeming deviations from the predictions of price theory, economists can usually explain those deviations without having to assume that the decision makers involved are irrational. If the deviations are a matter of degree (for example, an increase in the tax rate on incomes above $250,000 was followed by a much smaller increase in government revenues than predicted), there are a large number of hypotheses that can explain this deviation that are well short of questioning the rationality of the parties involved. To take just one such hypothesis, there may have been means by which those with incomes over $250,000 could shelter income from the tax authorities that had not been worth pursuing until the tax rate increased. Alternatively, one might argue that the deviation from the prediction of rational choice theory is a statistical fluke, due to some oddity of the data set, that the seeming anomaly is the result of the decision makers' not having had the appropriate information to reach the result predicted by the theory, that there was some theretofore unnoticed market failure, such as monopoly or monopsony, external costs or benefits, public goods, or informational asymmetry, that accounts for the discrepancy between the theory's predictions and the observed behavior. These statistical and structural problems are real and common, so that economists are not themselves being irrational in clinging fiercely to rational choice theory in the face of seeming anomalies in the theory's predictions.

Third, an economist may explain behavior that seems anomalous to rational choice theory by appeal to a slight emendation of the theory. Suppose, by way of example, that someone demonstrates that for a particular good, when the price rises, all other things held equal, the quantity demanded *increases*. Is this sufficient evidence on which to abandon the rational choice theory? Typically not. For instance, in the case of a good whose quantity demanded *rises* rather than falls when the price of the good increases, one might propose a new phenomenon called a "snob effect", which arises when consumers take an increased price for a good as a sign of its desirability, not as a sign to switch to cheaper alternatives. As a consequence, the demand curve for a good subject to a snob effect may slope upward, to indicate that an increase in the price of that good leads to an increase in the quantity demanded (Liebenstein, 1950).

Fourth, there is a strong presumption among economists in the evolutionary fitness of rational behavior - at least in the economic realm. That is, rational consumers will prosper, while irrational consumers will squander their resources and, perhaps, become money pumps for rational calculators. More importantly, rational profit-maximizing businesses will dominate those businesses that do not operate according to a rational plan.

Fifth and finally, Professor Gary Becker has shown that even if there were consumers who behaved irrationality, in the sense of having intransitive preferences, the standard predictions of price theory (such as that an increase in the relative price of a good will lead to a decline in the quantity of that good demanded) would still hold (Becker, 1962). Since that article appeared, there have been more formal demonstrations that the conclusions of price theory and of welfare economics are not much affected by the presence of even a large number of consumers with intransitive preferences. Therefore, while irrationality might still be an issue with respect to the behavior of certain individuals, it is not an issue with respect to aggregate behavior in markets and may, as a result, be ignored.

The point of all this is to suggest that there are plausible reasons why economists cling tenaciously to rational choice theory. The theory is extremely useful and powerful. Its predictions are frequently accurate and a valuable guide to the formulation of public policy. And it is facile enough to explain phenomena that seem anomalous without necessitating an abandonment of the theory.

4. The Use of Rational Choice Theory in Other Disciplines

Criticisms abound when scholars seek to use rational choice theory to describe non-market behavior, as has been the case in such oppressed disciplines as demography, history, biology, political science, international relations and law. None of these disciplines involves explicit market choices, but all of them have been revolutionized by the importation and use of rational choice theory.

Why has rational choice theory been so attractive to some scholars in these contiguous disciplines? The principal reason is that the theory is the most complete and coherent account of human decision making in the social sciences. Moreover, the acknowledged success of economics in the public policy arena in the past fifty years, which may be attributed in part to its grounding in a coherent theory of rational behavior, may have inspired emulation of the modeling aspect of economics by other disciplines in the hope that this will lead to academic and policy successes similar to those of economics.

But, as I noted, there have been sharp criticisms of rational choice theory in the study of non-market behavior. Why should this be the case? One possible answer is that traditional scholars are threatened by rational choice theory: it is an unfamiliar technique, wielded principally by young scholars and clearly threatens the academic standing of those who use traditional methods. But there is more to the objections than mere self-interest. Put in a light most favorable to the objectors, their query may be put this way: Rational choice theory may be fine for the consideration of explicit market decisions - such as which car to buy, whether to lease the car or to purchase it with a loan, which job to take and what terms and conditions to accept and how to invest one's savings. These are, after all, quantifiable decisions. They all involve money and that currency allows comparison among different economic courses of action. But what reason is there to believe that non-market decisions - such as whom to marry or how many children to have or how to care for each of them or whether to trust one's ally in foreign affairs and so on - are made according to the same calculations?' Put someone succinctly, the question is 'Why is the rational choice model suitable to market behavior but not to non-market behavior?' The question is a serious one and deserves an answer.

I can think of three factors that might make the rational choice model a better general model for market choices than for non-market choices. First, market choices are frequent and routine. Even if people make mistakes when they make their first market choices, they have an opportunity to learn through repeated transactions. Moreover, in those instances in which market transactions are rare in an individual's life - as, for example, the purchase of a house, there are many people who *have* made these purchases, so that there is the possibility of learning from others about the pitfalls of those rare transactions. Nonetheless, the general point bears making that market choices are more problematic for individuals, the rarer they are. Related to this matter is the fact that many non-market choices are so infrequent that people do not have repeated opportunities to learn and to make corrections. Love and marriage are examples. Even though one might consult others for their experiences with these infrequent decisions, each individual's circumstances with respect to many of these non-market choices are so highly particularized that the others' experiences may not be an appropriate guide to one's own best course of action.

Second, as already noted, market choices are mediated through a common medium - money - that makes commensurability easier. We do not have problems of 'comparing apples and oranges' in many market transactions because the choices almost always involve the purchaser's giving up money. Because the purchaser knows or could know the market price of other goods and services or can compute an opportunity cost, he or she can make a fairly accurate estimate of the comparative worth of very different courses of action, such as whether to purchase or lease a new car or whether to spend another year in school or get a job. By contrast, non-market choices usually do not involved a common measuring rod like money. Therefore, making comparisons across non-market alternatives or between a market and a non-market alternative may be very difficult. How does one compare the profound experience of parenthood with the cost of an exotic vacation?

Third, there are problems of transparency in non-market choices. Market choices involve relatively straightforward comparisons, save when they are complex and reserved for specialists, as in some complicated options valuations. There is, frequently, a single best (an optimal) decision. But many non-market choices are simply difficult to understand and have a variety of suitable outcomes. Consider the decision of whether or not to invite a friend to travel a long distance with one. There is no 'correct' answer to the question and there are lots of nuanced meanings, including misunderstandings, that may be read into the question and its answer.

Taken together, these issues of frequency, commensurability and transparency may suggest why rational choice theory is widely accepted as an explanation of market choices but has difficulties in acceptance as a model of non-market choices (Ulen, 1998).

B. The Application of Rational Choice Theory in the Law

The most important, but not the only, characteristic of law and economics is its use of rational choice theory to examine legal decisions. In this section I describe the general reasons why rational choice theory may be appropriate for the description and prediction of legal decision making and give examples of the use of the theory in the analysis of private law rules of contract and tort law and in the analysis of criminal law.

5. Why Rational Choice Theory is an Appropriate Model of Legal Decision Making

Rational choice theory is one of three distinguishing characteristics of law and economics. In light of the general criticism of the applicability of rational choice theory to non-market choices given above, one is entitled to ask why rational choice is appropriate for the discussion of legal matters, most of which are non-market choices.

The answer is that many legal decisions are indeed market-like choices. They may be said to be so on the ground that legal rules create implicit prices on different behaviors and that legal decision makers conform their behavior to those prices in much the same way as they conform their market behavior to the relative prices there. For example, the law imposes a monetary sanction (called 'compensatory money damages') on those who unjustifiably interfere with another's property, breach a contract, or accidentally injure another person or his property. These money amounts may be taken to be the 'prices' of engaging in certain kinds of behavior, such as a failure to take due care or to perform a contractual obligation. Presumably, rational decision makers will compare those legal prices with those of the alternatives and will comply with the law's duties (that is, not interfere with another's property without their permission, perform a contractual obligation, or take due care) if the price for doing so is greater than the price of not doing so. For example, if the benefit of breaching a contract is $10,000 and the money damages that the breacher can anticipate paying to the innocent party are $5,000, then there is likely to be breach of contract (Cooter and Ulen, 1997; Posner, 1998). It is the central innovation of law and economics to have recognized that many legal decisions have this market-choice-like quality and that, therefore, rational choice theory is an appropriate model of much legal decision making.

6. Private Law Examples of Rational Choice Theory

I shall here give only a few broad examples of rational choice theory in private law, rather than an exhaustive survey. One particular omission deserves mention. I shall have nothing to say about the Coase Theorem, the most famous example of the economic analysis of law and a superb example of rational choice theory in private law decision making, on the grounds that this *Encyclopedia* covers that theorem extensively elsewhere. Here I merely note that the bargaining behavior that the Coase Theorem posits will occur in the absence of transaction costs precisely because the parties are rational calculators in the manner assumed by rational choice theory. Notwithstanding the fact that I have not discussed the Coase Theorem, in Part C below I shall describe some criticisms of the assumptions of that theorem and then in Part D I shall some implications for the theorem of those criticisms. Here I shall give examples of rational choice theory as it informs the economic analysis of contract law and tort law.

6.1 Contract Law

In an economic analysis of contract law, the place to begin is with the question, Why do rational parties need the law's help in concluding consensual agreements? One might well argue that in the absence of transaction costs, parties seeking to conclude agreements would not need help from the law. They would costlessly conclude mutually beneficial terms. It follows that contact law aids parties to conclude agreements when transaction costs are positive.

What gives rise to positive transaction costs in contracting? There are two general sorts of reasons. First, there may be problems in the environment in which the parties negotiate and these problems can lead to inefficiencies. For example, there could be third-party effects and in the absence of legal intervention the contracting parties are not likely to pay attention to those external effects. Additionally, one of the contracting parties could be a monopolist and could, therefore, put the other party in a situation in which 'consent' would be meaningless. The law can correct for this social cost by insisting that parties reach roughly competitive terms in their agreement.

The second general source of transaction costs in contracting are problems that individual contractors may have. For example, some parties may have unstable or intransitive preferences because, say, they are very young, insane, or suffering from Alzheimer's disease. When people have unstable or intransitive preferences, there is no guarantee that they are in a position to gauge the benefit of bargaining and cannot, therefore, form mutually beneficial agreements. Predictably, contract law does not enforce agreements in which one of the parties has unstable preferences.

The transaction costs arising from factors of the contractual environment and individual transactors may be so high as to preclude contracting or to make it take place on inefficient terms. As a general corrective, contract law can present a set of pre-determined contract terms that take account of these transaction costs and save parties the costs of specifying these terms each time they negotiate to enter an agreement.

6.2 Tort Law

According to economic analysis, the tort liability system seeks to minimize the sum of prevention, accident and administrative costs. Potential injurers and potential victims are rational calculators who compare the expected costs and benefits of various states of the world (such as those arising from taking different kinds or amounts of precaution) and, given their tastes, maximize their utility subject to several constraints. By assumption, the transaction costs between potential injurers and victims are so high that they cannot form a contractual agreement regarding their obligations in the event of an accident. That being so, the potential injurer has virtually no incentive to take the expected costs of his failure to take adequate precaution into account. As a result, there are too many or too severe accidents and potential victims may inefficiently seek to protect themselves from uncompensated injury. Economic analysis of tort law focuses on using legal rules to induce the (rational) potential injurer to internalize these costs of failing to take adequate care. Specifically, by holding out the possibility that the potential injurer will be deemed liable for failure to take due care and, if liable, will have to pay the victim's damages arising from the accident, tort law induces the rational potential injurer to take the social-cost-minimizing level of care.

As an example of the rational-choice aspect of this analysis, consider the economic view of negligence *versus* strict liability. To be extremely terse about a complex matter, economic analysis suggests that some form of negligence is efficient when precaution is bilateral and that strict liability is efficient when precaution is unilateral. The intriguing novelty in this view is the implication that the negligence standard addresses itself to both potential victims and potential injurers in order to induce *both* of them to take care.

Imagine the calculations that a rational person will make when faced with some form of the negligence standard for determining liability. Assume that this person does not know whether she will be injured or will injure; for example, she could be an automobile driver. She knows that under the negligence standard the injurer who complies with the legal duty of care will not be held liable for the victim's injuries. Therefore, if she were to be an injurer, the best thing for her to do would be to comply with the legal duty of care. That action will minimize her expected liability and, being rational, she decides to comply with the legal duty of care. But suppose that she is the victim in an automobile accident. In that case she will almost certainly be injured by someone who has complied with the legal duty of care. (Why? Because every potential injurer is, like her, rational and will have recognized that his expected liability is zero if he complies with the legal duty of care. Being rational, he will seek to minimize his expected liability by taking the appropriate amount of care.) Having reasoned that she will be injured by a rational injurer who will not be found liable, she recognizes that if there is an accident in which she is the victim, she will have to bear her own accident losses. She must, therefore, take action so as to minimize those expected accident costs by taking the optimal amount of care (whose marginal cost equals its marginal benefit - the expected reduction in expected accident costs). Thus, negligence induces optimal care by both potential injurers and potential victims.

7. Public Law: The Decision to Commit a Crime

As a final example of rational choice theory as applied to legal decision making, consider the well-known Becker (1968) model of the decision to commit a crime. Becker hypothesized that criminals are rational calculators and that, therefore, they made their decisions about compliance with criminal law on the basis of a comparison of the expected costs and benefits of criminal and legal activity. The expected costs of crime result from multiplying the probabilities of the activity's being detected and of the perpetrator's being apprehended and convicted by the monetary value of the legal sanction and the value of any non-pecuniary losses he might suffer, such as a loss in reputation from being branded a criminal. The expected benefits of the crime result from multiplying the probability of success times the monetary and non-pecuniary benefits of the particular crime. These latter include both the value of the goods or the amount of money resulting directly from crime and such intangible but potentially valuable outcomes as being known in one's community as a law-breaker. According to the Becker model, the rational criminal will commit the crime if these expected costs are less than the expected benefits and will refrain from crime if the reverse is true. (For a critique of the Becker model's predictions, using the criticisms of Part C of this entry, see Wilson and Abrahamse, 1992).

C. Criticisms of Rational Choice Theory

Recent scholarship by some cognitive psychologists and by economists familiar with the cognitive psychological literature describes experimental results that are difficult to reconcile with rational choice theory. The experiments have questioned implications of that theory with regard to at least four different areas. First, subjects in carefully-designed experiments seem to reject mutually beneficial exchanges when they believe that the proposed division of the cooperative surplus violates widely-accepted norms of fairness. Rational choice theory predicts that this will not happen. Second, subjects in another series of experiments in which there are several stages of bargaining involved do not devise rational strategies. Third, most decision makers have cognitive limitations that cause systematic deviations in their behavior away from that predicted by the theory of rational choice. For instance, those engaged in a common-value auction fall prey to the 'winner's curse'; and people cling to the status quo, even though an alternative likely has much greater value. Fourth, experiments have shown that people do not make decisions about uncertain outcomes in the way that the theory of rational choice predicts.

I shall briefly summarize some of these results in this section before turning in Part D to a discussion of the important implications of this literature for the rational-choice-based economic analysis of the law.

8. Rational Bargaining

Rational choice theory makes two broad claims about bargaining. One is that whenever there is a cooperative surplus greater than the transactions costs of splitting that surplus, parties will find a means of dividing the surplus. The second is that there are certain situations in which people will not fully participate in bargaining behavior, such as in the provision of and payment for public goods. Experimental evidence questions both of these claims. People apparently willingly cooperate in circumstances in which rational choice theory predicts that they will not cooperate and they frequently do not bargain in circumstances in which the theory predicts that they will.

8.1 Cooperation in the Production of Public Goods

Rational choice theory predicts that for public goods - that is, goods that exhibit non-rivalrous consumption and for which the costs to private profit-maximizing suppliers of excluding non-paying beneficiaries are prohibitively high - rationally self-interested, utility-maximizing consumers will not pay for the units of a public good from which they benefit. They will, in the classic phrase, 'free ride', that is, consume the public good without paying for it.

However, a series of experiments reveals that people *do* willingly and voluntarily pay for their share of public goods (Thaler, 1992; Ulen, 1994). The experiments are variations on the following general set of rules. A group of people, usually college students, are brought together and each is given the same sum of money. They are told that they can invest some, none, or all of that money in something called a 'group exchange'. (The decision to invest in the group exchange is a secret one. That is, one does not know whether or not the other players have contributed. All one knows is that they have all been given the same amount of money and are all subject to the same rules.) The group is also told that the game operator will multiply the total sum invested by the group by a number that is larger than one but smaller than the number of people in the group and will then divide the resulting sum equally among *all* of the group members, whether they have invested in the group exchange or not. These rules make the group exchange into a public good. Presumably, the temptation on rational actors will be to contribute nothing to the group exchange and then benefit with an equal share of the sum generated by the game operator.

To see how this works, suppose that there are five people in the group and that each of them is given \$5. If no one contributes anything to the group exchange, then there is nothing for the game operator to multiply and nothing, therefore, for the group to divide. But suppose that only one person contributes nothing and the other four people in our example contribute their entire \$5 to the group exchange. Further, suppose that the group operator doubles the resulting \$20 to \$40 and then distributes that sum equally among all five players. Each, therefore, receives \$8. The incremental return to the four players who contributed \$5 is \$3, but that of the player who contributed nothing is \$8. This logic should be clear to all the subjects, so that none of them should contribute to the group exchange; all of them should seek to free ride. Thus, the prediction of the theory of rational choice is that no one will invest in the group exchange.

In laboratory experiments of this game, the predictions of rational choice theory are not borne out. Although not everyone contributes to the group exchange, a substantial number *do*. On average, subjects in the experiments contributed between 40 and 60 percent of their initial sum to the public good. When experimenters vary the conditions of the game - by, for example, increasing the number of times the game is played, giving the players some prior experience with the game, or increasing the size of the stakes - the general outcome is the same: contributions to the public good are well above what the theory of rational choice would predict. The only exception to the 40-60 percent contribution rate was when the subjects were graduate students in economics at the University of Wisconsin. The contribution rate for that group was only 20 percent (Marwell and Ames, 1981).

One variation of the experiment is particularly interesting: that of the players repeating the game several times. Rational choice theory would predict that with repeated plays the rate of contribution to the group exchange would decline (perhaps because the players would come to understand the disadvantages of contribution and the advantages of free riding). And that is what the experimenters found. (There is some controversy about whether the decline is rapid or gradual, but there is agreement that there is decline.) Were the reasons for the decline those given by rational choice theory? Plausible as the theory's conjecture sounds, it is not supported by the experimental results. The 40-60 percent cooperation rate of the earlier experiment is found to hold on the first trial of the game *even for experienced players* - that is, even for those players who have participated in other multiple-play public-goods experiments in which the contribution rate fell with repeated plays. Andreoni confirmed this surprising result in the following way. He assembled a group to play the public-goods experiment and announced the usual rules of the game and, further, that the game would be played for ten trials. He found, as expected, that the contribution rate declined over the course of those trials. At the end of the ten trials, he announced that the same players would play the game for an additional ten trials. When the game was re-started for the second run of ten trials, the participation rate rose back to the 40-60 percent range before declining again. (Andreoni, 1988)

These experimental results present a puzzle for rational choice theory: why do people cooperate when there appears to be a rational basis for *not* cooperating? One possibility is that people start any given interaction from the presumption that it is better to cooperate than not; they continue to cooperate until the evidence shows this to be ill-advised; and then they quit cooperating.

8.2 Rational Bargaining over a Cooperative Surplus

Rational choice theory offers no prediction about the particular proportions in which voluntary traders will divide a cooperative surplus; it merely suggests that if such a cooperative surplus exists and, very importantly, if there are no serious impediments to exchange (that is, no transaction costs), traders will find a way to divide that cooperative surplus so that both of them are better off than they would have been if they had not traded. The theory provides a complete explanation for exchanges that do take place and those that do not: if a voluntary exchange takes place, then there must have been a cooperative surplus to be divided and the impediments to exchange must have been trivial; if an exchange does *not* take place, then there was either no cooperative surplus to be divided (that is, the minimum price for which the seller was prepared to sell was greater than the maximum price the buyer was prepared to pay) or the costs of concluding an exchange were greater than the cooperative surplus. Rational choice theory offers no other reasons for a failure to exchange. Clearly, what would be troubling for rational choice theory would be exchanges that failed to materialize even though there was a cooperative surplus to be divided and there were no impediments to exchange.

Experimenters have probed these possibilities in a very wide-ranging series of experiments regarding the 'ultimatum bargaining game'. (Guth, Schmittberger and Schwarze, 1982). The game works as follows. There are two participants, call them Player 1 and Player 2. They do not know one another and are not allowed to communicate. The object is to divide a fixed sum of money, say, $20. Player 1 makes an offer to divide the sum; Player 2 then either accepts the division, in which case the players receive the actual division proposed by Player 1, or rejects it, in which case they each receive nothing. Thus, if Player 1 proposes that they each receive $10 and Player 2 accepts that proposal, that is what they actually receive. If Player 1 proposes that he receive $19 and Player 2 receive $1 and if Player 2 accepts that, that is what they each receive; if Player 2 rejects that division, they each receive nothing.

The prediction of rational choice theory is that Player 1 will recognize that the best thing for her to do is to propose a one-sided division of the fixed sum in her favor. This is because Player 2 will then be in the position of accepting whatever Player 1 proposes or getting nothing and the clearly rational thing for Player 2 to do is to accept something rather than nothing.

The experimental results do not confirm the prediction of rational choice theory. Those in the position to make the initial proposed division generally do *not* propose a one-sided division in their favor. Rather, in a wide-ranging number of experiments over many years and in many different countries, the modal (that is, most common) proposal is for a 50-50 split and the mean proposal has been for a 37-73 split. Nor was the prediction for the sheepish acquiescence of Players 2 to the proposed division confirmed. Most of them accepted the split (presumably because the modal proposal was an even split), but, interestingly, almost 25 percent of the proposals were rejected (with the most one-sided proposals being almost uniformly rejected) (Kahneman, Knetsch and Thaler, 1986).

There have been numerous variations on these basic versions of the ultimatum game. In every instance, no matter how complex the experimenters make the game, the results offer little support for rational choice theory's account of how people do or ought to behave.

8.3 The Endowment Effect or Status Quo Bias

Recall that rational choice theory predicts that in the absence of transaction costs and in the presence of a cooperative surplus, there will be an exchange. One of the most important discoveries in the experimental literature is an effect that suggests that bargains will not necessarily take place under the ideal conditions posited by rational choice theory. The reason is the presence of what is called an 'endowment effect' or 'status quo bias'. Thaler defines that effect as 'the fact that people often demand much more to give up an object than they would be willing to pay to acquire it'. (Thaler, 1992, p. 63). The closely related 'status quo bias' may be defined as a general preference for the current state of holdings over any alternative (Korobkin, 1994; Samuelson and Zeckhauser, 1988).

The endowment effect surfaced in laboratory experiments (Thaler, 1992; Korobkin, 1998). Experimenters intent on testing propositions about bargaining typically gave half the subjects something of value (for example, a lottery ticket, ballpoint pens, or a coffee mug) and the other half a sum of money. One member of each group was paired with a member of the other group. The pairs were then given an opportunity to exchange; the roles were then re-assigned and the participants again had an opportunity to exchange. This reversal of roles was done a number of times with the understanding that only one of the attempted exchanges would actually be executed by the experimenters. The subjects were given ample opportunity to learn the rules of the game.

The purpose of the experiments was to test two propositions about exchange suggested by rational choice theory. First was the proposition that when there are no impediments to exchange, goods and services will move to those who value them the most. Because there were no impediments in the experiments, the tickets, ballpoint pens and coffee mugs should end up in the hands of those who valued them the most. Sometimes that would be the subject to whom the items had been originally given and sometimes it would be to the person to whom cash had been given. Because the investigators did not know beforehand what the tastes and preferences of the subjects were, their prediction was that approximately half of the pairs would engage in an exchange.

Second was a proposition about the prices at which the exchanges would take place. Because of the role reversals and the repetition of the possible exchanges, each subject found herself alternately in the role of seller and buyer of the same object. The prediction of the experimenters was that the prices asked by subjects in their role as sellers ought to be roughly the same as the prices bid by them in their role as buyers.

The experiments confirmed neither of these propositions. First, far fewer transactions took place than the theory predicted - approximately half those anticipated. Second, the prices asked by those who were willing to sell and those bid by those who were willing to buy were not in equilibrium. The ratio of the median selling price and the median buying price was approximately 2 to 1. These results were invariant to the objects being exchanged and to other important factors.

9. Choice under Uncertainty

The rational choice theory of decision making under uncertainty posits that decision makers attempt to maximize their *expected* utility by combining three elements: their attitudes toward risk (risk neutrality, risk preferring, or, the most commonly-assumed attitude, risk aversion); their stable, well-ordered preferences for the possible outcomes; and estimates of the likelihood of the various possible outcomes. But some recent experimental results suggest that this is not an accurate description of how many people make decisions about uncertain outcomes.

9.1 Preference Reversals

Consider the following choice under uncertainty. There are two gambles, call them *H* and *L*. *H* entails a high probability of winning a small prize, say, a 90 percent chance of winning $4. *L* entails a low probability of winning a larger sum, say, a 10 percent chance of winning $40. When presented with these alternatives, most people choose *H*. The subjects were then asked to say for what price they would be willing to sell each gamble if they owned it (as, say, a lottery ticket). Surprisingly, most subjects put a higher price on *L* than on *H* (Lichtenstein and Slovic, 1971). This is surprising because the expected value (the product of the probability of winning and the value of winning) is almost identical in the examples given. What is curious about this is that although when put to a choice between *H* and *L* most people choose *H*, when asked to price the two gambles, most people attribute a higher selling price to *L* than to *H*, which indicates that they find *L* more valuable than *H*. The figures are dramatic. One scholar reports that in a recent replication of the experiment that used the values given above, 71 percent of the subjects preferred *H* but 67 percent priced *L* above *H* (Thaler, 1992, p. 84). If one had predicted an outcome on the basis of expected utility maximization, one would have confidently predicted that these choices would have been consistent. That is, if *H* were preferred to *L*, then the imputed selling price of *H* would have been higher than that of *L* and vice versa. But that consistency is not at all what the experimenters have found.

This curious phenomenon is called ‘preference reversal’. In so far as there is a simple explanation for these reversals, it is that people apparently use the payoffs rather than the expected values of gambles in pricing them. What is troubling about this explanation for rational choice theory is that if it is true, it can lead people to the sort of inconsistent and seemingly irrational choices shown in the experiments. In the extreme, of course, one can make sport of people who behave in this fashion by getting them to make preposterous offers for very low probability gambles that have huge monetary payoffs, a fact that may be evident to the organizers of state-operated lotteries (Grether and Plott, 1979).

Three possible explanations have been given for preference reversals: intransitive preferences, procedure invariance and violations of the independence axiom. Let us take these possibilities up in turn.

As we have already seen, one of the common definitions of rationality in economics is that preference orderings exhibit transitivity. It is easy to see that the preference-reversal phenomenon might imply intransitive preferences. A rational person ought to be roughly indifferent between the imputed cash value of *H* and *H* itself. Similarly, a rational person ought to be roughly indifferent between the imputed cash value of *L* and *L* itself. If, therefore, one prefers *H* to *L*, then she ought, by transitivity, to prefer the cash value of *H* to the cash value of *L*. But preference reversal means that when *H* is preferred to *L*, the cash value of *L* is preferred to the cash value of *H*. It turns out that this pattern of preferences is intransitive only if something called procedural invariance does not hold.

'Procedural invariance' refers to a result's being invariant to the particular procedure designed to measure it. And most scientific investigation presumes procedural invariance to hold. The distance from Berlin to Munich should be the same whether we start our measurement in Berlin and go south or in Munich and go north. In the context of choice under uncertainty, the phrase refers to the invariance of preference rankings when the investigator uses different means of eliciting the subject's preferences. It is standard in modern economics to say that *A* is preferred to *B* if *A* is selected when both *A* and *B* are available *or* if the subject has a higher reservation price for *A* than for *B*. That is, we can determine the preference ranking by two different procedures: either presenting the subject with the choice and seeing which she chooses or by asking the subject which good has the higher reservation price per unit. It is almost never stated as an axiom in microeconomics (but probably should be) that these different procedures must yield the same result. The notion is that the preference ranking of *A* and *B* is (or ought to be) independent of the procedure by which the investigator determines that ranking. As a result, the preference equivalence of the cash value of *H* and *H* itself and that of the cash value of *L* and *L* itself is the result of an assumption of procedural invariance.

The third possibility is that the subjects violate the independence axiom of expected-utility theory. That axiom says, in essence, that if you prefer *X* to *Y*, then you should also prefer the chance to win *X* with probability *p* to the chance to win *Y* with probability *p*. This seems as straightforwardly appealing as does the axiom of transitivity, but it turns out that the independence axiom is sometimes violated in decision making under uncertainty (Machina, 1990). The preference-reversal phenomenon would clearly be a violation of this axiom.

9.2 Intertemporal Choice

Decision making over uncertain outcomes frequently involves choosing between a current and a future outcome or between two future outcomes. There is a standard, rational-choice-based theory of this allocation of resources over time, but there is now experimental evidence that contradicts this theory. People seem not to be fully aware of the special problems and opportunities that the passage of time raises. As a result, they frequently make decisions about the allocation of resources over time that seem to be difficult to square with rational choice theory. Take the example of paying income taxes. Many taxpayers routinely have too much income tax withheld during the year so that they can receive a refund from the Internal Revenue Service after filing their tax returns in the Spring of the following year. This over-withholding constitutes an interest-free loan to the federal government. The taxpayers who currently do this would be better off (according to rational choice theory) if they were to reduce the amount withheld so that at the end of the year they neither owed money to nor were owed money by the IRS.

At the other extreme are examples of absurdly high discount rates. For example, people routinely ignore the warnings of dermatologists that over-exposure to the sun can cause skin cancer later in life, apparently preferring the current benefits of a suntan. But they may pay attention if the dermatologist tells them that the sun may cause large pores or blackheads in the near future. Most homeowners do not have nearly enough insulation in their attics and walls, even though the cost of installing more would lead to significant savings on energy use within one year. Nor do they buy more expensive energy-efficient appliances, even though the energy-use savings will more than make up for the increased purchase price within a year. Economists have calculated that the purchase of the lower-priced, less efficient appliances implies a discount rate of between 45 percent and 130 percent at low energy costs and between 120 percent and 300 percent at higher energy costs. Either set of discount rates is absurdly high.

Why do people make such anomalous decisions where intertemporal choice is involved? One of the most robust findings in the experimental literature is that discount rates decline sharply with the length of time that the subject must wait for her reward and with the size of the reward. These experimental results are not consistent with rational choice theory, which holds that discount rates should generally equal the market rate of interest, that the discount rates should be constant (that is, invariant to the period of time considered) and certainly invariant with respect to the amount of money involved. The difficulty posed by the declining discount rate as the date of the reward recedes further into the future is that it implies an anomalous preference reversal. This is because the individual's preference as between, say, Project *A* and Project *B* could initially be in favor of *A* (because it is, let us assume, the nearer in time) and then switch to *B*, *all other things remaining equal*, if the time at which *B* will be realized is brought forward (but is still realized after *A* is realized). If discount rates are constant, this sort of switching, all other things equal, cannot occur (Loewenstein and Elster, 1992).

The effect of the size of the reward on the discount rate is as strong as the effect of time delay. The general problem is that people perceive the difference between $100 today and $150 in a year as greater than the difference between $10 today and $15 in a year. As a result, many people are willing to wait for the extra $50 in the first instance but not for the extra $5 in the second instance. Rational choice theory cannot explain this robust experimental result. Shefrin and Thaler have proposed that the explanation lies in how people take mental account of small and large windfalls. They hypothesize that small windfall gains are put into a mental account that allows for immediate consumption, while large windfall amounts are put into a separate mental account for which there is a much lower propensity for immediate consumption. Thus, the opportunity cost of waiting for a small windfall may be perceived to be foregone consumption. But the opportunity cost of waiting for a large windfall will be foregone interest or investment. If foregone consumption is more difficult to resist than foregone interest or investment, that would explain the observed effect of the size of the award causing a decline in the discount rate (Shefrin and Thaler, 1988).

D. Implications of the Criticisms of Rational Choice Theory for the Economic Analysis of Law

As we have seen, law and economics has premised much of its scholarship on rational choice theory. Therefore, the implications of the literature critical of that theory for law and economics are profound. In this part I want to focus on four of those implications - on the relationship between transactions costs and the law, on the choice between mandatory and default rules in the law, on the best means of dealing with risky decisions by consumers and on some issues in tort law.

10. The Coase Theorem and Criticisms of Rational Choice Theory

The most famous piece of scholarship in law and economics is 'The Problem of Social Cost' by Professor Ronald Coase (1960). The broad inquiry to which that article is addressed is this: when may society rely upon bargaining to achieve the efficient use of resources and when may it not? That inquiry then leads to a discussion of how the law should be structured so as to encourage efficient resource use in those circumstances in which it is inappropriate to rely upon bargaining. The Coase Theorem says that when there are no impediments to exchange (that is, when transaction costs are zero), the efficient use of resources will result, regardless of the assignment of property rights. Appropriate legal policy depends on being able to identify impediments to exchange and to specify correctives when those impediments are significant. Law and economics scholarship has concentrated on search, bargaining and enforcement costs as the elements of transaction costs and has sought to identify the objective characteristics of transactions (for example, the number of people involved, whether the transaction is for a fungible or a unique item and so on) that cause these three elements of the costs of exchange to be high.

The literature reported in Section 8 has two important implications for the standard view of the Coase Theorem. First, the reported results on cooperation and fairness suggest that people are far more ready to cooperate and that they have a much stronger sense of what is an equitable outcome than rational choice theory predicts. These conclusions point in two very different directions on the Coase Theorem. On the one hand, the broad willingness to cooperate (as revealed in the public goods experiments) suggests that voluntary exchange may be able to achieve an efficient allocation in a *broader* range of circumstances than those of zero transaction costs and, further, that the need to intervene in private decision making to enhance efficiency, even when transaction costs are positive and significant, may be *less* than previously thought. For example, if people appear to be more willing to contribute to the provision of public goods than rational choice theory predicts, then there may be less need for the compulsory public subsidization of those goods or the level of subsidization can be less extensive. There are implications, too, regarding the need for or the most appropriate structure of environmental regulations - for example, people may be more willing to bestow the external benefits of environmentally-conscious activity than previously supposed.

On the other hand, the finding of the experimental literature that people appear to be extremely sensitive to the equitable distribution of resources suggests that *more* intervention in private decision making may be justifiable than previously thought. This is because the experiments suggest that people may be so sensitive to fairness issues that they would rather not cooperate than cooperate on terms that they consider to be excessively one-sided. This is a cause for the failure of bargaining that has not heretofore been given much weight. Even when transaction costs are very low, some otherwise efficient exchanges will *not* take place because some of the participants do not like the proposed division of the cooperative surplus. The experimental findings provide an *efficiency* justification for legal intervention in private decision making in order to prevent over-reaching by one of the parties that might forestall an otherwise efficiency-enhancing exchange.

The second major implication for the Coase Theorem of the criticisms reported in Section 8 arises from the endowment effect (or status quo bias). Recall that that effect suggested two anomalies in bargaining behavior: first, when transaction costs were very low, people were far more reluctant to transact than rational choice theory predicted and, second, subjects typically demanded twice as much to sell something they owned as they were willing to pay in order to acquire it. The troubling implication of those findings is that there may be cases in which there is no such thing as a uniquely efficient assignment of rights. Where society initially assigns an entitlement is where it is likely to remain; we should be far less sanguine about entitlements moving to their highest-valued use, even when transaction costs are zero, than we have been heretofore. (Indeed, status quo bias makes the notion of 'highest valuing use' less clear.)

11. Default and Mandatory Rules and the Criticisms of Rational Choice Theory

If one assumes, as does law and economics, that the law can increase the efficient use of resources by creating rules of conduct that correct for market failures, two issues that must be resolved are, first, the specification of a rule or standard and, second, whether that rule or standard is mandatory or may be waived by those affected. One of the areas of the law in which this issue has been central is corporation law. There the debate has been between those who favor non-waivable mandatory rules of corporate conduct and those who favor allowing corporations to opt out of some rules. Consider, for example, insider trading. Everyone admits that there are potential inefficiencies from allowing insider trading, although there are disagreements about the extent and likelihood of these inefficiencies. Most commentators, therefore, agree that there ought to be some legal regulation of the practice. However, there is disagreement about whether this regulation should take the form of a prohibition or merely a default rule from which those corporations that so choose might wish to opt out. Those who favor making the prohibition waivable argue that some corporations might wish to offer their managers partial compensation in the form of allowing them to trade on the basis of the inside information that they acquire in the course of working for the corporation. If that method of compensation is more efficient than the alternatives, then, the argument goes, those corporations and their managers ought to be allowed to opt out of the default rule. The other side argues that both private and public difficulties in policing the behavior of managers make the realization of those efficiencies illusory. Thus, they argue, the prohibition of insider trading should be non-waivable.

How are the findings of Part C relevant to this issue? Status-quo bias suggests that people will not make changes away from a default position unless the expected benefits from so doing substantially exceed the expected costs. That is, the default position has a strong anchoring effect. With respect to insider trading rules, the presence of status-quo bias might indicate that even if the prohibition on insider trading was waivable, very few corporations would take advantage of that waivability.

There is another relevant implication of status-quo bias. If most people are reluctant to leave the status quo, whatever that is, then the law ought to establish the starting position (that is, establish the status quo) at an efficient point. In the case of insider trading that might suggest that the appropriate starting point is a prohibition of the practice, not the freedom to engage in the practice unless one's employer has forbidden it. This sort of consideration no doubt has other applications in the law well beyond corporation law. For instance, it may say something about whether society should make the status quo one in which addictive drugs are legal or one in which they are illegal but one may (explicitly or implicitly) opt out of this illegality. (For the implications of status quo bias for a broad range of contract issues, see Korobkin, 1998.)

12. Risk Regulation and the Criticisms of Rational Choice Theory

The regulation of risk is a topic upon which there is very large and growing literature and about which there is a surprising lack of consensus. Many are convinced that the panoply of regulations dealing with risky behavior is not well conceived and the criticisms of rational choice under uncertainty contribute to an understanding of this position. Recall that, broadly speaking, people do not seem to do a very good job of appraising risky outcomes. For example, they tend to overestimate the value of low-probability, high-payoff gambles. And because of status-quo bias, they prefer a known, high risk to an unknown, low risk. These imperfections in the way people deal with risk may motivate them to demand legislative regulation of risk that reflects their own, not entirely coherent, views. For example, on an average day in the

United States 30 people are killed on the job, 56 are killed in accidents in the home, 133 die in automobile accidents and 4,000 die from cancer. Of those who die each day from cancer, 30 percent of those deaths are attributable to tobacco; 4 percent are attributable to cancers arising from occupational hazards; 1 percent to medical treatment; and 2 percent to air and water pollution (Breyer, 1993). All other things equal, these figures would suggest two predictions about current regulations designed to minimize the harms from risky activities: first, that a large amount of effort ought to be directed at reducing the risk of cancer and second, that a large portion of the cancer-reducing effort ought to be directed at tobacco-related cancers. Neither prediction is correct. Rather, the risk regulation of the United States government has a willy-nilly aspect with little rational regard for the value of the good it might be doing. For instance, there is no single implicit value of a life saved that is used by the federal government in regulating risk. Rather, the government's regulations imply that the value of a life saved ranges from $10,000 to $1 billion (Viscusi, 1992).

Just bringing coherence to risk regulation would be a substantial improvement in the efficient allocation of governmental resources. But the experiments on decision making under uncertainty described in Section 8 suggest an important new way of looking at the regulation of risk. Heretofore, much government risk regulation has been premised on the belief that individuals make errors in dealing with risk because they do not have correct information. If they had that information, they would make the appropriate maximizing decision. Thus, the government's role ought principally to be to disseminate accurate information to assist individuals and organizations in their decision making. But the material on intertemporal choice in Part C suggests that even if they had the appropriate information, some people would not make the right decision about risky activities.

How these insights should translate into a reform of risk regulation is a very broad issue. Here I want only to suggest that they might lead to principled justifications for far more paternalistic policies than those that rational choice theory typically recommends. For instance, where rational choice theory might suggest that the comparison of the costs and benefits of wearing motorcycle helmets ought to be left to motorcyclists so long as they are well-informed about the *true* costs and benefits, the findings about mistakes in intertemporal choice and in the assessment of risk imply that motorcyclists will always underestimate the benefits of wearing helmets and that, therefore, the best regulation for minimizing head injuries among motorcyclists may be one mandating helmet-wearing. These are significant differences in policy and we must wait on further empirical work to clarify the extent of the cognitive errors and the various policy choices before us.

13. Tort Law and the Criticisms of Rational Choice Theory

Finally, I come to the issue of whether the anomalies discussed in Part C affect the economic analysis of tort law. The connection between those anomalies and the economic analysis turns, I think, on this central issue: the economic analysis perceives that potential victims and potential injurers are capable of understanding and acting rationally in response to the implications of the tort liability system for their choices about which activities to pursue, how and when to pursue those activities, how cautious they should be, how much they should spend on warnings of danger to others and the like. If those whose behavior we seek to affect by imposing tort liability do not have the cognitive abilities to understand and act in accord with the law's desires, then we should not be surprised to learn that the tort liability system is not achieving its desired efficiency ends. For example, if decision makers make systematic errors when faced with uncertain outcomes or if they are systematically overconfident about their abilities to avoid an accident or injury, then they may behave in ways that are contrary to those anticipated by rational choice theory. The next sections seek to clarify how these imperfections might influence several issues in the economic analysis of tort liability.

13.1 The Choice Between Statutory Regulation and the Risk-Utility Test

There are two important points to be made about the efficiency of negligence and of strict liability. First, *within* negligence there are two very different means of determining whether someone had complied with a legal duty of care. In one set of circumstances compliance is determined by comparing the victim's or injurers actions with a clear rule - for example, a speed limit or manufacturing standard proposed by an administrative agency (or possibly by some respected private standard-setting group). This sort of negligence (negligence *per se*) is relatively easy for the court to determine and easy for potential injurers and victims to perceive and to follow. No sophisticated calculations are required and, therefore, the demands on the cognitive abilities of the potential victim and injurer are not large.

The other, more common form of negligence delegates to potential injurers and potential victims the determination of the appropriate amount of care to take. There is no hard-and-fast rule specifying the suitable amount of precaution; rather, each potential victim and potential injurer calculates what is appropriate in the understanding that, in the event of an accident, a court may check those calculations to see if they have been done reasonably. This standard of due care is frequently determined according to a 'risk-utility test' or the Hand Test. The court assumes that the parties who may injure or be injured compare the costs of precaution with the benefits of taking precaution (the reduction in the probability and severity of an accident) and that they will take all cost-justified precaution - that is, precaution that confers greater (expected) benefits than it costs.

The cognitive demands of the risk-utility test are substantial. In order to comply with the legal duties imposed by negligence, potential injurers and victims must independently form an estimate of the probability of an accident's occurring as a function of the amount of precaution they take and an estimate of the size of the accident losses that will result from various levels of precaution. An implication of the experiments noted in Part C above is that potential injurers and victims may make systematic errors in these calculations.

The potential shortcomings of human decision making with regard to risk may be the key to understanding when it is socially efficient to use the rule-like negligence *per se* and the due-care standard. Put simply, if one believes that those likely to be involved in a particular kind of accident are prone to cognitive errors and limitations, then the more appropriate method of achieving social efficiency (in the sense of minimizing the social costs of accidents) would be to state rules with which it is relatively easy to comply.

13.2 Strict Liability and Negligence

Recall that the law and economics literature has identified one principal factor that should figure in the efficient choice between negligence and strict liability: whether precaution is unilateral or bilateral. The presence of cognitive errors and limitations in the ability to perceive and act rationally upon risk complicates this distinction between unilateral and bilateral precaution. It is not unlikely that situations arise in which both the potential injurer and the potential victim *could* have taken precaution that would reduce the expected social costs of accidents but in which one of the two parties was very much less likely to have experience with the sort of calculations of risk and expectation that the economic theory supposes that both parties have. That is, a cognitive limitation in dealing with uncertain outcomes may be an independent factor in determining whether precaution was unilateral or bilateral and, therefore, in choosing between negligence and strict liability.

Consider, for example, product-related accidents. Suppose that we were free to decide for the first time which form of liability to use in those accidents and suppose further that we intend to use the economic theory exclusively in reaching our decision. Which form of liability - negligence or strict liability - ought we to use in order to minimize the social cost of product-related accidents? We might conclude that precaution is bilateral: producers can reduce the likelihood and severity of accidents by taking care in the design and manufacture of their goods and by warning consumers of any non-obvious dangers; consumers can reduce the expected social costs of accidents by taking care in the use of the product, by following the manufacturer's instructions, by using the product in a manner that it was intended that it be used and so on. But suppose that we make one more assumption - namely, that producers have much greater facility in making decisions about uncertain outcomes than do consumer because consumers are prone to the sort of miscalculations that we noted in Part C. We might now doubt that precaution is truly bilateral. Perfectly rational consumers might be able to calculate the appropriate level of risk and the expected level of accident costs, given different levels of precaution, but these are not, by assumption, perfectly rational consumers. They will make errors; importantly, they will make *more* and *more costly* errors than will producers. If so, then a situation that assumed the affected parties to be rational and that precaution was bilateral becomes one in which only one of the parties is reliably rational and there is, therefore, unilateral precaution. This makes out an argument for treating at least some product-related accidents under the strict liability rule. To put the point more generally, I am suggesting that the recognition that there may be cognitive limitations among potential victims and injurers should alter the search for the appropriate liability standard from one in which the law looks for the least-cost avoider to one in which the law looks for the least-cost decision maker or least irrational party.

14. Conclusion

We have seen how important rational choice theory is to law and economics. But we have also seen that there is an increasing body of experimental work that questions some of the assumptions of that theory. We must amend the rational-choice model, but precisely how we should amend the model is not yet clear. I want to conclude with a cautionary statement about the crucial questions that must be addressed in undertaking these emendations in rational choice theory and in drawing conclusions about law on the basis of these emendations.

Some may mistakenly think that we are put to a stark choice between, on the one hand, rational choice theory and, on the other hand, the extreme position that no coherent theory of human decision making is possible. That is a dangerous illusion. A synthesis is possible and is, I believe, coming. But it is not yet here and until it is, we must remain uncomfortably in the middle - somewhat skeptical about rational choice theory but not so skeptical that we abandon that theory. To see the dangers of moving too far, too fast in the application of Part C's findings, consider the experiments that suggest that cooperation in the provision of a public good is much more likely than rational choice theory predicts. This is, so far, merely suggestive; it is not a complete guide to behavior. Therefore, no one could responsibly use these experiments as a warrant for cutting the public subsidies for basic research and public television or for laxer enforcement of the intellectual property laws. Before we make policy pronouncements on the basis of these anomalies, we need to know much more. The implication of some of the experimenters is that their findings apply to *all* decision makers in *all* circumstances. But that seems highly unlikely. Surely there are important differences among circumstances and among people. There may be some people who always obey the predictions of rational choice theory; there may be some circumstances in which no one obeys those predictions. And there may be more subtle differences. For example, are there systematic differences in the dispensation to cooperate by age and gender? Are there objective circumstances about the manner in which the cooperation is solicited (for example, how long the people have known each other and whether they are allowed to communicate) that lead to a greater likelihood of cooperation? How robust is the finding that repeated playing leads to a diminution of the propensity to cooperate? These and many more questions need to be addressed.

Some day, perhaps soon, we shall have a complete account of human decision making than that provided by rational choice theory. And when we do, that account will greatly enhance our understanding of the law and our ability to draft the law for desirable ends.

Acknowledgements

The author would like to thank an anonymous referee for helpful comments.

Bibliography on Rational Choice Theory in Law and Economics (0710)

Andreoni, James (1988), 'Why Free Ride? Strategies and Learning in Public Goods Experiments', **38** *Journal of Public Economics*, 291-305.

Becker, Gary (1962), 'Irrational Behavior and Economic Theory', **70** *Journal of Political Economy*, 1-13.

Becker, Gary (1968) 'Crime and Punishment: an Economic Approach', **76** *Journal of Political Economy*, 169-217.

Breyer, Stephen (1993), *Breaking the Vicious Circle*, Cambridge, MA, Harvard University Press.

Coase, Ronald A. (1960), 'The Problem of Social Cost', **3** *Journal of Law and Economics*, 1-28.

Cooter, Robert D. and Ulen, Thomas S. (1997), *Law and Economics,* (2nd edn), Reading, MA, Addison-Wesley-Longman.

Dixit, Avinash and Nalebuff, Barry (1991), *Thinking Strategically*, New York, W.W. Norton & Co.

Grether, David and Plott, Charles (1979), 'Economic Theory of Choice and the Preference Reversal Phenomenon', **69** *American Economic Review*, 623-638.

Guth, Werner, Schmittberger, Rolf and Schwarze, Bernd (1982), 'An Experimental Analysis of Ultimatum Bargaining', **3** *Journal of Economic Behavior and Organization*, 367- 383.

Kahneman, Daniel, Knetsch, Jack and Thaler, Richard (1986), 'Fairness as a Constraint on Profit Seeking: Entitlements in the Market', **76** *American Economic Review*, 728-741.

Korobkin, Russell (1994), 'Policymaking and the Offer/Ask Price Gap: Toward a Theory of Efficient Entitlement Allocation', **46** *Stanford Law Review*, 663-708.

Korobkin, Russell (1998), 'The Status Quo Bias and Contract Default Rules', **83** *Cornell Law Review*, 608-687.

Lichtenstein, Sarah and Slovic, Paul (1971), 'Reversals of Preference between Bids and Choices in Gambling Decisions', **89** *Journal of Experimental Psychology*, 46-61.

Liebenstein, Harvey (1950), 'Bandwagon, Snob and Veblen Effects in the Theory of Consumers' Demand', **64** *Quarterly Journal of Economics*, 183-201.

Loewenstein, George and Elster, John (eds) (1992), *Choice Over Time*, New York, Russell Sage Foundation.

Machina, Mark (1990), 'Expected Utility Hypothesis', in John Eatwell, Milgate, Murray and Newman, Peter (eds), *The New Palgrave: Utility and Probability*, London, Macmillan Publishing.

Marwell, Gerald and Ames, Ruth (1981), 'Economists Free Ride, Does Anyone Else?', **15** *Journal of Public Economics*, 295-310.

Nozick, Robert (1993), *The Nature of Rationality*, Princeton, Princeton University Press.

Plous, Scott (1993), *The Psychology of Judgment and Decision Making*, New York, McGraw-Hill.

Posner, Richard A. (1998), *Economic Analysis of Law,* (4th edn), Boston, MA, Aspen Publishing Co.

Samuelson, William and Zeckhauser, Richard (1988), 'Status Quo Bias in Decision Making', **1** *Journal of Risk and Uncertainty*, 7-17.

Shefrin, Hersh and Thaler, Richard (1988), 'The Behavioral Life-cycle Hypothesis', **26** *Economic Inquiry*, 609-643.

Thaler, Richard (1992), *The Winner's Curse*, New York, W.W. Norton & Co.

Ulen, Thomas S. (1994), 'Rational Choice Theory and the Economic Analysis of Law', **19** *Law and Social Inquiry*, 487-522.

Ulen, Thomas S. (1998), 'The Growing Pains of Behavioral Law and Economics', *Vanderbilt Law Review* (forthcoming).

Viscusi, W. Kip (1992), *Fatal Tradeoffs: Public and Private Responsibilities for Risk*, New York, Oxford University Press.

Wilson, James Q. and Abrahamse, Alan (1992), 'Does Crime Pay?', **9** *Justice Quarterly*, 359-377.

0720
THE ENDOWMENT EFFECT

Christopher Curran
Associate Professor, Emory University

Abstract

This chapter reviews the literature on the endowment effect that challenges the validity of using neoclassical economic theory to evaluate legal issues. While a consensus does not yet exist, much of the research suggests that the endowment effect phenomena does not offer as much of a challenge to neoclassical economic theory as was once thought.
JEL classification: D0, D6
Keywords: Endowment Effect, Experimental Economics

1. Introduction

This essay discusses the issue of whether the results of recent experimental research on consumer behavior undermines the conclusions of neoclassical economics enough to render arguments based on that theory incorrect. This entry is not a thorough review of the rich experimental economics literature (see Kahneman, Knetsch and Thaler, 1991) for summary of much of this research and Conlisk, 1996, for a statement of the case for using the notion of bounded rationality in economics). Instead, we focus on the possibility that the phenomena known as the 'endowment effect' may provide evidence that questions the applicability of some of the basic assumptions made by economists about consumer rationality. After describing the endowment effect and some of the theories used to take account of this effect, we recount how some law and economics scholars use the endowment effect in their analyses.

2. The Endowment Effect

The endowment effect arises when consumer's willingness to accept (WTA) for a good is greater than their willingness to pay (WTP) for it. While economists have long recognized that an income effect may make cause the WTA to be greater than the WTP, they accepted the conclusion by Willig (1976) that these differences should be small. While psychologists had noted a difference between the WTP and WTA as early as the 1960s (see Coombs, Bezembinder, and Goode, 1967, and Slovic and Lichtenstein, 1968), economists only began to focus on the issue after observing this difference when using surveys to measure the value of environmental projects. When the economists asked consumers about both their WTP and their WTA in these surveys, they found that the reported WTA is much larger than the reported WTP - much larger than Willig's predictions suggest. Using students as subjects and goods such as coffee mugs, candy bars and trees as the commodities, experimental economists have been able to find evidence that their subjects often have a WTA that is substantially greater than their WTP (see, for example, Bishop, Heberlein and Kealy, 1983; Knetsch, 1984; Knetsch and Borcherding, 1979; Knetsch and Sinden, 1984; Brookshire and Coursey, 1987; Samuelson and Zeckhauser, 1988; Quattrone and Tversky, 1988; Donohue, 1989; Harless, 1989; Knetsch, 1989; Kahneman, Knetsch and Thaler, 1990; Ortona and Scacciati, 1992; Boyce et al., 1992; Shogren et al., 1994; Loewenstein and Adler, 1995; Sileo, 1995; Pratt and Zeckhauser, 1996, for evidence about, explanations of and implications of the endowment effect; Hoffman and Spitzer, 1993, offer an excellent summary of the results of both the empirical and theoretical research).

3. Format of the Experiments

The formats used these experiments follow a regular pattern. The experimental researchers randomly split the subjects into two groups. They give each of the members of one group some object - say a coffee mug or a candy bar - and then offer to buy the object back from them using some truth-revealing mechanism. The researchers then give the members of the other group money and then allow the subjects to purchase the object offered to the first group, again using a truth-revealing mechanism. (There are a large number of variations on the structure of the various experiments; see these studies or Hoffman and Spitzer, 1993, for more details of the different experiments.) The researchers report potentially conflicting evidence indicating (1) that the endowment effect is persistent and substantive, (2) that the endowment effect, while evident initially, tends to disappear over time and (3) that there is no difference in the WTP and the WTA.

4. Preference for the Status Quo

Studies that find evidence of the endowment effect suggest that consumers may have a greater preference for the status quo than what the assumption of rationality implies. Several criticisms have been leveled at the studies that find evidence of an endowment effect. For instance, some authors reject the use of hypothetical questions and experiments involving small amounts of money as revealing little about a subject's actual behavior in the market place (see Hoffman and Spitzer, 1993, p. 69, n. 23). Other authors question whether the subjects really understand what they are being asked and whether the effect will remain after repeated experiments. Unfortunately, the evidence on these points is mixed; while some studies find evidence that the WTP is equal to the WTA in experiments involving simple securities (see Kahneman, Knetsch and Thaler, 1990, pp. 1329-1330; Harless, 1989), other studies reach the opposite conclusion for simple securities (see, for instance, Knez, Smith and Williams, 1985) and for more complicated securities involving risk (see, for instance, McClelland and Schulze, 1991).

5. Prospect Theory

The experimental evidence has generated several attempts to provide a theoretical explanation of the endowment effect. We briefly review two contrasting explanations here, referring the reader to Hoffman and Spitzer (1993, pp. 85-96), Radin (1982), Heiner (1983) and Thaler (1980) for examples of and a fuller discussion of the theoretical literature generated by the endowment effect. The first of these explanations - usually identified as a version of 'prospect theory' - assumes that individuals have a preference for the status quo. Originally, Kahneman and Tversky (1979) suggested this model to describe human behavior in risky circumstances. (Also, see Tversky and Kahneman, 1991; Tversky and Wakker, 1995.) Later, Thaler (1980) and Kahneman, Knetsch and Thaler (1990) use elements from prospect theory to explain the endowment effect. Kahneman and Tversky (1979) assume that consumers have a value function that is positively sloped, concave for gains and convex for losses, implying that individuals are risk-averse with respect to gains and risk-loving with respect to losses. Figure 1 illustrates the value function suggested by Kahneman and Tversky (1979).

Figure 1
The Value Function Proposed in Prospect Theory

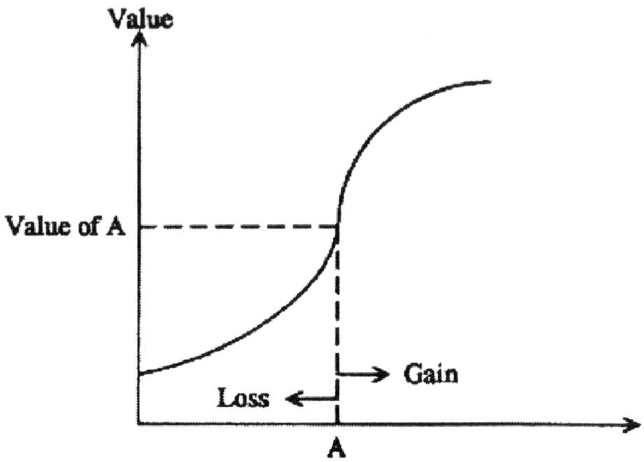

6. Prospect Theory and the Endowment Effect

Figure 2 illustrates how prospect theory might explain the endowment effect. We start with an individual owning quantity A of some good and ask how much he would be willing to pay to acquire the larger quantity B. Thus, the vertical distance between points D and C represents the WTP of this individual to acquire (B - A) units of the good. Now we compare this situation with the case where the individual already owns B units of the goods and is offered the opportunity to sell (B - A) units of the good. Since the individual actually owns B units of the good, we begin at point E (shown in this case to be valued higher than when the individual did not actually own the good, though it is not necessarily of higher value) and move to point F. Thus, the vertical distance between E and F is the individual's WTA, which in this case is greater than his WTP. The key point is that potential losses have a greater impact on the individual's value than do potential gains.

7. A Neoclassical Explanation for the Endowment Effect

The second explanation of the endowment effect, developed by Hanemann (1991), implies that we do not need to scrap neoclassical economic theory to generate large gaps between an individual's WTP and his WTA. Figure 3, which illustrates Hanemann's contribution, shows two indifference curves for some good X and wealth. Consider an individual's WTP to move from point A where he has X_0 of good X to point B where he has the same wealth and X_1 of good X.

Figure 2
A Prospect Theory Explanation of the Endowment Effect

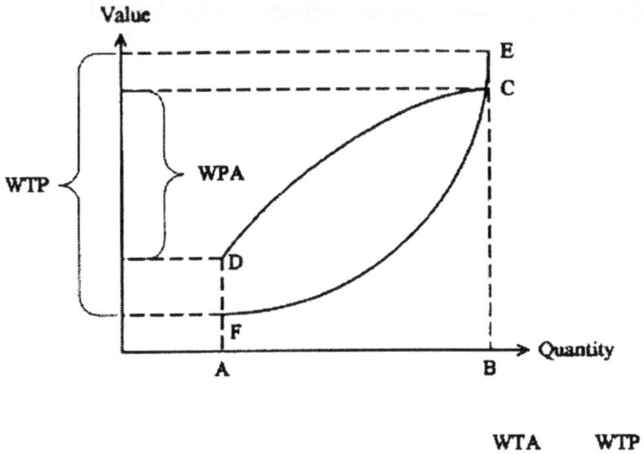

Since the individual is indifferent between being at point A and point C, the vertical distance between points B and C measures how much this individual is willing to pay to move to point B. Now consider how much this individual is willing to accept to move from point B to point A. Since the individual is indifferent between being at points B and D, the vertical distance between A and D measures his willingness to accept the move from point B to A. Figure 3 shows the case where the individual's WTA is greater than his WTP. As Hanemann (1991) proves, the size of this difference depends on the elasticity of substitution of the indifference curves - the more inelastic the indifference curves are, the larger is the spread between the WTA and the WTP. Put another way, the less substitutable a good is with money, the larger will be the endowment effect. More importantly, if Hanemann's hypothesis is correct, the endowment effect observed by experimental economists does not imply that the neoclassical analysis of welfare economics is fatally flawed. Shogren et al. (1994) report the results of experiments that lend support to Hanemann's hypothesis.

8. Reception of the Endowment Effect in Law and Economics Scholarship

Scholars in law and economics have given the endowment effect a mixed reception. Some authors such as Knetsch and Borcherding (1979), Hovenkamp (1991), Hoffman and Spitzer (1993) and Fischel (1995) accept the endowment effect as a real phenomena with serious implications for the study of legal issues while others such as Curran and Rubin (1995), while analyzing the implications of the endowment effect, seem to doubt its existence. A majority of legal scholars ignore the existence of an endowment effect.

9. The Hovenkamp Critique

Hovenkamp (1991) claims that the endowment effect has very significant implications for the study of law and economics because it potentially undermines the validity of traditional results from welfare economics. As Hovenkamp argues, the equality of WTP and WTA is central to the construction of demand curves, the estimation of consumers' surplus, the use of cost-benefits analyses and the use of indifference curves. He carries the argument further when he suggests that, when the endowment effect exists, 'the person has no indifference curve'. (Hovenkamp, 1991, p. 226). Thus, he concludes that an endowment effect that is 'substantial and ubiquitous could make [the tools of welfare economics] virtually useless'. (Hovenkamp, 1991, p. 227).

Figure 3
Hanemann's Explanation of the Endowment Effect

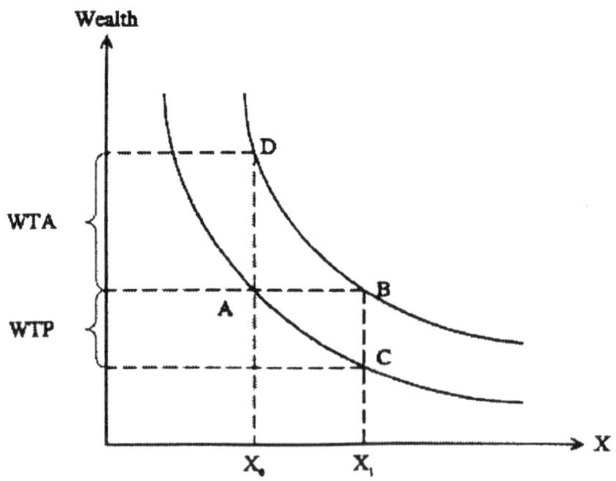

10. On Using WTP or WTA Measures of Value

Having rejected the traditional tools of neoclassical welfare analysis as virtually useless, Hovenkamp tackles the problem of whether courts should continue use the market price, which is equal to the WTP, as a measure of the value of property in cases involving eminent domain, environmental regulation and torts. While Hovenkamp's reasoning differs from that used in earlier studies by Knetsch and Sinden (1984) and Kennedy (1981), he reaches the similar conclusion that courts should use WTA as a measure of value. Moreover, Hovenkamp argues that in the presence of a large endowment effect, 'the wealth-maximizing state may find it appropriate to intervene on behalf of the poor more often than under traditional efficiency models'. Hovenkamp (1991, p. 228)

11. The Superiority of the WTA Measure of Value

It is useful to review Hovenkamp's reasoning. Consider an entitlement in a world with significant differences in individuals' WTP and WTA. There is an individual who has the largest WTA if he owns the entitlement - say individual A. Additionally, there is an individual - say individual P - who has the largest WTP for this entitlement. In a competitive world with transacting being costless, ownership of the entitlement will end up with individual P unless it originally belongs to some individual with a WTA that is higher than the WTP of individual P. Hovenkamp argues that, while this outcome is Pareto optimal, there exist other arrangements where the total wealth of society is higher. In particular, social wealth is maximized if entitlements begin in the hands of those who have the largest WTA - person A in our example. Thus, Hovenkamp concludes that entitlements should be assigned to those with the highest WTA.

12. The WTA Measure of Value and the Distribution of Income

Hovenkamp connects his analysis to income redistribution by arguing that, while there are no systematic differences in individuals' WTA associated with income differences, there is good reason to believe that an individuals WTP is a positive function of income. Moreover, Hovenkamp argues that the WTA-to-WTP ratio is much higher for the poor than it is for the rich, a point that Curran and Rubin (1995) implicitly do not accept in their criticism of Hovenkamp. By Hovenkamp's logic, transferring endowments to the poor from the rich will increase the total amount of social value.

13. Overcoming Practical Problems

One of the practical difficulties of using WTA as a measure of value when the WTA and WTP measures differ is the fact that no one ever observes WTA. Clearly, market prices are an accurate measure of the WTP of the purchaser and the WTA of the seller; they provide little information about the buyer's WTA once he is the owner. This measurement problem is especially important in thin markets where there are few substitutes for the good or where a good cannot be bought and sold. A piece of land that has sentimental value for the current owner is an example of a good with few substitutes while environmental goods like clear air and water are examples of goods that have no recognizable markets. Hovenkamp (1991, pp. 238-243) recognizes this difficulty with using WTA as a measure of value. He suggests, however, the fact that economic theory offers policymakers little aid in measuring WTA does not mean that they cannot use the concept. He suggests that policymakers should turn to psychologists and sociologists for aid in measuring WTA. Researchers in these fields, Hovenkamp contends, have many tools - surveys, questionnaires, interviews and tests - that would help in the measurement of WTA. Gathering this information is costly. When costs become prohibitive, Hovenkamp suggests that policymakers resort to generalizations. As an example of such a generalization, Hovenkamp (1991, p. 243) suggests the fact that biological organisms have 'a common set of survival needs and perhaps a common set of minimal needs for social productivity' implies that policymakers can assume that goods such as these have a WTA that is systematically greater than their WTP. Economists aware of the problems of rent-seeking common to governments - and well-documented in the public choice literature - probably will not share Hovenkamp's faith in the ability of policymakers to correctly identify what goods belong to the 'common set of survival needs'.

14. A Logical Problem

The fact that Hovenkamp rejects neoclassical economic theory presents him with a logical problem - what, if any, parts of the economic model can he use in his analysis? Clearly, Hovenkamp offers a theory that purports to differentiate among the various Pareto optimal points. However, Hovenkamp (1991, p. 230) does not explain what he means by 'Pareto optimality' in a world where indifference curves do not exist. Hovenkamp does not resolve this logical problem by constructing a completely new model of human behavior to replace the neoclassical economic model. Instead, he assumes that consumers' WTA is larger than their WTP and then borrows concepts from the neoclassical model when he needs them. While Curran and Rubin (1995) temper their analysis with expressions of concern, they also mix the results of neoclassical welfare economics in their criticism of Hovenkamp (for which Fischel, 1995, p. 200, criticizes them).

15. A Constitutional Solution to the WTP/WTA Disparity

Fischel attempts to skirt this problem by substituting 'constitutionalism' for welfare economics. Fischel argues that the participants at the Federal and the many state constitutional conventions knew about the endowment effect when they specified that the market price (WTP) and not the WTA was to be the measure of just compensation for eminent domain cases. Fischel argues that the participants of these constitutional conventions understood that using WTP as a measure of value would increase the ability of the government to exercise its eminent domain powers. Fischel suggests that one reason these individuals consistently choose to use the WTP measure of value is that they understood that using WTA as a measure of value would deter the development of the nation's infrastructure that is so important for economic growth. Moreover, he suggests that individuals may have an endowment effect when it comes to their earnings. Fischel posits that in resolving how to measure 'just' compensation in eminent domain constitution designers considered both (1) the public gain to society from the taking versus the private loss to the property owner and (2) the impact of the endowment effect on the property owner (of his land) and on the taxpayer (on his earnings). The resolution was to use WTP as a measure of value. Thus, since this resolution of the issue was by the conscience choice of the members of constitutional conventions, Fischel concludes that 'the offer/ask disparity may undermine welfare economics less than is usually supposed'. (Fischel, 1995, p. 187)

16. The Policymakers' Problem

Many may not find Fischel's assurances that the members of the various constitutional conventions considered and correctly solved the WTP/WTA disparity issue satisfactorily. The dilemma facing society is that in deciding whether to pursue a project, policymakers need to determine if the project is potentially Pareto improving. To make this determination, they have to estimate the costs of the project where these costs include the losses in value sustained by property owners affected by the project. Currently, in the United States courts use the market value of the property - that is, the WTP - plus some amount to cover any losses to the owner due to inconvenience. The advantage of using the WTP is that it is generally inexpensive to measure and avoids the strategic problems inherent in convincing an individual to reveal his true WTA. As long as the property is a close substitute for wealth, using WTP has the additional advantage of closely approximating WTA. However, in cases where the property involved has a great deal of sentimental value - for instance, when one's ancestors are buried on the land that is to be flooded in order to build a dam - the use of WTP may substantially underestimate WTA and may lead to the completion of projects that are not Pareto improving.

17. Reflections from Public Choice Research

Public choice research suggests further complications in restricting government project to those that are Pareto improving. (For examples of public choice research on income distribution see Hochman and Peterson, 1974; Gaertner and Pattanaik, 1988; Lee and McKenzie, 1990; Olson, 1987; Rowley and Peacock, 1975; Stigler, 1970; Tullock, 1971, 1983, 1986.) Interest groups and politicians often have incentives to engage in rent-seeking activities that would cause them to systematically ignore WTA measures in favor of the lower WTP measures. For instance, de Alessi (1960) recounts the many distortions created by government officials in an effort to use cost-benefit analysis to justify public projects. Thus, the fact that the members of the federal and various state constitutional conventions generally were politicians who either were members of various interest groups or may have been readily influenced by representatives of these interest groups undermines Fischel's constitutional justification for measuring value with market prices. On the other hand, it would be surprising if economic scholars find Hovenkamp's conclusion that sociologists and psychologist have tools for accurately measuring WTA to be very convincing.

18. Conclusion

The obituary for neoclassical economics surely is premature. As Hanemann (1991), Shogren et al. (1994) and Calfee and Rubin (1992) demonstrate, neoclassical economic theory predicts that the ratio of WTA to WTP can take on any value, depending of the elasticity of substitution between a good and wealth: the lower the elasticity of substitution, the larger the ratio of WTA to WTP will be. Moreover, as the leading proponent of experimental economics, Smith (1991, p. 894), observes, for all its deficiencies standard models of economic behavior based on individual rational choice are excellent predictors of actual behavior observed 'in the social context of exchange institutions'. It would seem rash to toss out all of neoclassical economic theory based solely on the evidence offered by the endowment effect.

Bibliography on the Endowment Effect (0720)

Alchian, Armen A. (1953), 'The Meaning of Utility Measurement', **43** *American Economic Review*, 26 ff.

Armentano, Dominick T. (1987), 'Comment: Efficiency, Liberty and Antitrust Policy', in Dorn, James A. and Manne, Henry G. (eds), *Economic Liberties and the Judiciary*, Fairfax, George Mason University Press, 309-316.

Baker, C. Edwin (1978), 'Counting Preferences in Collective Choice Situations', **25** *UCLA Law Review*.

Beavis, Brian and Rowley, Charles K. (1983), 'Evaluating Choice: A Note', **3** *International Review of Law and Economics*, 79-83.

Bishop, Richard, Heberlein, Thomas and Kealy, Mary Jo (1983), 'Contingent Valuation of Environmental Assets: Comparisons with a Simulated Market', **23** *Natural Resources Journal*, 619-648.

Boyce, Rebecca R., Brown, Thomas C., McClelland, Gary H., Peterson, George L. and Schulze, William D. (1992), 'An Experimental Examination of Intrinsic Values as a Source of the WTA-WTP Disparity', **82** *American Economic Review*, 1366-1373.

Brinig, Margaret F. and Crafton, Steven M. (1994), 'Marriage and Opportunism', **23** *Journal of Legal Studies*, 869-894.

Bromley, Daniel W. (1990), 'The Ideology of Efficiency: Searching for a Theory of Policy Analysis', **19** *Journal of Environmental Economics and Management*, 86-107.

Brookshire, David S. and Coursey, Don L. (1987), 'Measuring the Value of a Public Good: An Empirical Comparison of Elicitation Procedures', **77** *American Economic Review*, 554-566.

Bruce, Christopher J. (1984), 'Testing the Hypothesis of Common Law Efficiency: The Doctrine of Informed Consent', **6** *Research in Law and Economics*, 227-265.

Buchanan, James M. (1962), 'The Relevance of Pareto Optimality', **6** *Journal of Conflict Resolution*, 341-354.

Calabresi, Guido (1991), 'The Pointlessness of Pareto: Carrying Coase Further', **100** *Yale Law Journal*, 1211-1237.

Centi, Jean-Pierre (1987), 'Quel critère d'efficience pour l'analyse économique du droit (Which Efficiency Criterion for Economic Analysis of Law)', **2** *Revue de la Recherche Juridique*.

Coleman, Jules L. (1980), 'Efficiency, Exchange and Auction: Philosophic Aspects of the Economic Approach to Law', **68** *California Law Review*, 221-249.

Coleman, Jules L. (1980), 'Efficiency, Utility and Wealth Maximization', **8** *Hofstra Law Review*, 509-551.

Coombs, C.H., Bezembinder, T.G. and Goode, F.M. (1967), 'Testing Expectation Theories of Decision Making without Measuring Utility or Subjective Probability', **4** *Journal of Mathematical Psychology*, 72-103.

Cooter, Robert D. (1989), 'The Best Right Laws: Value Foundations of the Economic Analysis of Law', in Levit, Nancy and Hayman, Robert (eds), *Jurisprudence: Contemporary Readings, Problems and Narratives*, St Paul's, West, 1994.

Cotter, Thomas F. (1996), 'Legal Pragmatism and the Law and Economics Movement', **84** *Georgetown Law Journal*, 2071-2141.

Curran, Christophe and Rubin, Paul H. (1995), 'The Endowment Effect and Income Transfers', **17** *Research in Law and Economics*, 207-217.

Demsetz, Harold (1969), 'Information and Efficiency: Another Viewpoint', **12** *Journal of Law and Economics*, 1-22.

Dnes, Anthony W. (1984), 'Joint Production, National Income Definitions and Pricing in Linear Environmental Models', **18(4)** *Socio-Economic Planning Sciences*, 247-253.

Dobbs, I. (1981), 'Externality, Efficiency and the Pareto Principle', **1** *International Review of Law and Economics*, 167-181.

Egger, J.B. (1979), 'Efficiency is not a Substitute for Ethics', in Rizzo, Mario J. (ed.), *Time, Uncertainty and Disequilibrium*, Lexington, MA, Lexington Books, 117-125.

Fischel, William A. (1991), 'Exploring the Kozinski Paradox: Why is More Efficient Regulation a Taking of Property?', **67(3)** *Chicago-Kent Law Review*, 865-912.

Fischel, William A. (1995), 'The Offer/Ask Disparity and Just Compensation for Takings: A Constitutional Choice Perspective', **15** *International Review of Law and Economics*, 187-203.

Fischel, William A. and Shapiro, Perry (1988), 'Takings, Insurance and Michelman: Comments on Economic Interpretations of 'Just Compensation' Law', **17** *Journal of Legal Studies*, 269-293. Reprinted in Ellickson, Robert; Rose, Carol and Ackerman, Bruce (eds), Perspectives on Property Law, 2nd edn, 514-530, Boston, Little Brown, 1995.

Friedman, David D. (1988), 'Does Altruism Produce Efficient Outcomes? Marshall versus Kaldor', **17** *Journal of Legal Studies*, 1-13.

Frisch, R. (1959), 'On Welfare Theory and Pareto Regions', **9** *International Economic Review*, 39-92.

Gaertner, W. and Pattanaik, P.K. (eds) (1988), *Distributive Justice and Inequality: A Selection of Papers Given at a Conference, Berlin May 1986*, New York, Springer.

Gantner, Manfred (1993), 'Anmerkungen zur Universitätsreform aus finanzwissenschafltìcher Sicht (Notes on Reforming Universities from a Public Finance Perspective)', in Strasser, R. (ed.), *Beiträge zum Universitätsrecht*, Vienna, 119-139.

Gilson, Ronald J. and Kraakman, Reinier H. (1984), 'The Mechanisms of Market Efficiency', **70** *Virginia Law Review*, 549-644.

Glasner, David (1982), 'On the Difference Between Wealth and Liberty', **2** *International Review of Law and Economics*, 227-233.

Goldberg, Victor P. (1984), *Readings in the Economics of Contract Law*, Cambridge, Cambridge University Press. Reprinted in Feiwel, George (ed.), *Issues in Contemporary Microeconomics*, Macmillan Press, 395-402.

Grant, Robin F. (1989), 'Judge Richard Posner's Wealth Maximization Principle: Another Form of Utilitarianism?', **10** *Cardozo Law Review*, 815-845.

Hammond (1982), 'The Economics of Justice and the Criterion of Wealth Maximization' (Book Review)', **91** *Yale Law Journal*, 1493-1507.

Hanemann, W. Michael (1991), 'Willingness to Pay and Willingness to Accept: How Much Can They Differ?', **81** *American Economic Review*, 635-647.

Hanks, John L. (1986), 'On a Just Measure of the Efficiency of Law and Governmental Politics', **8** *Cardozo Law Review*, 1-38.

Harless, David W. (1989), 'More Laboratory Evidence on the Disparity Between Willingness to Pay and Compensation Demanded', **11** *Journal of Economic Behavior and Organization*, 359-379.

Hayashida, Seimei (1991), 'Koritsusei tai Ihosei: Minji Iho no Keizairiron (Efficiency vs. Unlawfulness: An Economic Theory of the Unlawfulness in the Civil Law in Japan)', **41** *Hokudai Hogaku Ronshu* (Hokkaido Law Review), 1364-1450.

Heiner, Ronald A. (1983), 'The Origin of Predictable Behavior', **73** *American Economic Review*, 560-595.

Hochman, Harold M. and Peterson, George E. (eds) (1974), *Redistribution through Public Choice*, New York, Columbia University Press.

Hoffman, Elizabeth and Spitzer, Matthew L. (1993), 'Willingness to Pay vs. Willingness to Accept: Legal and Economic Implications', **71** *Washington University Law Quarterly*, 59-114.

Hovenkamp, Herbert J. (1990a), 'Exchange on Public Choice', **57** *University of Chicago Law Review*, 840-843.

Hovenkamp, Herbert J. (1990b), 'Legislation, Well-Being and Public Choice', **57** *University of Chicago Law Review*, 63-116.

Hovenkamp, Herbert J. (1991), 'Legal Policy and the Endowment Effect', **20** *Journal of Legal Studies*, 225-247.

Johnsen, D. Bruce (1986), 'Wealth is Value', **15** *Journal of Legal Studies*, 263-288.

Jones, Peter and Sugden, Robert (1982), 'Evaluating Choice', **2** *International Review of Law and Economics*, 47-65.

Jones, Peter and Sugden, Robert (1983), 'Evaluating Choice: A Reply', **3** *International Review of Law and Economics*, 85-87.

Juhnjuhnwala, Bharat (1974), 'Kaldor-Hicks-Scitovsky Criteria: A Postmortem', **40** *Southern Economic Journal*, 493-496.

Kahan, Marcel (1992), 'Securities Laws and the Social Costs of "Inaccurate Stock Prices"', *Duke Law Journal*, 977-1044.

Kahneman, Daniel and Tversky, Amos (1979), 'Prospect Theory: An Analysis of Decision Under Risk', **47** *Econometrica*, 263-291.

Kahneman, Daniel, Knetsch, Jack and Thaler, Richard H. (1990), 'Experimental Tests of the Endowment Effect and the Coase Theorem', **98** *Journal of Political Economy*, 1325-1348.

Kahneman, Daniel, Knetsch, Jack and Thaler, Richard H. (1991), 'Anomalies: The Endowment Effect, Loss Aversion and Status Quo Bias', **5** *Journal of Economic Perspectives*, 193-206.

Kaldor, N. (1939), 'Welfare Propositions of Economics and Interpersonal Comparisons of Utility', **49** *Economic Journal*, 549-552.

Keenan, Donald C. (1981), 'Value Maximization and Welfare Theory', **10** *Journal of Legal Studies*, 409-419.

Kennedy, Duncan (1981), 'Cost-Benefit of Entitlement Problems: A Critique', **33** *Stanford Law Review*, 387-445.

Kirchner, Christian (1991), *Ökonomische Probleme des Zivilrechts*, Berlin, Springer-Verlag.

Knetsch, Jack L. (1984), 'Legal Rules and the Basis for Evaluating Economic Losses', **4** *International Review of Law and Economics*, 5-13.

Knetsch, Jack L. (1989), 'The Endowment Effect and Evidence of Nonreversible Indifference Curves', **79** *American Economic Review*, 1277-1284.

Knetsch, Jack L. (1990), 'Environmental Policy Implications of Disparities between Willingness to Pay and Compensation Demanded Measures of Values', **18** *Journal of Environmental Economics and Management*, 227-237.

Knetsch, Jack L. and Borcherding, Thomas (1979), 'Expropriation of Private Property and the Basis for Compensation', **29** *University of Toronto Law Journal*, 237-252.

Knetsch, Jack L. and Sinden, J.A. (1984), 'Willingness to Pay and Compensation Demanded: Experimental Evidence of an Unexpected Disparity in Measures of Value', **99** *Quarterly Journal of Economics*, 507-521.

Knez, Peter, Smith, Vernon L. and Williams, Arlington W. (1985), 'Individual Rationality, Market Rationality and Value Estimation', **75** *American Economic Review*, 397-402.

Kornhauser, Lewis A. (1980), 'A Guide to the Perplexed Claims of Efficiency in the Law', **8** *Hofstra Law Review*, 591-639.

Kraakman, Reinier H. (1988), 'Taking Discounts Seriously: The Implications of 'Discounted' Share Prices as an Acquisition Motive', **88** *Columbia Law Review*, 891-941.

Kronman, Anthony T. (1980), 'Wealth Maximization as a Normative Principle', **9** *Journal of Legal Studies*, 227-242.

Kübler, Friedrich (1990), 'Effizienz als Rechtsprinzip - Überlegungen zum rechtspraktischen Gebrauch ökonomischer Argumente (Efficiency as Legal Principle - Considerations for the Legal Practice Use of Economic Arguments)', in Baur, Jürgen F., Hopt, Klaus J. and Mailänder (eds), *Festschrift für Ernst Steindorff*, Berlin, De Gruyter, 687-704.

Lande, Robert H. (1982), 'Wealth Transfers as the Original and Primary Concern of Antitrust: The Efficiency Interpretation Challenged', **34** *Hastings Law Journal*, 67-151.

Lee, Dwight R. and McKenzie, Richard B. (1990), 'Second Thoughts on the Public-Good Justification for Government Poverty Programs', **19** *Journal of Legal Studies*, 189-202.

Lemley, Mark A. (1997), 'The Economics of Improvement in Intellectual Property Law', **75** *Texas Law Review*, 989-0.

Lipsey, Richard G. and Lancaster, K. (1956), 'On the General Theory of the Second Best', **24** *Review of Economic Studies*, 11-32.

Loewenstein, George and Adler, Daniel (1995), 'A Bias in the Prediction of Tastes', **105** *Economic Journal*, 929-937.

Macey, Jonathan R. and Miller, Geoffrey P. (1990), 'Good Finance, Bad Economics: An Analysis of the Fraud-on-the-Market Theory', **42** *Stanford Law Review*, 1059-1092.

Margolis, Stephen E. (1987), 'Two Definitions of Efficiency in Law and Economics', **16** *Journal of Legal Studies*, 471-482.

Markovits, Richard S. (1975), 'A Basic Structure for Microeconomic Policy Analysis in our Worse-Than-Second-Best World: A Proposal and Related Critique of the Chicago Approach to the Study of Law and Economics', *Wisconsin Law Review*, 950-1080.

Markovits, Richard S. (1980), 'Legal Analysis and the Economic Analysis of Allocative Efficiency', **8** *Hofstra Law Review*, 811-903.

McClelland, Gary H. and Schulze, William D. (1991), 'The Disparity Between Willingness to Pay Versus Willingness to Accept as a Framing Effect', in Brown, Donald R. and Smith, J.E. Keith (eds), *Frontiers of Mathematical Psychology: Essays in Honor of Clyde Coombs*, New York, Springer-Verlag, 166-192.

Medema, Steven G. (1993), 'Is There Life Beyond Efficiency? Elements of a Social Law and Economics', **51** *Review of Social Economy*, 138-153.

Medema, Steven G. and Samuels, Warren J. (1997), 'Ronald Coase and Coasean Economics: Some Questions, Conjectures and Implications', in Samuels, Warren J., Medema, Steven G. and Schmid, A. Allan (eds), *The Economy as a Process of Valuation*, Aldershot, Edward Elgar.

Miller, Geoffrey P. (1987), 'Economic Efficiency and the Lockean Proviso', **10** *Harvard Journal of Law and Public Policy*, 401 ff.

Milovanovic Milic (1994), 'Privatizacija i ekonomska efikasnost (Privatization and Economic Efficiency)', **1-2** *Ekonomska Misao*, 1-20.

Mishan, Ezra J. (1967), 'Pareto Optimality and the Law', **19** *Oxford Economic Papers*, 255-287.

O'Driscoll, Gerald P., Jr (1980), 'Justice, Efficiency and the Economic Analysis of Law: A Comment on Fried', **9** *Journal of Legal Studies*, 355-366.

Olson, Mancur (1987), 'Why Some Welfare-State Redistribution to the Poor is a Great Idea', in Rowley, Charles K. (ed.), *Democracy and Public Choice: Essays in Honor of Gordon Tullock*, Oxford, Blackwell, 191-222.

Ortona, Guido and Scacciati, Francesco (1992), 'New Experiments on the Endowment Effect', **13** *Journal of Economic Psychology*, 277-296.

Paz-Ares, Cándido (1993), 'Principio de Eficiencia y Derecho privado (Efficiency and Private Law)', in AA. VV., *Derecho, Moral y Eficiencia, III*, Jornadas de Filosofía del Derecho, Palma de Mallorca, Revisado en Estudios en homenaje a M. Brocheta Pont, Valencia 1995, III pp.

Posner, Richard A. (1980), 'The Ethical and Political Basis of the Efficiency Norm in Common Law Adjudication', **8** *Hofstra Law Review*, 487-507.

Pratt, John W. and Zeckhauser, Richard J. (1996), 'Willingness to Pay and the Distribution of Risk and Wealth', **104** *Journal of Political Economy*, 747-763.

Quattrone, George A. and Tversky, Amos (1988), 'Contrasting Rational and Psychological Analyses of Political Choice', **82** *American Political Science Review*, 719-736.

Radin, Margaret J. (1982), 'Property and Personhood', **34** *Stanford Law Review*, 957-1015.

Rizzo, Mario J. (1980), 'The Mirage of Efficiency', **8** *Hofstra Law Review*, 641-658.

Rothbard, Murray N. (1979), 'Comment: The Myth of Efficiency', in Rizzo, Mario J. (ed.), *Time, Uncertainty and Disequilibrium*, Lexington, MA, Lexington Books, 91-95.

Rowley, Charles K. and Peacock, Alan T. (1975), *Welfare Economics: A Liberal Restatement*, London, Martin Robertson, 198 p.

Rowley, Charles K. and Walker, Martin (1979), 'Pareto-Optimality and Gains-From-Trade: A Public Choice Interpretation', **34** *Public Choice*, 123-127.

Rozen, Marvin E. (1985), 'Maximizing Behavior: Reconciling Neoclassical and X-Efficiency Approaches', **19** *Journal of Economic Issues*, 661-685.

Ryssdal, Stray A.C. (1995), *Legal Realism and Economics as Behavior - A Scandinavian Look at the Economic Analysis of Law*, Oslo, Juridisk Forlag AS, Nerenius & Santérus Förlag AB Gad Jura AS.

Sager, Lawrence G. (1980), 'Pareto Superiority, Consent and Justice', **8** *Hofstra Law Review*, 913-937.

Samuels, Warren J. and Mercuro, Nicholas (1984), 'Posnerian Law and Economics on the Bench', **4** *International Review of Law and Economics*, 107-130.

Samuels, Warren J. and Mercuro, Nicholas (1986), 'Wealth Maximalization and Judicial Decision-Making: The Issues Further Clarified', **6** *International Review of Law and Economics*, 133-137.

Samuelson, W. and Zeckhauser, R. (1988), 'Status Quo Bias in Decision Making', **1** *Journal of Risk and Uncertainty*, 7-60.

Schwarzer, Stephan (1985), 'Wirtschaftsrecht und Ökonomische Effizienz (Commercial Law and Economic Efficiency)', *Wirtschaftspolitische Blätter*, 26-31.

Scitovski, T. (1951), 'The State of the Welfare Economics', **41** *American Economic Review*.

Shavell, Steven (1981), 'A Note on Efficiency vs. Distributional Equity in Legal Rulemaking: Should Distributional Equity Matter Given Optimal Income Taxation?', **71** *American Economic Review. Papers and Proceedings*, 414-418.

Shaviro, Daniel N. (1990), 'Exchange on Public Choice', **57** *University of Chicago Law Review*, 834-843.

Shogren, Jason F., Shin, Seung Y., Hayes, Dermot J. and Kleibenstein, James B. (1994), 'Resolving Difference in Willingness to Pay and Willingness to Accept', **84** *American Economic Review*, 255-270.

Sileo, Patrick W. (1995), 'Intransitivity of Indifference, Strong Monotonicity and the Endowment Effect', **66** *Journal of Economic Theory*, 198-223.

Slovic, P. and Lichtenstein, S. (1968), 'Relative Importance of Probabilities and Payoffs in Risk Taking', **78** *Journal of Experimental Psychology*, 1-18.

Smith, Vernon (1991), 'Rational Choice: The Contrast Between Economics and Psychology', **99** *Journal of Political Economy*, 877-897.

Stigler, George J. (1970), 'Director's Law of Public Income Redistribution', **13** *Journal of Law and Economics*, 1-10.

Stigler, George J. (1976), 'The Xistence of X-Efficiency', **66** *American Economic Review*, 213-216.

Stigler, George J. (1978), 'Wealth and Possibly Liberty', **7** *Journal of Legal Studies*, 213-217.

Stout, Lynn A. (1996), 'Insurance or Gambling? Derivatives Trading in a World of Risk and Uncertainty', **39** *Brookings Review*.

Stout, Lynn A. (1997a), 'How Efficient Markets Undervalue Stocks: CAPM and ECMH in A World of Uncertainty and Disagreement', **18** *Cardozo Law Review*.

Stout, Lynn A. (1997b), 'ATechnology, Transactions Costs and Investor Welfare: Is a Motley Fool Born Every Minute?', **75** *Washington University Law Quarterly*.

Symposium (1980), 'Symposium on Efficiency as a Legal Concern', **8** *Hofstra Law Review*, 485-972.

Thaler, Richard (1980), 'Toward a Positive Theory of Consumer Choice', **1** *Journal of Economic Behavior and Organization*, 39-60.

Tullock, Gordon (1971), 'Subsidized Housing in a Competitive Market: Comment', **61** *American Economic Review*, 218-219.

Tullock, Gordon (1980), 'Two Kinds of Legal Efficiency', **8** *Hofstra Law Review*, 659 ff.

Tullock, Gordon (1983), *Economics of Income Redistribution*, Boston, Kluwer-Nijhoff, 208 p.

Tullock, Gordon (1986), *The Economics of Wealth and Poverty*, New York, Columbia University Press, 210 p.

Tversky, Amos and Kahneman, Daniel (1991), 'Loss Aversion in Riskless Choice: A Reference-Dependent Model', **106** *Quarterly Journal of Economics*, 1039-1061.

Tversky, Amos and Wakker, Peter (1995), 'Risk Attitudes and Decision Weights', **63** *Econometrica*, 1255-1280.

Veljanovski, Cento G. (1981), 'Wealth Maximization, Law and Ethics - on the Limits of Economic Efficiency', **1** *International Review of Law and Economics*, 5-28.

Vukotic Veselin (1993), 'Privatizacija, Pravicnost i Efikasnost (Privatization, Justice and Efficiency)', **1-2** *Ekonomist*, 81-88.

Wang, William K.S. (1986), 'Some Arguments that the Stock Market is not Efficient', **19** *U.C. Davis Law Review*, 341-402.

Wetzstein, Michael E. and Centner, Terence J. (1992), 'Regulating Agricultural Contamination of Groundwater Through Strict Liability and Negligence Legislation', **22** *Journal of Environmental Economics and Management*, 1-11.

Other References

de Alessi, Louis (1960), 'Implications of Property Rights for Government Investment Choices', **59** *American Economic Review*, 13-24.

Calfee, John E. and Rubin, Paul H. (1992), 'Some Implications of Damage Payments for Nonpecuniary Losses', **21** *Journal of Legal Studies*, 371-409.

Conlisk, John (1996), 'Why Bounded Rationality?', **34** *Journal of Economic Literature*, 669-700.

Donohue, John J. III (1989), 'Diverting the Coasean River: Incentive Schemes to Reduce Unemployment Spells', **99** *Yale Law Yournal*, 549-609.

Willig, Robert D. (1976), 'Consumer Surplus Without Apology', **66** *American Economic Association*, 589-597.

0730
THE COASE THEOREM

Steven G. Medema
Associate Professor of Economics, University of Colorado at Denver

Richard O. Zerbe, Jr
University of Washington, Graduate School of Public Affairs

Abstract

The Coase theorem has evolved from an illustrative argument in Ronald Coase's 'The Problem of Social Cost' to a centerpiece of the modern law and economics movement. Along the way, the theorem has generated an enormous amount of controversy and discussion, including numerous theoretical attempts at proof and disproof and empirical and experimental analyses of the theorem's applicability. This chapter surveys the literature surrounding the Coase theorem and presents an outline of the major issues within the Coase theorem debate. In doing so, it attempts to assess the validity of the various challenges to the theorem's correctness and the implications of those challenges for the theorem's applicability, which is a separate issue. The analysis presented here illustrates the importance of transaction costs and property rights within the Coasean bargaining process and the need for further research along these lines to flesh out their implications law and economics.
JEL classification: K00
Keywords: Efficiency, Externalities, Invariance, Property Rights

1. Introduction

Ronald Coase's seminal essay, 'The Problem of Social Cost' (1960), is one of the most cited articles in the economics and legal literatures, and much of this attention is owed to a proposition that has come to be known as the Coase Theorem. While the Coase Theorem is by no means the only idea contained within that essay, it has captured the attention and interest of economists and legal scholars as have few other ideas. (For useful treatments of 'The Problem of Social Cost' as a whole, see Zerbe, 1976; Schlag, 1986; and Medema, 1996a; for context, see Coase, 1937, 1959.) Coase argued that, from an economic perspective, the goal of the legal system should be to establish a pattern of rights such that economic efficiency is attained. The legal system affects transactions costs and the goal of such a system is to minimize harm or costs, broadly conceived (Coase, 1960, p. 2). With this in mind Coase (1960, pp. 2-15) demonstrates the importance of transaction costs by considering the nature of bargaining or of contracts that could be struck by using an example of crop damage caused by straying cattle. He noted that negotiations among affected parties would result in an efficient and invariant outcome under the standard assumptions of competitive markets (especially, that the costs of transacting are zero), as long as rights are well-defined. Specifically, it is necessary to know whether the damaging business is liable or not for damage caused since without the establishment of this initial delimitation of rights there can be no market transactions to transfer and recombine them. But the ultimate result (which maximizes the value of production) is independent of the legal position if the pricing system is assumed to work without cost (Coase, 1960, p. 8).

This is as close as Coase comes in his essay to stating what has come to be known as the Coase Theorem.

A. Theorem(s) and Implications

2. Theorem(s)

Although Coase had set forth this idea already in 'The Federal Communications Commission' (Coase, 1959, p. 27), the first formal statement of the Coase Theorem did not come until 1966, when George Stigler (1966, p. 113) offered that 'The Coase theorem ... asserts that under perfect competition private and social costs will be equal'. Subsequently, the Theorem has been stated in numerous ways, including:

> if one assumes rationality, no transaction costs, and no legal impediments to bargaining, *all* misallocations of resources would be fully cured in the market by bargains. (Calabresi, 1968, p. 68, emphasis in original)

> in a world of perfect competition, perfect information, and zero transaction costs, the allocation of resources in the economy will be efficient and will be unaffected by legal rules regarding the initial impact of costs resulting from externalities. (Regan, 1972, p. 427)

> If transaction costs are zero the structure of the law does not matter because efficiency will result in any case (Polinsky, 1974, p. 1665).

> if there were (a) no wealth effects on demand, (b) no transaction costs and (c) rights to pollute or control pollution, the allocative solution would be invariant and optimal, regardless of the initial assignment of rights. (Frech, 1979, p. 254)

> In a world of zero transaction costs, the allocation of resources will be efficient, and invariant with respect to legal rules of liability, income effects aside (Zerbe, 1980, p. 84).

> a change in a liability rule will leave the agents' production and consumption decisions both unchanged and economically efficient within the following (implicit) framework: (a) two agents to each externality bargain, (b) perfect knowledge of one another's (convex) production and profit or utility functions, (c) competitive markets, (d) zero transactions costs, (e) costless court system, (f) profit-maximizing producers and expected utility-maximizing consumers, (g) no wealth effects, (h) agents will strike mutually advantageous bargains in the absence of transactions costs. (Hoffman and Spitzer, 1982, p. 73)

> when parties can bargain together and settle their disagreements by cooperation, their behavior will be efficient regardless of the underlying rule of law. (Cooter and Ulen, 1988, p. 105)

> a change in [law] affects neither the efficiency of contracts nor the distribution of wealth between the parties. (Schwab, 1988, p. 242)

While in many ways similar to one another, these statements of the Theorem contain important differences, many of which are at the heart of the theoretical debates over the Theorem.

Nonetheless, a casual reading of these statements reveals two general claims about the outcomes. The first is that, regardless of how rights are initially assigned, the resulting allocation of resources will be efficient. This proposition - the 'efficiency hypothesis' - is reflected in all statements of the Theorem. The second claim, which is not reflected in all statements of the Theorem, is that the final allocation of resources will be invariant under alternative assignments of rights. This is the so-called 'invariance hypothesis'. The debates over the correctness of the Coase Theorem, and/or its proper form, have turned on both of these hypotheses, and this struggle has been manifest in the current tendency to appeal to two different versions of the Theorem - the 'strong' version, which encompasses both the efficiency and the invariance propositions (reflected in the statements of the Theorem by Regan, Frech, Zerbe, and Hoffman and Spitzer, quoted above), and the 'weak' version, which encompasses the efficiency proposition alone (reflected in the statements of the Theorem by Calabresi, Polinsky, and Cooter and Ulen, quoted above).

3. Implications

For economists - Coase's target audience (Coase, 1988a, 1993) - the implication of the Theorem is that if remedies are considered in the unrealistic world in which competitive markets are normally considered, a world of zero transactions costs, the Pigouvian remedies said to be necessary for an efficient resolution of externality problems are not, in fact, necessary. All that is needed is a common law or statutory rule which assigns rights over the externality to one party or another. The market/pricing mechanism will then function in the same way as it does for ordinary goods and services over which rights are clearly defined. Furthermore, if rights are well-defined, the observed situation will be efficient (the parties having taken all Pareto-improving steps) and any further intervention (for example, Pigouvian remedies) will make matters worse rather than better.

If the implications for the economics of externalities are heretical, those for law are downright perverse, for the Theorem tells us that the form of legal rules does not matter - only their presence or absence. Thus, we will have the same amount of pollution (and thus clean air or water) and of outputs associated with the generation of pollution regardless of whether polluters or the victims of pollution are made liable for pollution damage. The same amount of effort will be devoted to precaution against causing torteous injury regardless of whether injurers or victims are liable for harm caused. The structure of law pertaining to breach of contract will have no impact on the allocation of resources through the contracting process. Attempts by judges to engage in social engineering from the bench will be fruitless, apart from distributional (as opposed to allocational) effects. Assuming that rights are alienable, the allocation of resources will be the same regardless of the rule of the law, and that allocation will be efficient. More generally, it is a matter of indifference whether courts impose property rules or liability rules (Calabresi and Melamed, 1972), and the entire issue of adherence to precedent becomes a moot point in terms of its effect on the allocation of resources.

B. Is the Coase Theorem Correct?

The Theorem has never been formally proved. Arguments regarding its correctness or incorrectness generally consist of attempts to demonstrate that it does or does not hold in a particular context or under a certain set of assumptions. Of particular import here is the framework within which the reallocations of rights contemplated by the Theorem are assumed to take place. Two basic frameworks can be identified: the 'quasi-competitive' framework, within which all relevant markets are assumed to be perfectly competitive and agents operate more or less along competitive lines in externality negotiations, and the 'game-theoretic' framework, within which there exists the potential for strategic behavior among affected parties. We examine each of these in turn.

4. The Quasi-Competitive Framework

Most of the analysis of the Theorem has taken place within the quasi-competitive framework, under which are two different types of treatment. First, there are discussions of small numbers externality negotiations within a more broad competitive context of full information, no strategic behavior, agents operating within competitive markets, and so on, with the result that parties strike mutually-beneficial bargains when they are available. This is analogous to the standard Edgeworth box analysis and is the environment contemplated by Coase in 'The Problem of Social Cost'. The second type of treatment actually assumes competitive markets in externality rights and analyzes the Theorem on that basis. In the latter case, the first optimality theorem of welfare economics suggests that the Coase Theorem is correct (Arrow, 1969).

4.1 Rents

One of the earliest but merely technical arguments raised against the Theorem is that it cannot hold under perfectly competitive conditions in the long run because it presupposes rents that may not exist. To consider the objection suppose that both the polluter and the victim are in a zero-profit, long-run equilibrium position. (For expositional simplicity, in the following discussion we will refer to the parties as 'polluters' and 'victims'. The analysis, of course, generalizes to all manner of externalities.) Then, the assignment of liability to the polluter will force the polluter to cease operations, since it lacks the resources with which to make liability payments to the victim. Similarly, if the victim is made liable, it will exit the market because it lacks the resources to bribe the polluter to reduce its harmful activity. Thus, it is argued, the Coase Theorem will only hold in the presence of 'non-transferable resources giving rise to Ricardian rents' (Wellisz, 1964, p. 351). It has been further argued that even the prior existence of rents would not ensure the validity of the Coase Theorem: the rents must be sufficient to support the externality - that is, sufficient to allow the polluter to pay damages (if he is liable) or the victim to pay the bribe (if the victim is liable); otherwise, a change in the direction of liability will cause the party bearing the cost of the externality to exit the industry (Tybout, 1972; Shapiro, 1974). Let us analyze these claims.

Suppose that the polluter is not earning rents and that he is liable for damage caused. Then, the polluter will be forced to go out of business in the long run, as he does not have the resources necessary to pay damages. This result is efficient since the externality existed inefficiently in the first place: the polluter was able to inflict damages on the victim only because he did not bear the full social cost of his actions. If the polluter is not liable for damages, the victims would be willing to offer a bribe up to the amount of damage to induce the polluter to cease operations, a bribe which the polluter would be willing to accept since it was not earning any rents in the first place. Thus, whether the polluter or the victim is earning no rents, we get the same, efficient, result regardless of the assignment of rights.

If neither party is earning rents sufficient to support the externality, the externality would not exist in the first place; the appearance of the externality would immediately drive the victim out of business and the externality would cease to exist. (See Wellisz, 1964, p. 350; Crain, Saurman, and Tollison, 1978 and Zerbe, 1980, pp. 89-90; 99.) Thus rents must exist for negotiation over rights to even be in the realm of possibility; that is, they are prior to the Coase Theorem analysis. But once they are satisfied, an efficient and invariant result will obtain.

The one case in which rents are not necessary is for externalities that are industry-wide in their emission and public bads in their effects (so that all firms in an industry are affected). Here, assuming that all firms are harmed equally (in terms of the effect on marginal and average costs), the externality acts in a manner analogous to an increase in input prices, causing an increase in marginal and average cost, a reduction in supply, and an increase in market price. The result will be invariant under alternative rules of liability.

4.2 Entry in the Long Run

One of the most discussed challenges to the Theorem concerns the effect of liability or bribe payments on entry into markets. If polluters are made liable for damages, the flow of liability payments into the victim industry will increase the rate of return in that industry. If one assumes that firms entering the market are also eligible for compensation, then entry will occur in the long run, leading to an increase in the output of the victim industry. When victims are liable, in contrast, the flow of bribe payments from victims to polluters raises the rate of return in the polluting industry, leading to entry into that industry and a corresponding increase in output. The arguments here are two: first, that the invariance proposition fails to hold because of the disparate entry effects of alternative legal rules; second, the efficiency proposition fails to hold because when polluters are liable the bribe-induced entry will result in too much victim output, relative to what is optimal, while when victims are liable the bribe-induced entry will result in too much polluter output, relative to what is optimal. (See Calabresi, 1965; Bramhall and Mills, 1966; Tybout, 1972; Baumol, 1972; Schulze and d'Arge, 1974; and Frech, 1979.)

The inefficiency issue is easily disposed of. First, if transaction costs are zero, agents are rational and there are no legal impediments to bargaining, then the long-run inefficiency will be cured through the same type of bargaining transactions that were employed to resolve the short-run inefficiencies caused by the externality (Calabresi, 1968, p. 67). That is, available gains from exchange will be exploited in the long run just as they are in the short run. Second, following Nutter (1968), any long-run misallocation will be cured by a single owner who will enter the market in order to exploit the potential for gain. Third, the above argument assumes the existence of a single efficient long-run equilibrium point (and thus that efficiency implies invariance), when, in fact, such need not exist. Here, the long-run equilibria are both efficient and thus the subsequent corrective negotiations or entrepreneurial actions are unnecessary. That is, long-run entry effects do not invalidate the efficiency argument.

The more difficult issue is that of invariance. While the above argument against invariance would appear to be straightforward, consider the following counter-argument. Suppose that ranchers are liable for damage done by their cattle. The flow of liability payments will then be capitalized into the value of farmland that adjoins ranching property and there will be no incentive for entry into farming in order to secure the bribe. In analogous fashion, any bribes that result from farmer liability will be capitalized into the value of ranchland that adjoins farms and there will be no incentive to enter ranching. Given this, the long-run entry effects that are said to invalidate the invariance proposition will not occur (Demsetz, 1972a; Frech, 1979).

The key to distinguishing between these competing claims regarding invariance has been provided by Holderness (1989), who pointed out that invariance turns on the issue of whether rights are assigned to open or closed classes of individuals or entities. An open class is defined as one into which entry is unrestricted, while a closed class is one which can be entered only if the right is purchased from a current class member (see also Demsetz, 1972b, 229-231). Consider first the assignment of rights within closed classes. Landowners constitute a closed class since one can become a landowner only by purchasing the land and the attendant bundle of rights from a current landowner. The assignment of rights to one class of owners creates at once a windfall gain for those having the right and a windfall loss for those not having it. However, in a competitive system these windfall gains and losses are immediately capitalized into the value of the land so that both types of land yield a normal rate of return. Since the rate of return for each of these types of land is unaffected by the assignment of rights, there are no incentives for entry or exit. Thus, the invariance proposition holds for closed classes (Holderness, 1989, pp. 183-184).

The invariance claim does not hold for open classes, however. Holdnerness's separation of open from closed classes calls attention since to a broad category of spurious objections all based on incomplete property right specification. Here, those who are not parties to the lawsuit through which the initial assignment of rights is generated can acquire that right costlessly merely by entering and this valuable right will not be capitalized into the price of any resource. Entry will indeed result (Holderness, 1989, p. 185). Similarly, the absence of a right reduces the returns to that activity, thereby inducing exit. The asymmetric entry/exit effects across alternative assignments of rights will thus result in different long-run outputs under alternative assignments of rights, thereby negating the invariance proposition.

This distinction illuminates the divergent results obtained by many of those offering support for or claiming to refute the invariance proposition. Those who have found the invariance proposition to be valid in this (the entry issue) context have either explicitly or implicitly assumed or worked with examples constituting closed classes. On the other hand, those finding against invariance have analyzed the problem in open-class contexts - primarily situations with two industries where entry is possible. The invariance proposition is applicable to closed class situations, such as externalities affecting land values, but is inapplicable to tort situations, such as accident law, where there is free entry into one or both classes and to assignments of rights which cover all (current and future) entrants into an industry.

The open class case, however, would seem to violate an underlying assumption of the Coase Theorem - fully-specified property rights. That is, rights in open classes are not delimited to the extent necessary to make market transactions possible; potential entrants are able to secure a valuable right without paying for it. This is consistent with Barzel's (1989, p. 2) definition of property rights as 'the powers to consume, obtain income from and alienate ... assets' and Allen's (1995, p. 2) definition of an 'economic property right' as '*one's ability, without penalty, to exercise a choice over a good, service, or person*' (emphasis in original). In fact, the assumption of zero transaction costs is said by some to mean that rights are fully specified (see Cheung, 1992; Allen, 1991, 1995) and the discussion in section 6, below). As such, the issue of incompletely specified rights, or open classes, goes to the issue of relevance rather than correctness.

4.3 Separable v. Non-separable Cost Functions

Another class of interesting objections is based on a failure to consider fully contract or merger possibilities. It has been argued, for example, that the validity of the efficiency (and invariance) proposition will turn on (in addition to other previously-recognized problems) the form of the cost function of the victim firm. It is well established that, if the victim's cost function is additively separable (that is, if $C_B = C(q_A, q_B) = C(q_A) + C(q_B)$), then the Coase Theorem holds - the outcome is both efficient and invariant under alternative assignments of rights (see Gifford and Stone, 1973; Marchand and Russell, 1973). Suppose instead, however, that the victim's (B's) costs of production are dependent upon both its own output and the output of the polluting firm (A), so that $C_B = C(q_A, q_B)$, where the pollution damage owing to firm A's output increases the costs of firm B.

With a non-separable cost function there is neither efficiency nor invariance. With a non-separable cost function, the level of pollution damage to B is a function not just of A's output, but of B's output as well and thus a given level of output by A causes B more harm (that is, causes a greater increase in B's costs) the more output B produces. In such a situation, the victim can and does contribute to its own damage without having to bear the cost, since it is fully compensated for all damage. As a result, the victim has no incentive to mitigate damages and produces an inefficiently high level of output. Moreover, the damage liability associated with this imposes a higher than optimal cost on the polluter, causing it to restrict its output below the optimal level (Marchand and Russell, 1973, pp. 613-615).

However, if both activities are controlled by a single owner, the result will be efficient and invariant regardless of the initial assignment of rights and irrespective of whether the victim's cost function is separable or non-separable (Marchand and Russell, 1973, pp. 614-616). Moreover, one can imagine a contract between owners that mimics the effect of single ownership assuming costs of monitoring and negotiation are zero. This demonstration is sufficient to negate the nonseparability critique, since the inefficiency contemplated will be exploited through merger, which can be achieved costlessly, or by an entrepreneur (see, for example, Nutter, 1968; Coelho, 1975 and Zerbe, 1980, pp. 87-88). Marchand and Russell (1975) have responded to this criticism by invoking difficulties in carrying out a merger - that is, by introducing transaction costs. But introducing transaction costs is no argument against the correctness of the Coase Theorem. A further argument that can be raised against the nonseparabilities critique is that it violates the assumption of fully-specified property rights (at least in the sense of Allen, 1991, 1995), since the victim is able to procure revenues from the polluter without giving up anything in return.

4.4 Non-Convexities at the Negotiation Starting Point

Perhaps the one seemingly insurmountable criticism of the invariance proposition comes from the recognition by Starrett (1972) that externalities will cause nonconvexities to exist in the production sets of victim firms. (See also Shapiro, 1974, 1977, 1978; Vogel, 1987.) The argument applies equally to consumption sets and thus to externalities to which consumers are party. This objection is similar to that of non-separable cost functions in calling attention to a contacting problem. This is an interesting objection because it points to the importance of information costs. In graphical terms, rather than generating a convex production set, such as in Panel a of Figure 1, the externality causes nonconvexities of the form illustrated in Panel b.

Figure 1

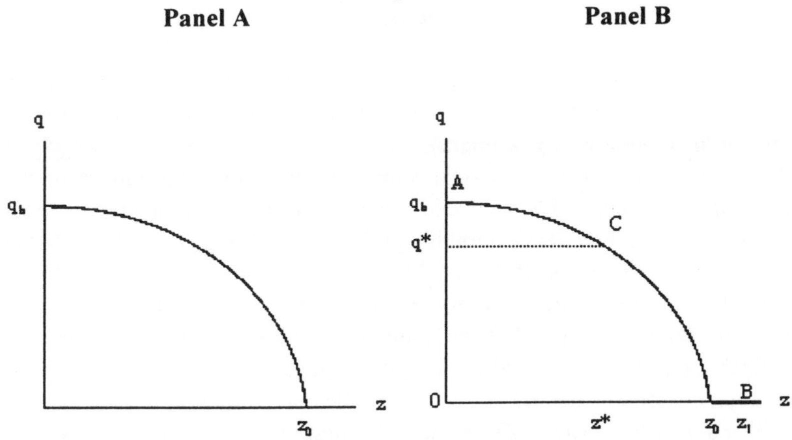

Here, q_B is the output of firm B, the victim and Z is the level of the externality. The analysis turns on the effect of increasing pollution damage on the victim's output. Panel (b) illustrates a situation of increasing marginal damage from pollution (given by the reduction in the victim's output due to the externality) with the recognition that, beyond some point (Z_0), marginal damage will be zero (Starrett, 1972, pp. 189-190).

The import of this for the Coase Theorem is as follows. Suppose that the polluter's (A's) profit-maximizing level of pollution in the absence of the legal rule is some level $Z_1 > Z_0$. With this level of pollution, B will produce no output. If the A has the right to pollute, the point $Z = Z_1$, $q_B = 0$ is the starting point for negotiation over the level of pollution. The minimum payment that the polluter is willing to accept to reduce pollution is the reduction in profits that would accompany the reduction in pollution. However, at (and around) Z_1, there is no benefit to the victim from a one unit reduction in pollution; the victim's output (q_B) would remain at zero with this one unit reduction in pollution. Thus, the victim would not be willing to offer a bribe payment to induce the polluter to reduce its pollution by one unit (to Z_1 - 1 units) - it is a cost with no attending benefit. Thus, the equilibrium when the polluter has the right to pollute will be at a pollution level $Z = Z_1$ and an output level for the victim of $q_B = 0$, a result which is due to the nonconvexity.

On the other hand, if the victim has the right to be free from pollution, the baseline from which negotiation begins is $Z = 0$. The victim will be willing to accept any bribe to allow positive levels of the pollution if the bribe is in excess of the lost profits due to pollution damage (or reduction in q_B). Thus, the parties will be able to negotiate to an efficient result along standard Coasean lines, but the final result will not (except by accident) be $Z = Z_1$ and $q_B = 0$. Thus, the invariance proposition does not hold in the presence of nonconvexities if the starting point for negotiation when the polluter has the right to pollute falls within the non-convex region of the victim's production set. However, if the initial level of pollution is some level $Z \leq Z_0$, the invariance proposition holds. (See Cooter, 1980 for a discussion of how legal rules can be specified to circumvent the nonconvexity problem).

The force of this critique is sufficiently powerful that the editors of the *Journal of Economic Theory* said that Starrett's demonstration that nonconvexities are inherent in externality problems 'destroy[s] the validity of the Coase Theorem' (Shapiro, 1977, p. 222). However, this judgment fails to understand the true nature of a fully transaction costs world. There is a Pareto-better point available, but the nonconvexity means that the parties will fail to reach it because the immediate marginal adjustments are not Pareto-better. Essentially, the point is that the victim will not be able to spend $15 for a change that will make it $20 better off because the first step along this path would involve spending a dollar to get a zero improvement in welfare and the victim, not being willing to take this first step, will never know that better things are on the horizon. The problem here is one of information: it is certainly the case that the victim would take this first, welfare-reducing step if it was certain that, in the end, it would be better off. If both victim and polluter knew of the existence of a superior position they could also merge to achieve it. Thus, the nonconvexities argument introduces imperfect information into the model. If, as most have maintained, information costs violate the zero transaction costs assumption of the Coase Theorem, fundamental non-convexities do not produce inefficiency. The non-convexity critique of the Theorem points to the importance of information costs, but, if these are considered as part of transactions costs, it does not point to the incorrectness of the Theorem itself.

4.5 Income, Taste and Preference Effects

An additional complication first hinted at by Buchanan and Stubblebine (1962) and Turvey (1963) and later more explicitly elaborated by Dolbear (1967) and Mishan (1965, 1967, 1971), within the economics literature, and by Kelman (1979) within the legal literature - is introduced when one or both parties to the externality are consumers, for, at this point, we are forced to take into account effects on demands that attend alternative assignments of rights. These effects arise first, from differences in tastes between parties and, second, from differences between the willingness to pay (WTP) and willingness to accept (WTA).

Differences in Tastes If tastes are different (that is, as long as indifference curves are not homothethic) a change in the income distribution will affect the pattern of demand and therefore the pattern of resource allocation, though not its efficiency. That is, alternative assignments of rights can have differential effects on the structure of demands for consumer goods. Since different assignments of rights result in different distributions of income, the composition of demands - and hence equilibrium prices and quantities across markets - will vary with alternative assignments of rights. For example, suppose that an economy produces only beef and fish and that fertilizer runoff used to produce grass, an input into beef production reduces fish production. Those that produce beef prefer to eat beef and those that produce fish prefer fish. A change in the liability rule from one in which beef producers are liable to one in which they are not will increase the income of beef producers and reduce the income of fish producers. This will then increase the demand for beef and reduce the demand for fish; thus, the relative production of beef and fish will not be invariant to the liability rule. This objection to the strong version of the Theorem is well recognized. But, we shall see that even this objection presupposes incomplete property rights.

Differences Between WTP and WTA A change in the law can change the sense of ownership and thus change the measure of value from the WTP to WTA or vice versa. Following Willig (1976), economists have tended to assume that any differences between willingness to accept (WTA) and willingness to pay (WTP) owing to a price change are small. This is now recognized as untrue in important cases. For environmental goods, researchers have demonstrated repeatedly that WTA questionnaires generate values from two to nineteen times greater than those elicited by WTP questions (Levy and Friedman, 1994, p. 495, n. 6; Hoffman and Spitzer, 1993, pp. 69-85). There are three reasons for the difference: income effects, substitution possibilities and loss aversion. (Hoffman and Spitzer, 1993) present an excellent survey of the WTA v. WTP issue, much of the evidence regarding which comes from the experimental literature. The present discussion touches on what we believe to be the most significant of these arguments.)

Let us first consider the implications of income effects. If most people experience diminishing marginal utility of income, the utility loss resulting from a reduction in income of a certain amount is greater than the utility gain associated with an increase in income of the same amount. Thus, if individuals bargain over utility, rather than over wealth *per se*, we would expect to see differences between WTA and WTP and thus negotiated solutions that vary with the initial assignment of rights (Hovenkamp, 1990). This is an income effect. For example (and assuming that A, the polluter, is a firm, so that wealth effects are irrelevant for it), if B (an individual) has the right to be free from pollution, then the amount of pollution generated will be a function of the payment that he is willing to accept to avoid pollution. If B does not have the right to be free from pollution (that is, A has the right to pollute), then the amount of pollution generated will be a function of the amount that B is willing to pay to avoid pollution. Since the maximum amount a person is willing to pay to avoid damages is a function of his budget constraint, while there is no such constraint on the amount that the individual is willing to accept, we will see (as long clean air is a normal good) a difference in the amount of pollution and thus in pollution-related output, depending on the initial assignment of rights (Mishan, 1971, p. 19). Thus, the invariance proposition will hold only when income effects are not present or when all relevant income elasticities of demand are zero.

The force of the income effects critique has been reflected in one of the few major modifications of the standard structure of the Coase Theorem: the addition of the assumption of no income effects or the qualifier 'income effects aside', as reflected in several of the statements of the Coase Theorem set out above. The use by some of the weak rather than the strong version of the Theorem is also attributable largely to the role that income effects play in negating invariance.

Consider next the issue of substitution possibilities. Recently, Hanemann (1991) showed that the poorer the substitutes for the good, the greater the divergence between the WTP and the WTA. Put another way, the divergence will be greater the more unique the good. The substantial divergence between WTP and WTA for unique goods arises in part from the fact that many of these goods have no close substitutes. Thus, for most people, the WTA to allow degradation of the Grand Canyon will be much greater than the WTP to prevent degradation for most people. A change in the law that results in a change from a WTP to a WTA criteria will have dramatic effects in the measure of value for the good. Zerbe (1998a) and Cohen and Knetsch (1992) have argued that the correct measure of damages as between the WTP and WTA is, however, a function of the psychological reference point which may not correspond with the legal reference point. For example, the Ellickson (1986) study of the response to differing range laws shows such a difference. In one half of Shasta County, California, open range was the legal rule and in the other half closed range was the rule. Yet in both parts of the County, in spite of opposite assignments of liability, people expected and provided similar remedies. Cattle owners took responsibility for the damages in all cases and this responsibility existed for many years and was enforced through social norms. The reference state was one of crops not being damaged by straying cattle.

A further argument against the invariance proposition comes from the influence that alternative assignments of rights may have on WTA v. WTP through effects on consumer tastes and preferences. Here, the assertion is that consumer tastes and preferences are not wholly exogenous to the structure of legal rules but are influenced by them (Zerbe and McCurdy, 1996). Prospect theory posits that individuals have a value (rather than utility) function which is convex for gains and concave for losses and that the degree of concavity is greater than the degree of convexity, so that losses of a given size are felt more acutely than gains of that same size (Kahneman and Tversky, 1979). The link between this idea and the WTA v. WTP argument is that the offer of money to relinquish a right would be treated as a loss, whereas the purchase of a right would be regarded as a gain. Since losses count more than gains, the minimum amount that an individual would be willing to accept to relinquish a right will exceed the amount that he is willing to pay to acquire it (Kahneman, Knetsch and Thaler, 1990). One reason for this loss aversion is suggested by what Thaler (1980) has called an 'endowment effect', owing to the fact that people value 'received income' more highly than 'opportunity income'. Because of this, people will be willing to forego more opportunity income to retain a right than they would spend in received income to acquire it and thus WTA will exceed WTP (Thaler, 1980; Kelman, 1979). Kelman attempts to apply this argument to the producer side as well, arguing that producers may value realized and opportunity income differently. However, doing so would contradict the assumption of profit maximization. Moreover, as Spitzer and Hoffman (1980, p. 1210) point out, a profit-maximizing entrepreneur could (and, following Nutter, 1968, would) arbitrage this difference, thus generating the outcome implied by the Coase theorem.

How important these forces are in creating a wedge between the WTP and the WTA is as yet uncertain. At this point, however, it seems reasonable to say that income and substitution effects and loss aversion are sufficient to invalidate the invariance, although not the efficiency, claim of the theorem.

The above possible exceptions to the Coase Theorem represent important cases, but do they really represent exceptions to the Coase Theorem? All of the objections to the Coase Theorem that rest on consumer preferences rest on a change in the distribution of wealth. Yet, these arguments at base reflect property rights that are not fully specified or are inefficiently specified. These conditions then violate the Coase Theorem assumptions that property rights are fully specified.

Consider first a change in the rule of liability. If property rights are fully defined (in the sense of complete ownership), this alteration of liability cannot take place without compensation; if it does, the right was not fully defined in the first place, in violation of the Theorem's assumptions. Thus, owing to the compensation, the distribution of wealth will be unaffected (Allen, 1995, p. 10). Allen's argument applies even to the income effects qualification. Of course, this rebuttal does not go to the case where non-existent rights are subsequently defined. However, in a world of zero transaction costs the definition of rights would be perfectly anticipated and thus reflected in resource values (Allen, 1995, pp. 10-11). In sum, when alternative assignments of rights influence the distribution of income and wealth, it must be the case that rights are less than fully defined and/or that transaction costs are positive. Indeed, Allen (1991, 1995) has argued that fully-defined rights and zero transaction costs are really the same thing (see the discussion in Section 6, below).

Perhaps the most intriguing case is one suggested by the recent literature in which legal ownership is different from psychological ownership (Zerbe, 1998a, 1998b). Evidence suggests that a sense of ownership attends certain environmental goods even if there is no individual ownership. A decision to cut down the last remaining stand of privately owned redwood trees, the Headwater Grove, may create a sense of loss among some that are non-owners of the grove. This loss is correctly measured by the WTA. If, however, a decision to measure the value of the grove is based on legal ownership the value to the public will be based on the WTP for preservation. Since for a normal good the WTP will be less than the WTA, the grove may be cut when it should not. Property rights are fully specified in this example so that it would appear to violate the strong version of the Theorem.

However, Zerbe (1998a, 1998b) has noted that, although property rights in this case are fully specified, they are inefficiently specified. He argues that '*efficiency requires that the legal measure of property and damage correspond to psychological reference points*'. (Posner's rule (1992, p. 52) for the allocation of rights is a subsidiary of this theorem. This rule is that where one class of claimants values the right more than other classes, efficiency requires that the right should go to the claimants that value it the most.) If there is not a correspondence between psychological and legal property rights, the use of WTP and WTA based on legal criteria can impose net losses. Imagine that a party, George, believes he owns a right or a property, M and that another party, Ronald, also believes that George owns property M. They discover that the law, however, holds that party George, not Ronald, owns M. Ronald suffers a loss of M psychologically and therefore economically, while George gains M. Since losses are, on the average, worth more than equivalent gains (due to income, substitution effects and loss aversion), on the average George will gain less than what Ronald loses. This is perfectly general, so that the application of law to affect a legal ownership different from psychological ownership must, on average, impose net losses. (This is true as long as Ronald and George may be regarded as equivalent in the sense that on average one does not have a greater income than the other or does not differ in some other relevant characteristic. Underlying this proof is the notion that we cannot speak of it being efficient to change preferences to be in accord with the law since this violates the proper context for benefit cost analysis - which requires that preferences be taken as they lie - and the very concept of efficiency. In any event benefit cost can not evaluate the advantages of a change in preferences since this does not take preferences as they lie.) Similarly, if one class of claimant psychologically possesses property so that its removal is felt as a psychological loss, as compared with a rival claimant who has a lesser psychological claim or no claim, efficiency requires that the law grant the right to the psychological possessor. But, in a zero transactions cost world this sort of inefficiency would not arise since the law would be made to correspond with the psychological sense of ownership.

5. The Game-Theoretic Framework

While the vast majority of the literature debating the validity of the Coase Theorem employs the quasi-competitive framework, a number of commentators have addressed the Theorem from a game-theoretic bargaining perspective, arguing that that the quasi-competitive framework is not appropriate or relevant for Coase Theorem-like bargains over rights owing to the small number of parties contemplated and the potential for strategic behavior. (See, for example, Davis and Whinston, 1962; Samuelson, 1966, p. 1141; Shoup 1971, p. 310; Regan 1972, p. 428; Cooter, 1982, pp. 16-17.) By placing the Theorem in a small numbers context but yet ignoring the potential for strategic behavior, it is presumed that the contemplated agreements 'can and will be reached because it is in the joint interest of the parties to do so' (Samuelson, 1985, p. 322). Yet, this fails to consider the possibility that what is rational for the group may not be rational for the individual and constitutes, in essence, an '*a priori* argument' for the Theorem (Regan, 1972, pp. 429-431).

Several commentators (for example, Davis and Whinston, 1965; Arrow, 1979; Aivazian and Callen, 1981; Samuelson, 1985 and Aivazian, Callen and Lipnowski, 1987) have suggested that the Coase Theorem, as envisioned by its proponents at least, lends itself quite naturally to the theory of cooperative games. It can be demonstrated that the Coase Theorem will always hold in a two-person cooperative game. However, this result is not particularly comforting since, by setting the problem in the context of a two-person cooperative game, efficiency is assured by definition (although there is no guarantee of invariance), making this more along the lines of an illustration of the Coase Theorem rather than a proof (Schweizer, 1988, pp. 246, 254). In fact, much of the quasi-competitive literature (especially the two-person analysis) can, without too much injustice, be described as cooperative game analysis. The situation is complicated when the cooperative game involves more than two players. While it has been suggested that the Theorem may not hold in such a context (Aivazian and Callen, 1981), this claim has been shown to be incorrect (Coase, 1981; De Bornier, 1986).

5.1 Noncooperative Game Theory

However, the most interesting and potentially most damaging, game-theoretic analysis of the Theorem has involved the use of noncooperative game theory. If parties have full information about each other's utility (or profit or production and cost) functions, the Coase Theorem will hold in a noncooperative setting.

The initial assignment of rights establishes the utility level of each player in the absence of further reallocations of resources and there are assumed to exist reallocations of resources which are efficiency enhancing, in the sense that the utility of one player can be increased without reducing the utility of the other player. However, neither party will agree to an alteration in the allocation of resources unless that reallocation increases its utility. The question, from the perspective of the noncooperative game, is whether there exists a sequence of permitted moves which will generate an efficient (Nash) equilibrium. Suppose that A is given the right to pollute. Then the victim, B, has an incentive to offer an alternative allocation of resources (for example, a combination of a bribe paid from B to A and a reduced level of pollution by A) to A, but B knows that A will accept this offer only if A's utility is increased under the new allocation. Since B knows A's utility function, he can determine the range of allocations sufficient to garner A's acceptance. And, since B's utility is higher with reallocation than without, he will not offer an allocation that A would reject, choosing instead that allocation from the group A will accept which maximizes his own utility. The resulting equilibrium is Pareto efficient, since, given the utility level of one player, the other player's utility is maximized. As Arrow (1979, p. 29) points out, however, this is not the competitive equilibrium. The same reasoning applies to the situation where the victim is given the right to be free from pollution (Arrow, 1979, pp. 27-29; Schweizer, 1988). In fact, it is not necessary for each party to enter the bargaining process with full information, only that each party perceives that there are net gains to it from providing full information *during* the negotiation process and thus will reveal such information during that process (Saraydar, 1983, p. 603, n. 12).

The problem, numerous commentators have pointed out, is that it is unlikely that the players will know each others' respective utility (or profit, production or cost) functions. This has a number of implications.

(a) Implication One: The Baseline Problem When victims are liable, the firm can influence the level of the bribe that it receives by making an upward adjustment in pollution emission at the time that the baseline level of pollution (against which subsidized/bribe-induced pollution reductions will be measured) is set or by choosing not to take cost-justified precautions. That is, the level of pollution on which the bribe is based may differ from the level of pollution that would have been emitted if the polluter was liable. The source of this incentive is the inability of the victim to ascertain with certainty the true baseline level of pollution. Moreover, disagreements over the baseline level of pollution may result in the failure to consummate bargains when the victim is liable. Conversely, if polluters are known to be liable for damages, then, in the absence of full information about actual damages and measures taken by the victim to

mitigate damages, the victim's moral hazard will result in too few resources being devoted to precaution/mitigation by the victim and too many resources being devoted to abatement by the polluter (Kamien, Schwartz and Dolbear, 1966; Tybout, 1972; Harris, 1990). With endogenous liability assignment, however, the moral hazard problems disappear, since a party does not know with certainty whether or not it will be forced to bear the costs of the externality. Thus each party will act efficiently to minimize expected costs by engaging in the appropriate level of precaution/preventive activity (Harris, 1990, pp. 701-702).

(b) Implication Two: Extortion Imperfect information raises the problem of extortion, which can arise in a number of forms. First and related to (a), above, polluters may threaten to emit higher levels of pollution in order to secure a larger bribe (Mumey, 1971). Second, as Shoup (1971, pp. 310-312) has pointed out, potential entrants may use extortion: if externality generators are not liable, 'entrepreneurs' may threaten to emit an externality in order to secure a bribe, or, symmetrically, if externality generators are liable, potential victims may threaten to 'come to the harm' in order to secure a bribe. If these threats necessitate the use of resources to establish credibility, the result will be inefficient. However, investing resources to establish credibility violates the zero transaction cost assumption of the Theorem. Jaffe (1975, p. 661) offers a further counter to Mumey's result. The polluter will not wish to invest resources in making a threat which will not be carried out and the mere potential that it can carry out a threat will induce a more generous bribe. Moreover, this extortion argument implicitly assumes both sufficient rents and an open class situation and, on the latter ground, is subject to the rebuttal noted above. Demsetz (1972a, p. 23) has also countered this criticism with the argument that competition for these gains will drive the price of extortion to zero, so that extortion is not a barrier to the attainment of the efficient equilibrium. It should also be noted that Coase (1959, p. 27, n. 54) recognized that the employment of resources 'solely to establish a claim' could preclude the attainment of the efficient result.

Third, since there are multiple ways to divide the gains from a bargain and each individual is interested in both achieving the benefits from cooperation and getting as large a share of the benefits as possible for himself, there will be threats of noncooperation in order to increase one's share of the gains. For these threats to be credible, however, they must occasionally be carried out and, when this is done the result will be sub-optimal (Regan, 1972, p. 429). One can see illustrations of what Regan (1972) has called the '*a priori* argument' for the Theorem in the challenges to the extortion argument. For example, it is argued that the limits of extortion are set by the size of the available rents: if one party tries to extort from the other an amount greater than this, the other party could simply transfer its resources into their next-best use. The extorting agent, being unwilling to forego the potential gain, will thus agree to a solution which garners for it an amount not in excess of the other party's rents. Thus, the only differential impact of alternative legal rules will be on the distribution of rents; the final allocation of resources will be unaffected (Boyd and Mohring, 1971; Demsetz, 1972a; Feldman, 1974).

(c) Implication Three: Private Information While Davis and Whinston (1965, p. 118) argued early on that information would be revealed through the bargaining process, the application of more complex strategic thinking suggests that private information, if revealed, may be used against one's self and thus adversely affect one's payoff. Given this, agents have an incentive to conceal information (through silence or lies) and to expend resources both to protect the value of their own private information and to acquire information from/about others. These costs and resultant delays and/or failures to consummate mutually-beneficial bargains, are likely to preclude the attainment of efficient negotiated solutions where information is asymmetrically distributed (Cooter, 1982; Sutton, 1986; Farrell, 1987). Cooter (1982, pp. 17-18) even goes so far as to argue that an equally strong case can be made that parties will never agree on the distribution of the surplus, even when transaction costs are zero, a proposition that he labels the 'Hobbes Theorem'. However, he maintains that the ever-present strategic element is not as 'insurmountable' as the Hobbes Theorem implies, nor as 'inconsequential' as the Coase Theorem implies; in fact, he argues, 'gains from trade in bargaining situations are realized more often than not' (Cooter, 1982, p. 19). Cento Veljanovski (1982, p. 60) offers a theorem similar to Cooter's Hobbes Theorem - the 'Johansen theorem', which holds that '[d]irect bargaining has an inherent tendency to dissipate the gains-from-trade through strategic behaviour' (see Johansen, 1979, pp. 515-520). Unlike Cooter, however, Veljanovski maintains that in a world of zero transaction costs the dissipation of gains is likely to be the more common outcome.

A number of commentators have demonstrated the potential for both agreement and non-agreement when information is imperfect. If neither party's utility function is a function of the other's private information, then an efficient result will be reached. However, if either party's utility function is a function of the other's private information, then there is no guarantee that an efficient result will be reached (Schweizer, 1988, pp. 259-263). (See also Arrow, 1979, pp. 29-31; Cooter, 1982, pp. 20-24; Samuelson, 1985; Illing, 1992). Our discussion here will draw primarily from Cooter's analysis. Arrow and Samuelson reach conclusions very similar to Cooter, using the assumption that the parties are uncertain about each others' utility functions. For example, Cooter (1982, pp. 20-24) points out that uncertainty regarding the opponent's response causes each player to form a rational expectation of this response in the sense of formulating a subjective probability distribution over his opponent's moves. Given this rational expectation regarding his opponent's strategy, each player chooses for himself the strategy that maximizes his expected utility based on a comparison of the greater share of the gains from taking a harder line in bargaining with the higher probability that this harder line will prevent an agreement from being reached. The problem is that, while each player will be playing the strategy that is optimal against the *distribution* of his opponent's possible strategies, this strategy is not necessarily optimal against the *particular* strategy played by the opponent. The outcome will be inefficient when players err in their predictions of the moves made by their opponents (Cooter, 1982, pp. 20, 23; Arrow, 1979, p. 31). In fact, Cooter contends that zero transaction (communication) costs actually decreases the possibility of reaching an agreement, in that it facilitates the transmission of threats and other strategic communications (Cooter, 1982, pp. 23), although, as Arrow (1979) has demonstrated, it is possible to design a collective decision rule that will induce a truthful revelation of preferences.

If the situation involves large bargaining groups, two more potential difficulties arise. First, individuals will have an incentive to free ride and thus the ability of the group to pay a bribe sufficient to induce the socially optimal level of output/pollution will be greatly reduced. Second, if there are differential damage effects across victims, we may observe the rise of coalitions within the victim group (for example, by level of damage), each applying pressure to encourage the result that best suits its interests. The greater is the number of coalitions, the smaller is the likelihood that the optimal solution will be reached (Wellisz, 1964, p. 354). However, as the number of parties approaches infinity (with large numbers of right-holders and large numbers of rights-seekers), the bargaining solution here will approach the efficient result of competitive equilibrium (Samuelson, 1985, p. 338).

In sum, the likelihood of incomplete information gives us little reason to believe that the Coase Theorem is correct when specified in a noncooperative bargaining context. But while the game-theoretic critiques of the Coase Theorem are suggestive of its demise, they have not gone unchallenged, largely on the grounds that it is incorrect to place the Theorem in such a context. At issue is what is meant by a world of zero transaction costs, to which we now turn.

6. The Issue of Transaction Costs

Perhaps the most sticky issue in the debate over the Coase Theorem is the meaning given to the assumption of zero transaction costs. Indeed, the very concept of transaction costs has been so vague and ill-defined that Stanley Fischer (1977, p. 322, n. 5) was once led to remark that 'almost anything can be rationalized by invoking suitably specified transaction costs'. Coase's (1960, p. 15) definition of transaction costs encompasses those costs associated with search, negotiation, monitoring and enforcement, which, as Dahlman (1979, p.

148) has noted, basically reduces to 'resource losses incurred due to imperfect information'. A bit more specificity (although even greater breadth) is found in more recent definitions within the property rights literature such as Barzel's (1989, p. 2) contention that transaction costs are the costs associated with the transfer, capture and protection of rights' and Allen's (1991, p. 3) statement that they encompass 'the resources used to establish and maintain property rights'. Under these latter definitions, zero transaction costs implies complete property rights (Allen, 1991, 1995; Cheung, 1992; see also Schlag, 1989).

If we take the Barzel/Allen definition as the basis upon which to evaluate the Coase Theorem, three implications immediately follow. First, there is an unspecified property right that lies at the heart of the private information examples. For example, Farrell (1987) constructs a problem in which parties A and B care about a time that is set. He notes that King Solomon would have little trouble finding the optimum value since he charges each party an amount equal to their effect on each other and that a 'bumbling bureaucrat' can under some circumstances find a superior (second best) result to that achieved under zero cost negotiations. The showing that a centralized authority can achieve an optimum is, however, equivalent to showing that there is an unspecified property right. When A is allowed to set the time (about which both A and B care), B will prefer to not participate in bargaining since his gain is greater when A just sets the time unilaterally and B pays nothing. The advantage that Solomon has is that he can force A and B to participate. Yet, in this example, B gets to use the time that A sets. For example, the time may represent the time for beginning a race. Farrell's example assumes that B is nevertheless allowed to participate in the race. But, if the race is owned the owner will in fact charge both A and B, yielding the Solomon solution. Another analogy can be made to ownership of a lake. The owner will charge each user at least the cost they impose on other users. Farrell implicitly assumes that government is the only owner of the lake. It is true that we can consider other examples in which the ownership of the resource seems more foreign to our usual thinking, as when the time represents a curfew or a time after which noise must be reduced-but there is a lack of ownership none the less. These are simply examples in which the absolute advantage of government with respect to certain sorts of enforcement costs may support government ownership, but enforcement costs are also transaction costs.

Second, nearly all of the challenges to the Theorem's correctness are invalidated under this conception of transaction costs, including entry, nonseparabilities, nonconvexities and even wealth effects, as noted above. This definition of transaction costs also invalidates other challenges to the Theorem which were not discussed in the preceding sections - those based on rent seeking (Jung et al., 1995; see Medema, 1996b) and the presence of risk (Posin, 1990; see Medema, 1995a and Posin's, 1995, response). Of particular importance here is the implication of the Barzel/Allen definition (and even Dahlman's definition) for the game-theoretic challenges, which rely on the existence of imperfect information. By any of these definitions, the presence of imperfect information has the effect of introducing transaction costs into the analysis through the behavior it induces and the game-theoretic challenges are correspondingly invalidated. (On this point see also Allen, 1995, pp. 12-13; Dahlman, 1979, pp. 158-159, n. 26; Hovenkamp, 1990, p. 787; Illing, 1992; Samuelson, 1985, p. 323; Zerbe, 1980, pp. 85-86). Indeed, Saraydar (1983), acknowledges that the imperfect information resulting from strategic behavior violates the assumption of zero transaction costs, but argues that such costs are virtually inevitable within a small numbers bargaining situation due to the incentive to distort information. Further evidence for this line of reasoning may be found within Coase (1960, pp. 31-33), who discusses the problem of moral hazard (along the lines of Harris, 1990) in the context of *positive* transaction costs.

Against these claims, defenders of the game-theoretic approach point out that giving this type of content to the idea of zero transaction costs basically renders the idea of bargaining meaningless and detaches the Theorem almost completely from reality, making it, in the words of one commentator 'more in common with astrology than with market analysis' (Veljanovski, 1982, p. 60). (See also Regan, 1972, pp. 429-430; Shoup, 1971, p. 310; Cooter, 1982, p. 17.) In the end, then, whether the game-theoretic and other challenges to the Coase Theorem go to its correctness or its relevance comes down to 'how one interprets the almost mystical world of zero transactions costs' (Zerbe, 1980, p. 85).

This takes us directly to the third implication of the Barzel/Allen definition - that '[t]ransaction costs are ubiquitous' (Allen, 1991, p. 4). The effect of this is to make the Theorem *per se* completely devoid of applicability to the real world. Coase (1981, p. 187) has made this point a bit more graphically, contending that the analysis of a world of zero transaction costs is akin to 'divining the future by the minute inspection of the entrails of a goose'. Indeed, by this definition the Theorem's efficiency proposition *must* hold, since any violation of it reflects a '[cost] associated with the transfer, capture, or protection of property rights'. It may be argued with some justice that all of this reduces the Coase Theorem to a mere tautology (Regan, 1972, pp. 429-30; Cooter, 1989, p. 67). So be it. Coase (1960, p. 15) never claimed that it was realistic, just that it follows logically from the same basic assumptions underlying Pigouvian theory circa 1960. And indeed, based on the foregoing analysis the correctness of the Theorem remains untouched, apart from the potential for taste and preference-induced divergences between WTA and WTP that may impact the invariance claim. The issue of relevance is a different matter altogether and one to which we now turn.

C. Relevance

A further facet of the extensive debate over the Coase Theorem has been the attempt to verify its predictions experimentally and empirically. Hovenkamp (1990, p. 794) has recently pointed out that '[c]onducting empirical tests of the Coase theorem is like conducting empirical tests of the Pythagorean theorem. Given the theorem's assumptions, the results flow out as a matter of logical necessity'. This is true; as such and given the impossibility of satisfying the zero transaction costs assumption in the world in which we live, the experimental and empirical tests go to the issues of relevance and applicability, rather than to the Theorem's correctness. In doing so, they begin to address the potential difficulties for the Theorem that are raised by the challenges discussed above, such as the effects of imperfect information, the potential for strategic behavior, nonconvexities and the presence of income or taste and preference effects.

7. Experimental Tests

The experimental tests of the Coase Theorem are among the most interesting of the various tests, since they offer the potential to mimic as closely as possible the conditions of zero transaction costs. At the same time, they can begin to capture the effects of factors such as imperfect information and isolate the import of these effects *vis-à-vis* situations in which they are absent.

7.1 Experimental Framework and Results

The most extensive experimental tests of the Theorem are those undertaken by Hoffman and Spitzer (at times with others - see Hoffman and Spitzer, 1982, 1985, 1986; Coursey, Hoffman and Spitzer, 1987; Harrison et al., 1987). The experiments undertaken by Hoffman and Spitzer all involve the same basic experimental framework. There is a range of possible outcomes, each with a different associated payoff. One party (the 'controller') is given the 'property right' and thus can determine the outcome unilaterally. Consider the following set of possible dollar payoffs (P_A, P_B) in the spirit of Hoffman and Spitzer: (5,0), (4,4) and (0,5). If A is the controller, he will chose (5,0) unless B induces him to choose a different outcome. The Coase Theorem predicts that (4,4) will be chosen, with the actual distribution of the joint payoff ($8) being a function of the negotiation process. And of course it is in B's interest to offer A up to $4 to choose (4,4) and in A's interest to accept any payment greater than $1 to do so.

In well over 500 experiments with various sizes of bargaining groups (including 1 · 1, 1 · 3, 2 · 2, 5 · 5, 1 · 9 and 1 · 19) conducted within this framework, the results were quite favorable. In all, the parties bargained to the efficient result 92 percent of the time, including 94 percent of the time under conditions of full information and 90 percent of the time under imperfect information. Moreover, the support for the Theorem's prediction was actually greatest in the 10 and 20 person situations - 98 percent, including 100 percent in 20 person negotiations, where the 19 people devised their own informal institutional arrangements (choosing representatives from the group as bargaining agents) to overcome the large numbers problems. Given how little the student subjects have at stake in these experiments, even those conducted under conditions of imperfect information suggest very low transaction costs. While this may seem quite unrealistic, these experiments do offer some fairly substantial support for the applicability of the Theorem when transaction costs are low.

One of the interesting issues raised by the early experiments came from the nearly equal division of the payoffs (± $1) in the vast majority of the cases. Individual rationality suggests, with respect to the above example, that the controller would not settle for less than $5 and could potentially induce the other party to agree to a $7.99 - $.01 split of the $8 payoff, as in, for example, a one-shot game. The fact that so many controllers settle for less than what should be their reservation price suggests either altruism - which contradicts entirely the theory of externalities, Coase Theorem or otherwise, since, if agents are altruistic, the individually rational behavior that is said to generate the externality in the first place would not occur (Harrison and McKee, 1985, p. 655) - or a potential problem with the experimental environment.

One hypothesis offered to explain this result is that participants in these experiments did not understand the full meaning and import of having a unilateral property right as controllers (Harrison and McKee, 1985). Another is that they did not feel a morally justified right to be the controller, since that position was determined on the basis of a coin flip rather than being, in some (for example, Lockean) sense, earned (Hoffman and Spitzer, 1985). Once measures were implemented to control for this - 'educating' subjects or having subjects 'earn' the position of controller by winning a preliminary game - the extent of individually rational behavior increased dramatically and without a significant drop-off in the rate at which efficient bargains were made - approximately 90 percent (Harrison and McKee, 1985; Hoffman and Spitzer, 1985, 1986). Even then, however, 20-30 percent of the experiments generated less than individually-rational outcomes, suggesting that the subjects behave more like Lockeans than like utilitarians or egalitarians. Rather than taking this as evidence against the Coase Theorem, Hoffman and Spitzer (1986, pp. 159-160) suggest that it speaks to the robustness of the Theorem across alternative hypotheses regarding individual behavior.

7.2 Criticisms re: Externality Problems

One of the criticisms of these early experiments was that they did not account for the possibility of 'affronts to dignity' and other such factors to which people would refuse to assign a monetary value or over which people would refuse to bargain (Kelman, 1985, pp. 1038-1039). In an attempt to deal with the 'affront to dignity' issue, Coursey, Hoffman and Spitzer (1987) conducted experiments that introduced a discomforting externality. This was accomplished by introducing the possibility that the 'victim' would have to hold one ounce of an unpleasant-tasting liquid in his or her mouth for twenty seconds. These experiments had two possible payoffs: (i) the 'polluter' gets $0 and the victim gets $10 and does not have to taste the liquid; (ii) the 'polluter' gets $20 and the victim gets $10 and does have to taste the liquid. The latter outcome, where the victim is exposed to the externality, is, of course, the efficient one. Out of 40 experiments, the efficient outcome was chosen 38 times - 22 out of 22 times when the polluter was the controller and 16 out of 18 times when the victim was the controller. The results with the polluter as the controller may not be surprising: when the 'polluter' has the right to pollute, polluting is efficient and there are substantial gains to the polluter from polluting, the polluter would be expected to pollute.

What may be a bit surprising, however, is the propensity for victims to sell their right to be free from the harm - here, for a 90 percent increase in payoff (from $10, the payoff to the victim without tasting, to $19.06, the average payoff to the victim when agreeing to taste), or roughly half of the gains to the polluter. In spite of the authors' claim to the contrary, these results further call into question the assumption of individual rationality (or the inducement thereof within the experimental environment), since, in half of the experiments, the 'polluters' paid the victims to taste the liquid even when the polluters had a unilateral right to force them to do so. And while the authors do not jump from a willingness to sell the right to avoid tasting bitter liquid to, say, the legalization of prostitution or pornography (although they do not entirely close the door on such matters, choosing instead to 'express no opinion' as to whether such activities should be allowed), they do suggest a presumption in favor of allowing individuals to transfer moderate amounts of dignity and/or moderate amounts of danger.

Based on their various findings, Hoffman and Spitzer (1986, p. 162, emphasis added) assert that their results '*produce a presumption in favor of the Coase Theorem*', by which they mean that 'a judge or a legislator should start his analysis by presuming that the parties can and will, in general, exhaust the gains from trade available through private bargaining' and that those who would argue against this 'must bear the burden of the proof'. Furthermore, they argue, the strength of the evidence for the optimality of the bargaining outcomes establishes a presumption in favor of injunctive over damages remedies because of the high probability that the parties will bargain to the efficient result (Hoffman and Spitzer, 1986, pp. 163-168). (See Calabresi and Melamed, 1972. For discussions of the relative efficacy of property rules and liability rules when transaction costs are positive, see also Polinsky, 1979; 1980; Ayres and Talley, 1995a, 1995b; Kaplow and Shavell, 1995, 1996.)

In making these claims, Hoffman and Spitzer clearly go too far. It is one thing to show that the Coase Theorem is largely confirmed in a laboratory setting that attempts more or less to mimic the zero transaction costs world, but it is quite another to say that the results thus generated establish 'a presumption in favor of the Coase Theorem' for efficiently resolving real-world externality problems with twenty or fewer parties. (It should be noted that the parties will always reach an efficient point, in the Pareto sense. That is, even if transaction costs are so large as to preclude rights transfers, that result is Pareto efficient, given transaction costs. See, for example, Samuels (1974), Buchanan (1983) and Calabresi (1991). However, the efficient result to which Hoffman and Spitzer's 'presumption' refers is the Pigouvian social optimum, which is equivalent to the Pareto optimal outcome when transaction costs are zero.) What may be established is that up to twenty-party externalities will be resolved efficiently through negotiations in many and perhaps even most, instances where transaction costs are very low and the stakes are very small. But transaction costs consist of far more than factors introduced by a twenty-second tasting of a foul liquid or adding parties to a bargain, particularly when the group consists of more-or-less homogeneous college students. The emphysema-ridden residents of the neighborhood are likely to have a far different view of pollution externalities than would others who are not so affected; the light sleepers are likely to look far differently at the neighborhood kennel than are the deep sleepers and so on. And how many groups are absent one or two members who are likely to impede any negotiated settlement? All of this is to say nothing of the information and coordination problems that may attend complicated real-world bargains. In sum, Hoffman and Spitzer develop some very nice results offering rather strong support for the Theorem when the conditions it assumes are nearly met. However, to move from this to claims of widespread applicability and presumptions in favor of the Theorem in real-world cases is a somewhat different matter, one requiring far more caution and future study than is implied by the authors.

7.3 Criticisms re: Invariance Proposition

Apart from transaction-cost-related issues of applicability, these experiments also fail to get at the invariance proposition *per se*. For example, might effects such as the normative sanction for rights, an affront to dignity, or wealth effects cause a divergence between WTA and WTP? These issues are side-stepped within the Hoffman and Spitzer experimental design that makes efficiency and invariance go hand-in-hand. While the evidence regarding the existence of a divergence between WTA and WTP is not uniform (see the survey by Hoffman and Spitzer, 1993, and the references cited therein), it seems to weigh in favor of the existence of a non-trivial divergence, one that is too large to be explained solely in terms of wealth effects. Attempts to measure the relationship between WTA and WTP have been done through surveys and through experiments. The survey evidence shows a substantial difference between WTA and WTP, although economists have been rather suspicious of these results because of their several potential biases. However, as we have noted, recent experimental treatments of this issue support the contention that WTA may be substantially greater than WTP, often more than twice as great (Levy and Friedman, 1994; Hoffman and Spitzer, 1993, pp. 69-85). While this literature is too vast to survey here, one set of experiments, undertaken by Kahneman, Knetsch and Thaler (1990), probes this issue in the context of the Coase Theorem and, in a number of different types of experiments, finds significant endowment effects. Using items such as mugs, pens, binoculars and chocolate bars, they find that individuals, when given the opportunity to exchange these items for cash, exhibit a strong reluctance to part with entitlements and thus that, contrary to standard assumption of economic theory, preferences are apparently not independent of entitlements (Kahneman, Knetsch and Thaler, 1990, p. 1339). The value that the subjects place on these objects 'appears to increase substantially as soon as the individual is given the object' (Kahneman, Knetsch and Thaler, 1990, p. 1342) and the resulting disparity between WTA and WTP does not dissipate in repeated trials (that is, with market experience). They suggest that this endowment effect is most likely to occur for items that are not easily replaceable, which makes the endowment effect particularly important for the Coase Theorem, since things like a nice view, or clean air or water, are not easily replaced and it thus can be expected that people will refuse to sell such goods even at prices somewhat greater than their reservation price for buying them.

Two implications of these WTA versus WTP experiments are particularly important. The most obvious is that the results provide strong evidence against invariance in the outcomes of bargains even when transaction costs are zero. Second, endowment effects reduce the gains from trade as compared with a world in which preferences are independent of endowments. Since fewer mutually advantageous exchanges are possible, the volume of trade is lower than it otherwise would be (Kahneman, Knetsch and Thaler, 1990, p. 1344). Given the size of the potential disparity between WTA and WTP, one can conceive of situations where each party's WTA is greater than the other party's WTP, so that no trade would occur, whereas if WTA were equal to WTP, we would see bargains consummated. Experiments run to test this implication in a Coase Theorem context revealed substantial under-trading relative to the Theorem's predictions (Kahneman, Knetsch and Thaler, 1990, pp. 1339-1341). Even when transaction costs are negligible, then, there does not seem to be much room for confidence in the generation of an invariant outcome when consumers are party to an externality.

7.4 Criticisms re: Different Contexts

Even less favorable to the Theorem's applicability are the results of an experiment by Stewart Schwab (1988), who looked at the Theorem in the context of labor law and labor-management negotiations. The graduate student subjects in Schwab's experiments were asked to negotiate a union contract over wages, vacation time and - the crucial aspect of the experiment - whether or not the company had the right to transfer work to its nonunion plant over the course of the three-year contract. The implications for the Coase Theorem lay in the contract presumption that was said to govern labor relations in the absence of a specific contract provision: in one group of experiments, subjects were told that the legal presumption was that the company must continue to use union workers unless the contract explicitly states otherwise (that is, includes a 'go clause'), while the other group was told that the presumption was that the company could transfer work to the nonunion plant during the course of the contract unless the contract explicitly stated otherwise (that is, includes a 'stay clause'). (These contract presumptions have actual counterparts in labor law B the *Milwaukee Spring* cases.)

Analysis of the results of these experiments shows that only about 20 percent of the contracts were fully efficient when wage levels, vacation time and the stay or go clause are accounted for, a vast difference from the roughly 90 percent efficiency of the Hoffman and Spitzer and the Harrison and McKee experiments. Out of 108 contracts, all but two had efficient wage levels, but only 31 percent had efficient vacation levels and only about 65 percent had a stay clause where it was efficient or a go clause where it was efficient. Schwab contends that three factors may account for these differences. First, parties in these experiments were bargaining over multiple contractual terms under a binding time constraint and thus may have found it difficult to make efficient choices on all items. Second, unlike many of the other experiments, subjects here were not given full and perfect information. This meant both that information had to be communicated during the negotiation process and that signaling and bluffing could occur, leading to inefficient agreements. Finally, the subjects did not know what the 'best' outcome was from the beginning and thus had to find their way to it and do so over a rather large bargaining range which, of course, could easily result in inefficient outcomes (Schwab, 1988, pp. 251-252).

Given these factors, the rather high rate of failure to reach efficient bargains is not particularly surprising. The environment of these experiments corresponds much more closely to a natural setting than do many of the other experimental treatments and the factors that exist in these natural settings are such as to weigh heavily against the attainment of efficient results. By the same token, however, these experiments go much more to the application of the insights of the Coase Theorem than to the testing of the Theorem *per se*, in that they introduce a variety of factors that are assumed away by the Theorem's assumption of zero transaction costs. Thus, earlier work, such as that by Hoffman and Spitzer, speaks favorably to the Coase Theorem on its own terms, while Schwab's results are rather pessimistic about the ability of parties to bargain to efficient results in more natural settings. However, Schwab's results take on a better cast when evaluated in light of what he calls the 'weak efficiency hypothesis', which says that the law will not affect the *rate* at which efficient bargains are consummated. (This is not to be confused with the 'weak' version of the Coase Theorem, noted above, which asserts efficiency but not invariance.) The form of the contract presumption does not have a significant effect on the inclusion of stay clauses or go clauses, nor on the efficiency of the contracts (Schwab, 1988, pp. 252-253).

8. Empirical Studies

There have been three studies that more or less take Coase's farmer-rancher example into the real world to look at the ability of parties to negotiate efficient solutions to animal trespass problems.

8.1 California Animal Trespass Laws 1850-90

Kenneth Vogel (1987) examines the response of farmers and ranchers to changes in California animal trespass laws between 1850 and 1890. At the time when, in 1850, California joined the Union, its principal industries were mining and cattle raising and, reflecting the importance of the cattle industry to the state, California had what was, in essence, strict nonliability for cattle trespass. This rule clearly favored the ranchers and the evidence strongly suggests that the rule was designed with that in mind. At the same time, however, it played a major role in hindering the development of agriculture in the state (Vogel, 1987, pp. 163, 167).

However, between 1851 and 1890 there were no less than 150 different laws enacted by the California legislature altering the rules that governed cattle trespass in ways that benefited farmers (Vogel, 1987, pp. 163-164). The Coase Theorem predicts that these alterations in the law will have no effect on the allocation of resources; that is, *ceteris paribus*, these changes in the law should have no effect on the level of resources devoted to ranching and farming, or on ranching and farming outputs. And, according to Vogel, this situation is particularly well-suited to testing the applicability of the Theorem to the real world since 'the externality is visible, the parties are, at least post hoc, easily identifiable and it is easy to measure, or use proxies to estimate, the damages' (Vogel, 1987, p. 181).

Contrary to the Theorem's prediction, however, the enactment of the various estray laws beginning in the 1860s was accompanied by an enormous increase in farm output, particularly for wheat farming, which became common in the valleys, while cattle were moved up into the foothills. Econometric analysis undertaken by Vogel shows that a number of variables attempting to capture the effects of legal change on crop outputs are significant and that these are uniformly positive in sign, which supports the claim that these legal changes did indeed influence the growth of agriculture (Vogel, 1987, p. 184).

Given the strength of the evidence, it remains to explain why the Coase Theorem fails here. Vogel suggests two reasons. First, transaction costs may be significant and, furthermore, are asymmetric across alternative assignments of rights; specifically, they are lower when ranchers are liable (Vogel, 1987, pp. 176, 187). When ranchers are not liable for the damage done by their cattle, the farmer wishing to keep the cattle off his land will have to negotiate with each rancher whose cattle might potentially stray onto his land in order to accomplish this. On the other hand, when farmers have the right to compensation for damages, the onus is on the ranchers to initiate negotiations and the rancher need only bargain with those farmers on whose land his cattle may be expected to stray. Second, there are nonconvexities as a result of the externality. If ranchers are not liable for trespass damages, the fact that each farmer has to negotiate with all ranchers whose cattle might stray onto his land in order to prevent damage means that '[i]f a farmer fails to contract with the rancher whose cattle actually use his land, all payments made to the other ranchers are useless' (Vogel, 1987, p. 176). The farmer will thus have little incentive to initiate such negotiations, with the result that efficiency will obtain only if it is efficient for cattle to be allowed to roam freely. This nonconvexity is not present when farmers are given the right (Vogel, 1987, pp. 174-176, 187). Taken together, these two factors can explain why output was lower when the ranchers were not liable.

In contrast to Hoffman and Spitzer, who use their experimental results to claim a presumption in favor of the Coase Theorem, Vogel (1987, pp. 186-187) argues that his results refute the general applicability of the Theorem. Yet, Vogel has not refuted the Theorem but rather has shown the importance for the case of straying cattle of transactions costs and pointed out the importance of assigning the legal rule to minimize transactions costs as both Coase (1960, p. 19) and Posner (1983, p. 71) suggest should be done. Given the enormous volume of legal change at the time, the nonconvexities present and the difficulty of ascertaining the source of the damage, Vogel's broad conclusion may be premature. Some degree of support for a more moderate view can be found in the study of contemporary trespass disputes undertaken by Robert Ellickson.

8.2 Effects of Open- v. Closed-Range Laws

Ellickson (1986, 1991) examines, among other things, the effects of open- versus closed-range laws on cattle trespass disputes in Shasta County, California. Under open-range laws, cattlemen are not usually responsible for accidental trespass damage, whereas they are strictly liable under closed range laws. Ellickson finds that cattlemen and their neighbors do in fact behave in a manner suggested by the Coase Theorem, cooperating to resolve their disputes regardless of who is liable. However, the evidence also suggests that it is not Coase Theorem-type mechanisms at work here; rather, individuals seem to rely on community norms to determine their behavior. For example, while the Theorem predicts that the cattleman would install a fence if he were liable (closed range) and that the neighboring farmer would do so if he were liable (open range), it is almost always the cattleman who installs the fence because both cattlemen and their neighbors believe that the cattleman is morally obligated to do so, since his cattle cause the damage. Moreover, the citizens seem to be very ignorant of the relevant law and ignore those aspects of the law that conflict with their view of the world. As such, they do not bargain 'in the shadow of the law' (see Mnookin and Kornhauser, 1979, and Cooter, Marks and Mnookin, 1982), but beyond it; community norms seem to have much more force than the legal rule in place. Ellickson suggests that this may be due to the fact that relations among the neighbors are both complex and continuing, because of which the transaction costs associated with acquiring information and litigating disputes are high and reliance on norms offers a lower-cost way of resolving these disputes. Ellickson (1989, 1991) also suggests that this norm-based behavior points to the need to revise certain of the behavioral concepts underlying law and economics.

8.3 Roaming Deer in Scottish Highlands

In a study that has interesting commonalities with that of Ellickson, Nick Hanley and Charles Sumner (1995) examine an externality situation owing to the roaming of red deer in the Scottish Highlands which cause damage to growing trees and, in the process, impose substantial costs on the owners of these forests, the value of the timber from which is diminished. In addition, the wandering deer may destroy growing crops on farmland and, when they stray onto sheep grazing land, reduce the forage for sheep, thus imposing costs on both farmers and sheep ranchers. The beneficiaries of the red deer population are estate owners, who derive substantial income and estate value from the presence of red deer on their estates (Hanley and Sumner, 1995, pp. 88-91).

Given the level of damage, the small number of parties, the ease of quantifying damage to forests and the relative ease with which estate owners could reduce the size of their herds, the situation seems to reflect an inefficiently-high deer population and a fertile ground for the working of Coase

Theorem-type mechanisms. Even so, an extensive study by Sumner (1993) failed to turn up any instances of Coasean bargaining between owners of deer estates and neighboring landowners. What one does observe, however, are Deer Management Groups which neighboring landowners have established 'to coordinate deer management across neighboring estates ... and forest/farmland, in order to reduce the level of the externality'. The advantage of such groups is that they 'effectively [internalize] the externality across members of the group', thereby avoiding the third-party effects that can result with bilateral bargaining (Hanley and Sumner, 1995, p. 93). It is interesting to note the parallel between the rise of the cooperative Deer Management Groups and the behavior of neighbors revealed in Ellickson's study of cattle ranching in Shasta County. While the law offers a low-cost option (free government culling) for dealing with red deer damage, groups of neighboring landowners in essence ignore the law and work out a solution amongst themselves, perhaps presumably because it is the case that the transaction costs associated with the cooperative efforts of the Deer Management Groups are lower than those that would attend bilateral negotiations of the Coasean variety (Hanley and Sumner, 1995, p. 93).

8.4 Implications for other Legal Rules: Divorce

The Coase Theorem has implications for all manner of legal rules, including, as Peters (1986, 1992) points out, the rules governing divorce. Since 1970, there has been a progressive movement in the US from divorce by mutual consent (requiring the agreement of both parties), to unilateral divorce, where the marriage can be terminated at the demand of either party. Intuitively, the rules governing divorce function to establish property rights with respect to dissolution of the marriage. Under unilateral divorce law, the spouse seeking divorce has property rights with respect to dissolution while, under mutual consent, the right rests with the spouse who does not wish to see a divorce occur (Peters, 1992, p. 690). The conventional wisdom was that unilateral divorce laws would make divorce easier (in economic terms, reduce transaction costs), thus increasing the divorce rates in states that adopted such laws. The Coase Theorem predicts that if bargaining costs are minimal and information is symmetric across parties, divorces will only be undertaken when they are efficient (that is, joint benefits exceed joint costs), regardless of the law governing divorce and that the legal rule will have no impact on the divorce rate.

Peters (1986) tests a model corresponding to the Coase Theorem environment against one that posits asymmetric information and thus predicts that divorce rates will differ across alternative legal rules and finds that the data support the predictions of the Theorem against the conventional wisdom: the move to a unilateral divorce rule does not affect the probability that a woman becomes divorced (Peters, 1986, pp. 446-448). Moreover, the level of alimony and child-support payments are 'significantly lower' in states with unilateral divorce rules (Peters, 1986, p. 449) and the labor force participation rates of married women in such states are higher, which, she argues, may represent an attempt by married women to self-insure against the possibility of becoming divorced without compensation (Peters, 1986, pp. 448-449, 451-452). Thus, both the divorce rates and the distribution of compensation are consistent with the Coase Theorem. However, a number of subsequent studies find that the evidence tends to support the conclusion that divorce rates are in fact higher in unilateral divorce states than in mutual consent states. (See, for example, Allen, 1992; Zelder, 1993a, 1993b; Brinig and Buckley, 1995; Friedberg, 1995, which also contain numerous citations to literature on both sides of the argument.) Within this debate, each side claims that the other's empirical work contains errors or biases that influence the results (see, for example, Peters, 1986, 1992; Allen, 1992).

Even if one is willing to accept the result that divorce rates are not impacted by the legal rules governing divorce, it remains to ascertain whether these results actually reflect the working of Coase Theorem-type mechanisms. There is plenty of reason to suggest that the answer is 'no', or at least 'not necessarily'. First, there is no evidence to suggest that 'unilateral' divorces are undertaken only when they are efficient. Rather, Peters infers that the efficiency proposition holds based on a questionable claim that transaction costs are low and the fact that the data confirm the model's invariance and distribution predictions. (For contrasting views on the potential magnitude of transaction costs here, see Peters (1992, p. 690) and Allen (1992, p. 684). Allen (1992, 1995) goes so far as to argue that, by working an uncompensated transfer of wealth from wives to husbands, the move to no-fault divorce violates the zero transaction costs/fully-specified rights condition assumed by the Theorem and thus that the rise in the divorce rate does not constitute a legitimate argument against the Theorem.) Furthermore, Peters fails to account for the fact that the Theorem predicts not just an invariant divorce rate, but an invariant allocation of household resources as well - just as the farmer-rancher example predicts an invariant allocation of resources devoted to farming and ranching. The fact that female labor force participation is higher in states with unilateral divorce rules thus speaks loudly against the claim of invariance.

8.5 Implications for Other Legal Rules: Pre-Trial Settlements

A similar problem attends the claim that the high rate at which suits are settled prior to trial supports the Coase Theorem (Hoffman and Spitzer, 1986, pp. 168-169). Glanter (1983, pp. 28-30) finds that roughly 90 percent of all lawsuits are settled before they go to trial and that, when they do not settle, it tends to be due to (i) cases that require a judicial decree to be settled; (ii) cases that are not costly to litigate, which reduces the incentive to settle; (iii) the placing by one or more parties of special value on having a judicial decree for reasons including, *inter alia*, precedent and reputation; (iv) cases that involve an issue that is not easily negotiated over, such as a 'fundamental value'; and (v) the high transaction costs associated with settlement as compared to going to trial - factors that lie outside of the bounds of the Coase Theorem. However, the high proportion of settlements does not imply that the parties have bargained to the Pareto optimal result contemplated by the Coase Theorem. There is no way to infer from the settlement data whether the parties have bargained to the socially optimal result contemplated within a zero transaction costs world, or if they simply have realized some of the potential gains from negotiation but hit a point where the transaction costs from further negotiation exceed the expected gains and choose to settle at a 'suboptimal' outcome because this settlement, although not optimal, is still better than going to trial.

8.6 Implications for Other Legal Rules: Unemployment

Perhaps the most unique empirical test of the Coase Theorem is Donohue's (1989a) analysis of the Illinois employment experiment (Spiegelman and Woodbury, 1987), which attempted to determine whether the payment of bonuses to unemployed workers for securing employment, or to employers for hiring unemployed workers, would reduce the duration of unemployment and the costs associated with the unemployment compensation system. While the experiment was conducted to ascertain how such bonuses might affect the duration of unemployment, its application to the Coase Theorem is straightforward. The efficiency hypothesis predicts that mutually advantageous bargains will be struck under either scheme and all workers and employers who satisfy the eligibility requirements will collect bonuses. The allocative invariance proposition suggests that members of the worker-payment group (WPG) will find jobs and collect bonuses at the same rate as members of the employer-payment group (EPG). The invariant distribution hypothesis predicts that members of the WPG and EPG groups will have the same aggregate compensation (wages plus bonus). The WPG workers would be expected to have lower wages than EPG workers, reflecting a bargaining away of a share of their bonus, as compared to EPG workers' higher wages as employers bargained away a share of their bonus.

Donohue's inquiry into the results of the Illinois experiment reveals that they contradict the predictions of the Coase Theorem on all counts. To begin with, the number of bonuses paid to WPG workers was about five times that paid to EPG employers. Furthermore, many workers and employers who met the requirements for bonuses failed to submit a voucher to receive their bonus - particularly employers. Given this, says Donohue, '[t]he conclusion that a number of individuals and employers acted inefficiently is hard to rebut' (Donohue, 1989a, p. 573). The experimental results also revealed that members of the WPG had a significantly greater improvement in obtaining employment, relative to the control group, than did members of the EPG, which, along with the differential bonus collection rates among the groups violates the allocative invariance prediction of the Theorem (Donohue, 1989a, pp. 569-577). Finally, there was no significant difference in wages across the WPG and EPG hirees, so that aggregate (wages plus bonus) compensation was higher for WPG workers than for EPG workers, in violation of the invariant distribution prediction of the Theorem. That is, it appears that workers did not bargain with employers over the wage or the bonus as a result of this program (Donohue, 1989a, pp. 586-590).

Donohue (1989a, pp. 591-601) asserts that transaction costs are extremely low here and thus that the Theorem fails in a case most favorable to its success. He offers two possible explanations for why the experiment failed to satisfy the predictions of the Coase Theorem, each of which goes to the issue of individual behavior/decision making in the context of such bargains. One possibility, to which Donohue lends a great deal of support, is ignorance on the part of workers, who seemed not even to realize that bargaining was possible and may not have understood that the bonuses could aid them in gaining employment. Moreover, there may have been an authoritarian effect which caused the workers to believe that the bonus was in effect inalienable - that the party designated to receive the bonus was in fact entitled to its full value, an effect that would also discourage the type of bargains envisioned by the Theorem (Donohue, 1989a, pp. 600-602).

Donohue's conclusions regarding the implications of the Illinois experiment for the Coase Theorem's applicability have been challenged by Ellickson (1989) and Lindgren (1990), both of whom contend that Donohue greatly underestimates the effect of transaction costs within this experiment. Acquiring this so-called 'free' money actually involves a substantial number of steps (and even more for employers than for workers), the aggregate effect of which is to make the process rather costly, *relative to the size of the bonus*. Lindgren (1990, pp. 581-582, 585), for example, lists the steps that participants in the WPG and EPG programs must go through in order to collect bonuses and offers several reasons why one would not anticipate an invariant distribution of income, or bargaining over the bonuses. In fact, Lindgren (1990, p. 583) suggests that the results do in fact match the predictions of the Coase Theorem (see also Ellickson, 1989, p. 625).

First, because costs are high relative to the bonuses, the insights underlying the Coase Theorem would lead one to predict that many workers or employers who are eligible for bonuses would not collect them. The Illinois study confirmed this prediction. Second, because costs are higher for employers than for workers, the insights of the Coase Theorem would lead one to predict that more workers in the worker-bonus group would be influenced to participate in the program, obtain work quickly and collect the bonuses. Again, the Illinois study confirmed these predictions (Lindgren, 1990, p. 583).

Indeed, if transaction costs were zero, the entire premise of the experiment would disappear, since job search is a positive transaction cost phenomenon (Lindgren, 1990, p. 578). Finally, the presence of stigma and institutional rigidity effects would lead one to predict minimal bargaining over wages and bonuses (in an amount different from the control group), a result again supported by the Illinois experiment. In fact, Ellickson finds the results of the Illinois experiment very consistent with his own study of Shasta County - that people often tend to rely on norms rather than 'legal rules' to govern their behavior, particularly when the stakes are low and there is an expectation of a continuing relationship, as among neighbors in Shasta County and between employers and employees in the Illinois experiment (Ellickson, 1989, pp. 627-628).

8.7 Implications for Other Legal Rules: Tenancy

The two earliest attempts to empirically validate the working of Coase Theorem-type mechanisms in real-world environments were undertaken by Cheung (1969a, 1973), who examined two of the classic illustrations of market failure caused by externalities - share tenancy arrangements in agriculture and the relationship between beekeepers and apple orchard owners. These studies undertake to examine the 'Stigleresque' version of the Theorem, which asserts the efficient internalization of externalities under conditions of perfect competition.

The standard view in the economics and tenancy literatures has long been that share tenancy leads to an inefficient allocation of resources, owing to (i) the short duration of the leases; (ii) the discouragement of effort on the part of the tenant, since a portion of each unit of output must be paid to the landowner as rent; and (iii) the disincentive for either party to make investments in the land that will maximize the land's productivity (see Cheung, 1969a, pp. 3-4, 7-8 and the references cited therein). As a result, one would expect to observe lower crop yields under share tenancy than under alternative cultivation arrangements. However, the Coase Theorem predicts that, if transaction costs are zero and there are well-defined and freely alienable private property rights in land, the allocation of resources will be 'the same whether the landowner cultivates the land himself, hires farm hands to do the tilling, leases his holdings on a fixed rent basis, or shares the actual yield with his tenant. In other words, different [observed] contractual arrangements do not imply different efficiencies of resource use Y' (Cheung, 1969a, p. 4).

An examination of share tenancy in China and Taiwan prior to the land reforms of 1949 shows that there was a well-developed system of private property rights in land in China and Taiwan at this time and that the market by and large comported with the dictates of competition. Furthermore, Cheung did *not* observe lower ratios of labor and other inputs, a lesser degree of improvements, or lower yields on tenant farms than on owner-cultivated farms or on farms employing wage labor, nor is there evidence that the market values of land under tenant cultivation are lower than the values of land under owner cultivation (Cheung, 1969a, pp. 56-61, 1980, p. 42). And, while it has been argued that, under share tenancy, certain types of activities - such as improvements to farms - would be contracted inadequately or not at all, Cheung (1980, p. 43) finds that these 'are precisely the activities stated in every written contract that I could find'. All of this evidence suggests quite strongly that charges that share tenancy is less efficient that other cultivation arrangements cannot easily be sustained.

Even though the theory assumes zero transaction costs where transaction costs are actually positive, it is able to explain 'much of the observed farming behavior' (Cheung, 1969a, p. 159). In this situation of well-defined property rights, transaction costs are not so high as to affect resource use at the margin, but, rather, affect the choice among alternative contractual arrangements - the use of alternative methods of cultivation reflecting the tradeoff between coordination costs and risk, each of which varies across alternative contractual arrangements (Cheung, 1980, p. 44). (For a related discussion, see Cheung, 1969b.) While Cheung's evidence does not conclusively demonstrate the optimality of share contracts, it certainly does lend strong support for the claim that, at a minimum, share contracting is no less efficient than other available contractual arrangements and thus that, under the appropriate (and not unrealistic) conditions, the mechanisms of the Coase Theorem can lead to a satisfactory resolution of externality problems through the market.

The other early study by Cheung of the working of Coase Theorem-type mechanisms is 'The Fable of the Bees ...' (1973), a study which responds to Meade's (1952) classic discussion of the positive reciprocal externalities that exist between beekeepers and the owners of apple orchards: apple blossoms provide valuable services to beekeepers, whose bees feed on them, while, at the same time, bees provide valuable pollination services to the apple-orchard owner. While Meade argued that a system of taxes and subsidies can and must, be imposed in order to achieve efficiency, contractual arrangements between farmers and beekeepers have long been routine in the US and the existence of a market for nectar and for pollination services can be readily observed in the state of Washington, the location of Cheung's study - in some cases merely by consulting the yellow pages of the telephone directory (Cheung, 1973, p. 19). The question, of course, is whether these markets generate an efficient allocation of resources. Cheung (1973, pp. 24-28) argued that a presumption can be established in the affirmative, since available data provides substantial support for the competitive nature of the market.

How is it that in this externality situation the market avoids the failure pointed to by Meade? To begin with, transaction costs are very low here. Since the value of resources devoted to pollination and nectar extraction is insignificant and farmers could easily and cheaply keep bees themselves (and sometimes do so), the gains from contracting with beekeepers are extremely small, which, in turn, suggests that contracting costs are minimal (Cheung, 1980, pp. 46-48). There is also a well-developed system of contractual relations between beekeepers and farmers, so well-developed, in fact, that, while written contracts (sometimes as simple as postcards) are used to secure an initial arrangement among the parties, oral agreements are standard for subsequent relations. Furthermore, these oral contracts are rarely breached, owing to the presence of 'extra-legal constraints' in the form of sanctions against those who do not honor their contracts (Cheung, 1973, p. 29). Yet, in spite of the informality of these contracts, they tend to be quite comprehensive, specifying 'the number and strength of the [bee] colonies, the rental fee per hive, the terms of delivery and removal of hives, the protection of bees from pesticide sprays and the strategic placing of hives'. And, where hives are placed merely for honey-generating purposes (that is, no pollination is involved), prices (often paid in honey) are not necessarily fixed - being allowed to vary with the honey yield (Cheung, 1973, p. 29). All of these various pieces of evidence lead Cheung to conclude that, contrary to Meade's story, 'the allocation of hives and nectar flows approximates that of a smoothly functioning market' wherein resources are efficiently allocated (Cheung, 1980, p. 50).

This having been said, Cheung notes that there are two factors which could potentially complicate these arrangements (relative to standard lease contracts), both of which relate to other levels of external effects. First, there are potential spillovers from one farmer contracting for pollination services, which could potentially lead neighbors to take strategic advantage by employing fewer hives themselves. Second, the use of pesticide sprays by one farmer may result in damage to the bees kept on nearby farms. But both of these issues are dealt with through either custom or explicit contracting (such as the payment of risk premiums for potential exposure to pesticides), depending on the circumstances. The reliance on customs here is an interesting parallel to Ellickson (1986, 1991), discussed above.

It should be obvious that it is not possible to confirm or refute the efficiency claims made by Cheung and, given this, the results cannot be said to show the applicability of the Theorem (here, the Stigler, 1966, version) *per se*. Yet, they offer important evidence that markets can successfully (if not fully efficiently) deal with potential externality problems under the appropriate conditions.

D. Importance

9. The Importance of the Coase Theorem

The importance of the Theorem lies not in whether it is correct, but in the detailed nature of the assumptions required to make it correct-in that is the nature of transactions costs. The interesting question about the Theorem then is the nature of the transactions costs associated with those situations in which the theorem is thought to not be correct. The legacy of the Theorem lies in the subsequent work attempting to detail the nature of transaction costs and their effect on the workings of the economic system. The richness and variety of types of economic arrangements can now be seen in the richness and variety of transaction costs and in mechanisms for reducing them.

In this sense the importance of the Coase Theorem lies not in its supposed correctness or incorrectness and the corresponding policy relevance or lack thereof, but, rather, in the positive transactions cost propositions that flow from it. These include both normative and positive propositions. Examples are Posner's (1992, p. 52) normative suggestion that at law '[s]ince transactions are never costless in the real world, efficiency is promoted by assigning the legal right to the party who would buy it ... if it were assigned initially to the other party' and the positive prediction of Lesser, Dobbs and Zerbe (1997) that suits at law in situations where negotiation costs are low will involve considerations of distribution not efficiency.

The Coase Theorem has helped to give rise to an extensive body of work, much of it summarized by Eggertsson (1990), concerned with economic behavior and institutions and to a more detailed and useful sense of what is meant by property. The Coase Theorem has made clearer the relationship between transactions cost and property rights and in doing so has begun to give a much stronger basis for understanding how legal regimes change in response to changes in constraints (North, 1981). One can now define the strength of property rights in terms of lower transaction costs for the exclusion, exchange and use of property.

In part of the economics literature at least (Eggertsson, 1990) the transactions cost approach has replaced the market failure model of public intervention that is expressed by Weimer and Vining (1992, p. 30):

> When is it legitimate for government to intervene in private affairs? In the United States, the normative answer to this question has usually been based on the concept of *market failure* - a circumstance where the pursuit of private interest does not lead to an efficient use of society's resources or a fair distribution of society's goods.

When the costs of transaction mechanisms are introduced there are departures from perfect markets. These departures are in fact externalities because they represent effects not taken into account in the decision making process. Externalities, then, are found everywhere there are transaction costs and are ubiquitous. Since the concept of market failure rests on externalities that are defined by transactions costs, the concept of market failure (and the concept of externality) does no work for us that is not already done by transaction costs (Zerbe and McCurdy, 1996). Externalities are in fact an unnecessary complication in the theory of government intervention.

Public goods represent a useful example of a situation in which the market failure model can be and to some extent is being, replaced by a transaction cost model. The older market failure approach is represented by Samuelson (1954), who saw public goods as a class of market failures. For example, in writing about the classic case of the lighthouse, Samuelson (1964, p. 45) writes:

> Here is a later example of government service: lighthouses. These save lives and cargoes; but lighthouse keepers cannot reach out to collect fees from skippers. So, says the advanced treatise, 'we have a divergence between private advantage and money cost ... and true social advantage and cost ... Philosophers and statesmen have always recognized the necessary role of government in such cases of 'external-economy divergence between private and social advantage'.

The transaction cost-property rights approach appears to provide a richer vehicle of analysis, as shown by Cheung, North and others. For example, Coase (1974a) shows that the British lighthouse system was once a well-functioning private system and that, in general, the system was more complex than that suggested by the simplistic market failure diagnostic.

The triumph of the transaction cost approach shows that the true legacy of the Coase Theorem lies not in its correctness, but in drawing attention to the role played by transaction costs within the economic system.

10. Conclusion

In light of the foregoing discussion, three things can be said about the Coase Theorem. First, it is correct, in the sense that it has withstood all of the challenges mounted against it to date. Efficiency will obtain, regardless of the initial assignment of rights and the result will be invariant keeping in mind that even income effects are irrelevant if one accepts the Barzel/Allen definition of zero transaction costs. Second, the Theorem, although correct, is unrealistic, as Coase recognized (see Coase 1960, p. 15, 1981, p. 187, 1988a, pp. 174-179). The latter point, of course, should have been obvious from the beginning, which raises the question as to why the debate over the Theorem has been so intense. A small part of the answer, within the economics profession at least, may lie in the interesting theoretical puzzle that the Theorem poses. Dwarfing this, however, is the normative debate that, implicitly or explicitly, pervades nearly all aspects of the Theorem's discussion.

Three prescriptions for legal-economic policy are said to flow from the Coase Theorem.

1. Rights-*cum*-market solutions are said to be preferable to Pigouvian remedies for the resolution of externality problems.
2. Property and contract are efficient; any interference with the outcomes so generated will make matters worse rather than better. It is this implication that makes the Coase Theorem, in the minds of some, 'the cornerstone of a laissez-faire legal and economic policy regarding contract and property law' (Hoffman and Spitzer, 1986, p. 151).
3. When transaction costs are positive, rights should be assigned to those who would possess them in the end-state if transaction costs were zero, as seen in the prescriptions of wealth maximization, or 'mimic the market'.

But the Coase Theorem says none of these things. The Theorem is a positive statement with no normative implications; it is an 'is' statement, not an 'ought' statement. Each of the above propositions rests on the assumption that efficiency is the goal of legal-economic policy. But the Coase Theorem goes merely to the presence of absence of efficiency; it does not tell us that it is all that matters or even that it matters at all. It is this normative leap that seems to underlie most of the hostility to the Coase Theorem - and, by extension, to law and economics generally. (See, for example, Baker, 1975; Kelman, 1979; the *Symposium on Efficiency as a Legal Concern, 1980*; *A Response to the Efficiency Symposium, 1980*; Schlag, 1986; Gjerdingen, 1986; Johnston, 1990 and Crespi, 1991.) For a response to these types of criticisms see Zerbe (1998a). Compounding the hostility to the normative use of the Coase Theorem are the use of incorrect definitions of economic efficiency by proponents of law and economics (Zerbe, 1998b).

Furthermore, even if one takes efficiency to be the goal of legal-economic policy, the Coase Theorem does nothing to establish the sanctity of property and contract or the superiority of the market over Pigouvian remedies, owing to the ubiquitous nature of transaction costs. If coordination is costless, the market will optimally allocate rights and resources, but so too will Pigouvian remedies. On the other hand, the Pigouvians fare no better in this debate since, after waving away the Coase Theorem on the grounds that transaction costs are positive, they tend to immediately fall back on the demonstration that Pigouvian remedies generate socially optimal outcomes, using models in which government is assumed to operate with full information and without cost. (But see Baumol, 1972, for a more judicious evaluation of Pigouvian remedies.)

Here, we come to the true import of the Coase Theorem. The Theorem is not, in the end, about markets or about costless bargaining; rather, it is about the costs of coordination. If coordination is costless, markets function perfectly; but so does government. If coordination is costly, markets function imperfectly; but so does government. The task for legal-economic policy thus becomes that of ascertaining the magnitude and influence of these costs and the resulting implications for alternative institutional-policy arrangements. The true and valuable legacy of the Theorem is all of the subsequent work on transactions costs that explore the costs of coordination under different regimes and in different situations. Like the Coase Theorem itself, this, too, is without direct normative implications. However, it has led to certain normative claims, as noted above. One, from an analytical perspective, is that the received conception of externalities should be abandoned. Another, this time from a policy perspective, is that judgments as to the appropriate form of government intervention should be made on the basis of what institutional arrangement produces the lowest combination of coordination costs. In this regard, it is interesting to note that much of the normative debate and the propositions we noted above in that regard can be turned into a series of positive predictions about which arrangements will promote economic efficiency. Where the affected parties could reach a solution through negotiation but choose litigation or regulation, the real issue is likely to be who is to be assigned property rights rather than how to realize gains from trade (see, for example, Lesser, Dobbs and Zerbe, 1997).

Finally, the meaningfulness of the Coase Theorem must be understood in epistemological terms. The 'correctness' of the Theorem is a matter of logical validity; in general, the Theorem is a conclusion derived from premises and the role of the assumptions constituting its premises is to rule out of consideration all those variables which would prevent the derivation of the conclusion as a matter of logic. The validity of the Theorem, therefore, is a function of the assumptions defining away certain limiting conditions. The empirical truth of the Theorem - its descriptive accuracy - is a separate matter from its logical validity. The Theorem considered empirically is a tendency statement, a statement that under certain conditions such and such behavior and allocative and so on results can be expected; that is, a law in the Marshallian sense. However, the logical and empirical aspects are closely related to one another in that changing the assumptional conditions of the Theorem is tantamount to changing the conditions in terms of which the Theorem is a tendency statement. The Theorem is a tendency or probability statement in a further empirical sense, to wit: the experimental literature indicates that the results expected on the basis of certain specifications of the Theorem are realized something less than one hundred percent of the time.

Given the foregoing, it becomes clear that much of the literature on the Coase Theorem not only overreaches in terms of the normative implications more or less improperly drawn from the Theorem, but fails to specify the meaningfulness of the Theorem in such terms - readily leading to practices which make claims for and take the Theorem far beyond what logicality and empiricism permit.

Acknowledgments

The authors would like to thank Douglas Allen, James Buchanan, Robert Cooter, Robert Ellickson, Elizabeth Hoffman, Richard Posner, Warren Samuels and participants in the Workshop in the History of Economic Thought and Methodology at Michigan State University for comments and suggestions on previous drafts of this chapter and for helping to clarify our thinking on certain points raised herein. The excellent research assistance of Mary Therese Cogeos is also gratefully acknowledged. Of course, the authors are solely responsible for any remaining errors.

Bibliography on The Coase Theorem (0730)

Aivazian, Varouj A. and Callen, Jeffrey L. (1980), 'Uncertain Externalities, Liability Rules and Resource Allocation: Comment', **70** *American Economic Review*, 1058-1059.

Aivazian, Varouj A. and Callen, Jeffrey L. (1981), 'The Coase Theorem and the Empty Core', **24** *Journal of Law and Economics*, 175-181.

Aivazian, Varouj A., Callen, Jeffrey L. and Lipnowski, Irwin F. (1987), 'The Coase Theorem and Coalitional Stability', **54** *Economica*, 517-520.

Allen, Douglas W. (1991), 'What are Transaction Costs?', **14** *Research in Law and Economics*, 1-18.

Allen, Douglas W. (1992), 'Marriage and Divorce: Comment', **82** *American Economic Review*, 679-685.

Allen, Douglas W. (1995), 'Property Rights, Transaction Costs and Coase: One More Time', in Medema, Steven G. (ed.), *Coasean Economics*, Boston, Kluwer Academic Publishers.

Arrow, Kenneth J. (1969), 'The Organization of Economic Activity: Issues Pertinent to the Choice of Market versus Nonmarket Allocation', in X (ed.), Joint Economic Committee, 91st Congress of the United States, 1st Session.

Arrow, Kenneth J. (1979), 'The Property Rights Doctrine and Demand Revelation under Incomplete Information', in Boskin, Michael J. (ed.), *Economics and Human Welfare: Essays in Honor of Tibor Scitovsky*, New York, Academic Press, 23-39.

Ayres, Ian and Talley, Eric (1995a), 'Distinguishing Between Consensual and Nonconsensual Advantages of Liability Rules', **105** *Yale Law Journal*, 235-253.

Ayres, Ian and Talley, Eric (1995b), 'Solomonic Bargaining: Dividing a Legal Entitlement to Facilitate Coasean Trade', **104** *Yale Law Journal*, 1027-1117.

Azqueta, Diego (1993), 'The Coase Theorem and Environmental Economics: A Survey of Some Unsettled Issues', **10** *Revista Española de Economia*, 59-71.

Baker, C. Edwin (1975), 'The Ideology of the Economic Analysis of Law', **5** *Philosophy and Public Affairs*, 3-48.

Barzel, Yoram (1989), *Economic Analysis of Property Rights*, Cambridge, Cambridge University Press, 122 p.

Baumol, William J. (1972), 'On Taxation and the Control of Externalities', **62** *American Economic Review*, 307-322.

Besen, Stanley M., Manning, Willard G., Jr and Mitchell, Bridger M. (1978), 'Copyright Liability for Cable Television: Compulsory Licensing and the Coase Theorem', **21** *Journal of Law and Economics*, 67-95.

Bigelow, John Payne (1993), 'Inducing Efficiency: Externalities, Missing Markets and the Coase Theorem', **34** *International Economic Review*, 335-346.

Boettke, Peter J. (1989), 'Information and the Coase Theorem: Comment', **3** *Journal of Economic Perspectives*, 195-198.

Boitani, Andrea and Grillo, Michele (1992), 'Some Reflections on Externalities, Coase Theorem and the Endogenous Determination of Property Rights', **43** *Metroeconomica*, 309-326.

Boyd, J.H. and Mohring, H. (1971), 'Externalities: 'Direct Interaction' vs. 'Asset Utilization' Frameworks', **38** *Economica*, 347-361.

Bramhall, David F. and Mills, Edwin S. (1966), 'A Note on the Asymmetry Between Fees and Payments', **2** *Water Resources Research*, 615-616.

Brinig, Margaret F. and Buckley, Francis H. (1995), *Divorce, Legal Rules and Free Spirits*, Mimeo, George Mason University School of Law.

Buchanan, James M. (1973a), 'The Institutional Structure of Externality', **28** *Public Choice*, 69-82.

Buchanan, James M. (1973b), 'The Coase Theorem and the Theory of the State', **13** *Natural Resources Journal*, 579-594.

Buchanan, James M. (1983), 'Rights, Efficiency and Exchange: The Irrelevance of Transaction Costs', in Neumann, M. (ed.), *Ansprache, Eigentums- und Verfagüngsrechte, Schriften des Vereins far Socialpolitik*, Berlin, Duncker and Humblot, 9-24. Reprinted in *Liberty, Market and State*, Harvester Press, 1986, 97-107. Reprinted in Medema, S.G. (ed.) (1995), *The Legacy of Ronald Coase in Economic Analysis*, Volume II, Chapter 8, 175-190, Aldershot: Edward Elgar.

Buchanan, James M. and Faith, Roger L. (1981), 'Entrepreneurship and the Internalization of Externalities', **24** *Journal of Law and Economics*, 95-111.

Buchanan, James M. and Stubblebine, W. Craig (1962), 'Externality', **29** *Economica*, 371-384.

Burrows, Paul (1970), 'On External Costs and the Visible Arm of Law', **22** *Oxford Economic Papers*, 39-56.

Calabresi, Guido (1965), 'The Decision for Accidents: An Approach to Non-Fault Allocation for Costs', **78** *Harvard Law Review*, 713-745.

Calabresi, Guido (1968), 'Transaction Costs, Resource Allocation and Liability Rules: A Comment', **11** *Journal of Law and Economics*, 67-73.

Calabresi, Guido (1991), 'The Pointlessness of Pareto: Carrying Coase Further', **100** *Yale Law Journal*, 1211-1237.

Calabresi, Guido and Melamed, A. Douglas (1972), 'Property Rules, Liability Rules and Inalienability: One View of the Cathedral', **85** *Harvard Law Review*, 1089-1128. Reprinted in Ackerman, Bruce A. (ed.), *Economic Foundations of Property Law*, Boston, Little Brown, 1975, 31-48.

Campbell, David (1996), 'On What is Valuable in Law and Economics', **8** *Otago Law Review*, 489-514.

Canterbery, E. Ray and Marvasti, A. (1992), 'The Coase Theorem as a Negative Externality', **26** *Journal of Economic Issues*, 1179-1189.

Chapman, Bruce (1982), 'Individual Rights and Collective Rationality: Some Implications for Economic Analysis of Law', **10** *Hofstra Law Review*, 455-481.

Chari, V. and Jones, L.R. (1991), 'A Reconsideration of the Problem of Social Cost: Free Riders and Monopolists', **July**, *Federal Reserve Bank of Minneapolis Staff Report*, 59 ff.

Cheung, Steven N.S. (1969a), *The Theory of Share Tenancy*, Chicago, IL, University of Chicago Press, 188 p.

Cheung, Steven N.S. (1969b), 'Transaction Costs, Risk Aversion and the Choice of Contractual Arrangements', **12** *Journal of Law and Economics*, 23-42.

Cheung, Steven N.S. (1970), 'The Structure of a Contract and the Theory of a Non-exclusive Resource', **13** *Journal of Law and Economics*, 49-70.

Cheung, Steven N.S. (1973), 'The Fable of the Bees: An Economic Investigation', **16** *Journal of Law and Economics*, 11-33.

Cheung, Steven N.S. (1974), 'A Theory of Price Control', **17** *Journal of Law and Economics*, 53-71.

Cheung, Steven N.S. (1978), *The Myth of Social Costs: A Critique of Welfare Economics and the Implications for Public Policy*, London, Institute of Economic Affairs, 93 p.

Cheung, Steven N.S. (1980), *The Myth of Social Cost*, San Francisco, Cato Institute.

Cheung, Steven N.S. (1983), 'The Contractual Nature of the Firm', **26** *Journal of Law and Economics*, 1-21.

Cheung, Steven N.S. (1992), 'On the New Institutional Economics', in Werin, Lars and Wijkander, Hans (eds), *Contract Economics*, Oxford, Basil Blackwell, 48-65.

Coase, Ronald H. (1937), 'The Nature of the Firm', **4** *Economica*, 368-405.

Coase, Ronald H. (1959), 'The Federal Communications Commission', **2** *Journal of Law and Economics*, 1-40.

Coase, Ronald H. (1960), 'The Problem of Social Cost', **3** *Journal of Law and Economics*, 1-44. Reprinted in Ackermann, Bruce A. (1975), *Economic Foundations of Property Law*, Boston, Little Brown, 17-22. Reprinted in Medema, Steven G. (1995), *The Legacy of Ronald Coase in Economic Analysis*, Vol. 2, Aldershot, Edward Elgar Publishing, 5-48. Reprinted in Coase, Ronald H. (1988), *The Firm, the Market and the Law*, Chicago, University of Chicago Press.

Coase, Ronald H. (1974a), 'The Lighthouse in Economics', **23** *Journal of Law and Economics*, 357-376.

Coase, Ronald H. (1974b), 'The Choice of the Institutional Framework: A Comment', **17** *Journal of Law and Economics*, 493-496.

Coase, Ronald H. (1981), 'The Coase Theorem and the Empty Core: A Comment', **24** *Journal of Law and Economics*, 183-187.

Coase, Ronald H. (1988a), *The Firm, the Market and the Law*, Chicago, IL, University of Chicago Press, 217 p.

Coase, Ronald H. (1988b), 'Blackmail' (The 1987 McCorkle Lecture), **74** *Virginia Law Review*, 655-676.

Coase, Ronald H. (1991), 'The Institutional Structure of Production', in Coase, Ronald H. (ed.), *Essays on Economics and Economists*, Chicago, IL, University of Chicago Press.

Coase, Ronald H. (1993), 'Law and Economics at Chicago', **36** *Journal of Law and Economics*, 239-254.

Coelho, Philip R.P. (1975), 'Externalities, Separability and Resource Allocation: Comment', **65** *American Economic Review*, 721-723.

Cohen, David and Knetsch, Jack (1992), 'Judicial Choice and Disparities Between Measures of Economic Values', **30** *Osgoode Hall Law Journal*, 131 ff.

Cooter, Robert D. (1980), 'How the Law Circumvents Starret's Nonconvexity', **22** *Journal of Economic Theory*, 499-504.

Cooter, Robert D. (1982), 'The Cost of Coase', **11** *Journal of Legal Studies*, 1-33. Reprinted in Donahue, Charles Jr, Kauper, Thomas E. and Martin, Peter W. (eds) (1992), *Property: An Introduction to the Concept and the Institution*. Reprinted in Ackerman, Bruce, Ellickson, Robert and Rose, Carol (eds) (1995), *Foundations of Property Law*. Reprinted in Medema, Steven G. (ed.) (1995), *The Legacy of Ronald Coase in Economic Analysis*, Aldershot, Edward Elgar Publishing, 96-128.

Cooter, Robert D. (1987), 'The Coase Theorem', in Eatwell, John, Milgate, Murray and Newman, Peter (eds), *The New Palgrave: A Dictionary of Economics*, London, Macmillan, 457-460. Reprinted in *The New Palgrave World of Economics* (forthcoming).

Cooter, Robert D. (1989), 'The Coase Theorem', in Eatwell, John, Milgate, Murray and Newman, Peter (eds), *The New Palgrave: Allocation, Information and Markets*, New York, W.W. Norton, 64-70.

Cooter, Robert D. and Ulen, Thomas S. (1988), *Law and Economics*, Glenview, IL, Scott, Foresman and Company.

Cooter, Robert D., Marks, Stephen and Mnookin, Robert H. (1982), 'Bargaining in the Shadow of the Law: A Testable Model of Strategic Behavior', **11** *Journal of Legal Studies*, 225-251.

Cotter, Thomas F. (1995), 'Owning What Doesn't Exist, Where it Doesn't Exist: Rethinking Two Doctrines from the Common Law of Trademarks', **3** *University of Illinois Law Review*, 487-541.

Cotter, Thomas F. (1996), 'Legal Pragmatism and the Law and Economics Movement', **84** *Georgetown Law Journal*, 2071-2141.

Coursey, Don L. and Stanley, L.R. (1988), 'Pretrial Bargaining Behavior within the Shadow of the Law: Theory and Experimental Evidence', **8** *International Review of Law and Economics*, 161-179.

Coursey, Don L., Hoffman, Elizabeth and Spitzer, Matthew L. (1987), 'Fear and Loathing in the Coase Theorem: Experimental Tests Involving Physical Discomfort', **16** *Journal of Legal Studies*, 217-248.

Crain, W. Mark, Saurman, David S. and Tollison, Robert D. (1978), 'The Coase Theorem and Quasi Rents: Correcting the Record', **6** *Public Finance Quarterly*, 259-262.

Crespi, Gregory Scott (1991), 'The Mid-Life Crisis of the Law and Economics Movement: Confronting the Problems of Nonfalsifiability and Normative Bias', **67** *Notre Dame Law Review*, 231-252.

d'Arge, Ralph C. (1973), 'Coase Theorem Symposium', **13** *Natural Resources Journal*, 557-560.

Dahlman, Carl J. (1979), 'The Problem of Externality', **22** *Journal of Law and Economics*, 141-162.

Daly, George (1974), 'The Coase Theorem: Assumptions, Applications and Ambiguities', **12** *Economic Inquiry*, 203-213.

Daly, George and Giertz, J. Fred (1975), 'Externalities, Extortion and Efficiency', **65** *American Economic Review*, 997-1001.

Davis, Otto A. and Whinston Andrew B. (1962), 'Externalities, Welfare and the Theory of Games', **70** *Journal of Political Economy*, 241-262.

Davis, Otto A. and Whinston Andrew B. (1965), 'Some Notes on Equating Private and Social Cost', **32** *Southern Economic Journal*, 113-126.

De Bornier, Jean Magnan (1986), 'The Coase Theorem and the Empty Core: A Re-examination', **6** *International Review of Law and Economics*, 265-271.

Demsetz, Harold (1971), 'Theoretical Efficiency in Pollution Control: Comments on Comments', **9** *Western Economic Journal*, 444-446.

Demsetz, Harold (1972a), 'When Does the Rule of Liability Matter?', **1** *Journal of Legal Studies*, 13-28.

Demsetz, Harold (1972b), 'Wealth Distribution and the Ownership of Rights', **1** *Journal of Legal Studies*, 223-232.

Demsetz, Harold (1978), 'On Extortion: A Reply', **68** *American Economic Review*, 417-418.

DeSerpa, Allan C. (1977), 'The Coase Theorem: A Diagrammatic Presentation', **15** *Economic Inquiry*, 600-604.

DeSerpa, Allan C. (1992), 'The Pure Economics of the Coase Theorem', **18** *Eastern Economic Journal*, 287-304.

Dick, Daniel T. (1976), 'The Voluntary Approach to Externality Problems: A Survey of the Critics', **2** *Journal of Environmental Economics and Management*, 185-195.

Dolbear, F. Trenery, Jr (1967), 'On the Theory of Optimum Externality', **57** *American Economic Review*, 90-103.

Dolbear, F. Trenery, Jr (1974), 'Externalities as Commodities: Comment', **64** *American Economic Review*, 341-343.

Donohue, John J. III (1988), 'Law and Economics: The Road not Taken', **22** *Law and Society Review*, 903-926.

Donohue, John J. III (1989a), 'Diverting the Coasian River: Incentive Schemes to Reduce Unemployment Spells', **99** *Yale Law Journal*, 549-609.

Donohue, John J. III (1989b), 'Reply to Professors Ellickson and Stigler', **99** *Yale Law Journal*, 635-636.

Eggertsson, Thrainn (1990), *Economic Behaviour and Institutions*, Cambridge, Cambridge University Press, 385 p.

Ellickson, Robert C. (1986), 'Of Coase and Cattle: Dispute Resolution among Neighbors in Shasta County', **38** *Stanford Law Review*, 623-687. Reprinted in **18** *Land Use and Environment Law Review*, 1987, 79-143.

Ellickson, Robert C. (1989), 'The Case for Coase and Against "Coaseanism"', **99** *Yale Law Journal*, 611-630.

Ellickson, Robert C. (1991), *Order Without Law: How Neighbors Settle Disputes*, Cambridge, MA, Harvard University Press.

Endres, Alfred (1976), 'Das Coase-Theorem bei langfristiger Betrachtung (The Coase Theorem in a Long Term Perspective)', **27** *Jahrbuch für Sozialwissenschaft*, 430-433.

Endres, Alfred (1977), 'Die Coase-Kontroverse (The Coase Controversy)', **133** *Journal of Institutional and Theoretical Economics*, 637-651.

Farrell, Joseph (1987), 'Information and the Coase Theorem', **1** *Journal of Economic Perspectives*, 113-129.

Farrell, Joseph (1990), 'Information and the Coase Theorem', in Baker, Samuel H. and Elliot, Catherine S. (eds), *Readings in public Sector Economics*, Lexington, MA and Toronto, D.C., Heath and Company, 165-174.

Faure, Michael G. (1986), 'Commentaar bij de Paper van Dr.Jan C. Bongaerts: Coase en Produktenaansprakelijkheid (Comment on the paper of Dr. Jan C. Bongaerts: Coase and Product Liability)', in Van Den Bergh, Roger (ed.), *Verslagboek Eerste Werkvergadering Recht en Economie*, Antwerpen, Handelshogeschool, 31-37.

Feldman, Robert (1974), 'Liability Rules and the Transfer of Economic Rents', **3** *Journal of Legal Studies*, 499-508.

Fischel, William A. (1978), 'A Property Rights Approach to Municipal Zoning', **54** *Land Economics*, 54-81. Reprinted in Beaton, Patrick W. (ed.) (1983), *Municipal Expenditures, Revenues and Services*, New Brunswick, Rutgers University Center for Urban Policy Research.

Fischel, William A. (1985), *The Economics of Zoning Laws: A Property Rights Approach to American Land Use Controls*, Baltimore, MD, John Hopkins University Press, 372 p.

Fischer, Stanley (1977), 'Long Term Contracting, Sticky Prices and Monetary Policy', **3** *Journal of Monetary Economics*, 317-323.

Frank, Robert H. (1991), *Microeconomics and Behavior*, New York, London, Montreal and Sydney, McGraw Hill, 694 p.

Frech, H. Edward III (1973), 'Pricing of Pollution: The Coase Theorem in the Long Run', **4** *Bell Journal of Economics and Management Science*, 316-319.

Frech, H. Edward III (1973), 'Biological Externalities and Evolution: A Comment', **39** *Journal of Theoretical Biology*, 669-672.

Frech, H. Edward III (1979), 'The Extended Coase Theorem and Long Run Equilibrium: The Non-Equivalence of Liability Rules and Property Rights', **27** *Economic Inquiry*, 254-268.

Frey, Bruno S. (1993), 'Review of: Environment and Economy: Property Rights and Public Policy', **31** *Journal of Economic Literature*, 1442-1443.

Friedberg, Leora (1995), 'Did No-Fault Divorce Raise Divorce Rates? Evidence from Panel Data', Working Paper, Massachusetts Institute of Technology.

Furubotn, Eirik G. (1995), 'Income Transfers, Entrepreneurial Effort and the Coase Theorem: The Case for Efficiency Reconsidered', **2** *European Journal of Law and Economics*, 99-118.

Ghosh, Shubha (1997), 'Takings, the Exit Option and Just Compensation', **17** *International Review of Law and Economics*, 157-176.

Gifford, Adam, Jr (1974), 'Externalities and the Coase Theorem: A Graphical Analysis', **14** *Quarterly Review of Economics and Business*, 7-21.

Gifford, Adam, Jr (1975), 'Externalities, Liability, Separability and Resource Allocation: Comment', **65** *American Economic Review*, 724-727.

Gifford, Adam, Jr and Stone, Courtney C. (1973), 'Externalities, Liability and the Coase Theorem: A Mathematical Analysis', **11** *Western Economic Journal*, 260-269.

Gjerdingen, Donald H. (1983), 'The Coase Theorem and the Psychology of Common Law Thought', **56** *Southern California Law Review*, 711-760.

Gjerdingen, Donald H. (1986), 'The Politics of the Coase Theorem and its Relationship to Modern Legal Thought', **35** *Buffalo Law Review*, 871-935.

Glanter, Marc (1983), 'Reading the Landscape of Disputes: What we Know and Don't Know (and Think we Don't Know) about Our Allegedly Contentious and Litigious Society', **31** *UCLA Law Review*, 4-71.

Goldberg, Victor P. (1974), 'Institutional Change and the Quasi-Invisible Hand', **17** *Journal of Law and Economics*, 461-492. Reprinted in Goldberg, Victor P. (ed.) (1989), *Readings in the Economics of Contract Law*, Cambridge, Cambridge University Press, 169-173.

Gould, J.R. (1973), 'Meade on External Economies: Should the Beneficiaries be Taxed?', **16** *Journal of Law and Economics*, 53-66.

Gould, J.R. (1975), 'Mohring and Boyd's Objection to the Coase Theorem: A Note', **42** *Economica*, 203-206.

Grady, Mark F. (1988), 'Common Law Control of Strategic Behavior: The Railroad and the Farmer', **17** *Journal of Legal Studies*, 15-42.

Greenwood, Peter H. and Ingene, Charles A. (1978), 'Uncertain Externalities, Liability Rules and Resources Allocation', **68** *American Economic Review*, 300-310.

Greenwood, Peter H. and Ingene, Charles A. (1980), 'Reply', **70** *American Economic Review*, 1060-1063.

Greenwood, Peter H., Ingene, Charles A. and Horsfied, James (1975), 'Externalities, Separability and Resource Allocation', **65** *American Economic Review*, 728-729.

Guellec, Dominique (1995), 'Externalites et Asymetries d'Information dans un Modele de Croissance (With English summary) (Externalities and Information Asymmetry in a Model of Growth)', **46(3)** *Revue Economique*, 837-846.

Hamilton, Jonathan H., Sheshinski, Eytan and Slutsky, Steven M. (1989), 'Production Externalities and Long-run Equilibria: Bargaining and Pigovian Taxation', **27** *Economic Inquiry*, 453-471.

Hanemann, W. Michael (1991), 'Willingness to Pay and Willingness to Accept: How Much Can They Differ?', **81** *American Economic Review*, 635-647.

Hanley, Nick and Sumner, Charles (1995), 'Bargaining Over Common Property Resources: Applying the Coase Theorem to Red Deer in the Scottish Highlands', **43** *Journal of Environmental Management*, 87-95.

Hansmann, Henry B. (1977), 'The Coase Proposition, Information Constraints and Long-Run Equilibrium: Comment', **67** *American Economic Review*, 459-461.

Harris, Frederick H. (1990), 'Economic Negligence, Moral Hazard and the Coase Theorem', **56(3)** *Southern Economic Journal*, 698-704.

Harrison, Glenn W. and McKee, Michael (1985), 'Experimental Evaluation of the Coase Theorem', **28** *Journal of Law and Economics*, 653-670.

Harrison, Glenn W., Hoffman, Elizabeth, Rustrom, E.E. and Spitzer, Matthew L. (1987), 'Coasian Solutions to the Externality Problem in Experimental Markets', **97** *Economic Journal*, 388-402.

Hatzis, Aristides N. (1991), 'Ronald H. Coase: Nobel Oikonomikon 1991', **68** *Epikentra*, 77-84.

Head, John G. (1974), 'Public Policies and Pollution Problems', **33** *Finanzarchiv*, 1-29.

Hellner, Jan (1978), 'Rättsekonomi, avbeställning och Coase-teorem (Law and Economics, Cancellation and Coase Theorem)', **24** *Juridiska Föreningen i Lund*, 101 p.

Hoffman, Elizabeth and Spitzer, Matthew L. (1982), 'The Coase Theorem: Some Experimental Tests', **25** *Journal of Law and Economics*, 73-98.

Hoffman, Elizabeth and Spitzer, Matthew L. (1985), 'Entitlements, Rights and Fairness: An Experimental Examination of Subjects' Concepts of Distributive Justice', **14** *Journal of Legal Studies*, 259-297.

Hoffman, Elizabeth and Spitzer, Matthew L. (1986), 'Experimental Tests of the Coase Theorem with Large Bargaining Groups', **15** *Journal of Legal Studies*, 149-171.

Hoffman, Elizabeth and Spitzer, Matthew L. (1993), 'Willingness to Pay vs. Willingness to Accept: Legal and Economic Implications', **71** *Washington University Law Quarterly*, 59-114.

Hoffman, Philip T. (1989), 'Institutions and Agriculture in Old Regime France', **145** *Journal of Institutional and Theoretical Economics*, 166-181.

Holderness, Clifford G. (1989), 'The Assignment of Rights, Entry Effects and the Allocation of Resources', **18** *Journal of Legal Studies*, 181-189.

Homa, M. (1974), 'Tentative Note on Liability Rules under the Coase System', **24** *Osaka Economic Papers*, 86-97.

Hovenkamp, Herbert J. (1990), 'Marginal Utility and the Coase Theorem', **75** *Cornell Law Review*, 783-810.

Hsiung, Bingyuang (1993), 'The Scale of the Market and the Scale of the Heart: Reconciling Coase and Buchanan on the Coase Theorem (In Chinese, with English summary)', **21** *Academia Economic Papers*, 331-356.

Illing, Gerhard (1992), 'Private Information as Transaction Costs: The Coase Theorem Revisited', **148** *Journal of Institutional and Theoretical Economics*, 558-576.

Inada, Ken I. and Kuga, Kigoshi (1973), 'Limitations of the " Coase Theorem " on Liability Rules', **6** *Journal of Economic Theory*, 606-613.

Jaffe, Jeffrey F. (1975), The "Coase Theorem": A Reexamination Comment', **89** *Quarterly Journal of Economics*, 660-661.

Johansen, L. (1979), 'The Bargaining Society and the Inefficiency of Bargaining', **32** *Kyklos*, 497-521.

Johnson, David B. (1973), 'Meade, Bees and Externalities', **16** *Journal of Law and Economics*, 35-52.

Johnston, Jason Scott (1990), 'Law, Economics and Post-Realist Explanation', **24** *Law and Society Review*, 1217-1254.

Jung, Chulho et al. (1995), 'The Coase Theorem in a Rent Seeking Society', **15** *International Review of Law and Economics*, 259-268.

Kahneman, Daniel and Tversky, Amos (1979), 'Prospect Theory: An Analysis of Decision Under Risk', **47** *Econometrica*, 263-291.

Kahneman, Daniel, Knetsch, Jack L. and Thaler, Richard H. (1990), 'Experimental Tests of the Endowment Effect and the Coase Theorem', **98** *Journal of Political Economy*, 1325-1348. Reprinted in Thaler, Richard H. (ed.) (1991), *Quasi Rational Economics*, New York, Russell Sage Foundation, 167-188.

Kamien, M.I., Schwartz, Nancy L. and Dolbear, F. Trenery, Jr (1966), 'Asymmetry Between Bribes and Charges', **2** *Water Resources Research*, 147-157.

Kaplow, Louis and Shavell, Steven (1995), 'Do Liability Rules Facilitate Bargaining? A Reply to Ayres and Talley', **105** *Yale Law Journal*, 221-233.

Kaplow, Louis and Shavell, Steven (1996), 'Property Rules versus Liability Rules: An Economic Analysis', **109** *Harvard Law Review*, 713-790.

Kelman, Mark G. (1979), 'Consumption Theory, Production Theory and Ideology in the Coase Theorem', **52** *Southern California Law Review*, 669-698.

Kelman, Mark G. (1980), 'Spitzer and Hoffman on Coase: A Brief Rejoinder', **53** *Southern California Law Review*, 1215-1223.

Kelman, Mark G. (1985), 'Comment (on Hoffman and Spitzer's Experimental Law and Economics)', **85** *Columbia Law Review*, 1037-1047.

Kessel, Reuben A. (1974), 'Transfused Blood, Serum Hepatitis and the Coase Theorem', **17** *Journal of Law and Economics*, 265-289.

Kneese, Allan V. and Maller, Koran G. (1973), 'Bribes and Charges in Pollution Control: An Aspect of the Coase Controversy', **13** *Natural Resources Journal*, 677-704.

Labus Miroljub (1995), *Osnovi Ekonomije: Savremene Teorije i Primena* (Foundation Economics: Contemporary Theories and Application), Jugoslovenska knjiga, Belgrade.

Ledebut, L.C. (1967), 'The Problem of Social Cost', **26** *American Journal of Economics and Sociology*, 399-415.

Lesser, Jonathan A., Dobbs, Daniel and Zerbe, Richard O., Jr (1997), *Environmental Economics*, Boston, Addison Wesley.

Levy, Daniel S. and Friedman, David D. (1994), 'The Revenge of the Redwoods? Reconsidering Property Rights and the Economic Allocation of Natural Resources', **61** *University of Chicago Law Review*, 493-526.

Liebermann, Yehoshua (1981), 'The Coase Theorem in Jewish Law', **10** *Journal of Legal Studies*, 293-303.

Liebhafsky, Harold H. (1973), 'The Problem of Social Cost: An Alternative Approach', **13** *Natural Resources Journal*, 615-676.

Lindgren, James (1989), 'Blackmail: On Waste, Morals and Ronald Coase', **36** *UCLA Law Review*, 597-608.

Lindgren, James (1990), ' "Ol' Man River, ... He Keeps on Rollin' Along": A Reply to Donohue's Diverting the Coasean River', **78** *Georgetown Law Journal*, 577-591.

Littlechild, Stephen C. (1978), 'The Problem of Social Cost', in Spadaro, Louis M. (ed.), *New Directions in Austrian Economics*, Kansas City, Sheed. Andres & McMeel, 77-93.

Macey, Jonathan R. (1988), 'Transaction Costs and the Normative Elements of the Public Choice Model: An Application to Constitutional Theory', **74** *Virginia Law Review*, 471-518.

Magnan De Bornier, Jean (1986), 'The Coase Theorem and the Empty Core: A Re-examination', **6** *International Review of Law and Economics*, 265-271.

Mailath, George J. and Postlewaite, Andrew (1990), 'Asymmetric Information Bargaining Problems with Many Agents', **57** *Review of Economic Studies*, 351-367.

Majone, Giandomenico (1995), 'The Development of Social Regulation in the European Community: Policy Externalities, Transaction Costs, Motivational Factors', **50** *Aussenwirtschaft*, 79-109.

Maloney, Michael T. (1977), 'The Coase Theorem and Long Run Industry Equilibrium: Note', **17** *Quarterly Review of Economics and Business*, 113-118.

Marchand, James R. and Russell, Keith P. (1973), 'Externalities, Liability, Separability and Resource Allocation', **63** *American Economic Review*, 611-620.

Marchand, James R. and Russell, Keith P. (1975), 'Externalities, Liability, Separability and Resource Allocation: Reply', **65** *American Economic Review*, 730-732.

Martins, Manuel Victor (1992), 'Ronald Coase: Na Fronteira de Economia e do Direito', **2** *Sub Judice*, 29-30.

McEwin, R. Ian (1981), 'Liability Rules, Insurance and the Coase Theorem', **6** *Australian Journal of Management*, 103-117.

Meade, James E. (1952), 'External Economies and Diseconomies in a Competitive Situation', **62** *Economic Journal*, 54-67.

Medema, Steven G. (1994), *Ronald H. Coase*, London, Macmillan.

Medema, Steven G. (1995a), 'Through A Glass Darkly, or Just Wearing Dark Glasses? Posin, Coase and the Coase Theorem', **62** *Tennessee Law Review*, 1041-1056.

Medema, Steven G. (1995b), *The Legacy of Ronald Coase in Economic Analysis. 2 vols*, Aldershot, Edward Elgar.

Medema, Steven G. (1996a), 'The Coase Theorem', in Coopera and Argyris (eds), *The Encyclopedia of Managerial Economics*, Oxford, Basil Blackwell.

Medema, Steven G. (1996b), 'Comment: The Coase Theorem, Rent Seeking and the Forgotten Footnote', **17** *International Review of Law and Economics*, 177-178.

Medema, Steven G. (1996), 'Of Pangloss, Pigouvians and Pragmatism: Ronald Coase on Social Cost Analysis', **18** *Journal of the History of Economic Thought*, 96-114.

Medema, Steven G. (1997a), 'The Trial of Homo Economicus: What Law and Economics Tells Us about the Future of Economic Imperialism', **27** *New Economics and its Writing: History of Political Economy Annual Supplement*, forthcoming.

Medema, Steven G. (1997b), 'The Coase Theorem, Rent Seeking and the Forgotten Footnote', **17** *International Review of Law and Economics*, 177-178.

Meran, Georg and Wolfstetter, Elmar (1987), 'Optimal Risk Shifting vs Efficient Employment in Illyria: The Labor Managed Firm under Asymmetric Information', **11** *Journal of Comparative Economics*, 163-179.

Miceli, Thomas J. and Sirmans, C.F. (1995), 'The Economics of Land Transfer and Title Insurance', **10** *Journal of Real Estate Finance and Economics*, 81-88.

Mishan, Ezra J. (1965), 'Reflections on Recent Developments in the Concept of External Effects', **31** *Canadian Journal of Economics and Political Science*, 3-34.

Mishan, Ezra J. (1967), 'Pareto Optimality and the Law', **19** *Oxford Economic Papers*, 255-287.

Mishan, Ezra J. (1971), 'The Post-war Literature on Externalities: An Interpretative Essay', **9** *Journal of Economic Literature*, 1-28.

Mishan, Ezra J. (1974), 'The Economics of Disamenity', **14** *Natural Resources Journal*, 55-86.

Mnookin, Robert H. and Kornhauser, Lewis A. (1979), 'Bargaining in the Shadow of the Law: The Case of Divorce', **88** *Yale Law Journal*, 950-997.

More, Daniel (197), 'The Coase Theorem and the Reciprocal Nature of Land-Use Conflicts in Pollution Cases', **4** *Studies in Law, Tel Aviv University*, 84-114.

Mumey, George A. (1971), 'The Coase Theorem: A Reexamination', **85** *Quarterly Journal of Economics*, 718-723.

Ng, Yew Kwang (1971), 'Recent Developments in the Theory of Externality and the Pigovian Solution', **47** *Economic Record*, 169-185.

Ng, Yew Kwang (1975), 'Coase's Theorem and First-party Priority Rule: Reply', **51** *Economic Record*, 272-274.

Ng, Yew Kwang (1977), 'Again on Externalities and Liability Rules: A Reply', **53** *Economic Record*, 542-544.

North, Douglass C. (1981), *Structure and Change in Economic History*, New York, W.W. Norton.

Norton, Seth W. (1987), 'The Coase Theorem and Suboptimization in Marketing Channels', **6** *Marketing Science*, 268-285.

Nutter, Warren G. (1968), 'The Coase Theorem on Social Cost: A Footnote', **11** *Journal of Law and Economics*, 503-507.

Ogus, Anthony I. (1991), 'Comment (on Staaf and Yandle, Collective and Private Choice; Constitutions, Statutes and the Common Law)', in Weigel, Wolfgang (ed.), *Economic Analysis of Law - A Collection of Applications*, Vienna, Österreichischer Wirtschaftsverlag, 267-269.

Parisi, Francesco (1991), 'Interpretazione Giuridica ed Analisi Economica - Il Teorema di Coase Trenta Anni Dopo (Legal Interpretation and Economic Analysis - The Coase Theorem Thirty Years Later)', *Rivista Critica del Diritto Privato*, 643-676.

Parisi, Francesco (1995), 'Private Property and Social Costs', **2(2)** *European Journal of Law and Economics*, 149-173.

Pejovich, Svetozar (1995), *Economic analysis of institutions and systems*, International Studies in Economics and Econometrics, vol. 33. Dordrecht and Boston: Kluwer Academic, 231 p.

Peters, H. Elizabeth (1986), 'Marriage and Divorce: Informational Constraints and Private Contracting', **76** *American Economic Review*, 437-454.

Peters, H. Elizabeth (1992), 'Marriage and Divorce: Reply', **82** *American Economic Review*, 686-693.

Polinsky, A. Mitchell (1974), 'Economic Analysis as a Potentially Defective Product: A Buyer's Guide to Posner's Economic Analysis of Law', **87** *Harvard Law Review*, 1655-1681.

Polinsky, A. Mitchell (1979), 'Controlling Externalities and Protecting Entitlements: Property Right, Liability Rule and Tax-Subsidy Approaches', **8** *Journal of Legal Studies*, 1-48.

Polinsky, A. Mitchell (1980), 'Resolving Nuisance Disputes: The Simple Economics of Injunctive and Damage Remedies', **33** *Stanford Law Review*, 1075-1112.

Posin, Daniel Q. (1979), 'The Coase Theorem: Through a Glass Darkly', **61** *Tennessee Law Review*, 868 ff.

Posin, Daniel Q. (1990), 'The Coase Theorem: If Pigs Could Fly', **37** *Wayne Law Review*, 89-120.

Posin, Daniel Q. (1991), 'Bringing Home the Bacon: A Response to Critics', **38** *Wayne Law Review*, 107 ff.

Posin, Daniel Q. (1995), 'Risk and the Error of the Coase Theorem', **62** *Tennessee Law Review*, 1057-1071.

Posin, Daniel Q. (1996), 'Silicone Breast Implant Litigation and My Father-in-Law: A Neo-Coasean Analysis', **70** *Tulane Law Review*, 2565-2582.

Posner, Richard A. (1983), 'Utilitarianism, Economics and Social Theory', in Posner, Richard A., *The Economics of Justice*, Cambridge, MA, Harvard University Press, 48-87.

Posner, Richard A. (1992), *Economic Analysis of Law, 4th edn*, Boston, Little Brown and Co.

Prudencio, Yves C. (1982), 'The Voluntary Approach to Externality Problems: An Experimental Test', **9** *Journal of Environmental Economy and Management*, 213-228.

Quirk, James P. (1987), *Intermediate Microeconomics, 3rd edn*, Chicago, Henley on Thames, Sydney and Toronto, Science Research Associates, 485 p.

Randall, Alan (1983), 'The Problem of Market Failure', **23** *Natural Resources Journal*, 131-148.

Randall, Allan (1972), 'Market Solutions to Externality Problems: Theory and Practice', **54** *American Journal of Agricultural Economics*, 175-183.

Randall, Allan (1974), 'Coasian Externality Theory in a Policy Context', **14** *Natural Resources Journal*, 35-54.

Regan, Donald H. (1972), 'The Problem of Social Cost Revisited', **15** *Journal of Law and Economics*, 427-437.

Roberts, John (1991), 'Review of: Managerial Dilemmas: The Political Economy of Hierarchy', **32** *Journal of Economic Literature*, 159-161.

Ryssdal, Stray A.C. (1995), *Legal Realism and Economics as Behavior - A Scandinavian Look at the Economic Analysis of Law*, Oslo, Juridisk Forlag AS, Nerenius & Santérus Förlag AB Gad Jura AS.

Ryssdal, Stray A.C. (1995), *An Economic Analysis of Civil Suits and Appeals*, Oslo, Juridisk Forlag AS, Nerenius & Santérus Förlag AB Gad Jura AS.

Samuels, Warren J. (1974), 'The Coase Theorem and the Study of Law and Economics', **14** *Natural Resources Journal*, 1-33.

Samuelson, Paul A. (1954), 'The Pure Theory of Public Expenditure', **36** *Review of Economics and Statistics*, 386-389.

Samuelson, Paul A. (1964), *Economics: An Introductory Analysis, 6th edn*, New York, McGraw-Hill.

Samuelson, Paul A. (1966), 'Modern Economic Realities and Individualism', in Stiglitz, Joseph E. (ed.), *The Collected Scientific Papers of Paul A. Samuelson*, Cambridge, MA, MIT Press, 1407-1418.

Samuelson, William (1985), 'A Comment on the Coase Theorem', in Roth, Alvin E. (ed.), *Game-Theoretic Models of Bargaining*, Cambridge, Cambridge University Press, 321-339.

Saraydar, Edward (1983), 'Bargaining Power, Dissimulation and the Coase Theorem', **139** *Journal of Institutional and Theoretical Economics*, 599-611.

Schap, David (1986), 'The Nonequivalence of Property Rules and Liability Rules', **6** *International Review of Law and Economics*, 125-132.

Schlag, Pierre (1986), 'An Appreciative Comment on Coase's the Problem of Social Cost: A View from the Left', **1986** *Wisconsin Law Review*, 919-962.

Schlag, Pierre (1989), 'The Problem of Transaction Costs', **62** *Southern California Law Review*, 1661-1699.

Schulze, William D. and d'Arge, Ralph C. (1974), 'The Coase Proposition, Information Costs and Long-run Equilibrium', **64** *American Economic Review*, 763-772.

Schulze, William D. and d'Arge, Ralph C. (1977), 'The Coase Proposition, Information Constraints and Long-Run Equilibrium: Reply', **67** *American Economic Review*, 462-463.

Schwab, Stewart J. (1987), 'Collective Bargaining and the Coase Theorem', **72** *Cornell Law Review*, 245-287.

Schwab, Stewart J. (1988), 'A Coasean Experiment on Contract Presumptions', **17** *Journal of Legal Studies*, 237-268.

Schwab, Stewart J. (1989), 'Coase Defends Coase: Why Lawyers Listen and Economists Do Not', **87** *Michigan Law Review*, 1171-1198.

Schwab, Stewart J. (1991), 'Coase, Rents and Opportunity Costs', **38** *Wayne State Law Review*, 55-74.

Schwab, Stewart J. (1993), 'Coase's Twin Towers: The Relation Between the Nature of the Firm and The Problem of Social Cost', **18** *Journal of Corporation Law*, 359-370.

Schweizer, Urs (1988), 'Externalities and the Coase Theorem: Hypothesis or Result?', **144** *Journal of Institutional and Theoretical Economics*, 245-266.

Shapiro, David L. (1974), 'Rent and the Coase Theorem', **7** *Journal of Economic Theory*, 125-128.

Shapiro, David L. (1977), 'A Note on Rent and the Coase Theorem: Editorial Addendum', **14** *Journal of Economic Theory*, 221-222.

Shapiro, David L. (1978), 'The Coase Theorem and Quasi Rents: Correcting the Record Reply', **6** *Public Finance Quarterly*, 262-264.

Shapiro, David L. (1984), 'A Note on Rent and the Coase Theorem', **7** *Journal of Economic Theory*, 125-128.

Shea, Koon Lam (1978), 'Coase Theorem, Liability Rules and Social Optimum', **114** *Weltwirtschaftliches Archiv*, 540-550.

Shogren, Jason F. (1992), 'An Experiment on Coasian Bargaining over Ex Ante Lotteries and Ex Post Rewards', **17** *Journal of Economic Behavior and Organization*, 153-169.

Shogren, Jason F. and Kask, Susan B. (1992), 'Exploring the Boundaries of the Coase Theorem: Efficiency and Rationality Given Imperfect Contract Enforcement', **39** *Economics Letters*, 155-161.

Shoup, Donald C. (1971), 'Theoretical Efficiency in Pollution Control: Comment', **9** *Western Economic Journal*, 310-313.

Silberberg, Eugene (1978), *The Structure of Economics. A Mathematical Analysi*, New York, McGraw-Hill.

Sinn, Hans-Werner and Schmoltzi, Ulrich (1981), 'Eigentumsrechte, Kompensationsregeln und Marktmacht Anmerkungen zum "Coase Theorem" (With English summary) (Property Rights, Compensation Rules and Market Power Comments on the "Coase Theorem ")', **196** *Jahrbuch fur Nationalokonomie und Statistik*, 97-117.

Spiegelman, Robert G. and Woodbury, Stephen A. (1987), 'Bonuses to Workers and Employers to Reduce Unemployment: Randomized Trials in Illinois', **77** *American Economic Review*, 513-530.

Spitzer, Matthew L. and Hoffman, Elizabeth (1980), 'A Reply to Consumption Theory, Production Theory and Ideology in the Coase Theorem', **53** *Southern California Law Review*, 1187-1223.

Staaf, Robert J. and Yandle, Bruce (1991), 'Collective and Private Choice: Constitutions, Statutes and the Common Law', in Weigel, Wolfgang (ed.), *Economic Analysis of Law - A Collection of Applications*, Vienna, Österreichischer Wirtschaftsverlag, 254-265.

Stake, Jeffrey E. (1995), 'Loss Aversion and Involuntary Transfers of Title', in Malloy, Robbin P. and Braun, Christopher K. (eds), *Law and Economics: New and Critical Perspectives*, New York, Lang, 331-360.

Starrett, David A. (1972), 'Fundamental Nonconvexities in the Theory of Externalities', **4** *Journal of Economic Theory*, 180-199.

Stigler, George J. (1966), *The Theory of Price, 3rd edn*, New York, Macmillan.

Stigler, George J. (1989), 'Two Notes on the Coase Theorem', **99** *Yale Law Journal*, 631-633.

Sumner, Charles (1993), 'Red Deer Management Problems in Strathyre Forest: Ecology, Economics and Land Use', MSc dissertation, Department of Environmental Science, University of Stirling.

Sutton, John (1986), 'Noncooperative Bargaining Theory: An Introduction', **53** *Review of Economic Studies*, 709-724.

Swan, Peter L. (1975), 'The Coase Theorem and 'Sequential' Pareto Optimality', **51** *Economic Record*, 268-271.

Thaler, Richard H. (1980), 'Toward a Positive Theory of Consumer Choice', **1** *Journal of Economic Behavior and Organization*, 39-60.

Turvey, Ralph (1963), 'On Divergences Between Social Cost and Private Cost', **30** *Economica*, 309-313.

Tybout, Richard A. (1972), 'Pricing Pollution and Other Negative Externalities', **3** *Bell Journal of Economics*, 252-266.

Tybout, Richard A. (1973), 'Pricing of Pollution: the Coase Theorem in the Long Run: Reply', **4** *Bell Journal of Economics*, 320-321.

Veljanovski, Cento G. (1977), 'The Coase Theorem: The Say's Law of Welfare Economics?', **53** *Economic Record*, 535-541.

Veljanovski, Cento G. (1982), 'The Coase Theorems and the Economic Theory of Markets and Law', **35** *Kyklos*, 53-74.

Ventura, Andrea (1990), 'Il Ruolo del Teorema di Coase nell'Analisi Economica del Diritto di G. Calabresi (The Role of the Coase Theorem in G. Calabresi's Economic Analysis of Law)', *Economia Pubblica*, 27-34.

Vogel, Kenneth R. (1987), 'The Coase Theorem and California Animal Trespass Law', **16** *Journal of Legal Studies*, 149-187.

Walsh, Cliff (1975), 'First-Party-Priority Revisited', **51** *Economic Record*, 275-277.

Wegehenkel, Lothar (1980), *Coase Theorem und Marktsystem* (Coase Theorem and the Market System), Tübingen, J.C.B. Mohr, 138 p.

Weimer, David L. and Vining, Aidan R. (1992), *Policy Analysis: Concepts and Practice, 2nd edn*, Englewood Cliffs, NJ, Prentice-Hall.

Weld, John (1973), 'Coase, Social Cost and Stability: An Integrative Essay', **13** *Natural Resources Journal*, 595-613.

Wellisz, Stanislaw (1964), 'On External Diseconomies and the Governement - Assisted Invisible Hand', **31** *Economica*, 345-362.

White, Barbara (1987), 'Coase and the Courts: Economics for the Common Man', **72** *Iowa Law Review*, 577-635.

Willig, Robert D. (1976), 'Consumer's Surplus Without Apology', **66** *American Economic Review*, 589-897.

Wohar, Mark (1988), 'Alternative Versions of the Coase Theorem and the Definition of Transaction Costs', **27** *Quarterly Journal of Business and Economics*, 3-19.

Woj, Carolyn (1985), 'Property Rights Disputes: Current Fallacies and a New Approach', **14** *Journal of Legal Studies*, 411-422.

X (1980), 'Symposium on Efficiency as a Legal Concern', **8** *Hofstra Law Review*, 485-972.

Zelder, Martin (1993a), 'The Economic Analysis of the Effect of No-Fault Divorce Law on the Divorce Rate', **16** *Harvard Journal of Law and Public Policy*, 241-267.

Zelder, Martin (1993b), 'Inefficient Dissolutions as a Consequence of Public Goods: The Case of No-Fault Divorce', **22** *Journal of Legal Studies*, 503-520.

Zelder, Martin (1997), 'The Cost of Accosting: A Reconciliatory Survey of Proofs and Disproofs of the Coase Theorem', in Medema, Steven G. (ed.), *Coasean Economics*, Kluwer, Academic Publishers.

Zerbe, Richard O., Jr (1976), 'The Problem of Social Cost: Fifteen Years Later', in Say, Lin, (ed.), *Theory and Measurement of Economic Externalities*, New York, Academia Press, 29-36.

Zerbe, Richard O., Jr (1980), 'The Problem of Social Cost in Retrospect', **2** *Research in Law and Economics*, 83-102.

Zerbe, Richard O., Jr (1998a), 'Is Benefit Cost Analysis Legal? Three Rules', **17** *Journal of Policy Analysis and Managment*, forthcoming.

Zerbe, Richard O., Jr (1998b), *A Foundation for Kaldor-Hicks Efficiency in Law and Economics: On the Kindness of Strangers*, Working Paper Graduate School of Public Affairs, University of Washington.

Zerbe, Richard O., Jr (1998c), 'An Integration of Equity and Efficiency', **73** *Washington Law Review*, forthcoming April 1998.

Zerbe, Richard O., Jr and McCurdy, Howard (1996), *The Failure of Market Failure*, Working Paper, University of Washington..

Zerbe, Richard O., Jr and Urban, Nicole (1988), 'Including the Public Interest in Theories of Regulation', **11** *Research in Law and Economics*, 1-23.

Zimbalist, Andrew (1994), 'Review of: Pay Dirt: The Business of Professional Team Sports', **32** *Journal of Economic Literature*, 167-168.

Zupan, Mark A. (1990), 'On Cream Skimming, Coase and the Sustainability of Natural Monopolies', **22** *Applied Economics*, 487-492.

Cases

Milwaukee Spring Div., 265 N.L.R.B. 206 (1982).
Milwaukee Spring Div., 268 N.L.R.B. 601 (1984).
UAW v. NLRB, 765 F.2d 175 (D.C. Cir. 1985).

0740
TRANSACTION COSTS

Douglas W. Allen
Associate Professor
Department of Economics - Simon Fraser University

Abstract

This chapter addresses the history, use and significance of the term transaction costs. Few words in the economic language have been more abused or fought over and this is shown to result from the emergence of two distinct definitions and uses. The 'Neoclassical' definition rests on the costs of trading across a market, while the 'property rights' definition centers on the costs of establishing and enforcing property rights. In articulating these two separate definitions and in demonstrating their relationship and separate uses, it is hoped that more progress can be made in the field of transaction cost economics.
JEL classification: K0, L0, L2, D0, D8
Keywords: Transaction Costs, Property Rights, Coase Theorem

1. Introduction

Transaction costs. Do another two words exist in the economic lexicon that generate as much friction? Conceptually introduced in Coase's 1937 paper 'The Nature of the Firm' as simply 'the cost of using the price mechanism' (Coase, 1988, p. 38), the words 'transaction costs' have evolved to the point where some skeptics claim they include any cost that is convenient and elusive enough to avoid critical examination (Niehans, 1987, p. 678). Advocates, on the other hand, have hailed the recognition of these costs as revolutionary and as important conceptually as 'marginalism' and 'substitution' (Cheung, 1983, p. 21).

The ambiguity that surrounds the concept of transaction costs stems, in large part, from the existence of two literatures simultaneously claiming ownership over the term. The 'property rights' literature begins with Coase and has consistently focused on the role transaction costs play in determining the distribution of property rights, broadly defined as all laws, rules, social customs and organizations that generate incentives for behavior. This literature has called into question fundamental concepts like efficiency and the nature of production. Though based in neoclassical economics, this literature has evolved beyond the neoclassical model and has produced the new sub-fields of 'law and economics', the 'new economic history' and the 'new institutional economics'. Though this field, through Coase, claims the discovery and rightful title to 'transaction costs', ironically the words are conspicuously absent from many of its titles. Indeed this literature is mostly responsible, though not solely, for the plethora of terms that either substitute for or refine the notion of transaction costs.

The 'neoclassical' literature on transaction costs begins in the early 1950s, although some might argue that it starts with Hicks (1935) or even Coase (1937). This literature defines transaction costs more narrowly, generally models them more explicitly and often analytically identical to transportation charges or taxes. The correspondence with familiar costs carries over to the types of issues examined, such as the effect of transaction costs on the volume of trade, abilities to arbitrage, the bunching of transactions, intermediation and the existence and efficiency of equilibrium - all standard neoclassical fare. Sometimes this literature examines issues of property right determination, such as the role of middlemen and the medium of exchange. In addition to the different approach and definition, the conclusions are often opposite from the property rights literature as well. This is especially true over questions of efficiency and this has increased the level of belittling rhetoric between the two camps. For example, it is common in the neoclassical literature, when reference is made to the Coase Theorem - the cornerstone of the property rights literature - to say 'the so-called Coase Theorem' (See Niehans, 1987 p. 678, for an example). The property rights literature is just as aggressive, claiming that the neoclassical camp often wants their cake and eat it too. For example, early criticisms over the monopoly model almost mocked the inconsistency of having a monopolist know its demand curve at zero costs, yet find it prohibitively costly to price discriminate (see Demsetz, 1969, or Barzel, 1977, for examples).

The likely cause of this dichotomous literature is twofold. First, there is the early introduction of costly transacting by Coase (1937) in the explicit context of institutional choice, at a time when the profession had little interest or ability to grapple with the issue. As Coase (1972) noted, his 1937 paper on the firm was often cited, but was little used. Second, there is Coase's failure in 1937 to define transaction costs with any precision, using instead the phrase 'the costs of the price mechanism'. At the same time, though Coase uses examples that suggest more than just the market is involved in transaction costs, he ultimately leaves the issue open for interpretation. As such, the property right literature did not truly begin until 1960, with Coase's publication of 'The Problem of Social Cost'. This latter article provided the necessary elaboration of Coase's 1937 publication in order to tie many existing ideas together and to provide a property rights research agenda (see Barzel and Kochin, 1992, or Medema, forthcoming, for elaborations on this point). In the intervening years, economists did what they could with the term transaction costs and the neoclassical approach was born.

The purpose of this chapter is to provide a broad picture of transaction costs: its history, definition, foundation, use, measurement and implications. As such, it is often necessary to sacrifice detail and the reader is directed to explore the references for further treatment. A theme throughout the chapter is the dichotomous use of the term 'transaction costs' in the two streams of literature already mentioned. It is ironic that a disagreement over ownership should engulf a term so closely related to property rights. Unfortunately, as with all cases of disputed ownership, useful output is lower for lack of definition.

2. A Tale of Two Histories, Part A: The Property Right Approach

In the beginning Coase created transaction costs. His critics might continue: 'And the term was formless and void and darkness was over the surface of the term'. For the believers in the property right approach, however, Coase (1937) is seminal. As an advanced undergraduate perplexed by economics' ability to conceptually organize the economy around prices, Coase was troubled that there was no room for any form of direct cooperation or direction. In his words 'we had a factor of production, management, whose function was to coordinate. Why was it needed if the pricing system provided all the coordination necessary?' (1992, p. 715). His solution was to recognize that there are 'costs of using the price mechanism'. When prices allocate resources at a cost, then they compete with other allocating mechanisms like firms and governments. Coase argued that, at times, firms and direct management supersede the market, while at other times market prices are used in directing goods and services. Readers interested in the genesis and a detailed account of the history of Coase's first great work are directed to Williamson and Winter (1991).

In this simple argument a charitable reading finds some basic elements that distinguish the property rights literature. First, all methods of allocating resources have costs and benefits and no single mechanism works for free and dominates all others - in modern language, all allocation mechanisms are 'second best'. Second, it is argued that 'rules', 'organizational forms' and 'methods of payments' are subject to economic analysis. Although it has been argued that Frank Knight (1921) indirectly made a similar case (see McManus, 1975; Barzel, 1987), Coase explicitly addressed this issue. And finally, Coase implicitly argues that positive transaction costs were both necessary and sufficient for an explanation of the firm.

Coase provides examples of what he meant by the costs of the price mechanism: discovering what the prices are, negotiating and closing a contract; and he hints at problems of enforcement, but he stops short of any definition. In fact, throughout all of his writings, Coase never goes beyond providing examples of transaction costs. Barzel and Kochin (1992, p. 25) have noted that 'the discussion of transaction costs in that [1937] paper is brief and cryptic' and even the most sympathetic reader would have to agree. Though the words 'transaction costs' are never used in his first work, Coase is still correct when, in his Nobel address, he states that: 'What I think will be considered in the future to have been the important contribution of this article is the explicit introduction of transaction costs into economic analysis'. (1992, p. 716).

It remains a strange fact of economic history that after the publication of 'The Nature of the Firm', neither Coase, nor any other writer in the profession, picked up the joint theme of transaction costs and property rights. Finally, in 'The Federal Communications Commission', Coase (1959) returns to the theme of the influence of transaction costs on property rights and this article provides the motivation for 'The Problem of Social Cost' (see Kitch (ed.), 1983, or Stigler, 1988, for discussions of how Coase came to write his most famous paper). Ironically, even Coase did not appreciate his accomplishment at the time of writing:

> I should add that in writing this article I had no such general aim in mind. I thought that I was exposing the weaknesses of Pigou's analysis of the divergence between private and social products, an analysis generally accepted by economists and that was all. It was only later and in part as a result of conversation with Steven Cheung in the 1960's that I came to see the general significance for economic theory of what I had written . . . (1992, p. 717)

A tremendous amount has been written regarding 'The Problem of Social Cost' and the literature it instigated. For friendly discussions of 'The Problem of Social Cost' see Cheung (1983), Barzel and Kochin (1992), Coase (1988, 1992) or Medema (1994, 1996a). For less friendly ones see Cooter (1982), Donohue (1989), Kelman (1979) and Samuels (1974). Regardless, for the purposes here, only two points require elaboration - namely, that Coase explicitly makes a connection between transaction costs and property rights in the context of the common law of liability and that Cheung (1969) generalized this argument to the context of contracts and contract choice.

Cheung has made many contributions to the property rights literature on transaction costs, but perhaps his most significant is generalizing Coase's original argument. The importance stems from the fact that Coase never defined transaction costs and has often used examples that suggest transaction costs arise only in market exchanges. Cheung, in analyzing share tenancy and providing the first contractual example of the Coase theorem, explicitly argues that contract choice depends on the transaction costs of the different contracts. These transaction costs are clearly *internal* and not just market costs. Cheung's work inspired Stiglitz (1974) and begins the principal agent literature, but it also establishes the precedent of thinking of transaction costs across markets *and* internal to the firm - a theme that is strongly articulated in Williamson (1975,

1979, 1985). This connection between transaction costs and property rights is summarized in 'the Coase Theorem', which is defined as follows:

> **Coase Theorem:** In the absence of transaction costs, the allocation of resources is independent of the distribution of property rights.

There are many attacks and defenses of the Coase Theorem, none of which are dealt with here (see Shapiro, 1974, for an example of an attack, Allen, 1997, for a defense and Zerbe, 1980, for a survey). The point is that for all property right approaches to transaction costs, the two concepts of property rights and transaction costs are fundamentally interlinked. In fact, it will be shown that they are two sides of the same coin and that this linkage distinguishes the property right approach from the neoclassical approach to the study of transaction costs.

Property Rights and Transaction Costs

The delineation of ownership is as old as human written records. The Mosaic laws as described in the Ten Commandments or the laws on takings in Exodus 22:1-15, as well as the host of other Levitical laws throughout the first five books of the Old Testament, are all attempts to legally define ownership. From the Hammurabi code to the English common law the notion of legal ownership, or legal rights, to property is well defined. In the words of Blackstone: 'The third absolute right; inherent in every Englishman, is that of property: which consists in the free use, enjoyment and disposal of all his acquisitions, without any control or diminution, save only by the laws of the land' (1803, p. 138).

Though it is difficult to identify where one idea begins, the modern attempt to go beyond a *legal* delineation of rights and begin talking about 'economic rights' seems to start with Alchian. Alchian's early work on tenure (1958) and the pursuit of individual utility within the context of regulated firms (Alchian and Kessel, 1962) hinge on the property right structures of the institutions in question. For example, managers and administrators of non-profit firms and universities, he argues, face a lower relative cost of private consumption on the job than their counterparts in the private sector. Because these firms are constrained in their ability to show profit, they are able to survive with higher costs. Alchian's insight was that the set of rules (the distribution of property rights) determined the level of output of the firm because they determined the incentives of each individual. This theme is manifest throughout Alchian's work and culminates in his famous article with Demsetz (Alchian and Demsetz, 1972). But perhaps Alchian's most significant contribution, articulated most clearly in Alchian (1965, 1979), is his emphasis on *economic* rather than *legal* rights. For Alchian, property rights are 'the rights of individuals to the use of resources' (1965, p. 817) not just under the law, but in reality. He makes clear that these rights are not solely dependent on the existence of the state, but that they depend on custom, reciprocity and voluntary restraints. This notion is now commonplace in the modern property rights literature and is explicitly found in Ellickson (1991) and Landa (1994). Although economic property rights are enhanced by the law, they are ultimately use rights and the greater extent one can exercise these uses and bear the consequences the greater are the property rights, regardless of the law. Property rights are therefore defined as:

> **Property Rights:** the ability to freely exercise a choice over a good or service.

The property rights literature argues there is a monotonic relationship between property rights and wealth. Given that trade is the transfer of property rights, there can be no trade (and hence no gains from trade) in the absence of property rights. Also, when property rights are perfectly defined, the Coase theorem states that the gains from trade are maximized. Assuming there is a continuum between these two extremes, as property rights become better defined, the gains from trade increase (see Anderson and Lueck, 1992 for an empirical example). Other things equal, individuals prefer better defined property rights to poorer defined ones because they prefer more wealth to less.

Increasing the ability to make choices of one individual can reduce the ability to make choices for others. Generally speaking individuals increase their property rights in three ways. First, the individual may steal the good in question. Second, the individual may privatize a good that was previously in the public domain. Finally, an individual may cooperate with other individuals with an agreement to divide the new wealth in some fashion.

When property rights are perfect, by definition no theft can take place and as a result, no effort is made to protect the rights (a point made in Cheung, 1974 and Barzel, 1985). However, when property rights are incomplete, individuals attempt to increase their ownership in an effort to increase their wealth. This attempt to capture property rights may be dissipating (as in the case of theft), or may be wealth generating (as in the case of assets brought out of the public domain). When there is an opportunity for theft, there is also an opportunity for protection. Hence, when property rights are incomplete, individuals are always in the process of maintaining their existing property rights and attempting to establish new ones. This leads to the property right definition of transaction costs.

> **Transaction Costs, #1:** the costs establishing and maintaining property rights.

This definition is first articulated in Allen (1991). Writers in the property rights literature have seldom defined transaction costs, relying mostly on examples of inspection, enforcing, policing and measurement which all hint at the protection of property rights and implicitly recognize the threat of appropriation or theft. For similar, but informal, definitions, see Cheung (1969, p. 16), McManus (1975, p. 336), Jensen and Meckling (1976, p. 308), Barzel (1985, p. 8), Goldberg (1989, p. 22) and Alchian and Woodward (1988, p. 66).

Transaction costs include any direct costs, as well as any concomitant inefficiencies in production or misallocation that resulted from them. For example, consider the Klein and Leffler (1981) example of a firm investing in a sunk asset as a guarantee of product quality. The firm does this to protect the wealth of its customer and as such it is clearly an attempt to maintain property rights. The transaction costs would include the cost of the investment and any increases in costs of production that it may have caused.

The property rights definition of transaction costs respects no boundaries between firms, markets, households, or any other theoretical constructs. When property rights are protected and maintained in any context, transaction costs exist. By explicitly recognizing this relationship it is clear that statements like 'if we assume zero transaction costs *and* complete property rights' are redundant. To say that a situation has zero transaction costs is to say that property rights are complete, according to this definition. Cheung (1992, p. 54) agrees with this, stating: 'the dual specifications of clearly delimited rights and zero transaction costs are redundant. If transaction costs are truly zero, the delineation of rights can be ignored'.

When it is costless to establish and maintain rights they are done so perfectly. If transaction costs are prohibitively high then property rights will neither be established nor maintained and property rights will be zero. The reverse, however, is not necessarily true. If property rights are complete in some situation, there are two possibilities, either transaction costs are zero, or costs may have been incurred to guarantee the property rights simply because the benefits of doing so exceed the costs - in which case transaction costs are positive. Further, when property rights are zero, transaction costs could also be zero. For example, if a property right could never be established, despite the resources devoted towards such a goal, no one would bother making any expenditures towards establishing property rights and the good would remain unowned. For example, there are no property rights over the planet Venus and no efforts have been made to establish any.

Transaction Cost Economics with the Property Rights Approach

An excellent survey of the property right literature is found in Eggertsson (1990a), while an excellent textbook treatment of this approach is found in Milgrom and Roberts (1992). Essentially the property rights literature is characterized by several features related to the above definition. First, the central question is always 'what explains the distribution of property rights?', where the 'distribution of property rights' has a broad meaning and includes all sets of rules, governance structures and organizations. Hence, families, firms, governments, non-profit institutions, contracts, are all viewed as sets of property rights. Lawyers forming a partnership to split the residuals, a farmer renting land from a landowner, or a judge deciding on a case, are all examples of different allocations of property rights. Every distribution of property rights has with it a set of production costs and a set of transaction costs. The distribution of property rights that maximizes the gains from trade net of all costs is the optimal distribution. This, in fact, is the grand hypothesis of transaction cost economics under the property rights approach. An account of transaction cost methodology is beyond the scope of this paper, but see Williamson (1979, 1985) for detailed accounts.

A second characterization is the reluctance to infer any policy implications from the analysis and to stress explanation. As stated earlier, this goes back to Coase's original idea that no single allocation mechanism dominates. Notions of 'market failure' lose meaning when there is no reason for prices to allocate everything. One might as well refer to 'government failure' or 'firm failure' in cases where prices do allocate.

This transaction cost approach dominates what is now called the 'New Institutional Economics', so named because it provides a theoretical framework and emphasis of testability to the institutional traditions of Veblen and Commons. Oliver Williamson is considered the founder of this literature, both in terms of vocabulary and content and he is one of the strongest proponents of applying the notion of transaction costs ubiquitously. His notion of a 'governance structure' as a distribution of property rights providing appropriate incentives to govern a relationship, is intended to apply within and outside firms. Williamson (1971) is the first to note the role sunk costs can play in causing contracting problems and incentives to vertically integrate. This idea is popularized in Klein, Crawford and Alchian (1978) and in Klein and Leffler (1981). The role of asset specificity and idiosyncratic capital is so attached to the name of Williamson that for many, transaction costs means little else. Although Williamson's understanding of the relationship between transaction costs and property rights is consistent with what is presented here, he also distinguishes between the 'property rights approach' and the 'transaction cost approach' to organizational problems. For Williamson, a property rights approach deals with grand private environmental rules, while the transaction cost approach deals with private incomplete contracts (see Williamson, 1990 for a discussion).

3. The Tale of Two Histories, Part B: The Neoclassical Approach

Although, Coase (1937) provides mostly market exchange examples and could be argued as the founder of the neoclassical approach to transaction costs, it could be better argued that this approach begins with Hicks' (1935) publication 'A Suggestion of Simplifying the Theory of Money', which predates Coase by two years. In his paper, Hicks begins what is known as a transaction demand for money, although he never calls it as such. For him, there are frictions in the economy and these apply to buying and selling capital assets yielding positive returns. When the returns were small, at the margin, relative to the costs of trading, individuals rationally hold cash balances yielding no return. In his words:

> The most obvious sort of friction and undoubtedly one of the most important, is the cost of transferring assets from one form to another. This is of exactly the same character as the cost of transfer which acts as a certain impediment to change in all parts of the economic system; it doubtless comprises subjective elements as well as elements directly priced. Thus a person is deterred from investing money for short periods, partly because of brokerage charges and stamp duties, partly because it is not worth the bother. (1935, p. 6)

Since money is used to facilitate exchange and since an exchange that needs 'facilitating' must be subject to transaction costs, it is not surprising that those concerned with money dealt with these costs. Indeed, Baumol (1952) and Tobin (1956) elaborate on the transaction demand for money and again treat transaction costs as the costs of trading. The first explicit statement of transaction costs as the cost of trading comes from Demsetz (1964) where he states that 'Transaction cost may be defined as the cost of exchanging ownership titles' (1988, p. 64). Although this type of definition refers to property rights, transaction costs only arise when an exchange of property rights takes place. This leads to the neoclassical definition of transaction costs:

> **Transaction Costs #2:** the costs resulting from the transfer of property rights.

This is a shortened version of the definition later given in Niehans (1987). The neoclassical approach to transaction costs dominates in finance and pure theory. The following is a partial list of papers that utilize a neoclassical approach: Brennan and Copeland (1988), Constantinides (1986), Dermody and Prisman (1993), Dumas and Luciano (1991), Fisher (1994), Gennotte and Jung (1994), George, Kaul and Nimalendran (1994), Guia-Abiad (1993), Hirshleifer (1973), Huberman (1990), Jouini and Kallal (1995), Lund (1993), Pesaran and

Timmermann (1994), Shaffer (1989), Stavins (1995), Wagner and Schulman (1994), Wilcox (1993) and Young (1989). A typical definition of transaction costs found in these papers would be as•follows:

> In general, transaction costs are ubiquitous in market economies and can arise from the transfer of any property right because parties to exchanges must find one another, communicate and exchange information. There may be a necessity to inspect and measure goods to be transferred, draw up contracts, consult with lawyers or other experts and transfer title. Depending upon who provides these services, transaction costs can take one of two forms, inputs or resources - including time - by a buyer and/or a seller or a margin between the buying and selling price of a commodity in a given market. (Stavins 1995, p. 134)

In the neoclassical approach, enforcement-type costs *within* firms are *not* transaction costs. Transaction costs consist of those costs that occur between firms or individuals from the process of market exchange. Hence, an economy made up of one giant firm, or a state run economy, would be a zero transaction cost economy by this definition. Because these transaction costs are just the cost of exchange, they are modeled in a more recognizable fashion, often in the form of a 'transaction function' (see Constantinides, 1979 for an example). These functions are similar to other neoclassical production functions and are usually assumed to depend on labor inputs. These functions may have increasing, constant, or decreasing returns to scale. Further, the transaction cost functions may have fixed or variable components. Although the analogy is not complete, in many ways transaction costs play a role very similar to transportation costs and taxes and, according to Niehans: 'transaction costs are analytically analogous to transportation costs'.

Being analytically similar means that many of the impacts of transaction costs are similar as well. Consider, for example, the impact of transaction costs on the volume of trade. If transaction costs increase with the quantity traded, this has the impact of increasing the relative price of the commodity being purchased. Since this holds for goods, in effect the budget constraint becomes kinked at the endowment point and, as a result, individual demands become less responsive to price changes and the volume of trade falls. These are often called 'proportional transaction costs' in the literature and their effect on multiperiod investment and consumption has also been examined. (See Bensaid et al., 1992; Boyle and Vorst, 1992; Constantinides, 1976; Davis and Norman, 1990; Eppen and Fama, 1969; Kamin, 1975; Leland, 1985; and Magill and Constantinides, 1976). Other similar results follow as well. Like per unit taxes, frictional per unit transaction costs drive a wedge between buying and selling prices, although neoclassical transaction costs are not necessary to explain price spreads. Glosten and Milgrom (1985), based on Copeland and Galai (1983), provide an adverse selection explanation for bid-ask spreads that assumes traders have zero friction costs.

Fixed transaction costs tend to bunch transactions together and provide an explanation for the demand for money (see Edirisinghe, Naik and Uppal, 1993, for an example). Differences in transaction costs across individuals lead to some specializing in the transaction function. Hence brokers and agents are those individuals with low transaction costs. Alchian and Allen (1964) were probably the first to note this (see also Niehans, 1969). Differences in the transaction costs across commodities provide an explanation for why some commodities are used as currencies of exchange (Niehans, 1969 and Alchian, 1977). In these last two cases, the question examined is close to the institutional type of question addressed by the property rights school. Neoclassical transaction costs have also been used to analyze the equity premium. The real average returns on US Treasury Bills is less than 1 percent, while for stocks it is closer to 7 percent. This difference is too large to explain with reasonable Arrow-Debreu models. Mehra and Prescott (1985) began a literature explaining this premium based on neoclassical trading costs. (See Aiyagari and Gertler, 1991, for an example and a survey of the literature.) Finally, all discussions of the existence of equilibrium with transaction costs utilize a neoclassical definition (See Bergstrom, 1976; Foley, 1970; Hahn, 1971; Hart and Kuhn, 1975; Heller and Starr, 1976; Kurz, 1974b; McKenzie, 1981; Radner, 1972; and Repullo, 1988).

Definitional Squabbles

For the most part, these two streams of literatures - the property rights approach and the neoclassical approach - flow independently. Those writing in the area of property rights follow the line of reasoning laid by Coase, Cheung and Williamson and use the broad notion of transaction costs. Those interested in the neoclassical issues of volume of trade and equilibrium generally stick to an Arrow-Debreu based general equilibrium model and use the narrow definition of straight exchange costs.

The major exception is Harold Demsetz. Demsetz was an early contributor to the theory of property rights and the role of enforcement costs in determining the distribution of property rights (See Demsetz, 1964, 1967 and 1972). Ironically though, he was also the first to articulate the neoclassical definition of transaction costs (Demsetz, 1968). For Demsetz, transaction costs remain 'the costs of coordinating resources through market arrangements' (1995, p. 4) and among property right economists he remains a staunch, though perhaps lonely, proponent of this view. Demsetz (1964) is the first to deal with the breadth of definition used for transaction costs. In Demsetz (1988) he acknowledges that this is mostly a question of semantics, since his collection of costs all fit under the rubric of 'governance' costs or the property rights definition. According to Demsetz, the clear meaning of transaction costs is the *cost of transacting*. To apply the term more broadly threatens to make the term tautological and useless. This view is summarized by Schlag, 'an overly expansive view of transaction costs threatens to make the Coase theorem tautological. On the other hand, an overly restrictive view of transaction costs can effectively invalidate the theorem' (1989, p. 1675).

Demsetz (1988, pp. 144-150) argues that a broad definition of transaction costs hinders any understanding of firms and markets. For example, Demsetz (1995) argues that the definition of a firm and its internal organization are two separate issues that have been confused since Coase. Demsetz defines the firm as a production unit, created to exploit gains from specialization. Since markets only transfer titles they complement firms and the Coasean notion of firms and markets substituting for one another does not arise. This is exactly the opposite way the property rights literature would define a firm (see Barzel, 1989, as an example). Coase has always put emphasis on the formal relations within a firm (for example, employer vs. employee) as a possible means of reducing transaction costs. Alchian and Demsetz (1972), on the other hand, downplay the role of authority within the firm. (See Medema, 1994, for a discussion of Coase vs. Alchian and Demsetz.)

Demsetz, *de facto*, takes a property rights approach to the internal organization of the firm, however. Demsetz (1995) discusses several transaction costs (definition #1) arguments for the firm without using the term, including: shirking, Knightean uncertainty, reduction of coordination costs and the agency problems from opportunism. Hence, in the end there is very little to quibble over and the definition to be used depends on the problem being addressed. Clearly, all of the costs mentioned by Demsetz fall under the umbrella of the property right definition of transaction costs, where a broad transaction cost definition is necessary in order to make clear that the Coase theorem does not apply.

4. The Distribution of Property Rights vs. The Volume of Trade

The economics profession is littered with various assertions and theorems stating that distributions of property rights do not matter. The Coase theorem is the most famous of these, but there are many others. For example, the Modigliani/Miller theorem (1958) is almost identical to the Coase theorem. This proposition states that if capital markets are perfect and firms and investors face the same rate of interest, then investors can unravel any corporate structure chosen by the firm. This means that the ratio of debt to equity financing, as well as the form of debt and equity within the firm, is irrelevant to the firms value. A similar result is found in the Ricardian Equivalence Theorem (1951). This theorem states that with perfect capital markets, the government's choice over taxation and debt is irrelevant to the level of household wealth, because taxpayers are able to unravel any financing decisions of governments.

In addition to these, there are a host of equivalence results regarding taxes, the most famous being that it is irrelevant whether the consumer or the producer is taxed, the result is the same in terms of both resource allocation and incidence of tax paid. Furthermore, both *ad valorem* and per unit taxes are equivalent in terms of resource allocation. Finally, in trade policy and again in terms of resource allocation, it is well known that tariffs and quotas can have identical effects.

All of these results are special cases of the Coase theorem because all taxes, debt obligations, equity shares and other policy instruments are delineations of property rights. A firm deciding on the optimal amount of debt versus equity is essentially assigning property rights over the stream of expected profits, including priority in case of unexpected shortfalls. A government deciding on a choice between taxation and debt is simply transferring property rights over time. In all of these cases, only a different distribution of property rights exists and given the Coase theorem, this does not alter the allocation of resources - when, as Coase stated, transaction costs are zero.

When transaction costs are not zero, these equivalence results do not occur. For example, Barzel (1976) shows how the tax equivalent result is altered when transaction costs are positive. When goods are complex bundles of commodities they become difficult to define under tax legislation and some attributes are possibly ignored. Under these conditions, taxes have the effect of altering the relative price of the taxed and untaxed attributes and therefore alter the mix or quality of the item that is produced. Lump sum taxes tend to increase the quality of good, while per unit taxes tend to lower quality. The result is that different forms of taxation can have vastly different effects on resource allocation. Furthermore, differences in the ability to avoid taxation implies that tax revenue is not neutral with respect to the location of the tax.

All these examples explain why the property rights approach requires a broad definition of transaction costs. Given the Coase theorem and all of its different manifestations, distributions of property rights are irrelevant. If we did live in a world of zero transaction costs (definition # 1), then firms truly would toss coins to decide debt levels, if indeed there were any firms, which would also be decided by a coin toss. And so on for governments and all other institutions. The importance of the Coase theorem then is that it points to transaction costs as the *necessary* factor in any explanation of the distribution of property rights. The definition of transaction costs, therefore, must be those costs that cause the Coase theorem to not apply. This also seems to be the reason why the neoclassical approach never analyzes questions of economic organization outside of the choice of medium of exchange. They have selected a definition of transaction costs that is too limited for this purpose. Many in the neoclassical literature have balked at this line of reasoning, suggesting that it is tautological. The difference of opinion stems from the different objectives each approach is interested in.

5. The Causes of Transaction Costs

Regardless of which stream of literature is examined, the underlying theme for transaction costs is the notion of ignorance. Hence, even though its treatment is different and the definition is narrower, the neoclassical approach still uses examples of transaction costs that are similar to the property rights approach. Niehans states that parties must

> find each other, they have to communicate and to exchange information . . . goods must be described, inspected, weighed and measured. Contracts are drawn up, lawyers may be consulted, title is transferred and records have to be kept. In some cases, compliance needs to be enforced through legal action and breach of contract may lead to litigation. (1987, p. 676)

Negotiation, fraud, communication and contract stipulation all come about because knowledge is incomplete and not common. Though its importance is recognized by everyone, the role of information leads to a great deal of confusion in the discussion of transaction costs. Information costs are a prerequisite to transaction costs and are a necessary condition for their existence. Information costs, however, are not always transaction costs. Steven Cheung once remarked that transaction costs are costs that do not exist in a Robinson Crusoe world (a definition consistent with definition #1). Clearly Crusoe faced many information problems, but until Friday showed up, he had no transaction cost problems.

Barzel has been a strong proponent of the distinction between information and transaction costs. Barzel (1977) states that 'transaction costs include those (costs) required to formulate and to police contracts' (p. 292), but goes on to point out that it is possible to have information problems resulting in speculation, sorting and signalling, which may appear to yield decreases in social value, but that these reductions are impossible when transaction costs are zero. With zero transaction costs, contracting is a perfect substitute for information because contracts can always be made over all contingencies. Barzel (1982, 1985) stresses that information costs are at the heart of transaction costs because they lead to measurement. Barzel (1977) notes that when the distinction between information costs and transaction costs is made, several other points follow rather obviously: costless information implies perfect property rights; individual honesty does not necessarily eliminate transaction costs; costly information means transaction costs can explain self-imposed constraints; and total costs, not just transaction costs or information costs, are required to be minimized.

It is not always appreciated that information costs are not sufficient for transaction costs. The mere presence of information costs lead to risky events which can be eliminated through contingent claim contracts. In addition to costly information a factor is required to eliminate the ability to write complete contingent claim contracts. There are several examples of what this factor might be. Knight was the first to suggest this with his distinction between risk and uncertainty; uncertainty arising in situations where moral hazard prevented individuals from assigning accurate probabilities to events and thereby eliminating the ability to contract over the risk. Barzel (1989) and Allen (1991) have stressed the idea that goods are complicated bundles of attributes that both are variable in nature and alterable by individuals. The inability to separate the contributions to quality by nature and man allows for cheating to take place in equilibrium. Other attempts to add to information costs include the notion of asymmetric information and opportunism (see Ackerlof, 1970, and Williamson, 1975, 1985).

6. Modelling Transaction Costs, Part A: Neoclassical Modelling

As may be expected, the two literatures have different methods by which transaction costs are modelled. In both cases, transaction costs considerably complicate the neoclassical model and the level of mathematical sophistication is quite demanding. The major point made here, however, is that neoclassical modeling is a direct extension of the Arrow-Debreu model, while property rights modeling involves some fundamental differences.

In an Arrow-Debreu world with complete contingent markets, trades only take place once. An early application of transaction costs in neoclassical models explained why markets had a 'sequence' over time - the general idea being that at any given time, a specific market may be too expensive to trade in and thus trade is postponed until some future date.

There are two general types of approaches in modeling neoclassical transaction costs. The first, used by Foley (1970), Hahn (1971, 1973) and Starrett (1973), involves a central transactor who takes buy and sell orders from each household and carries them out. In order to pay for his services, the 'broker' charges a margin between the buying and selling price for his efforts. The second approach requires households and firms to directly use resources in the purchase and sale of goods. Here the firms and households use some type of 'transfer technology'. (For early treatments, see Kurz, 1974a; Niehans, 1971; or Ulph and Ulph, 1977. See Repullo, 1988, for a later treatment using this style.)

Although the specific technologies are generally simple, they are usually sufficient to complicate the analysis greatly.

Three general approaches are taken to model the transaction technology. The first simply assumes that some general transaction function $T(x)$ exists (see Brennan and Copeland, 1988, for example). This function is often assumed to depend on the volume of trade, cash flows, number of traders and other such variables that reflect the 'size' of the transaction. The second assumes that transaction costs are fixed (see Leland, 1974; Mukherjee and Zabel, 1974; Brennan, 1975; Goldsmith, 1976; Levy, 1978; or Mayshar, 1979, 1981; for examples). Finally, proportional (or 'iceberg') transaction costs $k(x)$ are assumed, where k is a constant fraction and x again is a measure of the size of transaction (see Gennotte and Jung, 1994, or Constantinides, 1986, for examples). All of these technologies make their way into standard objective functions for firms and households. Though the subsequent analysis is usually complicated, the results are most often exactly analogous to the effects of transportation charges. Typically, these analyses show that the presence of transaction costs reduces the frequency and volume of trade.

7. Modelling Transaction Costs, Part B: Property Rights Modeling

The property rights approach to modeling is a vast, diverse and technically complex literature, well beyond the scope of this survey to treat it in any detail (see Holmstrom and Milgrom, 1994, or Hart and Moore, 1990). Unlike the neoclassical literature, where transaction costs enter and yield results which are somewhat predictable, modeling the distribution of property rights is fundamentally different. Rather than entering through a transaction technology, transaction costs arise through changes in incentives and manifest in changes in values in different property right distributions, with often surprising results. For example, Coase (1960) is perhaps the first surprising result, despite the lack of formalization. Cheung (1969) is another and perhaps the first case of a formal treatment of transaction costs from a property rights approach. Here two examples of property rights modeling are provided to highlight some differences.

The simple example of insurance, first discussed in Rothschild and Stiglitz (1976), demonstrates some differences. Consider a world where there are two types of behavior: careful and uncareful and all else equal, individuals prefer being uncareful. Furthermore, there is the chance that a fire may occur and the probability of this event depends on the behavior of the individual. If insurance companies can fully observe behavior they offer a full insurance contract and everyone takes it - no one has an incentive to be careless.

Thus far, we have a standard neoclassical problem and the introduction of risky events has changed little. Recall that the marginal rate of substitution of the individual for wealth in both states of the world is:

$$\left(\frac{\pi_a}{1-\pi_a}\right)\frac{U'(W_a)}{U'(W_b)}$$

where π_a is the probability of fire in state 'a', U the individual's affine utility function and W the wealth level in the two states. In the case of pure uncertainty the probabilities are determined by nature.

However, if the behavior of the individual is not observable, the probabilities are alterable by the individual and a transaction cost problem arises. As has been noted above the transaction cost problem requires: (1) the presence of uncertainty (here the probability of a fire) and (2) the ability of the individual to change his behavior without costless detection. Since the firm cannot observe behavior, this implies individuals all become careless, which alters the marginal rate of substitution! The introduction of costly information leads to preferences no longer being fixed and exogenous and this is an example of a fundamental difference between the two types of models. (Arnott and Stiglitz, 1988) explore the implications of shifting marginal rates of substitution.)

The solution to this particular problem has the insurance company offering an incomplete contract (an insurance contract with a deductible), which points to a second difference. Namely the possible non-existence of explicit transaction costs in equilibrium. The insurance company, by offering an incentive compatible contract, does not engage in any form of direct monitoring. Such monitoring is not necessary and many property right models have no actual resources used to establish and maintain property rights in equilibrium. In this case, the transaction costs are simply the lost gains from trade that result from the incomplete contract.

As a second example, consider a variation on the principal-agent model first introduced by Stiglitz (1974). In this model the effort of a risk-averse agent is unobservable and so a contract is reached that trades off incentives for risk avoidance. For example, consider the case of cropshare contracts, where a risk-averse farmer contracts with a risk-neutral landowner (Allen and Lueck, 1995). For a plot of land, output is $q=(e+\theta)$, where e is the unobservable labor effort and θ is a random variable with mean 0 and variance σ^2. Furthermore, assume that the farmer's income is $Y=\alpha q+\beta$ and his utility is $U=E(Y)+(r/2)Var(Y)$, where r is a measure of risk aversion, α is the share of output and β is a fixed side payment. Finally, assume that the cost of effort to the farmer is $c_0+c_1e+(c_2/2)e^2$.

For a given outputshare the effort which maximizes farmer utility is:

$$\hat{e}(\alpha) = \frac{\alpha - c_1}{c_2},$$

which represents the behavior of the farmer and becomes a constraint to the landowner designing the optimal contract. This incentive compatibility constraint represents another example of a fundamental distinction in modeling property right distributions - namely, the constraints often involve optimization problems. The next stage in this particular problem involves the landowner maximizing his expected income $E\,((1 - \alpha)\,(\hat{e} + \beta) + \beta)$ subject to the incentive constraint and a participation constraint.

Although the principal-agent model has been extended and broadly applied, (see Dewatripont, 1989; Freixas, Guesnerie and Tirole, 1985; Holmstrom, 1979, 1982; or Shavell, 1979, for examples), it has recently fallen out of favor for models where all parties are risk neutral (see Eswaran and Kotwal, 1985; Grossman and Hart, 1986; Leffler and Rucker, 1991; and Allen and Lueck, 1992a, for examples). Holmstrom and Milgrom (1991) develop an explicit principal-agent model where risk aversion is not required. The great advantage of risk neutrality is that it allows for several margins over which transaction cost behavior can take place. However, though there remains no single way to model transaction costs in the property rights approach, the bottom line remains that it does involve some fundamental differences from putting a 'T' in a cost function.

8. Direct Empirical Work

The empirical work in transaction cost economics is very large. On the property rights side, studies have examined vertical integration (Anderson, 1988; Fishback, 1986, 1992; Globerman, 1980; Globerman and Schwindt, 1986; Joskow, 1985; Levy, 1985; Mahoney, 1992; Masten, 1984; Masten, Meehan and Snyder, 1989, 1991; and Monteverde and Teece, 1982), long-term contracts (Crocker and Masten, 1988; Joskow, 1985, 1987; Leffler and Rucker, 1991; Masten and Crocker, 1985), franchising and share contracts (Allen and Lueck, 1992a, 1992b, 1993; Alston and Higgs, 1982; Alston, Datta and Nugent, 1984; Datta, O'Hara and Nugent, 1986; Lafontaine, 1993; Williamson, 1976; Zupan, 1989a, 1989b), marriage (Allen, 1990, 1991; Brinig, 1990; Brinig and Alexeev, 1993; Parkman, 1992), wildlife (Lueck, 1991), horse racing (Hall, 1986), price adjustments (Crocker and Masten, 1991; Goldberg and Erickson, 1987; Joskow, 1988b, 1990), economic history (North, 1981; North and Weingast, 1989; and North, 1990), rate of return regulation (Crew and Kleindorfer, 1985) and a host of other organizational issues (see Shelanski and Klein, 1995, for a more complete listing of references to the empirical literature).

Studies in the neoclassical approach are also numerous and mostly focus on asset arbitrage, the volume of trade, risk adjusted returns and the bundling of transactions (see Demsetz, 1968; Fisher, 1994; Frenkel and Levich, 1975; Litzenberger and Rolfo, 1984; Malkiel, 1966; Pesaran and Timmermann, 1994; Phillips and Smith, 1980; Protopapadakis and Stoll, 1983; Schultz, 1983; Smiley, 1976). It should be stressed that the empirical transaction cost literature seriously tests hypotheses and therefore by its existence refutes the assertion that transaction cost economics is tautological. However, most of property right and neoclassical empirical studies are of the comparative static variety and attempt to test transaction cost hypotheses using various proxies for asset specificity, uncertainty, measurement costs, friction and other transaction cost variables in reduced form equations. There are only two studies that have attempted to measure the *level* of transaction costs.

The first and perhaps most ambitious of these is Wallis and North (1986), who attempt to measure the entire transaction sector of the economy over 100 years. Understandably, the first problem they face is how to define transaction costs. Their property rights background leads them to define transaction costs as 'the resource costs of maintaining and operating the institutional framework associated with capturing the gains from trade'. In the end, however, they simply separate resources devoted to transacting as their measure and in doing so ironically come closer to a neoclassical definition. Although they acknowledge the conceptual problems this definition has with respect to firms, they settle for the following compromise:

> We divide occupations into those that provide primarily transaction services to the firm and, by elimination, those that provide primarily transformation services. The wages of employees in these 'transaction occupations' constitute our measure of the transaction sector within firms. (1986, p. 100)

This compromise would require all protective services (police, courts and so on) included in the non-transaction sector of the economy, which makes Wallis and North so uncomfortable, they switch its classification (pp. 102-103). The analysis of Wallis and North concludes that the transaction sector accounts for a significant part of the economy and that this has grown from 25 percent to 40 percent over the years 1870 to 1970.

Davis (1986), however, has pointed out that this estimate is not robust for even small changes in the line that separates 'transactions' from 'production'. In the end, the problem of definition seems overwhelming. Is a farmer a manager/marketing agent, or a grain-growing field hand? All jobs have elements of production and transaction in them and it seems an impossible task to separate them. This perhaps best explains why Wallis and North were both the first and the last to tackle transaction costs on such a grand scale.

A more sophisticated treatment of measuring the costs of organization is found in Masten, Meehan and Snyder (1991). They note that much of the empirical literature proxies only 'the hazards of market exchange' and ignores the internal costs of governance. Reduced form estimates are unable to distinguish between internal and external transaction costs.

Furthermore, attempts to directly measure transaction costs are subject to the problems faced by Wallis and North. Finally, Masten, Meehan and Snyder recognize the selection bias that occurs since the efficient organization structure is chosen and the other choices are not observed. Their solution is to utilize switching regression techniques and to adopt censured regression models used in labor economics. From this technique they obtain actual dollar estimates of organization costs and therefore can estimate the magnitude of individual coefficients and not just their relative impact. Masten, Meehan and Snyder apply this methodology to naval shipyard contracts and find that overall organization costs amount to 14 percent of total costs. They estimate that if an incorrect contractual agreements is chosen that this would lead to increases in organizational costs of up to 70 percent.

9. Conclusion

The essential element of transaction costs, that property rights must be protected, is found in most fields of economics and throughout the discipline's history. Adam Smith, in discussing foreign trade, endowments, corporate ownership structure and non-profit organizations repeatedly exploits concepts of costly information and the ability of individuals to exploit others' ignorance to their own advantage (see West, 1990, for an account of Smith's anticipation of modern economic ideas like principal-agent relations). In macroeconomics the notion of costly information lead to the rational expectations revolution and subsequent real business cycle models based on search and the disincentives found in unemployment insurance programs. Public choice models are founded on the premise that individuals can use the state as a mechanism to transfer wealth to themselves. In game theory, the prisoner's dilemma and other non-cooperative games are essentially transaction cost problems. And other fields like industrial organization, international trade, development and labor, all contain ideas that hinge on the protection of property rights.

Given its long history and prevalence, it is ironic that the definition of transaction costs would be so difficult to agree on. This paper has argued that two definitions prevail in the literatures: one that defines transaction costs as only occurring when a market transaction takes place; the other defining transaction costs as occurring whenever any property right is established or requires protection. I have called these the neoclassical and property rights definitions and have argued that which definition is useful depends on what question is being examined. Recognizing the distinction, though, is important for removing ambiguity and animosity.

Bibliography on Transaction Costs (0740)

Ackerlof, George A. (1970), 'The Market for Lemons: Qualitative Uncertainty and the Market Mechanism', **84** *Quarterly Journal of Economics*, 488-500.

Aivazian, Varouj A. and Callen, Jeffrey L. (1980), 'Uncertain Externalities, Liability Rules and Resource Allocation: Comment', **70** *American Economic Review*, 1058-1059.

Aivazian, Varouj A. and Callen, Jeffrey L. (1981), 'The Coase Theorem and the Empty Core', **24** *Journal of Law and Economics*, 175-181.

Aivazian, Varouj A., Callen, Jeffrey L. and Lipnowski, Irwin F. (1988), 'The Coase Theorem and Coalitional Stability', **54** *Economica*, 517-520.

Aiyagari, S.R. and Gertler, M. (1991), 'Asset Returns with Transactions Costs and Uninsured Individual Risk', **27** *Journal of Monetary Economics*, 311-331.

Alchian, Armen A. (1958), 'Private Property and the Relative Cost of Tenure', in Bradley, P. (ed.), *The Public Stake in Union Power*, Charlottesville, VA, University Press of Virginia, 350-371.

Alchian, Armen A. (1961), *Some Economics of Property Rights*, Rand Paper, Rand Corporation.

Alchian, Armen A. (1965), 'Some Economics of Property Rights', **30** *Il Politico*, 816-829.

Alchian, Armen A. (1977), 'Why Money?', **9** *Journal of Money, Credit and Banking*, 133-140.

Alchian, Armen A. (1979), 'Some Implications of Recognition of Property Right Transaction Costs', in Brunner, K. (ed.), *Economics and Social Institutions*, Boston, 233-252.

Alchian, Armen A. and Allen, W. (1964), *University Economics*, Belmont, Wadsworth Publishing Co.

Alchian, Armen A. and Demsetz, Harold (1972), 'Production, Information Costs and Economic Organization', **62** *American Economic Review*, 777-795.

Alchian, Armen A. and Kessel, R. (1962), *Aspects of Labor Economics (Competition, Monopoly and the Pursuit of Money)*, Princeton, Princeton University Press.

Alchian, Armen A. and Woodward, S. (1988), 'Review of Williamson's "The Economic Institutions of Capitalism"', **26** *Journal of Economic Literature*, 65-79.

Alfaro Aguila-Real, Jesús (1996), 'Los Costes de Transacción (Transaction Costs)', in Menéndez, Aurelio (ed.), *Estudios Homenaje*, Madrid, Tomo I, 131-162.

Allen, Douglas W. (1990), 'In Inquiry into the State's Role in Marriage', **13** *Journal of Economic Behavior and Organization*, 171-191.

Allen, Douglas W. (1991), 'What are Transaction Costs?', **14** *Research in Law and Economics*, 1-18.

Allen, Douglas W. (1997), 'Property Rights, Transaction Costs and Coase: One More Time', in Medema, Steven G. (ed.), *Coasean Economics: Law and Economics and the New Institutional Economics*, Dordrecht, Kluwer Academic Publishers, 105-118.

Allen, Douglas W. and Lueck, Dean (1992a), 'Contract Choice in Modern Agriculture: Cash Rent versus Cropshare', **35** *Journal of Law and Economics*, 397-426.

Allen, Douglas W. and Lueck, D. (1992b), 'The Back-Forty on a Handshake: Specific Assets, Reputation and the Structure of Farmland Contracts', **8** *Journal of Law, Economics and Organization*, 366-377.

Allen, Douglas W. and Lueck, D. (1993), 'Transaction Costs and the Design of Cropshare Contracts', **24** *Rand Journal of Economics*, 78-100.

Allen, Douglas W. and Lueck, D. (1995), 'Risk Preferences and the Economics of Contracts', **5** *American Economic Review, Papers and Proceedings*, 447-451.

Alston, L. and Higgs, R. (1982), 'Contractual Mix in Southern Agricultre since the Civil War: Facts, Hypotheses and Tests', **42** *Journal of Economic History*, 327-353.

Alston, L., Datta, S. and Nugent, J. (1984), 'Tenancy Choice in a Competitive Framework with Transaction Costs', **92** *Journal of Political Economy*, 1121-1133.

Andersen, E. (1988), 'Transaction Costs as Determinants of Opportunism in Integrated and Independent Sales Forces', **9** *Journal of Economic Behavior and Organization*, 242-264.

Anderson, Terry L. and Lueck, Dean (1992), 'Land Tenure and Agricultural Productivity on Indian Reservations', **35** *Journal of Law and Economics*, 427-454.

Arnott, R. and Stiglitz, J. (1988), 'The Basic Analytics of Moral Hazard', **90(3)** *Scandinavian Journal of Economics*, 383-413.

Babic, Blagoje (1994), *Prelaz u Tranziciji (Deception in Transition)*, Belgrade, Prometej.

Barzel, Yoram (1976), 'An Alternative Approach to the Analysis of Taxation', **84** *Journal of Political Economy*, 1177-1197.

Barzel, Yoram (1977), 'Some Fallacies in the Interpretation of Information Costs', **20** *Journal of Law and Economics*, 291-307.

Barzel, Yoram (1982), 'Measurement Cost and the Organisation of Markets', **25** *Journal of Law and Economics*, 27-48.

Barzel, Yoram (1985), 'Transaction Costs: Are They Just Costs?', **141** *Journal of Institutional and Theoretical Economics*, 4-16.

Barzel, Y. (1987), 'Knight's "Moral Hazard" Theory of Organization', **25** *Economic Inquiry*, 117-120.

Barzel, Yoram (1989), *Economic Analysis of Property Rights*, Cambridge, Cambridge University Press, 122 p.

Barzel, Yoram and Kochin, L. (1992), 'Ronald Coase on the Nature of Social Cost as a Key to the Problem of the Firm', **94** *Scandinavian Journal of Economics*, 19-31.

Baumol, William J. (1952), 'The Transactions Demand for Cash: An Inventory Theoretic Approach', **66** *Quarterly Journal of Economics*, 545-556.

Bensaid, B., Lesne, J.P. and Pages, H. (1992), 'Derivative Asset Pricing with Transaction Costs', **2** *Mathematical Finance*, 63-86.

Bergstrom, T. (ed.) (1976), 'How to Discard "Free Disposability" - At No Cost', **3** *Journal of Mathematical Economics*, 131-134.

Blackstone, W. (1803), *Commentaries on the Laws of England*, London, Strahan.

Bowers, James W. (1993), 'The Fantastic Wisconsylvania Zero-Bureaucratic-Cost School of Bankruptcy Theory: A Comment', **91** *Michigan Law Review*, 1773-1792.

Boyle, P.P. and Vorst, Ton (1992), 'Option Replication in Discrete Time with Transaction Costs', **47** *Journal of Finance*, 271-293.

Breeden, Charles H. and Toumanoff, Peter G. (1984), 'Transaction Costs and Economic Institutions', in Leube, K.R. and Zlabinger, A.H. (eds), *The Political Economy of Freedom*, München, Philosophia Verlag, 161-177.

Brennan, Michael J. (1975), 'The Optimal Number of Securities in a Risky Asset Portfolio when there are Fixed Costs of Transaction: Theory and Some Empirical Results', **10** *Journal of Financial and Quantitative Analysis*, 483-496.

Brennan, Michael J. and Copeland, T.E. (1988), 'Stock Splits, Stock Prices and Transaction Costs', **22** *Journal of Financial Economics*, 83-101.

Brinig, Margaret F. (1990), 'Rings and Promises', **6** *Journal of Law, Economics and Organization*, 203-215.

Brinig, Margaret F. (1993), 'The Law and Economics of No-Fault Divorce', **27** *Family Law Quarterly*, 453-470.

Brinig, Margaret F. (1994), 'The Effect of Transactions Costs on the Market for Babies', **18** *Seton Hall Journal on Legislation*, 553-579.

Brinig, Margaret F. and Alexeev, Michael V. (1991), 'Legal Rules, Bargaining and Transactions Costs: The Case of Divorce', in Nagel, Stuart and Mills, Miriam K. (eds), *Systematic Analysis in Dispute Resolution*, New York, Quorum Books, 91-105.

Brinig, Margaret F. and Alexeev, Michael V. (1993), 'Trading at Divorce: Preferences, Legal Rules and Transaction Costs', **8** *Ohio State Journal on Dispute Resolution*, 279-297.

Brinig, Margaret F. and Alexeev, Michael V. (1995), 'Fraud in Courtship: Annulment and Divorce', **2** *European Journal of Law and Economics*, 45-63.

Brousseau, Eric (1993), 'Les Theories des Contrats: Une Revue', **103(1)** *Revue d'Economie Politique*, 1-82.

Brousseau, Eric (1993), *L'Economie des Contrats; Technologies de l'Information et Coordination Interentreprises*, Paris, Presses Universitaires de France (PUF).

Brousseau, Eric (1995), 'Contracts as Modular Mechanisms: Some Propositions for the Study of 'Hybrid Forms'', **2(3)** *International Journal of the Economics of Business*, 409-439.

Brousseau, Eric and Bessy, Christian (1997a), 'Brevet, Protection et Diffusion des Connaissances: une Relecture Neo-institutionnelle des Proprietes de la Regle de Droit (Patent, Protection and Diffusion of Knowledge: A Neo Instititional Revision of the Characteristics of the Rule of Law)', **79(S)** *Revue d'Economie Industrielle*, 233-254.

Brousseau, Eric and Bessy, Christian (1997b), *Technology Licensing Contracts: Features and Diversity*, 14th Conference of the European Association of Law and Economics (EALE), Universitat Pompeu Fabra, Barcelona, Spain.

Brousseau, Eric and Bessy, Christian (1997c), *The Governance of Intellectual Property Rights: Patents and Copyrights in France and in the US*, Inaugural Conference for the International Society for New Institutional Economics, The Present and Future of the New Institutional Economics, Washington University, St. Louis, Missouri.

Campbell, David (1996), 'On What is Valuable in Law and Economics', **8** *Otago Law Review*, 489-514.

Centi, Jean-Pierre (1987), 'Quel Critère d'Efficience pour l'Analyse Economique du Droit? (Which Efficiency Criterion for Economic Analysis of Law)', **2** *Revue de la Recherche Juridique*.

Centner, Terence J. (1985), 'Are FmHA Loans Entitlements Protected by the Due Process Clause?', **34** *Drake Law Review*, 389-427.

Centner, Terence J. and Wetzstein, Michael E. (1987), 'Reducing Moral Hazard Associated with Implied Warranties of Animal Health', **68** *American Journal of Agricultural Economics*, 143-150.

Centner, Terence J. and Wetzstein, Michael E. (1988), 'Reducing Moral Hazard Associated with Implied Warranties of Animal Health: Reply', **70** *American Journal of Agricultural Economics*, 413-414.

Centner, Terence J. and White, F.C. (1987), 'FmHA's Efforts against Delinquent Borrowers: Property Interests and Transaction Costs', **12** *Western Journal of Agricultural Economics*, 35-41.

Cheung, Steven N.S. (1969), *A Theory of Share Tenancy*, Chicago, University of Chicago Press, 188 p.

Cheung, Steven N.S. (1970), 'The Structure of a Contract and the Theory of a Non-exclusive Resource', **13** *Journal of Law and Economics*, 49-70.

Cheung, Steven N.S. (1974), 'A Theory of Price Control', **17** *Journal of Law and Economics*, 53-71.

Cheung, Steven N.S. (1978), *The Myth of Social Costs: A Critique of Welfare Economics and the Implications for Public Policy*, London, Institute of Economic Affairs, 93 p.

Cheung, Steven N.S. (1983), 'The Contractual Nature of the Firm', **26** *Journal of Law and Economics*, 1-21.

Cheung, Steven N.S. (1992), 'On the New Institutional Economics', in Werin, Lars and Wijkander, Hans (eds), *Contract Economics*, Oxford, Blackwell, 48-65.

Chianale, Angelo (1992), *L'atto Pubblico: Contributo allo Studio dei Costi Transattivi* (The Document under the Seal of a Public Officer: Contribution to the Study of Transaction Costs), Torino, Giappichelli.

Chisholm, Darlene C. (1997), 'Profit-Sharing Versus Fixed-Payment Contracts: Evidence From the Motion Pictures Industry', **13** *Journal of Law, Economics and Organization*, 169-201.

Coase, Ronald H. (1937), 'The Nature of the Firm', **4** *Economica*, 386-405. Reprinted in Kronman, Anthony T. and Posner, Richard A. (eds) (1979), *The Economics of Contract Law*, Boston, Little Brown, 31-32.

Coase, Ronald H. (1959), 'The Federal Communications Commission', **2** *Journal of Law and Economics*, 1-40.

Coase, Ronald H. (1960), 'The Problem of Social Cost', **3** *Journal of Law and Economics*, 1-44. Reprinted in Ackermann, Bruce A. (1975), *Economic Foundations of Property Law*, Boston, Little Brown, 17-22. Reprinted in Medema, Steven G. (1995), *The Legacy of Ronald Coase in Economic Analysis*, Vol.2, Aldershot, Edward Elgar Publishing, 5-48. Reprinted in Coase, Ronald H. (1988), *The Firm, the Market and the Law*, Chicago, University of Chicago Press.

Coase, R. (1972), 'Policy Issues and Research Opportunities in Industrial Organization', in Fuchs, Victor (ed.), *Economic Research: Retrospective and Prospect (Vol.3)*, NBER General Series no. 96, Cambridge National Bureau of Economic Research, 59-73.

Coase, Ronald H. (1988), *The Firm, the Market and the Law*, Chicago, University of Chicago Press, 217 p.

Coase, Ronald H. (1991), 'The Institutional Structure of Production', in Coase, Ronald H. (ed.), *Essays on Economics and Economists*, Chicago, IL, University of Chicago Press.

Coase, Ronald H. (1992), 'The Institutional Structure of Production', **82(4)** *American Economic Review*, 713-719.

Coelho Philip R.P. (1975), 'Externalities, Liability Separability and Resource Allocation: Comment', **65** *American Economic Review*, 721-723.

Cohen, Lloyd R. (1991), 'Holdouts and Free Riders', **20** *Journal of Legal Studies*, 351-362.

Constantinides, G.M. (1976), 'Optimal Portfolio Revision with Proportional Transaction Costs: Extension to HARA Utility Functions and Exogenous Deterministic Income', **22** *Management Science*, 921-923.

Constantinides, G.M. (1979), 'Mutiperiod Consumption and Investment Behavior with Convex Transaction Costs', **25** *Management Science*, 1127-1137.

Constantinides, G.M. (1986), 'Capital Market Equilibrium with Transaction Costs', **94** *Journal of Political Economy*, 842-862.

Cooter, Robert D. (1982), 'The Cost of Coase', **11** *Journal of Legal Studies*, 1-33. Reprinted in Donahue, Charles Jr, Kauper, Thomas E. and Martin, Peter W. (1992), *Property: An Introduction to the Concept and the Institution*. Reprinted in Ackerman, Bruce, Ellickson, Robert and Rose, Carol (1995), *Foundations of Property Law*. Reprinted in Medema, Steven G. (ed.) (1995), *The Legacy of Ronald Coase in Economic Analysis*, Aldershot, Edward Elgar Publishing, 96-128.

Copeland, T.E. and Galai, D. (1983), 'Information Effects on the Bid Ask Spread', **38** *Journal of Finance*, 1457-1469.

Crew, M.A. and Kleindorfer, D.R. (1985), 'Governance Costs or Rate-of-Return Regulation', **141** *Journal of Theoretical and Institutional Economics*, 104-123.

Crocker, Keith J. and Masten, Scott E. (1988), 'Mitigating Contractual Hazards: Unilateral Options and Contract Length', **19** *Rand Journal of Economics*, 327-343.

Crocker, Keith J. and Masten, Scott E. (1991), 'Pretia ex Machina? Prices and Process in Long-Term Contracts', **34** *Journal of Law and Economics*, 69-99.

Datta, Samar, O'Hara, Donald and Nugent, Jeffrey (1986), 'Choice of Agricultural Tenancy in the Presence of Transaction Costs', **62(2)**, *Land Economics*.

Davis, L. (1986), 'Comment', in Gallman (ed.), *Long Term Factors in American Economic Growth*, Chicago, University of Chicago Press, 149-161.

Davis, M.H. and Norman, A.R. (1990), 'Portfolio Selection with Transaction Costs', **15** *Mathematical Operations Research*, 676-713.

Demsetz, H. (1969), 'Information and Efficiency: Another Viewpoint', *Journal of Law and Economics*, 1-22.

Demsetz, Harold (1964), 'The Exchange and Enforcement of Property Rights', **7** *Journal of Law and Economics*, 11-26.

Demsetz, Harold (1967), 'Toward a Theory of Property Rights', **57** *American Economic Review*, 347-359. Reprinted in Demsetz, Harold (1988), *Ownership, Control and the Firm: The Organization of Economic Activity*, Vol. I, Cambridge: Basil Blackwell, 104-116

Demsetz, Harold (1968), 'The Cost of Transacting', **82** *Quarterly Journal of Economics*, 33-53.

Demsetz, Harold (1972), 'When Does the Rule of Liability Matter?', **1** *Journal of Legal Studies*, 13-28.

Demsetz, Harold (1988), 'The Theory of the Firm Revisited', **4** *Journal of Law, Economics and Organization*, 141-161.

Demsetz, Harold (1995), *The Economics of the Business Firm*, Cambridge, Cambridge University Press.

Dermody, J.C. and Prisman, E.Z. (1993), 'No Arbitrage and Valuation in Markets with Realistic Transaction Costs', **28** *Journal of Financial and Quantitative Analysis*, 65-80.

Dewatripont, Mathias (1989), 'Renegotiation and Information Revelation over Time: The Case of Optimal Labor Contracts', **103** *Quarterly Journal of Economics*, 589-619.

Dnes, Antony W. (1992), "Unfair" Practices and Hostages in Franchise Contracts', **148** *Journal of Institutional and Theoretical Economics*, 484-504.

Dnes, Antony W. (1993), 'A Case-Study Analysis of Franchise Contracts', **22** *Journal of Legal Studies*, 367-393.

Dnes, Antony W. (1996), 'The Economic Analysis of Franchise Contracts', **152** *Journal of Institutional and Theoretical Economics*, 297-324.

Donohue, John J. III (1989), 'Diverting the Coasian River: Incentive Schemes to Reduce Unemployment Spells', **99** *Yale Law Journal*, 549-609.

Dudek, Daniel J. and Wiener, Jonathan Baert (1996), *Joint Implementation, Transaction Costs and Climate Change*, Paris, OECD.

Dugger, William M. (1983), 'The Transaction Cost Analysis of O.E. Williamson: A New Synthesis?', **17** *Journal of Economic Issues*, 95-114.

Dumas, B. and Luciano, E. (1991), 'An Exact Solution to a Dynamic Portfolio Choice Problem under Transactions Costs', **46** *Journal of Finance*, 577-595.

Edirisinghe, C., Naik, V. and Uppal, R. (1993), 'Optimal Replication of Options with Transactions Costs and Trading Restrictions', **28** *Journal of Financial and Quantitative Analysis*, 117-138.

Eggertsson, Thrainn (1990a), *Economic Behaviour and Institutions*, Cambridge, Cambridge University Press, 385 p.

Eggertsson, Thrainn (1990b), 'The Role of Transaction Costs and Property Rights in Economic Analysis', **34** *European Economic Review*, 450-457.

Ellickson, Robert C. (1991), *Order Without Law: How Neighbours Settle Disputes*, Cambridge, MA, Harvard University Press.

Eppen, G. and Fama, Eugene F. (1969), 'Cash Balance and Simple Dynamic Portfolio Problems with Proportional Costs', **10** *International Economic Review*, 119-133.

Eswaran, Mukesh and Kotwal, A. (1985), 'A Theory of Contractual Structure in Agriculture', **75** *American Economic Review*, 352-367.

Fischel, William A. (1980), 'Externalities and Zoning', **35** *Public Choice*, 37-43.

Fishback, Price V. (1986), 'Did Coal Miners Owe their Souls to the Company Store? Theory and Evidence from the Early 1900s', **46** *Journal of Economic History*, 1011-1029.

Fishback, Price V. (1992), 'The Economics of Company Housing: Historical Perspectives from the Coal Fields', **8** *Journal of Law, Economics and Organization*, 346-365.

Fisher, S. (1994), 'Asset Trading, Transaction Costs and the Equity Premium', **9** *Journal of Applied Econometrics*, 571-594.

Foley, D.K. (1970), 'Economic Equilibrium with Costly Marketing', **2** *Journal of Economic Theory*, 276-291.

Frech, H. Edward III (1973), 'Pricing of Pollution: The Coase Theorem in the Long Run', **4(1)** *Bell Journal of Economics*, 316-319.

Frech, H. Edward III (1979), 'The Extended Coase Theorem and Long Run Equilibrium: The Non-Equivalence of Liability Rules and Property Rights', **27(1)** *Economic Inquiry*, 254-268.

Freixas, X., Guesnerie, Roger and Tirole, Jean (1985), 'Planning Under Incomplete Information and the Ratchet Effect', **52** *Review of Economic Studies*, 173-191.

Frenkel, Jacob A. and Levich, R.M. (1975), 'Covered Interest Arbitrage: Unexploited Profits', **83** *Journal of Political Economy*, 325-338.

Frey, Bruno S. (1985), 'Comment on Barzel, Transaction Costs: Are they Just Costs?', **141** *Journal of Institutional and Theoretical Economics*, 17-20.

Gemtos, Petros A. (1991), 'Thesmikes Analyseis sten Oikonomike: E Theoria ton Praxiakon Dikaiomaton (Institutional Analyses in Economics: The Property Rights Theory)', **4** *Aissymnetes*, 27-48.

Gennotte, G. and Jung, A. (1994), 'Investment Strategies under Transaction Costs: The Finite Horizon Case', **40** *Management Science*, 385-404.

George, T.J., Kaul, G. and Nimalendran, M. (1994), 'Trading Volume and Transaction Costs in Specialist Markets', **49** *Journal of Finance*, 1489-1505.

Globerman, S. (1980), 'Markets, Hierarchies and Innovation', **14** *Journal of Economic Issues*, 977-998.

Globerman, S. and Schwindt, R. (1986), 'The Organization of Vertically Related Transactions in the Canadian Forest Products Industries', **7** *Journal of Economic Behavior and Organization*, 199-212.

Glosten, L. and Milgrom, Paul R. (1985), 'Bid, Ask and Transaction Prices in a Specialist Market with Heterogeneously Informed Traders', **14** *Journal of Financial Economics*, 71-100.

Goldberg, Victor P. (1989), 'Production Functions, Transactions, Costs and the New Institutonalism', in Goldberg, Victor P. (ed.), *Readings in the Economics of Contract Law*, Cambridge, Cambridge University Press, 21-23. Reprinted in Feiwel, George (ed.), *Issues in Contemporary Microeconomics,* Macmillan Press, 1985, 395-402.

Goldberg, Victor P. and Erickson, John R. (1987), 'Quantity and Price Adjustments in Long-Term Contracts: A Case Study of Petroleum Coke', **30** *Journal of Law and Economics*, 369-398.

Goldsmith, D. (1976), 'Transaction Costs and the Theory of Portfolio Selection', **31** *Journal of Finance*, 1127-1139.

Grossman, Sanford J. and Hart, Oliver D. (1986), 'The Costs and Benefits of Ownership: A Theory of Vertical and Lateral Integration', **94** *Journal of Political Economy*, 691-719.

Guia-Abiad, V. (1993), 'Borrower Transaction Costs and Credit Rationing in Rural Financial Markets: The Philippine Case', **31** *Developing Economies*, 208-219.

Hahn, F.H. (1971), 'Equilibrium with Transaction Costs', **39** *Econometrica*, 417-439.

Hahn, F.H. (1973), 'On Transaction Costs, Inessential Sequence Economies and Money', **40** *Review of Economic Studies*, 449-461.

Hall, Christopher D. (1986), 'Market Enforced Information Asymmetry: A Study of Claiming Races', **24** *Economic Inquiry*, 271-291.

Hansen, Robert G. and Thomas, Randall S. (1992), 'An Auction - Theoretic Analysis of Corporate Auctioneer's Liability Regimes', **4** *Wisconsin Law Review*.

Hart, D. and Kuhn, H. (1975), 'A Proof of Existence of Equilibrium Without the Free Disposal Assumption', **2** *Journal of Mathematical Economics*, 335-343.

Hart, Oliver D. and Moore, John (1990), 'Property Rights and the Nature of the Firm', **98** *Journal of Political Economy*, 1119-1158.

Heller, W. and Starr, R. (1976), 'Equilibrium with Non-convex Transaction Costs: Monetary and Non-monetary Economies', **43** *Review of Economic Studies*, 195-215.

Hennart, Jean-François, Anderson, E. and Anderson, Erin (1993), 'Countertrade and the Minimization of Transaction Costs: An Empirical Examination', **9** *Journal of Law, Economics and Organization*, 290-313.

Hess, James D. (1990), 'A Comparison of Alternative Approaches to Economic Organization: Comment', **146** *Journal of Institutional and Theoretical Economics*, 72-75.

Hicks, John R. (1935), 'A Suggestion for Simplifying the Theory of Money', **2** *Economica*, 1-19.

Hirshleifer, Jack (1973), 'Exchange Theory: The Missing Chapter', **11** *Western Economic Journal*, 129-146.

Holm, Hakan J. (1995), 'Computational Cost of Verifying Enforceable Contracts', **15** *International Review of Law and Economics*, 127-140.

Holmstrom, B. (1979), 'Moral Hazard and Observability', **10** *Bell Journal of Economics*, 74-91.

Holmström, Bengt (1982), 'Moral Hazard in Teams', **13** *Bell Journal of Economics*, 324-340.

Holmström, Bengt and Milgrom, Paul R. (1991), 'Multitask Principal-Agent Analyses: Incentive Contracts, Asset Ownership and Job Design', **7** *Journal of Law, Economics and Organization*, 24-52.

Holmström, Bengt and Milgrom, Paul R. (1994), 'The Firm as an Incentive System', **84** *American Economic Review*, 972-991.

Huberman, Gur (1990), 'Dividend Neutrality with Transaction Costs', **63** *Journal of Business*, 93-107.

Hutter, Michael (1986), 'Transaction Cost and Communication', in Graf Von Der Schulenburg, J.-Matthias and Skogh, Göran (eds), *Law and Economics and The Economics of Legal Regulation*, Dordrecht, Kluwer, 113-129.

Hwang, Chun-Sin and Kan, Steven S. (1994), *Principles of Economics, Cooperating for Mutual Prosperity and Progress* (in Chinese), Published by the authors and distributed by Shin Lu Bookstore, Taipei.

Hwang, Chun-Sin and Kan, Steven S. (1995), 'Democracy and the Principle for the Division of Labor in Government Organization (in Chinese)', in Chien, Sechin Y.S. and Tai, Terence H. (eds), *Philosophy and Public Norms*, Taipei, Academia Sinica, Sun Yat-sen Institute for Social Sciences and Philosophy, 163-200.

Jensen, M. and Meckling, W. (1976), 'Theory of the Firm: Manegerial Behavior, Agency Costs and Ownership Structure', **3** *Journal of Financial Economics*, 305-360.

Johnsen, D. Bruce (1992), 'The Incentive Effects of Soft Dollar Brokerage', in Lehn, Kenneth and Kamphuis, Robert (eds), *Modernizing US Securities Regulations: Economic and Legal Perspectives*, 511-519.

Johnsen, D. Bruce (1994), 'Property Rights to Investment Research: The Agency Costs of Soft Dollar Brokerage', **11** *Yale Journal on Regulation*, 75-113.

Johnsen, D. Bruce (1995), 'The Quasi-Rent Structure of Corporate Enterprise: A Transaction Cost Theory', **44** *Emory Law Journal*, 1277 ff.

Johnsen, D. Bruce, Habib, Michel A. and Naik, Narayan Y. (1998), 'Spin-offs and Information', *Journal of Financial Intermediation*, forthcoming.

Joskow, Paul L. (1985), 'Vertical Integration and Long-Term Contracts: The Case of Coal-Burning Electric Generating Plants', **1** *Journal of Law, Economics and Organization*, 33-80.

Joskow, Paul L. (1987), 'Contract Duration and Relationship-Specific Investments: Empirical Evidence from Coal Markets', **77** *American Economic Review*, 168-185.

Joskow, Paul L. (1988), 'Price Adjustment in Long-Term Contracts: The Case of Coal', **31** *Journal of Law and Economics*, 47-83.

Joskow, Paul L. (1990), 'The Performance of Long-term Contracts: Further Evidence from Coal Markets', **21** *Rand Journal of Economics*, 251-274.

Jouini, E. and Kallal, H. (1995), 'Martingales and Arbitrage in Securities Markets with Transaction Costs', **66** *Journal of Economic Theory*, 178-197.

Jovanovic, Aleksandra (1993), *Participativna Ekonomija: Uticaj Tipa Svojine na Ponasanje (Efikasnost) Preduzeca* (Participatory Economics: Influence of a Property Form on Behaviour (Efficacy) of a Firm), Belgrade, Pravni fakultet.

Jovanovic, Aleksandra (1994), 'Transakcioni Troskovi Privatizacije (Transaction Costs of Privatisation)', **43(9-10)** *Pravni Zivot*, 895-905.

Jovanovic, Aleksandra (1996), 'Ekonomski Efekti Nekih Ekonomskih Prava', in Svetislav, Taborosi (ed.), *Srbija u Tranziciji*, Belgrade, Pravni fakultet, 113-125.

Jovanovic, Aleksandra, Hiber, Dragor (1996), 'Postupak Izvrsenja na Imovini Drustvenog Preduzeca i Moralni Hazard (Execution Procedure on the Propery of a Social Enterprise and Moral Hazard)', in X (ed.), *Svojina i Slobode - Aspekti Tranzicije*, Belgrade, Institut ekonomskih nauka, 202-208.

Jovanovic, Aleksandra, Mijatovic Bosko (1996), 'Preduzece i Moralni Hazard (Firm and Moral Hazard)', **45(5-8)** *Pravni Zivot*, 404-415.

Kamin, J.H. (1975), 'Optimal Portfolio Revision with a Proportional Transaction Cost', **21** *Management Science*, 1263-1271.

Kan, Steven S. (1993), 'Entrepreneurship, Transaction Costs and Subjectivist Economics', **1(2)** *Journal of Enterprising Culture*, 159-182.

Kan, Steven S. and Hsiao, Ding-Way (1996), 'Contracts in Tsing Dynasty to Build Irrigation System at Lan-Yang Plain: A Transaction Cost Analysis', **59** *Journal of Agricultural Economics* (Chinese), 111-157.

Kan, Steven S. and Hwang, Chun-Sin (1994), *Principles of Economics: Cooperating for Mutual Prosperity and Progress* (in Chinese), Published by the authors and distributed by Shin Lu Bookstore, Taipei.

Kan, Steven S. and Hwang, Chun-Sin (1996), 'A Form of Government Organization from the Perspective of Transaction Cost Economics', **7** *Constitutional Political Economy*, 197-220.

Kaplow, Louis and Shavell, Steven (1996), 'Property Rules versus Liability Rules: An Economic Analysis', **109** *Harvard Law Review*, 713-790.

Kelman, Mark G. (1979), 'Consumption Theory, Production Theory and Ideology in the Coase Theorem', **52** *Southern California Law Review*, 669-698.

Kitch, Edmund W. (ed.) (1983), 'The Fire of Truth: A Remembrance of Law and Economics at Chicago, 1932-1970', **26** *Journal of Law and Economics*, 163-233.

Klein, Benjamin and Leffler, Keith B. (1981), 'The Role of Market Forces in Assuring Contractual Performance', **89** *Journal of Political Economy*, 615-641.

Klein, Benjamin, Crawford, Robert G. and Alchian, Armen A. (1978), 'Vertical Integration, Appropriable Rents and the Competitive Contracting Process', **21** *Journal of Law and Economics*, 297-326.

Knight, Frank (1921), *Risk, Uncertainty and Profit*, London, Houghton Mifflin Company.

Kurz, M. (1974a), 'Equilibrium in a Finite Sequence of Markets with Transaction Costs', **42** *Econometrica*, 1-20.

Kurz, M. (1974b), 'Arrow-Debreu Equilibrium of an Exchange Economy with Transaction Costs', **15** *International Economic Review*, 699-717.

Lafontaine, Francine (1993), 'Contractual Arrangements as Signaling Devices: Evidence from Franchising', **9** *Journal of Law, Economics and Organization*, 256-289.

Landa, Janet T. (1994), *Trust, Ethnicity and Identity: Beyond the New Institutional Economics of Ethnic Trading Networks, Contract Law and Gift-Exchange*, Ann Arbor, University of Michigan Press.

Leder, Mathias (1992), 'Der Transaktionskostenansatz - Möglichkeiten und Grenzen (The Transaction Cost Approach - Possibilities and Boundaries)', in Schlieper, Ulrich and Schmidtchen, Dieter (eds), *Makro, Geld und Institutionen*, Tübingen, 106-108.

Leffler, Keith B. and Rucker, Randal, R. (1991), 'Transaction Costs and the Organization of Production: Timber Contracts', **99** *Journal of Political Economy*, 1060-1087.

Leland, Hayne E. (1974), 'On Consumption and Portfolio Choices with Transaction Costs', in Balch, McFadden and Wu (eds), *Essays on Economic Behavior under Uncertainty*, Amsterdam, North-Holland, 184-191.

Leland, Hayne E. (1985), 'Option Pricing and Replication with Transaction Costs', **11** *Journal of Finance*, 1283-1301.

Lemley, Mark A. (1997), 'The Economics of Improvement in Intellectual Property Law', **75** *Texas Law Review*, 989 ff.

Levy, David T. (1985), 'The Transactions Cost Approach to Vertical Integration: An Empirical Examination', **67** *Review of Economics and Statistics*, 438-445.

Levy, H. (1978), 'Equlibrium in an Imperfect Market: A Constraint on the Number of Securities in the Portfolio', **68** *American Economic Review*, 643-658.

Litzenberger, R.H. and Rolfo, J. (1984), 'Arbitrage Pricing, Transaction Costs and Taxation of Capital Gains: A Study of Government Bonds with the Same Maturity Date', **13** *Journal of Financial Economics*, 337-361.

Lueck, Dean (1991), 'Ownership and the Regulation of Wildlife', **29** *Economic Inquiry*, 249-260.

Lueck, Dean and Allen, Douglas W. (1993), 'Transaction Costs and the Design of Cropshare Contracts', **24(1)** *Rand Journal of Economics*, 78-100.

Lund, J.R. (1993), 'Transaction Risk versus Transaction Costs in Water Transfers', **29** *Water Resources Research*, 3103-3107.

MacKaay, Ejan (1979), 'The Costliness of Information and its Effects on the Economic Analysis of Law', in Ziegel, Jacob B. (ed.), *Proceedings of the Seventh Annual Workshop on Commercial and Consumer Law*, Toronto, Canada Law Book.

Magill, M.J.P. and Constantinides, G.M. (1976), 'Portfolio Selection with Transactions Costs', **13** *Journal of Economic Theory*, 245-263.

Mahoney, J. (1992), 'The Choice of Organizatinonal Form: Vertical Financial Ownership versus Other Methods of Vertical Integration', **13** *Strategic Management Journal*.

Malkiel, B.G. (1966), *The Term Structure of Interest Rates: Expectations and Behavior Patterns*, Princeton, Princeton University Press.

Masten, Scott E. (1984), 'The Organisation of Production: Evidence from the Aerospace Industry', **27** *Journal of Law and Economics*, 403-417.

Masten, Scott E. and Crocker, Keith J. (1985), 'Efficient Adaptation in Long-Term Contracts: Take-or-Pay Provisions for Natural Gas', **75** *American Economic Review*, 1083-1093.

Masten, Scott E., Meehan, James W., Jr and Snyder, Edward A. (1989), 'Vertical Integration in the U.S. Auto Industry: A Note on the Influence of Transaction Specific Assets', **12** *Journal of Economic Behavior and Organization*, 265-273.

Masten, Scott E., Meehan, James W., Jr and Snyder, Edward A. (1991), 'The Costs of Organization', **7** *Journal of Law, Economics and Organization*, 1-25.

Mayshar, J. (1979), 'Transaction Costs in a Model of Capital Market Equilibrium', **87** *Journal of Political Economy*, 673-700.

Mayshar, J. (1981), 'Transaction Costs and the Pricing of Assets', **36** *Journal of Finance*, 583-597.

McKenzie, L. (1981), 'The Classical Theorems on Existence of Competitive Equilibrium', **49** *Econometrica*, 819-841.

McManus, J. (1975), 'The Cost of Alternative Economic Organizations', **8** *Canadian Journal of Economics*, 334-350.

Medema, Steven G. (1994), *Ronald H. Coase*, London, Macmillan.

Medema, Steven G. (1995a), 'Through a Glass Darkly, or Just Wearing Dark Glasses? Posin, Coase and the Coase Theorem', **62** *Tennessee Law Review*, 1041-1056.

Medema, Steven G. (1995b), *The Legacy of Ronald Coase in Economic Analysis*, 2 vols, Aldershot, Edward Elgar.

Medema, Steven G. (1996a), 'Of Pangloss, Pigouvians and Pragmatism: Ronald Coase on Social Cost Analysis', **18** *Journal of the History of Economic Thought*, 96-114.

Medema, Steven G. (1996b), 'Comment: The Coase Theorem, Rent Seeking and the Forgotten Footnote', **16** *International Review of Law and Economics*.

Medema, Steven G. (forthcoming), 'The Coase Theorem', in Coopera and Argyris (eds), *The Encyclopedia of Managerial Economics*, Oxford, Basil Blackwell.

Mehra, R. and Prescott, E. (1985), 'The equity Premium - A Puzzle', **15(2)** *Journal of Monetary Economics*, 145-161.

Milgrom, Paul R. and Roberts, Mark J. (1992), *Economics, Organization and Management*, Englewood Cliffs, NJ, Prentice-Hall.

Milovanovic Milic (1994), 'Privatizacija i Ekonomska Efikasnost (Privatization and Economic Efficiency)', **1-2** *Ekonomska Misao*, 1-20.

Modigliani, Franco and Miller, Merton H. (1958), 'The Cost of Capital, Corporation Finance and the Theory of Investment', **48** *American Economic Review*, 261-297.

Monteverde, Kirk and Teece, David J. (1982), 'Appropriable Rents and Quasi-Vertical Integration', **25** *Journal of Law and Economics*, 321-328.

Mukherjee, R. and Zabel, E. (1974), 'Consumption and Portfolio Choices with Transaction Costs', in Balch, McFadden and Wu (eds), *Essays on Economic Behavior under Uncertainty*, Amsterdam, North-Holland.

Niehans, J. (1969), 'Money in a Static Theory of Optimal Payment Arrangements', **1** *Journal of Money, Credit and Banking*, 706-726.

Niehans, J. (1971), 'Money and Barter in General Equilibrium with Transaction Costs', **61** *American Economic Review*, 773-783.

Niehans, J. (1987), 'Transaction Costs', in Eatwell, John, Milgate, Murray and Newman, Peter (eds), *The New Palgrave: A Dictionary of Economics*, London, Macmillan, 676-679.

North, Douglass C. (1981), *Structure and Change in Economic History*, New York, W.W. Norton.

North, Douglass C. (1990), *Institutions, Institutional Change and Economic Performance*, Cambridge, Cambridge University Press.

North, Douglass C. and Weingast, Barry R. (1989), 'Constitutions and Commitment: The Evolution of Institutions Governing Public Choice in Seventeenth Century England', **49** *Journal of Economic History*, 803-832.

Olson, A. (1987), 'Leaving Liablity Alone', **Aug 12** *Wall Street Journal*, 18 ff.

Ott, Claus (1991), 'Vorvertragliche Aufklärungspflichten im Recht des Güter- und Leistungsaustausches (Precontractual Obligation to Provide Information in the Law)', in Ott, Claus and Schäfer, Hans-Bernd (eds), *Ökonomische Probleme des Zivilrechts*, Berlin, Springer, 142-162.

Parkman, Allen M. (1992), 'Unilateral Divorce and the Labor-Force Participation Rate of Married Women Revisited', **82** *American Economic Review*, 671-678.

Pesaran, M.H. and Timmermann, A. (1994), 'Forecasting Stock Returns: An Examination of Stock Market Trading in the Presence of Transacton Costs', **13** *Journal of Forecasting*, 335-367.

Phillips, S.M. and Smith, C.W., Jr (1980), 'Trading Costs for Listed Options: The Implications for Market Efficiency', **8** *Journal of Financial Economics*, 179-201.

Protopapadakis, A. and Stoll, H.R. (1983), 'Spot and Futures Prices and the Law of One Price', **38** *Journal of Finance*, 1431-1455.

Provencher, Bill (1991), *A Quantitative Analysis of Private Property Rights in Groundwater*, University of California, Davis, Ph.D. Dissertation.

Radner, Roy (1972), 'Existence of Equilibrium of Plans, Prices and Price Expectations in a Sequence of Markets', **40** *Econometrica*, 289-303.

Repullo, R. (1988), 'The Core of an Economy with Transaction Costs', **40** *Review of Economic Studies*, 447-458.

Ricardo, D. (1951), 'Funding System', in Straffa, P. (ed.), *The Works and Correspondence of David Ricardo*, Cambridge, Cambridge University Press.

Rothschild, Michael and Stiglitz, Joseph E. (1976), 'Equilibrium in Competitive Insurance Markets: An Essay on the Economics of Imperfect Information', **90** *Quarterly Journal of Economics*, 629-649.

Rubin, Paul H. (1990), *Managing Business Transactions*, New York, Free Press.

Ryssdal, Stray A.C. (1995), *Legal Realism and Economics as Behavior - A Scandinavian Look at the Economic Analysis of Law*, Oslo, Juridisk Forlag.

Samuels, Warren J. (1974), 'The Coase Theorem and the Study of Law and Economics', **14** *Natural Resources Journal*, 1-33.

Schlag, Pierre (1989), 'The Problem of Transaction Costs', **62** *Southern California Law Review*, 1661-1699.

Schmidtchen, Dieter (1989), 'Evolutorische Ordnungstheorie oder: die Transaktionskosten und das Unternehmertum (The Theory of Evolutionary Order, or: Transaction Costs and Entrepreneurship)', *Ordo: Jahrbuch für die Ordnung von Wirtschaft und Gesellschaft*, 161-182.

Schultz, P. (1983), 'Transaction Costs and the Small Firm Effect', **12** *Journal of Financial Economics*, 81-88.

Shaffer, S. (1989), 'Structuring an Option to Facilitate Replication with Transaction Costs', **31** *Economic Letters*, 183-187.

Shapiro, David L. (1974), 'Rent and the Coase Theorem', **7(1)** *Journal of Economic Theory*, 125-128.

Shavell, Steven (1979), 'Risk Sharing and Incentives in the Principal and Agent Relationship', **10** *Bell Journal of Economics*, 55-73.

Shelanski, H and Klein, P. (1995), 'Empirical Research in Transaction Cost Economics: A Review and Assessment', **11** *Journal of Law, Economics and Organization*, 335-361.

Smiley, Robert H. (1976), 'Tender Offers, Transactions Costs and the Theory of the Firm', **58(1)** *Review of Economics and Statistics*, 22-32.

Starret, David A. (1973), 'Inefficiency and the Demand for "Money" in a Sequence Economy', **40** *Review of Economic Studies*, 437-448.

Stavins, R.N. (1995), 'Transaction Costs and Tradable Permits', **29** *Journal of Environmental Economics and Management*, 133-148.

Stigler, George J. (1988), *Memoirs of an Unregulated Economist*, New York, Basic Books, 228 p.

Stiglitz, Joseph E. (1974), 'Incentives and Risk Sharing in Sharecropping', **61** *Review of Economic Studies*, 219-256.

Stout, Lynn A. (1997), 'A Technology, Transactions Costs and Investor Welfare: Is a Motley Fool Born Every Minute?', **75** *Washington University Law Quarterly*.

Tobin, James (1956), 'The Interest-Elasticity of Transactions Demand for Cash', **38(3)** *Review of Economics and Statistics*, 241-247.

Ulph, A.M. and Ulph, D.T. (1975), 'Transaction Costs in General Equilibrium Theory - A Survey', **42** *Economica*, 355-372.

Ulph, A.M. and Ulph, D.T. (1977), 'Efficiency, Inessentiality and `Debreu Property' of Prices', in Schwödiauer (ed.), *Equlibrium and Disequilibrium in Economic Theory*, Dordrecht, Reidel, 337-359.

Wagner, W. and Schulman, E. (1994), 'Passive Trading: Point and Counterpoint', **20** *Journal of Portfolio Management*, 25-28.

Wallis, J. and North, C. (1986), 'Measuring the Transaction Sector in the American Economy, 1870-1970', in Gallman (ed.), *Long Term Factors in American Economic Growth*, Chicago, University of Chicago Press, 95-148.

Wegehenkel, Lothar (1980), *Transaktionskosten, Wirtschaftssystem und Unternehmertum* (Transaction Costs, Economic System and Entrepreneurship), Tübingen, Mohr, 77 p.

West, E.G. (1990), *Adam Smith and Modern Economics*, Hants, Edward Elgar.

Whincop, Michael J. (1996), 'Due Diligence in SME Fundraising: Reform Choices, Economics and Empiricism', **20** *University of New South Wales Law Journal*, 433-464.

Whincop, Michael J. (1997), 'Nexuses of Contracts, the Authority of Corporate Agents and Doctrinal Indeterminacy: From Formalism to Law-and-Economics', **20** *University of New South Wales Law Journal*.

Wilcox, J.W. (1993), 'The Effect of Transaction Costs and Delay on Performance Drag', **49** *Financial Analysts Journal*, 45-54.

Williamson, Oliver E. (1971), 'The Vertical Integration of Production: Market Failure Considerations', **61** *American Economic Review*, 112-123.

Williamson, Oliver E. (1975), *Markets and Hierarchies: Analysis and Antitrust Implication: A Study in the Economics of Internal Organization*, New York, Free Press, 286 p.

Williamson, Oliver E. (1976), 'Franchise Bidding for Natural Monopolies - in General and with Resect to CATV', **7** *Bell Journal of Economics*, 73-104.

Williamson, Oliver E. (1979), 'Transaction-Cost Economics: The Governance of Contractual Relations', **22** *Journal of Law and Economics*, 233-261.

Williamson, Oliver E. (1981), 'Contract Analysis: The Transaction Cost Approach', in Burrows, Paul and Veljanovski, Cento G. (eds), *The Economic Approach to Law*, London, Butterworths, 39-60.

Williamson, Oliver E. (1985), *The Economic Institutions of Capitalism: Firms, Markets, Relational Contracting*, New York, Free Press, 450 p.

Williamson, Oliver E. (1990), 'A Comparison of Alternative Approaches to Economic Organization', **146** *Journal of Institutional and Theoretical Economics*, 61-71.

Williamson, Oliver E. and Winter, S. (eds) (1991), *The Nature of the Firm, Origins, Evolution and Development*, Oxford, Oxford University Press.

Wittman, Donald A. (1982), 'Efficient Rules in Highway Safety and Sports Activity', **72** *American Economic Review*, 78-90.

Wohar, Mark E. (1988), 'Alternative Versions of the Coase Theorem and the Definition of Transaction Costs', **27(1)** *Quarterly Journal of Business and Economics*, 3-19.

Young, A.R. (1989), 'An Economic Rationale for Door Prizes', **8** *Marketing Science*, 375-380.

Zec, Miodrag, Mijatovic, Bosko and Nebojsa, Savic (eds) (1994), *Privatizacija Nuznost ili Sloboda Izbora* (Privatization Necessity or Freedom of Choice), Belgrade, Ekonomski institut and Jugoslovenska knjiga.

Zerbe, Richard O., Jr (1980), 'The Problem of Social Cost in Retrospect', **2** *Research in Law and Economics*, 83-102.

Zupan, Mark A. (1989a), 'Cable Franchise Renewals: Do Incumbent Firms Behave Opportunistically?', **20** *Rand Journal of Economics*, 473-482.

Zupan, Mark A. (1989b), 'The Efficacy of Franchise Bidding Schemes in the Case of Cable Television: Some Systematic Evidence', **32** *Journal of Law and Economics*, 401-456.

0750
PUBLIC GOODS AND CLUB GOODS

Patrick McNutt
Chairperson, Competition Authority, Dublin and Research Associate, Department of Political Science, University of Dublin

Abstract

Public goods contrast with private goods. Pure public goods have the unique characteristics of non-excludability and non-rivalry in consumption while private goods are sold to those who can afford to pay the market price. The under-supply equilibrium of a public goods provision is an important aspect of the provision of public goods. The economic theory of clubs represents an attempt to explain the under-supply equilibrium of a public goods provision. It raises many different and controversial issues which impinge on government policy in the public sector. In many respects, a club provision proffers an alternative to a central government provision of local public goods. The salient characteristic of a club, the excludability factor, may militate against an equal and democratic distribution of the club good. At the level of voluntary clubs, with which Buchanan was originally concerned, club theory can critically appraise the efforts at achieving optimal membership of the club and the maximum utility of club members. As the literature introduces increasing problems with cooperation then it behoves law and economics scholars to research and develop non-market and/or non-cooperative solutions to an optimal provision of public goods.
JEL classification: D60, D71, K00.
Keywords: Free Rider, Pareto Optimality, Club Goods, Excludability and Non-rivalry, Coase Theorem, Homogeneity

1. Introduction

Pure public goods as originally defined by Samuelson (1954) have the unique characteristics of non-excludability and non-rivalry in consumption. Public goods contrast with private goods; public goods are non-excludable and non-rivalrous in consumption while private goods are sold to those who can afford to pay the market price. The market price excludes some consumers while the property of rivalrous consumption ensures that not all consumers who can afford to pay the price, actually purchase the private good. The public goods property of non-rivalry ensures that a provision of the good for consumer A entails a provision for consumer B. Likewise, the property of non-excludability ensures that one cannot exclude consumer B from securing the benefits of the public good, consequently there is no incentive for consumer B to pay the costs of providing the public good. Therefore a consumer may 'free ride' (Kim and Walker, 1984) on the provision of the public good, securing the benefits but not paying the costs of provision.

A lighthouse signal is a classic example of a pure public good, where the provision is both non-rival and non-excludable. Local radio or community radio, theatre performances and untelevised sports events are interesting examples of a local public good, where the provision is non-rival but excludable. The market is not the only mechanism through which goods and services are provided in a modern economy (Coase, 1974); public goods and club goods are characterised by their provision wholly through a political process since by their very nature they are unmarketable.

A primary reason why market failure persists is reflected in the inability of citizens to act cooperatively and it is this lack of cooperation which mandates an allocative role for government in the economy. A public good that becomes excludable is a club good (McNutt, 1996). The economic analysis of clubs pioneered by Buchanan (1965) can be applied to the provision of local public goods, ranging from the supply of decentralised regional public goods (local health boards) to community projects and neighbourhood schemes, such as community sports clubs and residents associations.

In the theory of clubs, however, there is collective consumption but with an exclusion principle, for example, a membership fee. One can think of club goods as public goods *sans* non-excludability. There are economies of scale in that additional members reduce the average cost of the club good. But additional members also lead to crowding which in the long run could be regarded as the introduction of rivalrous consumption. Indeed the club goods have polar extremes as noted by Mueller (1989, p. 131): 'for a pure public good the addition of one more member to the club never detracts from benefits of club membership ... [for] a pure private good, say an apple, crowding begins to take place on the first unit'.

2. Excludability and Non-Rivalry

There are, therefore, two salient properties pertaining to the provision of public goods, namely, non-excludability in supply and non-rivalry in consumption. The latter implies that inter-citizen consumption is mutually exclusive, that is, the consumption by one citizen of the public good will not affect the consumption level of any other citizen. Radio broadcasts, clean air or defence spring to mind as examples of a non-rivalrous public good. Non-excludability is the hallmark of a political system where the central government funding emanates directly from citizen taxation. However, in the provision of some public goods, either local public goods or club goods, the citizens often prefer to act independently of government. The property of excludability in the supply of the public good is the *sine qua non* of club goods.

A prisoner's dilemma characterisation of the market failure problem would indicate a Pareto inferior outcome as long as a dominant strategy existed for the individual citizen. The incentive to cheat on collective decisions, otherwise known as the free rider problem, illustrates one dominant strategy which undermines the optimal provision of public goods. In the classic tradition of public choice, government intervention *per se* would represent an externality. It is the increasing trend towards local public goods in the provision of public sector output that has facilitated the application of club theory which exhibits a cooperative response to the resolution of a local or regional issue.

Buchanan (1965), who was one of the first scholars to consider the efficiency properties of voluntary clubs, derived the economic conditions under which an optimal provision of a local public good could be attained. This early work outlined a justification for club analysis in the explanation of why clubs would organise. Both Buchanan and Olson (1965) recognised independently that clubs enable members to exploit economies of scale in the provision of the public good and to share in the cost of its provision. They each addressed the issue of membership restrictions, with Olson distinguishing between exclusive clubs and inclusive clubs with *no* membership constraints.

Likewise, Tiebout (1956) had much earlier addressed a club-related issue in his work on population mobility and size of local government. His 'voting with the feet' hypothesis has many direct applications in the area of local public goods. Other scholars, notably Schelling (1969) and McGuire (1974) justified club formation on the basis of 'a taste for association'. This has since been translated in the club literature as the assumption of homogeneity (identical tastes), an assumption which has raised the policy issue as to whether or not mixed clubs are optimal. For example, if mixed clubs are not optimal then the policy of group segregation is optimal whereas the policy of busing, as practised in some US states, is suboptimal. The issue of optimality, however, is not completely resolved across the club literature.

3. Public Goods Paradox

To what extent the theory of clubs enables policymakers to escape the under-supply equilibrium in the optimal provision of public goods remains a challenging issue. In other words, the optimal provision of public goods generally is constrained by what can broadly be defined as the public goods paradox, that is, unless the spoils of the public good are divisible there is no incentive for the individual to participate in its provision. Club theory overcomes the problem of non-excludability in so far as members of the club use the club good. The non-excludability characteristic of a pure public good may constrain the realisation of economies of scale in any interest-group provision of the good unless the gains are divisible.

Table 1
An Economics Typology

	Excludable	Non-Excludable
Rival	Private good	Public good
Non-Rival	Local public good	Pure public good

The public good in Table 1 is characterised as non-excludable and rival. In other words, rivalness in consumption is the distinguishing feature between a public good and a pure public good. The good could be described as a common good in the absence of any rival behaviour between citizens; some examples include air quality, frontier land and outer space. Rivalrous behaviour, however, converts the common good into a public good as frontier land is zoned, air quality control becomes necessary and space stations are constructed.

Once property rights are established the good eventually becomes an excludable and rival private good. For example, if a toll-free congested bridge, a rival and non-excludable good, becomes a congested bridge with Pigou-Knight tolls, the good therefore becomes a rival and excludable private good. There are increasingly few examples remaining (Hummel, 1990) of a pure public good otherwise defined as a public externality. Medical knowledge is one example but the classic examples of national defence, the environment, outer space and unpolluted air are no longer regarded as pure public goods.

Table 2
An Economics A Law and Economics Typology

	Excludable	Non-Excludable
Rival	Private good	Private externality
Non-Rival	Club good	Public externality

To what extent they represent McNutt's (1996) 'collective good' thus warranting a citizen tax, depends upon how acceptable the good is to the citizens and the citizens' effective demand for that good. For example, should *peaceniks* who may regard defence as an unacceptable public good or Gaelic speakers who may regard the English-language public radio broadcasts as an unacceptable public good, be obliged to pay the requisite fee or charge to have the good supplied? While pollution represents the classic example of an externality, may we suggest pollution control as a modern example of a pure public good. This would include anti-smoking legislation, catalytic converters in car exhausts and CFC legislation. Albeit, the classic lesson from the literature (Van Zandt, 1993) is that an optimal provision of pure public goods may escape the policymaker.

The property of excludability, as noted in Table 2, is the essence of a club theory approach to the provision of public goods. If consumption of the public good is not contingent on payment, individuals have no incentive to reveal their true preferences. The individual becomes a free rider and if all individuals behave likewise the net result is an absence of effective demand for the good. Where consumption is non-rival, for example, exclusion could be easily applied. However, because the marginal cost to previous consumers of adding one extra consumer is zero, the price should be zero. In this case there is no need to exclude. However the administrative costs of the public good provision must be covered somehow and with non-rival consumption in the absence of exclusion, the usual market method cannot determine price.

Musgrave and Musgrave (1980) have argued in favour of the non-excludability characteristic; they have argued that with excludability, non-rivalrous goods can be effectively provided by private production. In a different context Ng (1979, p. 190) emphasised the non-rivalrous characteristic, particularly if we do not regard public production as a necessary and sufficient condition for a public good. Since free riders impact on these conditions it is rather difficult to compute exactly the individual's valuation of a public good. And this is particularly difficult if payment is not contingent to a particular preference revealation. Preference revelation mechanisms (Kormendi, 1980) for example, where individuals pay a price that equates with their revealed preference for the good, are presented as experimental attempts to minimise the problem. Another alternative to the market failure result in the provision of public goods is to be found in the general theory of clubs. Tanzi (1972) had shown that welfare costs may be involved in providing public goods which differ with respect to how individuals are excluded from consuming the good.

4. The Coase Theorem and Property Rights

In standard public goods analysis it is assumed that consumption of the public good can be extended to all consumers at a zero marginal cost. It is also assumed that a free rider problem exists or that individuals (Cohen, 1991) can only be excluded at some positive cost. Loehr and Sandler (1978, p. 27) consider the issue of a 'forced rider' in which people 'are forced to consume, whether they like them or not' a range of public goods, for example defence. They further comment that 'it is entirely possible that the welfare of some individuals might fall when a marginal unit of the public good is provided'. The Pareto optimality conditions would have to allow for subsidies for these individuals to ensure that the marginal utility to tax price ratios for all individuals are equal. The forced rider may influence the provision of the public good. This could be extended to local goods and services where forced riders may be involved in decision making.

Pigou (1920) had suggested that government intervention was necessary in order to abate the externality problem. The transactions costs of grouping concerned citizens together in order to resolve the externality problem was prohibitive. Coase (1960) argued that in the absence of transaction costs, concerned citizens could resolve the problem, independent of government. Theorem 1, the Coase Theorem and the liability rules amend the public choice analysis of the externality problem.

Theorem 1: In the absence of transactions costs and bargaining costs, concerned citizens will agree to resolve an externality problem and arrive at a Pareto optimal allocation of resources, independent of government.

The apportionment of blame and the allocation of property rights, that is, the right to clean air, the right to pollute, proffer an alternative, indeed a complement, to the introduction of Pigovian taxes. The idea behind liability rules was to apportion blame; an alternative to this procedure in tort law is to establish optimal conditions which may prevent the accident or property rights dispute occuring. The traditional response in public finance was either to compensate the offended party or tax the offending party. This required an apportionment of blame which may have induced unnecessary government expenditure and rent-seeking activity. The costs incurred must be weighted against an inter-citizen or club resolution of the initial dispute.

The costs of providing the public good must include the bargaining costs attributable to the resolution of the ensuing debate on the amount of public good supplied, if at all. The treatment of these bargaining costs are a cental feature in Buchanan and Tullock (1962) whose framework was used by Loehr and Sandler (1978) in considering the impact of bargaining costs in the provision of public goods. They illustrate the net indirect costs imposed on forced riders and the number of individuals required to reach agreement on public provision. They further represents costs imposed upon a person who 'bears some burden under all decision rules with the exception of unanimity'.

In this case if the individual was a forced rider he would agree to the decision only when adequately compensated, that is when net costs are zero where the entire population is in agreement. Loehr and Sandler further comment that their cost function is 'downward sloping since the greater the proportion of the population needed for agreement, the more likely persons similiar to himself (but not identical to him) will be wooed by the early proponents of the public action'. A point may be reached where the need to form larger and larger coalitions would force bargains between free riders and forced riders. A particularly interesting point in Loehr and Sandler (p. 31) is their comment that the cost curve need not end at zero when unanimity is reached.

In other words, some free riders, they argue, may still exist, even where everyone is in agreement on the policy'. Summation of all individual cost curves in their presentation creates a community cost curve which indicates that more and more decisive groups would imply a higher cost in terms of effort and bargaining. If the decisions have to be made at the point where community costs are at a minimum then we are abandoning Pareto optimality. The solution presented represents a second best solution. McNutt (1996) considered an inter-citizen resolution by adapting an earlier argument in Turvey (1968, p. 310) who had argued that the traditional interpretation of an externality is rather restrictive. How much group B suffers from A's externality depends not only on 'the scale of A's diseconomy but also on the precise nature of A's activity and B's reaction to it'. For example, the victim in Pigou's chimney example could reduce the disutility by installing an indoor clothes-line.

The Pigouvian solution of reducing the amount of smoke contrasts with the alternative solution of either building a higher chimney or using different smokeless fuel. McNutt (1996) shows that by allowing an inter-citizen resolution to a dispute, the cost may be less than the government cost. If citizens can agree on the resolution of an externality problem, the cost to the government of financing the inter-citizen solution may be less than a central government solution. An inter-citizen resolution like the Coase theorem offers an alternative to government action in the resolution of an externality problem. One policy implication of this result applies to traffic congestion in large cities. Rather than impose a tax on car owners who persist in driving to the city at rush hour, car-users should be encouraged to resolve the externalities of long tailbacks, car emissions and queues by acting collectively. Car pools with special motorway lane access, such as the HOV (heavy occupancy lanes with at least three passengers per vehicle) lanes in the US, would be socially more efficient than allowing as many fee paying cars to enter the city limits; citizens would prefer to incur the lower garage parking fee for the pooled car.

5. Tiebout-Oates World

It is useful to re-examine the conditions which independently underpin the Tiebout (1956) and Oates (1972) models of local public goods and adapt the

Loehr-Sandler model in a search for some common ground in a Tiebout-Oates type world. Forced riders, can leave the local neighbourhood; this assumes no relocation constraints; crucial to the question posed here is the failure of individuals to reveal their true preference for local public goods. In his analysis, Tiebout recognised the efficiency in the supply of public goods and further acknowledged that voting process was the only recourse to reveal the preferences of the sharing group. The optimal allocation is determined by a 'voting with the feet' exercise.

Tiebout had presented an earlier framework for the theory of clubs in assuming an infinite number of individuals who form themselves into many clubs of different sizes. Under certain conditions the infinity assumption allows each club to maximise its own benefit without violating Pareto optimality. The Buchanan-Ng framework may be preferable to the Tiebout framework in the case where location of consumers is exogenous, transport is costly and where there are few clubs. In the Tiebout model individuals can vote with their feet, moving to regions according to their preferences for public goods.

Nevertheless, in order to examine this model further we note two assumptions of the Tiebout model, namely (i) consumer-voters are fully mobile and (ii) they have full information on the differences on revenue and expenditure in the local areas. These two assumptions depend on the absence of relocation constraints such as employment, house purchase and school availability. It also presupposes a large number of alternative communities with which the consumer can effectively rank order each community. The remaining assumptions include the following: (iii) there are no external economies or diseconomies of scale in the supply of the public services; (iv) there is an optimal community size for every community service; and finally (v) communities below the optimal size attract the new residents.

This set of assumptions establish the classic Tiebout model and ensure the global optimality of excludable public goods provision. Mueller (1989, p. 157) outlines an illustrative proof of this global property. However the new residents can produce congestion in the new area and the resulting congestion costs and possible negative externalities if the community has grown beyond the optimal size, forces Mueller to conclude that in general the Tiebout model will not produce a Pareto optimal outcome. In his illustration he shows quite clearly how a non-Pareto though stable equilibrium can emerge. Empirical evidence to support the hypothesis has been forthcoming, for example, Cebula (1979) showed that inter-area differences in welfare benefits influenced migration decisions while Aronson and Schwartz (1973) in an earlier and original analysis showed that those towns likely to gain in relative population are those that offer residents equal or better services at an equal or lower tax rate.

6. A Marginal Decision Curve

McNutt (1996) offered an alternative interpretation to the global condition in a Tiebout-Oates world by considering the idea of a marginal decision (MD) curve. This differs from the average benefit curve employed initially by Mueller (1979); while both curves represent benefit, Mueller's curve assumes that benefit is a function of community size whereas McNutt's curve is a function of the number of internal members (who form an internal group) in the sharing group. The concept of an *internal group* is used to explain the formation of alliances in the provision of public goods. In many instances, for example, the alliance may expressly form to prohibit the supply of public goods as with defence or environmental quality. As illustrated by McNutt (pp. 198-199), the group MD schedules are mirror images of each other which reinforces the point that utility in the club is maximised by dividing the club good equally between each group. Let us take the example of tulips in a public square; tulips represent a public good, planted in the public square by the local authority. Assume that the tulips, for whatever reason, offend a sub-group of the individuals who spend the day in the square. For this sub-group the tulips represent an externality. The square itself is a public good, but the presence of tulips reduces the utility of this sub-group. Next we introduce the concept of internal member:

Definition: define the sub-group S of citizens such that there is an issue i which at least one member j of the group regards as an externality, then $j \in S$ is defined as an internal member of the set S. The set S is a proper subset of the set, C, of all individuals in the square.

If the committee responsible for planting tulips decides against planting tulips in the square, the internal group is defined as decisive. The significance of an internal group is in its ability to rank local public goods in descending order of preference. The important characteristic of an alliance supplied public good is jointness in supply, that is, the supply includes private benefits as well as public goods. The private good may include cultural or educational benefits but may also include private externalities as with the tulips example.

Club theorists may have underestimated how members of a sharing group become associated. Apart from similiar tastes, there is the possibility of an 'association by alliance', that is an alliance of internal citizens who expressly object to the supply of a public good. How this manifests itself in theory, is as follows: the 'sharing group', that is the group of all citizens who consume the good, is subdivided into group A which derives exactly half as much utility as group B, the internal group, in any provision of a local public good. Group B, an internal group, has a negative impact on the remaining members, $(MD_A) = 1/2\ (MD_B)$.

If the rule is to maximise the utility of the sharing group then emphasis will be in the directon of group B. Ironically the utility of the A group will decrease. The dominance of the internal group secures a reduction in the amount of local public good in order to maximise the utility of the sharing group, B. McNutt (1996, pp. 198-199) called this 'the tulips paradox', that is, in the local provision of a public good the presence of a decisive internal heterogeneous group with identical tastes may reduce the supply of the local public good in order to maximise the utility of the larger citizenry group.

7. A Buchanan-Ng Framework

There are two basic models across the literature on club theory, the Buchanan (1965) within-club model and the more general Oakland (1972) total economy model which will be developed in a later section. Buchanan's model is the classic treatment of clubs while the Oakland model is more general in extending club theory to include heterogeneous members, discrimination, variations in the utilisation of the public good and exclusion costs. Neither model, however, guarantees Pareto optimality in the provision of local goods, which ironically is the *raison d'être* of club theory as a methodological study of the allocative efficiency of (impure) public goods.

The assumptions underpinning the Buchanan model include the following: (i) individuals have identical tastes for both private and public goods; (ii) the size of the club good (a swimming pool), hence its total cost, is fixed; and (iii) equal sharing of costs. Mueller (1979) has argued that (iii) follows as an assumption from (i). In a simple model Buchanan determines the optimal size of the club membership. Mueller shows that with some algebraic manipulation, by deducting each individual's share (equal shares) of the cost of providing the good from private income to obtain 'net of public good income' and substituting this into an objective function with the amount of public good and club size as explanatory variables, the Buchanan model obtains the Samuelson condition for the efficient consumption of a public good.

The crucial assumption in the Buchanan model, and in club theory generally, is the assumption of identical tastes and incomes. The Tiebout model shows that it is inefficient to have individuals of differing tastes in the same club. Intuitively, think of ten women golfers in a golf club of 25 players. The result here is akin to Pauly's (1967) result, obtained much earlier, that no stable equilibrium will exist if the women golfers form a winning majority. This is particularly the case if the number of women golfers increased and the threat of exit by the male golfers becomes credible - they could leave and form an alternative club. The dynamics of the situation would suggest that a small membership size is optimal - in other words, there has to be a limited degree of publicness (an excludability factor) as additional members beyond the optimal membership size will impose a cost on existing members. Congestion may arise on the golf course, reducing the utility of existing members.

According to Ng the relevant Pareto optimality condition requires that any individual in the club must derive a total benefit in excess of the aggregate marginal cost imposed on all other consumers in the club. So the Buchanan-Ng theory is to optimise the membership; alternatively Oakland considers the degree of congestion or overcrowding to be important. Club theory has many interesting applications in the analysis of congestion and in establishing the optimal group size for (say) a local golf club to a local community. Buchanan's economic theory of clubs builds on three rather important assumptions: (i) that the benefits and costs are divisible amongst the club members. As more members join, average costs for the provision of the club declines, but marginal benefits begin to fall as more members contribute to congested levels of membership; (ii) it is costless to the club to exclude members. This conveneintly removes any distortion should exclusion be deemed necessary in order to attain an optimal (MC = MB) membership. Finally it is assumed that (iii) there is no discrimination across members. This is a rather difficult assumption to defend in practice, as in the case of golf clubs and swimming pools where there is evidence of sex discrimination. However, with these three fundamental assumptions, an individual quasi-concave utility function is maximised in order to find the optimal club size and the optimal quantity of the good.

The public good is not a pure public good, but rather there is an element of congestion as individuals consume the good up to its capacity constraint. What arises then is some exclusion mechanism in order to charge consumers a price for the provision and use of the good. Brown and Jackson (1990, p. 80) had commented that the purpose of a club 'is to exploit economies of scale, to share the costs of providing an indivisible commodity, to satisfy a taste for association with other individuals who have similar preference orderings'. For Buchanan and Ng the main club characteristic is membership or numbers of consumers and it is this variable that has to be optimised. For Tiebout an assumption of infinity of individual consumers presupposes costless exit from one region to another and the formation of many clubs. Oakland considered the degree of congestion as an important characteristic in the provision of a club good. There is room for all of the characteristics in a general theory of clubs that seeks to determine a Pareto-optimal distribution of public goods.

What appears not to have been examined in this context is the interpretation of an individual's income elasticity of demand as a proxy for tastes for a public good. In the Tiebout world high-income individuals may migrate to the same area which leaves relatively poorer individuals consuming only the public goods which they themselves can afford to provide. No one really objects to club membership when the public good is tennis courts, squash courts or golf clubs.

To avoid congestion in the club and to achieve economies of scale, a Pareto efficient outcome is arrived at by introducing an exclusion principle. But in a Tiebout world of clubs, right-handed golfers exiting to form an alternative club, is quite different to the world in which high-income individuals migrate to one area and low-income individuals to another area.

As Mueller (1979, p. 144) pointed out 'the voluntary association approach is likely to affect the distribution of income'. If individuals can vote with their feet and have positive income elasticities of demand for public goods they can benefit from living in a community with incomes higher on average than their own. But for the poorer individuals transport and mobility is costly and for the higher-income individuals the formation of interest groups (for example, regional or local environmental lobby) is a concomitant to the provision of the public good. Each militate against an egalitarian distribution of the public good. Any attempt to transfer across from rich to poor 'runs directly into the issue of the proper bounds of the polity and the rights of citizenship' according to Mueller. However, in order to reach levels of efficient voluntary provision in Paretian terms, cooperation is necessary.

8. Precis on General Models

The presumption is that a voluntary provision of the public good will lead to a suboptimal outcome. The general model further assumes the existence of a private good and an impure public good, with the private good acting as a numeraire. The members are heterogeneous, non-members are costlessly excluded and club members determine their utilisation rate of the club good by varying the number of visits (to the public park) and time spent at the club. Optimal provision in this general model, within which both members and non-members are considered in deriving the optimal conditions for a single club, requires, according to Sandler and Tschirhart (1980, p. 1489) 'that the marginal benefits from crowding reduction, resulting from increased provision, equal the marginal costs of provision (MRT)'. This is analogous to the earlier Pareto optimal condition (MRS = MRT) for public goods provision and not unlike the conclusion extracted by Buchanan. The utilisation condition in the general Oakland model requires an equal rate of utilisation for all members, although total toll payments (for utilisation) vary between heterogeneous members.

Oakland's model is identical to the Buchanan model under the following conditions: (i) all members are homogeneous and each consumes the available quantity (say) X of the public good, such that $X_i = X_j$; (ii) for the members S the crowding function must be an identity mapping, that is $C(S) = S$, this reduces the general Oakland utility function to the Buchanan function $U(Y_i, X_i, S)$, where S substitutes for $C(S)$. The insertion of a crowding function into the utility function is one major difference between the models in club theory. Sandler (1978) argued that by including a crowding function, crowding externalities such as poor view can be considered, (a) increases in the provision of the public good reduces crowding ($dc/dc < 0$) and (b) increases in member use of the good increases crowding, that is ($dc/dx_i > 0$). It has been argued that the general model implicitly assumes cardinality of the utility function. Sandler and Tschirhart (1980, p. 1490) in their review of club theory comment that since 'the general model requires an ordering of the population based upon club preferences', cardinality is implicit.

Cardinality may rule out particular functional forms of the utility function, that may be otherwise appropriate for club analysis, for example the transformation $W = \mathrm{Log}U$. In practice, however, populations cannot be ordered; this applied weakness in the Oakland model has been overcome by Hillman and Swan (1979) who proposed an ordinal representation that does not require an ordering of the population. Their model, a *ceteris paribus* type model, maximises an arbitrary members utility subject to the constancy of other members utility levels. Recall that Buchanan's model maximised individual utility $U(Y, X, S)$ subject to a production:cost constraint $F(Y, X, S) = O$. The Hillman and Swan (1979) result is akin to this basic Buchanan model when (i) $C(S) = S$ and (ii) F = $U[Y, X, C(S)]$. The (ii) condition is *the Buchanan constraint* in the optimization procedure; an analogy requires that the Hillman and Swan constraint be rewritten as $F = U[Y_l, X, C(S)] = O$. This may be unlikely but worthy of further research.

Both Tiebout (1956) and Oakland (1972) represent alternative frameworks to the approach adopted by Buchanan (1965) in accounting for the under-supply of public goods. Oakland looked at the degree of congestion while the Tiebout model is an application of club theory to community size. A Tiebout-Oakland public goods problem would manifest itself for those public goods for which congestion begins at a certain size of community. As the community gets larger, residential density increases (community congestion), reducing the utility of everyone living in the community. Two factors which are important in the context are: (i) that the total number of people may not be an integral multiple of N, the number of workers, that is there may be a fixed population as identified by Pauly (1967); and (ii) the number of communities may be fixed. The one exception, alluded to by Atkinson and Stiglitz (1980), is a frontier society.

If the communities are fixed, say, to two, an optimal provision of the public good may involve an equal treatment, a result which in Atkinson and Stiglitz (1980) yields a local minimum (maximum) solution with population shortage (excess), hence social welfare could be increased by moving to an unequal treatment. A similiar point was alluded to earlier in the discussion of the marginal decision curve. However, the general theory of clubs with the property of no discrimination of members assumes a group of homogeneous individuals. The

Tiebout world has heterogeneous individuals sorting themselves out into homogeneous populations with homogeneous tastes. Hence doctors and lawyers live in the same neighbourhood and there are golfers in the golf club and swimmers in the swimming club. Health and sports clubs have to acquire an optimal mix of members in order to minimise crowding and queues. A sorting mechanism has to be introduced such as a rota or a time schedule based on membership age. But is the sorting optimal? In answering this question we have to refer to the concept of homogeneity.

9. Homogeneity

In the literature there are at least two interpretations of homogeneity in the club literature; first (i) Tiebout's (1956, p. 419) homogeneity as captured in his work where he commented on 'restrictions due to employment opportunities are not considered'. In mixed communities doctors and lawyers do not have equal incomes since the respective income depends on labour supply. Consequently they are not perfect substitutes and the community needs both; the community is better off if they have the same tastes. Secondly, an Atkinson-Stiglitz (1980, p. 531) type homogeneity, which is a weaker version of the Tiebout homogeneity and argues 'that individuals are [not] always better off forming homogeneous communities with people of identical tastes'. In their argument, they consider a third public good produced as a compromise to a merged community forming from the separate communities. In the merged case the individual can enjoy the benefits of the economies of scale associated with three public goods (equivalent to our average cost reductions in the Buchanan model), but when these benefits are weighted against diminishing returns to labour N (equivalent to the declining benefits in a Buchanan model), the individual is better off.

An interesting dimension arises in the context of a heterogeneous population which can be translated into different marginal valuations. If, for example, the local authority does not tax the individuals according to their respective valuations, by imposing an equal tax, there may not be an optimal provision of the local public good in the merged community. Those who value the public good less, are essentially subsidised by the high-value individuals and receive a windfall gain in the provision of the good. The movement from separate communities to a merged community is not a Pareto improvement. Atkinson and Stiglitz (1980) arrive at a similar result, assuming no diminishing returns to labour, in looking at positive benefits, that is 'everyones taxes [are] cut'. Whether the sorting is optimal or not depends clearly on the assumptions of diminishing returns to labour, the existence of a windfall provision to individuals with lower valuations and on the assumption of homogeneity.

Pauly (1970b) and McGuire (1974) in their generalisation of the earlier work of Tiebout assume an indefinitely large number of individuals, forming clubs of different sizes. Pareto optimality is not violated with the assumption of infinity (uncountable infinity according to Ng, 1979) as each individual can join a club that suits his or her preference, thus maximising the individual (average) benefit or the benefit of the club. The applicability of this infinity framework is, according to Ng (1979, p. 212), suitable for the cases where the number of clubs for the same good is large and the population is mobile; he suggests group segregation in housing the nomadic life and sports clubs.

In the typology of public goods presented in Table 2 earlier, the club good is defined as a non-rival excludable public good. A different usage of rivalry has been discussed in the literature by Starrett (1988, p. 58) in the context of club theory and local communities. The spatial element in local communities, with competing use for a limited (same) space, generates 'club rivalry that is independent from the rivalries we have been discussing'. In what he refers to as a bare bones model, Starrett concludes with an optimality condition which suggests that efficient size will require that average provision cost equal the sum of the various marginal rivalry costs. In the model transport costs play the role of rivalry costs, as Starrett (1988, p. 59) argues 'transportation has no value to the members per se but must be incurred if they want to share the collective good'.

That each individual in the club is equal distance from Starrett's collective good, the assumption of radical symmetry, is dropped in an alternative model which allows for choice in the number of trips to the collective good (for example, the public park) and in the amount of residential land held by each individual. The first-best solution is an unequal division of land as individuals closer to the public good represent an externality to these further out in the residential area. The latter residents have larger tracks of land. Starrett's unsurprising conclusion is a formulation 'that treats equals equally' (p. 60); the reason, apart from the formal rigour of his model, is that in the real world the political system will impose this constraint on society. Of the Lagrangean optimisation results presented by him the one that is of interest is the condition for optimal club size.

Theorem 2: The Henry George Theorem states that if public expenditure is fixed and population varies, the population that maximises consumption per capita is such that rents equal the public good expenditure.

The Starrett (1988, p. 62) result which states that the supply of the public good should equal the pseudo-land rent in the optimal spatial club is in many respects similiar to the Henry George Theorem as derived by Atkinson and

Stiglitz (1980, p. 525). Optimization on club size leads to the Starrett result. In a Henry George world, each citizen had identical tastes, an assumption which is imported by Buchanan into his original club model. Since club rivalry involves spatial separation the marginal cost of rivalry is reflected in the marginal premia on limited space. Starrett concludes 'that in our bare-bones model this premia could be measured in terms of transport costs, [but] differential land rents turns out to be the right measure in broader contexts' (p. 62). The measure is right, relatively speaking, in that it secures an optimal club size. The different approaches within the general theory of clubs highlight the many different characteristics of a club and of a club good. The general theory of clubs offer a solution to the optimal provision of public goods.

10. Future Research and Controversies

In this final section we look at some of the more interesting areas of research within the public and club goods literature, areas of recent controversies indeed which have arisen across the literature. Many of the issues have an important bearing on the optimal provision of local public goods and consequently on local public finance.

10.1 Membership Homogeneity

Membership homogeneity has to be one of the more controversial issues within the club literature, particularly from a public policy perspective. For example, if mixed clubs with heterogeneous membership are found to be non-optimal, as outlined in our earlier discussion, serious policy implications for group housing or education schemes may arise. The literature is divided on the optimality of mixed clubs, with Ng (1973b) and Oakland (1972) arguing for the optimality of clubs and Berglas and Pines (1978), Helpman (1979), McGuire (1974) and Stiglitz (1977) arguing in favour of homogeneous clubs. The latter group, according to Sandler and Tschirhart (1980, p. 1492), 'have recognised that mixed clubs may be desirable when strong scale economies require a larger membership than possible with homogeneity'.

Mixed clubs, however, are not Pareto optimal due to an important assumption: the equal cost sharing assumption which states that in a mixed club, albeit all members pay the same membership fee, those members with higher valuations of the public good have a higher total payment as they use (visit the park) the good more frequently. Conversely mixed clubs are shown to be efficient when there are no second-best constraints imposed. Hence, by invoking second-best constraints requiring all members to share club costs equally, as alluded to in our argument on windfall gains or requiring all members to use the club equally irrespective of tastes as in McGuire (1974) and Porter

(1977), mixed clubs can always be shown to be less desirable than homogeneous clubs. It is the set of second best constraints that relegates the mixed clubs to second place in the efficiency comparisons. A scale of membership fees may (paradoxically) encourage the intense user of the good to use it less and while her less frequent user revisits frequently.

10.2 Pareto Optimality

Neither the within-club Buchanan model nor the Oakland economy model, ensure Pareto optimality. As Sandler and Tschirhart (1980, p. 1493) conclude '[within-club] may fail when the membership size is large relative to the entire population, [general model] will fail when multiple clubs are desirable'. The multiple clubs translates into a variable number of clubs and this requires that both the optimal number and optimal size of clubs be determined simultaneously. A rather different slant on the optimality controversy is whether or not Buchanan, in his original article, failed to consider Pareto optimality. Ng (1973b, p. 294) has argued that Buchanan did fail to give Pareto optimal conditions in maximising the 'average net benefits instead of total net benefits'; Ng (1979, p. 212) in defending his position has reiterated that his analysis aims 'at Pareto optimality or maximising total benefits of the whole population'. Both Berglas (1976) and Helpman and Hillman (1977) criticised Ng's (1973b) attack on Buchanan and questioned whether or not Ng had maximised total benefits of one club, which in general is non-Pareto optimal.

The Buchanan-Ng framework on clubs which concentrates on each particular club, is preferable, according to Ng (1979, p. 212), to 'the more general model (wherein) *these* conditions are not satisfied' (our italics). The conditions referred to are generally the infinity conditions outlined in our discussion. In contrast Berglas (1976) defended Buchanan on optimality and Helpman and Hillman (1977, p. 295) suggested that the issue is very much dependent 'on a recognition of the different types of club problems analysed' and a realisation of the difference between maximizing average net benefits (for the members) and maximising total net benefits for the club. Buchanan proceeded with the former, whereas Ng proceeded with the latter 'in maximising total net benefits for the entire economy' (p. 1493) according to Sandler and Tschirhart (1980). Other scholars have considered the issues arising from exclusion costs, member discrimination and the analysis of an efficient membership fee or toll for optimal club provisions. The interested reader is directed to the review by Sandler and Tschirhart (1980) and Mueller (1989) and the bibliographies contained therein. Game theory has helped to shed some light on the issues raised in the club literature and in particular Pauly (1967) to whom we referred earlier, defined the optimum club size as that size for which average net benefits are maximised. This is at variance with the non-game arguments by Ng (1973b), Helpman and Hillman (1977) and the Oakland general model. A direct comparison between the game and non-game outcomes is complicated by the different assumptions used. In particular the game approach does not admit the interdependency between the membership and the provisions which characterises the classic Buchanan type model; nor does it consider a simultaneous solution to membership, provision of the good and finance. In many cases the club fee is decided ex-post. The approaches do converge on the optimum number of clubs in the homogeneous case.

Pauly (1970a, p. 60) divided a mixed population into homogeneous groups, with each group divided into multiple clubs where average net benefits are maximised. He proved that the core was non-empty and existed 'if the clubs consist of identical members with equal payoffs and that clubs with higher average pay-offs have fewer members'. There has been an increase in game theoretic contributions, for example, Cornes and Sandler (1986), Sandler and Posnett (1991) and notaby Sugden (1981, p. 118) who has argued that where there is 'a consistent theory of non-Nash, utility-maximising behaviours, even less of the public good would be supplied than in a Nash equilibrium'. The conclusion is that public goods would never be supplied at all.

10.3 Profit-Maximising Clubs

However there are two more recent controversial developments to which we would like to turn our attention. The first concerns the issue of profit-maximising clubs, alluded to in the classic survey by Sandler and Tschirhart (1980). Berglas and Pines (1978) have demonstrated that a perfectly competitive industry with identical firms (each firm acts as a club) supplying the shared club good would achieve the same efficiency conditions as those of a private co-operative.

Hillman (1978) found that the non-discriminating monopolist provided smaller output and charged a higher price and operated more crowded facilities than the non-profit cooperative. In contrast Hillman and Swan (1979) have shown that a discriminating monopolist will always achieve an effecient outcome. Ng (1973a) argued that a government was necessary in order to achieve the efficient outcome, defined as maximising total benefits. He continued to argue, in the spirit of our earlier discussion, that since members under a monopolist will maximise net benefit rather than total benefit an efficient outcome is not attained in the absence of a centralised government.

Ng apparently underestimated the impact of short-run political objectives in guiding a government-run club, as later outlined by Sandler (1978). Scotchmer (1985, p. 39) has argued that with a homogeneous population, profit-maximising clubs will achieve an equilibrium that is 'within epsilon' of being efficient. There is entry in response to profits and with incumbent clubs making a conjectural variation on 'the price and facility response in other clubs when it changes its strategy', the number of clubs will be too large. The strategy space is defined by facility X and price P, not facility X and the member N. With the strategy space

(*X*, *P*) each club believes that it can get more clients at the expense of other clubs. The set of strategies is a Nash equilibrium if no club can charge (*X*, *P*) such as to make more profit, with the zero conjectural variation assumptions. The strategy space (*X*, *N*) is abandoned because the Nash equilibrium requires the assumption, deemed unlikely by Scotchmer (1985, p. 27), that 'the other [clubs] will change their prices in whatever manner necessary to maintain the clientiele'.

The earlier profit-maximising club literature explored by Berglas (1976) and Wooders (1980) had assumed that there was an efficient size sharing group and the conclusion has been that provided entry forces profits to zero, a club equilibrium will be efficient. However, these firms are competitive in the sense of being a 'utility-taker', whereas Scotchmer (1985) departs from this in arguing that firms take as fixed the strategies of other firms. It is essentially a non-cooperative game and the equilibrium is cast as a Nash equilibrium. For members the utility available in other clubs will change as membership changes.

10.4 Multi-Product Clubs

A further area of research which was introduced in the wake of new material on contestability theory is the idea of a multi-product club, footnoted initially by Sandler and Tschirhart (1980, p. 1513). In particular, they had suggested a role for the concept of economies of scope defined simply as complementarity in production. Within the literature, however, some scholars have considered this issue already, although the joint products include a private good and an impure (or indeed pure) public good. Examples would include the Samuelson constraint and the Henry George Theorem. However, in the area of local government, where communities and cities share multiple club goods, this application may prove to be useful. Berglas and Pines (1978) did, however, present a multiproduct club model, but did not consider the concept of economies of scope.

The essence of this assumption in any industry-type analysis is that the two products cannot independently be provided at a cheaper cost than joint production. It is important to recall that the relationship in the club literature between the average cost curve and the number of clubs is related to the definition of a single product monopoly. The condition of sub-additivity in the cost function had already been used in the club literature by Pauly (1970a, p. 55) in his argument that 'club characteristic functions may be sub-additive'. The many variants to the economic analysis implicit in Buchanan's original model have advanced our understanding of club theory and have helped to incorporate club theory into the economic analysis of local public finance.

11. Concluding Comment

The economic theory of clubs represents an attempt to explain the under-supply equilibrium of a public goods provision. It raises many different and controversial issues which impinge on government policy in the public sector. In many respects, a club provision proffers an alternative to a central government provision of local public goods. The salient characteristic of a club, the excludability factor, may militate against an equal and democratic distribution of the club good. At the level of voluntary clubs, with which Buchanan was originally concerned, club theory can critically appraise the efforts at achieving optimal membership of the club and the maximum utility of club members.

Game-theoretic approaches to public goods provision may give scholars the latitude within which they could abandon the conventional postulate of individual utility maximisation and critically evaluate how rational behaviour can be encouraged in the individual for the voluntary provision of the public good. Arguably, it is in the arena of an interchange between club provision and an interest group provision of a local public good that the contestable issue of sub-additivity may arise. The externalities, both private and public, to a certain degree may discourage rational individuals from contributing more in order to attain a Paretian outcome.

If the literature identifies increasing problems with cooperation then it behoves law and economics scholars to adopt an approach which will research and develop non-market and/or non-cooperative solutions to an optimal provision of public goods. This approach will contribute positively to an evaluation of the economics of the provision of excludable club goods. The approach will also precipitate a much wider debate on the policy issues of local neighbourhood supply and provision of public services; it may also impact on the theory of public goods provision generally by focusing more on the (intra-interest group) economies of organisation *per se* in an attempt to explain the under-supply equilibrium of a public goods provision.

Bibliography on Public Goods and Club Goods (0750)

Adelstein, Richard P. and Edelson, Noel (1976), 'Subdivision Exactions and Congestion Externalities', **5** *Journal of Legal Studies*, 147-163.

Aronson, J. Richard and Schwartz, E. (1973), 'Financing Public Goods and the Distribution of Population in a System of Local Government', **June**, *National Tax Journal*, 353-367.

Aronson, J. Richard (1978), *Public Finance*, New York, McGraw-Hill.

Atkinson, Anthony B. and Stiglitz, J.E. (1980), *Lectures in Public Economics*, Maidenhead, McGraw-Hill.

Becker, G. and Tomes, Nigel (1976), 'Child Endowments and the Quantity and Quality of Children', **84** *Journal of Political Economy*, 143-165.

Benson, Bruce L. (1994), 'Are Public Goods Really Common Pools: Considerations of the Evolution of Policing and Highways in England', **39** *Economic Inquiry*, 249-271.

Berglas, Eitan (1976), 'On the Theory of Clubs', **66** *American Economic Review*, 116-121.

Berglas, Eitan and Pines, D. (1978), *Clubs, Local Public Goods and Transportation Models: A Synthesis*, Foerder Institute, **32/78** Working Paper.

Bergstrom, T., Blume, L. and Varian, H.R. (1986), 'On the Private Provision of Public Goods', **29** *Journal of Public Economics*, 25-49.

Bonus, Holger (1980), 'Offentliche Güter und der Öffentlichkeitsgrad Von Gütern (Public Goods and the Publicness of Goods)', **136** *Journal of Institutional and Theoretical Economics*, 50-81.

Borcherding, Thomas E. (1978), 'Competition, Exclusion and the Optimal Supply of Public Goods', **21** *Journal of Law and Economics*, 111-132.

Bowen, H.R. (1943), 'The Interpretation of Voting in Allocation of Resources', **58** *Quarterly Journal of Economics*, 27-48.

Brennan, J. and Flowers, Marilyn R. (1980), 'All Ng Up on Clubs: Some Notes on the Current Status of Club Theory', **8(2)** *Public Finance Quarterly*, 153-170.

Brown, C.V. and Jackson, P.M. (1990), *Public Sector Economics*, Oxford, Basil Blackwell.

Brubaker, Earl D. (1975), 'Free Ride, Free Revelation, or Golden Rule?', **18** *Journal of Law and Economics*, 147-161.

Buchanan, James M. (1949), 'The Pure Theory of Government Finance: A Suggested Approach', **57** *Journal of Political Economy*, 496-505.

Buchanan, James M. (1965), 'An Economic Theory of Clubs', **32** *Economica*, 1-14.

Buchanan, James M. (1967), 'Public Goods in Theory and Practice: A Note on the Minasian-Samuelson Discussion', **10** *Journal of Law and Economics*, 193-197.

Buchanan, James M. and Tullock, Gordon (1962), *Calculus of Consent*, Ann Arbor, University of Michigan Press.

Cebula, R.J. (1979), 'A Survey of the Literature on the Migration of State and Local Government Policies', **34** *Public Finance*, 69-82.

Cheung, Steven N.S. (1973), 'The Fable of the Bees: An Economic Investigation', **16** *Journal of Law and Economics*, 11-33.

Coase, Ronald H. (1960), 'The Problem of Social Cost', **3** *Journal of Law and Economics*, 1-44. Reprinted in Ackermann, Bruce A. (1975), *Economic Foundations of Property Law*, Boston, Little Brown, 17-22. Reprinted in Medema, Steven G. (1995), *The Legacy of Ronald Coase in Economic Analysis*, Vol. 2, Aldershot, Edward Elgar Publishig, 5-48. Reprinted in Coase, Ronald H. (1988), *The Firm, the Market and the Law*, Chicago, University of Chicago Press.

Coase, Ronald H. (1974), 'The Lighthouse in Economics', **23** *Journal of Law and Economics*, 357-376.

Cohen, Lloyd R. (1991), 'Holdouts and Free Riders', **20** *Journal of Legal Studies*, 351-362.

Cornes, Richard and Sandler, Todd (1986), *The Theory of Externalities, Public Goods and Club Goods*, Cambridge, Cambridge University Press, 303 p.

De Geest, Gerrit (1992), 'The Provision of Public Goods in Apartment Buildings', **12** *International Review of Law and Economics*, 299-315.

De Jasay, Anthony (1989), *Social Contract, Free Ride: A Study on the Public Goods Problem*, Oxford, Oxford University Press, 256 p.

Demsetz, Harold (1970a), 'The Private Production of Public Goods', **13** *Journal of Law and Economics*, 293-306.

Demsetz, Harold (1970b), 'Reply to Professor Thompson', **16** *Journal of Law and Economics*, 413-415.

Demsetz, Harold (1973), 'Joint Supply and Price Discrimination', **16** *Journal of Law and Economics*, 389-405.

Dubin, Jeffrey A. and Navarro, Peter (1988), 'How Markets for Impure Public Goods Organize: The Case of Household Refuse Collection', **4** *Journal of Law, Economics and Organization*, 217-241.

Ekelund, Robert B., Jr and Hulett, Joe R. (1973), 'Joint Supply, the Taussig-Pigou Controversy and the Competitive Provision of Public Goods', **16** *Journal of Law and Economics*, 369-387.

Evans, Andrew (1970), 'Private Good, Externality, Public Good', **17** *Scottish Journal of Political Economy*, 79-89.

Frech, H. Edward III and Rochlin, Clifford B. (1979), 'Advertising as a Privately Supplied Public Good', **27(2)** *Economic Inquiry*, 414-418.

Frech, H. Edward III and Rochlin, Clifford B. (1982), 'A New Economic View of Advertising', **1** *Journal of Advertising*, 213-222.

Goldin, Kenneth D. (1977), 'Equal Access versus Selective Access: A Critique of Public Goods Theory', **29** *Public Choice*, 53-71.

Green, Jerry R. (1976), *Consumer Theory*, London, Macmillan.

Hansmann, Henry B. (1986), 'A Theory of Status Organizations', **2** *Journal of Law, Economics and Organization*, 119-130.

Hartog, Hendrik (1981), 'Property as Government in Eighteenth-Century America: The Case of New York City', **10** *Journal of Legal Studies*, 305-341.

Head, John G. (1974), *Public Goods and Public Policy*, Durham, NC, Duke University Press.

Helpman, Elhanan (1979), 'On Optimal Community Formation', **1** *Economic Letters*, 289-293.

Helpman, Elhanan and Hillman, Arye L. (1977), *On Optimal Club Size*, Foerder Institute, **91/76** Working Paper.

Hillman, Arye L. (1978), 'The Theory of Clubs: A Technological Formulation', in Sando (ed.), *Essays in Public Economics: The Kiryat Anavim Papers*, Lexington, Lexington Books.

Hillman, Arye L. and Swan, Peter L. (1979), 'Club Participation Under Uncertainty', Mimeo.

Holtermann, A. (1972), 'Externalities and Public Goods', **39** *Economica*.

Hummel, Jeffrey Rogers (1990), 'National Goods Versus Public Goods: Defense, Disarmament and Free Riders', **4** *Review of Austrian Economics*, 88-122.

Kaplow, Louis (1993), 'Should the Government's Allocation Branch be Concerned about the Distortionary Cost of Taxation and Distributive Effects?', Program in Law and Economics Discussion Paper, 122 ff.

Kim, O. and Walker, Martin (1984), 'The Free Rider Problem: Experimental Evidence', **43** *Public Choice*, 3 ff.

Knight, Frank H. (1924), 'Some Fallacies in the Interpretion of Social Cost', **38** *Quarterly Journal of Economics*, 582-602.

Kormendi, Roger C. (1979), 'A New Remedy for the Free Rider Problem? - Flies in the

Ointment', **1** *Research in Law and Economics*, 115-130.

Kormendi, Roger C. (1980), 'Further Thought on the Free Rider Problem and Demand Revealing Processes', **2** *Research in Law and Economics*, 219-225.

La Croix, Sumner J. (1989), 'Homogeneous Middleman Groups. What Determines the Homogeneity?', **5** *Journal of Law, Economics and Organization*, 211-222.

Lee, Dwight R. (1977), 'Discrimination and Efficiency in the Pricing of Public Goods', **20** *Journal of Law and Economics*, 403-420.

Lindahl, E. (1929), 'Just Taxation - A Positive Solution', in Musgrave, R.A. and Peacock, A.T. (eds), *Classics in the Theory of Public Finance*, New York, Macmillan.

Lipsey, Richard and Lancaster, K. (1956), 'The General Theory of the Second Best', **24** *Review of Economic Studies*, 11-32.

Loehr, W. and Sandler, Todd (1978), *Public Goods and Public Policy*, New York, Sage Publications.

MacKaay, Ejan (1995), 'Mededinging, welvaart en federalisme (Competition, Welfare and Federalism)', in Kanning, Walter (ed.), *Liber amicorum voor Arnold Heertje*, Leiden, Stenfert Kroese, 93-100.

Marchand, James R. and Russel, Keith P. (1973), 'Externalities, Liability and Resource Allocation', **63** *American Economic Review*, 611-620.

McGuire, T. (1974), 'Group Segregation and Optimal Jurisdiction', **82** *Journal of Political Economy*, 112-132.

McNutt, Patrick (1996), *The Economics of Public Choice*, Cheltenham, Edward Elgar.

Meade, James E. (1952), 'External Economies and Diseconomies in a Competitive Situation', **62** *Economic Journal*, 54-67.

Minasian, Jora R. (1967), 'Public Goods in Theory and Practice Revisited', **10** *Journal of Law and Economics*, 205-207.

Minasian, Jora R. (1979), 'Indivisibility, Decreasing Cost and Excess Capacity: The Bridge', **22** *Journal of Law and Economics*, 385-397.

Mishan, Ezra J. (1969), 'The Relationship Between Joint Products, Collective Goods and External Effects', **77** *Journal of Political Economy*, 329-348.

Mishan, Ezra J. (1971), 'The Postwar Literature on Externalities: An Interpretative Essay', **9** *Journal of Economic Literature*, 329-348.

Moffit, Robert (1990), 'The Econometrics of Kinked Budget Constraints', **4** *Journal of Economic Perspectives*, 119-139.

Mueller, D. (1979), *Public Choice*, Cambridge, Cambridge University Press.

Mueller, D. (1989), *Public Choice II*, Cambridge, Cambridge University Press.

Musgrave, P.B. and Musgrave, R.A. (1980), *Public Finance in Theory and Practice*, London, McGraw Hill.

Musgrave, Richard A. (1938), 'The Voluntary Exchange Theory of Public Economy', **35** *Quarterly Journal of Economics*, 213-237.

Ng, Yew Kwang (1973a), 'Optimal Club Size: A Reply', **45** *Economica*, 407-410.

Ng, Yew Kwang (1973b), 'The Economic Theory of Clubs: Pareto Optimality Conditions', **40** *Economica*, 291-298.

Ng, Yew Kwang (1979), *Welfare Economics, Introduction and Development of Basic Concepts*, London, Macmillan.

O'Driscoll, Gerald P., Jr (1976), 'The American Express Case: Public Good or Monopoly?', **19** *Journal of Law and Economics*, 163-175.

Oakland, W.H. (1972), 'Congestion, Public Goods and Welfare', **1** *Journal of Public Economics*, 339-357.

Oates, W. (1972), *Fiscal Federalism*, London, Harcourt Brace Jovanovich.

Olson, Mancur (1965), *The Logic of Collective Action: Public Goods and the Theory of Groups*, Cambridge, MA, Harvard University Press, 186 p.

Pauly, Martin (1967), 'Clubs, Commonality and the Core', **34** *Economica*, 314-324.

Pauly, Martin (1970a), 'Cores and Clubs', **9** *Public Choice*, 53-65.

Pauly, Martin (1970b), 'Optimality, Public Goods and Local Government', **78** *Journal of Political Economy*, 572-586.

Pearce, David W. (1977), *Environmental Economics*, London, Longman.

Pigou, A.C. (1920), *The Economics of Welfare*, London, Macmillan.

Porter, R. (1977), 'On the Optimal Size of Underpriced Facilites', **67** *American Economic Review*, 753-760.

Posner, Eric A. (1995), 'The Regulation of Groups: The Influence of Legal and Nonlegal Santions on Collective Action', **63** *University of Chicago Law Review*, 113-197.

Rothenberg, Jerome (1970), 'The Economics of Congestion and Pollution: An Integrated View', **60** *American Economic Review. Papers and Proceedings*, 114-121.

Samuelson, Paul A. (1954), 'The Pure Theory of Public Expenditure', **36** *Review of Economic Statistics*, 387-389.

Samuelson, Paul A. (1967), 'Pitfalls in the Analysis of Public Goods', **10** *Journal of Law and Economics*, 199-204.

Sanchez, Isabel (1991), 'Provisi¢n Voluntaria de Bienes Publicos: Resultados Experimentales (Volutantary Contributions to Public Goods: Experimental Results)', **11** *Revista de Economia Publica*, 2 ff.

Sandler, Todd (1977), 'Impunity of Defence: An Application to the Economics of Alliances', **30** *Kyklos*, 443-460.

Sandler, Todd (1978), 'Public Goods and the Theory of the Second Best', **33** *Public Finance*, 331-343.

Sandler, Todd and Posnett, J.W. (1991), 'The Private Provision of Public Goods: A Perspective on Neutrality', **19** *Public Finance Quarterly*, 22-42.

Sandler, Todd and Tschirhart, John (1980), 'The Economic Theory of Clubs: An Evaluative Survey', **18** *Journal of Economic Literature*, 1481-1521.

Schelling, Thomas C. (1969), 'Models of Segregation', **May** *American Economic Review*, 488-494.

Scotchmer, Suzanne (1985), 'Profit Maximising Clubs', **27** *Journal of Public Economics*, 25-45.

Seldon, Anthony (1986), *The Riddle of the Education Voucher*, London, Institute of Economic Affairs.

Shoup, D. Carl (1971), 'Theoretical Efficiency in Pollution Control: Comment', **9** *Western Economic Journal*, 310-313.

Starrett, David A. (1988), *Foundations of Public Economics*, Cambridge, Cambridge University Press.

Stiglitz, Joseph E. (1977), 'The Theory of Local Public Goods', in Feldstein and Inman (eds), *The Economics of Public Services*, London, Macmillan.

Sugden, Robert (1981), *The Political Economy of Public Choice*, Oxford, Martin Robertson.

Tanzi, V. (1972), 'A Note on Exclusion, Pure Public Goods and Pareto Optimality', **27** *Public Finance*, 75-79.

Thompson, Earl A. (1973), 'The Private Production of Public Goods: A Comment', **16** *Journal of Law and Economics*, 407-412.

Tideman, T. Nicolaus (1980), 'The Evaluation of Rules for Making Collective Decisions: A Reply to Kormendi', **2** *Research in Law and Economics*, 213-217.

Tiebout, Charles M. (1956), 'A Pure Theory of Local Government Expenditures', **64** *Journal of Political Economy*, 416-424. Reprinted in Cowen, T. (ed.) (1992), *Public Goods and Market Failures*, Chapter 9, London: Transaction Publishers.

Turvey, Ralph (1968), *Public Enterprise*, Harmondsworth, Pengiun.

Turvey, Ralph (1971), *Demand and Supply*, London, Allen and Unwin.

Van Zandt, David E. (1993), 'The Lessons of the Lighthouse: "Government" or "Private" Provision of Goods', **22** *Journal of Legal Studies*, 47-72.

Vasic B. Vukasin (1986), 'Makroekonomska Politika kao Javno Dobro (Macroeconomic Policy as a Public Good)', **3** *Ekonomist*, 429-430.

Williams, Stephen F. (1978), 'Running Out: The Problem of Exhaustible Resources', **7** *Journal of Legal Studies*, 165-199.

Wolf, Charles, Jr (1979), 'A Theory of Nonmarket Failure: Framework for Implementation Analysis', **22** *Journal of Law and Economics*, 107-139.

Wooders, M. (1980), 'The Tiebout Hypothesis: Near Optimality in Local Public Good Economies', **48** *Econometrica*, 1467-1485.

0760
NETWORK EXTERNALITIES

William H. Page
Mississippi College, School of Law

John E. Lopatka
University of South Carolina, School of Law

Abstract

A network exists when a product's value to the user increases as the number of users of the product grows. Each new user of the product derives private benefits, but also confers external benefits (network externalities) on existing users. Network externalities may cause markets to fail. Networks may not reach optimal size, because users fail to take account of external benefits. Markets in which incompatible standards compete may 'tip' in the direction of a standard that gains an early advantage, even if that standard is objectively inferior. Suppliers of network goods may compete to become the de facto standard or may attempt to make their products compatible. The theory of network externalities has been applied in numerous legal areas including antitrust (monopolization and cooperative standard-setting); intellectual property (the scope of protection for dominant software programs); and corporate law (the selection of contract terms).
JEL classification: K00
Keywords: Increasing Returns, Positive Feedback, Lock-In, Standardization

1. Introduction

The subject of network externalities has become popular in the economic and legal literature since the mid-1980s. The fundamental idea is that the act of joining a network confers a benefit on all other participants in the network. According to proponents, this seemingly simple phenomenon strongly influences competitive strategies and market outcomes in network markets. Network externalities can, for example, influence consumers' decisions whether to adopt a new technology and producers' decisions whether to standardize their products. Ultimately, the literature suggests, network externalities can cause markets to fail: 'equilibrium may not exist, or multiple equilibria may exist' and 'the fundamental theorems of welfare economics may not apply' (Katz and

Shapiro, 1994, p. 94). Networks may not reach optimal size, because purchasers do not take account of social benefits of their purchases, and markets may converge on an inferior standard that effectively excludes better products.

The theory of network externalities is well developed, especially for such a new field of inquiry. Its policy implications are less clear. Some economists claim that the inefficiencies associated with network externalities are common in some important markets, including computer hardware and software, transportation and telecommunications. And some argue that network externalities justify changes in the law of antitrust, corporations, economic regulation and intellectual property. Some of the proposed policy changes would involve greater government intervention in the market, some would involve less. Other scholars suggest that courts and policymakers should be cautious in relying on network externalities. They argue that the theoretical market failures associated with network externalities would only occur under rare conditions. They also challenge the empirical evidence that network externalities have actually thwarted the adoption of better technologies. Any real market failures in network markets, they argue, probably stem from familiar economic phenomena (like natural monopoly) that are better analyzed using conventional tools. Even if the market has failed, government intervention is inappropriate because network externalities cannot be identified in practice or government action is likely to be more costly than any benefits it may produce. In the following discussion, we will address both theoretical and policy issues, trying wherever possible to keep them distinct.

A. Types of Network Externality

The users of certain products can be thought of as forming networks, either because they are physically connected or because they have close market relationships. A network *externality* is a benefit conferred on users of such a product by another's purchase of the product. (A purchase may also impose external costs, but the literature focusses primarily on the sources and consequences of external benefits, or positive consumption externalities.) Some analysts distinguish between direct externalities, exemplified by communications networks, and indirect externalities, exemplified by the 'hardware/software paradigm' (Katz and Shapiro, 1985, 1994; Church and Gandal, 1992b). Note that the distinction between direct and indirect externalities refers to the source of benefit to participants in the network, not necessarily to the magnitude of the network effect.

2. Direct Externalities

Direct externalities typically occur in a physical, two-way communications network (Rohlfs, 1974). My purchase of a fax machine, for example, directly benefits existing fax machine owners, who now have an additional person with whom they may communicate. If there are n fax machines in the network, each owner has $n(n\text{-}1)$ potential interlocutors; an additional fax machine adds $2n$ (total) potential communications within the system, and thus enhances the value of membership, assuming that each owner may at some point wish to communicate with every other owner (Economides, 1996). Similar reasoning applies to telephones and internet access software, each of which expands the number of people who can communicate over a physical network. Users of the network thus receive increasing returns in consumption. (Notice that direct benefits do not accrue to users of a *one-way* physical network, like paging or electric power transmission, because the existing users of the networked goods may not interact with new users any more easily than those who are not on the network (Economides and White, 1994; Economides, 1996).) Producers of network goods may also receive increasing returns to scale in production, at least up to some critical mass.

The 'positive feedback effect' (Arthur, 1989, 1990) of increased network size makes the larger network that much more attractive to new purchasers, and the goods that permit access to the network that much more valuable. The value of the good to the purchaser also depends on the purchaser's expectations about the future size of the network. The demand for a fax machine is thus a function not only of the price of the product, but also of the expected size of the network to which the fax machine will be connected. This last point resolves the apparent paradox that, despite the downward slope of the demand curve, the marginal purchase of a good can yield a higher value than inframarginal goods: the value contributed by the expected size of the network offsets the reduction in value from the purchase of a marginal unit (Economides, 1996).

Direct network externalities might arise even in the absence of a physical network. Those who speak a language, for example, constitute a network. The value of knowing a language depends in part on how many others speak it. A student's decision to learn a language is influenced by the expected size of the network of speakers; and the student's learning the language directly benefits other speakers. Similarly, the value to an individual of a particular word processing program, say WordPerfect, likely will depend in part on the number of others who select WordPerfect and with whom the individual expects to exchange files. This effect is diminished to the extent that conversion between programs is possible, but, so long as conversion is imperfect or costly, the effect persists.

3. Indirect Externalities

Economists have also identified *indirect* externalities in the 'network' of users of systems of compatible devices, even if the devices owned by different users are not physically connected. A system can be any combination of a durable good and associated goods or services that perform some desired function. Katz and Shapiro (1994) illustrate this type of system with the hardware/software paradigm, which includes not only computer hardware and software, but many other product combinations, including cameras and film, phonographs and records, and television sets and programming. More broadly, a typewriter keyboard could be considered hardware, and the capability and experience of using that keyboard could be considered software. Owners of compatible hardware and software systems constitute a 'virtual network' (Katz and Shapiro, 1985, 1994; Arthur, 1989, 1990). At the extreme, any combination of complementary products can be described as a system, and those who purchase the system can be said to form a virtual network. Thus, a cappuccino machine, a coffee grinder, espresso coffee beans and milk form a system, and those who drink home-made cappuccino form a network.

Indirect externalities can arise in these markets only when, as is typical, the components are purchased at different times. For example, applications software programs are often purchased at various times over the useful life of a computer. In these circumstances, adoption of the hardware by one purchaser confers external benefits on other users of the same hardware, because it expands the installed base of the hardware, stimulating demand for compatible software. Suppliers may therefore take advantage of scale economies and provide more varieties of software. The availability of more diverse and inexpensive software enhances the value of the existing users' hardware. These indirect benefits stemming from strong complementarities are said to cause positive feedback in much the same way as direct benefits of expanded communication in physical networks.

Indirect network externalities may arise in many contexts. Participants in physical networks, both one-way and two-way, may receive indirect external benefits, if the increased size of the network results in more options and better service. Traders on a financial exchange may also receive indirect benefits from the array of services provided by the exchange (Economides, 1993a, 1996). And users of Discover cards benefit when more people carry Discover cards, because more merchants will accept a widely-adopted card (Evans and Schmalensee, 1996).

4. Network Effects versus Network Externalities

Liebowitz and Margolis (1994, 1995a) distinguish network *externalities* from network *effects*. A network effect exists when 'the net value of an action ... is affected by the number of agents taking equivalent actions' (Liebowitz and Margolis, 1994, p. 135). Network effects, so defined, are ubiquitous in the economy. Purchases of a good by one group of consumers may bid up its price and thereby affect other consumers of that good as well as consumers of complementary and substitute products. Liebowitz and Margolis point out that economists at one time misinterpreted these interactions as inefficiencies, but now recognize them to be pecuniary external economies and diseconomies, which the price system internalizes as wealth transfers between, say, purchasers and suppliers. Liebowitz and Margolis (1994, p. 135) would limit the term network externality to those specific network effects in which 'the equilibrium exhibits unexploited gains from trade regarding network participation'. Network externalities, so defined, do cause market failure, but are far less common than network effects generally.

Liebowitz and Margolis (1995a) accept the distinction between direct and indirect network effects, but argue that they are fundamentally different in their consequences for efficiency. They recognize that direct network effects in physical networks may (in limited circumstances) be true externalities. But they challenge the notion that indirect network externalities arise whenever complementary goods become more plentiful and cheaper as the number of users of the related product increases. They contend that much of what the literature calls indirect network externalities are merely positive pecuniary externalities that result in wealth transfers.

These theoretical points lead to very different policy conclusions. If the price of complementary goods decreases as a network grows because rents are transferred from input suppliers or producers to consumers, the market does not fail, and no state-sponsored remediation is necessary. If instead price falls due to positive technological externalities, remediation may be required, but only because of a conventional market failure in an upstream or downstream market, not network externalities.

Katz and Shapiro (1994), leading scholars in the field, have adopted the distinction between network effects and network externalities in theory, though they disagree in its application, and generally argue that true network externalities are more common than Liebowitz and Margolis suggest. Other scholars continue to use the term network externalities to encompass all network effects. (Economides, 1996; Klausner, 1995).

B. Effect of Externalities on Network Size

5. Physical Networks/Direct Externalities

The existence of positive network externalities in adoption of a technology in a physical network implies that the private marginal benefit of acquiring a network technology is lower than the social benefit. In deciding whether to buy a network good, the individual compares the price only with his private benefit, not the benefit that his purchase confers on other users. Consequently, the equilibrium size of a physical network under perfect competition, with direct network externalities, may be smaller than the social optimum (Katz and Shapiro 1994; Economides, 1996).

The size of a physical network is also affected by consumer expectations. Because information about other potential purchasers' future actions is always imperfect, consumers' expectations may result in a nonoptimal network size. For example, if all consumers expect no one else to purchase, then the network size will be zero, even if all consumers would benefit by joining the network; if all expect everyone to purchase, the size will be large (Katz and Shapiro, 1994). The importance of consumer expectations gives producers an incentive to convince consumers through a variety of practices that their networks will attract many users.

Some physical networks may be owned by a single firm. Firms that own a network may use their property rights to internalize consumption externalities. This result is most apparent in entirely internal networks. Fax machines, for example, faced an initial externality problem in that purchasers had no incentive to buy one unless others did also. If there were a high enough degree of uncertainty, the market might not have developed at all. But large firms apparently had enough incentives to purchase fax machines for purely internal communications to create a critical mass (Katz and Shapiro, 1994, p. 97, n. 4).

A single firm's ownership or sponsorship of a physical network with individual subscribers can also internalize network externalities. Consumer surplus is maximized if the sum of marginal private and social benefits of a purchaser equals marginal cost (Liebowitz and Margolis 1994; Katz and Shapiro, 1994). Liebowitz and Margolis argue that ownership of such a network can usually solve the problem of a suboptimal network size that flows from direct network externalities. The owner will set access prices that reflect the fact that additional users provide benefits to all other users. If marginal costs are assumed to increase, a network can reach an optimal size. Liebowitz and Margolis believe that the assumption of increasing marginal cost, typical to economic models, is appropriate here because economies of scale are exhaustible for many network commodities. In these circumstances, more than one network can coexist, so competition is possible. If, on the other hand, economies of scale are inexhaustible, the market is a natural monopoly, which may be inefficient but not because of something unique to the network character of the good.

Suppose that ownership of the network does imply a monopoly. Economides and Himmelberg (1995) argue that the incentive of the monopolist to restrict output overwhelms its incentive in increase consumer demand by influencing expectations about network size. The resulting monopoly equilibrium is at a lower network size than under competition. Katz and Shapiro (1994) argue that, if a monopolist charges a single access fee above marginal cost, external benefits will not be internalized. But price discrimination 'may well allow the network to internalize the adoption externalities: for example by setting access fees at or below cost and earning profits on usage fees' (p. 101). The network owner thus addresses the problem of buyer expectations about the future size of the network.

Liebowitz and Margolis (1994) recognize that not all networks that generate direct network externalities can be owned. For example, the network of speakers of Esperanto is not ownable and so may fail due to direct network externalities. But other market mechanisms may minimize any social cost in such cases. Intermediary organizations may, for example, facilitate communication among groups within the population. Network effects can also be internalized by the direct interaction of participants. For example; computer programmers working on a common project can agree to adopt the same language. These interactions will tend to internalize potential externalities when transactions are easy. Liebowitz and Margolis believe, therefore, that network externalities will not often result in a suboptimal size of a network, and to the extent that a network is inefficiently small, the reason can be traced to the conventional market failure associated with natural monopoly.

6. Virtual Networks/Indirect Externalities

The analysis of the effect of indirect externalities on the size of virtual networks is somewhat different. In these markets, externalities may arise because of the durable nature of the hardware component in the system. The purchaser of hardware knows he will be 'locked in' to the product for a time, because the cost of switching to different hardware will be substantial. (On the effects of switching costs, see Klemperer, 1987a, 1987b, 1989). Consumers then may be uncertain about the future availability and price of software for the product. If this uncertainty can be addressed, then the network externality problem disappears. If, for example, all of the components of the system are competitively supplied by firms with U-shaped average costs, the market will reach an efficient competitive equilibrium. The market is indistinguishable from any competitive market with complementary products (Katz and Shapiro, 1994). Note that this outcome differs from the inefficient outcome in physical network markets under competition discussed in the previous section.

Katz and Shapiro (1994) argue that network externalities can arise if hardware is supplied competitively at marginal cost, but differentiated software is provided at a price above marginal cost by firms subject to scale economies. Apparently responding to Liebowitz and Margolis, Katz and Shapiro (p. 100) state that 'if all goods were priced at marginal cost, these network externalities would be merely be pecuniary externalities, and market equilibrium in hardware/software markets would be efficient'. If, however, software is not priced at marginal cost, a suboptimal variety of software may result or software may be produced at an inefficiently high cost, and the resulting networks may be smaller than optimal because the marginal social benefit of additional sales is greater than the private benefit to the purchaser. In such circumstances, Katz and Shapiro argue, a subsidy to hardware suppliers (or software suppliers) can increase consumer welfare by expanding the supply and variety of software. Liebowitz and Margolis presumably would respond that the subsidy in this case is (theoretically) justified because of imperfect competition in software, rather than because of any indirect network externality.

If a monopolist supplies both hardware and software, consumers may fear that, once they are locked in to the durable good, the monopolist will exploit them by increasing prices of the software. (Farrell and Shapiro, 1988; Katz and Shapiro, 1994; Shapiro and Teece, 1994). Sponsorship arrangements by the monopolist may provide a solution. Thus, network externalities can be avoided if the seller can somehow commit to software prices in advance of purchase. If such commitment is possible, consumers would have no reason to fear lock-in specifically. They would, of course, be subject to monopoly pricing (either single-price or discriminatory), but any inefficiency would then be attributable to the monopoly, not to network externalities. (Katz and Shapiro, 1985, 1994).

The monopolist may attempt in various ways to approximate a commitment to future supply of compatible goods at prices consumers expect to pay. It may, for example, attempt to guarantee a competitive supply of compatible software, even inviting competitive firms to enter the market (Economides, 1996; Farrell and Gallini, 1988; Katz and Shapiro, 1994). It may also adopt a policy of leasing hardware, thereby assuring that customers would not be locked in, were it to raise software prices. Or it might engage in 'penetration pricing' of hardware, which would mean that, although consumers may pay high software prices, they will be compensated by lower hardware prices. Finally, it may rely on its reputation as a bond securing purchasers against exploitation (Katz and Shapiro, 1994). If it were to exploit purchasers, it would damage its ability to sell later generations of its hardware.

C. Competition Among Networks

7. Tipping and Lock-In

One of the most striking consequences of network externalities is their effect on the nature of competition between sellers of products embodying different, incompatible standards. The literature cites many examples: VHS and Beta standards for VCRs; phonographs and compact disc players; conventional versus high-definition television; and so forth. In such markets, network externalities may favor the market's adoption of a single seller's product as the de facto standard, such as VHS rather than Beta as a videotaping format. In corresponding theoretical models, one technology gets an early advantage (for whatever reason), and positive feedback of the larger network size leads new users to adopt that technology. It is suggested that the first mover in markets for information-based software receive continuously increasing returns to scale, reinforcing early successes and aggravating early defeats (Arthur, 1989, 1990, 1994, 1996). Ultimately, competing technology leaves the market. A market that settles on a single standard is said to have 'tipped'.

In other markets, network externalities and scale economies may be exhausted at a smaller network size, so that the market can accommodate more than one network. Moreover, consumers' heterogeneous preferences can result in multiple standards, such as the IBM-PC and the MacIntosh computer (Liebowitz and Margolis, 1995a; Katz and Shapiro, 1994, p. 106). Firms, therefore, might prefer to promote their own incompatible networks regardless of the resulting size. Or each firm might prefer its own standard, yet prefer compatibility with a rival's standard if only one standard can prevail.

The tendency of network markets to tip leads to particularly intense competition early in the market's existence (Farrell and Shapiro 1988). Competitors may employ aggressive strategies like 'penetration pricing' - in some instances giving the product away - in order to become the de facto standard. Katz and Shapiro (1994, p. 107) observe that in such cases firms are 'bidding for future monopoly profits'. After achieving dominance, the firm may recoup some or all of the expenses it incurred in the early competition. In such cases, what appears to be monopoly profit earned by the firm in later stages of production is actually recovery of the earlier expenditures. Another possibility is that a firm with an early lead may have an incentive to deter new entry by low pricing in order to build on its advantage (Farrell and Saloner, 1986a).

One implication of the network externalities literature is that the market may settle on a good with a lower *social* valuation. The literature cites numerous examples: the QWERTY typewriter keyboard (David, 1985); VHS and Beta videocassette formats (Arthur, 1990); and AM stereo (Besen and Johnson, 1986). Proponents of network externalities point out that a good's value to the user depends upon its inherent benefit (the value of the good to the purchaser even if no one else adopted it) plus its network benefit. The network benefits increase with the size of the network. Initial adopters will primarily take account of the good's (apparent) inherent benefit to them. If that inherent benefit is greater for good A than for good B, the initial adopters will choose A. As the size of network increases, it becomes still more advantageous to choose A over B, and all subsequent adopters will do so. But suppose that, although B offers lower inherent benefits, its *network* benefits increase at a higher rate than those of good A, and at some network size actually exceed those of A. In theory, B would offer greater social benefits if it were adopted by the market as a whole; but the market nevertheless chooses A (Farrell and Saloner, 1986b; Klausner, 1995). Katz and Shapiro (1994, p. 106) state that 'standardizing on a single system can be very costly if the system turns out to be inferior to another system'. This type of standardization may also affect innovation incentives in the market.

Once the market tips toward a single standard, it may remain on that standard and its successors for a long time. Markets may exhibit 'excess inertia' and remain locked into a standard, even though an objectively 'better' standard is available (Katz and Shapiro, 1985; Farrell and Saloner, 1986a). Present users face substantial switching costs; even though all users would be better off with the new standard, those benefits do not accrue to the present users who must pay for switching. New purchasers also may opt for the established standard because of the immediate benefit that the established network offers; they do not take account of the benefit that purchasing the new technology would confer on later purchasers. Even if they anticipate the new technology would be widely adopted, the benefits of that adoption to the purchaser may be so far in the future that they are substantially discounted (Farrell and Saloner, 1986b, p. 947, n. 14).

Theoretical models, however, demonstrate no inevitable tendency of markets to lock-in on inferior products. Changes in the assumptions underlying the models (for example, concerning communication and information in the market) may eliminate the outcome of excess inertia (Farrell and Saloner, 1985, 1986a; Liebowitz and Margolis, 1990). Moreover, markets may actually exhibit 'insufficient friction' (Katz and Shapiro, 1986b, 1994) or 'excess momentu' (Farrell and Saloner, 1986b), tipping suddenly and inefficiently to new technologies. Insufficient friction may be inefficient because consumers do not take account of the network benefits their purchase of the established product would confer on existing users. Given this external benefit, it may be socially preferable to stay with the established technology. Nevertheless, consumers, fearing that they will be stranded with an obsolete, unsupported technology (the 'penguin effect', Farrell and Saloner 1987), may jump to the new technology. Katz and Shapiro (1986b, 1992) suggest that sponsorship of proprietary technologies may lead to inefficient adoption of one technology over another through excess momentum. For example, if the incumbent technology is supplied competitively under a shared standard, a new, proprietary technology might be offered at 'penetration' prices in order to attract an installed base. The incumbent competitive suppliers would be unable to price below their marginal cost, because they can have no expectation of recoupment.

8. Criticism of the Tipping Scenario

Liebowitz and Margolis (1995a) dispute the suggestion that increasing returns to scale in high-technology markets lead to market failure. They point out that the frequently-observed relationship between increasing participation in a market with indirect network effects and falling prices is ambiguous. Such a relationship may result from scale economies, but it may also reflect technological progress. In the latter case, prices drop because advances in technology reduce industry costs, not because of a network effect.

Liebowitz and Margolis (1994) also criticize the suggestion that markets fail because the 'wrong' network is chosen, so that total net benefits are lower that they would have been under the losing technology. This kind of asserted failure is a function of models that assume inexhaustible scale economies, for only then does a single network survive. Liebowitz and Margolis argue that the marginal gains of network size are often exhausted at sizes above a critical mass that is small relative to the total market. If the benefits of size are exhausted, multiple networks can exist. In that event, not only are monopoly problems lessened, but the theoretical question shifts to whether the best *set* of networks emerge. And the inframarginal externality that may affect the discrete choice of a network 'is not different from other coordination problems that exist in many other market choices' (Liebowitz and Margolis, 1994, p. 141).

Liebowitz and Margolis are especially critical of claims that network externalities lead consumers to make discrete choices among networks, choices that do not maximize social welfare. Such externalities cannot be addressed by taxes and subsidies, because those policies can only affect the scale of a network. Rather, the assumed market failures occur because network externalities supposedly prevent value-increasing transitions from one technology to a superior one. At the extreme, the literature seems to suggest that economic actors may easily become forever stuck in technologies that are widely recognized as inferior to available alternatives. Liebowitz and Margolis (1994, p. 145) colorfully call this the 'Chicken Little view of market transitions'. They contend that economics has generally not done well in explaining transition, which affects all components of the economy, not just networks. Nevertheless, value-increasing transitions do occur, even if the process is not well understood.

Evans and Schmalensee (1996) note that, for example, the computer software market 'exemplifies Schumpeter's (1942) view of modern competition - one in which firms and industries are constantly created and destroyed through the process of innovation'.

Whatever the theoretical possibility of market failure brought about by network externalities, critics complain that empirical support has not been adduced. Proponents of network externalities, for example, have often pointed to the conventional QWERTY keyboard as an illustration of lock-in. The keyboard arrangement was chosen, it is said, to slow down the typist to avoid mechanical jamming; other arrangements permit faster typing. Even though technological improvements have eliminated the mechanical problems, users are locked-in to the inferior QWERTY arrangement - consumers wish to avoid the costs of learning a different arrangement, and producers will not supply alternative products because not enough consumers would purchase them. Liebowitz and Margolis (1990) argue forcefully, however, that the story is factually incorrect, for the QWERTY keyboard is not demonstrably inferior to the leading alternative. Similarly, Liebowitz and Margolis (1994) find evidence that the Beta videotaping format is no better than VHS. In all, Liebowitz and Margolis believe that real indirect network externalities are of limited theoretical importance and have not been established empirically. For a similar discussion of the complexity of the issue of objective 'superiority' of one technology to another, see Van Vleck (1995).

D. Compatibility and Standardization Among Network Goods

9. Compatibility and Standardization Among Network Goods

Many of the private and social consequences of network externalities depend upon whether products competing in a network market are compatible in a relevant sense. The term compatibility is used in the literature to refer to different relationships depending upon the context. For example, physical networks are said to be compatible if they allow direct interconnection; virtual networks are said to be compatible if various components of the system are 'interoperable', that is, they can work together; and various products, such as computer software, may be said to be compatible if consumers can use them without significant retraining (Lemley and O'Brien, 1997). For useful surveys of the issues surrounding compatibility and standardization in markets with network externalities, see Cohen (1996) and Katz and Shapiro (1994).

Whether systems are made compatible depends on a host of factors that may influence decisions of firms on questions of design and contracting with other producers. Compatibility may arise as a result of a single firm's product becoming the de facto standard in the market; or it may arise through collective standard-setting mechanisms. In addition, converters or adapters may make products compatible to varying degrees (Farrell and Saloner, 1992). In some instances, it may be to a firm's advantage to try to prevent compatibility with existing systems and compete with them to become the de facto standard for at least a part of the market. In other instances, firms may choose to make their products compatible with other products by licensing or by participation in coalitions or standard-setting organizations (Katz and Shapiro, 1994).

Compatibility, by expanding the size of networks, offers both private benefits and private costs to producers and consumers of network goods. Participants in compatible physical networks receive the direct external benefits of communicating with a larger number of consumers, and save the costs of owning two sets of hardware. Participants in compatible virtual networks receive the indirect benefits of a larger network, including a greater variety of components that may be mixed and matched to achieve an optimal system (Matutes and Regibeau, 1988), and a reduced risk of being stranded with obsolete technology. Producers receive the benefits associated with larger scale. Compatibility may impose costs, however, depending upon how it is achieved. If it is achieved by standardization, then there may be a reduction in the variety of systems and products available to first-time consumers (Gilbert, 1992). If it is achieved by adapters, the adapters themselves impose costs (Katz and Shapiro, 1994).

Whether firms have an incentive to create compatibility depends upon how the resulting changes in the terms of competition affect them. Compatibility reduces the risk that the market will tip to a rival's sponsored standard, and so may reduce the intensity of competition, at least in early stages when incompatible systems would be competing to become the market's de facto standard (Katz and Shapiro, 1986b). This tendency suggests that some firms (or coalitions of firms) may have an incentive to agree to adopt a compatible standard (Besen and Farrell 1994; Katz and Shapiro, 1994). But if systems are compatible, then the market may accommodate more firms, and so compatibility may actually increase competition over the long term (Katz and Shapiro, 1994). Firms that standardize reduce their chances of becoming the dominant firm.

When networks are incompatible, then competition is between physical networks or between systems of goods that comprise virtual networks. When virtual networks are compatible, however, competition is among the components of the system (Matutes and Regibeau, 1988; Economides 1988, 1996; Katz and Shapiro, 1994). In such situations, the firm's preference for compatibility depends upon the tradeoff between the increased demand that compatibility creates and the increased competition that it entails. Firms that believe they offer a better overall system (like Apple Computer in its earlier years, perhaps) may opt for incompatibility; firms that believe they offer a better individual component may opt for compatibility. In general, the 'winner take most' nature of competition between incompatible systems may lead firms with very promising (or highly regarded) technology to oppose compatibility, even when compatibility is socially preferable (Katz and Shapiro, 1994). The social optimum is not achieved because firms individually do not take account of the effects of compatibility on others.

E. Policy Implications

10. Policy Implications: General Remark

The many inefficiencies identified in the network externalities literature have led some to propose changes in government policies to accommodate the theory. But most economists have counselled caution in using the network externalities literature to justify greater government intervention. Katz and Shapiro (1994), for example, note that private market responses may correct any inefficiency. Furthermore, they point out that interest group pressures make government responses less likely to favor efficiency than powerful incumbent producers. And there is little reason to think the government has the ability to identify the correct market outcome better than market mechanisms (Arrow, 1995; Vita and Wellford, 1994; Lopatka and Page, 1995a, 1995b). Liebowitz and Margolis (1994) are even more insistent that the network externalities literature is far too limited in its theoretical implications and its empirical support to justify a more interventionist government policy.

Nevertheless, legal literature and to a lesser extent the case law have begun to take account of network externalities. A search of the WESTLAW 'Journals and Law Reviews' database reveals over references to 'network externalities' in diverse areas of law. And the concept has begun to be accepted by some policymakers and courts. The following sections will address some of these issues.

11. Antitrust: Monopolization

Because it predicts that a single firm may dominate a market, network externalities theory has been recruited to support claims of monopolization. It implies that a firm may have an incentive to make its network incompatible, to achieve higher sales volumes than its competitors during early stages of production, and to convince potential users that its standard eventually will prevail. The practices that a firm uses to influence the direction in which the market tips are likely to be attacked as exclusionary. For example, in *Eastman Kodak Co. v. Image Technical Services, Inc.* (1992), the Supreme Court held that an equipment manufacturer (without monopoly power in the equipment market) could have monopolized by requiring consumers to purchase its repair services as a condition of obtaining its replacement parts. The Court did not mention network externalities explicitly, but did treat the equipment, services, and parts as a sort of system. Recall that Katz and Shapiro (1994) specifically refer to 'durable equipment and repair services' as an example of the hardware/software paradigm, or an indirect network. The Court's reasoning closely resembles a network externalities analysis. It stated that purchasers were locked-in to Kodak equipment and would find it costly to predict the prices of aftermarket services and products at the time of equipment purchase. High switching costs and imperfect information are important features of network externalities theory.

The United States, in its amicus brief in *Kodak*, appeared to reject network externalities theory by arguing that Kodak could not extract monopoly profits in aftermarkets because it lacked monopoly power in the equipment market. But the Antitrust Division under the Clinton administration explicitly invoked network externalities theory in suing Microsoft for monopolizing the market in personal computer operating systems, although it limited the scope of its complaint to restraints in Microsoft's distribution contracts (*United States v. Microsoft*, 1995). In the litigation challenging the consent decree in that case, all sides (and the District Court) agreed that network externalities in the hardware and software markets had important antitrust implications and might justify stricter application of monopolization standards. A group of anonymous amici curiae filed a brief that was co-authored by Brian Arthur and Garth Saloner, both prominent theorists of network externalities. For a full analysis of the brief and the district court's opinion, see Lopatka and Page (1995a).

Network externalities theory has limitations as a policy guide in monopolization cases. (Lopatka and Page, 1995a, 1995b; Evans and Schmalensee, 1996; Gifford, 1996). It does not, for example, support breakup of a firm that achieves dominance. The theory predicts that networks will often grow large for efficiency reasons. Tipping does not necessarily imply that a producer is forever locked in, because new technology (and creative new producers) can benefit from the same phenomenon to leapfrog the old dominant firm. The very possibility of tipping is an important incentive to innovation and novel marketing strategies. And history contains enough examples of technological change sweeping away previously dominant firms to caution against government action to break up a market leader.

Lock-in may not even signal market failure. A firm may dominate because it in fact offers the best product. An antitrust court could not confidently declare that the wrong technology had triumphed (Vita and Wellford, 1994). While excess inertia is possible, theory does not tell us when it is present. Thus there is no justification for encouraging displacement of a dominant firm by weakening its locked-in position. Nor is there justification for detailed supervision of the dominant firm's practices. If the market is a natural monopoly, it is not well suited to antitrust regulation, regardless of network externalities.

For similar reasons, network externalities theory does not offer much assistance in identifying 'exclusionary' conduct that creates monopoly power. Some models suggest that markets can be tipped by trivial events or an early advantage, so that the development of the market is path dependent (Arthur, 1989; David, 1985). Microsoft's MS-DOS operating system may have achieved dominance because IBM selected it long ago for the IBM PC (Besen and Farrell, 1994). If historic accident determines market outcomes, however, none of Microsoft's subsequent competitive acts can be blamed for its dominant position. Some practices may be theoretically inefficient, but courts lack the knowledge to identify when they are so. Firms may, for example, use advertising to manipulate consumers' expectations about which standard will prevail (Besen and Farrell, 1994; Katz and Shapiro, 1994). Or they may use product preannouncements to discourage existing customers from switching to another supplier and to encourage prospective purchasers to wait (Farrell and Saloner, 1986b). But there is no effective way to distinguish these practices from efficient dissemination of information (Ordover and Willig, 1981).

Network externalities theory may actually provide efficiency explanations for apparently exclusionary practices. For example, vertical integration or exclusive contracts may allow a producer to establish a credible commitment to provide a supply of complementary goods. Similarly, a lease-only policy (sometimes suspect in antitrust law) may be an effort to assure consumers that they will not be locked in to a dying network.

Predatory pricing issues may also be influenced by network externalities. Katz and Shapiro (1994, p. 104), describe 'penetration pricing': 'by selling hardware below cost early on, the network sponsor is stimulating the demand for software, which may lead to a lower price of software if software is produced according to economies of scale or if the elasticity of demand for software is higher for marginal consumers than for the average hardware consumer' (see also Besen and Farrell, 1994). This pricing strategy may resemble predatory pricing; but its goal is to overcome network externalities in building an installed base. Below-cost pricing or even giveaways of some products, like computer software, may be a rational means of establishing an installed base of complementary product sold by the same firm. Farrell (1989) suggests that this sort of competitive below-cost pricing by sponsors of proprietary technologies will typically lead to the better technology being adopted. Thus, Lemley (1996) concludes that such a price war raises concerns only if it is asymmetric, that is, if one of the combatants has greater staying power.

Although network externality theory is susceptible to misuse in the analysis of monopolization, it may sometimes provide a helpful context for examining allegedly exclusionary conduct. For example, Lemley (1996) suggests that concealment of a proprietary claim to a market standard during a period in which that standard is being promoted for acceptance in the market or by standard-setting organizations may be monopolistic.

12. Antitrust: Horizontal and Vertical Agreements

Antitrust's traditional hostility to horizontal agreements may cast suspicion on some agreements in network industries. But antitrust has also recognized that some industries require cooperation in order to exist. (See, for example, *National Collegiate Athletic Ass'n v. Board of Regents*, 1984). Network industries often fall in this category (Carlton and Klamer, 1983; Evans and Schmalensee, 1996). Perfect competition may be inefficient (in physical networks) or entirely impractical (in virtual networks). Network externalities can often be internalized only by contract or joint ownership. Bank credit cards require cooperation among banks in order to compete with cards issued by a single firm (Carlton and Frankel, 1995). Telecommunications networks require agreements on interconnection and sharing of joint costs and revenues. Producers of both hardware and software must settle on standards to assure compatibility (Brown, 1993). Lemley (1996) mentions the Internet Engineering Task Force as an example of a necessary standard-setting organization. While these points suggest procompetitive explanations for some types of agreements, they do not exclude the possibility of such an organization being used as a cartel or an exclusionary device. Some network joint ventures may thus require continuing antitrust controls. Real estate multilisting services offer network benefits, but do not justify price fixing by participating realtors. And network externalities do not imply that standard-setting joint ventures should be permitted to exclude competitors (Anton and Yao, 1995).

Mergers and joint ventures have become common in network industries. Network externality theory offers a number of efficiency justifications for these arrangements. Physical networks may offer greater value to subscribers by merging, and may benefit from scale economies and greater information. Research and development joint ventures may permit firms to pool information and resources to create more advanced technology. These considerations do not, however, imply that antitrust scrutiny is inappropriate. A merger creating a network that is larger than is justified by scale economies may create an unnecessary danger of monopoly. In *Money Station, Inc. v. Board of Governors of Federal Reserve System*, the Board argued to the court that an acquisition of a small ATM network by a bank controlling the dominant ATM network was less likely to lead to anticompetitive effects because (p. 1133):

> Network externalities, such as the economies of ubiquity, tend to promote the consolidation of regional ATM networks. As a result, in various geographic areas, like the Mideast region, dominant ATM networks have been emerging throughout the EFT industry. One recent study indicates that the ten largest regional networks now account for 80 percent of all regional ATM transactions in the United States. In this light, the Board believes that, as a result of economic and market structure conditions, regions are likely to have one dominant ATM network.

The court properly questioned this reasoning as a way of avoiding competitive concerns about the merger. It is not clear that network externalities require dominance of a single firm.

13. Intellectual Protection for Proprietary Standards

The theory of network externalities suggests that a single product may emerge as the de facto standard in the market. Should the presence of network externalites, and the consequent danger of lock-in, affect the intellectual property protection given to a proprietary de facto standard? Menell (1987, 1989), relying in part on an analogy to the QWERTY story, has argued that network externalities justify limiting copyright protection to computer software that has become the industry standard. In *Lotus Development Corp. v. Borland International* (1995), the court adopted this reasoning, holding that Lotus 1-2-3's user interface was a 'method of operation', like the buttons on a VCR, and therefore not protectable expression under copyright law. One of the reasons the court offered was the need for compatibility. The court found it 'absurd' to suggest that 'if a user uses several different programs, he or she must learn how to perform the same operation in a different way for each program used'. A concurring judge added that 'if Lotus is granted a monopoly on this pattern, users who have learned the command structure of Lotus 1-2-3 or devised their own macros are locked into Lotus ...' Consequently, a competitor (Borland) should be allowed to copy Lotus's menu command structure.

This decision adopts a network externality theory raised by Borland and amici curiae in their briefs on appeal. It has been questioned by Dam (1995), who points out that 'compatibility' in this case is not the interoperability that allows use of competitive software or the inteconnection that allows communication across a physical network. Rather, compatibility in this case means only that a user may costlessly adopt a competing product. The argument is that the menu structure has become the de facto industry standard, and so free copying should be allowed to assure adequate competition. But it is questionable whether network externalities are at issue here. The users of Lotus 1-2-3 do not constitute a physical network, so there are no direct external benefits from expansion of the installed base. Furthermore, the case does not involve complementary products, so there are no apparent indirect network externalities from greater availability of compatible goods. There are at best so-called convenience externalities. There are switching costs between spreadsheets, but not evidently more than between products generally.

One difficulty with the use of network externalities to limit copyright protection is that it is difficult to limit the principle to computer software. It has been suggested that many popular copyrighted works, such as *Gone With the Wind*, create a network of users that may be exploited in spinoffs and sequels. Thus, the case of computer software does not appear to be unique among copyrighted products (Lunney, 1996). More generally, the application of the network externalities concept to negate copyright protection for popular software is similar to the antitrust argument that the successful firm has monopolized, and is questionable for the same reasons. Weakening copyright protection allows greater competition by clones, but reduces the payoff for innovators, by threatening loss of protection for successful firms.

14. Contract Terms and Other Norms

Some scholars have argued that social norms have network aspects. Conventional rules like those governing right of way for drivers at an intersection have greater value the more people adopt them. This extension of the concept of network externalities has been most fully developed by Klausner and Kahan (Klausner, 1995; Kahan and Klausner, 1996), who have argued that the adoption of corporate contract terms can create indirect network externalities. Common use and judicial interpretation of contract terms benefit the 'network' of firms adopting those terms by, for example, clarifying the meaning of the set of legal rules governing the firm. Larger network size generates positive feedback because it increases the stock of judicial precedent and the common understanding of the relevant rules. Network externalities thus modify the conception of the firm as a nexus of contracts. They imply that contract terms that maximize the value of the individual firm may not maximize social wealth. State corporation laws, by providing default rules for contractual provisions, are analogous to industry standards in physical networks like telecommunications, because they can facilitate the creation of networks. Their goal should be to promote the creation of an optimal mix of uniformity and diversity by providing 'open-ended' default rules menus of alternative provisions. Network externalities may also account for the dominance of Delaware corporation law. Some scholars have suggested that states compete in a race to the top for corporate charters by offering statutes that maximize firm value. But Delaware's dominance (despite the prevalence of similar laws) may reflect the positive feedback effect of its large network of incorporated firms. This result implies that Delaware law has become popular not because it offers optimal terms, but because it has become locked in.

Bibliography on Network Externalities (0760)

Allen, Beth (1982), 'Some Stochastic Processes of Interdependent Demand and Technological Diffusion Exhibiting Externalities Among Adopters', **23** *International Economic Review*, 595-608.

Anton, James and Yao, Dennis A. (1995), 'Standard-Setting Consortia, Antitrust, and High-Technology Industries', **64** *Antitrust Law Journal*, 247-265.

Antonelli, Christiano (1992), 'The Economic Theory of Information Networks', in Antonelli, Christiano (ed.), *The Economics of Information Networks*, Amsterdam, North Holland.

Antonelli, Christiano (1993), 'Externalities and Complementarities in Telecommunications Dynamics', **11** *International Journal of Industrial Organization*, 299-450.

Antonelli, Christiano (1994), 'Localized Technological Change and the Evolution of Standards as Economic Institutions', **6** *Information Economics and Policy*, 195-216.

Armstrong, Mark, et al. (1995), 'The Access Pricing Problem', **44** *Journal of Industrial Economics*, 132-150.

Arrow, Kenneth J. (1975), 'Vertical Integration and Communication', **6** *Bell Journal of Economics*, 173-183.

Arrow, Kenneth J. (1995), 'Declaration Appended to Memorandum of the United States of America in Support of Motion to Enter Final Judgment and in Opposition to the Positions of IDE Corporation and Amici (Jan. 17, 1995), United States v. Microsoft Corp., 159 F.R.D. 318 (D.D.C. 1995)'.

Arthur, W. Brian (1988), 'Self-Reinforcing Mechanisms in Economics', in Anderson, Philip W. et al. (eds), *The Economy as an Evolving Complex System*, Reading, MA, Addison-Wesley, 9-31.

Arthur, W. Brian (1989), 'Competing Technologies, Increasing Returns, and Lock-In by Historical Events', **99** *Economic Journal*, 116 ff.

Arthur, W. Brian (1990), 'Positive Feedbacks in the Economy', **262** *Scientific American*, 92 ff.

Arthur, W. Brian (1994), *Increasing Returns and Path Dependence in the Economy*, Ann Arbor, MI, The University of Michigan Press.

Arthur, W. Brian (1996), 'Increasing Returns and the New World of Business', **July** *Harvard Business Review*, 100 ff.

Artle, R. and Averous, C. (1973), 'The Telephone System as a Public Good: Static and Dynamic Aspects', **4** *Bell Journal of Economics*, 89-100.

Axelsson, B. and Easton, G. (eds) (1992), *Industrial Networks, A New View of Reality*, London, Routledge.

Baird, Douglas G. et al. (1994), *Game Theory and the Law*, Cambridge, MA, Harvard University Press.

Baker, Donald I. (1993), 'Compulsory Access to Network Joint Ventures under the Sherman Act: Rules or Roulette?', **1993** *Utah Law Review*, 999-1133.

Balcer, Yves and Lippman, Steven A. (1984), 'Technological Expectations and Adoption of Improved Technology', **34** *Journal of Economic Theory*, 292-318.

Banerjee, Abhijit V. (1992), 'A Simple Model of Herd Behavior', **107** *Quarterly Journal of Economics*, 797 ff.

Baumol, William J. and Sidak, J. Gregory (1994), 'The Pricing of Inputs Sold to Competitors', **11** *Yale Journal on Regulation*, 171-202.

Bensaid, Bernard and Lesne, Jean-Philippe (1996), 'Dynamic Monopoly Pricing with Network Externalities', **14** *International Journal of Industrial Organization*, 837 ff.

Bental, Benjamin and Spiegel, Menahem (1995), 'Network Competition, Product Quality and Market Coverage in the Presence of Network Externalities', **43** *Journal of Industrial Economics*, 197-208.

Berg, Sanford V. (1987), 'Public Policy and Corporate Strategies in the AM Stereo Market', in Gabel, H. Landis (ed.), *Product Standardization as a Tool of Competitive Strategy*, North Holland.

Berg, Sanford V. (1988), 'Duopoly Compatibility Standards with Partial Cooperation and Standards Leadership', **3** *Information Economics and Policy*, 35-53.

Besen, Stanley M. (1992), 'AM versus FM: The Battle of the Bands', **1** *Industrial and Corporate Change*, 375 ff.

Besen, Stanley M. and Farrell, Joseph (1994), 'Choosing How to Compete: Strategies and Tactics in Standardization', **8** *Journal of Economic Perspectives*, 117 ff.

Besen, Stanley M. and Johnson, Leland Law (1986), *Compatibility Standards, Competition, and Innovation in the Broadcasting Industry*, Rand Publication No. R-3453-NSF.

Bijl, Paul W.J. and Goyal, Sanjeev (1995), 'Technological Change in Markets with Network Externalities', **13** *International Journal of Industrial Organization*, 307-325.

Bolter, Walter et al. (1990), *Telecommunications Policy for the 1990s and Beyond*, New York, M.E. Sharpe, Inc.

Borenstein, Severin et al. (1995), 'Antitrust Policy in Aftermarkets', **63** *Antitrust Law Journal*, 455-482.

Braunstein, Yale and White, Lawrence (1985), 'Setting Technical Compatibility Standards: An Economic Analysis', **30** *Antitrust Bulletin*, 337 ff.

Brinig, Margaret F. (1995), 'A Maternalistic Approach to Surrogacy', **81** *Virginia Law Review*, 2377-2399.

Brinig, Margaret F. and Buckley, Francis H. (1996), 'The Market for Deadbeats', **25** *Journal of Legal Studies*, 201-232.

Brown, Jack E. (1993), 'Technology Joint Ventures to Set Standards or Define Interfaces', **61** *Antitrust Law Journal*, 921-936.

Cabral, Luis (1990), 'On the Adoption of Innovations with Network Externalities', **19** *Mathematical Social Sciences*, 229-308.

Carlton, Dennis W. and Frankel, Alan S. (1995), 'The Antitrust Economics of Credit Card Networks', **63** *Antitrust Law Journal*, 643-668.

Carlton, Dennis W. and Klamer, J. Mark (1983), 'The Need for Coordination among Firms, with Special Reference to Network Industries', **50** *University of Chicago Law Review*, 446-465.

Carlton, Dennis W. and Salop, Steven (1996), 'You Keep on Knocking but You Can't Come In: Evaluating Restrictions on Access to Input Joint Ventures', **9** *Harvard Journal of Law and Technology*, 319-352.

Choi, Jay Pil (1994), 'Irreversible Choice of Uncertain Technologies with Network Externalities', **25** *Rand Journal of Economics*, 382 ff.

Choi, Jay Pil (1996), 'Do Converters Facilitate the Transition to a New Incompatible Technology?: A Dynamic Analysis of Converters', **14** *International Journal of Industrial Organization*, 825 ff.

Chou, Chien-fu and Shy, Oz (1990), 'Network Effects Without Network Externalities', **8** *International Journal of Industrial Organization*, 259-270.

Church, Jeffrey and Gandal, Neil (1990), 'Complementary Network Externalities and Technology Adoption', **11** *International Journal of Industrial Organization*, 239-260.

Church, Jeffrey and Gandal, Neil (1992a), 'Integration, Complementary Products, and Variety', **1** *Journal of Economics and Management Strategy*, 651-675.

Church, Jeffrey and Gandal, Neil (1992b), 'Network Effects, Software Provision, and Standardization', **40** *Journal of Industrial Economics*, 85-104.

Church, Jeffrey and King, I.P. (1993), 'Bilingualism and Network Externalities', **26** *Canadian Journal of Economics*, 337-345.

Cohen, William E. (1996), 'Competition and Foreclosure in the Context of Installed Base and Compatibility Effects', **64** *Antitrust Law Journal*, 535-569.

Compton, Charles T.C. (1993), 'Cooperation, Collaboration, and Coalition: a Perspective on the Types and Purposes of Technology Joint Ventures', **61** *Antitrust Law Journal*, 861-897.

Conner, Kathleen R. (1995), 'Obtaining Strategic Advantage from being Imitated: When can Encouraging "Clones" Pay?', **41** *Management Science*, 209-225.

Conrad, Cecilia and Duchatelet, M. (1987), 'New Technology Adoption', **5** *International Journal of Industrial Organization*, 315-321.

Cowan, Robin (1990), 'Nuclear Power Reactors: A Study in Technological Lock In', **50** *Journal of Economic History*, 541-567.

Cowan, Robin (1991), 'Tortoises and Hares: Choice among Technologies of Unknown Merit', **101** *Economic Journal*, 801-814.

Cowan, Robin (1992), 'High Technology and the Economics of Standardization', in Dierkes, Meinolf and Hoffmann, Ute (eds), *New Technology at the Outset*, Frankfurt/M and New York, Campus, 279-300.

Crandall, Robert W. and Sidak, J. Gregory (1995), 'Competition and Regulatory Policies for Interactive Broadband Networks', **68** *Southern California Law Review*, 1203-1237.

Dam, Kenneth W. (1995), 'Some Economic Considerations in the Intellectual Property Protection of Software', **24** *Journal of Legal Studies*, 321-377.

David, Paul A (1985), 'Clio and the Economics of Qwerty', **75** *American Economic Review*, 332-337.

David, Paul A. (1986), 'Understanding the Economics of Qwerty', in Parker, W.N. (ed.), *Economic History and the Modern Economist*, Oxford, Basil Blackwell.

David, Paul A. and Bunn, Julie Ann (1988), 'The Economics of Gateway Technologies and Network Evolution', **3** *Information Economics and Policy*, 165-202.

David, Paul A. and Greenstein, Shane (1990), 'The Economics of Compatibility Standards: An Introduction to the Recent Research', **1** *Economics of Innovation and New Technology*, 3-41.

David, Paul A. and Steinmueller, W. Edward (1994), 'Economics of Compatibility Standards and Competition in Telecommunication Networks', **6** *Information Economics and Policy*, 217-241.

Desruelle, Dominique et al. (1996), 'Complementarity, Coordination and Compatibility: An Analysis of the Economics of Systems', **14** *International Journal of Industrial Organization*, 747 ff.

Domowitz, Ian (1995), 'Electronic Derivatives Exchanges: Implicit Mergers, Network Externalities, and Standardization', **35** *Quarterly Review of Economics and Finance*, 163-175.

Dowd, Kevin and Greenaway, David (1993), 'Currency Competition, Network Externalities and Switching Costs: Towards an Alternative View of Optimum Currency Areas', **103** *Economic Journal*, 1180-1189.

Dratler, Jay, Jr (1996), 'Microsoft as an Antitrust Target: IBM in Software?', **25** *Southwestern University Law Review*, 671-744.

Dybvig, Philip and Spatt, Chester (1983), 'Adoption Externalities as Public Goods', **20** *Journal of Public Economics*, 231-247.

Economides, Nicholas (1988), 'Desirability of Compatibility in the Absence of Network Externalities', **78** *American Economic Review*, 108-121.

Economides, Nicholas (1991), 'Compatibility and the Creation of Shared Networks', in Guerin-Calvert, Margaret and Wildman, Steven (eds), *Electronic Services Networks: A Business and Public Policy Challenge*, New York, Prager Pub. Inc.

Economides, Nicholas (1993a), 'Network Economics with Application to Finance', **2** *Financial Markets, Institutions, and Instruments*, 89-97.

Economides, Nicholas (1993b), 'A Monopolist's Incentive to Invite Competitors to Enter in Telecommunications Services', in Pogorel, Gerard (ed.), *Global Telecommunications Services and Technological Changes*, Amsterdam, Elsevier.

Economides, Nicholas (1996), 'The Economics of Networks', **14** *International Journal of Industrial Organization*, 673 ff.

Economides, Nicholas (1997), 'Network Externalities, Complementarities, and Invitations to Enter', *European Journal of Political Economy,* forthcoming.

Economides, Nicholas and Himmelberg, Charles (1995), 'Critical Mass and Network Evolution in Telecommunications', in Brock, Gerard (ed.), *Toward a Competitive Telecommunications Industry: Selected Papers from the 1994 Telecommunications Policy Research Conference*, Mahwah, NJ, Lawrence Erlbaum Association.

Economides, Nicholas and Salop, Steven (1992), 'Competition and Integration among Complements, and Network Market Structure', **40** *Journal of Industrial Economics*, 105-123.

Economides, Nicholas and White, Lawrence (1994), 'Networks and Compatibility: Implications for Antitrust', **38** *European Economic Review*, 651-662.

Economides, Nicholas and White, Lawrence (1995), 'Access and Interconnection Access Pricing: How Efficient is the Efficient Component Pricing Rule?', **40** *Antitrust Bulletin*, 557-579.

Economides, Nicholas and White, Lawrence (1996), 'One-Way Networks, Two-Way Networks, Compatibility, and Antitrust', in Gabel, David and Weiman, David (eds), *Opening Networks to Competition: The Regulation and Pricing of Access*, Amsterdam, Kluwer Academic Press.

Encaoua, David et al. (1996), 'Compatibility and Competition in Airlines: Demand Side Network Effects', **14** *International Journal of Industrial Organization*, 701 ff.

Evans, David S. and Schmalensee, Richard (1996), 'A Guide to the Antitrust Economics of Networks', **Spring** *Antitrust*, 36-39.

Farrell, Joseph (1989), 'Standardization and Intellectual Property', **30** *Jurimetrics Journal*, 35-50.

Farrell, Joseph (1996), 'Creating Local Competition', **49** *Federal Communications Law Journal*, 201-215.

Farrell, Joseph and Gallini, Nancy (1988), 'Second-Sourcing as a Commitment: Monopoly Incentives to Attract Competition', **103** *Quarterly Journal of Economics*, 673-694.

Farrell, Joseph and Saloner, Garth (1985), 'Standardization, Compatibility, and Innovation', **16** *Rand Journal of Economics*, 70-83.

Farrell, Joseph and Saloner, Garth (1986a), 'Economic Issues in Standardization', in Miller J. (ed.), *Telecommunications and Equity*, Amsterdam, North Holland.

Farrell, Joseph and Saloner, Garth (1986b), 'Installed Base and Compatibility: Innovation, Product Preannouncements, and Predation', **76** *American Economic Review*, 940-955.

Farrell, Joseph and Saloner, Garth (1986c), 'Standardization and Variety', **20** *Economic Letters*, 71-74.

Farrell, Joseph and Saloner, Garth (1987), 'Competition, Compatibility and Standards: The Economics of Horses, Penguins and Lemmings', in Gabel, H. Landis (ed.), *Competitive Strategies for Product Standards*, London, McGraw Hill.

Farrell, Joseph and Saloner, Garth (1988), 'Coordination Through Committees and Markets', **19** *Rand Journal of Economics*, 235-252.

Farrell, Joseph and Saloner, Garth (1992), 'Converters, Compatibility, and the Control of Interfaces', **40** *Journal of Industrial Economics*, 9-36.

Farrell, Joseph and Shapiro, Carl (1988), 'Dynamic Competition with Switching Costs', **19** *Rand Journal of Economics*, 123 ff.

Farrell, Joseph and Shapiro, Carl (1989), 'Optimal Contracts with Lock-In', **79** *American Economic Review*, 51 ff.

Farrell, Joseph and Shapiro, Carl (1992), 'Standard Setting in High-Definition Television', **1** *Brookings Papers on Economic Activity: Microeconomics 1*.

Fischel, William A. (1980), 'Externalities and Zoning', **35** *Public Choice*, 37-43.

Fischel, William A. (1994), 'Zoning, Nonconvexities, and T. Jack Foster's City', **35** *Journal of Urban Economics*, 175-181.

Gabel, H. Landis (1991), *Competitive Strategies for Product Standards*, London, McGraw Hill.

Gallini, Nancy and Karp, Larry (1989), 'Sales and Consumer Lock-in', **56** *Economica*, 279-294.

Gandal, Neil (1994), 'Hedonic Price Indexes for Spreadsheets and an Empirical Test for Network Externalities', **24** *Rand Journal of Economics*, 19-39.

Gandal, Neil (1995), 'A Selective Survey of the Literature on Indirect Network Externalities', **17** *Research in Law and Economics*, 23-31.

Gandal, Neil (1996), 'Compatibility Standards and Complementary Network Externalities in the PC Software Market', *Review of Economics and Statistics*, forthcoming.

Garud, Raghu and Kumaraswamy, Arun (1993), 'Changing Competitive Dynamics in Network Industries: An Exploration of Sun Microsystems' Open Systems Strategy', **14** *Strategic Management Journal*, 351-369.

Gifford, Daniel J. (1996), 'Microsoft Corporation, the Justice Department, and Antitrust Theory', **25** *Southwestern University Law Review*, 621-670.

Gilbert, Richard J. (1989), 'Mobility Barriers and the Value of Incumbency', in Schmalensee, Richard and Willig, Robert (eds), 1 *Handbook of Industrial Organization*, 475 ff.

Gilbert, Richard J. (1992), 'Symposium on Compatibility: Incentives and Market Structure', **40** *Journal of Industrial Economics*, 1 ff.

Gilbert, Richard J. and Sunshine, Steven C. (1995), 'Incorporating Dynamic Efficiency Concerns in Merger Analysis: The Use of Innovation Markets', **63** *Antitrust Law Journal*, 569-601.

Gillette, Clayton P. (1996), 'Rules, Standards, and Precautions in Payment Systems', **82** *Virginia Law Review*, 181-251.

Graham, Lawrence D. and Zerbe, Richard O., Jr (1996), 'Economically Efficient Treatment of Computer Software: Reverse Engineering, Protection, and Disclosure', **22** *Rutgers Computer and Technology Law Journal*, 61-142.

Gross, Irwin R. (1994), 'A New Framework for Software Protection: Distinguishing Between Interactive and Non-Interactive Aspects of Computer Programs', **20** *Rutgers Computer and Technology Law Journal*, 107-187.

Habermeier, Karl F. (1989), 'Competing Technologies, the Learning Curve, and Rational Expectations', **33** *European Economic Review*, 1293-1311.

Hanna, Ramsey (1994), 'Note: Misusing Antitrust: The Search For Functional Copyright Misuse Standards', **46** *Stanford Law Review*, 401-448.

Harbord, David and Hoehn, Tom (1994), 'Barriers to Entry and Exit in European Competition Policy', **14** *International Review of Law and Economics*, 411-435.

Hazlett, Thomas (1995), 'Predation in Local Cable TV Markets', **40** *Antitrust Bulletin*, 609-644.

Henriet, D. and Moulin, Herve (1996), 'Traffic Based Cost Allocation in a Network', **27** *Rand Journal of Economics*, 332-345.

Ignatin, Gary R. (1992), 'Note: Let the Hackers Hack: Allowing the Reverse Engineering of Copyrighted Computer Programs to Achieve Compatibility', **140** *University of Pennsylvania Law Review*, 1999-2050.

Johnston, Jason S. (1993), 'The Influence of The Nature of the Firm on the Theory of Corporate Law', **18** *Journal of Corporation Law*, 213-244.

Kahai, Simran K. et al. (1995), 'Deregulation and Predation in Long-Distance Telecommunications: An Empirical Test', **40** *Antitrust Bulletin*, 645-666.

Kahan, Marcel and Klausner, Michael (1996), 'Path Dependence in Corporate Contracting: Increasing Returns, Herd Behavior and Cognitive Biases', **74** *Washington University Law Quarterly*.

Kattan, Joseph (1993), 'Market Power in the Presence of an Installed Base', **62** *Antitrust Law Journal*, 1-21.

Katz, Michael L. and Shapiro, Carl (1985), 'Network Externalities, Competition, and Compatibility', **75** *American Economic Review*, 424-440.

Katz, Michael L. and Shapiro, Carl (1986a), 'Technology Adoption in the Presence of Network Externalities', **94** *Journal of Political Economy*, 822-841.

Katz, Michael L. and Shapiro, Carl (1986b), 'Product Compatibility Choice in a Market with Technological Progress', **38** *Oxford Economic Papers*, 146-165.

Katz, Michael L. and Shapiro, Carl (1992), 'Product Introduction with Network Externalities', **40** *Journal of Industrial Economics*, 55 ff.

Katz, Michael L. and Shapiro, Carl (1994), 'Systems Competition and Network Effects', **8** *Journal of Economic Perspectives*, 93-115.

Klausner, Michael (1995), 'Corporations, Corporate Law, and Networks of Contracts', **81** *Virginia Law Review*, 757-852.

Klemperer, Paul (1987a), 'The Competitiveness of Markets with Switching Costs', **18** *Rand Journal of Economics*, 138-150.

Klemperer, Paul (1987b), 'Markets with Consumer Switching Costs', **102** *Quarterly Journal of Economics*, 375 ff.

Klemperer, Paul (1989), 'Price Wars Caused by Switching Costs', **65** *Review of Economic Studies*, 405-420.

Krauss, Michael I. (1994), 'Regulation vs. Markets in the Development of Standards', **3** *Southern California Interdisciplinary Law Journal*, 781-808.

Kristiansen, Eirik Guaard (1996), 'R&D in Markets with Network Externalities', **14** *International Journal of Industrial Organization*, 769 ff

Lamberton, D.M. and Neumann, K.-H. (1994), 'The Economics of Standards', **6** *Information Economics and Policy*, 193-194.

Langlois, Richard N. (1992), 'External Economies and Economic Progress: The Case of the Microcomputer Industry', **66** *Business History Review*, 1-50.

Lehr, William (1996), 'Compatibility Standards and Industry Competition: Two Case Studies', **4** *Economics of Innovation and New Technology*, 97-112.

Lemley, Mark A. (1996), 'Antitrust and the Internet Standardization Problem', **28** *Connecticut Law Review*, 1041 ff.

Lemley, Mark A. and O'Brien, David (1997), 'Encouraging Software Reuse', **49** *Stanford Law Review*, 255 ff.

Lewis, Tracy R. and Yao, Dennis A. (1995), 'Some Reflections on the Antitrust Treatment of Intellectual Property', **63** *Antitrust Law Journal*, 603-619.

Liebowitz, S.J. and Margolis, Stephen E. (1990), 'The Fable of the Keys', **22** *Journal of Law and Economics*, 1-26.

Liebowitz, S.J. and Margolis, Stephen E. (1994), 'Network Externality: An Uncommon Tragedy', **8** *Journal of Economic Perspectives*, 133-150.

Liebowitz, S.J. and Margolis, Stephen E. (1995a), 'Are Network Externalities a New Source of Market Failure?', **17** *Research in Law and Economics*, 1-22.

Liebowitz, S.J. and Margolis, Stephen E. (1995b), 'Path Dependence, Lock-in, and History', **11** *Journal of Law, Economics, and Organization*, 205-226.

Liebowitz, S.J. and Margolis, Stephen E. (1995c), 'Policy and Path Dependence: From Qwerty to Windows 95', **33** *Regulation*.

Liebowitz, S.J. and Margolis, Stephen E. (1995d), 'Reply to Comments by Regibeau and Gandal', **17** *Research in Law and Economics*, 41-46.

Liebowitz, S.J. and Margolis, Stephen E. (1996), 'Should Technology Choice be a Concern of Antitrust Policy', **9** *Harvard Journal of Law and Technology*, 283-318.

Lopatka, John and Page, William H. (1995a), 'Microsoft, Monopolization, and Network Externalities: Some Uses and Abuses of Economic Theory in Antitrust Decisionmaking', **40** *Antitrust Bulletin*, 317-370.

Lopatka, John and Page, William H. (1995b), 'Posner's Program for the Antitrust Division: A Twenty-Five Year Perspective', **48** *SMU Law Review*, 1713-1747.

Lunney, Glynn S., Jr (1996), 'Lotus v. Borland: Copyright and Computer Programs', **70** *Tulane Law Review*, 2397-2436.

Matutes, Carmen and Padilla, A. Jorge (1992), 'Shared ATM Networks and Banking Competition', **38** *European Economic Review*, 1113-1138.

Matutes, Carmen and Regibeau, Pierre (1988), 'Mix and Match: Product Compatibility without Network Externalities', **19** *Rand Journal of Economics*, 221-234.

Matutes, Carmen and Regibeau, Pierre (1989), 'Standardization Across Markets and Entry', **40** *Journal of Industrial Economics*, 467-487.

Matutes, Carmen and Regibeau, Pierre (1992), 'Compatibility and Bundling of Complementary Goods in a Duopoly', **40** *Journal of Industrial Economics*, 37-54.

McAndrews, James and Rob, Rafael (1996), 'Shared Ownership and Pricing in a Network Switch', **14** *International Journal of Industrial Organization*, 727 ff.

Menell, Peter S. (1987), 'Tailoring Legal Protection for Computer Software', **39** *Stanford Law Review*, 1329-1372.

Menell, Peter S. (1989), 'An Analysis of the Scope of Copyright Protection for Application Programs', **41** *Stanford Law Review*, 1045-1071.

Menell, Peter S. (1994), 'The Challenges of Reforming Intellectual Property Protection for Computer Software', **94** *Columbia Law Review*, 2644-2254.

Morris, Charles R. and Ferguson, Charles H. (1993), 'How Architecture Wins Technology Wars', **March** *Harvard Business Review*, 89-91.

Owen, David R. (1996), 'Note: Interfaces and Interoperability in Lotus v. Borland: A Market-Oriented Approach to the Fair Use Doctrine', **64** *Fordham Law Review*, 2381-2423.

Perritt, Henry H., Jr (1995), 'Access to the National Information Infrastructure', **30** *Wake Forest Law Review*, 51-103.

Perrot, Anne (1993), 'Compatibility, Networks, and Competition: A Review of Recent Advances', *Transportation Science*.

Pirrong, Stephen Craig (1995), 'The Self-Regulation of Commodity Exchanges: The Case of Market Manipulation', **38** *Journal of Law and Economics*, 141-206.

Postrel, S.R. (1990), 'Competing Networks and Proprietary Standards: the Case of Quadraphonic Sound', **19** *Journal of Industrial Economics*, 221-234.

Rasmussen, Robert K. and Skeel, David A., Jr (1995), 'The Economic Analysis of Corporate Bankruptcy Law', **3** *American Bankruptcy Institute Law Review*, 85 ff.

Regibeau, Pierre (1995), 'Defending the Concept of Network Externalities', **17** *Research in Law and Economics*, 33-39.

Regibeau, Pierre and Rockett, Katherine (1996), 'The Timing of Product Introduction and the Credibility of Compatibility Decisions', **14** *International Journal of Industrial Organization*, 801 ff.

Ribstein, Larry E. (1995a), 'Linking Statutory Forms', **58** *Journal of Law and Contemporary Problems*, 58 ff.

Ribstein, Larry E. (1995b), 'Statutory Forms for Closely Held Firms: Theories and Evidence from LLCs', **73** *Washington University Law Quarterly*, 369 ff.

Ribstein, Larry E. and Kobayashi, Bruce H. (1995), 'Uniform Laws, Model Laws and Limited Liability Companies', **66** *University of Colorado Law Review*, 947-999.

Ribstein, Larry E. and Kobayashi, Bruce H. (1996), 'An Economic Analysis of Uniform State Laws', **25** *Journal of Legal Studies*, 131-99.

Robinson, Glen O. (1996), 'The New Communications Act: A Second Opinion', **29** *Connecticut Law Review*, 289-329.

Rohlfs, Jeff (1974), 'A Theory of Interdependent Demand for a Communications Service', **10** *Bell Journal of Economics*, 141-156.

Saloner, Garth (1990), 'Economic Issues in Computer Interface Standardization: the Case of UNIX', **1** *Economics of Innovation and New Technology*, 135-156.

Scharfstein, David S. and Stein, Jeremy C. (1990), 'Herd Behavior and Investment', **80** *American Economic Review*, 465 ff.

Shapiro, Carl (1995), 'Aftermarkets and Consumer Welfare: Making Sense of Kodak', **63** *Antitrust Law Journal*, 483-511.

Shapiro, Carl and Teece, David J. (1994), 'Systems Competition and Aftermarkets', **39** *Antitrust Bulletin*, 135 ff.

Shy, Oz (1996), 'Technology Revolutions in the Presence of Network Externalities', **14** *International Journal of Industrial Organization*, 785 ff.

Takeyama, L.N. (1994), 'The Welfare Implications of Unauthorized Reproduction of Intellectual Property in the Presence of Network Externalities', **42** *Journal of Industrial Economics*, 155-165.

Teece, David J. (1994), 'Information Sharing, Innovation, and Antitrust', **62** *Antitrust Law Journal*, 465-481.

Teter, Timothy T. (1993), 'Note: Merger and the Machines: An Analysis of the Pro-Compatibility Trend in Computer Software Copyright Cases', **45** *Stanford Law Review*, 1061-1098.

Thum, Marcel (1994), 'Network Externalities, Technological Progress, and the Competition of Market Contracts', **12** *International Journal of Industrial Organization*, 269-289.

Turnbull, Shann (1995), 'Innovations in Corporate Governance: The Mondragon Experience', **3(3)** *Corporate Governance: An International Review*, 167-180.

Turnbull, Shann (1997), 'Stakeholder Co-orporation', **29(3)** *Journal of Co-operative Studies*, 18-52.

Van Vleck, Va Nee L. (1995), 'Reassessing Technological Backwardness: Absolving the "Silly Little Bobtailed" Coal Car', **55** *Journal of Economic History*, 383 ff.

Veall, Michael R. (1995), 'On Product Standardization as Competition Policy', **18** *Canadian Journal of Economics*, 416-425.

Vita, Michael G., and Wellford, Charissa P. (1994), 'Regulating the Electromagnetic Environment: Alternative Approaches to Policy', in Fleming, James R. and Gemery, Henry A. (eds), *Science, Technology, and the Environment*, 238 ff.

Weiman, David F. and Levin, Richard C. (1994), 'Preying for Monopoly? The Case of Southern Bell Telephone Company, 1894-1912', **102** *Journal of Political Economy*, 103-126.

Wortman, Tara J. (1995), 'Note: Unlocking Lock-In: Limited Liability Companies and the Key to Underutilization of Close Corporation Statutes', **70** *New York University Law Review*, 1362-1408.

Other References

Jorde, Thomas M. and Teece, David J. (1993), 'Rule of Reason Analysis of Horizontal Arrangements: Agreements Designed to Advance Innovation and Commercialize Technology', **61** *Antitrust Law Journal*, 579-619.

Ordover, Janusz A. and Willig, Robert D. (1981), 'An Economic Definition of Predation: Pricing and Product Innovation', **91** *Yale Law Journal*, 8 ff.

Schumpeter, Joseph A. (1942), *Capitalism, Socialism and Democracy*, New York, Harpercollins.

Sheff, David (1994), *Game Over: How Nintendo Conquered the World*, New York, Vintage Books.

Cases

Eastman Kodak Co. v. Image Technical Services, Inc., 504 U.S. 45 (1992).

Lotus Development Corp. v. Borland Int'l, 49 F.3d 807 (1st Cir. 1995), aff'd by an equally divided Court, 116 S. Ct. 804 (1996).

Money Station, Inc. v. Board of Governors of Federal Reserve System, 81 F.3d 1128 (D.C. Cir. 1996).

National Collegiate Athletic Ass'n v. Board of Regents, 468 U.S. 85 (1984).

United States v. Eastman Kodak Co., 853 F. Supp. 1454 (W.D.N.Y. 1994).

United States v. Microsoft Corp., 159 F.R.D. 318 (D.D.C. 1995), rev'd, 56 F.3d 1448 (D.C. Cir. 1995).

0770
PATH DEPENDENCE

Stan J. Liebowitz
Professor of Economics and Associate Dean
School of Management, University of Texas at Dallas

Stephen E. Margolis
North Carolina State University

Abstract

What role does the past play in current economic conditions? Economic models usually determine equilibrium ending points without concern for intermediate disequilibrium conditions or the prior history of the system. That the past does play some role is obvious, but the nature of its impact requires careful delineation. Some path dependence theorists have argued that past decisions might have locked-in certain inferior outcomes. In making sense of this claim particular attention needs to be paid to the meaning of 'inferior'. Upon investigation, such claims have been found to be without empirical support (in private markets) and based on fairly narrow theoretical assumptions. In nonmarket contexts less is known.
JEL classification: K0, K2, L5.O3, L0
Keywords: Path Dependence, Network Externality, Network Effect, Lock-In

1. Introduction

Most generally, path dependence means that where we go next depends not only on where we are now, but also upon where we have been. History matters. Stochastic processes are path dependent if they exhibit memory: The probability distribution for the process at time t+1 depends upon more of the history of the system than just its state at time t.

As it has recently been applied in economics, path dependence means that equilibrium allocations depend on history. Economic allocations that are path dependent could not be predicted by knowledge of the efficient allocations, or the conditions that determine the efficient allocation, alone (Arthur, 1989). An expectation of path dependence accordingly is in conflict with economic models that derive an equilibrium without taking account of the process leading to equilibrium.

Path dependence has a natural appeal. How could an outcome not depend upon the events that occur in the process of adjustment to equilibrium? The usual answer is that small variations in adjustments are averaged out, or countered, under the influence of the forces tending toward some determinate equilibrium. To take a familiar example, we expect price and quantity to adjust toward the supply-demand intersection, even if price adjustment were momentarily misdirected. Path dependence arguments introduce conditions under which correcting adjustments are not inevitable and they appeal for attention to the peculiarities that may unravel the predictability suggested by conventional equilibrium models. As we discuss below, however, this appeal must be countered by the recognition that any theory is a simplification of reality. So it remains a crucial question whether theories that ignore the sequence of events leading to equilibrium are ignoring something important.

The phrase 'lock-in by historical events', (Arthur, 1989) offers what is perhaps the best expression of the alleged importance of path dependence for economics. Lock-in has special meaning here. In some sense, of course, we are always locked in to a number of things; to eating, breathing, and remaining in our solar system to name three. But this is not what lock-in means in this literature. The lock-in in path dependence is a lock-in to something bad, or at least a lock-out of something better. It constitutes an inferior economic outcome such as an inferior standard or product where superior alternatives exist, are known, and where the costs of switching are not high.

These historical events of interest, in Brian Arthur's terminology, are 'small' or 'insignificant'. The insignificance of these historical events is not their effects - for their consequences are alleged to be large - but rather that they may seem inconsequential at the time they occur. There is an implicit allegation that such events are neither inevitable, in which case they might be taken as instances of the stinginess of nature, nor the product of significant conflict or deliberation, in which case they are the avoidable consequence of human folly. As we will elaborate below, a part of the appeal of the path dependence literature is the implicit allegation that these lock-ins, these bad economic outcomes, are avoidable by small but prudent interventions.

Path dependence is an idea that spilled over to economics from intellectual movements that arose elsewhere. In physics and mathematics the related ideas come from chaos theory. One potential of the non-linear models of chaos theory is sensitive dependence on initial conditions: determination, and perhaps lock-in, by small, insignificant events. In biology, the related idea is called contingency - the irreversible character of natural selection. Contingency implies that fitness is only a relative notion: it is not survival of the fittest possible, but only of the fittest that happen to be around at the time. Scientific popularizations like James Gleick's book *Chaos*, Mitchell Waldrop's *Complexity* and Stephen J. Gould's *Wonderful Life* have moved these ideas into the public view.

While the warm reception given to path dependence in the social science is due in part to the attention given to these related ideas in the physical sciences, the analogy is incomplete. If, for example, turtles become extinct, they will not reappear suddenly when circumstances change to make it advantageous to have a shell. But if people stop using large gas guzzling engines because gasoline has become expensive, or extend patent protection to the 'look and feel' of software, they can always revert to their old ways if they came to regret the switch. Stephen J. Gould, who has made the affirmative case for contingency in biological evolution, nevertheless has noted the limitations of the analogy to social evolution. What may have also been lost in social sciences' borrowing of this concept are the active debates in the real sciences about the generality or applicability of chaos and contingency. Christian de Duve (1995), for example, argues that contingency applies only within important constraints in biological evolution.

Similarly, path dependence and chaos have an apparent unity that may be misleading. In chaos theory, small events or perturbations do tend to cause a system to evolve in very different ways but the system never settles down in any repeatable path or fixed equilibrium. The essence of the 'chaos theory' is that this seemingly endless pattern, which never finds an equilibrium, is not random but rather has a determinate structure. Path dependence in economics has imported the view that minor initial perturbations are important, but has grafted this on to a theory where there are a finite number of perfectly stable alternative states, one of which will arise based on the particular initial conditions. The potential for never-ending 'disequilibrium' that seems the essence of chaos theory is thus missing from the economic analysis of path dependence.

Path dependence challenges some parts of the law and economics literature. Some of the influence of economics on legal reasoning comes through efficiency results, or at least expectations of efficiency. To take one example, support for privity in contract can be found in economists' arguments that individuals' maximizing actions have the effect, under certain conditions, of maximizing total wealth. Path dependence (in its strong forms) is a challenge to these arguments. For the law itself, path dependence may seem self evident, given the role of precedent. In fact, those who have put forward the view that the law may tend toward efficiency have borne the burden of proof that precedent - or path dependence - would not overwhelm other factors. So for the law, what has seemed to require special argument is the absence of path dependence, not its presence. For this reason, the empirical issue of path dependence in market-based choices may be of particular importance for law and economics. If path dependence can interfere with efficiency even where precedent does not play an explicit role and where we might expect evolution toward efficiency, such influence would appear magnified in the law, where precedent has such an explicit role.

In the remainder of this entry, we examine the theoretical and empirical claims of the economic literature on path dependence. We start with a simple example of path dependence, offered to help fix ideas. Following that, we offer a taxonomy of path dependence claims that draws on our article in the *Journal of Law, Economics and Organization*. In our view, some of the confusion around path dependence has resulted from a failure to distinguish among types of path dependence claims. We offer a remedy here. Following that, we present a discussion of the means by which market behaviors would tend to unravel instances of path dependence that constitute inefficiencies. The possibility that profit-seeking activities may be able to undo harmful path dependence reduces the issue to an empirical one: Are there documented instances of harmful path dependence? We close on that issue.

2. The Allegation: The Inefficiency of Path Dependence

The allegation of path dependence, as it addresses the workings of laissez-faire markets, is that market choices can stick us on undesirable paths. Once we are stuck in such a rut, individual decisions are the best we can manage only from the rut in which we find ourselves. Accordingly, for any allocation decision that might be susceptible to path dependence, we lose the usual presumption that individual choices lead to an optimal outcome. Consider the following example of a choice that could be subject to path dependence. Suppose that it is important that we all drive on the right side of the road, unless we all drive on the left. Assume also that it matters fairly little which convention we adopt but that most of us would prefer a convention of right-hand-side driving. Suppose further that one early driver is observed driving on the left-hand-side of the road. (Perhaps he was avoiding a puddle from a leaking horse trough.) Others who were planning to drive make a quick determination that left-hand-side driving, though mildly objectionable, will be the safe way to go. Those drivers are also observed driving on the left, which causes still more left-hand-side driving, and so on. Notice then that *it could happen that* we each prefer to drive on the right, but that each of us ends up driving on the left. Each agent behaves in a privately optimal way, given his circumstances, but the aggregate outcome is inferior to a seemingly feasible alternative.

As we will see when we examine these issues in detail, the phrase ‘it could happen that’ is a crucial one. That something could happen does not mean that it does happen. Before we can get to that, some definitions.

3. Definitions of Path Dependence

There are three possible efficiency outcomes where past conditions or decisions exhibit a persistent influence on a dynamic process. First, such persistence might do no harm. That is to say, an initial action does put us on a path that cannot be left without some cost, but that path happens to be optimal (although not necessarily uniquely optimal). For example, a capricious decision to part one's hair on the left may lead to a lifetime of left-side parting, but the initial urge to part on the left might capture all there is to be taken into account. On a grander scale, our decision to use a particular system for powering the machinery in a plant may be a controlling influence for decades, but the long-term effects of the decision may be fully appreciated by the initial decision maker and fully taken into account. We have used the term *first-degree path dependence* to indicate instances in which persistence of prior conditions or decisions exists, but with no implied inefficiency. This taxonomy of path dependence claims appears in our 1995 paper in the *Journal of Law, Economics and Organization.* Mark Roe's 1996 *Harvard Law Review* paper also offers a related categorization of path dependence. In Roe, path dependence can be weak (the efficiency of the chosen path is tied with some alternatives), semi strong, (the chosen path is not the best but not worth fixing, or strong (the chosen path is highly inefficient, but we are unable to correct it).

Since information is always imperfect, a second possibility arises. When individuals fail to predict the future perfectly, it is possible, even likely, that decisions appearing efficient *ex ante* may not always appear to be efficient *ex post*. Here the inferiority of a chosen path is unknowable at the time a choice is made, but we later recognize that some alternative path would have yielded greater wealth. In such a situation, which we have termed *second-degree path dependence*, persistence of prior conditions or decisions leads to outcomes that are regrettable and costly to change. They are not, however, inefficient in any meaningful sense, given the assumed limitations on knowledge.

Related to this second type of path dependence is *third-degree path dependence*. In third-degree path dependence, persistence leads to an outcome that is inefficient - but in this case the outcome is 'remediable'. That is, there exists some feasible arrangement for recognizing and achieving a preferred outcome, but that outcome is not obtained. Williamson (1993b, p. 140) offers the term 'remediability' to describe the condition that such feasible alternatives exist, and urges remediability as the appropriate standard for public policy discussion. Similar positions have been argued by Demsetz, Coase, Calabresi and Dahlman, among others. In the framework that these authors have advocated, market failure is not demonstrated unless a specific policy recommendation can be shown in which the benefits exceed the costs, including all of the administrative costs of the policy. For actual policy purposes, it of course makes a difference whether the remediation remains possible: lost opportunities in the past are of not interest. But for the consideration of market failure, an opportunity for remediation in the past is of at least academic interest.

The three types of path dependence make progressively stronger claims. First-degree path dependence is a simple assertion of an intertemporal relationship, with no implied claim of inefficiency. Second-degree path dependence stipulates that intertemporal effects propagate error. Third-degree path dependence requires not only that the intertemporal effects propagate error, but also that the error was avoidable.

The essence of the distinction between third-degree path dependence and the weaker forms is the availability of feasible, wealth-increasing alternatives to actual allocations, now or at some time in the past. The paths taken under first- and second-degree path dependence cannot be improved upon, given the available alternatives and the state of knowledge. Third-degree path dependence, on the other hand, supposes the feasibility, in principle, of improvements in the path taken.

The existence of first- and second-degree path dependence is not in dispute. Clearly, this form of path dependence is very common. They are a reflection of ordinary durability and they have long been reflected in economic modeling. First-degree path dependence is recognized, for example, when we acknowledge that Robinson Crusoe and Friday may choose to make provision for the future. Ordinary durability installs (at least) this kind of persistence. Economists consider second-degree path dependence when we study decision making under uncertainty. While it may be of interest to identify these instances of persistence, first- and second-degree path dependence do not constitute a challenge to standing efficiency claims.

For these reasons, it is not surprising that the main focus of this literature rests on third-degree path dependence. The claim that the predictions of efficiency in standard economic methodology are likely to be wrong is a bold claim. Naturally, it is an empirical issue whether the path dependence literature acknowledges something important that neoclassical economics neglects by focusing on equilibrium positions rather than on the path toward equilibria. Some of the most prominent examples in this literature feature specific claims of inefficiency. For example, listen to Paul David: 'The accretion of technological innovations inherited from the past therefore cannot legitimately be presumed to constitute socially optimal solutions provided for us - either by heroic enterprises or herds of rational managers operating in efficient markets' (1992, p. 137).

Since it is only this third form of path dependence that can be understood as market failure, it is important to maintain the distinctions among these various forms. One must take care not to extend the plausibility of instances of ordinary durability - first- and second-degree path dependence - to third degree claims.

4. What forms of path dependence appear in the literature?

Brian Arthur's (1989) consideration of path dependence gives us the phrase of 'lock-in by historical events'. In his examples of the workings of positive-feedback models, which we examine in detail below, he finds that path inefficiency is possible where there are increasing returns. Arthur's version of path dependence is the third-degree form - so long as the information regarding the returns to each choice is available to relevant decision makers.

Thomas Schelling anticipated some of the kinds of problems that are considered in the path dependence literature. He discusses as 'interactive behaviors' problems in which outcomes depend heavily on the order in which actions occur. Inferior outcomes may prevail in these cases, even in the face of known preferred alternatives, illustrating the third-degree form (1978, pp. 36-8). Shelling offers these cases, however, as examples of nonmarket behavior, and he also notes that market institutions often arise as remedies for these problems (p. 33). Elsewhere he acknowledges the unfeasibility of some hypothetical improvements (p. 132).

The archetypal allegation of path dependence is the configuration of the typewriter keyboard. David's (1985) presentation is largely responsible for introducing this story to economists. According to this story, the standard 'QWERTY' keyboard arrangement, introduced in the 1870s, is dramatically inferior to an arrangement offered by August Dvorak in the 1930s. We are, however, regrettably locked into the inferior arrangement by a coordination failure: no one trains on the Dvorak keyboard because Dvorak machines are hard to find, and Dvorak machines are hard to find because no one trains on Dvorak keyboards. The process is said to be path dependent in that the timing of the adoption of QWERTY, and not its efficiency, explains its survival.

Some of David's claims for this case do not go beyond first-degree path dependence. Most readers will not question the observation repeated in David that 'One damn thing leads to another' (David, 1985, p. 332), because it asserts no more than first-degree path dependence. But David makes stronger claims. In accepting and repeating the claim that the cost of retraining in Dvorak is recovered ten days after the end of training (p. 332), for example, he positions the QWERTY case as an active example of third-degree path dependence. David's 1985 paper concludes: 'Competition in the absence of perfect futures markets drove the industry prematurely into standardization *on the wrong system* where decentralized decision making subsequently has sufficed to hold it' (emphasis in original). We stay with the wrong keyboard, according to David, not because sunk investments in QWERTY make the switch to the Dvorak arrangement an inferior choice, but because of 'decentralized decision making'. This attribution of the error to decentralized decision making clearly suggests that alternative, presumably centralized, decision mechanisms would correct this error. This is a third-degree claim. David's reader is likely to find the claim of path dependence in the third-degree form to be more palatable because of his earlier establishment of weaker forms of path dependence.

Paul Krugman has offered industrial location as an example of inefficient path dependence. If there were economies of having several firms in the same industry produce at a single location, we would expect firms to congregate somewhere. It could happen that firms simply congregate around the first location at which a plant is established. In such a circumstance, there would be no reason to think that the location chosen by such an industry is efficient. Krugman uses the example of the accumulation of carpet manufacturing firms around Dalton, Georgia (this city is the center of carpet production in the United States; Krugman offers it as an example of path dependence and as an example of the defects of traditional economic models). In such cases, it is argued, economics does not tell us which location would be chosen for an industry, and that it would only be by the sheerest of coincidences that the choice of location for a single plant would turn out to be the efficient location for an entire industry. There are several problems with this argument. First, there are some reasons to think that the first firm at a particular location would have chosen a location that is congenial to its industry. Second, most industries have multiple production sites, and therefore there would be competition among these candidate sites as a focus for industrial agglomeration. (For example, many carpet plants operate successfully in locations outside of Georgia, both in the Southeast and elsewhere.) Finally, locational choices may often involve a choice among a number of equally efficient alternatives. The fact that economics cannot explain the choice of a particular location over equivalently attractive alternatives is no evidence against the efficiency of the chosen outcome.

Path dependence along with the QWERTY story have moved out of academic writing and into the arena of public policy. In the *Los Angeles Times* (October 5, 1995), Steve Steinburg writes, regarding the adoption of an internet standard, '[I]ts all too likely to be the wrong standard. From Qwerty to Dvorak keyboards, to Beta vs. VHS cassettes, history shows that market share and technical superiority are rarely related'. In *The Independent* (September 5, 1995) Hamish McRae discusses the likelihood of 'lock-in' to inferior standards. He notes the Beta and VHS competition as well as some others, then adds, 'Another example is MS-DOS, but perhaps the best of all is the QWERTY keyboard. This was designed to slow down typists ... .' In *Fortune* (May 15, 1995) Tim Smith reports that QWERTY was intended to slow down typists, and then notes, 'Perhaps the stern test of the marketplace produces results more capricious than we like to think'. In a long feature series in the *Washington Post* (November 13, 1995), Steve Pearlstein argues that modern markets, particularly those linked to networks, are likely to be dominated by just a few firms. After introducing readers to Brian Arthur, he states, 'The Arthurian discussion of networks usually begins at the typewriter keyboard'. The QWERTY story has also been published in the *New York Times*, *The Sunday Observer*, and *The Boston Globe*, *The Encyclopedia Britannica*, and broadcast on PBS's Lehrer news hour. The story can be found in two very successful economics books written for laymen; Robert Frank's and Philip Cook's *Winner Take All Society* and Paul Krugman's *Peddling Prosperity*, where an entire chapter is devoted to the 'economics of QWERTY'. It also figures prominently in Dixit and Nalebuff's *Thinking Strategically* and appears in some of Stephen J. Gould's writings.

These popularizations generally constitute the third-degree form. For the academic writings as well, the simple observation of durability conveys little surprise. These are interesting tales precisely because they are tales of things gone wrong.

5. Market Actions and Path Dependence

We start with a simple numerical example of path dependence as an illustration of the basic case. Table 1 is reproduced from a 1989 paper by Brian Arthur that is often credited with starting the whole discussion. The table is the basis for an exercise by which Arthur seemingly demonstrates the likelihood of unsatisfactory lock-in where there are increasing returns.

Table 1
Adoption Payoffs

Number of Previous Adoptions	0	10	20	30	40	50	60	70	80	90	100
Technology A	10	11	12	13	14	15	16	17	18	19	20
Technology B	4	7	10	13	16	19	22	25	28	31	34

The story that goes with the table is that there are two technologies that are in competition with each other. A would-be adopter arrives on the scene and chooses between technologies A and B. Assume for now that an adopter receives a payoff (value), as shown in the table, that is determined by the total number of adopters of a given technology. So, for example, if there are 21 adopters of technology A, each would enjoy a payoff of 12. The payoffs increase with the number of adopters, which incorporates the increasing returns assumption. These increasing returns might be due to either economies in production, or network effects. (Network effects occur where the value of a product to a user increases as more consumers use the product.)

Arthur uses the table to illustrate the likelihood of undesirable lock-in. The first adopter on the scene, choosing between a payoff of 10 with technology A and a payoff of 4 with technology B, would be expected to choose technology A. The arrival of subsequent adopters will only serve to reinforce the advantage of choosing A. But notice that if the eventual number of adopters is large enough, technology B would yield greater returns. But the choices of individual adopters will lock us in to technology A.

Arthur's story of lock-in is simple - deceptively so. If we look at the table alone, it seems unavoidable that individuals' choices will lead to an irreversible choice of technology A and it seems undeniable that A is an unfortunate choice where the number of eventual adopters is large. The first adopter would rather have 10 than 4, and so would anyone else. We are locked in; the market fails. Each agent acts rationally, given the payoffs in the table, but as a group we end up with less than we might have had. Perhaps, the argument goes, some government action is needed to enforce a coordinated decision.

What is lacking from the table and is also lacking in the great outpouring of abstract modeling of path dependency, is an appreciation of both the variety of steps that people take to avoid such harms, and the restrictive conditions assumed in the table. These analyses make the common mistake of assuming that market organization and perfect decentralization are, or ought to be, the same thing.

Imagine for a moment that each of these technologies is owned, perhaps through patent or copyright. In that case, if the number of potential adopters is large, the owner of technology B would have a significant incentive to establish B as the technology of choice. Just as the owner of especially productive land is expected to capture the value of its advantages, the owner of a technology would be expected to capture the advantages that it offers over the next best alternatives. Given that, it is worthwhile for the owner of technology B to cut prices for early adopters or provide other incentives to induce adoptions of B. While the owner of A will have similar incentives, the total wealth potential of technology B is greater, so B would be able to offer greater incentives to become the technology of choice, under the assumption that B is the technology capable of yielding greater total benefits. Alternatively, if the technology is not owned, it would pay all would-be adopters to enter agreements to adopt the preferred technology.

More generally, the inefficiency that seems inescapable in the table is a profit opportunity for someone who can figure out the means to move the outcome from A to B and appropriate the difference. Such entrepreneurship can take various forms, some of which are familiar. Where a technology is not patentable or otherwise ownable, a firm may be able to create a format or a variant of the technology that is. Firms can advertise, they can lease out the goods that implement the technology, they can enter strategic alliances. On the consumer side, a large user of a technology may be able to profit from adopting technology B regardless of the choices of other users. For example, large firms with numerous typists would have switched to Dvorak if Dvorak really did offer significant advantages.

The model that gives us lock-in from the numbers in the table not only reduces producers to the role of mere spectators, but it also assumes that consumers have no foresight. For if consumers were aware of the entire table, all that is required to prevent lock-in to an inferior alternative is that adopters can make reasonable forecasts of the number of eventual adopters. If, for example, early adopters know that they will be joined by 100 more, they will see that everyone will be better off with technology B. The latecomers will see it that way too, and the early-comers know it. (For a more complete discussion of this example, including an alternative interpretation of the table, see our 1995 paper.)

The kind of foresight that we are talking about here is not the domain of gifted visionaries. It is the kind of foresight that led consumers to buy an FM radio (as opposed to AM) in the early 1960s, cassette players in the 1970s (as opposed to eight-track), and CD players in the 1980s (as opposed to analog phonograph recordings). It leads newlyweds to buy a service for eight even when they do not yet know three other couples in town. And in 1990, it led consumers to buy Windows-based computers even when most machines were still DOS-based .

Finally, this model of lock-in also imposes certain other theoretical restrictions that may or may not commonly occur in the world. For example, to obtain the lock-in that Arthur demonstrates, the technology that offers smaller benefits at low levels of use must enjoy greater economies of scale. That is, the returns functions must cross, or initial consumer decisions will not put us on wrong paths. Since changes in payoffs must be due to economies of scale or network effects, it must be presumed that these influences differ across technologies. While it is certainly possible that this could occur, the requirements for lock-in are far more stringent than might appear upon a casual reading. In particular, it would seem that network effects would most likely exert the same influence on either of two rival standards or technologies.

6. Cases

The extensive theoretical literature on path dependence formalizes the following type of claim: it is possible to specify models in which right-hand-side driving is widely preferred, but nevertheless we all end up driving on the left. Such models must always include assumptions, explicit or not, about expectations, ownership, information, network effects, production economies, communication, the possibility of side payments, the presence of large users and, more generally, entrepreneurship. Many of these are simply ignored, which is to say they are implicitly assumed away. The question then becomes whether this particular abstraction of reality captures what is important about the kinds of choices that path dependence is said to address. We are left then with an empirical question.

For empirical support, the literature of path dependence draws repeatedly on the same handful of stylized cases based on the popular histories of some well-known competitions between competing technological developments. First and foremost is the aforementioned story of the typewriter keyboard. In second place in this cannon is the competition between the Beta and VHS videotaping formats. After that is the eclipse of the Macintosh operating system by Microsoft's Windows.

Our paper 'The Fable of the Keys' (Liebowitz and Margolis, 1990) presents evidence on the typewriter keyboard story. In short, the received history is that the now-standard QWERTY keyboard arrangement is inefficient (some argue deliberately so) and that the Dvorak keyboard is known to be better. Our research shows that most of the claims for the superiority of the Dvorak keyboard can be traced to Dvorak's own writings. An often mentioned 'Navy Study', purporting to demonstrate the superiority of Dvorak, turns out to have been supervised by a Lieutenant Commander August Dvorak. A reading of the Navy study reveals that it was transparently rigged in favor of the Dvorak arrangement. In addition, a number of studies, using various methodologies, indicate that Dvorak offers little or no advantage over the QWERTY arrangement.

The allegation regarding the Beta and VHS competition is that the Beta format was superior, but that an early lead for VHS, strong producer alliances and better marketing led consumers to forsake their preferred alternative in order to be compatible with the majority of users. Simple versions of this history often ignore the fact that Beta had a two-year head start on VHS. Also overlooked is the fact that Sony, the creator of the Beta format, took great pains to try to forge a producer alliance, first offering its machine to the creators of VHS and then offering its machines to other Japanese and American producers, well before VHS had any significant market share. Beta's early adoption by Sanyo, Toshiba and Zenith runs counter to the claims that Sony was not interested in partners. Sony's failure to attract RCA to its coalition, however, gets to the true heart of the matter. Beta and VHS had almost identical performance, owing to common technological roots including the joint production of a previous generation of machines. Sony chose a small cassette for Beta, limiting the recording time, while Matsushita (the owner of JVC, the nominal creator of VHS) chose a larger cassette and a longer taping time. In negotiations, RCA told Sony that it preferred VHS since at that time Beta allowed recording time of only one hour, insufficient for movies or football games. Sony slowed down the tape, allowing the taping of two hour programs, albeit at lower quality. Matsushita in turn slowed down VHS to get four hours of taping time, and RCA entered an agreement to market the four-hour VHS machine. RCA's judgement that longer taping time was more important to consumers than smaller cassettes appears in retrospect to be correct. Everywhere that consumers had a choice they overwhelmingly chose VHS even though the price differential was negligible (RCA came in with a startlingly low $1000 price, but this was matched by Zenith's $996 price within the week). Picture quality seems not to have been the issue either. *Consumer Reports* product testing at the time indicated no clear advantage in picture quality for either format, finding VHS better in two tests, Beta better in one, and a tie in another (Klopfenstein, 1989, p. 28).

What this case actually demonstrates is not lock-in but rather the ability of markets to facilitate a switch from one path or standard to another. In spite of Beta's two-year head start, the market shifted very quickly to a format that offered an advantage to consumers. It is noteworthy that broadcasters eventually standardized on the Beta format. The main difference between the formats, other than the size of the cassette, is the way the cassette is threaded. The Beta method, although more complicated, offers some advantages in editing videotape and in special effects. This advantage is unimportant to most home users, but is important to broadcasters. Broadcasters and home users rarely exchange video tapes, so there is little benefit for compatibility between the two. It is interesting, therefore, that professional broadcast users standardized on Beta, which is advantageous to them, and home users adopted VHS, which, with its longer taping time, is preferable to them.

The third of these path dependence stories is computer operating systems. It is sometimes claimed that although Microsoft operating systems are inferior to the Macintosh operating system, Macintosh failed because consumers were so locked-in to DOS that they would not make the switch to the better system. This claim requires close examination along several dimensions. First, the superior operating system is not the one that is theoretically ideal, but the one that is most efficient given the cost of the hardware required to run it. That is, economic efficiency is what counts, not some form of engineering efficiency. When DOS was king, computer memory was expensive and processors were slow. The graphical interface of the Macintosh required far more computing power to update than the DOS interface, on the order of fifteen to one. To take advantage of graphical documents required much processing and storage capacity, making it more expensive to get reasonable performance from a Macintosh machine. As the price of memory fell and processors became faster, the DOS operating system took on the features of the Macintosh, until at the present time they (Windows95 and the Macintosh) are almost identical in functionality for the typical consumer. Often overlooked is the fact that the better operating system, the graphical operating system, did win, when it was justified by the cost. Again, it is worth noting that graphics professionals, for whom graphical processing was critical even at very high prices, moved to the Macintosh early on, when there was no good DOS alternative. That continues to be the market where the Macintosh has its greatest market share.

Van Vleck (1997) digs deeply into the claim, longstanding in the literature of economic history, that the British use of a small coal car (compared to the US and Germany) was an example of persistence of technological backwardness; a kind of path dependence. Van Vleck shows rather convincingly that the small coal car was an efficient response to differences in prevailing conditions in Great Britian.

Of particular relevance for law and economics is work by Bruce Kobayashi and Larry Ribstein on the adoption of uniform laws by states. For certain areas of the law, particularly where laws effect dealings with outsiders, standardization of statutes is efficient. Kobayashi and Ribstein (1996) studies the adoption of statutes that allow limited liability companies and find that while there are strong tendencies toward uniformity, the first form of a provision is not particularly to become the standard form. Again this is contrary to an expected influence from path dependence. In a related paper, Ribstein and Kobayashi (1996) do find evidence of an influence of efficiency in states' tendencies regarding uniformity of statutes. They show that uniformity is much more likely to be found in those areas of the law in which uniformity is particularly advantageous.

7. Path Dependence Outside of Markets

Our attention has been largely limited to the role of path dependence in market choices. Our observation is that where feasible improvements to an allocation can be identified, private actors will attempt to engage in exchanges that will allow them to profit from accomplishing these improvements. We do note, however, that many social choices do not take place in markets, and in fact may not even be recognized explicitly as choices.

The choice of religious and social institutions does not take place in an explicit market. The choice of government, for much of history, has not even been a choice for individual citizens. The institution of slavery was not a voluntary transaction. In these cases, the forces that would normally promote an efficient solution in the market do not necessarily come to the fore. A lack of ownership of alternative institutions is one problem, but a more important and fundamental problem is the absence of voluntary, feasible transactions. If the state or military controls the proceeds from productive activities, there may not be a feasible way to wealth-increasing improvements, since the beneficiaries can not write enforceable contracts to 'pay off' the despots who control the system.

Where there is no ownership of assets, or where coerced transactions are possible, the usual efficiency implications of market transactions can not be presumed. In such a world suboptimal solutions might have considerable permanence. For two differing analyses of path dependence for institutions, see North (1990) and Kiwit (1996). North's influential book, unfortunately, seems to accept at face value the claims of the path dependence literature that are based on false empirics.

These considerations have special importance with regard to path dependence and the law. For some aspects of the law, such as Antitrust, our finding that lock-ins are rare or nonexistent has fairly obvious implications. One of the concerns that has arisen in recent years, for example, is that high technology industries are particularly prone to path dependence because of network effects, and that therefore society might become ensnared in an inferior technology or standard. This argument has been made, both in the press and in arguments to the court, in connection with the many antitrust actions regarding Microsoft. Since these concerns can also be voiced for many technological standards, they might also made in connection with other antitrust cases, including the case that is currently being made against Intel. Our writing cautions that lock-in problems with choices of technologies or standards do not follow reliably, or even with much likelihood, from the simple presence of network effects.

The role of path dependence and lock-in is murkier in other areas of the law. With regard to statutory law, one might refer to legal institutions as a kind of market where suppliers of legal rules (legislators, judges) interact with demanders of these rules (constituents, plaintiffs). Yet even under this public-choice view of legal institutions, they are not the same as markets. The role of entrepreneur, of someone who can become rich by selling a better solution, does not have a complete analogy. Perhaps politicians do fill this role to some extent, but dollars and votes do not necessarily translate one to one. Nevertheless, the work of Kobayashi and Ribstein, cited above, shows that for several legal developments where path dependence might be expected to appear, it is not found.

Other writers, most prominently Richard Posner, have said much more regarding efficiency in the common law. Judges certainly could, where their decisions were not thoroughly circumscribed by precedent, seek out the global optima that are allegedly locked-out under theories of lock-in. But where legal efficiency is said to be the product of evolution to efficiency, the mechanisms for avoiding lock-in are less readily apparent. Indeed, litigators proposing novel legal theories may play the entrepreneurial role. Nevertheless, we are less sanguine that problems of path dependence are reliably avoided where law evolves from law and accordingly is less able to make the kinds of systematic jumps that allow markets to avoid lock-in.

Bibliography on Path Dependence (0770)

Arthur, W. Brian (1989), 'Competing Technologies, Increasing Returns, and Lock-In by Historical Events', **97** *Economic Journal*, 642-665.

Arthur, W. Brian (1990), 'Positive Feedbacks in the Economy', **262** *Scientific American*, 92-99.

Arthur, W. Brian (1994), *Increasing Returns and Path Dependence in the Economy*, Ann Arbor, Michigan, University of Michigan, Institute of Public Administration.

Berg, Sanford V. (1989), 'The Production of Compatibility: Technical Standards as Collective Goods', **42** *Kyklos*.

Besen, Stanley M. and Joseph Farrell (1994), 'Choosing How to Compete: Strategies and Tactics in Standardization', **8** *Journal of Economic Perspectives*.

Black, Bernard and Kraakman, Reinier H. (1996), 'A Self-Enforcing Model of Corporate Law', **109** *Harvard Law Review*, 1911-1979.

Blanchard, Olivier Jean and Summers, Lawrence H. (1987), 'Hysteresis in Unemployment', **31(2)** *European Economic Review*, 288-295.

Carlton, Dennis W. and Klamer, J. Mark (1983), 'The Need For Coordination among Firms, With Special Reference to Network Industries', **50** *University of Chicago Law Review*.

Cook, Philip J. and Frank, Robert H. (1996), *The Winner-Take-All Society : Why the Few at the Top Get So Much More Than the Rest of Us*, Penguin USA, reprint.

Chapman, Bruce (1994), 'The Rational and the Reasonable: Social Choice Theory and Adjudication', **61** *University of Chicago Law Review*, 41-122.

Chou, D. and Shy, O. (1990), 'Network Effects without Network Externalities', **8** *International Journal of Industrial Organization*, 259-270.

Church, J and Gandal, Neil (1992), 'Network Effects, Software Provision, and Standardization', **XL** *Journal of Industrial Economics*, 85-104.

Church, Jeffrey and Gandal, Neil (1993), 'Complementary Network Externalities and Technological Adoption', **11** *International Journal of Industrial Organization*, 239-260.

Cowan, Robin (1991), 'Tortoises and Hares: Choice among Technologies of Unknown Merit', **101** *Economic Journal*, 801-814.

Dam, Kenneth W. (1995), 'Some Economic Considerations in the Intellectual Property Protection of Software', **24** *Journal of Legal Studies*, 321 ff.

David, Paul A. (1985), 'Clio and the Economics of QWERTY', **75(5)** *American Economic Review*, 332-337.

David, Paul A. (1992), 'Heroes, Herds and Hysteresis in Technological History: Thomas Edison and the Battle of the Systems Revisited', **1** *Industrial and Corporate Change*, 129-180.

De Duve, Christian (1995), *Vital Dust: Life as a Cosmic Imperative*, New York, Basic Books.

Demsetz, H. (1973), 'Information and Efficiency: Another Viewpoint', **10** *Journal of Law and Economics*, 1-22.

Dixit, A. and Nalebuff, Barry (1991), 'Thinking Strategically', New York, Norton.

Economides, Nicholas (1989), 'Desirability of Compatibility in the Absence of Network Externalities', **79** *American Economic Review*, 1165-1181.

Farrell, Joseph and Saloner, Garth (1976), 'Installed Base and Compatibility: Innovation, Product Preannouncements, and Predation', **5** *American Economic Review*, 940-955.

Farrell, Joseph and Saloner, Garth (1985), 'Standardization, compatibility, and Innovation', **16(1)** *Rand Journal of Economics*, 70-83.

Franz, Wolfgang (1990), 'Hysteresis: An Overview', **2** *Empirical Economics*, 109-125.

Gould, Stephen J (1991), 'The Panda Thumb of Technology', in X (ed.), *Bully for Brontosaurus*, New York, Norton.

Hunt, Shelby D. and Morgan, Robert M. (1996), 'The Resource Advantage Theory of Competition: Dynamics, Path Dependencies, and Evolutionary Dimensions', **60** *Journal of Marketing*, 107-114.

Kahan, Marcel and Klausner, Michael (1996), 'Path Dependence in Corporate Contracting: Increasing Returns, Herd Behavior and Cognitive Biases', **74** *Washington University Law Quarterly*.

Kaplan, Steven N. and Ramseyer, J. Mark (1996), *Those Japanese Firms, with their Disdain for Shareholders: Another Fable for the Academy*, Washington University Law Quarterly.

Katz, Michael L. and Shapiro, C. (1986), 'Technology Adoption in the Presence of Network Externalities', *Journal of Political Economy*, 822-841.

Katzner, Donald (1993), 'Some Notes on the Role of History and the Definition of Hysteresis and Related Concepts in Economic Analysis', **15(3)** *Journal of Post Keynesian Economics*, 323-345.

Kiwit, Daniel (1996), 'Path-Dependence in Technological and Institutional Change - Some Criticisms and Suggestions', **7** *Journal des Economistes et des Etudes Humaines*, 69-93.

Klopfenstein, B.C. (1989), 'The Diffusion of the VCR in the United States', in Levy, M.R. (ed.), *The VCR Age*, California, Newsbury Park, Sage Publications.

Kobayashi, Bruce H. and Ribstein, Larry E. (1996), 'Evolutions of Spontaneous Uniformity: Evidence from the Evolution of the Limited Liability Company', **34** *Economic Inquiry*, 464-483.

Krugman, Paul R. (1994), *Peddling Prosperity*, New York, Norton.

Lardner, J. (1987), *Fast Forward*, New York, Norton.

Levinson, R.J. and Coleman, Mary T. (1992), *Economic Analysis of Compatibility Standards: How Useful is it,*, FTC working paper 1992.

Liebowitz, S.J. and Margolis, Stephen E. (1990), 'The Fable of the Keys', **22** *Journal of Law and Economics*, 1-26.

Liebowitz, S.J. and Margolis, Stephen E. (1994a), 'Network Externality: An Uncommon Tragedy', **8** *Journal of Economic Perspectives*, 133-150.

Liebowitz, S.J. and Margolis, Stephen E. (1994b), 'Are Network Externalities a New Source of Market Failure?', **16** *Research in Labor Economics*.

Liebowitz, S.J. and Margolis, Stephen E. (1995), 'Path Dependence, Lock-in and History', **11** *Journal of Law, Economics, and Organization*, 205-226.

Lopatka, John and Page, William H. (1995), 'Microsoft, Monopolization, and Network Externalities: Some Uses and Abuses of Economic Theory in Antitrust Decision Making', **Summer 1995** *The Antitrust Bulletin*, 317-369.

Mokyr, Joel (1991), 'Evolutionary Biology, Technological Change and Economic History', **43** *Bulletin of Economic Research*, 127-147.

Nelson, Richard R. and Winter, Sidney G. (1982), *An Evolutionary Theory of Economic Change*, Cambridge, MA, Belknap of Harvard University Press.

North, Douglass C. (1990), *Institutions, Institutional Change and Economic Performance*, Cambridge, Cambridge University Press.

Ribstein, Larry E. (1995), 'Statutory Forms for Closely Held Firms: Theories and Evidence from LLCs', **73** *Washington University Law Quarterly*, 369 ff.

Ribstein, Larry E. (1995), 'Linking Statutory Forms', **58** *Journal of Law and Contemporary Problems*, 58 ff.

Ribstein, Larry E. and Kobayashi, Bruce H. (1995), 'Uniform Laws, Model Laws and Limited Liability Companies', **66** *University of Colorado Law Review*, 947-999.

Ribstein, Larry E. and Kobayashi, Bruce H. (1996), 'An Economic Analysis of Uniform State Laws', **34** *Journal of Legal Studies*, 131-199.

Roe, Mark J. (1996), 'Chaos and Evolution in Law and Economics', **109** *Harvard Law Review*, 641-668.

Schelling, Thomas C. (1978), *Micromotives and Macro Behavior*, New York, Norton.

Van Vleck, Va Nee L. (1997), 'Delivering Coal By Road and Rail: The Efficiency of the "Silly Little Bobtailed" Coal Wagon', **57** *Journal of Economic History*, 139-160.

Vita, Michael G. and Wellford, Charissa P. (1994), 'Regulating the Electromagnetic Environment: Alternative Approaches to Policy', in Fleming, James R. and Gemery, Henry A. (eds), *Science, Technology, and the Environment.*

Williamson, Oliver E. (1993a), 'Contested Exchange Versus the Governance of Contractual Relations', *Journal of Economic Perspectives*, 103-108.

Williamson, Oliver E. (1993b), 'Transaction Cost Economics and Organization Theory', **2** *Industrial and Corporate Change*, 107-156.

Williamson, Oliver E. (1994), *The Politics and Economics of Redistribution and Inefficiency*, **17** *Greek Economic Review*, December 1995, pp. 115-136.

0780
NON-LEGAL SANCTIONS

Stephan Panther
Institute of Economics, AWM, Universität Hamburg

Abstract

The study of non-legal sanctions is a comparatively new area in law and economics, which is developing fast. Little universally agreed upon stock of knowledge exists and relevant contributions are spread in diverse fields. Therefore, the main aim of this review is to provide a systematic and integrated view of the topic. It is placed firmly in a New Institutionalist framework and a clear classificatory structure is developed. Non-legal sanctions are seen to flow from informal social norms, which are systematized using a game theoretic perspective. From this departure, the host of applications to diverse substantive areas of law can be presented clearly. Outstanding contributions are highlighted.
JEL classification: A12, A13, C70, K00
Keywords: Non-Legal Sanctions, Social Norms, Incomplete Contracts, Reputation, Relationship-Specific Assets, Informal Insurance

A. Introduction

1. The Limits of Legal Rules

Law and economics has focused on the analysis of the (efficiency) effects of formal legal rules, which are enforced by a specialized central agency, 'the state', employing legal sanctions. However, even in fully developed market economies with a high degree of division of labor, formal legal rules do not comprise the total picture. They would do so only if it were possible to *specify* and *enforce* a comprehensive set of property rights perfectly, and, building on this, perfectly specify and enforce contracts. In such a world, actors would only interact through voluntary contracts, not influencing each other in any other way. It is a perfectly secure world. Even if it is not characterized by perfect and complete information for every actor, actors' expectations concerning each others' behavior are sure to be fulfilled since an omniscient, omnipotent and benevolent government guarantees perfect enforcement. This world, of course, is utopian.

The world we live in knows only incompletely specified and enforced property rights and contracts. The arm of the law does not reach everywhere. Crimes remain unsolved, courts err and using them is costly, and hence some cases are simply never filed. Contracts do not contain provisions for all possible contingencies that might arise. Rulers, politicians and government officials are self-interested and hard to control and it actually might be a blessing that they are not omniscient and omnipotent. In our world, formal legal rules and legal sanctions no longer determine behavior with certainty. Other factors co-determine actions. Especially non-legal rules (social norms) and non-legal sanctions play prominent roles.

Before turning our attention to these (see also the comments on Lindenberg, 1990, and Schlicht, 1997, in Section 6 below), it should be noted that the other important factors shaping action are cognitive rules and schemata. After all, it is the subjective perception of rules and sanctions which matters for individual behavior, a point stressed by Opp (1985). Denzau and North (1994) discuss this issue in a neo-institutionalist framework. Lessig (1996) and Sunstein (1996) raise some cognitive issues in relation to law, the latter especially suggesting that the mere declaration of a rule as a law may influence the prevailing social norms.

2. A Framework for Classification

Since the term sanction is somewhat ambiguous, a note of clarification is necessary right at the start. Sociologists usually use it to describe both punishments and rewards, while legal scholars frequently only consider punishments (but see Ellikson, 1991, pp. 124-126). Fortunately, little in the following depends on this distinction in a fundamental way. I will generally follow the legal usage here, explicitly noting deviations.

Any system of sanctions faces the same issues. At a first level these are: who decides about the sanction, how, And who administers the sanction? All of these may be examined in greater detail. Ellikson (1991) (see also Ellikson, 1987), probably *the* seminal contribution on non-legal rules and enforcement, distinguishes five types of rules applicable to sanctioning systems (pp. 132-136). 'Constitutive rules' answer the first of the 'who' questions above, relating especially to the structural aspects of the question (for example, which court is in charge?). 'Controller-selection' rules give an answer to the second 'who' question in a systematic fashion (for example, first vs. second party control, see below). 'Procedural', 'remedial' and 'substantive' rules relate to the 'how' question above. 'Procedural rules' refer to the way information has to be obtained, weighted, interpreted, and so on by those who impose sanctions. 'Substantive rules' define the kind of behavior to be sanctioned, 'remedial rules' regulate the type and severity of the sanction. Together the latter two describe the criteria used in imposing sanctions.

I see the distinction between non-legal and legal sanctions as drawing on the last two types of rules only; a legal sanction is administered in accordance with criteria laid down in a legal rule. Of course, the law frequently delegates the decision over the precise content of the required behavior to other, possibly private, actors. Contract law is centered on this idea. It nevertheless remains clear when conduct is law abiding and when not. In modern western societies the law also regularly contains binding constitutive, procedural and controller selection rules, the existence of which is, however, not taken as part of the definition of a legal sanction here.

Social norms are to non-legal sanctions what laws are to legal sanctions. Coleman (1990), Elster (1989a) and Hechter (1987) are monographs containing comprehensive treatments of social norms from a methodological individualistic perspective. Coleman is the prime reference. Elster's treatment, while full of insight, is hampered by his non-consequentialist definition of norms. Opp (1985) is a systematic account in the form of an article, Opp (1979) provides a systematic comparison of sociological and economic accounts of norms as far as available at the date of publication.

All of the aspects of a sanctioning system just discussed may be regulated by a system of social norms. The main debate has, however, been on the issue of whether a mere substantial rule, a prescription or prohibition of an action, constitutes a social norm, or whether an attached remedial rule, the specification of a sanction in case of deviation, has to be present, too. The latter view is taken here, which is argued, for example, in Weise (1996). It is also implied by Coleman (1990, pp. 241-249), while Elster (1989a, pp. 98-100) favors the former. See Crawford and Ostrom (1995) for a comprehensive discussion.

Given the primary focus of this review on non-legal sanctions, we will classify social norms by the way they are enforced. While the following is *one* common classification, it is by no means universally accepted. It follows largely Ellikson (1991, pp. 123-136) and Kiwit and Voigt (1995). (See also James Coleman, 1990, pp. 241-249 for a somewhat different view.)

External norms are enforced through sanctions by non-specialized members of a society. Ellikson (1991) further distinguishes situations where sanctions are administered by those against whom a norm has been transgressed (*second party control*) from those where originally nonaffected parties are involved in sanctioning (*third party control*). Decisions about and enforcement of the sanction may lie with the same actor or may be separated. The non-specialized nature of enforcement does not imply anything about the severity of the sanction, which may range from expression of disapproval to ostracism to physical violence.

Internal norms have been internalized to such a degree that their transgression, while benefiting narrow self-interest, causes discomfort, psychic costs. In contrast to external norms, issues of policing do not arise here. The very actor who deliberates a deviation from a rule also sanctions himself (*first party control*). Cooter (1996) (Cooter, 1994, is an earlier version) contains a systematic treatment as a foundation for his public policy recommendations (see Section 13).

Borderline cases, where the term 'social norm' for the basis of a sanctioning system is somewhat stretched, are those where the relevant rules are codified and sanctions are decided about and possibly even enforced in an organized fashion by specially designed agents ('Third party control by organizations' in the terminology of Ellikson, 1991, 'formal private rules' for Kiwit and Voigt, 1995). As long as the rules are not given legal status, this is still a case of non-legal sanctions.

Recently, the term 'convention' (dating back as least as far as Weber, 1921[1978]) has reappeared in economic and New Institutionalist theory as a rival to the term 'social norm', as for example, in Sugden (1986) and Young (1996). The latter define 'convention' in game theoretic terms as a particular equilibrium in games with multiple equilibria. If external norms are modeled as games (see Sections 4 and 5), they constitute 'conventions' in this sense too. By way of contrast, I suggest limiting the use of the term 'convention' to norms which are self-enforcing in a narrow sense: self-enforcing even in the absence of any sanctioning action. This implies that deviating from equilibrium strategies is not profitable even if everybody else merely continues the behavior prescribed on the equilibrium path in the absence of deviation. The typical example is an equilibrium in a coordination game, driving on the prescribed side of the road being the notorious real world case. By this very definition, 'conventions' lie outside the scope of this paper.

3. Basic Relationships between Legal and Non-Legal Sanctions

A non-legal sanction may be complementary to a legal sanction, both requiring the same action in a certain situation. In this case, non-legal sanctions add to the effect of legal sanctions. Obviously it is also possible for legal and non-legal norms/sanctions to work in opposite directions, making them conflicting, just as a neutral case may arise.

When the non-legal and legal norms conflict, the question of the dynamic development of the two arises. No generally accepted theory exists. Taxonomically, one may distinguish three cases. First, social norms may regularly adapt to legal rules. In this vein, in an article also interesting because of its substantial focus (see Section 12), Ramseyer (1987) seems to suggest that norms follow legal incentives, making them effectively an appendix to formal institutions. The reverse position, social norms regularly forcing legal rules to adapt, is rarely taken in New Institutionalist thinking. The third position, the two influencing each other with the one or the other being dominant from time to time, seems to dominate. North (1990) offers a comprehensive treatment in a general New Institutionalist framework. He suggests the possibility of path-dependency in the institutional development caused by the persistence of non-legal rules. Kiwit and Voigt (1995) discuss this critically. Cooter (1996) discusses the development of internal norms using arguments from evolutionary game theory, also emphasizing the reciprocal interaction of external and internal norms. He sees the existence of network externalities in norm-adherence as a possible cause for path-dependency in their development. Adams (1996) adds the dependency of a norm on the context of other existing norms as another important reason for path-dependency: informal norms come in hierarchically connected systems, meta-norms helping to interpret more specific ones. All in all, social norms are likely to be interlinked with legal rules and with each other, making change a slow, gradual process occasionally interrupted by big jumps.

A special and particularly strong case of conflict occurs when non-legal sanctions involve actions prohibited by law, that is, the infringement of legal rights. This subcategory can be referred to as *extra-legal sanctions*. They are dominant in organized crime, and I refer the reader to Chapter 8400 (Organized Crime and Illegal Markets) in this encyclopedia. I will speak of non-legal sanctions, whenever the above conflict is not present. It is in this narrow definition that we will use the term from now on.

The last distinction draws our attention to an important final point. If non-legal sanctions do not violate legal rights, how are they possible? For a sanction to exist, the sanctioner needs to be able to act in a way that diminishes the utility of the wrongdoer. Thus, non-legal sanctions are only possible in a world where not all 'assets' of an actor consist of legally protected rights. In the terminology of Charny (1990, p. 392), the sanctioned party of the interaction has posted a 'bond' which can be confiscated by the sanctioning party. Böhm-Bawerk (1881), in an early treatment of related issues, termed these non-legal assets 'Verhältnisse' ('relationships'). In a world where property rights are perfectly specified and enforced, no such non-legal 'assets', and hence no non-legal sanctions, would be available.

We have now come full circle and will in the following Sections 4 to 6 turn to a survey of the theoretical literature on non-legal sanctions which tries to clarify the mechanisms involved in non-legal sanctioning systems. The following sections then survey the applications in several substantive fields.

B. Theory

4. External Norms: Second Party Control

If only the parties involved in an exchange are able to impose non-legal sanctions on each other, the non-legal assets used in the process may be termed *relation-specific prospective advantages* (Charny, 1990, p. 392). The sanctioning action usually consists in the termination of the exchange, at least for long enough periods to deter deviations in the first place. Eger (1995, Chapter 4) contains a systematic treatment of second party control, as do E. Posner (1995) (see also Section 13), Rubin (1993) and Kronman (1985) (discussed also in Section 11).

The most straightforward way to conceptualize relation-specific prospective advantages can be traced back to Williamson (1983) (but see the earlier work by Schelling, 1960, p. 135; see also Williamson 1985, Chapters 7 and 8). The central idea is the posting of 'hostages'. The exchange partner A, prone to undertake an opportunistic breach of agreement, takes an action which gives the trading partner B control over an asset which is valuable to A (but not necessarily to B). A prime example is relation-specific investment, which pays considerably less outside the present relation. By leaving the relationship after being cheated, a partner can thus sanction the cheater. The emphasis here lies in the direct, possibly deliberate, creation of relation-specific advantages by the parties to the exchange themselves.

The dominant conceptualization of a sanctioning system involving relation-specific prospective advantages is the idea of a repeated game. Taylor (1976) and Ullmann-Margalit (1977) are early exemplary versions which are often cited outside economics and game theory. The theory covers both bilateral and multilateral games. It relies on the game never definitely ending in any particular period. A deviator is punished by all others in the game, who are all second parties, since they are all hurt by his deviation. Here the relation-specific advantage consists in the value of repeating the exchange/cooperation with the established partner in comparison with the value of the next best alternative, given by the non-cooperation payoff. Besides the payoff difference between cooperation and outside-option, the time horizon determines the severity of the sanction possible. The latter is caught in the discount factor which determines the weight of future payoffs. In the context of repeated games it may also be interpreted as reflecting the exogenous chance that an actor 'dies', that is, leaves the game which leads to the separation of the partners.

A notorious problem with the idea of cooperation being sustained by repetition of exchange is the multiplicity of equilibria in repeated games, which in fact regularly have an infinite number of equilibria. No universally accepted theory of choosing among them exists, even though the idea that people eventually manage to coordinate on pareto optimal ones (that is, cooperative ones in this context) has intuitive appeal. We sidestep this issue and continue the discussion focusing on the cooperative equilibria made possible in the game structures under review.

Note that important additional questions arise in the multilateral case: How is information about deviations disseminated? Can it be trusted to be correct? How can actors be motivated to administer a sanction? The information issues are usually 'dealt with' by choosing appropriate assumptions, most frequently by the public observability of deviations. Before elaborating on the motivation question it should be noted that its relevance is not absolutely obvious. After all, in the situations treated in this section, everybody is a second party, that is, directly affected by a deviation. The main issue, however, is whether an action other than delivering the required sanction exists which is more advantageous to the actor in question. This will not be the case when the actions required for sanctioning constitute an equilibrium in the stage game (the one-period game which is repeated over time). Otherwise an actor is tempted to deviate from the punishment path. A host of formal contributions have dealt with this problem, Abreu (1988) being a central one. The idea of the formal solution is to punish the deviator from a punishment path (forgiving the original deviator) and anybody deviating from that punishment path, and so on.

Models of repeated interaction become more interesting if the factors determining the severity of the sanction, that is, determining the relative gain from cooperation, are explained endogenously. Klein and Leffler (1981) and Telser (1980) are early contributions in this vein. They center on the idea that raising the price paid to the supplier in an exchange, and thus ceteris paribus raising his profit, will make the exchange opportunity more valuable to him. If the supplier can manipulate the quality of the good and the buyer can detect this only ex post and if a high price is paid only if customers expect high quality, increased profit from the sales of high quality constitutes a relation-specific advantage. The underlying basic idea is fairly general and has been applied widely especially in the theory of efficiency wages. Within that body of theory the contributions by Akerlof (1982) and Shapiro and Stiglitz (1984) contain explicit formulations of the kind of non-legal sanction mechanism considered here.

Recently a closely related mechanism has been studied by Kranton (1996a) and Ghosh and Ray (1996) in the context of random matching games. A bilateral cooperation game (a kind of prisoners' dilemma in continuous strategies) is played between two actors, who can decide to continue the cooperation next period or leave the relationship. If they do leave, they are randomly matched with another unmatched player. What stops players from always trying to cheat each other and quit the relationship immediately afterwards? There exists an equilibrium where two newly matched players do not cooperate fully right from the start, but rather build up cooperation slowly. Leaving an exchange partner in such a situation is costly since a renewed buildup of cooperation is necessary. In this way, an existing relationship again offers relation-specific advantages.

Kranton (1996b) provides a different endogenous explanation of the possible size of non-legal sanctions in a relationship conceptualized as a repeated game. She considers a model where relational exchange and anonymous search markets are mutually exclusive alternatives for any particular actor. If actors cheat in an ongoing relationship they have to withdraw into the market forever. Payoffs in the search markets determine the severity of this sanction. The proportion of actors engaged in relational exchange also feeds back to the market, however, due to search externalities (thick market externality: more people on the market make search easier). The reciprocal influence of the two institutions may lead to either of them prevailing even if the other one is efficient. A related model is Kultti (1995). Pairwise lifelong credit contracts between agents are enforced by the threat of trading on a barter market. Agents come in two types and asymmetries in production possibilities and numbers of actors per type determine the result.

The related but distinct idea of the *reputation* of an actor has been introduced into the formal game-theoretic literature by Kreps et al. (1982). They consider a repeated prisoners' dilemma with a definite end known in advance. If for all agents non-cooperation were the equilibrium in a one shot game ('non-cooperative actors'), cooperation would not be possible. Non-cooperation would always result in the last period, since no sanction for deviation from the norm would be available in the future. This being so, non-cooperation would result in the second to last period, and hence in the third to last period, and so on. In the model of Kreps et al. (1982), cooperation is nevertheless sustainable, since actors come in two types, one of which will cooperate as long as the exchange partner has done so up to now, even in the last period ('cooperative actors'). Actors do not know each other's type. Non-cooperative actors find it worthwhile to camouflage themselves as cooperative actors almost up to the end of the game. If non-cooperative actors deviate, their exchange partner learns their true type immediately. In that sense they lose their reputation, which constitutes the relation-specific prospective advantage in this model.

However, this clearly does not transport all that there is to the common sense notion of reputation. The latter is centered on the idea of *public* information about an actor: the past behavior of an actor towards exchange partners becomes known to other actors who, when they deliberate a transaction, will take this information into account (see also Charny, 1990, for this definition of the concept). This usually includes the above notion of reputation as an estimate of the characteristics of an actor, but does not logically have to. A reputation for cheating simply means that an actor is publicly known to have cheated before (a qualified number of times?), whether this is due to special personal traits or not. When I want to clearly distinguish between the two notions of reputation, I will use the term *g-reputation* if I want to refer to the game theoretic usage of the term, and *cs-reputation* for the common sense notion. This common sense notion of reputation leads us to the next section.

5. External Norms: Third Party Control

When third parties administer sanctions, the information and motivation issues already relevant for multilateral second party control gain considerably in importance. In particular the motivation problem becomes more pointed: why should an actor sanction another, usually at least foregoing cooperation benefits in doing so, when the other has not deviated against him? The theoretical answers to these issues are as yet more exploratory than comprehensive.

Consider the contribution of Klein and Leffler (1981) mentioned in Section 4. In its simplest version, all demanders are identical in all respects and the behavior of the supplier is identical towards them. If the supplier cheats, he cheats all demanders and only second-party sanctions occur as a consequence. Nevertheless, it can and has been interpreted as a model of cs-reputation in the sense just introduced.

Suppose quality were stochastic (for example, reliability) and consequently not every buyer could observe quality in the period after purchase. Assume that the information transmission problem is solved. Upon receiving the information that quality is poor, a reputational equilibrium of the following kind is self-enforcing, needing no threats to would-be deviators from the punishment path: every demander expects poor quality and is only willing to pay the correspondingly lower price, and the supplier, knowing this, will actually provide poor quality at the lower cost. Since punishment strategies constitute an equilibrium, there is no motivation problem for sanctions to be administered.

Bendor and Mookherjee (1990) also assume that the information problem is solved. They model a multitude of actors engaged in simultaneous repeated bilateral exchanges. The motivation problem is dealt with by assuming a prisoners' dilemma structure on payoffs and calling for the equilibrium of the single shot stage game (the non-cooperative action) to be played as a punishment. Two of their results are worth mentioning: referring to the interpretation of discount factors as reflecting separation probabilities, they state that non-legal sanctions by second parties are sufficient in very stable societies, third-party sanctions are effective at intermediate levels of stability, and in a society with very unstable relationship only legal enforcement can sustain cooperation. Furthermore, for third-party control to be effective, either the payoffs from exchanges with different actors have to influence each other or they have to differ. If payoffs from exchanges are separable and symmetric, third-party enforcement is ineffective.

Kandori (1992) has tackled the information problem by trying to find minimal requirements for third-party sanctions to be effective. He looks at this question in a random matching game with bilateral exchange: every period, actors are reshuffled into new pairs. Kandori basically confirms the intuition about the role cs-reputation may play in such a situation: he finds conditions under which a 'label', determined by the past actions of an actor and known to the player he is matched with at the start of their trading period, is sufficient for cooperation to be sustained. The motivation problem reappears, since Kandori considers general payoff structures. Hirshleifer and Rasmusen (1989) discuss the somewhat related issue of ostracism.

Kandori (1992) and especially Ellison (1994) have analyzed another kind of equilibrium, which does not require any information transmission. Whenever a player has been cheated, he will cheat any other player in the game. In a contagious process, cooperation will eventually break down. This becomes interesting if one assumes a public randomization device (a public 'signal', for example, a campaign for 'moral renewal'). Using this idea, Ellison shows that such a contagious process can be of finite length. This is shown for prisoners' dilemma games and random matching of pairs. In addition, the result does not require 'too patient' players and equilibrium can even be stable in situations where deviations may occur by mistake. We may then find periods of widespread deviation alternating with periods of cooperation in a population.

6. Internal Norms

Internal norms provide first party sanctions. The actor deliberating a deviation from a rule foresees at the same time an internal non-legal sanction in the form of reduced utility. The potential importance of internal norms is fairly obvious. Nevertheless, they have been somewhat disreputable in mainstream economic theory, since their use amounts to explanation via preferences. Economists have been very skeptical about any direct way of obtaining data about preferences and in the absence of data, postulating a 'preference for something' can explain virtually any behavior. However, as survey techniques have become more and more sophisticated in other social sciences and experiments have gained general approval in economics, evidence on preferences can be obtained and tested far more reliably. This has put internal norms back on the research agenda of methodological individualistic theoreticians.

Despite their temporary disrepute, internal norms have very reputable ancestors. No one less than the 'founding father' of modern economics, Adam Smith, has been counted among those who have developed a full blown theory of internal norms. Elsner (1989) traces Smith's parsimonious theory which builds on the human faculty of being able to put oneself into another person's shoes and on the human desire for approbation from those around him. Along the same lines, McAdams (1995) introduces a theory of status closely connected to internal norms. He argues that the esteem of others as an end in itself is an important motivating force of actors, working both in groups which are close knit and in groups which only share a common observable trait.

Internal norms are closely tied to emotions, the relevant non-legal sanctions being regret, remorse, shame, guilt, embarrassment and the like (see, for example, Frank 1987, 1988; Huang and Wu, 1994; and Elster, 1996). Their role is straightforward if emotions are conceived as a direct sanction for breach of a substantive rule in the sense of Ellikson (1991). Their role, however, may also be important in enforcing second- and third-party non-legal sanctions, if an actor feels guilty, and so on if he does not sanction a deviator. In this context feelings of hatred, vengeance and anger also are important, a subject especially studied by Frank (1988).

Internal norms are also connected to cognitive issues. A comprehensive modern methodologically individualistic approach of human action - recognizing Smithian antecedents - is formulated by Lindenberg (1990). He stresses the role of socially learned 'framing effects': the preferences and the action space available to an actor depend on the way a situation is perceived, 'framed'. This may, for example, explain why opportunities for opportunistic behavior are used differentially in two situations even though 'objective' incentives are the same. Framing effects thus emphasize the conditionality of internal norms (see Section 11 for an application). Even closer to modern social psychology is Schlicht (1997) (Schlicht, 1993 is an earlier condensed version), which also goes well beyond a theory of internal norms, giving an explanation of various forms of rule-guided behavior broadly compatible with the theory of Lindenberg. Based on a fundamental cognitive propensity to perceive the world as governed by regularities, human actors are equipped with a preference for rule-guided behavior, deviation causing discomfort (cognitive dissonance), which requires corrective action. This may serve as a foundation for 'moralistic agression', the increased likelihood and severity of defense, if a subjectively established moral right has been infringed upon.

Another line of research has focused on the genesis of internal norms. Here evolutionary approaches dominate. Landes and Posner (1978) draw on sociobiological reasoning, while Witt (1986) provides an account combining results from the psychology of learning with elements of evolutionary game theory. The latter is also the base of the recent endeavor of Güth and Kliemt (1994).

C. Applications

7. Family

Comprehensive treatments of the role of non-legal sanctions in stabilizing the family as an institution are Ben-Porath (1980) and Pollak (1985). They integrate both external and internal norms in their analysis, Pollak emphasizing the insuring role of families. Both discuss the pros and cons of the organization of economic activities in families, but Ben-Porath discusses the role of other informal social relationships, especially friendship, too.

Becker, Landes and Michael (1977) consider the idea of relation-specific investments and the costs of finding a new partner in the context of marriage and its dissolution. Note that this application predates the work of Williamson on relation-specific investments and could be regarded as the first application of these ideas. Weitzman (1981a, 1981b), without explicit reference to Becker et al., contain nevertheless the same argument as an important building block of her comprehensive discussion of the social and economic implications of the marriage contract.

Several papers center around the idea of bequests and their manipulation by parents as a non-legal sanction against children. The 'Rotten Kid Theorem' (Becker, 1974, 1981, Chapter 8) shows under which conditions altruistic parents can assure family wealth maximizing behavior by selfish children. Becker and Murphy (1988) analyze public policies on education, old age security, divorce, marriage age, and so on as attempts to correct for defects in the sanctioning mechanism via bequests. Bernheim, Shleifer and Summers (1985) provide a general discussion of non-altruistically motivated parents leaving bequests. Pauly (1990), Zweifel and Strüwe (1994) and Richter (1995) include discussions of the demand for long-term-care insurance if parents desire to manipulate the behavior of children via bequests. Parents may decide rationally not to buy such insurance in order to leave intact the incentives of children to care for them in their old age.

8. Informal Insurance beyond the Family

As already noted, while the family is an important informal insurance institution it is by no means the only one. Other close-knit relationships also provide the basis for such arrangements. In particular, informal insurance in developing economies has attracted considerable attention in recent years. The articles are written in a fairly analytical style without losing sight of the underlying institutional setup. Most of them explicitly discuss non-legal sanctions. Fafchamps (1992), taking up many of the issues raised by Posner (1980), discusses the institutions of rural areas of developing countries with reference to the formal game-theoretic literature of repeated games emphasizing problems of asymmetric information. The article is nevertheless written in a very accessible style and remains largely informal.

Extending the partly empirical, partly theoretical study by Kimball (1988), Coate and Ravallion (1993) discuss informal insurance as a problem of second party sanctions in a repeated game framework. They discuss the maximum amount of risk-sharing possible in such an arrangement and compare with first best risk-sharing. Both Udry (1994) and Besley and Coate (1995) extend the analysis in the direction of community credit. Udry emphasizes the role played by sanctions imposed by village or family elders, serving a function very much like the formal arbitration procedures in Bernstein (1992) (see Section 11). Empirical results are given from a field study in Nigeria. Besley and Coate emphasize the role of third party sanctions in enforcing repayment in group lending. Again comparisons are made with first best arrangements. Finally Arnott and Stiglitz (1991) began the task of analyzing formal and informal institutions that exist side by side (see also Kranton, 1996b, discussed on p.1171) in the case of insurance arrangements. Their noteworthy result sees informal institutions surviving even if their existence is inefficient.

9. Pre-Legal Societies

Several contributions purport to study the entire system of rules governing a pre-legal society. Posner (1980) is an early and in many ways seminal contribution. He argues that many features of 'primitive societies' can be understood as the consequence of two factors: first, high uncertainty leading to a great need for insurance; and second, the absence of formal insurance due to high information and other transaction costs. The article derives an exceptionally rich picture from this basic argument, discussing a host of institutions and comparing them with modern legal rules. The argument reappears in Posner (1981) Chapters 6 and 7 and is applied to Homeric Greece in Chapter 5. The latter attempt is criticized in Versteeg (1989). Commenting on a historical case study on a New Guinean tribe, Benson (1988) emphasizes the ability of pre-legal societies to marshal change. Friedman (1979) provides a lively account of historical institutions in early medieval Iceland. Pointing out the conditions leading to their gradual decomposition, he also takes a less sanguine view than Benson on the potential of such a system today. Iannaccone (1992) may be useful in understanding the way religious communities close their ranks. Finally, Miller (1993) points out the role that sacred scriptures may play in regulating rituals.

10. Property

Several contributions inquire into the policing and sanctioning of property rights by informal sanctions. Here the well-known study by Ellikson (1991), already heavily referred to in Section 2, provides a prime example. The case study which forms the major part of this monograph studies the norms on cattle trespass in a small, close-knit community, enforced by first-, second- and third-party sanctions. Legal provisions concerning trespass have even been overruled by informal rules. The use of the legal system for regulating motorway accidents involving cattle shows that the legal system is relied upon more frequently if the social distance between the parties of a conflict becomes larger, if the stakes increase, or if costs can be shifted to third parties. Ellikson (1986) and Ellikson (1989) are separate publications based on this material. Also in the field of tort law, Ramseyer (1996) describes the working of the strict liability regime privately operated by some firms in Japan prior to 1995.

Ostrom (1990), a modern classic by any standard, deals with the non-legal, either semi-formal or informal enforcement of property rights in common pool situations. Her account is full of empirical material in field studies from different parts of the world, both successes and failures from the point of view of efficiency. As conditions for success, she identifies among other elements (see pp. 88-104) the involvement of appropriators in monitoring as well as graded sanctions, conditional on the severity and frequency of deviation from the rule. These are mentioned here because they are connected with two noteworthy effects not described so far. Monitoring has a direct private benefit to those involved: they gain information on the state of compliance in the system, which allows them to adopt a strategy of compliance conditional on the state of compliance in the system. In the same vein, sanctioning provides the information to the violator that the sanctioning system is well-functioning. This work has been extended through experimental research published in Ostrom, Gardner and Walker (1992, 1994).

Further work on aspects of non-legal enforcement of property rights are Anderson and Hill (1975), an early analysis of issues related to Ellikson (1991), as well as Benson (1986, 1989b). Finally, Anderson and Swimmer (1997) deliver an empirical analysis of the transaction cost determinants of the property rights regimes of about 40 North American Indian nations.

11. Contract

Both Charny (1990) and Rubin (1993) are comprehensive treatments of the issue of non-legal sanctions in relation to contracts (see also Kronman, 1985 for a somewhat earlier and more limited account). Both are written in an informal style, the latter being more of a systematization of the contributions up to the time of publication while the former offers more an original synthesis. Charny identifies three 'systems' of non-legal sanctions: third party decision making with reputational enforcement (external norms with formal decision making processes and third-party sanctions); reputational monitoring by market participants (external norms and third-party sanctions); and unilateral decision making (second-party sanctions). Internal norms play a minor but non-negligible role.

The role of formal decision making in non-legal sanctioning is explored in detail in Bernstein (1992) in a case study of the New York diamond trade. Her rich material includes a view on the development of non-legal enforcement embedded in an ethnic group into a more formal structure. The article by Matsumura and Ryser (1995) presents a case study and a model for the Japanese institution of public announcement of default on notes and the sanctioning system built around it. Their contribution is especially noteworthy for analytic consideration of incentive issues concerning the revelation of information. The role of clearing houses, which is central in this system, is also the topic of the historical study by Gorton and Mullineaux (1987) on nineteenth-century commercial banks. Taking a property rights perspective, Pirrong (1995) studies the limits of formal private enforcement in the light of a historical case study on the Chicago Board of Trade. He concludes that unequal distribution of gains may lead to the non-development of efficiency-enhancing institutions. Greif, Milgrom and Weingast (1994) and Milgrom, North and Weingast (1990) are other highly interesting historical case studies on formal medieval institutions backing up non-legal sanctioning mechanisms. The mix of authors makes for good history and good theory. The latter article concentrates on the growth of the 'Law Merchant', the autonomous, international merchant law system which is also studied in Benson (1989a). Benson argues in favor of the efficiency-promoting role of spontaneously evolved systems of rules. The analysis of Schwartz and Scott (1995) provides an antidote to the efficiency view on formal private rulemaking. In an analysis of the 'American Law Institute' and the 'National Conference of Commissioners on Uniform State Laws', two US institutions, they discover evidence of the capture of these institutions by interest groups.

The purely informal norm backed by third-party sanctions has also been dealt with in the area of contracts. Such reputational mechanisms requiring information transmission are most effective in closely knit (business) communities. The seminal paper in this area is Macaulay (1963), which goes well beyond analyzing bilateral relationships, for which it is usually credited. A very early economic study is Cheung (1973), discussing the pricing of the pollination services of bees, explicitly noting the relevance of social norms (p. 30). Allen and Lueck (1992) report on a modern field study concentrating on agricultural contracts. Ramseyer (1991), in an analysis of the Japanese banking industry, cautions against overestimation of the role of reputation and repeated deals.

Basically, business partners do not know whether the opposing party will defect and quit the market or whether it is there to stay. Legal rules, information gathering and formal private policing are used as remedies.

In a brilliant historical study, Greif (1994) has compared the community- and reputation-based enforcement mechanism of a medieval Jewish trader community in Islamic North Africa with the individualistic enforcement mechanism of their Genuese contemporaries combining analytical clarity with a host of interesting institutional issues. A notable result is the likely superiority of the communal system at any moment in time combined with its inferiority in the opening up of new trading areas.

The literature on second-party sanctions based on external norms is large. Concerning contract law, however, as may have become clear already in Section 4, it is largely identical with the literature on relational/long-term contracts which is dealt with in a chapter section in this encyclopedia. The relatively new models of the endogenous determination of the severity of the sanction via exit from and re-formation of relationships have, however, not yet found their way into this literature.

When we leave the framework of purely external norms and take internal sanctions into account, the theory of relational contracts developed by Macneil over the course of the last twenty years is a prime reference. Macneil can take credit for being the first to formulate a theory covering relational contract (which has been acknowledged by writers like Williamson). It has been changing considerably over time. A good, concise statement of its latest stage of development is Macneil (1987), along with Macneil (1983, 1985). The theory stresses the relevance of internalized solidarity and reciprocity norms in ongoing contractual relationships, apart from the disciplining role of other sanctions. His theory is not developed in close contact with economic reasoning and therefore is not always easy to understand from this frame of mind. Lindenberg and de Vos (1985) criticize it from a revisionist rational choice perspective, to which Macneil (1987) replies. Lindenberg (1988) presents a theoretical design of his own applying his 'framing' theory (see Section 6). The approach centers on the idea of 'weak solidarity' in long-lasting contract relationships. While selfish gain-maximization is the main aim, solidarity norms enter the decision as a secondary factor. By way of contrast, the 'strong solidarity' present in close-knit social units like families is characterized by the fulfillment of normative duties as the main aim and selfish aims as a secondary, distracting, factor. Lindenberg argues that 'strong solidarity' frequently is detrimental to contractual relationships.

Several other publications dealing with non-legal sanctions in relation to contracts also implicitly or explicitly refer to both internal and external norms. Experimental work supporting the importance of internal norms in contracts is presented by Hackett (1994). Very interesting work based on anthropological field studies on trading networks by South-East Asian Chinese is presented in Landa (1979, 1981). (See also Landa, 1983, on the Kula Ring, a classic anthropological example of gift exchange). An onion-like structure of 'relatedness' is described, ranging from the nuclear family to the ethnic group of Hokkien-Chinese to Non-Chinese, associated with declining levels of trustworthiness. The trading practices embedded in these relationships are discussed using information economics and the theory of money. Of particular interest is the borderline between credit and cash transactions. The argument is generalized in Carr and Landa (1983) where religious groups are included and a club-theoretic framework is used. Cooter and Landa (1984) deepen the analysis with respect to the question of the socially vs. privately optimal size of trading groups. They conclude that the socially optimal trading group is smaller than under free entry, but larger than a monopolistic trading group maximizing only the welfare of its members. This and other work has recently been republished in book form (Landa, 1994). While using the early analytical apparatus common at the time, it is nevertheless full of insights. La Croix (1989) builds upon the above work and, using the line of argument of Williamson (1983), discusses the kind of (ethnic, religious, and so on) 'bond' posted in a middleman group.

12. Corporations

Ramseyer (1987) provides an excellent discussion of the role of non-legal sanctions in explaining the relative rareness of hostile takeovers in Japan, embedded in a good general discussion of the role of culture and norms. He argues that the existing norms persist largely due to the fact that they are in line with the underlying economic incentives. Hostile takeovers are relatively unprofitable in Japan since the firms are highly leveraged. Hence banks have a good bargaining position for appropriating any efficiency gains the takeover might produce.

Black and Kraakman (1996) provide an excellent analysis of the possibility to design a self-enforcing corporate law. The aim of the effort is to protect the interests of minority shareholders in the absence of non-legal norms and effective legal enforcement, a situation prevailing especially in some of the former socialist countries. The approach centers on the idea of giving the parties concerned as much direct leverage as possible, minimizing the need for third-party involvement (courts, lawyers, officials, and so on). Core elements are reliance on procedural protection - like transaction approval by outside directors - bright line rules and strong legal remedies on paper which to some extent compensate for weak remedies in fact.

13. Crime and Criminal Enforcement

Felson (1986) provides a detailed account of how non-legal sanctions may support law enforcement. Combining elements of social control, routine activity and rational choice theory, he provides a minimal set-up for non-legal sanctions. A potential offender has to have at least one social contact, the 'intimate handler', whose disapproval affects the potential offender, be it intrinsically or instrumentally. Close kin are usually a case in point. This person has to be contactable by a person who might observe any potential offence, the 'guardian'. Felson then describes how the density of social ties in closely knit, locally concentrated communities provides a multitude of social relationships which can be turned into handler and guardian at any time, significantly lowering crime rates. The more sparsely knit or the more spatially dispersed the web of social contacts is, it is argued, the less effective are non-legal sanctions, causing crime rates to be higher in urban areas. The most recent exercise in tracing social influences on criminality, Glaeser, Sacerdote and Scheinkman (1996), can also be interpreted as modeling the effects of non-legal sanctions on crime rates.

Kunz (1976, 1993) emphasize somewhat different issues. It is asserted that a criminal subculture is stabilized by three elements which serve to reduce the probability and severity of official sanctions in such a subculture: a norm of mutual protection by non-cooperation with official authorities, enforced by non-legal, frequently extra-legal sanctions, and the promise of mutual support in case a member of the subculture has been exposed to legal sanctions

Opp (1989), reconstructing central sociological theories of crime in a rational choice framework, suggests further potential pathways for effects of non-legal sanctions, when discussing the theory of 'differential association'. Day-to-day interactions may influence the kind of norms internalized and thereby alter the subjective costs of committing a crime. Cognitive aspects are also stressed. Systematic differences in the day to day interactions of people may influence their knowledge about opportunities for criminal action or about ways to escape formal sanctions.

When discussing the 'labeling approach', Opp also treats the effects of 'stigma', non-legal disadvantages (that is, sanctions) suffered as a consequence of being convicted, on crime. The criminal career hypothesis maintains that rather than deterring, criminal punishment condones further crime by labeling the actor who committed the crime a 'criminal', stigmatizing him and thus pushing him into a criminal career. Opp points out that this hypothesis could be reconstructed in terms of an economic analysis if one assumes that the stigma accompanying criminal sanctions reduces post-punishment legal opportunities, that is, stigma reduces the opportunity cost of further offences. If stigma leads to more additional crimes due to criminal careers than it deters by raising the disutility of an offence in the first place, it may actually reduce the deterrent effect rather than increase it. Rasmusen (1996) considers other models of 'stigma'. The models analyze self-enforcing third-party sanctions, are adverse selection and moral hazard driven, and give rise to multiple equilibria. Karpoff and Lott (1993) include an empirical study of the interaction between criminal sanctions and the loss of reputation caused by these sanctions in the case of corporate fraud.

14. Non-Legal Sanctions and Public Policies

Several publications contain discussions of public policies and regulation from a non-legal sanctions perspective. Two questions are central: first, is a particular social norm enforced by non-legal sanctions likely to be efficient? Second, does the state have the means to improve upon a social norm?

The first question has two aspects, which are not always clearly distinguished: it is necessary for an efficient norm to prescribe an efficient behavior, that is, to contain an efficient substantive rule. However, this is not sufficient. In addition the informal enforcement of that behavior via informal first-, second-, or third-party control has to be efficient. If both aspects can be answered affirmatively, no public policy is required. This is the position taken in a public policy centered article by Rock and Wachter (1996). They discuss what they term a norm of 'no-dismissal-without-cause' in the non-union sector of the US economy overriding the legal status of 'employment at will' (Kamiat, 1996 is a critical comment.). In the same vein, Benson (1994), referring to external norms, argues that a large amount of the public activities considered as the provision of public goods could be, and historically have been, privately provided. He presents historical case studies for policing and road maintenance in Britain.

The deviation from efficiency that provides the most straightforward a priori case for state intervention is inefficient informal enforcement of an efficient substantive rule, calling for enforcement by the state. Along this line, Cooter (1996) is probably the most ambitious and systematic attempt to formulate a program of incorporating non-legal norms in law. He proposes to judge the efficiency of non-legal norms by evaluating the structure generating it, using the term 'structural approach' for this endeavor. Rubin (1994), building on his systematic exposition of private enforcement mechanisms (see also Section 11), discusses how governments of the Eastern European transition countries can build upon and support the autonomous development of non-legal sanctioning mechanisms. He favors legal enforcement of arbitration and the adoption of privately generated rules into the law. Giving this view an explanatory twist, Hägg (1994) sees firms demanding regulation and supervision in order to overcome problems remaining after the various forms of non-legal enforcement elaborated above in Sections 4 and 5 have been exhausted. A technical analysis is combined with some historical evidence.

Besides these rather general treatments, more specific analyses exist. Johnston (1996) analyzes a specific legal question. He discusses the influence of the US merchant law on business norms. Specifically, he looks at the requirement of a written contract for court enforcement of contracts worth more than $500. He finds evidence that the writing requirement is not complied with in contracts within repeated relationships, where non-legal enforcement is expected to be sufficient. He identifies requirement of written contract whenever this is the relevant business norm as a reasonable reform of the law. E. Posner (1996b) is a critical comment. Epstein (1992a) discusses the use of business customs as evidence of due care in tort cases, arguing in favor of such a presumption in cases where the tort occurs between parties of a voluntary agreement. Epstein (1992b) presents an essentially identical argument in the area of intellectual property. Finally, the discussion of public policy responses to non-legal sanctions in Charny (1990), centered around the problem of information costs and possibly unsophisticated actors in the market, argues in favor of enforcement of the norm that well-informed rational actors would have agreed upon. The general principles derived are applied to detailed problems of US contract law, however, this reviewer feels that the policy discussion is somewhat disconnected from the earlier comprehensive discussion of non-legal sanctions (see Section 11).

Social norms may, however, not always prescribe efficient behavior. If they do not, this calls for corrective interventions rather than enforcement of the norm. Cooter (1996) expects norms to require inefficient conduct if it is possible to externalize costs to third parties or if heavy network externalities are present in norm use. E. Posner (1996a) argues for more general skepticism concerning the efficiency of norms, inefficiencies being especially due to information problems and strategic behavior in norm creation and enforcement. McAdams (1995) proposes an interesting and original theory of racial discrimination based on his status-oriented theory of norms (see Section 6) and looks at the US anti-discrimination laws from this perspective. Epstein (1995) is a critical comment.

Let us now turn to the second fundamental issue. The above contributions are mute on the question of whether beneficial intervention is possible. Intervention, however, may be problematic for several reasons. Striking a classic note, Charny (1996) is skeptical as to whether the evaluation of the efficiency of norms can be undertaken with reasonable accuracy at all given the numerous factors at stake. More fundamentally, state intervention may cause counterproductive changes in the content or enforcement of social norms. In highly original research drawing on psychological material and self-conducted experiments, Frey (1993a) produces evidence showing that formal incentives may adversely affect internal norms. When a certain kind of behavior which has been sustained by internal norms becomes rational from the point of view of external incentives, for instance because of formal legal sanctions, the internal motivation to act might be crowded out under certain conditions. Whenever this is the case, internal norms and external incentives cannot simply be added, rather they substitute for each other over an initial range. Frey (1993b, 1993c) are applications in the field of the employment relation. Frey (1997) summarizes the entire research project. Chong (1996) provides a related survey of the interactions between incentives stemming from internal norms and other sources.

Concentrating on external norms, E. Posner (1995) is a well written, insightful and comprehensive informal discussion of the various channels through which public policy may influence non-legal sanctioning systems based on game theoretic reasoning. He especially emphasizes the effects of policies on the ability of groups to continue to enforce external norms encouraging cooperation. Various specific policy areas are discussed. Pildes (1996) also discusses various ways in which public policies can undermine efficiency enhancing norms, taking recourse to the concept of 'social capital' developed by Coleman (1990). In a similar vein, Bernstein (1996), in a detailed case study on US merchant law, shows that the policy of adopting 'business norms' into law can change those very norms adversely. Finally, Lindbeck (1995) discusses the effect of the welfare state in the presence of (external and internal) social norms. He argues that the disincentives of the welfare state will be cushioned temporarily by contrary social norms which will, however, be shaped over time by those very disincentives. Both multiple equilibria and vicious circles may result (see also Arnott and Stiglitz, 1991, discussed on p. 14).

More generally, in the presence of social norms stipulating non-legal sanctions, formal legal rules interact with those norms in a complex manner. Levmore (1996) and McAdams (1996) contain comprehensive and well-reasoned discussions of the role and interaction of norms and law in the area of communication. The former discusses the use of anonymous communication as a means to further the frankness of comments, a solution which is frequently dominated by the use of intermediaries. The latter discusses the prohibition of blackmail by criminal law, arguing that the ban is likely to reach a second-best optimum when combined with privacy laws, the benefit of a blackmail ban being essentially the use of information otherwise used for blackmail for public dissemination, leading to non-legal sanctions. Hasen (1996) discusses the relationship between social norms encouraging people to vote in a general election and state laws trying to enforce mandatory voting.

An interesting treatment of the interaction of legal and non-legal rules and sanctions concerning the use of the legal enforcement system, the courts, is included in Ramseyer and Nakazato (1989) (see also McAdams, 1996). Japanese are frequently said to be reluctant in using the modern legal system since it contradicts traditional norms both in form (publicity of conflict vs. traditional desire for harmony) and substance (universalism vs. traditional particularism). Their empirical findings of Japanese litigation rates related to automobile accidents contradict this by showing behavior in line with maximization of short-term gain. This reviewer, however, finds the identification of 'cultural' influences with irrationality in the early parts of the paper unfortunate. The beginnings of an explanation of the results which is in line with the theoretical structure elaborated in Sections 4 and 5 of this chapter are given in Section 5.

Finally, mandating certain conduct by law may itself create a relationship between law enforcers and the addressees of a law, which can be norm generating. In this vein, McMaster and Sawkins (1996) argue for considering the regulatory relationship itself as a relational contract using the term more or less in the sense of Macneil (see p. 1181).

Acknowledgments

I acknowledge the helpful comments of an anonymous referee.

Bibliography on Non-legal Sanctions (0780)

Abreu, Dilip (1988), 'Towards a Theory of Discounted Repeated Games', **56** *Econometrica*, 383-396.

Adams, Michael (1996), 'Norms, Standards, Rights', **12** *European Journal of Political Economy*, 363-375.

Akerlof, George A. (1982), 'Labor Contracts as Partial Gift Exchange', **97** *Quarterly Journal of Economics*, 543-569.

Allen, Douglas W. and Lueck, Dean (1992), 'The "Back Forty" on a Handshake: Specifik Assets, Reputation, and the Structure of Farmland Contracts', **8** *Journal of Law, Economics and Organization*, 366-376.

Anderson, C. Leigh and Swimmer, Eugene R. (1997), 'Some Empirical Evidence on Property Rights of First Peoples', **33** *Journal of Economic Behavior and Organization*, 1-22.

Anderson, Terry L. and Hill, Peter J. (1975), 'The Evolution of Property Rights: A Study of the American West', **18** *Journal of Law and Economics*, 163-179.

Arnott, Richard J. and Stiglitz, J.E. (1991), 'Moral Hazard and Nonmarket Institutions: Dysfunctional Crowding Out or Peer Monitoring?', **81** *American Economic Review*, 179-190.

Becker, Gary S. (1974), 'A Theory of Social Interaction', **82** *Journal of Political Economy*, 1063-1093.

Becker, Gary S. and Murphy, Kevin M. (1988), 'The Family and the State', **31** *Journal of Law and Economics*, 1-18.

Becker, Gary S., Landes, Elisabeth M. and Michael, Robert T. (1977), 'An Economic Analysis of Maritial Instability', **85** *Journal of Political Economy*, 1141-1187.

Ben-Porath, Y. (1980), 'The F-Connection: Families, Friends and Firms and the Organization of Exchange', **6** *Population Development Review*, 1-30.

Bendor, Jonathan and Mookherjee, D. (1990), 'Norms, Third Party Sanctions, and Cooperation', **6** *Journal of Law, Economics, and Organization*, 33-63.

Benson, Bruce L. (1984), 'Guns for Protection and other Private Sector Responses to the Fear of Violent Crime', in Kates, Don, Jr (ed.), *Firearms and Violence: Issues of Regulation*, Cambridge, MA, Ballinger, 329-356.

Benson, Bruce L. (1986), 'Guns for Protection and other Private Sector Responses to Government's Failure to Control Increasing Violent Crime', **8** *Journal of Libertarian Studies*, 75-109.

Benson, Bruce L. (1988), 'Legal Evolution in Primitive Societies', **144** *Journal of Institutional and Theoretical Economics*, 772-788.

Benson, Bruce L. (1989a), 'The Spontaneous Evolution of Commercial Law', **55** *Southern Economic Journal*, 644-661.

Benson, Bruce L. (1989b), 'Enforcement of Private Property Rights in Primitive Societies: Law without Government', **9** *Journal of Libertarian Studies*, 1-26.

Benson, Bruce L (1990), *The Enterprise of Law: Justice Without the State*, San Francisco, Pacific Research Institute for Public Policy.

Benson, Bruce L. (1991a), 'An Evolutionary Contractarian View of Primitive Law: The Institutions and Incentives Arising Under Customary American Indian Law', **5** *Review of Austrian Economics*, 65-89.

Benson, Bruce L. (1991b), 'Reciprocal Exchange as the Basis for Recognition of Law: Examples from American History', **10** *Journal of Libertarian Studies*, 53-82.

Benson, Bruce L. (1992a), 'The Evolution of Values and Institutions in a Free Society: The Under-Pinnings of a Market Economy', **5** *International Journal on the Unity of Sciences*, 411-442. Reprinted in Radnitzky, Gerard and Bouillon, Hardy (eds), *Values and the Social Order Vol.I*, Aldershot, Avebury, 87-125.

Benson, Bruce L. (1992b), 'Customary Law as a Social Contract: International Commercial Law', **2** *Constitutional Political Economy*, 1-27.

Benson, Bruce L. (1994), 'Are Public Goods Really Common Pools: Considerations of the Evolution of Policing and Highways in England', **39** *Economic Inquiry*, 249-271.

Benson, Bruce L. (1995), 'An Exploration of the Impact of Modern Arbitration Statutes on the Development of Arbitration in the United States', **11** *Journal of Law, Economics, and Organization*, 479-501.

Bernheim, B. Douglas, Shleifer, Andrei and Summers, Larry (1985), 'The Strategic Bequest Motive', **93** *Journal of Political Economy*, 1045-1076.

Bernstein, Lisa (1992), 'Opting Out of the Legal System: Extralegal Contractual Relations in the Diamond Industry', **21** *Journal of Legal Studies*, 115-157.

Bernstein, Lisa (1996), 'Merchant Law in a Merchant Court: Rethinking the Code's Search for Immanent Business Norms', **144** *University of Pennsylvania Law Review*, 1765-1823.

Besley, T. and Coate, Stephen (1995), 'Group Lending, Repayment Incentives and Social Collateral', **46** *Journal of Development Economics*, 1-18.

Black, Bernard and Kraakman, Reinier H. (1996), 'A Self-Enforcing Model of Corporate Law', **109** *Harvard Law Review*, 1911-1979.

Böhm-Bawerk, Eugen (1881), *Rechte und Verhältnisse vom Standpunkte der volkswirtschaftlichen Güterlehre* (Rights and Relationships from the Point of View of the Economic Theory of Goods), Innsbruck, Wagner.

Carr, Jack L. and Landa, Janet T. (1983), 'The Economics of Symbols, Clan Names and Religion', **12** *Journal of Legal Studies*, 135-156.

Chami, Ralph and Fischer, Jeffrey (1995), 'Community Banking, Monitoring and the Clinton Plan', **14** *Cato Journal*, 493-508.

Charny, David (1990), 'Nonlegal Sanctions in Commercial Relationships', **104** *Harvard Law Review*, 375-467.

Charny, David (1996), 'Illusions of a Spontaneous Order: "Norms" in Contractual Relations', **144** *University of Pennsylvania Law Review*, 1841-1858.

Cheung, Steven N.S. (1973), 'The Fable of the Bees: An Economic Investigation', **16** *Journal of Law and Economics*, 11-33.

Choi, Chong Ju (1993), 'Buying versus Creating Reputation', **13** *International Review of Law and Economics*, 99-101.

Chong, Dennis (1996), 'Values versus Interests in the Explanation of Social Conflict', **144** *University of Pennsylvania Law Review*, 2079-2134.

Coate, Stephen and Ravallion, Martin (1993), 'Reciprocity Without Commitment. Characterization and Performance of Informal Insurance Arrangements', **40** *Journal of Development Economics*, 1-24.

Coleman, James S. (1990), *Foundations of Social Theory*, Cambridge, MA, Belknap of Harvard University Press.

Cooter, Robert (1994), 'Structural Adjudication and the New Law Merchant: A Model of Decentralized Law', **14** *International Review of Law and Economics*, 215-231.

Cooter, Robert (1996), 'Decentralized Law for a Complex Economy: The Structural Approach to Adjudicating the New Law Merchant', **144** *University of Pennsylvania Law Review*, 1644-1696.

Cooter, Robert and Landa, Janet T. (1984), 'Personal Versus. Impersonal Trade: The Size of Trading Groups and Contract Law', **4** *International Review of Law and Economics*, 15-22.

Crawford, Sue E.S. and Ostrom, Elinor (1995), 'A Grammar of Institutions', **89** *American Political Science Review*, 582-600.

Denzau, Arthur and North, Douglass C. (1994), 'Shared Mental Models: Ideologies and Institutions', **47** *Kyklos*, 3-31.

Eger, Thomas (1995), *Eine ökonomische Analyse von Langzeitverträgen* (An Economic Analysis of Long-Term Contracts), Marburg, Metropolis.

Ellikson, Robert C. (1986), 'Of Coase and Cattle: Dispute Resolution among Neighbors in Shasta County', **38** *Stanford Law Review*, 623-687.

Ellikson, Robert C. (1987), 'A Critique of Economic and Sociological Theories of Social Control', **16** *Journal of Legal Studies*, 67-99.

Ellikson, Robert C. (1989), 'A Hypothesis of Wealth-Maximizing Norms: Evidence from the Whaling Industry', **5** *Journal of Law, Economics, and Organization*, 83-97.

Ellikson, Robert C. (1991), *Order Without Law*, Cambridge, MA, Harvard University Press.

Ellison, Glenn (1994), 'Cooperation in the Prisoners Dilemma with Anonymous Random Matching', **61** *Review of Economic Studies*, 567-588.

Elsner, Wolfram (1989), 'Adam Smith's Model of the Origins and Emergence of Institutions: The Modern Findings of the Classical Approach', **23** *Journal of Economic Issues*, 189-213.

Elster, Jon (1989a), *The Cement of Society: A Study of Social Order*, Cambridge, Cambridge University Press.

Elster, Jon (1989b), *Nuts and Bolts for the Social Sciences*, Cambridge, Cambridge University Press.

Elster, Jon (1996), 'Rationality and the Emotions', **106** *Economic Journal*, 1386-1397.

Epstein, Richard A. (1992a), 'The Path to The T.J. Hooper: The Theory and History of Custom in the Law of Tort', **21** *Journal of Legal Studies*, 1-38.

Epstein, Richard A. (1992b), 'International News Service vs. Associated Press: Custom and the Law as Sources of Property Rights in News', **78** *Virginia Law Review*, 85-128.

Epstein, Richard A. (1995), 'The Status-Production Sideshow: Why the Antidiscrimination Laws are Still a Mistake', **108** *Harvard Law Review*, 1085-1109.

Fafchamps, Marcel (1992), 'Solidarity Networks in Preindustrial Societies: Rational Peasants with a Moral Economy', **41** *Economic Development and Cultural Change*, 147-174.

Felson, Marcus (1986), 'Linking Criminal Choices, Routine Activities, Informal Control, and Criminal Outcomes', in Cornish, Derek B. and Clarke, Ronald V. (eds), *The Reasoning Criminal*, New York, Springer, 119-128.

Frank, Robert H. (1987), 'If Homo Economicus could choose his own Utility Function, would he want One with a Conscience?', **77** *American Economic Review*, 593-604.

Frank, Robert H. (1988), *Passions within Reason*, New York, W.W. Norton.

Frey, Bruno S. (1993a), 'Motivation as a Limit to Pricing', **14** *Journal of Economic Psychology*, 635-664.

Frey, Bruno S. (1993b), 'Does Monitoring Increase Work Effort?', **31** *Economic Inquiry*, 663-670.

Frey, Bruno S. (1993c), 'Shirking or Work Morale? The Impact of Regulating', **37** *European Economic Review*, 1523-1532.

Frey, Bruno S. (1997), *Not Just for the Money: an Economic Theory of Personal Motivation*, Cheltenham, Edward Elgar.

Friedman, David D. (1979), 'Private Creation and Enforcement of Law: A Historical Case', **8** *Journal of Legal Studies*, 399-415.

Ghosh, Parikshit and Ray, Debraj (1996), 'Cooperation in Community Interaction Without Information Flows', **59** *Review of Economic Studies*, 63-80.

Glaeser, E.L., Sacerdote, B. and Scheinkman, Jose A. (1996), 'Crime and Social Interactions', **111** *Quarterly Journal of Economics*, 507-548.

Gorton, Gary and Mullineaux, Donald J. (1987), 'The Joint Production of Confidence: Endogenous Regulation and Nineteenth Century Commercial-Bank Clearinghouses', **19** *Journal of Money, Credit, and Banking*, 457-468.

Greenberg, Stephanie W. and Rohe, William M. (1986), 'Informal Social Control and Crime Prevention in Modern Urban Neighborhoods', in Taylor, Ralph B. (ed.), *Urban Neighborhoods: Research and Policy*, New York, Praeger, 79-118.

Greif, Avner (1994), 'Cultural Beliefs and the Organization of Society: A Historical and Theoretical Reflection on Collectivist and Individualist Societies', **102** *Journal of Political Economy*, 912-950.

Greif, Avner, Milgrom, P. and Weingast, Barry (1994), 'Coordination, Commitment, and Enforcement: The Case of the Merchant Guild', **102** *Journal of Political Economy*, 745-776.

Güth, Werner and Kliemt, Hartmut (1994), 'Competition or Cooperation. On the Evolutionary Economics of Trust, Exploitation and Moral Attitudes', **45** *Metroeconomica*, 155-187.

Gutrie, James and Turnbull, Shann (1995), 'Audit Committees: Is There a Role for Corporate Senates and/or Stakeholders Councils?', **3(2)** *Corporate Governance: An International Review*, 78-89.

Hackett, Steven C. (1994), 'Is Relational Exchange Possible in the Absence of Reputations and Repeated Contact?', **10** *Journal of Law, Economics, and Organization*, 360-389.

Hägg, P. Goran T. (1994), 'The Economics of Trust, Trust Sensitive Contracts, and Regulation', **14** *International Review of Law and Economics*, 437-451.

Hasen, Richard L. (1996), 'Voting Without Law', **144** *University of Pennsylvania Law Review*, 2135-2179.

Hechter, Michael (1987), *Principles of Group Solidarity*, Berkeley, University of California Press.

Hirshleifer D. and Rasmusen, Eric (1989), 'Cooperation in a Repeated Prisoners' Dilemma with Ostracism', **12** *Journal of Economic Behavior and Organization*, 87-106.

Huang, Peter H. and Wu, Ho-Mou (1992), 'Emotional Responses in Litigation', **12** *International Review of Law and Economics*, 31-44.

Huang, Peter H. and Wu, Ho-Mou (1994), 'More Order without More Law: A Theory of Social Norms and Organizational Cultures', **10** *Journal of Law, Economics, and Organization*, 390-406.

Iannaccone, Laurence R. (1992), 'Sacrifice and Stigma: Reducing Free-riding in Cults, Communes, and other Collectives', **100** *Journal of Political Economy*, 271-291.

Johnston, Jason Scott (1996), 'The Statute of Frauds and Business Norms: A Testable Game-Theoretic Model', **144** *University of Pennsylvania Law Review*, 1859-1912.

Kamiat, Walter (1996), 'Labor and Lemons: Efficient Norms in the Internal Labor Market and the Possible Failures of Individual Contracting', **144** *University of Pennsylvania Law Review*, 1953-1970.

Kandori, Michihiro (1992), 'Social Norms and Community Enforcement', **59** *Review of Economic Studies*, 63-80.

Karpoff, Jonathan M. and Lott, J.R., Jr (1993), 'The Reputational Penalty Firms Bear from Committing Criminal Fraud', **36** *Journal of Law and Economics*, 757-802.

Katz, Avery (1996), 'Taking Private Ordering Seriously', **144** *University of Pennsylvania Law Review*, 1745-1764.

Kimball, Miles (1988), 'Farmers Cooperatives as Behavior Toward Risk', **78** *American Economic Review*, 224-232.

Kiwit, Daniel and Voigt, Stefan (1995), 'Überlegungen zum Institutionellen Wandel unter Berücksichtigung des Verhältnisses Interner und Externer Institutionen (On Institutional Change Acknowledging the Relationship Between Formal and Informal Institutions)', **46** *Ordo*, 117-147.

Klein, Benjamin and Leffler, Keith B. (1981), 'The Role of Market Forces in Assuring Contractual Performance', **89** *Journal of Political Economy*, 615-641.

Kranton, Rachel E. (1996a), 'The Formation of Cooperative Relationships', **12** *Journal of Law, Economics, and Organization*, 214-233.

Kranton, Rachel E. (1996b), 'Reciprocal Exchange: A Self Sustaining System', **86** *American Economic Review*, 830-851.

Kreps, David M., Milgrom, P., Roberts, John and Wilson, Robert (1982), 'Rational Cooperation in the Finitely Repeated Prisoners Dilemma', **27** *Journal of Economic Theory*, 245-252.

Kronman, Anthony T. (1985), 'Contract Law and the State of Nature', **1** *Journal of Law, Economics, and Organization*, 5-32.

Kultti, Klaus (1995), 'A Model of Pairwise Credit', **97(3)** *Scandinavian Journal of Economics*, 441-457.

Kunz, Harald (1976), *Die Ökonomik Individueller und Organisierter Kriminalität* (The Economics of Individual and Organized Crime), Köln, Carl Heimanns.

Kunz, Harald (1993), 'Kriminalität (Crime)', in Ramb, B.-T. and Tietzel, M. (eds), *Ökonomische Verhaltenstheorie*, München, Vahlen, 181-207.

La Croix, Summer (1989), 'Homogeneous Middleman Groups: What Determines the Homogeneity?', **5** *Journal of Law, Economics, and Organization*, 211-222.

Landa, Janet T. (1979), 'Money and Alternative Institutional Arrangements for Achieving Ordered Anarchy', **1** *Munich Social Science Review*, 5-27.

Landa, Janet T. (1981), 'A Theory of the Ethnically Homogeneous Middleman Group: An Institutional Alternative to Contract Law', **10** *Journal of Legal Studies*, 349-362.

Landa, Janet T. (1983), 'The Enigma of the Kula Ring: Gift Exchanges and Primitive Law and Order', **3** *International Review of Law and Economics*, 137-160.

Landa, Janet T. (1994), *Trust, Ethnicity and Identity: Beyond the New Institutional Economics of Ethnic Trading Networks, Contract Law, and Gift Exchange*, Ann Arbor, University of Michigan Press.

Landes, William M. and Posner Richard A. (1978), 'Altruism in Law and Economics', **68** *American Economic Review*, 417-421.

Lessig, Lawrence (1996), 'Social Meaning and Social Norms', **144** *University of Pennsylvania Law Review*, 2181-2189.

Levmore, Saul (1996), 'The Anonymity Tool', **144** *University of Pennsylvania Law Review*, 2191-2236.

Lindbeck, Assar (1995), 'Welfare State Disincentives with Endogenous Habits and Norms', **97** *Scandinavian Journal of Economics*, 477-494.

Lindenberg, Siegwart (1988), 'Contractual Relations and Weak Solidarity', **144** *Journal of Institutional and Theoretical Economics*, 39-58.

Lindenberg, Siegwart (1990), 'Homo Socio-Oeconomicus: The Emergence of a General Model of Man in the Social Sciences', **146** *Journal of Institutional and Theoretical Economics*, 727-748.

Lindenberg, Siegwart and de Vos, Henk (1985), 'The Limits of Solidarity: Relational Contracting in Perspective and some Criticism of Traditional Sociology', **141** *Journal of Institutional and Theoretical Economics*, 558-569.

Lipford, Jody and Yandle, Bruce (1997), 'Exploring the Production of Social Order', **8(1)** *Constitutional Political Economy*, 37-55.

Macaulay, Stewart (1963), 'Non-Contractual Relations in Business: A Preliminary Study', **28** *American Sociological Review*, 55-67.

MacNeil, Ian R. (1983), 'Values in Contract: Internal and External', **78** *Northwestern University Law Review*, 340-418.

MacNeil, Ian R. (1985), 'Relational Contract: What We Do and Do Not Know', *Wisconsin Law Review*, 483-525.

MacNeil, Ian R. (1987), 'Relational Contract Theory as Sociology', **143** *Journal of Institutional and Theoretical Economics*, 272-290.

Matsumura, Toshihiro and Ryser, Marc (1995), 'Revelation of Private Information about Unpaid Notes in the Trade Credit Bill System in Japan', **24** *Journal of Legal Studies*, 165-187.

McAdams, Richard H. (1995), 'Cooperation and Conflict: The Economics of Group Status Production and Race Discrimination', **108** *Harvard Law Review*, 1003-1084.

McAdams, Richard H. (1996), 'Group Norms, Gossip and Blackmail', **144** *University of Pennsylvania Law Review*, 2237-2292.

McMaster, Robert and Sawkins, John W. (1996), 'The Contract State, Trust Distortion, and Efficiency', **54** *Review of Social Economy*, 145-167.

Milgrom, P., North, Douglass C. and Weingast, Barry (1990), 'The Role of Institutions in the Revival of Trade: the Medieval Law Merchant, Private Judges, and the Champagne Fairs', **2** *Economics and Politics*, 1-23.

Miller, Geoffrey P. (1993), 'Ritual and Regulation: A Legal Economic Interpretation of Selected Biblical Texts', **22** *Journal of Legal Studies*, 477-501.

North, Douglass C. (1990), *Institutions, Institutional Change and Economic Performance*, Cambridge, Cambridge University Press.

Opp, Karl Dieter (1979), 'The Emergence and Effects of Social Norms', **32** *Kyklos*, 775-801.

Opp, Karl Dieter (1985), 'Sociology and Economic Man', **141** *Journal of Institutional and Theoretical Economics*, 213-243.

Opp, Karl Dieter (1989), 'The Economics of Crime and the Sociology of Deviant Behaviour: A Theoretical Confrontation of Basic Propositions', **42** *Kyklos*, 405-430.

Ostrom, Elinor (1990), *Governing the Commons: The Evolution of Institutions for Collective Action*, Cambridge, Cambridge University Press.

Ostrom, Elinor, Gardner, Roy and Walker, James M. (1992), 'Covenants With and Without a Sword: Self-Governance is Possible', **86** *American Political Science Review*, 404-417.

Ostrom, Elinor, Gardner, Roy and Walker, James M. (1994), *Rules, Games, and Common Pool Resources*, Ann Arbor, University of Michigan Press.

Pauly, Mark V. (1990), 'The Rational Non-Purchase of Long-Term-Care Insurance', **98** *Journal of Political Economy*, 153-168.

Pildes, Richard H. (1996), 'The Destruction of Social Capital Through Law', **144** *University of Pennsylvania Law Review*, 2055-2077.

Pirrong, Stephen Craig (1995), 'The Efficient Scope of Private Transactions Cost Reducing Institutions: The Successes and Failures of Commodity Exchanges', **24** *Journal of Legal Studies*, 229-255.

Pollak, Robert A. (1985), 'A Transaction Cost Approach to Families and Households', **23** *Journal of Economic Literature*, 581-608.

Posner, Eric A. (1995), 'The Regulation of Groups: The Influence of Legal and Nonlegal Sanctions on Collective Action', **63** *University of Chicago Law Review*, 133-197.

Posner, Eric A. (1996a), 'Law, Economics and Inefficient Norms', **145** *University of Pennsylvania Law Review*, 1697-1744.

Posner, Eric A. (1996b), 'Norms, Formalities, and the Statute of Frauds: A comment on "Discovering Contract"', **145** *University of Pennsylvania Law Review*, 1971-1986.

Posner, Eric A. (1998), 'Symbols, Signals, and Social Norms in Politics and the Law', **27 (2)** *Journal of Legal Studies*, 765-798.

Posner, Richard A. (1980), 'A Theory of Primitive Society, With Special Reference to Law', **23** *Journal of Law and Economics*, 1-53.

Posner, Richard A. (1981), *The Economics of Justice*, Cambridge, MA, Harvard University Press.

Ramseyer, J. Mark (1987), 'Takeovers in Japan: Opportunism, Ideology and Corporate Control', **35** *UCLA Law Review*, 1-63.

Ramseyer, J. Mark (1991), 'Legal Rules in Repeat Deals: Banking and the Shadow of Defection in Japan', **20** *Journal of Legal Studies*, 91-117.

Ramseyer, J. Mark (1994), 'Learning to Love Japan: Social Norms and Market Incentives', **31** *University of San Diego Law Review*, 263 ff.

Ramseyer, J. Mark (1996), 'Products Liability Through Private Ordering', **144** *University of Pennsylvania Law Review*, 1823-1840.

Ramseyer, J. Mark and Nakazato, Minoru (1989), 'The Rational Litigant: Settlement Amounts and Verdict Rates in Japan', **18** *Journal of Legal Studies*, 263-290.

Rasmusen, Eric (1996), 'Stigma and Self-Fulfilling Expectations of Criminality', **39** *Journal of Law and Economics*, 519-543.

Richter, Wolfram F. (1995), 'Optimal Provision Against the Risk of Old Age', **52** *Finanzarchiv*, 339-356.

Rock, Edward B. and Wachter, Michael L. (1996), 'The Enforceability of Norms and the Employment Relationship', **144** *University of Pennsylvania Law Review*, 1913-1952.

Rubin, Paul H. (1993), 'Private Mechanisms for the Creation of Efficient Institutions for Market Economies', in Somogyi, Laszlo (ed.), *The Political Economy of The Transition Process in Eastern Europe,*, Cheltenham, Edward Elgar.

Rubin, Paul H. (1994), 'Growing a Legal System in the Post-Communist Economies', **27** *Cornell International Law Journal*, 1-47.

Rubin, Paul H. (1996), *Promises, Promises: Contracts in Russia and Other Post-Communist Economies*, Shaftesbury Papers, Edward Elgar and the Locke Institute.

Schelling, Thomas C. (1960), *The Strategy of Conflict*, Oxford, Oxford University Press.

Schlicht, Ekkehart (1993), 'On Custom', **149** *Journal of Institutional and Theoretical Economics*, 178-203.

Schlicht, Ekkehart (1997), *On Custom in the Economy*, Oxford, Oxford University Press.

Schwartz, Alan and Scott, Robert E. (1995), 'The Political Economy of Private Legislatures', **143** *University of Pennsylvania Law Review*, 595-654.

Shapiro, C. and Stiglitz, Joseph E. (1984), 'Equilibrium Unemployment as a Worker Discipline Device', **74** *American Economic Review*, 433-444.

Sinden, J.A. (1994), 'Learning To Love Japan: Social Norms and Market Incentives', **31** *University of San Diego Law Review*, 263 ff.

Sugden, Robert (1986), *The Economics of Rights, Co-operation and Welfare*, Oxford, Basil Blackwell.

Sunstein, Cass R. (1996), 'On the Expressive Function of Law', **144** *University of Pennsylvania Law Review*, 2055-2077.

Telser, Lester G. (1980), 'A Theory of Self-Enforcing Agreements', **53** *Journal of Business*, 27-44.

Udry, Christopher (1994), 'Risk and Insurance in a Rural Credit Market. An empirical Investigation in Northern Nigeria', **61** *Review of Economic Studies*, 495-526.

Ullman-Margalit, Edna (1977), *The Emergence of Norms*, Oxford, Oxford Clarendon Press.

Versteeg, J. Russell (1989), 'Law and the Security of Homeric Society. A Response to Richard A. Posner', **10** *Journal of Legal History*, 265-284.

Weber, M. (1921), *Economy and Society*, Berkeley, University of California Press.

Weise, Peter (1996), 'Verhaltenskoordination durch Soziale Kräfte und Normen (Coordination of Behavior through Social Forces and Norms)', in Priddat, Birger and Wegener, Gerhard (eds), Zwischen Evolution und Institution (Between Evolution and Institution), Marburg, Metropolis, 187-209.

Weitzman, Lenore J. (1981a), 'The Economics of Divorce: Social and Economic Consequences of Property, Alimony and Child Support Awards', **28** *UCLA Law Review*, 1181-1268.

Weitzman, Lenore J. (1981b), *The Marriage Contract*, New York, NY, Free Press.

Williamson, Oliver E. (1983), 'Credible Commitments: Using Hostages to Support Exchange', **73** *American Economic Review*, 519-540.

Witt, Ulrich (1986), 'Evolution and Stability of Cooperation without Enforceable Contracts', **39** *Kyklos*, 245-266.

Young, Peyton H. (1996), 'The Economics of Convention', **10** *Journal of Economic Perspectives*, 105-122.

Zweifel, Peter and Strüwe, Wolfram (1994), 'Pflegeleistung und Pflegeversicherung in einem Zwei-Generationen Modell (Long-Term-Care and Long-Term-Care-Insurance in a Two-Generation Model)', **51** *Finanzarchiv*, 28-47.

Other References

Becker, Gary S. (1981), *A Treatise on the Family*, Cambridge, MA, Harvard University Press.

Williamson, Oliver E. (1985), *The Economic Institutions of Capitalism*, New York and London, The Free Press.

Taylor, Michael (1976), *Anarchy and Cooperation*, London et al., John Wiley.

0790
LEGAL ERROR

Warren F. Schwartz
Professor of Law
Georgetown University Law Center

Abstract

Important legal rules, most significantly the rule which makes an injurer liable if she is negligent, require that in order to avoid liability an injurer must take socially optimal care. Since the rule is cast in general terms and, consequently, does not specify what the injurer must do to avoid liability, the judge or jury deciding the case must determine what socially optimal care for the injurer was in the circumstances in which the injury occurred. Legal error occurs when the judge or jury set socially optimal care at too low or too high a level.

An injurer deciding what to do to minimize the sum of precaution costs and liability costs takes the possibility of error into account. The possibility that too little care will be required will tend to induce the injurer to take too little care. The effect of the possibility that too much care will be required depends on the causality rule which is applied. If an injurer who is held liable for failing to take that care determined to be required is liable for all harm which occurs, including that harm which would have occurred even if the required care had been taken, the possibility that excessive care may be required will tend to make an injurer take excessive care. If, however, an injurer is liable only for that harm which would not have occurred if the required care had been taken, the injurer will take optimal care even if liability will be imposed if more than optimal care is not taken. It is difficult to draw any confident conclusions as to the frequency with which each of the two causality rules are employed.

A second model is employed to analyze legal error. Under this model, an injurer does not choose a level of care but makes a binary choice between compliance and violation of the rule. Under this approach both errors in holding injurers who have complied with the rule liable or in exonerating injurers who have not complied with the rule will reduce the incidence of compliance with the rule.

The practical usefulness of the analysis of legal error is greatly reduced by the absence of evidence either as to the errors which actually occur or the effect of those errors on the incentives of injurers.
JEL classification: K00
Keywords: Legal Error, Causality in Torts, Implementing a Negligence Rule, Injurers Compliance Strategy

1. Introduction

Legal rules imposing liability on injurers for the harm they do to victims are often framed to require that injurers must exercise 'reasonable care' (or some equivalent term) to avoid causing harm to persons who may be injured by their actions. Rules cast in this form do not specify what injurers must do to avoid causing injury. The determination of what constituted 'reasonable care' in the circumstances which in fact obtained when the particular injurer caused harm to the particular victim is made by the judge or jury empowered to decide the claim for damages brought by the victim against the injurer.

A common example in the literature (Polinsky, 1989, p. 40) is the speed at which an automobile is driven. Since the 'reasonable care' standard does not specify a speed at which automobiles must be driven in various circumstances the judge or jury is required to decide what speed was 'reasonable'. If the speed at which the car was driven exceeds that determined to be reasonable the injurer is liable to the victim. Legal error occurs when the judge or jury incorrectly determines what speed was reasonable in the circumstances which obtained when the injury occured.

2. Legal Error

The analysis of legal error, in accordance with the standard economic interpretation of the negligence standard, posits that there is a socially optimal speed (or, more generally, of course, level of precautions to avoid causing harm) at which the total of (1) the cost of precautions to avoid causing harm (in the example, going more slowly), and (2) the expected harm to victims, is as low as possible. Intuitively, as the driver goes more slowly the benefit derived from her trip declines because she arrives at her destination at a later time; but so, too, does the expected harm she will cause others. Socially optimal speed is the one which maximizes the value of the trip to the driver net of the expected harm caused to others. This is posited as the speed which the 'reasonable care' standard obliges the driver not to exceed.

To facilitate exposition, reducing the speed at which a car is driven will be used throughout as the example of taking care to avoid causing harm. The analysis is, however, general, applying to all instances in which an injurer incurs costs to reduce the expected harm to victims by decreasing the probability that harm will occur or the magnitude of that harm which does occur.

The determination of what the socially optimal speed is in any particular set of circumstances is not straightforward. In principle, the judge or jury must determine both expected harm to victims and benefit to the injurer at different speeds and choose the speed which maximizes the value of the trip to the injurer net of expected harm to victims. As a result, sometimes the speed chosen by judge or jury may exceed the social optimum and sometimes it may be less than the social optimum. In either event, what has been designated legal error has occurred.

3. The Impact of Legal Error on Injurers Incentives

The analysis of legal error focuses on the question of how the behavior of injurers will be affected by the expectation that legal error will sometimes occur. This analysis takes two forms, depending on what is posited as the controlling rule with respect to the liability of an injurer for harm which would have occurred even if the injurer had taken the care (in the example driven at the speed) which she was legally obligated to take.

Calfee and Craswell and Goetz independently developed the analysis of the effects of legal error on the assumption that an injurer who is held to have failed to take the required level of care is liable for all harm which occurs, including that harm which would have occurred even if the mandated care had been taken. In the terms of our example, reducing speed to the socially optimal level does not necessarily mean that all expected harm will be eliminated. However, the analysis developed by Calfee and Craswell and Goetz proceeds on the assumption that the liability of the injurer includes that harm which would have occurred even if socially optimal care had been taken. Kahan and Grady proceed from a different assumption. They posit that an injurer is liable only for that harm which would have been prevented by taking the required care. The difference in the assumption made by Calfee and Craswell and Goetz on the one hand, and Kahan and Grady, on the other, leads to dramatically different conclusions as to the effect of legal error on the incentives of injurers. The Calfee and Craswell and Goetz analysis concludes that legal error impairs the incentives of injurers in two ways, one (to return to the example) tending to induce them to drive too fast and the other to induce them to drive too slowly. The actual speed chosen by an injurer depends on the relative strength of these two tendencies. Generally, unless the variance in the errors determining socially optimal care is very great, the tendency to take too much care will dominate and, in the terms of the example, the driver will go too slowly. By contrast, Kahan and Grady conclude that legal error can only operate to induce injurers to take too little care, in the terms of the example, drive too fast.

To understand the impact of legal error on injurers it is necessary to analyze how an injurer decides at what speed to drive. If there were no legal error, so that legally mandated speed were always set equal to socially optimal speed, the injurer, under the assumption underlying the analysis of Calfee and Crasswell and Goetz, has a powerful incentive to drive at the socially optimal speed. If she goes faster she becomes liable for all harm which occurs, including the harm which would have occurred even if she had driven at the socially optimal speed. And, she has no reason to go more slowly because it is unnecessary to do so to avoid all liability for harm to victims.

Legal error changes this calculation by introducing two possibilities: (1) Sometimes, even if the injurer drives at or below the socially optimal speed, she will be held liable for all harm which occurs. (2) Sometimes, even if the injurer exceeds the socially optimal speed, she will not be held liable.

To understand how these possibilities affect the choice of speed by the injurer it is necessary to analyze the decision process of an injurer seeking to adapt optimally to the possibility of legal error. The injurer wants to minimize the sum of two costs : (1) the costs of care to avoid causing harm (slowing down); and (2) expected liability. Expected liability, in turn, depends on the expected harm and the probability that the injurer will be held liable and be required to compensate victims for the harm done to them. Since expected liability depends both on harm caused and the probability of being held liable, and taking care (in the example, slowing down) affects both, the injurer considers both in deciding how much care to take (how fast to go).

The injurer first calculates the probability of being held liable at various speeds by anticipating the distribution of views as to what constitutes socially optimal speed which will be held by the decision makers to whom a claim for damages by a victim may be assigned. The probability of being held liable for going at any particular speed depends on the proportion of potential decision makers the injurer anticipates will conclude that socially optimal speed is less than the speed at which the car is driven. This is, of course, an exercise in prediction by the injurer with respect to the views that will be taken by judges and juries. The analysis simply shows how the behavior of the injurer will vary with her belief as to what the actual distribution of views will be.

The estimate of the injurer as to the probability of being held liable associated with various speeds becomes a crucial component in the injurers choice of the speed which is individually optimal because it will minimize the sum of the costs of care (slowing down) and expected liability. The analysis of the injurers choice of speed posits that the distribution of views of potential decision makers is such that the two possibilities noted above exist: (1) there is some probability that the injurer will be held liable even if the speed she chooses is at or below the social optimum; and (2) there is some probability that the injurer will not be held liable even if the speed she chooses exceeds the social optimum. More generally, it is posited that the lower (higher) the speed chosen the smaller (larger) is the probability of being held liable.

The first of these possibilities will tend to cause the injurer to choose too low a speed (take too much care) and the second to choose too high a speed (take too little care). The reason which induces the injurer to choose too low a speed simply is that if there is some probability that liability will be imposed even if the socially optimal speed is chosen, it is individually beneficial for the injurer further to decrease her speed and, thus, reduce the probability of being held liable. If the benefit, in the form of reducing the probability of being held liable, exceeds the cost of additional slowing down it will be in the interest of the injurer to do so. Since, under the Goetz and Calfee and Croswell analysis, liability extends to all harm, whether or not it would have been prevented by taking socially optimal care, reductions in the probability of being held liable are very valuable and, as a result, the incentive to take excessive care very strong.

The way in which the probability that the injurer may *not* be held liable even if she drives faster than the social optimum causes the injurer to choose a speed higher than the social optimum is somewhat more subtle. Decreasing speed is privately beneficial to the injurer (the impact on the probability of being held liable aside) if it decreases either the probability of causing harm or the severity of that harm which does occur.This is so because, as noted above, expected harm is one component of expected liability. In this respect the private perspective of the injurer and the social perspective are identical.The probability that the injurer will not be held liable even if she chooses a speed which exceeds the social optimum, however, causes the private calculation of the injurer to depart from the social optimum.This is so because the private value of reducing expected harm is not the entire reduction but, rather, the reduction multiplied by the probability of being held liable. Thus, if, for example, a reduction in speed is evaluated as costing the injurer four dollars but reducing expected harm by six it is socially desirable that the reduction in speed occur. However, if there is only a 50 percent chance that the injurer will be held liable the injurers private evaluation of the reduction in expected harm will be only three dollars and the injuer will prefer not to reduce speed even if it is socially desirable to do so.

Thus, in sum, legal error tends both to induce the driver to go too fast and too slowly. Which effect will dominate depends on the distribution of views of potential decisionmakers and the costs and benefits associated with different speeds. In general, absent great variance in the views of potential decisionmakers the tendency to go too slowly will dominate.

Kahan and Brady accept the conclusion of Calfee and Craswell and Goetz with respect to the impact of legal error in the form of failing to hold an injurer laible even though she has not taken optimal care.They agree that error of this kind will tend to cause injurers to take too little care (drive too fast).They, however, disagree with the conclusion that error in the form of holding injurers laible even though they have taken socially optimal care will induce injurers to take excessive care (drive too slowly).

The source of this disagreement is the difference between what is assumed to be the liability of an injurer for harm which would have occurred even if the injurer had taken the care she was legally required to take. Grady and Kahan posit that the injurer is liable only for the harm which would not have occurred if legally mandated care had been taken. They demonstrate that, on this assumption, an injurer will not be induced to take more than socially optimal care even if she anticipates that legal error in the form of setting the required level above socially optimal care will occur.

Kahan chooses an example which makes his position both clear and persuasive. He hypothesizes a case in which the issue is the height of a fence which is required to be built to protect people from being hit by cricket balls. He illustrates the difference between his position and that taken by Calfee and Craswell and Goetz by asking whether a person who builds a fence which is lower than is legally required would be liable for injury resulting from a ball flying so high that it would have sailed over the legally required fence if it had been in place. It seems quite plausible to answer no to this question since the failure to build the fence has not caused the injury.

But Kahan argues that if this is so the anticipation of legal error in the form of imposing liability on a person who builds a fence which is of socially optimal height, on the erroneous premise that a higher fence is socially optimal, will not induce the building of the higher fence. He reasons as follows. Suppose, for example, that a socially optimal fence is ten feet high but decision makers conclude that it is eleven feet high and, as a result, impose liability if the socially optimal ten foot fence is built. Indeed, suppose that there is no distribution of views but that this error is made by all decision makers. Kahan concludes that even on this strong assumption the socially optimal ten foot fence will be built.

He arrives at this conclusion by asking whether the cost of increasing the size of the fence from ten feet to eleven feet will, from the perspective of the person deciding how high a fence to build, be justified by the associated reduction in expected liability. The essential premise underlying his answer to this question is that if the legally mandated eleven-foot fence is not built, liability is limited to harm resulting from balls which would not have gone over it. If the socially optimal ten-foot fence is built it will block all balls flying no higher than ten feet. Thus the benefit achieved by increasing the size of the fence from ten feet to eleven feet is to avoid liability for those balls which would have gone over a ten-foot fence but be blocked by an eleven-foot fence. Since it is assumed that the ten-foot fence is socially optimal the cost of increasing the size of the fence above ten feet must exceed the associated reduction in liability. As a result, the ten-foot, socially-optimal fence, and not the erroneously mandated eleven-foot fence, will be built.

4. The Actual Consequences of Legal Error

It is not clear the extent to which the Calfee and Craswell and Goetz analysis, or that of Grady and Kahan, better captures the consequences of legal error. In principle, the account of Grady and Kahan appears to be persuasive. It may be, however, that because application of this approach requires a determination of the question of what harm would have occured even if required care had been taken, that the Calfee and Craswell and Goetz approach is taken when this question is particularly difficult to answer.

In the example used by Kahan it is easy to separate the harm which would have been prevented if different levels of care had been taken from that which would have occurred anyway. A ball flying so high that it would have gone over a fence of specified height is an easy concept to understand and apply.

The case of optimal speed for a car, and many others, are much more problematic. Suppose that a person is hit by a driver going faster than the required speed. It is true, and explicitly assumed in the standard analysis, that there will be some probability that the person would have been injured even if the driver had been going at or below the required speed. Taking this probability into account requires some means for distinguishing the harm which would have been prevented from the harm which would have occurred, if the required care had been taken. Moreover, the uncertainty as to exactly which victims would not have been harmed would require some probablistic method of awarding damages such as has been proposed with respect to cases where uncertainty of damages is present (Shavell, 1987, p. 115).

All of this may simply be too complicated to be worth dealing with. In principle, the issue of what harm would have occurred to the particular plaintiff even if required care had been taken is present in all cases. Often, however, the issue is ignored and the injurer is held liable for all harm which occurs when she fails to take the care required by the governing rule. Thus the approach of Grady and Kahan may reflect actual practice when it is feasible to determine what harm would have occurred even if the required care had been taken and the approach of Calfee and Craswell and Goetz taken when it is not feasible to do so.

5. The Impact of Litigation Costs

In order to focus on the impact on the incentives of injurers of errors in determining the controlling legal standard the analyses so far considered all assume that litigation is costless. This assumption implies that all victims who have any chance of prevailing will sue.

If, however, the assumption of litigation being costless is relaxed, an injurer has available an additional strategy for reducing expected liability (Menel). A victim will only sue if the expected recovery exceeds the cost of suing. Putting the possibility of strategic exploitation of the costliness of defense and uncertainty of outcome aside, the expected value of suing depends on the amount of damages which it is anticipated will be recovered and the probability of recovering. Although taking strategic possibilities into account complicates the analysis, it remains true that the probability of success is an important determinant of the value of a suit. Thus, if the victim-plaintiffs probability of success can be reduced, so, too, can the expected value of the action. If the expected value of the action can be reduced to an amount less than the costs of the suit, the suit will not be brought.

Since the probability of a plaintiff succeeding varies with the care taken (the speed at which the car is driven) the injurer can reduce her expected liability by choosing a level of care which reduces victims chances of success to so low a level that the expected value of suing becomes less than the cost of suing. As a result, increasing care (going more slowly) is individually beneficial for an injurer in that not only can it make it less likely that those victims who do sue will recover, but also it reduces the number of victims who have a sufficiently high chance of prevailing that they will sue.

6. Modeling the Compliance Decision as a Binary Choice

There is a second body of scholarship which analyzes legal error using a different conceptual framework than the one discussed above (Png, 1986; Polinsky and Shavell, 1989; Kaplow, 1994a). Under this framework, a person is posited as making a binary choice between complying with the law and violating it. As a result of various mistakes that may be made, including error in deciding what the applicable law is, there is some probability that she will be held liable even if she complies with the law and some probability that she will be exonerated even if she violates the law. Both of these possibilities make the alternative of violating the law relatively more desirable for the person making the choice than would be the case in the absence of legal error or other factors leading to the guilty being exonerated or the innocent convicted. Thus legal error, under this conception, decreases deterrence in the sense that fewer people choose to comply with the law than would be the case in the absence of legal error.

This underdeterrence result appears on first impression to be inconsistent with the overdeterrence, or excessive compliance, result reached by Calfee and Croswell and Goetz. The difference is, however, explained by the different way in which the compliance decision is conceptualized under the two approaches. As Calfee and Craswell and Goetz (and indeed Grady and Kahan) frame the question the compliance decision is a continuous one of choosing the optimal amount which should be done to avoid causing harm. The individual optimum is determined by the effectiveness of care in reducing expected harm and the probability of being held liable associated with different levels of care. In this framework overdeterrence means that individuals take excessive care and underdeterrence that individuals take too little care. By contrast, under the view which conceives of the compliance choice as a binary one, there can be no overdeterrence and underdeterrence which means that some people choose to violate rather than comply.

The essential difference between the two approaches derives from two interrelated consequences of positing the compliance choice as a binary one: (1) the person making a compliance choice cannot adapt her behavior to the legal system by taking into account the variations in the probability of being held liable associated with doing more or less to avoid the harm which the legal rule is designed to prevent. (2) Under the binary approach error consists of imposing liability on the innocent or convicting the guilty. There is no place in the analysis for different magnitudes of error. Under the continuous approach, however, legal error consists of arriving at a standard which departs from the social optimum. There are, consequently, more or less egregious errors, depending on how far the standard departs from the social optimum. Moreover, the magnitude and frequency of these errors matter because the person making a compliance choice takes them into account in choosing how much will be done to avoid causing the harm which the legal rule is designed to prevent. It is in this process of adaptation that the incentive to overcomply arises. By doing more than is socially optimal the probability of being held liable can be reduced. This possibility is not taken into account when the compliance choice is posited as a binary one.

7. The Existing Evidence as to the Incidence of Legal Error and its Impact on the Incentives of Injurers

The analysis of legal error provides insights essential to an understanding of legal systems. It is clear that policy objectives cannot be achieved by enlisting decision makers who will make no mistakes. Deciding what behavior is reasonable (or some equivalent term), in various circumstances, is not a simple undertaking and sometimes a defendant will be asked to do too much to avoid the harm the rule is designed to avoid and sometimes too little. The adaptation of injurers and victims to the inevitability of error by judges and juries constitutes an essential part of the process through which law affects behavior. Positive and normative analysis which ignores this adaptation to the expectation of error is seriously incomplete.

The analysis of legal error is particularly useful in providing a means for understanding and evaluating various procedural features. Most fundamentally, under all of the analyses discussed above, legal error causes the behavior of persons subject to a legal regime to depart from the social optimum. A change in the system which reduces error will, consequently, cause behavior better to conform to the social optimum. It is thus possible to decide whether the change should be made by comparing its costs with the value of the associated improvement in behavior. The analysis of legal error also provides another perspective for evaluating the costliness of litigation. In general, the higher the costs which a victim must incur in suing an injurer the greater must the probability of success be for the victim to sue. The greater the probability of success which must exist before a victim will sue, the greater are the opportunities for injurers to decrease their expected liability by choosing a compliance strategy which reduces the victims chances of succeeding below the level required for suit to be brought.

Although the analysis of legal error thus offers the possibility of better understanding a legal system, the subtlety and complexity of the analysis make it very difficult to utilize to predict outcomes in particular circumstances or make concrete proposals for legal reform. Theoretical analysis teaches that outcomes depend on: (1) the distribution of views of potential decision makers as to what an injurer must do to avoid causing harm in order to escape liability; (2) the controlling rule as to whether an injurer is liable for harm which would occur even if required care had been taken; (3) the costliness of litigation to injurers and victims and (4) the information that injurers and victims have about each of the first three factors and that victims have about what injurers know and injurers have about what victims know.

To predict how a change in the system will affect the universe of outcomes one must somehow gain reliable answers to these factual questions and properly analyze the complex adaptations which would occur if the system were changed.

At the present time, it seems fair to say that the analysis of legal error constitutes a fundamental aspect of our understanding of how legal systems function. It has, however, so far yielded neither useful predictions of outcomes nor the foundation for specific proposals for reform.

Bibliography on Legal Error (0790)

Ben-Shahar, Omri (1995), 'Informed Courts, Uninformed Individual and the Economics of Judicial Hindsight', **151** *Journal of Institutional and Theoretical Economics*, 613-630.

Bouckaert, Boudewijn and Schäfer, Hans-Bernd (1995), 'Mistake of Law and the Economics of Legal Information', in Bouckaert, Boudewijn and De Geest, Gerrit (eds), *Essays in*

Law and Economics II: Contract Law, Regulation, and Reflections on Law and Economics, Antwerpen, Maklu, 217-245.

Bundy, Stephen M. (1994), 'Valuing Accuracy: Filling out the Framework: Comment', **23** *Journal of Legal Studies*, 411-433.

Calfee, John E. and Craswell, Richard (1984), 'Some Effects of Uncertainty on Compliance with Legal Standards', **70** *Virginia Law Review*, 965-1003.

Craswell, Richard and Calfee, John E. (1986), 'Deterrence and Uncertain Legal Standards', **2** *Journal of Law, Economics, and Organization*, 279-303.

Goetz, Charles J. (1984), *Law and Economics: Cases and Materials*, St. Paul, West Publishing.

Good, I.J. and Tullock, Gordon (1984), 'Judicial Errors and a Proposal for Reform', **13** *Journal of Legal Studies*, 289-298.

Grady, Mark F. (1988),'Discontinuities and Information Burdens: Review of the Economic Structure or Tort Law by William M. Landes and Richard A. Posner', **56** *George Washington Law Review*, 658-pp.

Grady, Mark F. (1989), 'Untaken Precautions', **18** *Journal of Legal Studies*, 139-156.

Graham, John D. and Wiener, Jonathan Baert (1995), *Risk vs. Risk: Tradeoffs in Protecting Health and the Environment*, Cambridge, MA, Harvard University Press.

Gravelle, Hugh S.E. (1983), 'Judicial Review and Public Firms', **3** *International Review of Law and Economics*, 187-205.

Hylton, Keith N. (1990), 'Costly Litigation and Legal Error under Negligence', **6** *Journal of Law, Economics, and Organization*, 433-452.

Kahan, Marcel (1989), 'Causation and Incentives to Take Care under the Negligence Rule', **18** *Journal of Legal Studies*, 427-447.

Kaplow, Louis (1994a), 'The Value of Accuracy in Adjudication: An Economic Analysis', **23** *Journal of Legal Studies*, 307-401.

Kaplow, Louis (1994b), 'Optimal Insurance Contracts when Establishing the Amount of Loss is Costly', **19** *Geneva Papers on Risk and Insurance*, 139-152.

Kaplow, Louis and Shavell, Steven (1994), 'Accuracy in the Determination of Liability', **37** *Journal of Law and Economics*, 1-15.

Kaplow, Louis and Shavell, Steven (1996), 'Accuracy in the Assessment of Damages', **39** *Journal of Law and Economics*, 191-209.

Katz, Avery and Beckner, Clinton F., III (1995), 'The Incentive Effects of Litigation Fee Shifting when Legal Standards are Uncertain', **15** *International Review of Law and Economics*, 205-224.

Kobayashi, Bruce H. and Lott, John R., Jr (1992), 'Low Probability-High Penalty Enforcement Strategies and the Efficient Operation of the Plea Bargaining System', **12** *International Review of Law and Economics*, 69-77.

MacKaay, Ejan (1979), 'Les Notions Floues ou l'Économie de l'Imprécision (Fuzzy Concepts or the Economics of Imprecision)', **12** *Langages*, 33-50.

MacKaay, Ejan (1980), 'Le Nozione "Fluide" Ovvero l'Economia Delllmprecisione (Fuzzy Concepts or the Economics of Imprecision)', *Informatica e Diritto*, 253-274.

Ortiz, Daniel R. (1994), 'Neoactuarialism: Comment', **23** *Journal of Legal Studies*, 403-409.

Png, Ivan Paak-Liang (1986), 'Optimal Subsidies and Damages in the Presence of Judicial Error', **6** *International Review of Law and Economics*, 101-105.

Polinsky, A. Mitchell (1989), *An Introduction to Law and Economics (2nd edn)*, Boston, Little Brown.

Polinsky, A. Mitchell and Shavell, Steven (1989), 'Legal Error, Litigation, and the Incentive to Obey the Law', **5** *Journal of Law, Economics, and Organization*, 99-108.

Rasmusen, Eric (1995), 'Predictable and Unpredictable Error in Tort Awards: The Effect of Plaintiff Self Selection and Signaling', **15(3)** *International Review of Law and Economics*, 323-345.

Shavell, Steven (1987), *Economic Analysis of Accident Law*, Cambridge, MA, Harvard University Press.

Stith, Kate (1990), 'The Risk of Legal Error in Criminal Cases: Some Consequences of the Asymmetry in the Right to Appeal', **57** *University of Chicago Law Review*, 1-61.

0800
NORMS AND VALUES IN LAW AND ECONOMICS

Denis J. Brion
Professor of Law
Washington and Lee University - School of Law

Abstract

The discourse of law and economics, both as an intellectual enterprise and as a practice that takes place in the processes of the law, is rich with values. This article explores the substance and nature of these values. The values in law and economics discourse are not only heterogeneous in character but they can also be advanced for a heterogeneity of purposes.
JEL classification: K00
Keywords: Discourse, Values, Explanatory Discourse, Descriptive Discourse, Critique

1. Definitions

The discourse of law and economics, both as an intellectual enterprise and as a practice that takes place in the processes of the law, is rich with values. In order to explore the substance and nature of these values, begin with a standard definition of economics:

> Economics is the study of how people and society end up *choosing*, with or without the use of money, to employ *scarce* resources that could have alternative uses, to produce various commodities and distribute them for consumption, now or in the future, among various persons and groups in society. It analyzes the costs and benefits of improving patterns of resource allocation. (Samuelson, 1976, p. 3)

This definition proceeds from the assumption that resources are scarce, establishes the analytical focus as the allocation of resources to productive activities and the distribution of wealth among the members of society, and adopts efficiency in resource allocation as a fundamental criterion of evaluation.

Law might be defined in a material sense as the complex of constitutional provisions, bodies of legislative enactments, such as codes and statutes, and, particularly in common law systems structured with an independent judiciary, the continually developing body of judicial doctrine. Functionally, the law defines the scope, powers and limitations of such elements of governance as the obligatory institutions of public agencies and defines the permissible ambit of relations among legal persons and between legal persons and entities of governance.

Proceeding from these definitions, law and economics is the use of the analytical techniques and values of economic analysis either for explanation or for prescription. In the realm of explanation, it is the enterprise of developing models that, in economic terms, accounts for the phenomena of human activity - the ongoing decisions and actions of such legal institutions as legislative bodies and the judicial process, and such practices as the legally permissible interactions of individuals. In the realm of prescription, law and economics discourse advocates the application of economic principles in the decision making of legal institutions, both substantively and procedurally, and the use of economic principles in shaping the permissible scope of interactions among legal persons.

A. Norms and Values

The discussion which follows will first describe the values that underlie the explanatory discourse of law and economics and then describe the values that underlie prescriptive discourse. This discussion will reveal that law and economics discourse is a substantially heterogeneous enterprise. And it is heterogeneous because the values that underlie it do not resolve into a unified, mutually consistent whole (Rakoff, 1996; Trebilcock, 1993).

2. Explanatory Discourse

Explanatory discourse seeks to develop models that explain in economic terms how humans interact both outside of, and within, social and political institutions. This discourse has given considerable attention to interaction among individuals, and to action within such public institutions as the judicial system, legislative bodies and administrative agencies. In general, the analytical approach to these models defines the basic agent of economic action in terms of a *homo economicus* understanding of human nature - that the individual is a self-interested actor, competitive in nature, who undertakes to achieve the rational maximization of personal utility (Cooter and Ulen, 1997).

Early work in law and economics proceeded from *homo economicus* assumptions to address the economic aspects of individual interaction. *The Tragedy of the Commons* (Hardin, 1968) explained the resource-destructive course of activity when a number of individuals had access to a resource in circumstances in which entitlements to the resource were poorly defined. The seminal analysis in *The Problem of Social Cost*, which came to be known as the Coase Theorem, holds that, in the absence of transaction costs, the original assignment of entitlements does not affect the allocation of resources to production in circumstances of conflict in resource use (Coase, 1960). In addition to the basic assumptions about human nature, both of these analyses posited that the paramount criterion of evaluation of human interaction is efficiency, implicitly defined as putting resources to the most valuable use in production. And both of these analyses posit, implicitly or expressly, that the prior definition of a pattern of individual entitlements to resources makes possible market action that guides the allocation of these resources toward efficiency.

Other early work describes the adjudication of private disputes in a common law system as an efficient process. This occurs because parties to a conflict have an incentive to litigate prior doctrinal rules that are inefficient, which in turn tends to induce the judiciary to replace these rules with efficient rules. The result is a tendency for the substance of judicial doctrine to evolve toward a body of efficient rules (Goodman, 1978; Landes and Posner, 1987; Priest, 1977; Rubin, 1977).

Public choice analysis takes as its focus the political process and the processes of governmental institutions (Farber and Frickey, 1991), characterizing itself as a descriptive, rather than a normative, enterprise. (Brennan and Buchanan, 1988). Public choice analysis applies 'economic analysis to political decision making, including theories of the state, voting rules and voting behavior, apathy, party politics, logrolling, bureaucratic choice, policy analysis, and regulation' (Mercuro and Medema, 1997, p. 84). Early public choice analysis describes the legislative process as a market for political action, in which individuals, whether constituents or lobbyists, express their demand in self-interested terms and legislators supply political action on the same basis (Downs, 1957; Buchanan and Tullock, 1962). Other work analyzes other elements of the political process in the same way, such as voting generally (Black, 1958), bureaucratic action specifically (Niskanen, 1971), and the public processes of governance generally (Bartlett, 1973).

The mainstream of descriptive discourse thus proceeds from a small number of particular principles. Human nature is posited in terms of the self-interested, utility-maximizing *homo economicus*. The market is posited as the paradigm of human interaction, whether the subject of exchange is goods and services or it is public action. The criterion for the evaluation of human interaction is efficiency in the allocation of resources to productive activity. And the general mode of analysis adopts the static, equilibrium model of neoclassic microeconomics, with a tacit presumption of a relatively fixed endowment of resources to be allocated, and of individuals participating in market activity with relatively fixed, rationally ordered utility schedules (Ackerman, 1989).

Institutional analysis takes an alternative approach to deriving models to explain human interaction by looking to institutions rather than markets as the milieu of activity (Mercuro and Medema, 1997, pp. 101-156). Institutions are defined as 'widely followed habits of thought and the practices which prevail in any given period' (Veblen, 1899). This approach posits that human action is relational and interdependent, in contrast to the atomistic character of human action in the neoclassic market model (Schmid, 1989). There is mutual feedback between economic action and institutions, with each shaping the nature of the other; thus, in contrast to the neoclassic model that posits a process moving toward equilibrium, institutional analysis posits a process of ongoing evolution (Schmid, 1989). It describes economic action in terms of conflict rather than in terms of the resultant cooperation that is described as the consequence of action within a market model; and institutions are understood as the means for controlling this inherent conflict (Mercuro and Medema, 1997, p. 107) The criterion of evaluation is the efficacy of institutions in minimizing the transaction costs inherent in economic action, thereby serving to maximize wealth (Coase, 1988).

3. Prescriptive Discourse

The substantive content of the materials of the law - constitutional provisions, legislative enactments and judicial doctrine - is a principal focus of prescriptive law and economics discourse. This aspect of the discourse seeks to prescribe the substantive basis for choices made in legal processes, particularly in the judicial process. This discourse presents several different sets of underlying values. Three of these lie in the mainstream of prescriptive discourse; others provide minor, though substantial, themes in the flow of discourse.

In the general understanding, law and economics discourse is identified with what has come to be called the Chicago School (Mercuro and Medema, 1997, pp. 51-83). Chicago School analysis is not, however, homogeneous, either in terms of the prescriptions that it offers or in terms of its underlying values. One substantial element of Chicago School proceeds from a particular set of principles - private property is a right that emerges spontaneously from interactions among individuals because cooperation tends to increase individual welfare (Benson, 1993). Thus, private property occupies a paramount position in the scheme of social values; the preferred method for resource allocation is the free market in goods and services; the role of the state is taken to be minimal, principally, the protection of antecedent rights; wealth distribution is determined according to individual attributes; and the principal criterion of evaluation is Pareto efficiency (Malloy, 1990a, pp. 86-92).

According to this approach, the individual entitlement to property is to be given maximum protection from the encroachment of other individuals, and governmental action that erodes its use-value can occur only with full compensation (Epstein, 1985). In the law of tort, the basic determinant of liability is the liberty-based protection of the right to bodily integrity. (Cooter, 1987). In the law of bargain, classic contract law applies - broad freedom of alienation, strict enforcement against breach, and minimal judicial policing of the substance of contract terms (Campbell, 1996; Gray, 1989).

The philosophical underpinnings of this approach are captured by Robert Nozick's concept of the 'night watchman' state (Nozick, 1974; Epstein, 1995). This approach is based on the values of Individualism. The autonomy of the individual is the highest political and social value. By nature, humans seek to maximize their individual welfare and cannot be changed in a fundamental way by the action of coercive institutions. Economic resources are a source of plenty, to be developed through the trial and error process of individual action. The optimal social arrangement establishes the maximal freedom of individual action; and public institutions are properly confined to the function of protection of individual autonomy (Thompson et al., 1990).

A different element of Chicago School analysis proceeds from a different set of principles - it posits aggregate societal wealth maximization as the highest good; it rejects the concept of natural or inherent rights; it approves of market action as a second-order value that serves the primary goal of the maximization of aggregate societal wealth; and it adopts cost-benefit analysis as a basic analytical technique (Malloy, 1990a, pp. 60-68; Medema, 1993). This approach is most closely identified with the work of Richard Posner (Posner, 1981a, 1998). Collective institutions, both public (governmental) and private (large-scale capitalist enterprise) have a substantial role in achieving wealth maximization. Entitlements to resources are contingent, rather than a protected right of the individual holder; thus, resources are to be directed, whether by market action or by the supervening action of collective institutions, to the most productive user (Kaplow and Shavell, 1996). The function of the judicial process, under this approach, is to mimic the market in the resolution of disputes (Medema, 1993; Calabresi and Melamed, 1972). In consequence, the pattern of the distribution of wealth is analytically irrelevant.

Thus, in the law of tort, the basis of liability is the minimization of costs associated with instances of harm (Calabresi, 1970). In the law of bargain, efficient breach, although it destabilizes the entitlement distribution effected by an executory contract, is approved because it shifts resources to the higher valuing user (Goetz and Scott, 1977). In the law of property, least cost avoider analysis justifies shifting entitlements to the more productive user (Polinsky, 1989; Posner, 1998).

This element of Chicago School analysis is based on hierarchical values. The paramount criterion of evaluation is aggregate societal wealth. Collective institutions, both private and public, have a substantial role in directing resources toward wealth-producing activities. Entitlements are not protected from erosion or transfer in order to shift resources to more productive users, thereby subordinating individual rights to the social good. A substantial spread in the distribution of power and wealth is acceptable in order to achieve the maximization of aggregate wealth (Riley, 1989; Thompson et al., 1990).

A third mainstream approach, identified with Yale Law School, also rejects the concept of natural or inherent rights (Mercuro and Medema, 1997, pp. 79-83; Malloy, 1990, pp. 69-75) Although this approach accords a substantial role to both public and private collective institutions, public institutions have a paramount role. These institutions provide a milieu of discourse by which the paramount values of society are determined, and have a substantial role in directing economic and social arrangements to advance the realization of these values (Ackerman, 1980, 1984; Rose-Ackerman, 1992). Because these ends are collective rather than individualistic in nature, then this approach, like the second branch of Chicago School analysis, is substantially hierarchical in character. This approach, however, is unlike the hierarchical branch of Chicago School analysis in two respects. It tends to prefer more qualitative utility concepts of social welfare over more quantitative measures of aggregate wealth (Brownsword, 1997). And it treats the pattern of the distribution of wealth as a highly relevant consideration in the determination of social welfare (Rose-Ackerman, 1985).

By way of summary, the mainstream of law and economics prescriptive discourse is dominated by approaches that are grounded either in individualist values or in hierarchical values. These values are, however, mutually inconsistent. Thus, mainstream discourse is properly characterized more as a debate than as a collective enterprise refining a unitary social scientific model under the aegis of a monolithic set of values.

As this discourse has matured, other voices, based on other values, have entered the debate. A prominent alternative is the discourse of critical legal studies, which itself is considerably heterogeneous (Unger, 1986; Kelman, 1987). Moreover, it has tended to be reactive in nature, in the sense of seeking to reveal, and to criticize, the tendency of mainstream academic discourse and judicial doctrine to advance hierarchical values behind a rhetoric of individual values. Thus, there has been a tendency in a substantial body of critical legal studies discourse not to offer a coherent prescription for an alternative conceptualization of the substance and processes of the law.

Notwithstanding this tendency, one approach with a distinctive character has emerged (Unger, 1976, 1984). This approach posits that values are properly chosen in a social milieu, and that the proper milieu for this choice is the immediate community. The law, according to this approach, ought to encourage the altruistic and cooperative tendencies of human nature over its self-interested and competitive tendencies. And the distribution of wealth ought to tend toward equality, thereby creating a social order that is relational in nature rather than hierarchical or transactional.

Thus, the proper determinant of the use of property is not the self-interest of the title-holder but instead the emergent values of the community in which it is located. In the law of harms, liability is based on a breach of a duty of care toward the physical and psychic integrity of others rather than on a failure to exercise economic rationality in pursuing wealth-increasing personal gain. And the process of exchange ought to be relational - an interactive process for seeking mutual benefit and for seeking synergism in the creation of common benefit (MacNeil, 1980; Brownsword, 1997; Campbell, 1996, 1997). This approach is based on the values of communality. Consistently with these values, the character of human interaction is relational, rather than hierarchical, transactional, or competitive. Wealth is distributed so as to tend toward equality. And the relational milieu serves as a bulwark against the exploitation of the individual by others seeking to enhance their self-interest or hierarchical institutions seeking to amass and exercise power. A 'Social Law and Economics', similarly based in the egalitarian values of communality, emphasizes the equitable distribution of wealth, the broad assurance of human dignity, and solidarity (Medema, 1993; Veljanovski, 1981b).

There is, as well, another distinct set of values that emerges from law and economics discourse. Although much of the work of Richard Posner is grounded in hierarchical values, he has also offered an extended account of human action based on his concept of bioeconomics (Posner, 1992). According to this account, human action is determined, driven by natural appetites and attributes embedded in human nature. Human action, in this view, is the consequence of the individual engaging in the rational maximization of the satisfaction of these drives. Because it posits that human action is determined, this approach carries a strong affinity to the natural law tradition.

Other approaches offer a mix of values. A 'classic liberal' approach is based on the two paramount values of individual liberty and human dignity (Malloy, 1990a, pp. 93-101, 1990b, 1988). Under this approach, the free market is an important institution through which individuals exercise their entitlement to liberty. The State, as well, plays an important economic role -

protecting and advancing human dignity by protecting the entitlements of individuals from erosion by private action or by the action of collective institutions, and maintaining individuals in the holding of a minimum level of wealth. This approach thereby combines values derived from both individuality and hierarchy.

John Rawls's *A Theory of Justice* presents a noted example of a mixed approach (Rawls, 1971). His concept of the priority of liberty rests on an Individualist foundation. The presumption in favor of an equal distribution of wealth and the substantial role of the State both in maintaining a system of liberties and in intervening in the pattern of wealth distribution rest on a hierarchist foundation.

Margaret Jane Radin has developed another example of a mixed approach by her concept of 'property for personhood' (Radin, 1982, 1987, 1989). That certain kinds of property, central to the definition of the individual, are protected from private alienation or public expropriation rests on individualist values. That the definition of the individual, and thus the specification of which particular property has the required nexus with personhood, takes place in a social process rests on communitarian values, as does the egalitarian thrust of the concept that certain property provides a presumptively inalienable individual endowment.

4. Mutual Critique

Because law and economics discourse is underlain by a heterogeneity of values, this discourse takes on the character of debate - the offering of particular approaches to analysis and prescription, and the mutual critique of these approaches.

4.1 Explanatory Discourse

A foundational assumption of explanatory discourse is that the primal agent of economic action is *homo economicus* - the self-interested, competitive, rational, utility-maximizing actor. This model comes under challenge as failing to account for the capacity of individuals to exhibit egalitarian altruism, to seek and achieve social solidarity, and to give their loyalty to hierarchical organizations (Campbell, 1997; Huang and Wu, 1994; Kelman, 1983; Leff, 1974; Morse, 1997; Sen, 1977). Another basic assumption posits that individual action in a free market will, with minimal administrative cost, continuously move resources to the highest valuing users, thereby achieving an efficient allocation of resources to production. The appeal to an efficiency criterion comes under critique on the ground that, even under the approach of neoclassic analysis, there is no unique efficiency point; instead, there are different efficiency points corresponding to different patterns in the distribution of wealth (Dworkin, 1980b; White, 1987b). The proposition that individual action in a free market tends toward efficiency is challenged on the grounds that, because of inevitable distortions, the market instead yields a path-dependent stream of suboptimal goods and services (Eastman, 1996).

The proposition that legal rules ought to be chosen for their efficiency comes under critique on the grounds that their efficiency consequences cannot be determined - if analyzed on a partial equilibrium basis, they can lead to general inefficiency; and general equilibrium analysis entails insuperable information costs (Rizzo, 1980; White, 1987b). A similar critique is made of the use of judicial remedies to provide incentives to engage in efficient action that can lead to distortion if the distinction between prices and sanctions is not taken into account (Nance, 1997). And the account of common law adjudication as a process that generates efficient rules comes under critique on the grounds that systemic bias in the selection of disputes that come before courts prevents the development of efficient rules for the various classes of disputes that can arise (Hadfield, 1992), and that the pursuit of self-interest by the parties to litigation creates a tendency toward the development of inefficient rules (Cooter and Kornhauser, 1980).

Another aspect of explanatory discourse is the tendency to adopt a numerate approach to the enterprise of evaluation and, in general, to advance law and economics discourse as a scientific enterprise (Horwitz, 1980). Although this approach is well grounded in enlightenment rationalism (Toulmin, 1990), in law and economics discourse it proceeds in part from the problem that interpersonal comparisons of utility cannot be made because utility itself cannot be measured by a transitive scale of evaluation (Kaldor, 1939). To assess instead the state of social welfare in terms of wealth, a factor that is susceptible to measurement, however, is to adopt a criterion of aggregate economic welfare that is considerably narrower than utility (Weinrib, 1980; Hicks, 1939). Moreover, a numerate approach tends to accept the results of measuring those factors that are susceptible to measurement as the proper order of things (McCloskey, 1988), thereby implicitly engaging in the is-ought fallacy.

The use of cost-benefit analysis as a means to assess the wealth impact of a legislative measure or judicial decision follows the Kaldor-Hicks Test derived from the classic papers published by Nicholas Kaldor and John R. Hicks (Kaldor, 1939; Hicks, 1939). Because this test does not require compensation in the aftermath of decisions that redistribute the entitlement to resources, it can be shown that, because of the effects of changes in utility positions and schedules in the absence of compensation, the test does not accurately determine whether a welfare improvement has occurred (Scitovsky, 1941; Mishan, 1969; Coleman, 1980b). In addition, the test itself does not accurately capture the views expressed by Professors Kaldor and Hicks, who took the position that wealth distribution is a relevant consideration for the political decision maker, and that, on the assumption of declining marginal utility in consumption, the principle of utility maximization entails a presumption of relative equality in the distribution of wealth, offset by a degree of inequality in order to provide an incentive to produce (Kaldor, 1939).

An alternative approach to the dominant, neoclassic model conceptualizes economic action in dynamic terms, tending toward disequilibrium as technology, resource endowments, and perceptions of utility change (Klein, 1977; Malloy, 1994). Producers can be seen as possessing the power to create and manipulate demand, and not simply react to demand (Bartlett, 1973), and the ultimate productive resource is human intelligence and human inventiveness (Schultz, 1981; Reich, 1983, 1991). Because human capacity is susceptible to enhancement by the investment of maintenance and education, then wealth maximization can be understood more in terms of a dynamic process of investment in human capital than in the efficient allocation of material resources.

4.2 Prescriptive Discourse

Individualist and hierarchical approaches have tended to dominate prescriptive discourse. Thus, the discourse of critical analysis as well has tended to address the values that underlie these approaches. Also, the thrust of this analysis has tended to take an expectable form - the critique of the consequences of the realization of a particular approach from the standpoint of the values of another particular approach.

The individualist value of the paramount importance of the self-interested, atomistic individual comes under critique on the basis that its implementation will fail to serve the values of efficient resource allocation and wealth maximization (Campbell, 1996). This failure is especially acute in the efficient production of public goods (White, 1987; Olson, 1971). It also comes under critique because it precludes other-directed individual action, to the exclusion of both organizational action and egalitarian altruism (Radin, 1989; Sunstein, 1989). This, in turn, will prevent the formation of the hierarchically directed organizations necessary to achieve aggregate wealth maximization. It will also preclude the altruistic action necessary to achieve a relatively equal distribution of wealth required for broadly realized utility maximization and for participation in the economic action that generates particular economic values on a sufficiently broad basis (Kelman, 1983). And the transactional nature of the individualist approach comes under critique because it leads to conceptually unrestricted commodification, which leads in turn to the destruction of the integrity of persons and particular kinds of objects (Radin, 1989; Sunstein, 1989).

The hierarchist principle of aggregate wealth maximization comes under a multifarious critique. It is criticized as incoherent in terms of the specification of what counts as wealth (Dworkin, 1980a; Rizzo, 1980), that its maximization does not necessarily correspond to an efficient allocation of resources (White, 1987a), and that it provides a criterion of social welfare that is substantially inferior either to utility (Baker, 1975, 1980; Dworkin, 1980a) or to collective values (Driesen, 1997). It also comes under critique because it treats the pattern of distribution of wealth as irrelevant (Schwartz, 1979). Because wealth distribution is irrelevant under the hierarchical approach, the pursuit of wealth maximization can generate a wide disparity in the distribution of wealth (Baker, 1975; Kennedy, 1981; Kronman, 1980; MacPherson, 1985; Weinrib, 1980). Because the lack of wealth precludes an individual from expressing her utility preferences in the market, a wide disparity in the distribution of wealth leads to a distortion in the efficiency point that the market can generate (Leff, 1974). Also, the primacy of the principle of wealth maximization has the effect of eroding individual entitlements to resources, rendering these entitlements contingent rather than vested (Chapman, 1982; Kronman, 1980; Reich, 1996; White, 1987). One of the principal proponents of a cost minimization, wealth maximization approach to the law of tort, Guido Calabresi, has been careful to assert that the wealth maximization principle ought to be subordinate to other principles, such as utility maximization, equity in the distribution of wealth, and security in the holding by individuals of entitlements to resources (Calabresi, 1980).

5. Summary

By way of summary, a rich array of values underlies the discourse of law and economics. Descriptive models of economic action and the working of the legal and political processes offer a mix of approaches to the explanation of the phenomena of economic action. The dominant discourse presents models that are numerate in character and that adopt the equilibrium approach of neoclassic microeconomics. A minor theme in this discourse presents models that are more qualitative in character and that adopt an alternative dynamic approach.

The array of values that underlies prescriptive discourse is similarly heterogeneous. The dominant discourse offers approaches based on competing individualist and hierarchical values. Minor themes in this discourse offer approaches based on the values of communality and naturalism. And the discourse of critique proceeds as an implicit debate over these alternative sets of values.

B. Theory

6. Theory

Related to the substance of the values that underlie law and economics discourse and the heterogeneity of these values is the matter of the cause of this heterogeneity - the question whether this conflict might be a consequence of the particular natures of the categories of economics and of law, or the inevitable nature of a discourse that takes place across the boundary between distinct areas of intellectual endeavor or, perhaps, the particular way in which this discourse has proceeded.

That this heterogeneity of values falls into a particular pattern in law and economics discourse is replicated in other areas of discourse. Jurisprudential theories can be understood as falling into a pattern of hierarchical positivism and formalism, individualistic classical law, natural law, and communitarian Marxist theory (Barry, 1988; Epstein, 1988; Peller, 1988). On a more particular level, judicial doctrine in United States courts, rather than developing, as the formalist account might predict, toward an ever more complete structure of rules and principles, can be mapped onto this same pattern of underlying values. This pattern can be seen in the different conceptualizations of ownership of land that implicitly determine the outcomes in particular cases - ownership as 'sole and despotic dominion' (Blackstone, 1765/69:2), a vested entitlement of the individual protected from State interference [*Pennsylvania Coal Co. v. Mahon*, 260 U.S. 393 (1922)]; ownership as the nexus by which the individual is lodged in a hierarchical order, in which the State holds the power to impose substantial limits on the right to use [*Penn Central Transp. Co. v. City of New York*, 438 U.S. 104 (1978)]; ownership as a right subordinate to the natural biotic webs that define the physical and biological order of the natural environment [*Just v. Marinette County*, 201 N.W.2d 761 (Wis. 1972)]; and ownership as the nexus by which the individual is lodged in a local community, in which the always emergent matrix of communal values determines the limits on individual use [*Goldblatt v. Town of Hempstead*, 369 U.S. 590 (1962)]. In the criminal law as well, doctrine can be categorized in terms of the conceptualization of criminality - subjective criminality, harmful consequences and manifest criminality (Fletcher, 1978), underlain by, respectively, individualist, hierarchical, and communitarian values.

The political ideologies manifested in the deliberations and actions of legislative bodies and in public political discourse can be mapped onto a similar pattern. The libertarian ideology embraces the values of individualism. The moderate conservatism of business enterprise and the social welfare values of left of center ideology embrace the values of hierarchy. Interest group pluralism advances the values of communality. And 'Green' blocs and religious fundamentalists embrace the values of naturalism.

The related social science of anthropology offers an explanation of this phenomenon of values heterogeneity and the patterns into which values fall. In anthropological discourse, a cosmology is defined in terms of bias:

> Anything whatsoever that is perceived at all must pass by perceptual controls. In the sifting process something is admitted, something rejected and something supplemented to make the event cognizable. The process is largely cultural. A cultural bias puts moral problems under a particular light. Once shaped, the individual choices come catalogued according to the structuring of consciousness, which is far from being a private affair. (Douglas, 1982, p. 1)

A bias is necessarily based on values. Particular sets of values make up a cosmology. And, there is no single master cosmology; there are only alternatives that are available for choice - particular cosmologies based on the values of individuality, hierarchy, communality and naturalism (Douglas, 1978; 1982; Thompson et al., 1990). Consciousness, the mental world that distinguishes human beings from the rest of biological organisms, must be organized around some set of deep values. The individual comes to adopt a particular cosmology in the ongoing process of socialization that is the milieu of human existence. And from this cosmology the individual goes about the necessary function of constructing a mental world.

A critic of contemporary economic thinking, remarking on what he sees as its 'poverty', has asserted:

> The study of who gets what and why, unlike the study of plants or planets, cannot help being an ideologically charged undertaking. Despite the laborious techniques and scientific pretension, most brands of economics are covertly ideological. Marxian economics, with its labor theory of value, assumes the inevitability of class conflict, and hence the necessity of class struggle, Keynesianism, with its conviction that industrial capitalism is systematically unstable, offers an equally 'scientific' rationale for government intervention. Neoclassical economics, with its reliance on the efficiency of markets, is a lavishly embroidered brief for laissez-faire. (Kuttner, 1985)

Economics, and the academic enterprise of law and economics discourse, are not, however, impoverished by the heterogeneity of their underlying values. Instead, this heterogeneity enriches the discourse. Economics and law are, fundamentally, intellectual enterprises that address the deep question of how, and on what values, humans shall organize the mental worlds that they create. Law and economics discourse would be impoverished only if it failed to reflect the full variety of values-based ways in which humans create their worlds.

Law and economics discourse cannot accurately be considered to have failed because it has not evolved toward values-homogeneity. Values-heterogeneity is a consequence of its nature as an intellectual enterprise - it comprises an ongoing debate over essentially contested concepts (Gallie, 1956).

C. Debate

7. Debate

A final matter is the function of values in law and economics discourse. Not only are these values heterogeneous in character but also they can be advanced for a heterogeneity of purposes. Values can serve as the focus of theoretical debate over whether a unifying set of values can emerge within a particular culture. Such a debate would conform to the methods of systematic philosophy and its foundationalist project (Rorty, 1979). Alternatively, values can provide the means for refining a particular conceptualization of economic action in legal processes. Such an enterprise would conform to the methods of normal science (Kuhn, 1970). Additionally, values provide the deep basis for advocacy - the enterprise of achieving consensus, whether in academic discourse, political discourse or discourse in the judicial process. Finally, values are a necessary ingredient to the quasi-foundationalist enterprise of the pragmatic method, in which discourse is directed toward the 'cash value' of employing one or another set of values in order to solve a particular problem in the arena of human action (Cotter, 1996; James, 1987).

Bibliography on Norms and Values in Law and Economics (0800)

Ackerman, Bruce A. (ed.) (1975), *Economic Foundations of Property Law*, Boston, Little Brown.

Ackerman, Bruce A. (1980), *Social Justice in the Liberal State*, New Haven, CT, Yale University Press.

Ackerman, Bruce A. (1984), *Reconstructing American Law*, Cambridge, Harvard University Press.

Ackerman, Bruce A. (1989), 'Constitutional Politics, Constitutional Law', **99** *Yale Law Journal*, 453-547.

Adams, Michael (1991), 'Normen, Standards, Rechte (Norms, Standards, Rights)', *Juristenzeitung*, 941-955.

Adams, Michael (1994), 'Rechte und Normen als Standards', in Tietzel, M. (ed.), *Homo Oeconomicus, XI (3), Ökonomik der Standardisierung*, 501-553.

Adelstein, Richard P. (1989), 'Islands of Conscious Power: Louis D. Brandeis and the Modern Corporation', **63** *Business History Review*, 614-656.

Adelstein, Richard P. (1991), 'Deciding for Bigness: Constitutional Choice and the Growth of Firms', **2(1)** *Constitutional Political Economy*, 7-30.

Anderson, Elizabeth (1993), *Value in Ethics and Economics*, Cambridge, MA, Harvard University Press.

Armentano, Dominick T. (1987), 'Comment: Efficiency, Liberty, and Antitrust Policy', in Dorn, James A. and Manne, Henry G. (eds), *Economic Liberties and the Judiciary*, Fairfax, George Mason University Press, 309-316.

Arup, Christopher (1982), 'Accounting for the Social Costs of Technology Through the Legal Process', in Cranston, Ross and Schick, Anne (eds), *Law and Economics*, Canberra, Australian National University, 25-38.

Ault, David E. and Rutman, Gilbert L. (1985), 'Comment (on Bilmes' Paper)', **7** *Research in Law and Economics*, 149-156.

Baker, C. Edwin (1974), 'Utility and Rights: Two Justifications for State Action Increasing Inequality', **84** *Yale Law Journal*, 39-59.

Baker, C. Edwin (1975), 'The Ideology of the Economic Analysis of Law', **5** *Philosophy and Public Affairs*, 3-48.

Baker, C. Edwin (1980), 'Starting Points in the Economic Analysis of Law', **8** *Hofstra Law Review*, 939-972.

Bandow, Doug (1987), 'The Conservative Judicial Agenda: A Critique', in Dorn, James A. and Manne, Henry G. (eds), *Economic Liberties and the Judiciary*, Fairfax, George Mason University Press, 257-271.

Barry, Norman P. (1988), 'The Classical Theory of Law', **73** *Cornell Law Review*, 283-291.

Bartlett, Randall (1973), *The Economic Foundations of Political Power*, New York, NY, Free Press.

Bebchuk, Lucian Arye (1980), 'The Pursuit of a Bigger Pie: Can Everyone Expect a Bigger Slice?', **8** *Hofstra Law Review*, 671-709.

Benson, Bruce L. (1988), 'Legal Evolution in Primitive Societies', **144** *Journal of Institutional and Theoretical Economics*, 772-788.

Benson, Bruce L. (1989), 'Enforcement of Private Property Rights in Primitive Societies: Law Without Government', **9** *Journal of Libertarian Studies*, 1-26.

Benson, Bruce L. (1989), 'The Spontaneous Evolution of Commercial Law', **55** *Southern Economic Journal*, 644-661.

Benson, Bruce L. (1990), 'Customary Law with Private Means of Resolving Disputes and Dispensing Justice: A Description of a Modern System of Law and Order Without State Coercion', **9** *Journal of Libertarian Studies*, 25-42. Reprinted as 'Law and Order Without State Coercion', in Veljanovski, Cento (ed.), *Regulation, Regulators and the Market*, 1991, London, Institute of Economic Affairs, 159-179.

Benson, Bruce L. (1991a), 'Reciprocal Exchange as the Basis for Recognition of Law: Examples from American History', **10** *Journal of Libertarian Studies*, 53-82.

Benson, Bruce L. (1991b), 'An Evolutionary Contractarian View of Primitive Law: The Institutions and Incentives Arising Under Customary American Indian Law', **5** *Review of Austrian Economics*, 65-89.

Benson, Bruce L. (1992), 'The Evolution of Values and Institutions in a Free Society: The Under-Pinnings of a Market Economy', **5** *International Journal on the Unity of Sciences*, 411-442. Reprinted in Radnitzky, Gerard and Bouillon, Hardy (eds), *Values and the Social Order Vol.I*, Aldershot, Avebury, 87-125.

Benson, Bruce L. (1993), 'The Impetus for Recognizing Private Property and Adopting Ethical Behavior in a Market Economy: Natural Law, Government Law, or Evolving Self-Interest', **6** *Review of Austrian Economics*, 43-80.

Benson, Bruce L. (1994a), 'Legal Philosophy', in Boettke, Peter J. (ed.), *The Elgar Companion to Austrian Economics*, London, Edward Elgar, 270-275.

Benson, Bruce L. (1994b), 'Emerging from the Hobbesian Jungle: Might Takes and Makes Rights', **5** *Constitutional Political Economy*, 129-158. Translated into Spanish and republished (1995), *Las Instituciones y Los Derechos de Propiedad al Emerger de la Jungla Hobbesiana: La Fuerza Quita los Reprinted Derechos y los Crea Libertas*, 12, 35-75.

Bilmes, Jack (1985a), 'Rejoinder to Ault and Rutman's Comment', **7** *Research in Law and Economics*, 157-158.

Bilmes, Jack (1985b), 'Freedom and Regulation: An Anthropological Critique of Free Market Ideology', **7** *Research in Law and Economics*, 123-147.

Black, Duncan (1958), *The Theory of Committees and Elections*, Cambridge, Cambridge University Press.

Blackstone, William (1765/1769), 2. *Commentaries on the Law of England*. (Reprinted), Buffalo, William S, Hein & Co. (1992).

Bloustein, E.J. (1978), 'Privacy is Dear at any Price: A Response to Professor Posner's Economic Theory', **12** *Georgia Law Review*, 421-495.

Blum, Walter J. and Kalven, Harry, Jr (1967), 'The Empty Cabinet of Dr. Calabresi: Auto Accidents and General Deterrence', **34** *University of Chicago Law Review*, 239-273. Reprinted in Rabin, Robert L. (ed.) (1983), *Perspectives on Tort Law*, Boston, Little Brown, 178-190.

Bouckaert, Boudewijn (1984), 'Efficiëntie of Rechtvaardigheid: het Onvermijdelijk Dilemma? (Efficiency or Justice: the Unavoidable Dilemma?)', **29** *Tijdschrift voor Sociale Wetenschappen*, 101-133.

Bovens, M.A.P. and Witteveen, W.J. (1987), 'Bruce Ackerman over Sociale Rechtvaardigheid, de rol van de Rechter en "Law and Economics" (Bruce Ackerman on Social Justice, the Role of the Judiciary and "Law and Economics")', *Staatkundig Jaarboek, Ars Aequi Libri*, 255-278.

Bowers, James W. (1991), 'Whither What Hits the Fan? Murphy's Law, Bankruptcy Theory, and the Elementary Economics of Loss Distribution', **26** *Georgia Law Review*, 27-83.

Brennan, Geoffrey and Buchanan, James M. (1981), 'The Normative Purpose of Economic 'Science': Rediscovery of an Eighteenth Century Method', **1** *International Review of Law and Economics*, 155-166.

Brennan, Geoffrey and Buchanan, James M. (1988), 'Is Public Choice Immoral? the Case for the "Nobel" Lie', **74** *Virginia Law Review*, 179-189.

Breyer, Stephen G. (1987), 'Economics and Judging: An Afterword on Cooter and Wald', **50(4)** *Law and Contemporary Problems*, 245-252.

Brietzke, Paul H. (1997), 'How and Why the Marketplace of Ideas Fails', **31** *Valparaiso University Law Review*, 951-969.

Bromley, Daniel W. (1990), 'The Ideology of Efficiency: Searching for a Theory of Policy Analysis', **19** *Journal of Environmental Economics and Management*, 86-107.

Brown, John Prather (1973), 'Toward an Economic Theory of Liability', **2** *Journal of Legal Studies*, 323-349.

Brownsword, Roger (1997), 'Contract Law, Co-operation, and Good Faith: The Move from Static to Dynamic Market-Individualism', in Deakin, Simon and Michie, Jonathan (eds), *Contracts, Co-operation and Competition: Studies in Economics, Management and Law*, Oxford, Oxford University Press, 255-284.

Buchanan, James M. (1962), 'The Relevance of Pareto Optimality', **6** *Journal of Conflict Resolution*, 341-354.

Buchanan, James M. and Tullock, Gordon (1962), *The Calculus of Consent: Logical Foundations of Constitutional Democracy*, Ann Arbor, University of Michigan Press.

Buxbaum, Hertig and Hirsch, Hopt (eds), *European Economic and Business Law, Legal and Economic Analyses on Integration and Harmonization*, Berlin, Walter De Gruyter, 401 p.

Calabresi, Guido (1970), *The Cost of Accidents: A Legal and Economic Analysis*, New Haven, CT, Yale University Press.

Calabresi, Guido (1980), 'An Exchange about Law and Economics: A Letter to Ronald Dworkin', **8** *Hofstra Law Review*, 553-562.

Calabresi, Guido and Melamed, A. Douglas (1972), 'Property Rules, Liability Rules, and Inalienability: One View of the Cathedral', **85** *Harvard Law Review*, 1089-1128.

Calsamiglia, Albert (1988), 'Justicia, Eficiencia y Derecho (Equity, Efficiency and the Law)', **1** *Revista del Centro de Estudios Constitucionales*, 327 ff.

Campbell, David (1996), 'The Relational Constitution of the Discrete Contract', in Campbell, David and Vincent-Jones, Peter (eds), *Contract and Economic Organisation: Socio-legal Initiatives*, Aldershot, Dartmouth, 40-66.

Campbell, David (1997), 'The Relational Constitution of Contract and the Limits of Economics: Kenneth Arrow on the Social Background of Markets', in Deakin, Simon and Michie, Jonathan (eds), *Contracts, Co-operation and Competition: Studies in Economics, Management and Law*, Oxford, Oxford University Press, 529-596.

Campbell, David and Harris, Donald R. (1993), 'Flexibility in Long-term Contractual Relationships: The Role of Co-operation', **20** *Journal of Law and Society*, 166-191.

Cass, Ronald A. (1987), 'Coping with Life, Law, and Markets: A Comment on Posner and the Law-and-Economics Debate', **67** *Boston University Law Review*, 73-97.

Centi, Jean-Pierre (1987), 'Quel Critère d'Efficience pour l'Analyse Economique du Droit (Which Efficiency Criterion for Economic Analysis of Law)', **2** *Revue de la Recherche Juridique*.

Chami, Ralph and Fischer, Jeffrey (1995), 'Community Banking, Monitoring and the Clinton Plan', **14** *Cato Journal*, 493-508.

Chapman, Bruce (1979), 'Law, Morality and the Logic of Choice: An Economist's View', **29** *University of Toronto Law Journal*, 114-137.

Chapman, Bruce (1982), 'Individual Rights and Collective Rationality: Some Implications for Economic Analysis of Law', **10** *Hofstra Law Review*, 455-481.

Chapman, Bruce (1983), 'Rights as Constraints: Nozick vs Sen', **15** *Theory and Decision*, 1-10.

Chapman, Bruce (1987), 'Raising Johnny to be Good: A Problematic Case for Economic Analysis of Law', **34** *University of Toronto Law Journal*, 358-376.

Chapman, Bruce and Quinn, J.J. (1982), 'Efficiency, Liberty and Equality: Three Ethical Justifications for Regulatory Reform', **20** *Osgoode Hall Law Journal*, 512-535.

Coase, Ronald H. (1960), 'The Problem of Social Cost', **3** *Journal of Law and Economics*, 1-44.

Coase, Ronald H. (1988), *The Firm, The Market, and the Law*, Chicago, University of Chicago Press.

Cohen, Jane Maslow (1987), 'Posnerism, Pluralism, Pessimism', **67** *Boston University Law Review*, 105-175.

Coleman, Jules L. (1980a), 'Efficiency, Utility, and Wealth Maximization', **8** *Hofstra Law Review*, 509-551.

Coleman, Jules L. (1980b), 'Efficiency, Exchange and Auction: Philosophic Aspects of the Economic Approach to Law', **68** *California Law Review*, 221-249.

Coleman, Jules L. (1982a), 'The Economic Analysis of Law', in Pennock, J. Roland and Chapman, John W. (eds), *Nomos XXIV: Ethics, Economics and the Law*, New York, New York University Press, 83-103.

Coleman, Jules L. (1982b), 'Corrective Justice and Wrongful Gain', **11** *Journal of Legal Studies*, 421-440.

Coleman, Jules L. (1984), 'Economics and the Law: A Critical Review of the Foundations of the Economic Approach to Law', **94** *Ethics*, 649-679.

Coleman, James S. (1987), 'Norms as Social Capital', in Radnitzky, Gerard and Bernholz, Peter (eds), *Economic Imperialism: The Economic Approach Applied Outside the Field of Economics*, New York, Paragon House, 133-155.

Coleman, Jules L. (1988), *Markets, Morals and the Law*, Cambridge, Cambridge University Press, 393 p.

Coleman, Jules L. and Kraus, Jody S. (1986), 'Rethinking the Theory of Legal Rights', **95** *Yale Law Journal*, 1335-1371.

Commons, John R. (1932), 'The Problem of Correlating Law, Economics and Ethics', **8** *Wisconsin Law Review*, 3-26.

Cooter, Robert D. (1983), 'Justice and Mathematics: Two Simple Ideas', in Skurski, Roger B. (ed.), *New Directions in Economic Justice*, Notre Dame Press.

Cooter, Robert D. (1984), 'Prices and Sanctions', **84** *Columbia Law Review*, 1523-1560.

Cooter, Robert D. (1987a), 'Torts As the Union of Liberty and Efficiency: An Essay on Causation', **63** *Chicago-Kent Law Review*, 522-551.

Cooter, Robert D. (1987b), 'Liberty, Efficiency, and Law', **50** *Law and Contemporary Problems*, 141-163.

Cooter, Robert D. (1987c), 'Justice At the Confluence of Law and Economics', **1** *Social Justice Research*, 67 ff.

Cooter, Robert D. (1989), 'The Best Right Laws: Value Foundations of the Economic Analysis of Law', **64** *Notre Dame Law Review*, 817-837. Reprinted in Levit, Nancy and Hayman, Robert (eds) (1994), *Jurisprudence: Contemporary Readings, Problems, and Narratives*, St Paul, MN, West Publishing Co., West.

Cooter, Robert D. (1989), 'Rawls's Lexical Orderings are Good Economics', **5** *Economics and Philosophy*, 47 ff.

Cooter, Robert D. (1990), 'Merit Goods: Some Thoughts on the Unthinkable', in Brennan, Geoffrey and Walsh, Cliff (eds), *Rationality, Individualism, and Public Policy*, Canberra, Centre for Research in Federal Financial Relations, 186-192.

Cooter, Robert D. (1994), 'Structural Adjudication and the New Law Merchant: A Model of Decentralized Law', **14** *International Review of Law and Economics*, 215-231. Reprinted under the title, 'The Structural Approach to Decentralizing Law: A Theory of Games and Norms', in a book edited by Gerard Hertig.

Cooter, Robert D. (1996), 'Punitive Damages', in Gray, Christopher B. (ed.), *Philosophy of Law: An Encyclopedia*, New York, Garland Inc.

Cooter, Robert D. and Gordley, James (1994), 'The Cultural Case for Inequality: An Economic Model of Merit Goods Based on Aristotelian Ideas of Akrasia and Distributive Justice', in Cowan, Robin and Rizzo, Mario J. (eds), *Profits and Moralilty*, Chicago, University of Chicago Press, 150-175.

Cooter, Robert D. and Kornhauser, Lewis A. (1980), 'Can Litigation Improve the Law Without the Help of Judges?', **9** *Journal of Legal Studies*, 139-163.

Cooter, Robert D. and Rappoport, Peter (1984), 'Were the Ordinalists Wrong About Welfare Economics?', **22** *Journal of Economic Literature*, 507 ff. Reprinted in Blaug, Mark (ed.), *Pioneers in Economics Section IV*, Edward Elgar Publishing Limited, forthcoming.

Cooter, Robert and Ulen, Thomas S. (1997), *Law and Economics*, 2nd edn, Reading, MA, Addison-Wesley.

Cordato, Roy E. (1992), *Welfare Economics and Externalities in an Open Ended Universe: A Modern Austrian Perspective*, Boston, Kluwer Academic Publishers.

Cosentino, Fabrizio (1988), 'Autonomia Privata e Paternalismo del Legislatore nella Prospettiva dell'Analisi Economica del Diritto (Individual Autonomy and the Paternalism of the Legislator: An EAL Perspective)', *Rivista Critica del Diritto Privato*, 473-511.

Cotter, Thomas F. (1996), 'Legal Pragmatism and the Law and Economics Movement', **84** *Georgetown Law Journal*, 2071-2141.

Craswell, Richard (1993), 'On the Uses of 'Trust'', **36** *Journal of Law and Economics*, 487-500.

Dahl, Robert A. (1985), *A Preface to Economic Democracy*, Berkeley, University of California Press.

Dau-Schmidt, Kenneth G. (1984), 'Sentencing Antitrust Offenders: Reconciling Economic Theory with Legal Theory', **9** *Wm. Mitchell Law Review*, 75 ff.

Dau-Schmidt, Kenneth G. (1990), 'An Economic Analysis of the Criminal Law as a Preference Shaping Policy', *Duke Law Journal*, 1-38.

Dau-Schmidt, Kenneth G. (1995), 'Legal Prohibitions as More Than Prices: The Economic Analysis of Preference Shaping Policies in the Law', in Malloy, Robin P. and Braun, Christopher K. (eds), *Law and Economics: New and Critical Perspectives*, New York, Peter Lang, 153 ff.

De Beus, J.W. (1989), *Markt, Democratie en Vrijheid* (Market, Democracy and Liberty), Zwolle, Tjeenk Willink, 682 p.

De Geest, Gerrit (1990), 'Public Choice, Mensbeeld en Ideologie (Public Choice, Model of Man and Ideology)', **19** *Rechtsfilosofie en Rechtstheorie*, 109-122.

De Geest, Gerrit (1994), *Economische Analyse van het Contracten- en Quasi-Contractenrecht: een Onderzoek naar de Wetenschappelijke Waarde van de Rechtseconomie* (Economic Analysis of Contract Law and Quasi Contract Law: A Study on the Scientic Value of Law and Economics), Antwerpen, Maklu, 568 p.

De Meza, David and Gould, J.R. (1992), 'The Social Efficiency of Private Decision to Enforce Property Rights', **100** *Journal of Political Economy*, 561-580.

Demsetz, Harold (1979), 'Ethics and Efficiency in Property Rights Systems', in Rizzo, Mario J. (ed.), *Time, Uncertainty and Disequilibrium*, Lexington, MA, Lexington Books, 97-116.

Demsetz, Harold (1982), 'Professor Michelman's Unnecessary and Futile Search for the Philosopher's Touchstone', in Pennock, J. Roland and Chapman, John W. (eds), *Nomos XXIV: Ethics, Economics and the Law*, New York, New York University Press, 41-47.

Dion, Michel (ed.) (1992), *L'Ethique ou le Profit* (Ethics or Profit), Montréal, Fides.

Dobbs, I. (1981), 'Externality, Efficiency and the Pareto Principle', **1** *International Review of Law and Economics*, 167-181.

Donohue, John J. III (1988), 'Law and Economics: The Road not Taken', **22** *Law and Society Review*, 903-926.

Donohue, John J. III (1994), 'Liberal Law and Economics (Reviewing Rethinking the Progressive Agenda by Susan-Rose Ackerman)', **13** *Journal of Policy Analysis and Management*, 192 ff.

Douglas, Mary (1978), *Cultural Bias*, Occasional Paper No. 34.

Douglas, Mary (1982), 'Introduction to Grid/Group Analysis', in Douglas, Mary (ed.), *Essays in the Sociology of Perception*, London, Routledge & Kegan Paul., 1-8.

Downs, Anthony (1957), *An Economic Theory of Democracy*, New York, Harper and Row.

Driesen, David M. (1997), 'The Societal Cast of Environmental Regulation: Beyond Administrative Cost-Benefit Analysis', **24** *Ecology Law Quarterly*, 545-617.

Dworkin, Ronald M. (1980a), 'Why Efficiency?', **8** *Hofstra Law Review*, 563-590.

Dworkin, Ronald M. (1980b), 'Is Wealth a Value?', **9** *Journal of Legal Studies*, 191-226.

Eastman, Wayne (1996), 'How Cosean Bargaining Entails a Prisoners' Dilemma', **72** *Notre Dame Law Review*, 89-101.

Eger, Thomas (1991), 'Veränderungen von Rechtsnormen im Systemvergleich. Eine Okonomische Analyse (Changes of Legal Norms in Different Economic Systems. An Economic Analysis)', in Wagener, H.-J. (ed.), *Anpassung durch Wandel. Evolution und Transformation von Wirtschaftssystemen. Schriften des Vereins für Socialpolitik*, Berlin, Duncker and Humblot, 81-99.

Eger, Thomas and Weise, Peter (1990), 'Normen als Gesellschaftliche Ordner (Norms as Social Co-ordination Parameters)', in X. (ed.), *Ökonomie und Gesellschaft, Jahrbuch 8, Individuelles Verhalten und kollektive Phänomene*, Frankfurt/New York, 65-111.

Egger, J.B. (1979), 'Efficiency is not a Substitute for Ethics', in Rizzo, Mario J. (ed.), *Time, Uncertainty and Disequilibrium*, Lexington, MA, Lexington Books, 117-125.

Ehrlich, Isaac (1982), 'On Positive Methodology, Ethics, and Polemics in Deterrence Research', **22** *British Journal of Criminology*, 124-139.

Eidenmüller, Horst (1995), 'Marktwirtschaft, Privatrecht und Verteilungsgerechtigkeit (Market Economy, Private Law and Distributive Justice)', in Pies, I. and Leschke, M. (eds), *John Rawls' Politischer Liberalismus*, Tübingen, Mohr/Siebeck, 123-127.

Englard, Izhak (1982), 'The Failure of Economic Justice', **45** *Harvard Law Review*, 1162-1178.

Epstein, Richard A. (1985), *Takings: Private Property and the Power of Eminent Domain*, Cambridge, MA, Harvard University Press.

Epstein, Richard A. (1988), 'The Classical Legal Tradition', **73** *Cornell Law Review*, 292-299.

Epstein, Richard A. (1995), *Simple Rules for a Complex World*, Cambridge, MA, Harvard University Press.

Eschenburg, Rolf (1978), 'Vertragstheoretisches Denken in der Ökonomie (Contractual Theory in Economics)', **23** *Hamburger Jahrbuch für Wirtschaft und Gesellschaftspolitik*, 221-236.

Farber, Daniel A. (1989), 'Review Essay: Environmentalism, Economics and the Public Interest', **41** *Stanford Law Review*, 1021-1043.

Farber, Daniel A. and Frickey, Philip P. (1991), *Law and Public Choice: A Critical Introduction*, Chicago, University of Chicago Press.

Feinman, Jay M. (1988), 'Practical Legal Studies and Critical Legal Studies', **87(3)** *Michigan Law Review*, 724-731.

Ferber, Marianne A. and Nelson, Julie A. (eds) (1993), *Beyond Economic Man: Feminist Theory and Economics*, Chicago, University of Chicago Press.

Fletcher, George P. (1972), 'Fairness and Utility in Tort Theory', **85** *Harvard Law Review*, 537-573. Reprinted in Rabin, Robert L. (ed.) (1983), *Perspectives on Tort Law*, Boston, Little Brown, 239-255.

Fletcher, George P. (1978), *Rethinking Criminal Law*, Boston, Little Brown.

Fletcher, George P. (1987), 'Why Kant', **87** *Columbia Law Review*, 421-432.

Freeman, Donald (1981), 'Value Maximization and Welfare Theory', **10** *Journal of Legal Studies*, 409-419.

Friedman, Lawrence M. (1984), 'Two Faces of Law', *Wisconsin Law Review*, 13-35.

Gaakeer, Jeanne (1994), 'De Taal van het Recht en de Taal van de Economie, ofwel Integratie en het Gevaar van Steno (Law's Language and Economics' Language, or Integration and the Danger of Shorthand)', in Foqué, R. et al. (eds), *Geïntegreerde Rechtswetenschap*, Arnhem, Gouda Quint, 423-441.

Gallie, W.B. (1956), 'Essentially Contested Concepts', **56** *Proceedings of the Aristotelian Society*, 167-198.

Gemtos, Petros A. (1998), 'Oi Theoretikes Vaseis tes Oikonomikes Analyses tou Dikaiou (The Theoretical Bases of Economic Analysis of Law)', **46** *Nomiko Vema*.

Gjerdingen, Donald H. (1986), 'The Politics of the Coase Theorem and its Relationship to Modern Legal Thought', **35** *Buffalo Law Review*, 871-935.

Goetz, Charles J. and Scott, Robert E. (1977), 'Liquidated Damages, Penalties and the Just Compensation Principle: Some Notes on an Enforcement Model and a Theory of Efficient Breach', **77** *Columbia Law Review*, 554-594.

Goldberg, Victor P. and Olmstead, Alan L. (1975), 'Institutional Change and American Economic Growth - A Critique of Davis and North', **12** *Explorations in Economic History*, 193-210.

Goodman, John C. (1978), 'An Economic Theory of the Evolution of Common Law', **7** *Journal of Legal Studies*, 393-406.

Gordon, Scott (1980), *Welfare, Justice and Freedom*, New York, Columbia Univ Press.

Grady, Mark F. (1994), 'Modern Accident Law Does Not Fit Corrective Justice Theory', **2** *Annual Review of Law and Ethics*, 7 ff.

Grant, Robin F. (1989), 'Judge Richard Posner's Wealth Maximization Principle: Another Form of Utilitarianism?', **10** *Cardozo Law Review*, 815-845.

Gray, John H. (1989), 'Contractarian Method, Private Property, and the Market Economy', in Chapman, John W. and Pennock, J. Roland (eds), *NOMOS XXXI: Markets and Justice*, New York, New York University Press, 13-58.

Guest, Stephen F.D. (1984), 'Utilitarianism, Economics and the Common Law', **5** *Otago Law Review*, 656-663.

Hadfield, Gillian K. (1992), 'Bias in the Evolution of Legal Rules', **80** *Georgetown Law Journal*, 583-616.

Hammond (1982), 'The Economics of Justice and the Criterion of Wealth Maximization' (Book Review), **91** *Yale Law Journal*, 1493-1507.

Hanak, András (1979), 'Neoklasszicista Justitia (Neo-classicist Justice)', **12** *Jogtudományi Közlöny*, 855-859.

Hardin, Garrett (1968), 'The Tragedy of the Commons', **162** *Science*, 1243-1248.

Harrison, Jeffrey L. (1986), 'Egoism, Altruism, and Market Illusions: The Limits of Law and Economics', **33** *UCLA Law Review*, 1309-1363.

Harsanyi, John C. (1977), 'Morality and the Theory of Rational Behaviour', **44** *Social Research*.

Hasen, Richard L. (1996), 'Voting Without Law', **144** *University of Pennsylvania Law Review*, 2135-2179.

Hatzis, Aristides N. (1993), 'Comments on Bertrand Lemmenicier's paper 'Social Justice and its Controversies'', **4** *Journal des Economistes et des Etudes Humaines*, 263-268.

Hatzis, Aristides N. (1996), 'Neofileleutherismos', Dikaio kai Oikonomike Analyse ton Thesmon: Eisagoge ste Melete ton Neon Oikonomikon Theorion gia to Dikaio, ten Koinonia kai ten Politike (The so-called 'Neo-Liberalism', the Law and the Economic Analysis of Institutions: Introduction to the Study of the New Economic Theories on Law, Society and Politics)', **6** *Aissymnetes*.

Hatzis, Aristides N. (1997), *Eisagoge sten Oikonomike Analyse tou Dikaiou* (Introduction to the Economic Analysis of Law), Aristotle University of Thessaloniki School of Law and Economics, Department of History, Philosophy and Sociology of Law.

Hatzis, Aristides N. (1997), *Krise tou Dikaiou e Krise tes Theorias tou? Prolegomena se mia Oikonomike Theoria tou Dikaiou ton Symvaseon* (A Crisis of Law or a Crisis of Its Theory? Prolegomena of an Economic Theory of Contract Law), working paper presented in a workshop under the auspices of Panteios University.

Hayashida, Seimei (1993), 'Jissenteki Suiron to Ho to Keizaigaku (Practical Reasoning and Law and Economics)', *XXXHotetsugaku Nempo 1992 (Annual of Legal Philosophy 1992)*, 44-59.

Heertje, A. (1966), 'Conflictstof voor juristen en economen (Conflict Material for Lawyers and Economists)', **15** *Ars Aequi*, 14-16.

Heller, Thomas C. (1976), 'The Importance of Normative Decisionmaking: The Limitations of Legal Economics as a Basis for a Liberal Jurisprudence', *Wisconsin Law Review*, 385-502.

Hesse, Günter (1992), 'Innovative Anpassung in Sozio-ökonomischen Systemen - Ein Beispiel, Landnutzungssysteme und Handlungsrechte bezüglich Boden (Innovative Adaptation in Socio-Economic Systems - An Example, Land Use Systems and Property Rights)', in Bievert, B. and Held, M. (ed.), *Evolutorische Ökonomik, Neuerungen, Normen, Institutionen*, Frankfurt a.M./New York, 110-142.

Hicks, John R. (1939), 'The Foundations of Welfare Economics', **49** *Economic Journal*, 696-712.

Hol, A.M. (1990), 'Efficiëntie als Instrument en als Norm. Enkele Rechtstheoretische Kanttekeningen bij de Economische Analyse van het Recht (Efficiency as Instrument and Norm: Some Remarks from Legal Theory to the Economic Analysis of Law)', **39(10)** *Ars Aequi*, 632-644.

Hol, A.M. (1991), 'Rechten en Doeleinden. Enkele Morele Aspecten van Juridische Aansprakelijkheid (Rights and Goals. Some Moral Aspects of Legal Liability)', in X (ed.), *Dilemma's van Aansprakelijkheid*, Zwolle, Tjeenk Willink, 127-142.

Holler, Manfred J. (1984), 'Norm, Normsetzung und Wissenschaft (Norms, Norm Setting, and Science)', **39** *Universitas*, 1145-1152.

Holler, Manfred J. (1984), 'Moral, Markt und Norm. Thesen zur ökonomischen Theoriebildung (Morals, Market, and Norms. Theses on the Creation of Economic Theories)', in Holler, Manfred J. (ed.), *Homo Oeconomicus 2*, München, Leudemann, 512-558.

Horwitz, Morton J. (1980), 'Law and Economics: Science or Politics?', **8** *Hofstra Law Review*, 905-912.

Hovenkamp Herbert J. (1990), 'Marginal Utility and the Coase Theorem', **75** *Cornell Law Review*, 783-810.

Hovenkamp, Herbert J. (1991), 'Legal Policy and the Endowment Effect', **20** *Journal of Legal Studies*, 225-247.

Huang, Peter H. and Wu, Ho-Mou (1994), 'More Order without More Law: A Theory of Social Norms and Organizational Cultures', **10** *Journal of Law, Economics, and Organization*, 390-406.

Hurst, James Willard (1982), *Law and Markets in United States History: Different Modes of Bargaining Among Interests*, Madison, University of Wisconsin.

James, William H. ([1907]1987), 'Pragmatism', in Kuklick, Bruce (ed.), *William James: Writings 1902-1910*, New York, Library of America, 479-624.

Johnsen, D. Bruce (1986), 'Wealth is Value', **15** *Journal of Legal Studies*, 263-288.

Kaldor, Nicholas (1939), 'Welfare Propositions of Economics and Inter-Personal Comparisons of Utility', **49** *Economic Journal*, 549-552.

Kaplow, Louis and Shavell Steven (1996), 'Property Rules versus Liability Rules: An Economic Analysis', **109** *Harvard Law Review*, 713-790.

Katz, Avery (1996a), 'Positivism and the Separation of Law and Economics', **94** *Michigan Law Review*.

Katz, Avery (1996b), 'Taking Private Ordering Seriously', **144** *University of Pennsylvania Law Review*.

Keenan, Donald C. (1981), 'Value Maximization and Welfare Theory', **10** *Journal of Legal Studies*, 409-419.

Kelman, Mark G. (1979), 'Choice and Utility', *Wisconsin Law Review*, 769-797.

Kelman, Mark G. (1980), 'Consumption Theory, Production Theory and Ideology in the Coase Theorem', **52** *Southern California Law Review*, 669-698.

Kelman, Mark G. (1983), 'Misunderstanding Social Life: A Critique of the Core Premises of 'Law and Economics'', **33** *Journal of Legal Education*, 274-284.

Kelman, Mark G. (1987), *A Guide to Critical Legal Studies*, Cambridge, MA, Harvard University Press.

Kelman, Mark G. (1987), 'The Necessary Myth of Objective Causation Judgments in Liberal Political Theory', **63** *Chicago-Kent Law Review*, 579-637.

Kennedy, Duncan (1976), 'Form and Substance in Private Law Adjudication', **89** *Harvard Law Review*, 1685-1778. Reprinted in Kronman, Anthony T. and Posner, Richard A. (eds) (1979), The Economics of Contract Law, Boston, Little Brown, 100-107.

Kennedy, Duncan (1981), 'Cost-Benefit of Entitlement Problems: A Critique', **33** *Stanford Law Review*, 387-445.

Kerkmeester, Heico (1997), 'De Retoriek van de Rechtseconomie (The Rhetorics of Law and Economics)', in Feteris, E.T. et al. (eds), *Op Goede Gronden*, Nijmegen, Ars Aequi Libri, 207-213.

Klein, Burton H. (1977), *Dynamic Economics*, Cambridge, MA, Harvard University Press.

Kornhauser, Lewis A. (1980), 'A Guide to the Perplexed Claims of Efficiency in the Law', **8** *Hofstra Law Review*, 591-639.

Kornhauser, Lewis A. (1998), 'Private Ordering in the Shadow of the Law', in Garth, Levine, and Sarat (eds), *Justice and Power in the Study of Law and Society*, Northwestern University Press, forthcoming.

Kozyris, Phaedon I. (1991), 'Treis Provlematismoi sten Amerikanike Theoria tou Dikaiou (Three Conjectures in American Jurisprudence)', **39** *Nomiko Vema*, 715-728.

Kozyris, Phaedon I. (1996), 'Protaseis Dianemetikes Dikaiosynes sto 'Telos tes Istorias': Ta Kyria Erotemata me Apla Logia (Proposals of Distributive Justice in the 'End of History': Basic Questions Made Easy)', **3** *Kritike Epitheorese*, 23-81.

Kronman, Anthony T. (1980), 'Wealth Maximization as a Normative Principle', **9** *Journal of Legal Studies*, 227-242.

Kuhn, Thomas (1970), *The Structure of Scientific Revolutions*, Chicago, University of Chicago Press.

Kunz, Harald (1985), 'Zur Entstehung und Verhaltenswirkung sozialer Normen, mit einigen Argumenten für eine Okonomisch Rationale Kriminalpolitik (On the Evolution and the Incentive Effect of Social Norms, with Some Arguments for an Economic Rational Crime Policy)', **68** *Monatsschrift für Kriminologie und Strafsrechtsreform*, 202-215.

Kuttner, Robert (1985), 'The Poverty of Economics', **2** *Atlantic Monthly*, 74-84.

Landes, William M. and Posner Richard A. (1987), *The Economic Structure of Tort Law*, Cambridge, MA, Harvard University Press.

Lee, Dwight R. (1988), 'Politics, Ideology, and the Power of Public Choice', **74** *Virginia Law Review*, 191-198.

Leff, Arthur A. (1974), 'Economic Analysis of Law: Some Realism about Nominalism', **60** *Virginia Law Review*, 451-482.

Lutz, Mark A. (1988), *Social Economics: Retrospect and Prospect*, Boston, Kluwer Academic Publishers.

MacNeil, Ian R. (1980), *The New Social Contract: An Inquiry into Modern Contractual Relations*, New Haven, CT, Yale University Press.

MacPherson, C.B. (1985), *The Rise and Fall of Economic Justice and Other Papers*, Oxford, Oxford University Press.

Malloy, Robin Paul (1986), 'Equating Human Rights and Property Rights - the Need for Moral Judgment in an Economic Analysis of Law and Social Policy', **47** *Ohio State Law Journal*, 163-177.

Malloy, Robin Paul (1988a), 'Market Philosophy in the Legal Tension Between Children's Autonomy and Parental Authority', **21** *Indiana Law Review*, 889-900.

Malloy, Robin Paul (1988b), 'The Merits of the Smithian Critique: A Final Word on Smith and Posner', **36** *University of Kansas Law Review*, 266-274.

Malloy, Robin Paul (1988c), 'The Invisible Hand or the Sleight of Hand? Adam Smith, Richard Posner and the Philosophy of Law and Economics', **36** *University of Kansas Law Review*, 209 ff.

Malloy, Robin Paul (1990a), *Law and Economics: A Comparative Approach to Theory and Practice*, St. Paul, West Publishing Company.

Malloy, Robin Paul (1990b), 'Is Law and Economics Moral? - Humanistic Economics and a Classical Liberal Critique of Posner's Economic Analysis', **24** *Valparaiso University Law Review*, 147-161.

Malloy, Robin Paul (1990c), 'The Limits of Science in Legal Discourse - A Reply to Posner', **24** *Valparaiso University Law Review*, 175-181.

Malloy, Robin Paul (1994), 'Adam Smith and the Modern Discourse of Law and Economics', in Malloy, Robin Paul and Evensky, Jerry (eds), *Adam Smith and the Philosophy of Law and Economics*, Boston, Kluwer Academic Publishers, 113-150.

Malloy, Robin Paul and Evensky, Jerry (eds) (1994), *Adam Smith and the Philosophy of Law and Economics*, Boston, Kluwer Academic Publishers.

Markovits, Richard S. (1983), 'Legal Analysis and the Economic Analysis of Allocative Efficiency: A Response to Professor Posner's Reply', **11** *Hofstra Law Review*, 667-689.

McCloskey, Donald N. (1988), 'The Rhetoric of Law and Economics', **86** *Michigan Law Review*, 752-767.

McGee, Robert W. (1992), *Business Ethics and Common Sense*,Westport, CT, Quorum Books, 302 p.

McGee, Robert W. (1994), *A Trade Policy for Free Societies:The Case Against Protectionism*, Westport, CT, Quorum Books, 197 p.

McGee, Robert W. (1996a), *Essays on Accounting, Taxation and Public Finance*, Dumont Institute for Public Policy Research. http://www.hili.com/~dumontin

McGee, Robert W. (1996b), *Taxation, Ethics and Public Policy*, Dumont Institute for Public Policy Research. http://www.hili.com/~dumontin

McGee, Robert W. (1996c), *The New Prohibitionism: The Movement to Regulate Personal Behavior*, Dumont Institute for Public Policy Research. http://www.hili.com/~dumontin

McGee, Robert W. (1996d), *Economics and Ethics*, Dumont Institute for Public Policy Research. http://www.hili.com/~dumontin

McGee, Robert W. (1996e), *Essays in Law and Economics from a Right Perspective*, Dumont Institute for Public Policy Research. http://www.hili.com/~dumontin

McGee, Robert W. (1996f), *Some Thoughts on Accounting, Ethics and Public Policy*, Dumont Institute for Public Policy Research. http://www.hili.com/~dumontin

McGee, Robert W. and Block, Walter E. (1996), *A Rights Perspective on Law, Economics and Ethics*, Dumont Institute for Public Policy Research. http:/www.hili.com/~dumontin

Meade, James E. (1964), *Efficiency, Equality, and the Ownership of Property*, London, Allen and Unwin, 92 p.

Medema, Steven G. (1993), 'Is There Life Beyond Efficiency? Elements of a Social Law and Economics', **51** *Review of Social Economy*, 138-153.

Mercuro, Nicholas and Medema, Steven G. (1997), *Economics and the Law: From Posner to Postmodernism*, Princeton, Princeton University Press.

Michelman, Frank I. (1967), 'Property, Utility and Fairness: Comments on the Ethical Foundations of 'Just Compensation' Law', **80** *Harvard Law Review*, 1165-1258. Reprinted in Ackerman, Bruce A. (ed.) (1975), *Economic Foundations of Property Law*, Boston, Little Brown, 100 ff.

Michelman, Frank I. (1978), 'Norms and Normativity in the Economic Theory of Law', **62** *Minnesota Law Review*, 1015-1048.

Michelman, Frank I. (1979), 'A Comment on Some Uses and Abuses of Economics in Law', **46** *University of Chicago Law Review*, 307-315.

Michelman, Frank I. (1982), 'Ethics, Economics, and the Law of Property', in Pennock, J. Roland and Chapman, John W. (eds), *Nomos XXIV: Ethics, Economics and the Law*, New York, New York University Press, 3-40.

Miller, Edythe S. (1990), 'Economic Efficiency, the Economics Discipline, and the "Affected-with-a-Public-Interest" Concept', **24** *Journal of Economic Issues*, 719-732.

Mishan, Ezra J. (1969), *Welfare Economics: An Assessment*, Amsterdam, North-Holland.

Morse, Jennifer Roback (1997), 'Who is Rational Economic Man?', **14** *Social Philosophy and Policy*, 177-206.

Nance, Dale A. (1997), 'Guidance Rules and Enforcement Rules: A Better View of the Cathedral', **83** *Virginia Law Review*, 837-937.

Ng, Yew Kwang (1988), 'Economic Efficiency versus Egalitarian Rights', **41** *Kyklos*, 215-237.

Nieuwenhuis, J.H. (1984), 'Recht en Belang (Law and Interests)', *Flores Debitorem*, 65-74.

Nieuwenhuis, J.H. (1988), 'Ieder het Zijne (Each His Own)', **2** *RMThemis*, 73-84.

Nieuwenhuis, J.H. (1997), *De Ramp op het Pikmeer* (The Pikmeer Disaster), Deventer, Kluwer, 22 p.

Niskanen, William A. (1971), *Bureaucracy and Representative Government*, Chicago, Atherton.

Nozick, Robert (1974), *Anarchy, State, and Utopia*, New York, Basic Books.

Nutter, Warren G. (1968), 'Economic Welfare and Welfare Economics', **2** *Journal of Economic Issues*, 166-172.

O'Driscoll, Gerald P., Jr (1980), 'Justice, Efficiency, and the Economic Analysis of Law: A Comment on Fried', **9** *Journal of Legal Studies*, 355-366.

Ogus, Anthony I. (1980), 'Economics, Liberty and the Common Law', **18** *Journal of Society of Public Teachers of Law*, 42-57.

Olson, Mancur (1971), *The Logic of Collective Action: Public Goods and the Theory of Groups*, New York, Shocken, Books.

Parisi, Francesco (1995), 'Toward a Theory of Spontaneous Law', **6** *Constitutional Political Economy*, 211-231.

Parisi, Francesco (1996a), 'Law as a Voluntary Enterprise', in Ratnapala, S. and Moens, G. (eds), *The Jurisprudence of Liberty*, Butterworths, London, 111-128.

Parisi, Francesco (1996b), 'Normative Knowledge and Self-Enforcing Rules in International Law', **2** *International Legal Theory*, 27-30.

Parisi, Francesco (1998a), 'Opinio Iuris Revisited: A Law and Economics Perspective (forthcoming)', **4** *International Legal Theory*.

Parisi, Francesco (1998b), 'Spontaneous Emergence of Law: Customary Law', in X., *Encyclopedia of Law and Economics*, Edward Elgar and University of Gent.

Parisi, Francesco (1998c), 'Customary Law', in Barnett, W. A., Hinich, M.J., and Schofield, N.J. (eds), *Political Economy: Institutions, Competition, and Representation*, New York, Cambridge University Press, 572-578.

Parisi, Francesco (1998d), 'The Economics of Customary Law: Lessons From Evolutionary Socio-Biology', in Ott, Claus and von Wangenheim, Georg (eds), *Essays in Law and Economics IV*, Antwerpen, Maklu, 245-269.

Parisi, Francesco (1999), 'The Cost of the Game: A Topology of Social Interactions (forthcoming), *European Journal of Law and Economics*.

Pejovich, Svetozar (1990), *The Economics of Property Rights: Toward a Theory of Comparative Systems*, Boston, Kluwer Academic Publishers.

Peller, Gary (1988), 'The Classical Theory of Law', **73** *Cornell Law Review*, 300-309.

Pennock, J. Roland and Chapman, John W. (eds) (1982), *Ethics, Economics and the Law (Nomos 24)*, New York, New York University Press, 323 p.

Polinsky, A. Mitchell (1989), *An Introduction to Law and Economics*, Boston, Little Brown.

Posner, Richard A. (1979a), 'Utilitarianism, Economics, and Legal Theory', **8** *Journal of Legal Studies*, 103-140.

Posner, Richard A. (1979b), 'Some Uses and Abuses of Economics in Law', **46** *University of Chicago Law Review*, 281-306.

Posner, Richard A. (1980a), 'The Ethical and Political Basis of the Efficiency Norm in Common Law Adjudication', **8** *Hofstra Law Review*, 487-507.

Posner, Richard A. (1980b), 'The Value of Wealth: A Comment on Dworkin and Kronman', **9** *Journal of Legal Studies*, 243-252.

Posner, Richard A. (1981a), *The Economics of Justice*, Cambridge, MA, Harvard University Press, 415 p.

Posner, Richard A. (1981b), 'The Concept of Corrective Justice in Recent Theories of Tort Law', **10** *Journal of Legal Studies*, 187-206.

Posner, Richard A. (1984), 'Wealth Maximization and Judicial Decision-Making', **4** *International Review of Law and Economics*, 131-135.

Posner, Richard A. (1985), 'Wealth Maximization Revisited', **2** *Notre Dame Journal of Law, Ethics and Public Policy*, 1378-1401.

Posner, Richard A. (1986), 'The Ethical Significance of Free Choice: A Reply to Professor West', **99** *Harvard Law Review*, 1431-1448.

Posner, Richard A. (1988), 'Comment (on Donohue)', **22** *Law and Society Review*, 927-929.

Posner, Richard A. (1989), 'On Theory and Practice: Reply to "Richard Posner's Praxis"', **49** *Ohio State Law Journal*, 1077-1084.

Posner, Richard A. (1990a), 'Rebuttal to Malloy', **24** *Valparaiso University Law Review*, 183-184.

Posner, Richard A. (1990b), 'Law and Economics', **24** *Valparaiso University Law Review*, 163-173.

Posner Richard A. (1992), *Sex and Reason*, Cambridge, MA, Harvard University Press.

Posner Richard A. (1998), *Economic Analysis of Law* (5th edn), New York, Aspen Publishers, Inc.

Priest, George J. (1977), 'The Common Law Process and the Selection of Efficient Legal Rules', **6** *Journal of Legal Studies*, 65-82.

Radin, Margaret J. (1982), 'Property and Personhood', **34** *Stanford Law Review*, 957 ff.

Radin, Margaret Jane (1987), 'Market-Inalienability', **100** *Harvard Law Review*, 1849-1937.

Radin, Margaret J. (1989), 'Justice and the Market Domain', in Chapman, John W. and Pennock, J. Roland (eds), *NOMOS XXXI: Markets and Justice*, New York, New York University Press, 165-197.

Raes, Koen (1988), 'Rechtstheorie als Ideologiekritiek (Legal Theory as Ideological Criticism)', in Kamstra, O.W.M. et al. (eds), *Nederlandsche Rechtswetenschap*, Zwolle, Tjeenk Willink, 283-298.

Raes, Koen (1990), 'Het Recht van de Schaarste (The Law of Scarcety)', **16** *Recht en Kritiek*, 380-394.

Rahmsdorf, Detlev W. (1987), 'Ökonomische Analyse des Rechts, Utilitarismus und die Klassische Deutsche Philosophie (Economic Analysis of Law, Utilitarianism and the Classical German Philosophy)', **18** *Rechtstheorie*, 487-501.

Rahmsdorf, Detlev W. and Schäfer, Hans-Bernd (eds) (1988), *Ethische Fragen der Wirtschaftspolitik und des Rechts* (Ethical Questions of Political Economics and Law), Berlin, Dietrich-Reimer-Verlag, 219 p.

Raiteri, Monica (1988), 'Giustizia Distributiva e Funzione Giudiziaria: Qualche Osservazione nella Prospettiva della Analisi Economica del Diritto (Distributive Justice and the Judicial Function, Some Observations form the Viewpoint of the Economic Analysis of Law)', *Materiali per una Storia della Cultura Giuridica*, 209-228.

Rakoff, Todd D. (1996), 'Too Many Theories', **94** *Michigan Law Review*, 1799-1809.

Rawls, John (1971), *A Theory of Justice*, Cambridge, MA, Harvard University Press.

Reich, Charles A. (1996), 'Property Law and the New Economic Order: A Betrayal of Middle Americans and the Poor', **71** *Chicago-Kent Law Review*, 817-823.

Reich, Robert B. (1983), *The Next American Frontier*, New York, Times Books.

Reich, Robert B. (1991), *The Work of Nations: Preparing Ourselves for 21st Century Capitalism*, New York, Alfred A. Knopf.

Riley, Jonathan (1989), 'Justice under Capitalism', in Chapman, John W. and Pennock, J. Roland (eds), *NOMOS XXXI: Markets and Justice*, New York, New York University Press, 122-162.

Rizzo, Mario J. (1980), 'The Mirage of Efficiency', **8** *Hofstra Law Review*, 641-658.

Rorty, Richard (1979), *Philosophy and the Mirror of Nature*, Princeton, Princeton University Press.

Rose-Ackerman, Susan (1985), 'Inalienability and the Theory of Property Rights', **85** *Columbia Law Review*, 931-969.

Rose-Ackerman, Susan (1989), 'Law and Economics: Paradigm, Politics, or Philosophy', in Mercuro, Nicholas (ed.), *Law and Economics*, Boston, Kluwer Academic Publishers, 233-258.

Rose-Ackerman, Susan (1992), *Rethinking the Progressive Agenda: The Reform of the American Regulatory State*, New York, NY, Free Press.

Rubin, Paul H. (1977), 'Why is the Common Law Efficient?', **6** *Journal of Legal Studies*, 51-63.

Rubin, Paul H. and Keenan, Donald C. (1985), 'Limits of the Equity-Efficiency Tradeoff', *Public Choice*, 425-436.

Sager, Lawrence G. (1980), 'Pareto Superiority, Consent, and Justice', **8** *Hofstra Law Review*, 913-937.

Samuels, Warren J. (1981), 'Maximization of Wealth as Justice: An Essay on Posnerian Law and Economics as Policy Analysis', **60** *Texas Law Review*, 147-172.

Samuels, Warren J. (1992), 'The Persuasive Proposition, 'What is, is and Ought to be': A Critique', in Millberg, William S. (ed.), *The Megacorp and Macrodynamics: Essays in Memory of Alfred Eichner*, New York, Armonk, M.E. Sharpe, 273-285.

Samuelson, Paul A. (1976), *Economics*, New York, McGraw-Hill.

Schäfer, Hans-Bernd (1989), 'Allokationseffizienz als Grundprinzip des Zivilrechts (Allocative Efficiency as Basic Principle of Civil Law)', in Ott, Claus and Schäfer, Hans-Bernd (eds), *Allekationseffizienz in der Rechtsordnung*, Berlin, Springer, 1-24.

Schlag, Pierre (1986), 'An Appreciative Comment on Coase's the Problem of Social Cost: A View from the Left', **1986** *Wisconsin Law Review*, 919-962.

Schlicht, Ekkehart (1990), 'Individuelles Bestreben und Kulturelles Gefüge (Individual Striving in the Cultural Context)', in Weise, Peter (ed.), *Ökonomie und Gesellschaft Jahrbuch 8, Individuelles Verhalten und kollektive Phänomene*, Frankfurt am, Main, Campus, 112-127.

Schlicht, Ekkehart (1994), 'Die Emotive und die Kognitive Gerechtigkeitsauffassung (The Emotive and the Cognitive View of Justice)', **2** *Ökonomie und Gesellschaft*, 141-154.

Schmalbeck, Richard L. (1983), 'The Justice of Economics: An Analysis of Wealth Maximization as a Normative Goal', **83** *Columbia Law Review*, 488-525.

Schmid, A. Allan (1989), 'Law and Economics: An Institutional Perspective', in Mercuro, Nicholas (ed.), *Law and Economics*, Boston, Kluwer Academic Publishers, 57-85.

Schultz, Theodore W. (1981), *Investing in People: The Economics of Population Quality*, Berkeley, University of California Press.

Schwartz, Gary T. (1979), 'Economics, Wealth Distribution and Justice', *Wisconsin Law Review*, 799-813.

Schwartz, Gary T. (1981), 'The Vitality of Negligence and the Ethics of Strict Liability', **15** *Georgia Law Review*, 963-1004. Reprinted in Rabin, Robert L. (ed.) (1983), *Perspectives on Tort Law*, Boston, Little Brown, 71-79.

Scitovsky, Tibor (1941), 'A Note on Welfare Propositions in Economics', **9** *Review of Economic Studies*, 77-88.

Seidenfeld, Mark (1996), *Microeconomic Predicates to Law and Economics*, Cincinnati, OH, Anderson Publishing.

Seidl, Christian (1997), 'Das Wesen liberaler Rechte (On the Essence of Liberal Rights)', in Ott, Claus and Schäfer, Hans-Bernd (eds), *Ökonomische Analyse des Rechts, Fünftes Travemünder Symposium zur Analyse des Rechts*, Berlin, Springer.

Seita, Alex Y. (1989), 'Common Myths in the Economic Analysis of Law', *Brigham Young University Law Review*, 993-1112.

Sen, Amartya K. (1970), *Collective Choice and Social Welfare*, San Francisco, Holden-Day.

Sen, Amartya K. (1977), 'Rational Fools: A Critique of the Behavioral Foundations of Economic Theory', **6** *Philosophy and Public Affairs*, 317-344.

Sen, Amartya K. (1979), 'Personal Utilities and Public Judgments: Or What's Wrong with Welfare Economics?', **89** *Economics Journal*, 537-558.

Spitzer, Matthew L. and Hoffman, Elizabeth (1980), 'A Reply to Consumption Theory, Production Theory and Ideology in the Coase Theorem', **53** *Southern California Law Review*, 1187-1223.

Steiner, J.M. (1976), 'Economics, Morality and the Law of Torts', **26** *University of Toronto Law Journal*, 227-252.

Strowel, Alain (1987), 'Utilitarisme et Approche Economique dans la Théorie du Droit. Autour de Bentham et de Posner (Utilitarianism and Economic Approach in Legal Theory. On Bentham and Posner)', **18** *Revue Interdisciplinaire d'Etudes Juridiques*, 1-45.

Sunstein, Cass R. (1989), 'Disrupting Voluntary Transactions', in Chapman, John W. and Pennock, J. Roland (eds), *NOMOS XXXI: Markets and Justice*, New York, New York University Press, 279-302.

Symposium (1980), 'Symposium on Efficiency as a Legal Concern', **8** *Hofstra Law Review*, 485-972.

Symposium (1996a), 'Elizabeth Anderson's Value in Ethics and Economics', **106** *Ethics*.

Symposium (1996b), 'Law, Economics, and Norms', **144** *University of Pennsylvania Law Review*.

Symposium (1998), 'Problems of Market Liberalism', **15** *Social Philosophy & Policy*.

Thompson, Michael et al. (1990), *Cultural Theory*, Boulder, CO, Westview Press.

Thurow, L. (1970), 'Equity vs. Efficiency in Law Enforcement', **18** *Public Policy*, 451-459.

Toulmin, Stephen (1990), *Cosmopolis: The Hidden Agenda of Modernity*, Chicago, University of Chicago Press.

Trebilcock, Michael J. (1993), *The Limits of Freedom of Contract*, Cambridge, Cambridge University Press.

Tribe, Laurence H. (1985), 'Constitutional Calculus: Equal Justice or Economic Efficiency', **98** *Harvard Law Review*, 592-621.

Trimarchi, Pietro (1970), 'Sul Significato Economico dei Criteri di Responsabilità Contrattuale (Economic Meaning of Contract-Liability Criteria)', *Rivista Trimestrale di Diritto e Procedura Civile*, 512-531.

Tsibris, Michalis R. (1989), 'Oikonomike Analyse tou Dikaiou: To Epomeno Vema (Economic Analysis of Law: The Next Step)', **37** *Nomiko Vema*, 574-586.

Tullock, Gordon (1971), *The Logic of the Law*, New York, Basic Books.

Tullock, Gordon (1980), 'Two Kinds of Legal Efficiency', **8** *Hofstra Law Review*, 659 ff.

Tullock, Gordon (1982), 'Welfare and the Law', **2** *International Review of Law and Economics*, 151-163.

Unger, Roberto Mangabeira (1976), *Law in Modern Society: Toward a Criticism of Social Theory*, New York, NY, Free Press.

Unger, Roberto Mangabeira (1984), *Passion: An Essay on Personality*, New York, NY, Free Press.

Unger, Roberto Mangabeira (1986), *The Critical Legal Studies Movement*, Cambridge, MA, Harvard University Press.

Van Manen, Niels F. (1994), 'Eigenbelang, Chaos en Sociale Orde (Self-interest, Chaos and Social Order)', in Raes, Koen and Willekens, H. (eds), *Economische Verklaringen van het Recht*, Den Haag, VUGA, 75-92.

Varat, Jonathan D. (1986), 'Review Essay: Economic Ideology and the Federal Judicial Task (Review of the Federal Courts: Crisis and Reform by Richard A. Posner)', **74** *California Law Review*, 649-674.

Veblen, Thorstein (1899), *The Theory of the Leisure Class*, New York, MacMillan.

Veljanovski, Cento G. (1981), 'The Economic Theory of Tort Liability - Toward a Corrective Justice Approach', in Burrows, Paul and Veljanovski, Cento G. (eds), *The Economic Approach to Law*, London, Butterworths, 125-150.

Veljanovski, Cento G. (1981), 'Wealth Maximization, Law and Ethics - on the Limits of Economic Efficiency', **1** *International Review of Law and Economics*, 5-28.

Waldron, Jeremy (1990), 'Criticizing the Economic Analysis of Law (Book Review of Jules L. Coleman, Markets, Morals, and the Law)', **99** *Yale Law Journal*, 1441-1471.

Weinrib, Ernest J. (1980), 'Utilitarianism, Economics and Legal Theory', **30** *University of Toronto Law Journal*, 307-332.

Weise, Peter and Eger, Thomas (1990), 'Normen als Gesellschaftliche Ordner (Norms as Social Co-ordination Parameters)', **8** *Ökonomie und Gesellschaft*, 65-111.

White, Barbara (1987a), 'Coase and the Courts: Economics for the Common Man', **72** *Iowa Law Review*, 577-635.

White, James Boyd (1987b), 'Economics and Law: Two Cultures in Tension (Alumni Distinguished Lecture in Jurisprudence)', **54** *Tennessee Law Review*, 161-202.

Wittman, Donald A. (1979), 'A Diagrammatic Expositon of Justice', *Theory and Decision*, 207-237.

Wittman, Donald A. (1982), 'Efficient Rules in Highway Safety and Sports Activity', **72** *American Economic Review*, 78-90.

Wu, Ho-Mou and Huang, Peter H. (1994), 'More Order without More Law: A Theory of Social Norms and Organizational Cultures', **10** *Journal of Law, Economics, and Organization*, 390-406.

Zwier, Paul J. (1985), 'The Consequentialist/Nonconsequentialist Ethical Distinction: A Tool for the Formal Appraisal of Traditional Negligence and Economic Tort Analysis', **26** *Boston College Law Review*, 905-944.

0900
GENERAL STRUCTURE OF THE LAW

Donald Wittman
Department of Economics, University of California at Santa Cruz

Abstract

Economic theory can provide insight into the general structure of the law and the organization of topics in this encyclopedia. After arguing that all of law is contract law, I show how economics can be used to explain the choice between criminal law and tort law, liability rules and property rights, prior regulation and post liability, restitution and torts, and courts and legislatures.
JEL classification: K1
Keywords: Structure, Torts, Contracts, Criminal Law, Property Rules, Liability Rules

1. Introduction

Economic theory has a number of core concepts - supply and demand, perfect competition versus monopoly, and high and low transaction costs - among others. All of these concepts and the results derived from them can generate insight into the legal system. The question at hand is whether the theoretical distinctions can also explain the broad structure of the law. That is, can economic analysis provide a partial explanation for the organization of topics in the *Encyclopedia of Law and Economics* and the organization of legal subjects, more generally? For example, is there an economic explanation for invoking criminal sanctions in addition to civil penalties? Is there an economic explanation for the choice between property rights and liability rules? Do contract and constitutional law involve the same underlying theoretical apparatus or do they employ different theoretical constructs? The same can be asked with regard to torts and contracts, and other categorizations.

2. All of Law is Contract Law

The first and possibly the best response is that all areas of the law are guided by the same principle - to create efficient outcomes. An outcome is Pareto efficient if one person cannot be made better off without making someone worse off (we will not deal with the distinction between wealth maximization and the Pareto principle here). A useful way of conceiving such a result is to suppose that the parties write an optimal contract. In this way, contract law, torts and restitution can be viewed as different manifestations of contract law. For example, in automobile accidents, the law implicitly asks what kind of contract would have been drawn up between the victim and the injurer before the accident happened. The negligence standard finds a person negligent if she did not undertake cost effective preventive procedures. The hypothetical contract suggests that each party would agree to be non-negligent. In the same way, restitution can be seen as contract law for affirmative obligations between parties who otherwise are not transacting with each other.

The analysis can be extended to other areas. As a city grows, it is inefficient to allow pre-existing quarries, feedlots and the like to remain. To use the contract analogy, if a contract had been written thirty years earlier, the feedlot and the city's residents would have agreed to shut down the feedlot when the city expanded. In the United States, such nuisances can be shut down via a civil action or under a zoning regulation. Either way the nuisance owner is not compensated - the court's interpretation of the Constitution does not consider such a regulation a taking (see *Boehm v. Philadelphia*, 1915) nor do the courts require the plaintiffs to compensate the nuisance maker for moving costs (see *Ensign v. Walls, 1948*). Despite their greatly different genealogy, these two areas of law treat the situation in a similar way. And despite the fact that property law was developed before contract law, the concept of contracts enlightens our understanding of the limits of property.

Depending on one's taste, one can stretch the contract analogy still further. During the enlightenment, the concept of a social contract was very popular (see Rousseau) and this concept has been updated in the more recent past to explain constitutional theory (see the chapters in the encyclopedia devoted to this topic).

Economics as a discipline is a great generalizer that tends to cross subject headings. Demand curves are drawn for cars, food and marriage. Likewise in the law, an economic concept can be used in seemingly unrelated areas. For example, if party X acts inefficiently, it makes economic sense that a second party, Y, optimally mitigates the damages that might arise. For example, if a plumber installs a bathtub drain improperly so that bath water leaks into the ceiling below, economic efficiency dictates that the homeowner stops using the bathtub once the problem is discovered. The cost of not taking a bath is less than the benefit of not having the ceiling collapse. This is known as 'mitigation of damages' in contract law. Similarly, it makes no economic sense for a farmer to plant a crop in the presence of sulfur fumes from a nearby factory since sulfur fumes kill crops. Therefore the farmer will not be compensated for the cost of planting the crop, but only for the lost profits in not being able to plant the crop in the first place (*United Verde Extension Mining Co. v. Ralston*, 1931 - see Wittman, 1981). This is known as the doctrine of 'avoidable consequences' in tort law. Finally, in continental law, a passerby is required to rescue a person lying unconscious on a railroad track if the cost of rescue is trivial. Again, this is just mitigation of damages in a different disguise. So three totally different areas of law are guided by the same economic reasoning.

Having first argued that, at some fundamental level, economic theory provides a unified explanation of the law and then giving an example of an economic concept that is applied to seemingly unrelated legal subjects, I will now try to argue that economic theory can also provide an explanation for the differential structure of the law. Of necessity, the distinctions will be more in shades of gray rather than in black and white.

3. Property Rights, Liability Rules and Communal Rights: The Role of Transaction Costs

Transaction costs in its many guises is often the key to explaining structural differences in the law. Consider the choice between protecting an entitlement via a property right (voluntary transfer) and a liability rule (compensated involuntary transfer). If a state wants to build a highway from A to B, all landowners along the proposed highway have monopoly positions and each will try to extract all the surplus value for herself. Ordinary market mechanism are not viable (that is, they have extremely high transaction costs) in this case. So the state employs eminent domain (a type of liability rule). As another example, drivers do not negotiate with other drivers and pedestrians for the right to put these other people in danger - the transaction costs would be too high. Instead, they pay ex post for any involuntary transfer (see Demsetz, 1972, for an extended argument). On the other side, where market transaction costs are low, entitlements tend to be protected by a property right - I cannot cut down my neighbor's cherry tree and, if I threaten to do so, my neighbor can get an injunction to prevent such an action. Of course, if I pay him enough, he may let me engage in my obsession.

The standard explanation for not using a liability rule in this case is that it is an imperfect measure of relative value and shifts the costs of decision making onto third parties (courts). Kaplow and Shavell (1996) have argued that this explanation is flawed. Under the shadow of a court-imposed liability rule, the parties can negotiate an outcome that does reflect higher value. For example, if the courts say that the damage to my neighbor is only \$1,000 when I cut down his tree when in fact it is worth \$2,000 to him not having his tree cut down, then he will be willing to bribe me $500 not to cut down the tree and I will accept the bribe if cutting cherry trees is worth only $1,200 to me (since cutting it down will mean a loss of the $500 bribe plus the court imposed liability of $1,000).

But Kaplow and Shavell's argument ignores transaction costs. To illustrate, we consider the entitlement structure for movie stars. Paul Newman is both a movie star and an entrepreneur (he has his own line of spaghetti sauce and salad dressing). Paul Newman has the property right to use photographs of himself or his name in advertising, and he can sell that right if it maximizes the return on his human capital. In this way, sales are value maximizing. However, such a property right system involves some exchange costs. Paul Newman must be contacted and a price must be negotiated. These costs are not trivial, yet they are unlikely to be very large since this is not a case of bilateral monopoly (as hard as it is to believe, there are substitutes for Paul Newman, perhaps Tom Cruise). Furthermore only a few people might be involved.

If there were a communal right to Paul Newman's name in advertising, then his name would be overused. 'Paul Newman Bail Bonds' might bring in increased profits to the bail bondsman, but decrease the overall profits of products with Newman's name). Turning this communal right into Paul Newman's property right would be extremely expensive. Every time he bought out one person, another person would arise to make use of his name or picture. So the right would likely remain a communal right, with overuse but no exchange costs. If Paul Newman could buy back the rights, the transaction costs would be very high - he would have to buy the right from many to stop them from using his name (this should be compared to the case were Paul Newman is given the right and then sells it to a few).

When the law gives Paul Newman the property right to his name for advertising, even if the particular allocation is incorrect, it is easily remedied (the other party will just buy the right to Paul Newman's name if it is worth more to the other party than to Paul Newman). When Paul Newman's entitlement to use his name for advertising purposes is only protected by a liability rule, the court's assessment of the damage to Paul Newman may be off. If the court overestimates the cost, essentially Newman's entitlement to his own name is protected by a property right; if the court significantly underestimates the damage, then his entitlement is virtually a communal right. It is very hard to remedy such a mistake, and if it is corrected, very high transaction costs are involved as the actor must buy back the right from numerous contenders. Furthermore, the negotiated price depends on the court's valuation or expected valuation. This adds a needless level of cost and/or uncertainty. So transaction costs are a key to the choice between a property right and a liability rule.

Calabresi and Melamed (1972) provided the first economic explanation for the choice between property rules and liability rules. Since then, there has been a large literature on the subject. For alternative explanations see Polinsky and Shavell (1984) who emphasizes strategic bargaining in the absence of perfect information and Krier and Schwab (1995) who emphasize court misinformation. See Ayres and Talley (1995) who argue that liabilty rules may facilitate bargaining.

4. Taxes versus Quantity Regulation versus Liability Rules: The Role of Imperfect Information

This topic covers some of the same territory as the previous section but under the assumption that high transaction costs prevent negotiation between the two sides.

Consider the case where a factory pollutes the air and the efficient outcome is that the factory reduces the pollution rather than the neighbors undertake damage prevention. If there is perfect information, pollution taxes, quantity restrictions and liability for the damage can all be set to yield the same efficient outcome. We employ the standard diagram where smoke is on the horizontal axis and dollars are on the vertical axis (see Figure 1). Then the marginal cost of increased smoke to the neighbors is increasing and the marginal benefit to the firm of increased smoke is decreasing (since the marginal cost of smoke abatement rises). The optimal amount of pollution is where these two curves intersect. Setting a pollution tax (or per unit of smoke liability rule) equal to t, the dollar value at the intersection of the marginal cost and benefit curves, will encourage the factory to produce until the tax equals the marginal benefit; that is, the factory will produce the optimal amount, s^*. Similarly, a regulation that the factory produce no more than the optimal amount of smoke, s^*, will again result in the optimal amount of smoke. If the factory is liable (either to the victims or to the government) for the area under the marginal cost of smoke curve, it will again choose the optimal amount of smoke damage.

When there is imperfect information, the various methods need not result in the same outcome (see Figure 2).

Figure 1

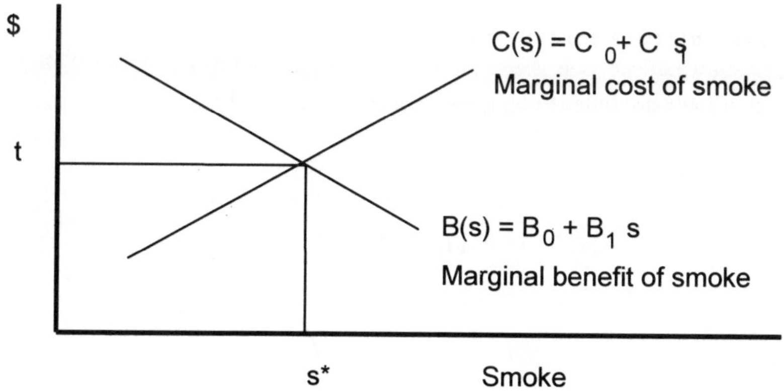

Assume that the marginal cost of smoke is $C(s) = C_0 + C_1 s + u$ and that the marginal benefit of smoke is $B(s) = B_0 + B_1 s + v$, where u and v are independently and symmetrically distributed random variables with mean zero. u and v are observed by the pollutee and the polluter, respectively, but not by anyone else, including the courts or other government agencies. Under quantity regulation, the level of smoke is set where the *expected* marginal benefit from smoke abatement equals the expected marginal cost. This level is denoted by $\bar{s}$. Thus $C_0 + C_1 \bar{s} = B_0 + B_1 \bar{s}$, or

$$\bar{s} = (B_0 - C_0) / (C_1 - B_1)$$

The optimal level of smoke is where actual marginal benefit equals actual marginal cost. This level is denoted by s^*. Thus $C_0 + C_1 s^* + u = B_0 + B_1 s^* + v$, or

$$s^* = (B_0 - C_0 + v - u) / (C_1 - B_1).$$

Quantity regulation causes deadweight losses whenever s* is not equal to $\bar{s}$ or v is not equal to u. The deadweight loss triangle is

$$0.5 \,|\, [s^* - \bar{s}]\, [B(\bar{s}) - C(\bar{s})] \,|$$

$$= |\, [0.5\, (v - u) / (C_1 - B_1)]\ [B_0 + B_1 \bar{s} + v - C_0 - C_1 \bar{s} - u] \,|$$

$$= | [0.5 (v - u) / (C_1 - B_1)] [B_0 + B_1 (B_0 - C_0) / (C_1 - B_1) + v - C_0 - C_1 (B_0 - C_0) / (C_1 - B_1) - u]|$$

$$= | 0.5 [(v - u) / (C_1 - B_1)] (v - u) |$$

Since u and v are independent, the expected deadweight cost is

$$0.5 (\sigma_v^2 + \sigma_u^2) / (C_1 - B_1).$$

Figure 2

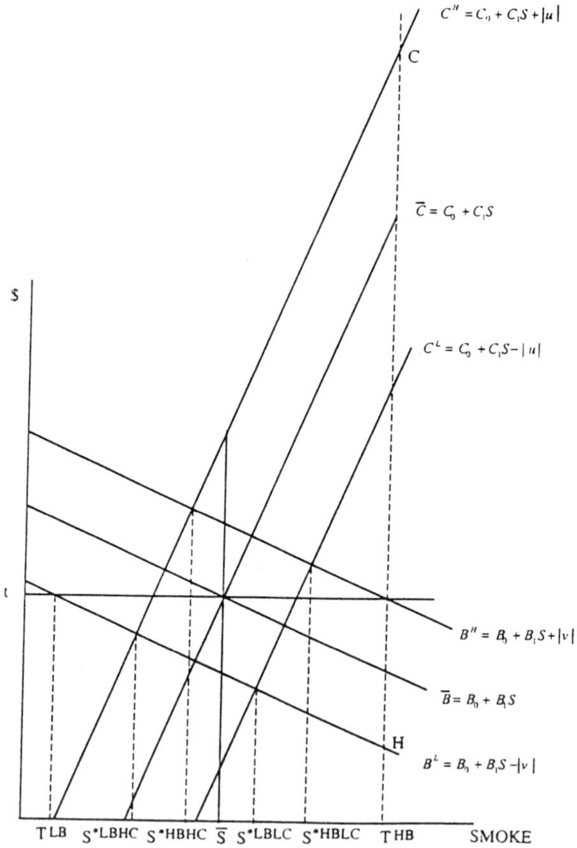

The Pigovian or pollution tax, t, is the level needed to induce efficient smoke production for the *expected* marginal benefit and cost

That is, $t = C_0 + C_1 \bar{s} = B_0 + B_1 \bar{s} = B_0 + B_1(B_0 - C_0) / (C_1 - B_1)$.

The polluter choose a level of output, s', where

$B_0 + B_1 s' + v = t = B_0 + B_1(B_0 - C_0) / (C_1 - B_1)$.

Equivalently,

$s' = (B_0 - C_0) / (C_1 - B_1) - v / B_1$

The deadweight loss triangle is

$0.5 \mid (s^* - s') [B(s') - C(s')] \mid$

$= 0.5 \mid [(v - u) / (C_1 - B_1) + v / B_1] (B_0 + B_1 s' + v - C_0 - C_1 s' - u) \mid$

$= 0.5 \mid [(v - u) / (C_1 - B_1) + v / B_1] [(C_1 / B_1) v - u] \mid$

$= 0.5 \mid [B_1 (v - u) + v (C_1 - B_1)] [(C_1 / B_1) v - u] / [(C_1 - B_1) (B_1)] \mid$

So the expected deadweight loss of the Pigovian tax is

$0.5 [(C_1^2 / B_1^2) \sigma_v^2 + \sigma_u^2] / (C_1 - B_1)$.

Hence the expected deadweight cost of a pollution tax to a quantity regulation is:

$[(C_1^2 / B_1^2) + \sigma_v^2 \sigma_u^2] / (\sigma_v^2 + \sigma_u^2)$

Quantity regulation is preferred to a pollution tax if and only if the cost curve is more elastic than the benefit curve ($\mid B_1 \mid < \mid C_1 \mid$). When $\mid B_1 \mid < \mid C_1 \mid$, the Pigovian tax works poorly because the marginal cost to the firm, t, is horizontal while the marginal cost to society is relatively vertical. Under regulation, the smoke constraint can be viewed as a vertical marginal cost curve to the firm which more nearly approximates the relatively vertical social marginal cost.

In contrast, strict liability (based on the expected marginal cost curve) is superior to the previous methods regardless of the slopes of the coefficients or the relative size of the error terms. Intuitively, strict liability is preferred because the marginal cost curve to the firm has the same slope as the marginal cost curve to society, in contrast to the Pigovian tax (which is horizontal) and the quantity regulation (which is implicitly vertical). More formally, the ratio of deadweight losses under a regulation relative to the deadweight losses under a liability rule is $1 + (\sigma_v^2 / \sigma_u^2)$ and the ratio of deadweight losses under a Pigovian tax relative to the deadweight losses under a liability rule is $(1 + C_1^2 \sigma_v^2 / B_1^2 \sigma_u^2)$

Furthermore, the liability rule alternative has lower information costs than either of the other two methods. The liability rule requires that the authority inform the polluter of two parameters C_0 and C_1 whereas quantity regulation and the effluent tax require only one parameter, s or t, respectively. Nevertheless, less information is needed to determine both C_0 and C_1 than is needed to determine s or t. Determining C_0 and C_1 requires surveying only a group of victims of pollution, while determining either s or t requires surveying groups of victims and polluters. For a more detailed discussion see White and Wittman (1983a).

Of course this discussion has not considered other transaction costs. For example, a system of regulation, once in place, requires relatively low court costs in comparison to strict liability for pollution (since the optimal amount of pollution is greater than zero). Although negligence liability has fewer court cases than strict liability, it more nearly approximates a quantity regulation in its effect.

5. Contracts, Specificatio, Contrat versus Tort, Delict, Responsibilite Civile: The Role of Information Transmission

Common law, Roman law and civil law distinguish between two groups (contracts, specificatio, contrat) and (tort, delict, responsibilite civile). These groups roughly correspond to low and high transaction cost situations. In contracts the parties are already transacting with each other; in many tort situations the parties first meet after the damage. But does the nature of the rules differ between these two groupings? A key difference may be the role of information transmission.

Contract law is often concerned with promoting efficient information exchange. *Hadley v. Baxendale* (1854) is the defining case. When the risk of loss is known to only one party to the contract, then the other party is not liable for the loss if it occurs. This creates the right incentives for the knowledgeable party to inform the other when it is cost effective for the other party to undertake additional precaution.

There are many applications of the basic principle. In trade between two parties involving a standard item, if the seller has superior information about the product, it is often economically efficient to have the seller inform the buyer. Even if it is not a standard product, such as selling a home, if the information can be obtained cheaply by the seller (say by living in the house), then it is economically efficient for the seller to transmit this information to the buyer rather than having potential buyers undertake repeated and costly inspections. Hence in many jurisdictions, home sellers are required to state what items are in disrepair (however, they are not required to state whether their neighbor's house will be up for sale in few weeks). Also, all easements on the property are required to be recorded and on the deed.

On the other side, there are many situations where such information transmission is not required. A geologist is not required by law to tell the present owner of the land that the land is likely to have significant oil deposits. To require such a disclosure would reduce the returns to specialized knowledge regarding oil discovery and ultimately result in a suboptimal amount of oil exploration. Thus in contracts, product liability, and real estate much of the law is devoted to determining the optimal amount of information transmission and then designing rules to promote that outcome.

In contrast, the issue of optimal information transmission is likely to be irrelevant for those tort cases involving harm between people who otherwise would have little contact (that is, for high transaction cost cases). And in such situations, the injurer is liable even for damages that are unforeseen. For example, if a drunk driver smashes into a person with an eggshell skull and as a consequence the victim suffers much greater damage than would ordinarily be the case, the drunk driver is still liable for the additional damage. It would not have helped if the victim carried around a big sign stating that he was especially susceptible to head injuries, and in general carrying around such a sign would not be cost effective. Furthermore, if drunk drivers were liable for less than the actual harm to eggshell skulls, then economic efficiency would require that drunk drivers be liable for more than the actual harm to 'rock skulls'.

However, the issue of information transmission is not entirely absent from high transaction cost situations. Automobiles are required to have brake lights, and in the United States mercaptane is added to natural gas (in this way, people in the vicinity of a natural gas pipe line leak can be warned of the danger by the smell).

Contract and torts differ in another important way. Contracts are written ex ante and, when possible, courts tend to rely on the written document rather than engage in their own cost-benefit analysis. The parties to the contact have a comparative advantage in determining the optimal contract. As a consequence, courts tend to hold the breacher strictly liable for the foreseeable damages rather than the courts determining on their own whether the breacher was negligent (of course, one might argue that the word breach is often synonymous with the word negligent). In contrast, the implicit contract in torts is determined by the courts ex post. As a result, the negligence rule is more likely to be invoked as the courts have to determine the efficient outcome on their own. See Posner (1992, Chapter 6) for further arguments along this line.

6. Crimes versus Torts: The Role of Limited Liability

The tort system deals with harms, so why do need a separate system for crimes? For example, why is assault a crime in addition to being a tort? Posner (1985, 1992, Chapter 7) has a well thought-out explanation for needing criminal law in addition to civil law. Essentially, criminals are often judgment proof (their wealth cannot cover their debts) and therefore the tort system is inadequate.

Most crimes involve a coerced transfer in the context of low transaction costs. The person who was shot in a robbery or gave up her wallet to avoid being shot was not a volunteer to the transaction. In order to prevent the conversion of a property right into a liability rule, a punitive damage should be imposed on the perpetrator beyond the payment for the actual harm, which itself may be very high (people do not like to be subjected to physical violence). But unlike breach of contract and many other types of torts, it is often hard to detect the perpetrator of a crime. If the criminal is not always caught, the price to be paid has to be multiplied by 1 over the probability of being punished. Also the criminal should pay for the cost of detection. This raises the price of the crime for those who are actually caught still higher. The resulting high price of a crime means that the criminal is often judgment proof. Because the person is judgment proof the victim of the crime or her heirs will not have sufficient incentive to find the criminal and bring him to court and the criminal will not be sufficiently deterred by the tort system. In turn, this means that people may undertake self-protection (bodyguards, extra locks, and so on) to avoid being robbed because they know they will not be sufficiently compensated if they are robbed. So the criminal should be liable not only for the robberies committed but also for the cost of prevention that others undertook to prevent the robbery from occurring (but see Kermit and

Lott, 1995, who argue to the contrary). This raises the optimal punishment still further beyond the capacity of the tort system

So the robber needs a non-monetary punishment such as a prison sentence to adequately deter and/or to physically restrain if deterrence is not sufficient. Hence the state enters into the equation. Unlike ordinary torts where the judgment itself involves no social cost but merely a transfer from one party to another, incarceration involves significant costs. So optimal punishment must take this into account.

It should be recognized that the judgment-proof explanation is not the whole story. Criminals may be jailed for petty crimes even when they are wealthy, wealthy anti-trust defendants may be both prosecuted for their crimes and sued for their torts, and there are victimless crimes that are not torts. Also the role of intention has not been fully analyzed. See Klevorick (1985a, 1985b) and Fletcher (1985) for further arguments against the economic model.

7. Prior Regulation versus Post Liability: The Role of Monitoring and Detection Costs

The legal system sometimes regulates the inputs and at other times charges for the output. For example, a person can be fined for drunk driving even in the absence of an accident and/or be found liable for the damage when there is an accident. To the economist, but perhaps not to the general public, the question is why society does not rely solely on sanctioning the output. Fining inputs involves monitoring and distortion costs. Since inputs only increase the likelihood of an accident, there are many more occurrences of the former than the latter. Hence, input monitoring is generally more expensive than output monitoring. Also there are many inputs into the production of the output. Imposing fines for only a few of the inputs will distort the choice set towards those activities that cannot be monitored.

There are several answers to the puzzle. A person may not be sufficiently deterred if they are judgment proof. The judgment-proof problem is much less likely to occur if inputs are sanctioned. The cost of input monitoring can be significantly reduced if there are only random checks. Also, it is sometimes easier to observe inputs than outputs. There may not be other witnesses to the scene of the accident besides those that were involved. Under such circumstances, it may be hard to disentangle the truth. Thus it may make more sense to monitor the inputs, such as drunk driving. See Wittman (1977) and Shavell (1984b) for more detailed arguments.

Not all people are adequately deterred by the threat of punishment for the outcome so they are prevented from further inputs. Drunk drivers sometimes lose their licenses and are put in jail if they continue to drive under the influence. Private parties can obtain injunctions rather than suing ex post for the resulting harm. Especially in criminal law, inputs are subject to sanction. If X shot at Y and missed, the law does not wait until X has killed Y before doing something about it. Of course, the punishment of attempts has to be less than the punishment for completions; otherwise the person would have more incentive to complete. See Posner (1992) for a more thorough exposition.

Another line of argument considers the defensive action by other parties. Others may undertake economically justified counter-measures to the inappropriate input so that the likelihood of an accident is significantly reduced. Such measures are costly and should be imposed on the party acting inappropriately even if there is no accident. For example, others may swerve out of the way or not even drive in the first place in order to avoid drunk drivers. Such defensive activity by others is costly and should be paid for by the drunk driver even though there was no accident. Hence there are fines for drunk driving, speeding, and so on. For a more thorough argument see Wittman (1981).

If both potential injurers and their victims are risk averse, then risk sharing may be optimal. A potentially fruitful line of research is to investigate how a division between input and output monitoring might improve risk allocation. This would go beyond the standard principal-agent models.

The choice of monitoring technology is applicable to goods as well as bads. In comparison to their counterparts in stores, the income of traveling salesmen are based more on sales than hours on the job. Paying household help by the hour is easier than calculating the value of all of the individual services which may vary from week to week. On the other side, hiring someone to come in and just clean your rugs (or windows) is based on the output.

Input and output monitoring need not be a choice between one or the other. Sometimes it makes sense to do both. But there is always a question of how much input monitoring is necessary - one might require pasteurization but not specify the shape of the bottle in which the milk is sold.

8. Torts versus Restitution: The Role of Court Transaction Costs

Torts compensate for non-negotiated harms while restitution compensates for non-negotiated benefits (Levmore, 1985).

In the absence of transaction costs, the distinction between harm and benefit and tort and restitution is more apparent than real. This can be illustrated by considering an example derived from *Miller v. Schoene* (1958). Cedar trees are vectors for pests that create damage to apple trees but not to the host cedars. In the state of Virgina, apples are an important agricultural crop while cedars are used mainly for ornamental purposes. Should owners of cedar trees be liable for the harm to apple orchards and the benefit to themselves if the cedar trees are not cut down or should apple growers be liable for the harm to the cedar growers and the benefit to the apple growers if they are? In the absence of transaction costs, this question cannot be answered. Either way, one side is harmed while the other side is benefited.

But in the real world there are transaction costs and such costs are asymmetrical in the two regimes of restitution and tort. In this situation the optimal outcome is clearly to have the cedar trees cut down. If cedar tree owners are liable for the damage to apple growers, they will cut down their trees and, except for mistakes, there will be no court cases. If apple growers (or the state) are liable for the benefit derived from cutting down cedar trees, then all of the cedar tree owners will go to court to collect for the benefit of cutting down their trees. This involves high transaction costs. Although courts can easily estimate that the total cost to all of the cedar tree owners is less than the benefit to all of the apple tree growers, determining the cost to each cedar tree owner is much higher. Furthermore, such a system would require apple growers to compensate all people who would have otherwise planted cedar trees but did not since the apple growers benefit from such a decision. This would make court costs astronomical.

Restitution for benefits has higher court transaction costs than torts for harm (hence the relative unimportance of the law of restitution in comparison to tort law). So when does it make sense to have restitution? We want restitution when the long-run entry of the desirable activity would be seriously eroded if compensation for the benefit did not exist - that is, we want compensation when the transaction costs of compensation are outweighed by the increased existence of the desired activity. Consider bounty hunters who track down people who fled on bail before their case went to trial. If bounty hunters were liable for not catching the criminal, no one would enter the business. So they are rewarded instead. Within the law of restitution proper, doctors can collect for services to an unconscious person found lying on the road even though the payment involves a transaction cost. The doctor bill is generally standard (there is no need for an expensive evidentiary hearing) and without such a payment doctors might just drive by. See Landes and Posner (1978) and Wittman (1984).

9. Contracts versus Constitutions: The Role of Monopoly

In contracts, when the question of monopoly arises, the standard remedy is to choose the competitive equilibrium price or behavior. For example, if a doctor comes upon an injured person in the middle of a desert, the doctor cannot take advantage of her monopoly position by demanding the person's life savings in return for rescue. She is only allowed to charge her customary rate, that is the competitive price, for such services. Much the same holds for breach of contract. Opportunism arises when one of the parties to a contract exploits the monopoly power temporarily gained through the contractual relationship. Again, the remedy is relatively simple - such opportunistic behavior is punished by the courts so that the parties have incentive not to breach in the first place.

In contrast, there is no easy solution to the problem posed by the monopoly of political power - no third party can enforce the contract between the government and the people. Thus creating an effective government while at the same time avoiding the dangers of monopoly power is the fundamental concern of democratic constitutional theory. The *Federalist Papers* were devoted to finding the proper balance between a well-functioning government and protection from tyranny.

Democracies need to prevent the majority from exploiting the minority via the majority's control of government and at the same time this protection should not allow the minority to exploit the majority. The conflict is always there. If all issues were resolved by simple majority rule, then the majority could exploit the minority, especially if there were a clear majority/minority cleavage in society (say along ethnic lines). Any tampering with simple majority rule (including such seemingly innocuous changes as having a majority rule legislature voted in by majority rule) will result in a bias for the status quo. See May (1952) who demonstrates that only a simple majority rule satisfies the conditions of anonymity (all people are treated alike), neutrality (if people reverse their preferences, the choice is reversed), and positive responsiveness. Consequently, any attempt to protect the minority will enable the minority to extort monopoly rents from the majority.

The problem is acute when unanimity is the decision rule. Although unanimity as an intellectual concept is at the foundation of constitutional theory, in practice it would be unworkable. Everyone would try to extract the gains from an agreement for herself. This monopoly holdout problem would make collective decision making impossible. In practice, something less than majority rule is required so that transaction costs are not too high (see Buchanan and Tullock, 1962).

Beyond the majority/minority issue is the agency problem. The government usually has a near monopoly on the means of coercive power. What is to prevent the military from over-throwing an election? Of course, this problem exists for all governments, not just those that are democratic (see Skepardas, 1997). This problem is thus more serious than the agency problem facing corporations - stockholders can throw out their managers and board of directors. Many ingenious solutions have been suggested. In the US the president is the commander and chief of the armed forces; each state can have their own militia, and the people have the right to bear arms. All of these are methods of breaking the monopoly of military power and creating a more competitive system. But clearly, there are costs. State militias are not a good way of organizing for modern warfare. And it is not clear that these safeguards are really necessary (many democratic governments do not guarantee the right to bear arms).

The constitution creates a competitive power arrangement. A federal system limits the power of the central government; and the competition between the states, amongst which the citizens can freely migrate, mitigates against the abuses of monopoly power by the states. The separation of powers between the legislative, executive and judicial branches is ultimately more important for being a separation of power than of powers. In this way, there is competition among the branches, each representing a different set of actors. In order for policy to be implemented, an agreement between these different centers of power is needed.

A second method of reducing the coercive power of a government, at least for those governments that obeys the constitution, is to place limits on the power of the government. Once again looking at the United States Constitution, we can observe various limits. Religious freedom is guaranteed. The takings clause prohibits taking of property without just compensation and juries are of one's peers. See Brennan and Buchanan (1980) for discussion of the appropriate limits on the state.

A constitution is an optimal social contract; it provides the underlying rules for making laws. Like any contract, there is a need to protect the parties from opportunism. Unlike the economic sphere, where a third party can enforce contracts and reduce opportunism, constitutions need built-in mechanisms that enforce but at the same time limit the ability of the government to coerce. In this section we have argued that this is the critical difference between contract law and constitutional law. As is always the case, there are other views. For example, Posner (1992, Chapters 23-28) and Wittman (1995, Chapter 10) argue that the United States constitution is efficiency enhancing while Beard (1948) argues that much of the constitution is merely a protection of the wealthy.

10. Courts versus Legislatures: The Role of Comparative Advantage

While there is considerable overlap between what courts and legislatures do (legislatures regulate some activity that could be decided in court, and courts in the United States decide whether certain legislative rulings are constitutional), there are critical differences. Legislatures are designed to resolve conflict among many disparate positions. Courts are designed to resolve disputes between two sides. Also courts are set up more for an ex post review of the facts. So it makes sense that each concentrates in its area of comparative advantage.

In the United States, and in many other countries as well, nuisances are mainly controlled by zoning and urban regulation rather than by the common law of torts. An important reason is that urban planning is multifaceted rather than two-sided.

Courts are more adept at deciding efficiency issues than questions of equity. Legislatures are designed to deal with issues of distribution - the political process of electing representatives and of resolving differences within the legislature is basically a means to resolve differences in values. Thus legislatures decide tax and expenditure policy while courts are more likely to determine the efficient incentives for optimal accident reduction and the facts relevant to a particular accident. .

There are interesting exceptions. In the United States, impeachment of the president is undertaken by the legislature rather than the courts.

11. Concluding Remarks

Finally, we should not forget a major reason for the subheadings in law is that there are returns to specialization. Both family law and bankruptcy law may use the same economic analysis, but the factual details still differ. Focusing in one area helps the practitioner if not always the theorist.

This contribution has shown how economic theory can provide insight into the 'general structure of the law'. There is considerable room for more research in this area. The answers provided are not complete and there are many more questions to be asked. Examples of the latter include: how and why state laws differ from federal laws, and how and why civil and criminal procedure differ.

Acknowledgments

I would like to thank Steven Shavell and the referee for helpful comments.

Bibliography on General Structure of the Law (0900)

Adelstein, Richard P. (1979), 'The Moral Costs of Crime: Prices, Information and Organization', in Gray, Charles M. (ed.), *The Costs of Crime*, Beverly Hills, CA, Sage Publications, 233-252.

Adelstein, Richard P. (1981), 'Institutional Function and Evolution in the Criminal Process', **76** *Northwestern University Law Review*, 1-99.

Adelstein, Richard P. (1992), 'Charles E. Lindblom', in Samuels, Warren J. (ed.), *New Horizons in Economic Thought: Appraisals of Leading Economists*, Cheltenham, UK, Edward Elgar, 202-226.

Ayres, Ian and Talley, Eric (1995), 'Solomonic Bargaining: Dividing a Legal Entitlement to Facilitate Coasean Trade', **104** *Yale Law Journal*, 1027 ff.

Backhaus, Jürgen G. (1996), *Good Economics, Bad Economics, and European Economics*, Meteor Research Memorandum, Maastricht, No. RM/96/007.

Beard, Charles A. (1948), *An Economic Interpretation of the Constitution of the United States*, New York, Macmillan.

Becker, Gary S. (1968), 'Crime and Punishment: An Economic Approach', **76** *Journal of Political Economy*, 169-217.

Benson, Bruce L (1990a), *The Enterprise of Law: Justice Without the State*, San Francisco, Pacific Research Institute for Public Policy.

Benson, Bruce L. (1990b), 'Customary Law with Private Means of Resolving Disputes and Dispensing Justice: A Description of a Modern System of Law and Order Without State Coercion', **9** *Journal of Libertarian Studies*, 25-42. Reprinted as 'Law and Order Without State Coercion', in Veljanovski, Cento (ed.) (1991), *Regulation, Regulators and the Market*, London, Institute of Economic Affairs, 159-179.

Benson, Bruce L. (1991a), 'Reciprocal Exchange as the Basis for Recognition of Law: Examples from American History', **10** *Journal of Libertarian Studies*, 53-82.

Benson, Bruce L. (1991b), 'An Evolutionary Contractarian View of Primitive Law: The Institutions and Incentives Arising Under Customary American Indian Law', **5** *Review of Austrian Economics*, 65-89.

Benson, Bruce L. (1992a), 'Customary Indian Law: Two Case Studies', in Benson, Bruce L. (1992), *Customary Law as a Social Contract: International Commercial Law*, **2** *Constitutional Political Economy*, 1-27.

Benson, Bruce L. (1992b), 'The Development of Criminal Law and its Enforcement: Public Interest or Political Transfers', **3** *Journal des Economistes et des Etudes Humaines*, 79-108.

Benson, Bruce L. (1992c), 'The Evolution of Values and Institutions in a Free Society: The Under-Pinnings of a Market Economy', **5** *International Journal on the Unity of Sciences*, 411-442. Reprinted in Radnitzky, Gerard and Bouillon, Hardy (eds) (1995), *Values and the Social Order Vol. I*, Aldershot, Avebury, 87-125.

Benson, Bruce L. (1993), 'The Impetus for Recognizing Private Property and Adopting Ethical Behavior in a Market Economy: Natural Law, Government Law, or Evolving Self-Interest', **6** *Review of Austrian Economics*, 43-80.

Benson, Bruce L. (1994a), 'Are Public Goods Really Common Pools: Considerations of the Evolution of Policing and Highways in England', **39** *Economic Inquiry*, 249-271.

Benson, Bruce L. (1994b), 'Emerging From the Hobbesian Jungle: Might Takes and Makes Rights', **5** *Constitutional Political Economy*, 129-158. Translated into

Spanish and republished (1995), *Las Instituciones y Los Derechos de Propiedad al Emerger de la Jungla Hobbesiana: La Fuerza Quita los Derechos y los Crea Libertas*, 12, 35-75.

Benson, Bruce L. (1994c), 'Legal Philosophy', in Boettke, Peter J. (ed.), *The Elgar Companion to Austrian Economics*, London, Edward Elgar, 270-275.

Benson, Bruce L. (1995a), 'Competition Among Legal Institutions: Implications for the Evolution of Law', in Gerken, Luden (ed.), *Competition Among Institutions*, London, Macmillan, 153-175.

Benson, Bruce L. (1995b), 'An Exploration of the Impact of Modern Arbitration Statutes on the Development of Arbitration in the United States', **11** *Journal of Law, Economics, and Organization*, 479-501.

Benson, Bruce L. (1995c), *Privatization in Criminal Justice*, Independent Policy Report, Oakland, Independent Institute.

Benson, Bruce L. and Wollan, Laurin A., Jr (1989), 'Prison Overcrowding and Judicial Incentives', **3** *Madison Paper Series*, 1-22.

Benson, Bruce L. and Wollan, Laurin A., Jr (1991), 'Increasing Judicial Responsibility Can Reduce Prison Overcrowding in America's Prisons: Opposing Viewpoints', in Tipp, Stacey L. (ed.), San Diego, Greenhaven Press, 139-144.

Bishop, William (1983), 'The Contract-Tort Boundary and the Economics of Insurance', **12** *Journal of Legal Studies*, 241-266.

Bouckaert, Boudewijn and De Geest, Gerrit (1995), 'Private Takings, Private Taxes, Private Compulsory Services: The Economic Doctrine of Quasi Contracts', **15** *International Review of Law and Economics*, 463-487.

Brennan, G. and Buchanan, James M. (1980), *The Power to Tax: Analytical Foundations of a Fiscal Constitution*, Cambridge, Cambridge University Press.

Brown, John Prather and Holahan, William L. (1980), 'Taxes and Legal Rules for the Control of Externalities when there are Strategic Responses', **9** *Journal of Legal Studies*, 165-178.

Buchanan, James M. and Tullock, Gordon (1962), *The Calculus of Consent: Logical Foundations of Constitutional Democracy*, Ann Arbor, University of Michigan Press.

Calabresi, Guido and Melamed, A. Douglas (1972), 'Property Rules, Liability Rules and Inalienability: One View of the Cathedral', **85** *Harvard Law Review*, 1089-1128.

Coleman, Jules L. (1987), 'Property, Wrongfulness and the Duty to Compensate', **63** *Chicago-Kent Law Review*, 451-470.

Cooter, Robert (1985), 'Unity in Torts, Contracts and Property: The Model of Precaution', **73** *California Law Review*, 1-51.

Craswell, Richard (1993), 'Property Rules and Liability Rules in Unconscionability and Related Doctrines', **60** *University of Chicago Law Review*, 1-65.

Dau-Schmidt, Kenneth G. (1990), 'An Economic Analysis of the Criminal Law as a Preference Shaping Policy', *Duke Law Journal*, 1-38.

De Geest, Gerrit (1994), *Economische Analyse van het Contracten- en Quasi-contractenrecht: een Onderzoek naar de Wetenschappelijke Waarde van de Rechtseconomie* (Economic Analysis of Contract Law and Quasi Contract Law: A Study on the Scientic Value of Law and Economics), Antwerpen, Maklu, 568 p.

Demsetz, H. (1972), 'When Does the Rule of Liability Matter?', **13** *Journal of Legal Studies*.

Dowd, Kevin (1996), *Competition and Finance: A New Interpretation of Financial and Monetary Economics*, Macmillan Press, 572 p.

Ellickson, R.C. (1973), 'Alternatives to Zoning: Convenants, Nuisance Rules, and Fines as Land Use Controls', **40** *University of Chicago Law Review*, 681-782.

Epstein, Richard A. (1975), 'Intentional Harms', **4** *Journal of Legal Studies*, 391-442.

Epstein, Richard A. (1979), 'Nuisance Law: Corrective Justice and its Utilitarian Constraints', **8** *Journal of Legal Studies*, 49-102.

Fletcher, George P. (1985), 'A Transaction Cost Theory of Crime?', **85** *Columbia Law Review*, 921-930.

Frech, H.E. III (1979), 'The Extended Coase Theorem and Long Run Equilibrium: The Non-Equivalence of Liability Rules and Property Rights', **27(1)** *Economic Inquiry*, 254-268.

Friedman, David D. (1991), 'Impossibility, Subjective Probability, and Punishments for Attempts', **20** *Journal of Legal Studies*, 179-186.

Grady, Mark F. (1994), 'Positive Theories and Grown Order Conceptions of the Law', **23** *Swedish Law Review*, 461 ff.

Hamilton, Alexander, Jay, John and Madison, James (1961), *The Federalist Papers*, New York, New American Library.

Kaplow, Louis (1990), 'A Note on the Optimal Use of Nonmonetary Sanctions', **42** *Journal of Public Economics*, 245-247.

Kaplow, Louis and Shavell, Steven (1995), 'Do Liability Rules Facilitate Bargaining? A Reply to Ayres and Talley', **105(1)** *Yale Law Journal*, 221-233.

Kaplow, Louis and Shavell, Steven (1996), 'Property Rules versus Liability Rules: An Economic Analysis', **109** *Harvard Law Review*, 715-790.

Kermit, Daniel and Lott, J.R., Jr (1995), 'Should Criminal Penalties Include Third Party Avoidance Costs?', **24** *Journal of Legal Studies*, 523-534.

Kitch, Edmund W. (1987), 'Law and the Economic Order', in Lipson, Leon and Wheeler, Stanton (eds), *Law and the Social Sciences*, New York, Russel Sage Foundation, 109-149.

Klevorick, Alvin K. (1985a), 'Legal Theory and the Economic Analysis of Law', **85** *Columbia Law Review*, 905-920.

Klevorick, Alvin K. (1985b), 'On the Economic Theory of Crime', **28** *Nomos*, 289 ff.

Kolstad, Charles D., Ulen, Thomas S. and Johnson, Gary V. (1990), 'Ex Post Liability for Harm vs. Ex Ante Safety Regulation: Substitutes or Complements?', **80** *American Economic Review*, 888-901.

Krier, James E. and Schwab, Stewart J. (1995), 'Property Rules and Liability Rules: The Cathedral in Another Light', **70** *New York University Law Review*, 440 ff.

Landes, William M. and Posner, Richard A. (1978), 'Salvors, Finders, Good Samaritans, and Other Rescuers: An Economic Study of Law and Altruism', **7** *Journal of Legal Studies*, 83-128.

Landes, William M. and Posner, Richard A. (1981), 'An Economic Theory of Intentional Torts', **1** *International Review of Law and Economics*, 127-154.

Levmore, Saul (1985), 'Explaining Restitution', **71** *Virginia Law Review*, 65-124.

Levmore, Saul (1986), 'Waiting for Rescue: An Essay on the Evolution and Incentive Structure of the Law of Affirmative Obligations', **72** *Virginia Law Review*, 879-941.

Long, Robert A., Jr (1984), 'A Theory of Hypothetical Contract', **94** *Yale Law Journal*, 415-434.

Macey, Jonathan R. (1987), 'Competing Economic Views of the Constitution', **56** *George Washington Law Review*, 50-80.

Mackaay, Ejan (1979), 'Les Notions Floues ou l'Économie de l'Imprécision (Fuzzy Concepts or the Economics of Imprecision)', **12** *Langages*, 33-50.

Mackaay, Ejan (1980), 'Le Nozione "Fluide" Ovvero l'Economia Dell'Imprecisione (Fuzzy Concepts or the Economics of Imprecision)', *Informatica e Diritto*, 253-274.

Mackaay, Ejan (1988), 'L'Ordre Spontané Comme Fondement du Droit - un Survol des Modèles de l'Émergence des Règles dans une Société Civile (Spontaneous Order as Foundation of Law - A Survey of Models of the Emergence of Rules in Civil Society)', **22** *Revue Juridique Themis*, 347-383.

Mackaay, Ejan (1989), 'L'Ordre Spontané Comme Fondement du Droit - un Survol des Modèles de l'Émergence des Règles dans la Société Civile (Spontaneous Order as the Foundation of Law - A Survey of Models of the Emergence of Rules in Civil Society)', **3** *Revue Internationale de Droit Economique*, 247-287.

Mackaay, Ejan (1991), 'Le Droit Saisi par le Jeu (Game-Theory Applied to Law)', *Droit et Société*, 57-81.

Mackaay, Ejan (1992), 'Le Droit Saisi par le Jeu (Game-Theory Applied to Law)', in Ost, François and Van De Kerkhove, Michel (eds), *Le Jeu: un Paradigme pour le Droit*, Paris, Librairie Générale de Droit et de Jurisprudence, 81-110.

Mattei, Ugo and Pulitini, Francesco (1990), 'Modelli Competitivi, Regole Giuridiche ed Analisi Economica (Competitive Models, Legal Norms and Economic Analysis)', *Quadrimestre*, 77-102.

May, K.O. (1952), 'A Set of Independent Necessary and Sufficient Conditions for Simple Majority Decision', **20** *Econometrica*, 680-684.

Miller, Jeremy M. (198), 'Economic Analysis of Legal Method and Law: The Danger in Valueless Values', **21** *Gonzaga Law Review*, 425-455.

Pennings, Joost, Heijman, Willem J.M. and Meulenberg, Matthew (1997), 'The Dimensions of Rights: A Classification of Environmental Rights and Production Rights', **4** *European Journal of Law and Economics*, 55-71.

Polinsky, A. Mitchell (1979), 'Controlling Externalities and Protecting Entitlements: Property Right, Liability Rule, and Tax-Subsidy Approaches', **8** *Journal of Legal Studies*, 1-48.

Polinsky, A. Mitchell and Shavell Steven (1994), 'Should Liability be Based on the Harm to the Victim or the Gain to the Injurer?', **10** *Journal of Law, Economics, and Organization*, 427-437.

Posner Richard A. (1985), 'An Economic Theory of the Criminal Law', **85** *Columbia Law Review*, 1193-1231.

Posner Richard A. (1987), 'The Constitution as an Economic Document', **56** *George Washington Law Review*, 4-38.

Posner Richard A. (1992), *Economic Analysis of Law* (4th edn), Boston, Little Brown.

Rasmussen, David W. and Benson, Bruce L. (eds) (1994), *The Economic Anatomy of a Drug War: Criminal Justice in the Commons*, Lanham, MD, Rowman and Littlefield..

Rose-Ackerman, Susan (1986), 'The Simple Economics of Tort Law: An Organizing Framework', **2** *European Journal of Political Economy*, 91-98.

Rose-Ackerman, Susan (1991), 'Regulation and the Law of Torts', **81** *American Economic Review. Papers and Proceedings*, 54-58.

Rose-Ackerman, Susan (1995), 'Public Law Versus Private Law in Environmental Regulation: European Union Proposals in the Light of United States and German Experience', in Eide, Erling and Van Den Bergh, Roger (eds), *Law and Economics of the Environment*, Oslo, Juridisk Forlag.

Rousseau, Jean Jacques (1954), *The Social Contract* (translated by Kendall, W.).

Rubin, Paul H. (1982), 'Common Law and Statute Law', **11** *Journal of Legal Studies*, 205-223.

Ryssdal, Stray A.C. (1995), *An Economic Analysis of Civil Suits and Appels*, Oslo, Juridisk Forlag.

Ryssdal, Stray A.C. (1995), *Legal Realism and Economics as Behavior - A Scandinavian Look at the Economic Analysis of Law*, Oslo, Juridisk Forlag.

Schap, David (1986), 'The Nonequivalence of Property Rules and Liability Rules', **6** *International Review of Law and Economics*, 125-132.

Shavell Steven (1984a), 'A Model of the Optimal Use of Liability and Safety Regulation', **15** *Rand Journal of Economics*, 271-280.

Shavell Steven (1984b), 'Liability for Harm versus Regulation of Safety', **13** *Journal of Legal Studies*, 357-374.

Shavell Steven (1985), 'Criminal Law and the Optimal Use of Nonmonetary Sanctions as a Deterrent', **85** *Columbia Law Review*, 1232-1262.

Shavell Steven (1986), 'The Judgment Proof Problem', **6** *International Review of Law and Economics*, 45-58.

Shavell Steven (1990), 'Deterrence and the Punishment of Attempts', **19** *Journal of Legal Studies*, 435-466.

Skepardas, Stergios (1997), *The Market for Protection and the Origin of the State*, Irvine Working Paper.

Spulber, Daniel F. (1988), 'Optimal Environmental Regulation under Asymmetric Information', **35** *Journal of Public Economics*, 163-181.

Staaf, Robert J. (1983), 'Liability Rules, Property Rights, and Taxes', **5** *Research in Law and Economics*, 225-231.

White, Michelle J. and Wittman, Donald A. (1981), 'Optimal Spatial Location Under Pollution: Liability Rules and Zoning', *Journal of Legal Studies*, 249-268.

White, Michelle J. and Wittman, Donald A. (1983a), 'Pollution Taxes and Optimal Spatial Location', *Economica*, 297-311.

White, Michelle J. and Wittman, Donald A. (1983b), 'A Comparison of Taxes, Regulation, and Liability Rules under Imperfect Information', **12** *Journal of Legal Studies*, 413-425.

Wiggins, Steven N. and Ringleb, A.H. (1992), 'Adverse Selection and Long Term Hazards: The Choice between Contract and Mandatory Liability Rules', **21** *Journal of Legal Studies*, 189-215.

Wittman, Donald A. (1977), 'Prior Regulation versus Post Liability: The Choice Between Input and Output Monitoring', **6** *Journal of Legal Studies*, 193-211.

Wittman, Donald A. (1981), 'Optimal Pricing of Sequential Inputs: Last Clear Chance, Mitigation of Damages and Related Doctrines in the Law', **10** *Journal of Legal Studies*, 65-91.

Wittman, Donald A. (1984a), 'The Geometry of Justice', *Theory and Decision*, 239-250.

Wittman, Donald A. (1984b), 'Liability for Harm or Restitution for Benefit?', **13** *Journal of Legal Studies*, 57-80.

Wittman, Donald A. (1985a), 'Should Compensation be Based on Costs or Benefits?', **5** *International Review of Law and Economics*, 173-185.

Wittman, Donald A. (1985b), 'Pigovian Taxes which Work in the Small Number Case', *Journal of Environmental Economics and Management*, 144-154.

Wittman, Donald A. (1995), *The Myth of Democratic Failure: Why Political Institutions Are Efficient*, Chicago, University of Chicago Press.

Yohe, Gary W. (1976), 'Polluters' Profits and Political Response: Direct Control versus Taxes: Comment', **66** *American Economic Review*, 981-982.

Cases

Boehm v. Philadelphia (1915), 59 Pa. Super. Ct 441.

Ensign v. Walls (1948), 323 Mich. 49; 34 N.W. 2d 549.

Hadley v. Baxendale (1854), 156 Eng. Rep 145.

Miller v. Schoene (1958), 276 U.S. 272.

United Verde Extension Mining Co v. Ralston (1931), 296 P. 262.